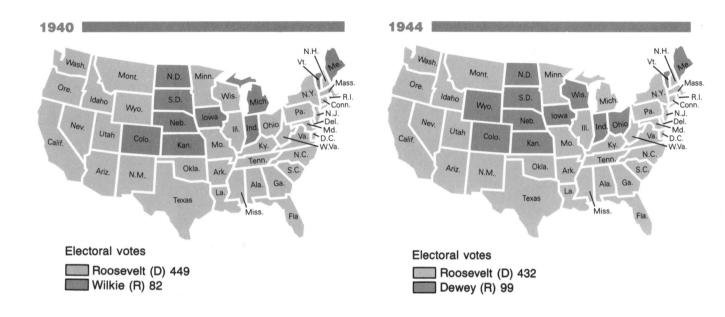

1940

Electoral votes

■ Roosevelt (D) 449
■ Wilkie (R) 82

1944

Electoral votes

■ Roosevelt (D) 432
■ Dewey (R) 99

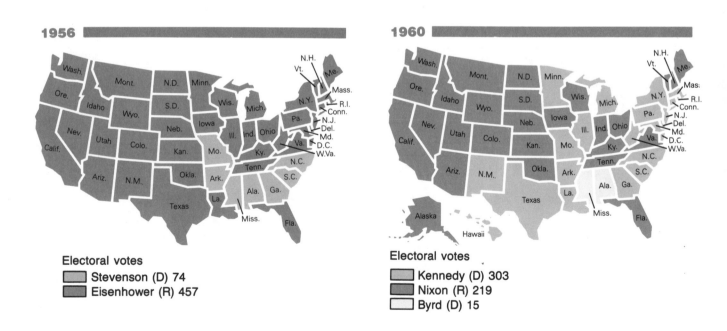

1956

Electoral votes

■ Stevenson (D) 74
■ Eisenhower (R) 457

1960

Electoral votes

■ Kennedy (D) 303
■ Nixon (R) 219
□ Byrd (D) 15

DEMOCRACY UNDER PRESSURE

An
Introduction
to the American
Political System

SEVENTH EDITION

DEMOCRACY UNDER PRESSURE

An Introduction to the American Political System

SEVENTH EDITION

Milton C. Cummings, Jr.

The Johns Hopkins University

David Wise

Author and political analyst

HARCOURT BRACE JOVANOVICH COLLEGE PUBLISHERS

Fort Worth   Philadelphia   San Diego   New York   Orlando   Austin   San Antonio
Toronto   Montreal   London   Sydney   Tokyo

Editor-in-Chief	**Ted Buchholz**
Acquisitions Editor	**David Tatom**
Developmental Editor	**John Haley**
Project Editor	**Margaret Allyson**
Senior Production Manager	**Kenneth A. Dunaway**
Senior Book Designer	**Don Fujimoto**
Photo Research/Permissions	**Susan Holtz**
Literary Permissions	**Van E. Strength**

Requests for permission to make copies of any part of the
work should be mailed to: Permissions Department,
Harcourt Brace Jovanovich, Publishers, 8th Floor, Orlando,
Florida 32887.

Address for Editorial Correspondence: Harcourt Brace
Jovanovich College Publishers, 301 Commerce Street, Suite
3700, Fort Worth, TX 76102.

Address for Orders: Harcourt Brace Jovanovich, Publishers,
6277 Sea Harbor Drive, Orlando, Florida 32887. 1-800-782-
4479, or 1-800-433-0001 (in Florida).

ISBN: 0-15-500198-1

Library of Congress Catalog Card Number: 92-72261

Printed in the United States of America

2 3 4 5 6 7 8 9 0 1   063   9 8 7 6 5 4 3 2 1

PREFACE

THERE is, without doubt, no better experience than revising a college text in government and politics to remind one of the astonishing pace of change that takes place within the American political system.

The election of Bill Clinton as president in 1992 marked an end to twelve years of Republican rule in the White House. In addition, the election of a Democratic president and Congress also meant an end to divided government. The departure of President George Bush, foreshadowed with substantial accuracy in the public-opinion polls during the campaign, undoubtedly reflected voter discontent with the disappointing state of the economy. The entry into the race of the independent candidate, Ross Perot, made the presidential election of 1992 particularly volatile. Perot's strong showing was widely perceived as the result of voter discontent with established political leaders and with "gridlock" in Washington — a "turn-the-rascals-out" mood that also changed the face of Congress, as the voters sent more women, minorities, and newcomers to Capitol Hill.

All of these swift currents and shifts in political power are charted in this revised edition. But if the focus of the 1992 election was on the domestic agenda, from the general need to revitalize the economy to specific programs such as health care for all Americans, the backdrop for the drama had changed beyond recognition.

The world in 1992 was dramatically different from the way it had appeared during the previous presidential election. In only a few short years, the Soviet Union and the communist system had collapsed. Beginning in 1989, the Berlin Wall came down, and the tide of democracy swept across Eastern Europe, leaving freedom in its wake — but also ethnic and national rivalries, civil war, economic dislocation, and political uncertainty. The Cold War had ended after more than four decades, and the danger of nuclear holocaust had receded.

Here at home, the changed nature of the international balance of power raised all sorts of questions that had not been fully discussed in the political arena. With the United States no longer facing a hostile superpower armed with nuclear weapons, the nation needed to redefine the concept of "national security." How much could defense spending safely be cut, and would the "peace dividend" really be put to work to meet domestic needs?

These issues, both domestic and international, are explored in this edition. The 1992 election and Bill Clinton's victory; the three-way televised debates between Clinton, Bush, and Perot and their vice-presidential running mates; the 1992 primary campaigns; the Republican challenge to President Bush by Patrick J. Buchanan; the field of Democratic candidates; the new uses of television in 1992; the role of professional campaign managers; how "soft money" circumvents the campaign spending law — all are here, along with a detailed case study of the presidential campaign and an analysis of significant trends in the 1992 elections.

With the publication of this Seventh Edition early in 1993, it has been more than two decades since *Democracy Under Pressure* first made its appearance. And what extraordinary years they have been: the end of the long war in Vietnam, the Watergate trauma and the impeachment inquiry; the resignation and pardon of the president of the United States; the energy crisis; the Carter years; the seizure of the American hostages in Iran and in Lebanon; the Soviet invasion of Afghanistan and the Soviet withdrawal almost a decade later; the election and reelection of Ronald Reagan, a conservative Republican president pledged to increasing the nation's military strength while cutting a broad range of social programs; and the Iran-contra affair. Then Bush's one-term presidency; his triumph in the Persian Gulf War, forcing Iraq's Saddam Hussein to withdraw from Kuwait; the failed coup attempt against Soviet president Mikhail S. Gorbachev, and, only four months later, his resignation and the end of the Soviet Union, and with it, the end of the Cold War; the emergence of Boris N. Yeltsin as the leader of Russia; the dramatic moves toward nuclear disarmament between the two sides; the continuing search for peace in the Middle East; and, at home, the increasing burdens of widespread layoffs, unemployment, plant closings, and economic recession.

This Seventh Edition of *Democracy Under Pressure* has been thoroughly and extensively revised not only to reflect these kaleidoscopic events, but to focus as well on the broader trends and on the newer interpretations of the American political system.

As in the past, the making of public policy is discussed throughout the book (and particularly in Part Three, "The Policymakers"), but a section introducing the student to policy analysis is included in Chapter One. This introduction to the policy process follows, in logical progression, the discussion of the concept of a political system.

Many new features and topics are incorporated into this edition. Among them are a detailed summary of the Persian Gulf War; a reorganized and expanded discussion of the role of women in American society; the controversy over the nomination of Justice Clarence Thomas, accused by Professor Anita Hill of sexual harassment, and how reaction to her treatment by members of the Senate Judiciary Committee resulted in a greater number of women running for Congress and other offices in 1992; a detailed summary and discussion of the 1990 census and what it reveals about demographic change in America; the passage of the 27th Amendment to the Constitution; the latest trends in fiscal federalism; the Exxon Valdez oil spill; the Endangered Species Act and the controversy over the spotted owl; the move by the voters toward term limits; and the budget crises in California and other states.

New data is provided on the decline of party allegiance, on the pattern of PAC spending in recent elections, and on the increasing cost of congressional campaigns. Examples from the 1992 campaign are used to illustrate how presidents attempt to use the powers of incumbency to win reelection.

Included as well are discussions of multiculturalism in America, the Rodney King case and the Los Angeles riots, Asian Americans as the fastest-growing segment of the population, passage of the Americans with Disabilities Act, an expanded section on Hispanic Americans, new data on the political power of gay Americans, and government spending on AIDS research.

The treatment of the presidency has been expanded to include an exploration of the president as popular leader of the nation and a discussion of the concepts of the personal presidency and the rhetorical presidency. John H. Sununu's departure as President Bush's chief of staff is reviewed, and there is a more detailed explanation of the Iran-contra affair and its impact on the 1992 election.

Our chapter on Congress has been revised to describe the House bank scandal, the new congressional budget procedures, the budget "summit" that proved so politically costly for President Bush when he reneged on his "no new taxes" promise, the savings and loan scandal, differing views on divided government, changing norms in the Senate, the latest data on marginal districts, and the attitude of the public toward Congress as an institution.

We cover in detail many significant new decisions by the United States Supreme Court dealing with abortion, libel, freedom of religion, search and seizure, and other important issues; the changes in the makeup of the Court; and the emergence of a centrist bloc of three justices. New material on the issue of capital punishment is included, along with an examination of the government's effort to prosecute organized crime.

We have expanded the discussion of the role of the news media in American politics, of the relationship between the president and the press, of the enormous impact of television on public opinion, and Ross Perot's unusual presidential campaign that relied almost entirely on television to reach the voters.

Our treatment of economic issues has been expanded to include a more detailed discussion of international trade and tariff issues, why American industry has become less competitive with other countries, and the political and economic problems presented at home by mounting deficits.

Finally, we have revised and expanded the discussion of foreign policy to include the dramatically changed nature of the world; the implications for America of the end of the Cold War, the democracy movement in the former Communist nations, the continued threat of nuclear proliferation, U.S. policy toward China, and the tragedy of Tiananmen Square; the invasion of Panama and the capture and imprisonment of Panamanian leader Manuel Noriega; the role of the United Nations; how the government controlled the information reaching the public during the Persian Gulf War; and global issues including overpopulation, famine, disease, and ethnic and religious conflicts.

Several structural features introduced in earlier editions have been retained. A Perspective at the end of each chapter, beginning with Chapter 2, provides a summary of key points for the reader. Important terms are defined in an updated Glossary. The Constitution is included, along with the Declaration of Independence, as well as a list of the presidents of the United States and the vote they received.

Once again, a Study Guide, keyed to the text, is available, both in book form, and now on computer disks as well, for those who wish to use it. The Study Guide, written by the authors with the editorial assistance of Robert W. Bernotas, has been revised and updated to parallel the changes in the content of the Seventh Edition. The Study Guide includes learning objectives, key points for each chapter, definitions, and self-tests with multiple-choice, true-false, short-answer, and fill-in-the-blank options, as well as a series of study exercises.

The package of instructional materials provided with the textbook includes an Instructor's Manual, prepared by Sue Lee of Northlake College, with chapter outlines and learning objectives keyed to the Study Guide and the textbook, as well as lecture suggestions, video resources, group projects, key points, and key terms.

Video tapes from the Annenberg/CPB collection, *The Constitution: That Delicate Balance*, are available as teaching aids and cover such subjects as the conflict between free press and national security, and between the requirements of the criminal justice system and the right of defendants to fair trial. Some of the thirteen one-hour tapes are provided without charge.

Interactive software is available in both IBM and Macintosh versions, providing simulations that cover topics including the Constitution, political participation and political campaigns, presidential choices, and public policy.

All adopters of the text are eligible to receive a free subscription to *The New Republic* magazine. Offering an intelligent analysis of major political issues each week, this magazine is ideal for stimulating class discussion of current policy issues. In addition, students may subscribe for approximately one-half the regular subscription price.

A test booklet keyed to the text, prepared by Evan Jones of St. Cloud State University, contains more than 2400 multiple-choice, true-false, and short-answer essay questions, with page references to the text. A computerized test bank offers instructors four ways to select questions, a range of formatting options, and the flexibility to edit or add questions. And finally, a customized test bank is available to instructors without access to a computer. An HBJ software specialist will compile questions in accordance with the instructor's criteria and mail or fax the test master within 48 hours.

As the title of this book indicates, the authors recognize that the American political system is under pressure, that its ability to cope with the problems facing the nation is being questioned by many individuals and groups in our society. In such a time, we continue to believe it useful to provide a book that focuses not only on the very considerable achievements of the American system of government but on its shortcomings too—a book that focuses on the reality as well as the rhetoric of American democracy. We have tried to do this in a textbook designed for the '90s.

In writing this book, we set three goals. First, we believe that a textbook should be lively and stimulating to read. So we have attempted to provide a text that is as clear and readable as possible without sacrificing scholarship or content.

Second, although we present American governmental and political institutions in their historical context, we have sought to relate politics and government to contemporary issues. At the same time, we have attempted to relate those contemporary issues to larger concepts. We have also included case studies on a number of topics.

Third, as we have indicated, we have attempted to focus on the gaps, where they exist, between American myths and American realities, between the political system's promise and its performance. Students and other citizens may not be disillusioned with the principles of American democracy, but they do ask that the political system practice those principles.

In examining the structure and processes of American politics and government, we have tried to ask: How is the political system supposed to work? How does it actually work? What might be done to make it work better? Each chapter is organized around a series of basic questions about the workings of the political system. The book does not, in every case, provide ready answers to those questions, but it raises them for the student's consideration and, if desired, for classroom discussion. At the same time, the book emphasizes the importance of each individual citizen for the quality of American society and American government. It provides examples of participation in the political process by students and other citizens. It examines the responsibilities as well as the rights of citizens in a democracy.

The authors deeply appreciate the assistance of the many people who helped to produce this book. We must begin with Kristin L. Kenney, who provided expert research and editorial assistance at every stage in the preparation of the revised manuscript for this Seventh Edition. Her contribution was invaluable and her dedication extraordinary. We also wish to thank our research assistants for previous editions: Norma W. Batchelder and Thomas A. Horne for the First Edition (1971), Freda F. Solomon for the Second Edition (1974),

Nancy D. Beers for the Third Edition (1977), M. J. Rusk-Pierce for the Fourth Edition (1981), Jessica Tolmach for the Fifth Edition (1985), and Robin G. Colucci for the Sixth Edition (1989). We wish to express our appreciation as well to Kate Sawyer, who kept our reference files up to date; and to John Fox Sullivan, president and publisher, and Rose Marie Pool, director of library services of the *National Journal*.

We are grateful as well to the many persons who gave us the benefit of their advice and assistance along the way. That list is long, and it includes Frederick L. Holborn, of the School of Advanced International Studies, The Johns Hopkins University; Dom Bonafede, of the American University; Dean John R. Kramer, of the Tulane University School of Law; Herbert E. Alexander, director of the Citizens' Research Foundation; Roger H. Davidson, of the University of Maryland; Walter J. Oleszek, of the Congressional Research Service of the Library of Congress; Harry Balfe, of Montclair State College; Harvey L. Schantz, of the State University of New York, Plattsburgh; Richard C. Wald, senior vice-president, ABC News; Richard M. Scammon, director, and Alice W. McGillivray, associate director, the Elections Research Center; Larry Hugick, managing editor of the Gallup Poll; Jane E. Kirtley, executive director of the Reporters Committee for Freedom of the Press; Kristine D. Frink, of the office of Representative Norm Dicks; Jonathan W. Wise, of the office of Senator Daniel P. Moynihan; Bonnie Hopper and Gloria Mundo of the U.S. Bureau of the Census; Francis J. Lorson, chief deputy clerk of the office of the clerk, United States Supreme Court, as well as the many scholars and colleagues whose help was acknowledged in earlier editions and to whom we remain indebted.

The authors are also grateful to those who read and commented on portions of the book, assisting us in the preparation of the Seventh Edition: Bill McKee of Oklahoma State University, Martin Mattingly of Tarrant County Junior College, Hugh Jones of Shippensburg University, Tom Heiting of Odessa College, Waino Peterson of College of the Sequoias, Bob Little of Brookhaven College, Mike Germaine of Valencia Community College, and David Sieg of Tidewater Community College.

A number of professors teaching the introductory American government course also offered us invaluable chapter-by-chapter comments on the Sixth Edition that helped us to plan the Seventh Edition: Jeffrey Tullis of the University of Texas, H. Brad Westerfield of Yale University, Francis E. Rourke of Johns Hopkins University, David Beam of Illinois Institute of Technology, James Magee of the University of Delaware, Charles Hamilton, John Tierney of Boston College, Lance Bennett of the University of Washington, Frank Sorauf of the University of Minnesota, Robert Peabody of Johns Hopkins University, M. Margaret Conway of the University of Florida, Robert X. Browning of Purdue University, and Gerald L. Houseman of Indiana University at Fort Wayne.

The comments of all these reviewers were consistently helpful; at the same time, responsibility for the final draft, including any errors or shortcomings, is ours.

Finally, we wish to express our thanks to members of the College Department of Harcourt Brace Jovanovich, Inc., beginning with David Tatom, acquisitions editor, who supervised this edition; Margaret Allyson, project editor, and Sara Schroeder, assistant project editor; John Haley, developmental editor; Margie Rogers, manuscript editor; Tom Torrans, proofreader; and Kristin Trompeter, assistant to the acquisitions editor. We shall always owe a special debt of gratitude to the late William A. Pullin, senior editor, who first proposed this project to us and gave it his continued support; to Virginia Joyner, our manuscript editor for the first two editions; to Harry Rinehart, designer for the first four editions; to Joanne D. Daniels, editor for the third and fourth editions; to Drake Bush, our editor for the last two editions; and to Bill M. Barnett, senior vice president. For this new edition, we are grateful as well to Susan G. Holtz, who supervised the selection of the many photographs and cartoons; to Molly Shepard, senior photo editor for the early chapters; to Van E. Strength, the literary permissions editor; to Ken Dunaway, the production manager; and to designer Don Fujimoto, who once again applied his creative talents to integrate the whole, type and graphics, into a result that captures in visual form the spirit and purpose of our examination of *Democracy Under Pressure*.

Milton C. Cummings, Jr.
David Wise

CONTENTS

PART ONE
THE AMERICAN DEMOCRACY

PART TWO
POLITICS U.S.A.

PART THREE
THE POLICYMAKERS

PART FOUR
GOVERNMENT IN OPERATION

PART FIVE
THE AMERICAN COMMUNITY

DEMOCRACY UNDER PRESSURE

An Introduction to the American Political System

SEVENTH EDITION

THE
AMERICAN
DEMOCRACY

THEY HAD been waiting in the chill night air for hours in front of the old State House in Little Rock, Arkansas, a crowd that grew to 40,000 people. They were singing "don't stop thinking about tomorrow," the words to a Fleetwood Mac tune that had become Arkansas Governor Bill Clinton's campaign song. And they sang "The Battle Hymn of the Republic."

It was election night, November 3, 1992, and not only in the crowd gathered at the State House, but across America there was an atmosphere of tension, of anticipation, and of high drama, as the returns began coming in from the small towns and great cities of America, sweeping like a great tide across the land. A

Chapter 1

Government and People

record-breaking number of voters had turned out, and in many communities they were lined up, waiting sometimes for as long as two hours to cast their votes.

For weeks, the public opinion polls had reported that Clinton, the Democratic challenger, had a solid lead over his rivals, President George Bush, the Republican candidate, who was seeking reelection, and billionaire Texas businessman Ross Perot, the feisty, unpredictable independent. But in the last week of the campaign, the gap in the polls between Bush and Clinton had narrowed, and the president, appearing to hit his stride at last, had barnstormed across the country, attacking his rivals with renewed energy and abandon. To many, it seemed too late.

Yet, as millions of Americans went to the polls and then turned on their television sets to watch, no one knew for sure. The only poll that mattered — the actual vote on election day — was being counted in a campaign that had been marked by an extraordinary level of invective, charges, and counter-charges.

Early in the evening, Georgia, and the normally Republican states of New Hampshire and Vermont, went for Clinton. Bush carried Indiana, but by a smaller margin than expected. Based on exit polls, the television network anchors were soon able to place New York, New Jersey, Illinois, and Michigan in Clinton's column. It was clear that the battleground states of the industrial North, many of them scarred by the recession and unemployment of the Bush years, were Clinton's. Yet for many minutes, Clinton's electoral vote total hung at

265, just five short of the 270 needed to win. At 10:49 P.M., NBC anchor Tom Brokaw looked into the eye of the camera and announced that Ohio, where the race had been close, had awarded its twenty-one electoral votes to Bill Clinton, who was now president-elect of the United States. Minutes later, the Clinton tide had reached across the Rockies to California.

In Houston, the president issued a gracious concession statement and asked the country to unite behind the winner. Ross Perot did the same, although he reminded his supporters he was still waiting in the wings if they were dissatisfied with Clinton's leadership.

At 11:21 P.M. local time, already after midnight in the East, Clinton, his wife, Hillary, his daughter, Chel-

sea, and his vice-presidential running mate, Senator Albert Gore, and the senator's family, appeared before the crowd and the TV floodlights. His voice still hoarse from months of campaigning, Clinton appealed for unity. "My fellow Americans," he said, "on this day with high hopes and brave hearts, in massive numbers, the American people have voted to make a new beginning. This election is a clarion call for our country to face the challenges of the end of the Cold War and the beginning of the next century."

He called for broad support "so we can turn this country around," and he added: "I ask you to join with us in creating a reunited states, a united country with a new sense of patriotism, to face the challenges of this new time. . . . We need more than new laws, new promises, or new programs. We need a new spirit of community, a sense that we're all in this together. If we have no sense of community, the American dream will continue to wither. Our destiny is bound up with the destiny of every American."

It was an extraordinary and electric moment, and to the crowd and the millions watching on television, there was a sense that the torch had been passed to a new, younger generation of Americans. Bill Clinton was forty-six, the first Democrat to be elected after twelve years of Republican rule during the presidencies of Ronald Reagan and George Bush.

In the classic phrase of American politics, it was, in the minds of many voters, "time for a change," and the vigorous southern governor, like a young California surfer, had caught the wave at its crest and had ridden it to victory.

November, 1991, the Berlin Wall comes down

Divided government, which had seemed to many to contribute to a sense of "gridlock" in Washington, had, for the moment, come to an end. At the same time the voters had chosen Bill Clinton, they had elected a solidly Democratic House of Representatives and maintained Democratic control of the Senate. And the election resulted in a slight gain in the number of Democratic governors. Four more women had been added to the Senate — two from California — and one new senator, Carol Mosely Braun, was the first African American woman to serve in that chamber. Ben Nighthorse Campbell, a Colorado Democrat, became the first Native American to be elected to the Senate in more than sixty years. In the new House, the number of women rose from twenty-eight to forty-seven.

Clinton would have his work cut out for him. Americans were in the grip of a lagging economy, layoffs, and high unemployment. Clinton had promised to revitalize the economy, provide medical care for some thirty-six million Americans who lacked health insur-

California's new senators: Barbara Boxer and Diane Feinstein

ance, and reform the welfare system. How he might accomplish these and other goals, and pay for new programs, remained to be seen. But at that moment of victory, in the night air of his native Arkansas, Bill Clinton held the support and the hopes of millions of Americans.

Clinton would preside over the United States in a world that looked entirely different from the way it had appeared only a few years earlier. During the Bush years, the Cold War that had held the world hostage since the end of the Second World War had ended. The Soviet Union, the Communist superpower, had collapsed. The fear of a nuclear holocaust had not been completely erased, but it had greatly diminished. America turned to dealing with its considerable problems at home.

There were enough of those. Not only the economy and health care, but the quality of education, and the interlocking problems of crime, drugs, poverty, homelessness, and the neglected inner cities. Only six months before the presidential election, Los Angeles had erupted in flames as riots broke out in the south central section of the city and spread to other neighborhoods. Providing jobs for the inner city and rebuilding urban areas were daunting challenges for any new president.

But the results of the 1992 election meant that America would move along a different path from that of the recent past. The inauguration of the new president in January 1993 marked the end of a Republican era, and a fresh start. Clinton and the Democrats brought a different philosophy to governing.

President Bush and his predecessor, Ronald Reagan, had believed in a minimum role for government. While Clinton had distanced himself from the traditional New Deal philosophy that there is a government solution to every social problem, he was much more willing than Bush to use the power of the federal government to try to meet domestic challenges.

Clinton's approach was a clear departure from that of the Reagan-Bush era, just as Ronald Reagan's credo had varied dramatically from that of most of his modern predecessors. Once an actor, later governor of California, Reagan was a conservative Republican who had first been elected president in 1980 on a pledge to reduce the reach and the scope of the federal government in the daily lives of Americans, while increasing the nation's military strength and cutting taxes.

In Reagan's first four years as president, social-welfare programs had indeed been cut back or their rate of growth slowed; income-tax rates had been cut, and

the defense budget had increased. But the percent and number of people living in poverty had also increased, and the federal budget deficit had grown to unprecedented levels.

Reagan's second term was marked by friendlier relations with the Soviet Union and its last leader, Mikhail Gorbachev. But Reagan's final years in the White House were clouded by the disclosure in 1986 that his administration had secretly sold arms to Iran to try to gain the release of American hostages in Lebanon, and that millions of dollars in profits from these sales had been diverted to the U.S.-backed contra rebels in Nicaragua. Even six years later, the Iran-contra scandal had created problems for President Bush during the 1992 campaign, as new evidence cast doubt on his oft-repeated claim that he was "out of the loop" on the arrangements to trade arms for hostages. After he lost the election, Bush pardoned former Secretary of Defense Caspar W. Weinberger and five other former government officials involved in the Iran-contra affair.

Los Angeles, 1992

**Closed U.S. steel plant,
Youngstown, Ohio**

By the early 1990s, America's perception of itself had changed. The almost boundless confidence of a nation that had pushed westward to the Pacific across a land of seemingly unlimited resources had given way, at least in the minds of many people, to a more cautious appraisal of America's ability to solve its problems.

At home, economic ills had become the number-one issue in the presidential election. In several areas of the country, smokestack industries had declined sharply, resulting in economic dislocation and hardship for the blue-collar workers who were laid off or dismissed in the steel, automobile, and other plants. Trade competition from Japan and other industrialized nations meant that the United States was no longer assured of economic pre-eminence in the world.

There were changes as well in the shape of American politics. Special-interest groups, often well financed and supporting a single issue, had become powerful actors in the nation's politics. Often such groups contributed to political candidates through political action committees (PACs), which had grown in number and importance even though some candidates declined to accept PAC money. Other trends were visible: the nation's political parties appeared to be declining in importance, and public confidence in the institutions of government was relatively low.[1]

---

[1] For example, according to a 1991 Gallup poll, only 18 percent of the public said they had "a great deal or quite a lot of confidence" in Congress. The comparable figure for the Supreme Court was 39 percent, and for the presidency, 50 percent. Source: *The Gallup Poll Monthly*, October 1991, p. 37.

Abroad, American influence and military power, while still enormous, did not always seem capable of achieving long-range goals. President Bush had dispatched half a million troops to the Persian Gulf; in the brief war fought early in 1991, the American military forced Iraq's dictator, Saddam Hussein, to withdraw from Kuwait. But during the 1992 election, Saddam was still in power in Iraq, and it was revealed that the United States had actually helped to strengthen Iraq's forces during the 1980s. And there was still no permanent peace in the Middle East among Israel and its neighbors.

Although the threat of nuclear war had receded, the danger of the spread of nuclear weapons to third-world countries had, if anything, increased. It seemed inevitable that more countries would acquire such weapons. At the same time, the United States found itself called upon to intervene in local or regional conflicts, or for humanitarian purposes. Late in 1992, for example, President Bush, with the support of the United Nations, dispatched the first of 28,000 Marines to restore order in Somalia and feed the starving people of that African nation.

Bill Clinton had been elected in 1992 at a moment in history when the American nation had passed through a long and extraordinarily turbulent period of assassination, civil unrest, war, abuse of presidential power, and economic hardship. The murder of President John F. Kennedy had been followed within two years by explosions of anger in the black areas of the nation's cities, by eight years of war in Vietnam, by the Watergate scandal and the resignation and pardon of Richard Nixon, by the seizure in Iran of American hostages who were held more than fourteen months until their release in 1981, by the painful combination of

An American in Vietnam

inflation and unemployment of the 1970s and part of the 1980s that had become an economic recession by the early 1990s, by the Persian Gulf War, and by the riots in Los Angeles in 1992.

The swirling currents of these events, over a period of three decades, had brought change not only to America but to the way Americans perceived their government and their political system. Anger at political leaders and disillusion with the political system characterized the national mood in the election of 1992, along with a desire for change.

Even before the Reagan-Bush years, many liberals and conservatives alike had questioned the effectiveness of government solutions to some social problems. Five decades earlier, President Franklin D. Roosevelt had ushered in an era of great social reform through federal government programs. John F. Kennedy and Lyndon Johnson had followed in his path. But many of the programs of Johnson's "Great Society" had not worked as their architects had envisioned, and in 1980 Reagan successfully assailed the "bureaucracy" and the government in Washington.

Despite the problems facing both individuals and the nation as a whole, there were some encouraging signs as well. The American political system had weathered the storm of Watergate, and that great crisis had been resolved within the framework of the Constitution. In the aftermath, at least some reform had occurred; a new campaign finance law had been enacted to try to regulate the abuses of political contributions, and

the law also provided for public financing of presidential campaigns. There were other signs of change. In 1984, Geraldine Ferraro was the Democratic candidate for vice-president, the first woman to be nominated for that office by a major political party. In that same year, the Reverend Jesse L. Jackson emerged as the first major African American candidate to seek the Democratic presidential nomination, as he did even more dramatically in 1988. More women, more African Americans, and more Hispanics were elected to Congress in 1992.

The new president might or might not succeed in achieving his goals. But beyond the policies of a particular president, broader questions were raised by the problems the nation had experienced over the past three decades.

After some two hundred years, was the American political system capable of meeting the social and economic needs of the American people and preserving their security? Could those goals be met and the huge federal deficit reduced as well? Were the nation's institutions outmoded or too slow to change with the times? Could America's industries remain competitive with those of other nations? At the same time, could Americans preserve the environment? In a multicultural society, with minority groups increasing in numbers, could Americans learn to put aside racial divisions and live in harmony? Was the American democracy still workable, even though it had been subjected to unusual pressures?

These and other questions will be explored in this book, but first it might be useful to examine the general relationship between people and government in a democratic system.

THE RECIPROCAL NATURE OF DEMOCRATIC POWER

In July 1945 a small group of scientists stood atop a hill near Alamogordo, New Mexico, and watched the first atomic bomb explode in the desert. At that instant the traditional power of government to alter the lives of people took on a terrifying new dimension. With the onset of the nuclear age and the development of intercontinental ballistic missiles (ICBMs), people have lived less than thirty minutes away from possible destruction. That is all the time it would take for ICBMs to reach their targets, destroying whole cities and perhaps entire nations. With the collapse of the Soviet Union in 1991 and the end of the Cold War, these concerns have diminished considerably, but not disappeared alto-

gether. The world seemed a safer place, but as of 1992 many of the missiles were still in their silos, in the United States, Russia, and China.

At the height of the Cold War, when America and the Soviet Union faced each other as hostile superpowers, the president of the United States was often described as a person with his finger "on the nuclear button." The existence of such chilling terminology, and of nuclear weapons, reflects the increasingly complex, technological, computerized society in which Americans live. As America has changed through the development of science, technology, and industrialization, government has changed along with it. Government has expanded and grown more complex; it is called on to perform more and more tasks.

The Impact of Government on People

Obviously, government can affect the lives of students or other citizens by sending them overseas to fight in a war in which they may be killed. Less obvious, perhaps, are the ways in which government pervades most aspects of daily life, sometimes down to minute details. For example, the federal government regulates the amount of windshield that the wipers on a car must cover and even the *speed* of the windshield wipers. (At the fast setting, wipers must go "at least 45 cycles per minute.")[2]

College students driving to class (perhaps over a highway built largely with federal funds) are expected to observe local traffic regulations. They may have to put a coin in a city parking meter. The classroom in which they sit may have been constructed with a federal grant. Possibly they are attending college with the aid of federal loans or grants. By 1992, for example, the government was spending $11.7 billion a year to assist six million college undergraduates and graduate students.

Clearly government's impact is real and far-reaching. Americans normally must pay three levels of taxes—local, state, and federal. They attend public schools and perhaps public colleges. They draw unemployment insurance, welfare benefits, Medicare, and social security. They must either obey the laws or pay the penalty of a fine or imprisonment if they break them and are caught and convicted. Their savings accounts and home mortgages are guaranteed by the federal gov-

[2] Motor Vehicle Safety Standards 104 (1991).

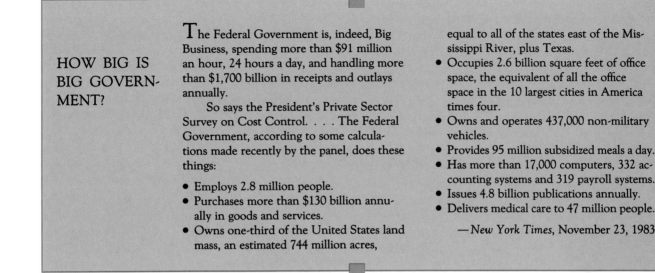

HOW BIG IS BIG GOVERNMENT?

The Federal Government is, indeed, Big Business, spending more than $91 million an hour, 24 hours a day, and handling more than $1,700 billion in receipts and outlays annually.

So says the President's Private Sector Survey on Cost Control. . . . The Federal Government, according to some calculations made recently by the panel, does these things:

- Employs 2.8 million people.
- Purchases more than $130 billion annually in goods and services.
- Owns one-third of the United States land mass, an estimated 744 million acres,

equal to all of the states east of the Mississippi River, plus Texas.
- Occupies 2.6 billion square feet of office space, the equivalent of all the office space in the 10 largest cities in America times four.
- Owns and operates 437,000 non-military vehicles.
- Provides 95 million subsidized meals a day.
- Has more than 17,000 computers, 332 accounting systems and 319 payroll systems.
- Issues 4.8 billion publications annually.
- Delivers medical care to 47 million people.

—*New York Times*, November 23, 1983

ernment. Their taxes support the armed forces and police, fire, health, and sanitation departments. To hunt, fish, marry, drive, fly, or build they must have a government license. From birth certificate to death certificate, government accompanies individuals along the way. Even after they die, the government is not through with them. Estate taxes must be collected and wills probated in the courts.

In the United States, "government" is extraordinarily complicated. There are federal, state, and local layers of government, metropolitan areas, commissions, authorities, boards and councils, and quasi-governmental bodies. Many of the units of government overlap. And all have an impact on the lives of individuals.

The Impact of People on Government

Just as government affects people, people affect government. The American system of government is based on the concept that power flows from the people to the government. Jefferson expressed this eloquently when he wrote in the Declaration of Independence, "to secure these rights, Governments are instituted among men, deriving their just powers from the consent of the governed." Abraham Lincoln expressed the same thought in his Gettysburg Address, speaking of "government of the people, by the people, for the people."

These are ideals, statements embodying the principles of democracy. As we shall note at many points in

this book, the principles do not always mesh with the practices. Yet, it remains true that if government in the United States has very real and often awesome powers over people, at the same time people, both individuals and the mass of citizens together, can have considerable power over the government.

The reciprocal nature of democratic power is a basic element of the American political system. As V. O. Key, Jr., the distinguished Harvard political scientist, put it: "The power relationship is reciprocal, and the subject may affect the ruler more profoundly than the ruler affects the subject." [3] Described below are several ways that people influence government.

Voting The first and most important power of the people in America is the right to vote in free elections to choose those who govern. At regular intervals, the people may, in the classic phrase of Horace Greeley, the nineteenth-century journalist and politician, "turn the rascals out." The fact that a president, member of Congress, governor, mayor, or school-board member may want to stand for reelection influences his or her performance in office. The knowledge of officials that they serve at the pleasure of the voters usually tends to make those officials sensitive to public opinion.

But isn't one person's vote insignificant when millions are cast? Not necessarily. That the individual's vote does matter even in a nation as big as the United States

---

[3] V. O. Key, Jr., *Politics, Parties, and Pressure Groups*, 5th ed. (New York: Crowell, 1964), p. 3.

Visitors at the Vietnam Veterans Memorial, Washington, D.C.

has been illustrated many times in close presidential elections.

Presidents are elected by electoral votes, but these are normally cast by the electors in each state for the candidate who wins the most popular votes in the state.[4] In 1960 a shift from John F. Kennedy to Richard M. Nixon of only 9,421 voters in Illinois and Missouri would have prevented either candidate from gaining a majority in the electoral college. And in 1968 and 1976, shifts of relatively small numbers of voters in a few states would have changed the outcomes of the presidential elections in those years.

Party Activity The political party is basic to the American system of government because it provides a vehicle for competition and choice. Without these, "free elections" would be meaningless. Despite an exceptionally strong showing by an independent candidate for president in 1992, for the most part, the two-party system has predominated in the United States. Since candidates for public office, even at the presidential level, are usually selected by their parties, people can influence government, and the choice of who governs, by participating in party activities. Whether political campaigns offer meaningful alternatives on the issues depends in part on who is nominated. And that in turn may be influenced by how many people are politically active. Political participation can take many forms, from

---

[4] See the description of the electoral college in Chapter 9.

ringing doorbells to running for local party committees or for public office.

Public Opinion   Candidates and elected officials are sensitive to what the public is thinking. This has been particularly true since the Second World War when sophisticated methods of political polling and statistical analysis were developed. But citizens do not have to wait around to be polled. They can make their opinion felt in a variety of ways: by participating in political activities, talking to other people, writing to their representatives in Congress, telephoning the members of their city council, writing to their newspapers, or testifying at public hearings. Even by reading the newspapers and watching television news broadcasts (or by not doing those things) people may indirectly influence government. A citizen who carefully follows public issues in the news media and magazines of opinion may help to influence government, since a government is less likely to attempt to mislead when it knows it is dealing with an informed public.

Interest Groups   When people belong to groups that share common attitudes and make these views felt, or when they organize such groups, they may be influencing government. These private associations, or interest groups, may be business and professional organizations, unions, racial and religious groups, or organizations of groups such as farmers or veterans. An interest group does not have to be an organized body. Students, for example, constitute a highly vocal interest group, even when they do not belong to a formal student organization.

Direct Action   In the late 1960s and early 1970s, as had happened before in American history, people sought to influence government by civil disobedience and sometimes by militant or violent action. Some civil rights leaders and student activists practiced "the politics of confrontation." The idea of direct and often disruptive action to achieve political ends appeared to have grown in part out of the civil rights movement (beginning with peaceful "sit-ins" to desegregate lunch counters in the South) and in part out of the organized opposition to the war in Vietnam. Demonstrations, marches, sit-ins, campus strikes, picketing, and protest characterized those years.

With the end of the war in Vietnam, this type of direct political action diminished considerably, but plainly it could return again if tensions in American society or in the world increased. In the 1980s, for example, several political leaders, both blacks and whites, were arrested in Washington, New York, and other cities while demonstrating at South African diplomatic missions to protest that country's policy of "apartheid," or racial separation. Farmers demonstrated

Police confront anti-abortion demonstrators, Wichita, 1991

in Washington for government assistance, and gay men and women, peace activists, and other groups held rallies on the Mall in the nation's capital to focus attention on their goals. And anti-abortion, "pro-life" groups have sought to prevent women from having abortions by blocking access to clinics.

WHAT IS GOVERNMENT?

The words "government," "politics," "power," and "democracy" ought to be clearly defined. The difficulty is that political scientists, philosophers, and kings have never been able to agree entirely on the meanings of these terms.

The ancient Greek philosopher Plato and his pupil Aristotle speculated on their meaning, and the process has continued up to the present day. Bearing in mind that no universal or perfect definitions exist, we can still discuss the words and arrive at a *general* concept of what they mean.

Government

Even in a primitive society, some form of government exists. A tribal chief emerges with authority over others and makes decisions, perhaps in consultation with the elders of the tribe. The tribal leader is governing.

Government, then, even in a modern industrial state, can be defined on a simple level as the individuals, institutions, and processes that make the rules for society and possess the power to enforce them. But rules for what? To take an example, if private developers wish to acquire a wildlife preserve for commercial use, and environmental groups protest, government may be called on to step in and settle the dispute. In short, government makes rules to decide who gets what of valued things in a society.[5] It attempts to resolve conflicts among individuals and groups.

David Easton, a political scientist at the University of Chicago, has written:

> Even in the smallest and simplest society someone must intervene in the name of society, with its authority behind him, to decide how differences over valued things are to be resolved.

This authoritative allocation of values is a minimum prerequisite of any society. . . . Every society provides some mechanisms, however rudimentary they may be, for authoritatively resolving differences about the ends that are to be pursued, that is, for deciding who is to get what there is of the desirable things.[6]

Easton's concept has come to be broadly accepted by many scholars today. In highly developed societies the principal mechanism for resolving differences is government. Government makes binding rules for society that determine the distribution of valued things.

Politics

Benjamin Disraeli, the nineteenth-century British prime minister and novelist, wrote in *Endymion* that "politics are the possession and distribution of power."

Disraeli's definition of *politics* comes very close to our definition of *government*. Disraeli was ahead of his time, for many political scientists today would agree in general with his definition, and they would add that there is little difference between politics and government.

For example, V. O. Key, Jr., equated politics with "the process and practice of ruling" and the "workings of governments generally, their impact on the governed, their manner of operation, the means by which governors attain and retain authority."[7] In other words, politics may be defined as the pursuit and exercise of power.

Such a definition might be confusing to those Americans who tend to look at politics as the pursuit of power, and government as the exercise of power. The conventional notion is that people engage in politics to get elected. But, in fact, those who govern are constantly making *political* decisions. It is very difficult to say where government ends and politics begins. The two terms overlap and intertwine, even if their meanings are not precisely the same.[8]

---

[5] A definition close to that suggested by the title of Harold D. Lasswell's *Politics: Who Gets What, When, How* (New York: McGraw-Hill, 1936).

[6] David Easton, *The Political System: An Inquiry into the State of Political Science* (New York: Knopf, 1953), pp. 136–37.

[7] Key, *Politics, Parties, and Pressure Groups*, p. 2.

[8] Of course, the word "politics" can also refer to a process that occurs in a wide variety of nongovernmental settings — in fact, in every form of social organization where different people, with competing goals and differing objectives, interact. Thus, one sometimes speaks of politics in the local PTA, the politics of a garden club, or the politics in the newsroom of a campus newspaper. In this book, however, we are talking about politics as it is more commonly understood, in its governmental setting.

August, 1991: Russian president Boris Yeltsin leads resistance to the coup attempt against Mikhail Gorbachev

Power

Power is the possession of control over others. People have sought for centuries to understand the basis of power, why it exists, and how it is maintained. Authority over others is a tenuous business, as many a deposed South American dictator can attest.

A century ago, Boss Tweed, the leader of Tammany Hall, the Democratic party machine in New York City, reportedly expressed a simple, cynical philosophy: "The way to have power is to take it." But once acquired, power must be defended against others who desire it. For seven years Nikita Khrushchev appeared to be the unquestioned ruler of the Soviet Union. One day in October 1964, he was summoned back to Moscow from his Black Sea vacation retreat and informed by his colleagues in the Presidium of the Communist party that he was no longer premier of the Soviet Union. It was reported that those who deposed him changed all

the confidential government and party telephone numbers in Moscow, so that Khrushchev could not attempt to rally support among elements still loyal to him.[9] Khrushchev was helpless, cut off from the tremendous power that was his only twenty-four hours before.

The coup against Khrushchev had its echo more than twenty-five years later when a group of hard-liners in the Kremlin attempted to overthrow Mikhail Gorbachev in August of 1991 while the Soviet leader was vacationing—again at a dacha on the Black Sea. The coup failed, thanks to the intervention of Russia's president, Boris N. Yeltsin, who mounted a tank to defy the coup-plotters. But four months later, Gorbachev had resigned, the Soviet Union had broken up, and Yeltsin emerged as the most influential leader of the former Soviet republics.

---

[9] *Observer* (London), November 29, 1964, p. 2.

It is a truism that power is often destructive of those who hold it. Lord Acton, the nineteenth-century British peer and historian, said that "power tends to corrupt and absolute power corrupts absolutely." The eighteenth-century French philosopher Montesquieu expressed a similar idea in *The Spirit of the Laws*: "Every man who has power is impelled to abuse it."

As Key has observed, power is not something that can be "poured into a keg, stored, and drawn upon as the need arises." [10] Power, Key notes, is *relational* — that is, it involves the interactions between the person who exercises power and those affected by that exercise of power.

If people, even in a primitive state, find it necessary to accept rulers who can authoritatively decide who gets what, then it follows that whoever governs possesses and exercises power in part because of that position. In other words, power follows office. To some extent, we accept the power exercised over us by others because we recognize the need to be governed.

Democracy

Democracy is a word that comes from two Greek roots, *demos*, the populace, and *kratia*, rule — taken together, rule by the people.[11] The Greeks used the term to describe the government of Athens and other Greek city-states that flourished in the fifth century B.C. In his famous *Funeral Oration*, Pericles, the Athenian statesman, declared: "Our constitution is named a democracy, because it is in the hands not of the few, but of the many."

All governments make decisions about the distribution of valued things. As was noted earlier, in a democratic government, power, in theory, flows from the people as a whole. This is one of the ideals on which the American democracy was founded. But the United States is too big for every citizen to take part in the deliberations of government, as in ancient Athens, so the distinction is sometimes made that America is a *representative* democracy rather than a direct one. Leaders are elected to speak for and represent the people.

Government by the people also carries with it the concept of *majority rule*. Everyone is free to vote, but normally whoever gets the most votes wins the election and represents *all* the people, including those who voted for the losing candidate. But in a system that is truly democratic, minority rights and views are also recognized and protected.

Every schoolchild knows the phrase from the Declaration of Independence, "We hold these truths to be self-evident, that all men are created equal." The concept of *equality* — that all people are of equal worth, even if not of equal ability — is also basic to American democracy. So are basic *rights* such as freedom of speech, press, religion, assembly, the right to vote, and the right to dissent from majority opinion. The idea of *individual dignity* and the importance of each individual is another concept basic to American democracy. And, American government is *constitutional* — the power of government is limited by a framework of fundamental written law. Under such a government — in theory — the police power of the state should not be used illegally to punish individuals or to repress dissent.

These are the ideals, noble, even beautiful, in their conception. But, this is not always what really happens. African Americans and other minorities in America are still struggling for full equality; a person may dissent from the dominant political view but lose his or her job as the price of nonconformity; the probing questions asked of people on welfare may leave them with little

---

[10] Key, *Politics, Parties, and Pressure Groups*, p. 2.

[11] There are, of course, many possible definitions of the word "democracy." The Greek word *demos* meant the populace, or the common people; hence democracy in this sense means government by the mass of people, as distinguished from those with special rank or status.

individual dignity; the police sometimes have their own views on freedom of assembly; and, as the Watergate scandal of the early 1970s revealed, the White House has committed many abuses in the name of national security. A few years later, congressional investigations disclosed other widespread violations of the constitutional rights of individuals by federal intelligence agencies. In the 1980s, the Iran-contra scandal revealed that officials in the White House itself had acted outside the law in the pursuit of foreign-policy objectives.

American democracy is far from perfect. "This is a great country," President John F. Kennedy once declared, "but it must be greater." [12] Every American has to judge for herself or himself how far America falls short of fulfilling the principles on which it was founded. Nevertheless, the ideals endure; the goals are there if not always the reality.

THE CONCEPT OF A POLITICAL SYSTEM

In today's electronic world, most people have listened to a stereo. Suppose for a moment that a visitor from outer space dropped in and asked you to describe a stereo system. You might say, "This is a compact disc player. I'm putting this CD in the little drawer that slides back in. This thing with all the knobs and buttons is an amplifier, and these big boxes over here are what we call speakers." Perhaps you might take the trouble to describe the details of each component at some length. At the end of your elaborate explanation, the visitor from space would still not know what a stereo was.

A better way to describe the compact disc player and the other components would be to explain that it is a *system for the reproduction of sound*, consisting of several parts, each of which performs a separate function and relates to the others. Having said that, you might turn on the power and play some music. Now the visitor would understand.

A Dynamic Approach

In the same way, it is possible either to describe people, government, politics, and power as isolated, static elements, or to look at them as interacting elements in a *political system*. The concept of a political system may provide a useful framework, or approach, for understanding the total subject matter of this book. Just as in the case of the stereo system, a political system consists of several parts that relate to one another, each of which performs a separate, vital function. If we think in terms of a system, we visualize all the pieces in motion, acting and interacting, dynamic rather than static. In other words, something is happening—just as when the compact disc is playing.

As David Easton says, "we can try to understand political life by viewing each of its aspects piecemeal," or we can "view political life as a system of interrelated activities." [13] One of the problems of trying to look at a political system is that government and politics do not exist in a vacuum—they are embedded in, and closely related to, many other activities in a society. But it is possible to separate political activity from other kinds of activity, at least for purposes of study.

Just as the CD player is part of a stereo system for the reproduction of sound, a political system also operates for a purpose: it makes the binding, authoritative decisions for society about who gets what.

Inputs, Outputs, and Feedback

We may carry the analogy of a stereo system to a political system even further. A sound system has *inputs, outputs,* and sometimes a loud whistling noise called *feedback*. Those are precisely the same terms used by political scientists in talking about a political system.

The *inputs* of a political system are of two kinds: demands and supports.

- "Demands," as the word indicates, are what people and groups want from the system, whether it be health care for the aged, loans for college students, equal opportunity for minorities, or higher subsidies for farmers.
- "Supports" are the attitudes and actions of people that sustain and buttress the system at all levels and allow it to continue to work. They include everything

---

[12] "Remarks of Senator John F. Kennedy, Street Rally, Waterbury, Connecticut, November 6, 1960," in *The Speeches of Senator John F. Kennedy, Presidential Campaign of 1960* (Washington, D.C.: U.S. Government Printing Office, 1961), p. 912.

[13] David Easton, "An Approach to the Analysis of Political Systems," *World Politics*, vol. 9 (April 1957), pp. 383–84. Our discussion of the concept of a political system relies chiefly on Easton's work, although it should not be read as a literal summary of his approach. For example, the analogy to a stereo system is the authors' own, and Easton's analysis of a political system is both much more detailed and broader in scope than the outline presented here.

from the patriotism drilled into schoolchildren to public backing for specific government policies.

The *outputs* of a political system are chiefly the binding decisions it makes, whether in the form of laws, regulations, or judicial decisions. Often such decisions reward one segment of society at the expense of another. The millionaire on New York's Park Avenue may be heavily taxed to clothe inner-city children on the South Side of Chicago. Or he may benefit from a tax loophole enacted by Congress and pay no taxes at all. The freeway that runs through a poor urban neighborhood may speed white commuters from the suburbs but dislocate black residents of the inner city. These decisions are "redistributive" measures in that something of value is reallocated by the political system. Sometimes even a decision *not* to act is an output of a political system. By preserving an existing policy, one group may be rewarded while another group is not.

Feedback in a political system describes the response of the rest of society to the decisions made by the authorities. When those reactions are communicated back to the authorities, they may lead to a fresh round of decisions and new public responses.

The concept of a political system is simply a way of looking at political activity. It is an approach, an analytical tool, rather than a general theory of the type developed to explain the workings of scientific phenomena. It enables us to examine not only the formal structure of political and governmental institutions, but also how these institutions actually work.

PUBLIC POLICYMAKING

There is a tendency in the study of American politics and government to concentrate on the institutions of government, such as the presidency, Congress, and the courts, and on the role of political parties, campaigns, and voters.

The *analysis of public policy* is another way of looking at government and politics. Instead of examining only institutions, policy analysis looks at what the institutions do.

A *policy* is a course of action decided upon by a government — or by any organization, group, or individual. It involves *a choice among competing alternatives.* When policies are shaped by government officials, the result is called *public policy.*

The analysis of public policy, therefore, focuses on how choices are arrived at and how public policy is made. It also focuses on what happens afterward. How well or badly is a policy carried out? What is its impact in its own policy area? And what effect does it have in other policy areas?

As Robert L. Lineberry has put it, policy analysts "focus, in systems language, on the outputs of the political system and their impact on the political, social, and economic environment." [14]

As Lineberry and other scholars have pointed out, if a problem does not get on the *public agenda* — the subjects that government policymakers try to deal with — no policy or output will be framed to deal with the problem. "Political issues emerge from contending defi-

---

[14] Robert L. Lineberry, *American Public Policy: What Government Does and What Difference It Makes* (New York: Harper & Row, 1977), p. 3.

nitions of a policy problem." [15] Thus, some people feel marijuana should be legalized, but unless a federal or state government acts, its possession and sale remain illegal.

But what happens when an issue does get on the public agenda and results in the creation of a public policy? Sometimes nothing. In 1964 President Lyndon Johnson declared his "war on poverty." A major new federal program was launched to try to deal with the problem. But three decades later, poverty had not been eradicated and had actually increased in America.

In other words, programs do not always work as intended. "Bills are passed, White House Rose Garden ceremonies held, and gift pens passed around by the president. At that point, when attention has waned, when the television cameras are gone and the reporters no longer present, the other face of policy emerges." [16] This second face of policy analysis, as Lineberry has suggested, is concerned with *implementation*, *impact*, and *distribution*.

Implementation is the action, or actions, taken by government to carry out a policy. "When policy is pronounced, the implementation process begins. What happens in it may, over the long run, have far more impact . . . than the intentions of the policy's framers." [17]

The *impact* of a policy can be measured in terms of its consequences, both in its immediate policy area and in other areas. For example, a government decision to combat inflation by tightening credit and raising interest rates may result in the closing of automobile plants

---

[15] Ibid., p. 24.

[16] Ibid., p. 69.
[17] Ibid., p. 71.

and worker layoffs because consumers have less money to use to buy cars. The closing of the auto plants may, in turn, lead to layoffs in the steel industry, since steel is a major supplier of the auto industry.

Distribution is concerned with the question of who wins and who loses from a given public policy. When the government builds post offices or maintains national parks, its policies are distributive, and people assume that everyone benefits. But a redistributive policy takes something away from one person and gives it to someone else. A welfare program that taxes more affluent members of society to assist the poor would be an example of such a policy. It is here in the area of redistributive policies that many of the major political battles are fought.

Public policies and policymaking are discussed throughout this book, and are the subject, in particular, of Part Four, "Government in Operation."

DEMOCRATIC GOVERNMENT AND A CHANGING SOCIETY

A political system relates to people, and the size of the population affects the outputs of the system. Of equal importance is the qualitative nature of the population: who they are, where they live, how they work, how they spend, how they move about. How the political system works, in other words, is affected to some extent by the surrounding social, economic, and cultural framework. As society changes, the responses of government are likely to change. Government reacts to basic alterations in the nature of a society; it tries to tailor programs and decision making to meet changing needs and demands. Population changes are also important politically; for example, the 1990 census data confirmed that the American population balance had continued to shift from the Northeast to the South and West. As a result, southern and western states gained more seats in Congress in 1992.

254,000,000 Americans

In 1990 federal census-takers fanned out across America, counting the population, as the Constitution requires every ten years. By the end of the year, 248.7 million people had been counted, a total that had risen to 254 million by 1992, according to Census Bureau

estimates. The Census Bureau predicts that by the year 2000 the figure may conceivably rise as high as 276 million.[18]

According to one study of population patterns in the United States, if the projections of some experts were realized, "we would have close to one billion people in the United States one hundred years from now."[19] Although the authors of the study add that birth control and other factors make it unlikely that such a staggering total will be reached by that time, they estimate that the United States *could* support a popula-

[18] U.S. Bureau of the Census, Current Population Reports, Supplement to *Projections of the Population of the United States, by Age, Sex, and Race: 1988 to 2080*, series P-25, no. 1018, January 1989, p. 33; figures rounded.

[19] Ben J. Wattenberg, in collaboration with Richard M. Scammon, *This U.S.A.* (New York: Doubleday, 1965), p. 18. Population projections have been lowered since this study was published.

Table 1-1
Profile of the United States Population, 1790–2010

	Population (in millions) Actual							Projected	
	1790	1870	1920	1960	1970	1980	1990	2000	2010
Total Population	4	39	106	179	203	226.5	248.7	276	301
Urban	—*	10	54	125	149	167	187	NA	NA
Rural	4	29	52	54	54	60	62	NA	NA
Nonwhite	1	5	11	20	25	32	49	48	58
White	3	34	95	159	178	195	200	228	243
Median age (years)	NA†	20	25	30	28.1	30	33	36	37
Primary and secondary school enrollment	NA	7	23	42	53	45	43	53	NA
College enrollment	NA	—*	.6	3	7	10	18	16	NA

* Less than 200,000
† NA: Not Available
SOURCE: U.S. Bureau of the Census, and National Center for Education Statistics, Department of Education. Projected totals are the most likely estimates as of 1989. Population figures rounded.

tion of one billion without people pushing one another into the ocean.

How the nation has expanded from a population of about 4 million in 1790, and what the future may hold, can be charted with Census Bureau statistics and projections to the year 2010, as shown in Table 1-1.

This dramatic increase in numbers of people — the "population explosion" — is taking place around the world. It raises questions that governments must ponder. Will there be enough food to eat? Enough room to live? Enough oil and other natural resources to meet humanity's future needs? Will the environment be destroyed?

Table 1-2
Who Are We?*

127.4 million females
121.2 million males
  18.3 million under five years
  31.2 million sixty-five and over
199.6 million white
  49.1 million nonwhite
118.8 million married
  28.9 million divorced or widowed
182.1 million old enough to vote
  17.9 million in college
  47.1 million in other schools
115.7 million employed
187.1 million urban dwellers
  59.0 million homeowners

* Data for 1990.
SOURCE: U.S. Bureau of the Census.

An interesting profile of the American public can be sketched with statistics that answer the question "Who are we?" (See Table 1-2.) A portrait of national origins can also be drawn. The great successive waves of immigration placed a stamp of diversity on America; even third- and fourth-generation Americans may think of themselves as "Irish" or "Italian." The 1990 census included a survey indicating that the ancestry groups of Americans included the following: German, 23.3 percent; Irish, 15.6 percent; English, 13.1 percent; African American, 12 percent; Hispanic, 8.6 percent; Italian, 6.0 percent; French, 4.1 percent; Polish, 4.0 percent; Asian Americans, 2.9 percent; Dutch, 2.5 percent; Scottish, 2.2 percent; and Native American, .08 percent.[20]

The United States is also a nation of more than 79.4 million Protestants, 57 million Catholics, and 5.9 million Jews.[21] Sometimes, prevailing notions about America's population are incorrect. For example, America is generally thought to be a nation of white, Anglo-Saxon Protestants. That group is influential in many areas of our national life. But as the national origin figures indicate, a majority of Americans stem from other than Anglo-Saxon stock.[22]

---

[20] Data provided by U.S. Bureau of the Census.
[21] The Census Bureau does not ask the religion of Americans in the decennial census, which has been taken every ten years in years that end in zero, but religious groups estimate their own membership. These are rounded figures based on the *Yearbook of American and Canadian Churches, 1991*, Constant H. Jacquet, Jr., and Alice M. Jones, eds. (Nashville: Abingdon Press, 1991), p. 270.
[22] See Wattenberg and Scammon, *This U.S.A.*, pp. 45–46.

creased. By the 1990s, Congress, although still concerned with price supports for farm products and the alarming number of farm foreclosures, was focusing more of its attention on such issues as budget deficits and the level of defense spending.

Americans move about a great deal. According to the Census Bureau, about 20 percent of Americans change their residence each year. In 1964 California surpassed New York as the most populous state in the Union. As a result, presidential candidates now spend more time than they used to campaigning in California. And in four of seven recent presidential election years, 1968, 1972, 1980, and 1984, Californians were elected president.

During and after the Second World War, as blacks migrated to northern cities, many whites in the central cities were moving to the suburbs. All these shifts and changing population patterns affect the American political system. The migration of millions of African American citizens to northern cities resulted in the election of black mayors in several large cities by the mid-1970s and in the election of more African American members of Congress. And the population shift from the cities to the suburbs increased the political power of suburbia. More members of Congress and state legislators now represent suburban areas than in the past, because lawmakers are apportioned according to population.

Although the accent in America is on youth, the median age of Americans is not eighteen or twenty-one but about thirty-three, and likely to go up as a result of a decline in the birth rate during the 1960s, combined with greater life expectancy.

The Mobile Society

A political system reacts not only to shifts in population totals but also to the *movement* of people geographically, socially, and economically.

For example, farm population declined from 30.5 million in 1930 to 3.9 million in 1990.[23] As the nation changed from a predominantly rural to an urban society (see Table 1–1), the importance of the "farm bloc" de-

Protest against farm loan policies, Ohio, 1985

---

[23] U.S. Bureau of the Census.

"And I say one bomb is worth a thousand words."

Drawing by Dana Fradon © 1980 The New Yorker Magazine, Inc.

Technological, Economic, and Social Change

In addition to the population explosion, America has experienced a knowledge explosion. Science and technology, computers, electronics, and high-speed communications are reshaping American society. Americans have split the atom and traveled to the moon and back. We listen for signals from other galaxies in outer space, and explore the inner space of the human brain. There appear to be no limits to technological potential — except the inability of human beings to control their own nature.

Technological change is soon reflected within the political system. Consider for a moment a single inno-

vation of the electronic age: television. Prior to the Second World War, television did not exist for the mass of Americans. Today, political candidates spend millions of dollars to purchase television time. Presidential nominees may deplore the "packaging" of political candidates by Madison Avenue, but they hire advertising agencies to do just that. Commercials are produced and presidents and candidates sold in the manner of detergents.

A considerable amount of the electronic-age technology is the by-product of defense research and development. In his farewell address to the nation in 1961, President Eisenhower, although himself a career soldier, warned of the dangers to liberty and democracy of the "military-industrial complex." What Eisenhower

WOMEN IN THE WORKPLACE: A BLUE-COLLAR GLASS CEILING, TOO

American women with college degrees surged into professional and executive occupations in the last decade, but those with less education were unable to break into many male-dominated blue-collar jobs, new census figures show. . . .

But . . . across the nation, less-educated women often remain in low-paying jobs in child care and office work. Two decades after women first broke into male-dominated trades such as construction and auto repair, they hold a tiny minority of those good-paying jobs, unable to overcome remarkably stubborn barriers.

Women hold a little less than 3 percent of jobs in the nation's construction trades, barely changed from 1980, and a little more than 4 percent of repair jobs. Women gained in other types of blue-collar employment. They doubled their share of jobs as postal carriers and now make up nearly half of all bus drivers and dispatchers.

Some specialists say that jobs such as firefighting and construction may be less attractive to women because of strong group cultures that can encourage hostility and harassment from men. . . .

Now, a third or more of medical, law, and business school graduates are women.

Women represent 46 percent of the nation's financial managers, 42 percent of biologists, 21 percent of physicians, and 39 percent of math professors.

By contrast, unfriendly craft unions and tradition-minded job counselors still control access to apprenticeships and training programs that lead to jobs in the blue-collar world, women's advocates say. . . .

"People say women don't want to go into construction because it's a dirty job," said Cynthia Marano, executive director of Wider Opportunities for Women, a national advocacy and training group. "Being a waitress and being a home health care aide are very dirty jobs."

—*Washington Post*, December 21, 1992

feared was that the Pentagon and the defense contractors who produce weapons for the military would gain "unwarranted influence" in the political system.

In the view of economist John Kenneth Galbraith, there already exists a "close fusion of the industrial system with the state," and in time "the line between the two will disappear." As a result of the technological revolution, Galbraith contends, a few hundred huge corporations are shaping the goals of society as a whole.[24] But government, too, exercises great power in the modern industrial state. Government is expected to help prevent either periodic economic recession or depression. Although economists argue over the best methods of managing the economy, they generally agree that the government has the major responsibility in promoting prosperity and full employment.

The past three decades also have been a time of rapid social change in America. At almost every level, wherever one looks, the change is visible — in manners and morals, in civil rights, in the theater, in literature,

and in the arts. The change could be seen as well in the continuing emphasis on a youth-oriented culture, and at the same time, the growing concern over problems of the elderly, whose ranks were increasing in numbers.

These social changes have been accompanied by new political concerns. Today, large numbers of people are disturbed about the pollution of the natural environment that has resulted from technological advance. Many American cities are blanketed in smog despite new laws. Some rivers are cleaner as a result of environmental legislation, but many are polluted by industrial and human waste. Across the land, toxic wastes have endangered communities, even forcing the relocation of an entire town, Times Beach, Missouri, in 1983. Pesticides are killing the wildlife in America.[25] Oil spills from tankers and offshore drilling, and medical waste are fouling beaches. The gasoline engine and power plants and other industries pour smoke and chemicals into the atmosphere. Acid rain, the greenhouse effect, and the deterioration of the ozone layer, are problems that transcend national boundaries.

[24] John Kenneth Galbraith, *The New Industrial State* (Boston: Houghton Mifflin, 1967), pp. 7–9, 392–93.

[25] See Rachel Carson, *Silent Spring* (Boston: Houghton Mifflin, 1962).

It is not only a matter of esthetics, of preserving the natural beauty of the land. Air and water pollution damage health and upset the delicate balance of nature, the total relationship between human beings and their environment. They raise serious questions about whether humanity will be able to survive the damage it is inflicting on the earth that sustains all life.[26]

The long-range problem of energy resources for the future, and the potential threat to the world's oil supply posed by Iraq's invasion of Kuwait in 1990, underscored the fact that environmental problems are, in the end, political problems. They pose for America questions of priorities and values. For example, will people ever be willing to use their cars less to conserve energy and reduce pollution? Do voters favor relaxation of environmental standards to increase the supply of oil and other energy sources? Or to preserve timber jobs in the Pacific northwest at the expense of the spotted owl? The environment and energy needs have created conflicting choices for individual citizens, for political leaders, and for society as a whole.

There were many other areas of conflict and change. Back in the 1960s, for example, to any white American who cared to listen, the message of the times was clear: black Americans would wait no longer to obtain the equality and freedom that are the rights of everyone under the American political system. This was the message preached peacefully by Dr. Martin Luther King, Jr., and expressed violently in the burning black neighborhoods of the nation's cities.

It is not possible to discuss or even list in a few pages all the social, economic, and cultural factors that are influencing the American political system today. Suggested here are simply some of the major changes, currents, and conflicts that have placed enormous pressures on American democracy. In later chapters, these will be taken up in more detail.

The Consent of the Governed

One of the characteristics of a viable political system is that it adapts to change. More than two hundred years after its creation, the ability of the American political

---

[26] We examine the problem of environmental pollution in more detail in Chapter 15.

"Then we agree! We're doing the best job that can be done considering that the country's ungovernable."

Drawing by Dana Fradon © 1978 The New Yorker Magazine, Inc.

system to adapt to relentless change, and to cope with recurring political crises, was being tested.

For a time, at least, the Vietnam War and the Watergate scandal were followed by a new atmosphere of questioning of presidential power by the public and by Congress. That kind of questioning is appropriate in a democracy. President Kennedy declared, in a speech at Amherst College in 1963, less than a month before his death, "men who create power make an indispensable contribution to the Nation's greatness, but the men who question power make a contribution just as indispensable." [27]

For many Americans, the presidency of Ronald Reagan brought a new sense of stability to a nation weary of turmoil and political upheaval. Reagan's election to two terms resulted in the longest presidential tenure since that of Dwight D. Eisenhower in the 1950s. Yet his successor, George Bush, proved a one-term president. Voting for change, the nation turned toward Bill Clinton.

The divisions in American society that had been caused by the war in Vietnam, the trauma of Watergate, and more recently, by the Iran-contra scandal, underscored and renewed a basic truth. The American political system rests on the consent of the governed, but that consent, to be freely given, required that the nation's political leaders earn and merit the trust of the people. In the long afternoon shadows of the twentieth century, such a bond of trust appeared to offer the best hope for the survival in America of democracy, a system that Winston S. Churchill once described as "the worst form of government except all those other forms that have been tried from time to time." [28]

[27] John F. Kennedy, "Remarks at Amherst College," October 26, 1963, in *Public Papers of the Presidents of the United States, John F. Kennedy, 1963* (Washington, D.C.: U.S. Government Printing Office, 1964), p. 816.

[28] *Parliamentary Debates*, House of Commons, Fifth Series, vol. 444 (London: His Majesty's Stationery Office, 1947), pp. 206–07.

Suggested Reading

Easton, David. *The Political System: An Inquiry into the State of Political Science*, 2nd edition* (University of Chicago Press, 1981). (Originally published in 1953.) The first edition was an early statement of the systems approach to the study of politics developed by Easton. See also his *A Framework for Political Analysis** (University of Chicago Press, 1979) and *A Systems Analysis of Political Life** (University of Chicago Press, 1979).

Galbraith, John Kenneth. *The New Industrial State*, 4th edition* (Houghton Mifflin, 1985). A very readable account of changes in the nature and role of the large corporation in the modern state. These changes, Galbraith argues, have had a major effect on political and social life in highly industrialized countries such as the United States.

Gore, Al. *Earth in the Balance: Ecology and the Human Spirit** (Houghton Mifflin, 1992). A strong warning that the quality of the environment and the world's ecosystems are in grave danger. The author, a United States senator, was elected vice-president of the United States in November, 1992.

Key, V. O., Jr. *Public Opinion and American Democracy* (Philadelphia Book Company, 1961). An important work in which the pre-1961 findings concerning public opinion and mass attitudes toward politics are analyzed in terms of their consequences for the actual workings of government.

Lineberry, Robert L. *American Public Policy: What Government Does and What Difference It Makes* (Harper & Row, 1978). A lucid, concise analysis of the making of public policy, its implementation, and its impact. Provides a useful introduction to policy analysis, illustrated by specific case studies.

Nicholas, H. G. *The Nature of American Politics*, 2nd edition* (Oxford University Press, 1986). A survey of major features of the American political system, written by a perceptive English observer. Contains a thoughtful discussion of what the author identifies as the special national style of politics in America.

Schattschneider, Elmer E. *The Semisovereign People* (Holt, Rinehart and Winston, 1975). (Originally published in 1960.) A lively and revealing analysis of the role of American interest groups and political parties in bringing public demands to bear on political officials.

Tocqueville, Alexis de. *Democracy in America*, 2 vols.,* Phillips Bradley, ed. (Knopf, 1945). (Available in many editions.) A classic analysis of American political and social life as seen through the eyes of a nineteenth-century French observer.

Wilson, Edward O. *The Diversity of Life* (Howard University Press, 1992). A wide-ranging survey of the development of life on earth over the last four billion years. Emphasizes the dangers which currently threaten to reduce the number of living species, and argues that it is important to maintain biodiversity.

---

* Available in paperback edition

E VERY EVENING in Washington an unusual ceremony takes place in the great domed Exhibition Hall of the National Archives. There, beneath a gold eagle in the ornate hall, are displayed the Declaration of Independence, the Constitution, and the Bill of Rights. The faded parchments are sealed in protective bronze-and-glass cases containing helium and a small amount of water vapor for preservation.

When the last visitor has left the building, a guard pushes a button. With a great whirring noise, the documents slowly sink into the floor. An electric mechanism

Chapter 2
The Constitutional Framework

gently lowers them into a "fireproof, bombproof vault" of steel and reinforced concrete twenty feet below. A massive lid clangs shut and the documents are safely put to bed for the night. The whole eerie process takes one minute.

Ideas, of course, cannot be preserved in a vault, but documents can. The documents, and the mystique that surrounds them, are part of what Daniel J. Boorstin has called the "search for symbols."[1] The quest for national identity, in which such symbols play a role, is a continuing process in America.

---

[1] Daniel J. Boorstin, *The Americans: The National Experience* (New York: Random House, 1965), pp. 325ff.

But the Constitution is much more than a symbol. The Constitution established the basic structure of the American government and a *written set of rules* to control the conduct of that government; in its own words, the Constitution is "the supreme Law of the Land." The United States was, in fact, the first nation to have a written constitution. It is a charter that has been continually adapted to new problems, principally through amendment and judicial interpretation by the Supreme Court — changes that often reflect the prevailing political climate.

Yet, today, the American political system is sometimes attacked for what its critics see as a failure to respond to urgent national problems. Urban decay and racial disorders in Los Angeles and elsewhere have led to renewed calls for programs to alleviate poverty, crime, and unemployment in the nation's inner cities. Nor were the problems only social and economic; some were political and constitutional. The growth of presidential power in the twentieth century, the Watergate scandal, resulting in the resignation of a president under threat of impeachment, and the Iran-contra affair —

with its disclosures of a secret foreign policy conducted from the White House — have, in recent times, placed great strains on the system of constitutional government. Even though the Constitution is reinterpreted to meet changed conditions, does that process take place fast enough? Is the constitutional framework that was constructed in 1787 sufficiently flexible to meet the needs of a complex, urban society today? Why, for example, did it take nearly one hundred years after the Civil War for the Supreme Court to apply the Constitution to outlaw racial segregation in public schools? Or why did 131 years pass after the nation was founded before the Constitution recognized the right of women to vote?

We will be exploring these questions, and such others as: Who were the framers of the Constitution? What political ideas influenced them? Were they merely interested in protecting their own economic positions? What political bargains were struck by the framers? Why does the United States have a federal system of government, and what does that mean? How did the Supreme Court acquire its power to interpret the Constitution? How does the Constitution affect people's lives today?

Bridget Mergens

THE CONSTITUTION AND THE DECLARATION OF INDEPENDENCE

The Constitution Today

In 1985 Bridget Mergens, a senior at Westside High School in Omaha, Nebraska, asked permission to organize a Christian Bible study group at the school. Although Westside already had other extracurricular activities — a chess club and a scuba diving club, for example — the principal and the school board refused to allow a Bible club.

Public schools are run by local governments, and the First Amendment to the Constitution, as interpreted by the United States Supreme Court, prohibits Congress or state or local governments from enacting any law regarding the "establishment of religion." The school principal said that granting official club status for Bridget Mergens's Bible group would violate the Constitution's "establishment clause."

Mergens, while still in her senior year in high school, took her case to court. She argued that under a 1984 federal law — the Equal Access Act — schools that

receive federal funds, and that allow extracurricular student groups to meet on school grounds, cannot discriminate against a group because of the subject it wishes to discuss. Mergens, in other words, contended that she had as much right to study the scriptures before or after classes as to learn how to scuba dive.

She lost her first round in the lower federal court, but won in a federal appeals court. Omaha school officials then took their case to Washington, to the United States Supreme Court. In June of 1990 the Supreme Court ruled, 8–1, that the Equal Access Act was constitutional and that Mergens's Bible club should have been allowed to meet in her public high school on the same basis as other extracurricular clubs.[2]

Justice Sandra Day O'Connor, writing the Court's opinion, said: "We think that secondary school students are mature enough and are likely to understand that a school does not endorse or support student speech that it merely permits on a nondiscriminatory basis.

"There is a crucial difference between government speech endorsing religion, which the establishment clause forbids, and private speech endorsing religion, which the free speech and free exercise clauses protect."[3]

---

[2] *Board of Education of Westside Community Schools* v. *Mergens,* 496 U.S. 226 (1990).

[3] *Ibid.*

A teenager had successfully taken her case to the highest court in the land (although she was 23 years old, married, and long out of high school when the Supreme Court ruled in her favor). In *Mergens*, the Supreme Court wrote another chapter in the continuing battle over the proper place of religion in the public schools. It interpreted the Constitution in favor of religious expression, even on school property, rejecting arguments that a Bible group violated the constitutional provision for separation of church and state.

In that same year, 1990, the Supreme Court, although by then generally described as politically conservative, nevertheless delivered one of its most controversial opinions in support of freedom of expression. It struck down a federal law that made it a crime to burn or deface the American flag. The emotionally charged issue of flag burning had first come before the court in an earlier case. In 1984, at the Republican National Convention in Dallas, Gregory Lee Johnson had taken part in a protest against the policies of President Reagan's administration. Johnson doused an American flag with kerosene and set it on fire while dozens of demonstrators chanted, "America, the red, white and blue, we spit on you." He was convicted of violating the Texas flag desecration law, fined $2,000, and sentenced to one year in prison. When the case reached the Supreme Court, the justices ruled, 5–4, that the Texas law and all federal and state laws protecting the flag violated the right of freedom of speech, contained in the First Amendment to the Constitution.[4]

Justice William J. Brennan, Jr., writing for the majority, said, "If there is a bedrock principle underlying the First Amendment, it is that the Government may not prohibit the expression of an idea simply because society finds the idea itself offensive or disagreeable. . . . We do not consecrate the flag by punishing its desecration, for in doing so we dilute the freedom that this cherished emblem represents."

In a concurring opinion, Justice Anthony M. Kennedy said, "The hard fact is that sometimes we must make decisions we do not like. We make them because they are right, right in the sense that the law and the Constitution, as we see them, compel the result."

Chief Justice William H. Rehnquist dissented, quoting the text of "The Star-Spangled Banner." Across the land, outraged citizens attacked the court for defending flag-burners, and President George Bush

Protesters burning the flag in Chicago

promptly announced that he would propose a constitutional amendment to prohibit flag-burning. But Congress rejected the proposed amendment and instead enacted a federal law barring flag-burning. Then in 1990, the Supreme Court, again by a vote of 5–4, struck down the new federal law, which had been used to prosecute flag-burners in two cases.[5] Once again, it ruled that the Constitution permits freedom of expression, even when that expression is offensive to many persons.

The highest court in the land interpreted the Constitution to mean that neither a state nor Congress itself could pass a law that violated the right of free speech in America. The case arose and was decided within the framework of the Constitution.

The Constitution directly affects many other facets of American life and politics. When in 1954 the Supreme Court outlawed officially supported segregation in the public schools, it did so on the grounds that

---

[4] *Texas v. Johnson*, 491 U.S. 397 (1989).

[5] *U.S. v. Eichman; U.S. v. Haggerty*, both 496 U.S. 310 (1990).

"separate-but-equal" schools violated the Constitution.[6] The enforcement of that constitutional decision —particularly as it related to the busing of schoolchildren— is still being contested in the political arena and the courts.

Abortion is another controversial political issue affected by Supreme Court rulings. In 1973, in *Roe* v. *Wade*, the Supreme Court ruled that state laws restricting abortions during the first three months of pregnancy were unconstitutional.[7] A decade later, the Supreme Court, reaffirming its 1973 decision, struck down various state laws that had been designed to make it more difficult to obtain legal abortions.[8] Then in 1992, the Court ruled on a Pennsylvania law that restricted abortion. By a narrow 5-4 margin, it reaffirmed the consitutional right to abortion first proclaimed in *Roe* v. *Wade*, while upholding most of the restrictions in the Pennsylvania law. (The Court's rulings on abortion are discussed in more detail on pp. 148–152).

As these selected examples illustrate, constitutional government affects the quality of American society here and now, today and tomorrow. Yet it is a story that has been unfolding for more than two centuries; it began, as much as anywhere, in the city of Philadelphia in June 1776.

---

[6] *Brown* v. *Board of Education of Topeka et al.*, 347 U.S. 483 (1954).
[7] *Roe* v. *Wade*, 410 U.S. 113 (1973); *Doe* v. *Bolton*, 410 U.S. 179 (1973).
[8] *Akron* v. *Akron Center for Reproductive Health, Inc.*, 462 U.S. 416 (1983).

We Hold These Truths . . . .

Early in May 1776 Thomas Jefferson rode down the mountain on horseback from Monticello, his Virginia home, and headed north to take his seat in the Continental Congress at Philadelphia. It had been just over a year since the guns blazed at Lexington and Concord, but the thirteen American colonies, although at war, were still under the jurisdiction of the British crown.

Independence was in the air, however, nourished by the words of an Englishman only recently arrived in America. His name was Thomas Paine, and his pamphlet, *Common Sense*, attacked George III, the British monarch, as the "Royal Brute." Paine's fiery words stirred the colonies.

On June 7 Richard Henry Lee, one of Jefferson's fellow delegates from Virginia, introduced a resolution declaring that the colonies "are, and of right ought to be, free and independent States." Four days later, after impassioned debate, the Continental Congress appointed a committee of five, including Jefferson, to "prepare a declaration."

At thirty-three, Jefferson was already known, in the words of John Adams of Massachusetts, as a man with a "peculiar felicity of expression," and the task of writing the declaration fell to him. Jefferson completed his draft in about two weeks. Sitting in the second-floor parlor of the house of Jacob Graff, Jr., a German bricklayer, Jefferson composed some of the most enduring words in the English language. His draft, edited some-

---

WHAT WAS EDITED OUT OF THE DECLARATION OF INDEPENDENCE

Jefferson's draft of the Declaration of Independence originally included an attack on slavery, and sought to blame that "execrable commerce" on King George III. But the Continental Congress cut the passage out of the final document in deference to the wishes of South Carolina and Georgia, and, Jefferson suspected, those Northerners who profited from carrying slaves in their ships. Had the passage remained in, the Declaration would have included these words:

he has waged cruel war against human nature itself, violating its most sacred rights of life & liberty in the persons of a distant people who never offended him, captivating & carrying them into slavery in another hemisphere, or to incure miserable death in their transportation thither. This piratical warfare, the opprobrium of infidel powers, is the warfare of the Christian king of Great Britain. Determined to keep open a market where MEN should be bought & sold. . . . suppressing every legislative attempt to prohibit or to restrain this execrable commerce . . . he is now exciting those very people to rise in arms among us, and to purchase that liberty of which he has deprived them, by murdering the people upon whom he also obtruded.

—Carl L. Becker,
The Declaration of Independence

what by Benjamin Franklin and John Adams, was submitted on June 28.

On July 2 the Continental Congress approved Richard Henry Lee's resolution declaring the colonies free of allegiance to the crown. The Declaration of Independence is not the official act by which Congress severed its ties with Britain. Lee's resolution did that. Rather, the Declaration "was intended as a formal justification of an act already accomplished."[9]

For two days Congress debated Jefferson's draft, making changes and deletions that Jefferson found painful. No matter; what emerged has withstood the test of time:

> We hold these Truths to be self-evident, that all Men are created equal, that they are endowed by their Creator with certain unalienable Rights, that among these are Life, Liberty, and the pursuit of Happiness — That to secure these Rights, Governments are instituted among Men, deriving their just Powers from the Consent of the Governed, that whenever any form of Government becomes destructive of these Ends, it is the Right of the People to alter or to abolish it, and to institute new Government. . . .

---

[9] Carl L. Becker, *The Declaration of Independence* (New York: Vintage Books, 1942), p. 5.

Thomas Jefferson

The Continental Congress approved the Declaration on July 4 and ordered that it be "authenticated and printed." Although the fact is sometimes overlooked, Jefferson and his colleagues produced and signed a treasonable document. They were literally pledging their lives.

Dr. Benjamin Rush of Philadelphia, one of the signers, asked John Adams many years later: "Do you recollect . . . the pensive and awful silence which pervaded the house when we were called up, one after another, to the table of the President of Congress to subscribe what was believed by many at that time to be our own death warrants?"[10]

---

[10] David Hawke, *A Transaction of Free Men* (New York: Scribner's, 1964), p. 209.

Jefferson composed the first draft of the Declaration of Independence on this portable writing desk.

The solemnity of the moment was breached only once. It is said that Benjamin Harrison of Virginia, whom Adams once described as "an indolent and luxurious heavy gentleman of no use in Congress or committee," turned to Elbridge Gerry of Massachusetts, a skinny, worried-looking colleague, and cackled: "I shall have a great advantage over you, Mr. Gerry, when we are all hung for what we are now doing. From the size and weight of my body I shall die in a few minutes, but from the lightness of your body you will dance in the air an hour or two before you are dead."[11]

THE POLITICAL FOUNDATIONS

Although Jefferson later said he had "turned to neither book nor pamphlet" in writing the Declaration of Independence, he was certainly influenced by the philosophy of John Locke (1632–1704) and others, by his British heritage, with its traditional concern for individual rights, and by the colonial political experience itself.

The Influence of John Locke

John Locke's philosophy of *natural rights* was political gospel to most educated Americans in the late eighteenth century. Jefferson absorbed Locke's writings, and some of the English philosopher's words and phrases emerged verbatim in the Declaration.[12]

Locke reasoned that human beings were "born free" and possessed certain natural rights when they lived in a state of nature before governments were formed. People contracted among themselves to form a society to protect those rights. All persons, Locke believed, were free, equal, and independent, and no one could be "subjected to the political power of another, without his own consent."[13] These dangerous ideas—dangerous in an age of the divine right of kings—are directly reflected in the language of the Declaration of Independence, written nearly a century later.

The English Heritage

The irony of the American Revolution is that the colonists, for the most part, rebelled because they felt they were being deprived of their rights as *English citizens.*

Many of the ideas of the Declaration of Independence in 1776, the Constitution, framed in 1787, and the Bill of Rights, added to the Constitution in 1791, evolved from their English heritage. The political and intellectual antecedents of the American system of government included such British legal milestones as the Magna Carta, issued by King John at Runnymede in 1215, in which the nobles confirmed that the power of the king was not absolute; the Habeas Corpus Act (1679); and the Bill of Rights (1689).

From England also came a system of *common law,* the cumulative body of law as expressed in judicial decisions and custom rather than by statute. The men who framed America's government were influenced by the writings of Sir Edward Coke, the great British jurist and champion of common law against the power of the king, and Sir William Blackstone, the Oxford law professor whose *Commentaries on the Laws of England* (1765–69) is still an important historical work.

If the *ideas* embodied in the American system of government are to be found largely in the nation's English heritage, it is also true that American *institutions* developed to a great extent from colonial foundations. The roots of much of today's governmental structure can be found in the colonial charters.

The Colonial Experience

Even before they landed at Plymouth in 1620, the Pilgrims—a group of English Puritans who had separated from the Church of England—drew up the Mayflower Compact. The Pilgrims had sailed from Holland intending to settle in the area that is now New York City, but landed instead just north of Cape Cod. In the cabin of the *Mayflower* forty-one male adults signed the compact, declaring that "we . . . doe by these presents solemnly & mutualy in the presence of God, and one of another, covenant & combine our selves togeather into a civill body politick."

The Mayflower Compact, as Samuel Eliot Morison noted, "is justly regarded as a key document in American history. It proves the determination of the small group of English emigrants to live under a rule of law, based on the consent of the people, and to set up their own civil government."[14]

---

[11] Ibid.

[12] For example, the phrase "a long train of abuses."

[13] Peter Laslett, ed., *Locke's Two Treatises of Government* (Cambridge: Cambridge University Press, 1960), p. 348.

A year earlier at Jamestown, Virginia, a group of settlers had established the first representative assembly in the New World. Puritans from the Massachusetts Bay Colony and another group from London framed America's first written constitution in 1639—the Fundamental Orders of Connecticut. The Massachusetts Body of Liberties (1641) embodied traditional English rights, such as trial by jury and due process of law (later incorporated into the Constitution and the Bill of Rights).

The political forms established by the Puritans contributed to the formation of representative institutions. Beyond that, Puritanism shaped the American mind and left its indelible stamp on the American character. The English Puritans who came to America were influenced by the teachings of John Calvin, the sixteenth-century French theologian of the Protestant Reformation. Theirs was a stern code of hard work, sobriety, and intense religious zeal. Even today, with rapidly changing, increasingly liberal sexual and moral codes, Americans do not always seem to be able to enjoy their new freedom entirely. The Puritan heritage is not easily forgotten.

The Colonial Governments The thirteen original colonies, some formed as commercial ventures, others as religious havens, all had written charters that set forth their form of government and the rights of the colonists. All had governors (the executive branch), legislatures, and a judiciary.

The eight *royal* colonies were New Hampshire, New York, New Jersey, Virginia, North Carolina, South Carolina, Georgia, and Massachusetts. They were controlled by the king through governors appointed by him. Laws passed by their legislatures were subject to approval of the crown. In the three *proprietary* colonies—Maryland, Delaware, and Pennsylvania—the proprietors (who had obtained their patents from the king) named the governors, subject to the approval of the crown; laws (except in Maryland) also required the crown's approval. Only in the two *charter* colonies, Rhode Island and Connecticut, was there genuine self-government. There, freely elected legislatures chose the governors, and laws could not be vetoed by the king.

Except for Pennsylvania, which had a unicameral legislature, the colonial legislatures had two houses.

The members of the upper house were appointed by the crown or proprietor (except in Connecticut and Rhode Island, where both houses were elected), and the members of the lower house were elected by the colonists. Appeals from the colonial courts could usually be taken to the Privy Council in London.

The Paradox of Colonial Democracy Democracy, in the modern sense, did not exist in colonial America. For example, by the 1700s every colony had some type of property qualification for voting. Women and blacks were not considered part of the electorate. In 1765, of the 1,850,000 estimated population of the colonies, 400,000 were blacks, almost all of them slaves. Consequently, "whatever political democracy did exist was a democracy of white, male property owners."[15]

In addition, many white persons were indentured servants during the colonial period. These were English, Scotch-Irish, and Western Europeans, including many convicts, who sold their labor for four to seven years in return for passage across the sea.

Even aside from slavery and indentured servitude, there was little social democracy. A tailor in York County, Virginia, in 1674 was punished for racing a horse because "it was contrary to law for a labourer to make a race, being a sport only for gentlemen."[16] In colonial New York, the aristocracy "ruled with condescension and lived in splendor."[17]

Nine of the thirteen colonies had an established, official state church. Although the colonists had in many cases fled Europe to find religious freedom, they were often intolerant of religious dissent. The Massachusetts Bay Colony executed four Quakers who had returned there after being banished for their religious convictions. In Virginia the penalty for breaking the Sabbath for the third time was death.[18] And although the colonial press and pamphleteers developed into a powerful force for liberty, the first newspaper to appear in America, *Publick Occurrences*, was immediately suppressed.[19]

Yet, despite their shortcomings, the colonial governments provided an institutional foundation for what was to come. Certain elements were already visible:

---

[14] Samuel Eliot Morison, "The Mayflower Compact," in Daniel J. Boorstin, ed., *An American Primer* (Chicago: University of Chicago Press, 1966), p. 19.

[15] Clinton Rossiter, *Seedtime of the Republic* (New York: Harcourt Brace Jovanovich, 1953), p. 35.

[16] Ibid., p. 87.

[17] Ibid., p. 88.

[18] Nat Hentoff, *The First Freedom: The Tumultuous History of Free Speech in America* (New York: Delacorte Press, 1980), pp. 160–61.

[19] The newspaper was published in Boston on September 25, 1690.

British tax stamps

The British had routed the French from North America and provided military protection to the colonies; England in turn demanded that its subjects in America pay part of the cost. At the same time, the colonies were expected to subordinate themselves to the British economy; ideally they would remain agricultural, develop no industry of their own, and serve as a captive market for British manufactures.

The colonists had no representatives in the British Parliament. They resented and disputed the right of London to raise revenue in America. Whether or not James Otis, the Boston patriot, cried, "Taxation without representation is tyranny!"—and there is reason to think he did not—the words reflected popular sentiment in the colonies.[21]

A series of laws designed to give the mother country a tight grip on trade, to restrict colonial exports, and to protect producers in England proved to be the economic stepping stones to revolution. In 1772 Samuel Adams of Massachusetts formed the Committees of Correspondence to unite the colonies against Great Britain. This network provided an invaluable political communications link for the colonies. Letters, reports, and decisions of one town or colony could be relayed to the next.

The committees resolved to hold the First Continental Congress, which met in Philadelphia in September 1774. The war began in April 1775. The Second Continental Congress met the following month, and by June 1776 Thomas Jefferson was busily writing in the second-floor parlor of the bricklayer's house in Philadelphia.

separation of powers, constitutional government through written charters, bicameral legislatures, elections, and judicial appeal to London, which foreshadowed the role of the Supreme Court. Equally important, in their relationship with England, the colonies became accustomed to the idea of sharing powers with a central government, the basis of the federal system today. It was, in Clinton Rossiter's apt phrase, the "seedtime of the republic."

THE AMERICAN REVOLUTION

"The Revolution," John Adams wrote in 1818, "was effected before the war commenced. The Revolution was in the minds and hearts of the people."[20]

A Growing Sense of Injury

In the eyes of the crown, the American colonies existed chiefly for the economic support of England. Economic conflicts with the mother country, as well as political and social factors, impelled the colonies to revolt.

The Articles of Confederation (1781–89)

The Declaration of Independence had proclaimed the colonies "free and independent states." During the war all the colonies adopted new constitutions or at least changed their old charters to eliminate references to the British crown. Seven of the new constitutions contained a bill of rights, but all restricted suffrage. All provided for three branches of government, but their dominant features were strong legislatures and weak

---

[20] In Charles Francis Adams, ed., *The Works of John Adams*, vol. 10 (Boston: Little, Brown, 1856), p. 282.

[21] Otis supposedly uttered his famous line in a speech to the Massachusetts Superior Court in 1761. But as Daniel J. Boorstin points out, the line does not appear in the original notes of the speech taken by John Adams. See Boorstin, *The Americans: The National Experience*, pp. 309, 360–61.

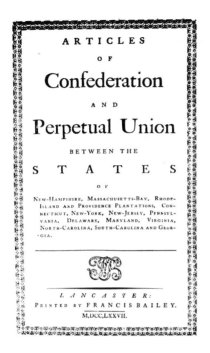

executives. Governors were elected by the people or by legislatures, and their powers were reduced. For the first time, the colonies began to refer to themselves as "states."

When Richard Henry Lee offered his resolution for independence in June 1776, he also had proposed that "a plan of confederation" be prepared for the colonies. The plan was drawn up by a committee and approved by the Continental Congress in November 1777, a month before George Washington withdrew with his troops for the long, hard winter at Valley Forge. The Articles were ratified by the individual states by March 1, 1781, and so were already in effect when the war ended with the surrender of Cornwallis at Yorktown that October. The formal end to hostilities came with the conclusion of the Peace of Paris in February 1783.

Article III of the Articles of Confederation really established a "league of friendship" among the states, rather than a national government. No executive branch, no president, no "White House" existed. Instead, Congress, given power to establish executive departments, created five: foreign affairs, finance, navy, war, and post office. Congress had power to declare war, conduct foreign policy, make treaties, ask for — but not demand — revenues from the states, borrow and coin money, equip the navy, and appoint senior officers of the army, which was made up of the state militias. Con-

gress was unicameral, and each state, regardless of size, had only one vote. The most important actions by Congress required the consent of nine states. There was no national system of courts.

While these were not inconsiderable powers, the most significant fact about the government created under the Articles was its weakness. Congress, for example, had no power to levy taxes or regulate commerce — the colonies had seen enough of these powers under English rule. Above all, Congress could not enforce even the limited powers it had. The functioning of government under the Articles depended entirely on the good will of the states. Because unanimous agreement of the states was required to amend the Articles, but in practice could never be obtained, there was no practical way to increase the powers of the government; the Articles were never amended.

By 1783 the American states had achieved their independence not only from Great Britain but also from each other. They had won their freedom, but they had been unable to form a nation. Yet the Articles did represent the idea of some form of national government, for under them, "Congress waged war, made peace, and kept alive the idea of union when it was at its lowest ebb."[22] As historian Merrill Jensen has emphasized, the Articles "laid foundations for the administration of a central government which were to be expanded but not essentially altered in function for generations to come."[23]

TOWARD A MORE PERFECT UNION

The Background

Under the inadequate government of the Articles of Confederation, the states came close to losing the peace they had won in war. They quarreled among themselves over boundary lines and tariffs. For example, New Jersey farmers had to pay heavy fees to cross the Hudson River to sell their vegetables in New York. With no strong national government to conduct foreign policy, some states even entered into negotiations with foreign

[22] Alpheus T. Mason, "America's Political Heritage: Revolution and Free Government — A Bicentennial Tribute," in M. Judd Harmon, ed., *Essays on the Constitution of the United States* (Port Washington: Kennikat Press, 1978), p. 17.

[23] Merrill Jensen, *The New Nation* (New York: Knopf, 1950), pp. 347–48.

George Washington

powers. General Washington worried that Kentucky might join Spain.[24] There was real concern over possible military intervention by European powers.

By 1786 severe economic depression had left many farmers angry and hungry. Debtor groups demanded that state governments issue paper money. The unrest among farmers and the poor alarmed the upper classes. They feared, in today's terms, a revolution of the left. These political and economic factors, combined with fear of overseas intervention, generated pressure for the creation of a new national government.

Virginia, at the urging of James Madison, had invited all the states to discuss commercial problems at a meeting to be held at Annapolis, Maryland, in September 1786. The Annapolis conference was disappointing. Representatives of only five states turned up. But one of those delegates was Alexander Hamilton, a brilliant thirty-one-year-old New York attorney who was one of a small group of men pushing for a convention to create a stronger government. There had been talk of such a meeting since 1780, when Hamilton wrote to a friend listing the "defects of our present system."[25]

At Annapolis, Hamilton and Madison persuaded the delegates to call upon the states to hold a constitutional convention in Philadelphia in May 1787. In the interim a significant event took place. Angry farmers in western Massachusetts, unable to pay their mortgages or taxes, late in 1786 rallied around Daniel Shays, who had served as a captain in the American Revolution. They were seeking to stop the Massachusetts courts from foreclosing the mortgages on their farms. Armed with pitchforks, the farmers marched on the Springfield arsenal to get weapons. They were defeated by the militia. Fourteen ringleaders were sentenced to death, but all were pardoned or released after serving short prison terms. Shays escaped to Vermont.

Shays's Rebellion, coming on the eve of the Philadelphia convention, had a tremendous effect on public opinion. Aristocrats and merchants were thoroughly alarmed at the threat of "mob rule." The British were amused at the American lack of capacity for self-government. The revolt was an important factor in creating the climate for a new beginning at Philadelphia.

The Philadelphia Convention

On February 21, 1787, Congress grudgingly approved the proposed Philadelphia Convention "for the sole and express purpose of revising the Articles of Confederation." Beginning in May, the delegates met and, disregarding Congress's cautious mandate, worked what has been called a "miracle at Philadelphia."[26]

The Delegates Because the story of how a nation was born is in large part a story of people, it might be useful to focus briefly on some of the more prominent delegates who gathered at Philadelphia. First was George Washington, who had commanded the armed forces during the Revolution. A national hero, a man of immense prestige, Washington was probably the only figure who could have successfully presided over the coming struggle in the convention. When Washington arrived in Philadelphia, a crowd gathered and bells rang out. He immediately paid a call on Benjamin Franklin, internationally famous as a scientist-diplomat-statesman. Then eighty-one and suffering from gout, Franklin arrived at the sessions in a sedan chair borne by four convicts from the Walnut Street jail. Alexander Hamil-

---

[24] William H. Riker, *Federalism: Origin, Operation, Significance* (Boston: Little, Brown, 1964), pp. 18, 20.

[25] Letter to James Duane, in Clinton Rossiter, *1787: The Grand Convention* (New York: Macmillan, 1966), p. 53.

[26] Catherine Drinker Bowen, *Miracle at Philadelphia* (Boston: Little, Brown, 1966).

ton was there, as a delegate from New York, but he took surprisingly little part in the important decisions of the convention. From Virginia came James Madison, often called the "Father of the Constitution," who had long advocated a new national government. A tireless note-taker, Madison kept a record of the debates. Without him there would have been no detailed account of the most important political convention in the nation's history.

Gouverneur Morris, a colorful man who stumped about on a wooden leg, shatters the image of the delegates as stuffy patriarchs. His wit offended some, but his pen was responsible for the literary style and polish of the final draft of the Constitution. From Massachusetts came Elbridge Gerry, and Rufus King, a lawyer with a gift for debating; from South Carolina, John Rutledge, a leading figure of the revolutionary period and later a justice of the Supreme Court, General Charles Cotesworth Pinckney, Oxford-educated war hero and aristocrat, and his second cousin, Charles Pinckney, an ardent nationalist.

Twelve states sent delegates to Philadelphia. Only Rhode Island boycotted the convention; an agrarian party of farmers and debtors controlled the Rhode Island state legislature and feared that a strong national government would limit the party's power. Of the fifty-five men who gathered at Philadelphia in the Pennsylvania State House (now Independence Hall), eight had signed the Declaration of Independence, seven had been chief executives of their states, thirty-three were lawyers, eight were businessmen, six were planters, and three were physicians. About half were college graduates.[27] The delegates, in sum, were generally men of wealth and influence; the Constitution was not drafted by small farmers, artisans, or laborers.

It was a relatively young convention. Jonathan Dayton of New Jersey, at twenty-six, was the youngest delegate. Alexander Hamilton was thirty-two. Charles Pinckney was twenty-nine. James Madison was thirty-six. The average age of the delegates was just over forty-three. (At eighty-one, Franklin pulled the average up.)

The Setting The convention of 1787 had many of the earmarks of a modern national political convention but for one factor: to preserve their freedom of debate, the delegates worked in strictest secrecy. The press and public were not allowed in the room. In other respects the setting would be a familiar one today: the weather was intolerably hot and the speeches interminable. And just as in a modern convention, a plush tavern and inn, the Indian Queen, soon became a sort of informal headquarters.

Philadelphia was not a pleasant place two hundred years ago. It was a crowded city of open sewers, foul smells, and rotting animal carcasses. The clatter of wagon wheels on the rough cobblestones was so bad that, when the sessions got underway, at the request of the delegates the city spread a load of gravel outside the hall to muffle the noise.

The convention opened on May 14, 1787, but it was not until May 25 that a quorum of delegates from seven states was reached. The delegates gathered in the East Room of the State House, the same chamber where the Declaration of Independence had been signed eleven years before. "Delegates sat at tables covered in green baize — sat and sweated, once the summer sun was up. By noon the air was lifeless, with windows shut for privacy, or intolerable with flies when they were open."[28] For almost four months the stuffy East Room was to be home.

The Great Compromise On May 29 Edmund Randolph, the thirty-three-year-old governor of Virginia, took the floor to present fifteen resolutions that

Gouverneur Morris

---

[27] Charles Warren, *The Making of the Constitution* (New York: Barnes & Noble, 1967), pp. 55–60.
[28] Bowen, *Miracle at Philadelphia*, p. 23.

George Washington presiding at the Constitutional Convention in Philadelphia, 1787.

stunned the convention. The resolutions, which Madison had helped to draft, went far beyond mere revision of the Articles—they proposed an entirely new national government under a constitution. Randolph was moving swiftly to make the Virginia Plan, as his proposals are known, the main business of the convention.

As John P. Roche has noted, the Virginia Plan "was a political master-stroke. Its consequence was that once business got underway, the framework of discussion was established on Madison's terms. There was no interminable argument over agenda; instead the delegates took the Virginia Resolutions—'just for the purposes of discussion'—as their point of departure."[29] The Virginia Plan called for:

1. A two-house legislature, the lower house chosen by the people and the upper house chosen by the lower. The legislature would have the power to annul any state laws that it found unconstitutional.

2. A "national executive"—the makeup was not specified, so there might have been more than one

president under the plan—to be elected by the legislature.

3. A national judiciary to be chosen by the legislature.

The convention debated the Virginia Plan for two weeks. As the debate wore on, the delegates from the smaller states became increasingly alarmed. It had not taken them long to conclude that the more heavily populated states would control the government under the Virginia Plan. "The Virginia Plan," one writer has contended, "would mean nothing less than a second American revolution."[30]

On June 15 William Paterson of New Jersey, a lawyer, "a squat man with a bulbous nose, a receding chin

---

[29] John P. Roche, "The Founding Fathers: A Reform Caucus in Action," *American Political Science Review*, vol. 55, no. 4 (December 1961), p. 803.

[30] Fred Barbash, *The Founding: A Dramatic Account of the Writing of the Constitution* (New York: The Linden Press/Simon and Schuster, 1987), p. 58.

AN AMERICAN KING

Charles Pinckney rose . . . to urge a "vigorous executive." He did not say a "President of the United States." It took the Convention a long while to come around to *President*. Always they referred to a chief executive or a national executive, whether plural or single. James Wilson followed Pinckney by moving that the executive consist of a single person; Pinckney seconded him.

A sudden silence followed. "A considerable pause," Madison wrote . . . *A single executive*! There was menace in the words,

some saw monarchy in them. True enough, nine states had each its single executive—a governor or president—but everywhere the local legislature was supreme, looked on as the voice of the people which could control a governor any day. But a single executive for the national government conjured up visions from the past—royal governors who could not be restrained, a crown, ermine, a scepter!

—Catherine Drinker Bowen,
Miracle at Philadelphia.

and traces of his native Ireland in his voice,"[31] rose to offer an alternative plan. He argued that the convention had no power to deprive the smaller states of the equality they enjoyed under the Articles of Confederation. Paterson proposed what became known as the New Jersey Plan, which called for:

1. Continuation of the Articles of Confederation, including one vote for each state represented in the legislature. Congress would be strengthened so that it could impose taxes and regulate trade, and acts of Congress would become the "supreme law" of the states.
2. An executive of more than one person to be elected by Congress.
3. A Supreme Court, to be appointed by the executive.

The Paterson plan would have merely amended the Articles. The government would have continued as a weak confederation of sovereign states. But many of the delegates at Philadelphia were determined to construct a strong *national* government, and for this reason the Paterson plan was soon brushed aside. As both the weather and tempers grew warmer, the convention swung back to consideration of the Virginia Plan. But little progress was made.

The fact was that the convention was in danger of breaking up. "I *almost* despair," Washington, presiding over the deadlock, wrote to Hamilton in New York.

The impasse over the makeup of Congress was broken on July 16 when the convention adopted the

Great Compromise, often called the Connecticut Compromise because it had been proposed by Roger Sherman of that state. As adopted after much debate, the Connecticut Compromise called for:

1. A House of Representatives apportioned by the number of free inhabitants in each state plus three-fifths of the slaves.
2. A Senate, or upper house, consisting of two members from each state, elected by the state legislatures.

The plan broke the deadlock because it protected the small states by guaranteeing that each state would have an equal vote in the Senate. Only in the House, where representation was to be based on population, would the larger states have an advantage.

Catherine Drinker Bowen has suggested that the delegates might never have reached agreement "had not the heat broken." On Monday, July 16, the day the compromise was approved, "Philadelphia was cool after a month of torment; on Friday, a breeze had come in from the northwest. Over the weekend, members could rest and enjoy themselves."[32]

With the large state versus small state controversy resolved by this compromise, the convention named a committee to draft a constitution. Then the convention adjourned for eleven days, and General Washington went fishing.

On August 6 the convention resumed its work. The committee brought in a draft constitution that called for a "congress," made up of a house of represen-

---

[31] Ibid., p. 69.

[32] Bowen, *Miracle at Philadelphia*, p. 186.

tatives and a senate; a "supreme court"; and a "president of the United States of America."

The broad outline of the Constitution as it is today was finally clear. But much work remained:

> And so the men of Philadelphia persevered through the hot [summer] days, filling out the details now that the grand design had been set in the Connecticut Compromise, sawing boards to make them fit, as Benjamin Franklin said. Some of the boards required much sanding and smoothing, as the delegates thrashed out irksome but vital aspects of the relations between the national and state governments, the enumerated powers of Congress, the jurisdiction of the courts, the reach of impeachment, the amending clause, and procedures for ratifying the Constitution itself. . . . They deliberated as if the eyes of the world were on them.[33]

The Other Compromises As debate continued, the convention made other significant compromises. Underlying the agreement to count three-fifths of all slaves in apportioning membership of the House of Representatives was a deep-seated conflict between the mercantile North and the agrarian South, where the economy was based on slave labor. Of the fifty-five delegates to the convention, at least twenty-five owned slaves.[34] The men of the North argued that if slaves were to be counted in determining representation in the House, then they must be counted for tax purposes as well. In the end, the South agreed.

The slave trade itself was the subject of another complicated compromise. On August 22 George Mason of Virginia attacked "the infernal traffic" and its evil effect on both individuals and the nation. Slavery, he said, would "bring the judgment of heaven on a Country. As nations can not be rewarded or punished in the next world they must in this. By an inevitable chain of causes & effects providence punishes national sins, by national calamities."[35]

Charles Cotesworth Pinckney of South Carolina warned that his state would not join the Union if the slave trade were prohibited. The issue was settled by an agreement that Congress could not ban the slave trade until 1808. This compromise is contained in Article I of the Constitution, which obliquely refers to slaves as "other persons."[36]

In yet another compromise, the South won certain trade concessions. Southerners were worried, with reason, that a northern majority in Congress might pass legislation unfavorable to southern economic interests. Because the South relied almost entirely on exports of its agricultural products, it fought for, and won, an agreement forbidding the imposition of export taxes.

Even today, the United States is one of the few nations that cannot tax its exports.

We the People On September 8 a Committee of Style and Arrangement was named to polish the final draft. Fortunately it included Gouverneur Morris. Morris, probably aided by James Wilson,[37] drafted the final version, adding a new preamble that rivals Jefferson's eloquence in the Declaration of Independence:

> "We the People of the United States, in Order to form a more perfect Union, establish Justice, insure domestic Tranquility, provide for the common defence, promote the general Welfare, and secure the Blessings of Liberty to ourselves and our Posterity, do ordain and establish this Constitution for the United States of America."

On September 17 the long task was finished. The day was cool, and the trace of autumn in the air must have reminded the delegates of how long they had labored. Thirty-nine men signed the Constitution that afternoon. Benjamin Franklin had to be helped forward to the table, and it is said that he wept when he signed. According to Madison's notes, while the last members were signing, Franklin observed that often, as he pondered the outcome during the changing moods of the convention, he had looked at the sun painted on the back of Washington's chair and wondered whether it was rising or setting. "But now at length I have the happiness to know," Franklin declared, "that it is a rising and not a setting sun."[38]

The Constitutional Framework

The Constitution was not perfect, but it represented a practical accommodation among conflicting sections and interests achieved at a political convention. And the central fact of the Constitution is that it created the potential for a strong national government where none

---

[33] James MacGregor Burns, *The Vineyard of Liberty: The American Experiment* (New York: Knopf, 1982), p. 40.

[34] Barbash, *The Founding*, p. 149.

[35] In Carl Van Doren, *The Great Rehearsal* (New York: Viking Press, 1948), p. 153.

[36] Acting on President Jefferson's recommendation, Congress did outlaw importation of slaves in 1808. But the illegal slave trade flourished up to the Civil War. Perhaps 250,000 slaves were illegally imported to America between 1808 and 1860. The slavery issue was not settled until the end of the Civil War and the ratification on December 18, 1865, of the Thirteenth Amendment, which declared that "neither slavery nor involuntary servitude, except as a punishment for crime whereof the party shall have been duly convicted, shall exist within the United States."

[37] Warren, *The Making of the Constitution*, pp. 687–88.

[38] In Van Doren, *The Great Rehearsal*, p. 174.

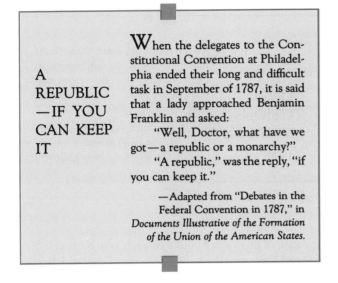

A REPUBLIC —IF YOU CAN KEEP IT

When the delegates to the Constitutional Convention at Philadelphia ended their long and difficult task in September of 1787, it is said that a lady approached Benjamin Franklin and asked:

"Well, Doctor, what have we got—a republic or a monarchy?"

"A republic," was the reply, "if you can keep it."

—Adapted from "Debates in the Federal Convention in 1787," in *Documents Illustrative of the Formation of the Union of the American States.*

that federal laws are supreme over any conflicting state laws. But the states also exercise control within their borders over a wide range of activities.

The Constitution thus brought into being a *federal system*, also known as *federalism*, in which the powers and functions of government are shared by the national government and the states. This system is discussed in detail in Chapter 3.

The National Government The Constitution divided the national government into three branches— legislative, executive, and judicial. It created a government, therefore, based on the principles of *separation of powers* and *checks and balances*. Each of the three branches is constitutionally equal to and independent of the others. In this way the framers thought to prevent any single branch from becoming too powerful. (In fact, however, the twentieth century has seen the presidency become the most powerful branch of the federal government, at least in foreign affairs.)

In creating a government based on these ideas, the framers were influenced by the French political philosopher Baron de Montesquieu (1689–1755). In *The Spirit of the Laws*, published in 1748, Montesquieu advocated a separation of powers into legislative, judicial,

had existed before, and provided the written framework to control the power and operation of that government.

The Federal System The structure of the government created by the Constitution is deceptively simple at first glance, yet endlessly intricate. Article VI declares that the laws passed by Congress "shall be the supreme Law of the Land." This important *supremacy clause* means

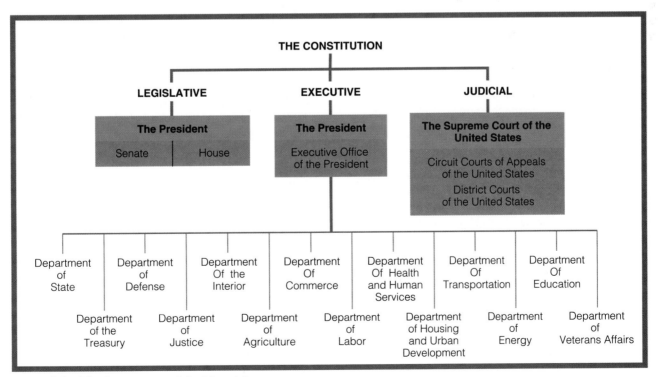

Figure 2-1 The Government of the United States

and executive branches. "When the legislative and executive powers are united in the same person, or in the same body of magistrates, there can be no liberty," he wrote.[39]

Yet the term "separation of powers" is somewhat misleading. Although the Constitution established institutional checks and separated powers, the United States is also a government of *shared powers*. The branches of the government are separated, but their powers and functions are fused or overlapping. The Constitution provided many ways in which the three branches would interact. For example, although Congress makes the laws, the president submits legislation to it, and he may convene Congress in special session. The president also may veto bills passed by Congress. Clearly, the president is involved in the legislative function.

Similarly, Congress is involved in the executive process in its watchdog role and through its power to create federal executive agencies and to advise on and consent to the appointment of high-level federal officials. Because Congress appropriates money to run the federal government, it may delve deeply, through its committees, into the operations of executive agencies.

Through the process of *judicial review*, the courts decide whether the laws passed by Congress or actions taken by the president are constitutional. (See pp. 494–495 for a detailed discussion of judicial review.) President Woodrow Wilson called the Supreme Court "a kind of Constitutional Convention in continuous session."[40] The president participates in the judicial process through his power to nominate federal judges, including members of the Supreme Court. And Congress can pass laws to overrule Supreme Court decisions.

The notion of three separate-but-equal branches of government has been eroded by the pressures of the twentieth century. In the past, American presidents have at varying times exercised great powers, as Lincoln did during the Civil War. But in modern times, power, especially military–diplomatic power, has been largely concentrated in the hands of the president. The power of Congress to declare war, for example, has greatly diminished in importance since the Second World War. And in a nuclear attack the president obviously would have no time to consult Congress. But even in

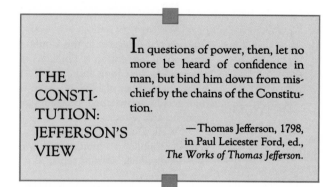

THE CONSTITUTION: JEFFERSON'S VIEW

In questions of power, then, let no more be heard of confidence in man, but bind him down from mischief by the chains of the Constitution.

—Thomas Jefferson, 1798,
in Paul Leicester Ford, ed.,
The Works of Thomas Jefferson.

the case of protracted conflicts, such as in Korea (1950–53) and Vietnam (1964–73), Congress never did declare war. Frustration in Congress over the president's ability to wage war without congressional approval led in 1973 to the passage of the War Powers Resolution, which sets a time limit on the use of combat forces abroad by a president.[41]

In other areas as well, the lines between the three branches of government have become blurred. Today, for example, the complex task of managing the economy has been delegated in part to independent regulatory commissions and agencies that do not fall neatly into any of the three categories—legislative, executive, and judicial—envisioned under the Constitution and in fact exhibit features of all three.

In sum, although the three branches of government are based on separated powers, they also share powers. And among the three branches (as among human beings) there is a never-ending tug-of-war for dominance, a process that Alpheus T. Mason has called "institutionalized tension."[42]

The "Great Silences" of the Constitution Some issues were so difficult and potentially divisive that the framers did not attempt to settle them at all. Because they were trying to construct a political document that stated general principles, they chose to avoid some sensitive problems.

The framers compromised over the vital moral and political issue of whether to abolish the importation of slaves while forming "a more perfect union"; the un-

---

[39] Baron de Montesquieu, *The Spirit of the Laws*, vol. 1 (New York: Hafner, 1949), p. 151.

[40] Edward S. Corwin, Harold W. Chase, and Craig R. Ducat, *The Constitution and What It Means Today* (Princeton: Princeton University Press, 1978), p. 5.

[41] The War Powers Resolution is discussed in detail on pp. 374–375.

[42] Alpheus T. Mason, *The Supreme Court: Palladium of Freedom* (Ann Arbor: University of Michigan Press, 1962), p. 8.

derlying question of whether to abolish slavery itself was not faced at Philadelphia. Five Southern states might not have ratified the Constitution if the framers had abolished the slave trade in 1787. The delegates compromised in order to achieve enough unity to form a new nation, but America paid a high moral and political price. The question of slavery, avoided at Philadelphia, led in time to a bloody civil war. And today, two centuries later, black men and women in America are still struggling for the full freedom and equality denied to them by the framers.

The framers also made no explicit statement in the Constitution defining the full scope of the powers of the national government. The history of the Supreme Court is the history of whether the Constitution is to be loosely or strictly interpreted.

But even the Supreme Court's power of judicial review is nowhere expressly provided for in the Constitution (although some scholars argue it is conferred in general terms). "Without some body to act as umpire," Archibald Cox has written, "the several parts must inevitably fall to squabbling and the enterprise launched at Philadelphia break up on the reefs. Yet the Constitution nowhere specifically and explicitly stated who, if anyone, was to have the final word."[43] The power of the Supreme Court to declare acts of Congress unconstitutional, although exercised in several early opinions, was not firmly set forth and established until 1803, when the Court ruled in the case of *Marbury v. Madison.*[44] Chief Justice John Marshall, in his historic opinion, argued that since the Constitution was clearly "superior" to an act of Congress, "It is emphatically the province and duty of the judicial department to say what the law is. . . . A law repugnant to the Constitution is void."

The Constitution says nothing whatever about how candidates for office shall be chosen. The development of political parties, nominating conventions, and primaries all occurred without any formal constitutional provision for them.

Similarly, the cabinet is not specifically established in the Constitution but has evolved through custom, beginning during Washington's first administration. As Richard F. Fenno, Jr., has noted, the cabinet is "an extralegal creation," limited in power as an institution by the very fact that it has no basis in law.[45]

Motives of the Framers Were the framers of the Constitution selfless patriots who thrust aside all personal interests to save America? Or were they primarily rich men who were afraid of radicals like Daniel Shays? In short, did they form a strong government to protect themselves and their property, or did they act from nobler motives?

The debate has raged among scholars. More than seventy-five years ago, the historian Charles A. Beard analyzed in great detail the economic holdings of the framers and concluded that they acted to protect their personal financial interests. The Constitution, said Beard, was "an economic document drawn with superb skill by men whose property interests were immediately at stake."[46]

Later scholars, reacting to Beard, have reached opposite conclusions. Forrest McDonald has asserted that of the fifty-five delegates, "a dozen at the outside, clearly acted according to the dictates of their personal economic interests." He concluded that an "economic interpretation of the Constitution does not work" and that it is "impossible to justify" Beard's analysis.[47] Similarly, Robert E. Brown has suggested that "we would be doing a grave injustice to the political sagacity of the Founding Fathers if we assumed that property or personal gain was their only motive."[48]

Was It Democratic? The argument is sometimes advanced that the Constitution was framed to guard against popular democracy and unchecked majority rule. "The evils we experience flow from the excess of democracy," Elbridge Gerry of Massachusetts told the convention.[49]

The word "democracy" today generally has a favorable, affirmative meaning, but to the framers of the

[43] Archibald Cox, *The Court and the Constitution* (Boston, Mass.: Houghton Mifflin Company, 1987), p. 42.

[44] *Marbury v. Madison,* 1 Cranch 137 (1803). Judicial review is discussed on pp. 494–495.

[45] Richard F. Fenno, Jr., *The President's Cabinet* (Cambridge: Harvard University Press, 1959), pp. 19–20.

[46] Charles A. Beard, *An Economic Interpretation of the Constitution of the United States* (New York: Macmillan, 1935), p. 188. Originally published in 1913.

[47] Forrest McDonald, *We the People* (Chicago: University of Chicago Press, 1958), pp. vii, 350, 415.

[48] Robert E. Brown, *Charles Beard and the Constitution* (Princeton: Princeton University Press, 1956), p. 198.

[49] Bowen, *Miracle at Philadelphia,* p. 45. Elbridge Gerry, Edmund Randolph, and George Mason were the only three framers who refused to sign the Constitution. Much later, Gerry gave his name to a famous but controversial practice. While he was governor of Massachusetts in 1812, the legislature carved up Essex County to give maximum advantage to his party. One of the districts resembled a salamander. From then on, the practice of redrawing voting districts to favor the party in power became known as "gerrymandering." (See p. 451.)

THE CONSTITUTION: "DEFECTIVE FROM THE START"

In May of 1987, as the nationwide celebration of the 200th anniversary of the Constitution approached, the then Supreme Court Justice, Thurgood Marshall, broke dramatically with the almost universal acclaim the document had been receiving. Marshall, who later retired in 1991, voiced his strong dissent in a speech in Hawaii to a group of lawyers:

> Supreme Court Justice Thurgood Marshall yesterday sharply attacked the Founding Fathers and the planned celebration of the Constitution's bicentennial, urging Americans not to go overboard in praising a document that sanctioned slavery and denied women the right to vote.
>
> Marshall, the Court's only black justice [at that time], said the Constitution was "defective from the start, requiring several amendments, a civil war and momentous social transformation to attain the system of constitutional government, and its re-

spect for the individual freedoms and human rights, we hold as fundamental today." . . .

The preamble's first three words, "we the people," Marshall said, did not include "the majority of American citizens," women and blacks. . . . "The men who gathered in Philadelphia in 1787 could not have envisioned" the "bloody civil war" and amendments that freed slaves and gave blacks the right to vote, followed by the women's suffrage movement that led to the 19th Amendment giving women the right to vote in 1920.

"They could not have imagined, nor would they have accepted, that the document they were drafting would one day be construed by a Supreme Court to which had been appointed a woman and the descendant of an African slave."

—*Washington Post*, May 7, 1987.

Constitution, it was a term of derision. "Remember," John Adams warned, "democracy never lasts long. It soon wastes, exhausts, and murders itself. There never was a democracy yet that did not commit suicide."[50]

From a contemporary viewpoint some of the provisions of the Constitution appear highly undemocratic. For example, slavery was permitted to flourish. In addition, because the Constitution leaves voting qualifications to the states, persons without property, women, and many African Americans were long disenfranchised. Until the passage of the Seventeenth Amendment in 1913, senators were elected by state legislatures, although by 1912 in at least twenty-nine states an attempt was made to reflect popular choice.[51] The framers had deliberately avoided direct election of senators, for the Senate was seen as a check on the multitudes. Madison assured the convention that the Senate would proceed "with more coolness, with more system, and with

more wisdom, than the popular branch." And, of course, the Constitution interposed an electoral college between the voters and the presidency.

But to stress only these aspects of the Constitution would be to overlook the basically representative structure of the government it created — particularly in comparison with other governments that existed in 1787 — and the revolutionary heritage of the framers. The Constitution perhaps originally reflected considerable distrust of popular rule, but it established a balanced institutional framework within which democracy could evolve.

The Fight over Ratification

When the convention had finished its work, a successful outcome was by no means certain. The political contest over ratification of the Constitution lasted for more than two and a half years, from September 1787 until May 29, 1790, when Rhode Island finally joined the Union. But the Constitution went into effect in June 1788 when it was ratified by nine states.

---

[50] Charles Francis Adams, ed., *The Works of John Adams*, vol. 6 (Boston: Little, Brown, 1851), p. 484.

[51] Edward S. Corwin et al., eds., *The Constitution of the United States of America, Analysis and Interpretation* (Washington, D.C.: U.S. Government Printing Office, 1964), p. 1356.

The Articles of Confederation had required that any amendment be approved by Congress and the legislatures of all thirteen states. No such unanimity could ever be achieved. In effect this created a box from which the framers could not climb out. So they chose another route — they simply ignored the box and built an entirely new structure. Defending the convention's action, Madison reminded his countrymen of the right of the people, proclaimed in the Declaration of Independence, to alter or abolish their government in ways "most likely to effect their safety and happiness."[52]

Article VII of the Constitution states that "ratification of the Conventions of nine States shall be sufficient for the Establishment of this Constitution." Why conventions and not legislatures? Because the Constitution took power away from the states, the framers reasoned that the state legislatures might not approve it. Second, if the Constitution were approved by popularly elected conventions, it would give the new government a broad base of legitimacy.

The great debate over the Constitution soon divided the participants into two camps: the Antifederalists, who opposed it, and the Federalists. Although the debate was vigorous, relatively few people actually participated in the ratification process. The voters could not vote for or against the Constitution. Their choice was confined to selecting delegates to the state ratifying conventions. Only an estimated 160,000 persons voted for delegates to the ratifying conventions, out of a total population of about 4,000,000.

Some historians tend to pay more attention to the Federalists — because they won — but those opposed to the Constitution had a strong case. The convention, after all, had met in complete secrecy, in a "Dark Conclave," as the Philadelphia *Independent Gazetteer* termed it. What is more, the Constitution, as its opponents argued, was extralegal. The framers had clearly exceeded their mandate from Congress to revise the Articles of Confederation. Above all, the Constitution included no bill of rights.

The Federalists argued that the states faced anarchy unless they united under a powerful central government. The omission of a bill of rights was difficult to justify, however. The question had not been raised until near the end of the Philadelphia Convention, and the weary delegates were not inclined to open a new debate.

Furthermore, many delegates felt that a bill of rights would be superfluous since eight states had bills of rights. Hamilton argued that "the Constitution is itself . . . a Bill of Rights."[53]

But during the struggle over ratification, the Antifederalists warned that without a bill of rights in the new Constitution, individuals in the states would have no protection against a powerful national government. Ultimately, as the price of winning support in the state conventions, the Federalists had to promise to enact a bill of rights as the first order of business under a new government.

Richard Henry Lee's *Letters of the Federal Farmer* was among the most effective of the various Antifederalist attacks circulated among the states. In New York, Hamilton, Madison, and John Jay, writing as "Publius," published more than eighty letters in the press defending the Constitution. Together in book form they are known today as *The Federalist*, the classic work explaining and defending the Constitution.

By January 9, 1788, a little more than three months after the Philadelphia Convention, five states had ratified the Constitution: Delaware, Pennsylvania, New Jersey, Georgia, and Connecticut. Massachusetts, a key and doubtful state, ratified next, thanks to the efforts of Sam Adams and John Hancock. Maryland and South Carolina followed suit, and on June 21, 1788, New Hampshire became the ninth state to ratify.

The Constitution was now in effect, but Virginia and New York were still to be heard from. Without these two powerful states, no union could succeed. Washington, Madison, and Edmund Randolph, who finally decided to support the Constitution that he had not signed, helped to swing Virginia into the Federalist camp four days later. In part because of *The Federalist* papers, New York ratified on July 26 by a narrow margin of three votes. North Carolina finally ratified in 1789 and Rhode Island in 1790. (See Table 2–1.) By that time George Washington was already serving as president of the United States of America.

AMERICA: A CASE STUDY IN NATION BUILDING

"The United States was the first major colony successfully to revolt against colonial rule," Seymour Martin

---

[52] James Madison, "The Federalist, No. 40," in Edward Mead Earle, ed., *The Federalist* (New York: Random House, Modern Library), p. 257.

[53] Alexander Hamilton, "The Federalist, No. 84," in Earle, ed., *The Federalist*, p. 561.

Table 2-1
The Ratification of the Constitution

State	Date	Vote in the Ratifying Convention
Delaware	December 7, 1787	Unanimous
Pennsylvania	December 12, 1787	46–32
New Jersey	December 18, 1787	Unanimous
Georgia	January 2, 1788	Unanimous
Connecticut	January 9, 1788	128–40
Massachusetts	February 6, 1788	187–168
Maryland	April 28, 1788	63–11
South Carolina	May 23, 1788	149–73
New Hampshire	June 21, 1788	57–47
Virginia	June 25, 1788	89–79
New York	July 26, 1788	30–27
North Carolina	November 21, 1789	194–77
Rhode Island	May 29, 1790	34–32

Lipset has written. "In this sense, it was the first 'new nation.'"[54]

The Declaration of Independence and the success of the American Revolution influenced the philosophers and political leaders of the French Revolution. Jefferson's words were translated into many languages, influencing liberals during the nineteenth century in Germany, Italy, and South America. Even today, the ideas expressed in the Declaration of Independence have relevance in a world in which millions of people are still groping toward political freedom.

Problems of a New Nation

The turmoil that has accompanied the growth of the new countries of Africa and Asia demonstrates that independence does not necessarily bring political maturity and peace. From Vietnam to Zimbabwe, as colonialism has given way to the forces of nationalism, political independence often has been accompanied by political instability. The same has proved true in some of the countries of Eastern Europe, notably Yugoslavia, following the collapse of the Soviet Union and its communist system in 1991. Yet America had a successful revolution. And, despite the Civil War, two world wars, a depression, periodic inflation and unemployment, Vietnam, Watergate, the Iran-contra affair, huge budget

deficits, the recession of the early 1990s, and other issues that confront the nation today, it has survived. How did the revolutionary leaders of America carve out an enduring new nation where none had existed before?

The process was slow and difficult. As Lipset has observed:

A backward glance into our own past should destroy the notion that the United States proceeded easily toward the establishment of democratic political institutions. In the period which saw the establishment of political legitimacy and party government, it was touch and go whether the complex balance of forces would swing in the direction of a one- or two-party system, or even whether the nation would survive as an entity. It took time to institutionalize values, beliefs, and practices, and there were many incidents that revealed how fragile the commitments to democracy and nationhood really were.[55]

The United States, in other words, went through growing pains similar to those of the new nations of Africa and Asia today. If some contemporary new nations have encountered difficulty in establishing political freedom and democratic procedures, so did America. For example, the Federalists under President John Adams wanted no organized political opposition and used the Alien and Sedition acts, passed in 1798, to suppress their opponents. At least seventy persons were jailed and fined under the Sedition Act, which made almost any criticism of the government, the president, or Congress a crime.

The Process of Nation Building

Lucian Pye has conceived of the process of nation building as a series of crises: identity, integration, penetration, participation, and distribution.[56]

The first crisis in the making of a new nation, as Pye views it, is for a people to gain "a sense of common *identity* as either subjects or citizens of a common political system."[57] For many years most colonists probably thought of themselves as English, or as New Yorkers or Virginians, rather than as Americans. And it took time and a series of conflicts between the colonies and the

---

[54] Seymour Martin Lipset, *The First New Nation* (New York: Basic Books, 1963), p. 2.

[55] Ibid., p. 16.

[56] Lucian W. Pye, "Transitional Asia and the Dynamics of Nation Building," in Marian D. Irish, ed., *World Pressures on American Foreign Policy* (Englewood Cliffs, N.J.: Prentice-Hall, 1964), pp. 154–72.

[57] Ibid., p. 162.

British government before a developing sense of American nationhood emerged.[58]

By then the process of *integration* was also underway. Integration, in this sense, describes the way that various groups in the nation relate to one another and to the national governmental system. In the prerevolutionary period, integration was taking place rather rapidly; the Committees of Correspondence, which enabled the colonists to coordinate their responses to the British, served as a significant integrating device.

Penetration is the ability of a government to reach all layers of society in order to carry out public policies, to act directly on the people. Since 1789 the scope and importance of the national government's penetration has increased greatly, as every individual who has submitted a federal income tax form is aware.

Participation, or bringing increasing numbers of people into the political process, began in the 1780s and has continued ever since. Through successive broadenings of the franchise and other measures, popular participation in the national government has been enlarged substantially, although not always peacefully. Women, African Americans, and other groups often have had to fight for the right to participate in the political system.

Distribution describes the government's control over the outputs of the political process: "What are the rewards of the political system, and who is to receive them?"[59] When the framers prohibited export taxes in the Constitution, they were concerned with problems of distribution. Distribution lies at the very heart of the process of government and politics.

It is, of course, difficult to pinpoint just when a nation passes through these various stages. Nevertheless, the processes Pye has identified can be observed in the American experience. As a result, the historical development of the American nation — with all its crises and problems — remains relevant to the emerging nations in today's world.

THE CONSTITUTION THEN AND NOW

The Constitution, Chief Justice Marshall said in *McCulloch* v. *Maryland*, was "intended to endure for ages to come, and consequently to be adapted to the various crises of human affairs."[60] This opinion, delivered in 1819, embodied the principle of loose or *flexible construction* of the Constitution; that is, the Constitution must be interpreted to meet changing conditions.

The members of the Supreme Court have generally reflected the times in which they have lived. Successive Supreme Courts have read very different meaning into the language of the Constitution. But the Court is not the only branch of the government that interprets the Constitution. So does Congress when it passes laws. So does the president when he makes decisions and takes actions. In addition, the Constitution has been amended twenty-seven times. The inputs of the American political system have resulted in a continual process of constitutional change. (The Constitution follows Chapter 16 of this book.)

What It Says

The Legislative Branch Article I of the Constitution vests all legislative powers "in a Congress of the United States, which shall consist of a Senate and House of Representatives." This article spells out the qualifications and method of election of members of the House and Senate. It gives power of impeachment to the House but provides that the Senate shall try impeachment cases. It empowers the vice-president to preside over the Senate with no vote, except in the case of a tie.

It provides that all tax legislation must originate in the House. It allows the president to sign or veto a bill and Congress to override his veto by a two-thirds vote of both houses.

Section 8 of this article gives Congress the power to tax, provide for the "general welfare" of the United States, borrow money, regulate commerce (the "commerce clause"), naturalize citizens, coin money, punish counterfeiters, establish a post office and a copyright and patents system, create lower courts, declare war, maintain armed forces, suppress insurrections and repel invasions, govern the District of Columbia, and make all "necessary and proper laws" (sometimes called the "elastic clause") to carry out the powers of the Constitution.

Section 9 provides certain basic protections for citizens against acts of Congress. For example, it says that the writ of *habeas corpus* shall not be suspended unless

---

[58] Richard L. Merritt, *Symbols of American Community* (New Haven: Yale University Press, 1966).

[59] Pye, "Transitional Asia and the Dynamics of Nation Building," p. 167.

[60] *McCulloch* v. *Maryland*, 4 Wheaton 316 (1819).

**"The executive Power shall be
vested in a President of
the United States of America."**

required by the public safety in cases of rebellion or invasion. One of the most important guarantees of individual liberty, the writ is designed to protect against illegal imprisonment. It requires that a person who is detained be brought before a judge for investigation so that the court may literally, in the Latin meaning, "have the body."

The article also prohibits Congress or the states from passing a "bill of attainder" — legislation aimed at a particular individual — or an "ex post facto" law, imposing punishment for an act that was not illegal when committed. It provides that only Congress may appropriate money drawn from the Treasury, a provision that is the single most important check on presidential power. The article also outlaws titles of nobility in America.

The Executive Branch   Article II states, "The executive Power shall be vested in a President of the United States of America." The framers did not provide for direct popular election of the president. Rather, they established the electoral college, with each state having as many electors as it had representatives and senators. The electors were to choose the president and vice-president. Alexander Hamilton argued that by this means the presidency would be filled by "characters preemi-

nent for ability and virtue." The electors, he thought, being "a small number of persons, selected by their fellow-citizens from the general mass, will be most likely to possess the information and discernment requisite."[61]

The election of 1800 was thrown into the House of Representatives because Jefferson and his vice-presidential running mate, Aaron Burr, although members of the same party, each received the same number of electoral votes. On the thirty-sixth ballot, the House chose Jefferson as president. Afterward, the electoral system was modified by the Twelfth Amendment to provide that electors must vote separately for president and vice-president.

The rise of political parties meant that in time the electoral college became largely a rubber stamp. As it works today, the voters in each state choose between slates of electors who usually run under a party label. All the electoral votes of a state normally go to the candidate who wins the popular vote in that state; electors on the winning slate routinely vote for their party's candidates for president and vice-president. But the electors do not

---

[61] Alexander Hamilton, "The Federalist, No. 68," in Earle, ed., *The Federalist,* pp. 441–42.

have to obey the will of the voters. For a variety of reasons (discussed in Chapter 9), there sometimes has been pressure to modify or abolish the electoral college system. However, a proposed constitutional amendment to provide for direct, popular election of the president failed to pass the Senate in 1970 and again in 1979.

The Constitution makes the president commander in chief of the armed forces, gives him the right to make treaties "with the Advice and Consent" of two-thirds of a quorum of the Senate, to appoint ambassadors, judges, and other high officials, subject to Senate approval, and to summon Congress into special session.

The Judiciary Article III states, "The judicial Power of the United States, shall be vested in one supreme Court, and in such inferior Courts" as Congress may establish. It also provides for trial by jury. The Supreme Court's vital right of judicial review of acts of Congress stems from both the *supremacy clause* of the Constitution (see below) and Article III, which asserts that the judicial power applies to "all Cases . . . arising under this Constitution."

Other Provisions Article IV governs the relations among the states and between the states and the federal government. Article V provides methods for amending the Constitution and for ratifying these amendments. Article VI states that the Constitution, laws, and treaties of the United States "shall be the supreme Law of the Land." This is the powerful *supremacy clause* by which laws of Congress prevail over any conflicting state laws. Article VII declares that the Constitution would go into effect when ratified by conventions in nine states.

The Amendment Process

The framers knew that the Constitution might have to be changed to meet future conditions. It had, after all, been created because of the need for change. So they provided two methods of proposing amendments: by a two-thirds vote of both houses of Congress or by a national convention called by Congress at the request of legislatures in two-thirds of the states.

Once proposed, an amendment does not take effect unless ratified, either by the legislatures of three-fourths of the states or by special ratifying conventions in three-fourths of the states.

No amendment has ever been *proposed* by the convention method. In the mid-1960s, the late Senator Everett McKinley Dirksen of Illinois, the Republican Senate leader, encouraged the states to petition Congress to call a constitutional convention. The general purpose was to amend the Constitution to overturn the Supreme Court's "one person, one vote" decisions that had forced the reapportionment of state legislatures.[62] By 1970 thirty-three state legislatures, only one short of the required two-thirds, had petitioned Congress to call a convention. Dirksen's campaign failed, but the large number of petitions led several senators and legal scholars to warn that a constitutional convention might run wild and make sweeping changes in the structure of the federal government, because no precedent exists for setting an agenda of such a convention.

Similar warnings were voiced a decade later when another movement began to call a convention, this time to propose an amendment to require a balanced federal budget. President Carter cautioned that such a conclave would be "completely uncontrollable." Nevertheless, the Constitution clearly permits a convention to be held if two-thirds of the state legislatures should request it. By 1992, thirty-two state legislatures had petitioned

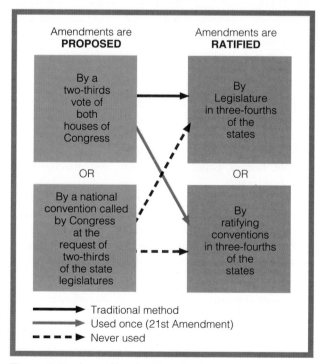

Figure 2-2 Amending the Constitution

---

[62] See discussion in Chapter 9, pp. 347–349.

Congress for a convention to propose a balanced budget amendment, short of the necessary two-thirds of the states.[63] But there was considerable support in Congress, and in the Bush administration, for an amendment to require a balanced budget. Advocates of the measure pressed Congress to propose such an amendment and send it to the states for ratification. Senior citizens and other groups, alarmed that an amendment might result in cuts in the Social Security program, opposed the change, as did the House Speaker, Thomas S. Foley, Democrat, of Washington. In June, the amendment was rejected in the House, receiving nine votes less than the necessary two-thirds.

Of the twenty-seven amendments ratified by 1992, only the Twenty-first Amendment, repealing Prohibition, was ratified by state conventions; the rest were ratified by state legislatures. Some of the amendments add to the Constitution; others supersede or revise the original language of the Constitution.

The Bill of Rights

The amendments to the Constitution fall into three major time periods. The first twelve, ratified between 1791 and 1804, were remedial amendments designed to perfect the original instrument. The next three grew out of the great upheaval of the Civil War and were designed to deal with the new position of blacks as free men and women. Amendments in the third group were all passed in the twentieth century and deal with a wide range of subjects, in part reflecting more recent pressures toward change in American society.

The first ten amendments are the Bill of Rights.[64] The provisions of the first four are: (First Amendment) freedom of religion, speech, press, assembly, and peti-

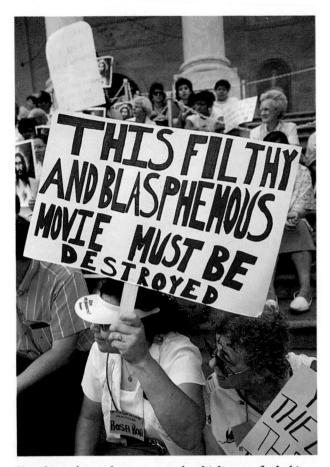

Freedom of speech, even speech which some find objectionable, is guaranteed by the First Amendment.

tion; (Second Amendment) the right to bear arms; (Third Amendment) protection against quartering of soldiers in private homes; and (Fourth Amendment) protection against unreasonable search and seizure of people, homes, papers, and effects, and provision for search warrants.

The Fifth Amendment provides that no person can be compelled "to be a witness against himself" or to stand trial twice for the same crime. It also lists other rights of accused persons, including that of indictment by a grand jury for major crimes and the general provi-

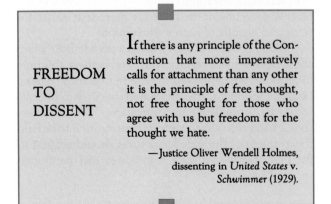

FREEDOM TO DISSENT

If there is any principle of the Constitution that more imperatively calls for attachment than any other it is the principle of free thought, not free thought for those who agree with us but freedom for the thought we hate.

—Justice Oliver Wendell Holmes, dissenting in *United States* v. *Schwimmer* (1929).

---

[63] But many of the state petitions were more than ten years old and their validity was in question.

[64] Some scholars regard only the first eight or nine amendments as the Bill of Rights. The first ten amendments were passed by the First Congress on September 25, 1789, and went into effect when ratified by three-fourths of the states on December 15, 1791. The Bill of Rights is discussed in detail in Chapter 4.

sion that no person shall "be deprived of life, liberty, or property, without due process of law." The Sixth Amendment calls for a speedy and public trial by jury in criminal cases and sets forth other protections, including the right to have a lawyer.

The Seventh Amendment provides for jury trial in civil cases, and the Eighth Amendment bars excessive bail or fines, or cruel and unusual punishment. The Ninth Amendment provides that the enumeration of certain rights in the Constitution shall not deny other rights retained by the people, and the Tenth Amendment reserves to the states, or to the people, powers not delegated to the federal government.

These ten amendments were designed to protect Americans against the power of the *federal* government. Nothing in the Constitution specifically provides that *state* governments also must abide by the provisions of the Bill of Rights. But in interpreting the Fourteenth Amendment, ratified in 1868 after the Civil War, the Supreme Court in the twentieth century gradually has extended the protection of almost all of the Bill of Rights to apply to the states.

The Later Amendments

The Eleventh Amendment (1795)[65] was added to guarantee that a sovereign state would never again be hauled into federal court by a private citizen or foreign citizen. In *Chisholm* v. *Georgia*,[66] the Supreme Court had ruled for two South Carolina citizens who had sued the state of Georgia on behalf of a British creditor to recover confiscated property.

The Twelfth Amendment (1804), as already discussed, was adopted after the deadlocked election of 1800. It provided that presidential electors vote *separately* for president and vice-president.

The next three amendments resulted from the Civil War. The Thirteenth Amendment (1865) forbids slavery. It also outlaws involuntary servitude in the United States and its territories except as punishment for a crime. Its purpose was to free the slaves and complete the abolition of slavery in America. Lincoln's

---

[65] Date after each amendment refers to date of ratification.
[66] *Chisholm* v. *Georgia*, 2 Dallas 419 (1793). However, citizens can sue states in state courts if they are deprived of their rights under the Constitution or federal laws, and states can appeal such cases to the federal courts. *Scheuer* v. *Rhodes*, 416 U.S. 232 (1974); *Maine* v. *Thiboutot*, 448 U.S. 1 (1980).

Emancipation Proclamation, which was issued during the war, applied *only* to areas in rebellion and under Confederate control and therefore did not actually free any slaves.

The Fourteenth Amendment (1868) was adopted to make the former slaves citizens. But it has had other unintended and far-reaching effects. The amendment says that no state "shall abridge the privileges or immunities of citizens"; nor "deprive any person of life, liberty, or property, without due process of law"; nor deny anyone "the equal protection of the laws." The famous "due process clause" of the amendment has been used by the Supreme Court to protect the rights of individuals against the police power of the state in a broad spectrum of cases. The "equal protection of the laws" provision was the basis for the landmark 1954 Supreme Court decision outlawing segregation in public schools.

The Fifteenth Amendment (1870) barred the federal and state governments from denying any citizen the right to vote because of race, color, or previous condition of servitude. It did not, however, prevent some states from disenfranchising blacks by means of restrictive voting requirements, such as literacy tests.

Forty-three years elapsed after the adoption of the Fifteenth Amendment before another was ratified. The Sixteenth Amendment (1913) allowed Congress to pass a graduated individual income tax, based in theory on ability to pay. The tax has been, of course, the largest single source of federal revenue.

The Seventeenth Amendment (1913) provided for direct election of senators by the people, instead of by state legislatures.

The Eighteenth Amendment (1919) established Prohibition by outlawing the manufacture, sale, or transportation of alcoholic beverages. It provides a classic instance of a government output doomed to failure because ultimately the input of popular *support* was lacking. Prohibition led to the era of bathtub gin, "flappers," speakeasies, and bootlegging. It was marked by widespread defiance of the law by otherwise law-abiding citizens and by the rise of organized crime, which quickly moved to meet public demand for illicit liquor. Partly as a result of Prohibition, organized crime remains entrenched in America today, exercising political influence in some areas of the country. Prohibition was repealed in 1933.

The Nineteenth Amendment (1920) guaranteed women the right to vote. Women in many states could vote even before the amendment was proposed, but it

The Nineteenth Amendment, ratified in 1920, guaranteed women the right to vote.

provided a constitutional basis for this major expansion of the electorate. Even so, it may seem surprising today that female suffrage was not constitutionally adopted until the year 1920, in time for that year's presidential election.

Under the Twentieth (or "lame duck") Amendment (1933), the terms of the president and vice-president begin on January 20 and the terms of members of Congress on January 3. Prior to that time a president and members of Congress defeated in November would continue in office for four months until March 4 (formerly the date of presidential inaugurations). Injured by the voters, the defeated incumbents sat like "lame ducks."[67] The amendment also provides alternatives in case of the death of the president-elect before Inauguration Day or in case no president has been chosen.

The Twenty-first Amendment (1933) repealed Prohibition but permitted states to remain "dry" if they so desired.

The Twenty-second Amendment (1951) limits presidents to a maximum of two elected terms. It was proposed after President Franklin D. Roosevelt had won a fourth term in 1944. Before then, through hallowed tradition established by George Washington, no president had been elected more than twice.

The Twenty-third Amendment (1961) gives citizens of the District of Columbia the right to vote in presidential elections; they did so for the first time in 1964. When the amendment was adopted, the capital

---

[67] The phrase apparently originated as London stock exchange slang. It was used to describe a stock jobber or broker who could not make good his losses and would "waddle out of the alley like a lame duck." Abraham Lincoln is sometimes credited with introducing the phrase in America. When a defeated senator called on Lincoln and asked for a job as Commissioner of Indian Affairs, Lincoln was quoted as saying afterward: "I usually find that a Senator or Representative out of business is a sort of lame duck." George Stimpson, *A Book about American Politics* (New York: Harper & Row, 1952), pp. 527–28.

had a population of 800,000 — larger than that of thirteen of the states.

The Twenty-fourth Amendment (1964) abolished the poll tax as a prerequisite for voting in federal elections or primaries. It applied to only five Southern states that still imposed such a tax, originally a device to keep blacks (and in some cases poor whites) from voting.

The Twenty-fifth Amendment (1967) was spurred by President Dwight D. Eisenhower's 1955 heart attack and by the murder of President Kennedy in Dallas, Texas, on November 22, 1963. It defines the circumstances in which a vice-president may take over the leadership of the country in case of the mental or physical illness or disability of the president. It also requires the president to nominate a vice-president, subject to majority approval of Congress, when that office becomes vacant for any reason.[68]

The Twenty-sixth Amendment (1971) gave persons eighteen years of age or older the right to vote in all elections — federal, state, and local. The amendment was proposed by Congress in March 1971 and ratified in June. As a result, 1972 was the first presidential election year in which persons eighteen through twenty were able to vote in elections at every level of government.

The Twenty-seventh Amendment (1992) prohibited Congress from voting itself a pay raise; the amendment provides that any vote to increase congressional salaries cannot take effect until after the next Congress is elected. The amendment was first submitted to the states in 1789. Until 1984, only ten states had ratified

---

[68] The amendment was used for the first time in October 1973 when President Nixon nominated House Republican leader Gerald R. Ford to replace Vice-President Agnew, who had resigned. Congress confirmed Ford in December. When Nixon resigned in August 1974, Ford became president, again under the amendment. The amendment was used a third time when President Ford that same month nominated Nelson A. Rockefeller of New York to be vice-president. Congress confirmed Rockefeller in December 1974.

The assassination of President John F. Kennedy, November 23, 1963.

A STUDENT GETS THE CONSTITUTION AMENDED

In 1789, it bothered James Madison that under the new Constitution he had helped to create, members of Congress could vote to increase their own salaries. They would, he warned, be able "without control to put their hand into the public coffers, to take out money to put in their pockets." There was, Madison said, "a seeming indecorum in such power that leads me to propose a change."

Madison proposed an amendment to the constitution. It said: "No law varying the compensation for the services of the Senators and Representatives shall take effect, until an election of Representatives shall have intervened." The proposed amendment was sent to the states as part of the original Bill of Rights.

There it languished; after a century, only seven states had ratified the amendment. Enter Gregory D. Watson, a student of government at the University of Texas in Austin, who came across it in 1982 while researching a paper. Watson made passage of Madison's amendment a personal crusade, and under his prodding, beginning in the mid-eighties, one state legislature after another ratified the proposal. Finally, on May 7, 1992 Michigan became the 38th state to ratify, providing the necessary three-fourths of the states.

Although some scholars argued that the amendment was invalid because of the passage of time, six days later the Archivist of the United States pronounced the 27th Amendment part of the Constitution. By that time Gregory Watson was an aide to a Democratic state legislator in Texas. "I always knew in my heart of hearts that this day would come," he said.

—Adapted from the *New York Times*, May 8, 1992.

the amendment. During the late 1980s and early 1990s, public indignation over congressional pay raises and perquisites led many other states to approve the amendment, and in May of 1992, Michigan became the 38th state to ratify, providing the necessary three-fourths vote. Some scholars questioned the validity of the amendment, arguing that the states had taken too long to act — 203 years. Since 1919, Congress has set deadlines, usually seven years, for states to ratify proposed amendments, but it did not do so in this case.

Several other constitutional amendments have been suggested in recent years. In 1978 Congress approved and sent to the states a proposed constitutional amendment that would treat the District of Columbia as a state for purposes of representation in Congress and the electoral college. (The Twenty-third Amendment gave district residents the right only to vote for president, and a 1970 law permitted the district a nonvoting delegate in the House.) Congress set a seven-year time limit for approval of the amendment. By 1985 only sixteen states had ratified the proposal, and it expired.

A proposed amendment, designed to guarantee equal rights for women under the law, was approved by Congress in 1972 and sent to the states for ratification. "Equality of rights under the law shall not be denied or abridged by the United States or by any State on ac-count of sex," the amendment read. It was proposed to nullify the many state laws that discriminate against women in jobs, business, marriage, and other areas.

After an initial burst of support, the Equal Rights Amendment (ERA) ran into increasing difficulty. By 1977 only thirty-five states — three short of the necessary thirty-eight — had approved the amendment.[69] With time running out, Congress extended the deadline for ratification from 1979 to June 30, 1982. But by that date, no additional states had ratified, and ERA was defeated. Undaunted, supporters of the Equal Rights Amendment reintroduced it in Congress. In November of 1983, however, the amendment failed by six votes to achieve the necessary two-thirds majority in the House.

In 1982 foes of legalized abortion introduced a proposed amendment to the Constitution that would allow states to prohibit abortions. The "pro-life" amendment was designed to overturn a 1973 Supreme Court ruling that legalized abortions. The proposed amendment was defeated in the Senate in 1983.

Proposals for a constitutional amendment to require a balanced federal budget were introduced beginning in the early 1980s, even as state legislatures were

---

[69] Confusing the picture further, several states attempted to rescind their approval of the amendment.

petitioning Congress to call a national convention for the same purpose. A proposed balanced-budget amendment was approved in 1982 by the necessary two-thirds of the Senate, but later that year it was rejected by the House. As already discussed, new efforts in support of such an amendment were under way in Congress in 1992.

In 1984, the Senate rejected a proposed constitutional amendment, supported by President Reagan, to permit organized, spoken prayers in the public schools. The Senate also voted down a proposed constitutional amendment to allow silent prayer in the public schools.

Presidents Bush and Reagan repeatedly urged Congress to enact a proposed constitutional amendment to give presidents the power to veto *parts* of appropriations bills passed by Congress. The Constitution does not provide for such an *item veto*; the president can veto only an entire bill. And there was little prospect that Congress would increase the president's power in this manner.

A Document for the Living . . .

At 4 P.M. in Philadelphia on September 17, 1987, the moment when, two hundred years earlier, the delegates had finished signing their names to the Constitution, former Chief Justice Warren E. Burger rang a replica of the Liberty Bell. It was a signal for bells to ring throughout Philadelphia, in the capitals of the fifty states, and in U.S. diplomatic missions around the world.

Philadelphia was bedecked with balloons, flags, and parade floats for the bicentennial celebration. Tall ships sailed the Delaware River. President Reagan spoke at Independence Hall, recalling the convention two hundred years before. "In a very real sense it was then, in 1787, that the revolution truly began," he said.

What Alexander Hamilton called "the American drama" had begun its third century. The world of the framers had changed beyond measure. But that process of change had been foreseen.

"The Constitution belongs to the living and not to the dead," Thomas Jefferson wrote. He added:

> Some men look at constitutions with sanctimonious reverence and deem them like the ark of the covenant, too sacred to be touched. They ascribe to the men of the preceding age a wisdom more than human, and suppose what they did to be beyond amendment. . . . Laws and institutions must go hand in hand with the progress of the human mind. . . . As new discoveries are made, new truths disclosed, and manners and opinions change . . . institutions must advance also, and keep pace with the times.[70]

Through a variety of ways, including amendments and judicial review, the oldest written national constitution in the world remains the vital framework of the American political system. But are constitutional principles enough? Today, many Americans are asking that the nation's institutions fulfill the promise of its ideals, and that principles be translated into reality. Constitutional democracy was born at Philadelphia, but, in a real sense, the work was only begun.

PERSPECTIVE

The Constitution and the Bill of Rights provide the basic framework of American government. The Constitution established the structure of the government

---

[70] "Letter to Samuel Kercheval, 1816," in Saul K. Padover, ed., *The Complete Jefferson* (New York: Duell, Sloan & Pearce, 1943), p. 291.

and a written set of rules to control the conduct of the government. The Declaration of Independence, approved by the Continental Congress on July 4, 1776, proclaimed that "all men are created equal" and that government derived its just powers from "the consent of the governed." Many of the ideas contained in these documents were drawn from the colonists' English heritage.

Before the Constitution was framed, a weak central government had been established under the Articles of Confederation. During the Constitutional Convention of 1787, the Virginia Plan, favored by the large states, and the New Jersey Plan, favored by the small states, were debated. The Great Compromise, also called the Connecticut Compromise, was finally adopted as an alternative. That compromise provided for a House of Representatives, to be based on population in each state, and a Senate, to consist of two members from each state — a solution that satisfied both the large and the small states. The convention also compromised over the slavery issue by delaying a ban on the importation of slaves until 1808 and by counting three-fifths of all slaves in apportioning the House of Representatives.

The Constitution divided the national government into three branches: legislative, executive, and judicial. The government is based on the principles of separation of powers and checks and balances, even though in practice many powers and functions overlap and are shared. The Constitution also created a federal system, in which the powers and functions of government are shared by the national government and the states. The Constitution was ratified in 1788, but only after a long debate and political struggle between the Federalists and the Antifederalists. In 1791 the states ratified a Bill of Rights intended to protect individuals from the power of the federal government. These first ten amendments to the Constitution included provisions for freedom of religion, speech, press, assembly, and petition; the right to bear arms; protection against unreasonable search and seizure; the right to due process of law and protection against self-incrimination and double jeopardy; the right to a speedy and public trial by jury in criminal cases; and protection against cruel and unusual punishment. Through 1992, the Constitution had been amended twenty-seven times. The Supreme Court interprets the Constitution. Exercising judicial review, the Supreme Court decides whether laws passed by Congress and acts of the president are constitutional.

Suggested Reading

Beard, Charles A. *An Economic Interpretation of the Constitution of the United States** (Free Press, 1986). (Originally published in 1913.) The classic argument suggesting that delegates to the Philadelphia Convention were influenced primarily by economic motives in framing the Constitution. A number of later scholars have taken issue with Beard's interpretation.

Becker, Carl L. *The Declaration of Independence** (Random House, 1958). (Originally published in 1942.) A perceptive discussion of the Declaration of Independence and the events leading up to it.

Boorstin, Daniel J. *The Americans: The Colonial Experience** (Random House, 1958). An analysis of the impact of the colonial period on U.S. political ideas and institutions.

Burns, James MacGregor. *The American Experiment, Vol. I: The Vineyard of Liberty** (Knopf, 1982). An historical analysis, rich in narrative, of the shaping of the republic and the development of liberty in America. Covers the period from the framing of the Constitution to the Emancipation Proclamation.

Corwin, Edward S., et al., eds. *The Constitution of the United States of America, Analysis and Interpretation* (U.S. Government Printing Office, 1964). A comprehensive and detailed line-by-line exposition of the Constitution. See also Corwin, revised by Harold W. Chase and Craig R. Ducat, *The Constitution and What It Means Today*, 14th edition* (Princeton, 1979).

Earle, Edward Mead, ed. *The Federalist** (Random House, Modern Library). A classic collection of essays written by Alexander Hamilton, James Madison, and John Jay, prominent supporters of the proposed Constitution during the struggle over ratification. *The Federalist* papers were published in the press under the pseudonym "Publius"; they remain an important exposition of the federal government's structure.

Farrand, Max. *The Framing of the Constitution of the United States** (Yale University Press, 1913). A good general account of the Constitutional Convention by the scholar who compiled in four volumes the basic documentary sources on the convention proceedings.

Kelly, Alfred H., and Harbison, Winfred A. *The American Constitution: Its Origins and Development*, 7th edition* (Norton, 1991). A good general history of American constitutional development beginning with the colonial period.

Lipset, Seymour Martin. *The First New Nation** (Norton, 1979). An important historical and sociological study of America that seeks to trace the relationship between a nation's values and the development of stable political institutions. Compares the early American experience with that of today's emerging nations.

Mason, Alpheus T., ed. *The States Rights Debate: Anti-federalism and the Constitution*, 2nd edition* (Oxford University Press, 1972). A valuable series of essays and documents tracing the historical tension between states' rights and national supremacy in the federal system, as it was reflected in the Constitutional Convention and in the fight over ratification.

Rossiter, Clinton, *Seedtime of the Republic* (Harcourt Brace Jovanovich, 1953). A penetrating analysis of American political and social history in the colonial and revolutionary periods, with emphasis on the political ideas that were to condition the formation of the American nation.

Rossiter, Clinton. *1787: The Grand Convention* (Norton, 1987). (Originally published in 1966.) A very readable account of the Philadelphia Convention, the battle for ratification of the Constitution, and the first years of the new republic. Makes interesting observations on the personal characteristics and objectives of the framers of the Constitution.

Rutland, Robert A. *The Birth of the Bill of Rights*, 1776–1791, Bicentennial edition* (Northeastern University Press, 1991). A study of how Americans came to rely on legal guarantees in an effort to preserve their personal freedom. English common law, colonial charters and statutes, and specific events in the thirteen colonies are discussed as important factors that led to the Bill of Rights.

Storing, Herbert J. *What the Anti-Federalists Were For** (University of Chicago Press, 1981). A detailed analysis of the position of the Antifederalists in the struggle over the ratification of the Constitution. Traces how the views of the Antifederalists helped to bring about the enactment of the Bill of Rights.

---

* Available in paperback edition.

I T USED TO BE SAID that the French minister of education could, by glancing at the clock in his office, tell at any given moment what book was being read by every schoolchild in France.

The tale may be a bit exaggerated, but no official in Washington could even begin to perform the same feat. France has a centralized, *unitary* system of government. The nation is divided into administrative units called departments, uniformly administered from Paris. Educational and other policies are set by the central government.

In contrast, the United States has a *federal* system of government, in which power is constitutionally shared by a national government and fifty state govern-

Chapter 3

The Federal System

ments. Within the states, of course, are thousands of local governments — and schools are controlled by local and state governments or independent school districts.

The constitutional sharing of power by a national government and regional units of government (states, in the case of the United States) characterizes and defines a federal system or *federalism*. The terms "federalism" and "the federal system" are used interchangeably to describe this basic structure of government in the United States. (These terms should not be confused with "the federal government," which simply refers to the national government in Washington.)

To say that power in America is shared by the national and state governments may, at first glance, seem merely to be stating the obvious. Yet no principle of American government has been disputed more than federalism. Should that be doubted, one need only recall that more than 500,000 people died during the Civil War settling problems of federalism.

More recently, the rioting that erupted in the streets of Los Angeles in April of 1992 provided dramatic testimony to the nature of the federal system. The disorders were triggered when a jury that included no blacks in a state court in California acquitted four white police officers in the savage beating of a black motorist. Local police in Los Angeles were slow to respond and failed to restore order, so the governor called out the national guard. When that, too, appeared inadequate to restore order, the president placed the national guard under federal authority and dispatched thousands of

federal agents and armed troops to the nation's second-largest city. All three layers of government—local, state, and national—were drawn into, and reacted to, the crisis. And all three layers would have to play a role in any long-term solutions to the problems of the nation's inner cities.

The question of *how* power is to be shared in the federal system is central to the political process in the United States. It is a subject of continuing political debate. It has been reflected in many important decisions of the Supreme Court. The migrant worker in the lettuce fields of California, the family on welfare in New York, the West Virginia coal miner, the spouse seeking a Nevada divorce, the murder suspect fighting

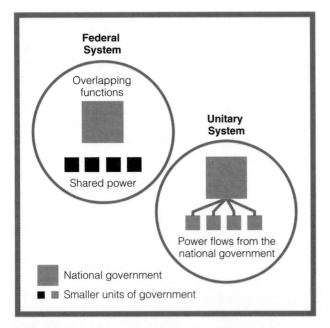

Figure 3-1
Federal and Unitary Systems of Government Compared

extradition, the slum dweller hoping for an apartment in a federal housing project — these people do not think of their problems in terms of the federal system. Yet the relationship among national, state, and local governments vitally touches their lives. To a considerable extent, federalism affects who wins and who loses as a result of government decisions in American society. It affects the outputs of the political system.

Federalism is one answer to the problem of how to govern a large nation. Although there are all sorts of institutional arrangements in the 193 nations of the world, governments tend to be either centralized and unitary, or federated. In the twentieth century, federal-

ism has become a popular style of government. By 1964, one study concluded, "well over half the land mass of the world was ruled by governments that with some justification, however slight, described themselves as federalisms." [1] The list of federal systems includes Switzerland, Canada, Australia, Mexico, India, and Germany.[2] Unitary systems, in which all power is vested in a central government, include Britain, France, Israel, and South Africa.

FEDERALISM: THE PROS AND CONS

What are the arguments for and against a federal system? Federalism permits diversity. Since problems and circumstances vary from one community to another, the argument can be made that a number of governments dealing directly with local problems, and accountable to local voters, may perform better than a single, remote bureaucracy. Local governments, by this reasoning, may have a better idea than the national government of how to cope with local problems.

Another argument advanced for a federal system of government is that it allows more levels of government, more points of access to the government, and as a result, more opportunities for political participation. A system in which there are *multiple points of access* to government may offer advantages to individuals or groups seeking benefits from the political system. Because

---

[1] William H. Riker, *Federalism: Origin, Operation, Significance* (Boston: Little, Brown, 1964), p. 1.
[2] The former Soviet Union was a federal system. When it broke up in 1991, it was replaced by a Commonwealth of Independent States, a very loose grouping of eleven of the fifteen former Soviet republics. Although the future of the Commonwealth was uncertain, it, too, could be roughly characterized as a federal system.

Table 3-1
The Federal System

Scholars and political leaders alike have debated the relative merits and drawbacks of federalism since the founding of the republic. Here are some of the major arguments that have been made:

Advantages	Disadvantages
Permits diversity and diffusion of power	Makes national unity difficult to achieve and maintain
Local governments can handle local problems better	Local governments may block national policies
More access points for political participation	May permit economic inequality and racial discrimination
Protects individual rights against concentrated government power	Law enforcement and justice are uneven
Fosters experimentation and innovation	Smaller units may lack expertise and money
Suits a large country with a diverse population	May promote local dominance by special interests

FEDERALISM UNDER CHALLENGE

Federal assistance to states and localities through grant-in-aid programs, once applauded by respected observers and commentators, has become the object of searching examination. Once regarded as essential institutional innovations, the programs are now criticized for causing bureaucratic nightmares. Once said to be the best hope for social progress, federal involvement is now blamed for increased poverty, escalating medical costs, urban decay, and educational retrogression. What was once accepted as a growing presence has been sharply curtailed, a victim of antigovernment sentiments and pressing budget deficits. . . . Yet federalism works well when national, state, and local governments together take the time to design and implement programs that meet broad social needs not easily addressed by local jurisdictions alone.

—Paul E. Peterson, Barry G. Rabe, and Kenneth K. Wong, *When Federalism Works*

Americans have a federal system, they may vote at frequent intervals for mayors, town-council and school board members, governors, other state officials, and, at the national level, members of the House of Representatives and senators elected from the states.

Some analysts also argue that because power is diffused and fragmented among many different units in a federal system, there is better protection for individual rights than in a highly centralized government. Concentrated power is dangerous, supporters of federalism often maintain.

Advocates of a federal system also stress that the existence of many units of government allows for more experimentation and innovation in solving problems. For example, new social programs are sometimes originated in one state and then adopted in another, or even nationally. Many of the social programs of Franklin D. Roosevelt's New Deal were copied from some of the states, a pattern that was repeated during the 1960s and 1970s. And, during the Reagan era, when the federal government was trying to cut back spending for social programs, a number of states took the lead in education, economic development, and other important areas.

In addition, advocates of federalism argue that it is well-suited to the United States, a nation covering a large geographic area with a highly diversified population of more than 254 million people.

But critics contend that a federal system also has distinct disadvantages. Federalism may serve as a mask for privilege and economic or racial discrimination.[3] In the past, at least, in some areas of the South and in other sections of the country, the federal system has permitted

[3] Riker, *Federalism: Origin, Operation, Significance*, pp. 152–53.

WASHINGTON: COLOR-BLIND IN A BLIZZARD?

While a trivial matter, one example indicates the difficulty of keeping too many strings tied to the center nail, of seeking too much uniformity, or setting one pattern for all of the diverse nation. The state of Wyoming had a slight hassle with the U.S. Bureau of Public Roads over the color of paint to be used to mark the sides and center line of Wyoming highways. Wyoming had painted a solid yellow line to mark the shoulder of the road and an intermittent yellow line for the center. The Bureau of Public Roads said the lines must be standardized with the rest of the country, which meant white lines except in the no-passing stretches. After much haggling Wyoming inevitably gave in, but with a parting comment: "Let them come out here and find one of their white lines during one of our blizzards." The highway engineers had found that in the blowing blizzards of Wyoming's winters, drivers could see yellow lines, but not white ones. In this encounter they learned that yellow lines could not be seen from Washington.

—Terry Sanford, *Storm Over the States*

state and local governments to repress blacks. Inequalities may occur when special interests exercise considerable influence on the politics and economy of a state or locality. For example, West Virginia, although the nation's third leading coal producer, is a relatively poor state, a fact usually attributed in part to its dependence on a single industry. Along with abandoned strip mines, pockets of poverty scar the hillsides; in 1991 West Virginia ranked forty-ninth in the nation in per capita income.[4] Although the energy shortage of the 1970s increased the price of coal and brought greater prosperity to the state, industry pressures tended to keep taxes low. That in turn affected West Virginia's ability to provide social services for its residents.

Critics also argue that under the federal system, local or special interests — for example, the automobile industry, oil companies, or in the past, white supremacists in the Deep South — have often been able to frustrate efforts to solve national problems like segregated public schools, poverty, pollution, and energy needs. The same local officials whose understanding of local problems is often cited as a benefit of federalism may be in a position to thwart national policies. Government that is "closer to the people" may not serve all the people equally. Nor is it necessarily the case that local governments can solve problems more efficiently; they may lack the national government's skill and money. In fact, because the federal government collects most of the taxes in America, it can be argued that the system of federalism has often left cities and states unable to pay for local services.

Other arguments are sometimes made against a federal system: its very diversity may make it difficult to achieve and maintain national unity; it can be more difficult and costly to make a complex system work; and law enforcement and justice may be administered unevenly.

The relations between the states and the federal government are thus a source of continuing conflict and controversy in the American political system and raise a number of questions of fundamental importance. Who benefits and who loses under the federal system? Does federalism restrict progress in solving national problems? Do the advantages of federalism outweigh the price of fragmented government? Why does the United States have a federal system? What are the problems it has created? What are the consequences of federalism in American politics? In the performance of the states?

THE CHECKERBOARD OF GOVERNMENTS

Average Americans complain that they are being squeezed by high taxes on at least three levels of government — national, state, and local. They are confronted by a bewildering checkerboard of overlapping governments and local districts. One study of the federal system found that a resident of Park Forest, Illinois, paid taxes to eleven governmental units, starting with the United States of America and ending with the "South Cook County Mosquito Abatement District."[5] Moreover, states have different laws and rules for deal-

---

[4] U.S. Department of Commerce, *Survey of Current Business* (Washington, D.C.: U.S. Government Printing Office, April, 1992), p. 73.

[5] Morton Grodzins, *The American System* (Chicago: Rand McNally, 1966), pp. 3–4.

FEDERALISM: IT DOESN'T ALWAYS WORK

BOOTHBAY HARBOR, MAINE, Sept. 3 (AP) — A seal that lay wounded on a beach for 14 hours because of a dispute between state and federal officials died early today. The animal, which had been shot in the stomach, died at the laboratory of the State Department of Sea and Shore Fisheries. State wardens said they couldn't aid the seal because a new federal law placed jurisdiction for marine mammals with the U.S. Marine Fisheries Service.

At the Newagen Inn, a resort near where the seal was beached . . . guests tried to get help, but failed. . . . Several of the guests placed a towel under the seal and then kept placing water on the towel to keep the seal moist. . . . The harbor seals killed in Maine this summer were probably shot by fishermen who complain that the seals tear holes in their nets.

—*Washington Post*, September 4, 1973

ing with such matters as taxation, criminal justice, education, marriage, and licensing of professions and businesses.

The Census Bureau has counted a total of 83,186 governments in the United States: some 3,000 counties; 19,200 municipalities; 16,700 townships; 14,700 school districts; 29,500 special districts (for natural resources, fire protection, housing development, and other services); 50 states; and one national government.[6]

But knowing how many governments exist in America tells little about how the federal system operates — how the various levels of government relate to one another. One way to visualize the system as a whole was suggested by Morton Grodzins:

> The federal system is not accurately symbolized by a neat layer cake of three distinct and separate planes. A far more realistic symbol is that of the marble cake. Wherever you slice through it you reveal an inseparable mixture of differently colored ingredients. There is no neat horizontal stratification. Vertical and diagonal lines almost obliterate the horizontal ones, and in some places there are unexpected whirls and an imperceptible merging of colors, so that it is difficult to tell where one ends and the other begins. So it is with federal, state, and local responsibilities in the chaotic marble cake of American government.[7]

Cooperation — and Tension

Is the American federal system essentially cooperative — or is it competitive? In fact, federalism can be seen both as a rivalry between the states and Washington, and as a partnership. A system of 83,186 governments could not operate without a substantial measure of cooperation, but a great tension is built into the system as well.

---

[6] U.S. Bureau of the Census, *1987 Census of Governments*, Vol. 1, No. 1. The total represents the actual number of governments in 1987; the other figures are rounded.

[7] Morton Grodzins, "Centralization and Decentralization in the American Federal System," in Robert A. Goldwin, ed., *A Nation of States* (Chicago: Rand McNally, 1963), pp. 1–4.

"A great tension is built into the system . . .": federal troops on guard at Central High School in Little Rock, Arkansas, September 1957

In 1975, for example, New York City was in deep financial trouble; there was a real possibility that the city would default on its bonds. The administration of President Gerald R. Ford at first declined to help. New York State took control of the city's finances, but the specter of default remained. Finally, Ford relented and recommended to Congress that it aid New York City. Congress passed a bill providing billions in federal loans for the city. Ultimately, the federal government did not permit the nation's biggest metropolis to go broke, but the political struggle over aid to New York City was protracted and bitter.

There have been other dramatic examples of tension within the federal system. Several times in recent decades the president of the United States has deployed armed federal troops in states experiencing civil disorders. In 1957 President Eisenhower sent troops into Little Rock, Arkansas, to enforce court-ordered integration of the previously all-white Central High School. In the fall of 1962 two men were killed on the campus of the University of Mississippi at Oxford during rioting over the admission of James H. Meredith, a black student. President Kennedy deployed 16,000 federal troops in Mississippi to enroll Meredith and protect him as he attended classes. In June 1963 Governor George Wallace carried out a campaign pledge to "stand in the schoolhouse door" to try to prevent two black students from entering the University of Alabama. Wallace backed down after President Kennedy federalized the state's national guard to enforce the order of a federal court. In 1967, President Johnson dispatched 4,700 federal paratroopers to quell racial disorders in Detroit; and in 1992, President Bush sent 4,500 troops and 1,000 federal law enforcement agents to Los Angeles after rioting broke out there.

Although presidents tend to use the rhetoric of cooperation when they talk about federal–state relations, there is clearly an underlying tension among competing levels of government. Sometimes the tensions arise from social issues, as in the armed confrontations over racial desegregation. Often, as in the case of the "bailout" of New York City, they are rooted in disagreements over how tax revenues should be shared or used.

Political and ideological tensions arise as well— between those who look to the federal government to solve major national social and economic problems (often northern Democrats and liberal Republicans), and those who tend to see the government in Washington as a threat to individual liberty and initiative and regard the states as a bulwark against an expanding federal "octopus" (often conservative Republicans and some southern Democrats).

The Changing Federal Framework

The federal system has been viewed differently at various times. During much of the nineteenth century and until 1937, the concept of *dual federalism* was accepted, in which the Supreme Court saw itself as a referee between two competing power centers—the states and the federal government—each with its own responsibilities.

This orthodox view of the federal system prevailed until the New Deal of Franklin D. Roosevelt. During the 1930s the Roosevelt administration responded to the Great Depression with a series of laws establishing social-welfare and public-works programs. In 1937 the Supreme Court began holding these programs constitutional. With the federal government thrust into a position of expanded power, a new view of federalism emerged, that of *cooperative federalism*. In this view, the various levels of government are seen as related parts of a single governmental system, characterized more by cooperation and shared functions than by conflict and competition. For example, the federal government provides most of the money to build major highways, but the program is administered by state and local governments. Some scholars have argued that, historically, the

1935: President Franklin D. Roosevelt signs the Social Security Act

American federal system has always been characterized by such shared functions at the federal, state, and local levels.[8]

One student of the federal system, Michael D. Reagan, has suggested that it no longer makes sense to think of federalism "as a wall separating the national and state levels of government." Rather, he maintains, extensive federal financial aid to the states has created "*a nationally dominated system of shared power and shared functions.*"[9]

President Lyndon Johnson coined the term *creative federalism* to describe his own view of the relationship between Washington and the states. During his administration, Congress enacted "Great Society" legislation that further expanded the role of the federal government. President Nixon launched what he termed the *new federalism*, designed to return federal tax money to state and local governments.

In recent years yet another concept, that of *regulatory federalism*, has emerged as a new description of the changing pattern of federal–state relations. Beginning in the 1960s, a series of federal laws dealing with the environment and a broad range of other concerns imposed various requirements on the states. For example, a 1974 law barred the release of any federal highway-construction funds to states with laws that did not conform to the maximum speed limit of fifty-five miles per hour set by Congress at that time.[10] In 1978, Congress amended the law to allow Washington to withhold up to ten percent of certain highway funds from states where more than half the drivers were found to be exceeding the fifty-five-miles-per-hour limit. Under this act, the federal government for a time withheld highway funds from Arizona because its drivers were speeding.[11] (In 1987, Congress passed legislation that permitted the states to raise the maximum speed limit to sixty-five miles per hour on rural portions of the interstate highway system.)

The Clean Air Act of 1970 set federal air-quality standards for the whole country, but required the states to draft plans to enforce those standards; to a lesser extent, similar requirements were contained in the 1990 amendments to the act.[12] The term *regulatory federalism* thus describes the emergence of such federal programs aimed at, or implemented by, state and local governments. (The concept of regulatory federalism is discussed in greater detail later in this chapter.)

In the 1980s, President Reagan also adopted the slogan of "new federalism" to put forth his own programs to change the pattern of federal–state responsibilities. In his 1982 State-of-the-Union message, Reagan proposed a broad restructuring of federal–state relations. He asked that the welfare and food-stamp programs and certain other social programs costing billions of dollars be shifted to the states, with the federal government in return paying the state share of the Medicaid program of health payments to the poor. Congress displayed no enthusiasm for the Reagan-style new federalism and did not approve the plan.

President Reagan had taken office determined to change the nature of federal–state relations in America; he was critical of domestic social-welfare programs and sought to reduce the amount of money that Washington made available to states and localities for those purposes. But one study of federal grants during the Reagan years found that the administration had "only partial success in altering the shape of the federal system."[13] Although federal grants to the states were reduced by more than 4 percent, and many smaller programs were consolidated, "these changes have proved only marginal adjustments in a system that has remained largely intact."[14]

Political scientist Donald F. Kettl has contended that Reagan's promise to relax federal rules and return more power to state governments was in reality "a Trojan horse . . . to disguise budget cuts." Reagan, he concluded, left the federal system "even more entangled in regulation and the problems that accompany it."[15]

All these changes in the patterns and language of federalism reflect the fact that the United States has to a great extent become a national society. People often

[8] Grodzins, *The American System;* Daniel J. Elazar, *American Federalism: A View from the States* (New York: Crowell, 1966); Daniel J. Elazar, *The American Partnership* (Chicago: University of Chicago Press, 1962).
[9] Michael D. Reagan, *The New Federalism* (New York: Oxford University Press, 1972), pp. 4, 145.
[10] *Regulatory Federalism: Policy, Process, Impact and Reform* (Washington, D.C.: Advisory Commission on Intergovernmental Relations, 1984), p. 9.
[11] Data provided by the Federal Highway Administration, U.S. Department of Transportation. Several other states have had their federal highway funds temporarily frozen because of speeders, but Congress, reluctant to crack down on the states, in recent years has ordered the funds released.
[12] *Ibid.*
[13] Paul E. Peterson, Barry G. Rabe, and Kenneth K. Wong, *When Federalism Works* (Washington, D.C.: The Brookings Institution, 1986), p. 228.
[14] *Ibid.*, p. 218.
[15] Donald F. Kettl, *The Regulation of American Federalism* (Baltimore: The Johns Hopkins University Press, 1987), p. 174.

TROUBLED WATERS: THE SECOND BATTLE OF NEW ORLEANS

NEW ORLEANS—Twelve Mile Point is just above the Huey P. Long Bridge on the Mississippi River. The river is 2,000 feet wide there, very deep and a main thoroughfare of one of the last independent breeds of riverboat kings.

Twelve Mile Point is also where a 600-foot cargo ship collided with a tug towing eight barges on a moonless evening in October 1986. No one was injured, but the collision set off one of the greatest river battles between the locals and the federals since Mark Twain plied these waters on the eve of the Civil War.

The ship was piloted by Capt. Robert M. (Mickey) Karr. . . . Why Karr had trouble at Twelve Mile Point has been debated at length, and the debate has escalated into a war between the National Transportation Safety Board (NTSB) and river pilots about states' rights.

The pilots handle ship traffic on the 143-mile stretch of the river between New Orleans and Baton Rouge, through a thicket of oil refineries, past such old sugar plantations as White Hall and a place known as Kamikaze Alley, named because of the erratic maneuvering sometimes required when a huge barge fleet moored there.

"Piloting is an art, it's not a science," [Capt. Martin] Gould said after NTSB probers returned to Washington. "The government can't treat it from a scientific approach. If they do, they're making a mistake."

This kind of mood about accident investigations extends throughout piloting, in part because river pilots have remained independent of federal regulation since 1851, when the Supreme Court, in deciding a Philadelphia case, ruled that the states should regulate pilots. Since then, the Coast Guard has tried to gain jurisdiction but has never succeeded. The Coast Guard investigates all marine accidents but has no jurisdiction on the Mississippi River, a state waterway. Therefore, its recommendations have no teeth.

The pilots said the dispute is a matter of principle. To them, it is about an abuse of power by a federal agency, despite the fact that NTSB recommendations are not binding. "This is America," Gould said. "I have a hell of a hard time understanding how Washington could allow these people to have that kind of power."

—Laura Parker, "Federal Probers, Clannish Pilots Collide on River," *Washington Post*, January 2, 1988

look to Washington to solve problems. Today, for example, most people expect the federal government—not their mayor or town-council members—to deal with large-scale periodic economic difficulties, such as inflation and unemployment. But the need for solutions to major national problems has not resolved the larger question of how to make a federal system work. As one study viewed the problem:

> The basic dilemma . . . is how to achieve goals and objectives that are established by the national government, through the action of other governments, state and local, that are legally independent and politically may be hostile. Those state and local governments are subject to no federal discipline except through the granting or denial of federal aid. And that is not very useful, because to deny the funds is in effect to veto the national objective itself.[16]

THE HISTORICAL BASIS OF FEDERALISM

"A Middle Ground"

In April 1787, a month before the Constitutional Convention opened at Philadelphia, James Madison set forth his thoughts on the structure of a new government in a letter addressed to George Washington.

Madison argued that while the states could not each be completely independent, the creation of "one simple republic" would be "unattainable." Madison wrote: "I have sought for a middle ground which may at once support a due supremacy of the national authority, and not exclude the local authorities wherever they can be subordinately useful."[17]

---

[16] James L. Sundquist with David W. Davis, *Making Federalism Work* (Washington, D.C.: The Brookings Institution, 1969), p. 12.

[17] Letter to George Washington, April 16, 1787, in Saul K. Padover, ed., *The Complete Madison* (New York: Harper & Brothers, 1953), p. 184.

Essentially, Madison had forecast the balanced structure that emerged from a compromise five months later. The bargain struck at Philadelphia in 1787 was a federal bargain. The Constitutional Convention created the federal system, with its sharing of power by the states and the national government. The delegates to the convention agreed to give up some of the states' independence in order to achieve enough unity to create a nation. Yet America probably got a federal system of government because no stronger national government would have been acceptable to the framers or to the states.

There are a number of reasons why a stronger central government would have been unacceptable. First, public opinion in the states almost certainly would not have permitted adoption of a unitary form of government. Loyalty to the states was strong. The Articles of Confederation showed just about how far people had been willing to go in the direction of a central government prior to 1787—which was not very far. The diversity of the American people, regional interests, even the state of technology—transportation was slow and great distances separated the colonies—all militated against the establishment of a central government stronger than the one framed at Philadelphia. Finally, federalism was seen as an effective device for limiting national power by distributing authority between the states and the national government.

A Tool for Nation Building

The collapse of European colonial empires since the Second World War confronted successful rebels in Africa and Asia with an urgent problem: how to organize their new nations. William H. Riker holds that large emerging nations face two alternatives: they can unite under a central government, in which case they have "merely exchanged one imperial master for a lesser one"; or they can join "in some kind of federation, which preserves at least the semblance of political self-control." He adds, "In this sense, federalism is the main alternative to empire as a technique of aggregating large areas under one government."[18]

The framework of federalism in the United States first permitted a disunited people to find a basis for political union, and then allowed room for the development of a sense of national identity. As a result, "The

United States of America" is not only the name of a country—to an extent, it is also a description of its formal governmental structure.

THE CONSTITUTIONAL BASIS OF FEDERALISM

Federal Powers: Enumerated, Implied, Inherent, and Concurrent

The Constitution established the framework for the American federal system. Under it, the three branches of the federal government are granted certain specifically *enumerated powers*. Congress, for example, has the power to coin money; the president is commander in chief of the armed forces.

In addition, the Supreme Court has held that the national government also has broad *implied powers*. These flow from its enumerated powers and the "elastic clause" of the Constitution, which gives Congress power to make all laws "necessary and proper" to carry out its enumerated powers. For example, the right of the United States to establish a national banking system is an implied power flowing from its enumerated power to collect taxes and regulate commerce.[19]

The Supreme Court also has held that the national government has *inherent powers* that it may exercise simply because it exists as a government. One of the most important inherent powers is the right to conduct foreign relations. Since the United States does not exist in a vacuum, it must, as a practical matter, deal with other countries, even though the Constitution does not spell this out. The Court made clear in the *Curtiss-Wright* case that the "war power" of the United States government is an inherent power. It said, "The power to declare and wage war, to conclude peace, to make treaties, to maintain diplomatic relations with other sovereignties, if they had never been mentioned in the Constitution, would have vested in the federal government as necessary concomitants of nationality."[20]

Finally, the federal government and the states also have certain *concurrent powers*, which they exercise independently. The power to tax, for example, is enjoyed by both the federal and state governments. Of course, a state cannot exercise a power that belongs only to the federal government under the Constitution, nor can a state take actions that conflict with federal law.

---

[18] Riker, *Federalism: Origin, Operation, Significance*, pp. 4–5.

[19] McCulloch v. Maryland, 4 Wheaton 316 (1819).
[20] United States v. Curtiss-Wright Export Corp., 299 U.S. 304 (1936).

These various powers are complex concepts. They developed slowly as the nation grew and found it necessary to adapt the Constitution to changing conditions.

The Supreme Court as Umpire

The Supreme Court serves as an arbiter in questions of state versus national power. The federal system could not function efficiently without an umpire.

The Court's attitude has changed radically over the decades; sometimes the Court has supported states' rights, and sometimes it has supported expanded federal power. But in every period, the Court has served as a major arena in which important conflicts are settled within the federal framework.

McCulloch v. Maryland The most important of these Supreme Court decisions was that of Chief Justice John Marshall in *McCulloch v. Maryland* in 1819. His ruling established the doctrine of *implied powers* and gave the federal government sanction to take giant steps beyond the literal language of the Constitution.

James W. McCulloch might otherwise not have gone down in American history. But as it happened he was cashier of the Baltimore branch of the National Bank of the United States, which had been established by Congress. The National Bank had failed to prevent a business panic and economic depression in 1819, and some of its branches were managed by what can only be termed crooks. As a result, several states, including Maryland, tried to force the banks out of their states. Maryland slapped an annual tax of $15,000 on the National Bank. McCulloch refused to pay, setting the stage for the great courtroom battle of the day. Daniel Webster argued for the bank, and Luther Martin, attorney general of Maryland, for his state.

The first question answered by Marshall in his opinion for a unanimous Court was the basic question of whether Congress had power to incorporate a bank. Marshall laid down a classic definition of national sovereignty and broad constitutional construction. "The government of the Union . . . is emphatically and truly a government of the people. In form and substance it emanates from them. Its powers are granted by them, and are to be exercised directly on them, and for their benefit." [21]

Chief Justice John Marshall:
"Let the end be legitimate. . . . "

Marshall conceded that the Constitution divided sovereignty between the states and the national government but said that "the government of the Union, though limited in its powers, is supreme within its sphere of action." Although the power to charter a bank was not among the enumerated powers of Congress in the Constitution, he said, it could be inferred from the "necessary and proper" clause. In short, Congress had "implied powers."

"Let the end be legitimate," Marshall wrote, "let it be within the scope of the Constitution, and all means which are appropriate, which are plainly adapted to that end, which are not prohibited, but consist with the letter and spirit of the Constitution, are constitutional." Congress, Marshall said, had the right to legislate with a "vast mass of incidental powers which must be involved in the Constitution, if that instrument be not a splendid bauble."

On the second question of whether Maryland had the right to tax the National Bank, Marshall ruled against the state, for "the power to tax involves the power to destroy." No state, he said, possessed that right because this implied that the federal government de-

---

[21] *McCulloch v. Maryland* (1819).

pended on the will of the states. Marshall ruled the Maryland law unconstitutional.

Thus, at an early stage in the nation's history, Marshall established the key concepts of implied powers, broad construction of the Constitution, and national supremacy. More than one hundred years were to pass before these powers were exercised fully, but the decision laid the basis for the future growth of national power.

The Division of Federal and State Power Under the Tenth Amendment, "The powers not delegated to the United States by the Constitution, nor prohibited by it to the States, are reserved to the States respectively, or to the people."

At first glance, this amendment might seem to limit the federal government to powers *specifically* enumerated and "delegated" to the federal government by the Constitution. But in deciding *McCulloch v. Maryland*, Chief Justice Marshall emphasized that the Tenth Amendment (unlike the Articles of Confederation) does not use the word "expressly" before the word "delegated."

This omission was not accidental. In 1789, during the debate on the first ten amendments, James Madison and others blocked the attempt of states' rights advocates to limit federal powers to those "expressly" delegated.[22] During the debate, Madison objected to insertion of the key word "because it was impossible to confine a Government to the exercise of express powers; there must necessarily be admitted powers by implication, unless the Constitution descended to recount every minutia."[23]

The Supreme Court that followed the Marshall Court took a much narrower view of the powers of the federal government. Under Roger B. Taney, who served as chief justice from 1836 to 1864, the Court invoked the Tenth Amendment to protect the powers of the states. And in 1871 the Supreme Court ruled that the amendment meant that the federal government could not tax the salaries of state officials, a decision the Court later overruled.[24]

For two decades after the First World War, the Court invoked the Tenth Amendment to invalidate a series of federal laws dealing with child labor and regulating industry and agriculture. And in 1935 the Court cited the amendment in declaring unconstitutional the National Industrial Recovery Act, a major piece of New Deal legislation designed to reduce unemployment.[25]

But in the watershed year of 1937, the Court swung around and upheld the Social Security program and the National Labor Relations Act as valid exercises of federal power.[26] And in 1941 it specifically rejected the argument that the Constitution in any way limited the power of the federal government to regulate interstate commerce. The decision upheld the Fair Labor Standards Act. Speaking for the Court, Chief Justice Harlan Fiske Stone called the Tenth Amendment "a truism that all is retained which has not been surrendered."[27]

Thus, more than 120 years after *McCulloch v. Maryland*, the Supreme Court had finally swung back to John Marshall's view of the Constitution as an instrument that gave the federal government broad powers over the states and the nation. In 1976, however, the Supreme Court, in a 5–4 decision it later reversed, struck down a federal law extending federal minimum-wage and maximum-hour provisions to some 3.4 million state and municipal workers. The Court held that Congress had infringed too far upon "the separate and independent existence" of the states.[28] But seven years later the Supreme Court appeared to change direction again in a case involving Bill Crump, a supervisor for the Wyoming Game and Fish Department, who was forced to retire at age 55. Crump argued that a federal law prohibiting age discrimination in employment protected him. The Supreme Court agreed, thereby extending the federal law to cover state and local government employees.[29] Finally, in 1985, the Supreme Court reversed its 1976 decision by holding 5–4 that federal minimum-wage standards covered public transit workers.[30] The landmark case, *Garcia v. San Antonio*

[22] Alfred H. Kelly and Winfred A. Harbison, *The American Constitution* (New York: Norton, 1955), p. 176.
[23] In Walter Berns, "The Meaning of the Tenth Amendment," in Goldwin, ed., *A Nation of States*, p. 138. For a spirited defense of the opposite view, see "The Case for 'States' Rights'" by James J. Kilpatrick in the same volume.
[24] *Collector v. Day*, 11 Wallace 113 (1871). This decision was overruled by the Supreme Court in 1939 in *Graves v. O'Keefe*, 306 U.S. 466 (1939).

[25] *Schechter Poultry Corporation v. United States*, 295 U.S. 495 (1935).
[26] *Steward Machine Co. v. Davis*, 301 U.S. 548 (1937); *National Labor Relations Board v. Jones & Laughlin Steel Corp.*, 301 U.S. 1 (1937).
[27] *United States v. Darby*, 312 U.S. 100 (1941).
[28] *The National League of Cities v. Usery*, 426 U.S. 833 (1976).
[29] *Equal Employment Opportunity Commission v. Wyoming*, 460 U.S. 226 (1983).
[30] *Garcia v. San Antonio Metropolitan Transit Authority*, 469 U.S. 528 (1985).

Metropolitan Transit Authority, confirmed and greatly strengthened the federal government's power to regulate the states.

Nevertheless, many advocates of a states'-rights position continue to rely on the Tenth Amendment as the constitutional foundation for their argument. In general, they see the Constitution as the result of a compact among the states. A more widely accepted view today is that the national government represents the *people*, and that sovereignty rests not with the states but with "we the people," who created the Constitution and approved it.

Restrictions on the States

The *supremacy clause* of the Constitution (Article VI, Paragraph 2) makes it clear that the Constitution and the laws and treaties made under it are supreme over state constitutions or laws.

In addition, the Constitution places many restrictions on the states: they are forbidden to make treaties, coin money, pass bills of attainder or ex post facto laws, impair contracts, grant titles of nobility, tax imports or exports, keep troops or warships in peacetime, engage in war (unless invaded), or make interstate compacts without congressional approval. The Bill of Rights, as interpreted by the Supreme Court, and the Fourteenth and Fifteenth amendments place additional restrictions on the states.

Local governments derive their powers from the states and are subject to the same constitutional restrictions as are the states. If a state cannot do something, neither can a locality, since "in a strictly legal sense . . . all local governments in the United States are creatures of their respective states."[31]

Federal Obligations to the States

The Constitution (in Article IV) defines the relations of the federal government to the states. For example, the United States must guarantee to every state "a republican form of government." In addition, the federal government must protect the states against invasion and against domestic violence on request of the governor or legislature. Presidents have, on several occasions, intervened in the states with force either at the invitation of, or over the objections of, the governor.

Congress may admit new states to the Union, but the Constitution does not spell out any ground rules for their admission. In practice, when a territory has desired statehood, it has applied to Congress, which has passed an "enabling act" allowing the people of the territory to frame a constitution. If Congress approved the constitution, it passed a joint resolution recognizing the new state. (If in the future Congress should admit another state, it could follow this procedure, or adopt a new one.) As the frontier expanded westward, Congress steadily admitted new states until 1912, when New Mexico and Arizona, the last contiguous continental territories, became states. The forty-eight states became fifty in 1959 with the admission of Alaska and Hawaii — the only states of the Union that do not border on another state.

Interstate Relations

Article IV of the Constitution also requires the states to observe certain rules in their dealings with one another. First, states are required to give "full faith and credit" to the laws, records, and court decisions of another state. In practice, this simply means that a judgment obtained in a state court in a civil (not a criminal) case must be recognized by the courts of another state. If, for example, a person in New York loses a lawsuit and moves to California to avoid paying the judgment, the courts there will enforce the New York decision.

Sometimes, however, states fail to meet their obligations to one another. For example, a couple legally married in one state might not be legally married in another. In the famed *Williams v. North Carolina* cases[32] — the dispute went up to the Supreme Court twice — a man and a woman left their respective spouses in North Carolina, went to Nevada, got six-week divorces, and married each other. When they returned home, the state of North Carolina successfully prosecuted them for bigamy, convictions that were upheld when the case reached the Supreme Court the second time.[33]

Second, the Constitution provides that the citizens of each state are entitled to "all privileges and immunities" of citizens in other states. As interpreted by the

---

[31] Daniel J. Elazar, *American Federalism: A View from the States*, p. 164.

[32] *Williams v. North Carolina*, 317 U.S. 287 (1942), 325 U.S. 226 (1945).

Supreme Court, this hazy provision has come to mean that one state may not discriminate against citizens of another. But in practice, states do discriminate against persons who are not legal residents. For example, a state university often charges higher tuition fees to out-of-state students. States usually charge nonresidents much higher fees for fishing and hunting licenses than they do residents.

Finally, the Constitution provides for extradition of fugitives who flee across state lines to escape justice. A state may request the governor of another state to return fugitives, and normally the governor will comply with such a request. But in several instances in the past, northern governors refused to surrender blacks who had escaped from chain gangs or prisons in the South.

One famous example arose in the Scottsboro case, which began in 1931 when nine black youths were pulled off a freight train in Alabama by a mob and accused of raping two white girls. There was considerable doubt that the crime had even been committed. The Supreme Court reversed death sentences imposed on eight of the defendants, but all drew long prison terms. In 1948 one defendant, Haywood Patterson, escaped from an Alabama prison and fled north. He was later arrested in Detroit by the FBI, and the state of Alabama demanded his return. Governor G. Mennen Williams of Michigan refused to extradite him.[34]

Interstate Compacts

The Constitution permits the states to make agreements with one another with the approval of Congress. These *interstate compacts* were of minor importance until the twentieth century, but the spread of metropolitan areas — and metropolitan problems — across state borders and the increasing complexity of modern life have brought new significance to the agreements.

The Port Authority of New York and New Jersey was created by an interstate compact between the two states and approved by Congress in 1921. The powerful and quasi-independent authority operates, among other things, John F. Kennedy International Airport and La Guardia Airport in New York and Newark Airport in New Jersey. It also controls and runs the bridges and tunnels leading into Manhattan, and the world's largest bus terminal, near Times Square. Air and water pollution, pest control, toll bridges, and transportation are matters on which states have entered into agreements with one another, with varying degrees of success.

THE GROWTH OF STRONG NATIONAL GOVERNMENT

The late Senator Everett McKinley Dirksen of Illinois, a legislator noted for his Shakespearean delivery and dramatic flair, once predicted sadly that the way things were going, "The only people interested in state boundaries will be Rand McNally."[35]

While this may be an exaggerated view of trends in the American federal system, Dirksen's remark reflected the fact that the national government has been gaining increased power. The formal structure of American government has changed very little since 1787, but the balance of power within the system has changed markedly.

The Rise of Big Government

A century ago, the federal government did not provide social security, medical insurance for millions of citizens, vast aid to public and private education, or billions of dollars in welfare payments. Nor did it have independent regulatory agencies to watch over various segments of the economy.

As American society has grown more complex, as population has surged, the national government's managerial task has enlarged. People demand more services and government grows bigger in the process. Six cabinet departments — Housing and Urban Development; Transportation; Energy; Health and Human Services;

[33] Despite the confusion of the divorce laws, the situation had improved somewhat since an earlier landmark case, *Haddock v. Haddock*, 201 U.S. 562 (1906). In the words of one constitutional scholar: "The upshot [of that Supreme Court decision] was a situation in which a man and a woman, when both were in Connecticut, were divorced; when both were in New York, were married; and when the one was in Connecticut and the other in New York, the former was divorced and the latter married," in Edward S. Corwin et al., eds., *The Constitution of the United States of America, Analysis and Interpretation* (Washington, D.C.: U.S. Government Printing Office, 1964), p. 750.
[34] Patterson was later charged with stabbing a man, went to prison, and died there in 1953. The other Scottsboro prisoners were freed on parole by 1950. Clarence Norris, believed to be the last survivor of the nine defendants, was finally pardoned by the state of Alabama in 1976.

[35] *New York Times*, August 8, 1965, section 4, p. 2.

Education; and Veterans Affairs — have been created since 1965.

The power to tax and spend for the general welfare is a function of the national government that has expanded enormously in the twentieth century. The government's role in the regulation of interstate and foreign commerce has also vastly increased.

Much of the growth of big government and of federal social welfare programs took place during the New Deal in the 1930s and during Lyndon Johnson's "Great Society" in the 1960s. Although conservatives periodically attack these programs as "handouts" that create dependence on government, the major programs are so well established that no new administration in Washington is likely to be able to abolish them. President Reagan, however, came into office in 1981 determined to make substantial cuts in federal spending in the field of social welfare. He had repeatedly pledged to do so in his campaign for the presidency.

And the Reagan administration did indeed enact billions of dollars in cuts in domestic spending — in social welfare and food programs designed to assist the poor, as well as in a broad range of other programs aimed at helping low-income families, including Medicaid,

housing subsidies, and student loans. Together, these spending cuts came to be known popularly as "the Reagan revolution."

But how big were the reductions in domestic spending? The Reagan White House claimed it had reduced federal domestic programs by $232 billion during the administration's first four years, compared to projected spending by the previous Democratic administration.[36] But in the public debate over budget cuts there was "confusion as to exactly what had been accomplished." [37] In part, this was because federal spending actually increased in many of the programs that the Reagan administration claimed it had cut. In most cases, the "cuts" were reductions in what *might* have been spent. Nevertheless, the Reagan program did have a measurable impact on government spending and on the outputs of the political system. The budget cuts "landed

[36] Testimony of David A. Stockman, director, Office of Management and Budget, to House Budget Committee, February 22, 1984, p. 12.

[37] John W. Ellwood, "Introduction," in John William Ellwood, ed., *Reductions in U.S Domestic Spending: How They Affect State and Local Governments* (New Brunswick: Transaction Books, 1982), p. 3.

A dinner party in Dallas . . .

and a homeless family in California.

heavily on the poor and near poor. Education and training, community development, welfare, nutrition, housing assistance and other anti-poverty programs suffered most." [38] As one study suggested, "there can be no doubt about one of the central consequences of Reagan administration policies: income in the United States will be distributed more unevenly than before between the rich and the poor." [39]

By the end of the decade of the 1980s, the accuracy of that prediction had been dramatically confirmed. According to one survey of incomes by the Congressional Budget Office, for the 2.5 million people in the top one percent in America, incomes rose by about 75 percent between 1980 and 1990, to an average of more than $500,000 a year.[40] Just the increase in wealth for this richest one percent was equal to the total income of the 50 million people in the poorest 20 percent of the nation.[41]

The role of the federal government, particularly in the field of social-welfare programs, will probably continue to be debated in America. Although a particular administration may reduce the share of the pie allocated to social programs, the pie itself — the federal budget — keeps growing. Many Americans still tend to look to the national government to solve national problems.

[38] *New York Times*, February 16, 1988, p. D19.
[39] Joel Havemann, "Sharing the Wealth: The Gap Between Rich and Poor Grows Wider," *National Journal*, October 23, 1982, p. 1788.
[40] *National Journal*, December 8, 1990, p. 2957.
[41] *Ibid.*
[42] *Budget of the United States Government, Fiscal Year 1993* (Washington, D.C.: U.S. Government Printing Office, 1992), p. 239.

Big Government and Foreign Policy

The responsibility of the federal government for the conduct of foreign affairs in the nuclear age has increased the size of the national government. In fiscal 1993, for example, the budget request for national defense totaled $286 billion, a substantial 19 percent of the total federal budget, and, except for Social Security, the largest single item.[42] The State Department, the Central Intelligence Agency, the United States Information Agency, the National Security Agency, and related agencies have expanded along with the Pentagon.

With the collapse of the Soviet Union in 1991, the military threat to the United States had diminished dramatically, and the Democratic-controlled Congress pressed President Bush to make substantial cuts in defense spending. Although the president proposed major cutbacks in the production of strategic arms, such as the B-2 stealth bomber and nuclear warheads for the Trident II submarines, the 1993 defense budget request was only $6 billion less than projected spending on defense a year earlier. Despite the shifts in the international balance of power, the United States continued to spend hundreds of billions on the military. Defense industries and military bases provided jobs for many Americans and enjoyed strong support in Congress, where members are sensitive to the concerns of their districts. Partly as a result, the so-called "peace dividend" — the funds allocated to national defense that might be spent on domestic needs because of the end of the Cold War — seemed elusive, or at least slow to materialize.

**U.S. F16s over Kuwait
during the Gulf War**

THE IMPACT OF FEDERALISM ON GOVERNMENT AND POLITICS

America's government institutions and its political system developed within a framework of federalism, and they reflect that fact. Federalism has also placed its stamp on a broad range of informal activities in American society, including the operations of many private groups.

Federalism and Government

The nature of representation in Congress reflects the impact of federalism. Each state, no matter how small, has two senators who represent the constituents of their state. Members of the House represent districts within the states, but they also constitute an informal delegation from their states. Senators and representatives, when elected, must reside in the states they represent. In the event of a deadlock in the electoral college, the House of Representatives votes by state to select the president, with each state having one vote.

Federalism also affects the court system. State and local courts exist side by side with federal courts in the United States and handle the vast majority of cases. But even the federal district courts and circuit courts are organized along geographic lines that take into account state boundaries. And, under the custom of "senatorial courtesy," before the president appoints a federal dis-

trict or circuit court judge, the White House privately submits the name to the senators representing the home state of the nominee. If the state has a senator from the same party as the president, and that senator objects, the name is usually dropped.[43]

Many powerful interest groups are in a sense federations of state associations and groups. This is true, for example, of the American Medical Association, the American Bar Association, and to some extent the American Federation of Labor-Congress of Industrial Organizations (AFL-CIO).

Federalism and American Politics

When Governor Bill Clinton of Arkansas sought the Democratic nomination for president in 1992, his first big test came in February in the presidential primary in New Hampshire. He lost to former Massachusetts Senator Paul E. Tsongas. In March Clinton recovered from that defeat with resounding victories in Florida, Texas, and other Southern and border states on "Super Tuesday," and he went on to win the nomination. Four years earlier, in 1988, George Bush's big win in New Hampshire started his bandwagon rolling toward the Repub-

---

[43] As the system of senatorial courtesy has operated in recent years, some presidents have notified both home-state senators of potential nominees, even when one or more senator does not belong to the president's party. However, in practice, only an objection by a member of the president's party is likely to affect a nomination.

Bill Clinton campaigns in the 1992 New Hampshire primary with his wife, Hillary

lican presidential nomination and his election to the White House in November.

Often, although not always, the victory that comes to a national political candidate in a noisy convention hall in the heat of July or August gains its first momentum in the snows of New Hampshire in February or March. Other key primary states also may play an important role; in 1992 Clinton's victories in Illinois, New York, and Pennsylania helped to secure his position as the front-runner for the Democratic presidential nomination.

As the primary contests illustrate dramatically, federalism affects party politics in the United States. National political parties are organized along federal lines. The United States has no national party system such as that in Britain, for example. Rather, a federation of fifty state parties is precariously held together by a national committee between presidential nominating conventions.

The governors' chairs in the fifty states are political prizes. As a result, fifty centers of political power in the states compete with the locus of national power in Washington.

To a party out of power nationally, the existence of state political machinery takes on special importance. By building up state parties and demonstrating leadership ability on the state level, the "out" party may consolidate its position and prepare for the next national election. Often a strong governor or a former governor will emerge as a contender for the party's presidential nomination.

Although state political parties constitute basic political units in the United States, state political systems vary greatly. In some states, such as New York, there is lively competition between Democrats and Republicans. Other states have often been dominated by one party, as in the case of the Democrats in Arkansas. The makeup of the electorate in the states may differ from that of the nation as a whole. For example, proportionately, there are fewer Democrats in Kansas and Nebraska than in the national electorate.

State governments also vary in what they do and in the quality of their performance. How good are the schools in a state? Does the state have effective programs in the fields of health services, penology, welfare, law enforcement, and pollution control? As anyone who has driven across America knows, some states just look (and are) wealthier; they have better state roads, for example. Some have adopted innovative social programs that have led the way for other states and the federal government.

Policy Outcomes in the States   Since state governments do vary in quality, does the nature of a political system in a state affect the types of public policies adopted in the state? In other words, does the politics of a state make a difference in the lives of the people of that state?

Political scientists have done a good deal of research on this question, and their answers have varied. One analysis suggested that states with active two-party competition were more likely to enact broad social welfare programs because both parties would compete for the votes of a state's "havenots." [44]

Later studies found that socioeconomic factors (whether a state was rich or poor in per-capita income), rather than political factors, seemed to account for most of the differences in state welfare-spending and for differences in spending, taxing, and services among the states. [45] But another study concluded that if taxing and spending in a state were measured in terms of their *redistributive* impact — who gets what and who pays for it — then the politics of the state was considerably more important than its economics. Lower socioeconomic groups did fare better, for example, in states with certain political characteristics, such as higher levels of political participation. [46] More recent studies have suggested that

other variables, in addition to politics and economics, may affect the policies of a state government. Religion, demographic factors, and in particular the actions of bureaucrats and the organization of a state government's bureaucracy, may all play important roles. [47]

But, at least some researchers have concluded that politics *does* make a difference in the quality and type of government provided by the states. In other words, the fact that America has a federal system directly affects people's lives because it affects the performance of the states in which they live. Not only the structure of government but the whole political process is federalized.

FEDERALISM TODAY

The *Budget of the United States Government, Fiscal Year 1993* is a red-, white-, and blue-covered volume the size of a telephone book and nearly two and a half inches thick. To the nonexpert, it seems a bewildering mass of statistics and gobbledygook, filled with phrases such as "object classification" and "unobligated balance lapsing."

Buried in the budget's somewhat mysterious statistics are figures that add up to a substantial total of federal aid to state and local governments. For 1993, the

[47] Virginia H. Gray, "The Determinants of Public Policy: A Reappraisal," in Thomas R. Dye and Virginia Gray, eds., *The Determinants of Public Policy* (Lexington: D.C. Heath, 1980), p. 217.

[44] V. O. Key, Jr., *Southern Politics in State and Nation* (New York: Knopf, 1949), p. 307.

[45] Richard E. Dawson and James A. Robinson, "Inter-Party Competition, Economic Variables and Welfare Policies in the American States," *Journal of Politics*, vol. 25 (1963), pp. 265–89; Thomas R. Dye, *Politics, Economics, and the Public: Policy Outcomes in the American States* (Chicago: Rand McNally, 1966), p. 293; Thomas R. Dye, *Understanding Public Policy*, 2nd ed. (Englewood Cliffs: Prentice-Hall, 1975), p. 304.

[46] Brian R. Fry and Richard F. Winters, "The Politics of Redistribution," *American Political Science Review*, vol. 64, (June 1970), pp. 508–22.

amount was estimated at $199.1 billion.[48] The following figures show the sharp increase in federal aid to state and local governments since 1950:

1950: $ 2.3 billion	1980: $ 91.5 billion
1960: $ 7.0 billion	1985: $105.9 billion
1970: $24.1 billion	1990: $135.4 billion
1975: $49.8 billion	1993 estimate: $199.1 billion

Despite these dollar increases, as a percentage of the total federal budget, federal aid to state and local governments has actually declined in recent years. In 1980, for example, such grants amounted to 15 percent of the federal budget, but in 1993 the total had dropped to 13 percent.

Any analysis of American government must take into account the huge sums of money flowing from people and corporations in the states to Washington in the form of taxes, and back out again in the form of federal aid. It is here that federalism moves from the realm of theory into practical meaning in terms of dollars and cents.

[48] *Budget of the United States Government, Fiscal Year 1993* (Washington, D.C: U.S. Government Printing Office, 1992), Part One, p. 438.

Figure 3-2
The Federal Aid Pipeline: 1992 Grants to States and Localities

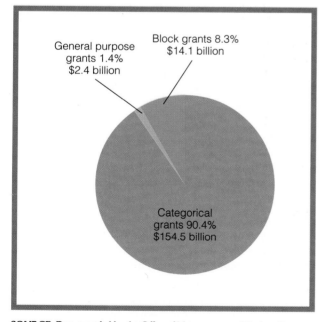

General purpose grants 1.4% $2.4 billion

Block grants 8.3% $14.1 billion

Categorical grants 90.4% $154.5 billion

SOURCE: Data provided by the Office of Management and Budget. Percentages are rounded; dollar figures are 1992 estimates.

The federal government channels money to states and local communities in three ways:

Categorical grants, also known as *grants-in-aid*, are earmarked for specific purposes only, such as pollution control, schools, or hospitals, for example.

Block grants are for general use in a broad area, such as community development.

General purpose grants, the smallest category, may be used by states and localities mostly as they wish.

By far the largest amount of federal aid (about 90 percent of the total) comes in the form of categorical grants. Block grants rank next, and then general purpose aid. (See Figure 3–2.)

Categorical Grants

In fiscal 1993, as in previous years, the great bulk of federal aid to states and local communities came in the form of categorical grants-in-aid. A categorical grant is "money paid or furnished to state or local governments to be used for specific purposes"[49] in ways spelled out by law or administrative regulations. In 1991 there were 543 separate grant programs administered by federal agencies. Not surprisingly, many state and local officials complained that the maze of federal grants-in-aid created a burdensome amount of paperwork for them.

Typical categorical grants are in the fields of education, pollution control, highways, conservation, and recreation. The Medicaid and Food Stamp programs are examples of two very large categorical grants. In 1992, categorical grants again amounted to about 90 percent of all federal aid to states and localities. To be eligible for federal aid, the state and local governments must sometimes meet *matching requirements*. That is, Washington requires the recipients to put up some of their own funds in order to get the federal money.

When communities and states match federal money, they usually do so according to a formula that takes into account their ability to pay. Poor states pay less than rich states. This process is called *equalization*.

It is in the administration of federal grants that the gears of national, state, and local governments mesh or collide. Federal fiscal aid is the primary means by which local, state, and federal governments interrelate. In

[49] *Fiscal Balance in the American Federal System*, vol. 1, Advisory Commission on Intergovernmental Relations (Washington, D.C.: U.S. Government Printing Office, 1967), p. 137.

"It's too bad you can't get
federal matching funds,
whatever they are."

Drawing by D. Fradon,
© 1969 The New Yorker Magazine, Inc.

dealing with such programs as slum clearance, education, or welfare services, mayors, governors, and lesser
officials communicate with one another and with administrators and legislators in Washington. Because of
these aid programs, the lines of the federal system criss-
cross, linking various levels of government that must
cope with common problems, from pollution to poverty. The result is both cooperation and conflict. For
example, cities and states collaborate in a wide range of
programs such as law enforcement and highway planning. But as a group, mayors tend to distrust state governments; they argue that the states are receiving too
large a share of federal revenues at a time when the cities
are desperate for funds.

Block Grants

In addition to categorical grants, since the 1960s, aid to
the states and local communities has also flowed from
Washington in the form of block grants. These grants
are used "within a broad functional area largely at the
recipient's discretion." [50]

In 1992, block grants accounted for about 8 percent of all federal aid to states and localities. Among the
major block grants included in the federal budget for
that year were programs for community development,
social services, health care, employment and training,
and education. Together, the block grants amounted to
$14.1 billion.

Revenue Sharing: The End of the Experiment

Between 1972 and 1986, the federal government turned
over $83 billion in federal tax monies to state and local
governments to spend at will under a program known as
general revenue sharing. The program was controversial — critics feared that local governments might use
the money to build golf courses instead of health clinics,

---

[50] *Summary and Concluding Observations: The Intergovernmental
Grant System,* Advisory Commission on Intergovernmental Relations (Washington, D.C.: U.S. Government Printing Office, 1978),
p. 3.

and some did. But revenue sharing proved very popular with local communities, and provided more than half the money for some municipal budgets. However, many members of Congress objected to appropriating federal funds without controlling how the money was spent. Representative Jack Brooks, a Texas Democrat and chairman of the House committee with jurisdiction over the program, called revenue sharing a "snake."[51] In 1985, President Reagan proposed to end revenue sharing, and a year later it died.

A study by the Brookings Institution suggested that a major goal of some advocates of revenue sharing

—increased decision-making at the local level—had not been achieved in most communities. The study also concluded that "troubled central cities [were] not in any major way" helped by revenue sharing.[52]

Where the Money Goes

How was the $199.1 billion total in federal aid spent in fiscal 1993? Federal budget estimates show that almost all of it was allocated to eight major categories: health; income security; education, training, employment and social services; transportation; community and regional development; natural resources and the environment; general government; and agriculture, in that order. (Figure 3-3 and Table 3-2 show where the money goes.)

[51] *National Journal,* August 11, 1979, p. 1331.
[52] Richard P. Nathan, Charles F. Adams, Jr., and associates, *Revenue Sharing: The Second Round* (Washington, D.C.: The Brookings Institution, 1977), pp. 106, 164.

Figure 3-3
Federal Grants to State and Local Governments, 1980–1993

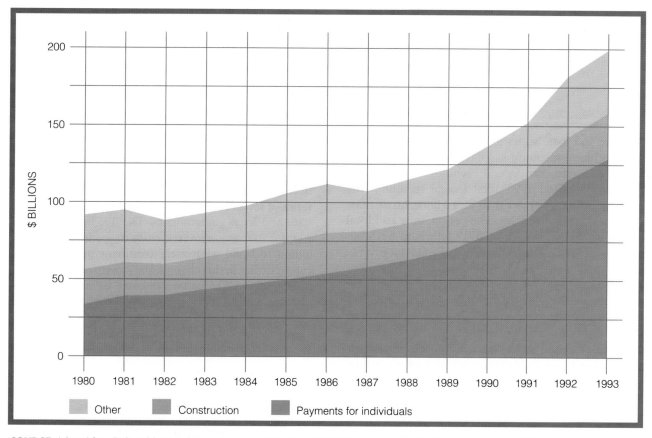

SOURCE: Adapted from *Budget of the United States Government, Fiscal Year 1993* (Washington, D.C.: U.S. Government Printing Office, 1992), Part One, pp. 435, 438–439. Construction grants are for highways, airports, mass transit, community development, and other facilities. Other grants are for education, training, employment, and social services.

Table 3-2
Where the Money Goes: Federal Aid Grants to State and Local Governments, by Function, 1993 (in billions of dollars)

Percent	Category	Total	Major Items
44.0	Health	$ 88.5	Medical assistance
22.0	Income security	44.1	Unemployment compensation, retirement
15.0	Education, training, employment, and social services	29.9	Aid to elementary and secondary schools, job training, and foster care
11.0	Transportation	22.3	Highways
2.0	Community and regional development	4.9	Housing and urban renewal
2.0	Natural resources and the environment	4.0	Construction of sewage treatment plants
1.0	General government	2.3	Collection of taxes
1.0	Agriculture	1.3	Crop insurance, animal and plant health programs
1.0	Other	1.8	National defense, energy, veterans benefits, and administration of justice
Total 100		$199.1	

SOURCE: Adapted from *Budget of the United States Government Fiscal Year 1993* (Washington, D.C.: U.S. Government Printing Office, 1992), Part One, pp. 436, 438. Figures and percentages are estimated and rounded.

Fiscal Headaches in the Federal System

As state and local authorities are quick to point out, state and local spending also has been increasing at an even faster rate than federal spending. For example, between 1986 and 1990, total federal spending rose from $1.1 trillion to more than $1.4 trillion, an increase of 27 percent. During the same period, state and local expenditures increased from $717 billion to $976 billion, an increase of 36 percent.[53] Yet the federal government collects 81 percent of the most important "growth" tax — the income tax.[54] Revenues from income taxes directly reflect economic growth, providing the federal government with increased tax receipts in an expanding economy. By contrast, local governments rely mainly on real estate taxes, and state governments depend heavily on sales taxes; both sources of revenue tend to grow less rapidly than the economy as a whole.

Although more states were taxing personal income, in 1991 there were still seven states that did not.[55]

Regulatory Federalism

Beginning in the 1960s and continuing to the present, a series of federal laws have imposed strict standards on state and local governments. The 1983 Clean Water Act, for example, required cities to spend nearly $120 billion to build wastewater treatment plants. As discussed earlier in this chapter, the growth of such federal programs aimed at, or implemented by, state and local governments has been termed *regulatory federalism*.[56]

Legislation with this kind of impact on state and local governments includes the 1964 Civil Rights Act, the 1965 Highway Beautification Act, the 1970 Occu-

[53] U.S. Bureau of the Census, *Governmental Finances in 1985–86*, no. 5, pp. 2, 6, and *Governmental Finances: 1989–90*, no. 5, pp. 2, 6.

[54] U.S. Bureau of the Census, *Governmental Finances: 1989–90*, p. 2.

[55] Data provided by the Advisory Commission on Intergovernmental Relations.

[56] David R. Beam, "Washington's Regulation of States and Localities: Origins and Issues," in *Intergovernmental Perspective*, Summer 1981, vol. 7, no. 3 (Washington, D.C.: Advisory Commission on Intergovernmental Relations, 1981), p. 10. For a discussion of some of the complex issues related to regulatory federalism, see Mel Dubnick and Alan Gitelson, "Nationalizing State Policies," in *The Nationalization of State Government*, Jerome J. Hanus, ed. (Lexington: D.C. Heath, 1981), pp. 39–74.

Smog in Los Angeles: a target of regulatory federalism

pational Safety and Health Act, as well as many other laws dealing with clean air and water, endangered species, education, employment, persons with disabilities, and age discrimination.

Some of these laws apply directly to the states or local governments. The Equal Employment Opportunity Act of 1972, for example, bars job discrimination by states or localities on the basis of race, religion, sex, and national origin.

Other laws cut across all federal programs. The 1964 Civil Rights Act, for instance, prohibits discrimination under any program that receives federal money. Other laws "cross over" and impose rules in one area of government activity to influence policy in another area; the laws holding back federal highway funds for states that refused to adopt and enforce the nationwide speed limits set by Congress is one such example. Another was the 1984 law withholding up to 10 percent of federal highway funds from states with a drinking age under twenty-one. And finally, some laws, such as the Clean Air Act of 1970, and its 1990 amendments, set standards but required the states to implement them.

Many of these federal laws were passed to meet national goals, such as providing cleaner air and water. And often, those goals were supported by states and communities. But the complex federal requirements contained in these laws, and the extensive paperwork that goes with them, have given rise to intergovernmental tensions, and to a continuing debate over the nature of regulatory federalism.

THE FUTURE OF FEDERALISM

Clearly, the shape of relations among Washington, the state houses, and city halls has changed considerably over time and continues to be characterized by both conflict and cooperation.

But new ideas have been introduced into the mix. The state of Minnesota, for example, has dramatically modified state and local fiscal relations. Minnesota revamped its system of school aid to ensure equal funds for students throughout the state, regardless of the wealth of the school districts where they lived. The reforms also guaranteed property-tax relief to homeowners and businesses, and helped cities and counties by beginning a program of state revenue sharing for local governments.[57]

By 1991 thirty-six states and the District of Columbia had adopted a "circuit breaker" system of property-tax relief for low-income homeowners and for the aged. Persons in these categories below certain income ceilings were guaranteed property-tax reductions.[58]

The vast problems of urban areas provide one of the greatest challenges to the American federal system.

---

[57] *State-Local Finances: Significant Features and Suggested Legislation,* Advisory Commission on Intergovernmental Relations (Washington, D.C.: U.S. Government Printing Office, 1972), pp. 6–8.

[58] *Significant Features of Fiscal Federalism 1992* (Washington, D.C.: Advisory Commission on Intergovernmental Relations, February 1986), Vol. I, Table 41, p. 126.

Some efforts have been made at new approaches. For example, increasing attention is now being paid to solving problems on a metropolitan-area-wide basis. Many communities, especially in urban areas, have ignored traditional political jurisdictional lines to pool their efforts in attacking common problems (such as pollution) that respect no political boundaries, and in planning to take advantage of federal grants. Federal legislation such as the Transportation Assistance Act of 1982 has been designed to assist and encourage area-wide solutions to urban problems.

Yet serious dislocations and new problems of regulatory federalism continue to plague the federal system. Many critics of the federal structure question whether states are willing or able to meet their responsibilities. By contrast, defenders of the states have noted that most of the successful programs of the New Deal "had been anticipated, by experiment and practice, on the state level or by private institutions." [59]

The states, many still caught in a fiscal squeeze, may find it difficult to play such an innovative role today. Some cities are in financial difficulty at the very time that more services are being demanded by the inner-city residents who are least able to pay for them. And the dramatic growth of regulatory federalism, with all of its new rules, has imposed new burdens on state and local governments.

"America's federal system," the Advisory Commission on Intergovernmental Relations has warned, "is on trial as never before in this century of crisis and change." [60] The problems that confronted America in the 1990s raised the fundamental question of whether a federal system born in compromise more than two centuries ago can adapt itself to the needs of a technological, urban society in an age of onrushing change.

PERSPECTIVE

The United States has a federal system of government in which power is constitutionally shared by a national government and fifty state governments. Some countries have a unitary system in which policies are set by a single central government.

Advocates of a federal system argue that it permits diversity, and that local officials may perform better than the federal bureaucracy since problems vary from one locality to another. Other arguments made for a federal system are that its many levels of government allow more points of access for citizens, and that it protects individual rights, fosters experimentation and innovation, and is suited to a large country such as the United States.

A federal system also has disadvantages, however; it may make national unity harder to achieve, local governments may frustrate national policies, or the system may serve as a mask for privilege and economic or racial discrimination. In addition, law enforcement and justice may be uneven, and local governments may lack skill and money and may be dominated by special interests.

The rioting that erupted in the streets of Los Angeles in April of 1992 after a jury that included no blacks acquitted four white police officers on trial for the beating of a black motorist provided dramatic testimony to the nature of the federal system. All three layers of government — local, state, and national, were drawn into, and reacted to, the crisis.

The American federal system was created at the Constitutional Convention of 1787. The delegates reached a compromise: they would give up some of the states' independence in order to achieve enough unity to create a nation. Under the Constitution, the three branches of government are granted certain specifically enumerated powers. Congress, for example, has the power to coin money, and the president is commander in chief of the armed forces. The Supreme Court has held that the national government also has broad implied powers, as well as inherent powers that it may exercise simply because it exists as a government. The federal government and the states also independently exercise concurrent powers.

The Supreme Court is the umpire of the federal system. The case of *McCulloch v. Maryland* (1819) established the key concepts of implied powers, broad construction of the Constitution, and supremacy of the national government. The *supremacy clause* of the Constitution makes it clear that the Constitution prevails over state laws. Under the federal system, local governments in the United States derive their powers from the states and are subject to the same constitutional restrictions as the states.

The formal structure of American government has changed very little since 1787, but the balance of power within the system has changed markedly. A century ago, the federal government did not provide social secu-

---

[59] Nelson A. Rockefeller, *The Future of Federalism* (Cambridge: Harvard University Press, 1962), p. 15.

[60] *Ninth Annual Report*, Advisory Commission on Intergovernmental Relations (Washington, D.C.: U.S. Government Printing Office, 1968), p. 13.

rity, medical insurance for millions of citizens, vast aid to public and private education, or billions of dollars in welfare payments. As American society has grown more complex, with a highly diversified population of more than 254 million people, the national government's managerial task has grown larger. The power to tax and spend for the general welfare is a function of the national government that has expanded enormously in the twentieth century.

There have been sharp increases in federal aid to state and local governments since 1950, but as a percentage of the federal budget, aid has actually declined in recent years. In 1980, for example, such grants amounted to 15 percent of the federal budget, but in 1993 the total had dropped to 13 percent. There are three kinds of federal aid to the states: categorical grants, which are earmarked for specific purposes; block grants, which are for use in a broad general area; and general purpose grants, which may be used by states and localities mostly as they wish.

Most of the federal aid to state and local governments falls into eight categories: health; income security; education, training, employment and social services; transportation; community and regional development; natural resources and the environment; general government; and agriculture. State and local authorities are quick to point out that state and local spending has been increasing at an even faster rate than federal spending. Yet states and local governments depend on federal aid in part because the federal government collects a major share of all taxes.

The vast problems of urban areas provide one of the greatest challenges to the American federal system.

Suggested Reading

Advisory Commission on Intergovernmental Relations, *Regulatory Federalism: Policy, Process, Impact and Reform* (Advisory Commission on Intergovernmental Relations, 1984). A study of the emergence of regulatory programs of the federal government that state and local governments are required to implement.

Davis, S. Rufus. *The Federal Principle* (University of California Press, 1978). An examination of the history of federalism from the Hellenic age through the twentieth century. Contains an interesting analysis of the American model of federalism created at the Constitutional Convention of 1787.

Derthick, Martha. *Between State and Nation: Regional Organizations of the United States** (The Brookings Institution, 1974). An analysis of the theory and actual operation of regional organizations in the American federal system. The Appalachian Regional Commission, the Tennessee Valley Authority, and the Delaware River Basin Commission are among the regional organizations discussed.

Elazar, Daniel J. *American Federalism: A View from the States*, 3rd edition (Harper & Row, 1984). A good general treatment of American federalism. The book emphasizes some of the problems and areas of controversy in contemporary intergovernmental relationships, and traces the historical roots of cooperation and shared functions among the various layers of government in the federal system.

Ellwood, John W., ed. *Reductions in U.S. Domestic Spending: How They Affect State and Local Governments* (Transaction Books, 1982). A critical analysis of the early impact of the Reagan administration's budget cuts for social welfare programs. Examines the effects of the cuts on state and local governments.

Grodzins, Morton. *The American System* (Transaction Books, 1983). (Edited by Daniel J. Elazar.) A comprehensive analysis of American federalism by a leading authority on the subject.

Hanus, Jerome J. *The Nationalization of State Governments* (Lexington Books, 1981). A collection of five essays that examines intergovernmental relations in the federal system. Focuses on the political impact of federal grant-in-aid policies on both state and national policymaking.

MacMahon, Arthur W. *Administering Federalism in a Democracy* (Oxford University Press, 1972). A thoughtful examination of American federalism that emphasizes its administrative aspects. Analyzes federal grants-in-aid, the impact of Supreme Court decisions, and the role of state and local governments in administering federal programs.

Reagan, Michael D., and Sanzone, John G. *The New Federalism*, 2nd edition* (Oxford University Press, 1981). An excellent study of the pattern of federalism in the United States. The book questions traditional definitions of a federal system and examines the development of federal grants-in-aid, the limited ability of state governments to finance public services, and the dominant role of the federal government in the American federal system.

Riker, William H. *Federalism: Origin, Operation, Significance* (Little, Brown, 1964). A historical and comparative analysis of federalism. Riker examines with great clarity the conditions that give rise to federalism and maintain it. He is sharply critical of certain aspects of American federalism and argues that historically it permitted the oppression of blacks.

Wheare, K. C. *Federal Government*, 4th edition (Greenwood, 1980). (Originally published in 1963.) A perceptive comparative analysis of federal governmental systems. Based primarily on a comprehensive examination of the workings of federalism in Australia, Canada, Switzerland, and the United States.

---

* Available in paperback edition.

D ONALD AGUILLARD, a twenty-five-year-old high school biology teacher in Lafayette, Louisiana, was upset about a law just passed by the state legislature. In his biology class, Aguillard taught the widely accepted theory of evolution developed more than a century earlier by Charles Darwin. The theory holds that human beings evolved over many millions of years and are descended from other primates.

The year was 1981. The new law in Louisiana would have required Donald Aguillard and any other teacher who taught evolution to give equal time to "creation science," the fundamentalist belief that in six days God created the universe and all life forms, including human beings, less than 10,000 years ago.

Chapter 4

Civil Liberties and Citizenship

"It would have required me to teach something I didn't believe in," Aguillard said.[1] The young man drafted a letter to the American Civil Liberties Union, which decided to challenge the law in court. Aguillard was asked to join the suit, and he agreed.

He won in the lower federal courts, and the governor of Louisiana, Edwin Edwards, appealed to the United States Supreme Court. The issues had been fought years before at the state level. In Tennessee, another high school biology teacher, John T. Scopes, had been prosecuted in 1925 for teaching evolution in violation of a state law. His conviction and fine of $100 were later overturned on a technicality. Now, more than half a century later, the issue had arisen again.

---

[1] Telephone interview with the authors, December 8, 1987.

In June of 1987 the United States Supreme Court ruled 7–2 that the Louisiana statute violated the Bill of Rights and was unconstitutional.[2] The law, Justice William Brennan wrote for the majority, "embodies the religious belief that a supernatural creator was responsible for the creation of humankind." Therefore, the Court held, the state law "advances a religious doctrine," which is prohibited by the First Amendment of the Constitution.[3]

In deciding cases under the Bill of Rights, the Supreme Court often has the difficult task of attempting to

---

[2] *Edwards v. Aguillard*, 482 U.S. 578 (1987).
[3] Ibid.

---

balance competing constitutional principles, and the rights of the individual against those of society as a whole. The questions raised in this process are many and complex. Should freedom of the press and freedom of expression be absolute rights under the First Amendment? What if free speech conflicts with the rights of others? Should prayers be allowed in public schools? What does the law say now about government wiretapping and "bugging"? What are the legal rights of student demonstrators? Can police search your home or car without a warrant? What are your rights if you are arrested? Will the federal Bill of Rights be of any help to you if you are arrested by state or local police? These are some of the questions to be explored in this chapter.

Donald Aguillard

INDIVIDUAL FREEDOM AND SOCIETY

The Supreme Court's decisions in the area of civil liberties and individual rights often illustrate the tension between liberty and order in a free society. Freedom is not absolute, for as Supreme Court Justice Oliver Wen-

dell Holmes, Jr., once said, "The right to swing my fist ends where the other man's nose begins." But the proper balance in a democracy between the rights of an individual and the rights of society as a whole can never be resolved to everyone's satisfaction.

The rights of the individual should not always be viewed as competing with those of the community; in a free society, the fullest freedom of expression for the individual also may serve the interests of society as a whole. As John F. Kennedy observed, "The rights of every man are diminished when the rights of one man are threatened." [4]

The nineteenth-century British philosopher John Stuart Mill advanced the classic argument for diversity of opinion in his treatise *On Liberty:* "Though the silenced opinion be an error, it may, and very commonly does, contain a portion of truth; and since the general or prevailing opinion on any subject is rarely or never the whole truth, it is only by the collision of adverse opin-

---

[4] John F. Kennedy, "Radio and Television Report to the American People on Civil Rights," June 11, 1963, in *Public Papers of the Presidents, John F. Kennedy, 1963* (Washington, D.C.: U.S. Government Printing Office, 1964), p. 468.

LIBERTY AND JUSTICE FOR ALL?

"The way they say it, it's as if there is liberty and justice, but there isn't."

Twelve-year-old Mary Frain, sitting pensively on a wooden rocker in her Jamaica, Queens, home, gave this explanation yesterday as one of her reasons for objecting to the daily Pledge of Allegiance to the flag in school.

The crank calls and angry letters have almost disappeared from the life of the introverted seventh grader who, with a classmate, Susan Keller, won a federal court decision on Dec. 10 permitting students in city schools to remain in their seats during the flag-saluting ceremony.

Because of the pressure, Susan Keller soon transferred to another school. But Mary still refuses to stand in the morning when most of the children in her honors class at Junior High School 217 at 85th Avenue and 148th Street stand to recite the pledge.

At home, following a quick lunch, the

youngster discussed the impact of the court case on her life.

"Like when we walked along the halls, the kids used to call us commies. We had phone calls. One was obscene. Some just laughed or breathed when you picked it up. But it's dying down now. . . ."

Mary persisted, she said, because of strong objections to the wording of the pledge.

"Liberty and justice for all?" she said. "That's not true . . . for the blacks and poor whites. The poor have to live in cold miserable places. And it's obvious that blacks are oppressed."

The girl would compromise her position if the pledge were rephrased to be spoken as a "goal." "Like if when you say it you're making a vow to make it liberty and justice for all," she explained.

—*New York Times*, January 31, 1970

ions that the remainder of the truth has any chance of being supplied."[5]

In American society, the Supreme Court is the mechanism called upon to resolve conflicts between liberty and order, between the rights of the individual and the rights of the many. In doing so, the Court operates within the framework of what James Monroe called that "polar star, and great support of American liberty," the Bill of Rights.

THE BILL OF RIGHTS

The first ten amendments to the Constitution constitute the Bill of Rights.[6] These vital protections were omitted from the Constitution as drafted in 1787. (See Chapter 2.) The supporters of the Constitution, it will be recalled, promised to pass a Bill of Rights in part so that they might win the struggle over ratification.

Although the Bill of Rights is the fundamental charter of American liberties, it is the Supreme Court that ultimately decides how those rights shall be defined and applied. It should be remembered that the Supreme Court does not operate in a vacuum. Its nine justices are human beings and actors in the drama of their time. As former Chief Justice Earl Warren once declared, "Our judges are not monks or scientists, but participants in the living stream of our national life."[7] Individual liberties may depend not only on what the Court says in particular cases but on what the political system will tolerate in any given era.

Although the Bill of Rights was passed to guard against abuses by the new *federal* government, the Supreme Court has ruled over the years, case by case, that virtually all the safeguards of the Bill of Rights apply as well to *state* and *local* governments and agencies.

Alpheus T. Mason, a leading constitutional scholar, observed that the fundamental rights of a free society gained "no greater moral sanctity" by being written into the Constitution, "but individuals could thereafter look to courts for their protection. Rights formerly natural became civil."[8]

---

[5] John Stuart Mill, *On Liberty* (New York: Appleton-Century-Crofts, 1947), p. 52.
[6] As noted in Chapter 2, some scholars regard only the first eight or nine amendments as the Bill of Rights.
[7] Earl Warren, "The Law and the Future," *Fortune*, November 1955, p. 107.
[8] Alpheus T. Mason, *The Supreme Court: Palladium of Freedom* (Ann Arbor: University of Michigan Press, 1962), p. 58.

Freedom of Speech

"Congress shall make no law respecting an establishment of religion, or prohibiting the free exercise thereof; or abridging the freedom of speech, or of the press; or the right of the people peaceably to assemble, and to petition the Government for a redress of grievances."

These forty-five words are the First Amendment of the Constitution. Along with "due process of law" and other constitutional protections, these words set forth basic American freedoms. As Justice Benjamin N. Cardozo once wrote, freedom of thought and of speech is "the matrix, the indispensable condition, of nearly every other form of freedom."[9] (Although the Constitution states that "Congress shall make no law" abridging First Amendment freedoms, the Supreme Court has interpreted this to mean that state and local authorities cannot do so, either.)

Yet the courts have frequently placed limits on speech. Several types of expression do not enjoy constitutional immunity from government regulation. These include fraudulent advertising, obscenity (which courts have had vast difficulty in defining), child pornography, libel, and, in some cases, street oratory. The Supreme Court, for example, has ruled that police are justified in arresting a sidewalk speaker if he is too effective in stirring his audience.[10] Three decades before that decision, Supreme Court Justice Oliver Wendell Holmes, Jr., had established the classic "clear and present danger" test to define the point at which speech loses First Amendment protection:

> The character of every act depends upon the circumstances in which it is done. . . . The most stringent protection of free speech would not protect a man in falsely shouting fire in a theater and causing a panic. . . . The question in every case is whether the words used are used in such circumstances and are of such a nature as to create a clear and present danger that they will bring about the substantive evils that Congress has a right to prevent.[11]

Later, in the Gitlow case, the Court went even further, ruling that some speech could be prohibited if it threatened the overthrow of the government or in other ways injured the public welfare, a doctrine that came to be known as the "bad tendency" test.[12] The

---

[9] *Palko v. Connecticut*, 302 U.S. 319 (1937).
[10] *Feiner v. New York*, 340 U.S. 315 (1951).
[11] *Schenck v. United States*, 249 U.S. 47 (1919).
[12] *Gitlow v. New York*, 268 U.S. 652 (1925).

Justice Oliver
Wendell Holmes, Jr.

Court's free-speech yardstick shifted again during the New Deal and the Second World War, then appeared to swing back to the "clear and present danger" test in the 1950s. Thus, even so fundamental a right as free speech, while broadly protected by the Constitution, has been limited by the Supreme Court according to the circumstances and the times.

In reconciling the requirement of free speech with other social rights and needs, the Supreme Court often has tried to draw a line between "expression" and "action." But that is not always an easy matter. In the major "draft-card burning" case, in 1968, David P. O'Brien had argued that when he burned his card to protest the

Vietnam war, his action was "symbolic speech," protected by the Constitution. But the Court rejected this argument, 7–1. Chief Justice Warren, in his majority opinion, declared: "We cannot accept the view that an apparently limitless variety of conduct can be labeled 'speech.' " [13]

On the other hand, as noted in Chapter 2, the Supreme Court has ruled that neither the states nor Congress may prohibit the burning of an American flag, even though many persons find that form of free expression deeply offensive.[14] And the Court unanimously ruled unconstitutional a St. Paul, Minnesota "hate crime" law that had sought to prohibit speech or action aimed at persons because of their race, religion, or gender. (*R. A. V. v. St. Paul*, 112 S. Ct. 2538, 1992). The case arose when a 17-year-old white high-school dropout was arrested for burning a cross on the lawn of a black couple. While it found the cross-burning "reprehensible," the Court said the city law violated the First Amendment because it prohibited only certain kinds of speech on a selective basis. The ruling cast doubt on the constitutionality of similar "hate crime" laws across the nation. And in an earlier case, the Supreme Court struck down a Massachusetts law under which Valarie Goguen had been arrested and sentenced to six months in jail for wearing an American flag patch

---

[13] *United States* v. *O'Brien*, 391 U.S. 367 (1968).
[14] *Texas* v. *Johnson*, 491 U.S. 397 (1989), which struck down a state law that barred flag-burning; and *U.S.* v. *Eichman* and *U.S.* v. *Haggerty*, both 496 U.S. 310 (1990), which invalidated the federal law prohibiting flag-burning.

SMOKEY BEAR: NO FLAG BURNING IN THE NO-SMOKING SECTION

The Supreme Court's ruling in 1989 that burning the American flag is a form of symbolic speech protected by the First Amendment was not greeted happily by President Bush or his administration. The following is a letter written at the time by the legal office of the Department of the Interior to Major Carl Holmberg of the United States Park Police:

Carl—
Just a quick note on the recent Supreme Court flag desecration decision in order that you can plan for the demonstrations around the 4th of July.

While it is now apparently the law that the demonstrators may roll Old Glory and fire her up like a Marlboro if they want, we don't have to permit it in the no-smoking section. As you know, the park regulations at 36 C.F.R. 2.13 prohibit the lighting or maintaining of fires except in designated areas or receptacles. This regulation is still in effect. It doesn't matter if they want to burn the American Flag or the *Washington Post*, unauthorized fires are still prohibited in the parks.

Richard G. Robbins

—*Washington Post*, July 1, 1989

on the seat of his blue jeans.[15] Although the Court majority based its conclusion on a finding that the law was unconstitutionally vague, Justice Byron R. White concurred in the decision on the grounds that the law restricted freedom of expression.

Later, however, the Supreme Court upheld the right of the government to revoke the passport of Philip Agee, a former agent of the Central Intelligence Agency who had exposed the names of CIA officers and agents overseas. Because Agee's disclosures were designed to obstruct intelligence operations, the Court said, "they are clearly not protected by the Constitution."[16] By its ruling, the Court seemed to say that in some cases expression amounted to action.

The right of free expression by students and student demonstrators was affirmed as far back as 1969, when the Court ruled that a thirteen-year-old Iowa girl, Mary Beth Tinker, could not be suspended from her junior high school for wearing a black arm band to class in protest against the war in Vietnam. "In our system," the Court held, "state-operated schools may not be enclaves of totalitarianism. School officials do not possess absolute authority over their students."[17] In winning the fight for her constitutional rights, Mary Beth Tinker had made a much broader point for all students in America. For the Court concluded: "It can hardly be argued that either students or teachers shed their constitutional rights to freedom of speech or expression at the schoolhouse gate."

But the Supreme Court also has made it clear that student rights to free expression are not unlimited. In 1983, Matthew Fraser, a seventeen-year-old high school student near Tacoma, Washington, gave a speech on behalf of a candidate for the student government. In it, he described his friend as "a man who is firm — he's firm in his pants . . . his character is firm . . . a man who will go to the very end, even the climax, for each and every one of you." The school suspended Matthew Fraser for disruptive conduct. In 1986, the Supreme Court ruled in favor of the school officials, holding 7 – 2 that students may be suspended for using "vulgar and offensive" language.[18]

And in 1988, in a major decision on student rights, the Supreme Court upheld, 5 – 3, the power of school administrators to censor a high school newspaper, stu-

dent plays, and other activities in certain circumstances. The case arose when the principal of a high school in Hazelwood, Missouri, a suburb of St. Louis, removed from the school newspaper two pages that contained articles about teenage pregnancy and the effect of divorce on children.[19] The Court ruled that where an activity was "part of the school curriculum," school administrators had broad powers of censorship. Justice Byron R. White's majority opinion noted that *Spectrum*, the student paper, was published as part of a journalism class. Justice William Brennan, in a sharp dissent, argued that the "First Amendment permits no such blanket censorship authority," and that school officials could not act as "thought police."[20]

In 1987, the Court held 5 – 4 that public employees could not be fired for exercising their constitutional rights of free speech. The case arose in 1981 when Ardith McPherson, a clerk-typist employed by the county government in Houston, Texas, heard of the assassination attempt against President Reagan. McPherson, a black, speculated to a friend that the president might have been shot by a black angered by the administration's cuts in welfare and social programs. She added: "If they go for him again, I hope they get him." A passing supervisor overheard the remark and McPherson was fired, although she said the comment was not serious. Justice Thurgood Marshall, writing for the Court majority, said that the remark, taken in context, was "political speech" for which, under the Constitution, Ardith McPherson could not be fired.[21]

In 1982 the right of students to read books in the school library gained support from the Supreme Court. Steven Pico, a student at Island Trees, a New York City high school, sued the school board when eight books, including Desmond Morris's *The Naked Ape* and Eldridge Cleaver's *Soul on Ice*, were removed from the library shelves after objections by some members of the community. The Court, ruling that the First Amendment limits the power of a school board to ban books, declared: "Our Constitution does not permit the official suppression of *ideas*."[22] Despite the Court's decision, censorship of books in public schools, sometimes under pressure from conservative groups, appears to be increasing.[23] Not long before the Island Trees case, for

[15] *Smith v. Goguen,* 415 U.S. 566 (1974).
[16] *Haig v. Agee,* 453 U.S. 280 (1981).
[17] *Tinker v. Des Moines School District et al.,* 393 U.S. 503 (1969).
[18] *Bethel School District No. 403 v. Fraser,* 478 U.S. 675 (1986).

[19] *Hazelwood School District v. Kuhlmeier,* 484 U.S. 260 (1988).
[20] Ibid.
[21] *Rankin v. McPherson,* 483 U.S. 378 (1987).
[22] *Board of Education, Island Trees Union Free School District v. Pico,* 457 U.S. 853 (1982).
[23] *Washington Post,* May 10, 1982, p. A2.

example, a school in St. David, Arizona, banned the works of Mark Twain, Ernest Hemingway, Joseph Conrad, and Homer.

In 1991, the Supreme Court struck down a New York State law that was designed to prevent criminals from profiting from books or movies about their crimes.[24] The Court ruled that the law violated the First Amendment because it restricted a certain kind of speech, writing about one's own criminal conduct. The case concerned Henry Hill, a Mafia figure whose story was told in the book, *Wiseguy*, and the movie, *GoodFellas*.

In 1987 the Supreme Court ruled that the First Amendment protects the right of individuals "verbally to oppose or challenge police action." It struck down as unconstitutionally overbroad a city law in Houston, Texas, that allowed the police to arrest almost anyone who might annoy them while they were on official business.[25]

On the other hand, the Supreme Court has ruled, in effect, that some rock music is too loud. In 1989, it upheld a New York City noise-control ordinance governing rock concerts in Central Park.[26]

Preferred Freedoms and the Balancing Test Different philosophies, often identified with particular justices, have emerged as the Supreme Court has struggled with problems of freedom of expression.

For example, Justices Hugo Black and William O. Douglas established themselves as advocates of the "absolute" position. Black argued that "there *are* 'absolutes' in our Bill of Rights"[27] that cannot be diluted by judicial decisions. He maintained, for instance, that obscenity and libel are forms of speech and therefore cannot be constitutionally limited. But a majority of the Court took the position that the rights of the First Amendment must be "balanced" against the competing needs of the community to preserve order and to preserve the state. This view was championed by Justice Felix Frankfurter and others.

In performing this delicate balancing act, however, some members of the Court have argued that the basic freedoms should take precedence over other needs. Thus, Justice Harlan Fiske Stone argued that the Con-

stitution had placed freedom of speech and religion "in a preferred position."[28]

Despite these mixed views, the Supreme Court, while reluctant to narrow the scope of basic liberties, has generally not hesitated to balance such freedoms against other constitutional requirements.

Freedom of the Press

Closely tied to free speech, and protected as well by the First Amendment, is freedom of the press. However, the courts do not always rule in favor of the press, despite the First Amendment.

The press plays a vital role in a democracy because it is the principal means by which the people learn about the activities of the government. A democracy rests on the consent of the governed, but in order to give their consent, the governed must be informed. For example, in developing political opinions or in choosing among candidates in an election campaign, most voters rely on the news media — television, newspapers, and magazines — for their information.

Because of the importance of a free press in a democratic society, the Supreme Court has rarely permitted advance censorship of the press. It has been reluctant to permit officials at any level of government to tell the press what it may or may not print.

The strong tradition of a free press in the United States rests on the principle, rooted in English common law, that normally there must be no governmental "prior restraint" of the press. The Supreme Court had dealt with this issue more than half a century ago, when it ruled that a Minneapolis weekly newspaper could not be suppressed because of articles attacking city officials as "corrupt" and "grafters."[29] The Court held that even "miscreant purveyors of scandal" were protected from prior restraint by the First Amendment. But the Court said that the press might be censored in advance by the government in "exceptional cases" relating to national security, during wartime, for example — and it gave as one illustration a news story that might report the sailing date of a troopship. Moreover, in 1971 the federal government, claiming that national security was endangered, had tried to stop the *New York Times* from continuing to publish a series based on a secret history of the Vietnam war — the so-called Pentagon Papers. For

---

[24] *Simon and Schuster v. New York State Crime Victims Board*, 112 S. Ct. 501 (1991).

[25] *Hill v. City of Houston*, 483 U.S. 1001 (1987).

[26] *Ward v. Rock Against Racism* 491 U.S. 781 (1989).

[27] Hugo L. Black, "The Bill of Rights," *New York University Law Review*, vol. 35 (April 1960), p. 867.

[28] *United States v. Carolene Products Co.*, 304 U.S. 144 (1938).

[29] *Near v. Minnesota*, 283 U.S. 697 (1931).

**General Manuel
Noriega**

ernment warned that publication of the article would violate the Atomic Energy Act of 1954, which prohibits the disclosure of "restricted data" about nuclear weapons.

The magazine, a liberal monthly journal of opinion, countered that the article disclosed no secrets. According to the magazine, the writer, Howard Morland, had been given no access to classified data and had pieced the story together by interviewing scientists and touring nuclear plants with the knowledge and permission of the government. The *Progressive* said it wished to publish the article to show that the government had cloaked its atomic weapons policy in excessive secrecy and to inform the public about an issue affecting the survival of the human race.

The First Amendment to the Constitution, on its face, might seem to prohibit the government from censoring an article in advance—even an article about the hydrogen bomb. The amendment states that "Congress shall make no law . . . abridging the freedom . . . of the press." But the Supreme Court, the ultimate arbiter of what the Constitution means, has always balanced the First Amendment against other social needs and other parts of the Constitution. And so Judge Warren of the district court argued that a hydrogen bomb, if used, would not leave people alive to enjoy their rights under the First Amendment. "You can't speak freely when you're dead," he said.[31] The battle lines were drawn; despite the First Amendment, a publication had been censored in advance by the government.

As the *Progressive* case unfolded, additional facts emerged. A government physicist stated that the magazine article contained no information that could not be

fifteen days, the federal courts restrained publication. Finally, the Supreme Court ruled 6–3 that the *Times* and other newspapers that had been restrained were free to publish.[30] Justice Hugo Black, in the strongest of the opinions on the majority side, wrote: "The press was protected so that it could bare the secrets of government and inform the people."

The Supreme Court made it clear in 1990, however, that it will not, in every instance, prohibit censorship. It voted 7–2 to let stand a lower court order that barred CNN from broadcasting tape recordings of conversations between Manuel Antonio Noriega, Panama's deposed dictator, and his lawyer.

More often, however, the press has triumphed in the continuing tension between official secrecy and the First Amendment. One of the most dramatic cases took place in the city of Milwaukee, Wisconsin, more than a decade ago.

The Progressive and the H-Bomb   On March 9, 1979, in Milwaukee, Federal District Court Judge Robert W. Warren issued an order restraining the *Progressive* magazine from publishing an article on how the hydrogen bomb works.

The United States government had gone into court to block publication of the article, which it claimed would help other countries to build thermonuclear bombs, bringing civilization "one step closer to its potential destruction in a nuclear holocaust." The gov-

[31] *New York Times*, March 10, 1979, p. 1.

[30] *New York Times Company v. United States* 403 U.S. 713 (1971).

learned from the diagrams published by the *Encyclopedia Americana* with an article by Dr. Edward Teller, a physicist known as the "father of the H-bomb."

The *Progressive* appealed, but the United States Supreme Court declined to intervene. Finally, in September the government announced it was dropping its suit against the *Progressive* because a newspaper in Madison, Wisconsin, had published the very facts the government was trying to suppress. In November the *Progressive* finally published the Morland article.[32] But for six months the federal government had succeeded in imposing prior restraint on the press.

Despite the outcome in the *Progressive* case and in the Pentagon Papers case, the issue remained unresolved. The press is protected by the First Amendment, but how far that protection extends is not clear. In the case of the Noriega tapes, a television network was prohibited from airing material. These battles illustrate one facet of the continuing struggle between the press and the government in American democracy.

During the 1970s, the Supreme Court, under Chief Justice Warren Burger, had issued a series of rulings against the press. By 1980 the Court had permitted the jailing of Myron Farber, a *New York Times* reporter, for refusing to turn over his notes to the judge in a murder case; had allowed police to search a newspaper office for photographs of demonstrators; had made it much easier for individuals to sue the press for libel; and had required that a former Central Intelligence Agency officer turn over to the government the income from a book he wrote criticizing the agency's record in Vietnam.

As these cases show, freedom of the press is a relative term, applied differently by the Supreme Court at different times. In the Pentagon Papers case, the Court protected the right of the press to publish important information that the government preferred to suppress. In a series of later decisions, the Court ruled that the press must yield to the needs of the process of criminal justice. And yet in other decisions, the Court has expanded the rights of the press — supporting access by reporters to criminal trials, for example.

As already noted, the Supreme Court has been reluctant to impose "prior restraint" on the press. And the Court has ruled unanimously that it is unconstitutional to compel a newspaper to provide free space for a political candidate to reply to editorial-page criticism.[33]

The Court thereby rejected the argument that the First Amendment required citizen "access" to newspapers to present differing viewpoints.

"In the First Amendment," Justice Black wrote in the Pentagon Papers case, "the Founding Fathers gave the free press the protection it must have to fulfill its essential role in our democracy. The press was to serve the governed, not the governors." [34]

While the Court has thus usually protected the press under the First Amendment, it also has placed limitations on freedom of the press in several areas.

Free Press and Fair Trial When basic rights collide, the Supreme Court may be called upon to act as a referee. In recent years the Supreme Court has shown increasing concern over pretrial and courtroom publicity that may prejudice the fair trial of a defendant in a criminal case. The issue brings into direct conflict two basic principles of the Bill of Rights — the right of an accused person to have a fair trial and the right of freedom of the press.

The use of television has complicated the problem of a fair trial. In two cases the Supreme Court struck down convictions in which the defendants' televised confessions of murder were presumed to have influenced the jury.[35] In 1966 the Supreme Court reversed the conviction of a Cleveland, Ohio, osteopath found guilty of bludgeoning his wife to death, ruling that the defendant's constitutional rights had been prejudiced by publicity that gave the trial the "atmosphere of a 'Roman holiday' for the news media." [36] Similar excessive courtroom publicity influenced the 1966 decision of the Texas Court of Criminal Appeals to reverse the conviction of Jack Ruby for the murder of Lee Harvey Oswald, the accused assassin of President Kennedy. Before Ruby could be retried, he died of illness in January 1967.

It is entirely possible that some jurors are influenced for or against a defendant by news stories. However, in the television age, public figures in particular cannot avoid considerable pretrial publicity. And in 1981 the Supreme Court ruled that states could permit trials to be televised. The possibility that television might impair the judgment of a juror, the Court ruled,

---

[32] Howard Morland, "The H-Bomb Secret: How We Got It — Why We're Telling It," *The Progressive*, November 1979, p. 14.

[33] *Miami Herald Publishing Co.* v. *Tornillo*, 418 U.S. 241 (1974).
[34] *New York Times Company* v. *United States* (1971).
[35] *Irvin* v. *Dowd*, 366 U.S. 717 (1961); *Rideau* v. *Louisana*, 373 U.S. 723 (1963).
[36] *Sheppard* v. *Maxwell*, 384 U.S. 333 (1966).

did not justify "an absolute constitutional ban on broadcast coverage."[37]

In the mid-1970s the press was increasingly coming under judicial restraints in the form of "gag orders" issued by courts to restrict news gathering and publication. In 1976 the Supreme Court heard arguments in a Nebraska case that was viewed as a critical test of freedom of the press.

On October 18, 1975, in Sutherland, Nebraska (population 840), six members of the James Kellie family were found murdered, and a twenty-nine-year-old unemployed handyman, Erwin Charles Simants, who lived next door, was arrested and charged with murder in the course of a sexual assault. Details of the crime were considered so lurid that a local judge issued an order prohibiting the press from reporting a pretrial hearing. A coalition of news organizations in Nebraska took their case to the Supreme Court.

In June 1976 the Supreme Court unanimously ruled that the Nebraska gag order violated the First Amendment's provision for freedom of the press.[38] Some judges, however, soon found other ways to restrain the press. In a number of instances, judges closed their courtrooms to the press in pretrial proceedings. In 1979, in the *Gannett* case, the Supreme Court upheld this practice for a time. It ruled, 5–4, that the public and the press could be barred from pretrial hearings if a judge found a "reasonable probability" that publicity would harm a defendant's right to a fair trial.[39] Although the Sixth Amendment guarantees "the right to a speedy and public trial," Justice Potter Stewart, writing for the Court, said that a defendant could waive this right. If the judge agreed, the courtroom could be closed. The press and many members of the legal profession immediately protested the decision.

Following the *Gannett* case, the Supreme Court agreed to decide whether it is constitutional for a judge to conduct an *entire* trial in secret in the belief that publicity might impair a defendant's right to a fair trial. The case was brought by two Richmond, Virginia, newspapers who challenged the secret trial of a man accused of murdering a motel manager.

In 1980 the Supreme Court ruled in favor of the press in the Richmond case. In a 7–1 decision, the Court said that trials must be open to the public and the press except in the most unusual circumstances. "We

hold that the right to attend criminal trials is implicit in the guarantees of the First Amendment," the Court declared.[40] But under the *Gannett* decision, pretrial proceedings could still be closed. Since a majority of cases are disposed of in such pretrial proceedings, at this point the victory of the press was by no means total.

Nevertheless, the Supreme Court continued to rule in favor of open proceedings in three later decisions. It held that the press may not be excluded from a trial during testimony by a minor who claimed to be the victim of a rape.[41] It ruled that the jury selection process must be totally open to the press and public.[42] Finally, it held that even pretrial hearings must be open to the press where, as in California, the proceedings resemble a trial—a decision that modified and, in effect, overruled the *Gannett* case.[43] The practical result has been to open pretrial hearings in all states to the press and public.

Despite these rulings, the issue of free press and fair trial remains unresolved and a subject of ongoing controversy.

Confidentiality: Shielding Reporters and Their Sources The right to have a fair trial often conflicts with the First Amendment in another important area—that of confidentiality for reporters and their news sources.

Journalists argue that they must offer confidential sources complete anonymity, particularly in the case of investigative reporting, when disclosure of the name of a source might lead to reprisals against that person. (The importance of investigative reporting—which relies in part on confidentiality of sources—was dramatically illustrated during the Watergate affair, when reporters Bob Woodward and Carl Bernstein of the *Washington Post* uncovered many details of the break-in at Democratic party headquarters by burglars employed by the president's campaign, and the cover-up of that crime by the Nixon administration.) But what if a news reporter has information vital to the defense in a criminal trial, or which the government needs to prove its case? Do reporters have the "privilege" under the First Amendment of refusing to surrender such evidence? The Supreme Court has said no.

In its 1972 decision in the Caldwell case, the Court explored the question of whether reporters have the

[37] *Chandler and Granger v. Florida*, 449 U.S. 560 (1981).
[38] *Nebraska Press Association v. Stuart*, 427 U.S. 539 (1976).
[39] *Gannett Co., Inc. v. De Pasquale*, 443 U.S. 368 (1979).

[40] *Richmond Newspapers, Inc. v. Virginia*, 448 U.S. 555 (1980).
[41] *Globe Newspaper Co. v. Superior Court*, 457 U.S. 596 (1982).
[42] *Press-Enterprise Co. v. Superior Court*, 464 U.S. 501 (1984).
[43] *Press-Enterprise Co. v. Superior Court*, 478 U.S. 1 (1986).

New York Times reporter Earl Caldwell

New York Times reporter Myron Farber goes to jail.

constitutional right to protect their sources. Specifically, the Court ruled that the First Amendment did not exempt news reporters from appearing and testifying before state and federal grand juries. The decision came in the case of Earl Caldwell, a reporter for the *New York Times*, and in two related cases.[44] Caldwell had declined to appear before a federal grand jury to testify about the Black Panthers in the San Francisco area. He argued that merely appearing would destroy his relationship of trust with his confidential news sources. But the Supreme Court said that the investigation by a grand jury

of possible crimes was of greater importance to the public than the protection of news sources. The courts had generally taken this position even before the Supreme Court ruled. But some reporters have gone to jail rather than reveal their sources, and many members of the press feel that compelling reporters to testify abridges their First Amendment rights.[45]

The issue of reporters' sources arose again in 1978 during the dramatic murder trial of Dr. Mario Jascalevich, a New Jersey physician. Dr. Jascalevich had been

---

[44] *United States* v. *Caldwell; Branzburg* v. *Hayes; In the Matter of Paul Pappas*, all 408 U.S. 665 (1972).

[45] Earl Caldwell did not go to jail because the term of the federal grand jury seeking his testimony had expired by the time the Supreme Court ruled.

REPORTERS' SOURCES: THE JUSTICES DISAGREE

The issue in these cases is whether requiring newsmen to appear and testify before state or federal grand juries abridges the freedom of speech and press guaranteed by the First Amendment. We hold that it does not. . . .

Citizens generally are not constitutionally immune from grand jury subpoenas; and neither the First Amendment nor other constitutional provision protects the average citizen from disclosing to a grand jury information that he has received in confidence. . . .

We are asked . . . to grant newsmen a testimonial privilege that other citizens do not enjoy. This we decline to do.

—Justice Byron R. White in *United States* v. *Caldwell* (1972)

The Court's crabbed view of the First Amendment reflects a disturbing insensitivity to the critical role of an independent press in our society. . . . The Court in these cases holds that a newsman has no First Amendment right to protect his sources when called before a grand jury. The Court thus invites state and federal authorities to undermine the historic independence of the press by attempting to annex the journalistic profession as an investigative arm of government.

—Justice Potter Stewart, dissenting in *United States* v. *Caldwell*

indicted after a series of articles by Myron Farber of the *New York Times* suggested that a "Dr. X" had murdered patients at a small New Jersey hospital by injecting them with curare, a paralyzing drug used by South American Indians to poison their hunting arrows.

The defense demanded Farber's notes, and the judge ordered them turned over to the court for inspection. Farber refused, citing the First Amendment and New Jersey's press shield law, which was designed to protect reporters from revealing their sources. The court sent Farber to jail for contempt and fined the *Times*.

The jury acquitted Dr. Jascalevich after a long trial. But the Supreme Court, as already noted, declined to overturn Farber's conviction.[46] The *Times* reporter spent a total of forty days in jail, but he never revealed his source. The newspaper was fined $285,000 and incurred an estimated $1 million in legal costs.[47]

Usually, the press tries to protect its sources of information. But in 1991, the Supreme Court ruled that news organizations could be sued if they broke their promises of confidentiality to a source.[48] The case arose in Minnesota when Dan Cohen, an adviser to the Republican candidate for governor, leaked to reporters the minor criminal record of an opposition candidate. Although the news organizations promised not to reveal Cohen's name, editors of two newspapers — over the objections of their reporters — identified Cohen as the source of the stories. The editors did so because they reasoned that his role as the leaker was in itself newsworthy. The day the stories were printed, Cohen was fired from his job at an advertising agency. He sued the newspapers and was awarded $200,000. The Supreme Court ruled that the First Amendment did not give the press the right to break its promises to news sources. The Cohen case was an exception, however, since, as already discussed, normally the press vigorously attempts to shield the identity of its news sources.

To assist the press in protecting its sources, by 1992 twenty-eight states had passed shield laws for the news media. And Congress had made periodic efforts to enact a federal immunity law for journalists. But many journalists preferred no legislation, arguing that a shield law, even though well-intentioned, would violate the First Amendment by defining — and thus limiting — reporters' rights.

Television and Radio: A Limited Freedom   Radio and television do not enjoy as much freedom as other segments of the press, because, unlike newspapers, broadcast stations are licensed by the Federal Communications Commission. The FCC does not directly regulate news broadcasts, but stations are required to operate in the public interest. For example, broadcasters must provide "equal time" to political candidates. Otherwise the FCC may revoke their licenses, although the commission, in the past, has seldom exercised its power to do so. Potentially, however, the federal government has powerful leverage over the operations of the broadcasting industry.

Why is the government able to regulate broadcasters but not the written press? The reason advanced most often is that the broadcast spectrum has a limited number of spaces and that stations would overlap and interfere with each other if the government did not regulate them. As the Supreme Court has stated, "Unlike other modes of expression, radio (and television) is not available to all."[49] This *scarcity theory* has been criticized because, in fact, there are more broadcasting stations than newspapers in the United States. And later technology such as the rapid growth of cable television and satellite broadcasts have opened up even more outlets to the public.[50]

The First Amendment clearly protects the written press. But the framers of the Constitution did not foresee the invention of television. The result "is a major paradox: TV news, which has the greatest impact on the public, is the most vulnerable and least protected."[51]

In 1969 the Supreme Court specifically rejected the claim of the broadcasting industry that the free press provisions of the First Amendment protected it from government regulation of programs. The Court did so in upholding the FCC's "fairness doctrine," which at that time required radio and television broadcasters to present all sides of important public issues. Justice Byron White ruled for the Court that "it is the right of viewers and listeners, not the right of the broadcasters, which is paramount"; a licensed broadcaster has no First Amendment right to "monopolize a radio frequency to the exclusion of his fellow citizens."[52]

---

[46] *New York Times Company v. New Jersey*, 439 U.S. 997 (1978).
[47] *Washington Post*, October 25, 1978, p. 1.
[48] *Cohen v. Cowles Media Co.*, 111 S. Ct. 630 (1991).

[49] *National Broadcasting Co. v. United States*, 319 U.S. 190 (1943).
[50] See Norman Dorsen, Paul Bender, and Burt Neuborne, *Political and Civil Rights in the United States*, 4th ed., vol. 1 (Boston: Little, Brown, 1976), pp. 774–77.
[51] David Wise, *The Politics of Lying: Government Deception, Secrecy, and Power* (New York: Random House, 1973), p. 273.
[52] *Red Lion Broadcasting Co., Inc. v. Federal Communications Commission*, 395 U.S. 367 (1969).

In 1987, however, the FCC abolished the fairness doctrine on the grounds that it unconstitutionally restricted the First Amendment rights of broadcasters. The decision did not affect the FCC's power to license and regulate radio and TV stations, nor did it change the rule requiring broadcasters to give "equal time" to political candidates.

Although the Supreme Court has declined to extend full freedom of the press to broadcasters, it has held that the First Amendment protects the right of broadcasters to report news events.[53] The Court did so by ruling in favor of a Philadelphia radio station sued for libel by a distributor of nudist magazines after the station reported his arrest. Here the Supreme Court was extending some constitutional protection to broadcasters, but just how much was by no means clear.

In 1978 the Supreme Court ruled in the "seven dirty words" case that the government has the right to prohibit the broadcasting of "patently offensive" language.[54] The case began at 2 P.M. one afternoon in New York City, when a station owned by the Pacifica Foundation broadcast a monologue by comedian George Carlin called "Filthy Words." In it, Carlin gave a detailed analysis of "the words you couldn't say on the public airwaves . . . the ones you definitely wouldn't say, ever." Soon after, a man wrote to the FCC complaining that he heard the broadcast while driving with his young son. The FCC reprimanded the station, but later indicated it would permit such broadcasts at times of the day "when children most likely" would not be listening. It therefore prohibited "indecent speech" over the airwaves between 6 A.M. and 8 P.M. However, in 1988 Congress enacted a total, twenty-four-hour ban on broadcasting indecent speech, a rule that a federal appeals court struck down in 1991 as overbroad. The following year the Supreme Court upheld that decision,[55] but the daytime ban continued.

Freedom of Information

Freedom of the press is diminished if the news media are unable to obtain information from official agencies of government. Beginning in 1955, Congressman John E.

Moss, a California Democrat, pushed for legislation to force the federal government to make more information available to the press and public. As a result, the "Freedom of Information Act" was signed into law by President Johnson in 1966. It requires federal executive branch and regulatory agencies to make information available to journalists and other persons unless it falls into one of several confidential categories. Exempted from disclosure, for example, are national security information, personnel files, investigatory records, and the "internal" documents of an agency. The law provides that individuals can go into federal district court to force compliance by the government.

The Freedom of Information Act was strengthened in 1974 with a number of amendments. One permits federal courts to review whether documents withheld by the government on grounds of national security were properly classified in the first place; another provision requires the government to respond within ten days to persons who make requests. The law has resulted in the release of considerable amounts of information to the public. Nonetheless, a House subcommittee noted that "foot dragging by the federal bureaucracy" had hindered the release of information under the act.[56] Often, federal agencies have refused to release meaningful information under the act unless citizens go into federal court and sue, an expensive and time-consuming process.

While encouraging a greater flow of government information to the public through the act, Congress also has responded to demands for tighter control over federal files on individuals. The Privacy Act of 1974 provides that the government may not make public its files about an individual, such as medical, financial, criminal, or employment records, without that person's written consent. The law also generally gives citizens the right of access to information about themselves in government files.

In the field of national security and foreign policy, government secrecy is supported by a formal *security classification* system. Under executive orders issued by every president since Truman in 1951, thousands of officials can stamp documents Top Secret, Secret, or Confidential if, in their judgment, disclosure would jeopardize national security. Under this system, millions

---

[53] *Rosenbloom v. Metromedia*, 403 U.S. 29 (1971).

[54] *Federal Communications Commission v. Pacifica Foundation*, 438 U.S. 726 (1978).

[55] *Federal Communications Commission v. Action for Children's Television*, 112 S. Ct. 1282 (1992).

[56] U.S. Congress, House, Committee on Government Operations, *Administration of the Freedom of Information Act*, 92nd Cong., 2nd sess., Twenty-first Report (Washington, D.C.: U.S. Government Printing Office, 1972), p. 8.

of government documents are classified every year. Beginning with President Kennedy, these orders provided that at least some secret documents be automatically declassified after a certain number of years. In 1982, however, President Reagan issued an executive order that eliminated automatic declassification on new documents, and in other ways made it easier for the government to classify information.[57]

In addition, President Reagan issued a directive in 1983 designed to reduce leaks of government information to the press. It would have required that hundreds of thousands of government workers be subject to lie detector tests. Congress opposed the directive, and the President suspended the provision for lie detector tests. Another provision obliged 122,400 officials with access to sensitive intelligence information to sign agreements to submit for government review books and articles containing such information, even after the officials returned to private life.[58] Although Congress also opposed these prepublication agreements, they were still in force in 1992.[59]

In 1980 the Supreme Court ruled that CIA employees who sign secrecy agreements were not free to publish books about their experiences without prior agency approval.[60] The Court ruled that Frank W. Snepp III, a former CIA officer in Vietnam, had to give the government the royalties earned from his book, *Decent Interval*, even though it contained no classified information. The Court declined to consider Snepp's argument that the agreement violated his First Amendment rights.

Obscenity

Long before the 1990s, X-rated movie houses, showing endless varieties of sexual intercourse, in color, were commonplace in most large American cities and many smaller communities. Explicit videotapes could be rented or purchased for home viewing. In books, magazines, films, and on television, human sexuality was described and depicted, often in graphic terms.

All this seemed a far cry from the not so distant past, when the books of Edgar Rice Burroughs were almost removed from a Downey, California, elementary school library because of persistent reports that Tarzan and Jane were unmarried. (When it was established that the jungle king and his mate were in fact husband and wife, the books were left on the shelves.)

Today, changing standards of public morality have resulted in freer acceptance of sex in art, literature, and motion pictures by some—but certainly not all—segments of the public. In 1957 in *Roth v. United States*, the Supreme Court held for the first time that "obscenity is not within the area of constitutionally protected speech or press."[61] Justice William J. Brennan, Jr., ruled for the Court that material that is "utterly without redeeming social importance" is not protected by the Constitution. Brennan went on to give his definition of obscene matter: "whether to the average person, applying contemporary community standards, the dominant theme of the material taken as a whole appeals to prurient interest."[62]

The Court, however, has had continued difficulty in defining obscenity. D. H. Lawrence, whose book *Lady Chatterley's Lover* was banned in the United States from 1928 until 1959, once said: "What is pornography to one man is the laughter of genius to another."[63]

Justice Potter Stewart, concurring in one Supreme Court decision, said he would not attempt to define "hard-core" pornography, "but I know it when I see it."[64] This somewhat subjective approach was further refined in the case of a book commonly known as *Fanny Hill* and first published in 1749. Justice Brennan, speaking for the Court, applied and expanded the Court's opinion in the Roth case in concluding that *Fanny Hill* was not obscene.[65]

The practical effect of these cases was to remove almost all restrictions on content of books and movies as long as the slightest "social value" could be

[57] Executive Order 12356, *National Security Information*, April 2, 1982.
[58] National Security Decision Directive-84, *Safeguarding National Security Information*, March 11, 1983.
[59] *Washington Post*, December 24, 1987, p. A13, and data provided by the Information Security Oversight Office.
[60] *Snepp* v. *United States*, 444 U.S. 507 (1980).
[61] *Roth* v. *United States* and *Alberts* v. *California*, 354 U.S. 476 (1957).
[62] *Webster's New International Dictionary* defines "prurient" as "itching, longing; uneasy with desire, or longing; or persons, having itching, morbid, or lascivious longings; or desire, curiosity, or propensity, lewd."
[63] D. H. Lawrence, "Pornography and Obscenity," in Diana Trilling, ed., *The Portable D. H. Lawrence* (New York: Viking, 1947), p. 646.
[64] *Jacobellis* v. *Ohio*, 378 U.S. 184 (1964).
[65] *A Book Named "John Cleland's Memoirs of a Woman of Pleasure"* v. *Attorney General of Massachusetts*, 383 U.S. 413 (1966).

"No one could claim that Judge Walker doesn't approach these obscenity hearings with an open mind."

Drawing by Stevenson
© 1969 The *New Yorker* Magazine, Inc.

demonstrated. Nevertheless, the Supreme Court affirmed the federal conviction of publisher Ralph Ginzburg, who went to prison for mailing obscene material. The divided Court based its 5–4 decision not on the material itself but on the way it had been advertised and exploited for "titillation" rather than "intellectual content." [66]

Then, in 1973, came the landmark case of *Miller* v. *California*, which set new standards for defining obscenity.[67] Chief Justice Burger, who wrote the majority opinion in the 5–4 decision, explained that the case began when unsolicited mail arrived at a restaurant in Newport Beach, California. The envelope, "opened by the manager of the restaurant and his mother," included an advertising brochure for a book entitled *Sex Orgies Illustrated*.

The Court set a new three-part test for judging works dealing with sexual conduct:

1. Whether the average person, "applying contemporary community standards," would find that the work, taken as a whole, "appeals to prurient interest."

2. Whether the work depicts "in a patently offensive way" sexual conduct prohibited by state law.

3. Whether the work as a whole "lacks serious literary, artistic, political, or scientific value."

The Court seemed to rule, in effect, that local communities should be permitted to set their own standards. Justice Burger wrote: "It is neither realistic nor constitutionally sound to read the First Amendment as requiring that the people of Maine or Mississippi accept public depiction of conduct found tolerable in Las Vegas or New York City." [68] The decision appeared to clear the way for state legislatures to pass laws giving local communities greater control over books, movies, magazines, and other materials.

But in a series of subsequent decisions, the Supreme Court made it clear that there were limits to the right of communities to ban material as obscene. And in 1987 the Court shifted away from the "community standards" yardstick by ruling that the social value of a work must be judged from the standpoint of a "reasonable person," not the entire community. "The proper inquiry," Justice Byron R. White wrote for the majority, "is not whether an ordinary member of any given community would find serious literary, artistic, political or scientific value in allegedly obscene material, but whether a reasonable person would find such value in the material, taken as a whole." [69]

Even earlier, the Supreme Court's decisions had demonstrated that the Miller ruling did not give communities free reign to censor sexually explicit works. In 1974 the Court unanimously had refused to uphold the

[66] *Ginzburg v. United States*, 383 U.S. 463 (1966).
[67] *Miller v. California*, 413 U.S. 15 (1973).
[68] Ibid.
[69] *Pope v. Illinois*, 481 U.S. 497 (1987).

NUDE DANCING: THE SUPREME COURT REQUIRES A BARE MINIMUM

In 1991, the Supreme Court decided by a vote of 5–4 that states could ban nude dancing. The case, *Barnes* v. *Glen Theatre*, had been brought by the owners of the Kitty Kat Lounge in South Bend. Following are excerpts from the majority opinion:

By William H. Rehnquist, the Chief Justice of the United States:

Indiana's requirement that the dancers wear at least pasties and a G-string is modest, and the bare minimum necessary to achieve the state's purpose."

By Justice Antonin Scalia, concurring:

"The purpose of Indiana's nudity law would be violated, I think, if 60,000 fully consenting adults crowded into the Hoosierdome to display their genitals to one another, even if there were not an offended innocent in the crowd."

—*Barnes* v. *Glen Theatre* (1991)

conviction of a movie theater manager in Albany, Georgia, because the film *Carnal Knowledge* showed "a woman with a bare midriff." Justice William H. Rehnquist, who wrote the Court's opinion, declared that local juries did not have "unbridled discretion" under the *Miller* case to declare what was obscene.[70]

The Supreme Court restricted censorship by local communities in other cases as well. In 1975, for example, the Court ruled that the city of Jacksonville, Florida, could not prevent drive-in theaters from showing films including nudity.[71] On the other hand, the Court upheld the conviction of William Hamling, who had published an illustrated version of the report of the President's Commission on Obscenity and Pornography.[72]

In 1982 the Supreme Court held that child pornography is not a category of speech protected by the Constitution. It ruled that works that visually depicted sexual conduct by children could be banned by state law, even though the material might not meet the legal test of obscenity under the *Miller* case.[73] In 1984 Congress passed a law strengthening the federal penalties against child pornography.

In 1986 the Court reaffirmed a lower court decision that struck down an Indianapolis law that sought to ban pornography on the grounds that such material discriminated against women by portraying them as sex objects.[74] Later, the Court struck down an attempt by Congress to ban the "dial-a-porn" industry, ruling that a part of a law barring "indecent" speech on the telephone was unconstitutional.[75] But the Court ruled that the First Amendment does not protect nude dancing; it held in 1991 that states may prohibit such entertainment. The case had been brought by the owners of the Kitty Kat Lounge, an adult club in South Bend, Indiana, featuring live performances.[76]

Libel

A person defamed by a newspaper or other publication may be able to sue for libel and collect damages because the First Amendment does not protect this form of "free speech." Libel is a published or broadcast report that exposes a person to public contempt or injures the person's reputation. For example, some years ago a New York newspaper suggested that one Stanislaus Zbyszko, a wrestler, was built along the general lines of a gorilla. Near the article, it ran a picture of a particularly hideous-looking anthropoid. The New York State courts held this to be libelous.[77]

[70] *Jenkins* v. *Georgia*, 418 U.S. 153 (1974).
[71] *Erznoznik* v. *City of Jacksonville*, 422 U.S. 206 (1975).
[72] *Hamling* v. *United States*, 418 U.S. 87 (1974).
[73] *New York* v. *Ferber*, 458 U.S. 747 (1982).

[74] *Hudnut* v. *American Booksellers Association, Inc.*, 475 U.S. 1001 (1986).
[75] *Sable Communications of California, Inc.* v. *Federal Communications Commission*, 492 U.S. 115 (1989).
[76] *Barnes* v. *Glen Theatre*, 111 S. Ct. 2456 (1991).
[77] Robert H. Phelps and E. Douglas Hamilton, *Libel* (New York: Macmillan, 1966), p. 62.

Truth has always been an absolute defense in libel cases. That is, if a publication can show that a story is true, the person claiming to have been libeled cannot recover damages. More recently, under the *New York Times* rule, the Supreme Court has made it almost impossible to libel a public official, unless the statement is made with "actual malice" — that is, "with knowledge that it was false or with reckless disregard of whether it was false or not." [78] Ruling against Alabama officials who had brought a libel suit against the *Times*, the Supreme Court held in 1964 that in a free society "debate on public issues should be uninhibited, robust and wide-open, and . . . may well include vehement . . . attacks on government officials." [79] Later Court decisions expanded the *New York Times* rule to include not only officials but "public figures" such as political candidates and persons involved in events of general or public interest. [80]

But in the 1970s the Supreme Court greatly narrowed its definition of a public figure. It ruled that a lawyer who represented the family of a youth shot and killed by a police officer in Chicago was not a public figure; it upheld his lawsuit against a publication that had falsely accused him of being a "Communist-fronter." [81] Similarly, the Court ruled in favor of Mrs. Russell A. Firestone and against *Time* magazine, which inaccurately reported that her husband had been granted a divorce on grounds of adultery (although the judge did note that some of her reported but unsubstantiated extramarital escapades "would have made Dr. Freud's hair curl"). Despite the extensive publicity surrounding the divorce, the Court ruled that Mrs. Firestone was not a public figure. The two decisions left the press vulnerable to libel suits by persons who might — or might not — be considered public figures. [82]

The Supreme Court narrowed the definition of a public figure even further in 1979. Senator William Proxmire, a Wisconsin Democrat, gave one of his derisive "Golden Fleece" awards to a scientist who had received half a million dollars in federal funds to study aggression in monkeys. The purpose of the study was to help select crew members for submarines and space-

craft. Proxmire charged in a Senate speech and in news releases and newsletters that the scientist, Dr. Ronald R. Hutchinson, had "made a monkey out of the American taxpayer." Hutchinson sued the senator for libel. The Supreme Court said the scientist had not become a public figure by accepting federal funds, and it ruled that while the Constitution protected Proxmire's speeches in the Senate, his press release describing the monkey research was not immune. [83]

Similarly, the Court ruled that Ilya Wolston, a former State Department interpreter, did not become a public figure by pleading guilty to contempt of court after refusing to appear before a grand jury investigating Soviet espionage. Wolston had sued the *Reader's Digest* for publishing a book that included him in a list of "Soviet agents." "A private individual is not automatically transformed into a public figure just by becoming involved in . . . a matter that attracts public attention," the Court held. [84]

The same year, the Supreme Court permitted a libel award against a novelist. [85] The Court let stand a $75,000 judgment against the author of *Touching*, a novel about nude encounter groups. The suit had been brought by a California psychologist who said he was the recognizable model for one of the characters in the book.

Moreover, in 1979 the Supreme Court ruled 6–3 that journalists who are sued for libel could be forced to produce files or notes that disclosed their "state of mind" — their thoughts and motivations — in preparing a news story. [86] The information, the Court said, was needed by public figures attempting to prove that stories had been prepared with "actual malice." The case arose in a suit against CBS and the producer of "60 Minutes." In the majority opinion, Justice Byron R. White said the Court could not require a libel plaintiff to prove malice, as it had done in the *New York Times* case, and then "erect an impenetrable barrier" to the collection of vital evidence.

Another legal action against CBS was widely publicized. General William C. Westmoreland, the former U.S. military commander in Vietnam, sued the network for $120 million because in a documentary broadcast it had charged that a "conspiracy" existed within the highest levels of the American military to conceal the

[78] In the Supreme Court's decision, the word "malice" is not used in its commonly understood meaning of "ill will" or "spite."

[79] *New York Times Co.* v. *Sullivan*, 376 U.S. 254 (1964).

[80] *Curtis Publishing Co.* v. *Butts* and *Associated Press* v. *Walker*, 388 U.S. 130 (1967); *Rosenbloom* v. *Metromedia* (1971).

[81] *Gertz* v. *Robert Welch, Inc.* 418 U.S. 323 (1974).

[82] *Time* v. *Firestone*, 424 U.S. 448 (1976).

[83] *Hutchinson* v. *Proxmire*, 443 U.S. 111 (1979).

[84] *Wolston* v. *Reader's Digest*, 443 U.S. 157 (1979).

[85] *Mitchell* v. *Bindrim* and *Doubleday* v. *Bindrim*, 444 U.S. 984 (1979).

[86] *Herbert* v. *Lando*, 441 U.S. 153 (1979).

strength of the communist enemy in Vietnam. After the trial had gone on for almost five months, Westmoreland, faced with strong testimony against him and mounting legal bills, dropped the lawsuit.

In 1985 Ariel Sharon, former defense minister of Israel, lost a $50-million libel suit against *Time*, although the jury found that the news magazine had defamed him by printing a false account of his role in the 1982 Beirut massacre of Palestinian refugees.

In 1987 the Supreme Court ruled in favor of the *Washington Post* and overturned a $2-million libel award against the newspaper that had been won in a lower court by the president of the Mobil Oil Corporation.[87] The *Post* had reported that the executive "set up" his son in a shipping company that did business with Mobil. The decision made it easier for newspapers to carry out investigative reporting, because it made it less likely that public figures would sue.

And in 1988, the Supreme Court overturned a $200,000 award to the Rev. Jerry Falwell for "emotional distress," which the conservative television evangelist claimed he had suffered when *Hustler* magazine published a parody that portrayed Falwell as a drunk having sex with his mother in an outhouse. Although the Court found that the parody was "doubtless gross and repugnant in the eyes of most," it ruled that a public figure was not protected against satire or political cartoons, however "outrageous" or offensive.[88] On the other hand, the Supreme Court has held that expressions of opinion, such as in a newspaper column, may be libelous if false and defamatory.[89]

In 1990, a jury awarded $34 million to Richard A. Sprague, a former city district attorney, who had sued the *Philadelphia Inquirer* for libel, charging that it had falsely implied that he had stopped a homicide investigation of the son of a police captain.[90]

In 1991, the Supreme Court dealt with the knotty problem of whether, and to what extent, reporters may alter quotations of persons they interview. The case arose when Jeffrey Masson, director of the Sigmund Freud archives, claimed that quotes attributed to him by journalist Janet Malcolm in the *New Yorker* magazine had been altered or fabricated, which the writer denied. The Court ruled that even "deliberate alteration" of quotes is not grounds for libel unless the alteration resulted "in a material change in the meaning" of the statement.[91]

Despite some victories by the press, in the 1990s the threat of libel actions had become a major problem for the news media, publishers, and writers. In a number of cases, huge multimillion-dollar damages had been awarded by juries to plaintiffs in libel cases. Most of these big awards were later overturned or reduced by the courts, but some First Amendment students argue that large punitive damages and legal costs in libel cases inhibit press freedom.

Privacy

Closely related to the issue of libel is the "right" to privacy. Although not specifically provided for in the Constitution, it has been recognized to a considerable extent by the courts. Justice Louis Brandeis wrote that the makers of the Constitution sought to give Americans "the right to be let alone . . . the right most valued by civilized men."[92]

Today that right has been defined and protected by a series of Supreme Court decisions and by legislation. Nevertheless, in an era of computerized data banks and sophisticated surveillance techniques, the right of individuals to be free of intrusion into their privacy remains a subject of continuing concern and conflict. The government, corporations, credit firms, the press, insurance companies, schools, banks, and other institutions all, to some degree, have been accused of infringing on privacy.

The concept of a right of privacy was first given expression by the Supreme Court in the 1965 case of *Griswold* v. *Connecticut*.[93] The head of the state's Planned Parenthood League, along with a physician who was also a professor at Yale Medical School, prescribed contraceptives and provided birth control information to married couples. They were convicted and fined under a state law. The Supreme Court, however, ruled that guarantees in the Bill of Rights cast "penumbras," or shadows, that may encompass other rights not specifically mentioned. "Various guarantees create zones of privacy," the Court said. The police must be kept out of the bedroom, the Court added, citing "a right of privacy older than the Bill of Rights."

[87] *Tavoulareas* v. *Washington Post Company*, 484 U.S. 870 (1987).
[88] *Hustler Magazine Inc.* v. *Falwell*, 485 U.S. 46 (1988).
[89] *Milkovich* v. *Lorain Journal Co.*, 497 U.S. 1 (1990).
[90] *News Media and the Law*, Summer 1990, Vol. 14, No. 3, p. 3.
[91] *Masson* v. *New Yorker Magazine*, 111 S. Ct. 2419 (1991).
[92] *Olmstead* v. *United States*, 277 U.S. 438 (1928).
[93] *Griswold* v. *Connecticut*, 381 U.S. 479 (1965).

PRIVACY: THE SECRET ZONE

Generally speaking, the concept of a right to privacy attempts to draw a line between the individual and the collective, between self and society. It seeks to assure the individual a zone in which to be an individual, not a member of the community. In that zone he can think his own thoughts, have his own secrets, live his own life, reveal only what he wants to the outside world. The right of privacy, in short, establishes an area excluded from the collective life, not governed by the rules of collective living. It is based upon premises of individualism, that the society exists to promote the worth and the dignity of the individual. It is contrary to the theories of total commitment to the state, to society, or to any part thereof.

—Thomas I. Emerson,
The System of Freedom of Expression

In other cases, the Supreme Court, in the past, at least, has reiterated the right to privacy in very clear language. In the controversial case of *Roe* v. *Wade*, for example, the justices ruled that the concept of privacy included the right to a legal abortion. "The Constitution does not explicitly mention any right of privacy," the Court declared. But "the Court has recognized that a right of personal privacy, or a guarantee of certain areas or zones of privacy, does exist under the Constitution." [94]

And in yet another decision, the Court ruled that Robert Eli Stanley, a Georgia resident, had the right to watch pornographic movies in his own home.[95] The case arose when police with a warrant searched Stanley's home for evidence of bookmaking activity, found three reels of eight-millimeter film, and viewed them on a projector in Stanley's living room.

What if the right of the press to report the news under the First Amendment conflicts with the individual's right to be left alone? Sometimes the Supreme Court has sided with the individual, sometimes with the press.

A landmark invasion-of-privacy case began in 1952, when James Hill and his family were held hostage by three escaped convicts for nineteen hours in their suburban Philadelphia home. Later a novel and a play, both called *The Desperate Hours*, appeared. *Life* magazine said the play was based on the Hills' experience. But in the play the family was molested, while the Hills had not been harmed. The family sued the magazine. The Supreme Court ruled against the family, holding that the press could only be liable for "*calculated* falsehood" and not for inadvertent errors.[96] The lawyer who unsuccessfully argued the case for the Hills in the Supreme Court was Richard M. Nixon, later president.

In other cases, individuals have successfully defended their right to privacy against the news media. After a construction worker in West Virginia died when a bridge collapsed, a Cleveland newspaper referred to his family as "hillbillies." The Court upheld a $60,000 judgment against the paper for invasion of privacy.[97] But in a Georgia case, the court ruled in favor of a television station that broadcast the name of a young woman who had been raped and killed by six teenage boys. The victim's father sued the TV station, but the court said his privacy had not been invaded because the broadcaster had obtained his daughter's name from public court records.[98]

Congress has passed a series of laws relating to personal privacy. The Privacy Act of 1974, as already discussed, gives individuals a degree of control over government files maintained about them. The Fair Credit Reporting Act (1970) regulates credit agencies, department stores, and banks. And the Family Education Rights and Privacy Act (1974) gives parents or pupils the right to see school records and instructional material.

Freedom of Assembly

In addition to protecting free speech, the First Amendment protects the right of the people "peaceably to assemble." The Supreme Court has held this right to be

---

[94] *Roe* v. *Wade*, 410 U.S. 113 (1973).
[95] *Stanley* v. *Georgia*, 394 U.S. 557 (1969).

[96] *Time* v. *Hill*, 385 U.S. 374 (1967).
[97] *Cantrell* v. *Forest City Publishing Co.*, 419 U.S. 245 (1974).
[98] *Cox Broadcasting Corp.* v. *Cohn*, 420 U.S. 469 (1975).

SUPREME COURT TO PICKETS: WELCOME

The Supreme Court April 20 unanimously struck down a law that bars demonstrations in front of its own building in Washington, D.C.

The First Amendment protects the freedom of individuals to use leaflets or picket signs to express their views while standing on the sidewalks adjacent to the Supreme Court building, the justices held.

The case of *United States* v. *Grace* arose after Thaddeus Zywicki and Mary Grace in 1980 were asked to leave the sidewalk outside the court, where they were picketing. They promptly challenged a 1949 [Federal law] that prohibits the "display [of] . . . any flag, banner, or device designed or adapted to bring into public notice any party, organization, or movement" in the building or grounds of the U.S. Supreme Court. . . .

Justice Byron R. White, writing for the court, said the picketing ban "is no more necessary for the maintenance of peace and tranquility on the public sidewalks surrounding the building than on any other sidewalks in the city."

—Congressional Quarterly,
Weekly Report, April 4, 1983

"equally fundamental" to the right of free speech and free press.[99] It ruled in 1897 that a city can require a permit for the "use of public grounds." [100] But a city, in requiring licenses for parades, demonstrations, and sound trucks, must do so in the interest of controlling traffic and regulating the use of public streets and parks; it cannot — in theory — exercise its licensing power to suppress free speech.[101] The legitimate responsibility of public officials and police to control traffic or prevent a demonstration from growing into a riot is sometimes used as a device to suppress free speech because there is a thin, and not always readily distinguishable, line between crowd control and thought control.

In 1977 the heavily Jewish suburb of Skokie, Illinois, passed three local ordinances designed to prevent a march there by the American Nazi Party, an anti-Semitic group. The American Civil Liberties Union, although a liberal group opposed to the Nazis, went into court to defend the Nazis' right to march. Leaders of the Nazis ultimately called off plans to demonstrate in Skokie, the home of several thousand survivors of Hitler's Nazi regime. A few months later, in October 1978, the Supreme Court let stand a lower court ruling that Skokie's ordinances had violated the constitutional guarantees of free speech — possessed even by Nazis.[102]

In 1983 the Supreme Court permitted people to picket and to display flags and signs on the sidewalk outside the Supreme Court itself. The case was brought by two persons who had been asked to leave when they picketed the Court.[103]

Freedom of Religion

President Jefferson wrote in 1802 that the freedom of religion clause of the First Amendment was designed to build "a wall of separation between Church and State." The wall still stands, but in several areas the Supreme Court has modified its contours.

Many of the American colonies were settled by groups seeking religious freedom but intolerant of religious dissent. Gradually, however, religious tolerance increased. When the Bill of Rights was passed, its first words were: "Congress shall make no law respecting an establishment of religion, or prohibiting the free exercise thereof."

The "Free Exercise Clause" This clause of the First Amendment protects the right of individuals to worship or believe as they wish, or to hold no religious beliefs. It also means that people cannot be compelled by government to act contrary to their religious beliefs, unless religious conduct collides with valid laws. In that difficult area, the courts have had to try to resolve the conflict between the demands of religion and the demands of law.

---

[99] *De Jonge* v. *Oregon*, 299 U.S. 353 (1937).
[100] *Davis* v. *Massachusetts*, 167 U.S. 43 (1897).
[101] *Hague* v. *C.I.O.*, 307 U.S. 496 (1939).
[102] *Collin* v. *Smith*, 439 U.S. 916 (1978); see also *National Socialist Party* v. *Village of Skokie*, 432 U.S. 43 (1977).

[103] *United States* v. *Grace*, 461 U.S. 171 (1983).

For example, in a number of instances the Supreme Court has attempted to define the grounds that may be invoked by conscientious objectors to military service. Ever since the draft began during the Civil War, the law has provided some form of exemption for those whose religious beliefs would not permit them to serve in the armed forces. In 1965 the Supreme Court ruled that a "sincere and meaningful" objection to war on religious grounds did not require a belief in a Supreme Being.[104]

Then, in June 1970, with the war in Vietnam still in progress, the Court extended this protection to persons opposed to war for reasons of conscience. It ruled that Elliott Ashton Welsh II, a twenty-nine-year-old computer engineer from Los Angeles, could not be imprisoned for his refusal on ethical and moral grounds to serve in the armed forces. Welsh — and therefore other young Americans — the Court ruled, did not have to base his refusal on a belief in God or religious training. The government must exempt from military service, the Court declared, "all those whose consciences, spurred by deeply held moral, ethical, or religious beliefs, would give them no rest or peace if they allowed themselves to become part of an instrument of war."[105] The draft law, the Supreme Court ruled, did not require military service by "those who hold strong beliefs about our domestic and foreign affairs or even those whose conscientious objection to participation in all wars is founded to a substantial extent upon considerations of public policy."[106] But a year later the Court held that the draft law and the Constitution did not permit conscientious objection to *particular* wars.[107]

In the *Flag Salute* cases, the Court initially ruled in 1940 that children of Jehovah's Witnesses could not be excused from saluting the American flag on religious grounds.[108] But three years later the Court reversed itself and decided in favor of Walter Barnett, also a member of the Jehovah's Witnesses, whose seven children had been expelled from West Virginia schools for refusing to salute the flag. Justice Robert H. Jackson, speaking for the Court, held that "the flag salute is a form of utterance" protected by the First Amendment. "If there is any fixed star in our constitutional constellation," Jackson said, "it is that no official, high or petty, can prescribe what shall be orthodox in politics, nationalism, religion or other matters of opinion." Because the

Court's decision rested on the "free speech clause," it protects anyone who refuses to salute the flag for whatever reason. The Supreme Court also ruled that members of the Amish church could not be forced to send their children to school beyond the eighth grade. And it held that a state could not deny unemployment compensation to a member of the Seventh-day Adventist Church who refused to take a job that required her to work on the Sabbath.[109]

In 1962 a group of Navajo Indians was arrested in the California desert for using peyote in a religious ceremony of the Native American Church. Peyote, a variety of cactus containing the hallucinogenic drug mescaline, is a narcotic under California law. But in 1964 the California Supreme Court ruled that the state could not prohibit the religious use of the drug by the Navajos.[110]

The California case did not reach the United States Supreme Court, but in 1990, the Court upheld an Oregon law that banned the use of peyote in religious ceremonies.[111] Once again, the case centered on the use of the drug in religious rites by two members of the Native American Church. Despite the Supreme Court's decision, individual states could decide whether or not to outlaw the religious use of the hallucinogen.[112] At the time of the Supreme Court's 1990 ruling, federal law and twenty-four states, many with large Native American populations, did permit the sacramental use of peyote.

Not every religious practice is protected by the First Amendment, however. During the nineteenth century the Supreme Court outlawed polygamy.[113] Although George Reynolds proved that as a Mormon he was required to have more than one wife, the Supreme Court sustained his conviction. The Court ruled that religious conduct could not violate the law, adding, rather gruesomely: "Suppose one believed that human sacrifices were a necessary part of religious worship?"

And the Supreme Court has denied tax-exempt status to schools that practice racial discrimination

---

[104] *United States* v. *Seeger*, 380 U.S. 163 (1965).

[105] *Welsh* v. *United States*, 398 U.S. 333 (1970).

[106] Ibid.

[107] *Gillette* v. *United States* and *Negre* v. *Larsen*, 401 U.S. 437 (1971).

[108] *Minersville School District* v. *Gobitis*, 310 U.S. 586 (1940).

[109] The Jehovah's Witnesses won their fight in *West Virginia Board of Education* v. *Barnette*, 319 U.S. 624 (1943). (Walter Barnett's name was misspelled in court records.) The Amish prevailed in *Wisconsin* v. *Yoder*, 406 U.S. 205 (1972), and a member of the Seventh-day Adventist Church won her case in *Sherbert* v. *Verner*, 374 U.S. 398 (1963).

[110] William Cohen, Murray Schwartz, and DeAnne Sobul, *The Bill of Rights: A Source Book* (New York: Benziger Brothers, 1968), pp. 267–68.

[111] *Oregon* v. *Smith*, 494 U.S. 872 (1990).

[112] After the Supreme Court ruling, Oregon enacted a new law permitting the religious use of peyote.

[113] *Reynolds* v. *United States*, 98 U.S. 145 (1878); *Davis* v. *Beason*, 133 U.S. 333 (1890).

Nursery school children taking time out to pray

based on religious beliefs. The Court in 1983 upheld the power of the Internal Revenue Service to revoke the tax exemption of Bob Jones University, which interpreted the Bible to ban interracial dating and marriage.[114]

The "Establishment Clause" This clause of the First Amendment means, in the words of Justice Black, that "neither a state nor the federal government can set up a church. Neither can pass laws that aid one religion, aid all religions, or prefer one religion over another." [115]

Despite the constitutional separation between church and state, religion has always been a significant factor in American life. Since 1865 the nation's coins have borne the motto "In God We Trust"; many major presidential speeches end with a reference to the Almighty; the pledge of allegiance contains the phrase

"one nation under God"; public meetings often open with invocations and close with benedictions; and a chaplain opens the daily sessions of the U.S. Senate and the House of Representatives. In 1983, the Supreme Court upheld the practice of opening state legislative sessions with a prayer.[116]

In 1984 the Supreme Court narrowly upheld the right of cities to include the nativity scene as part of an official Christmas display.[117] The decision came in the case of a crèche owned by the city of Pawtucket, Rhode Island. In this and other cases, the Court has held that not every expression of religion in a public forum violates the "establishment clause" of the First Amendment.

Yet hardly any subject generates more emotion than church-state relations. In 1962 the Supreme Court outlawed officially composed prayers in the public

---

[114] *Bob Jones University* v. *United States* and *Goldsboro Christian Schools, Inc.* v. *United States,* 461 U.S. 574 (1983).
[115] *Everson* v. *Board of Education,* 330 U.S. 1 (1947).

[116] *Marsh* v. *Chambers,* 463 U.S. 471 (1983).
[117] *Lynch* v. *Donnelly,* 465 U.S. 471 (1984).

schools.[118] The initial school-prayer case arose after the Board of Regents of New York State composed a "non-denominational" prayer that it recommended local school boards adopt.[119] The parents of ten children in New Hyde Park, New York, objected and went to court. In ruling the prayer unconstitutional, Justice Hugo Black, speaking for the Court, declared that the First Amendment means "that in this country it is no part of the business of government to compose official prayers for any group of the American people to recite as part of a religious program carried on by government."[120]

In 1963 the Court outlawed daily Bible reading and recitation of the Lord's Prayer in public schools.[121] These decisions by the Court brought down a tremendous storm of protest upon its marble pillars. Ten years later, 10 percent of the nation's schools — and almost 28 percent in the South — were openly defying the Court's prayer ban, according to one study.[122]

It was under the "establishment clause" that the Court banned prayers in public schools. President Reagan, a strong supporter of prayer in public schools, urged Congress to pass a constitutional amendment to overrule the Supreme Court. Attempts to do so were defeated in the Senate in 1982, and the Senate in 1984 also rejected a proposed constitutional amendment to permit silent prayer in public schools.

By 1985, 25 states had passed laws providing for a period of silent meditation in public schools. Over the years such statutes were struck down by federal courts in several states, but upheld in Massachusetts. Then in 1985 the Supreme Court overturned an Alabama law that permitted a one-minute period of silence or "voluntary prayer" in the public schools.[123] The Court said the statute sought to encourage religion in the classroom, but indicated it might uphold such laws that did not mention prayer. Two years later, however, the Court, on technical grounds, refused to uphold a "moment of silence" law in New Jersey.[124]

In 1967 Frederick Walz, a New York lawyer, purchased a small, weed-covered plot of land on Staten Island taxed by the city at $5.24 a year. Walz then brought suit on the grounds that state tax exemption for churches raised his own tax bill and violated the constitutional barrier against "establishment of religion." In 1970 the Supreme Court rejected his arguments.[125] The Court held that if church property were taxable, disputes would arise over assessments, and the result would be "excessive government entanglement" of church and state.

But in most cases the Supreme Court has been careful to reject laws that seemed to favor religion. In 1985 the justices, by a vote of 8 – 1, struck down a Connecticut statute that allowed employees to refuse to work on their Sabbath. The Court held that the law violated the establishment clause by advancing "a particular religious practice."[126]

The main constitutional argument over church–state relations, however, centers on the question of whether, and to what extent, the government can aid church-related schools. In 1990, for example, 2.5 million students, 5.4 percent of all schoolchildren, were enrolled in Roman Catholic schools.[127]

In 1947 the Supreme Court ruled as constitutional a New Jersey statute under which the parents of both public and parochial students were reimbursed by the local school district for the fares paid by their children to get to school on public buses.[128] This was the celebrated Everson case. The fare payments, the Court held, did no more than "help parents get their children, regardless of their religion," safely to and from school.

In 1960 John F. Kennedy became the first Roman Catholic to be elected president. Politically, it would have been awkward for him to propose federal aid to church-supported schools. In 1961 Kennedy submitted a bill to aid elementary and high schools that *omitted* aid to parochial schools, "in accordance with the clear prohibition of the Constitution." President Kennedy relied on *Everson* in reaching this conclusion. He argued that the Supreme Court, in that instance, had permitted aid to the child, not to the school. The Catholic Church hierarchy attacked the bill, which went down to defeat in a tangle of religious controversy.

Congress in 1965, during the Johnson administration, passed the first general bill authorizing federal aid

---

[118] *Engel v. Vitale*, 370 U.S. 421 (1962).
[119] "Almighty God, we acknowledge our dependence upon Thee, and we beg Thy blessings upon us, our parents, our teachers, and our country."
[120] *Engel v. Vitale* (1962).
[121] *Abington School District v. Schempp* and *Murray v. Curlett*, 374 U.S. 203 (1963).
[122] *New York Times*, April 20, 1980, "Spring Survey of Education," p. 3, quoting a survey by Prof. Richard B. Dierenfield of Macalester College.
[123] *Wallace v. Jaffree*, 472 U.S. 38 (1985).
[124] *Karcher v. May*, 484 U.S. 72 (1987).

[125] *Walz v. Tax Commission of the City of New York*, 397 U.S. 664 (1970).
[126] *Estate of Thornton v. Caldor, Inc.*, 472 U.S. 703 (1985).
[127] Data provided by the National Center for Educational Statistics, Department of Education.
[128] *Everson v. Board of Education* (1947).

to elementary and secondary schools. It provided aid, through the states, to children in both public and church-supported schools. By emphasizing assistance to children in low-income areas, it avoided much of the religious controversy that had surrounded previous attempts to pass an education bill.

Enrollments have dropped sharply in Roman Catholic and other church-affiliated schools in recent years, partly because of higher tuition fees imposed to meet greater operating costs. Hundreds of church schools have been forced to close. Since the *Everson* case in 1947, more than two-thirds of the states have enacted various kinds of aid to parochial schools, ranging from free lunches to driver-education programs. Some of these programs have been upheld. For example, the Supreme Court has ruled that a state may lend textbooks to parochial school students.[129] It struck down a program of religious instruction in public schools by visiting teachers,[130] but upheld a "released time" program allowing public school students to attend religious classes outside of school.[131]

In 1971, in the case of *Lemon v. Kurtzman*, the Supreme Court declared unconstitutional certain state programs of direct aid to parochial schools.[132] In its decision, the Court outlined a three-part test of constitutionality for such state laws: the statute must have a secular purpose, its primary effect cannot be either to advance or inhibit religion, and it cannot foster excessive government entanglement with religion. The effect of the *Lemon* case was to limit severely state aid to church-affiliated schools throughout the nation. In 1973 the Supreme Court ruled that state programs of income tax credits and tuition reimbursements to parents of parochial school students violated the "establishment clause" of the First Amendment. The Court struck down such programs in New York and Pennsylvania.[133] In 1975 the Court disapproved the direct loan

to church-related schools of materials such as films and laboratory equipment, and the provision of other services, including counseling and testing.[134] But the Court has permitted counseling and diagnostic services off the school premises.[135]

Although the Supreme Court had curtailed state aid to church schools, it appeared to reverse direction in 1983 when it upheld a Minnesota law giving all of the state's taxpayers a deduction for tuition, transportation, textbooks, and other instructional material, even though almost all of the benefits went to taxpayers who sent their children to religious schools.[136] But in 1985, the Court ruled that public funds may not be used to pay teachers to provide remedial or special instruction to pupils in religious schools.[137]

The Supreme Court has been less reluctant to approve some forms of government aid to private colleges and universities. It upheld a federal law providing construction funds for private colleges, including church-related colleges.[138] And the Court has approved state aid for general, nonreligious purposes to church-related colleges.[139]

In deciding cases that relate to freedom of religion under the First Amendment, the Supreme Court has always faced a dilemma, because the two clauses of the amendment in a sense clash with each other. That is, in protecting the rights of a particular religious group to engage in "free exercise" of its faith, the Court might be viewed as favoring a religion in violation of the "establishment clause." Recognizing this dilemma, the Court has attempted to exercise what it has called a "benevolent neutrality," in order to protect freedom of religion without sponsorship of a particular faith.

The Supreme Court tackled the complex issue of separation of church and state again in 1992 when it ruled that prayers may not be included in public school graduation ceremonies.[140] The case arose when a rabbi in Providence gave a nondenominational invocation and benediction at a high school graduation ceremony. Daniel Weisman, whose daughter Deborah was among the graduates, filed suit, claiming that the prayer violated the Constitution's prohibition on the "establishment" of religion.

[129] *Board of Education v. Allen*, 392 U.S. 236 (1968).
[130] *Illinois ex rel. McCollum v. Board of Education*, 333 U.S. 203 (1948).
[131] *Zorach v. Clauson*, 343 U.S. 306 (1952).
[132] *Lemon v. Kurtzman*, the Pennsylvania case, and *Earley v. DiCenso* and *Robinson v. DiCenso*, the Rhode Island cases, all 403 U.S. 602 (1971). In *Lemon*, the Court set forth a three-pronged test of whether a given practice was constitutional or violated the separation of church and state: whether it had a secular purpose, whether it had the principal effect of advancing or inhibiting religion, and whether it complied with the "excessive government entanglement" standard the Court had cited in the *Walz* case.
[133] *Sloan v. Lemon*, 413 U.S. 825 (1973); *Committee for Public Education and Religious Liberty v. Nyquist*, 413 U.S. 756 (1973); *Levitt v. Committee for Public Education and Religious Liberty*, 413 U.S. 472 (1973).

[134] *Meek v. Pittenger*, 421 U.S. 349 (1975).
[135] *Wolman v. Walter*, 433 U.S. 229 (1977).
[136] *Mueller v. Allen*, 463 U.S. 388 (1983).
[137] *Aguilar v. Felton*, 473 U.S. 402 (1985), and *Grand Rapids v. Ball*, 473 U.S. 373 (1985).
[138] *Tilton v. Richardson*, 403 U.S. 672 (1971).
[139] *Roemer v. Maryland Public Works Board*, 426 U.S. 736 (1976).
[140] *Lee v. Weisman*, 112 S. Ct. 2649 (1992).

The Supreme Court agreed. In a 5–4 decision, it ruled that the First Amendment did not permit prayers at graduation ceremonies. Such prayers, the Court reasoned, coerced students to participate in a religious activity—or miss their graduation. No school, the Court held, "can persuade or compel a student to participate in a religious exercise. That is being done here, and it is forbidden by the Establishment Clause of the First Amendment."

Loyalty and Security

Should those who would destroy the Bill of Rights enjoy its protection?

This dilemma was at the heart of a great public debate that began with the end of the Second World War. In this area two constitutional principles clashed: the right to individual freedom of expression and the government's responsibility to protect national security.

With the collapse of the Soviet Union in 1991, it might be hard for many Americans to understand the atmosphere that prevailed four decades earlier. The emergence of the Soviet Union as a rival power to the United States, the onset of the Cold War, and the division of the world during the 1950s into two armed nuclear camps created fear of communism at home and generated pressures to curb dissent and root Communists or "radicals" out of government posts.

Some political leaders, notably the late Senator Joseph R. McCarthy, a Wisconsin Republican, exploited public concern for political benefit. During the early 1950s McCarthy's freewheeling investigations of alleged Communists in the State Department and other agencies injured many innocent persons, destroyed careers, and created a widespread climate of fear in the federal government and in the nation. Few dared to raise their voices against him. When he attacked the Army in 1954, a series of public hearings exposed McCarthy's methods to the blinding light of television and led to his censure by the Senate later that year. After that, McCarthy lost influence. He died in 1957.

Against this background, two opposing views crystallized in the Court and within American society. One view was that a nation, like an individual, has the right to self-preservation; it must take action against internal enemies, and it need not wait until the threat is carried out, for that may be too late. The other view was that the First Amendment guarantees free speech for everyone, that if Americans have confidence in the democratic

Senator Joseph R. McCarthy

system they need not fear other ideologies or the clash of ideas.

The effort to suppress dissent did not begin with "McCarthyism." As early as 1798, the Alien and Sedition acts had provided a maximum fine of $2,000 and two years in prison for "malicious writing" against the government of President John Adams. The first person to be convicted under the acts was Matthew Lyon, a Vermont congressman whose "crime" was to accuse President Adams of "a continual grasp for power . . . an unbounded thirst for ridiculous pomp, foolish adulation and selfish avarice." After Jefferson became president in 1801, the various Alien and Sedition acts were repealed or permitted to expire.

In 1940 Congress passed the Smith Act, which made it unlawful for any person to advocate overthrowing the government "by force or violence." In 1951 the Supreme Court upheld the constitutionality of the Smith Act and the conspiracy conviction of eleven Communist party leaders.[141] In later decisions, however, the Supreme Court severely restricted the use of the act.[142]

After the outbreak of the Korean War, Congress passed the Internal Security Act of 1950, known as the

---

[141] *Dennis* v. *United States,* 341 U.S. 494 (1951).

[142] *Yates* v. *United States,* 354 U.S. 298 (1957); *Scales* v. *United States,* 367 U.S. 203 (1961); *Noto* v. *United States,* 367 U.S. 290 (1961); *Elfbrandt* v. *Russell,* 384 U.S. 11 (1966).

McCarran Act. It required Communist "front" organizations to register with the Attorney General. The Supreme Court held that the Communist Party could be compelled to register under the McCarran Act, but it was never actually forced to do so.[143] And the Court ruled that to require *individual* Communists to register would violate the Fifth Amendment.[144]

As the postwar years have shown, however, freedom of expression has varied sharply with the political climate; even a "fixed star" may be viewed through a very different telescope in each decade.

Due Process of Law

"The history of liberty," Justice Felix Frankfurter once wrote, "is largely the history of the observance of procedural safeguards."[145] A nation may have an enlightened system of government, but if the rights of individuals are abused, then the system falls short of its goals.

The Fifth and Fourteenth amendments to the Constitution provide for "due process of law," a phrase designed to protect the individual against the arbitrary power of the state. Sometimes, the distinction is made between *substantive due process* (laws must be reasonable) and *procedural due process* (laws must be administered in a fair manner).

Until 1937 the Supreme Court used the concept of substantive due process to protect the "liberty" of businesses against regulation by Congress and the states. It adopted the view that laws regulating industry must be reasonable. After 1937, the Court abandoned substantive due process as it upheld laws passed by Congress during the New Deal to regulate business. In so doing, the Court took the view that economic regulation was the responsibility of Congress and the legislatures, not of the judicial branch. But in the area of civil rights, civil liberties, and privacy, the Court has continued to apply substantive due process.

Searches and Seizures   Due process begins at home, for the right of individuals to "be secure in their persons, houses, papers, and effects, against unreasonable searches and seizures" is spelled out in the Fourth Amendment and marks a fundamental difference between a free and a totalitarian society.

The Fourth Amendment also provides important protections against the government. In the United States, as a general principle, police are not authorized to search a home without a search warrant signed by a judicial officer and issued on "probable cause" that the materials to be seized are in the place to be searched. Until 1980, police could lawfully enter a home without a warrant to make a valid arrest, and they could conduct a limited search at the same time. But in April of that year, the Supreme Court ruled that the Fourth Amendment prohibited police from entering a home without a warrant to make a routine arrest.[146] Police must obtain a warrant except in emergency circumstances, the Court held. Justice John Paul Stevens ruled, in effect, that a family's home is its castle: " . . . the Fourth Amendment has drawn a firm line at the entrance to the house. Absent exigent circumstances, that threshold may not reasonably be crossed without a warrant." The decision invalidated the laws of twenty-three states.

Public school students are not afforded the same Fourth Amendment protections as are other citizens, however. Under a 1985 Supreme Court decision, school officials do not need a warrant, or "probable cause" to believe a crime has taken place, in order to search students.[147] The case involved a fourteen-year-old girl whose purse was opened by a school official who found marijuana, a pipe, and letters indicating the student sold marijuana. The Court ruled 6–3 that officials needed only "reasonable grounds" to conduct a search.

Although the Constitution is designed to protect against unreasonable government intrusion, in actual practice constitutional principles are sometimes violated. Two innocent families in Collinsville, Illinois, found that out in April 1973 when federal narcotics agents kicked in the doors of their homes, terrorized them at gunpoint, and ransacked their houses in a drug raid based on false information. The agents had no search or arrest warrants. Subsequent investigations disclosed that dozens of other such raids, sometimes fatal to the victims, had been carried out by federal, state, and local narcotics agents.[148] During the Nixon administration, it was disclosed that agents employed by the White House had burglarized the office of a psychiatrist who had treated Daniel Ellsberg, the former government official who leaked the Pentagon Papers to the news media. This was in addition to the illegal entry into

---

[143] *Communist Party v. Subversive Activities Control Board*, 367 U.S. 1 (1961).
[144] *Albertson v. Subversive Activities Control Board*, 382 U.S. 70 (1965).
[145] *McNabb v. United States*, 318 U.S. 332 (1943).
[146] *Payton v. New York*, 445 U.S. 573 (1980).
[147] *New Jersey v. T.L.O.*, 469 U.S. 325 (1985).
[148] *New York Times*, July 1, 1973, section 4, p. 6.

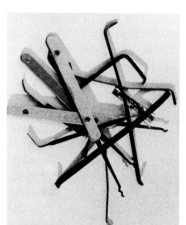

Lockpicks carried by one of the burglars at the Watergate

the Democrats' Watergate headquarters by burglars working for President Nixon's campaign. It also was disclosed that Nixon himself had approved for a time a plan that included "surreptitious entry" of the homes or offices of persons suspected by the government of being a threat to internal security—even though the President had been warned, in writing, that this was "clearly illegal" and "amounts to burglary." In 1975 the FBI admitted it had conducted hundreds of illegal break-ins against dissident groups and individuals, and a presidential commission found that the CIA also had engaged in illegal burglaries.[149]

In 1969 the Supreme Court ruled that police lacking a search warrant could not ransack a home in the course of making a lawful arrest but must confine their search to the suspect and the immediate surroundings.[150] The decision overturned the conviction of Ted Steven Chimel of California, who had been serving a five-year-to-life term for stealing rare coins—which police found after searching his home without a search warrant.

Automobiles have less protection against search and seizure than do homes. Under Supreme Court rulings, police may search an automobile without a warrant if they have probable cause to believe it contains illegal articles, and also may search any containers and packages found in such a car, even in a locked trunk.[151] "When a legitimate search is underway," the Court held, police could not be expected to make "nice distinctions . . . between glove compartments, upholstered seats, trunks and wrapped packages." [152]

Police who stop a car for a traffic violation may order the occupants to get out.[153] And police may search a car and its contents if they have lawfully arrested its occupants.[154] That case arose in New York State when Roger Belton and three friends were stopped by a state trooper for speeding. The officer smelled burnt marijuana and saw an envelope on the floor marked "Supergold." He arrested all four people and, while searching

---

[149] *New York Times*, September 26, 1975, p. 1, and *Report to the President by the Commission on CIA Activities within the United States* (Washington, D.C.: U.S. Government Printing Office, 1975), pp. 167–68, 298. This report is generally known as the Rockefeller Report.

[150] *Chimel v. California*, 395 U.S. 752 (1969).
[151] *Carroll v. United States*, 267 U.S. 132 (1925); *Texas v. White*, 423 U.S. 67 (1976); *United States v. Ross*, 456 U.S. 305 (1982).
[152] *United States v. Ross*, (1982).
[153] *Pennsylvania v. Mimms*, 434 U.S. 106 (1977).
[154] *New York v. Belton*, 453 U.S. 454 (1981).

PAMPERING THE FOURTH AMENDMENT

Los angeles, nov. 18—President Reagan told a story in Florida Wednesday . . . to illustrate his view that courts foolishly adhere to technicalities in allowing some evidence to be thrown out of court if it is obtained illegally. Police in California a few years ago found heroin in the diapers of a baby but the case was thrown out, Reagan said, "because the baby hadn't given its permission to be searched."

The President . . . has been embarrassed in the past when some of his stories have failed to check out. But the diaper case turns out to be . . . true. They are still talking in Colton, Calif., 60 miles east of Los Angeles, about the Dec. 29, 1969, search of the home of Robert Garcia Cordova and Ramona Padilla, and the packet of heroin found in the diapers worn by Padilla's 9-month-old daughter. . . . Municipal Court Judge Theodore G. Krumm ruled that the baby had not been named in the search warrant and so her diapers had been illegally examined.

—*Washington Post*, November 19, 1982

Belton's jacket, found cocaine. The Court ruled the search was justified because it was limited to an area where a suspect might reach for a weapon or evidence.[155]

The Supreme Court has also ruled that police may stop drivers at roadside checkpoints to see if they are intoxicated.[156] That decision, in 1990, was the first in which the Court has upheld the right of police, in enforcing the law, to detain individuals without any suspicion of wrongdoing. Until then, some basis for police action was required.

For example, police may "stop and frisk" a suspect on the street without a warrant if they are reasonably suspicious that the person is armed or dangerous.[157] A police officer also may "stop and frisk" a criminal suspect on the basis of an informant's tip that the officer considers to be reliable.[158] And police may arrest someone in a public place without a warrant on "probable cause" that the person has committed a crime.[159]

Cherished constitutional principles are usually established in cases involving criminals and other people who are not pillars of the community. In 1957 Cleveland police, with no search warrant, barged into the house of a woman named Dollree Mapp. They did not find the fugitive or the betting slips they were after but seized some "lewd and lascivious books and pictures." She was tried and convicted for possession of these items. But the Supreme Court ruled that a state could not prosecute a person with unconstitutionally seized evidence, a decision that protected not only Mapp but every American.[160]

The Supreme Court had long held that the federal government could not use illegally seized evidence in court, a principle known as "the exclusionary rule."[161] The *Mapp* case meant that the states, too, were subject to this rule.

But the Burger Court, in a series of decisions over several years, narrowed the impact of the exclusionary rule. Finally, in 1984, the Supreme Court for the first time created a "good faith" exception to the rule, permitting courts to consider illegally seized evidence in some cases when police reasonably believed that their search was constitutional.[162] The Court's 6–3 decision was immediately hailed by President Reagan and other conservatives who contended that the exclusionary rule had interfered with law enforcement.

The Supreme Court had been chipping away at the exclusionary rule for a decade. In 1974 the Burger Court held that a witness before a grand jury could not refuse to answer questions based on evidence seized unlawfully.[163] The following year the Court seemed to move even farther away from the exclusionary rule, leading Justice William J. Brennan, Jr., to warn in a dissent that the rule faced "slow strangulation."[164] Then in 1976 the Court curtailed the power of federal courts to overturn state court convictions because of illegally seized evidence,[165] thereby further limiting the exclusionary rule. The trend continued. In 1980 the Supreme Court ruled that evidence illegally seized by the government could be used to discredit statements made by a defendant during cross-examination at a trial.[166]

In 1983 the Supreme Court ruled in an Illinois drug case where police had arrested a couple on an anonymous tip and, armed with a search warrant, seized 350 pounds of marijuana in their home and car. Once again, the opinion narrowed the exclusionary rule. The Court, in deciding against the defendants, held that judges who issue warrants no longer need to examine closely the truthfulness of such anonymous tips and instead should exercise "common sense."[167]

The following year, the Supreme Court ruled that illegally obtained evidence may be admitted at a trial if the prosecution can show that the evidence would "inevitably" have been discovered by lawful means.[168]

Less than a month after that decision, the Burger Court created the "good faith" exception in cases where police relied on search warrants that turned out to be flawed. In Sunset Canyon, California, police searched the home of Antonio Leon and discovered cocaine. The search warrant had been issued without "probable cause" as required by the Fourth Amendment. The Supreme Court upheld the police.[169] In a second case,

---

[155] *Ibid.*
[156] *Michigan v. Sitz*, 496 U.S. 444 (1990).
[157] *Terry v. Ohio*, 392 U.S. 1 (1968).
[158] *Adams v. Williams*, 407 U.S. 143 (1972).
[159] *United States v. Watson*, 423 U.S. 411 (1976).
[160] *Mapp v. Ohio*, 367 U.S. 643 (1961).
[161] *Weeks v. United States*, 232 U.S. 383 (1914).

[162] *United States v. Leon*, 468 U.S. 897 (1984), and *Massachusetts v. Sheppard*, 468 U.S. 981 (1984).
[163] *United States v. Calandra*, 414 U.S. 338 (1974).
[164] *United States v. Peltier*, 422 U.S. 531 (1975).
[165] *Stone v. Powell* and *Wolff v. Rice*, 429 U.S. 874 (1976).
[166] *United States v. Havens*, 446 U.S. 620 (1980).
[167] *Illinois v. Gates*, 462 U.S. 213 (1983).
[168] *Nix v. Williams*, 464 U.S. 417 (1984).
[169] *United States v. Leon* (1984).

after the fatal beating of a Roxbury, Massachusetts, woman, police searched the home of her friend Osborne Sheppard and found incriminating evidence, which was used to convict him of murder. Later, it turned out that police had used the wrong form in filling out the search warrant. Once again, the Supreme Court ruled against the defendant.[170] And in 1987 the Court held that evidence seized improperly as the result of "honest mistakes" by police may be used at trial.[171]

Most legal scholars expected the "good faith" exception would be extended far beyond the circumstances in these two cases. Justice William J. Brennan, Jr., a liberal, and one of three dissenters in these key exclusionary rule cases, declared: "It now appears that the Court's victory over the Fourth Amendment is complete."

In a controversial 1978 decision, the Supreme Court had permitted police to search newspaper offices and seize evidence of a crime, even though the newspaper was an innocent "third party" not suspected of any wrongdoing.[172] The case arose in 1971 on the campus of Stanford University. A group of antiwar demonstrators at the university hospital attacked police, two of whom were seriously injured. The university newspaper, the *Stanford Daily*, published photographs of the incident. The next day, armed with a warrant, police swooped down on the paper's newsroom and searched its photo labs, filing cabinets, desks, and wastepaper baskets. The Supreme Court ruled that the First Amendment does not bar newsroom searches for criminal evidence.

In the aftermath of the *Stanford* case, sheriff's deputies and other law enforcement officials raided a television station newsroom in Boise, Idaho, in 1980, searching for and seizing videotapes of a prison riot. The local prosecutor said he needed the tapes to identify the riot leaders. Reacting to these incidents, Congress enacted a law barring most such newsroom searches. The law, the Privacy Protection Act of 1980, ordinarily requires federal, state, and local authorities to use subpoenas, rather than searches, in seeking evidence from journalists, authors, scholars, and others who write for publication.

The Uninvited Ear In the technological age, the right of privacy has been threatened by highly sophisticated wiretapping and eavesdropping devices.

In Washington practically anyone of importance assumes, or at least jokes, that his or her telephone is tapped. (One leading columnist began his telephone conversations: "Hello, everybody.") As a Senate committee has demonstrated, even the olive in a martini may be an electronic bug. With infrared light, persons in a room may be photographed through the wall of an adjoining room. Infrared light also may be used to pick up speech as far as *thirty-four miles* away. A person who swallows a "radio pill" becomes for a time a human broadcasting station, emitting signals that enable an investigator to follow the subject from some distance away.[173]

Modern technology has made possible a new form of government intrusion into the private lives of individuals, a threat that Justice Potter Stewart has called "the uninvited ear." Many prosecutors and law enforcement officials insist that wiretapping and electronic bugs are essential tools in cases involving espionage, kidnapping, and organized crime. Other observers believe that the use of such devices inevitably will be abused by government authorities and result in the violation of constitutional liberties.

Despite Justice Holmes's denunciation of wiretapping as "dirty business," the Supreme Court for almost forty years (1928–1967) held that the practice did not violate the Fourth Amendment's protection against unreasonable search and seizure.[174] But Section 605 of the Federal Communications Act of 1934 outlawed wiretapping, and three years later the Supreme Court held that wiretap evidence could not be used in federal courts.[175] Finally, in 1967, the Court caught up with modern technology by ruling that a conversation was tangible and could be seized electronically, and that placing a bug or tap did not have to involve physical "trespass" to violate the Fourth Amendment. The Court also ruled that police could not eavesdrop without a court warrant. The case involved Charles Katz, a Los Angeles gambler who made interstate telephone calls to bookmakers from a public phone booth to bet on college basketball games. Unknown to Katz, the FBI had taped a microphone to the top of his favorite phone booth on Sunset Boulevard. Because the FBI had no warrant, the Supreme Court held that Katz's constitu-

[170] *Massachusetts v. Sheppard* (1984).
[171] *Maryland v. Garrison*, 480 U.S. 79 (1987).
[172] *Zurcher v. Stanford Daily*, 436 U.S. 547 (1978).

[173] Alan F. Westin, *Privacy and Freedom* (New York: Atheneum, 1967), pp. 70, 87.
[174] *Olmstead v. United States* (1928).
[175] *Nardone v. United States*, 302 U.S. 379 (1937); *Benanti v. United States*, 355 U.S. 96 (1957).

THE CON-
STITUTION
PROTECTS
TELEPHONE
BOOTHS

The Fourth Amendment protects people, not places. . . . No less than an individual in a business office, in a friend's apartment, or in a taxicab, a person in a telephone booth may rely upon the protection of the Fourth Amendment.

One who occupies it, shuts the door behind him, and pays the toll that permits him to place a call, is surely entitled to assume that the words he utters into the mouthpiece will not be broadcast to the world.

—Justice Potter Stewart,
in *Katz v. United States* (1967)

tional rights had been violated and threw out his conviction.[176]

Technology creates continuing dilemmas for the Supreme Court's justices. Cordless telephones came into widespread use in the 1980s, but conversations over those phones can often be overheard. Unbeknownst to the Scott Tyler family of Dixon, Iowa, their nearby neighbors, Sandra and Rich Berodt, were listening in to their conversations. One day, Tyler, a food distributor, told a business associate that he would have "a light load" for him. Sandra Berodt thought he had said "a white load," and, mistakenly convinced that her neighbor was dealing in cocaine, called the sheriff's office. The Tylers' conversations were then taped, and based in part on what was overheard, Scott Tyler was charged with stealing $35,000 in merchandise from his company, convicted, and jailed for four months. The Tylers sued the Berodts for listening in on their conversations, but when the case reached the Supreme Court in 1990, the Court let stand a lower court decision that the Tylers had no "reasonable expectation of privacy" when they used their cordless phone.[177] The Fourth Amendment may protect telephone booths, but it does not protect cordless phones.

When public concern over crime increases, so do pressures to employ wiretaps and electronic eavesdrop-

ping devices. In the late 1960s "law and order" became a growing political issue. In 1968 Congress passed the Omnibus Crime Control and Safe Streets Act permitting court-authorized wiretapping and bugging by federal, state, and local authorities in a wide variety of cases, and the use of such evidence in trials.

In 1969, when the Nixon administration came to power, Attorney General John N. Mitchell claimed that the Justice Department had power, even without court approval, to tap and bug domestic groups it considered to be a threat to internal security. In 1972, however, the Supreme Court ruled, in an 8–0 decision, that this highly controversial policy violated the Fourth Amendment of the Constitution.[178] In 1973 President Nixon confirmed that early in his first term, in a supposed effort to plug news "leaks" and protect "national security," he had authorized wiretaps of a total of seventeen White House aides, other officials, and news reporters. Warrantless wiretapping and bugging had taken place under other presidents as well, including Lyndon Johnson and John F. Kennedy.

In 1978 Congress passed the Foreign Intelligence Surveillance Act, which, for the first time, required a court order even for wiretapping and bugging in national security investigations. The law also established a special, seven-judge court to issue such warrants. The only exception in the law permits the government to

[176] *Katz v. United States*, 389 U.S. 347 (1967). *Katz* overruled the *Olmstead* decision. In a related case, *Berger v. New York*, 388 U.S. 41 (1967), the Supreme Court invalidated a New York State law that permitted police to engage in electronic surveillance with a court warrant; the Court held that the state law was too broad in setting standards for electronic eavesdropping.
[177] *Tyler v. Berodt*, 493 U.S. 1022 (1990).

[178] *United States v. United States District Court for the Eastern District of Michigan*, 407 U.S. 297 (1972). In this case, sometimes also known as the *Keith* case, the Supreme Court did not address itself to the question of whether the president had power to order electronic surveillance against foreign intelligence activities or agents.

THE RIGHT TO LOOK DIFFERENT

Edward Lawson, a thirty-seven-year-old bachelor and head of his own consulting firm, liked to take long walks in San Diego, often at night. Over a two-year period, police stopped him fifteen times for vagrancy and arrested him three times.

Lawson, who wore his hair in long dreadlocks that came down over his shoulders, was black. The arrests took place in predominantly white neighborhoods.

The police stopped Lawson under a state law that required individuals to provide "credible and reliable" identification to a police officer who had reason to be suspicious of their presence. Lawson sued and fought his case all the way up to the United States Supreme Court.

In 1983, the Court decided 7–2 that the California law violated the Fourteenth Amendment, which provides that no state may deprive any person of liberty—as had happened to Edward Lawson—without "due process of law."

The California statute, Justice Sandra Day O'Connor wrote for the majority, allows innocent people "to continue to walk the public streets 'only at the whim of any police officer' who happens to stop" them. The statute, the Court ruled, was unconstitutional.

—Adapted from *Kolender, Chief of Police of San Diego, et al., v. Lawson* (1983)

eavesdrop on the communications of foreign powers without a warrant. The special court did not appear to be any great obstacle to government wiretapping, however. As of the end of 1990, the panel of rotating judges to whom requests come had approved 5,955 wiretapping applications and had rejected none.[179]

Because the 1968 Omnibus Crime Control Act required police to obtain court warrants to eavesdrop in domestic criminal investigations, the two laws, taken together, prohibit virtually all electronic surveillance without a warrant. But in 1979 the Supreme Court held that a break-in by government agents to plant a court-authorized bug is constitutional; it said that Congress had not ruled out "covert entry" to carry out electronic surveillance.[180]

Rights of the Accused "Due process of law" may mean little to average Americans—unless and until they are arrested. This is because most of the important procedural safeguards provided by the Constitution, as interpreted by the Supreme Court, concern the rights of accused persons.

Before anyone may be brought to trial for a serious federal crime, there must be a grand jury indictment, a finding that enough evidence exists to warrant a criminal trial. The Constitution does not require states to use grand juries, and in most state cases, in place of an *indictment*, a criminal *information* is filed with the court by the prosecutor in order to bring a defendant to trial. The Bill of Rights entitles suspects or defendants to be represented by a lawyer; to be informed of their legal rights and of the charges against them; to have a speedy and public trial by jury; to summon witnesses to testify in their behalf; to cross-examine prosecution witnesses; and to refuse to testify against themselves. In addition, they may not be held in excessive bail, or subjected to cruel and unusual punishment or to double jeopardy for the same offense. These rights are contained in the Fifth through Eighth amendments.

Under Chief Justice Earl Warren, the Supreme Court, in a series of split decisions in the mid-1960s, greatly strengthened the rights of accused persons, particularly in the period immediately following arrest. It is in the station-house stage that police traditionally attempt to extract a confession from suspects. It is also the very time at which accused persons may be most disoriented, frightened, and uncertain of their rights. The Court came under severe political attack for these decisions, which many law enforcement authorities argued would hamper their ability to fight crime. The Warren Court rulings came at a time of rising violence and unrest in America. Many citizens, worried about "law and order," focused their criticism on the Court and on the judicial system, which was often accused of "coddling criminals." Supporters of the Warren Court decisions and of civil liberties argued that there is no better

---

[179] Data provided by U.S. Department of Justice.
[180] *Dalia v. United States*, 441 U.S. 238 (1979).

test of a democracy than the procedural safeguards it erects to protect accused persons from the police power of the state.

A landmark case of the Warren era began in Chicago on the night of January 19, 1960. A man named Manuel Valtierra was shot in the back and killed. Police picked up his brother-in-law, Danny Escobedo, a laborer. He was questioned, released, picked up ten days later, and interrogated again. He asked to see his lawyer, but the request was refused. During the long night at police headquarters, Danny Escobedo confessed. In 1964, by a vote of 5–4, the Supreme Court reversed his conviction, freeing him after four-and-a-half years in prison. Justice Arthur Goldberg ruled for the Court that under the Sixth Amendment, a suspect is entitled to counsel even during police interrogation once "the process shifts from investigatory to accusatory."[181] Nor can the government use incriminating statements made by a suspect to an informer imprisoned with him or her before a trial; the Supreme Court has ruled that use of such evidence deprives the suspect of the right to have an attorney present, unless, the Court ruled in 1990, the incriminating statements concern a separate crime for which the prisoner has not been indicted.[182]

As far back as 1957, the Court had laid down the *Mallory* rule, requiring that a suspect in a federal case be arraigned without unnecessary delay.[183] In 1966, in *Miranda* v. *Arizona*, the Supreme Court extended the protection it had granted to suspects with the *Escobedo* decision. Ernesto A. Miranda, an indigent twenty-three-year-old man, described by the Court as mentally disturbed, was arrested in March 1963, ten days after the kidnapping and rape of an eighteen-year-old woman near Phoenix. The woman picked Miranda out of a police lineup, and after two hours of interrogation—during which he was not told of his right to silence and a lawyer—he confessed. The Supreme Court struck down Miranda's conviction; in a controversial 5–4 decision, the Court ruled that the Fifth Amendment's protection against self-incrimination requires that suspects be clearly informed of their rights before they are asked any questions by police.

Chief Justice Warren declared for the narrow majority that statements made by an accused person may not be used against him in court unless strict procedures

Ernesto Miranda after his arrest on parole violations

are followed: "Prior to any questioning, the person must be warned that he has a right to remain silent, that any statement he does make may be used against him, and that he has a right to the presence of an attorney, either retained or appointed."[184] Although a defendant may knowingly waive these rights, Warren ruled, he cannot be questioned further if at any point he asks to see a lawyer or indicates "in any manner" that he does not wish to be interrogated.

The chief justice, declaring that *Miranda* went to "the roots of our concepts of American criminal jurisprudence," argued eloquently that the "compelling atmosphere" of a "menacing police interrogation" was designed to intimidate the suspect, break his will, and lead to an involuntary confession in violation of the Fifth Amendment. That is why, he concluded, "procedural safeguards" must be observed in the police station. In a strong dissent Justice John Harlan said: "It's obviously going to mean a gradual disappearance of

[181] *Escobedo* v. *Illinois*, 378 U.S. 478 (1964).
[182] *United States* v. *Henry*, 447 U.S. 264 (1980); *Illinois* v. *Perkins* 496 U.S. 292 (1990).
[183] *Mallory* v. *United States*, 354 U.S. 449 (1957).

[184] *Miranda* v. *Arizona*, 384 U.S. 436 (1966).

THE POLICE DON'T ALWAYS KNOCK

WINTHROP, MASS. —Fifteen burly policemen, carrying rifles and handguns, broke down two doors and poured into the home of the William Pine family last Tuesday. The men wore no uniforms, did not offer any identification and did not speak, Mrs. Pine said today in an interview, except for a few brusque orders followed by a rough shove to the living room couch. Bewildered, Mrs. Pine and her daughter screamed over and over:

"Please don't kill us, please don't kill us."

"Just don't move," came the only reply. State and Federal agents and the nar-cotics squads of several communities had been surveying the house next to the Pine residence for the last two and a half months, where they believed a lucrative heroin factory was in operation. When the time came, they raided the wrong house.

"I thought they were all maniacs that had come to kill us," Mrs. Pine said. " . . . they never told us who they were or that they were police officers even after they left," she said. "I didn't know police operated like that in America. I'm ashamed that this could happen here."

—*New York Times*, January 15, 1973

confessions as a legitimate tool of law enforcement." After the decision many police began carrying "Miranda cards" to read suspects their rights.

With the election of President Nixon, the era of the Warren Court came to an end. In 1969 Nixon named a new chief justice, Warren E. Burger. Within four years, Nixon had appointed three more Supreme Court justices who were, as a group, generally more conservative than their predecessors. Particularly in the area of criminal justice, the pendulum gradually began to swing back from the liberal philosophy of the Warren Court.

In 1971 the Burger Court handed down a decision that greatly narrowed the scope of the *Miranda* ruling. The Court held that if a statement were made by a suspect without proper *Miranda* warnings, it still could be used to discredit his or her testimony at a trial.[185] In a further qualification of its *Miranda* decision, the Supreme Court later ruled that juries did not have to be convinced "beyond a reasonable doubt" in deciding whether a confession was voluntary and therefore admissible as evidence in court.[186] The Burger Court also upheld the admission of hearsay evidence to convict a defendant in a state court.[187] And in 1972 the Court

diluted the Fifth Amendment's safeguard against self-incrimination; it upheld a law that diminished the immunity from prosecution granted to a witness compelled to testify.[188]

The Burger Court retreated even farther from *Miranda* in three later decisions. It ruled that evidence obtained by police after an incomplete warning of legal rights was given to a defendant could nevertheless be used against him or her.[189] The Court also weakened *Miranda* by allowing prosecutors to use incriminating statements obtained by police after a defendant had demanded to see a lawyer.[190] And it held that even after suspects exercise the right to remain silent about one crime, they still can be questioned about another.[191]

Despite these decisions, in 1976 the Burger Court did reinforce the *Miranda* decision. Two men arrested for selling marijuana in Ohio were advised of their rights but later contended at their trial that they had been framed by an informer. The prosecutor emphasized that the defendants had not told that story at the time of their arrest. But the Court ruled silence by suspects after being advised of their *Miranda* rights could not later be used against them.[192] However, in 1980 the Court ruled that if a defendant took the stand at a trial, he or she could be questioned about prearrest silence.[193]

---

[185] *Harris* v. *New York*, 401 U.S. 222 (1971). The defendant claimed at his trial that he had sold baking soda, not heroin, to an undercover narcotics agent. The prosecution then read a statement the defendant had made, without police warnings, just after his arrest, admitting the sale and making no mention of baking soda.
[186] *Lego* v. *Twomey*, 404 U.S. 477 (1972).
[187] *Dutton* v. *Evans*, 400 U.S. 74 (1970).

[188] *Kastigar* v. *United States*, 406 U.S. 441 (1972).
[189] *Michigan* v. *Tucker*, 417 U.S. 433 (1974).
[190] *Oregon* v. *Hass*, 420 U.S. 714 (1975).
[191] *Michigan* v. *Mosley*, 423 U.S. 96 (1975).
[192] *Doyle* v. *Ohio* and *Wood* v. *Ohio*, 426 U.S. 610 (1976).
[193] *Jenkins* v. *Anderson*, 447 U.S. 231 (1980).

In 1977 the Burger Court, in a grisly Iowa murder case, reaffirmed the right of counsel provided by the Sixth Amendment. The suspect, Robert Anthony Williams, with no lawyer present, led police to the body after a detective drew him into conversation about the crime during a long automobile ride. The Supreme Court by a narrow 5–4 margin reversed the conviction.[194] But when the same defendant was found guilty at a second trial, the Supreme Court upheld his conviction ruling that the body would have been discovered even without the help of Williams. In 1979 the Court ruled in a murder case that even when suspects had been advised of their *Miranda* rights, incriminating admissions could not be used against them if police held them for questioning without valid grounds for arrest in the first place.[195] Two years later, the Court extended *Miranda* to include psychiatric interviews with defendants,[196] as well as to prohibit any police interrogation without a lawyer, once a suspect has asked for one.[197]

On the other hand, the Court appeared to permit the use of subtle psychology on suspects unless police were aware that their actions or words were "reasonably likely" to make a suspect confess.[198] The case arose when Thomas Innis, a murder suspect, led police to a hidden weapon after officers remarked that it would be too bad if a child "would pick up the gun and maybe kill herself." The Court said that this was not the sort of "interrogation" forbidden by *Miranda*.

And in 1984, in another retreat from *Miranda*, the Supreme Court held that where "public safety" is endangered, police can question suspects without advising them of their rights.[199] The case arose when police in Queens, New York, cornered a rape suspect in a supermarket. Without advising the man of his *Miranda* rights, they asked where he had hidden his gun, and he told them. The Court ruled that the suspect's statement, "The gun is over there," was admissible.

In 1985 President Reagan's Attorney General, Edwin Meese III, publicly attacked the Supreme Court's *Miranda* decision as "infamous" and wrong.[200] And the Court, under Chief Justice William H. Rehn-

quist, whom President Reagan appointed in 1986, continued to narrow the scope of suspects' rights. In four cases in its 1987 term, for example, the justices ruled in favor of police and against the rights of criminal defendants.[201] In 1990, however, the Rehnquist court, although generally perceived as unsympathetic to the rights of defendants, surprised its critics by ruling that a suspect who asks for and consults with a lawyer cannot be questioned again after the lawyer leaves.[202] Despite that decision, the Court continued to narrow the protections of *Miranda*. The following year it ruled that even if a confession is coerced, it can be used in a trial if other evidence is adequate to sustain a guilty verdict.[203]

Ernesto Miranda was stabbed to death in a barroom quarrel in Phoenix, Arizona, on February 1, 1976. Fernando Rodriguez Zamora was arrested on a murder charge for allegedly handing the knife to the assailant, who fled. The police read Zamora his rights. They used a "Miranda card."

•   •   •

The right of an indigent defendant to have a lawyer in a state court might seem basic, but in fact it was not established by the Supreme Court until 1963 in the celebrated case of *Gideon v. Wainwright*.[204]

---

[194] The Supreme Court reversed Williams's conviction in *Brewer* v. *Williams*, 430 U.S. 387 (1977). His conviction at the second trial was upheld by the Court in *Nix* v. *Williams* (1984).
[195] *Dunaway* v. *New York*, 442 U.S. 200 (1979).
[196] *Estelle* v. *Smith*, 451 U.S. 454 (1981).
[197] *Edwards* v. *Arizona*, 451 U.S. 477 (1981).
[198] *Rhode Island* v. *Innis*, 446 U.S. 291 (1980).
[199] *New York* v. *Quarles*, 467 U.S. 649 (1984).
[200] *Washington Post*, August 26, 1985, p. A6.

[201] *New York Times*, May 31, 1987, section 4, p. 1.
[202] *Minnick* v. *Mississippi*, 111 S. Ct. 486 (1990). The decision extended the principle established in *Edwards* v. *Arizona*.
[203] *Arizona* v. *Fulminante*, 111 S. Ct. 1246 (1991).
[204] *Gideon* v. *Wainwright*, 372 U.S. 335 (1963).

Clarence Earl Gideon

Clarence Earl Gideon petitioned the Supreme Court in 1962 from the Florida State Prison at Raiford, where he was serving a five-year term for breaking into a poolroom in Panama City, Florida, and allegedly stealing some beer, wine, and coins from a cigarette machine and a jukebox. A drifter, a man whose life had had more than the normal share of disasters, Gideon nevertheless had one idea fixed firmly in his mind—that the Constitution of the United States entitled him to a fair trial. And this, he insisted in his petition, he had not received. Clarence Earl Gideon had not been provided with a lawyer by the court. In 1942 the Supreme Court had ruled that the right of counsel was not a "fundamental right," essential to a fair trial in a state court and that it was not guaranteed by the "due process clause" of the Fourteenth Amendment.[205] But in *Gideon*, two decades later, the Court changed its mind. Justice Black declared for the majority: a person "who is too poor to hire a lawyer cannot be assured a fair trial unless counsel is provided for him." A few months later, Gideon won a new trial and this time—with the help of a lawyer—he was acquitted.

The landmark *Gideon* decision left open a question of vital importance to millions of poor persons arrested each year for misdemeanors and so-called petty offenses, crimes carrying maximum penalties of six months in jail. Because Gideon had been convicted of a felony, the decision in his case did not clarify whether defendants accused of lesser offenses also were entitled to free counsel. Then in 1972 the Supreme Court overruled the conviction of Jon Richard Argersinger, a Tallahassee, Florida, gas station attendant who had not been offered an attorney when he pleaded guilty to carrying a concealed weapon, a misdemeanor.[206] The decision meant that no persons—unless they voluntarily give up their right to a lawyer—may be sentenced to jail for any offense, no matter how minor, unless they have been represented by an attorney at their trial.

An Expanding Umbrella of Rights

The Bill of Rights was passed as a bulwark against the new *federal* government. It did not apply to the *states*. Congress, in fact, rejected a proposal by James Madison to prohibit the states from interfering with basic liberties.

Because America has a federal system of government, this created a paradox: the same constitutional rights established under the federal government were often meaningless within a state. It was as though the Bill of Rights were a ticket valid for travel on a high-speed train but no good for local commuting. Not until 1925 did the Supreme Court systematically begin to apply the Bill of Rights to the states. By 1970 the process was virtually complete. But even today, there is no written provision in the Constitution requiring the states to observe the Bill of Rights.

In 1833 the Supreme Court ruled in *Barron* v. *Baltimore* that the provisions of the Bill of Rights did not apply to the state governments and "this Court cannot so apply them." [207] Near the end of the Civil War, Congress passed the Fourteenth Amendment, which for the first time provided that "No State shall . . . deprive any person of life, liberty, or property, without due process of law." Did Congress thereby mean to "incorporate" the entire Bill of Rights into the Fourteenth Amendment and apply the Bill of Rights to the states? The argument never has been settled, but the point—thanks to the decisions of the Supreme Court in this century—is rapidly becoming moot.

In the *Gitlow* case in 1925, the Court held that freedom of speech and press were among the "fundamental personal rights" protected by the Fourteenth Amendment from abridgment by the states.[208] The Court thus began a process of *selective incorporation* of the Bill of Rights. Two years later, the Court confirmed that freedom of speech was locked in under the Fourteenth Amendment.[209] In 1931 freedom of the press was specifically applied to the states.[210] In 1932, in the first of the Scottsboro cases, the Court partially incorporated the Sixth Amendment by requiring that a defendant in a capital case be represented by a lawyer.[211] Two years later, it applied freedom of religion to the states.[212] In 1937 freedom of assembly was held to apply to the states.[213]

Later that same year came the landmark incorporation decision of *Palko* v. *Connecticut*.[214] Frank Palko

---

[205] *Betts* v. *Brady*, 316 U.S. 455 (1942).
[206] *Argersinger* v. *Hamlin*, 407 U.S. 25 (1972).

[207] Chief Justice John Marshall, in *Barron* v. *Baltimore*, 7 Peters 243 (1833).
[208] *Gitlow* v. *New York* (1925).
[209] *Fiske* v. *Kansas*, 274 U.S. 380 (1927).
[210] *Near* v. *Minnesota* (1931).
[211] *Powell* v. *Alabama*, 287 U.S. 45 (1932).
[212] *Hamilton* v. *Regents of the University of California*, 293 U.S. 245 (1934).
[213] *De Jonge* v. *Oregon* (1937).
[214] *Palko* v. *Connecticut* (1937).

had been sentenced to life imprisonment for killing two policemen. Under an unusual Connecticut statute, the state could appeal and did; a new trial resulted in a death sentence. Palko appealed to the Supreme Court, contending that the second trial had placed him in double jeopardy, in violation of the Fifth Amendment. Justice Benjamin Cardozo ruled that the Fourteenth Amendment *did* require the states to abide by the Bill of Rights where the rights at stake were so fundamental that "neither liberty nor justice would exist if they were sacrificed." But Cardozo added that while procedural rights such as the immunity against double jeopardy were important, "they are not of the very essence of a scheme of ordered liberty," and therefore not binding to the states. The distinction was not helpful to Frank Palko; he was executed.

In 1947 the *Everson* case incorporated the principle of separation of church and state, and in 1961 *Mapp* established that the Fourth Amendment applied to the states. In 1962 the Court carried the Eighth Amendment's protection against cruel and unusual punishment to the states; it further extended this protection in 1972 when it held that capital punishment as then administered constituted cruel and unusual punishment in violation of the Eighth Amendment.[215] In rapid succession, other rights were applied to the states: the Fifth Amendment's protection against self-incrimination;[216] and the Sixth Amendment's rights to counsel,[217] to a speedy trial,[218] to confrontation of an accused person by the witnesses against him,[219] to compulsory process for obtaining witnesses,[220] and to trial by jury in all serious criminal cases.[221]

In 1969, on Earl Warren's final day as chief justice, the Court, in *Benton v. Maryland*,[222] finally applied the Fifth Amendment's prohibition of double jeopardy to the states; it ruled that John Dalmer Benton should not have been tried twice for larceny. The Court thus overruled Justice Cardozo's decision in the *Palko* case.

The process of incorporation had in effect come full circle in the thirty-two years between *Palko* and *Benton*. Of the portions of the Bill of Rights that could apply to the states, almost every significant provision —

with the exception of the Fifth Amendment's right to indictment by grand jury for major crimes — had been applied.[223] Thus, through the slow and shifting process of selective incorporation, the Supreme Court has brought the states almost entirely under the protective umbrella of the Bill of Rights.

Balancing Liberty and Order

At a time when democracy is under pressure, when the American political system is being tested to determine whether it can meet the problems of an urbanized, complex, and changing society, the Bill of Rights is more important than ever.

The Bill of Rights and the Supreme Court remain a buffer between popular emotion and constitutional principle. For it is precisely in times of stress and upheaval that fundamental liberties require the most protection. As Justice Jackson put it so eloquently, freedom to differ over "things that do not matter much" is a "mere shadow" of freedom. "The test of its substance is the right to differ as to things that touch the heart of the existing order."[224]

While the Supreme Court may at times be more zealous than other institutions in protecting civil liberties, it is by no means insensitive to public pressure. As John P. Frank has noted: "The dominant lesson of our history . . . is that courts love liberty most when it is under pressure least."[225] It is not enough, therefore, to leave the protection of fundamental liberties to the courts. Public support for civil liberties is a vital factor in the preservation of those liberties.

It is in the field of civil liberties and civil rights that some of the most sensitive demands and supports (inputs) are fed into the political system. For example, in weighing the rights of defendants versus the suppression of crime by society, the federal government is

---

[215] *Robinson v. California*, 370 U.S. 660 (1962); *Furman v. Georgia*, 408 U.S. 238 (1972).
[216] *Malloy v. Hogan*, 378 U.S. 1 (1964).
[217] *Gideon v. Wainwright* (1963); *Argersinger v. Hamlin* (1972).
[218] *Klopfer v. North Carolina*, 386 U.S. 213 (1967).
[219] *Pointer v. Texas*, 380 U.S. 400 (1965).
[220] *Washington v. Texas*, 388 U.S. 14 (1967).
[221] *Duncan v. Louisiana*, 391 U.S. 145 (1968).
[222] *Benton v. Maryland*, 395 U.S. 784 (1969).

[223] The Supreme Court, in *Hurtado v. California*, 110 U.S. 516 (1884), and later cases, declined to apply to the states the requirement of a grand jury indictment. Four other provisions of the Bill of Rights have not been incorporated to apply to the states — these have not been tested at the Supreme Court level. They are the right to a jury trial in civil cases where the amount in dispute exceeds $20 (Seventh Amendment); the ban on "excessive bail" and "fines" (Eighth Amendment); the right of the people "to keep and bear arms" (Second Amendment); and the ban on peacetime quartering of soldiers in private homes (Third Amendment). See Henry J. Abraham, *Freedom and the Court: Civil Rights and Liberties in the United States*, 4th ed. (New York: Oxford University Press, 1982), pp. 81–83.
[224] *West Virginia Board of Education v. Barnette* (1943).
[225] In Mason, *The Supreme Court: Palladium of Freedom*, p. 171n.

making some highly important allocations of values (outputs). And in Supreme Court decisions on topics such as abortion, school desegregation, the rights of suspects, and school prayers, the public reaction (feedback) is formidable.

In applying the First Amendment and in balancing the claims of individual rights versus those of society, the Supreme Court generally moved during the 1960s in the direction of freer expression, reflecting the attitudes of a more permissive society. However, the Warren Court's decisions on the rights of defendants collided with a public alarmed about crime. In the 1970s, under Chief Justice Warren Burger, the Court appeared to shift away from the philosophy expressed in the Miranda case. But the Burger Court, although often more conservative in tone, also defended civil liberties by expanding the right to counsel, by forbidding government wiretapping of domestic groups without a warrant, and by other rulings. It held, for example, that all charges must be dismissed against defendants who are denied their constitutional right to a speedy trial.[226] By the 1990s, the Rehnquist Court in some, but by no means all, decisions had expanded the rights of free expression and of the press even as it continued, in most instances, to limit the rights of criminal defendants.

As always, the Court was charting new waters against a background of strong public sentiment. The delicate balance between liberty and order is constantly shifting, from issue to issue and from one decade to the next. Even with the Constitution as ballast, this will always be so.

CITIZENSHIP

Who Is a Citizen?

Although the Constitution as framed in 1787 uses the phrase "citizen of the United States," the term was not defined until the adoption of the Fourteenth Amendment in 1868. It provides that: "All persons born or naturalized in the United States . . . are citizens of the United States and of the State wherein they reside."

The amendment rests on the principle of *jus soli* (right of soil), which confers citizenship by place of birth. Congress by law has also adopted the principle of *jus sanguinis* (right of blood), under which the citizenship of a child is determined by that of the parents. All persons born in the United States, except for the children of high-ranking foreign diplomats, are citizens. But in addition, children born abroad of American parents, or even of one American parent, may become citizens if they and their parents meet the complex and varying legal requirements.

An immigrant who wishes to become a citizen may become "naturalized" after residing in the United States

---

[226] *Strunk v. United States,* 412 U.S. 434 (1973).

Citizenship day ceremony on Ellis Island

continuously for five years, or three years in the case of the spouse of a citizen. The oath of citizenship is administered by a federal judge, but the processing of applications for citizenship is handled by the Immigration and Naturalization Service of the Department of Justice. Children under age eighteen of naturalized citizens normally derive their American citizenship from their parents. Generally speaking, naturalized citizens enjoy the same rights as native-born Americans, although no naturalized citizen may be elected president or vice-president.

Loss of Citizenship

It is sometimes believed that persons lose their citizenship if imprisoned for a year and a day, but this is not so; the laws of most of the fifty states deprive persons convicted of certain crimes of the right to vote, but no state may deprive Americans, native-born or naturalized, of their citizenship. In general, the Supreme Court has barred congressional attempts to deprive natural-born Americans of their citizenship as punishment for crimes. For example, in 1958 the Court ruled that desertion from the armed forces during wartime was not grounds for deprivation of citizenship, because such a penalty would constitute "cruel and unusual punishment," forbidden by the Eighth Amendment.[227] In 1963 the Supreme Court struck down a law that provided automatic loss of citizenship for leaving the country in wartime to evade the draft.[228] As a result, the young men who went to live in Canada during the late 1960s to avoid military service in the Vietnam War did not lose their citizenship. In January 1977 President Carter granted a blanket pardon to most Vietnam draft evaders, although not to military deserters.

In 1964 the Supreme Court held that naturalized citizens enjoyed the same rights as native-born Americans.[229] It voided a law that had provided that naturalized persons lost their citizenship for living three years in their country of national origin.

In 1967, in the landmark case of *Afroyim* v. *Rusk*,[230] the Court ruled that Congress had no power to take away American citizenship unless it is freely renounced. An American, the Court said, had "a constitutional

right to remain a citizen in a free country unless he voluntarily relinquishes that citizenship." Specifically, the Court held that Beys Afroyim, a naturalized citizen, could not be deprived of citizenship for voting in an election in Israel.

A Nation of Immigrants

The McCarran-Walter Act, passed in 1952 over President Truman's veto, preserved the "national origins" system of immigration quotas first imposed by Congress in the 1920s to curb the wave of immigration that followed the First World War. Opponents of the national origins quota system argued that it was based on racial prejudice and designed to give preference to white, northern Europeans over immigrants from southern and eastern Europe. For example, in 1965, before the system was changed, the quota for all countries totaled 158,503. Of this, 108,931 (70 percent) was allotted to three countries — Great Britain, Ireland, and Germany. Italy, where thousands of young people desired to come to the United States, had a quota of 5,666. India had a quota of 100, as did most of the Asian and African nations. (From 1917 until 1952 Chinese and all other Asians were completely excluded.)

The Immigration Act of 1965 abolished the national origins quota system and substituted a new annual ceiling that Congress in 1980 set at 270,000 a year. The law also permitted a varying number of refugees to enter each year above that total.

By the mid-1980s, Congress struggled to cope with immigration reform legislation in response to problems created by the increasing flow of immigrants who entered the United States illegally, particularly from south of the border. In 1986 Congress passed a major immigration bill designed to reduce the flow of undocumented immigrants by punishing employers who knowingly hired them, and by granting legal status to those who arrived before January 1, 1982. Government and civilian demographers estimated that there were more than 4 million persons in the country illegally, and some analysts put the figure much higher.[231]

In 1990, Congress enacted a comprehensive revision of the immigration laws, setting a new annual ceiling of 675,000 immigrants beginning in 1994. The new law was also designed to allow more Europeans to

---

[227] *Trop* v. *Dulles,* 356 U.S. 86 (1958).
[228] *Kennedy* v. *Mendoza-Martinez,* 372 U.S. 144 (1963).
[229] *Schneider* v. *Rusk,* 377 U.S. 163 (1964).
[230] *Afroyim* v. *Rusk,* 387 U.S. 253 (1967).

[231] *New York Times,* May 7, 1987, p. A16.

immigrate to America and to attract workers with special skills. And it eliminated the provisions of the McCarran-Walter Act that had excluded people from the United States because of their political beliefs or ideology. In 1991, the State Department began a three-year lottery program to allow 40,000 immigrants annually from Ireland and other countries from which immigration had been reduced when the national origins system was abolished in 1965.

By the early 1990s, however, America had tightened the restrictions on political refugees seeking asylum on its shores. A decade earlier, thousands of Cuban and Haitian refugees who streamed into Florida by boat in 1980 were admitted outside any quotas and given special status. Vietnamese "boat people" who escaped from Vietnam during the same period were admitted to the United States under the parole authority of the Attorney General.

But by 1992, thousands of Haitian refugees who tried to escape by boat were forcibly turned back by the Coast Guard. The Refugee Act of 1980 defined those who may claim political asylum as persons with "a well-founded fear of persecution" based on race, religion, nationality, or their political opinions. Washington interpreted the law narrowly, to bar those whom it claimed were simply seeking better economic conditions. And the Supreme Court made it more difficult for refugees seeking to escape conscription by guerrilla forces. A young Guatemalan, Jairo Elias-Zacarias, had refused the demand of armed guerrillas that he join them; he fled his village, crossing the Mexican border to Arizona, where he was arrested. The Court ruled that Elias–Zacarias had not shown that he escaped because of his "political opinion" and ordered him sent back to Guatemala.[232]

The Supreme Court in recent years has considerably enlarged the rights of legal aliens, however, by providing them with access, equal to that of citizens, to welfare benefits, Medicaid, and the right to practice law (although not to state employment as troopers or teachers).[233] And the children of illegal aliens have the same right to attend public schools as the children of citizens.[234]

Haitian refugees intercepted by U.S. Coast Guard

Change, Citizen Action, and Dissent

The Bill of Rights is really a list of promises by the government to the people. There is no similar list of constitutional obligations of the people to the government. Nevertheless, for a democracy to work, citizens must be willing to participate in the political process.

When Americans work for a better environment, support political candidates, or speak out or organize on public issues, whether they dissent from established policy or support it, they are fulfilling a responsibility of citizenship. Freedom to dissent is an important aspect of democracy. In fact, it may be argued that one of the most important responsibilities of citizenship is to exercise the rights protected by the Constitution, including those of free speech and dissent.

Voting in elections, actively participating in political party activity and community programs, forming and

---

[232] *Immigration and Naturalization Service v. Elias-Zacarias*, 112 S. Ct. 812 (1992).

[233] *Graham v. Richardson*, 403 U.S. 365 (1971); *In re Griffiths*, 413 U.S. 717 (1973); *Foley v. Connelie*, 435 U.S. 291 (1978); *Ambach v. Norwick*, 441 U.S. 68 (1979).

[234] *Plyler v. Doe*, 457 U.S. 202 (1982).

expressing political opinions, either singly or through groups—all are necessary to the workings of a healthy democracy.

Many Americans lament that the system is not responsive enough to their interests. Often, they are right. But sometimes those who feel this way fail to take as simple a step as registering to vote. Frequently it does seem that the political system is slow to respond to pressures for change, and that ordinary citizens have no way to express themselves to influence political leaders. Yet, at times, individual citizens have shown that it is not only possible to "fight City Hall" but, occasionally, to win.

In Los Angeles two decades ago, a social worker named John Serrano, the son of a Mexican shoemaker, was told by a principal to get his children out of the barrio of East Los Angeles and into a better school "if you want to give them a chance." Serrano took the advice and moved out to a suburb, but he did not forget the encounter. It seemed to him unjust that schools in a poor Mexican-American neighborhood should be worse than those in wealthier neighborhoods. He joined forces with John E. Coons, a University of California law professor, who had been opposing inequalities in public school funding. Serrano, with the parents of a group of other Los Angeles schoolchildren, signed a complaint and went to court. On August 30, 1971, the Supreme Court of the State of California decided the case of *Serrano* v. *Priest*. It ruled that John Serrano was right, that a system of financing public schools through local property taxes "invidiously discriminates" against the poor because it makes the quality of a child's schooling depend on where he lives.

The implications of the California decision were dramatic. If extended elsewhere, it would mean a sweeping change in the way public schools are financed across America. Other states would have to find a way to equalize spending on education in all their school districts, because every state but Hawaii relies heavily on real estate taxes to pay for public schools.

Dozens of lawsuits were filed in other states to try to bring about just such a change. Then, in March 1973, the Supreme Court ruled on the issue in a similar case that arose in Texas.[235] The Court held 5–4 that the Texas system did not violate the Fourteenth Amendment "merely because the burdens or benefits . . . fall unevenly depending upon the relative wealth of the political subdivisions in which citizens live."

Despite the Supreme Court's decision, John Serrano's lawsuit had set in motion forces that could not be stopped. Many states were adopting alternative methods of school financing as a result of the California decision. In 1989, the Texas Supreme Court unanimously ruled that the state's system would have to be changed because of "glaring disparities" between rich and poor school districts.[236] By 1992, forty states had modified their systems for financing public schools.[237] The United States Supreme Court's ruling had slowed down the momentum of change, but pressures for equality of school district financing continued. In California, and in America, John Serrano had demonstrated that one citizen can make a difference.

PERSPECTIVE

In a democratic society, freedom is not absolute. The proper balance between the rights of one individual and the rights of society as a whole never can be resolved to everyone's satisfaction. In the American political system, the Supreme Court is the mechanism called upon to resolve conflicts between liberty and order and between the rights of the individual and the rights of society. The Court operates within the framework of the Bill of Rights, the fundamental charter of American liberty. The Bill of Rights is part of the Constitution, but the Supreme Court decides how those rights will be defined and applied. Individual liberties may depend not only on what the Court rules but on what the political system will tolerate in any given era.

The First Amendment is designed to protect freedom of religion, speech, press, assembly, and petition. In interpreting the First Amendment, different Supreme Court justices have adopted different philosophies. For example, Justice Hugo Black argued that "there *are* 'absolutes' in our Bill of Rights" that cannot be diluted by judicial decisions. However, a majority of the Court has held that First Amendment rights must be "balanced" against the competing community needs to preserve order and to preserve the government.

Although the Court has generally hesitated to impose prior restraint on the press, it has limited freedom

---

[235] *The San Antonio Independent School District* v. *Rodriguez*, 411 U.S. 1 (1973).

[236] *New York Times*, October 4, 1989, p. B9.
[237] Data provided by Education Commission of the States.

of the press in other ways — sometimes requiring journalists to reveal sources; permitting individuals to sue the press for libel; recognizing the right of privacy; banning "obscene" material; supporting the right of public schools to censor student newspapers; and upholding the power of the government to regulate radio and television. And in recent years the Court has shown increasing concern over pretrial and courtroom publicity. This issue brings two principles of the Bill of Rights into conflict — the right of an accused person to have a fair trial and the right of freedom of the press.

The First Amendment contains two clauses protecting freedom of religion. The "free exercise clause" protects the right of individuals to worship or believe as they wish, or to hold no religious beliefs. The "establishment clause," in the words of Justice Hugo Black, means that "neither a state nor the federal government can set up a church. Neither can pass laws that aid one religion, aid all religions, or prefer one religion over another." In deciding cases that relate to freedom of religion, the Supreme Court has always faced a dilemma because the two clauses of the amendment in a sense clash with each other. That is, in protecting the rights of a particular religious group to engage in "free exercise" of its faith, the Court might be viewed as favoring a religion in violation of the "establishment clause." Recognizing this dilemma, the Court has attempted to exercise what it has called a "benevolent neutrality," in order to protect freedom of religion without sponsorship of a particular faith. In 1962 and 1963 the Supreme Court outlawed the daily reading of school prayer, and in 1985 it struck down an Alabama law that permitted a one-minute period of silence or "voluntary prayer" in the public schools.

On the other hand, the Court's decision in the *Everson* case (1947) allowed states to provide various kinds of aid to church-related schools for the purpose of helping the child. Since 1971, however, when the Supreme Court outlined a three-part test of constitutionality for such state laws, it has declared certain state programs of aid to parochial schools unconstitutional. But it has allowed states to give tax deductions for tuition paid to religious schools. It also ruled that members of the Amish church could not be forced to send their children to school beyond the eighth grade. This complex issue of separation of church and state arose again in 1992 when the Supreme Court ruled that prayers may not be included in public school graduation ceremonies. The Court said that prayer did in fact violate the Constitution's barrier against establishment of religion.

The Fourth Amendment protects the right of individuals to "be secure in their persons, houses, papers, and effects, against unreasonable searches and seizures." In the United States, as a general principle, police are not authorized to search a home without a search warrant signed by a judicial officer and issued on "probable cause" that the materials to be seized are in the place to be searched. Nor may police make routine arrests without a warrant of persons in their homes. But in 1985 the Court ruled that school officials do not need a warrant or "probable cause" to search students. The "exclusionary rule" bars the use of illegally seized evidence in court, but the Supreme Court, in a series of decisions, has gradually weakened that rule.

The right of privacy, or what Justice Brandeis called "the right to be let alone," in the electronic age has been threatened by sophisticated wiretapping and eavesdropping devices. But in 1968 and 1978 Congress passed laws requiring court warrants for electronic surveillance in domestic criminal cases and in national security cases.

The Bill of Rights entitles suspects or defendants to be represented by a lawyer; to be informed of their legal rights and of the charges against them; to have a speedy and public trial by jury; to summon witnesses to testify in their behalf; to cross-examine prosecution witnesses; and to refuse to testify against themselves. The Fifth through Eighth amendments also protect the accused from being held in excessive bail, or subjected to cruel and unusual punishment, or being tried twice for the same offense.

In the mid-1960s, the Warren Court strengthened the rights of the accused. In the *Escobedo* case (1964), the Court ruled that under the Sixth Amendment a suspect is entitled to counsel even during police interrogation once the process shifts from "investigatory to accusatory." In the *Miranda* case (1966), the Court held that suspects must be clearly informed of their rights — including the right to remain silent and have a lawyer present — before they are asked any questions by police. In the *Gideon* case (1963), the Court ruled that even poor defendants must be provided with a lawyer. But in several cases dealing with the rights of criminal defendants, the Burger Court retreated from the Warren Court's decisions. The Rehnquist court continued to narrow the scope of suspects' rights. In 1990, however, the Supreme Court ruled that a suspect who asks for and consults with a lawyer cannot be questioned again after the lawyer leaves.

The Bill of Rights was passed as a safeguard against the new federal government. It did not apply to the states. But between 1925 and 1970, through the process of "selective incorporation," the Supreme Court brought the states and local governments almost entirely under the Bill of Rights.

Under the Fourteenth Amendment, anyone born or naturalized in the United States is a citizen. The Supreme Court has held that Congress may not take away a person's citizenship unless it is freely renounced. In 1986 Congress passed a major immigration bill designed to reduce the flow of undocumented immigrants by punishing employers who knowingly hire them, and by granting legal status to illegal aliens who arrived before January 1, 1982. In 1990, Congress enacted a comprehensive revision of the immigration laws designed to allow more Europeans to immigrate to America and to attract workers with special skills. But the government tightened the restrictions on political refugees seeking asylum in America.

Suggested Reading

Abraham, Henry J. *Freedom and the Court: Civil Rights and Liberties in the United States*, 5th edition* (Oxford University Press, 1988). A detailed examination of the Bill of Rights. Analyzes how the Supreme Court, through decisions in specific cases, has gradually enlarged the area of constitutional freedom in the United States.

Berns, Walter. *Freedom, Virtue, and the First Amendment* (Louisiana State University Press, 1957). A provocative analysis that takes sharp issue with some of the major court decisions designed to protect freedom of expression in the United States.

Dorsen, Norman; Bender, Paul; and Neuborne, Burt. *Political and Civil Rights in the United States*, 4th edition (Little, Brown, 1976). A clear, comprehensive discussion of political and civil liberties in the United States, containing extensive excerpts of the Supreme Court's decisions in major constitutional cases. Published with biennial supplements covering the most recent Supreme Court decisions.

Hentoff, Nat. *The First Freedom: The Tumultuous History of Free Speech in America** (Dell, 1981). A lively, clearly written analysis of the history of the First Amendment. Contains a detailed discussion of leading Supreme Court cases involving free speech, freedom of the press, and freedom of religion.

Jackson, Robert H. *The Supreme Court in the American System of Government** (Harvard University Press, 1955). A very useful general discussion of the Supreme Court's role in the American political system. Jackson was an associate justice of the Supreme Court.

Lewis, Anthony. *Gideon's Trumpet** (Random House, 1964). A detailed and readable account of the Supreme Court case that established the right of a poor man to have a lawyer when charged with a serious criminal offense in a state court. Sheds light on the role of the Court in safeguarding the rights of defendants.

Lewis, Anthony. *Make No Law: The Sullivan Case and the First Amendment* (Random House, 1991). A significant study of libel law and First Amendment issues by a columnist for *The New York Times* who covered *New York Times* v. *Sullivan* when he was a reporter for the newspaper.

Mason, Alpheus T. *The Supreme Court: Palladium of Freedom* (University of Michigan Press, 1962). A concise discussion of the Supreme Court's place in the American political system by a distinguished scholar of constitutional law. Emphasizes the Bill of Rights and the Court's role in protecting minority views.

McCloskey, Robert G. *The Modern Supreme Court.** (Harvard University Press, 1972). (Edited by Martin Shapiro.) This book, left partly unfinished at the time of Professor McCloskey's death, analyzes important periods in the recent history of the Supreme Court. Professor McCloskey had completed sections on the Stone (1940–1945) and Vinson (1946–1952) periods. For the years 1953–1969, the editor has reprinted some of the journal articles in which McCloskey analyzed aspects of the Warren Court.

Mill, John Stuart. *On Liberty** (Appleton-Century-Crofts, 1947). (Originally published in 1859.) A classic examination of the problem of balancing individual rights and the rights of the community.

Salisbury, Harrison E. *Without Fear or Favor** (Ballantine, 1981). A useful and revealing study of the *New York Times* and its relationship to, and battles with, the federal government. Salisbury, a former foreign correspondent for the *New York Times*, analyzes the legal struggle over the publication of the Pentagon Papers and examines in detail the CIA's relationship with the *New York Times* and the news media in general.

*The Supreme Court and Individual Rights** (Congressional Quarterly, 1980). A useful survey of the impact of Supreme Court decisions on individual rights. Focuses on First Amendment rights and the guarantees of political participation, due process, and equal protection.

White, G. Edward. *Earl Warren: A Public Life** (Oxford University Press, 1987). A biography of the man who served as chief justice of the United States from 1953 to 1969. The book sheds light on the personal and intellectual leadership Warren provided as a member of the Supreme Court.

*Available in paperback edition.

AMERICA IS a multicultural society, made up of many different groups with distinct ethnic, racial, and religious identities. Even a cliché like "the melting pot," or a political slogan like the Reverend Jesse L. Jackson's "Rainbow Coalition," succeed in capturing a truth — that the United States is a land of astonishing diversity. Yet the rights proclaimed in the Declaration of Independence and those set forth in the legal language of the Constitution are not enjoyed equally by all Americans. For many minority groups, the equality promised by these fundamental American charters has been an elusive goal rather than an achieved fact, a vision of a possible future rather than a description of the often bleak present. For example, despite the

Chapter 5

The Struggle for Equal Rights

civil rights laws enacted by Congress in the 1960s and decisions of the Supreme Court, even today many of the more than 30 million African Americans do not enjoy full social and economic equality. Almost one out of three blacks in the United States is poor — by official definition of the federal government — as opposed to one out of nine whites.[1] African Americans, it is true, have made some economic gains in recent years. For example, 53.2 percent of black families — more than half — earn $20,000 a year or more.[2] But, at the same

---

[1] Adapted from U.S. Bureau of the Census, Current Population Reports, *Poverty in the United States: 1990*, series P-60, no. 175, August, 1991, p. 4. The poverty level for a family of four in 1990 was defined by the federal government as an income of less than $13,359.

time, the gap in income levels and living standards has widened between the growing African American middle class and the millions of blacks still below the poverty line. Economic gains registered by some African Americans were little comfort to the unemployed black youth in an inner-city slum, the worker frozen out of a construction job by a white union, or even to a middle-class black seeking to move into a hostile white suburb.

In America today, the infant mortality rate for African American children is more than twice as high as it is for whites. By age 15, black students are more than twice as likely as white students to be two or more grades behind in school. Unmarried mothers accounted for more than 90 percent of births to African American teenagers. Among young black males, homicide is the leading cause of death.[3] In 1992, the rate of black unemployment was 14.1 percent, more than double that of whites.[4] And the median income of black families was less than two-thirds that of white families.[5]

[2] Adapted from U.S. Bureau of the Census, Current Population Reports, *Money Income of Households, Families, and Persons in the United States: 1990*, series P-60, no. 174, August, 1991, p. 70.

[3] *The State of America's Children 1991* (Washington, D.C.: Children's Defense Fund, 1991), pp. 93, 94, 97, 144.
[4] Bureau of Labor Statistics, U. S. Department of Labor.
[5] U. S. Bureau of the Census.

A MISSISSIPPI MEMORY

The earliest memory of my life is of an incident which occurred when I was three-and-a-half years old in Holly Springs, Mississippi. My father was registrar and professor of religion and philosophy at Rust College, a Negro Methodist institution there.

One hot summer day, my mother and I walked from the college campus to the town square, a distance of maybe half a mile. I remember it as clearly as though it were a few weeks ago. I held her finger tightly as we kicked up the red dust on the unpaved streets leading to the downtown area. When we reached the square she did her shopping and we headed for home. Like any other three-and-a-half-year-old on a hot day, I got thirsty.

"Mother," I said, "I want a Coke." She replied that we could not get Cokes there and I would have to wait until we got home where there was lots of Coke in the icebox.

"But I want my Coke now," I insisted. She was just as insistent that we could not get a Coke now. "Do as I tell you," she said, "wait 'til we get home; you can have a Coke with plenty of ice."

"There's a little boy going into a store!" I exclaimed as I spied another child who was a little bigger than I. "I bet he's going to get a Coke." So I pulled my mother by the finger until we stood in front of what I recall as a drugstore looking through the closed screen doors. Surely enough, the other lad had climbed upon a stool at the counter and was already sipping a soft drink.

"But I told you you can't get a Coke in there," she said. "Why can't I?" I asked again. The answer was the same, "You just can't." I then inquired with complete puzzlement, "Well, why can *he*?" Her quiet answer thundered in my ears. "He's white."

We walked home in silence under the pitiless glare of the Mississippi sun. Once we were home she threw herself across the bed and wept. I walked out on the front porch and sat on the steps alone with my three-and-a-half-year-old thoughts.

—James Farmer,
former National Director of CORE,
in Esquire, May 1969

This statistical portrait does not sketch in the daily indignities, the rebuffs, the humiliations, and defeats that African Americans may face. Some three decades ago, author James Baldwin could write: "The brutality with which Negroes are treated in this country simply cannot be overstated, however unwilling white men may be to hear it."[6]

And despite substantial changes for the better since Baldwin wrote those words, the African American citizen in many cases remains on the outside of American society, looking in. It is true that black income, political power, education, and employment opportunities have increased since the civil rights movement of the 1960s, especially for the black middle class. But William Julius Wilson and other scholars have suggested that, even with the gains of the civil rights movement, conditions have actually deteriorated for blacks in the inner cities.[7]

The African American still has a greater chance than a white American of being born in a ghetto and of living in crowded, substandard housing. The black child's school still may be largely segregated if it is lo-

---

[6] James Baldwin, *The Fire Next Time* (New York: Dial Press, 1962), p. 82.

[7] William Julius Wilson, *The Truly Disadvantaged: The Inner City, the Underclass and Public Policy* (Chicago: University of Chicago Press, 1987).

cated in a black neighborhood, since the 1954 Supreme Court decision in the *Brown* case outlawed only official, government-backed segregation of public schools. And the school also may be old, overcrowded, and below the standards of public schools in white neighborhoods.

If the African American youth does not succumb to rats, crime, crack cocaine, heroin, gang warfare, AIDS, and other soul-destroying forces of the ghetto, perhaps he or she will obtain work. But often the work will be menial and low-paying. Black families may have to buy shoddy merchandise at high credit rates from neighborhood merchants. The food at the local chain supermarket — if any large chains operate branches in the neighborhood at all — may be of poorer quality and priced higher than the same items at the chain's branches in white neighborhoods. If the African American man or woman raises a family, the children may face the same bleak future, continuing the cycle of poverty and despair.

Even if a black youth climbs out of the ghetto, gets a job as a skilled worker, or goes to college and enters a profession, his or her troubles are not necessarily over. On moving to a white neighborhood, black families may encounter hostility and social ostracism. Under the best of economic circumstances, African American parents still must face the problem of explaining to their children the divisions in American society between white and black.

But it is not only African Americans who are struggling for equal rights in the United States. For the nearly two million Native Americans, the rhetoric of equality has a particularly ironic sound. Often living in poverty, with an unemployment rate about twice the national average, they are outcasts in a land that once was theirs.

The nation's Hispanic community, the second fastest-growing segment of the population, is another large group that has been denied full equality in American society. The term "Hispanic" usually includes Mexican Americans — by far the largest group — as well as Puerto Ricans, Cubans, and persons of Central or South American or other Spanish origin. The Bureau of the Census reported in March 1991 that there were 21.4 million Hispanics in the United States, including undocumented immigrants. And the Hispanic population was growing more than five times as fast as the population as a whole.[8]

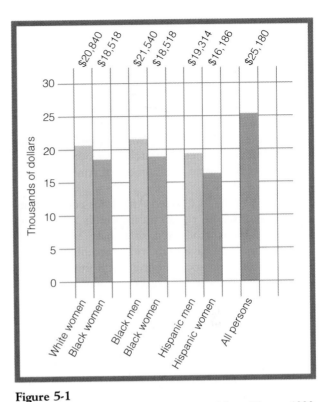

Figure 5-1
Median Income of Selected Minorities in United States, 1990
SOURCE: U.S. Bureau of the Census.

According to the census survey, there were 13.4 million Mexican Americans in the United States. Although Mexican Americans make up a sizable population bloc in five southwestern states, they are underrepresented politically. Many are migrant workers living in abysmal conditions.

Puerto Ricans, all of whom are American citizens, form another important segment of the Hispanic community. Yet many of the approximately 2.4 million Americans of Puerto Rican background who live on the mainland suffer discrimination and poverty, and are locked in the *barrios*, or slums, of the great cities.

Asian Americans, who make up the fastest-growing minority group in America, have often been the targets of hostility and bias, sometimes by other ethnic groups. Asian Americans are now the third largest minority in the nation, ranking in size right after African Americans and Hispanics.

The Women's Liberation movement that emerged as an important social and political force during the 1970s reflected the growing awareness that women, although constituting a majority of the population, were, in effect, another "minority group." Discrimination based on sex is built into many public and private

---

[8] U.S. Bureau of the Census, and *Washington Post*, March 11, 1992, p. A5.

institutions. Some indication of the problem may be seen in the gap in earnings between men and women. In 1990, for example, the median income of men was $27,866, while that of women was $19,816.[9]

Gay men and women, although gradually gaining acceptance in many American communities, still face formidable obstacles, ranging all the way from subtle bias in the workplace to physical violence on the streets. But gay and lesbian voters have become an important political force in a number of American communities.

The 43 million disabled Americans comprise another group whose rights, until recently, were often neglected. Many other minorities have suffered discrimination. Jews have been widely accepted in many areas of American society but are still unwelcome in some private clubs, in the executive suites of some corporations, and in some residential areas. Prejudice against Catholics was a major issue in John F. Kennedy's 1960 presidential campaign. Italian Americans are often the victims of subtle discrimination because of the stereotype, reinforced by movies and television, that they are members of, or somehow linked to, organized crime. Poles, Arab Americans, and other groups are still victims of racial slurs and discrimination. And discrimination is not limited to ethnic or religious minorities. Children, the elderly, and persons with AIDS also have sometimes been deprived of their rights.

All these inequalities cast a shadow over the future of America. Racial polarization in American society has been reflected in the nation's political issues and alignments. For example, as African Americans and other minority groups pressed for greater equality and opportunity, white blue-collar workers in many cases reacted with hostility. Many in this group held strong beliefs that "they," the blacks, were "asking too much," while "we had to make it on our own." Studies of the nation's ethnic patterns have noted, however, that other nationality groups, as members of the white majority, have been more easily assimilated into American society. Blacks and Hispanics migrating outward from the inner city frequently moved into white, ethnic neighborhoods. White factory or construction workers who had saved their money to buy modest houses in such neighborhoods often felt their housing investments, their schools—and perhaps their jobs—threatened by the

newcomers. Ugly racial incidents sometimes resulted. Social tension and racial protest put continuing pressure on American institutions.

By the 1990s, the increasing use of the term "multiculturalism" among many scholars, political leaders, and members of the news media reflected the fact that America was made up of many different groups of diverse backgrounds and cultures. But as these groups vied for political and economic power that had often been denied to them, critics raised the question of whether there might be serious disadvantages for America in all of this—a danger that the country might fragment into many separate ethnic groups and lose its national identity and unity.

Yet, in a society marked by diversity, the problems remained. Would the nation mobilize its energies to remove some of the causes of racial unrest—poverty, hunger, discrimination, slums, powerlessness, and unemployment? Or would the public support cuts in the government programs created to alleviate these problems? What is the history of the struggle for equal rights in America? How have government and private institutions contributed to discrimination? How did the civil rights movement of the postwar decades evolve? What steps has government taken to ensure the civil rights of minorities? Can African Americans and other minority groups achieve integration only at the cost of losing their ethnic and cultural identity? Does the emphasis on multiculturalism in American society weaken national unity? These are some of the problems we will explore in examining the continuing struggle for equality in America.

SOME GROUPS IN PROFILE

Native Americans

Who is a Native American? In the 1990s, the term was gradually replacing the more familiar "Indians," which some individuals and tribal groups found objectionable.[10] (As of 1992, the federal government still maintained a Bureau of Indian Affairs, which used the term "Indians.") Since there is no accepted demographic definition, a Native American is whoever tells the censustaker he or she is one. According to the 1990 census,

---

[9] U.S. Bureau of the Census, Current Population Reports, *Money Income of Households, Families, and Persons in the United States: 1990*, series P-60, no. 174, August, 1991, p. 5.

[10] The term "Indians" reflected the widespread belief in the time of Columbus that the peoples who lived in North America before the Europeans came inhabited the outer edge of the Indies, or what is now known as Asia.

there were almost 2,000,000 Native Americans, including 23,797 Aleuts and 57,000 Eskimos, in America. (The Eskimos and Aleuts of Alaska are two culturally distinct groups and prefer the term Alaska Natives.) An estimated 950,000 Native Americans lived on or near reservations.[11]

Native Americans are American citizens (Congress conferred citizenship on all Indians in 1924), and there is no requirement that a Native American live on a reservation, an area of land "reserved" for their use and held in trust by the federal government. There are 278 reservations in 33 states in the United States, varying in size from small settlements in California of only a few acres, to the 16-million-acre Navajo reservation spreading through Arizona, New Mexico, and Utah.

The federal government spends more than $4 billion a year on aid to Native Americans.[12] But the Bureau of Indian Affairs does not have responsibility for assisting those who are living off the reservation, of whom more than one fourth are living in poverty.[13] And the plight of those Native Americans living on the reservation is little better.

Few reservations can support their population; unemployment among Native Americans averages 45 percent on the reservations, and only 25 percent of those who do find work earn more than $7,000 a year.[14] Many live in shacks, adobe huts, even abandoned automobiles. Incidence of illness and disease is significantly higher among Native Americans than among the white population; for example, in 1988 the tuberculosis rate was more than five times higher than that of the population as a whole.[15] Unsanitary housing, unsafe water, and

---

[11] Data provided by Bureau of Indian Affairs, U.S. Department of the Interior.

[12] In fiscal 1991, a dozen agencies of the federal government spent an estimated $4.7 billion on programs for Native Americans. Data provided by the Office of Management and Budget.

[13] U.S. Bureau of the Census, General Social and Economic Characteristics, *1980 Census of Population, United States Summary*, p. 162.

[14] Bureau of Indian Affairs, U.S. Department of the Interior, *Indian Service Population and Labor Force Estimates*, January 1991.

[15] Indian Health Service, U.S. Department of Health and Human Services, *Trends in Indian Health 1991*, p. 53.

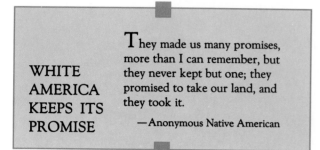

WHITE
AMERICA
KEEPS ITS
PROMISE

They made us many promises, more than I can remember, but they never kept but one; they promised to take our land, and they took it.

—Anonymous Native American

malnutrition all contribute to ill health among Native Americans. The percentage of Native American teenagers enrolled in school is only half the national average, and the proportion who graduate from college is less than half that of other Americans.[16] The suicide rate among Native Americans is higher than that of all Americans, and among Native Americans aged fifteen to twenty-four, nearly twice as high as the national average.[17] Although the rate of deaths from alcoholism among Native Americans has decreased in recent years, it is more than five times as high as the national average.[18]

The federal government has been deeply involved in the history of the white man's broken promises to the Native Americans. Until 1871 the government treated Indian tribes as separate, sovereign nations. After that, the government stopped making treaties with the tribes and adopted a policy of breaking down the tribal structure. The Dawes Act of 1887 divided reservations into small allotments; but the land not distributed to individuals was put up for public sale. Between 1887 and 1934, some 90 million acres of land were removed from tribal hands in one way or another. When the Indian Reorganization Act of 1934 ended the practice of breaking up the reservations, the tribes regained some of their vitality.

In 1953 Congress adopted a policy declaration designed to end the special trustee relationship between the federal government and Native Americans. This policy of "forced termination" was almost unanimously opposed by the Native Americans, who feared that without federal protection their lands and cultural identity would vanish. Finally in 1974 Congress passed

the Indian Self-Determination and Education Assistance Act, which ended the policy of forced termination and gave Native American tribes control over federal programs on their reservations.

In recent years, Native Americans have had some success in recovering lands taken by the government. In 1980, after a long court case, Congress passed the Maine Indian Claims Settlement Act. Under it, the federal government agreed to pay the claimants $84 million and return 300,000 acres as compensation for 12.5 million acres of land originally taken by the federal government. Later that year, 60,000 Sioux were awarded $122.5 million by the U.S. Supreme Court in compensation for 7,000,000 acres taken by Congress in the Black Hills.[19] In 1988, the Puyallups dropped their claim to valuable land in Tacoma, Washington, in return for $162 million in cash, acreage, and jobs. And in 1991, President Bush signed legislation to recognize the Aroostook Band of the Micmacs in Maine, who had been omitted from the 1980 settlement in that state.

Beset by poverty, disease, illiteracy, substandard housing, and the threat of forced cultural assimilation, Native Americans felt they had long overdue claims on the American political system. Beginning in the 1960s, Native Americans added their voices to the protests of other minorities. In 1972 several hundred Native Americans came to Washington and occupied the Bureau of Indian Affairs (BIA). The protesters arrived in a caravan they called "The Trail of Broken Treaties." They pitched a twenty-foot-high tepee on the lawn, flew the American flag upside down at half-staff, and for six days barricaded themselves inside the bureau to dramatize their demands. Even before the occupation of the building, much of the militancy had been directed at the BIA, which makes decisions affecting the lives of Native Americans but has traditionally been controlled by white executives.

In 1973, 200 armed supporters of the American Indian Movement (AIM) seized the tiny village of Wounded Knee on the Pine Ridge Indian Reservation in South Dakota. The militants had chosen their target carefully and with a shrewd understanding of modern mass communications. For Wounded Knee was the site of the massacre of at least 153 Sioux by the United States Army in 1890, and it was part of the title of a best-selling book.[20] The town's occupation stirred na-

---

[16] Data provided by Indian Health Service, U.S. Department of Health and Human Services.
[17] *Trends in Indian Health 1991*, p. 32.
[18] Data provided by Indian Health Service, U.S. Department of Health and Human Services.

[19] *United States v. Sioux Nation of Indians*, 448 U.S. 371 (1980).
[20] Dee Brown, *Bury My Heart at Wounded Knee* (New York: Holt, Rinehart and Winston, 1970).

1973: The Second Battle of Wounded Knee

tional attention and attracted network television coverage. For seventy days, U.S. marshals surrounded the village; although the marshals were determined to avoid another massacre, two Native American supporters were killed in exchanges of gunfire, and one federal agent was paralyzed by a bullet.

In one sense, the occupation was a protest against poverty, federal policy, and the paternalism of the Bureau of Indian Affairs. But the seizure also involved an internal political struggle among the protesters. After more than two months, the militants surrendered under a peace agreement. The Second Battle of Wounded Knee was over, but the broader problems faced by Native Americans remained.

Hispanic Americans

Like Native Americans, Americans of Hispanic origin must contend with the twin problems of discrimination and poverty.

Of the total Hispanic American population of 21.4 million, almost two-thirds, or 13.4 million, are Mexican Americans. The majority of the Mexican Americans in the United States live in five states of the Southwest, where they compose the largest single minority group. California has the largest Mexican American population, followed by Texas. Other Mexican Americans are concentrated in smaller numbers in New Mexico, Arizona, and Colorado.

Table 5-1
Number of Hispanic Americans in California and the Southwest, 1990

State	Number of Hispanics
California	7,688,000
Texas	4,340,000
New Mexico	579,000
Arizona	688,000
Colorado	424,000

SOURCE: U.S. Bureau of the Census. Figures are rounded.

AMERICA THE BEAUTIFUL

For a child born with brown skin in one of the southern tier of states, of farm-migrant parents who speak a different language from most Americans, the future is already charted.

The young Chicano—or Mexican American—migrant will move with his parents through the citrus groves of Florida or California, stoop over the beans and tomatoes in Texas, hoe sugarbeets in western Kansas, crawl through the potato fields of Idaho and Maine and pick cherries in Michigan, moving with the season and the harvests.

He will sleep, crowded with his family in shells of migrant housing without heat, refrigeration or sanitary facilities. He will splash barefoot through garbage-strewn mud infested with internal parasites and drink polluted water provided in old oil drums.

By the age of 12 he will have the face of an adult and his shoulders will form in a permanent stoop. He will acquire the rough dry skin and the pipestem arms and legs that indicate a lack of vitamins and proteins. He will be surrounded by children infected with diseases of the intestines, blood, mouth, eyes and ears and thus condemned to poor learning records at school—when they are able to attend school at all.

That was the picture of the Chicano's life painted at a Senate subcommittee hearing last week. Dr. Raymond M. Wheeler, a Southern physician who had served on a team studying health conditions of the migrants, told the Senators: "The children we saw have no future in our society. Malnutrition since birth has already impaired them physically, mentally and emotionally."

—*New York Times*, July 26, 1970

According to one Census Bureau study, more than 28 percent of all Hispanic and Mexican American families were living in poverty—compared to a national average of 13.5 percent. The median income for Mexican Americans was $8,874 a year.[21] Unemployment was substantially higher than that of the rest of the population. Fewer than half of adult Mexican Americans had completed high school, much lower than the rate for the nation as a whole.[22]

Between 1951 and 1964, hundreds of thousands of Mexican migrant laborers entered the United States temporarily as farm workers under the "bracero" program enacted by Congress. Millions of others have entered the country illegally to join the ranks of the migrants.

Many migrants, whether legal or not, live and work under the most difficult conditions. They perform backbreaking stoop labor in the fields under the hot sun, risking injury from insecticides used to protect the crops. Often they must live in shacks without electricity or running water, their health endangered by open sewage and other unsanitary conditions. Migrant Mexican American workers have a life expectancy much shorter than the national average, and a much higher birth rate and infant mortality rate.

Farm workers are not covered by the National Labor Relations Act, and they have encountered great obstacles in organizing labor unions. In 1970 Cesar Chavez and his United Farm Workers won a five-year strike against grape growers in central California. Chavez's effort, aided by a nationwide boycott of table grapes by consumers in sympathy with the strike, helped to focus national attention on "La Causa," as the grape workers called their movement, and on "La Raza," the Mexican Americans themselves. In 1975 California passed legislation generally providing for farm workers the same rights held by union members in other industries. The landmark farm labor bill was a victory for Chavez.

During the 1960s, Chavez had emerged as an extraordinary figure, a quiet but determined man who became a symbol of the *Chicanos* (as many Mexican Americans proudly call themselves) while leading his union in the fight against the grape growers. Chavez's childhood reads like a passage in John Steinbeck's Depression-era novel, *The Grapes of Wrath*. His parents were Mexican migrant workers. Following the seasons, the family traveled back and forth between California's

---

[21] *New York Times*, January 19, 1992. Data from Census Bureau as of 1989.
[22] Ibid.

Cesar Chavez

Imperial and San Joaquin valleys. By the time Chavez finished the eighth grade he had attended *thirty-seven* schools. Eventually the family settled in a slum neighborhood near San Jose called, appropriately, by its residents "Sal Si Puedes" ("get out if you can"). Chavez began organizing his union in 1962; within six years, the United Farm Workers had 17,000 members. But by the early 1980s, Chavez and his union faced serious problems, and the UFW had lost some of its power.

Chavez's career has been closely linked to his cultural identity as a Mexican American. A biographer captured some of this while describing Chavez speaking to a group of Mexican American students:

> In the Union we're just beginning, and you're just beginning. Mexican American youth is just beginning to wake up. Five years ago we didn't have this feeling. Nobody wanted to be *chicanos*, they wanted to be anything but *chicanos*. But three months ago I went to San Jose State

"WHAT IS THE WORTH OF A MAN?"

In 1979 Cesar Chavez led a strike by his United Farm Workers against the lettuce growers of California. On February 9, in the Imperial Valley, Rufino Contreras, a young lettuce worker taking part in the strike, was shot to death during a clash between pickets and non-union workers. He left a widow and two young children. Two foremen and an equipment operator, all employees of the owner of the farm where Contreras died, were charged with murder, but the case was later dismissed.

Reporter Laurie Becklund of the *Los Angeles Times* attended the funeral and filed this account:

> CALEXICO — Rufino Contreras, the 27-year-old lettuce picker who was shot to death on Saturday, was buried here Wednesday morning after an outdoor mariachi funeral mass in which he was mourned as a martyr by more than 7000 United Farm Workers of America members and their families.
>
> "Rufino is not dead," UFW President Cesar Chavez said in his eulogy. "Wherever farm workers organize, stand up for their rights and strike for justice, Rufino Contreras is with them."

> Sitting in . . . the front row of a flower-filled shrine where the Mass was celebrated was Rosa Contreras, the young man's widow. . . . Clutching her 5-year-old son to her, she seemed oblivious to the labor leader's words.
>
> "Mis hijos," she said time after time, leaning her head back and moaning, tears running down her thin, youthful face. "My children, children of my heart. Where is their father; where are you, Fino?"
>
> "What is the worth of a man?" Chavez asked during his eulogy. "Rufino and his father and his brother together gave the company 20 years of their labor. . . ." The cries of Contreras's young widow could be heard throughout the eulogy. . . . She grabbed hold of [her son] and cried into his shoulder as if he were a man.
>
> Her other child, Nancy Berenice, 4, smiled when she saw her mother. She did not know she was supposed to cry.
>
> —*Los Angeles Times*, February 15, 1979

"A MESSAGE TO OUR PEOPLE"

BELL GARDENS, Calif., Dec. 29 — The problem with Bell Gardens, a city official said not long ago, is that "we just have too many people."

With that in mind, the City Council passed a zoning ordinance last year to control population density. But the five-member City Council was all white, while almost 90 percent of the 42,000 people squeezed into the 2.5 square miles of this gritty industrial suburb were Hispanic. The residents, most of them recent arrivals from Mexico, saw the Council's move as an attempt to drive them from their low-cost homes. Several hundred existing housing units would be affected by the ordinance.

So the immigrant population of Bell Gardens rose up and seized political power, registering voters, drawing up petitions and ousting the white mayor and three other white City Council members in a special election earlier this month.

Local politicians were stunned. . . . "They didn't think we could do it," said Josefina Macias, a school attendance assistant who was a leader of the recall movement. "We've awakened the community. They were just asleep. This sends a message to our people everywhere that they can take hold of their government."

—*New York Times*, December 30, 1991

College and they had a beautiful play in which they let everybody know that they were *chicanos*, and that *chicanos* mean something and that they were proud of it.[23]

The percentage of Hispanics, including Mexican Americans, in the general population is not reflected in the makeup of Congress. In California, for example, where Mexican Americans constitute about 16 percent of the population, only three of the forty-five members of Congress serving in 1992 — Edward R. Roybal, Matthew G. Martinez, and Esteban E. Torres — were Mexican Americans.

Hispanics have joined the ranks of other minority groups fighting for full equality in American society. In 1974 and 1982 Mexican Americans were elected governor of New Mexico, and in 1986, Bob Martinez, a Republican, was elected as Florida's first governor of Hispanic descent; later he served as the nation's "drug czar" under President Bush. By 1992 there were 14 Hispanic members of Congress; the first Hispanic member of the cabinet, Lauro F. Cavazos, had served as secretary of education, and Catalina Vasquez Villalpando was Treasurer of the United States. In the nation, 4,202 Hispanics had been elected to public office.[24]

Mexican Americans and other Hispanics have registered additional political gains, electing mayors in recent years in Denver, Santa Fe, and San Antonio, and electing members of state legislatures in Texas, California, New Mexico, Colorado, and Florida, as well as in Illinois and New York. But many Mexican Americans, desiring to preserve their own identity, have not felt the need to participate in American politics. "We are another country," said Miguel Garcia of East Los Angeles. "We have our own culture, our own language. We feel different from the rest of America."[25] Yet, when Hispanic Americans have organized politically, they often have made their voices heard. In Parlier, California, a small town near Fresno, the local council refused to appoint a Mexican American as chief of police. The Hispanic community organized, defeated three members of the council, and elected as mayor Andrew Benitez, a twenty-two-year-old Mexican American.[26]

Undocumented Immigrants

Although the precise number of undocumented immigrants in the United States is not known, the federal government has estimated that as many as 4 million or more persons are in the country illegally.[27] The majority

---

[23] Peter Matthiessen, *Sal Si Puedes: Cesar Chavez and the New American Revolution* (New York: Random House, 1969), p. 109.

[24] Harry P. Pachon, "An Overview of Hispanic Elected Officials in 1991," in *1991 National Roster of Hispanic Elected Officials* (Washington, D.C., National Association of Latino Elected and Appointed Officials Educational Fund, 1991), p. vii.

[25] *Washington Post*, March 29, 1978, p. A6.
[26] *New York Times*, April 21, 1978, p. 14.
[27] *New York Times*, May 7, 1987, p. A16.

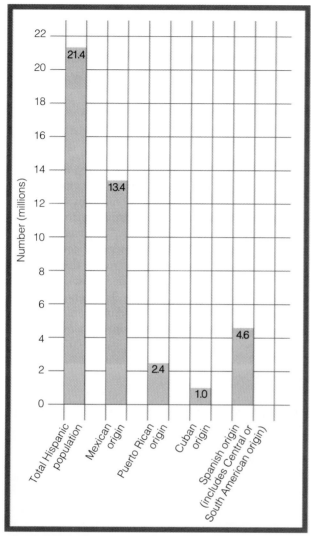

Figure 5-2
Hispanic Americans: 1991
SOURCE: U.S. Bureau of the Census.

a figure presumably far lower than the actual total. The Census Bureau estimated that another 2 million undocumented immigrants arrived during the 1980s.[29]

Some employers, particularly growers and farm owners in California and Texas, have hired undocumented workers as a source of cheap labor. But labor unions and some other groups argued that undocumented persons in the United States undermine minimum wage, health, and safety laws, and other benefits enjoyed by U.S. workers. The United States Supreme Court has ruled that states can bar the employment of persons who are in the United States illegally.[30] But the Court declared unconstitutional a state law in Texas barring the children of undocumented persons, most of them Mexicans, from attending public schools.[31]

In 1986, as noted in Chapter 4, Congress passed a major immigration bill designed to reduce the flow of undocumented immigrants by punishing employers who knowingly hired them, and by granting legal status to undocumented aliens who arrived before January 1, 1982. But Hispanic groups argued that sanctions against employers would only increase job discrimination against Hispanics.

Puerto Ricans

Puerto Rico has commonwealth status and Puerto Ricans are American citizens, with a nonvoting Resident Commissioner in the United States House of Representatives. As Americans, Puerto Ricans living on the island use U.S. currency, mails, and courts, and may receive U.S. welfare benefits and food stamps. They pay no federal taxes unless they move to the mainland. Islanders cannot vote in U.S. elections, but in 1980, for the first time, they were able to vote in primaries to express their presidential preference and to select delegates to the Democratic and Republican national conventions. They sing their own national anthem, have their own flag, and are Spanish-speaking.

Yet many of the island's residents who come to the mainland seeking a better life encounter not only a language barrier but economic and racial discrimination as well. Puerto Ricans who migrate to the mainland frequently settle in cities. If the newcomers find employment at all, it is generally in unskilled, low-paying

are Mexicans or other Latin Americans. The Census Bureau has estimated that about 70 percent of all undocumented persons are Hispanic.[28] During the 1980 census the government for the first time made a major effort to count undocumented persons, but the task was difficult. Many naturally tended to avoid census-takers or did not trust the Census Bureau's promise that the information would remain confidential. In the end, the census counted only 2 million undocumented persons,

---

[28] U.S. Bureau of the Census, Current Population Reports, *The Hispanic Population in the United States: March 1991*, series P-20, no. 455, October, 1991, p. 21.

[29] *Washington Post*, March 11, 1991, p. A5.
[30] *DeCanas* v. *Bica*, 424 U.S. 351 (1976).
[31] *Plyler* v. *Doe*, 457 U.S. 202 (1982).

jobs in hotels, restaurants, and factories. Often forced to live in substandard housing, Puerto Ricans sometimes face hostility from inner-city blacks who regard them as an economic threat. The population of Puerto Rico was 3.6 million in 1991. In the same year the U.S. Census Bureau reported that there were 2.4 million persons of Puerto Rican origin in the continental United States.[32] Of this total, about a million lived in New York City, and there were large Puerto Rican communities in Chicago, Philadelphia, Newark, and Bridgeport and Hartford, Connecticut. As in the case of many other minorities, the median income of Puerto Rican families was half that of other Americans, and the unemployment rate often much higher.

On the island itself, there has been an ongoing debate over Puerto Rico's political status, which has focused on three choices: continuing as a commonwealth; statehood; or independence. The commonwealth status for Puerto Rico was established in 1952 under Luis Muñoz Marín's Popular Democratic party. In 1967 voters in Puerto Rico voted 60 percent for commonwealth status, 39 percent for statehood, and less than 1 percent for independence.[33]

In 1976, however, the New Progressive party, which favored statehood, came to power when Carlos Romero Barceló was elected governor. Romero Barceló was reelected in 1980, but was defeated in 1984 by former governor Rafael Hernández Colón, the pro-commonwealth candidate of the Popular Democratic party, who was narrowly reelected in 1988. Two years later, Congress considered legislation to allow Puerto Ricans to vote to determine their future status; the House passed the measure but it expired in a Senate committee in 1991.

Few Puerto Ricans favor outright independence. One group that does, the Puerto Rican Armed Forces of National Liberation (FALN), claimed responsibility for more than fifty bombings in the mid-1970s in New York City and elsewhere on the mainland, which caused a number of deaths. In 1979 President Carter freed four Puerto Rican nationalists from jail. They had served long prison terms after attempting in 1950 to assassinate President Truman and firing shots at members of Congress on the floor of the U.S. House of Representatives.

Like other minority groups, Puerto Ricans in the United States have evidenced growing cultural pride and political awareness in recent years. In several cities, Puerto Rican citizen groups have organized to work for such goals as better education — particularly bilingual school programs — and employment.

Asian Americans

The 7.3 million Asian Americans counted in the 1990 census made up the fastest-growing minority group in the United States. Over a decade, the number of Asian Americans more than doubled, growing from 3.5 million in 1980, an increase of almost 108 percent. By the beginning of the 1990s, Asian Americans constituted 3 percent of the population and were the third-largest minority, ranking in size just after African Americans (about 12 percent) and Hispanics (9 percent).

The largest group of Asian Americans were persons of Chinese heritage, who comprised almost 23 per-

[32] U.S. Bureau of the Census, Current Population Reports, *The Hispanic Population in the United States: March 1991*, series P-20, no. 455, October, 1991, p. 2.

[33] Some supporters of independence boycotted the referendum, however.

Table 5-2
Asian Americans in the United States, 1990

Asians or Pacific Islanders, by Group	Total	Percent
	7,273,662	100.
Chinese	1,645,472	22.6
Filipino	1,406,770	19.3
Japanese	847,562	11.7
Asian Indian	815,447	11.2
Korean	798,849	11.0
Vietnamese	614,547	8.4
Hawaiian	211,014	2.9
Samoan	62,964	0.9
Guamanian	49,345	0.7
Other Asian or Pacific Islander	821,692	11.3

SOURCE: Data provided by U.S. Bureau of the Census.

Army Specialist Melissa Rathbun-Nealy

cent of the total, followed by Filipino Americans and Japanese Americans. (See Table 5-2). California, the nation's fastest-growing state, had 39 percent of all Asian Americans in the United States. Although many persons of Chinese, Japanese, and other Asian descent live in California and other western states, there has been a rapid increase in the Asian population in New York and Texas. The result was some surprising statistics. For example, there were more Asian Americans in New York (694,000) than in Hawaii (685,000).

Immigration from Vietnam, India, and Korea increased at the fastest rate during the decade and helped to swell the tide of newcomers from Asia. Although the stereotype of the Korean grocer or Asian owner of a retail store had some basis in fact, it was also true that Asian Americans included a successful professional class of scientists, engineers, and physicians. The rapid increase in the numbers of Asian Americans was bound to have a continuing political and cultural impact, not only in California, but in many other areas of the country as well.

Women

Early in 1991, the United States was at war in the Persian Gulf. The images that flashed across the television screens in American living rooms showed women as well as men risking their lives in that war. More than 35,000 women served in the Gulf, fifteen died, and two

were taken prisoner.[34] The nightly news showed pictures of Army Major Marie Rossi, who was killed when her helicopter went down in Saudi Arabia, and Army Specialist Melissa Rathbun-Nealy, an Army POW who fell into Iraqi hands but was safely released after the war.

When the conflict began, women were officially barred from combat; as a practical matter, they were exposed to the hazards of war. In 1991, after the war had ended, Congress voted to relax the restrictions somewhat, by letting women in the Air Force and Navy fly combat missions. But many women in the military, and civilians as well, remained angered by the broader, more general ban on the use of women in combat. In 1992, more than 220,000 women served in the military, making up more than 11 percent of the nearly two million total personnel in the armed services.

---

[34] Of the total of fifteen dead, four were killed by enemy action—including three women who died when an Iraqi Scud missile hit their barracks—and eleven died in accidents or of natural causes.

A GOVERN-
MENT OF MEN?

What goes largely unexamined, often even unacknowledged (yet is institutionalized nonetheless) in our social order, is the birthright priority whereby males rule females. Through this system a most ingenious form of "interior colonization" has been achieved. It is one which tends moreover to be sturdier than any form of segregation, and more rigorous than class stratification, more uniform, certainly more enduring. However muted its present appearance may be, sexual dominion obtains nevertheless as perhaps the most pervasive ideology of our culture and provides its most fundamental concept of power.

This is so because our society, like all other historical civilizations, is a patriarchy. The fact is evident at once if one recalls that the military, industry, technology, universities, science, political office, and finance — in short, every avenue of power within the society, including the coercive force of the police, is entirely in male hands. As the essence of politics is power, such realization cannot fail to carry impact.

—Kate Millett, *Sexual Politics*

The war in the Persian Gulf was perhaps the most dramatic testimony thus far of the fact that the role of women in American society was changing rapidly. That had become clear even seven years earlier, in 1984, when Geraldine Ferraro, a 48-year-old member of Congress from New York, accepted the Democratic nomination for vice-president at San Francisco. The cheering delegates at the national convention and the millions who watched televison knew they were witness to an historic moment in American politics.

For the first time, a major party had selected a woman for the second highest office in the land. Walter F. Mondale, the Democratic presidential nominee, had chosen the Queens Democrat several days before in a move that electrified the nation and gave his campaign new momentum for a time.

The Mondale-Ferraro ticket was defeated by President Reagan and Vice-President George Bush. But by 1992 women had occupied high office in all three branches of the government. In that year, a woman associate justice, Sandra Day O'Connor, sat on the Supreme Court. Two women served in the cabinet, and 31 women were members of Congress.[35] Women comprised 18 percent of state legislators, and served as mayors in 151 cities.[36]

Much of the progress toward equal rights and full participation in American society achieved by women in recent decades can be credited to the Women's Liberation movement. The movement, which began in the 1970s, changed the way that Americans think and act about the role of women in the family and in society. Women proved they could combine careers and child-rearing, and by the 1990s, the two-income family in which both husband and wife worked, was as common as it had been rare a few decades earlier.

Although the organized effort to end sex discrimination in American society was generally known as Women's Liberation, or the women's movement, it encompassed many different groups. And it drew support from many people of both sexes who were not actively engaged in the Women's Liberation movement but agreed with the objectives of full equality for women.

Yet the gains made by women on the political front could hardly conceal the barriers faced by women in almost every aspect of American society and the glaring economic inequalities between men and women. How many women were chief executive officers of the top 500 American corporations, for example? The answer in 1992 was dismaying: exactly one.[37] Many women in the corporate world faced a "glass ceiling," an unacknowledged obstacle that limited how high they could rise.

Despite impressive advances, American women still struggled for equality in the marketplace. The median income of women was only 71 percent of that of

---

[35] In 1992, there were 29 women in the House (including one non-voting delegate from the District of Columbia) and two in the Senate.

[36] Data provided by Congressional Caucus for Women.

[37] She was Linda J. Wachner, the head of Warnaco, Inc., a manufacturer of lingerie and men's sportswear. The company was the only one headed by a woman to appear on the "*Fortune* 500" list of major American corporations. Data provided by National Association for Female Executives.

DIANE JOYCE WINS HER CASE

In Santa Clara County, California, south of San Francisco, Diane Joyce had a job shoveling asphalt and patching potholes for the county road agency. After four years, she applied for a promotion to a desk job as a dispatcher.

At the time, in 1980, not one of the agency's 238 skilled positions was held by a woman. Two years earlier, the county had enacted a voluntary affirmative action program to correct the statistical imbalance.

Paul Johnson, a white male, who had worked for the transportation agency for thirteen years, also applied for the job. He scored two points higher than Diane Joyce on an examination for the position. Joyce got the job, and her male competitor sued.

Eventually, the case made its way to the United States Supreme Court. Although the Court had previously upheld the principle of affirmative action to remedy past discrimination against blacks and other minorities, it had never ruled specifically whether women might be entitled to preferential treatment.

In 1987, the Court decided 6–3 in favor of Diane Joyce. It held that it was permissible for Santa Clara County to take sex and race into account in making its employment decisions because of a "conspicuous imbalance" in the number of men and women assigned to certain jobs. "We therefore hold," Justice William Brennan wrote for the majority, "that the agency appropriately took into account as one factor the sex of Diane Joyce in determining that she should be promoted to the road dispatcher position."

"I knew I could do the job from the beginning," Joyce said.

—*Johnson v. Transportation Agency*, Santa Clara County (1987), the *Washington Post*, March 26, 1987, and *Time*, April 6, 1987

---

men. The stereotype of the female office worker as a secretary was all too real. In 1991, 61.7 million women workers in the United States composed 46 percent of the labor force. Yet women held 80 percent of all clerical jobs. Only 43 percent of working women, but 65 percent of working men, earned $15,000 or more in 1990.[38] These statistics reflected the fact that many companies do not promote women to executive-level jobs. And even when women were hired in professional and executive positions, they earned considerably less than their male counterparts. (See Figure 5-3.) On the other hand, more women were entering the prestigious professions of law and medicine; beginning in the 1970s, the number of women graduating from medical and law schools rose dramatically, from 1,500 in 1970 to 20,672 in 1990.[39]

Although the last legal barriers to equal employment of women by the federal government were removed in 1962, the bureaucracy was not exempt from the bias against employment of women prevailing in private industry. In 1990, for example, women comprised just under half of all federal white-collar workers, but held only 41 percent of the professional, administrative, and technical jobs.[40]

One of the most significant social developments of the past two decades has been the dramatic increase in the number of employed women, who for the first time outnumber those at home. By 1992, 55 percent of adult American women held jobs outside the home. (By comparison, in 1970, 41 percent held jobs outside the home.)[41]

Clearly, and despite the continuing barriers, American women, if they so chose, were no longer limited to home, kitchen, and children (even though some TV commercials persist in showing stereotyped women comparing laundry detergents and floor waxes). As Carol A. Whitehurst has suggested, "Women, today, seldom think in terms of career versus marriage, but

---

[38] U.S. Bureau of the Census, Current Population Reports, *Money Income of Households, Families, and Persons in the United States: 1990*, series P-60, no. 174, August, 1991, pp. 160, 162, 164, 167.

[39] Data provided by National Center for Education Statistics, U.S. Department of Education.

[40] Office of Personnel Management, *Federal Civilian Workforce Statistics*, Affirmative Employment Statistics, September 30, 1990, Table 3.

[41] Bureau of Labor Statistics, U.S. Department of Labor, *Employment and Earnings*, January, 1992, Table 3, p. 164.

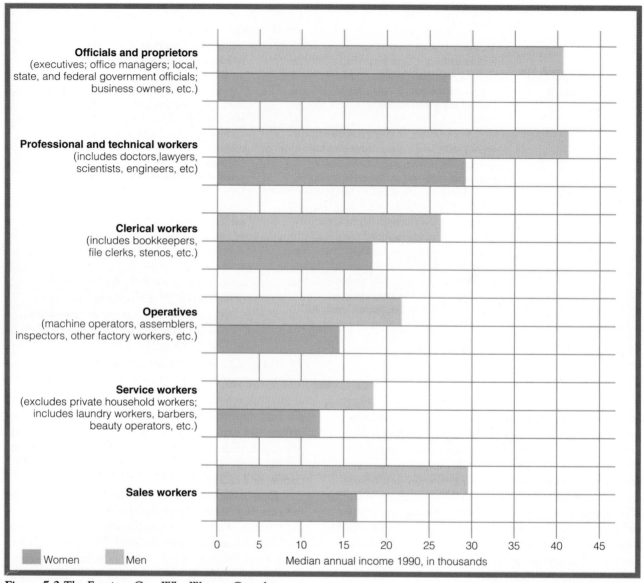

Figure 5-3 The Earnings Gap: Why Women Complain
SOURCE: U.S. Bureau of the Census.

instead believe that they can successfully combine the two. As an increased number of women enter the labor force and the time spent on motherhood shortens, careers become more attractive to women, and old negative images of women with careers begin to decline." [42]

In June of 1983 Sally K. Ride, a thirty-two-year-old physicist from Encino, California, became the first

American woman to travel in outer space. She was a crew member of the space shuttle Challenger, which lifted off from Cape Canaveral, Florida, on a successful six-day mission. In August 1984 Judith A. Resnick became the second American woman in space as a crew member aboard the space shuttle Discovery; in January 1986 she died tragically with five other astronauts and Christa McAuliffe, a New Hampshire schoolteacher, when the space shuttle Challenger blew up shortly after launch. In October 1984, Dr. Kathryn D. Sullivan became the first American woman to walk in space. De-

[42] Carol A. Whitehurst, *Women in America: The Oppressed Majority* (Santa Monica: Goodyear Publishing Company, Inc., 1977), p. 69.

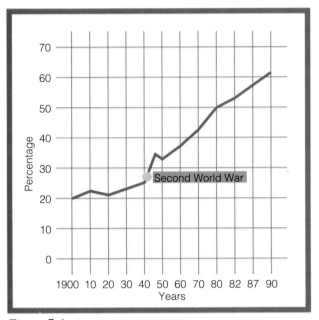

Figure 5-4
How Many Women Work: The Percentage of Women over Age 16 in the Labor Force

spite these gains for women in some areas, the Constitution did not specifically guarantee equal rights for women. For more than a decade, the women's movement struggled but failed to pass a constitutional amendment to secure those rights.

In 1972, Congress proposed such an amendment to eliminate discrimination against women. The Equal Rights Amendment (ERA) said simply: "Equality of rights under the law shall not be denied or abridged by the United States or by any state on account of sex." Congress provided that the amendment would have become part of the Constitution if ratified by legislatures of three-fourths of the states within seven years, a deadline later extended until 1982. The Equal Rights Amendment was aimed at state laws that discriminate against women in such areas as marriage, property ownership, and employment. It would also have nullified certain laws favoring women, and would have made women legally subject to military service if there were a draft.

In some states opponents of the ERA argued that the amendment would mean "unisex" public toilets or other mingling of the sexes in public facilities. Charges of this kind frightened many voters, even though supporters of the amendment contended that the right of privacy, which has been recognized by the Supreme Court, would permit reasonable separation of sexes in public facilities. But perhaps the most effective argument used by opponents of the ERA was that the amendment somehow represented an attack on the sanctity of the home, that it undermined the concept of the man as head of the household and the woman as homemaker, receiving special protection under the law. The battle over the ERA thus represented a philosophical conflict between the older, more traditional concept of the role of women and a newer view of women as both liberated and fully equal. In 1982, the amendment fell three states short of the thirty-eight necessary to win ratification.

By 1992, sixteen states had equal rights provisions in their constitutions. And the issue of equal rights for women was receiving increasing attention in state courts. In Illinois, for example, a court ruled that a mother may not be automatically preferred over the father in awarding custody of children in a divorce. A court in the state of Washington ruled that it was unconstitutional under the state ERA to bar girls from playing football with boys.

In 1972, Congress enacted a law barring discrimination because of a person's sex by schools and colleges that receive federal funds. As a result of the law, Title IX of the Education Amendments of 1972, many schools upgraded their athletic programs for women, for example. In 1984, however, the Supreme Court ruled that the law applied only to the specific departments or programs that received federal money, not to the educational institution as a whole.[43] This narrower view of the law had been supported by the Reagan administration, reversing the policy of three previous administrations. In 1988 Congress, over President Reagan's veto, passed a law to undo the Supreme Court decision. As a result, federal anti-discrimination laws once again apply to an entire institution if any department or program receives federal funds.

Laws benefiting women were to some extent a reflection of the growth of the feminist movement in America. The women's movement, one study concluded, "has developed a sophisticated organizational structure and has established itself as a significant presence in national policy making."[44] Feminists, the same study suggested, had an important impact on the adoption of Title IX, as well as on the passage of other laws

---

[43] *Grove City* v. *Bell*, 465 U.S. 555 (1984).
[44] Joyce Gelb and Marian Lief Palley, *Women and Public Policies* (Princeton: Princeton University Press, 1982), p. 4.

providing equal credit opportunities for women and extending disability benefits to pregnant women.[45]

Such laws, whether at the federal or state level, were designed to secure equal *legal* rights for women. But the issue of women's rights was much broader than that.

Rulings by the Supreme Court — even passage of an equal rights amendment — would not ensure immediate equality for women. "So widespread and pervasive are discriminatory practices against women, they have come to be regarded, more often than not, as normal," a presidential task force reported. "American women are increasingly aware and restive over the denial of equal opportunity, equal responsibility, even equal protection of the law. An abiding concern for home and children should not, in their view, cut them off from the freedom to choose the role in society to which their interest, education, and training entitle them."[46]

In 1981 the Supreme Court ruled that the government may exclude women from the military draft and registration for it. "The Constitution requires that Congress treat similarly situated persons similarly, not that it engage in gestures of superficial equality."[47]

In 1980 more than half of the first women graduates of the United States Military Academy at West Point were assigned to combat branches at their own request. They were barred by law, however, from assignments likely to involve close combat.[48]

As already noted, during the Persian Gulf war in 1991, the debate over whether women should serve in combat became somewhat moot. Officially, women were barred from combat in that conflict; in reality they were exposed to the dangers of war.

Two major groups represent women's rights, the National Women's Political Caucus and the National Organization for Women. The Caucus, with 25,000 members in forty-five states, was founded in 1971. It helped to increase the number of women delegates to the national party conventions in 1972 and the total of women elected to public office that year. The Caucus emphasizes political goals, including the election and appointment of more women to public office, and the

improvement of social conditions for minorities and the poor through legislation. The organization has worked to defeat state legislators who voted against ratification of the Equal Rights Amendment.

The number of women holding public office has increased noticeably since the women's movement began. Yet, in the entire history of the United States, through 1992, 134 women had served in the Congress compared to more than 12,000 men.[49]

President Carter named three women to cabinet posts: Juanita Kreps to Commerce, Patricia Harris to Housing and Urban Development and later to Health and Human Services, and Shirley Hufstedler to Education. President Reagan named Margaret M. Heckler as Secretary of Health and Human Services, Elizabeth Hanford Dole as Secretary of Transportation, Ann McLaughlin as Secretary of Labor, and Jeane J. Kirkpatrick as American ambassador to the United Nations. President Bush named Mrs. Dole as Secretary of Labor and replaced her with Lynn Martin. He also named Barbara Hackman Franklin as Secretary of Commerce. In 1992 there were three women governors, in Texas, Kansas, and Oregon. The number of women in state legislatures had more than quadrupled, from 305 (4.1 percent) in 1969 to 1,349 (18 percent).[50]

The National Organization for Women (NOW), founded in 1966, shares some of the political aims of the National Women's Political Caucus but places more emphasis on issues pertaining specifically to the status of women. NOW, with more than 250,000 members, has worked to improve equal employment opportunities for women, campaigned for the Equal Rights Amendment, defended the rights of lesbians, and supported the reform of laws dealing with women. NOW opposes all aspects of sex discrimination and is pledged to "take action to bring women into full participation in the mainstream of American society now, assuming all the privileges and responsibilities . . . in fully equal partnership with men."

Many issues sometimes seen as primarily affecting women are not "women's issues" at all, but concern the entire society. One example is the issue of sexual harassment, which dramatically came to the attention of millions of Americans in the fall of 1991 when the Senate

---

[45] Ibid., p. 5.

[46] *A Matter of Simple Justice*, The Report of the President's Task Force on Women's Rights and Responsibilities (Washington, D.C.: U.S. Government Printing Office, 1970), p. iii.

[47] *Rostker v. Goldberg*, 453 U.S. 57 (1981).

[48] *New York Times*, January 25, 1980, p. 1.

[49] Data on women provided by Center for Women in American Politics. Of the 134 women who have served in Congress, 16 were elected to the Senate, 120 to the House, and two served in both the House and Senate.

[50] Data provided by Congressional Caucus for Women.

Anita Hill

Clarence Thomas

Judiciary Committee was considering the nomination to the Supreme Court of Judge Clarence Thomas. Anita Hill, a thirty-five-year-old law professor at the University of Oklahoma and a former aide to Thomas, stunned the nation with her graphic testimony to the Senate committee accusing Thomas of sexual harassment. According to Hill, Thomas spoke to her about pornographic materials, sex organs, and sexual acts, and repeatedly asked to date her. Thomas denied all of Hill's charges, accused the committee of conducting a televised, "high-tech lynching," and was eventually confirmed by the panel, and then by the full Senate, 52–48. Senators and television viewers who followed the hearings were left puzzled as to whether Thomas or his accuser was telling the truth, but there was no doubt that the hearings had sensitized many American men to an issue that they had not taken seriously before. One poll taken at the time reported that 53 percent of men said they had engaged in behavior that women might interpret as sexual harassment; the same survey reported that 38 percent of women felt they had been subjected to sexual harassment at work.[51]

---

[51] *New York Times*, October 11, 1991, p. A1.

The Senate hearings had a noticeable political effect as well. In the midst of the hearings, seven women members of the House marched up the steps of the Capitol in an attempt to explain their viewpoint to their Senate colleagues; they did not succeed, but the photographs and television images of the determined Congresswomen made an indelible impression in the mind of the public. Many women were outraged at the treatment of Hill by a group of white male Senators, and particularly by Senator Arlen Specter's controversial charge that Hill had committed "flat-out perjury."

As a result, more women participated in the 1992 elections, both as campaign workers and as candidates. For example, there were 130 women candidates for the House of Representatives that year, almost double the number in any previous year, and 18 women candidates for the Senate. Senator Specter, who ran for re-election in 1992, found himself in an unusually difficult campaign as a result of his aggressive questioning of, and comments about, Hill. His opponent, Lynn H. Yeakel, a previously unknown fund-raiser for women's charities, won the Democratic primary in a race in which she emphasized the issue of Specter's treatment of Hill. In Illinois, Carol Moseley Braun won the Democratic nomination for Senate, defeating Senator Alan J.

Lynn Yeakel

Carol Moseley Braun

Dixon, an entrenched incumbent. She, too, had entered the race because of her anger over the confirmation of Justice Clarence Thomas. In California, two women, Dianne Feinstein, the former mayor of San Francisco, and Congresswoman Barbara Boxer, won Democratic primary contests for two separate nominations for United States Senate seats.

Abortion By 1992, probably no issue divided American society as sharply as the controversy over abortion. For more than two decades, abortion has been a politically volatile social issue. On one side are a majority of

"pro-choice" women and men who support the right of a woman to have an abortion to terminate a pregnancy. Many women feel that state regulation of pregnancies violates their right of privacy. "Pro-choice" groups, such as the Planned Parenthood Federation of America, argue that women have the right to control their reproductive systems and to make decisions about their own bodies.

Other, "pro-life" Americans — including many women — strongly disagree. Legalized abortion has been deplored by the Roman Catholic Church; many Americans feel abortions are a form of murder and violate the rights of unborn children. To an extent, therefore, the moral and legal arguments revolve around the question of when life begins. The anti-abortion forces argue that life begins the moment of conception, but that view has not been accepted either by the pro-choice forces or by the United States Supreme Court.

In 1973 a Supreme Court decision gave dramatic evidence of the shifting social attitudes in America and the concerns of the women's movement. In the case of *Roe* v. *Wade*, the Court ruled 7–2 that no state may interfere with a woman's right to have an abortion during the first three months of pregnancy.[52] The decision in effect struck down laws restricting abortion in forty-six states. Reaffirming its decision, the Supreme Court in 1983 invalidated various state laws designed to make it more difficult to obtain legal abortions.[53] Again in 1986 the Supreme Court narrowly reaffirmed its landmark decision in *Roe* v. *Wade* by establishing a constitutional right to abortion. It did so by voting 5–4 to strike down a Pennsylvania law that discouraged abortions.[54] A year later, the Court invalidated an Illinois law that would have required teenagers to notify their parents before having abortions.[55]

The Supreme Court's 1973 guidelines in *Roe* v. *Wade* had severely limited the power of a state government to regulate abortions. During the first three months, or trimester of a pregnancy, the decision was up to the woman and her physician. During the last six months, the state could regulate abortion procedures, but only during the last ten weeks could a state ban abortions (except where necessary to preserve the life or health of the mother). The Court reasoned that a child

[52] *Roe* v. *Wade*, 410 U.S. 113 (1973); *Doe* v. *Bolton*, 410 U.S. 179 (1973).

[53] *Akron* v. *Akron Center for Reproductive Health, Inc.*, 462 U.S. 416 (1983).

[54] *Thornburgh* v. *American College of Obstetricians and Gynecologists*, 476 U.S. 747 (1986).

[55] *Hartigan* v. *Zbaraz*, 484 U.S. 171 (1987).

THE REAL JANE ROE

Norma McCorvey, a slight, green-eyed carnival worker known as "Pixie" to her friends, was raped by three men as she returned to her motel one night in 1969.

Her pregnancy set off a social revolution. McCorvey, then 21, did not want the baby. The product of a broken home in Dallas, she was a high school dropout, a bride and mother at 16, a divorcee within a year, a troubled and impoverished young woman who considered herself one of life's losers.

Under the pseudonym of Jane Roe, her case, *Roe* v. *Wade*, became the landmark 1973 Supreme Court decision overturning anti-abortion laws in Texas and in other states . . . one of the most contro-

versial and hotly debated in the court's history. . . .

Few court decisions have had a more immediate impact on such a personal aspect of American life. According to the Alan Guttmacher Institute, a research affiliate of the Planned Parenthood Federation of America:

An estimated 13 million abortions, involving 9 million American women, have been performed during the decade.

The number of abortions performed annually grew from 744,600 in 1973 to 1.55 million in 1980. . . .

—*Washington Post*, January 23, 1983

born during the last ten weeks of normal pregnancy is presumed to be capable of survival. In the wake of the Supreme Court's decision, medical authorities have estimated more than 1.5 million American women a year have abortions to terminate unwanted pregnancies.

As a result of the Supreme Court's decision in *Roe* v. *Wade*, the National Right to Life Committee was formed. This committee and other "pro-life" groups

sought to overturn the Supreme Court's ruling by bringing about an amendment to the Constitution to prohibit abortions. By 1992 only nineteen of the thirty-four states needed had passed resolutions calling for a constitutional convention to consider an anti-abortion amendment. But anti-abortion groups became a powerful force in a number of political campaigns, where they have opposed candidates who favor legalized abortion.

Although abortions became legal after *Roe* v. *Wade*, the Supreme Court's decision did not settle the question of who should pay for abortions. In 1977 the Court ruled that states did not have to spend Medicaid funds for elective abortions—those not "medically necessary" to preserve the health of the mother.[56] In the meantime, Congress in 1976 had passed a controversial amendment sponsored by Representative Henry J. Hyde, an Illinois Republican. The Hyde amendment banned federal Medicaid payments for abortions, even those medically necessary, except in cases of rape or incest or where the mother's life was "endangered." In 1980 the Supreme Court, by a vote of 5–4, upheld the Hyde amendment.[57] The result was that poor women could no longer count on the government paying for abortions; Medicaid had been paying for an estimated 300,000 abortions a year.

[56] *Maher* v. *Roe*, 432 U.S. 464 (1977).
[57] *Harris* v. *McRae*, 448 U.S. 297 (1980).

SOME GROUPS IN PROFILE / 151

In the meantime, anti-abortion groups remained highly vocal and in some cases highly militant. In Wichita, Kansas, in 1991, "pro-life" activists of Operation Rescue caused turmoil for 46 days by attempting to block the entrances to abortion clinics, a tactic designed to discourage women from entering to have abortions. Anti-abortion activists adopted the same strategy in Washington, D.C., Philadelphia, Buffalo, and other cities. "Pro-choice" activists in turn attempted to keep the entrances to the clinics open.

By the 1992 presidential election year, the continued political opposition to legalized abortion, along with a decided conservative shift in the makeup of the Supreme Court, had combined to create a climate in which the future of a woman's right to a legal abortion was in doubt. Three years earlier, in 1989, the Supreme Court in a Missouri case, *Webster* v. *Reproductive Health Services*, ruled 5–4 that states may impose sharp restrictions on abortions.[58] Although it stopped short of overturning *Roe* v. *Wade*, the Court held that states could regulate abortions at any stage of pregnancy, including the first three months. "For today, at least," Justice Harry A. Blackmun said in a dissent, "the law of abor-

tion stands undisturbed. . . . But the signs are evident and very ominous, and a chill wind blows."[59]

Later Supreme Court decisions seemed to march in the same anti-abortion direction. In 1990, the Court ruled in cases from Minnesota and Ohio that states may require teen-age girls to notify both parents before having an abortion.[60] And in 1991 the Court, by a vote of 5–4, upheld federal rules that barred employees of federally funded family planning clinics from discussing abortion with their patients.[61] In the spring of 1992, with a presidential election in the offing—and abortion looming as a volatile campaign issue—the Bush administration partially relaxed the rules to permit physicians at such clinics, but not other staff members, to counsel pregnant women on abortions.

Meanwhile, early in 1992, the Supreme Court agreed to hear arguments on a restrictive Pennsylvania statute, setting the stage for a major test of *Roe* v. *Wade* and of abortion rights in a congressional and presidential election year.[62] The Pennsylvania law required a

---

[58] *Webster v. Reproductive Health Services,* 492 U.S. 990 (1989).

[59] *Washington Post,* July 4, 1989, p. A1.
[60] *Hodgson v. Minnesota* 497 U.S. 417 (1990), and *Ohio v. Akron Center for Reproductive Health* 497 U.S. 502 (1990).
[61] *Rust v. Sullivan* 111 S. Ct. 1759 (1991).
[62] *Planned Parenthood of Southeastern Pennsylvania v. Casey* 112 S. Ct. 2791 (1992).

THE SUPREME COURT REAFFIRMS ROE

On June 29, 1992, the last Monday of its term, the Supreme Court reaffirmed, 5–4, the essential principles of *Roe* v. *Wade*, its 1973 decision establishing the constitutional right of women to have abortions in the early stages of pregnancy. At the same time, the Court upheld most restrictions on abortion contained in a Pennsylvania law. Following are excerpts from the majority opinion:

Our obligation is to define the liberty of all, not to mandate our own moral code. . . . These matters, involving the most intimate and personal choices a person may make in a lifetime, choices central to personal dignity and autonomy, are central to the liberty protected by the Fourteenth Amendment. At the heart of liberty is the right to define one's own concept of existence, of meaning, of the universe, and of the mystery of human life. . . .

An entire generation has come of age free to assume Roe's concept of liberty in defining the capacity of women to act in society, and to make reproductive decisions. . . . A decision to overrule Roe's essential holding under the existing circumstances would address error, if error there was, at the cost of both profound and unnecessary damage to the Court's legitimacy, and to the Nation's commitment to the rule of law. It is therefore imperative to adhere to the essence of Roe's original decision, and we do so today.

—*Planned Parenthood of Southeastern Pennsylvania v. Casey,* 1992.

married woman to tell her husband of her intent to have an abortion, compelled women to wait 24 hours before having an abortion, required doctors to counsel women on alternatives to, and the risks of, abortion, and made it compulsory for minors to get the consent of one parent or a judge before undergoing an abortion.

In June of 1992, on the last day of its term, a narrowly divided Court reaffirmed, 5-4, the constitutional right to an abortion that it had first established in *Roe v. Wade*. At the same time the Court upheld most of the restrictions in the Pennsylvania law, although it struck down the requirement that a woman notify her husband before having an abortion. The majority opinion, written by Justices Sandra Day O'Connor, Anthony M. Kennedy, and David H. Souter, held that "an entire generation" had come of age relying on the liberty of women to make reproductive choices. For the Court to overrule its own decision in *Roe v. Wade* under political pressure, the opinion said, would damage the public confidence in the Court, the "legitimacy" on which the Court's power rests.

In deciding the important Pennsylvania case, the Supreme Court relied on a new standard to judge the constitutionality of the state statute—whether its provisions created an "undue burden" that placed a "substantial obstacle" in the path of a woman seeking an abortion. In a separate opinion, Justice Blackmun joined the majority in upholding the essential principles of *Roe v. Wade*, the decision he had written almost two decades before. There had been little reason to hope that abortion rights would survive, he said. "But now, just when so many expected the darkness to fall, the flame has grown bright."

Gay Rights

According to the Kinsey Institute for Sex Research, 2 percent of American women and 4 percent of American men are exclusively homosexual, and 13 percent of women and 37 percent of men have had some homosexual experience during or after adolescence. A more recent study based on Kinsey data concluded that a somewhat lower figure, about 20 percent of American men, had such experience at some time in their lives.[63]

Although no one knows the size of the gay population in the United States, it is "certainly in the millions."[64]

Like other minority groups, gay men and lesbian women often have been discriminated against in employment, housing, and other areas. Some of this stems from a long-standing general bias against gays by many individuals; in other cases, discrimination is fueled by the opposition of conservative or religious groups who feel that homosexuality violates moral or religious precepts.

In recent years, however, changing public attitudes, the increased political power of gays, and the willingness of more gay men and women to express their sexual preferences openly—to "come out of the closet"—have given gays a greater degree of both visibility and acceptance in American society.

For example, a poll conducted by the Gallup organization in June 1992 found that 74 percent of all Americans favored equal job opportunities for homosexuals, and 57 percent thought it acceptable for gay persons to serve in the armed forces. Yet in the same Gallup survey, only 41 percent of those polled thought gay persons should be hired as elementary school teachers. Under half, 48 percent, believed that homosexual relations between consenting adults should be legal.[65] And in an earlier Gallup poll, 66 percent of Americans said they would not vote for a homosexual for president.[66]

Through a combination of court decisions, legislative action, and changing public perceptions of homosexuals, many jurisdictions have protected gay rights. By 1992, 88 communities, including such major population centers as New York, San Francisco, Boston, Detroit, Los Angeles, and Washington, D.C., had passed local laws or taken executive action to protect gay rights in employment, housing, and other areas. Twenty-one counties and eighteen states—including California, New York, Illinois, Michigan, Ohio, Pennsylvania, Massachusetts, Wisconsin, and Connecticut—had taken similar action. In 1986, however, the Supreme Court ruled 5-4 that the Constitution does not protect homosexual relations between consenting adults, even in the privacy of their homes.[67] The Court did so in upholding a Georgia law that prohibited oral or anal sex.

[63] Robert E. Fay, Charles F. Turner, Albert D. Klassen, and John H. Gagnon, "Prevalence and Patterns of Same-Gender Sexual Contact Among Men," *Science*, Vol. 243, January 20, 1989, pp. 338-48. The conclusions of the authors were based on their interpretation of a Kinsey survey taken in 1970.

[64] Elizabeth Ogg, *Changing Views of Homosexuality* (New York: Public Affairs Committee, Inc., 1978), p. 3; National Women's Political Caucus, "Gay Rights: A Position Paper."
[65] *The Gallup Poll News Service*, June 12, 1992, pp. 2-3.
[66] Gallup Opinion Index, Report No. 160, November 1978, p. 26
[67] *Bowers v. Hardwick*, 478 U.S. 186 (1986).

The justices did not rule whether the same law could be applied to heterosexuals.

The case arose when Michael Hardwick, a gay bartender in Atlanta, had failed to pay a ticket for drinking in public. A police officer with a warrant was admitted to his home, and found Hardwick in his bedroom having sex with another man. Hardwick was arrested for violating the Georgia sodomy law. Gay rights groups viewed the Supreme Court's ruling as a setback for homosexual rights. Because it upheld the right of police to enter the bedroom, many groups saw the decision as a violation of the concept of privacy that the Court had expanded in recent years.

Even before the ruling, however, twenty-five states, including California, Illinois, Ohio, and New York, had removed criminal sanctions from private sex acts by consenting adults. Yet the laws concerning gays were uneven. In the state of Washington, a teacher who had not engaged in open homosexual conduct was fired when his homosexuality became known; the U.S. Supreme Court let the decision stand.[68] In Delaware he could not have been dismissed on those grounds. Most public universities permit students to use meeting rooms to discuss gay rights, although some universities deny use of their facilities for this purpose. Laws protecting gay rights were repealed in Miami after a nationally publicized battle; and in St. Paul, Minnesota; Wichita, Kansas; and Eugene, Oregon. Despite these votes, the controversy in Miami and other cities had the effect of focusing increased public attention on the legal and civil rights of gays.

The first avowed homosexual member of Congress, Representative Gerry E. Studds, a Massachusetts Democrat from Cape Cod, was easily reelected several times, by increasingly bigger margins, despite his censure by the House in 1983 for having had sexual relations ten years earlier with a male congressional page. Representative Barney Frank, another Massachusetts Democrat, was investigated by the House Ethics committee in 1989 after confirming published reports of his relationship with a male prostitute who lived in his home for a time. The panel suggested that Frank be reprimanded, and the full House did so in 1990, rejecting calls that he be expelled or censured. Frank, too, was reelected that year.

But it was the crisis over the deadly acquired immune deficiency syndrome (AIDS), that led to the first

major congressional action benefiting gays. The disease devastated the homosexual community, although it was by no means limited to gays, since the virus associated with AIDS could be transmitted not only by sexual contact between homosexuals but also by heterosexual sex, contaminated blood transfusions, needles used by drug addicts, and by infected pregnant mothers to their babies.[69] Prodded by gay activists, Congress in 1983 authorized $30 million for a quick federal response to public health emergencies, including AIDS. In October 1988, Congress passed its first comprehensive AIDS legislation. The $1 billion package included funds for research, new drugs, home health care for AIDS patients, and anonymous testing. Similar bills have been enacted in later years. For fiscal 1992, for example, Congress appropriated $1.9 billion for these purposes.

In October 1987, more than 200,000 gay men and women from across the nation gathered on the mall in Washington, the scene of many political protests. They carried signs that read, "Get Ready for the Gay 90s," "Dyke from Ohio," and "Condoms, Not Condemnation." They had come to march for an end to discrimination against homosexuals and for more funds to fight AIDS.

Under the Civil Service Reform Act of 1978, most federal agencies could not discriminate against homosexuals in their hiring practices, although the FBI, the

---

[68] *Gaylord v. Tacoma*, 434 U.S. 879 (1977).

[69] By March 1992, the AIDS epidemic in the United States had exceeded 218,300 cases. Of that total, more than 141,200 persons had died. More than 12,800 heterosexual AIDS cases had been reported. By that time, it was estimated that there were one million Americans carrying the HIV virus. Data from Centers for Disease Control.

CIA, and other "sensitive" government agencies could as a rule dismiss or refuse to hire gay persons.

The armed forces have exercised the right to dismiss or exclude homosexuals, and in general the courts have not interfered with this policy. Between 1982 and 1991, 13,307 men and women in all branches of the military were dismissed because they were found to be gays.[70]

In the past, federal law permitted the Immigration and Naturalization Service to bar gay persons from the United States. In 1980, however, the Justice Department ruled that homosexual aliens would not be barred unless they made a voluntary declaration of their homosexuality.

The law barring foreign homosexuals from entering the United States was passed three decades ago, long before the American Psychiatric Association, in 1973, removed homosexuality from its list of mental disorders, and urged that gays be given the same legal protections as other citizens. Despite changing public views toward gays, however, a substantial number of Americans continued to regard homosexuality as offensive to their personal, community, or religious standards.

On the other hand, in many states, political leaders could ignore gay power only at their peril. In San Francisco, with its large gay population, no mayor could be expected to win election without the support of members of the gay community. In New York, Denver, Washington, D.C., Houston, and Austin, gays had become an important political group. By 1990, the Human Rights Campaign Fund, started in 1980 to elect officials who support gay rights, was the 20th largest political action committee in the nation with a campaign chest of nearly $2.3 million.[71]

Disabled Americans

Until relatively recently, the estimated 43 million Americans with disabilities were a kind of invisible minority, their rights of equal treatment and equal access more often than not overlooked or neglected.

A person in a wheelchair has as much need and right to enter a shopping mall or a restaurant as anyone else; but often no ramp was available, and a set of stairs difficult or impossible to navigate blocked the way. In employment, transportation, access to other public facilities, and in other ways, the disabled have been disadvantaged.

In 1990, Congress acted to remove these everyday barriers to a normal life for persons with disabilities. The Americans with Disabilities Act, enacted in that year and signed into law by President Bush, was the most significant anti-discrimination law since the 1964 Civil Rights Act. The act defined disabled persons as anyone with "a physical or mental impairment that substantially limits one or more of the major life activities." The law, with provisions to take effect over a period of years, bans discrimination against such persons in employment, public accommodations, transportation, and telecommunications. Under the law, employers of more than fifteen persons cannot refuse to hire qualified disabled persons. New buses, taxis, and trains, hotels, restaurants, stores, schools, parks, museums, movie and other theaters, as well as auditoriums, doctors' offices, and health clubs must be accessible to disabled persons. Banks must lower ATM machines to accommodate persons in wheelchairs, restaurants must provide menus in Braille for the blind or visually impaired. Public and other telephones, to the extent possible, must allow hearing- or voice-impaired persons to place and receive calls. In every aspect, the law sought to accommodate the rights of disabled Americans far beyond what had ever been done before.

BLACK AND WHITE: AN AMERICAN DILEMMA

On March 3, 1991, officers of the Los Angeles Police Department cornered a twenty-five-year-old motorist, Rodney G. King, after a wild automobile chase through city streets. Police said he had been speeding. As officers surrounded the man, four of them began beating him repeatedly with their metal batons and kicking him. He was clubbed more than fifty times and shocked with a Taser electric stun gun as he lay on the ground near his car. Fifteen officers stood by and witnessed the savage beating, making no move to intervene.

Unknown to the police, a resident of a nearby apartment building turned on his video camera. In millions of homes on television news broadcasts, and later in a courtroom in California, the famous video tape was played again and again. Rodney King's skull was fractured in at least nine places. His eye socket was shat-

[70] *Washington Post*, August 19, 1991, p. A8.
[71] *National Journal*, January 6, 1990, p. 18.

Rodney King is beaten by Los Angeles police on the famous video tape

tered, his leg was broken, his cheekbone fractured, and he suffered other injuries.

Rodney King was black. The four officers who beat him were white. All four were later tried for assault with a deadly weapon and excessive use of force, and two were also charged with falsifying police reports. In their defense, the officers contended that King had aggressively resisted arrest. On April 29, 1992, all four were acquitted by a jury that included no blacks in suburban Simi Valley, the community to which the trial had been moved.[72]

Within a few hours of the startling verdict, the predominantly black area of south central Los Angeles erupted in violent anger. Some white motorists and truck drivers were dragged from their vehicles and beaten as television crews in helicopters photographed the carnage. One of the drivers died from the blows.

More than 3,700 fires were set, stores looted. In three nights of destruction, 60 persons died, the majority of them black and Hispanic, and more than 2,300 were injured. Close to 14,000 persons were arrested.

The violence spread to other parts of Los Angeles and to other cities as demonstrations turned ugly in Atlanta, San Francisco, Seattle, Las Vegas, and elsewhere. Los Angeles Mayor Tom Bradley declared a curfew, Governor Pete Wilson called out the National Guard. The city of the angels was turned into a virtual war zone. A pall of dark smoke hung over the nation's second-largest city, closing all but one runway at Los Angeles International Airport. Freeways were clogged as thousands of frightened residents fled the city. Most businesses and offices shut down.

On the third day, President Bush sent in 1,000 federal law enforcement agents and ordered 4,500 federal troops to stand by; some later joined the National Guard in patrolling the streets. The president spoke to the nation on television, with a plea for racial harmony and a promise to restore law and order, and he said the

---

[72] The jury was deadlocked on one charge against one officer, Laurence M. Powell, for excessive use of force. Prosecutors then moved to retry Powell.

1992: Los Angeles riots

"PEOPLE, CAN WE ALL GET ALONG?"

During the third day of the riots in Los Angeles in the spring of 1992, Rodney G. King, the man at the center of the storm, went on television with a plea for racial harmony and an end to the violence:

LOS ANGELES, May 1 — People, I just want to say, can we all get along? Can we get along? Can we stop making it horrible for the older people and the kids?

I mean, we've got enough smog here in Los Angeles, let alone to deal with setting these fires and things. It's just not right; it's not right. And it's not going to change anything. We'll get our justice. They've won the battle, but they haven't won the war. We'll have our day in court, and that's all we want.

I'm neutral. I love everybody. I love people of color. You know, I'm not like they're making me out to be. We've got to quit. We've got to quit. After all, I mean, I can understand the first upset, for the first two hours after the verdict. But to go on — to keep going on like this and to see this security guard shot on the ground, it's just not right. It's just not right because those people will never go home to their families again.

I mean, please, we can get along here. We can all get along. We've just got to. I mean, we're all stuck here for a while. Let's try to work it out. Let's try to beat it. Let's try to work it out.

—*Washington Post*, May 2, 1992.

Justice Department was reviewing whether the police officers might be prosecuted for their actions under federal civil rights laws. Rodney King, whose terrible beating had begun it all, also went on television with an emotional plea for peace. "People," he said, "I just want to say, can we all get along? Can we get along?" Gradually, the violence subsided, but the scars remained.

For months before the trial of the four officers, the white police chief, Daryl F. Gates, who had been accused of encouraging brutality among his officers, refused to resign. Finally, not long before the riots, he was replaced by Philadelphia's police chief, Willie L. Williams, a black. But Gates was still in command when the city erupted after the trial verdict. He was criticized by some political leaders for responding too slowly to the riots. Two hours after the violence broke out, he went to a cocktail party.

The nation was shaken to the core by the terrible events in Los Angeles. Since the videotaped evidence had seemed clear, millions of persons, black and white, were baffled by the jury's decision. President Bush said he had been "stunned" by the verdict. Few Americans condoned the violence, even if they understood the emotions that had fueled it. Some political leaders called for social programs to get at the root causes of poverty and hopelessness in the inner city. Democrats pummeled Republicans for neglecting urban problems during the Reagan and Bush administrations.

If not for the damning video tape, would Americans have ever known about the savage beating of Rodney King? Obviously not. The fact that a motorist, even one who was breaking the law by speeding, could be treated this way by police in the nation's second-largest city, shocked many white Americans. It might have come as less of a shock to those African Americans who had direct, personal experience with the racial prejudice that still existed among individuals in many segments of American society, including, in some cases, the police.

Perhaps no white man or woman can ever fully comprehend what it is like to be born with black skin in America. In his prophetic 1962 book *The Fire Next Time*, author James Baldwin tried to tell:

Long before the Negro child perceives this difference, and even long before he understands it, he has begun to react to it, he has begun to be controlled by it. . . . He must be "good" not only in order to please his parents and not only to avoid being punished by them; behind their authority stands another, nameless and impersonal, infinitely harder to please, and bottomlessly cruel. And this

Rodney King appealing for peace

filters into the child's consciousness through his parents' tone of voice as he is being exhorted, punished, or loved; in the sudden, uncontrollable note of fear heard in his mother's or his father's voice when he has strayed beyond some particular boundary. He does not know what the boundary is, and he can get no explanation of it.[73]

Another writer, Ralph Ellison, argued that the black adult is unseen by the white world. "I am an invisible man," he wrote. "I am a man of substance, of flesh and bone, fiber and liquids — and I might even be said to possess a mind. I am invisible, understand, simply because people refuse to see me."[74]

Ellison wrote those words in 1952. If African American men and women in America are visible today, it is because a revolution in civil rights has taken place since that time. Yet black Americans still have not been able to reach the goal of full equality in American society.

It is paradoxical, and tragic as well, that a nation founded on the principle that all people are created equal should have "a race problem." This is the paradox that the Swedish sociologist Gunnar Myrdal termed the "American Dilemma" in his classic study half a century ago.[75] "The American Negro problem is a problem in the heart of the American," Myrdal wrote. "The American Dilemma . . . is the ever-raging conflict between,

[73] Baldwin, *The Fire Next Time*, p. 40.
[74] Ralph Ellison, *Invisible Man* (New York: Random House, 1952), p. 3.
[75] Gunnar Myrdal, *An American Dilemma: The Negro Problem and Modern Democracy* (New York: Harper & Row, 1962). Originally published in 1944.

on the one hand, the valuations preserved on the general plane which we shall call the 'American Creed,' where the American thinks, talks, and acts under the influence of high national and Christian precepts, and on the other hand . . . group prejudice against particular persons or types of people." [76]

Author Charles E. Silberman has argued that in one sense "Myrdal was wrong. The tragedy of race relations in the United States is that there is no American Dilemma. White Americans are not torn and tortured by the conflict between their devotion to the American creed and their actual behavior. . . . What troubles them is not that justice is being denied, but that when racial conflicts erupt their peace is . . . shattered and their business interrupted." [77]

The tension between black and white Americans is not only a problem for the African American still seeking a rightful place in American society but a problem for all citizens, a moral contradiction that strikes at the roots of American democracy. Two decades after Myrdal had summarized his views, and again in 1992, the "fire next time" predicted by James Baldwin visited American cities in the form of racial disorders, and social conflict remained a continuing threat to the nation's future.

By the 1980s a substantial black middle class had emerged in the United States, and black incomes were growing. But this created even deeper divisions among blacks. William Julius Wilson has suggested that economic class, rather than race, may have become more important in determining the status of blacks in America. "As the black middle class rides on the wave of political and social changes . . . the black underclass falls behind." [78] Other scholars have disagreed with Wilson's interpretation, arguing that "The biggest problem that black Americans face is that they are in a country that has historically oppressed black people because they are *black*." [79] Wilson himself later said he might avoid the use of the term "underclass" in the future because it enabled some analysts to blame the poor for their plight.

The unprecedented migration of blacks from the South to northern cities in the years after the Second World War had helped to create explosive ghetto conditions in those cities. And the poverty of the inner city continued to exist in the midst of what is, for many Americans, an affluent society. Blacks in America, Silberman has noted, are "an economic as well as a racial minority." No matter how "assimilated" the black American is, because of his skin color, "he cannot lose himself in the crowd. He remains . . . an alien in his own land." [80]

THE HISTORICAL BACKGROUND

"The Negro," Gunnar Myrdal observed, "was brought to America for the sake of the white man's profit. He was kept in slavery for generations in the same interest." [81]

The African American

Unlike most other immigrants, who came to these shores seeking freedom, African Americans came in slavery. Theirs was a forced immigration. While the Irish American, the Italian American, or other Americans might regard their forebears' country of national origin with pride, until the 1960s few black Americans identified with African culture. In part this was because black Americans absorbed the whites' concept of Africa as a land of jungles and savages. Only in relatively recent years have substantial numbers of scholars explored the history and culture of West Africa. Although interpretations of that history vary, one study placed "the western Sudan among the important creative centers in the development of human culture." [82]

It was there, south of the Sahara in the western Sudan, that the majority of the slaves brought to America were captured, to be transported across the sea under cruel conditions. The slaves, chained together and lying on their backs, were packed in layers between the decks in spaces that sometimes measured less than two feet. Often, only a third survived the voyage "and

---

[76] Ibid., p. lxxi.

[77] Charles E. Silberman, *Crisis in Black and White* (New York: Random House, 1964), p. 10.

[78] William Julius Wilson, *The Declining Significance of Race: Blacks and Changing American Institutions* (Chicago: University of Chicago Press, 1978), p. 22.

[79] Lucius J. Barker and Jesse J. McCorry, Jr., *Black Americans and the Political System*, 2nd ed. (Boston: Little, Brown, and Company, 1980), p. 342.

[80] Silberman, *Crisis in Black and White*, pp. 43–44.

[81] Myrdal, *An American Dilemma: The Negro Problem and Modern Democracy*, p. lxxvi.

[82] August Meier and Elliott M. Rudwick, *From Plantation to Ghetto* (New York: Hill and Wang, 1966), p. 5.

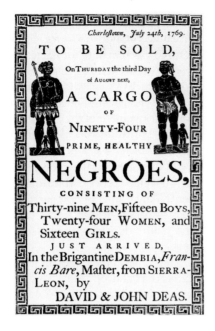

Charleſtown, July 24th, 1769.

TO BE SOLD,

On THURSDAY the third Day of AUGUST next,

A CARGO

OF

NINETY-FOUR

PRIME, HEALTHY

NEGROES,

CONSISTING OF

Thirty-nine MEN, Fifteen BOYS, Twenty-four WOMEN, and Sixteen GIRLS.

JUST ARRIVED,

In the Brigantine DEMBIA, *Francis Bare*, Maſter, from SIERRA-LEON, by

DAVID & JOHN DEAS.

loss of half was not at all unusual."[83] It was not surprising that the slaves sometimes mutinied aboard ship.

No one knows how many slaves were brought to North and South America and the West Indies between the sixteenth and the mid-nineteenth centuries, but the figure has been estimated at 15 million. It easily may have been twice that.

An African American Heritage

In the 1950s a white or black child reading a textbook in American history scarcely would have realized that African Americans were a significant part of the American past. Beginning in the 1960s, however, interest in the cultural heritage of African Americans was accompanied by new studies of the role of blacks in the nation's history.

Perhaps the first person to fall in the American Revolution was a black man, Crispus Attucks. A forty-seven-year-old runaway slave, later a sailor, he was the first of five men killed by British soldiers in the Boston Massacre of 1770, five years before the Revolutionary War began.[84] African Americans took part in the battles of Lexington, Concord, and Bunker Hill; they were

---

[83] Ibid., p. 33.

[84] John Hope Franklin, *From Slavery to Freedom* (New York: Knopf, 1967), p. 128.

with Washington at Valley Forge. About 5,000 blacks served in the Continental Army. And 186,000 blacks served in the Union ranks during the Civil War.

Black explorers, soldiers, scientists, poets, writers, educators, public officials—the list of such men and women who made individual contributions is long and distinguished; moreover, blacks as a group have contributed to the culture of America and participated in its historical development. Yet from the start, the role of African Americans was overlooked or neglected. "We hold these truths to be self-evident," the Declaration of Independence says, "that all men are created equal." But that soaring language was not meant to include the African American, who was recognized by the framers at Philadelphia as only "three-fifths" of a person. The American Dilemma, even as the republic began, was engraved in the new nation's Constitution but had scarcely touched its conscience.

Dred Scott, Reconstruction, and "Jim Crow"

Citizens of a state automatically are "citizens of the United States" under the Constitution. But until after the Civil War, this in reality meant free white persons. The citizenship status of free blacks—there were almost 100,000 in the early 1800s—remained a subject of political dispute. The Supreme Court ruled on the question in the famous *Dred Scott* decision of 1857.

Dred Scott

Chief Justice Roger B. Taney

Dred Scott was a slave who had lived in the North for four years. Antislavery forces sought to bring Scott's case before the Supreme Court on the grounds that his residence on free soil had made him a free man. To sue for freedom, Scott first had to prove he was a citizen. But Chief Justice Roger B. Taney ruled that Dred Scott and black Americans "are not included, and were not intended to be included, under the word 'citizens' in the Constitution." [85]

It took a civil war and a constitutional amendment to reverse Taney's decision. In 1865, eight months after the surrender at Appomattox, the states ratified the Thirteenth Amendment, abolishing slavery. The Fourteenth Amendment, ratified in 1868, reversed the *Dred Scott* decision by making citizens of the freed slaves. The Fifteenth Amendment, ratified in 1870, was designed to give former slaves the right to vote.

During the Reconstruction era (1863 – 1877), Congress passed a series of civil rights measures. Two laws enacted in 1870 make it a crime for police to violate a person's civil rights or for anyone to conspire to do so. The statutes were seldom invoked until the 1960s, when the federal government used them to prosecute and convict police in brutality cases where local authorities had failed to act, or where the offenders had received light sentences. Of the laws passed during Reconstruction, the last, the Civil Rights Act of 1875, was

the strongest. The law was aimed at providing equal public accommodations for blacks. But this postwar trend toward equality for African Americans was short-lived. In the *Civil Rights Cases* of 1883, the Supreme Court struck down the 1875 Civil Rights Act, decreeing that the Fourteenth Amendment protected citizens from infringement of their rights by the *states* but not by *private individuals*. Discrimination by one citizen against another was a private affair, the Court held.

Thus, less than two decades after the Civil War, the Supreme Court had seriously weakened the Fourteenth Amendment and neutralized the efforts of Congress to pass civil rights laws to protect black citizens. The Court decisions were also a sign of what was to come.

After 1883 the atmosphere was ripe for the rise of segregation and of "Jim Crow" laws designed to give legal recognition to discrimination.[86] Segregation, the separation of black and white Americans by law, became the new way of life in the South. "Jim Crow" was accompanied by lynchings and terror for African Americans.[87]

Plessy v. Ferguson

In 1896 the Supreme Court put its official seal of approval on racial segregation in America. The great constitutional test of legal discrimination began on a June day in 1892, when Homer Adolph Plessy bought a ticket in New Orleans, boarded an East Louisiana Railroad train, and took his seat — in a coach reserved for whites. He was asked to move, refused, and was arrested.

Plessy was chosen for this test by opponents of the state's Jim Crow railroad law, which required equal but separate accommodations for white and black passengers. The Supreme Court ruled that the Louisiana statute did not violate the Fourteenth Amendment.

Yet the case of *Plessy* v. *Ferguson* is remembered as well for the ringing dissent of a single justice, a former slaveholder from Kentucky, John Marshall Harlan. Shocked by the activities of the Ku Klux Klan, Harlan had become a champion of civil rights for blacks. And he declared: "Our Constitution is color-blind, and nei-

---

[85] *Dred Scott* v. *Sandford*, 19 Howard 393 (1857).

[86] In 1832 Thomas D. "Daddy" Rice, a blackface minstrel, had introduced a song and dance about a slave named Jim Crow ("Weel a-bout and turn a-bout/And . . . jump Jim Crow"), and the term came to be applied to the anti-black laws of the 1890s.

[87] There were about 100 lynchings a year in the 1880s and 1890s; 161 lynchings took place in 1892.

ther knows nor tolerates classes among citizens. . . . The thin disguise of 'equal' accommodations for passengers in railroad coaches will not mislead any one, nor atone for the wrong this day done." [88]

Despite Harlan's eloquent dissent, the doctrine of "separate but equal" remained the law of the land for fifty-eight years, until 1954, when the Supreme Court finally ruled that it had no place in American life.

The Case of Linda Carol Brown

In the city of Topeka, Kansas, more than half a century after *Plessy*, Oliver Brown, a black man and a welder by trade, was disturbed by the fact that his eight-year-old daughter, Linda Carol, attended an elementary school twenty-one blocks away from her home. Only black students attended the school, for Topeka elementary schools were segregated by local option under state law. To go the twenty-one blocks to Monroe Elementary

School, Linda Carol caught a school bus each morning at 7:40 A.M. The difficulty was that the bus arrived at the school at 8:30 A.M., but the doors of the school did not open until 9 A.M. Often, it meant that the children had to wait outside in the cold. To get home in the afternoon, she had to walk past the railroad tracks and cross a busy and dangerous intersection. Oliver Brown tried to enroll his children at Sumner Elementary School, which was only seven blocks from the Brown home. He was unable to do so. Sumner was a school for white children. With the help of the National Association for the Advancement of Colored People (NAACP), Oliver Brown took his case to court.

Brown v. Board of Education

On May 17, 1954, Chief Justice Earl Warren delivered the unanimous opinion of the Supreme Court in the case of *Brown v. Board of Education of Topeka, Kansas*.

The issue before the Supreme Court was very simple: the Fourteenth Amendment guarantees equal protection of the laws. The plaintiffs argued that segregated schools were not and could never be equal, and were therefore unconstitutional.

Chief Justice Warren asked: "Does segregation of children in public schools solely on the basis of race, even though the physical facilities and other 'tangible' factors may be equal, deprive the children of the minority group of equal educational opportunities? We believe that it does." Such segregation of children, the chief justice added, "may affect their hearts and minds in a way unlikely ever to be undone. . . . We conclude that in the field of public education the doctrine 'separate but equal' has no place. Separate educational facilities are inherently unequal. Therefore, we hold that the plaintiffs . . . are, by reason of the segregation complained of, deprived of the equal protection of the laws guaranteed by the Fourteenth Amendment." [89]

The Supreme Court did not attempt in 1954 to enforce its decision. The Court, as Justice Robert Jackson pointed out, "is dependent upon the political branches for the execution of its mandates, for it has no physical force at its command." [90]

---

[88] *Plessy* v. *Ferguson*, 163 U.S. 537 (1896).

Linda Carol Brown, 1954

---

[89] *Brown* v. *Board of Education of Topeka, Kansas*, 347 U.S. 483 (1954).

[90] In Robert H. Jackson, *The Supreme Court in the American System of Government* (Cambridge: Harvard University Press, 1955), p. 11.

Much of the South reacted to the *Brown* decision by adopting a policy of massive resistance. How, then, would the Court's ruling be implemented? A year later, in May 1955, the Supreme Court itself faced the problem, unanimously ordering local school authorities to comply with the decision "with all deliberate speed." [91] But compliance was very slow, and in some instances there were direct armed confrontations between federal and state power.

Little Rock, Oxford, and Alabama

In September 1957 nine black children attempted to enter the previously all-white Central High School in Little Rock, Arkansas, under a federal court order. Governor Orval Faubus called out the National Guard to block integration of the school, but the troops were withdrawn by direction of the court. The black students braved a screaming mob of whites. President Eisenhower reluctantly dispatched federal paratroopers to Little Rock to quell the violence. Central High was (and is) integrated.

Violence continued to flare in the South during the Kennedy administration. When James Meredith, a black student, enrolled in the University of Mississippi at Oxford in 1962, two men were killed and several injured in the rioting that took place on the campus. President Kennedy dispatched federal marshals and ordered 16,000 troops to restore peace and protect Meredith. The following year, Alabama's Governor George Wallace attempted to block the enrollment of two black students at the University of Alabama at Tuscaloosa. Wallace backed down only after Kennedy federalized the Alabama National Guard.

The School Decision: Aftermath

Fifteen years after the *Brown* decision, only 20 percent of black students in the South attended integrated public schools (defined by the federal government as at least 50 percent white). Faced with continued defiance, the Supreme Court ruled unanimously in October 1969 that school districts must end segregation "at once" and operate integrated systems "now and hereafter." [92] It was the first major Supreme Court decision presided over by the new chief justice, Warren Burger. Through federal court rulings and the efforts of the federal government in working with local school boards, the pattern gradually changed. But even as more schools became integrated, the question of public school desegregation, in the North as well as in the South, remained a volatile issue.

And in Topeka, Kansas, where it had all begun, a federal judge in 1979 reopened the *Brown* case after a group of parents complained that, twenty-five years later, the city's schools were still segregated. "The wheel has turned all the way around," Charles Scott, Jr., attorney for the parents, said, "and nothing has changed." [93] Among the group of parents who filed the complaint was Linda Carol Brown, now the mother of two children in the Topeka public school system. In 1987 a federal district court ruled that the school district, while not perfectly balanced, "has achieved a high level of integration" and was in compliance with the law.

Busing: The Controversy Continues

By the mid-seventies the familiar yellow school bus had become the symbol of a deeply divisive political and social issue in the United States. The *Brown* decision left many unanswered questions, among them whether the Constitution required busing of schoolchildren to achieve desegregation. In April 1971 the Supreme Court ruled unanimously that in some circumstances it did; the Court held that busing could be used "as one tool of desegregation." [94]

The Court has not upheld busing in every case, however. It struck down plans to bus children to desegregate schools in Richmond and Detroit,[95] but upheld a busing plan in Boston, the scene of prolonged violence over busing that began in 1974.

Although 18 million public school children rode school buses in the United States, many parents, both white and black, objected to busing to achieve desegre-

---

[91] *Brown v. Board of Education of Topeka, Kansas*, 349 U.S. 294 (1955). John Marshall Harlan, grandson of the justice who dissented in *Plessy v. Ferguson*, was by this time a member of the Supreme Court and participated in the second Brown decision.

[92] *Alexander v. Holmes County Board of Education*, 396 U.S. 19 (1969).
[93] *Washington Post*, November 30, 1979, p. 1.
[94] *Swann v. Charlotte-Mecklenburg County Board of Education*, 402 U.S. 1 (1971).
[95] *School Board of the City of Richmond, Virginia v. State Board of Education*, 412 U.S. 92 (1973); and *Milliken v. Bradley*, 418 U.S. 717 (1974).

gation. White parents often have opposed the busing of their children into largely black, inner-city schools. A number of parents, black and white, objected to long bus rides into unfamiliar neighborhoods for their children.

In the cities of the North, school segregation often has been the result not of law but of *de facto* segregation —residential patterns that created black neighborhoods and, along with them, black schools. It was this kind of segregation that created one of the most difficult questions facing Americans. Millions of whites had moved to the suburbs, some at least partly in search of better schools; even those who did not consider themselves racists often reacted with hostility to the idea of busing their children back to the inner-city schools they had fled. On the other hand, to many black students trapped in ghetto schools, the school bus appeared to offer the only immediate means to quality education.

As the issue continued to trouble the nation, some black educators concluded that quality education did not depend on busing and desegregation. Wilson Riles, the superintendent of education in California, rejected the idea "that a black child can't learn unless he is sitting next to a white child," and political scientist Charles

Hamilton called busing black children "a subtle way of maintaining black dependency on whites." [96]

As in the case of school busing, the 1954 *Brown* decision did not deal with the issue of *de facto* segregation. But the question was involved in a case in Denver decided by the Supreme Court in 1973.[97] The Court ruled that where a school board had intentionally segregated a "substantial portion" of students, local authorities must desegregate the entire school system. The Supreme Court ruling in the Denver case warned the North that it could not operate deliberately segregated schools by manipulating school boundaries, any more than the South could.

And the Supreme Court reaffirmed its Denver decision in 1979, when it approved sweeping crosstown busing plans in two Ohio cities, Dayton and Columbus.[98] In 1991, however, the Supreme Court ruled 5–3

---

[96] Diane Ravitch, "Busing: The Solution That Has Failed to Solve," *New York Times*, December 21, 1975, section 4, p. 3.
[97] *Keyes* v. *School District No. 1*, 413 U.S. 189 (1973).
[98] *Dayton Board of Education* v. *Brinkman*, 443 U.S. 526 (1979); *Columbus Board of Education* v. *Penick*, 443 U.S. 449 (1979).

in an Oklahoma City case that busing need not continue once a school district had made good faith efforts to end racial segregation.[99] Chief Justice William H. Rehnquist, writing for the majority, said that court-supervised busing was not meant to continue indefinitely, but had been "intended as a temporary measure to remedy past discrimination." [100]

Some four decades after the *Brown* decision, most minority students still attended segregated schools across the nation. "In 1986 more than 71 percent of Latino students and 63 percent of blacks were enrolled in schools that had a minority population of more than 50 percent," according to one survey.[101] Moreover, one third of the students in both groups attended "intensely segregated schools — those in which 90 percent or more of the students came from minority groups." [102] In the continuing struggle over school desegregation, it had become very clear in the years following the *Brown* decision that racial problems were not confined to any one section of the nation.

THE CIVIL RIGHTS MOVEMENT: FREEDOM NOW

The Montgomery Bus Boycott

On the evening of December 1, 1955, Rosa Parks, a forty-three-year-old seamstress, boarded a bus in Montgomery, Alabama, as she did every working day to return home from her job at a downtown department store. When half a dozen whites got on at a bus stop, the driver asked black passengers near the front of the bus to give up their seats to the whites and move to the rear. Three other black passengers got up; Rosa Parks did not. She was arrested and fined $10, but her quiet refusal launched a boycott of the Montgomery bus line by a black population that had had enough. It was a remarkable year-long protest, and it catapulted to national fame the twenty-seven-year-old Baptist minister who led it. His name was Dr. Martin Luther King, Jr.

During the boycott King went to jail, and his home was bombed, but he won. The boycott ended in November 1956 as a result of a federal court injunction

prohibiting segregation of buses in Montgomery. The victory set the pattern for other boycotts and for direct action throughout the South.

King, who led the civil rights movement and remained its symbolic head until his assassination in 1968, was an apostle of nonviolence, an eloquent man who attempted, with some success, to stir the American conscience. King grew up in comfortable middle-class surroundings in Atlanta, where his father was pastor of the Ebenezer Baptist Church. And it was in Atlanta in 1957, following the Montgomery boycott, that King formed the Southern Christian Leadership Conference (SCLC) as a vehicle for his philosophy of nonviolent change, which had been influenced by the teachings of Gandhi.

Until then, the principal black organization in the United States had been the NAACP, which stressed legal action in the courts as the road to progress. It was a lawyer's approach, and it had won many important struggles. King's battleground was the streets rather than the courts, and he sought through nonviolent confrontation to dramatize the issue of civil rights for the nation and the world.

The civil rights movement came of age at a time when many blacks were growing impatient with the slow pace of "gradual" change. Their desire was for "freedom now" — rather than at some unspecified time in the future.

Sit-ins and Freedom Rides

In February 1960 four black college students in Greensboro, North Carolina, sat down at a lunch counter at Woolworth's and asked politely for cups of coffee. They were refused service. They continued to sit for the rest of the morning. They came back the next day, and the next. Soon other students, white and black, joined them. They were spattered with mustard and ketchup and spat upon and cursed by whites. But at Greensboro the sit-in movement was born.

It spread to seven other states. The new tactics were a success. Within six months, not only the Woolworth's in Greensboro but hundreds of lunch counters throughout the South were serving blacks. In 1961 the sit-in technique was adapted to test segregation on interstate buses and in bus terminals. Black and white Freedom Riders rode into Alabama, where they were savagely beaten, slashed with chains, and stoned in attacks by whites. One bus was burned. But the Freedom

[99] *Board of Education v. Dowell* 111 S. Ct. 630 (1990).
[100] Ibid.
[101] *The State of America's Children 1991* (Washington, D.C.: Children's Defense Fund, 1991.), p. 84.
[102] Ibid.

The police dogs of Birmingham, 1963

As some civil rights workers have said, "What good is a seat in the front of the bus if you don't have the money for the fare?"

"We're in a new stage of the movement," Dr. King's widow, Coretta Scott King, said the other day, discussing civil rights developments over the last 10 years. "The issue now is jobs and money. In many ways, that's a harder nut to crack than the blatant discrimination that we were struggling against back in the old days."

—*New York Times,* April 2, 1978

Riders succeeded in publicizing the fact that segregation on interstate transportation, although outlawed by the Supreme Court, was then still a reality.[103]

Birmingham and the Dream

In the spring of 1963 Dr. King organized mass demonstrations against segregation in industrial Birmingham, Alabama. When arrests failed to stop the demonstrators, the authorities used high-pressure fire hoses, police dogs, and cattle prods. The demonstrators sang "We Shall Overcome" and continued to march. Photographs of the police dogs unleashed by Birmingham

Police Commissioner Eugene "Bull" Connor went out on the news wires. Another photograph showed police kneeling on a black woman and pinning her to the sidewalk. The scenes outraged much of the nation and the world.

Late in August King led a massive, peaceful "March on Washington for Jobs and Freedom." Some 200,000 Americans, black and white, jammed the mall between the Lincoln Memorial and the Washington Monument. The nationally televised, orderly demonstration had a powerful effect on the nation, but even more powerful were the words of Dr. King, who articulated the vision of what America could be and might become:

> I have a dream that one day this nation will rise up and live out the true meaning of its creed. . . .
>
> I have a dream . . . that my four little children will one day live in a nation where they will not be judged by the color of their skin but by the content of their character. . . .

---

[103] The Supreme Court had barred segregation on interstate transportation in a series of decisions, on buses in *Morgan* v. *Commonwealth of Virginia,* 328 U.S. 373 (1946); on trains in *Henderson* v. *United States,* 339 U.S. 816 (1950), which held that an interstate railroad could not segregate a dining car; and in other cases.

When the anti-abortion mothers march around the Capitol, when the farmers jam the streets with their tractors, they are, consciously or otherwise, imitating the moral theater Martin Luther King staged for the mass audience of television. Sometimes it works, and often it doesn't, but a range of political strategies, now regarded as orthodox and acceptable, was considered outrageous [and] sometimes illegal when King introduced it.

—*Washington Post,* April 2, 1978

**Dr. Martin Luther King, Jr.,
at the March
on Washington,
August 1963:
"I have a dream. . . ."**

So let freedom ring. . . . From every mountainside, let freedom ring . . . to speed up that day when all of God's children, black and white men, Jews and Gentiles, Protestants and Catholics, will be able to join hands and sing in the words of that old Negro spiritual, "Free at last! Free at last! Thank God Almighty, we are free at last!" [104]

In Birmingham, eighteen days later, a bomb was thrown into the Sixteenth Street Baptist Church on a Sunday morning. Four black girls attending Bible class died in the explosion. But from the agony of Birmingham that summer, from the impressive March on Washington, and from the powerful words of Dr. King, there emerged the strongest civil rights legislation since Reconstruction.

---

[104] *The Negro in American History*, vol. 1, *Black Americans 1928–1968*, with an introduction by Saunders Redding (Chicago: Encyclopaedia Britannica Educational Corp., 1969), pp. 175–76.

The Legislative Breakthrough

During the Eisenhower administration, Congress had passed the Civil Rights Act of 1957, the first such legislation since 1875. It created a United States Commission on Civil Rights and strengthened the civil rights section of the Justice Department. The law proved to be of limited value in protecting civil rights, however.

The Civil Rights Act of 1964 In 1963 President Kennedy proposed a comprehensive civil rights bill. After Kennedy's assassination that November, the House acted, but southerners in the Senate staged a fifty-seven-day filibuster. In June the Senate invoked cloture to cut off debate — the first time it had ever done so on a civil rights bill — and passed the measure. On July 2 President Johnson signed the Civil Rights Act of 1964 into law. The principal provisions were designed to:

"LORD, HOW DARE WE CELEBRATE?"

Aᴛʟᴀɴᴛᴀ, Jan. 17 — The ceremony was to honor the achievements of the Rev. Martin Luther King Jr., but the Rev. Bernice King, the slain civil rights leader's youngest child, found no cause for joy.

"Lord, how dare we celebrate?" she repeated as she recited chapter and verse of the nation's woes: 23 million Americans functionally illiterate, "more than 40 mil-

lion Americans...without health care...young African-American boys...killing other young African-American boys over failed drug transactions," a recession in which "nobody is even sure whether their job is secure . . . Lord, how dare we celebrate?"

—Washington Post, January 18, 1992

1. Prohibit racial or religious discrimination in public accommodations that affect interstate commerce, including hotels, motels, restaurants, cafeterias, lunch counters, gas stations, motion picture houses, theaters, and sports arenas.

2. Prohibit discrimination because of race, color, sex, religion, or national origin by employers or labor unions.

3. Bar voting registrars from adopting different standards for white and black applicants.

4. Permit the Attorney General to bring suit to enforce desegregation of public accommodations; and allow individuals to sue for their rights under the act.

5. Permit the executive branch of the federal government to halt the flow of funds to public or private programs that practice discrimination.

6. Extend the life of the Civil Rights Commission; create a Community Relations Service to conciliate racial disputes and an Equal Employment Opportunity Commission to enforce the fair employment section of the act.

The 1964 act did not cover violence directed at black Americans or at civil rights workers, white or black. Two days after President Johnson signed the bill into law, the bodies of three young civil rights workers —two of them from the North—were found in a shallow grave near Philadelphia, Mississippi.[105] In a civil rights act passed in 1968, Congress provided criminal penalties for injuring or interfering with civil rights workers or any persons exercising their civil rights; if the injury results in death, the maximum penalty is life imprisonment. The 1968 law also made it a federal offense to cross state lines with intent to incite a riot.

At the same time, Congress passed the Fair Housing Act, the first federal open housing law in the twentieth century. In 1970, when the law went fully into effect, it prohibited discrimination in the rental or sale of all privately owned single-family houses rented or sold through real estate agents or brokers.

---

[105] In 1967 seven men were convicted of conspiracy against the slain civil rights workers under an 1870 federal statute. Because the murders of the rights workers did not constitute a federal crime, the conspiracy statute was the only weapon available to the Justice Department. The seven, including an Imperial Wizard of the Ku Klux Klan and the deputy sheriff of Neshoba County, were given prison sentences ranging from three to ten years.

Table 5-3

Voter Registration in the South before and after the Voting Rights Act of 1965

	Percent of Voting-Age Population Registered					
	1964	1972	1976	1980	1986	1990
Black	43.3	56.6	63.1	56.5	64.6	59.0
White	73.2	67.8	67.9	65.8	63.2	62.5

SOURCES: 1968 *Congressional Quarterly Almanac*, pp. 772, 1055; *Congressional Quarterly, Revolution in Civil Rights*, p. 70; *The Voting Rights Act: Ten Years After*, Report of the U.S. Commission on Civil Rights (Washington, D.C.: U.S. Government Printing Office, 1975), p. 43; and U.S. Bureau of the Census.

The Voting Rights Act of 1965 During the Reconstruction era, state governments in the South were controlled by northern radical Republicans. After the white South regained control over its governments, particularly in the 1890s and thereafter, blacks were systematically denied the right to vote. What the Ku Klux Klan could not accomplish by intimidation, a broad range of other obstacles did. Literacy tests rigged to keep black voters from the polls, the all-white primary (which rested on the theory, rejected by the Supreme Court in 1944, that political parties were private clubs), the poll tax, and gerrymandering of election districts were all deliberate attempts to keep black voters in the South from gaining political power and challenging or changing the existing order. In short, the Fifteenth Amendment was being systematically flouted.

Only 12 percent of black Americans of voting age were registered in the eleven southern states in 1948. And, although the figure rose to 43.3 percent by November 1, 1964, it was still far below the 73.2 percent white registration in the same states.[106] (See Table 5-3.)

In Dallas County, Alabama, exactly 335 blacks out of a black population of 15,115 were registered to vote at the start of 1965. Martin Luther King chose Selma, the county seat, as the place where he would dramatize the voting rights issue. Dr. King called for a fifty-mile march from Selma to Montgomery, the state capital. But state troopers acting under orders of Governor Wallace used tear gas, whips, and night sticks to break up the march. President Johnson federalized the National Guard, and the march resumed under protection of the troops. Through the heat, the mud, and the rain, their ranks swelling in numbers and in pride, the marchers walked

---

[106] Southern Regional Council data in 1965 *Congressional Quarterly Almanac*, p. 537.

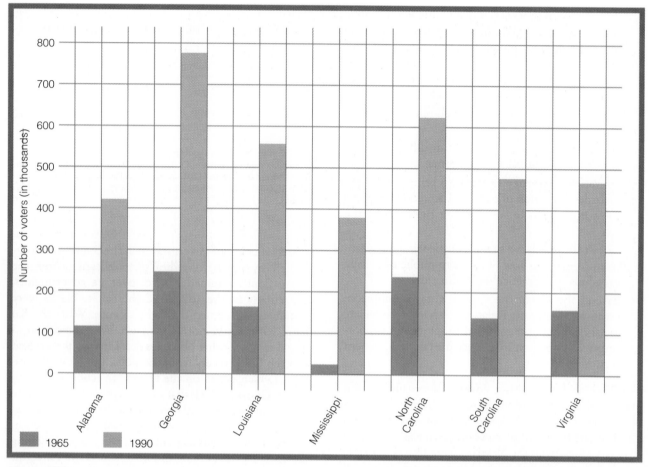

Figure 5-5
Increase of Black Voter Registration in the Seven Southern States Covered by the 1965 Voting Rights Act
SOURCE: U.S. Bureau of the Census.

on until, joined by Dr. King, they reached the steps of the Alabama Capitol building.

In the midst of the struggle in Selma, and before the marchers had finally reached Montgomery, President Johnson went on nationwide television to address a special joint session of Congress, and to urge new legislation to assure black Americans the right to vote. Then, in a dramatic moment in that speech, the president from Texas invoked the song and the slogan of the civil rights movement. "And we shall overcome," he said slowly. Thunderous applause greeted the remark, and Congress responded to Johnson's appeal with a second landmark civil rights measure.

The Voting Rights Act of 1965, passed after the Senate once again imposed cloture to crush a filibuster, covered six southern states — Alabama, Georgia, Louisiana, Mississippi, South Carolina, and Virginia — as well as Alaska, and parts of North Carolina, Arizona, and Idaho. Through an automatic "triggering" formula,

the act suspended literacy tests in areas where less than half the voting-age population had registered for, or had actually voted in, the 1964 election. It gave the federal government power to appoint federal examiners to require enrollment of qualified voters in such areas. Even outside of such areas, the attorney general could go into federal court to seek the appointment of examiners.

The effect of the Voting Rights Act was immediate. Within two years, black registration increased by more than 1,280,000 in the eleven states of the South. In Mississippi, black registration jumped from 6.7 percent of eligible voters to 59.8 percent.[107]

At the same time, however, in some southern states, black registration drives following passage of the Voting Rights Act also spurred new white registration. As a result, despite the percentage increase in black

---

[107] United States Commission on Civil Rights, *Political Participation*, May 1968, pp. 171, 222.

March on Montgomery, Alabama, 1965

registration, in actual numbers, there were more new white voters in those states than new black voters.

In 1970 the Voting Rights Act (which would otherwise have expired that year) was extended for five years and its scope broadened to include areas of California, Oregon, four New England states, and parts of New York City. In 1975 Congress again extended the act, for seven years, and broadened its basic provisions to protect language minorities — Spanish-speaking Americans, Native Americans, Asians, and Alaska natives. The revised law covered about a dozen more states. Literacy and character tests were permanently banned throughout the nation. Then, in 1982, Congress extended the Voting Rights Act for twenty-five years. This assured Americans that the protections built into the act would remain law through the year 2007.

The Voting Rights Act encouraged blacks to run for office. In 1967, two years after passage of the act, approximately 1,000 blacks sought party, state, and local offices in the South; nearly 250 were elected.

By 1984, registration and turnout of black voters nationwide was a major theme of the Reverend Jesse L. Jackson's campaign for the Democratic presidential nomination. Even before that, blacks in large numbers were registering to vote. In Illinois, for example, over an eighteen-month period, 200,000 new voters registered and helped to elect Representative Harold Washington in 1983 as Chicago's first black mayor.

Of the 30 million black Americans in 1990, more than 20.4 million were eligible to vote and 7.9 million, about 39 percent, did so — a relatively high percentage for a non-presidential election year. Only 4.4 million blacks had voted in 1966; by 1980, 8 million voted. Major black registration drives were mounted in many areas of the country in 1984, and 10.3 million blacks turned out to vote in the elections that year.[108]

In 1988, 10.1 million blacks voted.[109] In that year, Jackson emerged as a serious contender in the race for the Democratic presidential nomination. His string of impressive primary victories was largely due to his support by 90 percent or more of the black voters in several states. At the same time, Jackson won more than 25 percent of the white voters in some states. His enormous appeal and support among black voters was the most dramatic illustration of how the Voting Rights Act, and the increased participation of blacks in elections, had influenced the shape of politics in America in little more than two decades.

The Urban Riots

The black pall of smoke that hung over Los Angeles during the riots of April, 1992, did not mark the first time that fire, racial anger, and destruction had visited the city's streets. Even as the major civil rights laws of

---

[108] U.S. Bureau of the Census, Current Population Reports, *Voting and Registration in the Election of November 1990*, series P-20, no. 453, October, 1991, p. 4.

[109] U.S. Bureau of the Census, Current Population Reports, *Voting and Registration in the Election of November 1988*, series P-20, no. 440, October, 1989, p. 17.

the mid-1960s were taking effect, black protest in America entered a new phase. The great expectations aroused by the civil rights movement and legislative action by Congress had brought no visible change of status to the millions of black Americans in city slums. Frustration and poverty characterized the ghettos. Combined with summer heat and police incidents, the mixture proved volatile and tragic.

Los Angeles was sweltering in a heat wave on the night of August 11, 1965, when a highway patrolman stopped a young black driver for speeding and arrested him. A crowd gathered, more police arrived, and trouble flared. By the time the police had left, the residents of Watts, the city's black ghetto, were in an angry mood. Two days after the incident, arson, looting, and shooting broke out. The Watts riot had begun. Cries of "Burn, baby, burn!" filled the air. When it was all over, 34 persons were dead, more than 1,000 had been injured, and $35 million in damages had been done.

The Watts explosion was the most dramatic event in a pattern of major violence that was to afflict dozens of American cities. Watts was followed by disorders in Chicago and Cleveland in 1966, and by even more destructive riots in Newark and Detroit in 1967. Outbreaks occurred in Washington and more than one hundred other cities after the assassination of Martin Luther King in April 1968. A total of 13,600 federal troops was dispatched to Washington, where rioters had set fires only a few blocks from the White House. For twelve days, armed troops occupied the capital of the United States.

During the Detroit riot, President Johnson went on nationwide television to plead for calm and to announce the appointment of a National Advisory Commission on Civil Disorders. The commission reported in March 1968:

> Our nation is moving toward two societies, one black, one white—separate and unequal. . . . Certain fundamental matters are clear. Of these the most fundamental is the racial attitude and behavior of white Americans toward black Americans. . . . Race prejudice has shaped our history decisively; it now threatens to affect our future. White racism is essentially responsible for the explosive mixture which has been accumulating in our cities since the end of World War II.[110]

To meet these problems, the commission recommended a massive national effort to eliminate racial barriers in employment, education, and housing, and to create new jobs. The commission's findings were controversial—many Americans disagreed with the emphasis on white racism as the cause of the urban riots. Few could disagree, however, with the gravity of the problems underscored by the explosions in the cities in the 1960s and in 1992.

During the 1970s there were noticeably fewer outbreaks of large-scale urban violence. But in May of 1980, a major racial disorder in Miami reminded Americans that the underlying problems remained. The rioting was touched off when a white jury acquitted four white police officers of murdering a black Miami man who had been beaten to death by police. For two nights, arson, looting, and sniper fire racked the black areas of downtown Miami. When it was over, fourteen persons were dead, and more than three hundred injured. There were additional disorders in Miami in 1982 and 1984.

Black Power, Black Pride

During the late 1960s, advocates of direct, militant action had to a considerable extent drowned out the voices of more moderate black leaders. Black Power advocates and members of the militant Black Panthers often found it easier to capture the attention of the public and the press than did the moderates. And the assassination of Martin Luther King and other leaders committed to nonviolence weakened the position of the moderates.

Stokely Carmichael, a black leader who had popularized the phrase "Black Power," defined the term as "a call for black people in this country to unite, to recognize their heritage, to build a sense of community."[111] While there were various definitions of Black Power, a common theme was the need for African Americans to exercise political control of their communities, both in the urban ghettos and in rural areas of the South. Economically, the term was tied to the creation of independent, black-owned and black-operated businesses. Spiritually, it meant racial pride; it also gave rise to slogans such as "Black is Beautiful," and to the emphasis on "soul" and "soul brothers."

Black Panthers and local police were killed in a series of shootings in several cities. The most widely publicized case took place in 1969, when Chicago police raided an apartment before dawn, allegedly in a search for weapons, and shot to death Fred Hampton, chair-

---

[110] *Report of the National Advisory Commission on Civil Disorders* (New York: Bantam Books, 1968), pp. 1, 10.

[111] Stokely Carmichael and Charles V. Hamilton, *Black Power* (New York: Random House, 1967), p. 44.

man of the Illinois Black Panther party.[112] Many Americans were dismayed by police excesses against Panthers, but deeply disturbed as well by the existence of armed militant groups, and the use of violence to gain political objectives.

Although militants had for a time commanded an audience, the majority of black Americans sought full social and economic equality and dignity within the American system rather than apart from it. Along with many white Americans, they still believed in Martin Luther King's dream.

AFFIRMATIVE ACTION: THE SUPREME COURT RULES

The civil rights movement and the legislation enacted in the sixties did not settle a larger constitutional question: Were government and private "affirmative action" programs — designed to favor minorities and remedy past discrimination — constitutional?

John F. Kennedy, in an executive order issued in 1961, was the first president to call for affirmative action by the government. The order prohibited discrimination by contractors who received federal money, and instructed them to hire and promote members of minority groups.

The Civil Rights Act of 1964 barred discrimination by universities or others who received federal assistance. The act also outlawed discrimination by employers or unions. Many universities, employers, and unions went a step further and established affirmative action programs that gave *preference* in admissions or jobs to minorities. The programs were based on the theory that members of these groups were disadvantaged as a result of past discrimination. Merely guaranteeing minorities equal opportunity, it was argued, would not solve the problem, because members of such groups often would be at a disadvantage when competing with whites who had not suffered discrimination. Advocates of affirmative action, therefore, pressed for positive steps to aid minorities to compensate for the past and bring about equality of opportunity *and* equality of results.

Bakke and Weber: The Battle Is Joined

Opponents of affirmative-action programs argued that they were a form of "reverse discrimination" against whites. Since the Fourteenth Amendment to the Con-

stitution extended equal protection of the laws to everyone, and the 1964 Civil Rights Act outlawed any form of discrimination, were programs unconstitutional and illegal if they favored a black or a Hispanic over a white person?

As with many constitutional questions, these arguments and counterarguments ebbed and flowed and eventually focused on the case of one person — a white man named Allan Paul Bakke. Born in 1940, Bakke graduated from college in 1963 with an engineering degree and a 3.51 grade average. He joined the Marines, served in Vietnam, and later went to work on the moon program for the National Aeronautics and Space Administration (NASA). But what he wanted most was to be a doctor. Nights and weekends, he was a hospital volunteer.

In 1973 and 1974 Bakke applied to the medical school of the University of California at Davis. He did not get in. Davis had a special admissions program that reserved sixteen out of one hundred places in the medical school each year for minorities. In both years, minority students were admitted with much lower scores than Bakke's. Bakke sued. He contended that he had been excluded on the basis of his race in violation of the Constitution and the 1964 act.

The California Supreme Court upheld Bakke and ordered him admitted to medical school. The University of California appealed. In an historic ruling in June 1978, the United States Supreme Court, by a vote of 5–4, ordered Bakke admitted to the medical school at Davis. At the same time, the Court upheld the right of universities to give special preference to blacks and other minorities as long as they do not use rigid racial "quotas" such as the one at Davis.

The majority based its decision not on the 1964 law, but on the Fourteenth Amendment's guarantee of equal protection of the laws. Associate Justice Lewis F. Powell, Jr., who provided the key swing vote in the case, delivered the majority opinion: "Preferring members of any one group for no reason other than race or ethnic origin is discrimination for its own sake. This the Constitution forbids."

At the same time, Powell said that flexible admission programs, such as Harvard's, that "take race into account," but do not set a "fixed number of places" for minorities, were constitutional.[113]

In September, Bakke, by then thirty-eight, married, and the father of two young children, entered

---

[112] *New York Times*, May 23, 1970, p. 12.

[113] *Regents of the University of California* v. *Allan Bakke*, 438 U.S. 265 (1978).

the medical school at Davis, California. The Supreme Court had interpreted the Constitution to protect the rights of an individual. Allan Bakke had won his case—but so had America's minorities, who could continue to be given some preference by colleges and universities under the standard defined by the Supreme Court.

The *Bakke* decision left unsettled the question of affirmative action in employment. But a year later, the Supreme Court ruled in the case of Brian Weber, a blue-collar worker in a small town in Louisiana, who suddenly found himself in the vortex of a major constitutional test. Weber, a thirty-two-year-old white man, was employed as a lab technician for the Kaiser Aluminum and Chemical Corporation in Gramercy, Louisiana. He was also an officer of his local union, and had helped to establish on-the-job training programs for workers at the plant. Workers selected for such training in a skilled craft could expect to earn more money.

Weber applied and was rejected for the training program, which set aside half the jobs for black workers. Several of the blacks selected had less seniority than Weber, who took his case to court and lost. The Supreme Court ruled 5–2 that the history of the 1964 Civil Rights Act showed that it was designed to help minorities and not to prohibit private affirmative action programs. The Court added: "It would be ironic indeed if a law triggered by a Nation's concern over centuries of racial injustice and intended to improve the lot of those who had been excluded from the American dream for so long . . . constituted the first legislative prohibition of all voluntary, private . . . efforts to abolish traditional patterns of racial segregation." [114] Then in 1980 the Supreme Court ruled that Congress could constitutionally require that 10 percent of federal public works contracts be awarded to minority-owned business firms in order to remedy past discrimination.[115]

Four years later, the Supreme Court ruled that affirmative action plans to protect recently hired black employees must yield to seniority when layoffs are necessary.[116] The case arose over personnel practices in the Memphis fire department. But in 1986, the Supreme Court upheld affirmative action in employment in cases involving sheet-metal workers in New York and firefighters in Cleveland.[117] And in 1987, in its broadest endorsement of affirmative action to date, the Court ruled that employers may promote women and minorities ahead of white males, even where there is no evidence of prior discrimination.[118] It did so in the case of Diane Joyce, who had been a road repair worker in Santa Clara, California. (See box, p. 143).

Beginning in the late 1980s, however, a series of nine Supreme Court decisions made it more difficult for workers to sue employers for discrimination. By that time, late in the Reagan administration, the Supreme Court had become generally conservative, and increasingly minority groups looked to the legislative branch, rather than to the courts, for remedies. Faced with the series of Court decisions, civil rights groups lobbied on Capitol Hill for a law to protect workers against discrimination by employers. Congress sought to counter the Court decisions with new legislation, touching off a two-year struggle with President Bush, who argued that employers would adopt hiring quotas for minorities to protect themselves against lawsuits. Bush's critics charged that the warning about "quotas" was designed to alarm white workers already facing layoffs and dismissals in a recession. After vetoing one measure, Bush in 1991 signed a civil rights bill that overturned the Court's rulings and—in the wake of the Clarence Thomas hearings—allowed victims of sexual harassment to collect limited money damages.

EQUAL RIGHTS: A BALANCE SHEET FOR THE 1990s

By 1992 there were 26 African Americans in the House of Representatives, and 7,480 black elected officials throughout the nation. An African American served in the cabinet, and another sat on the Supreme Court. A black American, General Colin L. Powell, was chairman of the Joint Chiefs of Staff, the most powerful military position in the nation. By that time, black mayors served in 14 cities, including New York—where David N. Dinkins had become that city's first black mayor—Los Angeles, Detroit, New Orleans, Atlanta, Newark, Baltimore, Denver, Kansas City, Seattle, and Washington, D.C., where Sharon Pratt Kelly was the first African American woman to be elected mayor of a major city.[119]

[114] *United Steelworkers of America* v. *Weber*, 443 U.S. 193 (1979).
[115] *Fullilove* v. *Klutznick*, 448 U.S. 448 (1980).
[116] *Firefighters Local Union No. 1784* v. *Stotts et al.*, 467 U.S. 561 (1984).
[117] *Sheet Metal Workers* v. *Equal Employment Opportunity Commission*, 478 U.S. 421 (1986); *Firefighters* v. *Cleveland*, 478 U.S. 501 (1986).
[118] *Johnson* v. *Transportation Agency, Santa Clara County*, 480 U.S. 616 (1987).
[119] *Black Elected Officials: A National Roster 1991* (Washington, D.C.: Joint Center for Political Studies, 1991).

L. Douglas Wilder, the grandson of slaves, was the governor of Virginia, the first elected African American governor in U.S. history. The Reverend Jesse L. Jackson, a black, had again run for the Democratic presidential nomination in 1988 and gained the support of a substantial number of white voters. Ron H. Brown was chairman of the Democratic National Committee, the first black ever to run a major political party in America. And Martin Luther King Day, January 15, was a federal holiday observed in many states.

Within the civil rights movement, as Michael B. Preston has suggested, the emphasis had "shifted from protest to politics." [120] In the 1980s, "the increase in black elected officials nationwide [provided] ample proof that electoral politics is currently the dominant game in the black search for equality." [121]

The American political system, in the civil rights legislation passed in the mid-1960s, had demonstrated its ability to respond to peaceful pressures for change. Black voters in the South, who began to come to the polls in increasing numbers, were better protected by federal law. Public accommodations were finally, by federal law, open to all Americans. And the nation had become aware that 30 million black Americans would no longer wait.

But these gains reflected only part of the picture. The ghettos of the nation still existed. About 1.5 percent of all elected officials were black. In jobs, housing, education, and income, the black man or woman still sat, figuratively, in the back of the bus. A Census Bureau survey reported that median family income for blacks was $21,423 in 1990, compared with $36,915 for whites. [122] Those figures alone told much of the story. Moreover, 31.9 percent of black Americans, almost one-third, were below the poverty line compared with 10.7 percent of whites. [123] The unemployment rate for blacks was 14.1 percent in 1992 compared with 6.5 percent for whites. For black teenagers, traditionally a group acutely hit by unemployment, the rate was much higher — 36.5 percent in 1992, compared with 18.5 percent for whites of the same age. [124]

Still, some economic gains had been registered by blacks by the 1990s. In 1960 only 17 percent of black families had incomes of $20,000 or more; the figure had risen to 53.2 percent in 1990. Despite these gains, the median income for black families in 1990 was only 58 percent of the median income for white families. [125] In 1989 blacks composed just over 3 percent of the nation's physicians, lawyers, dentists, and engineers. [126] Because many blacks continued to be economically disadvantaged, economic issues were of increasing interest to traditional civil rights groups.

Other minority groups were not sharing equally in the benefits of American society. On average, women earned only 71 cents for every dollar men earned. Hispanic Americans and Native Americans, as we have seen, lagged far behind the society as a whole by every economic yardstick.

Although racial prejudice existed among many groups in America, it was often more strongly expressed among low-income whites, for this group felt most immediately threatened by blacks, economically and socially. Belatedly, more attention both in and out of government began to be focused on the problems of low-income whites and blue-collar workers.

For example, a study by a White House panel found that the purchasing power of blue-collar workers had remained almost static for five years. "These men are on a treadmill," the report said. It called blue-collar workers "the forgotten people." They live close to high-crime areas — but cannot afford to flee, the report said. They see welfare programs at close hand, yet their wages "are only a notch above the liberal states' welfare payments." To remedy these conditions, the study called for more job-training programs, more adult education, and tax subsidies of day-care centers for children of working mothers. [127]

While inequalities remained between whites and blacks, there were some signs of change. For example, more African Americans had migrated to the suburbs. Between 1970 and 1987, the black suburban population more than doubled. Only 7.1 million blacks lived in suburbia, however, or about 25 percent of the total

[120] Michael B. Preston, "Black Politics and Public Policy in Chicago: Self-Interest versus Constituent Representation," in Michael B. Preston, Lenneal J. Henderson, Jr., and Paul Puryear, eds. *The New Black Politics: The Search for Political Power* (New York: Longman, 1982), p. 159.

[121] Ibid.

[122] U.S. Bureau of the Census, Current Population Reports, *Money Income of Households, Families, and Persons in the United States: 1990*, series P-60, no. 174, August, 1991, p. 3.

[123] Ibid., p. 2.

[124] Data provided by Bureau of Labor Statistics, U. S. Department of Labor.

[125] Adapted from U.S. Bureau of the Census, Current Population Reports, *Money Income of Households, Families, and Persons in the United States: 1990*, series P-60, no. 174, August, 1991, p. 3.

[126] U.S. Bureau of the Census, *Statistical Abstract of the United States 1991*, p. 395.

[127] *New York Times*, June 30, 1970, pp. 1, 20.

RACISM: A
PORTRAIT IN
BLACK AND
WHITE

Blacks and whites tend not to agree on what racism is. . . .

"In general, white people today use the word 'racism' to refer to the explicit, conscious belief in racial superiority," wrote [Professor Judith] Lichtenberg. "For the most part black people mean something different by racism: they mean a set of practices and institutions that result in the oppression of black people. Racism, in this view, is not a matter of what's in people's heads but of what happens in the world."

Blacks and whites generally have conflicting definitions of racism because the phenomenon affects their groups differently. Blacks traditionally have been on the receiving end of racism and have, as a result, become far more attuned to it Whites, on the other hand, traditionally have been the sources of racism, or at least the passive beneficiaries of it.

As a result of these divergent perceptions and experiences, "whites and blacks have developed two different languages of race, and central to the differences of the language are different definitions of racism," said Robert Blauner, a University of California at Berkeley sociologist and author of "Black Lives, White Lives."

"In these two different languages of race, the black language of race sees race and racism as absolutely central to American culture and the way society is organized, whereas whites . . . don't see race and racism as central."

—*Washington Post*, June 8, 1992

black population. By contrast, approximately 101 million whites, or almost half of all whites, lived in the suburbs. And 57 percent of blacks lived in the central cities.[128]

America today is a multicultural society, a land of diversity, and often, conflict among groups. Some see danger in diversity, and a loss of national identity. The liberal historian Arthur M. Schlesinger, Jr., for example, has warned that the emphasis on ethnic differences may fragment the nation. What Schlesinger has termed the "cult of ethnicity," could, in his view, divide the country into "separate ethnic and racial communities."[129]

Despite that danger, the need remained to remedy the persistent inequalities that mocked the ideals of American society. Although minorities had registered political and economic gains, serious racial divisions persisted, and substantial numbers of blacks, Hispanics, Native Americans, and other groups remained outside the mainstream of American affluence.

More than a century after the Civil War, many Americans were still struggling for equality and justice. In 1963, in an address to the nation about civil rights for blacks, President Kennedy declared: "This is not a sectional issue. . . . We are confronted primarily with a moral issue. It is as old as the scriptures and is as clear as the American Constitution." America, he said, "will not be fully free until all its citizens are free."[130]

How America responds to this moral issue might well decide its future. The continued struggle for equality for all Americans remained a great domestic challenge, testing the nation's political system and the minds and hearts of the American people.

PERSPECTIVE

America is a multicultural society, made up of many different groups with distinct ethnic, racial, and religious identities. Yet despite the historic civil rights laws passed by Congress in the 1960s, and despite landmark decisions of the Supreme Court, many minority groups still do not enjoy full social and economic equality. Almost one out of three African Americans in the United States is poor, according to federal statistics, as opposed to one out of nine whites.

---

[128] Data provided by U.S. Bureau of the Census.
[129] Arthur M. Schlesinger, Jr., *The Disuniting of America: Reflections on a Multicultural Society* (New York: W. W. Norton & Co., 1992), p.15.

[130] "Radio and Television Report to the American People on Civil Rights," June 11, 1963, *Public Papers of the Presidents of the United States, John F. Kennedy 1963* (Washington, D.C.: U.S. Government Printing Office, 1964), p. 469.

Native Americans are among the most disadvantaged of all minorities. Unemployment among Native Americans on the reservations is high, life expectancy low. Many live in shacks, adobe huts, and abandoned automobiles.

The nation's Hispanic community—which includes Mexican Americans, Puerto Ricans, Cubans, and persons of Central or South American or other Spanish origin—is growing more than five times as fast as the population as a whole. The Census Bureau estimated there were 21.4 million Hispanics in the United States in 1991. Hispanics constitute another group that struggles with discrimination and poverty.

The 7.3 million Asian Americans counted in the 1990 census make up the fastest-growing minority group in the United States. By the beginning of the 1990s, Asian Americans constituted 3 percent of the population and were the third-largest minority, ranking just after African Americans (about 12 percent) and Hispanics (9 percent).

The Women's Liberation movement that emerged in the 1970s can be credited with much of the progress made by women toward equal rights and full participation in American society. Women have proved they can combine careers and child-rearing; by the 1990s, the two-income family in which both husband and wife worked was as common as it had been rare a few decades earlier. Today, more than half of adult American women work outside the home. However, bias based on sex is built into many public and private institutions. Women's salaries are often much lower than those of men performing the same work.

Many issues sometimes seen as primarily affecting women are not "women's issues" at all, but concern the entire society; one example is the issue of sexual harassment. In the fall of 1991 when the Senate Judiciary Committee was considering the nomination to the Supreme Court of Judge Clarence Thomas, Anita Hill, a law professor and a former aide to Thomas, stunned the nation with her graphic testimony to the Senate committee accusing Thomas of sexual harassment. Thomas denied all of Hill's charges, accused the committee of conducting a televised, "high-tech lynching," and was eventually confirmed by the panel, and then by the full Senate, 52–48. Many women were outraged at the treatment of Hill by a group of white male Senators. As a result, more women participated in the 1992 elections, both as campaign workers and as candidates.

The Supreme Court has provided evidence of shifting social attitudes in America, and the strength of the women's movement. In 1973 the Court ruled in *Roe* v. *Wade* that no state may interfere with a woman's right to have an abortion during the first three months of pregnancy. By 1992, however, the future of a woman's right to a legal abortion was in doubt. The Supreme Court ruled in 1989 that states may regulate abortions at any stage of pregnancy, including the first three months, and in 1990, that states could require teen-age girls to notify both parents before having an abortion. The major test of *Roe* v. *Wade* came in 1992 when the Court ruled on a restrictive Pennsylvania statute. A narrowly divided Court reaffirmed, 5–4, the constitutional right to an abortion that it had first established in *Roe* v. *Wade*. At the same time the Court upheld most of the restictions in the Pennsylvania law, although it struck down the requirement that a woman notify her husband before having an abortion.

Through a combination of court decisions, legislative action, and changing public perceptions, homosexuals have gained greater protection for their rights. By 1992, eighty-eight communities and eighteen states had passed local laws or taken executive action to protect gay and lesbian rights in employment, housing, and other areas. The laws concerning gays are not uniform, however. Many cities lack or have repealed laws protecting homosexuals. But in San Francisco, New York, Washington, D.C., and several other cities, gays had become an important political group.

Until relatively recently, the estimated 43 million Americans with disabilities were a kind of invisible minority, their rights of equal treatment and equal access more often than not overlooked or neglected. In employment, transportation, and in other ways, the disabled have been disadvantaged. In 1990, Congress acted to remove these everyday barriers to a normal life by passing the Americans with Disabilities Act, the most significant anti-discrimination law since the 1964 Civil Rights Act.

Unlike most other immigrants who came to these shores seeking freedom, African Americans came as slaves. In the *Dred Scott* decision (1857), the Supreme Court ruled that blacks were not citizens under the Constitution. The decision was later reversed by the Fourteenth Amendment, which in 1868 made citizens of the freed slaves.

The Supreme Court ruled in *Plessy* v. *Ferguson* (1896) that a state law requiring equal but separate accommodations for white and black railroad passengers did not violate the Fourteenth Amendment. This doctrine of "separate but equal" remained the law of the land until 1954, when Chief Justice Earl Warren delivered the unanimous decision of the Supreme Court in the historic school desegregation case of *Brown v. Board of Education of Topeka, Kansas.* The justices ruled that school segregation violated the Fourteenth Amendment's requirement of equal protection of the law for individuals. Yet, some four decades later, public school segregation still exists in many cities of the North and South. School segregation in the North often resulted from patterns of residential segregation. In some instances, the Court has approved busing of students to achieve desegregation. In 1991, however, the Court ruled in an Oklahoma City case that busing need not continue once a school district had made good faith efforts to end racial segregation.

Dr. Martin Luther King, Jr., a black minister, led the civil rights movement that began in the 1950s. Largely in response to that movement, several important civil rights bills were enacted by Congress in the mid-1960s. The Civil Rights Act of 1964 prohibited racial or religious discrimination in public accommodations. The Voting Rights Act of 1965 suspended literacy tests in southern counties in which blacks were being denied the right to vote. The 1965 law was later amended to apply to other minorities as well, and to states in the North and West. In 1968, laws were passed to prevent discrimination in housing, and to protect persons exercising their civil rights.

Protests by minority groups in the inner cities of America have sometimes turned violent. The urban riots of the 1960s were repeated in Los Angeles in 1992 after a jury that included no blacks acquitted four white police officers on trial for the beating of Rodney G. King, a black motorist.

In the wake of the civil rights movement, affirmative-action programs were established to give preference in university admissions or jobs to minorities. The programs were based on the theory that members of these groups were entitled to special preference because they were disadvantaged as a result of past discrimination. Opponents of affirmative action argued that such programs were a form of reverse discrimination against whites. These arguments eventually focused on the case of Allan Bakke. In 1973 and 1974 Bakke applied to medical school at the University of California at Davis. He did not get in. But in both years, minority students were admitted with much lower scores than Bakke's. Bakke sued. In 1978 the Supreme Court ordered Bakke admitted to medical school, but upheld the right of universities to give preference to minorities as long as they do not use rigid "quotas," such as the one at the University of California at Davis.

A year later, in the Weber case (1979), the Supreme Court upheld affirmative action in employment. Beginning in the late 1980s, a series of nine Supreme Court decisions made it more difficult for workers to sue employers for discrimination. Congress sought to counter the Court decisions with new legislation, touching off a two-year struggle with President Bush, who argued that employers would adopt hiring quotas for minorities to protect themselves against lawsuits. After vetoing one measure, Bush in 1991 signed a civil rights bill that overturned the Supreme Court's rulings and — in the wake of Senate hearings on the nomination of Clarence Thomas to the Supreme Court — allowed victims of sexual harassment to collect limited money damages.

By 1992, 26 members of the House of Representatives, one cabinet member, and a Supreme Court justice were African American. As of 1990, the proportion of black families with incomes of $20,000 or more had risen to 53.2 percent. But the median income of black families was only 58 percent of that of white families. Moreover, in 1990, 31.9 percent of black Americans, almost one-third, were below the poverty level.

Despite political and economic gains by African Americans, serious racial divisions persisted, and substantial numbers of blacks, Hispanics, Native Americans, and other groups remained outside the mainstream of American affluence.

Suggested Reading

Baldwin, James. *The Fire Next Time** (Dial Press, 1963). An examination of the status of blacks in America by a leading black writer. Baldwin argues for "total liberation" of blacks and maintains that blacks are the key to America's future.

Barker, Lucius J., and McCorry, Jesse J., Jr. *Black Americans and the Political System*, 2nd edition (Little, Brown, 1980). A comprehensive analysis of how black people have fared in the American political system. Includes discussions of how Congress, the courts, the presidency, and political parties have responded to the problems that African Americans face.

Brown, Dee. *Bury My Heart at Wounded Knee** (Holt, Rinehart and Winston, 1970). A powerful, detailed, and highly readable account of how Native Americans were driven from their villages and hunting grounds, often brutally, by white Americans as the frontier pushed westward. The book, which became a national best-seller, contains excellent descriptions of major Native American chiefs and tribal leaders.

Carmichael, Stokely, and Hamilton, Charles V. *Black Power** (Random House, 1967). The political definition of Black Power. Carmichael, the black leader who popularized the term, and Hamilton, a political scientist, urged black Americans to seek community control and use other such political tools.

Edsall, Thomas Byrne, with Edsall, Mary D. *Chain Reaction: The Impact of Race, Rights, and Taxes on American Politics* (Norton, 1991). A study of the rise to power of the presidential wing of the Republican party from 1968 to 1988. Argues that during this period the Republicans were able to forge a new coalition of voters, and to win five out of six presidential elections, by capitalizing on the twin issues of race and taxes.

Ellison, Ralph. *Invisible Man** (Modern Library, 1992). (Originally published in 1952.) In this novel a black writer describes the identity problem of blacks in a white society. The "invisible man" cannot be seen, Ellison argued, because whites refuse to acknowledge his existence.

Franklin, John Hope. *From Slavery to Freedom*, 6th edition* (Knopf, 1988). A classic study of black history in America written by a distinguished black historian.

Garcia, F. Chris, ed. *Latinos and the Political System** (University of Notre Dame Press, 1988). A wide-ranging set of essays on the involvement in United States politics of three major groups of Americans of Hispanic descent — Mexican Americans, Cuban Americans, and Puerto Ricans. Focuses on the history and demography of Hispanic Americans, and on the effects of their political participation on American public policies.

Gelb, Joyce, and Palley, Marian Lief. *Women and Public Policies*, revised and expanded edition* (Princeton University Press, 1987). An examination of the development of women's groups and their impact on the American political system. Traces the role of women in bringing about changes in several policy areas.

Hacker, Andrew. *Two Nations: Black and White, Separate, Hostile, Unequal* (Scribner's, 1992). A searching examination of race relations in the United States at the beginning of the 1990s. Contains extensive statistical data comparing the social and economic status of blacks and whites in America.

Jaynes, Gerald David, and Williams, Robin M., Jr. *A Common Destiny: Blacks and American Society* (National Academy Press, 1989). A comprehensive review, sponsored by the National Research Council, of the position of African Americans in American society since the Second World War. Emphasizes political participation, employment and income, family patterns, education, health, crime and the criminal justice system, and the important role of social, political, and religious institutions within the black community.

Jordan, Winthrop D. *White over Black: American Attitudes toward the Negro, 1550–1812** (University of North Carolina Press, 1968). A detailed examination of the attitudes of white people toward blacks during the first two centuries of slavery in North America. The book draws extensively on newspaper accounts, speeches, pamphlets, letters, and court records of the day.

Meier, August, and Rudwick, Elliott M. *From Plantation to Ghetto*, 3rd edition* (Hill and Wang, 1976). A history of blacks in America with emphasis on black protest movements, particularly in the twentieth century. Includes a discussion of the African heritage of American blacks.

Myrdal, Gunnar. *An American Dilemma: The Negro Problem and Modern Democracy** (Pantheon, 1975). (Originally published in 1944.) A classic study of race relations in the United States until the time of the Second World War. Traces the history of blacks in America and stresses the gap between the American creed of equality for all and the actual treatment black Americans have received. This book, by an eminent Swedish sociologist, has had a major influence on American thought about race relations.

Preston, Michael B.; Henderson, Lenneal J., Jr.; and Puryear, Paul L., eds. *The New Black Politics: The Search for Political Power*, 2nd edition (Longman, 1987). A collection of essays by leading scholars of black politics. Focuses on the shift from civil rights protests to electoral politics in the black search for equality.

Schlesinger, Arthur M., Jr. *The Disuniting of America: Reflections on a Multicultural Society.* (Norton, 1992). An essay on America as a multicultural nation. The author argues that too much emphasis on the culture of spearate ethnic groups will result in a fragmented society that loses it sense of national unity and American identity.

Whitehurst, Carol A. *Women in America: The Oppressed Majority* (Random House, 1977). A comprehensive analysis of the role of women in American society. Explores the status of women in the world of work, education, politics, and the home.

Woodward, C. Vann. *The Strange Career of Jim Crow*, 3rd revised edition* (Oxford University Press, 1974). A classic study of the establishment and consequences of segregation laws in the South after the Civil War.

* Available in paperback edition.

PART TWO

POLITICS U.S.A.

WHEN MARIE ANTOINETTE, according to legend, responded to the bread shortage in France by remarking, "Let them eat cake," she was showing an unwise disregard for public opinion. In due course, her head was cut off on the guillotine.

After President Lyndon Baines Johnson sent half a million men to fight in Vietnam, he discovered that public opinion had turned against him. In 1968, he announced that he would not run for president again and retired to his ranch in Texas.

Chapter 6

Public Opinion and Interest Groups

When his successor, Richard Nixon, became entangled in the Watergate scandal, his popularity dropped almost 40 points, the House Judiciary Committee voted to impeach him, and in 1974 he was forced to resign.

When in 1986 it became known that President Reagan had sold arms to Iran in an effort to free American hostages who had been seized in Lebanon, and that millions of dollars in profits had been diverted to the contras in Nicaragua, his approval rating dropped 16 points, plummeting from 63 to 47 percent in little more than a month.[1]

---

[1] *Gallup Report*, Jan.–Feb. 1987, no. 256–57, p. 43.

In March 1991, just after American forces dispatched to the Persian Gulf by President Bush forced Iraq's Saddam Hussein to withdraw from Kuwait, Bush's approval rating, buoyed by a wave of patriotic feeling, soared to 89 percent in the polls.[2] Only a year later, in February of 1992, with the administration plagued by economic recession and broad voter dissatis-

faction, Bush's popularity had plunged 50 points to 39 percent.[3] A few months later, his approval rating dropped even lower.

All governments are based, to some extent, on public opinion. Even dictators must pay some attention to public opinion, if only in order to repress it. In a democracy, public opinion is often described as a controlling force. "Public opinion stands out, in the United States," the English statesman James Bryce wrote, "as the great source of power, the master of servants who tremble before it."[4] But in fact, the role of public

---

[2] Gallup poll, February 28–March 3, 1991.

[3] Gallup/*USA Today*/CNN poll, February 19–20, 1992.

[4] James Bryce, *The American Commonwealth*, vol. 1 (New York: Putnam, Capricorn Books, 1959), p. 296.

opinion in a democracy is extremely difficult to define. Who is the public? What is public opinion? Does a person's opinion matter? Do political candidates and leaders manipulate public opinion? What role do the mass media play in the formation of public opinion? Should government leaders try to follow public opinion or their own judgment? What influence should, or does, public opinion have on government? On policymaking? Who governs? These are questions that continue to divide philosophers, politicians, pollsters, and political scientists.

PUBLIC OPINION

Although people often speak about opinions held by "the public," the phrase is not very useful because there are few questions on which every citizen has an opinion. The concept of "special publics" was developed by political scientists "to describe those segments of the public with views about particular issues." [5] In short, there are many publics.

What is opinion and when does it become public opinion? People have opinions on many subjects — music, fashions, and movies, for example. Sometimes such views are loosely referred to as "public opinion." In a narrower context, however, only opinions about public matters constitute public opinion.

Public opinion may thus be defined as the expression of attitudes about government and politics.

Public opinion would mean little, however, if it had no effect. Many political scientists, therefore, talk about public opinion as a process of interaction between the people and the government. V. O. Key, Jr., for example, defined public opinion as "those opinions held by private persons which governments find it prudent to heed." [6] Floyd Allport conceived of public opinion as enough people expressing themselves so strongly for or against something that their views are likely to affect government action. [7] And W. Lance Bennett has suggested that public opinion is *situational*, because the people who hold and express opinions are constantly changing, as do the issues and conditions to which the

public responds. [8] In the language of a political system (discussed in Chapter 1), public opinion can be thought of as one of the inputs of the system that may affect the outputs, or binding decisions, of the government. However, government officials try very hard to shape and manipulate public opinion to support their policies; to the extent that they succeed in this effort, public opinion *also* may be thought of as an output of the political system.

Private opinions become public — provided they are expressed — when they relate to government and politics. Not all privately held opinions about government and politics are expressed publicly, however; because of pressures for conformity, people may sometimes find it more prudent to keep their views private. [9] The phrase *political opinion* is sometimes used to refer to opinions on political issues — a choice among candidates or parties, for example.

How Public Opinion Is Formed

Walter Lippmann, in his classic study of public opinion, observed that each individual, in viewing distant events, tends to form a "picture inside his head of the world beyond his reach." [10] And, Lippmann noted, the mental snapshots do not always correspond with reality. How do individuals form their opinions about government and politics? As might be expected, the answer is as varied as the range of opinions people hold. The views of a sixty-year-old white Protestant dairy farmer in Wisconsin may vary sharply from those of an unemployed African American youth in South Central Los Angeles. We know this instinctively, without being told. But *why* may their opinions differ? A person's political background, and such factors as the influence of family and schools, certainly play a part. So do such variables as age, social class, income, religion, sex, ethnic background, geography, group membership, and political party preference.

Political Socialization: The Family and the Schools
Over the years, a person acquires a set of political atti-

---

[5] V. O. Key, Jr., *Public Opinion and American Democracy* (New York: Knopf, 1961), p. 10.

[6] Ibid., p. 14.

[7] Floyd H. Allport, "Toward a Science of Public Opinion," *Public Opinion Quarterly*, vol. 1, January 1937, p. 23.

[8] W. Lance Bennett, *Public Opinion in American Politics* (New York: Harcourt Brace Jovanovich, 1980), pp. 12–13.

[9] Allport, "Toward a Science of Public Opinion," p. 15.

[10] Walter Lippmann, *Public Opinion* (New York: Free Press, 1965), pp. 18–19. Originally published in 1922.

A well-armed Georgia family

tudes and forms opinions about social issues. In other words, a person undergoes *political socialization.*

The family plays a significant role in this process. In the view of Robert E. Lane, the family "incubates" political attitudes and opinions.[11] And the "crucial period" of a child's political, social, and psychological development is between the ages of nine and thirteen.[12]

Through watching television programs, and in various other ways, children acquire rudimentary ideas about politics at an early age. For example, 63 percent of fourth-graders questioned in one study identified with a political party. Almost every one of the children interviewed thought of party affiliation as a family characteristic: "All I know is *we're* not Republicans."[13] Children may acquire not only party preferences by listening to their parents, but "an orientation toward politics" and a set of "basic values and outlooks, which in turn may affect the individual's views on political issues long after he has left the family fold."[14]

How then to explain the students who protested the Vietnam war on college campuses in the 1970s, even though in some cases their parents may have supported the war? The answer is that children, obviously, do not always follow the political leanings of their parents and may even come to hold completely opposite views. That should not be surprising. A family is a group, and its influence on political attitudes may tend to diminish as children grow older and come into contact with other groups. A classic study of Bennington College students during the 1930s illustrates the point. Bennington had always been a very liberal college with a politically liberal faculty. During the Great Depression, however, "the families that could afford to send their daughters to an expensive private college tended to be conservative Republicans. The result was that women whose parents identified with the Republican party . . . were exposed to a faculty who were by and large Roosevelt Democrats. With each year of residence at the college, each successive class of students became more liberal and identified more strongly with Franklin D. Roosevelt than the class behind it."[15]

These and similar findings have led some political scientists to question the long-established emphasis on the family as the primary political influence on children. After studying a national sample of high school seniors, M. Kent Jennings and Richard G. Niemi concluded that the political "similarity between students and their parents was often modest."[16]

Elementary schools also have a part in the political socialization of children. Every country indoctrinates its schoolchildren with the basic values of its political system. American children salute the flag in school, sing patriotic songs, learn about George Washington's cherry tree (an invention of a literary charlatan named Parson Weems), and acquire some understanding of democracy and majority rule. In junior high or high school they are required to take "civics" courses.

But the extent of the influence of schools on opinion formation also has been questioned. The same study that found a divergence in views between parents and older children also reported that in high school, "Students gravitated toward the opinions of their friends more so than toward those of their social studies teachers."[17]

---

[11] Robert E. Lane, *Political Life* (New York: Free Press, 1959), p. 204.
[12] Fred I. Greenstein, *Children and Politics* (New Haven: Yale University Press, 1965), p. 1.
[13] Ibid., pp. 71–73.
[14] Key, *Public Opinion and American Democracy*, pp. 301, 305.

[15] Bennett, *Public Opinion in American Politics*, pp. 165–66, citing Theodore M. Newcomb's study in Theodore M. Newcomb, *Personality and Social Change* (New York: Dryden Press, 1943).
[16] M. Kent Jennings and Richard G. Niemi, *The Political Character of Adolescence* (Princeton: Princeton University Press, 1974), p. 319.
[17] Ibid., p. 328.

The political socialization of students continues in college — as the Bennington study suggests — and not only in the political science courses they may take. They also learn from the political environment on the campus. The high degree of political involvement, conflict, and controversy that characterized many American campuses in the 1960s and early 1970s, during the war in Vietnam, obviously had some influence on the political opinions of college students, whether or not they participated personally in the protest demonstrations.

While the gradual process of political socialization does have some general effect on the opinions people hold, a number of sociological and psychological factors also may have an influence on public opinion. Whether a person is young or old, rich or poor, farmer or city dweller, or westerner or southerner may affect the opinions he or she holds. This can be measured easily by taking almost any controversial public issue and analyzing the findings of public opinion polls. For example, in January of 1992, the Gallup poll asked people whether abortions should be legal. Nationally, 31 percent of those interviewed said abortion should be legal under all circumstances, 14 percent were opposed, and 2 percent had no opinion. But, among college graduates, 42 percent said abortion should always be legal, 10 percent were opposed, and 1 percent had no opinion.[18] In other words, a much higher proportion of college graduates favored legal abortion. On any issue — from legalizing pot to school busing — opinions often vary with such factors. Which factors are more important than others vary with the individual, and their relative significance is difficult to measure with precision. But a number can be identified.

Social Class Differences in social class, occupation, and income do appear to affect people's opinions on public matters. For example, one study indicates that people who identify with the working class are more likely to favor federal social-welfare programs than are people who identify with the middle class.[19] Another

---

Table 6-1

How Race, Religion, and Sex Influence Voter Attitudes
Nationwide surveys taken by the Gallup poll have shown that voter prejudice against blacks, Jews, Catholics, and women in politics has declined dramatically in recent years.

Beginning in 1958, the Gallup poll asked voters whether they would vote for a black for president. Following are the answers received in selected years.

	Yes	No	No Opinion
1958	38%	53%	9%
1965	59%	34%	7%
1969	67%	23%	10%
1978	77%	18%	5%
1983	77%	16%	7%
1987	79%	13%	8%

Voters also were asked whether they would vote for a Jew for president. Following are the answers received in selected years:

	Yes	No	No Opinion
1937	46%	46%	8%
1958	62%	28%	10%
1969	86%	8%	6%
1978	82%	12%	6%
1983	88%	7%	5%
1987	89%	6%	5%

Voters also were asked whether they would vote for a Catholic for president. Following are the answers received in selected years:

	Yes	No	No Opinion
1937	64%	28%	8%
1958	68%	25%	7%
1969	88%	8%	4%
1978	91%	4%	5%
1983	92%	5%	3%
1987	NA*	NA	NA

Voters also were asked whether they would vote for a woman for president. Following are the answers received in selected years:

	Yes	No	No Opinion
1937	31%	65%	4%
1958	52%	44%	4%
1969	54%	39%	7%
1978	76%	19%	5%
1983	80%	16%	4%
1987	82%	12%	6%

Voters also were asked whether they would vote for a homosexual for president. Following are the answers received:

	Yes	No	No Opinion
1983	29%	64%	7%
1987	NA	NA	NA

* NA: Not available.
SOURCE: Adapted from The Gallup Poll: Public Opinion 1935–1971, vols. 1–3 (New York: Random House, 1972); Gallup Opinion Index, March 1976, p. 20, and November 1978, p. 26; and Gallup Report, September 1983, pp. 9–14, and July 1987, no. 262, pp. 16–20.

---

[18] *The Gallup Poll Monthly*, January 1992. Respondents were asked, "Do you think abortions should be legal under any circumstances, legal only under certain circumstances, or illegal in all circumstances?"

[19] Lloyd A. Free and Hadley Cantril, *The Political Beliefs of Americans* (New Brunswick: Rutgers University Press, 1967), p. 216. See also extensive data of the Survey Research Center, University of Michigan, 1956, quoted in Key, *Public Opinion and American Democracy*, Chapter 6.

survey found that community leaders were more tolerant of Communists, atheists, and nonconformists than were people of lower social and economic status.[20] And a 1992 Gallup poll showed that 70 percent of people with incomes under $20,000 favored distributing condoms in high schools to prevent AIDS, a measure favored by a lower proportion, 59 percent, of those with incomes over $50,000.[21]

One study of political learning suggests that children brought up in homes of lower economic status are taught to accept authority more readily than children reared in upper-class homes. This study found that upper-class children are therefore more likely to criticize political authority, that they receive more political information from their parents, and that they are more likely to become politically active.[22]

Religion, Sex, and Ethnic Factors Religion, sex, race, and ethnic background also may influence the opinions people hold. To appeal to voters from ethnic groups, political parties in New York and other large cities customarily run a "balanced ticket" — one that includes an

---

[20] Samuel A. Stouffer, *Communism, Conformity, and Civil Liberties* (Gloucester: Peter Smith, 1963).
[21] *The Gallup Poll Monthly*, April 1992, p. 6.
[22] Greenstein, *Children and Politics*, pp. 155–56.

Irish candidate, an Italian candidate, and a Jewish candidate. In a primary election for mayor of New York City in 1969, the victorious Democratic candidate, Mario Procaccino, repeatedly emphasized that he was once an immigrant boy from Bisaccia, Italy. In a sentence that reached artistic perfection in its wide-ranging ethnic appeal, he told the crowds: "I couldn't get a job on Wall Street because my name was Procaccino and I was a Catholic, and my father was a shoemaker right in the heart of black Harlem."

Although Americans like to think they form their opinions without reference to race, creed, sex, or color, studies of their political behavior have demonstrated that this has not been the case in years past. (See Table 6-1.) For example, no Catholic was elected president until 1960. But in public opinion polls today Americans say they are much more willing to accept members of minority groups or women as political leaders.

There may be a gap, however, between how people say they will vote and their actual behavior in the voting booth. In 1988, for example, the Reverend Jesse L. Jackson, an African American candidate, won several important Democratic presidential primaries and caucuses, and demonstrated substantial strength among white voters. But many party leaders and voters said they felt a black could not be elected president. Jackson did not receive the nomination.

Jesse Jackson campaigning in Iowa, 1988

A voter's religious or ethnic background may affect party preference or political leanings. In a 1992 survey, nearly 60 percent of the Jews questioned and almost 42 percent of the Roman Catholics identified themselves as Democrats, compared to 36 percent of the Protestants.[23] In another survey, Jewish and black voters questioned were more inclined to support governmental social-welfare programs than were other groups.[24] In a third survey, more Catholics would vote for a woman or a Jew for president than would Protestants.[25]

Religious affiliation may also affect public opinion on *specific* issues — Quakers may favor disarmament; Jews may support aid to Israel; and Catholics may oppose the use of federal funds for abortions for the poor. Similarly, ethnic identification may help to shape public opinion on certain issues — Americans of Italian descent may be offended by the depiction of fictional gangsters with Italian names on publicly licensed television stations; African Americans may favor stronger legislation aimed at preventing housing discrimination.

Geographic Factors People's opinions are sometimes related to where they live. Democrats have traditionally been more numerous in the rural South and the big cities of the North; Republicans have been stronger in the Midwest and rural areas. Yet sectional and geographic differences among Americans are often exaggerated; on some broad questions of foreign policy, for example, sectional variations are likely to be minimal. And, on many issues, differences in outlook between the cities and suburbs have replaced the old sectional divisions. Whether people come from an urban or rural background may be more significant today than their geographic roots.

Group Influence Although the shape of a person's opinions on public questions is initially influenced by the family, in later life, other groups, friends, associates, and peers also influence individual views. In numerous experiments psychologists have discovered that people tend to "go along" with the decision of a group even when it contradicts accepted standards of morality and behavior. In a classic and controversial experiment at Yale University, Stanley Milgram placed subjects in groups of four, three of whom were secretly Milgram's

assistants. The one unwitting subject was told to administer powerful electric shocks to the person serving as the "learner" in the experiment whenever the "learner" made an error in performing a laboratory task. In fact, no electricity was being administered, but the subject did not know that, and the "learner" shouted, moaned, and screamed as the supposed voltage became higher. The results were surprising: egged on by their colleagues, 85 percent of the subjects administered shocks beyond 120 volts, and 17.5 percent went all the way to the maximum, a shock of 450 volts.[26]

On occasion, group influence may even prevent the expression of opinion. Almost everyone has been in a situation at one time or another where he or she hesitates to express a political opinion because those listening might disagree or even be hostile. The author Mark Twain said he exposed to the world "only my trimmed and perfumed and carefully barbered public opinions and conceal carefully, cautiously, wisely, my private ones." [27] An individual who expresses an opinion is vulnerable, because "social groups can punish him for failing to toe the line." [28] If a view seems too risky to express, an individual may keep it private. But if public opinion changes, people may voice previously hidden feelings.[29]

Various types of groups may influence people. A group whose views serve as guidelines to an individual's opinion is known as a *reference group*. There are two types of reference groups. Groups that people come into face-to-face contact with in everyday life — friends, office associates, or a local social club — are known as *primary groups*, since their influence is direct. *Secondary groups*, as the term implies, may be more remote. These are organizations or groups of people such as labor unions or fraternal, professional, or religious groups.

[23] Gallup poll, July 1992, p. 1.
[24] Free and Cantril, *The Political Beliefs of Americans*, p. 148.
[25] *Gallup Report*, September 1983, no. 216, pp. 11, 12.

[26] Stanley Milgram, "Group Pressure and Action Against a Person," *Journal of Abnormal and Social Psychology*, vol. 69 (1964), pp. 137–43. In a somewhat similar experiment, Solomon Asch, a psychologist at Swarthmore College, placed subjects among groups of college students whose members, unknown to the subjects, deliberately responded incorrectly when they were asked to match up black lines of varying lengths on white cards. Influenced by the group's false judgments, the subjects gave incorrect answers 37 percent of the time. S. E. Asch, *Psychology Monograph*, vol. 70, no. 416 (1956).
[27] Mark Twain, *The Autobiography of Mark Twain*, Charles Neider, ed. (New York: Harper & Row, 1959), p. 386.
[28] Elisabeth Noelle-Neumann, "The Spiral of Silence: A Theory of Public Opinion," *Journal of Communication*, vol. 24 (Spring 1974), p. 43.
[29] Ibid., p. 45.

Ross Perot appearing on
"Larry King Live"

Mass Media In the television age, the images that flash into people's living rooms obviously have a major impact on public opinion. So do newspapers, magazines, and other media that bring news about government and politics to the public.

In the 1992 presidential campaign, for example, the impact of television seemed even greater than ever. When Texas businessman Ross Perot first revealed his presidential ambitions, he chose to do so on "Larry King Live," a popular television talk show on CNN. As Perot zoomed upward in the polls in the spring of that year, surpassing his rivals, President Bush and Governor Bill Clinton of Arkansas, he seemed to be on TV everywhere. Perot did not run in any primaries; he used the talk shows and morning television shows to get his personality and views across to the American public. The impact of mass media on the formation of public opinion is discussed in greater detail beginning on page 198.

Party Identification In any campaign, voters are influenced by a candidate's personality and appearance and by the nature of the issues that arise. But how they vote and what they think about public issues may also be closely linked to their political party affiliation. Political scientists make distinctions, therefore, among *candidate* orientation, *issue* orientation, and *party* identification.[30]

As an example of how party identification may relate to opinions, in 1987 more than one-third of all Republicans (36 percent) favored a decrease in spending for social welfare programs. But only 13 percent of Democrats favored such a decrease.[31]

There is evidence, however, that party ties are becoming somewhat less important; the number of Americans who consider themselves political independents has increased in recent years. The loosening of party loyalties was never more dramatically illustrated than during the 1992 presidential election campaign. As has been noted, during the spring of that year, polls showed deep voter dissatisfaction both with President Bush, the announced Republican candidate for re-election, and Governor Bill Clinton of Arkansas, the front-runner for the Democratic presidential nomination. In May, there was a sudden groundswell of support among many voters for a new candidate, Ross Perot, who was unaffiliated with either major party. Portraying himself as an outsider unencumbered by the conventional political machinery, Perot suddenly leapt ahead of both major-party candidates in some polls. Perot dropped out as the Democrats nominated Clinton. Once again the

---

[30] Angus Campbell, Philip E. Converse, Warren E. Miller, and Donald E. Stokes, Survey Research Center, University of Michigan, *The American Voter* (New York: Wiley, 1960).
[31] *Gallup Report*, August 1987, no. 263, p. 25.

presidential campaign was a two-man race. Both Clinton and Bush rose in the polls after their parties' national conventions, which helped to rally rank-and-file party members to their cause. Although Perot had pulled out in July, he continued his efforts to get on the ballot in every state, and did, paying his "volunteers" $7 million. Then, in October, he announced he was a candidate again, turning the campaign into a three-way contest once more. Since Perot ran without benefit of a political party, in 1992 it seemed as though party labels were less of an advantage than in the past to candidates for the presidency. Nevertheless, and despite the deep voter discontent in that year, about two-thirds of all adult Americans identify with one of the two major parties.

Although children may later come to hold views different from those of their parents, party loyalty tends to be passed on from one generation to the next. These factors will be discussed in more detail in the next three chapters.

The Qualities of Public Opinion

Public opinion has identifiable *qualities*. Like pictures, public opinions may be sharp or fuzzy, general or detailed — and they may fade. In analyzing the qualities of opinions, political scientists speak of *direction*, *intensity*, and *stability*.

There was a time when political scientists would describe people as being "for" or "against" something. But after the Second World War, when public opinion polling evolved into a more exact science, pollsters and analysts discovered that simple "yes" or "no" answers sometimes masked wide gradations in opinion on a given subject. In other words, it is possible to measure opinions in *direction* along a scale.[32] Thus people speak of liberals and radicals as being to "the left" and conservatives to "the right," with moderates in "the center." If radical political opinions are thought of as being at one end of a line and conservative at the other end, the opinion of one individual may be located at a given point along the line. One person may favor government control of all medical programs; another may prefer federal health programs limited to the aged and needy; and a third person may favor wholly private health care.

Public opinion varies in *intensity* as well as direction. A person may have mild opinions or more deeply felt views. An automobile owner may be only mildly in sympathy with attempts to reduce gasoline consump-

---

[32] Key, *Public Opinion and American Democracy*, p. 11.

"Grayson is a liberal in social matters, a conservative in economic matters, and a homicidal psychopath in political matters."

Drawing by Lorenz
©1974 The New Yorker Magazine, Inc.

Another quality of public opinion is its degree of *stability*. Opinions change — sometimes slowly, sometimes rapidly and unpredictably — in response to new events or personalities. As already discussed, public opinion about President Bush fluctuated greatly during his time in office, rising to great heights during the Persian Gulf War early in 1991, and then plunging downward when the reality of the faltering economy took over. These sharp variations in voter attitudes can be recorded with some degree of precision. Public opinion may be measured and its qualities analyzed. The measuring tool is the political poll.

Political Polls

In the week before the 1980 election, most political observers and pollsters were terming the contest "too close to call." But during that final week, Ronald Reagan's campaign poll-taker, Richard Wirthlin, assured the Republican nominee that he would defeat President Carter by 8 or 9 percentage points in the popular vote. As it turned out, Reagan won the election by 10 points.

Today, virtually all presidential candidates rely on advice from a poll-taker. The data gathered by political polls are not always reliable, however. In 1948 the Gallup and Roper polls wrongly predicted that Governor Thomas E. Dewey of New York, the Republican candidate, would defeat President Harry S Truman. Dewey

tion by holding down the speed limit. By contrast, a "right to life" anti-abortion activist may hold very strong opinions. Robert E. Lane and David O. Sears have suggested that there may be "something congenial" about extreme views and intensity of opinion "which suggests a mutual support." [33] That is, people well to the left or right may hold their political opinions more fiercely than others.

---

[33] Robert E. Lane and David O. Sears, *Public Opinion* (Englewood Cliffs: Prentice-Hall, 1964), p. 106.

1992: THE POLLS PREDICT A WINNER

Although in 1992 President Bush, who was behind in the public opinion polls, discounted their accuracy—and assailed "nutty pollsters"—the final polls by all the major survey organizations were remarkably close to each other and to the actual outcome.

For example, the last ABC News Poll before election day reported Bill Clinton leading with 44 percent, Bush with 37 percent, and independent candidate Ross Perot with 16 percent. The Gallup poll for CNN/USA Today reported Clinton ahead 44 to 36, with 14 for Perot, and the Harris Poll had Clinton leading 44 to 38, with 17 for Perot.

On election day, the actual vote was Clinton 43 percent, Bush 38 percent, and Perot 19 percent. Since polls usually have a margin for error of 3 percent, the results in 1992 were very close to the mark. Some polls report only "likely voters," and how those voters are identified could account for some of the differences in the results.

Pollsters are careful to point out that their polls are not predictions of election outcomes, but snapshots of the electorate at a given moment. Since several of the polls were taken over a two- or three-day period ending November 1, two days before the election, they could not forecast the outcome precisely in any event.

—Based on data in *New York Times*, November 3, 1992, and *Congressional Quarterly*, Weekly Report, November 7, 1992.

---

lost. "I never paid any attention to polls myself," Truman later wrote in his typically direct style.[34]

The art of political polling has come a long way since 1948, and the margin of error has been greatly reduced. But polls may still be wrong or in conflict with one another. For example, several polls just before the 1988 New Hampshire presidential primary showed then Vice-President George Bush and Senator Robert Dole in a dead heat, although the final Gallup poll showed Dole ahead by 8 points. In the actual vote in New Hampshire, Bush defeated his rival by 9 percentage points, a 17-point error for Gallup.[35]

Even when polls are accurate, they may be so swiftly overtaken by events as to appear to be misleading. In February 1984, the *New York Times* published a page-one story reporting that the latest nationwide *New York Times*/CBS News Poll showed that Walter Mondale, the choice of 57 percent of those polled, "now holds the most commanding lead ever recorded this early in a Presidential nomination campaign by a nonincumbent."[36] On the same day the story appeared, the voters of New Hampshire gave Senator Gary Hart a dramatic victory over Mondale, catapulting Hart into the national spotlight and touching off a string of primary victories for the Coloradan.

Despite some well-publicized errors, political polls are substantially accurate more often than not, and frequently useful as a guide to voter sentiment. Politicians are convinced of their value.[37] Today, polls—before,

"And don't waste your time canvassing the whole building, young man. We all think alike."

Drawing by Stevenson
©1982 The New Yorker Magazine, Inc.

---

[34] Harry S Truman, *Memoirs by Harry S Truman: Years of Trial and Hope*, vol. 2 (Garden City: Doubleday, 1956), p. 177.

[35] "New Hampshire Confounded Most Pollsters," *Washington Post*, February 8, 1988, p. A1.

[36] *New York Times*, February 28, 1984, p. 1.

[37] Louis Harris estimated in 1968, for example, that 80 percent of all candidates for the U.S. Senate used polls.

COUNTING
THE BEANS

The federal government's Crop Reporting Board, among its various duties, must count the number of soybeans in America. It can't, so it takes a random sample. The results are closely guarded, so that speculators in the commodities markets cannot profit from advance information. The following news story describes how the board works:

WASHINGTON — The Agriculture Department's Crop Reporting Board . . . works primarily for the nation's farmers, who decide how much to plant, or breed, based on the board's predictions. . . .

Across the United States, the board employs 3,500 part-time "enumerators," as they are called. . . . The enumerators might be assigned

to estimate the soybean crop. They cannot count every bean, so instead they select random-sample plots and use probability tables, much the way opinion pollsters do, to predict a total. . . .

For the soybean crop, enumerators in several states pick out sample plots three feet long and two rows wide. Then they get down on all fours and, yes, they count the beans. . . .

The results of all those bean counts, top-secret totals that cannot be discussed on pain of going to jail, are sent to Washington, where they are locked into a safe at the Crop Reporting Board.

—*New York Times*, February 20, 1984

during, and even after Election Day — are a standard part of political campaigns. In a presidential election year, millions of dollars are paid to the more than 200 polling organizations in the United States.[38]

How Polls Work A political polling organization may question only 1,500 people, or even fewer, to measure public opinion on a given issue or to determine which candidate leads in a campaign.[39] Many people find it difficult to accept the idea that public opinion in an entire nation may be measured from such a small sample. Behind some of the skepticism is the belief that each individual is unique, and that his or her thoughts cannot be so neatly categorized. If only 1,500 Americans are polled in a population of 254,000,000, each person questioned is, in effect, "speaking for" 169,333 people. How, it may be asked, can the views of one individual represent the opinions of so many fellow citizens?

The answer lies in the mathematical law of *probability*. Toss a coin 1,000 times and it will come up heads about 500 times. The same principle of probability is

used by insurance companies in computing life expectancy. And it is used by poll-takers in measuring opinion. Because the group to be measured, known as the *population* or the *universe*, is usually too large to be polled individually on every issue, the poll-taker selects at random a sample of the population. The *random sample*, also called a *probability sample*, must be representative of the universe being polled. When the *Literary Digest* polled owners of automobiles and telephones in 1936 — a time when many Americans had neither — it was not sampling a representative group of Americans. As a result, its prediction that Franklin Roosevelt would lose the presidential election proved incorrect. If the sample is of sufficient size and properly selected at random, the law of probability will operate, and the results will usually be accurate within a 4-percent margin of error.

One way to conceptualize the principles involved in polling is to think of a huge jar of white marbles to which a smaller number of yellow marbles are added. Suppose the jar is thoroughly shaken so that all the marbles are completely mixed together. If a scoop is then used to remove enough of the marbles, the sample should contain the same proportion of yellow to white marbles as exists in the entire jar.

Take another example. Suppose that one out of every four Americans has blue eyes. For the same reason that a flipped coin comes up heads half the time, or the same percentage of yellow marbles can be scooped from

---

[38] Major political polling organizations include the American Institute of Public Opinion (the Gallup poll) and Louis Harris & Associates, Inc. (the Harris survey), which publish their findings in newspapers and magazines. A number of pollsters also take private polls for political clients. In addition, there are many smaller state and regional polls, as well as polls conducted by newspapers and television networks.

[39] The Gallup poll normally uses a national sample of 1,000 persons. Louis Harris interviews 1,250 people.

the jar each time, the probability is that a random sample will catch in its net the same percentage of blue-eyed persons as exists in the whole population. Using this technique, we can estimate the number of blue-eyed Americans from a random sample. Similarly, we can estimate the number of Americans who support abortion or who oppose capital punishment.

But a true random sample of the entire United States would be very difficult (and very expensive) to take. A survey researcher would, in theory, have to have a list of everyone in the population, and then select at random the names of people to be questioned. To simplify the task, most polling organizations use *cluster sampling*—interviewing several people from the same neighborhood. As long as the geographic areas are chosen at random, the clustering will not result in an unacceptable margin of error.[40] Poll-takers often combine the cluster technique with the selection in a series of stages or steps of geographic areas to be polled, with each unit selected becoming successively smaller. For example, in pinpointing the location for an interview, the pollster might start by selecting regions of the country, and then choose counties or other smaller areas at random within those regions. From there, still selecting at random, the researcher would scale down to a city, a neighborhood, a precinct, a block of houses, an apartment building, and then one apartment, where the actual interview would take place. The desirable size of the sample does not depend very much on the size of the population being measured, and beyond a certain point, increasing the number of persons polled reduces the sampling error only slightly.

A less reliable method of polling is based on the *quota sample*. For example, an organization that wanted to test ethnic opinion would instruct its staff to interview African Americans, Italians, Jews, Poles, Hispanics, and so on, in proportion to their percentage in the population as a whole. Under this method the interviewer has considerable discretion in the choice of persons selected to be questioned. The poll-taker might select only well-dressed or cooperative individuals, thus skewing the results. Therefore, quota sampling is less useful than random sampling as a method of measuring political opinion.

The method of selecting the sample is not the only factor that may affect the reliability of a poll. The way in which questions are phrased, the personality of the interviewer, and the manner in which poll data are interpreted may all affect the result.[41] Perhaps 10 to 20 percent of the people interviewed refuse to answer or answer only reluctantly. A Gallup poll completed two days before the 1992 election showed 6 percent "undecided"—a fairly normal percentage of persons in this flexible category. How this undecided vote is interpreted and allocated can drastically affect the accuracy of a political poll.

Political polls do not necessarily predict the outcome of an election. A poll only measures opinion at the moment the survey is taken. A poll taken four days before an election, for example, will not always match the vote on Election Day. In 1992, a Gallup poll was taken on October 31 through November 1 and published on November 2, one day before the election; with the percent undecided allocated among the three major candidates, it gave Bill Clinton 49 percent, George Bush 37 percent, and Ross Perot 14 percent. Clinton won the election with six percentage points less than the poll had reported. The actual vote for the two major-party candidates was 43 percent for Clinton, and 38 percent for Bush. Independent candidate Ross Perot received 19 percent of the vote but carried no states.[42]

An intriguing question often raised is whether there is a danger that political polls themselves may create a "bandwagon effect" and influence the outcome of an election. Do some voters or convention delegates, out of a desire to be with the winner, jump on the bandwagon of the candidate who is leading in the polls?

Whether or not a "bandwagon effect" really exists has been debated by political scientists for some time. For example, Bernard Hennessy found "little evidence" of such an effect, arguing that indifferent voters would not care who won or even remember poll results, and concerned voters would not cast their ballot for a candidate simply because of a poll.[43]

But other scholars have suggested that indeed there may be a bandwagon effect. As already noted, people often compare their views to the dominant public opinion before speaking out. Elisabeth Noelle-Neu-

---

[40] Herbert F. Weisberg and Bruce D. Bowen, *An Introduction to Survey Research and Data Analysis* (San Francisco: Freeman, 1977), p. 24.

[41] For a discussion of the pitfalls and problems of public-opinion polling, see Michael Wheeler, *Lies, Damn Lies, and Statistics: The Manipulation of Public Opinion in America* (New York: Liveright, 1976).

[42] *New York Times*, November 3, 1992, p. A13; and *National Journal*, November 7, 1992, p. 2539.

[43] Bernard Hennessy, *Essentials of Public Opinion* (North Scituate: Duxbury Press, 1975), pp. 70–71.

mann argues that there exists a "spiral process which prompts . . . individuals to perceive the changes in opinion and to follow suit. . . ."[44]

During past presidential campaigns, the television networks were criticized for projecting primary results in some states before the polls there had closed. The networks based their predictions either on mathematical projections of early returns, or on "exit polls" taken as people left the voting booths. Critics of these practices argued that such early "calls" of an election contest would discourage some voters from bothering to cast their ballots.

It is also possible that polls may create other effects. For example, a candidate may need to make a reasonably strong early showing in the polls in order to attract and raise the money needed to campaign. Many contributors want to back a winner.

On the other hand, if the polls suggest that a candidate is running behind, supporters of that candidate may be more inclined to go to the polls. Conversely, if the candidate's rating in the polls is high, some potential supporters may become complacent and stay home on Election Day. Such theories, based on present evidence, are debatable, but the possible effect of polls on voting is a subject that merits further exploration.[45]

In any event, polls today are a permanent part of the political landscape and an important tool of the "new politics."

What Americans Believe

Do Americans agree on anything? Some people say that there is an underlying consensus in America, a basic agreement among its citizens on fundamental democratic values and processes, that permits democracy to flourish. But the supposed consensus often melts away and disappears on closer examination. For example, Americans say they believe in fair play and justice, but they do not necessarily stick by those principles when their own interests are threatened. White homeowners may know that it is "fair" for a black family to buy the house next door, but they may oppose the sale if they

believe that the value of their property would go down if the neighborhood becomes racially mixed.

On the whole, Americans seem to be pragmatic, approaching each issue as it comes up and judging it on its merits. Most Americans do not have a fixed, coherent set of political beliefs. People may have clear preferences on specific issues, but often their convictions are not interrelated. A voter who is "liberal" on one issue may be "conservative" on another. For example, a majority of Americans have agreed that "the Federal Government should act to meet public needs" in such fields as education, medical care, public housing, urban renewal, unemployment, and poverty.[46] But when the same Americans are asked questions about their general concepts of the proper role of government, they are "pronouncedly conservative." Thus, a clear majority agreed with the statement: "We should rely much more on individual initiative and not so much on governmental welfare programs."[47] On some issues, in short, Americans seem to have a "split personality."

Why should Americans hold such seemingly contradictory opinions? One explanation may lie in the competing fundamental values of *individualism* and *equality* that observers such as Alexis de Tocqueville saw in America as far back as the early nineteenth century. The belief in "rugged individualism" may cause some Americans to complain about "welfare chiselers." The belief in equality may explain why the same individuals favor government social programs.[48]

Some political research has suggested that the pattern of beliefs in America is changing, and that voters are becoming more aware of political issues and thinking about them more coherently. One study, *The Changing American Voter*, found "long-term tendencies of the public to move in one direction or another" on the issues.[49] Since the 1960s, the study found, voters have begun to evaluate candidates and parties more in terms of their issue positions, with this being reflected to some extent by how citizens vote.[50] "The role of party has declined as a guide to the vote," the study reported. "And, as party has declined in importance, the role of issues appears to have risen."[51]

---

[44] Elisabeth Noelle-Neumann, "Turbulences in the Climate of Opinion: Methodological Applications of the Spiral of Silence Theory," *Public Opinion Quarterly*, vol. 41, no. 2 (Summer 1977), p. 144.

[45] For a pollster's view of the question, see Dr. George H. Gallup, "Polls and the Political Process," *Public Opinion Quarterly*, vol. 29 (Winter 1965–66), p. 546.

[46] Free and Cantril, *The Political Beliefs of Americans*, p. 13.

[47] Ibid., p. 30.

[48] See Bennett, *Public Opinion in American Politics*, pp. 141–50.

[49] Norman H. Nie, Sidney Verba, and John R. Petrocik, *The Changing American Voter*, enlarged ed. (Cambridge: Harvard University Press, 1979), p. 348.

[50] Ibid.

[51] Ibid., p. 156.

Political Participation

One way people can influence government is through the force of public opinion. An even more direct way people can make their opinions felt is by voting. Yet, one of the more surprising facts about America is that almost half the people — and sometimes more than half — do not bother to vote.

In 1992 the Census Bureau estimated that 189,044,000 citizens in the United States were old enough to vote. Of that total, approximately 123,200,000 registered to vote. Of these, about 104,000,000 actually cast their ballots for president on Election Day, November 3. That means about 55 percent of the population of voting age actually voted.

In off-year, nonpresidential elections, usually well under half of the voting-age population goes to the polls to vote for senators and representatives. In 1970, for example, 43.5 percent cast their ballots for members of the House. In 1974 only 35.9 percent voted for members of the House. For 1978 the figure was down to 34.9 percent. It rose to 38.0 percent in 1982, then dropped to 33.4 percent in 1986. There was no significant change in 1990, with 33.1 percent voting for members of the House.[52]

These figures, not uncommon for American elections, raise important questions about the nature of "government by the people." "Every regime lives on a body of dogma, self-justification, glorification and propaganda about itself," E. E. Schattschneider has written.

> In the United States, this body of dogma and tradition centers about democracy. The hero of the system is the voter who is commonly described as the ultimate source of all authority. The fact that something like forty million adult Americans are so unresponsive to the regime that they do not trouble to vote is the single most truly remarkable fact about it. . . . What kind of system is this in which only a little more than half of us participate? Is the system actually what we have been brought up to think it is?[53]

Some people do not vote because they may feel the system holds no benefits for them, or because they feel there is no difference between the candidates. For some, therefore, nonvoting may be a form of protest. Others are nonvoters because they are apathetic about politics and political issues.

Americans not only fail to participate fully in the political system, it has been argued that they are often poorly informed about government and many public issues. One study found only 26 percent of the American public to be "well informed" on specific questions dealing with international affairs (such as the identity of four major world leaders).[54]

Public knowledge about many specific questions concerning domestic politics is equally limited. One Gallup poll reported that only 46 percent of the voters knew the name of their representative in Congress.[55] Another survey showed that only 62 percent knew their representative's party affiliation; and only 21 percent knew how he or she had voted on any major bill.[56] According to a Gallup poll published in 1986, only 45 percent of the public knew that the First Amendment or the Bill of Rights protects freedom of the press.[57] A nationwide survey of seventeen- and eighteen-year-olds found that only 45 percent knew who represented them in Congress; only 65 percent could name the three branches of the federal government; only 32 percent could name the chief justice of the United States; and only 67 percent knew that the Democrats controlled the House of Representatives.[58]

In a Gallup poll of college seniors conducted in 1989, 24 percent of the students did not know that Franklin D. Roosevelt was president during World War II, 23 percent thought that Soviet ruler Joseph Stalin coined the phrase "Iron Curtain" (it was British statesman Winston Churchill), and two-thirds thought that the words "government of the people, by the people, for the people shall not perish from the earth," appear in the U.S. Constitution, rather than Lincoln's Gettysburg address.[59]

Schattschneider has concluded, "An amazingly large number of people do not seem to know very much

---

[52] U.S. Bureau of the Census, *Statistical Abstract of the United States: 1991*, p. 270; and Elections Research Center, Washington, D.C.

[53] E. E. Schattschneider, *The Semisovereign People* (New York: Holt, Rinehart, and Winston, 1960), p. 99. By 1988 the number of nonvoters totaled about 91 million.

[54] Free and Cantril, *The Political Beliefs of Americans*, p. 61.

[55] Gallup poll, *Washington Post*, August 1, 1982, p. A19.

[56] Quoted in David S. Broder, *The Party's Over: The Failure of Politics in America* (New York: Harper & Row, 1971), p. 184. Note, however, that substantially more voters are able to identify and evaluate their representatives in Congress when presented with the names on a list. See Chapter 12.

[57] Gallup poll in *People and the Press* (Los Angeles: Times Mirror, 1986), p. 19.

[58] Gallup poll, 1978, conducted for the National Municipal League. Data provided by the National Municipal League.

[59] Gallup poll conducted for the National Endowment for the Humanities, *Boulder Daily Camera*, October 9, 1989, p. 1.

Secret Service agents
moments after assassination
attempt on President Reagan,
March 30, 1981,
Washington, D.C.

about what is going on." [60] One effect of the lack of public knowledge is to give government officials wider latitude in making policy decisions — since they may assume that the public will neither know nor care very much about the results of those decisions.

On the other hand, ignorance about political matters is not always the fault of the public. The government, in an effort to place its policies in the best possible light, sometimes issues misleading information or engages in outright deception.[61] For example, the Kennedy administration initially denied that CIA-supported exiles had invaded Cuba in 1961; the Johnson administration suppressed crucial information about events in the Tonkin Gulf in 1964; and in 1983 the Reagan White House denied that American military forces had invaded or planned to invade the Caribbean island of Grenada even as the troops prepared to land. Later, President Reagan ordered that his arms-for-hostages dealings with Iran be hidden from Congress and the public. And the Bush administration concealed the extent of United States military and economic support for Iraq in the years before the Persian Gulf War of 1991.

Some scholars challenge the traditional assumption that many voters are politically ignorant. They suggest that the degree of information possessed by the public is "situational"; that is, it may vary from one election to another. For example, when differences between candidates are sharper, the public seems to absorb more information. "Voters *can* take stands, perceive party differences, and vote on the basis of them. But whether they do or not depends heavily on the candidate and the parties." [62]

Violence

On the afternoon of March 30, 1981, as President Reagan left the Washington Hilton Hotel, John W. Hinckley, Jr., fired a .22-caliber revolver, seriously wounding the president and three other persons. A Secret Service

[60] Schattschneider, *The Semisovereign People*, p. 132.

[61] See David Wise, *The Politics of Lying: Government Deception, Secrecy, and Power* (New York: Random House, 1973).

[62] Richard G. Niemi and Herbert F. Weisberg, *Controversies in American Voting Behavior* (San Francisco: Freeman, 1976), p. 168. See also Bennett, *Public Opinion in American Politics*, pp. 27–30, 43–48, and 90–91.

man pushed the chief executive into his limousine, and he was taken to the hospital, where surgeons removed a bullet from his lung. Reagan recovered from his wounds. His twenty-five-year-old assailant, tried and found not guilty by reason of insanity, was committed to a mental hospital for an indefinite period.

As the television networks played and replayed the videotape of that terrible moment when the president was shot, it seemed all too familiar to the people of America. Assassination and violence have several times loomed over the political landscape in recent years.

Democracy operates on the premise that at least a substantial number of citizens will participate peacefully in the political system. The "consent of the governed" implies that public opinion plays a role in the political process. But if the system fails to respond to the demands placed upon it, or if participation is slow to bring change, individuals or groups may vent their anger against the system in violent ways. Or unbalanced persons, acting out of personal frustration, may choose political targets.

Sometimes the violence is viewed at least in part as a form of political or social protest, such as the rioting that broke out in Los Angeles in April of 1992 after a jury with no blacks acquitted four white police officers in the beating of a black motorist, Rodney G. King. At other times, organized groups, such as the radical Weather Underground in the 1960s or the Puerto Rican nationalists, have engaged in bombings for stated political ends. And all too often in American history, deranged assassins have struck at political leaders.

The United States has had a violent past, for Americans have not always sought to bring about political change through lawful or peaceful means. The American Revolution, the Civil War, the frontier, racial lynchings, and the Ku Klux Klan are some examples. Clearly, assassination and violence are not new forms of American political behavior. Four American presidents have been assassinated—Lincoln, Garfield, McKinley, and Kennedy—and serious attempts have been made against the lives of six others—Jackson, Theodore Roosevelt, Franklin Roosevelt, Truman, Ford, and Reagan.

But political assassination and violence occurred with tragic frequency during the 1960s. The assassinations of President Kennedy in 1963; of his brother Robert Kennedy, a presidential candidate, in 1968; and of Dr. Martin Luther King, Jr., that same year—all had dramatic impact on the political process. So did the racial violence in the cities.

The Warren Commission, the presidential panel that studied President Kennedy's assassination, concluded that it had been carried out by Lee Harvey Oswald, who "acted alone," a finding challenged in many books, and in a popular film, *JFK*, by those who contend that shots were fired by more than one person and that Kennedy was the victim of a conspiracy. Similar conspiracy theories circulated for many years after the assassination of President Lincoln in 1865. But most political assassinations in American history appear to have been the acts of unbalanced persons venting their rage and frustration on the national leader. Such purposeless acts differ in motivation from the planned assassination of a political leader by conspirators or revolutionists. Planned assassinations may be viewed as an attempt to go outside the political system. They are not a form of "participation" in the political system, but rather a rejection of that system.

As a presidential study panel reported, "Assassination, especially when the victim is a president, strikes at the heart of the democratic process. It enables one man to nullify the will of the people in a single, savage act. It touches the lives of all the people of the nation."[63]

Mass Opinion in a Democracy

Suppose the president of the United States could push a button every morning and receive, along with his scrambled eggs and coffee, a printout summarizing the precise state of public opinion on a given spectrum of issues during the preceding twenty-four hours. And suppose he tried to tailor his policies to this computerized intelligence. Would that be good or bad?

Good, one person might respond. After all, democracy is supposed to be government by the people, and if the president knows just what people are thinking, he can act in accordance with the popular will.

Bad, another might answer. The president is elected to exercise his best judgment and lead the nation, not to follow the shifting winds of public opinion. After all, if the people are not satisfied with a president's leadership and decisions, they may elect a new one every four years.

Both arguments have merit. A president or a member of Congress usually tries to lead and shape public

[63] "Assassination," *To Establish Justice, To Insure Domestic Tranquility*, Final Report of the National Commission on the Causes and Prevention of Violence (Washington, D.C.: U.S. Government Printing Office, 1969), p. 120.

FOR AN "ELECTRONIC TOWN HALL"

Twenty-three years ago, Ross Perot had a simple idea. . . . Mr. Perot gave his idea a name that draped the old dream of pure democracy with the glossy promise of technology: "the electronic town hall."

Although Mr. Perot has repeatedly said he would not try to use the electronic town hall as a direct decision-making body, he has on other occasions suggested placing a startling degree of power in the hands of the television audience.

He has proposed . . . passing a constitutional amendment that would strip Congress of its authority to levy taxes, and place that power directly in the hands of the people, in a debate and referendum orchestrated through an electronic town hall. . . .

To many who support Mr. Perot, and even to many who do not, the idea of an electronic town hall has a powerful appeal. It holds the promise of a magical, technological, answer to all they have come to hate about the ways of Washington — the endless, gridlocked repetition of arguments . . . the corruptive influence of lobbyists and interest groups, the insulation of the political elite from the rest of the population, the shallowness of a debate framed by the forces of journalism.

—New York Times, June 6, 1992.

opinion and at the same time to follow it. No president can totally ignore public opinion during the four years between elections. But if our hypothetical president did try to rule according to computer printouts, it would soon become apparent that there was no way to please everybody. The president also would discover that if the policies suggested by the poll data failed to work, those policies—and the president—would soon become highly unpopular.

Nevertheless, modern political candidates and leaders are highly attuned to techniques for measuring and influencing public opinion. In the 1980s, President Ronald Reagan sampled opinion daily, much as the hypothetical president described above. (See boxes, this page.)

When Ross Perot, the billionaire Texas businessman, launched his presidential campaign in the spring of 1992, he spoke of running "electronic town meetings"

A TV SET CANNOT GOVERN

Many who study the relationship between the public and public policy—demographers, poll takers and political scientists—fear that Mr. Perot's idea would make worse the very ills it proposes to correct. It is, they say, an awkward, unworkable hybrid—New England town hall meets Brave New World. . . .

One who believes that strongly is the former astronaut Frank Borman, the man Mr. Perot hired to guide the concept in its first, failed go-around.

"I would not now be in favor of an electronic town hall," Mr. Borman said. . . . "You realize as you get older that a lot of issues are very profound and difficult to understand. I don't think you can take an extremely complex issue and air it completely in a half-hour or hour of television so that people will gain an informed understanding. I don't think you can govern 250 million people with a TV set."

Mr. Borman said he had come to believe that an electronic town hall would become a "national platform" for demagoguery with "enormous potential for manipulating the emotions of people," and could intimidate Congress, "already a pretty sorry group," into abandoning itself utterly to satisfying whatever seemed the people's will that week. "I have come to see," he said, "that greatness in governing is not achieved by simply following the will of the masses."

—New York Times, June 6, 1992

from the White House, in which through television, he would as president find out what the public was thinking and what they wanted. Under various proposals that have been made for such meetings, a president would speak to the nation on TV, and the public would respond either by dialing an 800 number, pushing special buttons on their television sets, or mailing in ballots. Perot, who made his fortune in the computer industry, was fascinated with the idea of using technology to interact with the voters. For example, Perot said that if elected he would not raise taxes unless consultation with the public persuaded him that there was a "grass roots consensus" to do so.[64] Critics of electronic government argued that a president who merely responded to the public whim would have abdicated his leadership, and that, in any event, a televised "town meeting" would bring responses only from the more politically activist citizens, a group that would not be representative of the entire electorate.

Political polls, television spot commercials, and professional campaign managers are all part of the efforts at mass persuasion employed today. (These techniques are discussed in detail in Chapter 8.)

Political leaders often attempt to "manage" public opinion or to manipulate it in their favor by the use of such techniques, and by the conscious use of symbols. When a president addresses the nation on television in a military crisis, the dramatic format of the Oval Office of the White House and a nationwide TV address are impressive symbols of his power, designed to engender public support. When the president travels to a distant city to make a speech, the presidential seal goes with him, and an aide unobtrusively hangs it on the rostrum just before the chief executive appears. Ronald Reagan, a veteran movie actor, used his polished skills as a performer to good advantage on television, both as a campaigner and as president. Ross Perot did not enter any primary elections but relied almost entirely on television talk shows and commercials to reach the people; he was in that sense the first true media candidate for president of the United States.

Public officials, political candidates, professional campaign consultants, media advisers, and government information officers customarily engage in political persuasion designed to influence or even manipulate the electorate. Indeed, as Dan Nimmo has suggested, "The

political communicator not seeking to persuade others to his views is more rare than the whooping crane."[65]

Leaders may court public opinion, but it remains an elusive concept. The truth is that the role of public opinion in a democracy has never been satisfactorily defined. The people, Walter Lippmann has argued, "can elect the government. They can remove it. They can approve or disapprove its performance. But they cannot administer the government. They cannot themselves perform. . . . A mass cannot govern."[66]

Certainly the public does not possess nearly so much information as the president, who daily receives a massive flow of intelligence and other data from all over the globe to aid him in his decision making. On the other hand, as E. E. Schattschneider has pointed out, *"nobody knows enough to run the government.* Presidents, senators, governors, judges, professors, doctors of philosophy, editors, and the like are only a little less ignorant than the rest of us."[67]

The unstated premise of opinion polls, Schattschneider adds, is that "the people really do decide what the government does on something like a day-to-day basis."[68] Obviously, that is rarely the case. It is reasonable to assume, however, that presidents and legislators, because they hope to be re-elected, do take public opinion into consideration in reaching major policy decisions. In addition, they try to influence public opinion to win support for the decisions they have made.

Public opinion in a democracy, then, may be seen as a broad but flexible framework for policymaking, setting certain outer limits within which government may act. As Key has observed, "Unless mass views have some place in the shaping of policy, all the talk about democracy is nonsense."[69]

MASS MEDIA AND PUBLIC OPINION

In a modern society, the public forms its opinions largely on the basis of what the mass media — newspapers, television, radio, and magazines — present to it. Consequently, the quality of the mass media, the

---

[64]Interview with Dan Rather, *CBS Evening News*, June 3, 1991.

[65] Dan Nimmo, *Political Communication and Public Opinion in America* (Santa Monica: Goodyear, 1978), p. 98.

[66] Walter Lippmann, *Essays in the Public Philosophy* (Boston: Little, Brown, 1955), p. 14.

[67] Schattschneider, *The Semisovereign People*, p. 136.

[68] Ibid., p. 133.

[69] Key, *Public Opinion and American Democracy*, p. 7.

"Damn it, Turner, you were supposed to orchestrate public opinion!"

Drawing by Stevenson
©1982 The New Yorker Magazine, Inc.

amount of time and space they devote to public affairs, their editorial stands, ownership patterns, and objectivity are all factors with potential influence on public opinion.

The television age, with the enormous impact of TV on public opinion, has brought a recognition that the press is an actor in the political process, not merely a mirror held up to reflect events. This was dramatically illustrated near the start of the 1992 presidential primary campaign when the leading Democratic candidate, Bill Clinton, was accused of having had an extramarital affair. The charge came from Gennifer Flowers, an Arkansas state employee and part-time cabaret singer who sold her story to the *Star*, a national tabloid newspaper. Clinton, with his wife, Hillary, at his side, immediately went on the CBS television program, "60 Minutes," to deny Flowers' charge while admitting some past marital "wrongdoing."[70] The mainstream press, once the story had broken in the tabloid newspaper, gave extensive coverage to the charges, and the "character issue" was to plague Clinton for months.

Democratic presidential candidate Bill Clinton is accused of an affair by singer Gennifer Flowers

---

[70] *Washington Post*, January 27, 1992, p. A1.

Figure 6-1
Confidence in Institutions: Percentage of Americans Who Have
a "Great Deal" or "Quite a Lot" of Confidence in Major U.S. Institutions

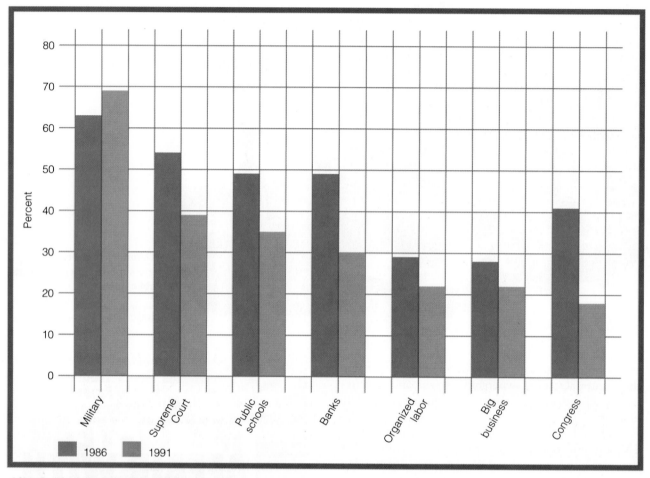

SOURCE: *The Gallup Poll Monthly*, October 1991, p. 37.

Four years earlier, in 1988, former Senator Gary Hart, then the front-runner for the Democratic presidential nomination, was forced to drop out of the race when the *Miami Herald* reported that he had spent the weekend with a young woman later identified as Donna Rice, a Miami model; it soon developed that Hart also had sailed to Bimini with Rice aboard a yacht unfortunately named the *Monkey Business*. It is unlikely that his campaign would have collapsed so quickly without the influence of TV. Television brought the Hart scandal into every corner of the land and quickly made it national news.

Television links the nation electronically, so that voters in one part of the nation immediately know what is happening hundreds or even thousands of miles away in another section of the country.

With that kind of power and influence in American politics, the press itself has inevitably become a target for criticism. To some extent this has occurred because the press today, as already noted, is widely perceived as a participant in the political process, not merely as a neutral bystander. For example, during the 1988 presidential campaign, Dan Rather, the anchor of the CBS Evening News, sharply questioned Vice-President George Bush, the Republican front-runner, about his role in the Iran-contra scandal. Bush displayed an aggressive style in his replies. The nine-minute clash on the evening news brought criticism of Rather, but it also helped Bush overcome a widespread public perception of him as a "wimp" who lacked the strength of character to be president.

In recent years the press has sometimes been attacked by government officials and others, and has come under government pressure. Some critics contend that the press is biased, unfair, or inaccurate in its reporting of public issues. Some of this type of criticism stems from conservatives who feel the press is too "liberal." But even among the general public, only about one-quarter to a third of the people have a high degree of confidence in the news media. (See Table 6-2.)

According to one survey, 76 percent of those questioned saw a high degree of political bias in news coverage. Only 28 percent thought that news organizations deal fairly with all sides in covering political and social issues, and 68 percent thought the news media tended to favor one side. Although 54 percent thought that news organizations "get the facts straight," 44 percent thought that news is "inaccurate." On the other hand, 82 percent of the public view network TV news favorably (the network anchors all get high believability ratings), and 77 percent regard daily newspapers favorably. Moreover, 68 percent of the public thinks that criticism by the news media keeps political leaders from doing "wrong" things.[71]

Under President Nixon, criticism of the news media was encouraged by various government actions and by attacks on the press by high administration officials. In a celebrated speech in November 1969, Vice-President Spiro T. Agnew assailed "a small band of network commentators and self-appointed analysts" who had discussed a televised address to the nation by President Nixon.[72] A week later, Agnew attacked the *Washington Post* and the *New York Times*, both eastern newspapers often critical of the administration.

Possibly some of these government pressures on the press were designed to divert public attention from the question of the government's own truthfulness; the Nixon administration in time became ensnared in scandals that led to the resignation of both Nixon and Agnew. At the same time, pressures on the press also seemed designed to persuade the news media to temper their criticism and present news about the government in a more favorable light. In this respect, the television

Table 6-2
Level of Confidence in News Media, by Selected Groups, October 1991
According to poll data, the majority of Americans do not have a high degree of confidence in newspapers or television.

	Confidence in Newspapers		
	A great deal/Quite a lot	Some	Very Little/None
National	32%	44%	22%
Men	35%	42%	22%
Women	31%	46%	20%
Republican	34%	41%	22%
Democrat	35%	42%	21%
Independent	29%	49%	21%

	Confidence in Television		
	A great deal/Quite a lot	Some	Very Little/None
National	24%	46%	29%
Men	27%	44%	28%
Women	22%	47%	30%
Republican	24%	42%	33%
Democrat	26%	45%	27%
Independent	23%	49%	27%

SOURCE: *The Gallup Poll Monthly*, October 1991, p. 39.

networks are potentially in a vulnerable position, since they are composed of stations licensed by the federal government. Jeb Stuart Magruder, while an assistant to President Nixon, suggested in a memo that the administration could "get the media" by such tactics as threatening Internal Revenue Service investigations of news organizations.

The government's pressures on the press and the issue of press "fairness" stirred debate in the 1970s. During the Watergate investigation, however, there was wide recognition of the fact that the press, and particularly the *Washington Post*, had played a significant role in uncovering the massive abuse of power by the Nixon White House. The disclosures by the press helped to shape public opinion and were one factor among many leading to Nixon's resignation as president.

In the wake of Watergate, Americans became much more aware of the role of investigative reporting. Although the practice has led to some abuses and considerable criticism, a 1982 Gallup poll reported that four out of five Americans, or 79 percent, favored investigative reporting, and only 18 percent disapproved.[73]

---

[71] Gallup poll conducted for Times Mirror, November 1989, in "The People & the Press," Part V, pp. 13, 14, 17, and 20.
[72] *New York Times*, November 14, 1969, p. 1.
[73] *Gallup Report*, January 1982, no. 196, p. 31.

Because of the power of the press to influence public opinion, presidents and other political leaders are — despite the attacks on the press during the Nixon years — often cautious in their criticism of the news media. For example, although President Carter occasionally criticized the news media, he was generally restrained, even during the flood of adverse publicity in 1980 about his brother Billy's payments from the government of Libya. President Reagan sometimes had harsh words for the press, but got along well with reporters on a personal level and usually avoided sharp confrontation with them, as did President Bush.

Although the press is powerful, so are political leaders. Presidents are well aware that their actions and words tend to dominate the news. They know that the press is obliged to report what they say and do, and that the news presidents generate has a strong impact on public opinion.

In fact, one of the major criticisms of the press is that it tends to rely too heavily on "official sources," ranging all the way from local police to the office of the mayor or governor, to the president's press secretary.

Official sources frequently have a vested interest in manipulating the press and shaping opinion to support policy. But because these same official sources control the flow of information to the public, the press often becomes dependent on such sources.

To an extent, at least, press and government have a relationship that is at once adversarial and mutually dependent. Politicians want to get re-elected, the press wants to report the news, and sometimes those two forces collide. At the same time, each side needs the other. The public, in turn, relies on the press for its information about government, but is often critical of both. Out of the three-way interaction among the press, the government, and the voters, public opinion emerges and plays its key role in the political process.

News Leaks and "Backgrounders"

Officials at every level of government frequently "leak" stories to the press, divulging information on condition that the officials remain anonymous. The motives for such leaks vary greatly — a political leader may be launching a "trial balloon," an idea for a new policy or program, in order to test public reaction. If the reaction is unfavorable, the administration can deny the program was ever even contemplated. Or a story may be leaked to attack a political opponent in a campaign, or to under-

mine an opponent, or to increase public support and sympathy for a political leader. The military services regularly leak "secrets" about other countries' weaponry to inflate their budgets.

But another kind of leak, the unofficial leak at a lower level, often plagues presidents and other political leaders. In Washington, for example, presidents — infuriated by some disclosure or other in the press — periodically call in the Federal Bureau of Investigation to try to find the source of the leak. President Reagan once said he had "thought of the guillotine" for leakers. But the culprits are almost never uncovered.

Sometimes Congress is equally upset by leaks. After the confirmation of Supreme Court Justice Clarence Thomas, the Senate tried to discover the source of the original stories revealing that Anita F. Hill had accused Thomas of sexual harassment. A special counsel was appointed, but the senators backed away from forcing two reporters to reveal their sources of the stories, and the investigation failed to reveal the leakers.

But there is a great deal of hypocrisy surrounding the periodic outcries over leaks; the same officials who order lie detector tests for government employees to try to stop leaking of classified information may turn around and invite a correspondent to lunch to reveal similar information. And when high officials, including presidents, leave office, they often write books and, in effect, sell secrets to the public in their memoirs.

Although disclosures of information are often deplored, neither government nor the news media could really operate without the institution of the news leak. For the press, one astute observer has commented, the leak is "its lifeline to unauthorized truth."[74]

When a leak takes place in a group setting, it is known as a "backgrounder." Officials in Washington often meet reporters to discuss government policies and plans with the mutual understanding that the information can be attributed only to unnamed "officials" or sometimes not attributed to any source at all.

Max Frankel, when chief of the Washington Bureau of the *New York Times*, filed an affidavit in the Pentagon Papers case explaining that officials and reporters "regularly make use of so-called classified, secret, and top secret information . . . without the use of 'secrets' . . . there could be no adequate diplomatic, military, and political reporting of the kind our people take for granted, either abroad or in Washington. . . ."

---

[74] Quoted in Wise, *The Politics of Lying*, pp. 287, 394.

The *Times* correspondent cited several instances where he had been given secret information. "I remember President Johnson, standing beside me, waist-deep in his Texas swimming pool, recounting for more than an hour his coversation the day before . . . with Prime Minister Kosygin of the Soviet Union . . . for my 'background' information, and subsequent though not immediate use in print. . . . This is the coin of our business and of the officials with whom we regularly deal. . . . The government hides what it can . . . and the press pries out what it can. . . . Each side in this 'game' regularly 'wins' and 'loses' a round or two."[75]

Television

With some 185 million television sets in American homes, the potential for creating an informed public through TV is vast. Entertainment is the economic heart of the television industry, however, and news and public-affairs programs occupy only a small part of the broadcast day. The three major broadcast networks,

[75] Ibid., pp. 105–106.

CBS, NBC, and ABC, occupy a leading position in the industry, but in recent years CNN, the Cable News Network, has taken its place alongside them. In the 1980s, cable television grew rapidly, reaching 56.2 million homes by 1992. Even so, a substantial share of all television revenues goes to the three networks and their eighteen wholly owned TV stations. Advertising on the three major networks exceeds $8 billion a year.[76] The networks sell popular packaged shows to affiliates across the nation, and charge large fees for airing sponsors' commercials during "prime time"—the after-dinner hours when millions of persons are tuned in to network programs.

For prime-time shows, the typical cost of a minute of commercial time is $150,000.[77] Audience rating figures are the controlling statistics in the broadcast industry, and news programs are not as profitable as popular mass-entertainment shows. Nevertheless, all three networks have evening television news programs that reach a combined total audience of more than 40

[76] Data provided by *Broadcasting Magazine*.
[77] For top-rated prime-time shows, the cost of a minute of commercial time ranges as high as $600,000. Data provided by the ABC television network.

Figure 6-2
Audiences Reached by Leading Media

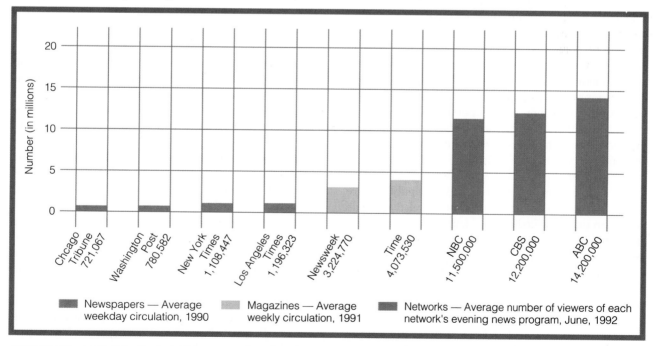

SOURCE: *Editor and Publisher Yearbook*, 1991; average paid circulation for 6-month period ending September 30, 1990 (newspapers); Audit Bureau of Circulations, report of average paid circulation for six months ended December 31, 1991 (magazines); and Nielsen Media Research (networks).

Clarence Thomas appearing before the Senate Judiciary Committee, 1991

million persons each night. Other news programs reach millions of viewers on CNN, which broadcasts news 24 hours a day, on the Public Broadcasting System (PBS), and over C-Span, and other cable and satellite systems.

In addition to news programs, Sunday panel-shows like "Meet the Press" air political issues, and the networks and public television broadcast a wide range of news documentaries. The networks and many local stations maintain their own news staffs.

Because television reaches millions of homes, news programs have a strong influence on public opinion. During the war in the Persian Gulf in February of 1991, and the unsuccessful coup against Soviet leader Mikhail Gorbachev in August, not only the public but even high government officials relied on CNN to bring them minute-by-minute developments.

In an earlier era, news reports of the fighting in Vietnam, which brought that conflict into American living rooms night after night, were a major factor in swinging public opinion against the war.

Similarly, the televised Senate Watergate hearings in 1973 played a major role in making the public aware of a scandal to which the voters had paid relatively little attention in the preceding presidential election. A year later, millions of Americans were able to watch the debates of the House Judiciary Committee as it voted to impeach President Nixon. In 1987, the country was fascinated as Marine Lieutenant Colonel Oliver North; his secretary, Fawn Hall; Vice Admiral John Poindexter; and other actors in the Iran-contra scandal testified on TV to congressional committees. In October 1991, millions of viewers were mesmerized by the televised Senate hearings into charges of sexual harassment

brought by Anita Hill against Supreme Court nominee Clarence Thomas. An estimated 52 million persons or more viewed the second televised debate between George Bush and Michael Dukakis four weeks before the 1988 presidential election. Television coverage of hearings, political debates, and conventions conveys an immediacy and has an impact that no other medium can approach.

Newspapers

A farmer in Nebraska and an attorney in Manhattan may both read newspapers, but the treatment of news about government and politics may be very different in the pages they read. The New Yorker probably reads the *New York Times*, which places heavy emphasis on national and international news gathered by its own reporters. The Nebraskan may read a small-town daily that concentrates on crop reports, wheat prices, and local events, and that relies on the wire services for sketchy reports about national and world events.

There are a number of excellent newspapers in the United States. A partial list would include the *New York Times*, the *Washington Post*, the *Los Angeles Times*, *The Wall Street Journal*, the *St. Louis Post-Dispatch*, the *Christian Science Monitor*, the *Chicago Tribune*, and the *Baltimore Sun*. But for most Americans, who live outside the circulation area of such publications, the outstanding fact about their newspaper is often not its excellence but how limited is its coverage of national and world news.

Moreover, daily newspapers have been disappearing. In 1909 there were 2,600 dailies in the United States. By 1955 there were 1,785, by 1986, only 1,657, and in 1991 only 1,586.[78]

As a result, more and more cities have no competing newspapers — either there is only one daily newspaper or else all the papers are controlled by one owner. By 1992, only 41 cities in America had competing daily newspapers. Because of a growing trend toward concentrated ownership of all media, there were dozens of communities in which one person or company owned or controlled all the local newspaper and television and radio outlets. As a result, the public often has less choice in selecting its sources of information. This has proved dramatically true in New York City; for example, it had eight major newspapers in 1948 and three in 1992. On the other hand, as the number of newspapers has declined, the number of electronic information-sources has increased; there were 1,497 television and 11,164 radio stations in the United States in 1992, more than double the number two decades earlier. And as already noted, cable-television programming has expanded dramatically.

Magazines

Citizens who feel that their local newspaper and broadcast outlets fail to provide them with enough news on public issues may, of course, subscribe to a weekly news magazine. Only a small percent of the population does so, however. The circulation of *Time* is 4,073,530; *Newsweek* 3,224,770; and *U.S. News & World Report* 2,237,009. Smaller magazines that comment on public affairs have relatively tiny circulations and are usually struggling to survive. For example, as of 1991, the *Atlantic* had a circulation of 458,838; *Harper's* was 203,180; and the New Republic's was 94,060.[79]

The Press in a Democratic Society

In short, Americans do not read much about public affairs. In one study of newspaper reading habits, 47 percent of the people interviewed said they only read the headlines; fully 20 percent said the part of the news-

paper they were most interested in was the comic strips.[80]

Despite its shortcomings — the lack of quality newspapers in many communities, for example — a free press in the United States is essential to the functioning of democracy, and a vital link between the public and the government. That is why the press is protected by the First Amendment. Public opinion is formed on the basis of what the news media present to the public. Democratic government rests broadly on public opinion and presupposes a fairly well-informed public. American presidents have always had to worry about adverse public judgments on the quality of their performance in office. In the course of four years, opinions *are* formed about the merits of a president and his staff. (The role of the press in political campaigns is discussed in Chapter 8, and the relationship between the president and the press is discussed in Chapter 10.)

Aside from its role of informing the general public, the American press, particularly the quality newspapers, magazines, and television news-programs, does an excellent job of informing those who are politically aware — politicians, opinion leaders, political scientists, lawyers, journalists, college students, and others who are attuned to politics.

Information about public affairs, in other words, is available to those who want it. There is nothing about democracy that guarantees an alert, educated public. Like voting and other forms of political participation, knowledge of public affairs — the basis of intelligent public opinion — is largely up to the individual.

INTEREST GROUPS IN A PLURALIST SOCIETY

Who Governs?

Who governs in a democracy? Three different answers are possible. It can be said that "the people" govern through political leaders nominated as candidates of political parties (or running as independents) and elected by the voters.

Another view is that a "power elite," a "power structure," or an "establishment" actually runs things. This was the view advanced more than two decades ago by sociologist C. Wright Mills in *The Power Elite*. Mills

---

[78] Date provided by Newspaper Association of America.
[79] Magazine circulation figures from Audit Bureau of Circulations, 1991.

[80] Lane, *Political Life*, pp. 284–85.

argued that a small group, "possessors of power, wealth and celebrity," occupies the key positions in American society.[81] This theory holds that *elites* rule, that power in America is held by the few, not by the masses of people. Many other social scientists have interpreted American society in terms of elite theory.[82] And "the establishment" is an expression that has come into everyday usage to describe elite power. Political writer Richard H. Rovere, in a semi-humorous vein, described the "American Establishment" as a loose coalition of leaders of finance, business, the professions, and the universities, who hold power and influence in the United States regardless of what administration occupies the White House.[83]

Although elites do exist in almost every field of human activity, many scholars reject the concept that a single economic and social elite wields ultimate political power. In his classic study of community power in New Haven in the late 1950s, Robert A. Dahl provided a third answer to the question of "Who governs?" He examined several specific public issues and traced the process by which decisions were made on those issues. He concluded that the city's economic and social "notables" did not run New Haven. Some individuals and groups were particularly influential in the making of one type of decision—educational policy, for example. But in other policy areas, very different individuals and groups often played the most important role. The city was dominated by many different sets of leaders: "It was, in short, a pluralist system." [84]

Other scholars have criticized Dahl's approach on the grounds that the wielders of power cannot always be identified by examining key decisions. For example, truly powerful persons might prevent certain issues from ever reaching the public arena.[85] On such issues, those favoring the status quo are the winners, because no decisions are made that might lead to change. In short, the power to set the *agenda*, to determine which

public-policy questions will be debated, or even considered, may prove at least as important as the power to decide on the issues themselves.

Nevertheless, the *pluralist* character of American democracy is widely, although not universally, recognized. *Pluralism* is a system in which many conflicting groups within the community have access to government officials and compete with one another in an effort to influence policy decisions. Pluralism supposes, of course, that many individuals are active in groups and associations to advance their interests, and that these multiple interests and memberships overlap and, in many cases, conflict. For example, the same person who favors new school construction as a member of the PTA may oppose higher taxes as a member of a neighborhood association. As we shall see, however, many groups have been badly underrepresented or left out of the pluralist system. Minorities, the poor, the powerless, consumers, and others who do not belong to organized interest groups do not always fare well in a pluralist society. And many Americans do not join groups.

It has been argued that pluralism really consists of competing groups of elites, so that even a pluralist system falls far short of the classic democratic model. Some scholars who contend that America is ruled by the few are critical of elite power, and argue that the political system must be opened up to give more people access to it. Other scholars claim that only elites are dedicated to democratic principles, and that the masses of voters have little allegiance to freedom, the right of dissent, First Amendment values, or equal opportunity. But this latter view diminishes the importance of the ordinary voter and citizen, and reflects little confidence in representative democracy.

To an extent, the debate over whether America is an elite or pluralist democracy may pose the question in terms that are too rigid. As with most things, there is a mix. Elites do exercise power in and out of government, but competing groups also play an important role. And the voters retain the ultimate power of replacing elected leaders—from the school board member to the president of the United States.

Interest Groups: A Definition

Interest groups are private groups that attempt to influence the government to respond to the shared attitudes of their members.

---

[81] C. Wright Mills, *The Power Elite* (New York: Oxford University Press, 1959), pp. 8, 13.

[82] See, for example, Peter Bachrach, *The Theory of Democratic Elitism* (Boston: Little, Brown, 1966); G. William Domhoff, *Who Rules America?* (Englewood Cliffs: Prentice-Hall, 1967); and *The Higher Circles* (New York: Vintage Books, 1970).

[83] Richard H. Rovere, *The American Establishment* (New York: Harcourt Brace Jovanovich, 1962), p. 6.

[84] Robert A. Dahl, *Who Governs?* (New Haven: Yale University Press, 1961), p. 86.

[85] See Peter Bachrach and Morton S. Baratz, "Two Faces of Power," *American Political Science Review*, vol. 56, no. 4 (December 1962), pp. 947–52.

WHAT DO I DO? THIS CONGRESSMAN SAYS HE ALREADY SOLD HIS SOUL TO A POLITICAL ACTION COMMITTEE.

By Mike Peters for the
Dayton Daily News

Public opinion, as we have seen, is the expression of attitudes on public questions. When people organize to express attitudes held in common, and to influence the government to respond to those attitudes, they become members of interest groups.

When one group wins, another may lose. David B. Truman has pointed out that interest groups may make "certain claims upon other groups in the society" by acting through "the institutions of government."[86]

In the nineteenth century, political cartoonists were fond of drawing potbellied men in top hats and striped pants to represent Big Business. Muckrakers assailed oil, steel, and railroad barons as members of interest groups in league against the public welfare. Partly as a result of this muckraking tradition, many people tend to regard all interest groups as evil, business-dominated organizations plotting against the commonweal. And it is true that powerful interest groups, employing well-paid lobbyists in Washington, often bring about legislation that benefits corporate America, sometimes at the expense of the broader public. But it is also true that today many public-interest groups champion consumers, the environment, or other causes that benefit the public as a whole.

Many political scientists now consider interest groups a normal and vital part of the political process, conveyors of the demands and supports fed into the political system. Whether such groups are called "interest groups," "pressure groups," or "lobbies" — and

there is some disagreement over which label is best — their purpose is much the same, to influence government policies and actions. These groups should not be confused with political parties, which also seek to influence government — but by electing candidates to office. As we noted in Chapter 1, the members of some interest groups — college students, for example — may not even be formally organized as a group.

Who Belongs?

The tendency of Americans to come together in groups was noticed in the early nineteenth century by Alexis de Tocqueville. "In no country of the world," he observed, "has the principle of association been more successfully used or applied to a greater multitude of objects than in America."[87]

There are more than 100,000 clubs and associations in the United States. Not everyone belongs to a group, however. In America, "more than one-third of the population has no formal group association."[88] And nearly one-half of those who do belong to groups are affiliated with social, fraternal, or church-connected organizations that have little relation to politics.[89] Not all organizations are interested in influencing government, so only a minority of Americans belong to interest groups. One survey reported that only 31 percent of the population belonged to groups that sometimes take a stand on housing, better government, school problems, or other public issues.[90] That well over one-third of Americans belong to no groups at all raises basic questions about pluralist democracy that will be discussed later in this chapter.

Although interest groups vary tremendously in size, goals, budget, and scope of interest, they often employ the same techniques to accomplish their objectives. Some of these techniques are described below.

How They Operate

A few years ago, the Federal Trade Commission proposed a set of rules designed to protect people who buy used cars. The rules would have required the dealers to reveal to a buyer any major defects in a car.

The nation's used-car dealers, led by the National Automobile Dealers Association, mounted a massive

[86] David B. Truman, *The Governmental Process* (New York: Knopf, 1951), p. 37.
[87] Alexis de Tocqueville, *Democracy in America*, vol. 1, Phillips Bradley, ed. (New York: Vintage Books, 1945), p. 198.
[88] Robert H. Salisbury, *Governing America: Public Choice and Political Action* (New York: Appleton-Century-Crofts, 1973), p. 90.
[89] Ibid.

[90] Lane, *Political Life*, p. 75.

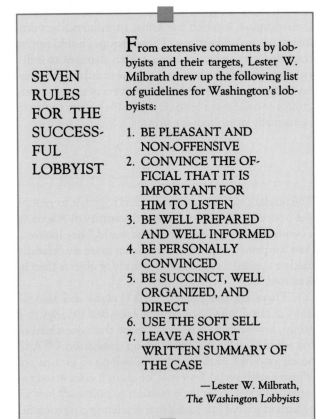

SEVEN
RULES
FOR THE
SUCCESS-
FUL
LOBBYIST

From extensive comments by lobbyists and their targets, Lester W. Milbrath drew up the following list of guidelines for Washington's lobbyists:

1. BE PLEASANT AND NON-OFFENSIVE
2. CONVINCE THE OFFICIAL THAT IT IS IMPORTANT FOR HIM TO LISTEN
3. BE WELL PREPARED AND WELL INFORMED
4. BE PERSONALLY CONVINCED
5. BE SUCCINCT, WELL ORGANIZED, AND DIRECT
6. USE THE SOFT SELL
7. LEAVE A SHORT WRITTEN SUMMARY OF THE CASE

—Lester W. Milbrath,
The Washington Lobbyists

lobbying campaign in Congress to overturn the FTC proposal. According to Ralph Nader's Congress Watch, the auto dealers' group gave campaign contributions of $770,000 to members of the House.

Congress voted to kill the rules that would have helped car buyers know what they were buying. "This says a lot about the contamination of the political arena by campaign contributions," said Representative Toby Moffett, Democrat of Connecticut.[91] Another opponent of the congressional action, Representative Barbara A. Mikulski, Democrat of Maryland, who was later elected to the United States Senate, said the rules would have protected car buyers from "Happy Harry and Smiling Sam," gypsy dealers. She added: "People should know if they're getting a car in reasonable condition or a four-wheel-drive lemon." [92]

It was a blatant but effective case of lobbying by an industry group. It won, and the consumers lost.

But if the used-car dealers triumphed, consumers won in another battle that began in New York State in

the mid-1980s, when beer prices rose as much as 31 percent. The reason: brewers ordered their distributors to carve out exclusive territories and avoid competition with other distributors — competition that would have meant lower prices. In Washington, senators who had received substantial contributions from the beer industry introduced legislation in Congress to exempt such practices nationwide from provisions of the federal antitrust laws. Consumer activists, working with the states, defeated the measure, saving the nation's beer-drinkers from higher prices.[93]

Lobbying One of the most powerful techniques of interest groups is *lobbying*, communication with legislators or other government officials to try to influence their decisions. Originally, the term "lobby-agent" was used to describe someone who waited in the lobbies of government buildings to buttonhole lawmakers. The term "lobbying" first came into use in the New York State capital at Albany, and was being used in Washington by the early 1830s.

Although the term is often used to mean direct contact with lawmakers, in its broadest sense lobbying is not confined to efforts to influence the legislative branch. Lobbyists also seek to influence officials of the executive branch, regulatory agencies, and sometimes the courts. And lobbyists spend much of their time monitoring events in Washington, in order to alert their clients to government actions or plans that may affect them.

One way that lobbyists influence officials is simple: they get to know them. By paying personal visits to members of Congress and government officials, by attending hearings of congressional committees, government agencies, and regulatory commissions, and by forming friendships with staff members and bureau-

---

[93] David Bollier, *Citizen Action and Other Big Ideas: A History of Ralph Nader and the Modern Consumer Movement* (Washington: Center for Study of Responsive Law, 1991), p. 14.

PUBLIC
OPINION
AND FREE
GOVERN-
MENT

All free governments, whatever their name, are in reality governments by public opinion. . . .

—James Russell Lowell,
address, Birmingham,
England, October 6, 1884.

---

[91] *New York Times*, May 27, 1982, p. 1. Data on contributions from Congress Watch.

[92] Ibid. Mikulski was elected to the U.S. Senate in 1986.

THE "ZING AND GLAMOR" OF LOBBYING

The life of a Washington lobbyist is not all fancy restaurants and high living, as this account by Marvin Caplan, a lobbyist for the AFL-CIO, demonstrates:

Tomorrow the House is scheduled to vote on a proposed anti-busing amendment to the Constitution (they can't vote today because of the congressional golf tournament). . . .

While the debate on the anti-busing amendment is going on, I and my fellow lobbyists are off the House floor, jammed into the narrow spaces marked for us on either side of the hall by brass stanchions and red velvet ropes. We compare notes, catch every unchecked or doubtful member who chances by and kibbitz. . . .

A bulletin from the front: Debate, scheduled for one hour, has been extended for one more. Four of us go to the coffee shop in a basement tunnel of the House—our

"Plastic Palace"—for a quick lunch of sandwiches, styrofoam bowls of bean soup and coffee. The debate's still on when we return. Now we just stand about waiting, sweltering in our cramped spot. Being a lobbyist sometimes has all the zing and glamor of guard duty in the Lincoln Tunnel.

At about 2:30 two bells ring. The doors to the House floor fling open. Several of us dash to the Republican side to greet members as they step off the elevators and urge "No" votes as they dash by. The sharp-eyed among us read the vote as it ticks off on the electronic scoreboard on the low wall around the spectators' gallery. The amendment doesn't come close to getting the two-thirds majority needed to pass. To a brief burst of handclapping in the House chamber, it is defeated, 216 to 209.

—*Washington Post, August 12, 1979*

crats, lobbyists make their presence felt. Lester Milbrath found that more than half the Washington lobbyists thought the personal presentation of viewpoints was the most effective way of reaching members of Congress.[94] Senators and representatives are busy people — often the lobbyists' chief value is that in support of their arguments they present carefully researched background material that may help a member of Congress decide how to vote on complex bills.

Money: The Lobbyist's Tool   When Michael K. Deaver, President Reagan's close friend and deputy chief of staff, left the White House in the spring of 1985, he set up his own lobbying firm in Washington. Foreign governments, defense contractors, corporations, and others seeking access to the center of power flocked to hire Deaver at fees ranging into millions of dollars. By early 1986, Deaver appeared on the cover of *Time* in a photograph that showed him telephoning someone from his richly appointed limousine. But the photograph and the cover headlines, "Who's This Man Call-

ing?" and "Influence Peddling in Washington," spelled trouble for Deaver.

Federal law prohibits ex-government employees from appearing before their former agencies to represent clients for a period of one year after leaving government service. Deaver was summoned to testify and explain

---

[94] Lester W. Milbrath, *The Washington Lobbyists* (Chicago: Rand McNally, 1963), pp. 212–13.

THE 116 CLUB: LOBBYING OVER LUNCH

An inconspicuous row house tucked away in a once-notorious alley on Capitol Hill has evolved into a headquarters of subterranean power, a place where Senators, Representatives and Federal officials do their lobbying.

The refurbished building houses the 116 Club, a name few Washingtonians have heard. It is the lunch and cocktail-hour watering hole where the city's most influential lobbyists present their employers' points of view to Government decision-makers away from the prying eyes of newsmen and the public.

"It's the sort of club where people in high places can be comfortable without feeling that they're in a fishbowl," explained a club member. "The membership is the innermost of the 'in' group."

Membership is about 200, including 116 "legislative relations specialists" — lobbyists — 60 Government workers who are mostly staff aides to Congressional committees and Federal regulatory agencies, and 30 nonresident members.

A few Senators and Representatives also belong, but their names, like those of other members, are closely guarded.

"I don't want to reveal any member's name," Robert H. Miller, the chairman of the club's board of governors, told a recent guest of the club. "This is a private club. . . ."

"Much of the major Congressional legislation affecting billions and billions of dollars is either written or influenced there," a club member said. . . .

Frequent visitors, and the few members who were willing to discuss the club's affairs privately, insist that the most powerful men in Congress often lunch at the club. In keeping with the bipartisan attitude, the figures of both an elephant and a donkey decorate the mantelpiece of the club's dining room.

—*New York Times*, November 6, 1974

his lucrative activities. In 1987, a federal jury convicted Deaver of lying to Congress and to a grand jury about his lobbying. He was fined $100,000 and sentenced to three years' probation.

Blatant lobbying at a high level did not begin with Michael Deaver. And sometimes even a president is lobbied. For example, in 1969 America's dairy industry wanted the price supports for milk raised. A Washington attorney for the largest of the milk cooperatives, the Associated Milk Producers, Inc. (AMPI), went to see an attorney for President Richard Nixon. The dairy group agreed to contribute campaign funds to the president. In due course, the attorney for the milk producers delivered a little satchel containing $100,000 in cash to the president's lawyer. The milk producers later pledged to contribute $2 million to Nixon in the 1972 presidential campaign. Soon afterward, the president invited the dairy leaders to the White House, posed for pictures with them, and thanked them for their political support.

In the spring of 1970 the dairy industry won a large price increase. The following year, however, the secretary of agriculture ruled against any further price in-

creases. The milk industry lobbied Congress furiously and generated thousands of letters to senators and representatives, urging legislation to boost milk prices. Secretary of the Treasury John Connally of Texas, a supporter of the dairy industry, warned the president that a veto of such legislation might cost him six farm states in the presidential election.[95] Nixon met with the dairy leaders again. He decided to increase milk prices — provided the milk producers kept their $2-million campaign pledge.

Less than two weeks after his original decision, the secretary of agriculture reversed himself and announced that milk prices would be increased after all. With a satchel full of cash and a promise of $2 million, lobbyists for a powerful industry had directly influenced the president of the United States.[96]

---

[95] Connally was indicted by the federal government but acquitted in 1975 on charges that he had accepted a total of $10,000 from AMPI in return for urging Nixon to raise milk price-supports.

[96] For more detailed accounts of the milk producers' lobbying, see Carol S. Greenwald, *Group Power* (New York: Praeger Publishers, 1977), pp. 3–8; and U.S. Senate, 93d Cong., 2d sess., *The Final Report of the Select Committee on Presidential Campaign Activities*, pp. 579–929.

The success of the dairy industry in winning price increases worth more than $300 million is a dramatic illustration of how lobbying by interest groups can affect — even reverse — public policy. In the policy-making process, interest groups play a key role.

As was demonstrated in the case of the dairy industry, money is often a useful tool for the lobbyist for an interest group. The public often thinks of the lobbyist as someone who hands out money to buy the votes of legislators. That may happen. A direct bribe, however, is a violation of federal law. Under a 1962 statute, a person who bribes a member of Congress, or a member of Congress who takes "anything of value" in exchange for a vote, may be fined $20,000 and imprisoned up to fifteen years. The language of the statute is broad enough to cover any kind of valuable favor, not just money. Bribery is illegal and risky, and there are better, legal ways to channel money to legislators. For example, lobbyists are expected to purchase tickets or whole tables of tickets to fund-raising dinners for political parties and candidates. Lobbyists may take a senator to lunch at an expensive restaurant in Washington. They may arrange a weekend on a yacht or a free trip to a resort. Christmas may bring a legislator a ham, a case of Scotch, or a pair of gold cuff links.

But lunches and small favors are only minor props in the drama of influencing lawmakers. Many members of Congress are practicing lawyers, insurance agents, bankers, and business executives. For example, in 1992, 244 members — or almost half — of the 102nd Congress were lawyers. It is not difficult for interest groups with nationwide chapters and members to channel legal or insurance fees or bank loans to members of Congress. Unless such payments can be shown to be outright bribes, they are legal; in any event, they are difficult to trace.

For the most part, lobbyists for interest groups are able to exert influence by means of campaign contributions and fund-raising. The American Medical Association (AMA), representing more than 297,000 physicians, is an example of a highly active interest group that has spent millions of dollars opposing national health

THE BILLBOARD LOBBY: CASH AND SUNSHINE FOR CONGRESS

Last January, Vernon Clark, chief lobbyist for the nation's largest billboard companies, produced a proposal to repeal most of the Highway Beautification Act, which has forced the removal of more than 100,000 roadway signs.

For years, the $650 million-a-year billboard industry has been nibbling away at the edges of the act, reducing its impact one chunk at a time. Clark's proposal would devour it in a final gulp. . . . So far, it has been a lobbyist's dream: a bill that is passing through the congressional maze almost exactly as it was written by an industry group. . . .

Over the past four years, Clark's group, the Outdoor Advertising Association of America (OAAA), has paid $20,500 in speaking fees to 10 members of the House Public Works and Transportation Committee, including $4,000 to [Chairman James J.] Howard. . . .

Shortly after Clark distributed his amendment in January . . . the outdoor advertisers paid for several members of Congress — including Howard . . . to fly to their annual convention in Palm Springs, Calif. This gave the industry a chance to discuss the issue with legislators in the relaxed atmosphere of the Canyon Hotel Racquet and Golf Resort. It is legal under congressional rules for business groups to pay for such trips.

Howard said through a spokesman that the amendment has nothing to do with these speaking invitations. At the Palm Springs convention, he said, "we listened to the concerns of businessmen, but we did not sit down and draft bills. There's very little lobbying that goes on."

— *Washington Post,* August 10, 1982

Even after heavy pressure and months of lobbying, the changes that the billboard industry wanted, which would have made it virtually impossible for cities to remove billboards from the sides of roads, did not go through. Lobbies do not always win.

insurance and other medical legislation. The American Medical Political Action Committee (AMPAC), the AMA's political arm, contributed almost $2.4 million to congressional candidates in the 1990 election.

Why does AMPAC contribute generously to Congress? During the Carter presidency, the administration proposed a bill to hold down hospital costs, which it estimated could save consumers $27 billion over five years. The AMA opposed the bill. The measure was referred to a health subcommittee in the House. Its chairman, Representative Dan Rostenkowski, Democrat of Illinois, and ten other members had received contributions from the AMA. The subcommittee voted to kill the Carter bill, and the Ninety-fifth Congress took no action to contain hospital costs.[97]

Many large interest groups are deeply involved in politics. For example, the AFL-CIO Committee on Political Education (COPE) contributes money to candidates, runs voter-registration drives, publicly endorses candidates, publishes their voting records for union members, and often provides volunteers to assist in political campaigns. During 1990 COPE contributed $838,000 to candidates for Congress. Although ostensibly nonpartisan, COPE in fact has mainly aided Democrats, just as the AMA is Republican-oriented.

The popular image of a Washington lobbyist as a glamorous figure who entertains powerful senators and dines at the best places is not always accurate. As most lobbyists are quick to point out, much of their work consists of solid research, long hours of committee hearings, and conversations with lawmakers in their offices. Whatever their technique, lobbyists have a substantial influence on political decision-making.

Mass Propaganda and Grass-Roots Pressure One of the ways in which interest groups try to influence public opinion in order to influence government is through mass-publicity campaigns. Using television, magazine, and newspaper advertising, and direct mailings to the general public and specialized audiences, interest groups seek to create a favorable climate for their goals. With the aid of a public relations firm, an interest group can utilize all the latest techniques of Madison Avenue. But it takes a great deal of money to

influence public opinion enough to create a response from government, and only affluent interest groups can afford programs aimed at the manipulation of mass public-opinion.[98]

A classic example of an apparently successful campaign by an affluent group was the publicity campaign of the American Automobile Association (AAA) in 1968 against a bill that would have allowed bigger trucks on the nation's roads. The AAA ran newspaper advertisements showing a triple-trailer truck with a huge boar's head devouring the highway as John Q. Motorist sat helplessly by, trapped in a monstrous traffic jam. The ad urged that the bill be defeated for reasons of safety and "because of the irreparable damage bigger trucks will do to our highways and bridges." With the public alarmed and the nation's bridges in apparent danger of imminent collapse, Congress abandoned the trucking bill. Presumably the AAA's publicity barrage influenced this outcome. But the AAA's victory was only temporary; in 1975 a bill became law permitting larger trucks on the roads.

In addition to such mass-propaganda campaigns, many interest groups approach some members of the public directly to try to create various forms of grass-roots pressure that will affect government. To influence senators, for example, an interest group might persuade powerful bankers in the senators' states to telephone them in Washington. Lobbyists may ask close personal friends of the senators to get in touch with them. Or lobbyists may try to get great numbers of legislators' constituents to write or wire them.

Both mass propaganda and grass-roots pressure were employed by highly organized evangelical-Christian groups in the 1980 political campaign. For example, the Reverend Jerry Falwell and his Moral Majority organization vigorously supported Ronald Reagan for president and several conservative candidates for Congress.

Today, many interest groups use computerized mailing lists to contact their members and supporters; the National Rifle Association, an aggressive group opposed to gun controls, reportedly can barrage Congress with a half a million letters on seventy-two hours' notice. The NRA had 2.8 million members, a budget of $86 million, and a full-time staff of 466 persons; in 1990

---

[97] "How Money Talks in Congress" (Washington, D.C.: Common Cause, 1979), pp. 12–13.

[98] V. O. Key, Jr., *Politics, Parties, and Pressure Groups*, 5th ed. (New York: Crowell, 1964), p. 130.

it contributed to more than 100 Senate and House races.[99]

Members of Congress are well aware that interest groups may be behind a sudden flood of postcards or letters on a pending bill. In addition, legislators know that, since most people do not write letters to their representatives in Congress, the mail they receive reflects the feelings of only a small percentage of their constituents. One study showed that only 17 percent of the general public writes letters to members of Congress.[100] Nevertheless, grass-roots pressure remains a popular form of trying to influence government, in part because interest groups, never certain which techniques are the most effective, tend to try them all.

The Washington Lawyers: Access to the Powerful

Members of prestigious Washington law firms are among the capital's most effective lobbyists. Often, large corporations pay big fees to Washington lawyers, not only for their expert knowledge of how the bureaucracy works, but for their political access and friends inside the government and in Congress as well. On more than one occasion, Washington lawyers have been able to orchestrate the passage of legislation designed to help their clients: "The lawyer's historic role was that of advising clients how to *comply* with the law. The Washington lawyer's present role is that of advising clients how to *make* laws, and to make the most of them."[101]

One of the most renowned of Washington lawyers, Clark M. Clifford, served in the cabinet and as an adviser to Democratic presidents. Aware of his stature, bureaucrats and members of Congress tended to return his telephone calls, giving Clifford the kind of political "clout" that corporate clients want—and pay large fees

to obtain. President Kennedy, who received a good deal of free advice from Clifford, once joked: "All he asked in return was that we advertise his law firm on the backs of one-dollar bills."[102]

Public Interest Groups

Corporate lawyers and lobbyists have increasingly faced a new kind of opponent in recent years. Beginning in the 1960s, public interest groups and public interest lawyers have also waged successful battles to influence public policy. In the fields of the environment, consumer protection, health, minority rights, and many other areas, these public interest groups have brought class action and other lawsuits, lobbied Congress, and through the powerful weapon of publicity, added new issues to the government agenda. During the Reagan years, however, public interest groups often found themselves on the defensive, battling against an unsympathetic administration.

One public interest group is Common Cause, a national citizens' lobby with approximately 270,000 members. Common Cause received major credit for passage of the election-reform laws of the 1970s.

The best-known public interest lobbyist, Ralph Nader, by 1992 headed a network of lawyers, lobbyists,

Ralph Nader

---

[99] NRA membership and staff size as of 1992; budget for fiscal 1991. Data provided by the National Rifle Association.

[100] Donald Devine, *The Attentive Public* (Chicago: Rand McNally, 1969), p. 119. Data from 1964.

[101] Joseph C. Goulden, *The Superlawyers: The Small and Powerful World of the Great Washington Law Firms* (New York: Weybright & Talley, 1972), p. 6.

[102] Ibid., p. 70. In the early 1990s, however, Clifford's reputation was tarnished by his involvement in the scandal and investigations surrounding the Bank of Commerce and Credit International (BCCI). In July 1992, Clifford was indicted on federal and state charges for his role in the bank affair.

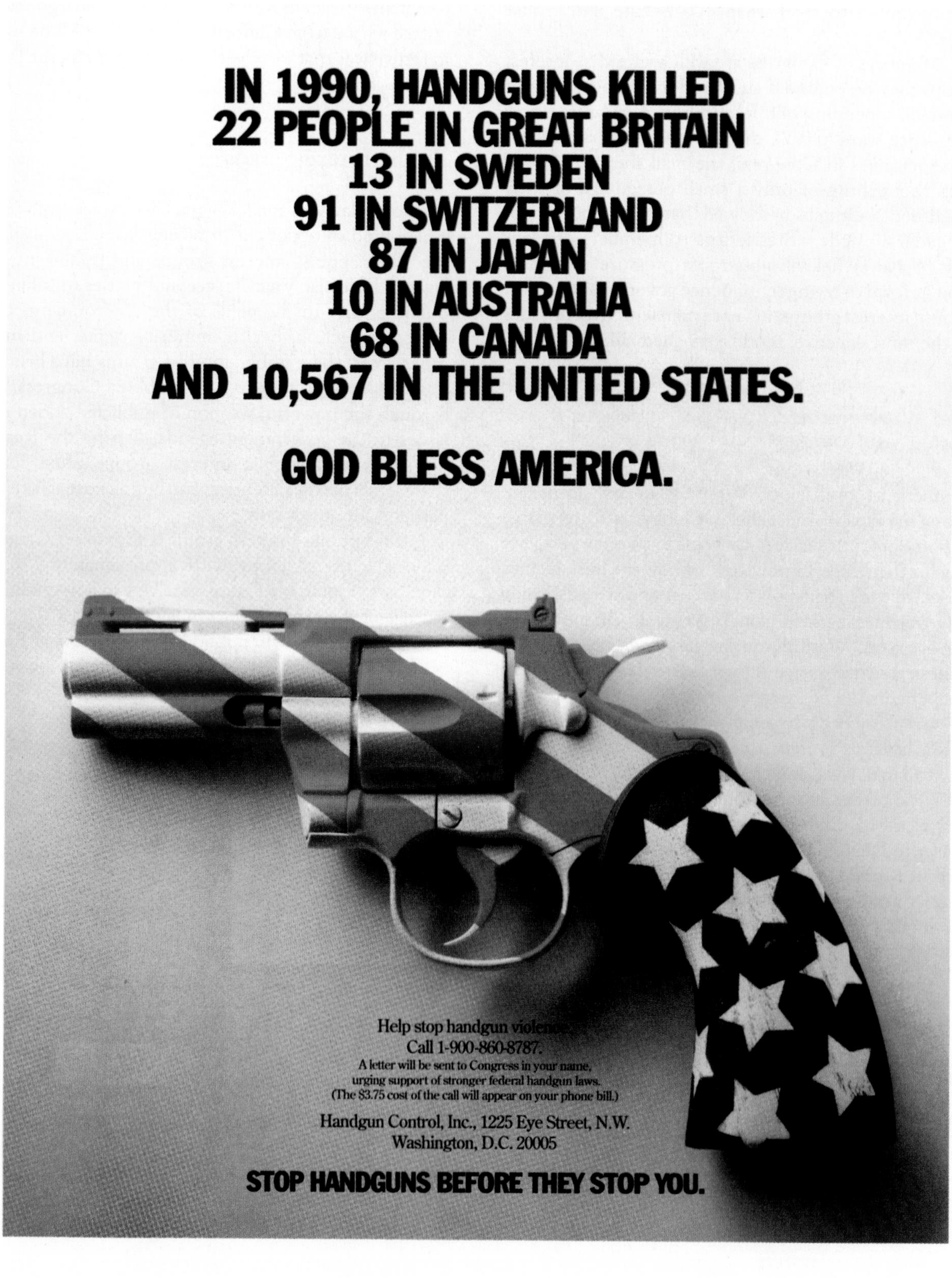

IN 1990, HANDGUNS KILLED
22 PEOPLE IN GREAT BRITAIN
13 IN SWEDEN
91 IN SWITZERLAND
87 IN JAPAN
10 IN AUSTRALIA
68 IN CANADA
AND 10,567 IN THE UNITED STATES.

GOD BLESS AMERICA.

Help stop handgun violence.
Call 1-900-860-8787.
A letter will be sent to Congress in your name,
urging support of stronger federal handgun laws.
(The $3.75 cost of the call will appear on your phone bill.)

Handgun Control, Inc., 1225 Eye Street, N.W.
Washington, D.C. 20005

STOP HANDGUNS BEFORE THEY STOP YOU.

and political analysts working in more than three dozen organizations. The Nader-affiliated public interest groups included Congress Watch, which concentrates on consumer affairs, the environment, transportation, congressional reform, and other legislation; the Center for Study of Responsive Law, a Nader clearinghouse for studies and reports by Nader task forces; the Freedom of Information Clearinghouse, which seeks to obtain government records under the Freedom of Information Act; the Center for Auto Safety; the Critical Mass Energy Project group, which monitors nuclear power; the Health Research Group, which works to improve medical care and food and drug safety; and the Public Interest Research Groups (PIRGs) in several states. The PIRGs enlist students and other citizens in a variety of public interest and consumer projects.

In addition to lobbying and working for consumers, the Nader organizations have produced a number of studies and books, including profiles of each member of Congress and reports on antitrust enforcement, land use, the U.S. Department of Agriculture, chemical additives to food, air pollution, corporate power, and many other subjects. Nader's activities are financed by foundations, income from the sale of these books, contributions from the public, and Nader's own funds, earned in lecturing and writing.

Single-issue Groups

In recent years, the "single-issue" interest group has become an increasingly significant phenomenon on the American political scene. These groups concentrate their efforts on lobbying for or against a particular issue, often with devastating effect.

The National Right to Life Committee and the National Rifle Association are examples of single-issue lobbies that have campaigned for such specific issues as ending legalized abortions and blocking gun-control legislation. Beyond lobbying on the issues, such groups may influence election results.

Former Senator Dick Clark, Democrat of Iowa, whose defeat was attributed to anti-abortion and anti-gun-control groups, has shed light on how single-issue lobbying works in actual practice. Shortly before the election, he got a call from an official of the Machinists and Aerospace Workers Union, which opposed the bill to deregulate natural gas. Clark planned to vote in favor of the bill. As Clark recalled it:

He said to me, "OK, if that's the case, we won't support you." I responded, "Look at my voting record as a whole. Don't make a decision like this based on a single vote." His reply was: "We don't give a . . . about your overall voting record. We're interested in this bill—period."[103]

Political Action Committees

Often, single-issue lobbies work through political action committees (PACs, pronounced "packs")—which are sometimes independent organizations, but more often the political arms of corporations, labor unions, or interest groups—established to contribute to candidates or to work for general political goals.

In 1980 a powerful conservative political action committee based in Arlington, Virginia, distributed to voters in five states little cards that looked not unlike those that come in packages of bubble gum. But the cards did not contain pictures of baseball players; beneath the words, "Target '80," each had a photograph of one of five United States senators inside a red border. On the backs of the cards appeared "ratings" of the senators by both conservative and liberal groups and notations such as:

"Favors sellout of Taiwan."
"Voted for New York City bailout."

The cards were directed against five "super-liberal" Democratic senators—Alan Cranston of California, George McGovern of South Dakota, Birch Bayh of Indiana, John Culver of Iowa, and Frank Church of Idaho. All five incumbents were the target of an intensive campaign to defeat them, waged by the National Conservative Political Action Committee (NCPAC). And all but Cranston lost their seats in the 1980 Reagan sweep.

A key figure in the NCPAC campaign was Richard Viguerie, a direct-mail specialist, who with the aid of computerized mailing lists, had been extremely successful in raising money directly from the public for various conservative causes. By Election Day, 1980, NCPAC had spent $2.8 million nationwide.

Some of the money went for television commercials, such as one used in Indiana that opened with a picture of a large baloney on a cutting board. Suddenly, a meat cleaver sliced through the baloney and a voice intoned: "One very big piece of baloney is Birch Bayh

---

[103] *Newsweek*, November 6, 1978, p. 48.

Table 6-3
PACs: The Top Ten
These ten political action committees gave the most to candidates in the 1990 congressional campaigns.

Political Action Committee	Amount Contributed (in millions)
Realtors Political Action Committee (National Association of Realtors)	3.09
American Medical Political Action Committee (American Medical Association)	2.38
Democratic Republican Independent Voter Education Committee (Teamsters)	2.34
National Education Association Political Action Committee (National Education Association)	2.32
UAW Voluntary Community Action Program (United Auto Workers)	1.79
Committee on Letter Carriers Political Education (National Association of Letter Carriers)	1.73
American Federation of State, County & Municipal Employees—PEOPLE, Qualified (American Federation of State, County & Municipal Employees)	1.55
National Association of Retired Federal Employees Political Action Committee (NARFE-PAC) (National Association of Retired Federal Employees)	1.53
Association of Trial Lawyers Political Action Committee (National Association of Trial Lawyers)	1.53
Carpenters Legislative Improvement Committee (United Brotherhood of Carpenters & Joiners of America)	1.49

SOURCE: Data provided by the Federal Election Commission, December 1991.

telling us he's fighting inflation." A price tag reading $46 billion appeared on the baloney and the voice added: "That's how much deficit spending Bayh voted for last year alone." After a pause, the voice continued: "So, to stop inflation, you'll have to stop Bayh first. Because if Bayh wins, you lose." Bayh lost.

By 1982, however, the political winds had changed. NCPAC spent nearly $4 million that year to defeat 38 incumbents it considered too liberal. Only one, Senator Howard W. Cannon, Democrat of Nevada, was defeated.[104] In several instances, PACs have failed to pass or to block important legislation. For example, in 1982, Senator Robert J. Dole, Republican of Kansas, successfully sponsored a tax increase bill bitterly opposed by big-business PACs. "About half of the $100 billion tax increase in the bill fell on business. . . . After observing the Gucci-clad lobbyists outside a Senate mark-up session one night . . . Dole said: 'They'll be barefoot by morning.' "[105]

Several factors account for the growth of PACs. The Federal Election Campaign Act of 1974 permitted unions and corporations to establish political committees to contribute $5,000 to each candidate in a primary or general election. The law was immediately challenged by Senator James Buckley of New York. In 1976, in the case of *Buckley* v. *Valeo*, the Supreme Court

upheld many of the law's provisions. But the Court ruled unconstitutional a provision of the law that had placed limits on "independent expenditures" made on behalf of candidates without their cooperation.[106]

The Supreme Court's decision—and a 1975 ruling of the Federal Election Commission allowing the Sun Oil Company to set up a PAC—opened the way for vastly increased expenditures by PACs in political campaigns. These may range all the way from bumper stickers and buttons to television spots endorsing a candidate.

For example, when Senator Dole sought the Republican presidential nomination in 1988, a PAC called Campaign America spent $6 million in the two years before the first presidential primary, much of it designed to help Dole. Campaign America, which had been established by Senator Dole, insisted its purpose was to support Republican candidates generally, but the PAC paid tens of thousands of dollars to a staff of political consultants who went to work on the Dole campaign, and it aided the senator's campaign in other ways.[107]

Even though direct contributions by a PAC to a federal candidate are still limited to $5,000 in each election, the number of political action committees is so

---

[104] *USA Today*, November 4, 1982, p. 5A.

[105] *Washington Post*, "PAC Power? They Keep On Losing," March 27, 1983, pp. B1–2.

[106] *Buckley* v. *Valeo*, 424 U.S. 1 (1976). The federal campaign-spending laws and the impact of Supreme Court decisions are discussed in detail in Chapter 8.

[107] Dan Morgan, "PACs Stretching Limits of Campaign Law," *Washington Post*, February 5, 1988, p. 1.

large that PAC contributions totaled just under $150 million in the 1990 congressional campaigns.[108]

Supreme Court decisions also have encouraged corporate political activity. In 1978 the Court overturned a Massachusetts law that prohibited corporations from spending money to influence the outcome of public referenda. The Court ruled that the state law violated the corporation's First Amendment rights.[109] In 1980 the Supreme Court ruled that a public utility could insert with its monthly bills statements on controversial political issues.[110]

A Harvard University study prepared for Congress identified other reasons for the growth of PACs. The study gave as one reason the changes in the federal election laws that have made it more difficult to raise campaign funds from individuals. And the study suggested that the decline in the power of political parties has forced candidates to turn to interest groups for money.[111]

Undoubtedly the publicity given to PACs in recent years has encouraged the formation of even more such committees. Changes in the structure of Congress may have also contributed. In the 1970s Congress reduced the power of its committee chairmen; as a result, power became fragmented among hundreds of subcommittees, each of which is cultivated by various lobbyists.

As the Harvard study noted, "PAC money is *interested* money."[112] That is, the PACs often give contributions to committee chairpersons with specific legislative outcomes in mind. In 1986, the twenty-two House committee chairmen received 44 percent of their money from PACs. Interest groups clearly try to put their money where it will have the most influence; for example, between 1987 and 1990, PACs representing the banking industry gave members of the House Banking Committee more than $3 million.[113]

In the mid-1980s, the tobacco industry fought hard to defeat a bill that would have abolished federal price supports for tobacco. Over a three-year period, PACs supported by the tobacco companies gave more than $1.3 million to members of the House. All ten members of the Tobacco and Peanut Subcommittee, who had received an average of $7,900 each in such contributions, voted against the bill. The measure was defeated; tobacco won.[114]

Fred Wertheimer, who analyzes political spending for Common Cause, has suggested that PAC contributions follow an "investment pattern," aimed at strengthening the group's long-term influence with members of Congress.[115] That pattern is reflected in the top-heavy support by PACs for incumbents. In 1990, for example, members of Congress received almost 80 percent of all PAC contributions, compared to only 10 percent received by challengers.[116]

In 1974 there were 608 PACs. By 1992 there were approximately 4,100.[117] Beyond question, the explosive growth and influence of political action committees, often tied to single-issue lobbying, is having a significant, controversial, and sometimes disturbing influence on politics and policy in America.

Regulating Interest Groups

Because the First Amendment to the Constitution protects free speech and the right to petition the government, the efforts of interest groups to influence Congress are constitutionally protected. Nevertheless, public concern over lobbying abuses led Congress, beginning early in this century, to try to impose legal controls on interest groups. Not until 1946, however, did Congress pass a general bill that attempted to control lobbying.

The Federal Regulation of Lobbying Act of 1946 requires individuals and groups to register with the clerk of the House and the secretary of the Senate if they solicit or collect money or any other thing of value

[108] Data provided by Federal Election Commission, December 1991.

[109] *First National Bank of Boston v. Bellotti*, 435 U.S. 765 (1978).

[110] *Consolidated Edison v. Public Service Commission*, 447 U.S. 530 (1980).

[111] Institute of Politics, John F. Kennedy School of Government, Harvard University, "An Analysis of the Impact of the Federal Election Campaign Act, 1972–78," prepared for the Committee on House Administration, U.S. House of Representatives (Washington, D.C.: U.S. Government Printing Office, 1979), p. 4.

[112] Ibid.

[113] Data provided by Congress Watch.

[114] Daniel Gross and Olivier Sultan, "Public Funding vs. Private Funding," *Public Citizen's Congress Watch*, The Democracy Project, May 1991, pp. 6–7.

[115] Fred Wertheimer, "Of Mountains: The PAC Movement in American Politics" (Paper written for the Conference on Parties, Interest Groups and Campaign Finance Laws, Washington, D.C., September 1979), pp. 5–8.

[116] The remaining 10 percent of PAC contributions in 1990 went to candidates for House seats where no incumbent was seeking re-election. Data provided by Federal Election Commission, December 1991.

[117] Data provided by Federal Election Commission, January 1992.

WHO LOBBIES FOR THE POOR?

The poor are powerless because they are a minority of the population, are often difficult to organize, and are not even a homogeneous group with similar interests that could be organized into an effective pressure group. . . .

Although every citizen is urged to be active in the affairs of his community and nation, in actual practice participation is almost entirely limited to organized interest groups or lobbies who want something from government.

As a result, legislation tends to favor the interests of the organized: of business-men, not consumers, even though the latter are a vast majority; of landlords, not tenants; doctors, not patients. . . . while the American political structure often satisfies the majority, it also creates *outvoted minorities* who can be tyrannized and repressed by majority rule, such as the poor and the black, students, migrant workers and many others.

—Herbert J. Gans, "We Won't End the Urban Crisis Until We End Majority Rule," *New York Times Magazine*, August 3, 1969

"to be used principally to aid . . . the passage or defeat of any legislation by the Congress of the United States." In 1954 the Supreme Court narrowed the scope of the act by exempting grass-roots lobbying aimed at the public.[118] Because of this decision and the loose wording of the statute, many interest groups simply do not register on the grounds that lobbying is not their "principal purpose." Moreover, although the law contains penalties, it has no enforcement provision. As a result, there have been few prosecutions since its enactment in 1946.

In 1991, the General Accounting Office, which serves as a watchdog for Congress, reported that it had studied 13,500 entries in *Washington Representatives*, a book that lists lobbyists and consultants. The GAO found that only 3,700 had registered.[119] Of the estimated 60,000 to 80,000 lobbyists active in Washington, only about 6,000 have registered in recent years.[120]

In sum, the Lobbying Act does not effectively regulate lobbying of Congress. And, of course, it does not apply at all to lobbying of the executive branch or the independent regulatory commissions. In the years that followed 1946, Congress periodically considered bills to strengthen the regulation of lobbying, but as of 1992 none had passed.

Interest Groups and the Policy Process

The view persists in American politics that interest groups are undemocratic, and that they work for narrow goals against the general welfare. Some do. But an interest group like Common Cause represents no narrow economic interest; it works for its conception of the public welfare on a wide spectrum of issues. So have the organizations formed by consumer advocate Ralph Nader. It may be more realistic to view interest groups simply as one part of the total political process. Citizens have every right under the Constitution to organize to influence their government. Interest groups compete for the government's attention and action—but so do individual voters, political parties, and the press.

On many major issues, there are likely to be interest groups arrayed on opposite sides. Those who accept democratic pluralism and the politics of interest groups believe that out of these conflicting pressures some degree of balance may be achieved, at least much of the time.

Interest groups perform certain functions in the American political system that cannot be performed as well through the conventional structures of government, which are based largely on geographic representation.

The kind of *representation* that interest groups provide supplements the representation provided by Congress. Interest groups may also permit the *resolution of inter-group conflicts*. In collective bargaining, for example, differences between two powerful interest groups—management and labor—are resolved. Inter-

---

[118] *United States* v. *Harris*, 347 U.S. 612 (1954).
[119] *Washington Post*, July 17, 1991, p. A21.
[120] Ibid.

est groups also perform a *watchdog* function; they can sound the alarm when new government policies threaten to injure the interests of their members. Finally, interest groups perform the function of *idea initiating*, that is, they generate new ideas that may become government programs. So important are these functions, Lester Milbrath has concluded, "if we had no lobby groups and lobbyists we would probably have to invent them." [121]

Some very serious criticisms can be leveled at interest groups, however. Perhaps the most comprehensive criticism of interest-group politics has been formulated by Theodore J. Lowi. [122] Lowi questions the assumption of many scholars and political leaders that the interest-group process in a pluralist society provides a desirable, or satisfactory, way for the American government system to work. What are the effects of interest groups on public-policy formation? Lowi argues that there is no assurance that the "pulling and hauling among competing interests" will result in policy decisions that are adequate to meet the social and political problems now facing the United States. In Lowi's view, interest-group pluralism has not resulted in "strong, positive government" but in "impotent government" that can "neither plan nor achieve justice." [123] For example, if business groups succeed in weakening environmental legislation, the interests of the larger public may be diminished.

As we have seen, most Americans do *not* belong to interest groups. Those who do tend to come from the better-educated, middle- or upper-class backgrounds that produce citizens with a high degree of political motivation. "The flaw in the pluralist heaven," E. E. Schattschneider has observed, "is that the heavenly chorus sings with a strong upper-class accent. Probably about 90 percent of the people cannot get into the pressure system." [124]

Some of the widespread voter disenchantment with government and political candidates that marked the 1992 presidential election year might be attributed, at least in part, to the feeling of many ordinary voters that they had been left out of the political system.

Disadvantaged groups — the poor, blacks, Hispanics, slum dwellers, migrant workers — often have nei-ther the knowledge nor the money to organize to advance their interests. Interest-group politics, in other words, is biased against minorities and in favor of business organizations and other affluent groups.

The ordinary American consumer is not as well represented in interest-group politics as are manufacturers. Americans who drive to work in a costly but possibly unsafe car, who are assailed by noisy commercials, swim at a beach polluted by oil, inhale pesticides and smog-filled air, and who eat food enhanced with dangerous additives may be forgiven if they wonder what interest group represents *them*.

There are hundreds of business groups represented in Washington, but a much smaller number of consumer organizations. One reason is that the interest of consumers is so general that it does not lend itself to organized expression as readily as the narrower interest of a special group, such as physicians or truckers. And as Mancur Olson, Jr., has pointed out, unless the number of individuals in a group is very small, or unless there is coercion or some special incentive to make individuals work together in their mutual interest, many people will not organize or act to achieve common or group interests through the political process. [125]

Even organized, active interest groups do not represent all they claim to represent. The leaders of an interest group tend to formulate policy positions for the group as a whole. Consequently, the public stance of an interest group often represents the views of an oligarchy rather than the views of the rank and file. The American Medical Association (AMA), for example, is more conservative than are many of its 297,000 members. Moreover, at least half of the nation's 615,000 physicians do not even belong to the AMA.

Despite all their flaws, interest groups do supplement formal channels of representation, and allow for the expression of public opinion in an organized manner. But if American democracy is to become more responsive to the needs of its citizens, the nation's legislators must find new ways to heed the voice of the ordinary citizen: the consumer, the poor, the African American and other minorities, and the powerless — groups that are much less likely to have a steel-and-glass office building and a team of registered lobbyists to speak for them in Washington.

---

[121] Milbrath, *The Washington Lobbyists*, p. 358.

[122] Theodore J. Lowi, *The End of Liberalism: Ideology, Policy, and the Crisis of Public Authority*, 2nd ed. (New York: Norton, 1979).

[123] Ibid., p. xvi.

[124] Schattschneider, *The Semisovereign People*, p. 35.

[125] Mancur Olson, Jr., *The Logic of Collective Action: Public Goods and the Theory of Groups*, revised ed. (Cambridge: Harvard University Press, 1971), p. 2.

PERSPECTIVE

Public opinion is the expression of attitudes about government and politics. All governments are based, to some extent, on public opinion. In a democracy, public opinion may be seen as a process of interaction between the people and the government, a broad but flexible framework for policymaking.

Political socialization is the process by which a person acquires a set of political attitudes and forms opinions about social issues. The family and the school play a part in the political socialization of children. The "crucial period" of a child's political, social, and psychological development is between the ages of nine and thirteen.

Many other factors also influence the opinions people hold. Among the most important are: differences in social class, occupation, and income; religion, sex, race, and ethnic factors; sectional and geographic differences; and the views of reference groups (such as a political party) or primary groups (such as friends, office associates, or a local club); and television, newspapers, magazines, and other media. The qualities of public opinion — direction, intensity, and stability — may be measured by political polls.

Often useful as a guide to voter sentiment, political polls are a standard part of political campaigns. They measure opinion by taking a random sample of a larger population, or universe. Because of the mathematical law of probability, the results of the poll usually reflect the opinions of the larger group. Although generally reliable, polls are sometimes wrong and do not necessarily predict the outcomes of elections.

In presidential elections, often only a little more than half of the voting-age population votes. In off-year, nonpresidential elections, usually well under half of the voting-age population votes for members of Congress.

Americans have not always sought to express their opinions or to bring about political change through lawful or peaceful means. If the political system fails to respond to the demands placed on it, or if participation is slow to bring about change, individuals or groups may vent their anger against the system in violent ways.

Modern political candidates and leaders are highly attuned to techniques for measuring and influencing public opinion. Political polls, television spot commercials, and professional campaign managers are all part of the efforts at mass persuasion employed today.

The quality of the mass media (including newspapers, television, radio, and magazines), the amount of time and space they devote to public affairs, their editorial stands, ownership patterns, and objectivity are all factors that may have great influence on public opinion. Government officials frequently "leak" stories to the press, divulging information on condition that the officials remain anonymous. The motives for such leaks vary greatly, and although disclosures of information are often deplored, neither government nor the news media could really operate without the institution of the news leak.

Who governs in the United States? One view is that the people govern through political leaders nominated as candidates of political parties (or running as independents) and elected by the voters. Another view is that elites rule; power is held by the few rather than the masses of people. Another view emphasizes the pluralist character of American democracy; that is, conflicting groups within the community have access to government officials and compete with one another in an effort to influence policy decisions. But some issues may never reach the public agenda for debate.

Interest groups are private groups that attempt to influence the government to respond to the shared attitudes of their members. When people organize to express attitudes held in common, and to influence the government to respond to those attitudes, they become members of interest groups. Lobbying, mass propaganda, and grass-roots pressure are among the techniques employed by interest groups to achieve their objectives. One of the most powerful techniques is lobbying, communication with legislators or government officials to try to influence their decisions.

Single-issue lobbies often work through political action committees (PACs) — which are sometimes independent organizations, but more often the political arms of corporations, labor unions, or interest groups. Although PACs are limited in the amount they can contribute directly to a candidate's campaign, the Supreme Court has ruled that they may make unlimited "independent expenditures" on behalf of candidates.

Interest groups perform certain functions in the American political system that cannot be performed as well through the conventional structures of government. They provide a representation that supplements Congress. They may permit the resolution of intergroup conflicts, and they may perform watchdog and idea-initiating functions.

But most Americans do not belong to interest groups. Disadvantaged groups often have neither the knowledge nor the money to organize to advance their interests. And the ordinary American consumer is not as well represented in interest-group politics as are business and industry. Many voters feel that they have been left out of the political system.

Suggested Reading

Almond, Gabriel A., and Coleman, James S., eds. *The Politics of the Developing Areas** (Princeton University Press, 1960). An influential book that explores and develops, among other topics, the concept of "political socialization."

Armbruster, Frank, and Yokelson, Doris. *The Forgotten Americans: The Values, Beliefs and Concerns of the Majority* (Arlington House, 1972). An informative portrait of the social and political attitudes of the American public from the 1930s through 1971. Based on a review of hundreds of public opinion surveys covering a wide range of issues.

Berry, Jeffrey M. *Lobbying for the People** (Princeton University Press, 1977). A useful and readable analysis of the political and organizational behavior of public interest groups. Using case studies, Berry profiles the activities and strategies of two public interest lobbying organizations in considerable detail.

Cobb, Roger W., and Elder, Charles D. *Participation in American Politics*, 2nd edition* (Johns Hopkins University Press, 1983). A very useful introduction to the agenda-building process. Presents a variety of case studies to illustrate how issues get on the political agenda.

Dahl, Robert A. *Who Governs?** (Yale University Press, 1961). An influential and detailed exploration of the nature of political power, based on a study of political decision-making in New Haven, Connecticut. Dahl maintains that there is a pluralism of power — rather than a single "power elite" — in the United States.

Greenstein, Fred I. *Children and Politics*, revised edition* (Yale University Press, 1967). A study of the attitudes of young children toward politics and of how political attitudes are formed. Based on interviews with schoolchildren in New Haven, Connecticut.

Jennings, M. Kent, and Niemi, Richard G. *The Political Character of Adolescence** (Princeton University Press, 1974). An important study of political learning among high school students. The authors find that the divergence between the political attitudes of children and their parents increases as children grow older.

Key, V. O., Jr. *Public Opinion and American Democracy* (Philadelphia Book Co., 1961). A detailed analysis of public attitudes about government and politics and their relation to the way government operates.

Lane, Robert E. *Political Life* (Free Press, 1965). (Originally published in 1959.) A comprehensive summary of political participation and public attitudes toward politics in the United States. Analyzes the factors that encourage and discourage political participation by the public.

Lippmann, Walter. *Public Opinion** (Free Press, 1965). (Originally published in 1922.) A basic work on how public opinion operates. As a distinguished political columnist, Lippmann helped to mold American public opinion for half a century.

Lowi, Theodore J. *The End of Liberalism: Ideology, Policy, and the Crisis of Public Authority*, 2nd edition* (Norton, 1979). A stimulating analysis of the theory and practice of interest-group politics in the United States. Lowi is strongly critical of the consequences of the interest-group bargaining process as it has developed since the New Deal.

Mills, C. Wright. *The Power Elite** (Oxford University Press, 1956). One of the best-known statements of the view that there is a unified "power elite" in the United States. In Mills's view, wealth, prestige, and power in America are concentrated in the hands of a hierarchy of corporate, government, and military leaders.

Olson, Mancur, Jr. *The Logic of Collective Action: Public Goods and the Theory of Groups*, revised edition* (Harvard University Press, 1971). An important analysis of the role of groups in the American political process. Based on an application of economic analysis to the relationships between individual self-interest and group membership and activity. Examines the consequences these relationships have for politics.

Paletz, David L., and Entman, Robert M. *Media Power Politics* (Free Press, 1981). A wide-ranging examination of the role of the mass media in American politics. Argues that the media have a major impact on what happens in the political arena.

Truman, David B. *The Governmental Process*, 2nd edition (Knopf, 1971). An influential study of interest groups in the United States. Develops and modifies a general theory of groups and applies it to American politics.

Weissberg, Robert. *Public Opinion and Popular Government* (Prentice-Hall, 1976). An interesting analysis of the role public opinion plays in determining which policies are adopted by government. Presents detailed results of polls conducted by Gallup, Harris, and other polling organizations on such topics as defense spending, health care, gun control, and racial integration.

Wheeler, Michael. *Lies, Damn Lies, and Statistics* (Liveright, 1976). A critical study of how public opinion polls may be used, abused, and misinterpreted. Discusses the influence opinion polls have on American politics and business.

---

* Available in paperback editions

WHEN THE Democrats met in New York City in July 1992 to nominate Bill Clinton as their candidate for president, the delegates to the national convention and the news media knew that much would depend on how well Clinton came across to the American people on television as he delivered his acceptance speech.

Clinton, the governor of the small state of Arkansas, had begun his quest for the presidency nine months earlier, on October 3, 1991, when he announced that he planned to run for president. At the time, Clinton himself later said, "Even my mother didn't think I had a chance." [1] Now, in the summer of 1992, he faced the task of defining himself and his views to the delegates, and to a vast audience watching on television. Clinton

Chapter 7

Political Parties

also faced the challenge of becoming as well known to the American voters as his Republican opponent, the incumbent president, George Bush.

As expected, Clinton sharply attacked his Republican opponent for the poor performance of the American economy under the Bush administration. "What is George Bush doing about America's economic problems?" he asked. "Well, he promised us 15 million new jobs by now. And he's over 14 million jobs short. We can do better." [2]

Clinton also threw down a challenge to "the forces of greed and the defenders of the status quo: your time has come — and gone," he said. "It's time for a change in America." [3]

---

[1] Speech, Mason District Democratic Committee Annual Crab Roast, Fairfax County, Virginia, September 12, 1992.
[2] *New York Times*, July 17, 1992, p. 14.
[3] Ibid., p. 14.

However, Clinton also had some words that delegates to Democratic conventions were not used to hearing from their presidential nominee. "But we Democrats," Clinton declared, "have some changing to do, too. It is time for us to realize that there is not a government program for every problem. And if we really want to use government to help people, we've got to make it work." [4] Clinton aimed his speech squarely at "all the people who do the work, pay the taxes, raise the kids and play by the rules—the hard-working Americans who make up our forgotten middle class." [5]

[4] *New York Times*, July 17, 1992, p. 15.
[5] Ibid., p. 14.

In the space of a few moments, a Democratic presidential nominee had made statements that might as easily have been said by any Republican candidate over the last twenty years. There was good reason for Clinton to strike a moderate, pragmatic tone.

In 1992, as had been true for many years in the past, there were more people in America who called themselves Democrats than there were people who identified with any other group — either Republicans or independents. But the gap between the two parties had narrowed; the number of people who identified themselves as Republicans had increased during the 1980s. In addition, close to a third of the voters called themselves independents. And there were also a sizable number of "Reagan Democrats," the blue-collar and middle-class

voters who normally supported the Democratic party but who voted for Reagan in 1980 and 1984.

As the fall campaign progressed, Clinton and his vice-presidential running mate, Senator Albert Gore, frequently contended that they were leading a "new Democratic party" in the 1992 election contest: "Our policies are neither liberal nor conservative, neither Democratic nor Republican. They are new. They are different." [6] As a result, Clinton often seemed to be competing with George Bush for some of the same groups of voters, and competing as well with Ross Perot, the independent candidate who became a major factor in the 1992 race.

On November 3, 43.7 million persons cast their votes for Clinton and slightly more than 38 million voted for Bush. Perot polled 19.2 million votes, an unusually strong showing for an independent. In the electoral college, however, all of the votes went to Clinton or Bush. The Democratic nominee carried 32 states and the District of Columbia, and won 370 electoral votes to 168 for Bush.

The drama of 1992 provided one set of answers to some recurring questions about American political parties: Have political parties declined in importance? Are they truly responsive and responsible instruments of democracy? Do they offer a genuine choice on the major issues facing the nation? Do they nominate the most able men and women to run the nation and its states and communities in the nuclear age? Are parties boss-controlled elitist organizations closed to outsiders? Are national conventions a circus and a farce, or useful tools of representative government? In discussing the role, history, organization, and performance of American political parties, we shall explore all of these questions.

WHAT IS A PARTY?

"As there are many roads to Rome and many ways to skin a cat," Frank J. Sorauf has written, "there are also many ways to look at a political party." [7] A political party is a group of men and women meeting in a small community in Connecticut to nominate a candidate for town council. It is a group of ward heelers in Chicago turning out to cheer at a political rally. It is congres-

sional leaders having a private breakfast at the White House with the president to discuss the administration's legislative proposals. It is the delegates to a national political convention exploding in a frenzy of noise, emotion, confetti, and balloons after the name of their candidate for president is placed in nomination. It is the millions who vote on Election Day.

As Sorauf has concluded, the nature of a political party is somewhat in "the eye of the beholder." [8] Nevertheless, it is possible to identify some of the elements that make up a major political party. There are the *voters*, a majority of whom consider themselves Democrats or Republicans; the *party leaders outside of government*, who frequently control the party machinery and sometimes have important power bases; the *party activists*, who ring doorbells, serve as delegates to county, state, and national conventions, and perform the day-to-day, grass-roots work of politics; and finally, the *party leaders in the government*, including the president, the leaders in Congress, and party leaders in state and local governments.

When someone speaks of "the Democratic party" or "the Republican party," that person may really mean any of these diverse elements — or all of them. Because a political party is like a big circus tent, encompassing so many different acts, it is as difficult to define in a shorthand way as it would be to define a circus. But, in very general terms, *a major political party is a broadly based coalition that attempts to gain control of the government by winning elections*, in order to exercise power and reward its members.

---

[6] Gov. Bill Clinton and Sen. Al Gore, *Putting People First: How We Can All Change America* (New York: Times Books, 1992), p. viii.

[7] Frank J. Sorauf, *Political Parties in the American System* (Boston: Little, Brown, 1964), p. 1.

[8] Ibid.

Today, political parties are less powerful than in the past, as party allegiances among the voters have declined and as competing groups—political action committees, professional campaign management firms, and interest groups—have increasingly come to share many of the traditional roles of parties. Nevertheless, political parties continue to perform vital functions in the American political system. The best way to look at political parties is not in terms of what they are but in terms of what they do. One of the major problems of government has been the management of the transfer of power. In totalitarian governments, power, once seized, is seldom peacefully relinquished. Usually the change comes unexpectedly. A democracy, however, provides orderly institutional arrangements for the transfer of power.

In normal circumstances, in the United States, a president, running as the nominee of a political party, is elected every four years and serves one or two terms. American political parties thus perform "an essential function in the management of succession to power."[9] They serve as a vehicle for choice, offering the electorate competing candidates for public office, and often, alternative policies. The element of choice is absolutely vital to democratic government. Where the voters cannot choose, there is no democracy. The parties operate the machinery of choice: nominations, campaigns, and elections.

Within the framework of a political system (the concept discussed in Chapter 1), political parties help to mobilize the demands and supports that are fed into the system, and participate as well in the authoritative decision making, or outputs, of the government.

In a presidential election, the party in power traditionally defends its record and attacks its opponents, while the party out of power suggests that it is time for a change. For example, in 1992 President Bush defended the record of his administration, blamed the Democratic Congress for blocking his programs, and sharply called into question Governor Clinton's "character" and fitness for the presidency. Repeatedly he asked the voters whether they could "trust" Clinton.

As we have seen, the Democrats and their candidate, Bill Clinton, sought to make the state of the economy under twelve years of Republican rule the central issue of the campaign. By seeking to mobilize mass opinion behind their slogans and policies, political parties

channel public support for, or against, the government. In so doing, they normally serve as an essential bridge between the people and the government. They provide a powerful means for the public's voice to be heard— and politicians must listen if they wish to survive in office. Parties thus help to hold officials accountable to the voters. They also help to recruit candidates for public office.

Because a political party consists of people expressing attitudes about government, it might seem to fit the definition of an interest group. But a political party runs candidates for public office. It is therefore much more comprehensive than an interest group. Instead of seeking only to *influence* government, often on a narrow range of issues, a major party attempts to win elections and *gain control* of the government.

The major political parties try to form "winning coalitions" by maneuvering "to create combinations powerful enough to govern."[10] In the process, they may serve to reconcile the interests of conflicting groups in society. The political party can fill the natural role of broker or mediator among interest groups, organized or not, because in order to win elections, it usually tries to appeal broadly to many groups of voters.

Parties also play a key role in the governmental process. When the Clinton administration succeeded the Bush administration in January 1993, Washington real estate agents were happy; it meant that Republicans would be selling their houses and Democrats would be buying them. Following a presidential election, the White House staff, the cabinet, and the more important policymakers and officials of the various executive branch departments are for the most part appointed from the president's party. To the victors belong the White House limousines.

Political parties play a vital role in the legislative branch as well. The president appeals to party loyalty through the party's legislative leaders in order to get his programs through Congress (although he may face a Congress, or at least one house, controlled by the opposition party). And both major parties have "Whips" in Congress—legislative leaders who are responsible for rounding up their party's members for important votes. Because political parties are involved in the governmental process, they serve to link different parts of the government: the president communicates with party leaders in Congress; the two houses of Congress

---

[9] V. O. Key, Jr., *Politics, Parties, and Pressure Groups*, 5th ed. (New York: Crowell, 1964), p. 9.

[10] Ibid., p. 167.

communicate in part through party leaders; and relationships among the national, state, and local governments depend to a considerable degree on ties among partisan officials and leaders.

In sum, political parties perform vital functions in the American political system. They (1) manage the transfer of power, (2) offer a choice of rival candidates and programs to the voters, (3) serve as a link between government and people by helping to hold elected officials accountable to the voters, (4) help to recruit candidates for office, (5) may serve to reconcile conflicting interests in society, (6) staff the government and help to run it, and (7) link various branches and levels of government.

THE DEVELOPMENT OF AMERICAN POLITICAL PARTIES

The framers of the Constitution created the delicately balanced machinery of the federal government and provided for regular elections of a president and Congress, but they said not a word about political parties. The reason was simple: in the modern sense, they did not exist.

Yet James Madison, the "father of the Constitution," foresaw that Americans would group together in factions. In *The Federalist* No. 10, he predicted that the task of regulating conflicting economic interests would involve "the spirit of party and faction in the necessary and ordinary operation of the government."

In his farewell address, George Washington warned against "the baneful effects of the spirit of party." His vice-president, John Adams, had declared: "There is nothing I dread so much as the division of the Republic into two great parties, each under its leader." [11] Yet the American party system began to take just such a shape in the 1790s during Washington's administration.

Federalists and Democratic-Republicans

The Federalist party, organized by Alexander Hamilton, Washington's secretary of the treasury, was the first national political party in the United States. The Federalists stood for strong central government, and their

[11] Wilfred E. Binkley, *American Political Parties* (New York: Knopf, 1963), p. 19.

These political buttons for George Washington were intended to be sewn on clothing.

appeal was to banking, commercial, and financial interests.

Thomas Jefferson built a rival coalition that became known as the Republican party, or Democratic-Republicans. [12] It was primarily an agrarian party of small farmers, debtors, southern planters, and frontiersmen. Being a practical politician, Jefferson sought to expand his coalition; in 1791 he made a famous trip to New York state, allegedly on a "butterfly hunting" expedition but actually to form an alliance with Aaron Burr and the Sons of Tammany, the political organization that was to dominate New York City. In the part-

[12] The name tends to be confusing to anyone attempting to trace the origins of the American party system. Today's Democratic party, the oldest political party in the world, claims the Jeffersonian Republican, or Democratic-Republican, party as its political and spiritual ancestor, a fact that Democratic orators remind us of endlessly and annually at Jefferson-Jackson Day dinners. Today's Republican party invokes Abraham Lincoln, not Jefferson.

nership of rural America and the cities, the Democratic party was born.

Jefferson's triumph in the election of 1800 inaugurated a twenty-eight-year period of ascendancy by the Jeffersonian Democratic-Republicans. In fact, the Federalists never again tried for the presidency after 1816 when James Monroe, the Democratic-Republican candidate, was overwhelmingly elected. Monroe's victory launched the brief Era of Good Feelings, in which there was little partisan activity.

Democrats and Whigs

By 1824 the Democratic-Republicans had split into several factions and the first phase of party government in the United States came to an end. The election in 1828 of Andrew Jackson, the hero of the War of 1812, opened a new era of two-party rivalry, this time between Democrats and Whigs. Jacksonian democracy soon came to symbolize popular rule and the aspirations of the common man.

The rival Whigs, led by Henry Clay, William Henry Harrison, and Daniel Webster, were a coalition of bankers, merchants, and southern planters held together precariously by their mutual distaste for Jacksonian democracy. The Whigs won two presidential elections between 1840 and 1854, and the two-party system flourished.[13] As Clinton Rossiter has noted, "Out of the conflict of Democrats and Whigs emerged the American political system — complete with such features as two major parties, a sprinkle of third parties, national nominating conventions, state and local bosses, patronage, popular campaigning, and the presidency as the focus of politics."[14]

During the 1850s, the increasingly divisive issue of slavery caused the Democratic party to split between North and South. The Whigs, crushed by Democrat Franklin Pierce's landslide victory in 1852, were equally demoralized. The nation was about to be torn apart by civil war, and the major political parties, like the Union itself, were disintegrating.

Democrats and Republicans

The Republican party was born in 1854 as a party of protest against the extension of slavery into the territories. The Kansas-Nebraska Act, passed that year, permitted slavery to move westward with the frontier and aroused discontent in the North and West.

In February 1854, a group of Whigs, Free-Soilers, and antislavery Democrats gathered in a church at Ripon, Wisconsin, to recommend the creation of a new party to fight the further expansion of slavery.[15] The name "Republican party" was suggested at the meeting. The political organization that resulted from

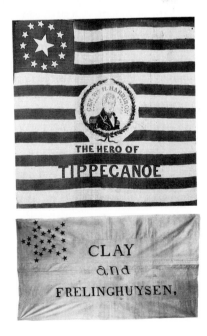

---

[13] Four Whig presidents occupied the White House. Only two were elected, however — William Henry Harrison in 1840 and General Zachary Taylor in 1848. Both died in office and were succeeded by their vice-presidents, John Tyler and Millard Fillmore.

[14] Clinton Rossiter, *Parties and Politics in America* (Ithaca: Cornell University Press, 1960), pp. 73–74.

[15] The party birthplace is also claimed by Jackson, Michigan, where the Republicans held their first state convention five months later.

the meeting took the place of the Whigs as the rival party of the Democrats, but it was a new party and not merely the Whigs masquerading under another label.

The first Republican presidential candidate, John C. Frémont, the "Pathfinder of the Rockies," was unable to find the trail that led to the White House in the election of 1856. But in 1860 the Republicans nominated Abraham Lincoln. By that time, the Democratic party was so badly divided over the issue of slavery that its northern and southern wings each nominated separate candidates for president. A fourth candidate ran as the nominee of the Constitutional Union party. The four-way split enabled Lincoln to win with only 39.8 percent of the popular vote. His election was a rare fusion of the man and the times. Lincoln preserved the Union; in the process, he ensured the future of the Republican party. By rejecting slavery, the Republicans had automatically become a sectional party, representing the North and West. And North and West meant Union, emancipation, and victory. The Democrats and the South meant slavery, secession, and defeat. Having been on the losing side of the bloody and tragic Civil War, the Democrats were a long time in recovering; the party was trapped and tangled in the folds of the Confederate flag.

For twenty-five years after 1860, the Republicans consolidated their strength and ruled America, becoming known by the 1870s as the Grand Old Party, a term later shortened to GOP. But by 1876 the Democrats had recovered sufficiently to give the Republicans spirited two-party competition for two decades. Twice, in 1884

and 1892, the Democrats elected Grover Cleveland as president.

America was changing. After the Civil War, the nation gradually became industrialized; railroad tracks pushed westward, spanning the continent; immigrants from Europe poured in. As the rail and steel barons amassed great fortunes, small farmers found themselves squeezed economically and outnumbered by workers. Agrarian discontent was reflected in the rise of minor parties like the Grangers, the Greenbackers, and the Populists.

The Populists, or People's party, were a protest party of western farmers. In 1892 their presidential candidate, James B. Weaver, showed surprising strength. By 1896 the spirit of Populism had captured the Democratic party, which nominated William Jennings Bryan for president. Bryan, running on a "free silver" platform, lost to Republican William McKinley, who defended the gold standard and conservative fiscal policies. The election resulted in a major realignment of the parties, from which the Republicans emerged stronger than ever as a coalition of eastern business interests, urban workers, midwestern farmers, and New England Yankees.

Theodore Roosevelt held the coalition together while he was president from 1901 to 1909, but his attempt to move the Grand Old Party in a more progressive direction alarmed its conservative business wing. In 1912 the Republican party split apart. The conservative wing renominated William Howard Taft, who had been Roosevelt's handpicked successor. The other wing, the Progressive ("Bull Moose") party, nominated Roosevelt. The Republican split resulted in victory for Woodrow Wilson, the Democratic nominee.

Wilson's two terms proved to be a short Democratic interlude. A nation weary of the First World War chose to "return to normalcy" in the 1920s with the Republican administrations of Warren G. Harding and Calvin Coolidge, two of the less distinguished presidents to occupy that office. Big Business dominated; it was the era of the Teapot Dome scandal, flappers, bathtub gin, and the Prohibition "speakeasy." In 1928 Republican Herbert Hoover defeated Al Smith, the first Roman Catholic nominee of a major party. A year later, the stock-market crash and the onset of the Great Depression dealt the Republican party a blow comparable to the effect of the Civil War on the Democrats.

The result of these events was the election of Franklin D. Roosevelt in 1932, the New Deal, and twenty years of uninterrupted Democratic rule under Roosevelt and his successor, Harry S Truman. Roose-

velt put together a new, grand coalition composed of the South, the big cities of the North, labor, immigrants, blacks, and other minority groups.

In 1952, in the midst of the Korean War, the Republicans nominated General Dwight D. Eisenhower and recaptured the presidency. But the Eisenhower magic could not be transferred to Richard Nixon, who narrowly lost the presidency to John F. Kennedy in 1960. The "New Frontier" seemingly opened a new era of Democratic supremacy. But Kennedy was assassinated in 1963. In 1964 Barry Goldwater, a conservative from Arizona, captured control of the GOP from its long-dominant and more liberal eastern, internationalist wing. The result was Republican disaster. Lyndon Johnson, who had succeeded to the presidency after Kennedy's death, was elected in his own right with 61.1 percent of the total vote—the greatest share of the popular vote in history.

But American political parties have extraordinary resiliency: "Each one is a citadel that can withstand the impact of even the most disastrous national landslide and thus provide elements of obstinacy and stability in the two-party pattern." [16] The Republican party survived the Goldwater debacle. It regrouped around Richard Nixon, who accurately gauged the temper of the nation in 1968. Lyndon Johnson, unable to hold the Democratic coalition together in the face of war and urban riots, did not choose to run. With the Democrats divided into at least three camps, Nixon triumphed, restoring the Republican party to power and demonstrating anew the strength of the American two-party system. Nixon's landslide victory in 1972 was an even more dramatic illustration of the point, a triumph soon overshadowed by the scandal of Watergate, the

---

[16] Rossiter, *Parties and Politics in America*, p. 7.

resignation of Vice-President Spiro Agnew, and Nixon's own resignation in 1974 on the brink of impeachment. Then in 1976 Jimmy Carter, starting from a very modest political base as the former governor of Georgia, captured the Democratic nomination, succeeded in reunifying the Democratic party, and went on to win the White House in a very close race against the incumbent, President Gerald R. Ford. The Democrats controlled both Congress, where they maintained their majority, and the executive branch. Yet, only six years after Nixon's resignation, the Republican party surged back to power in 1980, capturing the White House under Ronald Reagan and gaining control of the Senate for the first time in more than a quarter of a century. Reagan's landslide victory in 1984 consolidated Republican control of the presidency.

This ability of American political parties to survive adversity and rise again rests in part on the fact that many areas of the country and many congressional districts are dominated by one party; even when a party is defeated nationally, it will still have durable pockets of power across the nation. This remains true despite the spread of two-party politics to more states in recent years. For example, Reagan carried forty-nine states in winning re-election to the presidency in 1984, and his party kept control of the Senate, but the Democrats retained thirty-four of the state governorships and continued to control the House of Representatives.

The Democrats recaptured control of the Senate in 1986. As a result, President Bush, a Republican, faced a Congress with both houses controlled by the Democrats during his four years in office after 1988. The election in 1992 of a Democratic president, Bill Clinton, and a Democratic Congress brought to a close twelve years of Republican control of the White House. The Democratic victory demonstrated once again the ability of American political parties to regroup and return to power.

THE TWO-PARTY SYSTEM

Under the two-party system, to become the nominee of one of the two major parties is at least half the battle. In areas where one party dominates, it is equivalent to election. Throughout most of the nation's history, two major political parties have been arrayed against each other. The Democrats, in one guise or another, have endured. During successive eras they have been challenged by the Federalists, the Whigs, and the Republi-

cans. Minor or third parties have joined the struggle, with greater or lesser effect, but the main battle has been, historically, a two-party affair. As Allan P. Sindler has observed, "From 1828 to the present with few exceptions the two parties together have persistently polled upward of 90 percent of the national popular vote — that is, there has been little multi-partyism." [17]

In 1968 George Wallace formed the American Independent party and ran for president outside the two-party framework. He received 13.5 percent of the popular vote. Although a substantial showing for a minor-party candidate, it was nowhere near enough to win. In 1976 Eugene McCarthy, an independent candidate, received less than 1 percent of the popular vote. In 1980 Representative John B. Anderson, an Illinois Republican, won a place on the ballot in every state as an independent and waged a vigorous campaign for president. But he received only 6.6 percent of the popular vote and no electoral votes.

In 1992, Ross Perot, who also ran as an independent, made the strongest showing of any candidate who was not a major-party nominee since Theodore Roosevelt ran as the head of the Progressive (Bull Moose) party in 1912. Unlike most minor-party and independent candidates, Perot did not run short of funds to advertise his candidacy in the closing weeks of the campaign. A successful businessman and a billionaire, Perot financed most of his campaign with his own money.

With more than 19 million votes (19 percent), Perot was a major factor in the 1992 campaign, and in most states his presence on the ballot drew votes from both Clinton and Bush. In all, about one in five voters chose Perot, the independent. Perot's strong showing as an outsider may have reflected the fact that America's major parties were weaker in 1992 than they had been in earlier years. It may also have reflected voter discontent with the established political parties and political leaders.

The Roots of Dualism

In the states and in many local communities, one party may dominate, as the Democrats did for decades in the Solid South and the Republicans did in Kansas and Vermont. But on the whole, America has been a two-party nation. Why this should be so is a subject of mild

---

[17] Allan P. Sindler, *Political Parties in the United States* (New York: St. Martin's Press, 1966), p. 15.

dispute because there is no wholly satisfactory simple answer. Among the explanations that have been offered are these:

Tradition and History   The debate over ratification of the Constitution split the country into two groups. Dualism, therefore, is as old as the nation itself. And, once established, human institutions tend to perpetuate their original form. To some extent, Americans accept the two-party system because it has almost always been there.

The Electoral System   Many features of the American political system appear compatible with the existence of two major parties. In the United States, the single-member district system prevails in federal elections. For example, only one member of Congress may be elected from a congressional district, no matter how many candidates run — it is a case of winner take all. The same is true of a presidential election; normally in each state the candidate who receives the most popular votes wins all of the state's electoral votes. Under such a system, minor parties lacking a strong geographical base have little chance of poaching on the two-party preserve; they tend to lose and, having lost, to disappear.[18] (By contrast, a system of proportional representation with multimember districts, as in Italy, encourages the existence of many parties by allotting seats to competing parties according to the percentage of votes that they win.)

Patterns of Belief   A majority of the American voters stand somewhere near the middle ground on many issues of American politics. Ideological differences among Americans in the past have normally not been strong enough to produce a broad range of established minor parties representing widely varying shades of political opinion, as is the case in many Western European nations.

As noted earlier, American presidential candidates generally try to make very broad-based appeals. Although there are more Democratic than Republican voters in America, neither party enjoys the support of a majority of the electorate, and both must therefore look outside their own ranks for victory. To put together a winning coalition, a presidential candidate usually appeals to the great mass of voters in the ideological center. As a result, in some elections it may appear that there is very little difference between the two major parties. Since both parties woo the same voters, it is not surprising that, to an extent, they look alike. But they have important differences as well.

A classic study of national convention delegates found that the opinions of Democratic and Republican leaders diverged sharply on many important issues. What is more, these opinions were found to conform to party images: Republican leaders identified with "business, free enterprise, and economic conservatism in general," and Democrats were friendly "toward labor and toward government regulation of the economy." Differences of opinion among party leaders were found to be much sharper than the differences of opinion among ordinary members of the rank and file of the two parties.[19]

A more recent survey of party leaders, conducted in 1992, also found pronounced differences between the attitudes of Democratic and Republican leaders. For example, among delegates to the 1992 Democratic convention, 87 percent agreed that "the government should institute and operate a national health care program." But among delegates to the Republican convention that year, only 12 percent favored a government health care program.[20]

In one study of changes in American political parties, Everett Carll Ladd, Jr., and Charles D. Hadley suggested the emergence of a "two-tiered" party structure.[21] "There has been too much cultural change, too fast," they argued, with the result that middle-class white voters have tended to express their resistance to social change by voting for Republican presidential candidates but for Democrats for congressional and state offices. As the authors have expressed it, "in the two-

---

[18] The two parties need not be the same in all areas of the country, however. In some states, historically, minor parties have competed successfully with one of the two major national parties. For example, in Minnesota during the 1920s and 1930s, the Farmer-Labor party — not the Democratic party — was the chief competitor of the Republican party in state and congressional elections. Since a merger in 1944, the Democratic-Farmer-Labor party has been the principal rival to the Republicans in Minnesota.

[19] Herbert McCloskey, Paul J. Hoffmann, and Rosemary O'Hara, "Issue Conflict and Consensus among Party Leaders and Followers," *American Political Science Review*, vol. 54, no. 2 (June 1960), pp. 415–26. The study was based on interviews with delegates who attended the 1956 Democratic and Republican National Conventions.

[20] *Washington Post* and ABC News Delegate Survey, in *Washington Post*, August 16, 1992, p. A18.

[21] Everett Carll Ladd, Jr., with Charles D. Hadley, *Transformations of the American Party System: Political Coalitions from the New Deal to the 1970s*, 2nd ed. (New York: W. W. Norton, 1978), p. 262.

tiered system . . . resistance to social and cultural change deemed excessive is expressed in balloting for its great national fulcrum, the presidency; while general support for extending the managerial/welfare state is sustained by maintaining the Democratic majority at the subpresidential level. . . ." [22] Not every election conforms to this two-tiered model, however. In 1976 the voters elected a Democrat as president, and four years later the Republicans won the Senate as well as the presidency, as they did again in 1984. And in 1992, the Democrats won the presidency and both houses of Congress.

The Decline of Party Loyalties and Party Influence

The fading of party loyalties among many voters has been one of the most visible features of American politics in recent years. Beginning in 1974, about a third of the voters described themselves as independents. Only about two-thirds of the voters called themselves Republicans or Democrats.[23] As Ladd and Hadley have noted, "All measures lead to the same conclusion. There has been a long-term decline of party allegiance, and a dramatic drop-off over the last decade." [24] Political scientist Martin P. Wattenberg has made the point even more strongly: "Once the central guiding forces in American electoral behavior, the parties are now perceived with almost complete indifference by a large proportion of the population." [25]

Of course, candidates and issues, not just party affiliations, influence voters. But the diminishing influence of parties is a significant change from the past. One observer, Austin Ranney, has suggested that something approaching a "no-party system" has emerged in presidential politics.[26] The results of the 1984 election seemed to bear out this general movement away from party loyalties. The Republican candidate, President

"How would you like me to answer that question? As a member of my ethnic group, educational class, income group, or religious category?"

Drawing by D. Fradon © 1969 The New Yorker Magazine, Inc.

Reagan, won more than 58 percent of the vote even though less than one-third of the electorate described itself as identifying with the Republican party. In 1992, nearly one out of five voters cast their ballots for Ross Perot, who represented no party.

Various reasons have been suggested for the decline of party ties: a more educated electorate, less dependent on parties for guidance; an increase in "split-ticket" voting by persons who may, for example, vote for a Republican candidate for president and a Democrat for governor; the increasing importance of television and the news media generally; and the breaking up of the old loyalties and alignments within the major parties.[27]

In addition, as already noted, political parties themselves have become less powerful. Other groups such as political action committees, professional campaign managers, and interest groups have taken over some of the functions of parties. Urban political machines have declined. And candidates no longer rely on parties to run their campaigns to the extent that was true in the past. As Frank J. Sorauf has observed, "All the campaign assets . . . [candidates] once received from the party organizations and their workers — skills,

[22] Ibid., pp. 262, 268.

[23] Gallup Opinion Index, Report No. 131, June 1976, p. 11; Report No. 180, August 1980, p. 31; and Gallup Report, December 1986, no. 255, pp. 27–28.

[24] Ladd with Hadley, Transformations of the American Party System: Political Coalitions from the New Deal to the 1970s, p. 329.

[25] Martin P. Wattenberg, The Decline of American Political Parties 1952–1980, (Cambridge: Harvard University Press, 1984), p. xv.

[26] Austin Ranney, "The Political Parties: Reform and Decline," in Anthony King, ed., The New American Political System (Washington, D.C.: American Enterprise Institute for Public Policy Research, 1979), p. 245.

[27] Ladd with Hadley, Transformations of the American Party System: Political Coalitions from the New Deal to the 1970s, pp. 329–33.

information, pulse readings, manpower, exposure—
they now can get from pollsters, the media, public relations people, volunteer workers, or even by 'renting a
party' in the form of a campaign management firm." [28]
The "fairly primitive campaign skills" of parties "have
been superseded by a new campaign technology, and
more and more they are finding themselves among the
technologically unemployed." [29]

Despite the fading of party loyalties and influence,
however, political parties in America have by no means
become extinct. And even though the number of unaffiliated voters has risen, there are still many more
Americans who call themselves Democrats or Republicans than who term themselves independents.

The Democrats

One way to perceive the differences between the two
major parties is to examine their images. In the public's
imagination, the "typical" Democrat lives in a big city in
the North. He or she is a Catholic, a Jew, an African
American, an Hispanic American, a Pole, an Italian, or a
member of some other minority group. The imaginary
Democrat drinks beer, belongs to a union, works on an
assembly line, goes bowling, and has a fairly low income.

Genus Republican's habitat, by contrast, is the
hedge-trimmed suburbs. He or she lives in a split-level
house with a picture window, commutes to the city, and
belongs to a country club that has no members from
minority groups. The male of the species is almost certainly a white Protestant. He drinks martinis and eats
white bread. His wife drives a station wagon. He owns
his own company or is a corporate executive. He golfs
on weekends. He is rich, or at least comfortable, equally
at home in the boardroom or the locker room. That, at
any rate, is the popular image.

Like any caricature, these portraits are greatly
overdrawn. For example, one study of shifts in the
American electorate concluded that the Democrats'
base "has changed somewhat from the New Deal
era . . . they have lost ground among some of their old
constituencies, such as trade unionists, big-city whites,
and Southern whites; while they have made up for such
losses with gains among the upper-middle-class. . . ."
The study suggested the Republicans have "lost their
grip on the American establishment, most notably
among young men and women of relative privilege." [30]

Table 7-1

Family Income and Party Identification

Family Income	Democrat	Republican
$0–$15,000	51%	22%
$15,000–$24,999	43	28
$25,000–$39,999	41	30
$40,000 and over	34	37

SOURCE: *The Gallup Poll* press release, August 7, 1988.

Republicans could no longer count on the automatic
support of this affluent group; in 1992, both parties
battled for the support of "yuppies"—young, up-
wardly mobile professionals with substantial incomes.

Still, the image of each party and of individual
Democrats and Republicans, at least to an extent,
mirrors reality: studies have shown that the Democrats
usually, although not always, enjoy greater voter support from labor, Catholics, Jews, African Americans,
ethnic minorities, young people, and from those who
have not attended college, who have low incomes, and
who live in the cities. Republicans are more likely to be
Protestant, white, suburban, rural, wealthy, older, college educated, and professionals or business executives.
"Republicans tend to see themselves as middle class,
and Democrats are much more apt to consider themselves as working class." [31]

In other words, whether a person identifies with
the Democratic or Republican party may be related to
socioeconomic factors. For example, one survey found
that about half of the people interviewed with low incomes considered themselves Democrats, but only
about 22 percent of this group thought of themselves as
Republicans. (See Table 7–1.)

There are also philosophical and ideological differences between the parties. Democrats tend to believe
more in the ability of government to solve problems
than do Republicans. And Democrats, political scientist
Jo Freeman has observed, believe in "the inclusion of all
relevant groups and viewpoints," while Republicans see
themselves as "insiders who represent the core of
American society and are the carriers of its fundamental
values." [32]

[28] Frank J. Sorauf, *Party Politics in America*, 5th ed. (Boston: Little,
Brown, 1984), p. 420.

[29] Ibid.

[30] Ladd with Hadley, *Transformations of the American Party System, Political Coalitions from the New Deal to the 1970s*, pp. 258,
268.

[31] Sorauf, *Party Politics in America*, p. 148.

[32] Jo Freeman, "The Political Culture of the Democratic and Republican Parties," *Political Science Quarterly*, vol. 101, no. 3,
1986, p. 337.

THE TWO-PARTY SYSTEM / 235

Since 1932, in presidential elections, the Democratic party has, in spirit, been the party of Franklin D. Roosevelt. The vast social-welfare programs launched by the New Deal changed the face of America and gave the Democratic party an identity that has persisted for many years. Truman's "Fair Deal," Kennedy's "New Frontier," and Johnson's "Great Society" were all patterned on Roosevelt's New Deal. All sought to harness federal funds and federal energies to solve national problems.

Despite the success of Roosevelt's grand coalition, the Democratic party continues to display some of the characteristics of a bivalve, with two distinct halves. The southern, more moderate wing of the party differs significantly from the northern, urban, liberal wing. Normally, the overriding desire for power and electoral victory is the muscle that holds the two halves together. Sometimes the muscle fails. For example, in 1948 southern Democrats walked out of the national convention over the civil rights issue.

For decades the Democrats could count on the eleven states of the Old Confederacy as a solid Democratic bloc. But the South is no longer a one-party Democratic enclave. In 1972, for the first time, it voted solidly for a Republican, Richard Nixon. In the South in 1980, Jimmy Carter, the Democratic nominee, carried only his home state of Georgia against his Republican opponent, Ronald Reagan. And in 1984, Walter Mondale, the Democratic candidate for president, carried not a single state in the South. In 1988, Massachusetts Governor Michael Dukakis, the Democratic nominee, failed to carry any southern states. Governor Bill Clinton of Arkansas, a Democrat and a southerner, carried four southern states when he won the presidency in 1992. Since 1952, every Republican presidential candidate has won some southern electoral votes. (See Table 7–2.)

In political campaigns, Republicans like to label the Democrats as "spenders." On the whole, Democrats have been more willing to appropriate federal funds for social action. As a result of this political reality, the Democratic party since 1933 has been the party of social security, Tennessee Valley Authority, Medicare, and federal aid to education. It has, in short, often been the party of social innovation.

In addition to differences of substance, the two parties show perceptible differences in style. "I don't belong to any organized party," the humorist Will Rogers once quipped. "I'm a Democrat."[33] Democrats do tend to be uninhibited and occasionally raucous, fighting among themselves; Republicans are normally more sedate.

Of course, these differences do not always hold true. In 1988 the Democrats gathered in unusual harmony to nominate Michael Dukakis, the accepted frontrunner; it was the Republican convention, thrown into turmoil by the controversy surrounding Bush's choice of Senator Dan Quayle for vice-president, that provided unexpected color and excitement. Usually, however, it is the Democrats who brawl and squabble.

"A gathering of Democrats *is* more sweaty, disorderly, offhand, and rowdy than a gathering of Republicans . . . ," Clinton Rossiter has noted. "A gathering of Republicans *is* more respectable, sober, purposeful, and businesslike than a gathering of Democrats. . . ."[34] The Democratic donkey brays, snorts, kicks up its heels, balks, fusses, and is a very different animal in appearance, substance, and temperament from the Republican elephant.

The Republicans

"Fundamentally," Theodore H. White once wrote, "the Republican Party is white, middle-class and Protestant. . . . Two moods color its thinking. One is the old Protestant-Puritan ethic of the small towns of America. . . . The other is the philosophy of private enterprise, the sense that the individual, as man or corporation, can build swifter and better for common good than big government. From middle-class America the Republicans get their votes; from the executive leadership and from the families of the great enterprises they get their funds."[35]

[33] Quoted in Andrew Hacker, "Is the Party Over?" *The New York Times Book Review,* November 26, 1978, p. 12.
[34] Rossiter, *Parties and Politics in America,* p. 117.
[35] Theodore H. White, *The Making of the President 1968* (New York: Atheneum, 1969), p. 33.

Table 7-2
Republican Inroads in the South, 1950–92

Year	Number of Congress-persons		Number of Senators		Governors		Number of States Voting for Presidential Nominee	
	D	R	D	R	D	R	D	R
1950	103	2	22	0	11	0		
1952	100	6	22	0	11	0	7	4
1954	99	7	22	0	11	0		
1956	99	7	22	0	11	0	6	5
1958	99	7	22	0	11	0		
1960	99	7	22	0	11	0	7	3*
1962	95	11	21	1	11	0		
1964	89	17	21	1	11	0	6	5
1966	83	23	19	3	9	2		
1968	80	26	18	4	9	2	1	5†
1970	79	27	16(1)‡	5	9	2		
1972	74	34	14(1)‡	7	8	3	0	11
1974	81	27	15(1)‡	6	8	3		
1976	82	26	16(1)‡	5	9	2	10	1
1978	77	31	15(1)‡	6	8	3		
1980	69	39	11(1)‡	10	6	5	1	10
1982	82	34	11	11	9	2		
1984	73	43	12	10	9	2	0	11
1986	77	39	16	6	6	5		
1988	78	38	14	8	6	5	0	11
1990	77	39	15	7	8	3		
1992	77	48	13	9	8	3	4	7

* The eight Mississippi electors voted for Harry Byrd.
† George Wallace won five states on the American Independent ticket.
‡ Harry Byrd, Jr., was elected in Virginia in 1970 and 1976 as an Independent.
SOURCE: House, governor, and president figures in *Congressional Quarterly*, Politics in America 1945–1966 (Washington, D.C.: Congressional Quarterly Service, 1967), pp. 101, 123, 117–21. Senate figures in Richard Scammon, *America Votes 7* (Washington, D.C.: Governmental Affairs Institute, 1968), pp. 12, 31, 74, 82, 147, 205, 289, 357, 371, 379, 404. Data since 1968 from *Congressional Quarterly*, Weekly Reports; and *New York Times*.

"Yes, son, we're Republicans."

Drawing by M. Richter © 1991 The
New Yorker Magazine, Inc.

Despite the success of the Republicans in five out of the six presidential elections between 1968 and 1988, since the New Deal the Republican party has, in terms of party identification, enjoyed the support of only a minority of American voters; people who identify themselves as Democrats have, in recent decades, outnumbered people who say they are Republicans. In the face of such figures, the Republican party's constant task is to broaden its popular appeal and turn its minority into a majority, or at least a plurality. The Republican party won the presidency in 1980, 1984, and 1988 precisely because it was able to attract large numbers of Democrats and independents.

The familiar Democratic charge that "the Republican party is the party of Big Business" is partially accurate, just as it is true that, nationally, the Democrats have traditionally been the party of organized labor. The preference of business for the Republican party may be measured by analyzing campaign contributions. For example, in 1992 corporations and business executives contributed $28.7 million to the national Republican party but only $11.1 million to the Democratic party.[36]

During the Eisenhower years, federal regulatory agencies were markedly friendly to the broadcasting networks, airlines, and other businesses they were supposedly regulating. It can be argued that "it does make a difference to the television industry, the railroads, or the stock exchanges whether Democrats or Republicans have a majority in the independent commissions."[37]

Like the Democrats, the Republicans have a split personality. The scar left when Theodore Roosevelt bolted the party in 1912 has never entirely healed; in modern times the battle of Republican conservatives (the political heirs of William Howard Taft) against Republican liberal-moderates (the heirs of Theodore Roosevelt) has continued, although in muted form during the strongly conservative Reagan years.

The struggle broke out in 1952 in the convention battle between Senator Robert A. Taft of Ohio (the son of William Howard Taft) and General Eisenhower, who was backed by the eastern liberals. Then in 1964 Goldwater and the conservative wing won control of the party from the Eastern Establishment led by Nelson Rockefeller. In 1968 the ideological split was still highly visible, with liberals Rockefeller and George Romney

on one side, Ronald Reagan of California at the conservative end of the spectrum, and Richard Nixon near the center. Again in 1976 the split was reflected in the battle between President Ford and Ronald Reagan for the party's presidential nomination, the most serious challenge to a Republican president within his own party since the revolt against William Howard Taft. It was doubtful that a cleavage that ran so deep would disappear altogether. Despite Ford's nomination in 1976, the right wing of the Republican party remained a strong force within the GOP, ready to recapture the party, as it did in 1980. The Republican split was still visible that year, when Reagan was opposed in the primaries by three moderates, George Bush, John B. Anderson, and Howard H. Baker, Jr. This time, however, with Reagan as their standard-bearer, the conservative wing won the White House. Again in 1992 President Bush was challenged for the Republican nomination by Patrick J. Buchanan, a strongly conservative columnist.

In the 1980s and early 1990s, the Republican party also often drew support from conservative Christian religious groups. In 1988, a former television evangelist, Pat Robertson, challenged Vice-President George Bush in the Republican primary elections. In 1992 Robertson supported Bush.

Although fundamentalist religious groups varied in their methods and goals, they shared common social views; ". . . the New Right is generally concerned with what is seen as the breakdown of family, community, religion, and traditional morality in American life,"

[36] "Soft Money Update: September 1992," Center for Responsive Politics, September 29, 1992, p. 1.
[37] Rossiter, *Parties and Politics in America*, p. 131.

sociologist Jerome L. Himmelstein has written. "Abortion, the Equal Rights Amendment, busing, affirmative action, sexual permissiveness, drugs, prohibitions on school prayer, the secular curriculum in public schools, and many similar things are opposed on the grounds that they contribute to . . . social breakdown and moral decay." [38]

Minor Parties and Independent Candidates

Minor parties have been active throughout most of the nation's history, from the Anti-Masons of the 1830s and the Barnburners of the 1840s, to the Know-Nothings of the 1850s, the Greenbackers of the 1880s, the Populists of the 1890s, the Progressives of the 1920s, and the American Independents in 1968.

In 1968 the third-party movement of Alabama's George Wallace scared major-party supporters because of the possibility that Wallace would carry enough states to prevent either major-party candidate from gaining a majority of electoral votes. Wallace would then have been in a position to bargain with his electoral votes, or to throw the outcome into the House of Representatives. (The electoral college machinery is discussed on pp. 345–347.)

Although Wallace appeared on the ballot in every state, usually as the candidate of the American Independent party, he carried only five southern states; his forty-six electoral votes were not enough to deadlock the presidential election. His 13.5 percent of the popular vote was considerably less than the 21.1 percent received by the Know-Nothings[39] in 1856, the 27.4 percent polled by Theodore Roosevelt's Bull Moose party in 1912, or the 16.6 percent received by Robert La Follette's Progressives in 1924. In 1972 John G. Schmitz, the candidate of the American Independent party, received more than a million votes, or 1.4 percent of the popular vote.

In recent years, several candidates have run as independents for the presidency, without bothering to organize a third party. In 1992, Ross Perot, a billionaire, accepted no federal funds and invested an estimated $60

Copyright © 1992. Reprinted with special permission of King Features Syndicate.

million of his own money in his independent campaign, which relied heavily on television. In one Gallup poll taken in early June, 39 percent of those interviewed said that they would vote for or were leaning toward Perot.[40] His final share of the vote on November 3rd—19 percent—was very large. Even so, Perot did not carry a single state.

Other independent candidates for president have been much less well funded than Perot, and they have polled a much smaller share of the vote. In 1980 independent candidate John B. Anderson, like Perot, carried no state. But with 6.6 percent of the popular vote, Anderson did better than many others have, including Eugene McCarthy, who got less than 1 percent of the popular vote in 1976.

Almost two dozen minor parties ran candidates for president in 1992, but they had no hope of affecting the outcome. V. O. Key, Jr., has suggested that minor parties fall into two broad categories, "those formed to propagate a particular doctrine," and "transient third-party movements" that briefly appear on the American scene and then disappear. The Prohibition party and the Socialist party are examples of doctrinal parties that "have been kept alive over long periods by little bands of dedicated souls." [41] Among the transient third-party movements, Key perceived two types: parties of economic protest, such as the Populists, the Greenbackers, and the Progressives of 1924; and "secessionist parties" that have split off from one of the major parties, such as the Progressives in 1912 and the Dixiecrats in 1948.

---

[38] Jerome L. Himmelstein, "The New Right," in Robert C. Liebman and Robert Wuthnow, eds., *The New Christian Right: Mobilization and Legitimation* (New York: Aldine Publishing, 1983), p. 16.

[39] The anti-Catholic, anti-Irish Native American party was so secretive that its members pretended ignorance of party affairs; as a result editor Horace Greeley dubbed it the Know-Nothing party.

[40] *The Gallup Poll News Service*, volume 57, no. 10, July 12, 1992, p. 2.

[41] Key, *Politics, Parties, and Pressure Groups*, p. 255.

Figure 7–1
Minor-Party and Independent Vote, 1880–1992*

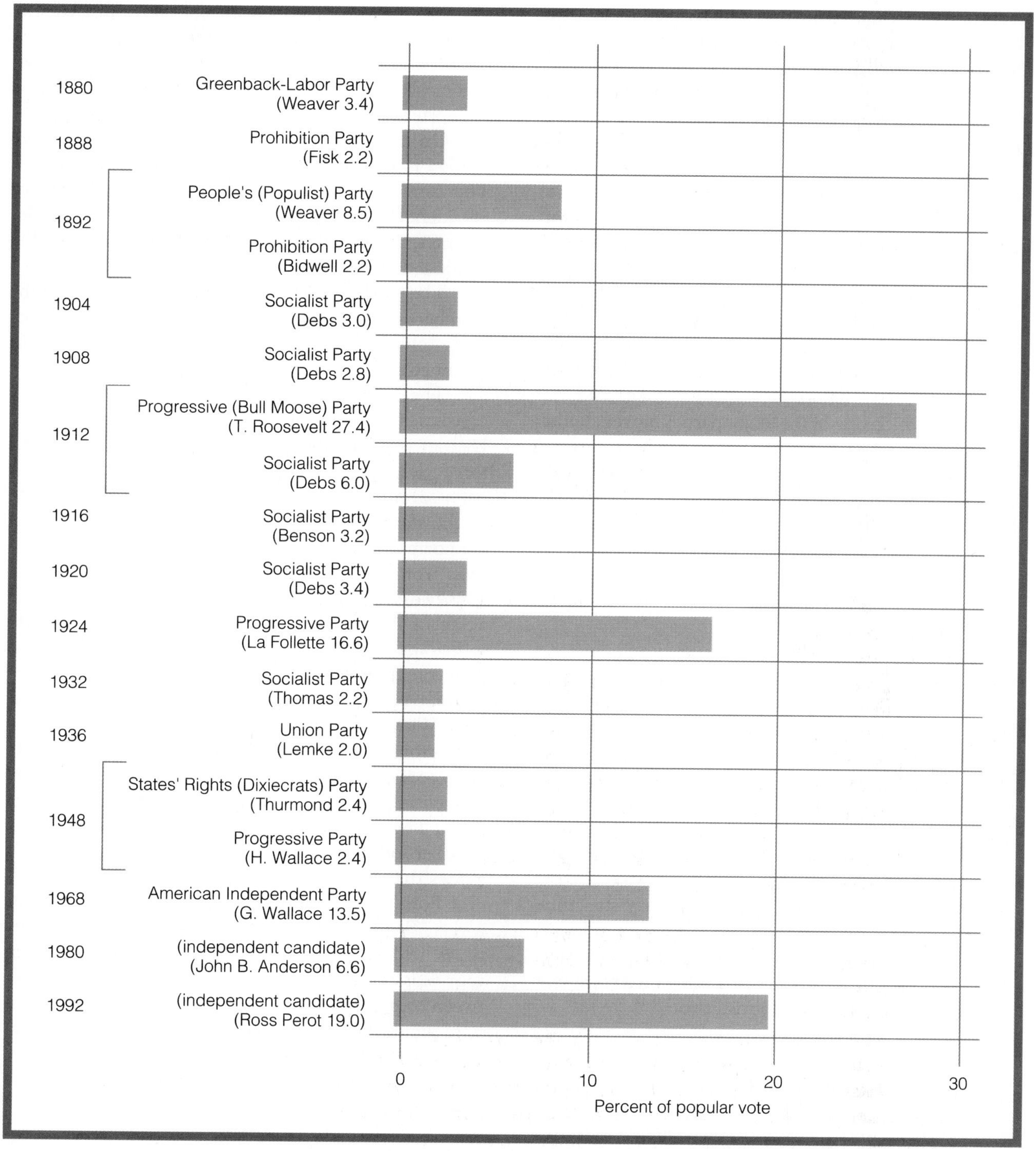

* Includes only those minor parties and independent candidates for president that polled 2 percent or more of the popular vote.
SOURCE: Neal R. Peirce, *The People's President* (New York: Simon and Schuster, 1968), pp. 305–07, reprinted by permission of Simon and Schuster; Donald B. Cole, *Handbook of American History* (New York: Harcourt Brace Jovanovich, 1968), pp. 304–05; *Politics in America*, 4th ed. (Washington, D.C.: Congressional Quarterly, 1971), p. 91; *New York Times*, January 6, 1981, p. A14; and *Washington Post*, November 5, 1992, p. A26.

Sometimes minor parties have a strong nativist streak. Just as the Wallace campaign played upon white fears of African Americans, more than a century ago the Know-Nothings, or Native American party, exploited fear of Irish immigrants and other "foreigners." The party platform in 1856, when Millard Fillmore ran as the Know-Nothing candidate, warned: "Americans must rule America."

In certain states minor parties have gained a powerful position. The Liberal party and the Conservative party in New York have sometimes held the balance of power in elections in that state. Nationally, however, minor parties have never consistently enjoyed much power or influence. On some occasions they have influenced the policies of the major parties—as when Populism captured the Democratic party in 1896.

"One of the persistent qualities of the American two-party system," Clinton Rossiter has concluded, "is the way in which one of the major parties moves almost instinctively to absorb (and thus be somewhat reshaped by) the most challenging third party of the time. In any case, it is a notable fact that no third party in America has ever risen to become a major party, and that no major party has ever fallen to become a third party." [42]

PARTY STRUCTURE

One could draw a neat organizational chart of a major political party, with the national chairperson and national committee at the top of the pyramid, and state and local party machinery arrayed below. The chart would be technically correct but highly misleading. In fact, the national party exists more on paper than in reality, in theory more than in fact.

American political parties are *decentralized* and only loosely organized. Rather than as a pyramid, with all power flowing from the top down, party structure "may be more accurately described as a system of layers of organization. Each successive layer—county or city, state, national—has an independent concern about elections in its geographical jurisdiction." [43]

National Political Parties

A national political party is somewhat like a sports trophy that a team may win and retain for a time but must return eventually so that it may be awarded to a new team. Thus, President Gerald R. Ford led the Re-

publican party in 1976, but after his defeat, he was obliged to give up control of the party machinery. Four years later, it belonged to Ronald Reagan. In 1992, Bill Clinton's capture of the Democratic presidential nomination and his election in November put the Democratic party organization firmly in the hands of Clinton supporters.

On paper, the party's quadrennial *national convention* is the source of all authority within the party. The convention nominates the party's candidates for president and vice-president; it writes a platform, settles disputes, writes rules, and elects the members of the national committee.

The *national chairperson* is formally elected by the members of the national committee. In practice he or she is chosen or retained by the party's presidential nominee at the end of the national convention.

The *national committee* of the Democratic party consists of two men and two women from each state, the District of Columbia, Puerto Rico, and some of the territories, plus 200 additional members chosen under party formulas based on population and party strength in the states, and fifty members elected at large. The Democratic National Committee includes representatives from Congress, Democratic governors, mayors, county officials, state legislators, youth, and women, for a total of 411 members. The Republican National Committee includes all GOP state party chairpersons, plus one woman and one man from each state, the District of Columbia, and the territories, for a total of 167 members. Within each state, members of the national committee for each party are selected under state law by state party convention, by the state delegation to the national convention, by state committees, or in primary elections. The national convention formally "elects" the members of the national committee, but in fact it simply ratifies the choices of each state.

Both parties' national committees meet only twice a year. Beginning in 1974 the Democrats have sometimes held additional midterm national conventions at four-year intervals to try to strengthen the party between presidential elections; however, the party did not hold a midterm convention in 1986 or 1990. In the past, national committees have sometimes been little more than the permanent offices in Washington that house

---

[42] Rossiter, *Parties and Politics in America*, pp. 5–6.
[43] Key, *Politics, Parties, and Pressure Groups,* p. 316.

the national chairperson and the staff. But more recently, the national committees of both parties have become more active between presidential elections. Between elections, the chief functions of the national committee staff are public relations, patronage, research, and fund-raising.

In the early 1980s, with President Reagan in the White House, the Democrats worked hard to revitalize their party machinery. Like the Republicans, the Democrats sought to build computerized mailing lists of potential party contributors and to provide better campaign services to party candidates.

As a rule, presidential nominees either largely ignore the machinery of the national committee and build a personal organization to run their campaign, or they take over the national committee machinery and make it their own. In theory, the national chairperson's main job is to manage the presidential campaign; in practice, however, the candidate's real campaign manager is seldom the party chairperson. In 1992, for example, James A. Baker III resigned as secretary of state to run the presidential campaign of Vice-President George Bush. Bill Clinton's campaign was managed by David Wilhelm, a Chicago political consultant.

Independent of the national committees, and serving as further evidence of the decentralization of American party politics, are the *congressional leaders* of each party, elected by their colleagues, and the *congressional and senatorial campaign committees.* Both major parties have campaign committees in the House and Senate; their members are chosen by party members in each branch of Congress. The congressional committees channel money, speakers, advice, and assistance to party members who are up for election.

In both the Republican and Democratic parties, there is often a good deal of conflict between the party leaders in Congress and the leaders of the more presidentially oriented national party organization, a built-in tension often reflected in rivalry and jealousy between the congressional campaign committees and the national committee.

State and Local Parties

Party organization and election laws vary tremendously in the states, with the result that one can find kaleidoscopic variety in almost any given phase of American politics below the national level. Just as the national party in power is controlled by the president, the state party is often dominated by the governor. In the case of some large northern industrial states, the mayor of a large city may wield considerable influence. On the other hand, the state party may be led by a party chairperson who is not obligated to, and was elected without the support of, the incumbent governor. And, of course, a state chairperson may head a party that is out of power and does not control the governor's office.[44] Some state party organizations are the fiefdom of a single party boss—either an elected official or a party leader outside government. But this is less often the case today than in the past.

Political scientist David R. Mayhew has classified a number of states as having "traditional party organizations" that are independent, long-entrenched, highly organized, seek to nominate candidates to a wide range of public offices, and offer jobs and other tangible rewards to their followers. But he notes that in other state parties there is "persistent factionalism" in which two or more party organizations "commonly operate in the same party in the same city or county, normally competing against each other in primaries for a broad range of offices. . . ."[45]

Republicans or Democrats may consistently dominate within a state, or power may be divided between the two parties. But even within one party, there are great variations in party politics from state to state. The Democratic party in Alabama is very different from that in Michigan. In both parties, liberals may control one state, conservatives or moderates another. And these local differences tend to make American political parties decentralized, fragmented, and weak.

State politics often reflects geographic cleavages. In New York the Democratic party traditionally controls New York City, while Republicans dominate "upstate," the areas outside the city. In Illinois the Democrats, strong in Chicago's Cook County, must contend with a heavy downstate Republican vote. In Michigan, Democrats are strong in Detroit, but Republicans dominate many other areas of the state.

The state parties are bound together within the national political party by a mutual desire to have a "winner" at the head of the national ticket. Often (although not always), a strong presidential candidate will sweep state and local candidates into office on his

[44] Robert J. Huckshorn, *Party Leadership in the States* (Boston: University of Massachusetts Press, 1976), pp. 69–95.
[45] David R. Mayhew, *Placing Parties in American Politics* (Princeton: Princeton University Press, 1986), pp. 17–77, 78.

THE OLD POLITICS—MACHINE STYLE

George Washington (Boss) Plunkitt, a political leader in New York City at the turn of the century, explained his philosophy for attracting votes:

What holds your grip on your district is to go right down among the poor families and help them in the different ways they need help. I've got a regular system for this. If there's a fire in Ninth, Tenth, or Eleventh Avenue, for example, any hour of the day or night, I'm usually there with some of my election district captains as soon as the fire engines. If a family is burned out I don't ask whether they are Republicans or Democrats; and I don't refer them to the Charity Organization Society, which would investigate their case in a month or two and decide they were worthy of help about the time they are dead from starvation. I just get quarters for them, buy clothes for them if their clothes were burned up, and fix them up til they get things runnin' again. It's philanthropy, but it's politics, too—mighty good politics. Who can tell how many votes one of these fires brings me?

—Boss Plunkitt, in William L. Riordon, *Plunkitt of Tammany Hall*

coattails. In 1980 Reagan's electoral sweep may have helped to defeat a number of well-known Senate and House Democratic liberals and to give the Republicans control of the Senate. But in 1984, Reagan's coattails spread less wide; despite his decisive reelection, the Republicans suffered a net loss of two Senate seats and made only limited gains in the House.

The layer of party organization below that of the national committees is the state committees. Like national committee members, members of the state committees are chosen in many different ways, including county conventions and direct primaries.

At the grass roots of each major political party is a third layer of party organization, consisting of the county committees, county chairpersons, district leaders, precinct or ward captains, and party workers. The local party organization is held together in part by the paste of patronage—the rewarding of party faithfuls with government jobs. The old-style, big-city political machines depended almost entirely on patronage; even today a substantial portion of party workers may be found on town, city, and county payrolls.

Although big-city machines still exist, the cigar-chomping, derby-hatted political "boss" of the late nineteenth and early twentieth centuries has in most areas enjoyed his "last hurrah." At one time, Frank Hague, the Democratic boss of Jersey City, could blatantly declare: "I am the law." Edward J. Flynn, the boss of the Bronx, could rise to considerable power within the national Democratic party. Carmine De Sapio, the leader of Tammany Hall, was able to dominate New York City politics in the 1950s. But Frank J. Sorauf has suggested, "The defeat of Carmine De Sapio and the Tammany tiger by the reformers in the fall of 1961 may stand as one of the great turning points in American politics." [46] Chicago's mayor Richard J. Daley, long a power in national Democratic politics, drew substantial support from the city's business community. He gave them what they wanted, "a new downtown area, an expressway . . . confidence in the city's economic future," and in the process made it almost impossible for Republican candidates to find any support among business leaders. [47] Daley, often described as the last of the big-city bosses, died in 1976.

The urban machines drew their power from the vast waves of immigrants to America's cities. The machines offered all sorts of help to these newcomers—from food baskets to city jobs. In return, all the boss demanded was the newcomer's vote. Each ward captain knew precisely how many votes he could deliver—the captain who did not would soon find he was no longer a municipal inspector of sewers. Since the 1930s, social security, welfare payments, food stamps, unemployment benefits, and general prosperity have cut the ground out from under the city machines: the social services formerly provided by the party clubhouse now flow from the impersonal bureaucracy in Washington.

---

[46] Sorauf, *Political Parties in the American System*, p. 53.

[47] David Halberstam, "Daley of Chicago," in William J. Crotty, Donald M. Freeman, and Douglas S. Gatlin, *Political Parties and Political Behavior* (Boston: Allyn and Bacon, 1971), p. 286. Reprinted from *Harper's Magazine*, August 1968.

And the establishment of the direct primary and internal party reforms have, in some cases, impaired the power of the bosses to control nominations.

However, the local party can still sometimes find a city job for a loyal worker, for "the power to hire is still an important power resource." [48] And urban machines can help the poor deal with complex city bureaucracies.[49] Or a city machine can award municipal construction contracts to party activists or financial contributors. But people participate in politics at the grass-roots level today for a variety of reasons, not only economic motives. The woman in Ohio who telephoned her neighbors and urged them to vote for Bush in 1992 may have wanted to feel that she was personally participating in the election of a president. The volunteers who rang doorbells for Clinton or for Perot that year did so in many cases for the sheer excitement of being involved in a political campaign. The suburban man who serves as a precinct captain may be active in politics because he enjoys the added prestige he acquires in the eyes of his neighbors. (He is the person who can get a new streetlight installed or the potholes filled in.) He may even be a party worker because he likes to attend the party's national convention as a delegate every four years.

Increasingly, two new kinds of activists are taking part in American politics at various levels, including service as delegates to national conventions. These are the issue activists — persons committed to a particular issue, such as civil rights or women's rights — and activ-

ists who work in the organizations of political candidates. These new breeds are, to some extent at least, replacing the "ward heelers" and party regulars of yesteryear.

The number of political activists at any level is fairly small, however. Perhaps only 10 percent of the population could be classified as "politically involved." (See Table 7-3.) If we apply the percentages shown in the table for 1988 to the 1988 voting-age population of 182,628,000 we find that in round numbers 16.4 million Americans spent money to help the campaign for one of

---

[48] Raymond E. Wolfinger, "Why Political Machines Have Not Withered Away and Other Revisionist Thoughts," *The Journal of Politics*, vol. 34 (1972), p. 384.

[49] Ibid., pp. 384–86.

Table 7-3
Political Participation

	1964	1968	1972	1976	1978	1980	1982	1984	1986	1988
Do you belong to any political club or organization?	4%	3%	NA*	NA*	NA*	3%	3%	NA*	NA*	NA*
Did you give any money or buy tickets or do anything to help the campaign for one of the parties or candidates?	11	12	10	9	13	8	NA*	13%	10%	9%
Did you go to any political meetings, rallies, dinners, or things like that?	8	14	9	6	10	8	9	8	7	7
Did you do any other work for one of the parties or candidates?	5	5	5	4	6	4	6	4	3	3
Did you wear a campaign button or put a campaign bumper sticker on your car?	17	15	14	8	9	7	8	9	7	NA*

* NA: Not Available.
SOURCE: Survey Research Center/Center for Political Studies, University of Michigan, in William H. Flanigan and Nancy H. Zingale, *Political Behavior of the American Electorate*, 4th ed. (Boston: Allyn and Bacon, 1979), p. 163. Reprinted with permission; and data for 1978 through 1986 and for campaign buttons and bumper stickers from the American National Election Studies, Center for Political Studies, Institute for Social Research, University of Michigan. Data for 1988 from the Survey Research Center/Center for Political Studies, University of Michigan, in William H. Flanigan and Nancy H. Zingale, *Political Behavior of the American Electorate*, 7th edition (Washington: CQ Press, 1991), p. 182.

the parties or candidates, 12.8 million attended political gatherings or functions, and 5.5 million did political work for parties or candidates.[50]

THE NATIONAL CONVENTION

Television has brought American politics into the living room. Perhaps nowhere is this more apparent than in the hoopla and drama of the presidential nominating convention. Viewers at home have a better and closer view of a national convention than the delegates. Network television reporters, sprouting antennae and electronic gear and looking like Martians, roam the convention floor interviewing political leaders and generating excitement. In darkened rooms just off the convention floor, TV directors follow the action on glowing monitors. They bark crisp orders; the camera cuts to Bob Schieffer of CBS or Andrea Mitchell of NBC. The latest gossip, the newest floor rumor, is fed back in living color to millions of American homes.

True, the television viewer will miss some of the drama of the convention hall, the actual feel of the crowd, the vast size of the amphitheater. On the other hand, he or she can sit back in the comfort of home and watch democracy in action as the Democrats and Republicans choose their candidates for the most powerful office in the world.

But is that really what the viewer is seeing? Are the delegates actually choosing the nominee, or are they merely ratifying what has been a foregone conclusion for weeks or months? Do the delegates have meaningful power and independent judgment, or are they robots legally bound to vote for the winner of their state's primary? Are some of them puppets taking orders from political bosses? Would it perhaps be better, after all, to watch a late movie? The answers to these questions depend entirely on what convention, what delegation, and which delegates one has in mind. Depending on the year and the circumstances, one can actually answer "yes" or "no" to each question.

The national convention has been roundly denounced as a carnival and a bore, and vigorously defended as the most practical method of choosing political candidates in a democracy. It may be all three.

Today, Nelson W. Polsby has suggested, "national conventions survive primarily as spectacle. . . . More and more conventions are designed as entertainment, although . . . they may still conduct business of great

---

[50] For a general discussion of political participation, see pp. 194–195.

THE NATIONAL CONVENTIONS: CORN PONE AND APPLE PIE

With the increasing importance of presidential primaries, national conventions are today much less important in the process of selecting a presidential nominee. But their earlier colorful atmosphere was captured in this vivid word picture by one observer half a century ago:

The national nominating convention is something unknown to the Constitution and undreamed of by the founding fathers. It is an American invention, as native to the U.S.A. as corn pone or apple pie. A Democratic or a Republican national nominating convention, once it gets going, emits sounds and lights that never were on land or sea. . . . At different hours of the day or night, it has something of the painted and tinselled and tired gaiety of a four-ring circus, something of the juvenile inebriety and synthetic fraternal sentiment of a class reunion, something of the tub-thumping frenzy of a backwoods camp meeting. . . . What goes on beneath the surface and behind locked doors is something both realistic and important. For it is here, unexposed to the public eye, that the deals and bargains, the necessary compromises are arranged — compromises designed to satisfy as well as possible all of the divergent elements within the party.

—Carl Becker, "The Will of the People," *Yale Review*, March 1945

importance to the future of the party."[51] And, of course, the conventions are spectacles carefully tailored for television; delegates, party leaders, candidates, and nominees are all reaching for the wider audience watching on TV. But, in 1992, the television networks cut back drastically on their convention coverage. The gavel-to-gavel coverage of the past was replaced by telecasts only of the main events each night.

The Democratic National Convention in New York City in 1992 nevertheless provided moments of television drama. First, Governor Mario Cuomo of New York launched an all-out attack on the economic record of the incumbent Republican administration and called for the election of Bill Clinton, "a new captain with a new course."[52] Then, almost immediately after being nominated, Bill Clinton was seen walking with his family through the streets of Manhattan to Madison Square Garden where he acknowledged the cheers of the Democratic National Convention. But probably the two most dramatic events of the convention week occurred outside the convention hall. On the morning of the convention's final day, Ross Perot announced that he was withdrawing from the presidential race — although he later reentered the campaign. And throughout the convention week the Democrats' Clinton-Gore ticket registered a surge in the polls — the so-called "convention bounce" — that put them well ahead of the Republican team of Bush and Quayle.

A month later in Houston, the Republicans, still behind in the polls, gathered to renominate their candidates for president and vice president. There were fights over some of the planks in the party platform; but the central event was President Bush's acceptance speech, which most observers felt he delivered very effectively. When the convention was over, there was some improvement in the Republicans' standing in the polls, even though the Bush-Quayle ticket was still behind their Democratic opponents. The national conventions of both major parties can play an important role in rallying voter support for their party's candidates.

The national nominating convention evolved slowly in American politics. Until 1824, nominations for president were made by party caucus in Congress. As a presidential aspirant that year, Andrew Jackson knew he did not have enough strength in the congressional caucus to gain the nomination, so his supporters boycotted the caucus. The Tennessee Legislature nominated Jackson, who received the most popular and electoral votes. But no candidate received a majority of

---

[51] Nelson W. Polsby, *Consequences of Party Reform* (New York: Oxford University Press, 1983), p. 77.
[52] *Washington Post*, July 16, 1992, p. A9.

the electoral votes, and the selection of a president fell to the House of Representatives. Jackson lost when the House chose John Quincy Adams. Jackson's efforts, however, successfully dethroned "King Caucus"; in the election of 1832, presidential candidates of all political parties were nominated by national conventions for the first time.

The early conventions provided no surprises, but in 1844, on the eighth ballot, the Democrats chose James K. Polk, a "dark horse" — a term used to describe a candidate who is initially thought to have only an outside chance of gaining the nomination. Polk won the election and proved an able president. Polk's nomination "marked the coming of age of the convention as an institution capable of creating as well as of ratifying consensus within the party." [53]

---

[53] Key, *Politics, Parties, and Pressure Groups*, p. 398. Polk was, in fact, the first "dark horse" to be nominated for president by a national political convention.

Nominating a Presidential Candidate

Because the choice of a presidential candidate is usually determined by the outcome of the presidential primaries and caucuses, national conventions today have become less important. As noted earlier, one symbol of their declining role is the fact that the major TV networks no longer provide gavel-to-gavel coverage, as in the past.

National party conventions normally take place over four days in July or August. The convention city is often hot and overcrowded; delegates spend long hours waiting for elevators and attempting to do such ordinarily simple things as ordering breakfast in a hotel coffee shop or getting through to someone on the telephone. Rival candidates set up headquarters in hotel suites. As the convention opens, rumors fly of deals and of switches by key delegations. There are press conferences, television interviews, parades, bands, and other forms of confusion and diversion. In trailers next to the convention hall, the key staff members of major candidates set up command posts, which are linked by telephone or walkie-talkies to their lieutenants on the floor. In a matter of seconds, instructions can be relayed to supporters in the various state delegations.

Major decisions are often made outside the convention hall. Behind the scenes, if the nomination has not already been determined in the primaries, presidential candidates and their lieutenants apply a combination of carrot and stick to party leaders and delegates, alternately pleading and pressuring for their support. The candidates know that state delegations seek to provide the winning margin of victory to a nominee, thereby earning his gratitude and, perhaps, future rewards. The psychological pressure on delegates is always the same: hop aboard this or that bandwagon before it is too late to matter.[54]

The convention, on its first day, normally hears the report of its credentials committee, the body that decides what delegates shall be seated. Often, rival delegations claim to represent the party in a state, or one faction may charge irregularities in the selection of delegates. The credentials committee must decide these disputes, subject always to the approval of the convention. In the evening the keynote speaker fills the air with the customary rhetoric. Sometimes, the keynote speech is unusually effective, as was that of Governor Mario Cuomo of New York at the 1984 Democratic convention or the keynote address by Governor Ann Richards of Texas at the Democratic Convention of 1988. A good keynote speech stirs the delegates and sets the tone for the rest of the convention; it may also catapult the speaker into national prominence, possibly as a contender for the party's nomination in the future.

On the second day the party platform is debated and voted on. The outcome of these struggles over credentials and the platform often signals which party faction has the votes to win the nomination for its candidate.

On the third day the nominations and balloting for the presidential nominee usually begin. Traditionally, a candidate's name is not mentioned until the very end of the nominating speech. ("I give you the name of the next president of the United States, ____ ____ ____!") The name is a signal for a carefully planned "spontaneous" demonstration on the floor, often employing professional demonstrators and organized to

the split second by experts armed with noisemakers, walkie-talkies, and stopwatches.

Despite time limits on oratory, the nominating and seconding speeches sometimes go on to the near limits of delegate endurance. Then the roll of states is called in alphabetical order for the balloting. In both parties, the candidate who wins a simple majority of the convention votes is nominated. Front-runners attempt to win on the first ballot, and 1952 is the last year in which a major-party presidential nomination was not settled on the first ballot. In some years since 1952, however, particularly 1968 and 1976, lesser candidates and dark horses have hoped that nobody would win on the first ballot; they would then have had a chance of picking up increased delegate strength on the second, third, or subsequent ballots.

It is the traditional privilege of the presidential nominee to select the vice-presidential nominee.[55] The fourth day of the convention is normally devoted to the routine nomination of and balloting for vice-president, the acceptance speeches of both candidates, and their climactic appearance with their families before the cheering delegates and television cameras. This moment of high personal and political drama underscores the fact that a national convention also serves the function of a party pep rally, generating enthusiasm for the ticket and, in effect, kicking off the presidential campaign.

Beneath the hoopla and the ballyhoo of a national party convention, serious business has taken place. Rival political leaders have clashed and fought, differences on issues within the party have been publicly aired, and a major political party has produced its nominees for the highest offices in the land.

The Delegates

Who are the few thousand men and women formally entitled to select the presidential nominees of the two major parties? In general, they represent a cross section of the party, but a generally affluent cross section, since the cost of travel to a convention city, of hotels and meals, mounts up to hundreds of dollars. The delegates

---

[54] Political candidates have a way of remembering who was for them when. Early backers enjoy a special status.

[55] In 1956 Adlai Stevenson, the nominee of the Democratic National Convention, threw open the choice of a vice-presidential candidate to the delegates. In the floor balloting, Senator Estes Kefauver of Tennessee narrowly defeated Senator John F. Kennedy of Massachusetts to become Stevenson's running mate.

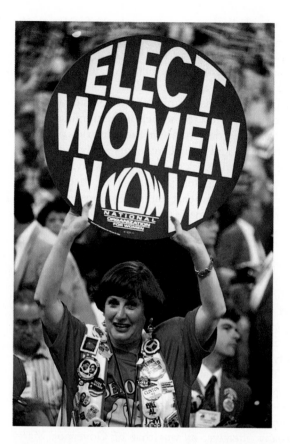

usually include governors, senators, members of Congress, mayors, state legislators, state party officials, and activists and contributors at the grass-roots level. Because of reforms instituted by the Democratic party, the 1972 national convention for the first time included substantial numbers of women, blacks, youths, and Spanish-speaking delegates.

Delegates to national party conventions are chosen by a variety of methods. In 1992 forty states and the District of Columbia held Democratic presidential primaries, and thirty-nine states plus the District of Columbia held Republican presidential primaries in which voters in one or both parties expressed their preference for a presidential nominee and chose all or some convention delegates. In the remaining states, delegates were chosen by other methods — caucuses, district conventions, state conventions, and, in a few cases, by state committees. In some instances, the results of the primaries were binding on the delegates; in others, the delegates went to the conventions unpledged to any particular candidate.

In 1976 the Democrats abandoned "winner-take-all" primaries, in which the presidential candidate who

won a primary, no matter how slim the margin of victory, could win all of a state's convention delegates. Instead the Democrats adopted a system of proportional representation, but with loopholes permitting a "winner-take-all" system at the district level in some states. In 1972 and previous years more delegates were chosen in the majority of states that did *not* hold presidential primaries. By 1980, however, more than two-thirds of the regular delegates to the Democratic National Convention were elected in primaries, with the rest selected by the other methods. In 1992, of the 4,319 delegates to the Democratic convention, 2,505, or 53 percent, were elected in primaries.

The procedures for selecting delegates have not always been democratic. For example, for many years, in some states, African Americans, women, and young people were systematically excluded from Democratic party delegations to national conventions. After the divisive 1968 national convention, reform elements within the Democratic party sought means to democratize the delegate-selection process.

A Democratic reform commission reported in 1970 that in at least twenty states there had been no

Table 7-4
Delegates, by Selected Groups, to the Democratic National
Convention, 1968–92

	Women	African Americans	Youth*
1968	13%	5.5%	4%
1972	38	15	21
1976	34	9	14.8
1980	49.9	14.9	NA
1984	50	18	8
1988	49	21	5
1992	49.7	17	4

*Eighteen to thirty years of age.
SOURCE: The Party Reformed, Final Report of the Committee on Party
Structure and Delegate Selection (Washington, D.C.: Democratic National
Committee, July 7, 1972), pp. 7–8; New York Times, July 12, 1976, p. C5;
1980 data from Democratic National Committee; 1984 data from New York
Times, July 15, 1984, p. 26; 1988 data from Washington Post, July 12, 1988,
p. A27; 1992 data from Washington Post, July 12, 1992, p. A13, and the
Democratic National Committee.

adequate rules for selection of delegates to the 1968
convention, "leaving the entire process to the discretion of a handful of party leaders." [56] The commission
issued guidelines designed to eliminate such abuses, but
it had no authority to enforce them. Somewhat to the
surprise of everyone, even commission members, the
panel's reform guidelines were followed by most state
Democratic party organizations. As a result, a TV
viewer watching the 1972 national convention at Miami
Beach could hardly fail to notice the substantial numbers of young delegates, women, and African Americans. (See Table 7–4.)

[56] *Mandate for Reform, Report of the Commission on Party Structure
and Delegate Selection to the Democratic National Convention*
(Washington, D.C.: Democratic National Committee, 1970), pp.
10–11.

Both major parties apportion delegates under complicated formulas based on population and party
strength within each state. The Republican National
Convention of 1992 had 2,210 regular delegates, each
casting one vote, and an equal number of alternates.
The Republicans allot a bonus of four delegates to each
state that votes Republican in the preceding presidential, senatorial, gubernatorial, or state legislative race.
The Democrats base the size of state delegations on
population and the size of the Democratic vote in each
state.

Delegates who are chosen by state and local party
organizations are sometimes under the control of party
leaders. But the growth of primaries and caucuses that
choose delegates pledged to vote for a particular candidate has greatly reduced the power of party leaders to
control national conventions.

But by 1980, many Democrats felt that grass-roots
party reform had gone too far. The Democratic National Convention that year created a Commission on
Presidential Nominations to revamp the nominating
process once again. The panel, known as the Hunt
Commission for its chairman, Governor James B. Hunt,

Jr., of North Carolina, recommended new rules designed to give party regulars — officeholders and party officials — much more power to nominate a presidential candidate. The party adopted these proposals; in 1992 in New York City, about one-fifth of the Democratic delegates were party and elected officials. For example, all but 61 of the 325 Democrats in the House and Senate were delegates to the 1992 Democratic Convention.[57]

Until 1968 the Democrats permitted one form or another of the unit rule, which in some cases allowed the majority of a state delegation to cast the state's entire vote. The opponents of this system argued that it made boss rule easier. In 1968 the Democrats voted to drop the unit rule at all party levels for the 1972 convention. Thus, another tool of the "old politics" fell by the wayside.

Do Conventions Decide?

Despite the tumult and the shouting, the results of most recent national conventions have been unsurprising, and the outcomes known in advance. Given that fact, are national conventions real arenas of democratic decision or mere rubber stamps?

In an analysis of sixty-five national nominating conventions from 1832 to 1960, the Brookings Institution, an independent research organization, identified five types of nominations:[58]

1. *Confirmation.* An existing president or party titular leader is confirmed as the party's choice.
2. *Inheritance.* A political understudy or previous leader inherits the party mantle.
3. *Inner group selection.* Dominant party leaders get together and agree on the nominee.
4. *Compromise in stalemate.* A deadlocked convention turns to a dark horse or unexpected candidate.
5. *Factional victory.* One of several competing factions within the party succeeds in nominating its candidate.

Although twenty-two conventions during this period were "confirming," fully nineteen, the second highest number, fell into the category of "factional victory," evidence that genuine competition had characterized national nominating conventions a substantial

share of the time. Only three of the nineteen conventions — those nominating McKinley in 1896, Dewey in 1944, and Kennedy in 1960 — had outcomes that were generally anticipated in advance of the convention.[59]

The struggle for nomination at a convention can, of course, take many different shapes. The phrase "smoke-filled room," often used to describe the selection of a candidate by political bosses operating in secret, grew out of the 1920 GOP convention. There, a group of Republican leaders met in Suite 404 of Chicago's Blackstone Hotel and ended a convention stalemate by selecting Warren G. Harding of Marion, Ohio, who *looked* like a president but was otherwise a mediocre chief executive. The Democrats set a record at their 1924 convention in New York, the longest ever held. The weary delegates finally chose John W. Davis, a New York corporation lawyer and former congressman from West Virginia, on the 103rd ballot; but the voters preferred the Republican candidate, Calvin Coolidge. Franklin D. Roosevelt led the field at the Democratic National Convention in 1932, but he was not nominated until the fourth ballot. In 1940, with the galleries chanting "We want Willkie," the Republicans nominated Wendell L. Willkie, Wall Street lawyer and a true dark horse. The Taft-Eisenhower convention battle in 1952 reflected the greatest split in the Republican party since 1912.

Since 1960, however, national conventions have filled more of a ratifying than a selecting function. For example, George McGovern's delegate strength going into the 1972 Democratic Convention was sufficiently great to make his nomination reasonably certain. In 1976 Gerald Ford had to fight for the Republican nomination against Ronald Reagan, but shortly before the convention it appeared that Ford had enough delegates to win, and he did. Carter's nomination in 1976 was preordained after his primary victories. The 1980 Republican National Convention merely ratified Ronald Reagan as the party's choice. And it was clear that year, even before the convention met, that the Democrats would renominate Jimmy Carter, the incumbent president. Similarly, in 1988 Bush's nomination was assured and Dukakis was the clear choice of the Democrats before they gathered at Atlanta.

In 1992 President Bush was challenged for the Republican nomination by Patrick Buchanan, the con-

---

[57] *Washington Post,* July 12, 1992, p. A12.

[58] Paul T. David, Ralph M. Goldman, and Richard C. Bain, *The Politics of National Party Conventions,* Kathleen Sproul, ed. (New York: Vintage Books, 1964), pp. 127–38. A paperback condensation of the study originally published by the Brookings Institution.

[59] Ibid., p. 286.

servative columnist, but by the end of the March primaries it seemed clear that Bush would be renominated. On the Democratic side, Bill Clinton emerged as the Democratic front-runner after a series of eleven mainly southern primaries between March 7th and March 17th. And after Clinton won the New York state primary in April, his nomination also seemed assured. This "ratifying" trend since 1960 does not mean that conventions have lost all power to decide or that vigorous battles will not take place in the future. But three factors have combined to diminish the decisional role of the convention in recent years.

First, preconvention campaigns by presidential hopefuls have gained in intensity and length.

Second, extensive coverage by television and other media has focused national attention on these preconvention campaigns and increased their importance. Consequently, they have become, to some extent, elimination races. In 1984, for example, Mondale's victories over Senator Gary Hart of Colorado in a series of primaries all but removed Hart from the race.

Third, there are many more presidential primaries than there were two decades ago. The results of these primaries may determine the nominee weeks or months before the national convention meets.

As a result of the intense press coverage now given to presidential primaries and to preconvention campaigning, one or another candidate has tended to gain a clear lead before the convention in the public mind, in the political polls, and often, within the rank and file of the party. William R. Keech, in a study made public in 1972, concluded that the surviving front-runner within each party usually receives the nomination. With one exception, the candidate ranking highest in support among the party rank and file, as measured by the last Gallup poll before the national convention, had emerged as the nominee in major-party nominations since 1936.[60] Nevertheless, as long as the institution of the national convention remains, the potential exists for a sharply contested battle for the nomination if two or more candidates enter the arena with roughly equal support and resources.

National conventions nominate candidates for president who go before the voters every four years. But many Americans do not participate in selecting the convention delegates who make this crucial choice. In 1992, for example, 20.2 million people voted in the Democratic primaries and 13.0 million in the Republican primaries, for a total of 33.2 million people, or about 18 percent of the number of Americans of voting age. Moreover, Austin Ranney has concluded that those who do vote in the presidential primaries are "quite unrepresentative" of the party identifiers who do not participate.[61] Even fewer people choose the delegates who are selected in other ways. Most people, for example, have never attended a district or state party convention where delegates are chosen.

The Future of the Convention System

From time to time various proposals have been made to revamp the national nominating convention or even replace it with some presumably more representative or more dignified procedure. One of the recurrent proposals is for a *national presidential primary*, in which the voters could directly choose the presidential candidates of the major parties. Those who advocate a national primary argue that it would be more democratic because it would reflect the choice of more voters.

The plan has some possible drawbacks, however: there is no assurance that voters in a national primary would be typical of nonvoting party rank-and-file members. Critics have also argued that if too many candidates entered the primary, the candidate who polled the most votes might be one who enjoyed intense but limited support, and who could not, therefore, win a general election. Or, no single candidate might receive a majority of the votes. In such a case, if a runoff were held, the candidate who initially led the field in the primary might lose.[62] Moreover, a national presidential primary might work against lesser-known candidates —John B. Anderson of Illinois, for example, in 1980. Such candidates benefit from a nominating process that is spread out over several months, allowing them to gain greater public recognition. And, it has been suggested, a national primary would further weaken American

[60] William R. Keech, "Presidential Nominating Politics: Problems of Popular Choice," paper prepared for the 1972 annual meeting of the American Political Science Association (Washington, D.C.: American Political Science Association, 1972), pp. 1–3. The exception was Senator Estes Kefauver, who led in the poll in 1952 but lost the Democratic nomination to Adlai Stevenson.

[61] Austin Ranney, "Turnout and Representation in Presidential Primary Elections," *American Political Science Review*, vol. 66 (March 1972), p. 27.

[62] For a discussion of the pros and cons of a national presidential primary, see Judith H. Parris, *The Convention Problem* (Washington, D.C.: The Brookings Institution, 1972), pp. 172–77.

political parties by bypassing party organizations, while increasing the power of the news media to influence the electoral process.[63]

Nelson W. Polsby has suggested that political parties deserve a continuing role in the selection of presidential nominees, for "no better institutions have evolved to conduct nominating politics."[64] Moreover, Polsby argues, political parties, because of their varied roles, are "crucial for the proper general functioning of the political system."[65]

In any event, the convention system, having survived since 1832, is not likely to disappear in the television age, at a time when it has grown into a sort of political Super Bowl. Nor is it at all clear that the national convention should be replaced. The Brookings Institution study concluded, "The continuing contributions made by the conventions to the survival and stability of the American political order are unique, indispensable, and, granted our form of Constitution, probably irreplaceable. . . . The services of the convention as a general conclave for the selection and recognition of top leadership in each party, and for its

[63] Austin Ranney, *The Federalization of Presidential Primaries* (Washington, D.C.: American Enterprise Institute for Public Policy Research, 1978), pp. 33–38.

[64] Polsby, *Consequences of Party Reform*, p. 182.

[65] Ibid.

replacement when necessary, could be abandoned only at serious national peril." [66]

POLITICAL PARTIES AND DEMOCRATIC GOVERNMENT

At best, Americans have always had a somewhat ambivalent attitude toward politics and politicians. "Politics," Clinton Rossiter has noted, "is sin, and politicians, if not sinners, are pretty suspicious fellows." [67]

In 1952 General Eisenhower enjoyed the support of many voters who felt he was "above politics" or "not a politician." The same was true of Ronald Reagan when he ran for governor of California for the first time in 1966, in a campaign that emphasized his nonprofessional political status. And certainly Ross Perot benefited from his outsider status in 1992.

Among many voters, the image of the politician as an unprincipled opportunist persists. The initial reaction of many Americans to the Watergate scandal was not shock at the illegal acts committed by the Nixon administration but the view that "they all do it."

Since political parties are vital to the functioning of American democracy, it is somewhat paradoxical that politics and politicians — especially with their access to the image-making resources of Madison Avenue — do not enjoy greater prestige.

The truth about politics and its practitioners may lie somewhere between Aristotle's view that "the good of man" is the object of politics and the classic statement of Simon Cameron, the Republican boss of Pennsylvania, that "an honest politician is one who, when he is bought, will stay bought."

Possibly Americans would have a more generous view of the craft of politics if it were more widely understood that parties and democracy are mutually dependent. Competition among political parties is the essence of democracy. Political parties in America, as we have seen, provide a vehicle of political choice, manage the transfer of power, help to hold politicians accountable to the voters, recruit candidates, staff and link branches of the government, and may sometimes resolve social conflict.

The rest of the world also has a vital stake in the politics of American democracy; certainly the party nominee chosen by the electorate to be president has greater power than any other leader in history. How an American president uses that power, including the nuclear weapons under his control, is of direct concern to all other nations, as well as to the voters at home.

The "brokerage" role of political parties in mediating among interest groups (whether such groups are organized or not), and in resolving social conflict, is of tremendous importance in a democracy under pressure. Both major political parties try to form a broad base by appealing to diverse groups in society. As a result, when one party loses power and another wins the presidency, the change tends to be accepted, or at least tolerated, by the voters. At the same time, the party out of power plays a valuable role as the opposition party, offering alternative programs in Congress and serving as a rallying point for its followers. The "out" party keeps alive the possibility of change for another four years. In these ways parties help to keep conflict manageable, for if substantial numbers of voters violently opposed the election results, the political system could not work.

A Choice, Not an Echo?

In his classic complaint about the similarity of American political parties, James Bryce concluded that "neither party has any principles, any distinctive tenets." The similarities of American parties are often lamented, but, as noted earlier, there are significant differences as well.

Some of these differences can be measured by comparing contrasting party platforms in presidential elections. Although the conventional view is that platforms are "meaningless," Gerald M. Pomper has concluded that platforms in fact "are reasonably meaningful indications of the party's intentions" and serve to identify the parties with "certain policies" [68]

Moreover — as surprising as it might be to many people — in a majority of cases, Pomper concluded, political parties actually carry out the promises contained in their platforms. Analyzing 1,795 platform pledges over a ten-year period (1968–78), Pomper determined that "almost two-thirds" of these promises were fulfilled.[69]

---

[66] David, Goldman, and Bain, *The Politics of National Party Conventions,* p. 339.

[67] Rossiter, *Parties and Politics in America,* p. 34.

[68] Gerald M. Pomper with Susan S. Lederman, *Elections in America: Control and Influence in Democratic Politics,* 2nd ed. (New York: Longman, Inc., 1980), p. 152.

[69] Ibid., pp. 161 and 164. See also Paul T. David, "Party Platforms as National Plans," in *Public Administration Review,* vol. 31, no. 3 (May/June 1971), pp. 303–15.

While it is true that American parties are not sharply ideological, it is also true that many American voters have not been sharply ideological. The argument is often made that major parties should offer a more pronounced choice on issues, not merely a choice between candidates; but it is by no means clear that extreme polarization of the parties on issues that divide American society is desirable. "The difference between Democrats and Republicans," Max Lerner has observed, "while it is more than the difference between Tweedledum and Tweedledee, is not such as to split the society itself or invite civil conflict. . . . The choices between the two are usually substantial choices but not desperate ones." [70]

Are Parties Accountable to the Voters?

When Americans go to the polls, they do not elect parties; they elect officials who usually run as the candidates of political parties. By its very nature, the American political system holds these officials accountable to the voters while holding the parties only indirectly accountable.

The most frequent criticism of the American party system is that the parties are not "responsible" to the electorate, that there is no way to make them keep the promises outlined in their platforms, and that, in any event, they lack the internal discipline to whip their programs through Congress.[71] One difficulty is that party platforms "are written for use in *presidential* campaigns, yet they consist mainly of proposals for legislation that will be meaningless unless there is congressional action." [72] Yet, as Gerald Pomper has noted, political parties often do carry out platform pledges.

In a parliamentary system of government, such as that in Great Britain, political parties are more closely linked to the popular will because the voters choose a majority party that is responsible for the conduct of both the executive and legislative branches of government. Since few critics of the American party system advocate parliamentary government for the United States, party accountability in America is likely to remain a matter of degree.

Many political scientists do not agree on the need for or desirability of greater party responsibility. For example, party cohesion strong enough to pass programs in Congress could only be achieved by reducing the importance and independence of individual legislators. But advocates of strong, responsible parties point to several ways that party responsibility can be strengthened, short of adopting the British system of parliamentary government: attempting to achieve greater discipline within parties by rewarding cooperative members with campaign funds, and electing the chairpersons of congressional committees on the basis of party loyalty rather than seniority.

To an extent, however, a measure of party responsibility already exists. When American parties embark on courses of action that displease large numbers of voters, the voters may retaliate. In 1964 Barry Goldwater, the Republican candidate, was the "hawk" who advocated "total victory" over communism. President Johnson, on the other hand, presented himself as a "dove," promising: "We are not about to send American boys nine or ten thousand miles away from home to do what Asian boys ought to be doing for themselves." [73] In less than a year, however, Johnson was sending combat troops to Vietnam. Many of his supporters felt misled; it turned out that they had voted for a "dove" and elected a "hawk." But in the election of 1968, Johnson found it prudent not to run again, and the nation sent a Republican to the White House. George Bush's rejection in 1992 by an electorate angry and frustrated over the state of the nation under his presidency is further evidence that a measure of accountability is not wholly lacking in American politics.

A LOOK AHEAD

Attempting to predict the future of American political parties is a perilous business. Like life itself, politics is often unpredictable; those who forecasted the eclipse of the Republican party in 1964 were required to watch the elephant ride into the White House in 1968 and again in 1972. Although similar predictions of Republican doom were heard after Nixon's resignation over the

---

[70] Max Lerner, *America as a Civilization*, vol. 1 (New York: Simon and Schuster, 1967), pp. 389–90.

[71] See, for example, Report of the Committee on Political Parties of the American Political Science Association, *Toward a More Responsible Two-Party System* (New York: Holt, Rinehart and Winston, 1950).

[72] David, Goldman, and Bain, *The Politics of National Party Conventions*, p. 344.

---

[73] Public Papers of the President, *Lyndon B. Johnson, 1963–64*, book 2 (Washington, D.C.: U.S. Government Printing Office, 1965), p. 1391.

'LOCKED OUT' OF THE POLITICAL SYSTEM

Challenging conventional assumptions, a new report asserts that Americans are angry, but not apathetic, about a political process they see controlled exclusively by politicians, special interests and the media and have turned their energies to community organizations to solve problems.

The diagnosis of public apathy toward politics and government "widely misses the mark," said David Mathews, Health, Education and Welfare Secretary in the Ford administration and now head of the Kettering Foundation, which sponsored the study. "What it misses is deep-seated anger about the process itself."

Matthews said citizens "feel locked out" of the political process. "And they know who locked them out."

Americans believe they are victims of a "hostile takeover" of the political process by a professional political class that speaks a unique language and deals in the art of avoidance when it comes to issues, the report states. As a result, citizens increasingly doubt that government can solve the problems they see facing the country.

Richard Harwood, who conducted the research for the report, said citizens "believe there's no room left for their voice."

—*Washington Post*, June 5, 1991

Watergate scandal in 1974, the GOP with Ronald Reagan as its candidate won the presidential elections of 1980 and 1984, and, with Bush, won in 1988. And the Democrats, whose prospects seemed bleak at the outset of the 1992 campaign, triumphed in November.

One fact seems clear. Over a period of time, political parties must respond to the pressures for, or against, change, or pay the price of defeat. And it seems likely that in times of substantial social stress in America, minor parties of the right and left will continue to arise. Possibly, more "non-party" candidates will seek the presidency as did Ross Perot in 1992 and John B. Anderson in 1980. Yet, in one form or another, the two-party system has flourished since the beginning of the republic and will probably survive.

The increased importance of television and of pre-convention campaigns probably makes the last-minute selection of an unknown candidate by a national convention less likely than in the past. Candidates will probably continue to rely more on television, which can reach millions of people, than on old-fashioned stump campaigning. Political commercials and professional campaign managers skilled in media techniques now play a major role in campaigns. So do political polls.

Political parties mirror the society in which they function. If government can be made more responsive to the public, political parties may play a vital part in that process, for they are uniquely situated to translate the hopes of the American people into action by the American government.

PERSPECTIVE

A major political party is a broadly based coalition that attempts to gain control of the government by winning elections. Political parties perform vital functions in the American political system. They manage the transfer of power, offer a choice of rival candidates and programs to the voters, and serve as a link between government and people by helping to hold elected officials accountable to the voters. In addition, they may reconcile conflicting interests in society, they staff the government and help to run it, and they link various branches and levels of government. Relationships among the national, state, and local governments depend to a considerable degree on ties among party officials and leaders.

The elements that make up a major political party include the voters; the party activists, people who serve as delegates to political conventions and perform the day-to-day, grass-roots work of politics; the party leaders outside of government, who frequently control the party machinery; and finally, the party leaders in the government, including the president, the leaders in Congress, and the party leaders in state and local governments.

Today, political parties are less powerful than in the past, as party loyalties among the voters have declined and competing groups have come to share many of the traditional roles of parties. In 1992 there were more persons in America who called themselves Democrats than there were people who identified with any other group — either Republicans or independents. But the number of people who identified themselves as Republicans had increased during the 1980s. In addition, almost one-third of the voters identify with no political party and called themselves independents. Whether a person identifies with the Democratic or Republican party may be related to socioeconomic factors.

Throughout most of the nation's history, two major political parties have been arrayed against each other. The Democrats, in one guise or another, have endured. During successive eras they have been challenged by the Federalists, the Whigs, and the Republicans. Minor or third parties, or independent candidates like Ross Perot, have joined the struggle, with greater or lesser effect; but the main battle, historically, has been a two-party affair.

Democrats usually, although not always, enjoy greater voter support than Republicans from labor, Catholics, Jews, African Americans, other minorities, young people, and from persons who have not attended college, who have low incomes, and who live in the cities. Republicans often receive greater support among voters who are Protestant, white, suburban, rural, wealthy, older, college educated, and professionals or business executives.

Several explanations have been offered for the existence of the two-party system. The debate over ratification of the Constitution split the country into two groups. Dualism, therefore, is as old as the nation itself. In the United States, a single-member district system prevails in federal elections. Under such a system, minor parties lacking a strong geographical base have little chance of poaching on the two-party preserve. And ideological differences among Americans in the past have normally not been strong enough to produce established minor parties representing widely varying shades of political opinion.

Yet minor parties have been active throughout most of the nation's history, from the Anti-Masons of the 1830s to the American Independent party in 1968. In certain states minor parties have gained a powerful position. Nationally, however, minor parties have never consistently enjoyed much power or influence. In 1992, Ross Perot, a billionaire, accepted no federal funds and invested an estimated $60 million of his own money in his independent campaign for the presidency. On election night, however, Perot did not carry a single state.

A party's quadrennial national convention is theoretically the source of all authority within the party. The convention nominates the party's candidates for president and vice-president. In recent years, however, conventions have tended to select the candidate who has won the most delegates in the primaries and caucuses and is already the front-runner. The party convention also writes a platform, settles disputes, writes rules, and elects the members of the national committee. Although both the 1992 Democratic National Convention in New York City, and the Republican National Convention in Houston, provided moments of television drama, one symbol of the declining role of national conventions is the fact that the major TV networks no longer provide gavel-to-gavel coverage, as in the past.

The national chairperson is formally elected by the members of the national committee, although in practice he or she is chosen or retained by the party's presidential nominee at the end of the national convention. Between elections, the chief functions of the staff of the national committee are public relations, patronage, research, and fund-raising.

Independent of the national committees are the congressional leaders of each party, elected by their colleagues, and the congressional and senatorial campaign committees. The congressional committees channel money, speakers, advice, and assistance to party members who are up for election.

Political parties are vital to the functioning of American democracy. There are significant differences among parties that are evident from their campaign platforms. Furthermore, platform promises are often carried out. There is, in addition, evidence that parties are, in some measure, responsible to the voters. When parties embark on courses of action that displease large numbers of voters, the voters may retaliate. Over a period of time, political parties must respond to the pressures for, or against, change, or pay the price of defeat.

Suggested Reading

American Political Science Association, Committee on Political Parties. *Toward a More Responsible Two-Party System: A Report* (Johnson Reprint Corporation, 1970). (Originally published in 1950.) Statement of the case for stronger, more disciplined, and more centralized political parties in the United States. This report, by sixteen authorities on political parties, initiated a lively debate among political scientists over the nature of American political parties.

Bartels, Larry M. *Presidential Primaries and the Dynamics of Public Choice* (Princeton: Princeton University Press,

1988). An illuminating analysis of how the present system for nominating presidential candidates works.

Beck, Paul Allen, and Sorauf, Frank J. *Party Politics in America*, 7th edition* (HarperCollins, 1992). A comprehensive analysis of political parties in the United States. Examines political party organization, the behavior of party supporters in the mass electorate, the role of parties in contesting elections, and the impact of parties on government.

Binkley, Wilfred E. *American Political Parties*, 4th edition (Knopf, 1963). A comprehensive treatment of the historical development of the American party system. Emphasizes the building of coalitions by American political parties.

Crotty, William J. *Decision for the Democrats: Reforming the Party Structure* (Johns Hopkins University Press, 1978). A detailed study of the reform movement within the Democratic party in the years following the 1968 Democratic Convention. Traces the major changes that were made in party structure and procedures, and summarizes their consequences.

Crotty, William J., and Jacobson, Gary C. *American Parties in Decline*, 2nd edition* (Little, Brown, 1984). A revealing analysis of the declining influence and significance of political parties in the United States. Discusses the weakened role of party in the electorate, in election campaigns, and in Congress.

David, Paul T.; Goldman, Ralph M.; and Bain, Richard C. *The Politics of National Party Conventions*, revised edition* (University Press of America, 1984). A detailed examination of the historical development of national party conventions. Stresses the functions that the national conventions perform in the American party system.

Duverger, Maurice. *Political Parties: Their Organization and Activity in the Modern State*, 3rd edition (Methuen, 1964). An influential comparative analysis of political parties in a number of countries. Among other topics, Duverger, a French political scientist, examines the nature of party organization in different types of parties and explores the relationship between the electoral system in a country and the type of party system that flourishes there.

Epstein, Leon D. *Political Parties in the American Mold** (University of Wisconsin Press, 1986). A thoughtful analysis of the historical development and current operation of political parties in America.

Epstein, Leon D. *Political Parties in Western Democracies* (Transaction Books, 1980). A useful comparative study of political parties in various countries, with special stress on those in Great Britain and the United States. Examines the historical development of parties, recruitment of party leaders, and the contribution of the parties to governing.

Herrnson, Paul S. *Party Campaigning in the 1980s* (Harvard University Press, 1988). An interesting analysis of the activities of the national parties in congressional election campaigns during the 1980s. Argues that the parties have been innovative in their use of new campaign techniques, and that they play a significant role in election contests for Congress.

Keech, William R., and Matthews, Donald R. *The Party's Choice* (The Brookings Institution, 1977). An analysis of the process by which presidential candidates were nominated between 1936 and 1976.

Key, V. O., Jr. *Politics, Parties, and Pressure Groups*, 5th edition (Crowell, 1964). A comprehensive analysis of political parties and interest groups. The extensive footnotes serve as a useful guide to much of the scholarly work on political parties and interest groups up to 1963. Examines the nature of the American party system, party structure and procedures, the relations between parties and the voters, and the impact of parties on government.

Ladd, Everett Carll, Jr., with Hadley, Charles D. *Transformations of the American Party System: Political Coalitions from the New Deal to the 1970s*, 2nd edition* (Norton, 1978). An interesting analysis of the changes in the American party system that have taken place since the New Deal. Emphasizes the changing makeup of the Democratic and the Republican electoral coalitions.

Liebman, Robert C., and Wuthnow, Robert, eds. *The New Christian Right: Mobilization and Legitimation** (Aldine Publishing Company, 1983). A collection of essays analyzing the activities of and impact of evangelical Christians in American politics. Includes a discussion of the Moral Majority and the emergence of religious leaders as political candidates.

Mayhew, David R. *Placing Parties in American Politics** (Princeton University Press, 1986). A thoughtful and detailed analysis of the American party structure on the state level. Mayhew points out that while some states have strong, unified traditional party organizations, in many other states parties are much weaker.

Mazmanian, Daniel A. *Third Parties in Presidential Elections* (The Brookings Institution, 1974). A comprehensive examination of American third parties: the conditions that cause them to arise, the factors that impede their success, and their role in the American party system.

Polsby, Nelson W. *Consequences of Party Reform** (Oxford University Press, 1983). A study of reforms in the presidential nominating system and of changes in the way that campaigns and parties are financed. Analyzes the results of these reforms and evaluates proposals for further change.

Ranney, Austin. *Curing the Mischiefs of Faction: Party Reform in America** (University of California Press, 1975). A thoughtful analysis of the theory and practice of party reform in the United States. Emphasizes three main periods when major changes were made in American party institutions: 1820–1840; 1890–1920; and 1956–1974.

Wattenberg, Martin P. *The Decline of American Political Parties, 1952–1984*, revised edition* (Harvard University Press,

1990). A clear, concise study of the diminishing importance of political parties and the growing impact of candidate images in American elections. Argues that American voters have become indifferent to parties because of an increasing belief that parties no longer play a significant role in the governing process.

*Available in paperback edition.

AMERICANS WATCHING television one night in 1992 saw an interesting ten-second commercial. It was not an advertisement for a detergent, a toothpaste, or a breakfast cereal. Rather, it sought to sell the voters the Democratic candidate for president of the United States.

The commercial for Bill Clinton opened with a close-up of President Bush's mouth. "Read my lips," Bush intoned. It was a none-too-subtle reminder by the

Chapter 8

POLITICAL CAMPAIGNS AND CANDIDATES

Clinton camp of Bush's "no new taxes" promise of four years earlier, a pledge he later broke. In a time of high unemployment and a weak economy, the commercial also showed Bush promising the voters in 1988 that they would be "better off four years from now." The announcer's voice cut in: "Well, it's four years later. How're you doin'?"

Television commercials are an important aspect of modern political campaigns; candidates at the presidential level and below routinely advertise their qualifications on TV. For a moment, through the medium of television, the consciousness of millions of viewers had been touched by Clinton's message.

In the 1992 presidential campaign, all three candidates — Bill Clinton, President George Bush, and Texas businessman Ross Perot — also appeared, to a much greater extent than in any past campaign, on the major television talk and entertainment shows. Wearing dark glasses, and looking like one of the stars of the "Blues Brothers," Clinton played the saxophone one night on the "Arsenio Hall Show." President Bush went on "Larry King Live" on CNN to attack Clinton's patriotism and his participation in demonstrations against the Vietnam War while a student in England. Ross Perot appeared so often on "Today" that he became almost as familiar to viewers as Bryant Gumbel, Katherine Couric, and Willard Scott. Perot, in fact, based almost his entire campaign on television appearances and commercials.

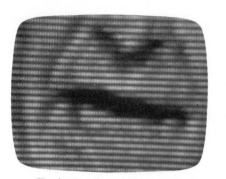

(Bush) Read my lips . . .

(Announcer) Remember?

(Bush) You will be better off four years from now than you are today . . .

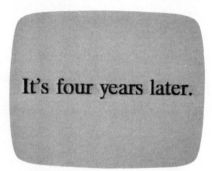

(Announcer) Well, it's four years later.

How're you doin'?

It is not surprising in the television age that candidates for political office try to sell themselves and their ideas on TV. Once nominated, candidates must appeal to the voters. And television offers the surest means of reaching the largest number of people.

As a result, television has dramatically changed American political campaigns since 1948. The day is long past when a William McKinley could campaign from his front porch in Canton, Ohio. Today's candidates hire an advertising agency or a special team of consultants to prepare TV "spots" — commercials that may air for ten seconds or longer. The candidates may debate their opponents on television, as the two major presidential rivals did in 1960, 1976, 1980, 1984, 1988, and 1992, or appear in carefully staged, televised question-and-answer sessions designed to display their warm personalities and firm grasp of the issues. Or they may buy an expensive half-hour of prime TV time for a sincere talk to the American people. As they whirl around the country, their campaign appearances in each state are carefully tailored for the statewide and local evening television news broadcasts, and, if possible, the nightly network news programs that reach a national audience. Television, in short, is an integral part of a modern political campaign.

For every candidate, between nomination and election there stands the campaign. In American politics, the campaign is the battleground of power. Victory may depend on how well the battle is fought, for a third or more of the voters decide how to vote during the campaign. Mostly because of the wide use of television, campaigns are expensive: in 1988 candidates at all levels spent $2.7 billion, a figure that rose to an estimated 3 billion in 1992.[1]

But political candidates do not always have equal financial and creative resources. In the era of electronic mass media, disturbing questions have arisen. Will the candidate with the best "image" — the most attractive appearance, the cleverest television advisers, the

---

[1] Herbert E. Alexander and Monica Bauer, *Financing the 1988 Election*, (Boulder, CO: Westview Press, 1991), p. 4. Estimate for 1992 provided by Herbert E. Alexander, director, the Citizens' Research Foundation.

In the 1992 presidential campaign, candidates appeared on talk shows and entertainment programs much more than in the past. Here Bill Clinton performs to the amusement of Arsenio Hall.

smoothest packaging—win the election? Do Americans vote for the carefully sanitized "image" of the candidate, rather than the person? Does the candidate with the most money always win? Should one candidate enjoy a financial advantage over another in a democracy? If not, what can be done about it? Do political polls influence the voters and affect the outcome of elections? Above all, amid the hoopla, the oratory, and the television commercials, can the voters make a reasonable choice for themselves and for the nation?

These questions have no easy answers. And yet, however imperfect campaigns may be, however raucous and divisive, they are a vital part of the American political system. Campaigns, in the words of the historian Henry Adams, are "the dance of democracy."

HOW CAMPAIGNS ARE ORGANIZED

Campaigns are organized chaos. On a national level, large numbers of people, professionals and volunteers, are thrown together for a relatively short period of time to mount an incredibly complex effort to elect a president. The candidate is rather like someone in the eye of a hurricane: jetting around the country—stumping, speechmaking, and handshaking—besieged by the crowds and camera crews, the press and the voters, local politicians and aides. The candidate may arise at 5 A.M.

and not get to sleep until 2 A.M. the next morning, with a dozen cities and thousands of miles traversed in-between. Physically exhausted, hands cut and bruised from the crowds, the candidate is expected to keep smiling throughout this ordeal and to remain alert—ready to respond instantly to any new issue or crisis. In some remote cornfield of Iowa, a television reporter may ask for comment on a sudden and complicated development in the Middle East. The candidate worries that an

inappropriate word or phrase might cost the election. An assassin may lurk in the hotel kitchen. In the jet age, the pressures on the candidate are constant and cruel.

The candidate, flying from one appearance to the next at five hundred miles an hour, obviously must have an elaborate campaign organization with a headquarters staff to plan and coordinate the total effort. Ultimate success may depend on many variables — the candidate's charisma, smile and appearance, TV makeup, advertising agency, and experience; the issues, the number of registered Democrats and Republicans, a sudden foreign-policy crisis, an ill-advised remark, the weather on Election Day — but not the least of these factors is the quality of the candidate's campaign organization.

The Republican party's 1992 manual for campaign workers tells a good deal about the work of politics. The titles and subheadings of the volume suggest the wide range of problems faced in organizing a campaign: "Absentee Ballots," "Communications Basics," "Direct Mail," "Door-to-Door Activities," "Election Law," "Fundraising," "Get-Out-the-Vote," "Graphics," "Media Kits," "Newspaper," "Phone Banks," "Postal Regulations," "Printing and Production," "Radio," "Speeches," and "Television." [2]

---

[2] Republican National Committee, *Campaign Encyclopedia* (Washington, D.C.: Republican National Committee, 1992).

HOW TO WIN AN ELECTION: REPUBLICAN VERSION

Voter Canvass. A volunteer often says something like this: "Hello, I'm _____ (Name), a neighbor of yours, and I'm here to tell you about _____, who's a candidate for _____ (Office). He is running for office because he believes _____ (Vision). Can _____ count on your vote on Election Day, _____ (Date) _____?"

The best time of day to canvass is when people are home. . . . Don't be afraid to walk during the dinner hour since it may be the only time to find people at home. Keep the visit short and cordial — apologize if you interrupt dinner. Never enter a person's home — you're not a salesman. When the person comes to the door, take a step back so you're less threatening to the voter. Notice children, if they're present, it makes a great impression and wins votes from parents. . . . Skip places that have dogs (Avoid potential bites!). Stick to sidewalks and driveways rather than cutting across lawns.

Television. If your event is outside, note the location of the sun before selecting the podium site. The sun should never be behind the speaker nor directly in the speaker's eyes. . . . Make-up is appropriate. Most women already wear make-up to avoid reflections; men should use a little light powder or pancake make-up, close to their natural skin tone, to minimize shine and hide any five o'clock shadow. . . . Avoid flashy, distracting clothing. Men should avoid plaids and narrowly striped shirts; women should avoid layers of jewelry and necklines with no place to anchor a clip microphone.

Dealing with Reporters. Contrary to many people's opinion, reporters are just like everybody else. . . . *Don't treat reporters like the enemy.* . . . Most reporters try to be fair. Our evaluation of what's fair or unfair is made through tinted glass: as Republican partisans we're not the most objective people ourselves. . . . *don't feed the media material you know they won't use.* If you "cry wolf" too many times, the media will start to ignore you altogether. . . . *Be honest and accurate.* . . . Lying will get you in trouble. . . . If all else fails, respond with a simple "no comment.". . . . Remember: NEVER TELL A REPORTER SOMETHING YOU DON'T WANT REPORTED. If the story is juicy enough, "off-the-record" has no meaning.

Speeches. Greet the audience visually. Wave like Ronald Reagan. Walk like an Olympic athlete. . . . *Save and polish your applause lines.* Applause lines are like diamonds. Formed under pressure, cut and polished until they shine.

Newspaper. A coordinated letter-to-the-editor program, run by a volunteer, can be another effective way to communicate your message.

Communications Basics. Don't feel compelled to respond to a reporter's exact ques-

A presidential candidate must have a campaign manager and a small group of top-level aides to give overall direction to the campaign. The candidate must have someone in charge of fund raising, for a national campaign costs millions of dollars; a media team to handle advertising and television; a press secretary; representatives to handle advance details of personal appearances; speech-writers; regional and state coordinators; and citizens' groups to enlist volunteer support. And the campaign staff must attempt to coordinate the work of national, state, and local party organizations so that there is a unified effort at all levels.

In 1992, Bill Clinton's campaign was run by a group of political operatives, many of them relatively young and unknown, who had been recruited by the Arkansas governor. His campaign chairman was Mickey Kantor, 52, a Los Angeles lawyer long active in Democratic politics. David Wilhelm, a Chicago political consultant, served as campaign manager. The communications director, George Stephanopoulos, 31, and like Clinton, a former Rhodes scholar, was in charge of the candidate's traveling staff and often appeared on television as a Clinton spokesperson. James Carville, an unconventional, behind-the-scenes campaign operative in ragged blue jeans, who grew up in a small town in Louisiana's Cajun country, was perhaps Clinton's most important political adviser. Paul Begala drafted many of the candidate's speeches.

continued . . .

tion. . . . The basic rule is: A reporter can ask any question he wants; you can answer any question you want. . . . *Don't exaggerate resume items.* Every single item contained in a campaign biography must be the truth, the whole truth, and nothing but the truth. Failure to follow this rule will mean likely defeat.

Phone banks. Cold-call prospecting—Cold-call prospecting is a telemarketing program which has been proven to produce a good list of prospective donors and at the same time make enough money to cover phone bank expenses. . . . The script you use will depend on whether you're calling as follow-up to a direct mail piece, making a cold-call prospect call, calling to enhance an event, or as a boiler-room operation.

Graphics. What guidelines should I follow when designing a logo? *Use credible colors.* Traditional campaign colors, such as dark blue, red, green and burgundy invoke trust. . . . Avoid using pink—it's too feminine.

Fundraising. It is important that the decoration chairman be well acquainted with novelty/florist/gift shops in the area, so that "freebies" can be arranged. . . . Flowers, as we all know, are not cheap. . . .

Get-Out-the-Vote. What activities can be implemented on Election Day? 1. *Victory Squads.* Victory squads are teams of volunteers who actually knock on the doors of favorable voters and urge them to vote. . . . each team has a car and driver that can take the voter to the polls while a volunteer babysits or watches the house.

2. *Sign waving.* In some states, it has become standard for volunteers (and sometimes candidates) to wave signs at key intersections to rouse interest in the election. Since there's no way to differentiate Republican cars from Democrat cars, it's best to do this activity in or around Republican areas. Be careful you don't cause accidents. Attractive young people may get the attention of drivers but can also be traffic hazards. . . .

To ensure an honest vote, you'll want to be sure only qualified voters cast their ballots on Election Day. . . . While most problems are with machine malfunctions, the practice of "voting dead people and vacant lots" is still all too prevalent. Therefore, it's important that Republican volunteers be visible in each precinct to help avoid voter fraud.

What Should I [the Candidate] Do on Election Day? Take time to have dinner with your family and friends. Election night has a habit of being the longest night of the year; rest and collect your thoughts. Prepare your remarks for a victory speech.

—Republican National Committee, *Campaign Encyclopedia, 1992*

HOW TO WIN AN ELECTION: DEMOCRATIC VERSION

Scheduling. It is up to the candidate's aide to make sure the campaign train runs on time. . . . When the candidate wants to make just one more call, the aide must disconnect the phone. And when the candidate cannot bear to face the last event of the day, it is up to the aide to sympathize while driving the candidate to it.

Campaign Headquarters and Volunteers. Make sure your headquarters is "user friendly." . . . Volunteers won't come back to places if they are afraid. In marginal areas, provide escorts to bus stops and parking areas. . . .

Adequate lighting and temperature control. Volunteers will not want to work in a dark or cold office. Comfortable chairs. Don't expect volunteers to submit to a torture test.

Candidate activity. Have the candidate canvass each undecided household. . . . Targeted issue literature should be left for people who aren't home. After visiting each house, the candidate should note on the 3x5 card. . . . something specific about the house, such as "German shepherd almost bit off my leg." . . . Each night the candidate should write a short note to each household visited that day. Open with "So glad to have met you," or "So sorry you were out." Then, mention something specific about each home, such as "Your German shepherd is a wonderful watchdog."

The Press. Always tell the truth, and don't play games with the press. Your credibility is more important than one negative story. A lie can lead to a career-long war with the press. . . . Do not try to fight or "punish" a reporter by not speaking to him or her. Remember the old adage: "Don't get into a fight with anyone who buys ink by the barrel and paper by the ton."

Fund Raising. Each person or group will have certain threshold questions that must be answered before a decision is made to give to the party. . . . Stated simply, you are looking for each prospect's "hot button," the lever that will create a link with the party and eventually turn that prospect into a contributor. . . . Focus on motivations. Few people will donate to your campaign just because you asked. To loosen your prospect's purse strings, appeal to basic human motivations like pride, idealism, altruism, obligation, compassion and, from the dark side, fear and ego gratification. . . . Let each prospect know it is socially acceptable to contribute to the Democratic party.

Get Out the Vote. On Election Day, plant gates (when shifts change), main intersections and transit stops (during rush hours), and office building plazas (during lunch hours) are all good places to find voters. . . . Remember, there are many voters we do not want to remind about Election Day. . . . Don't shoot yourself in the foot.

Tools and Techniques. Encourage targeted voters to turn out. Provide basic voting information such as poll locations and hours. Offer rides to voters and arrange for baby-sitting.

Literature Drop. The door-to-door distribution of literature is a cheap way to get campaign brochures or tabloids to voters. Never place campaign literature in a mailbox. It's against the law. Make sure volunteers understand the importance of tightly securing each piece of literature that is distributed. Literature that is strewn across lawns does not leave a good impression with voters.

—Democratic National Committee
campaign manual, 1988

President Bush's campaign was managed backstage by James A. Baker III, his closest political confidant, who gave up his post as Secretary of State to return to the White House when the midsummer polls showed Bush in deep trouble. Under Baker's direction, a close-knit group of advisers with varied professional backgrounds and experience filled the formal campaign posts. Polltaker Robert M. Teeter, a longtime Republican political consultant, served as the campaign chairman. A former Secretary of Commerce, Robert A. Mosbacher, Sr., was chief fund-raiser, and Frederic V. Malek, a veteran of the Nixon and Ford administrations,

James A. Baker III

nications system available to a president aboard *Air Force One* and everywhere else he moves, and with a huge White House staff to support his campaign, a president almost inevitably has the logistical edge over a rival.

A president's campaign appearances, even more than the challenger's, are carefully planned; several days before a presidential appearance in a town or city, the Secret Service checks over locations for security, and the political advance staff determines the best way to display the crowds for the television cameras, the most pleasing backdrops, and other details — all designed to maximize the political benefit to the chief executive. It should be noted, however, that the advantages of incumbency do not guarantee reelection; as Jimmy Carter, Gerald Ford, and George Bush discovered. All told, ten incumbent presidents have been defeated in general-election contests.

In 1992, President Bush sought to exploit many of the benefits of incumbency. When Hurricane Andrew devastated south Florida, Bush visited the scene and sent in federal troops and emergency aid for disaster relief — although he was criticized for responding too slowly. In Texas, a key state with 32 electoral votes, Bush announced at a General Dynamics plant in Fort Worth that he had approved the $6 billion sale of up to 150 F-16 fighter jets to Taiwan. In St. Louis, he was

was the campaign manager. Mary Matalin, his deputy for political operations, often attacked the Democratic candidate in sharp language that sometimes went beyond Bush's own rhetoric early in the campaign. Charles Black, a political public relations specialist, served as a senior adviser.

An incumbent president who runs for reelection normally enjoys certain advantages. He may benefit from the trappings of his high office, and from the aura of the presidency that surrounds him. He may award lucrative defense contracts to plants in key states that he needs to win for reelection. With the elaborate commu-

" . . .The advantages of incumbency." President Bush seeking reelection in 1992 announces at a General Dynamics plant in Texas his approval of the sale of F-16 fighter planes to Taiwan.

cheered by employees of McDonnell Douglas when he announced the sale of 72 F-15 fighter planes, worth $9 billion, to Saudi Arabia. "There is going to be one Santa Claus this election season," a Republican official was quoted as saying, "and [campaign manager] Baker is determined it will be Bush." [3]

CAMPAIGN STRATEGY

Aiming for the Undecided

Studies have shown that many voters are committed to one candidate or another in advance of the campaign. For example, in 1988 well over half of a sample of voters reported they had made up their minds *before* the fall campaign got underway. Vice-President Bush was running for president that year, but over much of the summer, many voters appeared to favor the less well-known Democratic candidate, Governor Michael Dukakis of Massachusetts. Nevertheless, a large group of voters — almost 40 percent — decided during the campaign. (See Table 8-1.) On election day, Bush won decisively. The percentage of undecided voters is sometimes higher in campaigns where no incumbent is a candidate.

Nelson W. Polsby and Aaron B. Wildavsky have contended that, for the majority of citizens in America, "campaigns do not function so much to change minds as to reinforce previous convictions." [4] Even so, when a third or more of the people *do* make up their minds during a campaign, their votes may well determine the outcome. For example, if 100 million votes are cast in a

presidential election, one third, or 33 million votes, is a sizable bloc by any standards.

The undecided voters may hold the key to victory in close elections. Since about two-thirds of all American voters identify with one of the two major parties, political candidates try to preserve their party base — to hold on to their natural constituency — while winning over voters from the other party, the independents, and the undecided.

While some poll data suggest that political campaigns do not influence the choice of a majority of voters, political analysts have concluded that campaigns may influence "a small but crucial proportion of the electorate. . . . Clearly, professional politicians drive themselves and their organizations to influence every remaining undecided voter in the hope and expectation that they are providing or maintaining a winning margin." [5]

And a number of scholars have disagreed with the view that campaigns have minimal influence on voters. Dan Nimmo and Robert L. Savage have argued that "there is a close relationship between candidate images and voting behavior." [6] They have concluded that while candidates' images usually emerge early in a campaign and remain about the same, those images can and do change during campaigns; as examples they cite John F. Kennedy in 1960 and Hubert Humphrey in 1968, whose images improved as their campaigns progressed. [7] In arguing that "campaigns make a difference," Nimmo and Savage emphasize that this is particularly true for independent voters, who are more likely than other voters to shift their impressions of the candidates during campaigns. [8]

Nimmo and others view political campaigns as "a process of communication" in which voters do not respond automatically on the basis of their socio-economic backgrounds or party loyalties. Rather, Nimmo contends, voters tend to "construct" their own individual view of the campaign; they arrive at a decision

Table 8-1
Presidential Elections: When the Voter Decides*

	1964	1968	1972	1976	1980	1984	1988
Decided how to vote							
Before conventions	40	33	43	33	42	49	31.7
During conventions	25	22	17	20	17	17	28.7
During the campaign	33	38	35	45	40	29	39.5
Don't remember not ascertained	3	7	4	2	1	5	.1

*Figures are rounded.
SOURCE: Data provided by University of Michigan, Institute for Social Research, Center for Political Studies, American National Election Studies.

---

[3] *Washington Post*, September 14, 1992, p. A10.
[4] Nelson W. Polsby and Aaron B. Wildavsky, *Presidential Elections*, 6th ed. (New York: Scribner's, 1984), p. 148.
[5] William H. Flanigan and Nancy H. Zingale, *Political Behavior of the American Electorate*, 5th ed. (Boston: Allyn and Bacon, 1983), p. 158.
[6] Dan Nimmo and Robert L. Savage, *Candidates and Their Images: Concepts, Methods, and Findings* (Pacific Palisades: Goodyear, 1976), p. 208.
[7] Ibid., pp. 136–37.
[8] Ibid., p. 143.

"I'm going to do a flip-flop on Africa. Can you make it look good"?

Drawing by Weber

by interpreting the symbols offered to them, often by drawing upon their own experience.[9]

Norman H. Nie, Sidney Verba, and John R. Petrocik in *The Changing American Voter* argued that campaigns may affect voting because "the public responds to the political stimuli offered it." The behavior of voters, they concluded, is influenced not only by psychological and sociological factors, "but also by the issues of the day and by the way in which candidates present those issues."[10]

Similarly, Walter DeVries and Lance Tarrance have emphasized that in many elections the outcome is determined by "ticket-splitters." They defined the term as a voter likely "to be basically a Republican or Democrat, but one who occasionally splits off to vote for a candidate of another party."[11] To convince the ticket-splitters, DeVries and Tarrance contend, candidates

must use campaigns to communicate their views on the issues.[12]

Increasingly, in campaigns today the strategists for the candidates "target" certain groups of voters. Some of these targets are geographic; a candidate may select specific states for special effort; or the campaign may target specific categories of voters, such as white southerners, young voters, African Americans, Hispanics, or other demographic groups.

Which Road to the White House?

Long before they can get into a general-election campaign, aspiring presidential candidates must, as a rule, enter the bruising arena of the primaries. In 1992, Bill Clinton's victories in Florida, Texas, and other southern and border states on "Super Tuesday" were important to his successful drive for the Democratic presidential nomination.

Conversely, former President Gerald R. Ford's decision not to enter the primaries in 1980 may have been the decisive factor in his failure to win the Republican nomination. And that same year, Carter's defeat of Senator Edward M. Kennedy in key primaries ensured Carter's renomination as his party's presidential candidate. The candidate who wins the most primaries does not necessarily gain the nomination; in 1984 Walter Mondale actually won fewer primaries than Senator Gary Hart of Colorado — eleven to Hart's sixteen. But it was Mondale who got the party's nomination.

[12] Ibid., p. 111.

The Clinton-Gore bus tour, 1992

[9] Dan Nimmo, *Political Communication and Public Opinion in America* (Santa Monica: Goodyear, 1978), pp. 361–72. See also David L. Swanson, "Political Communication: A Revisionist View Emerges," in *The Quarterly Journal of Speech*, vol. 64 (1978), pp. 211–22.

[10] Norman H. Nie, Sidney Verba, and John R. Petrocik, *The Changing American Voter*, Enlarged Edition, A Twentieth Century Fund Study (Cambridge: Harvard University Press, 1979), p. 319.

[11] Walter DeVries and Lance Tarrance, Jr., *The Ticket-Splitter: A New Force in American Politics* (Grand Rapids: William B. Eerdmans, 1972), p. 37.

SHOULD YOU BE A CANDIDATE?

Before the campaign can begin, there must be a candidate. And that job is not easy, as the following excerpt from a Republican party manual suggests:

The person who cannot answer virtually all of the following questions in the affirmative should not be running.

1. Does your family fully support your candidacy? Are they prepared to assume much more responsibility at home and put in extra time campaigning? Can they tolerate the verbal abuse you may receive and long hours you will spend away from home? Will your children accept and understand your frequent absence from home?
2. Can you afford to run? Can you expect enough contributions to keep out of serious personal debt? Is your business in good hands while you campaign? If you are employed, do you have a job to go back to in the event you lose?
3. Can your personal background stand intensive scrutiny? Are you fully prepared to have the public know about your debts, personal and organizational associations, past relationships with members of the opposite sex, family background, sources of income, health history, partners, etc.?
4. Are you strong enough physically and emotionally to stand up to the rigors of a tough campaign? Can your health tolerate long hours, poor food, erratic rest, continuing pressure, rejection and frustration? Most important, could your ego tolerate a loss if it should come?

—Candidate Recruitment, Republican National Committee campaign manual, 1980

For relatively unknown political candidates, the primary route may prove an attractive means of demonstrating their strength and gaining nationwide exposure in the media. For example, Jimmy Carter was not widely known in 1976, and his primary election victories that year were essential to his successful campaign for the Democratic presidential nomination; Carter's triumphs throughout the spring proved that he was a viable candidate and, of course, won him many convention delegates. In 1980 George Bush lost several key primaries to Ronald Reagan. But the fact that Bush also won some primaries may have helped to persuade Reagan to select him as his vice-presidential running mate. Then in 1984 Gary Hart's upset victory in the New Hampshire primary catapulted him to national prominence and almost derailed Mondale's campaign.

Even for a presidential aspirant who is far out in front, entering the primaries is almost always necessary in order to win the nomination. Today, most candidates feel compelled to take the primary route. One presidential candidate who found another way to gain the public's attention was Ross Perot, the Texas businessman who disdained the primaries in 1992 but captured an enormous amount of free television time and media attention by challenging the major-party candidates.

Perot built an organization of "volunteers," many of them paid, but did not run on a party label.

With preconvention campaigns so crucial, most candidates find it necessary to have a well-financed campaign organization already in operation long before the national convention. In 1992, for example, the preconvention campaign organizations of both Bush and Clinton were hardly distinguishable in size from those of major-party nominees in a general election.

Where and How to Campaign

Once nominated, candidates must decide how and where their precious time (and money) can be most profitably spent. Typically, candidates tend to spend more time campaigning in pivotal states such as New York, California, Pennsylvania, Illinois, Ohio, Texas, and Michigan. Their strategists know that the contest normally will be won or lost in the populous states with big electoral votes.

The candidate who logs the most miles on the campaign trail may not harvest the most votes. In 1960 Richard Nixon pledged to become the first candidate to take his presidential campaign to all fifty states. He did,

President Theodore Roosevelt campaigning

but at great physical and political cost; he lost to John F. Kennedy. By contrast, in 1968 Nixon moved at a relatively serene pace that preserved his physical energies. He concentrated on ten populous "battleground states," on those states in the South that might be captured from George Wallace, and on the border states.[13] This time, Nixon won.

Television has, of course, influenced the pattern of political campaigning. Aside from the advantage offered by television in reaching large numbers of voters, it also can reduce the risk to the safety of the candidate. In the light of the assassinations of President John F. Kennedy and Robert Kennedy, the attempt on the life of George Wallace, the two attempts against President Ford, and the attack on President Reagan in which he was seriously wounded, precautions would seem sensible. Yet candidates are under great pressure to mingle with the voters and to show themselves in person: "Rightly or wrongly, presidential candidates judge that they must be personally seen by audiences throughout the country,

through such rituals as motorcades, shopping center rallies and whistle-stop campaigns."[14]

Political candidates also worry about timing in a campaign. Generally speaking, candidates attempt to gear their campaign to a climactic windup in the last two weeks. Often in the final weeks of a presidential campaign, the airwaves are saturated with a "media blitz" of television commercials.

Political campaigns help to weld political parties together; for instance, campaign rallies and personal appearances by the candidate generate enthusiasm among partisan workers and volunteers. Candidates are concerned about maintaining their momentum and a certain level of excitement, not only with the voters, but for the sake of their own party organization as well.

The President as Candidate

Although three incumbent presidents — Ford, Carter, and Bush — were defeated in the elections of 1976, 1980, and 1992, an incumbent at least starts out with a great potential advantage over an opponent in a presidential campaign. As noted earlier, not only do the prestige and power of the office follow the president on the hustings, but all the visible trappings go along as well: *Air Force One*, the gleaming presidential jet, lands for an airport rally, the band plays "Hail to the Chief," and the voters are enveloped by the aura and mystique of the presidency. Just before a president speaks, an aide hangs a portable presidential seal on the lectern.

Aside from prestige, an incumbent president already has a huge organized staff and all the advantages of White House communications and other facilities, including extensive arrangements for handling the press. And he may be able to dominate the news by taking actions as president that are carefully timed for maximum political advantage. For example, during the 1984 campaign, President Reagan addressed the United Nations in New York, met with Soviet foreign minister Andrei Gromyko at the White House, and visited a B-1 bomber factory in Palmdale. Reagan used that setting to attack his opponent, Walter Mondale, for "weakening America's armed forces."[15] On television and in news

---

[13] Theodore H. White, *The Making of the President 1968* (New York: Atheneum, 1969), pp. 326–33.

[14] "Assassination," in *To Establish Justice, To Insure Domestic Tranquility*, Final Report of the National Commission on the Causes and Prevention of Violence (Washington, D.C.: U.S. Government Printing Office, 1969), p. 132.

[15] *New York Times*, October 23, 1984, p. A24.

photos, the president was seen posing in front of the huge bomber with thousands of Rockwell International workers in the background. It was a show that Mondale, the challenger, could not hope to match.

An incumbent president can use the power of his office in other ways as well. For example, in presidential election years when an incumbent is running, federal grants may flow in large amounts to states in which key primaries will take place. In other words, a president may use the levers of bureaucracy to try to win votes. He may also seize on a foreign-policy crisis to gain political advantage and display his leadership as commander-in-chief.

An incumbent president may be in such a strong position that he will decide to restrict his campaigning, allow the dignity of his office to work for him, and, in effect, campaign from the White House. He may adopt the "lofty, nonpartisan pose." [16] In 1976 President Ford attempted for a time to campaign from the White House, but when Carter accused him of trying to "hide in the Rose Garden," he soon took to the campaign trail. Yet Carter himself stayed close to the Rose Garden during the early primaries in 1980, claiming that the hostage crisis in Iran required his full attention to presidential duties in the White House.

Until 1968 the president-as-candidate enjoyed another advantage: he alone had the Secret Service to plan his movements and provide security. Candidates other than a president (or vice-president) had to move through the crowds unprotected, or at best with a private, and often amateur, bodyguard or a few local police. After Robert Kennedy was fatally shot during the preconvention campaign of 1968, however, President Johnson assigned Secret Service agents to all the candidates, a practice that Congress speedily made law. [17]

THE ISSUES

Political candidates in most cases develop a central theme for their campaign. Sometimes it emerges as the battle progresses; often it is well thought out in advance. Candidates attempt to choose their terrain, staking out certain issues that they believe will give them the advantage over their opponents.

But to a great extent the campaign theme is shaped by the candidate's status — candidate of the "out" party, incumbent president, or political heir to an incumbent. For example, in 1976 Carter was able to attack the record of eight years of Republican rule in the White House. He won the presidency. But in 1980 it was Reagan's turn to attack Carter's record, and this time, Reagan emerged as the winner. In 1984, Reagan, now the incumbent president, offered economic recovery, personal popularity, patriotism, and a sometimes militant foreign policy — a combination that proved irresistible to the voters. In 1988, Vice-President Bush defended the record of the Reagan-Bush administration, which had occupied the White House for almost eight years, and offered himself to the voters as the logical heir to a generally popular president, Ronald Reagan. Bush won. By 1992, however, the economy was in shambles and a younger and more charismatic Democratic opponent, Bill Clinton, took a commanding lead in the early polls. Many voters held Bush responsible for the high unemployment and economic doldrums, and Clinton won the election.

But even a popular president cannot always transfer his appeal to a successor. As Polsby and Wildavsky have noted, "One of the most difficult positions for a candidate is to try to succeed a President of his own

---

[16] V. O. Key, Jr., *Politics, Parties, and Pressure Groups*, 5th ed. (New York: Crowell, 1964), p. 471.

Robert F. Kennedy campaigning in Detroit, 1968

---

[17] The law authorizes Secret Service protection, unless declined, for "major presidential or vice-presidential candidates." The secretary of the Treasury, after consultation with an advisory committee that includes leaders of Congress, decides who qualifies as a candidate under this definition. The law does not specifically provide protection for preconvention candidates, but the precedent was set in 1968 when the Secret Service guarded a total of twelve candidates: six presidential candidates before the conventions and six party nominees (for president and vice-president).

President Johnson and Hubert Humphrey

party. . . . No matter how hard he tries to avoid it he is stuck with the record made by the President of his own party." [18] There is evidence that some incumbent presidents are a bit reluctant to expend their prestige on behalf of the heir apparent — who may not always want help. In 1968, for example, President Johnson's attitude toward Vice-President Hubert Humphrey, the Democratic nominee, seemed ambivalent at first, although in the end he publicly supported him. But Humphrey lost the election.

Sometimes, the substantive issues in a campaign become submerged as the candidates devote more time to attacking each other than to discussing policies and programs. The 1988 presidential race was marked by this sort of "negative campaigning" as Bush attacked his Democratic opponent, and Dukakis — some thought too late — responded. Polls indicated that a large number of voters were exasperated at the negative nature of the 1988 presidential campaign.

Again in 1992, Bush, behind in the polls, lashed out at his Democratic opponent. He repeatedly charged that Clinton had been less than candid about his efforts to avoid the draft during the war in Vietnam, and he attacked Clinton for participating in antiwar demonstrations in London. "I simply do not understand," Bush said, "when Americans are in a prison camp in Hanoi and Americans are dying on the battlefield . . . an American citizen organizing demonstrations in a foreign land." [19] Bush also assailed Clinton for visiting Moscow as a student, darkly implying that his Democratic opponent was somehow unpatriotic for traveling to the Soviet capital. The tactics backfired, and Bush quickly dropped his questions about the Moscow trip after Democrats accused him of adopting the tactics of the late Senator Joseph R. McCarthy, who sought to label his targets as Communists or their sympathizers.

It also was disclosed that a Bush administration political appointee in the State Department had ordered a search of the London embassy's files to dig up information about Clinton during his student days, and had sent officials in Washington to the National Archives records center in Suitland, Maryland, to examine Clinton's passport file and that of his mother. Because motherhood ranks right up with apple pie among American icons, Clinton was able to use the episode to good advantage on the stump. In several speeches during the last days of the campaign, he spoke of "political hacks rifling through my mother's files, trying to find dirt." [20]

Bread and Butter Issues

Peace and pocketbook issues have tended to dominate presidential campaigns. On domestic issues the Democrats can point to a wide range of social legislation passed during Democratic administrations. Not all of these programs have worked equally well, and some, such as the welfare program, have been widely criticized. Nevertheless, Democratic candidates since the New Deal have been able to campaign on the party's efforts toward achieving social progress at home. And, perhaps remembering the Great Depression that began in 1929 under a Republican president, voters have, in some years, tended to associate prosperity with Democrats. (See Figure 8–1.)

Bread and butter issues do not always work for the Democrats, however. In 1980, for example, double-digit inflation and continued high unemployment made the economy one domestic issue that President Carter preferred not to emphasize; it proved, in fact, one of the weakest issues for the Democratic incumbent. In 1984, a decline in both unemployment and the rate of inflation

[18] Polsby and Wildavsky, *Presidential Elections*, 2nd ed. (New York: Scribner's, 1968), p. 129.

[19] *New York Times*, October 14, 1992, p. A19.
[20] *New York Times*, October 28, 1992, p. A16.

Figure 8-1
Political Party Rated Best for Prosperity
Question: "Which political party — the Republican or Democratic — will do a better job of keeping the country prosperous?"

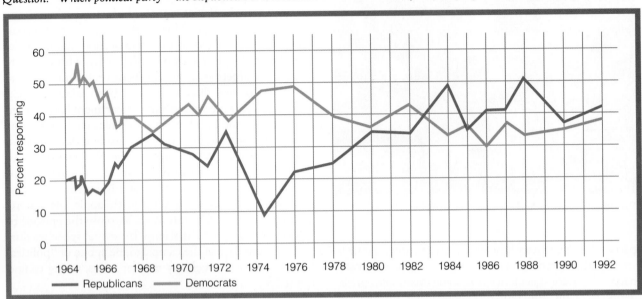

SOURCE: *Gallup Opinion Index*, Report no. 106 (April 1974), p. 21; Report no. 135 (October 1976), p. 5: Report no. 159 (October 1978), p. 21; Report no. 181 (September 1980), p.8; Report no. 223 (April 1984), pp. 18–19; and Gallup poll news release (September 23, 1984). 1985–1992 data provided by Gallup Organization.

worked in favor of the Republicans. Except for enormous budget deficits, President Reagan could point to an improved economy. This time, the Republicans had captured the economic issue. And in 1988, George Bush, the Republican vice-president, was able to claim that the Reagan administration had brought general prosperity and lower interest rates. His Democratic opponent, Michael Dukakis, argued that it was a false prosperity that squeezed the middle class. In November, the voters chose Bush. By 1992, with the economy troubled and unemployment high, the Democrats had regained a powerful domestic issue for the presidential campaign, an issue, perhaps more than any other, that helped the party and its candidate, Bill Clinton, to recapture the White House.

Foreign-Policy Issues

In the area of foreign affairs, the Republicans often have an advantage. (See Figure 8-2.) Because the Democrats were in power during the First World War, the Second World War, Korea, and Vietnam, the Republicans have often been able to tag the Democrats, fairly or not, as the "war party." Richard Nixon in 1968 was able to promise

new leadership to bring an end to the war in Vietnam. Although Nixon did not succeed in ending the American combat role in the Vietnam War until more than two months after his reelection in 1972, his trips to Beijing and Moscow earlier that year, and the appearance of progress toward a Vietnam peace agreement during the campaign, once again provided the Republican candidate with an advantage in the area of foreign policy. Yet it is also true that foreign-policy issues are not always the Republicans' strongest ground. For example, in 1980, even though President Carter lost the election, most observers felt that he had effectively emphasized the "war or peace" issue by suggesting that Reagan might be more likely than he to involve the country in a military action.

In 1992 President Bush, the Republican candidate, was able to emphasize that the Cold War had ended during his administration, and the danger of nuclear annihilation had receded. And he reminded the voters that Iraq and its dictator, Saddam Hussein, had been forced to retreat from Kuwait in the Persian Gulf War. The Democrats sought to counter Bush's claims of foreign policy successes by charging that he had not disclosed his role in the Iran-contra scandal, that his administration had secretly helped to arm Iraq, and that

Figure 8–2

Political Party Rated Best for Peace

"Looking ahead for the next few years, which political party do you think would be more likely to keep the United States out of war*—the Republican or the Democratic Party?"

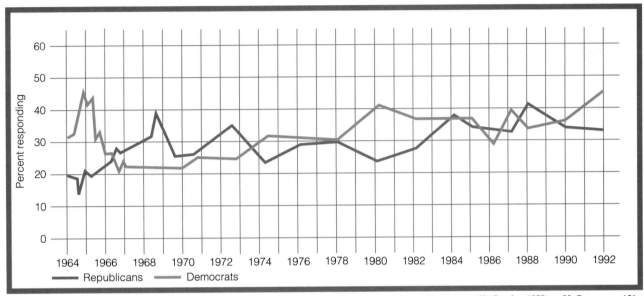

SOURCE: *Gallup Opinion Index*, Report no. 106 (April 1974), p. 19; Report no. 135 (October 1976), p. 6; Report no. 159 (October 1978), p. 22; Report no. 181 (September 1980), p. 7; Report no. 223 (April 1984), pp. 18–19; and Gallup poll news release (September 23, 1984), 1985–1992 data provided by Gallup Organization.
* Prior to 1992, the question was phrased, ". . . Keep the United States out of World War III. . ."

the administration had covered up its knowledge of more than $5 billion in fraudulent loans to Iraq by the Atlanta branch of an Italian bank.

Although presidents customarily present foreign-policy decisions in lofty terms unrelated to their election prospects, the truth is that foreign affairs and domestic politics are closely intertwined. That is, in making foreign-policy choices, presidents often have one eye on potential voter reaction at election time. This was well-illustrated by a remark made by President Bush early in 1992 as he campaigned in the New Hampshire presidential primary:

> If I'd'a listened to the leader of the United States Senate, George Mitchell, Saddam Hussein would be in Saudia Arabia and you'd be paying twenty bucks a gallon for gasoline. Now try that one on for size.[21]

The Imponderables

A sudden foreign-policy crisis, a personal scandal, a chance remark — these are among the many imponder-

ables that may affect voter attitudes in political campaigns.

In 1884, when Grover Cleveland was the Democratic nominee, his Republican opponents chanted: "Ma, Ma, where's my Pa? Gone to the White House, Ha, ha, ha." The slogan was a gleeful reference to the illegitimate child that Cleveland was accused of fathering.[22] It was soon overshadowed, however, by another slogan. A few days before the election, a Protestant minister supporting James G. Blaine, the Republican candidate, referred to the Democrats as the party of "rum, Romanism, and rebellion." The insult to Roman Catholics may

---

[21] President Bush, quoted on NBC Nightly News, January 15, 1992.

[22] The story broke during the campaign in a Buffalo, New York, newspaper under the headline: "A Terrible Tale — A Dark Chapter in a Public Man's History." Ten years earlier, Maria Crofts Halpin, an attractive widow, had given birth to a son, whom she named Oscar Folsom Cleveland, charging Cleveland with the baby's paternity. Cleveland said he was not certain he was the father, but he had assumed full responsibility for supporting the child; when the scandal broke, he telegraphed his friends in Buffalo — "Tell the truth." Because of his open attitude, Cleveland managed to minimize the damage to his presidential campaign. After Cleveland's election, the Democrats celebrated their first presidential victory in twenty-eight years by singing: "Hurrah for Maria, Hurrah for the kid, We voted for Grover, And we're damned glad we did!"

have cost Blaine New York State and thereby the election.

In 1948 Thomas Dewey's campaign train, the *Victory Special*, lurched backward into the crowd while the Republican nominee was orating at Beaucoup, Illinois. "Well, that's the first lunatic I've had for an engineer," snapped Dewey. The remark was widely publicized and did not sit well with the railroad unions. Overnight, "Lunatic Engineers for Truman" and similar groups sprang up to plague the Republican candidate along the right-of-way of the *Victory Special*.

In 1952 Richard Nixon's place as the vice-presidential candidate on the Republican ticket was endangered when newspapers reported the existence of the "Nixon fund," some $18,000 contributed by a group of California businessmen to meet Nixon's political expenses as a United States senator. Nixon went on nationwide television and, in his famed "Checkers" speech, defended his use of the $18,000 fund, listed his personal finances, noted that his wife Pat wore a "respectable Republican cloth coat," and announced that, come what may, his family intended to keep a black-and-white cocker spaniel named Checkers, which had been given to his two children.[23] Although the speech was a patently emotional appeal for which Nixon was often assailed by later critics, it turned the tide of public opinion and impressed General Eisenhower, the Republican presidential nominee. Nixon stayed on the ticket.

Mudslinging and charges of corruption are common in campaigns. Under the unwritten rules of the

1952: Richard M. Nixon delivers his "Checkers" speech on television

seamier side of American politics, a candidate may attempt to "get something" on an opponent. (The information might not be publicized, however, if the other side possesses equally damaging information, or if it is

---

[23] Checkers died in September 1964, and is buried at Westhampton, Long Island. He was not the first canine to gain fame in a presidential campaign. Running for a fourth term in 1944, Franklin D. Roosevelt ridiculed the Republicans for charging that he had sent a destroyer to fetch his dog: "The Republican leaders have not been content to make personal attacks upon me — or my wife — or my sons — they now include my little dog, Fala. . . . I am accustomed to hearing malicious falsehoods about myself but I think I have a right to object to libelous statements about my dog." See Robert E. Sherwood, *Roosevelt and Hopkins* (New York: Harper & Row, 1948), p. 821.

"BE SURE TO CRY SCANDAL!"

The following is an excerpt from a publication of the Republican National Committee that advised GOP candidates on campaign techniques:

Researching Scandals in the Democratic Party. With proper research and publicity, exposure of scandals can serve as a public service and as a source of votes. . . . Most scandals evolve from "tips," usually coming from newsmen, victims of the "scandal," public reports such as those of the State Auditor, or abused factions within or on the fringes of the wrongdoer's organization. . . .

Publicizing the Scandal. A "believable" springboard from which to break the scandal must be found. A newsman, a disenchanted insider, or a local prosecutor are possible means for breaking the scandal to the public.

Once the public has been informed that a scandal in fact does exist, it must be kept continually aware that its trust has been violated. . . . Question the principals of the opposition at every opportunity — at public gatherings as well as in the press. In other words, take advantage of every possible form of publicity — and be sure to cry, SCANDAL!

—Republican National Committee, *Research Techniques for Republican Campaigns* (1969)

felt that the opponent can successfully cry "smear.") Because mudslinging, rumors, and scandals presumably influence some voters, their use in political campaigns persists. It is often near the end of a campaign that a candidate's supporters try to leak such stories to the newspapers to damage a rival.

Perhaps the most startling and disturbing surprise development of any modern presidential campaign occurred in June 1972, when five men, wearing surgical rubber gloves and carrying electronic eavesdropping equipment, were arrested inside the Washington headquarters of the Democratic National Committee in the Watergate building. One of the men, James W. McCord, Jr., a former CIA agent, turned out to be director of security for President Nixon's campaign organization. Three weeks before the election, a federal grand jury in Washington indicted the five men plus two former White House aides, E. Howard Hunt, Jr., and G. Gordon Liddy, on charges of burglary, illegal wiretapping, and bugging.

The case immediately raised a host of questions about who had sent the men on their espionage mission to the Democratic headquarters. The White House and President Nixon repeatedly denied involvement. But one of the Watergate defendants, it developed, had $89,000 in his bank account that had been delivered to the Republican campaign committee and "laundered" through Mexico to disguise its origin.

The charges of espionage and financial irregularities seemed to have little impact on the voters in the 1972 election.[24] The Watergate case and the issue of

political espionage began to grow into a major scandal only well after the presidential election campaign. Early in 1973, five of the defendants pleaded guilty, and two others were convicted by a federal jury. Within months, the scandal had reached the president; several of his top aides resigned and some went to prison. A year later Nixon, facing impeachment, resigned in disgrace, his presidency shattered less than two years after his reelection by a landslide.

In 1984 a joke by President Reagan at the start of the presidential campaign caused him some embarrassment. Preparing for his weekly radio broadcast, Reagan was asked for a "voice check" by technicians. The president replied: "My fellow Americans, I'm pleased to tell you today that I've signed legislation that would outlaw Russia forever. We begin bombing in five minutes." The remark was not broadcast, but it was recorded by two networks and became public, arousing a storm of controversy. The comment was denounced by the Soviet Union, criticized by Walter Mondale, the Democratic candidate, and apparently triggered a partial Soviet military alert.[25]

In 1988, Bush's selection of Senator Dan Quayle of Indiana as his running mate caused an unanticipated storm over Quayle's military service during the war in Vietnam—he had served in the Indiana National Guard at home—a controversy that served to focus attention on Quayle's youth and relative lack of experience. Dukakis sought to exploit the doubts over Quayle, and some of his supporters wore lapel buttons that asked: "President Quayle?"

---

[24] A Gallup poll published in October showed that 52 percent of the voters had heard of the Watergate scandal, but only about a third were able to recite the key facts of the situation. Eight out of ten persons who knew about the incident said it was not a strong reason for voting for Nixon's Democratic opponent, Senator George McGovern. Source: Gallup poll, *Washington Post*, October 8, 1972, p. A5.

[25] *Washington Post*, August 14, 1984, p. A6, and October 12, 1984, p. A10.

Reprinted by permission: Tribune Media Services

At the very start of the 1992 presidential election year, Gennifer Flowers, a former lounge singer, claimed in the *Star*, a supermarket tabloid, that she had engaged in a twelve-year affair with Governor Bill Clinton. In an appearance with his wife, Hillary, on "60 Minutes," the CBS television program, Clinton denied Flowers' allegations but conceded marital "wrongdoing." For a time, however, the charges of infidelity threatened to derail Clinton's presidential hopes. Afterward, Clinton's supporters worried about what they termed "the bimbo factor"—fear that one or more other supposed lovers would surface during the campaign. Several months later, President Bush angrily denied rumors of long duration, finally published, that he had had an extramarital affair with Jennifer Fitzgerald, a former aide. After that, the private lives of the candidates receded as a campaign issue.

Hillary Clinton herself became a campaign issue during the primary battles because of an unguarded remark. A successful lawyer, Hillary Clinton had combined a career and motherhood and was a strong personality in her own right. When former California Governor Jerry Brown, a contender for the Democratic nomination, charged that her law firm in Arkansas had

benefited from her marriage to Governor Clinton, she replied: "I suppose I could have stayed home, baked cookies and had teas." To her detractors, it appeared that she was criticizing women who chose a more traditional role (although it was clear from the rest of her remarks that she was not).

The Republicans had some unexpected gaffes as well in 1992, thanks to Vice-President Dan Quayle. In a speech upholding "family values," Quayle caused a nationwide uproar when he attacked Murphy Brown, a fictional television character, for having a baby as a single, unmarried mother. Not long afterward, Quayle visited a school in Trenton, New Jersey, and coached a twelve-year-old student, William Figueroa, to add an "e" to the word "potato." Political cartoonists had a field day. The schoolboy, an instant celebrity, appeared on the David Letterman show. The principal got a call from the Potato Museum in Great Falls, Virginia. "Potatoe" T-shirts sprouted on college campuses.

Ross Perot was moving up rapidly in the polls after he reentered the race in October when, nine days before the election, he dropped a bombshell. In campaign appearances and on the CBS program "60 Minutes" Perot charged that President Bush's campaign had engaged in "dirty tricks" and had planned to leak a fake, computer-generated photograph to embarrass his daughter and had also planned to disrupt her church wedding. According to news reports, Perot believed that the supposed photograph would have depicted his daughter, Carolyn, in a sexual pose with another woman.

Perot claimed the alleged Republican plot was the real reason he had pulled out of the race in July. But he offered no proof of his charges, which were based in part on information from a man long regarded by the

Mike Peters reprinted by permission of UFS, Inc.

news media as a fabricator of bizarre tales of intrigue. Bush's press secretary labeled the allegations "crazy," compared Perot to people who believe in U.F.O.'s, and called the independent candidate "paranoid." [26] Perot's bizarre and unsupported claims may have hurt his campaign; his charges certainly raised questions about his temperament and fitness for the presidency in the minds of some voters and on the nation's editorial pages.

World crises that erupt suddenly during a campaign are still another category of imponderables that may affect voter decisions. In general, foreign-policy crises tend to help the party in power because of voter reluctance to "change horses in midstream." The Tonkin Gulf crisis of 1964, many details of which are disputed, created an atmosphere of wartime tension that, in the short run, may have benefited the election campaign of President Johnson. On the other hand, a foreign crisis that leads to a war, as in Korea or Vietnam, or that damages the prestige of the country, such as the seizure of American hostages in Iran, may, in the long run, erode the strength of the party in power and lead to retribution at the polls.

---

[26] *New York Times*, October 27, 1992, p. A1.

CAMPAIGN TECHNIQUES

Television and Politics

The little girl in the television commercial stood in a field of daisies, plucking the petals and counting, as birds chirped in the background. Then, as the little girl reached number ten, a doomsday voice began a countdown. When the voice reached zero, there was a rumbling explosion and a huge mushroom cloud filled the screen. As it billowed upward, President Lyndon Johnson's voice boomed out: "These are the stakes. To make a world in which all of God's children can live or to go into the dark. We must either love each other or we must die." A message was then flashed on the screen reading: "Vote for President Johnson on November 3."

Millions of Americans saw the famous "Daisy Girl" commercial during the 1964 campaign, even though it was shown only once before being withdrawn

"Ten, nine, eight, seven . . .   six, five, four, three . . .   two, one . . .

These are the stakes. To make a world in which all of God's children can live . . .

or to go into the dark. We must either love each other or we must die . . .

The stakes are too high for you to stay home."

because of the controversy it created. To many it seemed to suggest that Barry Goldwater, the Republican candidate, might lead the nation into nuclear war. As Theodore White has noted, "The film mentioned neither Goldwater nor the Republicans specifically — but the shriek of Republican indignation fastened the bomb message on them more tightly than any calculation could have expected."[27]

The marriage of television and politics took place in 1948, the first year in which a small but significant number of Americans viewed parts of the national nominating conventions on TV.[28] Since less than 200,000 homes had television sets in 1948, however, the real impact of television was not felt until the 1952 and 1956 Eisenhower-Stevenson campaigns. By 1956 almost 35 million homes had TV sets. In 1960, of America's 53 million households, 46.6 million, or 88 percent, had sets. By this time, television was playing a central role in presidential campaigns.

The Kennedy-Nixon Debates It was in 1960 that the major-party candidates were first able to reach vast audiences in a series of televised debates. Congress made the debates possible. Under Section 315 of the Federal Communications Act, broadcasters are required to provide "equal time" to all legally qualified candidates. The television networks argued that if the major-party candidates debated on TV, this provision would force the networks to give time to minor-party candidates. Congress in 1960 suspended the "equal time" provision, clearing the way for four debates between Senator John F. Kennedy and Vice-President Richard Nixon, his Republican opponent. Most observers believed that the debates helped Kennedy to win the election, in part because Nixon looked pale and haggard in the first debate and wore "Lazy Shave" powder as makeup. By contrast, Kennedy, looking tanned and vigorous, presented a much more telegenic image to the public.

The millions of voters watching the first debate may have remembered little of what the candidates said, but they noticed that Nixon did not look as pleasing as Kennedy. As White put it, "Probably no picture in

---

[27] Theodore H. White, *The Making of the President 1964* (New York: Atheneum, 1965), p. 322.

[28] 1948 was not the first year in which the national conventions were televised. But because very few people owned TV sets in the 1940s, less than one hundred thousand persons saw television broadcasts of the 1940 and 1944 conventions.

1960: John F. Kennedy and Richard M. Nixon in television debate

American politics tells a better story . . . than that famous shot of the camera on the vice-president as he half slouched, his 'Lazy Shave' powder faintly streaked with sweat, his eyes exaggerated hollows of blackness, his jaw, jowls, and face drooping with strain." [29]

The Carter-Ford Debates In 1976, for the first time since the presidential campaign of 1960, the major-party candidates reached millions of viewers in a series of televised debates. The debates were credited by some analysts with providing Jimmy Carter with his narrow margin of victory over President Ford, the Republican incumbent.[30]

As president, Ford was better known than Carter at the start of the 1976 campaign, and thus in theory had more to lose by debating his opponent. Normally, an incumbent president, or the better known of two candidates, has little incentive to debate an opponent; the television exposure only serves to help his rival become better known. But Ford, behind by thirty-three points in the polls, sought to regain the initiative by challenging his opponent to debate, and Carter accepted.[31]

Carter benefited from Ford's erroneous pronouncement in the second debate that the Soviet Union did not dominate Eastern Europe. Despite complaints by some viewers that the debates were "dull," they drew tremendous audiences and became the central drama of the election campaign.

The 1980 Debates Again in 1980 voters were able to watch the major candidates debate. First, Ronald Reagan, the Republican nominee, debated John B. Anderson, the independent candidate.

The second and main debate of the 1980 presidential campaign took place between Reagan and President Carter, the incumbent, one week before the election. Both candidates performed well, but Reagan gained ground by displaying an affable, apparently relaxed manner, thereby offsetting Carter's previous warnings that the Republican nominee was an aggressive hawk who might lead the country into a military adventure. Reagan hammered away at the economy. Near the end of the ninety-minute debate, he urged voters to ask themselves: "Are you better off than you were four years ago? Is it easier for you to go and buy things in the stores than it was four years ago?" [32] It was an effective sales pitch; polls showed that Reagan had won the debate.

The 1984 Debates Again in 1984, the public had a chance to view the major-party candidates in televised debates. Twice, President Reagan debated his Democratic opponent, Walter Mondale, and Vice-President George Bush debated his Democratic opponent, Geraldine Ferraro.

Mondale performed impressively in the first presidential debate. Reagan seemed confused at times, groping for words and facts, and even his supporters conceded that his closing statement was weak. Polls reported that Mondale had won.[33] Perhaps even more disturbing for the Reagan campaign was the emergence, for the first time, of the "age issue." The president's poor performance made some people wonder whether, at age seventy-three, he was getting too old for the job.

In their second debate Reagan showed less of the hesitation that had characterized his first performance. He demolished the age issue with a quip ("I am not going to exploit for political purposes my opponent's youth and inexperience"). In a sense, Reagan won the debate merely by not making any major mistakes.

Mondale's campaign never regained the momentum it had briefly enjoyed after the first debate. Reagan's "comeback" performance in the second debate ended any lingering hope that Mondale might have entertained of overtaking the president.

The 1988 Debates In 1988, Bush and Dukakis debated twice on television. In the first debate, both candidates did well, although Bush stumbled on the abortion issue, seeming to suggest that if abortion once again became illegal, women who had abortions might be subject to criminal penalties.[34] Dukakis challenged Bush on

---

[29] Theodore H. White, *The Making of the President 1960* (New York: Atheneum, 1961), p. 289.

[30] Although in 1976 Congress did not suspend the "equal time" provision again, the debates were made possible by a 1975 FCC ruling that debates could be broadcast as long as they were not sponsored by the television networks or held in a TV studio, and were telecast in their entirety. In 1983, the FCC eased the rules for presidential debates even further, holding that broadcasters could stage political debates in their studios as "bona fide news events." The ruling applied to political debates in campaigns at any level, from school board to president.

[31] The Democrats nominated Carter on July 14. The Gallup poll of July 16–26 showed Carter leading Ford, 62 to 29 percent, with 9 percent undecided. Source: *Gallup Opinion Index*, Report no. 134 (September 1976), p. 8.

[32] *New York Times*, October 30, 1980, p. B19.

[33] A Gallup poll taken after the debate found that Mondale had won, 54 to 35 percent. Gallup poll news release, October 22, 1984.

[34] *Washington Post*, September 26, 1988, p. A19.

issues such as national health insurance, housing, and homelessness. Bush attacked his opponent's alleged liberal ideology. "He's out of the mainstream," Bush declared. ". . . do we want this country to go that far left?" [35]

In the vice-presidential debate, although Senator Dan Quayle defended his record, he seemed uncertain when asked repeatedly what he would do if, as vice-president, he suddenly became president. A majority of voters thought Senator Lloyd Bentsen of Texas, the Democratic candidate, had bested his rival. At one point, when Quayle compared his experience in Congress to that of John F. Kennedy, Bentsen snapped: "Senator, you're no Jack Kennedy." [36] A CBS poll reported Bentsen the winner by more than two to one. [37]

Bush and Dukakis held their second and final debate in Los Angeles. With Bush ahead in the polls, political observers felt Dukakis had to score a breakthrough in the second debate, and to demonstrate more warmth to "connect" with the voters. He failed to do so. Once again, the debate illustrated the importance of TV

images in politics. At the conclusion of the ninety-minute encounter, Dukakis ducked away almost immediately; Bush remained on stage, shaking hands and smiling broadly, and the television cameras brought that image into millions of American homes. Polls taken after the debate agreed that Bush had won decisively. [38]

The 1992 Debates Although Bill Clinton challenged President Bush to a series of televised debates, Bush at first refused, citing differences over the format of the debates. By declining to debate, Bush found himself on the defensive for several days. The Clinton camp had taken to dressing volunteers in chicken suits to heckle the president at campaign stops, implying he was afraid to face his Democratic opponent. The giant fowl were known as "Chicken George," and they appeared to annoy the president greatly. At a midwest appearance, Bush got into an argument with one of the chickens, accusing the bird of polluting the Arkansas River.

Then Bush, who was lagging in the polls, countered by suddenly challenging Clinton to four debates. After more haggling over format, both camps finally

---

[35] Ibid., p. A22.
[36] *Washington Post*, October 6, 1988, p. A1.
[37] *Washington Post*, October 7, 1988, p. A14.

[38] *New York Times*, October 15, 1988, p. A8.

SPIN CONTROL: "CALL AND PRAISE THE PRESIDENT'S PERFORMANCE"

After every televised presidential debate, members of the candidates' staffs — so called 'spin doctors' — circulate among the news media to try to persuade reporters that their candidate won, or at least did not lose. The staffers try to put a favorable 'spin,' or twist, on events to help their candidate. The spin doctors' marching orders are supposed to be confidential, but in 1992, by mistake some copies of the Bush-Quayle instructions for action after the October 15 debate were faxed to the news media. Here are some excerpts:

Call your local political reporter and give the spin. Don't wait for him or her to call you — call ASAP. Remember, they are under a tight deadline due to the hour of the debate. *It is vital that you call right away and give your reaction.*

If there are any talk-radio shows on the air, call and praise the president's performance. Please use the talking points. It is im-

perative that all surrogates are giving the same message. . . . Issue a news release declaring the president the winner. . . .

The instructions include these "talking points":

Tonight was a clear win, a big win for the president. Bill Clinton came in a cautious and weak third place. . . .

The president forcefully stated that character is a key issue in this campaign. The person the American people choose to be president must be of unquestioned character and integrity. President Bush is known for his strength of character. . . .

Tonight the president asked the key issue in this campaign. *If a major domestic or international crisis breaks out, who is it you trust to solve the crisis and get the job done? The answer is George Bush.*

—*Washington Post*, October 17, 1992

agreed on three presidential debates plus one vice-presidential debate, all sandwiched into a nine-day period in mid-October. Since Ross Perot had jumped back into the race, he was invited to take part.

The first debate among the presidential rivals took place in St. Louis on October 11. A panel of reporters asked the questions. Bush once again attacked Clinton for organizing antiwar demonstrations in England as a student. Clinton accused Bush of questioning "my patriotism." Then in a dramatic moment, Clinton declared: "When Joe McCarthy went around this country attacking people's patriotism, he was wrong. And a senator from Connecticut stood up to him named Prescott Bush. Your father was right to stand up to Joe McCarthy; you were wrong to attack my patriotism. I was opposed to the war, but I love my country." [39]

Bush emphasized his experience and argued that the economy was not as bad as Clinton said it was.

However, Bush failed to do what he needed to do to catch up with Clinton—he scored no major points against his opponent. The unexpected star of the evening was Ross Perot, whose biting, homespun comments and humor contrasted with the more ponderous arguments of the two major-party candidates. Asked how, if elected, he planned to get his program passed by Congress, Perot replied: "Now, all these fellows with thousand-dollar suits and alligator shoes running up and down the halls of Congress that make policy now—the lobbyists, the PAC guys, the foreign lobbyists, and what-have-you, they'll be over there in the Smithsonian, you know, because we're going to get rid of them, and the Congress will be listening to the people." [40]

The vice-presidential debate took place in Atlanta on October 13. Vice-President Quayle went on the attack immediately, aggressively pressing Albert Gore, his

---

[39] *Washington Post*, October 12, 1992, pp. A1, A14.

[40] Ibid., p. A18.

Debate among Dan Quayle, James Stockdale, and Albert Gore

Democratic rival, and assailing Clinton's honesty and character. Repeatedly Quayle charged: "Bill Clinton has trouble telling the truth." And he asked: "Do you trust Bill Clinton to be your president?" [41]

Senator Albert Gore in turn assailed the Bush administration for the sorry state of the economy. "When the recession came they were like a deer caught in the headlights — paralyzed into inaction, blinded to the suffering and pain of bankruptcies and people who were unemployed. . . . It is time for a change." [42] Admiral James B. Stockdale, a hero of the Vietnam War who had been imprisoned and tortured by North Vietnam for more than seven years, took part as Perot's vice-presidential running mate. Clearly unused to the cruel arena of national politics, he performed poorly. Although most viewers felt sympathy for his plight, his exposure to a national TV audience undoubtedly hurt Perot; many viewers thought Stockdale was obviously unqualified to serve as president, should circumstances require it.

The second presidential debate took place in Richmond, Virginia, on October 15. This time, the debate had an informal talk show format, with a single modera-

tor, Carole Simpson of ABC, and questions from the audience. Bush attacked Clinton for taking "different positions" on issues and said: "You can't turn the White House into the Waffle House."

But then a voter arose and asked whether all three candidates could "focus on the issues and not the personalities and the mud." The plea worked; from that moment on the president and his two rivals largely concentrated on the economy, the cities, gun control, term limits, health care, the national debt, foreign policy, education, and minorities. All three candidates appeared relaxed, they interacted well with the questioners, and many observers considered it the best hour and a half in the history of televised presidential campaign debates. This time, Perot's one-liners seemed less charming than in the first debate. And again, Clinton had shown himself to be extremely articulate, confident, and knowledgeable. The encounter did nothing to help Bush close the gap in the opinion polls.

The third and final presidential debate took place on October 19 in East Lansing, Michigan. President Bush was more forceful, in this, his last chance to try to chip away at Clinton's lead. He repeatedly contended that Clinton had shown a "pattern" of attempting to straddle important issues. "When you're President of the United States, you cannot have this pattern of say-

---

[41] *Washington Post*, October 14, 1992, pp. A14, A15.
[42] Ibid., p. A15.

1992: Perot, Clinton, and Bush in their second televised debate, Richmond, Virginia

ing well, I'm for it but I'm on the other side of it."[43] Returning to this theme repeatedly in the last debate, Bush seemed to have found a line of attack that he was to use with increasing effectiveness during the final two weeks of the campaign, as he narrowed the gap in the polls, gaining ground on his Democratic rival.

As in the previous debates, however, Clinton was well-prepared and fast on his feet, and performed well. Clinton blamed Bush for the "failed" economy. "More people are working harder for less," he said, "100,000 a month losing their health insurance, unemployment going up, our economy slowing down. We can do better."[44] Both candidates went out of their way to avoid clashing with Ross Perot, the independent, obviously hoping to win over Perot supporters to their cause.

Record-breaking audiences watched the presidential and vice-presidential debates, reflecting widespread interest that had not been visible early in the campaign. It was estimated that 81 million people watched the first debate, 84 million viewed the second presidential debate, 91 million saw the third, and 76 million tuned in for the vice-presidential debate.[45]

In one sense, it may be unfair to the candidates and the voters to have so much depend on the impression that the presidential office-seekers make in one or more ninety-minute televised debates. Candidates often misstate some facts, which many viewers at home probably do not realize. On the other hand, the televised debates give millions of voters an opportunity they would not otherwise have to watch the candidates in action, to hear and contrast their views on a wide range of domestic and foreign issues, and to make judgments about the candidates' style and character.

Studies of the effect of televised debates on elections have reached varying conclusions. To an extent, some studies suggest, viewers see what they wish to see; that is, their perception of the candidates and issues hews close to their "original voting preference."[46] But other studies suggest that debates may have "a measurable direct influence on the outcome of the election."[47]

In 1992, as in some past election years, once again the tradition of televised debates had given the voters a chance to see the candidates interact, and the debates may have helped the viewers to make their own choice about who was best qualified to lead the nation as president of the United States.

Madison Avenue: The Packaging of the President

By 1992 there were television sets in about 93.1 million homes in America; 98 percent of all homes with electricity in the United States had TV sets—more than had bathtubs or telephones. The ability of political candidates to reach increased numbers of voters through television was reflected in a dramatic rise in campaign spending for TV broadcasts. In 1972 $10.8 million was spent for political broadcasts at the presidential level. In 1976, even with their budgets limited under the new federal elections law, the two major candidates spent $16.9 million on television advertising. By 1984, the total had more than doubled to $41.3 million.[48] And in 1988, the presidential candidates spent $52.5 million, or 57 percent of their total campaign outlays, on TV ads.[49] Spending for political advertising by candidates at all levels was much higher, of course, amounting to $227.9 million in 1988, a total that rose to an estimated $300 million in 1992.[50]

The increasing use of television and Madison Avenue techniques has, of course, raised the question of whether political candidates can be merchandised and packaged like toothpaste. To some extent the answer must be yes; many of the advertising executives who handle political "accounts" think in just those terms.

As a professional actor for most of his adult life, President Reagan enjoyed an added advantage on television. "Reagan," the *Washington Post* reported in 1980, ". . . calls upon his actor's training to get misty on cue, near the end of his talks. . . . His Sunday night closer was an anecdote . . . about looking into the faces of young people in Kansas City and feeling all warm and lumpy about it."[51]

Besides praising the candidate, television ads often jab at opponents. This kind of commercial that strongly

---

[43] *New York Times*, October 20, 1992, p. 21.
[44] Ibid., p. 23.
[45] Audience estimates from ABC research department, quoted in *Washington Post*, October 21, 1992, pp. B1, B6.
[46] Sidney Kraus and Dennis Davis, *The Effects of Mass Communication on Political Behavior* (University Park: The Pennsylvania State University Press, 1976), p. 59.
[47] Ibid.

[48] Adapted from Herbert E. Alexander and Brian A. Haggerty, *Financing the 1984 Election* (Lexington: Lexington Books, 1987), pp. 345, 369.
[49] Alexander and Bauer, *Financing the 1988 Election*, p. 98.
[50] Ibid. Estimate for 1992 from *New York Times*, October 27, 1992, p. A19.
[51] *Washington Post*, October 21, 1980, p. B4.

attacks a rival candidate is known as "negative advertising," a technique that has become increasingly popular in political campaigns in recent years. In 1982, for example, the Republican Senate candidate in Tennessee, Robin Beard, tried to portray his opponent, Senator Jim Sasser, as "soft" on Fidel Castro. In Beard's television commercial, an actor made up to look like Castro lit his cigar with an American bill and sneeringly said, "Muchas gracias, Señor Sasser." [52]

In 1984, several of President Reagan's commercials portrayed happy Americans in various everyday activities — going to work, raising flags, getting married, painting a picket fence. "It's morning again in America," a syrupy-voiced announcer intoned, "and under the leadership of President Reagan, our country is prouder . . . and stronger . . . and better. . . ." The commercials were primarily designed to win votes for Reagan by making Americans feel good about themselves.

In 1988, negative advertising was in vogue well before the general election. During the Democratic primaries, Representative Richard A. Gephardt, the Missouri Democrat, ran a TV commercial that attacked Governor Dukakis for suggesting that farmers "have to diversify and grow blueberries, flowers and Belgian endive." [53] The commercial helped Gephardt win in South Dakota, an agricultural state.

That fall, both Dukakis and Bush ran commercials sharply attacking each other. One Bush commercial, aimed at the Massachusetts prison furlough program, showed a group of inmates streaming through a revolving door. "As Massachusetts crime statistics flash on screen, an announcer attacks Dukakis' revolving door prison policy [that] gave weekend furloughs to first-degree murderers not eligible for parole. While out, many committed other crimes like kidnaping and rape, and many are still at large.'" [54] To underscore the point, Bush partisans enlisted the aid of a Maryland man who, with his fiancée, had been brutally assaulted by a Massachusetts convict, Willie Horton, a convicted murderer who was out on a furlough. The man, and a woman whose brother had been slain by the same convict, made a number of campaign appearances in California, a key state in presidential elections.

In addition, a conservative, pro-Bush political action committee aired television commercials featuring a photograph of Willie Horton and linking him to Dukakis. Because Horton was a black, the Dukakis camp charged that the Republicans were injecting "racism" into the campaign, an accusation that Bush denied. So effective was the commercial, that the name "Willie Horton" entered the political lexicon and became synonymous with negative, attack commercials.

The appearance of Bush on a boat in Boston harbor, charging that the Massachusetts governor's own seaport was one of the most polluted in the nation, was another television image that stuck with the voters. Somehow, when Dukakis tried the same tactic, it didn't work. He rode in a tank, wearing a helmet, to emphasize his commitment to a strong national defense, a campaign appearance that to many appeared silly and contrived.

In 1992, all three presidential candidates aired television commercials. One Bush ad, which outraged the Clinton camp, strongly suggested that Clinton would raise taxes on middle-class Americans. First the commercial showed a steamfitter in appropriately blue-collar clothes, holding a huge wrench. Beneath his photo appeared the words "$1,088 More in Taxes." Then a picture of a scientist flashed on the screen with the words "$2,072 More in Taxes." Clinton had proposed raising taxes on persons earning more than $200,000, an income achieved by few, if any, steamfitters and not many scientists. When the Clinton campaign protested, Charles Black, a senior Bush campaign strategist, told reporters that the commercial said Clinton's plan "could" raise taxes for the persons portrayed. [55]

The Clinton advertising team immediately launched a counterattack in the war of the commercials. The Clinton ad showed four television screens each with a clip from the the offending steamfitter ad. "George Bush is running attack ads," the announcer intoned. "He says all these people would have their taxes raised by Bill Clinton. Scary, huh? 'Misleading,' says the *Washington Post*. And *The Wall Street Journal* says, 'Clinton has proposed to cut taxes for the sort of people featured in Bush's ad.' So why's he doing it? Because George Bush had the worst economic record of any President in 50 years. George Bush is trying to scare you about Bill Clinton. But nothing could be more frightening than four more years." [56]

---

[52] *Washington Post*, October 30, 1982, p. 1.
[53] *Washington Post*, February 25, 1988, p. A10.
[54] *Washington Post*, October 5, 1988, p. 1.

[55] *Washington Post*, October 2, 1992, p. A1.
[56] *New York Times*, October 3, 1992, p. 8.

A Ross Perot commercial

Independent candidate Ross Perot spent millions on his commercials in 1992, beginning with a series of half-hour talks in which he flipped charts and offered his analyses of the lagging economy, the deficit, and the national debt. Later, Perot offered more conventional commericals, emphasizing his family and designed to make voters feel warm and fuzzy about a man who came across to many persons as having rather opposite qualities. Except for a few public appearances, Perot campaigned for president almost entirely through commercials and talk shows.

Quite aside from commercials, how a candidate comes across on television generally can make an enormous difference in a political campaign. In 1984, for example, Walter Mondale sometimes seemed either wooden or shrill on television. The circles under his eyes made him look fatigued. By contrast, "Reagan is never shrill or threatening. He is the narrator of one of his commercials and his strong, confident voice, as smooth and mellow as 20-year-old scotch, soothes and

reassures as he extols the accomplishments of his first term: 'Americans are working again and so is America. . . . Now it's all coming together. With our beloved nation at peace, we are in the midst of a springtime of hope for America. Greatness lies ahead.' " [57]

What is the impact of television in a political campaign? Thomas E. Patterson and Robert D. McClure have argued that the "nightly network newscasts of ABC, CBS, and NBC present a distorted picture of a presidential election campaign. These newscasts pay only limited attention to major election issues. These newscasts almost entirely avoid discussion of the candidates' qualifications for the Presidency. Instead . . . [they] devote most of their election coverage to the trivia of political campaigning that make for flashy pictures. Hecklers, crowds, motorcades, balloons, rallies, and gossip — these are the regular subjects of network campaign stories." [58]

In a study of the impact of television on voters in Summit County, Ohio, Harold Mendelsohn and Garrett J. O'Keefe found that persons who made up their minds late in a campaign were more likely than others to be influenced by television commercials. Similarly, they reported that "switchers," those who changed their minds during the course of a campaign, were more likely to be influenced by commercials. [59]

---

[57] *Washington Post*, October 5, 1984, p. A4.
[58] Thomas E. Patterson and Robert D. McClure, *The Unseeing Eye: The Myth of Television Power in National Politics* (New York: G.P. Putnam's Sons, 1976), pp. 22-23.
[59] Harold Mendelsohn and Garrett J. O'Keefe, *The People Choose a President: Influences on Voter Decision Making* (New York: Praeger, 1976), p. 171.

The impact of television on American politics should not be underestimated, but it is easy to exaggerate the influence of Madison Avenue and "the tube." The idea that a few advertising executives in New York can manipulate the mass of voters ignores other important factors — such as party identification or the voters' personal economic circumstances — that affect how people cast their ballots. In the midst of a recession, the millions of dollars spent by the Bush-Quayle campaign on television commercials did not, in the end, persuade enough voters to reelect the president and vice-president.

With the increased importance of television, however, there is at least a danger that a candidate with more money or more skilled media advisers or a better television style will enjoy a substantial advantage over a rival. (Under federal election laws the two major-party presidential candidates in 1992 accepted public funding and were held, in theory, to equal spending levels. But loopholes in the laws allowed these rules to be circumvented, and there was no such restriction in congressional and state campaigns.)

Moreover, with access to an audience of millions of voters through the electronic media, a political candidate may be tempted to display an "image" that masks the real person, to present the issues in capsulized, simplistic form, and to become a performer rather than a leader. But the candidate who goes too far in this direction takes the risk that the voters may "see through" the slickness and, in effect, switch channels — by voting for the opposing candidate. And even the cleverest media advisers must work within the existing political framework; their advertising campaigns are limited by the issues that seem important to the voters, by campaign spending laws, by party loyalties, and by the strengths and weaknesses of their client, the candidate. There are, in short, limits to the ability of Madison Avenue to package and sell a candidate.

Professional Campaign Managers

James Carville, a Washington political consultant, gained national recognition in 1992 when he served as a key behind-the-scenes adviser to Arkansas governor Bill Clinton. During the campaign, a reporter asked Carville to assess his job. He replied: "Let's say you ask a politician what time it is. Some pols will tell you the time. Some will tell you how to build a clock. Bill Clinton will tell you how to build a Swiss village. The consultant's job is to say: 'Governor, just tell them it's time for a change.' " [60]

Today, and for the past three decades, political consultants and professional campaign managers have been part of almost every major campaign. When Rep-

---

[60] *New York Times*, July 16, 1992, p. A11.

BY OHMAN FOR THE OREGONIAN

Copyright © 1990 by Jack Ohman/*The Orgeonian*

James Carville, key campaign advisor to Bill Clinton

resentative John B. Anderson of Illinois decided to run for president in 1980, he hired David Garth, a professional campaign manager with a reputation for a high degree of success.

A colorful, cigar-smoking New Yorker, Garth at one point scribbled a note on a sign-up sheet at Anderson headquarters in Washington. The sheet encouraged campaign workers to enter an upcoming softball game. "We don't have time for softball," Garth wrote. "We're playing hardball." [61]

Garth was quick to defend his craft against critics who argue that professional campaign managers manipulate the voters. "What is not manipulation?" he asked. "One of the great stupidities is that somehow what we do is manipulation, which it is, and that nothing else is. . . . When Roosevelt sat down to discuss his next fireside chat did they say 'You go ahead and say just what you think is right'? What I'm trying to say is, what happens behind the scenes hasn't changed in politics." [62]

Increasingly, at all levels of politics, candidates have turned to professional campaign managers and consultants. The firms earn large fees for their varied services, which include advertising, public relations, research on issues, public opinion sampling, organizing focus groups to test voter reaction, fund raising, telephone solicitations, computer analysis, and speech-writing.

As Larry Sabato has pointed out, however, the importance of campaign consultants can be overstated. "In most elections the new campaign techniques, and the consultants themselves, probably do not make the difference between winning and losing, although they make some difference and in at least a few cases can convincingly be given credit or blame for the margin of victory or defeat." But because consultants are often treated favorably in the press, and are skilled at self-promotion, "the perception is that consultants and technology make the difference in a greater percentage of elections than they likely do." [63]

Sabato suggests that members of the press, who value consultants as key sources of information, tend to treat them "with kid gloves. . . . There is a desperate need for the press to stop treating consultants as the gods of the political wars and to end their sweetheart arrangement." [64] And he adds: "Political consultants and the new campaign technology may be producing a whole generation of officeholders far more skilled at running for office than in the art of governing. Who can forget Robert Redford as a newly elected, media-produced U.S. senator at the end of the film *The Candidate* asking pathetically, 'Now what do I do?'" [65]

In the spring of 1965, when Ronald Reagan was thinking about running for governor of California, he approached the Spencer-Roberts political management firm to see whether it would handle his campaign. Such was the reputation of the California firm that aspirants for political office sought out Spencer-Roberts rather than vice versa. George Christopher, the former mayor of San Francisco (who eventually opposed Reagan in the primary), had also approached Spencer-Roberts. After meeting with Reagan, the political management firm "accepted" him, rather than Christopher, as a client.[66]

[61] *New York Times*, September 19, 1980, p. B1.
[62] Ibid.

[63] Larry J. Sabato, *The Rise of Political Consultants: New Ways of Winning Elections* (New York: Basic Books, Inc., 1981), p. 15.
[64] Ibid., pp. 310–11.
[65] Ibid., p. 337.
[66] James M. Perry, *The New Politics* (New York: Clarkson N. Potter, 1968), pp. 25–26.

CREATING THE REAGAN MYTH

Four years ago, in the midst of another presidential campaign, three experienced political strategists sat in a highly confidential meeting and mapped Ronald Reagan's way to a landslide victory. . . .

The meeting was run by Stuart Spencer, the California political consultant who almost 20 years earlier helped transform Ronald Reagan from a B-grade movie actor into the governor of California, and who is now providing similar services to Republican vice-presidential nominee, Sen. Dan Quayle. Spencer . . . consented to have the discussion taped so that an internal memo could be drafted. The result is a series of recordings that allow the listener to be virtually a fly on the wall in the innermost sanctum of the campaign. . . .

As the June 30, 1984, meeting began, the strategists had already sensed that something crucial was missing. "The problem," Spencer told the others, "is we've been talking to everybody at the White House over the past few days — and the Reagan administration fired all its bullets very early and very successfully in the first two years. All their plans, all their priorities, all their programs. They've run out of ammunition. The most striking thing I discovered is that they don't have a goddam thing in the pipeline. They don't have an idea."

[Robert] Teeter concurred. "Days digging around, and we found nothing," he said. "This is a national election. We've got to find something to say." . . .

Spencer suggested that perhaps they could have Reagan say something about "acid rain and all that stuff," since he was vulnerable on environmental issues. But [Kenneth] Khachigian threw up another red flag. "We're better off without it. If you get the old man going on it, he does 'killer trees,'" he warned, referring to Reagan's embarrassing assertion in 1980 that trees caused pollution. . . .

The three men had no doubt that Reagan would agree to their campaign strategy, even though he hadn't helped draft it. The president's political career was in many ways the product of a revolution in American politics which, well before 1984, had turned campaigns into sophisticated marketing operations run by experts more professional than the candidates themselves. Reagan supplied the broad vision and vocal cords. But from the start, Spencer's consulting firm had done the coaching and packaging, marketing him brilliantly to the most media-oriented state in the country and, later, to the most media-oriented nation in the world. . . .

"The President was never really involved in any of the planning or strategy of the campaign," conceded his campaign manager, Edward J. Rollins. . . . "The truth of the matter is that Ronald Reagan is the perfect candidate. He does whatever you want him to do. And he does it superbly well."

—*Washington Post*, September 18, 1988, adapted from Jane Mayer and Doyle McManus, *Landslide: The Unmaking of the President, 1984–1988*

Spencer-Roberts managed Reagan's successful campaign against incumbent governor Edmund "Pat" Brown, providing a wide range of public relations and other professional services. For example, because Reagan was an actor, some voters felt he was simply playing the part of a candidate and memorizing his speeches. Spencer-Roberts advised Reagan to hold question-and-answer periods after each of his speeches to demonstrate to the voters that he had a real grasp of the issues. The firm's advice helped elect Reagan governor.

From its beginnings in California in the 1930s, campaign management has rapidly grown to the status of being a profitable nationwide industry. Some firms handle only Republican candidates, and others specialize in managing Democrats. Almost inevitably, public relations firms that have branched out into campaign management have evolved from technicians giving advice on press releases to strategists helping candidates make major campaign policy decisions. As Stanley Kelley, Jr., has observed: "It is hard to see why the same trends which have brought the public relations man into political life will not also push him upward in political decision-making. His services are valuable because effective use of the mass media is one of the roads to power in contemporary society, and it is difficult clearly to separate strategic and tactical considerations in that use." [67]

One political scientist, Dan Nimmo, has contended that the use of professional campaign managers raises disturbing questions about American politics. The campaign consultants, he has observed, tend to approach elections as "contests of personalities" rather than choices between political parties or principles. And, he warns, the professional image makers "can make a candidate appear to be what he is not. . . ." [68]

The Polls

Public opinion polls, as pointed out in Chapter 6, are widely used in political campaigns, not only by the news media, but by the candidates themselves. Political candidates are always concerned about their standing in the polls published by the press, but the use of public opinion surveys has become much more sophisticated than a simple comparison of the relative standing of competing candidates. Politicians may order a confidential poll to be taken well before a campaign in order to gauge their potential strength; they may decide whether to run on the basis of the findings.

---

[67] Stanley Kelley, Jr., *Professional Public Relations and Political Power* (Baltimore: Johns Hopkins Press, 1956), p. 212.
[68] Dan Nimmo, *The Political Persuaders* (Englewood Cliffs: Prentice-Hall, 1970), pp. 197–98.

"The President is closing in the polls, but he still needs hurricanes in several key states."

Drawing by Steiner © 1992 The New Yorker Magazine, Inc.

Once candidates are committed to running in a primary or running in a general-election campaign, they may commission private polls to test voter sentiment; these assist them in identifying the issues and planning their campaign strategy. After the campaign is under way, additional private polls are taken to measure the success of the candidate's personal appeal and handling of the issues; both the candidate's style and positions on the issues may be adjusted accordingly. If elected, officials may rely on polls to measure voter reaction to their performance in office.

In the 1992 presidential campaign, President Bush sought to model himself on President Harry S Truman, a Democrat who attacked a "do-nothing" Congress controlled by the Republicans and won the 1948 election despite the fact that the polls showed him behind. (It was soon disclosed that in 1948 Bush had voted not for Truman but for Truman's Republican opponent, Governor Thomas E. Dewey of New York.)

Bush, too, trailed Clinton in the polls by a sizable margin for most of the campaign. Bush also attacked the Democratic-controlled Congress, but there the analogy ended. Political polling had become much more sophisticated since 1948, although not infallible. During the campaign, Bush was never ahead of Clinton in the polls, although he was able significantly to reduce Clinton's lead in the final week of the campaign. And, unlike Truman, he lost.

Political leaders often complain about polls, but almost all candidates rely on them. After Ronald Reagan was first elected president in 1980, it was revealed that during his campaign he had employed a highly sophisticated, computerized polling system. With fresh data flowing in constantly from national-sample interviews and surveys in twenty states, Reagan's staff was able to track shifts in opinion among the electorate, and to take action based on the information. As his chief poll-taker, Richard Wirthlin described it, "Tracking allows you to watch a campaign almost the same way you watch a movie." [69]

In 1988, Dukakis trailed Bush in the polls during the fall campaign. Some Dukakis supporters argued that the polls helped Bush by persuading voters that the contest was really over before election day, that they might as well get on the bandwagon and vote for a winner. Or, Dukakis supporters who thought the race was over might not vote at all. "The business of polls is really having a terrible effect. . . . It's terrible,"

---

[69] *Time*, September 15, 1980.

Dukakis complained in Ohio in mid-October, after a *Wall Street Journal*/NBC News poll showed Bush ahead by seventeen points.[70] The Democratic nominee argued that matters had reached the point where "polls drive the process."[71]

In 1992, it was Bush's turn to complain about the polls, which showed him trailing Clinton during the entire general election campaign. In the week after the final televised debate, Bush—again modeling himself on Harry Truman—took a whistle-stop train tour through three southern states. He told the crowd gathered along the tracks:

"Don't believe these crazy polls. Don't believe these nutty pollsters. Don't let these guys tell you what you think. You have a debate, you see what you think, and then two seconds later some crackpot comes on and tells you what you think. We don't need that in the United States."[72]

But whether polls influence voters and affect election outcomes is not entirely clear. It might also be argued that polls are merely a mirror reflecting public opinion at a given moment. And candidates who are leading in the polls also may worry that their supporters will be less inclined to bother to vote. (For further discussion of the possible impact of polls on elections, see Chapter 6, pp. 192–193.)

There is a close interrelationship among the various tools and techniques of the "new politics." The images candidates try to project on television may be tailored to the advice provided by professional campaign managers, who in turn rely on polls they have taken or commissioned. Many of these expensive, interlocking, and highly professionalized services were relatively new in the campaigns of the 1960s; today they are taken for granted.

The Press

After he lost the governor's race in California in 1962, Richard Nixon held a famous news conference in which he declared: "You won't have Nixon to kick around any more, because, gentlemen, this is my last press conference. . . ." The press, Nixon added, should recognize "that they have a right and a responsibility, if they're against a candidate, to give him the shaft, but also recognize if they give him the shaft, put one lonely reporter on the campaign who will report what the candidate says now and then."[73]

Nixon was exhausted and upset when he made these remarks, but his comments reflected his feelings after the 1960 presidential campaign and the 1962 California contest that he had been treated unfairly by the press. The complaint was not a new one; in 1807 President Jefferson had lamented "the falsehoods of a licentious press."

Modern candidates for political office can ill afford to ignore the press. In 1960 a mutual hostility developed between the press and Nixon, who allowed himself to be interviewed by only a few favored correspondents. By contrast, John F. Kennedy and his staff cultivated the friendship of the reporters assigned to his campaign, and a friendly atmosphere prevailed on his press plane. Eight years later, Nixon ran for president again, this time successfully. Determined not to repeat his earlier mistake, Nixon in 1968 paid great personal attention to the creature comforts of the reporters traveling with him; his staff was available to the press and conspicuously affable.[74]

But sometimes campaign staffs try to shield their candidates from the press, to avoid news conferences where a candidate may say something embarrassing. In 1988, for example, when Republican candidate George Bush arrived at Newark International Airport during

---

[73] Earl Mazo and Stephen Hess, *Nixon: A Political Portrait* (New York: Harper & Row, 1968), p. 282.

[74] See White, *The Making of the President 1960*, pp. 336–38, and *The Making of the President 1968*, p. 327.

---

[70] *Washington Post*, October 18, 1988, p. 1.

[71] Ibid.

[72] Bush statement while campaigning in South Carolina, October 20, 1992, broadcast by NBC News on the "Today" show, October 21, 1992.

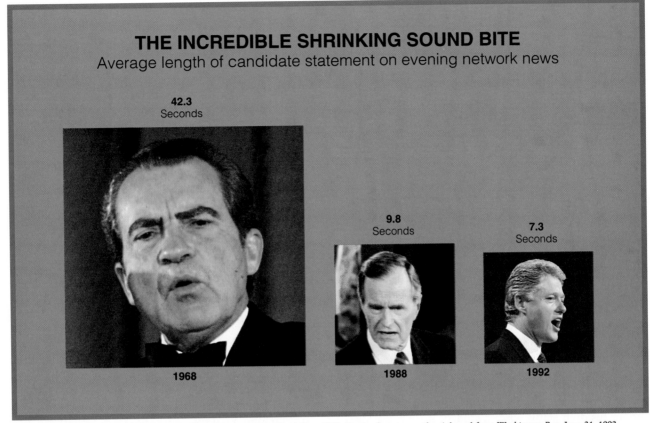

THE INCREDIBLE SHRINKING SOUND BITE
Average length of candidate statement on evening network news

42.3 Seconds

1968

9.8 Seconds

1988

7.3 Seconds

1992

Source: Kiku Adatto. Harvard University; Center for Media and Public Affairs. 1992 data for first six months. Adapted from *Washington Post*, June 21, 1992.

the campaign, reporters and photographers were kept fifty yards away—behind police barricades. A *Washington Post* article captured the scene: "'Come over here,' journalists bellowed at the vice president, trying to get him to answer impromptu questions. Bush cupped an ear, in a manner made familiar by his mentor, President Reagan, and disappeared instead into his limousine."[75]

Reporters covering Bush were so frustrated in their attempts to question him about his running mate, Dan Quayle, that they produced two small bullhorns to amplify their questions. Bush smiled at the ploy, but did not answer.[76]

In most presidential election years, more newspapers have endorsed Republican presidential candidates than Democratic candidates in their editorials. "Democratic candidates probably have to work a little harder at cultivating good relations [with the press] in order to help counteract the editorial slant of most papers. But Republicans have to work a little harder to win the sympathies of reporters of liberal tendency who dominate the national press corps."[77]

No doubt personal bias does color reporting at times. However, it is also true that the personal politics of news reporters may not be reflected in their stories, since many news reporters attempt to adhere to professional standards of fairness in covering the candidates. For example, despite charges by the Nixon administration that reporters have a Democratic and liberal bias, it was the intense coverage of Senator Thomas F. Eagleton's medical history—perhaps more than any other factor—that forced him to resign from the Democratic ticket in 1972. The highly publicized Eagleton story was helpful to Nixon and very damaging to George McGovern's campaign for president. Again in 1984, the supposedly liberal press intensely scrutinized the finances of Geraldine Ferraro, the Democratic vice-presidential

[75] *Washington Post*, September 21, 1988, p. 1.
[76] *New York Times*, October 8, 1988, p. A35.

[77] Polsby and Wildavsky, *Presidential Elections*, 6th ed., p. 187.

THE CAMPAIGN: "SOME KIND OF A CROSS-COUNTRY RACE"

Reporters and candidates live at a breakneck pace during presidential campaigns. A sense of the hectic nature of life on the campaign trail was captured by author Timothy Crouse in a conversation with reporter James Doyle of the *Washington Star:*

Doyle was slouching in an armchair by the picture window of his bedroom, dead tired from a week on the road. . . . He took a gulp of beer and looked out the window at the sun setting on the river.

"A lot of people," he said, "look at this coverage as if it were some kind of a cross-country race — you gotta get two paragraphs in when he stops at Indianapolis and two more when he stops at Newark. If you do it that way, without mak-ing any meaning out of it, it is going to come out like some crazy disjointed trip across the country.

"The problem is, if you try to write every day, you get caught up in sheer exhaustion. It's as simple as that. You do it by rote, because that's all you've got the energy for. It's the lack of sleep, the keeping up with deadlines, the disorientation from all this flying around — your mind just goes blank after a while. When it comes time to write the story, all you can do is just kind of a level job of stumbling through the day's events. I don't think I know how to cover a campaign."

—Timothy Crouse, *The Boys on the Bus*

candidate, and her husband. The controversy bogged down the Mondale-Ferraro campaign for weeks in its critical early stages. And in 1992, the press spent more time on the question of whether Clinton told the truth about his draft status while a student during the Vietnam War than it did, until just before the election, on the question of whether Bush told the truth about the extent of his involvement in the Iran-contra scandal while vice-president.

National political correspondents and columnists play an influential role in interpreting political developments and even in recruiting candidates. Speculation in the press about who may or may not become a candidate and published stories analyzing the relative strengths and abilities of rival contenders may affect what happens at the conventions and on Election Day.

In contrast, editorial support of political candidates by newspapers has a less demonstrable effect on the outcome of presidential campaigns. (See Table 8–2.) During the New Deal years, Roosevelt was consistently opposed by one-half to two-thirds of the nation's daily newspapers; Harry Truman in 1948 and John Kennedy in 1960 were endorsed by only 15 percent of the daily papers, but both won. So did Jimmy Carter in 1976 with endorsements from only 12 percent of the daily papers.

Despite the emphasis on television in politics, there are some 115 million daily-newspaper readers in the United States, and the impressions they receive in political campaigns are formed in part by what they read. As a result, candidates must include the written press in their calculations of campaign techniques and strategy, even if they rely on television for direct mass appeal to the electorate.

Table 8-2
Political Division of Daily Newspapers in Presidential Elections, 1932–92*

Year	Republican	Democratic	Independent or Neutral
1932	55.5%	38.7%	5.8%
1936	60.4	34.5	5.1
1940	66.3	20.1	13.6
1944	60.1	22.0	17.9
1948	65.2	15.4	19.4
1952	67.3	14.5	18.2
1956	59.0	17.0	24.0
1960	54.0	15.0	31.0
1964	34.7	42.4	22.9
1968†	60.8	14.0	24.0
1972	71.4	5.3	23.3
1976	62.0	12.0	26.0
1980‡	42.2	12.0	42.0
1984	57.7	9.4	32.7
1988	31.2	13.3	55.4
1992§	14.9	18.3	66.8

* Figures represent percentages of total number of papers replying to questionnaires. The number responding varied from year to year.
† Wallace had the support of 1.2 percent.
‡ Anderson had the support of 3.8 percent.
§ Perot had the support of .12 percent.
SOURCE: Data for 1932–1960 from William B. Dickinson, Jr., "Politicians and the Press," in Richard M. Boeckel, ed., *Editorial Research Reports*, vol. 2, no. 2 (September 2, 1964), p. 659. Data for 1964–1984 from *Editor & Publisher*, October 31, 1964; November 2, 1968; November 4, 1972; October 30, 1976; November 1, 1980; November 3, 1984; November 5, 1988; and November 7, 1992.

CAMPAIGN FINANCE

When Abraham Lincoln ran for Congress in 1846, it cost him 75 cents: "I made the canvass on my own horse; my entertainment, being at the houses of friends, cost me nothing; and my only outlay was 75¢ for a barrel of cider, which some farm-hands insisted I should treat to." [78]

Clearly, times have changed. The immense cost of American political campaigns can be seen at a glance from these figures, which represent total spending at all levels in presidential years since 1972:

$425 million in 1972	$1.8 billion in 1984
$540 million in 1976	$2.7 billion in 1988
$1.2 billion in 1980	$3.0 billion in 1992[79]

By the presidential election of 1976, the nature of political spending in the United States had been significantly reshaped by Watergate, Congress, and the Su-

SOFT MONEY

© 1980 Herblock

preme Court. For the first time, under the Federal Election Campaign Act of 1974 and its 1976 amendments, both major candidates, Jimmy Carter and Gerald Ford, financed their election campaigns in 1976 with federal funds; each candidate spent the approximately $22 million allotted to him under law. Major-party presidential candidates have continued to use federal funds since then. In 1988, for example, Bush and Dukakis each received $46.1 million in public money.[80] And in 1992,

[78] Carl Sandburg, *Abraham Lincoln: The Prairie Years*, vol. I (New York: Harcourt Brace & Co., 1926), p. 344.
[79] Alexander and Bauer, *Financing the 1988 Election*, p. 4; and 1992 estimate provided by Herbert E. Alexander, director, Citizens' Research Foundation.
[80] In addition, the two Democratic and Republican presidential candidates in 1988 could accept $8.3 million apiece from their national parties, so that the total federal spending ceiling was $54.4 million for each candidate.

Bush and Clinton each received $55.2 million in public funds.[81] Ross Perot, a billionaire, emphasized that he was spending his own money to pay for his campaign, and he accepted no federal funds. During the campaign he estimated he would spend $60 million to seek the presidency; if so, that would make him the single largest self-contributor in American history.

The presidential election of 1976 was the first in which the law sought to provide effective limits on the size of contributions to candidates. In 1972 Max Palevsky, a California millionaire, gave almost $320,000 to George McGovern, the Democratic candidate. In 1976 he could give only $1,000 to Jimmy Carter. The conclusion that might logically be drawn is that a candidate who receives a $1,000 contribution will feel less obligated to the donor than one who receives $320,000. And that result is what the new law was designed to achieve. But, as will be seen, loopholes developed that greatly weakened the impact of the law.

By the 1988 presidential campaign, so-called "soft-money" and "independent expenditures" on behalf of the presidential candidates totaled as much or more than the funds allotted under the Federal Election Campaign Act. These two types of campaign spending amounted to a huge loophole in the law.

"Soft money" is a term that describes funds raised by the two major political parties, not subject to the limits of federal law, and spent by them in the states to aid candidates *indirectly* in a variety of ways.

"Independent expenditures" are funds spent for or against a candidate by committees not formally con-

nected to a candidate. The groups that raise and distribute these funds are not subject to federal spending regulations.

This gigantic loophole in the law undercut the post-Watergate efforts at reform. Once again, big contributors in corporations and both parties were making contributions of $100,000 or more, gifts to party or "independent" committees that would be illegal if made to the candidates directly. And "soft money" helps candidates — it could be used in 1992, for example, to pay for a billboard that said "Vote Democratic," but not for one that said "Vote for Clinton."

Many critics argued that the interpretation of the 1974 law permitting such unrestricted use of "soft money" was illegal. Others called it "the loophole that ate the law," because political committees could not only accept large donations but did not have to make them public.[82] (See box, below.) Nevertheless, in the 1992 presidential campaign both parties relied heavily on this source of funding. By the start of the 1992 campaign, Republican party officials had raised $41 million in "soft money" and the Democratic party had raised $21 million.[83] The money came from business, individuals, and labor unions. Once again, "fat cats" — big contributors — and special interests were influencing election campaigns.

Money in election campaigns is a subject cloaked by a good deal of secrecy, and a vast amount of confusion. Over the years Congress has attempted to control the sources, amounts, and reporting of campaign ex-

---

[81] *New York Times*, July 10, 1992, p. A18.

[82] *Washington Post*, July 27, 1988, p. A4.
[83] Source: News release, Center for Responsive Politics, "Soft Money Update, September 1992," pp. 1–2.

THE LOOPHOLE THAT ATE THE LAW

The two major presidential candidates each will get $46 million in public funds to run their campaigns, but the amount spent on the presidential race this fall could double that, specialists say.

Much of the additional money will be in the form of unregulated and often unreported contributions from wealthy individuals, corporations, and labor unions not permitted to contribute directly to the campaigns.

But that's only the start. Tens of millions of dollars more will be raised and spent to benefit each presidential candidate, and the total could surpass the public funding, party and outside experts agree. . . .

The most controversial area of this fund-raising is soft money. Some critics call it the loophole that ate the law because political committees are permitted to accept large donations without making them public.

—Charles R. Babcock, *Washington Post*, July 27, 1988

penditures, but it was not until 1974 that the first comprehensive attempt to regulate campaign finance was enacted.

Despite this law, no politician or political scientist would accept the officially reported campaign spending figures as fully reflective of actual political campaign costs. Of the iceberg that is campaign finance, only a portion shows above the surface. Partly as a result, an atmosphere of public cynicism and mistrust has tended to surround the subject of money and politics. Voter attitudes on the subject are reflected in such statements as: "Money wins elections," "Politicians can be bought," or "Politics is a rich man's game."

Widespread financial abuses in President Nixon's 1972 campaign, revealed by the Senate Watergate committee and by the press, increased broad-gauge sentiment for public financing of elections and related reforms. The result was the Federal Election Campaign Act of 1974. (Provisions of the act are summarized on page 298.)

Money *is* important. It did not, however, win the Democratic nomination for Averell Harriman in 1956, nor did it put Nelson Rockefeller in the White House in 1960, 1964, or 1968 — and neither man lacked money. Since the Second World War, the Republicans have generally spent more than the Democrats on national campaigns. Therefore, if money *alone* had determined

the result of presidential elections, the Democrats could not have won. There are, in other words, some limits to the influence of money in elections.

Regulating Campaign Finance

Despite many loopholes that still remain, a series of laws enacted in the 1970s have somewhat strengthened the regulation of campaign spending in federal elections. The previous patchwork of federal legislation had also sought to require disclosure of gifts and expenditures, and to limit amounts spent, but the laws had fallen short of achieving these goals. Most states have campaign financial reporting laws, but they vary greatly and few are stringent.

The Federal Election Campaign Act of 1971 required disclosure of the names of all persons giving more than $100 to a federal campaign, placed limits on what candidates could spend, and repealed the Corrupt Practices Act of 1925, which had failed to limit political spending and did not apply to primary elections. In addition, the law repealed certain provisions of the Hatch Act of 1940, which sought to limit political contributions and spending in federal elections. These provisions had been evaded in actual practice by various subterfuges.

As far back as 1907 Congress prohibited corporations from contributing to candidates for office in federal elections. The Taft-Hartley Act of 1947 bars gifts by labor unions or corporations to federal election campaigns, but the law did not stop unions or corporations from financing political campaigns; they simply set up separate political arms to make campaign contributions, such as the AFL-CIO Committee on Political Education (COPE), and BIPAC, the Business-Industrial Political Action Committee.

In 1971 Congress for the first time let individuals take a limited federal income-tax credit for political contributions. In addition, Congress provided that, starting in 1973, taxpayers could specify that $1 of each person's federal income taxes go into a campaign fund to be distributed among the candidates in the next presidential election. The checkoff law was designed to provide public financing of presidential campaigns in order to free political parties of dependence on private contributions. Beginning in 1974, this option was included in the standard income-tax forms to make it more convenient for taxpayers.

The New Rules As already noted, the Federal Election Campaign Act of 1974 rewrote the laws of campaign finance in the United States. The law was modified by the Supreme Court in *Buckley* v. *Valeo*, an important ruling in January 1976 that opened the way to "independent expenditures." [84] Amendments enacted later that year and in 1979 made further changes. The law as of 1992 provided as follows:

Contribution limits. Individuals may give up to $1,000 to each candidate in each federal election and each primary; up to $5,000 per year to a political action committee, such as those sponsored by corporations or labor unions; and $20,000 per year to a national political-party committee. Total contributions by one person are limited to $25,000 a year. Political action committees that qualify may contribute up to $5,000 to a candidate in each election and each primary.

Public financing. Presidential—but not Senate or House —candidates have the option of accepting federal money to pay for general elections or primaries, as did both major

party candidates in 1992. To qualify for public funds in the primaries, a candidate must raise $5,000 in each of twenty states in contributions of $250 or less, for an overall total of $100,000. In addition, public funds may be used to help each major political party to finance its national convention.

Spending limits. Presidential candidates who accept federal funds are limited to a spending ceiling, set at $55.2 million each for Bush and Clinton in 1992, and in the general election they can accept no private contributions. For each candidate in the presidential primaries who accepted federal funds, the spending limit in 1992 was $33.1 million in both private contributions and federal matching funds.[85]

Disclosure. Candidates must file periodic reports with the government disclosing the names and addresses of all donors of more than $200 and listing all expenditures of more than $200.

Federal Election Commission. The law created a new bipartisan, six-member Federal Election Commission (reconstituted after the Supreme Court decision) to enforce the campaign finance laws and administer the public financing machinery.

The 1974 law had sought to limit campaign expenditures in all federal elections and to restrict individual spending by candidates or their families. But the Supreme Court, ruling that these limits, in general, restricted freedom of expression, struck them down — except for presidential candidates who accept public financing. The Court upheld the limits on contributions, ruling that this imposed less of a burden on free expression.

However, the Supreme Court ruling in *Buckley* v. *Valeo*, the key decision in 1976, permitted "independent expenditures" to be made by committees not formally connected with a candidate. This opened up one part of the enormous loophole in the law discussed earlier in this chapter.

As Elizabeth Drew, a political writer, has noted, "The law that established public financing of Presidential campaigns was intended to remove the role of private money from Presidential contests, but great rivers of private money, much of it untraceable, still flow into them." That is because the "'independent' committees working on a Presidential candidate's behalf . . . are independent in name only." [86]

How Much Does It Cost?

In many districts it costs several hundred thousand dollars to run for Congress; in 1988 the average cost of a

---

[84] *Buckley* v. *Valeo*, 424 U.S. 1 (1976).

[85] The Federal Election Campaign Act of 1974 set the limits for each presidential candidate at $10 million in the primaries and $20 million in the general elections. But the 1976 amendments contained an escalator clause keyed to the cost-of-living index; that is why the dollar totals were higher in subsequent years.

[86] Elizabeth Drew, *Politics and Money: The New Road to Corruption* (New York: Macmillan, 1983), pp. 1 and 2.

House race was $400,000.[87] In 1990, the average was $407,000.[88] But House races can cost more than $1 million in some cases. In 1978, one House candidate, Carter Burden, spent more than $1 million — the first time that threshold had been crossed. By 1986, the number of House races that cost more than $1 million had risen to fifteen.[89] In 1990, 168 candidates reported spending more than half a million dollars on their election campaigns.[90] And in 1990, eleven candidates for the House spent $1 million or more.[91]

To run for the United States Senate, a candidate may spend several million dollars. In 1988, the average cost of Senate campaigns was almost $4 million.[92] In 1990, the average cost of running for the Senate was $3.9 million.[93] All told, House and Senate candidates of both parties spent $457 million in 1988.[94]

The cost of Senate races sometimes soars beyond $10 million. In 1986, Senator Alan Cranston, a Democrat from California, spent $10.9 million to win reelection, and Republican Senator Robert Packwood of Oregon spent $6.2 million and also won reelection.[95] And the cost of Senate races keeps spiraling upward; in 1990, Senator Jesse Helms, the North Carolina Republican, spent $17.8 million to win reelection.[96]

Gubernatorial races also often prove to be very expensive. In 1980 Jay Rockefeller, a member of one of America's wealthiest families and heir to the Standard Oil fortune, spent about $12 million in winning reelection as governor of West Virginia. Almost all of the money was his own.[97]

The Rockefeller campaign was a dramatic example of the enormous financial resources that may be enjoyed by a wealthy candidate, although it paled beside Ross Perot's spending in his campaign for president in 1992. As noted, the 1974 campaign finance act sought to limit

1992: Tipper Gore and Hillary Clinton at the Democratic National Convention

such personal spending in federal elections, but the Supreme Court invalidated those provisions except for presidential (and vice-presidential) candidates who accept public funds.

Running for president is vastly more expensive than running for Congress (although the per capita cost per voter in congressional races is often comparable or sometimes even greater than in presidential campaigns). The cost of nominating and electing a president in 1980, including the preconvention campaigns and the national conventions, was about $275 million.[98] The cost of the 1984 presidential election was even higher, about $325 million, despite the ceiling on the use of public funds.[99] (See Figure 8–3.) And for 1988, the total cost of electing a president had soared to about $500 million.[100] In 1992, the estimated total was not expected to go substantially higher than $500 million, in part because President Bush had no serious challengers for renomination, which held down the cost of the presidential primary campaigns.

Although presidential candidates have been accepting public funds to finance their campaigns, as already noted, as much or more *private* money may be contributed to presidential campaigns through state and local party committees, independent expenditures, and other categories. Of the $500 million spent on the

[87] Alexander and Bauer, *Financing the 1988 Election*, p. 53.
[88] Data provided by Center for Responsive Politics.
[89] *Washington Post*, October 22, 1984, p. A9, and *Common Cause News*, April 7, 1987.
[90] Norman J. Ornstein, Thomas E. Mann, and Michael J. Malbin, *Vital Statistics on Congress 1991–1992* (Washington, D.C.: Congressional Quarterly, Inc., 1992), p. 76.
[91] Larry Makinson, *The Price of Admission: Campaign Spending in the 1990 Election* (Washington, D.C.: Center for Responsive Politics, 1991), p. 35.
[92] Alexander and Bauer, *Financing the 1988 Election*, p. 53.
[93] Data provided by Center for Responsive Politics.
[94] Alexander and Bauer, *Financing the 1988 Election*, p. 53.
[95] *Common Cause News*, February 13, 1987.
[96] Makinson, *The Price of Admission: Campaign Spending in the 1990 Election*, p. 22.
[97] *Washington Post*, November 30, 1980, p. A1.

[98] Alexander and Bauer, *Financing the 1988 Election*, p. 13. Most of the balance of the $500 million total, just under $274 million, was spent on the primary campaigns and the national conventions.
[99] Ibid.
[100] Ibid.

Figure 8–3
Major-Party Campaign Spending in Presidential Elections, 1956–92*

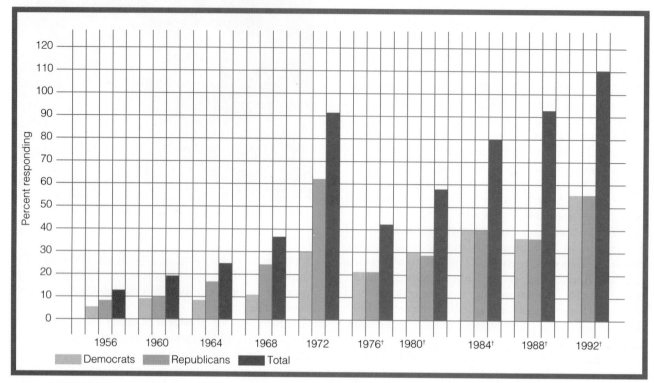

* Figures are for the postconvention campaigns.
† Both major-party presidential candidates accepted public funding in 1976, 1980, 1984, 1988, and 1992. Lower totals for those years reflect limits set for such candidates by the Federal Election Campaign Act of 1974.
SOURCE: Herbert E. Alexander, *Financing Politics: Money, Elections, and Political Reform*, 3rd ed. (Washington, D.C.: Congressional Quarterly Press, 1984). p. 7. Data for 1984, 1988, and 1992 provided by the Federal Election Commission. In 1992, in addition to the totals that include the full spending by major-party national committees shown above, independent candidate Ross Perot said he expected to spend $60 million of his own money to finance his presidential campaign.

presidential election of 1988, for example, in addition to the $92.2 million in public funds spent by the Democrats and Republicans, $116.1 million was spent on the general election campaign by nonpublic sources. Of that total, both major parties spent $61.6 million, including about $45 million in "soft money," $10.2 million went for "independent expenditures," and $27.5 million was spent by labor, corporations, and associations.[101]

Individuals, corporations, and labor unions have channeled money to state parties for voter registration and get-out-the-vote drives, compilation of lists of target voters, promotion of entire party slates, and other "party-building" activities — the so-called "soft money" permitted under amendments to the 1974 law.[102] The

"soft money" also has been used for partisan advertising; even though it must be spent at the state level, considerable benefit may be gained by the party's presidential candidate.[103]

Alexander Heard, author of a number of authoritative studies of campaign finance, has concluded that money is particularly important in "the shadow land of our politics" where it is decided who shall be a nominee of a political party: "Cash is far more significant in the nominating process than in determining the outcome of elections." [104]

---

[101] Adapted from Alexander and Bauer, *Financing the 1988 Election*, p. 12.

[102] Alexander, *Financing Politics: Money, Elections, and Political Reform*, p. 126.

[103] Drew, *Politics and Money: The New Road to Corruption*, pp. 14–18.

[104] Alexander Heard, *The Costs of Democracy* (Chapel Hill: University of North Carolina Press, 1960), pp. 14, 35.

Where Does the Money Go?

Today, radio and television costs are by far the biggest single item in campaign spending at the presidential level. In 1980 about $30.7 million, or more than a third of all presidential campaign expenditures, was spent on political broadcasting.[105] By 1984, the total had risen to $41.3 million.[106] In 1988, the presidential candidates spent $52.5 million on television advertising.[107] In 1992, by late-October, one week before election day, the three presidential candidates had spent more than $40 million to purchase TV time on the three broadcast networks. The breakdown showed that Clinton spent only $5.4 million on network television ads compared with $17.5 million spent by President Bush and $19.8 million by Ross Perot.[108]

Political committees also spend money on other forms of publicity and advertising. They must pay for polls and data processing, printing costs, telephone bills, headquarters costs, and salaries of party workers. A great deal of money is spent on Election Day to pay poll workers, to provide transportation to get the voters to the polls — and, sometimes, illicitly, to pay voters. Alexander Heard has estimated that Election Day spending accounts for "as much as one-eighth of the total election bill in the United States." [109]

Where Does the Money Come From?

By the 1980s, *political action committees* (PACs) had become a powerful and controversial source of campaign money. PACs are independent organizations, or more often, political arms of corporations, unions, or

"Senator, according to this report, you're marked for defeat by the A.D.A., the National Rifle Association, the A.F.L.-C.I.O., the N.A.M., the Sierra Club, Planned Parenthood, the World Student Christian Federation, the Clamshell Alliance . . ."

Drawing by Dana Fradon
© 1980 The New Yorker Magazine, Inc.

interest groups. (See Chapter 6 for a detailed discussion of PACs and single-issue groups.) PAC spending in all 1984 campaigns at the federal level totaled $267 million. That total increased to $340 million in 1986 and to an estimated $425 million in 1988.[110]

Although in the past business PACs may have contributed more to Republican candidates, that pattern has changed. PACs now tend to give to candidates already serving in Congress (and who therefore have a better chance of winning), not to their challengers. "The big news in 1988 was the shift in giving by business PACs," Herbert E. Alexander and Monica Bauer reported. "PACs have tended to move away from ideology and instead have become incumbent-oriented. . . . Three out of four PAC dollars in 1988 went to incumbents of both parties." [111]

By 1992 the number of PACs had increased rapidly to some 4,100, up from 600 two decades earlier. The growth of PACs was due, in part, to the 1976 Supreme Court decision permitting "independent expenditures" in political campaigns by groups not formally connected with a candidate.[112] PACs often contribute to political

[105] Adapted from Alexander, *Financing Politics: Money, Elections, and Political Reform*, p. 13.

[106] Adapted from Alexander and Haggerty, *Financing the 1984 Election*, pp. 345, 369.

[107] Alexander and Bauer, *Financing the 1988 Election*, p. 98.

[108] *New York Times*, October 27, 1992, p. A19.

[109] Heard, *The Costs of Democracy*, p. 394.

[110] Data provided by Herbert E. Alexander, director, Citizens' Research Foundation.

[111] Alexander and Bauer, *Financing the 1988 Election*, pp. 68–69.

[112] *Buckley* v. *Valeo* (1976).

campaigns because they hope a candidate will support legislation that will benefit a specific industry, union, or interest group. Elizabeth Drew has suggested that PAC money in turn has led candidates "to solicit and accept money from those most able to provide it, and to adjust their behavior in office to the need for money — and the fear that a challenger might be able to obtain more." [113]

The reasons why people give money to campaigns vary widely. Some contributors simply believe in a party or a candidate and wish to express their support. Others give because they do expect some tangible benefit or reward from the winning candidate. Others hope to buy access to a public official; for some who long for social recognition, an invitation to a White House dinner may be reward enough. [114]

Some of America's wealthiest families have contributed heavily to political campaigns. The bulk of the contributions from these families — whose wealth is rooted in the oil, steel, auto, railroad, and other large industries — went to the Republican party. While the contribution limits in the 1974 act have reduced the influence of individual donors, wealthy individuals and families can still contribute substantially to congressional and presidential candidates, since the law permits an aggregate contribution of $25,000 a year by each person. And the federal law does not apply in state or local elections, where wealthy individuals can make their presence felt.

Both major parties rely on a variety of sources to raise money: PAC contributions, individual contributions from the public, $100-a-plate and even $1,000-a-plate dinners, direct mail solicitation, televised appeals, contributions from members of labor unions and corporation executives, and corporate advertising in convention programs and political booklets.

An unadvertised source of campaign funds is the underworld. In some communities close ties exist between organized crime and politics; elected officials may take graft to protect criminal operations, and sometimes the payoffs take the form of campaign contributions. Heard has guessed that perhaps "15 percent of political campaign expenditures at state and local levels" comes from the underworld. [115]

Campaigns, Money, and Democracy

The reforms in the election laws during the 1970s sought to limit contributions, to provide meaningful public disclosure of campaign gifts and spending (in place of laws that invited evasion), to broaden the base of campaign giving through tax incentives, and to provide government subsidies. These reforms were based on the beliefs that candidates should not have to depend on big contributors to whom they might become obligated and that roughly equal resources should be available to candidates for public office.

The case for reform was compelling, since inadequate controls only served to reinforce voter cynicism about politics. But the growth and influence of "independent expenditures" and "soft money" have mocked these reforms. Because of the limited success of the 1974 law, there were pressures for further change.

Many analysts feel that special-interest money from PACs has achieved undue influence in the electoral process. In 1988 Michael Dukakis refused to accept PAC money in the primary election campaigns. Almost eight years earlier, President Carter, in his farewell address to the nation, warned that "single-issue groups and special-interest organizations" had become "a disturbing factor in American political life." [116]

As presidential candidates have relied more on public funding, PAC money has been diverted elsewhere. In 1992, as in previous campaigns, millions of dollars in special-interest money that might otherwise have gone into the presidential campaign was funneled into congressional campaigns through political action committees.

The growth and power of the PACs threatened to undermine the reforms of the federal election laws. The increase in "independent expenditures" and "soft money" had diminished the impact of the Federal Election Campaign Act. Various suggestions have been made for controlling PACs and plugging loopholes in the law. Some analysts also have suggested that public financing, available since 1976 in presidential campaigns, be extended to congressional campaigns.

Many problems remain. Loopholes in the law and the fact that some candidates have unequal financial resources, for example, tend to undermine public confidence in the American political process. And campaigns

---

[113] Drew, *Politics and Money: The New Road to Corruption*, p. 1.
[114] For a discussion of the complex motives for campaign giving, see Heard, *The Costs of Democracy*, Chapter 4.
[115] Heard, *The Costs of Democracy*, p. 163.

[116] *New York Times*, January 15, 1981, p. B10.

are a vital part of that process, for, within limits, they give the voters a chance to decide who shall govern.

PERSPECTIVE

For every candidate, between nomination and election there stands the campaign. In American politics, the campaign is the battleground of power. Victory may depend on how well the battle is fought during the campaign. Mostly because of the wide use of television, campaigns are expensive.

Campaigns are organized chaos. On a national level, large numbers of people, professionals and volunteers, are thrown together for a relatively short period of time to mount an incredibly complex effort to elect a president. A presidential candidate must have an elaborate campaign organization with a headquarters staff to plan and coordinate the total effort. A candidate's staff typically includes a campaign manager and a small group of top-level aides to give overall direction to the campaign, a person in charge of fund raising, a media team to handle advertising and television, a press secretary, representatives to handle advance details of personal appearances, speech-writers, regional and state coordinators, and citizens' groups to enlist volunteer support. And the campaign staff must attempt to coordinate the work of national, state, and local party organizations.

Studies have shown that many voters are committed to one candidate or another in advance of the campaign. But often a third or more of the people make up their minds during the campaign, and their votes may well determine the outcome of the election. In close elections, the undecided voters may hold the key to victory. Political candidates try to preserve their party base while winning over voters from the other party, the independents, and the undecided. Campaigns, therefore, are an important part of the political process.

Presidential candidates must, as a rule, enter the primaries to win their party's nomination. For relatively unknown political candidates, the primary route may prove an attractive means of demonstrating their strength and gaining nationwide exposure in the media. One presidential candidate who found another way to gain the public's attention was Ross Perot, the Texas businessman who did not enter the primaries in 1992, but captured an enormous amount of free television time and media attention by challenging the major-party candidates — Bill Clinton, the Democratic candidate, and President George Bush, the Republican candidate. Perot built an organization of "volunteers," many of them paid, but did not run on a party label.

An incumbent president may lose the election, but he starts out with a potential advantage over an opponent in a presidential campaign. Not only do the prestige and power of the office follow the president on the hustings, but all the visible trappings go along as well. He already has a large, highly organized staff, and all the advantages of White House communications and other facilities. He may be able to dominate the news by taking actions as president that are timed for maximum political advantage.

Peace and pocketbook issues have tended to dominate presidential campaigns. Democratic candidates since the New Deal have campaigned on the party's efforts to achieve social progress at home. In the area of foreign affairs, the Republicans often have an advantage. However, a sudden foreign-policy crisis, a personal scandal, a chance remark—these and other imponderables—may affect voter attitudes in political campaigns. Sometimes the issues become submerged as the candidates attack each other in what is known as "negative campaigning."

In 1960, for the first time, the major-party presidential candidates were able to reach vast audiences in a series of televised debates. In 1992, record-breaking audiences watched the presidential and vice-presidential debates, reflecting widespread interest that had not been visible early in the campaign.

The ability of political candidates to reach increased numbers of voters through television commercials has been reflected in a dramatic rise in campaign spending for TV broadcasts. In 1992, as in other recent elections, the major candidates paid for large numbers of television commercials to get their message to the voters. All three candidates also appeared, to a much greater extent than in any past campaign, on the major television talk and entertainment shows. With access to an audience of millions of voters through the electronic media, a political candidate may be tempted to display an "image" that masks the real person, to present the issues in capsulized, simplistic form, and become a performer rather than a leader.

At all levels of politics, candidates have turned to professional campaign managers and consultants. The firms earn large fees for their varied services which include advertising, public relations, research on issues, public opinion sampling, fund raising, telephone solicitations, computer analysis, and speech-writing. Opinion polls are widely used in political campaigns, not only by the news media, but by the candidates themselves to test voter sentiment, and to assist them in identifying the issues and planning their campaign strategy.

By the presidential election of 1976, the nature of political spending in the United States had been signifi-

cantly reshaped by Watergate, Congress, and the Supreme Court. For the first time, under the Federal Election Campaign Act of 1974 and its 1976 amendments, both major candidates, Jimmy Carter and Gerald Ford, financed their election campaigns in 1976 with federal funds. Major-party presidential candidates have continued to use federal funds since then, as did Bush and Clinton in 1992. But candidates also rely heavily on "soft money" and "independent expenditures" that amount to as much or more than the allotted federal funds. Ross Perot, a billionaire, emphasized that he was spending his own money to pay for his campaign, and he accepted no federal funds.

The Federal Election Campaign Act of 1974 revamped the laws governing campaign finance in the United States. As of 1992, after various modifications, the law provided: (1) individuals could give up to $1,000 to each candidate in each federal election or primary; (2) total contributions by one person were limited to $25,000 per year; (3) presidential candidates had the option of accepting federal money to pay for general elections or primaries; (4) candidates who accepted federal funds were then limited to a spending ceiling and could accept no private contributions for the general election; and (5) candidates were required to file periodic reports with the government disclosing the names and addresses of all donors of more than $200 and listing all expenditures of more than $200. But loopholes—particularly the use of "soft money" and "independent expenditures"—had substantially weakened the impact of the law.

By the 1980s, political action committees (PACs) had become a powerful and controversial source of campaign money. By 1992 the number of PACs had increased rapidly to some 4,100. PACs are independent organizations or, more often, political arms of corporations, unions, or interest groups. PACs often contribute to political campaigns because they hope a candidate will support legislation benefitting a specific interest.

Suggested Reading

Alexander, Herbert E. *Financing Politics: Money, Elections, and Political Reform*, 3rd edition (Congressional Quarterly Press, 1984). A comprehensive analysis of how campaign money is raised, spent, and regulated. Examines campaign financing in the 1976 and later national elections, traces the impact of election law reforms, and speculates on the role of money in politics during the 1980s.

Barber, James David. *The Pulse of Politics: Electing Presidents in the Media Age** (Transaction Publications, 1992). An interesting study of presidential campaigns and presidencies in the twentieth century. Emphasizes the role played by journalists and the news media in presidential politics.

Bibby, John F. *Politics, Parties, and Elections in America*, 2nd edition** (Nelson-Hall, 1992). An overview of the role of the Republican and Democratic parties in recruiting leaders, nominating candidates, and contesting elections. Argues that political parties are still a strong force in American elections even though many voters do not vote for the candidate of their party.

Cramer, Richard Ben. *What it Takes: The Way to the White House* (Random House, 1992). A colorful portrait of the lives of six 1988 presidential hopefuls and their families, by a Pulitzer Prize-winning journalist. Examines the forces that drove Joseph Biden, Gary Hart, Michael Dukakis, Richard Gephardt, George Bush, and Bob Dole to seek the presidency, and how political candidates sacrifice privacy for power.

Drew, Elizabeth. *Politics and Money: The New Road to Corruption* (Macmillan, 1983). A thoughtful and disturbing analysis of campaign finance. Drew emphasizes the loopholes that now exist in the 1974 Federal Election Campaign Act, and argues that the raising and spending of campaign funds is corrupting the democratic process.

Heard, Alexander. *The Costs of Democracy* (University of North Carolina Press, 1967). (Originally published in 1960.) A comprehensive and useful analysis of the relationships between money and politics. Examines the motives for campaign contributions, who contributes, techniques for raising money, past efforts to regulate campaign financing, and some of the political consequences of various campaign financing practices. Makes specific policy recommendations.

Jamieson, Kathleen Hall. *Dirty Politics: Deception, Distraction, and Democracy* (Oxford University Press, 1992). A careful analysis of deceptive television ads and other manipulative practices used in modern election contests. Argues that the news media focuses too much attention on the polls and the candidates' campaign strategy and gives too little attention to the candidates' proposals.

Kelley, Stanley, Jr. *Professional Public Relations and Political Power* (Johns Hopkins Press, 1956). An influential early analysis of the use of public relations techniques on behalf of candidates for public office and in campaigns focused on specific political issues. Kelley traces the rise of professional public relations firms that are involved in politics, examines the political role of public relations specialists, and assesses the consequences for American politics.

McGinniss, Joe. *The Selling of the President, 1968** (Pocket Books, 1984). (Originally published in 1969.) A critical, behind-the-scenes description of Richard Nixon's use of television in the 1968 presidential campaign by a writer who had extensive access to the advertising, television, and political advisers of the Republican candidate.

Maisel, Louis Sandy. *Parties and Elections in America: The Electoral Process** (Random House, 1987). An excellent general analysis of how election campaigns are conducted in America. The author was himself a major-party candidate for the U.S. House of Representatives.

Nimmo, Dan. *The Political Persuaders: The Techniques of Modern Election Campaigns* (Prentice-Hall, 1970). A valuable survey of campaign techniques in the television age. Includes discussions of campaign management, political polls and statistical analysis of the electorate, and the use of mass media to try to influence voters.

Polsby, Nelson W., and Wildavsky, Aaron B. *Presidential Elections*, 8th edition** (Free Press, 1991). An excellent, concise analysis of the basic strategic considerations affecting the conduct of presidential election campaigns.

Sabato, Larry J. *The Rise of Political Consultants: New Ways of Winning Elections* (Basic Books, 1981). A lively discussion of the role of professional political consultants, whose wide-ranging services have become a familiar part of modern election campaigns. Discusses the new campaign technology and the problems that have accompanied the rise of consultants.

Schram, Martin. *The Great American Video Game: Presidential Politics in the Television Age** (William Morrow, 1987). A lively account of how the 1984 presidential campaign was covered on national and local television. Provides examples of how campaign managers try to manipulate the news in order to benefit their candidate.

Wayne, Stephen J. *The Road to the White House, 1992: The Politics of Presidential Elections*, 4th edition** (St. Martin's Press, 1991). A clearly written analysis of the strategy and tactics of winning the American presidency. Includes sections on campaign finance, delegate selection, national conventions, the media, and voting.

White, Theodore H. *The Making of the President 1972* (Atheneum, 1973); *The Making of the President 1968* (Atheneum, 1969); *The Making of the President 1964* (Atheneum, 1965); *The Making of the President 1960** (Atheneum, 1961). Colorful detailed accounts of American presidential campaigns, set against the background of the social and cultural forces at work in American society. White, a leading political analyst, had access to many of the political figures he wrote about.

---

* Available in paperback edition.

THERE COMES a moment in every campaign when the bands are silent and the cheering stops. The candidate has given the last speech, made the last promise, answered the last question from reporters, smiled at the red light on the TV camera for the last time. There is nothing left to do but to board the campaign plane and fly home to await the verdict of the voters.

There is a certain majesty and mystery in this moment, for until the votes are counted, no one — not the candidates, the voters, the poll-takers, the news reporters, not even the computers blinking and buzzing in the control centers of the television networks — knows what the precise outcome will be.

Chapter 9

Voting Behavior and Elections

In a democracy, the people choose who shall govern, and that choice is expressed in the voting booth. Although the right to vote is basic to the American political system, it is not as common elsewhere as might be thought. Only about half of the world's countries hold regular free elections in which the people may choose among rival candidates.

Chapter 1 examined the reciprocal nature of power in a democracy: government makes authoritative, binding decisions about who gets what in society, but derives its power from the people. People may influence government in a number of ways — by taking part in political activity, by the opinions they hold, by belonging to interest groups, by direct action. But a fundamental way that people influence government is through the ballot box; voting is a very powerful "input" in the political system.

For example, as the presidential election of 1992 demonstrated, one of the most potent weapons of popular control in a democracy is the ability of the electorate to remove a party from power. In that year, Governor Bill Clinton of Arkansas, the Democratic challenger, defeated the Republican incumbent, President George Bush.

In the federal system that exists in the United States, the voters choose at all levels of government. In a presidential year, for instance, the voters select many of the more than 500,000 local, state, and federal elected officials, including the president and vice-president, 435 members of the House, one-third of the Senate, and 12 state governors.

American voters normally may choose among two or more competing candidates for the same office. In a democracy, voting is an act of choice among alternative candidates, parties, and, depending on the election, alternative policies.

Under a democratic form of government, then, the voter is theoretically supreme. Yet, as we have seen, there is often a gap between democratic theory and practice. For example, candidates for public office — at least below the presidential level — may compete with vastly unequal financial resources. TV commercials may attempt to manipulate the voters and create "images" of candidates, rather than informing the electorate. What the voters perceive may sometimes be distorted if one

side or the other engages in unethical campaign practices or "dirty tricks." Some voters may be unenthusias-
tic about the nominees of *both* major parties and may
believe that their choice is between the lesser of two
evils. In some years, they may choose to support a
minor-party or independent candidate. Or they may
easily come to feel that, for them, voting is a waste of
time.

In this chapter we shall examine some central
questions about voting in a democratic society: Do
enough people vote? Why do large numbers of people
fail to vote? How do voters make up their minds? What
do elections mean in a democracy — do voters speak in a
voice that can be understood by those whom they elect?
Do their votes influence government policies?

WHO VOTES?

The voter may have the final say in the United States —
but how many people vote? To those who hold an idealized view of representative democracy, the statistics are
bound to be disappointing. In some elections there are
as many nonvoters as voters.

The Voter

Half or more of the Americans of voting age have voted
for president in each election since 1928. But in nonpresidential election years, considerably less than half
have bothered to vote for members of Congress. In the

Figure 9–1
Voter Participation in Presidential and House Elections, 1960–92

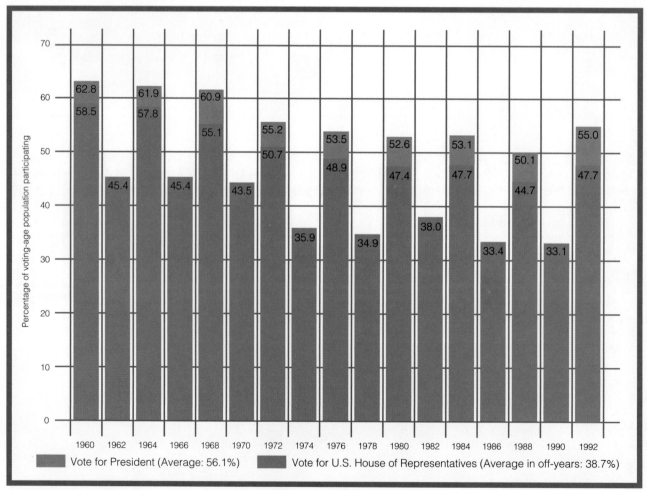

SOURCE: *Statistical Abstract of the United States: 1991* (Washington, D.C.: U.S. Government Printing Office, 1991), p. 270; data for 1990 provided by the
Elections Research Center, Washington, D.C., and data for 1992 provided by the Committee for the Study of the American Electorate, Washington, D.C.,
and *Congressional Quarterly,* Weekly Report, November 7, 1992, pp. 3600–3607.

Figure 9–2
Voter Participation in Presidential Elections, 1880–1992

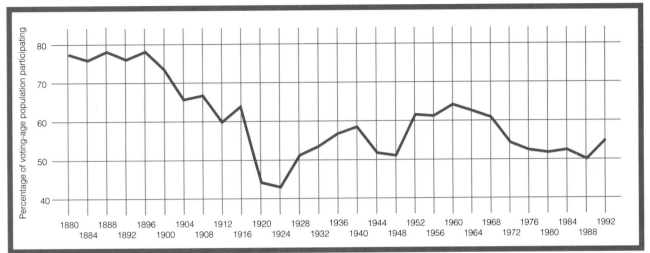

SOURCE: Figures for 1880 to 1916 in Robert E. Lane, *Political Life* (New York: The Free Press, 1965), p. 20. Reprinted with permission of Macmillan Publishing Co. Inc. from *Political Life* by Robert E. Lane. Copyright © 1959 by the Free Press. Figures for 1920 to 1948 in *Statistical Abstract of the United States 1969*, p. 368. Data for 1952 to 1980 from *Statistical Abstract of the United States: 1984*, p. 262. Data for 1984 from *Washington Post*, January 8, 1985, p. A3. Data for 1988 from *New York Times*, November 13, 1988, p. 32, and data for 1992 provided by the Committee for the Study of the American Electorate, Washington, D.C.

eight off-year congressional elections since 1962, an average of only 38.7 percent voted for the House of Representatives. By contrast, in the nine presidential elections from 1960 through 1992, an average of 56.1 percent cast their ballots for president. During these elections, voter turnout declined in every presidential year but two; the 1988 turnout was the lowest since 1924. In 1992, however, the voter turnout for president increased substantially — from 50.1 percent in 1988 to 55 percent four years later. (See Figure 9–1.)

Although twentieth-century Americans have made great technological progress, their forebears in the horse-and-buggy era scored much higher in voting participation. A much larger proportion of voters took part in presidential elections in the 1890s than in 1992. In the election of 1896, for example, almost 80 percent of all of the eligible voters cast their ballots. The drop in turnout is often attributed to the fact that the adoption of women's suffrage in 1920 brought into the electorate a large new group unaccustomed to voting. But the decline in voter participation had begun well before then. After voter turnout dipped to a low point in the early 1920s, it moved to generally higher levels in 1928 and in subsequent elections. (See Figure 9–2.) Despite this trend, voting participation in the United States is substantially lower than it is in many other countries of the world, including Great Britain, Germany, France, and Canada. (See Table 9–1.) Because other nations

calculate voter turnout in varying ways, however, the comparison with the United States is not precise.

Socioeconomic Factors It is clear that who votes varies with factors of geography, age, sex, education, ethnic background, religion, income, social class, and occupation. This does not necessarily mean that people

Table 9-1
Voter Participation in Other Countries

Nation	Election Date	Turnout
Australia*	1990	96%
Belgium	1991	85
Canada	1988	76
France	1988	84
Germany	1990	78
Great Britain	1992	78
Greece	1990	82
India	1989	61
Ireland	1990	64
Netherlands	1989	85
New Zealand†	1990	85
Portugal	1991	69
Switzerland	1991	46

* Compulsory registration and voting
† Compulsory registration
SOURCE: Data for 1988–1991 from *Electoral Studies*, Vol. 8, No. 3 (1989); Vol. 9, No. 3 (1990); Vol. 10, No. 3 (1991). Data for 1992 provided by David E. Butler.

vote or do not vote *because* of such social, demographic, and economic factors; it merely means that these factors often coincide with higher or lower voting participation.[1] For example, regional differences in voter participation may be associated with social and economic factors in those areas, the degree of two-party competition, and, in some cases, differences in the election laws governing registration and voting.

Middle-aged people vote more than the young or the very old. Although some college students and young people take an active part in election campaigns, poll data indicate that over 50 percent of Americans between the ages of eighteen and twenty-four did not register to vote in 1988.[2] In the past, studies showed that voting and political participation increase slowly with age, peak in the mid-forties and fifties, and decline after age sixty.[3]

During the first several decades after the women's suffrage amendment was ratified in 1920, men voted more than women. By 1988, however, the percent of women who turned out to vote was nearly 2 percent higher than that of men.[4] Because there are more women than men in the U.S. population, in absolute numbers there are likely to be more women than men voters in future elections. Sandra Baxter and Marjorie Lansing concluded in a 1980 study, "A major shift has occurred in the voting balance in the last decade: more women than men have gone to the polls to vote for president."[5]

College graduates vote substantially more than people with high-school or grade-school educations. One survey found that 77.6 percent of college-educated Americans reported that they voted in the 1988 presidential election, but only 54.7 percent of those with four years of high school and 36.7 percent of those with

Table 9-2

Voter Turnout by Group and Region, 1988

Voting Groups	Percent Voting
College education	77.6%
Managerial and professional people	75.2
Government workers	75.2
$35,000 and over	72.6
45–64 years	67.9
65 years and over	68.8
Nonagricultural industrial workers	58.6
White	59.1
Female	58.3
Northeast	57.4
Male	56.4
West	55.6
High school education	54.7
South	54.5
Farm workers	53.0
African American	51.5
Service workers	47.2
Operators, fabricators, and laborers	41.3
Unemployed	38.6
Grade school education	36.7
18–24 years	36.2
Below $5,000	34.7

SOURCE: U.S. Bureau of the Census, Current Population Reports, Population Characteristics, *Voting and Registration in the Election of November 1988*, series P-20, no. 440, October 1989, pp. 2, 4, 56, 60.

grade-school educations said they voted.[6] Education seems to cause the greatest variation in voter turnout of all the factors.[7]

Income, education, social class, and occupation are closely related; the higher the level in all these categories, the more likely a person is to vote. (See Table 9-2.)

Jews vote more than Catholics, and Catholics vote more than Protestants. Churchgoers are more likely to vote than nonchurchgoers, a phenomenon perhaps associated with the willingness of the churchgoer to participate in organized activity and the inclination of some religious groups to get involved in politics. African Americans vote less than whites — but historically African American voters in the South were often prevented from voting by legal subterfuge, violence, or intimida-

[1] See Lester W. Milbrath and M. L. Goel, *Political Participation*, 2nd ed. (Chicago: Rand McNally, 1977), for detailed citations of studies of political participation.

[2] U.S. Bureau of the Census, Current Population Reports, Population Characteristics, *Voting and Registration in the Election of November 1988*, series P-20, no. 440, October 1989, p. 4.

[3] Milbrath and Goel, *Political Participation*, p. 114; and Raymond E. Wolfinger and Steven J. Rosenstone, *Who Votes?* (New Haven: Yale University Press, 1980), pp. 37–38. However, Wolfinger and Rosenstone add that "The decline in turnout among people over sixty . . . is explained not by their greater age but by differences in education, marital status, and sex," p. 47.

[4] U.S. Bureau of the Census, Current Population Reports, Population Characteristics, *Voting and Registration in the Election of November 1988*, series P-20, no. 440, October 1989, p. 1.

[5] Sandra Baxter and Marjorie Lansing, *Women and Politics: The Invisible Majority* (Ann Arbor: University of Michigan Press, 1980), p. 1.

[6] U.S. Bureau of the Census, Current Population Reports, Population Characteristics, *Voting and Registration in the Election of November 1988*, series P-20, no. 440, October 1989, p. 2.

[7] For a discussion of the "very strong relationship between rates of voting and years of education," see Wolfinger and Rosenstone, *Who Votes?*, pp. 17–20 and 34–36.

tion. As was noted in Chapter 5, the number of black registered voters in the South increased dramatically after passage of the Voting Rights Act of 1965.

Voter Attitudes Voter turnout does vary with demographic and social differences, but other research has identified additional factors that seem to influence participation at the polls. This research has focused on voter *attitudes*.

For example, a strong Democrat or a rock-ribbed Republican is more likely to get out and vote than a citizen whose party loyalties are casual. The higher the *intensity of partisan preference*, therefore, the more likely it is that the person will vote. Similarly, the *degree of interest* people have in the campaign and their *concern over the election outcome* appear to be related to whether they vote. If people think the election is close, they are more likely to vote, because they may feel their votes will count. And, if people think they can understand and influence politics, they are more likely to vote than are those who regard politics and government as distant and complicated. The greater a person's *sense of political effectiveness*, in other words, the greater the chance that he or she will vote. Americans, moreover, are indoctrinated with the importance of voting long before they are old enough to do so. Thus the voter's *sense of civic duty* also bears on whether he or she goes to the polls.[8]

The Nonvoter

Some 35 to 45 percent or more of Americans do not vote in presidential elections. Who are they? Why don't they vote? The preceding section indicated that the nonvoter is more likely to be less educated, rural, nonwhite, southern, very young or very old, a person "whose emotional investment in politics . . . is on the average much less than that of the voter."[9] Although a

Drawing by Locher for the *Chicago Tribune*

rough portrait of the nonvoter can be sketched in these terms, the picture does not explain *why* he or she does not vote.

As noted earlier, and in Chapter 6, about 55 percent of the voting-age population — or about 104 million people — voted in the 1992 election. However, millions of Americans of voting age did not. In 1988 about 50 percent of the voting-age population — or 91.6 million people — voted. After that election the *New York Times*/CBS News poll released the following breakdown of nonvoters and the reasons they gave for not voting (with the percentages from the sample projected into numbers of people):

---

[8] Angus Campbell, Philip E. Converse, Warren E. Miller, and Donald E. Stokes, *The American Voter* (New York: Wiley, 1960), pp. 96–101. Our discussion of voter attitudes is based in part on Chapter 5 of this landmark study of voting conducted at the Survey Research Center, University of Michigan.

[9] Ibid., p. 111.

THE VOTERS: "THEY FEEL THEY ARE ISOLATED . . ."

"The great story of 1992 is the degree to which voters feel disconnected from their political system by the insulation of a professional political class, comprising politicians, the press and the pressure elite," said Will Marshall, director of the centrist, Washington-based Progressive Policy Institute. "People are yearning to be part of a democratic conversation with their Government, their leaders, and they now feel they are isolated by the political class, which has arrogated the conversation to itself."

— *New York Times*, June 6, 1992

33.8 million were not registered

11.9 million did not like the candidates

11.9 million were too busy, had to work, or had problems getting child care

5.5 million chose not to vote

3.6 million did not care or were not interested

3.6 million had just moved and had not met the residence requirements

2.7 million were sick or their child was sick

1.8 million thought their vote did not matter

1.8 million had never voted

.9 million thought the voting process too complicated

.9 million had no transportation

.9 million were out of town

6.3 million mentioned a variety of other reasons[10]

Even taking into account the fact that some people had good reasons for not voting, a nation with some 91.6 million persons who do not turn out in a presidential election would seem to fall somewhat short of the idealized model of popular democracy. But some political scientists believe that what might work in a simple, agrarian society does not apply in a modern, highly industrialized society like the United States today.[11] The harassed parent with five young children may well find it difficult to get to the polls on Election Day. Most people spend more time worrying about money, sex, illness, crime, the high cost of living, automobile repairs, and a host of other things than they do worrying about politics.

So if we ask whether enough people vote in the United States, we must also ask: How much is enough? A turnout of some 50 to 60 percent in a presidential election may not meet the classic standards of democracy, but it may be the best that can be expected in the United States today. In any event, it is reality; it is what we have.

One overall pattern that emerges from all the data about the voter and the nonvoter in the United States is that those who are more advantageously situated in the social system vote more than the "have-nots," or less advantaged. If members of all social groups in the United States voted in equal proportions, candidates might have to offer programs that appealed more to the disadvantaged groups that do not now come to the polls. In short, if everybody voted, the candidates and policies

of the American political system might be somewhat different from what they are today.

HOW THE VOTER DECIDES

We have an idea who votes and who does not. The next question is: Why do people vote the way they do? How people make up their minds to vote for one candidate instead of another is obviously of great interest to politicians, campaign managers, advertising executives, and pollsters. But the question also has much broader implications for all citizens and for democratic government; the kind of society in which we live depends in part on whether voters flip a coin in the voting booth or choose on a somewhat more rational basis — satisfaction or dissatisfaction with the incumbent administration, for example.

Although American voters have been extensively analyzed, we still do not know *precisely* why they behave the way they do. We do not know which of many factors ultimately causes a person to stay home or to vote for one candidate or party instead of another. To say, for example, that many Catholics are Democrats does not mean a person is a Democrat *because* he or she is a Catholic. And, although party loyalty appears to be related to voting habits, we do not know, for example, that a Vermont farmer votes Republican *because* he identifies with the Republican party. Psychologists know that it is extremely difficult to judge people's motives from their behavior; even asking voters to explain their actions may not produce satisfactory answers.

So there are limits to the ability of political scientists to interpret the behavior of voters. Even allowing for these limits, however, a great deal has been learned about voting habits in recent decades.

Two basic approaches have been followed in studying how the voters decide:

1. *Sociological.* This method focuses on the social and economic background of the voters — their income, class, ethnic group, education, and similar factors — and attempts to relate these factors to how they vote.

2. *Psychological.* This method attempts to go beyond socioeconomic factors and find out what is going on inside the minds of the voters, to measure their *perceptions* of parties, candidates, and issues. This second approach is based on the premise that how the voter responds depends less on *static* factors,

---

[10] Adapted from the *New York Times*/CBS News poll taken November 10–16, 1988. The total number of responses is smaller than the 91 million nonvoters in 1988.

[11] Milbrath and Goel, *Political Participation*, p. 143.

such as social class, than on *dynamic* changing factors of issues and politics. In short, voting behavior may change as the issues and candidates change.

The difference between these two approaches is not as great as it might seem at first glance: how the voters currently perceive the issues may well be shaped by their social and economic backgrounds. The social psychologists who followed the second approach beginning in the 1950s built on the foundations laid by the political sociologists in the 1940s.

The Sociological Factors

In the first of two classic voter studies, six hundred residents of Erie County, Ohio, were interviewed during the 1940 presidential election.[12] The study found a pattern that has been repeated over and over again in American national elections. Wealthier people usually voted Republican, and poorer people voted Democratic: "Different social characteristics, different votes." [13]

But the voter is a member of several groups simultaneously. Sometimes the claims of one group conflict with those of another. For example, the study concluded that rich people are more likely to vote Republican, Catholics are more likely to vote Democratic. What of wealthy Catholics? Such persons are said to be "cross-pressured" because their social affiliations are pulling them in opposite directions. The study found that these voters were more likely than others to delay their decision and change their minds during a campaign. In 1948 the same research method was used in a study of how one thousand voters in Elmira, New York, made up their minds during the Truman-Dewey campaign.[14] This more detailed study also concluded that social class influenced voting behavior.

Today, however, many of the more recent voter analyses, whether following the sociological or the psychological approach, are based on national rather than local poll data. From these various studies, it is possible to draw a picture of the American voter in terms of his or her social class and other sociological factors. (A breakdown of how different groups have voted in presidential elections is summarized in Table 9-3.)

Social Class, Income, and Occupation Upper-class and middle-class voters are more likely to vote Republican than are voters of lower economic and social status, who tend to be Democrats. The vote of union members has usually gone Democratic.

Professional and business people are more apt to support Republicans than Democrats. For example, with the exception of 1964—when Republicans in droves deserted Goldwater for Johnson—business and professional people voted heavily Republican in the seven elections from 1960 to 1984. (See Table 9-3.) Among persons in the highest income brackets, Republican candidates usually draw more votes than do Democrats. In a 1992 survey, for example, the one income group where George Bush had a substantial lead over Bill Clinton was among voters with an annual family income of $75,000 or more.[15]

Education In 1992 Bill Clinton received 43 percent of the votes of college graduates, compared to 40 percent voting for Bush. In the past, however, college graduates have tended to vote for Republicans rather than Democrats. A majority of college-educated voters were in the ranks of the GOP during the elections of Kennedy, Nixon, and Reagan, and during Bush's 1988 race for the presidency. Although Nixon averaged 43.4 percent of the popular vote in 1968, he received 54 percent of the votes of college graduates; by contrast, only 33 percent of voters with a grade-school education voted for Nixon. (See Table 9-3.) In 1992, Clinton, who received 43.2 percent of the total popular vote, was supported by 56 percent of voters with a grade-school education.

Religion and Ethnic Background In a 1992 survey, 59.5 percent of Jews, 41.8 percent of Catholics, but only 36 percent of Protestants said they considered themselves Democrats.[16] In 1960, Jews, Catholics, and Protestants voted 81, 78, and 38 percent, respectively,

[12] Paul F. Lazarsfeld, Bernard Berelson, and Hazel Gaudet, *The People's Choice* (New York: Columbia University Press, 1968). Originally published in 1944.
[13] Ibid., p. 21.
[14] Bernard R. Berelson, Paul F. Lazarsfeld, and William N. McPhee, *Voting* (Chicago: University of Chicago Press, 1966). Originally published in 1954.
[15] In this high-income group, George Bush received 46 percent of the votes of those polled, while Bill Clinton received 38 percent, and Ross Perot received 16 percent. Exit polls conducted by Voter Research and Surveys, an association of CNN, CBS News, and ABC News. *National Journal*, November 7, 1992, p. 2543.
[16] Gallup poll, July 1992.

Table 9-3
Votes by Groups in Presidential Elections, 1960–92

	1960 Dem.	Rep.	1964 Dem.	Rep.	1968 Dem.	Rep.	Wallace	1972 Dem.	Rep.	1976* Dem.	Rep.	McCarthy	1980 Dem.	Rep.	Anderson	Other
National	50.1%	49.9%	61.3%	38.7%	43%	43.4%	13.6%	38%	62%	50%	48%	1%	41%	50.8%	6.6%	1.4%
Men	52	48	60	40	41	43	16	37	63	53	45	1	38	53	7	2
Women	49	51	62	38	45	43	12	38	62	48	51	†	44	49	6	1
White	49	51	59	41	38	47	15	32	68	46	52	1	36	56	7	1
Nonwhite	68	32	94	6	85	12	3	87	13	85	15	†	86	10	2	2
College education	39	61	52	48	37	54	9	37	63	42	55	2	35	53	10	2
High school education	52	48	62	38	42	43	15	34	66	54	46	†	43	51	5	1
Grade school education	55	45	66	34	52	33	15	49	51	58	41	1	54	42	3	1
Professional and business people	42	58	54	46	34	56	10	31	69	42	56	1	33	55	10	2
White-collar workers	48	52	57	43	41	47	12	36	64	50	48	2	NA†	NA†	NA†	NA†
Manual workers	60	40	71	29	50	35	15	43	57	58	41	1	48	46	5	1
Union members	65	35	73	27	56	29	15	46	54	63	36	1	50	43	5	2
Farmers	48	52	53	47	29	51	20	NA†	NA†	NA†	NA†	NA†	31	61	7	1
Under 30	54	46	64	36	47	38	15	48	52	53	45	1	47	41	11	1
30–49 years	54	46	63	37	44	41	15	33	67	48	49	2	38	52	8	2
Over 49	46	54	59	41	41	47	12	36	64	52	48	†	41	54	4	1
Protestants	38	62	55	45	35	49	16	30	70	46	53	†	39	54	6	1
Catholics	78	22	76	24	59	33	8	48	52	57	42	1	46	47	6	1
Republicans	5	95	20	80	9	86	14	5	95	9	91	†	8	86	5	1
Democrats	84	16	87	13	74	12	14	67	33	82	18	†	69	26	4	1
Independents	43	57	56	44	31	44	25	31	69	38	57	4	29	55	14	2

*Figures for some groups do not add to 100% because of the vote for other minor-party candidates.
† Less than 1 percent
‡ Not available

for Kennedy. Because Kennedy was the first Roman Catholic to be elected president, the 1960 election was carefully analyzed to assess the effect of his religion on the result. The Michigan Survey Research Center concluded that Kennedy won a "bonus" from Catholics of 4.3 percent of the two-party vote (2.9 million votes) but lost 6.5 percent (4.4 million votes) from Protestant Democrats and independents. His religion cost him a net loss of 2.2 percent, or 1.5 million popular votes.[17] On the other hand, the heavy Catholic vote in big northern industrial states probably helped him win in the electoral college.[18] It cannot be demonstrated, however, that Kennedy won *because* he was a Catholic.

Various studies have shown that voters of Irish, Italian, Polish, Eastern European, and Slavic descent often favor Democrats, although President Reagan made strong gains among several of these groups in 1980 and 1984. Black Americans, who generally had voted Republican until the New Deal, shifted away from the party of Lincoln to give approximately 94 percent of their votes to the Democrats in 1964. And in the next

seven presidential elections from 1968 to 1992, the support among nonwhites for the Democratic presidential nominee never dropped below 82 percent. In a 1992 survey, Clinton received 83 percent of the vote from African Americans.[19]

Primary Groups In addition to conventional social groups, voters are influenced by personal contacts with much smaller "primary" groups, such as families, co-workers, and friends. Sometimes these influences may change a voter's mind. However, because people of sim-

[17] Angus Campbell, Philip E. Converse, Warren E. Miller, and Donald E. Stokes, "Stability and Change in 1960: A Reinstating Election," *American Political Science Review*, vol. 55, no. 2 (June 1961), pp. 269–80. Actual votes were obtained by applying percentages to the 1960 total two-party vote.

[18] See Ithiel de Sola Pool, Robert P. Abelson, and Samuel L. Popkin, *Candidates, Issues, and Strategies* (Cambridge: Massachusetts Institute of Technology Press, 1964), pp. 68, 117–18.

[19] Voter Research and Surveys exit polls for 1992 in *National Journal*, November 7, 1992, p. 2543.

1984 Dem.	1984 Rep.	1988 Dem.	1988 Rep.	1992 Dem.	1992 Rep.	Perot
41%	59%	46%	54%	43.2%	37.8%	19.0%
36	64	44	56	41	37	22
45	55	48	52	46	38	16
34	66	41	59	39	41	20
87	13	82	18	77	11	12
39	61	43	57	43	40	17
43	57	46	54	40	38	22
51	49	56	44	56	28	16
34	66	NA†	NA†	NA†	NA†	NA†
47	53	NA†	NA†	NA†	NA†	NA†
46	54	NA†	NA†	NA†	NA†	NA†
52	48	NA†	NA†	NA†	NA†	NA†
NA†	NA†	NA†	NA†	NA†	NA†	NA†
40	60	37	63	40	37	23
40	60	45	55	42	37	21
41	59	49	51	46	39	15
39	61	36	64	41	41	18
39	61	51	49	47	35	18
4	96	7	93	7	77	16
79	21	85	15	82	8	10
33	67	43	57	39	30	31

SOURCE: Data provided by the Gallup poll.

ilar social background tend to associate with one another, primary groups often merely reinforce the political views that are already held by the voter.

Geography In general, the Democrats still draw their strength from the big cities of the North and East. Outside the South, voters in rural areas are more likely to be Republicans. But the Democrats can no longer count on the South in presidential contests. In 1972, for example, President Nixon polled 71 percent of the popular vote in the South, and for the first time since Reconstruction, the Republican presidential ticket carried all eleven states of the Old Confederacy. In 1976 the Democratic candidate, Jimmy Carter, was a former governor of the Deep South state of Georgia, and he carried every southern state except Virginia. But in 1980 Republican Ronald Reagan polled 51 percent of the popular vote in the South. And in 1984, Reagan won every state in the South by a decisive margin; he also polled 62.4 percent of the popular vote in the region.[20] This trend contin-

ued when George Bush won every southern state in 1988 and polled 58.7 percent of the vote in the South.

In 1992 the Democrats nominated a pair of southerners for president and for vice-president, and this time the presidential race in the South was much closer. The Clinton-Gore Democratic ticket received 41.5 percent of the popular vote in the region, while Bush and Quayle won 42.7 percent for the Republicans, and Ross Perot and James B. Stockdale polled 15.8 percent. Clinton carried four states in the South in 1992; the remaining seven went to Bush.

The suburbs, originally Republican strongholds after the Second World War, are today more a mixture of Democrats and Republicans. Democratic strength has grown in suburbia as lower- and middle-class whites and many blacks have left the cities, but Republicans still dominate many suburbs.

Sex Until 1980, in most presidential elections, whether voters were men or women did not seem to have a significant influence on how they voted.[21] In 1980, however, it was different. The election that year provided the most striking example of a difference in voting behavior between men and women since voter polls began in the 1930s. In 1980 men voted for Ronald Reagan over Jimmy Carter by a dramatic margin of 15 percentage points or more. By contrast, women— perhaps because they perceived Reagan as being more likely to engage in a military adventure than Carter— split their votes more evenly between the two candidates.[22] (Virtually all surveys on the subject have shown that women are substantially less likely than men to favor military action.)[23]

[20] *Congressional Quarterly*, Weekly Report, February 10, 1973, p. 308; *Congressional Quarterly*, Weekly Report, November 6, 1976, p. 3118; *New York Times*, January 6, 1981, p. A14; and *New York Times*, December 22, 1984, p. 10. Vote totals are for the eleven states of the Old Confederacy: Alabama, Arkansas, Florida, Georgia, Louisiana, Mississippi, North Carolina, South Carolina, Tennessee, Texas, and Virginia.

[21] For a comparison of voting between men and women in the Eisenhower era, see Campbell, Converse, Miller, and Stokes, *The American Voter*, p. 493.

[22] The Gallup poll data in Table 9-3 indicated that Reagan ran 15 percentage points ahead of Carter among men. The ABC News exit poll, based on interviews of 9,341 voters leaving voting precincts on Election Day, reported that Reagan's margin over Carter was 19 percentage points among men. Both the Gallup poll and the ABC News exit poll found that among women who were interviewed, Reagan ran 5 percentage points ahead of Carter.

[23] Baxter and Lansing, *Women and Politics: The Invisible Majority*, p. 57.

At the beginning of 1984, some Republican electoral strategists were worried that this "gender gap" might seriously hamper President Reagan in his bid for reelection. But when Reagan won his sweeping victory in November 1984, women voters as well as the men gave him a solid reelection margin. There was still a substantial difference in the voting preferences of men and women in 1984, however. Reagan won the votes of 64 percent of the men, compared with 55 percent of women. In 1992 there again was a "gender gap" in the vote for president. The polls indicated that Clinton had a fairly narrow lead over Bush among male voters. Among women who voted, by contrast, Clinton's lead was sizable. The 1980, 1984, and 1992 elections all suggested that men and women may vote differently — when the images and issue positions of the candidates coincide with differences in political attitudes between men and women.

Age In most national elections since 1960, younger voters were more likely to vote Democratic than Republican. Older voters seemed to find the GOP attractive. From 1960 to 1980, the Democrats consistently got a higher percentage of the vote from those under age thirty than from voters fifty and older. In 1984, however, this pattern changed. During the 1984 campaign, many observers noted that Ronald Reagan, the oldest person ever to serve as president, was showing surprising strength among the nation's youngest voters. And the final returns confirmed this trend. Reagan, the Republican, ran as strongly among voters under thirty (60 percent) as among the older age groups. In 1992 Bill Clinton was the third-youngest candidate to become president. Clinton polled 47 percent of the vote from those who were under twenty-five, and 42 percent among voters in their fifties. (See Table 9–12.)

The Psychological Factors

It would be wrong to give too much weight to sociological factors in determining how voters behave. To do so would be to ignore the very important question of people's changing attitudes toward politics. After the Second World War, a group of scholars at the University of Michigan conducted new studies of voting behavior, concentrating on the psychology of voting — on how individuals perceive and evaluate politics.

The Michigan researchers noted that social characteristics of the population change only slowly over a period of time. The percentage of Catholics or Jews in the United States does not change overnight, for example. Yet the electorate may behave very differently from one election to the next. Long-term factors such as social class did not seem adequate to explain such sudden shifts; candidates and issues, which change in the short term, provided a more likely explanation: "It seemed clear that the key to the finer dynamics of political behavior lay in the reactions of the electorate to these changes in the political scene." [24]

In measuring voter attitudes, the Michigan electoral analysts identified three powerful factors: *party identification, candidates,* and *issues.*

Party Identification Many Americans display persistent loyalties to the Democratic or Republican parties. Voters may form an attachment to one party or the other and often do not change. Most national elections have taken place within the framework of this basic division in the electorate. However, in the 1992 election year, many voters, dissatisfied with the candidates and platforms of the major parties, turned their loyalties to independent candidate Ross Perot.

Since the late 1930s there have been substantially more Democrats than Republicans in the United States. (See Table 9–4.) In fact, in 1964, 1976, and 1980, Democrats outnumbered Republicans by *more* than two to one. By 1984 this Democratic advantage in party identification had narrowed considerably. The Gallup

---

[24] Campbell, Converse, Miller, and Stokes, *The American Voter*, p. 17.

"My God! I went to sleep a Democrat and I've awakened a Republican."

Drawing by Dana Fradon © 1984 The New Yorker Magazine, Inc.

Table 9-4
Party Identification
Among the American Electorate, 1940–92

Year	Percentage of Voters Identifying Themselves as:		
	Democrats	Republicans	Independents
1940	42%	38%	20%
1950	45	33	22
1960	47	30	23
1964	53	25	22
1966	48	27	25
1968	46	27	27
1970	45	29	26
1972	43	28	29
1974	44	23	33
1976	46	22	32
1980	47	23	30
1984	41	29	30
1986	40	30	30
1988	43	29	28
1990	40	32	28
1992	38	29	33

SOURCE: *Gallup Opinion Index*, Report No. 131, June 1976, p. 11; *Gallup Opinion Index*, Report No. 180, August 1980, p. 31; *Gallup Report*, December 1986, no. 255, pp. 27–28; the Gallup poll, August 7, 1988; the Gallup poll, January 1992; and the Gallup poll, January–June 1992.

poll reported that between 1980 and 1984 the number of voters who called themselves Democrats dropped by six percentage points, while the number of Republicans increased by six percentage points. And other polls in 1984 reported that the gap between Republicans and Democrats was only two or three percentage points. By 1988, however, Democrats outnumbered Republicans by 43 percent to 29 percent. In 1992, Gallup polls taken during the first half of the year suggested that 38 percent of the electorate considered themselves to be Democrats, compared with 29 percent who said they were Republicans and 33 percent who called themselves independents.

Although party identification remains a key factor in American politics, there are signs that it may be growing somewhat less important. In the 1972 presidential election, according to the University of Michigan election analysts, "issues were at least equally as important as party identification" as an explanation of the vote.[25] Moreover, as shown in Table 9–4, the number of people who identified with either of the two major parties dropped from 80 percent in 1940 to 67 percent in 1992, as the number of independents rose from 20 to 33 percent. And in most elections since the Second World War, there also has been extensive ticket splitting by many voters. For example, a person may vote for a Republican presidential candidate and a Democratic senator or representative. In 1988 Bush won by a large margin despite the Democratic advantage in party identification.

The Candidates Between 1952 and 1992 the GOP won seven of the eleven presidential elections that were held. How was this possible, given the higher percentage of those who identify with the Democratic party?

The answer is that although people may identify with a party, and frequently vote for its candidates, they do not always vote that way. Short-term factors, such as changes in candidates or issues, may cause enough voters to switch from the party they normally favor to have a decisive impact on the outcome of the election. In 1952 and 1956 Dwight Eisenhower, the Republican candidate, easily defeated Adlai Stevenson, a Democrat. Eisenhower's personal appeal, his smile, his image as an outstanding military hero of the Second World War, and—in the second election—his popularity as president all helped to offset normal party loyalties.

Clearly, the personal impression a candidate makes on the voters may have a powerful influence on the election returns. Thus, dour Calvin Coolidge looked like he had been "weaned on a pickle." Thomas E. Dewey, in the classic phrase of Alice Roosevelt Longworth, resembled "the bridegroom on a wedding cake." Nixon in 1968 remained "Tricky Dick" to many strong Democratic partisans. Humphrey "talked too much." Ford struck many voters as "well-meaning but dull." Carter was often seen as "decent but ineffective." Ronald Reagan, particularly during his highly successful 1984 reelection campaign, was a "leader who inspired confidence" for many voters. In 1988 George Bush, for a time at least, had difficulty overcoming his image as a rich "Ivy League" patrician who was ill at ease among the common folk. In 1992 Ross Perot was viewed by many voters as a folksy, feisty candidate who was willing to "face the hard issues," and to "tell it like it is." And Bill Clinton was seen favorably by many voters as "an ordinary guy" who enjoyed mingling with the people. Appearance, personality, and popularity of the candidates obviously bear some relation to the number of votes they receive.

[25] Arthur H. Miller, Warren E. Miller, Alden S. Raine, and Thad A. Brown, "A Majority Party in Disarray: Policy Polarization in the 1972 Election," *American Political Science Review*, vol. 70, no. 3 (September 1976), p. 770.

The Issues   Two central questions should be asked about the role issues play in a political campaign: Do voters vote according to their opinions about public issues? If so, do their policy preferences later affect the direction of the government? Both points will be discussed later in this chapter. For now, it is enough to note that a voter must be aware of the existence of an issue and must have an opinion about it if he or she is to be directly motivated by it.[26]

If an issue is to have a direct effect on an individual's voting behavior, a voter must not only recognize the issue and have a minimum degree of feeling about it, he or she also must come to think that one candidate or the other is closer to his or her own position. Research shows, however, that human beings are sometimes highly selective in accepting political messages. If they do not happen to be tuned in to the proper "wave length," the messages may be received only as so much noise. Increasing the volume may only make the voter flick the "off" switch. Like mechanisms that control the body's blood pressure and temperature, this mental fuse "seems to protect the individual citizen from too strenuous an overload of incoming information."[27] In some elections, even among voters who do hold opinions on public issues, only 40 to 60 percent can perceive differences between the parties on those issues.[28]

On certain *major* issues, or on issues that affect them directly, the voters do seem to "tune in" and form definite party preferences. It was noted in Chapter 8 that, in some years, many people have tended to associate prosperity with Democrats while others have thought the Republicans were more likely to keep the peace.

When one group of voters is directly affected by a political issue, its members may listen carefully to the political debate. For example, in 1964 Barry Goldwater voted against the first major civil rights bill since Reconstruction. Partly because black voters seemed to know in general where Goldwater stood on civil rights, they turned out in unprecedented numbers to vote for his Democratic opponent, Lyndon Johnson.

Moreover, issues may be more important in some elections than in others. Research by Norman H. Nie,

Sidney Verba, and John R. Petrocik suggests that substantial "issue voting" took place during the elections of 1964, 1968, and 1972. Issues such as the Vietnam War, race, and several controversial social issues sharply divided the voters during those election years.[29] Arthur H. Miller also found widespread issue voting in the 1972 election, ranking it as a more important influence that year than party identification or the voters' attitudes toward the candidates. But in 1976 the relative importance of issues declined. The data "clearly show," Miller concluded, "that in 1976 party identification had a greater impact than issues or candidates."[30] And in 1980, the public's evaluation of the candidates played a very important role.[31]

In 1992, one survey found 43 percent of those polled said that the "economy/jobs" was one of the issues that mattered most in deciding how to vote. Among that sizable bloc of voters, 53 percent voted for Clinton, compared to 24 percent who supported Bush and 23 percent who voted for Perot. In addition, among the one-fifth of the voters who said that "health care" was an issue that was important in deciding how to vote, 67 percent voted for Clinton.[32]

Retrospective Voting

The relative importance of candidates, issues, and party identification thus appears to vary from election year to election year. But in most elections another factor also seems to be at work — many voters appear to make up their minds by looking back at what has happened under the country's current political leadership and making a rough judgment about their leaders' performance in office. Morris P. Fiorina and other political scientists have explored this concept of *retrospective voting*. Fiorina points out that citizens "typically have one comparatively hard bit of data: they know what life has been like during the incumbent's administration."

---

[26] Issues also may have an *indirect* effect on voters. For example, if a candidate takes a position pleasing to labor union leaders, the union leaders may work enthusiastically on a voter registration drive among union members. That in turn may result in more votes for the candidate.

[27] Campbell, Converse, Miller, and Stokes, *The American Voter*, pp. 171–72.

[28] Ibid., p. 180.

---

[29] Norman H. Nie, Sidney Verba, and John R. Petrocik, *The Changing American Voter*, Enlarged Edition (Cambridge: Harvard University Press, 1979), pp. 96–109, 156–73.

[30] Arthur H. Miller, "Partisanship Reinstated? A Comparison of the 1972 and 1976 U.S. Presidential Elections," *British Journal of Political Science*, vol. 8, part 2 (April 1978), p. 152.

[31] See Gregory B. Markus, "Political Attitudes During an Election Year: A Report on the 1980 NES Panel Study," *American Political Science Review*, vol. 76, no. 3 (September 1982), pp. 538–60, especially p. 560.

[32] Voter Research and Surveys exits polls for 1992 in *National Journal*, November 7, 1992, p. 2544.

They need *not* know the precise economic or foreign policies of the incumbent administration in order to see or feel the *results* of those policies. And is it not reasonable to base voting decisions on results as well as intentions? In order to ascertain whether the incumbents have performed poorly or well, citizens need only calculate the changes in their own welfare. If jobs have been lost in a recession, something is wrong. If sons have died in foreign rice paddies, something is wrong. If polluters foul food, water, or air, something is wrong. And to the extent that citizens vote on the basis of such judgments, elections do not signal the direction in which society should move so much as they convey an evaluation of where society has been. Rather than a prospective decision, the voting decision can be more of a retrospective decision.[33]

VOTING PATTERNS

Although the act of voting represents an individual decision, the result of an election is a group decision. On Election Day as the sun moves west across the continent's four time zones, the tides and patterns of electoral choice are already beginning to form. The polls have closed in the East as voters in California and elsewhere along the Pacific Coast are still casting their ballots.[34] The results from the first precincts in New England trickle in, then more, and in time, the decision takes shape much as a photograph gains definition in the developing trays of a darkroom.

Sometimes the resulting picture is sharp, quickly seen, and its meaning clear; other times it is as blurred as an impressionist painting. Yet the trained eye analyzing the results of American elections can detect patterns and trends, interrelationships, currents, sectional nuances, and sometimes national meaning.

Control

For national political parties, the prize is control of the presidency. But party success or failure is measured in terms of states won or lost. Broad voting patterns on the national level can easily be seen by comparing political maps in presidential years, such as those found inside the front and back covers of this book. Some political

results are geographically dramatic — for example, Franklin D. Roosevelt's 1936 landslide, in which the map is solidly Democratic except for Maine and Vermont. And Ronald Reagan's strong electoral victory in 1984 also covered nearly every part of the map; the Democrats that year carried only one state, Walter Mondale's Minnesota, and the District of Columbia. By contrast, GOP bedrock strength in the Midwest is illustrated by the maps of the elections of 1940, 1944, and 1948; in each case the Plains states are a Republican island in a Democratic sea.

Landslides such as 1936 and 1984 leave behind a rather homogeneous map. But the "checkerboard" effect of 1960 and 1968 reflects the fact that the nation was narrowly divided in those elections. The election of 1976 was also close, but the concentration in the South and the Northeast of most of the states carried by Carter underscores the regional bases from which Carter assembled his victory.

In 1992, when the Democrats' Bill Clinton won a solid victory over George Bush, the Democratic tide spread over most regions of the country. But there were still a sizable number of states that Bush carried — concentrated mainly in a belt of territory in the center of the country running from Texas northward to the Canadian border, in the Southeast, and in the Rocky Mountain section of the West.

---

[33] Morris P. Fiorina, *Retrospective Voting in American National Elections* (New Haven: Yale University Press, 1981), pp. 5–6.

[34] In the past, sometimes the major television networks projected the winner of a presidential race before the polls had closed in the West. In 1980 President Carter conceded while the polls were still open in California, Oregon, Washington State, Alaska, and Hawaii.

Coalitions

The broad outline of the national vote can be shown on a map, but much that is politically significant is less visible. Electoral victories are built not merely on simple geographic foundations; they also are formed by alliances of segments of the electorate and of interest groups, and by unorganized masses of voters who coalesce behind the winner. Politicians and political scientists are interested, therefore, in *coalitions* of voters.

Roosevelt's New Deal brought together a coalition of the South, the urban North, minority groups, and labor unions. Nixon's winning coalition in 1968 included part of the South, most of the Midwest, the West, whites, Protestants, businesspeople, and white-collar workers. Long-term trends in American politics can be traced by analyzing the makeup of winning and losing coalitions.

Congress

In analyzing these alignments, however, congressional as well as presidential voting patterns should be considered. Although, as will be shown, the two are often linked, in most presidential elections since the New Deal days, the Democratic party has been stronger in congressional elections than in contests for the presidency. In the period from 1932 to 1992, Republican

presidential nominees were elected to seven four-year terms in the White House. Yet during that same period, the Republicans won full control of Congress for a total of only four years (1947–1948 and 1953–1954). In presidential election years since the 1940s, the Democratic presidential nominee has received fewer votes than the total vote polled by Democratic candidates for the House of Representatives in every presidential election except 1964. And in 1992 Ross Perot won more than 19 million votes as an independent candidate for president, in an election in which all the Senate races and all but one of the 435 seats in the House of Representatives were won by a Democrat or a Republican.

Coattails

The entire House of Representatives and a third of the Senate are elected every two years. In a presidential election year, the vote for president may affect the vote for Congress and also can have an effect on state and local offices, although there are signs that in recent years the impact of the presidential vote on contests for other offices may be lessening.

The interrelationship between the vote for president and for members of the House is illustrated in Figure 9–3. Some individual members of Congress are strong enough to withstand the tides of presidential

Figure 9–3
Presidential and House Vote, 1928–92

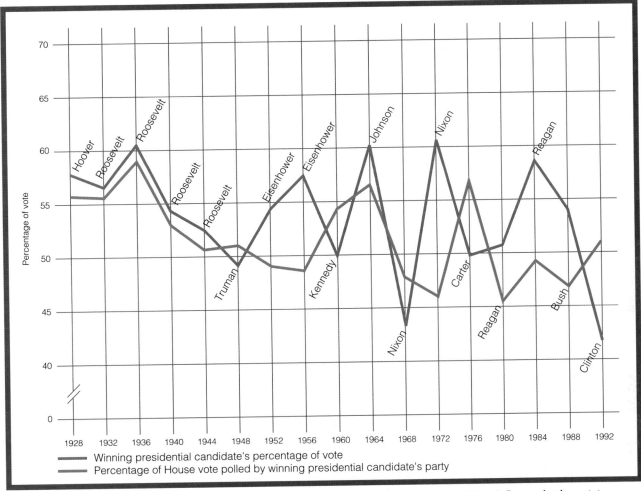

Winning presidential candidate's percentage of vote
Percentage of House vote polled by winning presidential candidate's party

SOURCE: Congressional Quarterly, *Politics in America* (Washington, D.C.: Congressional Quarterly Service, May 1969), p. 41. Reprinted with permission; 1972 and later data from *Congressional Quarterly*, Weekly Reports.

voting, but at times a president has been able to carry into office with him a majority of his own party in the House.

The fortunes of presidential and senatorial candidates are also sometimes linked, especially in the more competitive two-party states. In this century, however, three presidents have been elected along with a Congress controlled by the opposition party in both wings of the Capitol—Eisenhower in 1956, Nixon in 1968 and 1972, and Bush in 1988. (See Table 9–5.) The 1980 and 1984 elections left the Republicans in control of the Senate and the presidency, but the Democrats remained the majority party in the House. In 1992 the Democrats

took control of both the executive and legislative branches for the first time in twelve years.

As Table 9–6 shows, the president's party generally loses strength in midterm congressional elections. In off-year elections since 1920, the party in power has lost an average of thirty-one seats in the House; in some of those election years, the party's losses were well above average, as in 1922 and 1938. Occasionally, the party in power may actually gain a few seats, as in 1934, or suffer only minor losses, as in 1962 and 1990.

Why the voters normally reduce the strength of the party of the president they elected two years earlier has been the subject of considerable scholarly research.

Table 9-5

Major-Party Lineup; President and Congress, 1932–92*

Election Year†	President and Party		Congress	House D R	Senate D R	President's Popular Vote Percentage
1932	Roosevelt	D	D	313–117	59–36	57.4%
1934	Roosevelt	D	D	322–103	69–25	
1936	Roosevelt	D	D	333–89	75–17	60.8
1938	Roosevelt	D	D	262–169	69–23	
1940	Roosevelt	D	D	267–162	66–28	54.7
1942	Roosevelt	D	D	222–209	57–38	
1944	Roosevelt	D	D	243–190	57–38	53.4
1946	Truman	D	R	188–246	45–51	
1948	Truman	D	D	263–171	54–42	49.6
1950	Truman	D	D	234–199	48–47	
1952	Eisenhower	R	R	213–221	47–48	55.1
1954	Eisenhower	R	D	232–203	48–47	
1956	Eisenhower	R	D	234–201	49–47	57.4
1958	Eisenhower	R	D	283–154	66–34	
1960	Kennedy	D	D	263–174	64–36	49.5
1962	Kennedy	D	D	259–176	68–32	
1964	Johnson	D	D	295–140	67–33	61.1
1966	Johnson	D	D	248–187	64–36	
1968	Nixon	R	D	243–192	58–42	43.4
1970	Nixon	R	D	255–180	54–44†	
1972	Nixon	R	D	243–192	56–42	60.7
1974	Ford	R	D	291–144	60–37§	
1976	Carter	D	D	292–143	61–38	50.0
1978	Carter	D	D	277–158	58–41	
1980	Reagan	R	D/R	243–192	46–53	50.8
1982	Reagan	R	D/R	269–166	46–54	
1984	Reagan	R	D/R	253–182	47–53	58.8
1986	Reagan	R	D	258–177	55–45	
1988	Bush	R	D	260–175	55–45	53.9
1990	Bush	R	D	267–167*	56–44	
1992	Clinton	D	D	259–175*	57–43	43.2

* Does not include independents and minor parties.

† Presidential years appear in boldface.

‡ In 1970 Harry Byrd, Jr., of Virginia was elected as an Independent and is therefore not included in this and subsequent totals until his retirement in 1982. However, he received committee assignments as a Democrat. Also in 1970 James Buckley was elected as a Conservative from New York. He generally voted Republican but is not included in this table. In 1976 he was defeated.

§ The total became Democrats 61, Republicans 37, after a disputed Senate contest in New Hampshire was won by the Democratic candidate in a new, special election in September 1975.

* After the 1990 and 1992 elections, there was one independent in the House.

SOURCE: Adapted from *Congressional Quarterly*, Politics in America (Washington, D.C.: Congressional Quarterly Service, 1979), pp. 120–21; *Congressional Quarterly*, Weekly Reports; and *National Journal*, November 7, 1992, p. 2555.

It is clear that substantially fewer voters turn out in off years. (See Figure 9–1.) Angus Campbell has suggested that in presidential elections that stimulate a high degree of public interest, the normally "less involved peripheral voters" tend to turn out and vote for the winner, as do many independents and people who switch from the opposing party. In the midterm elections, the peripheral voters tend to "drop out," and many independents and party switchers move back to their usual positions. The result is a decline in the proportion of the vote for the president's party.[35] Barbara Hinckley, in an analysis of midterm House results from 1954 through 1966, found that the "midterm loss was concentrated" in marginal House districts where the president ran

Table 9-6
Midterm Loss in House of Representatives of Party in Control of Presidency, 1922–90

Size of Loss (Average Loss: 31 seats)	Net Number of Seats Lost or Gained Since Previous Election	Year	Incumbent President
Massive	−75	1922	Harding
	−71	1938	Roosevelt
	−55	1946	Truman
	−49	1930	Hoover
	−48*	1974	Ford
Above average	−47	1958	Eisenhower
	−47	1966	Johnson
	−45	1942	Roosevelt
	−29	1950	Truman
	−26	1982	Reagan
	−18	1954	Eisenhower
	−12†	1970	Nixon
Below average	−12	1978	Carter
	−10	1926	Coolidge
	−8	1990	Bush
	−5	1986	Reagan
	−4	1962	Kennedy
	+9	1934	Roosevelt

* Republicans lost five House seats in special elections in 1974; their net loss on Election Day in 1974 was forty-three seats.
† Republicans lost three House seats in special elections in 1969; their net loss on Election Day in 1970 was nine seats.
SOURCE: Adapted from *Congressional Quarterly*, Weekly Reports.

ahead of his party's winning congressional candidate in the preceding election.[36] In the ensuing off-year election, when the party's presidential nominee was not heading the ticket, these members of Congress were particularly vulnerable to defeat.

But why are the midterm losses of the president's party sometimes very large and sometimes quite small? Edward R. Tufte has suggested that such variations are related to two factors: ". . . the vote cast in midterm congressional elections is a referendum on the performance of the president and his administration's management of the economy." The size of the midterm loss, Tufte added, "is substantially smaller if the President has a high level of approval, or if the economy is performing well, or both."[37]

[35] Angus Campbell, "Surge and Decline: A Study of Electoral Change," in Angus Campbell, Philip E. Converse, Warren E. Miller, and Donald E. Stokes, *Elections and the Political Order* (New York: Wiley, 1966), pp. 44–45, 59, 61–62.

[36] Barbara Hinckley, "Interpreting House Midterm Elections: Toward a Measurement of the In-Party's 'Expected' Loss of Seats," *American Political Science Review*, vol. 61, no. 3 (September 1967), p. 699.

[37] Edward R. Tufte, "Determinants of the Outcomes of Midterm Congressional Elections," *American Political Science Review*, vol. 69, no. 3 (September 1975), p. 824.

"The Untouchable Incumbent.
Incumbents . . . evolved in the manner of the porcupine. They grew longer and longer quills."

SOURCE: Drawing by Jeff MacNelly from *A Political Bestiary* by Eugene J. McCarthy and James J. Kilpatrick, McGraw-Hill Book Company, 1979

Nevertheless, the kind of campaigns that individual House candidates run in local congressional districts also shape the midterm verdict. In 1982, for example, near the bottom of a severe recession, the approval rating in the polls for President Reagan, a Republican, was 42 percent. Republican House candidates took great pains to demonstrate their independence from the Reagan administration's economic policies, and Republican strategists targeted their campaign contributions into districts where GOP House incumbents faced close races. In November, Republicans lost twenty-six seats in the House — the largest midterm loss for a president in his first term in the twentieth century. Nevertheless, as Thomas Mann and Norman Ornstein have argued, "the losses would have been much deeper had national economic conditions alone determined the net shift in House seats." [38]

Although the "coattail" effect in presidential voting exists, it can be overstated. In 1984, for example, the

Republicans made a net gain of only fourteen seats in the House of Representatives and actually lost strength in the Senate — despite the Reagan landslide in the presidential voting. The absence of presidential coattails was seen again in 1988 when the Republican party lost seats in the House, despite the election of George Bush. And in most elections, many candidates of the party that loses nationally are able to survive. This is because voters are selective: some do not vote for all candidates on the ballot; others pick and choose and split their tickets. At times the coattail effect may work in reverse, as when a local candidate pulls a larger vote than the national ticket. [39]

Sometimes, candidates for governor may ride into the statehouse on a sufficiently long presidential coat-

---

[39] For an additional discussion of the coattail phenomenon, see Warren E. Miller, "Presidential Coattails: A Study in Political Myth and Methodology," *Public Opinion Quarterly*, vol. 19, no. 1 (Spring 1955), pp. 353–68.

Table 9-7
Party Control of Governorships

Following Elections of*	Democrats	Republicans
1946	23	25
1948	30	18
1950	23	25
1952	18	30
1954	27	21
1956	28	20
1958	35	14
1960	34	16
1962	34	16
1964	33	17
1966	25	25
1968	19	31
1970	29	21
1972	31	19
1974	36	13†
1976	37	12†
1978	32	18
1980	27	23
1982	35	15
1984	34	16
1986	26	24
1988	28	22
1990	28	20†
1992	30	18†

*Presidential years appear in boldface.
† After the 1974 and 1976 elections, there was an independent governor in Maine. After the 1990 and 1992 elections, independents held the governorship in Alaska and Connecticut.
SOURCE: *Congressional Quarterly*, Politics in America (Washington, D.C.: Congressional Quarterly Service, 1969), p. 69; *Congressional Quarterly Weekly Reports*; and *National Journal*, November 11, 1992, p. 2578.

---

[38] Thomas Mann and Norman Ornstein, "Election '82: The Voters Send a Message," *Public Opinion*, December/January 1983, p. 8.

Table 9-8
How the Governors Are Elected (through 1994)

Four-year Term	
Election in presidential years	9
Election in even-numbered years at midterm	34
Election in odd-numbered years	4
Total, four-year terms	47
Two-year Term	
Election in even-numbered years	3
Total, all states	50

SOURCE: Data provided by the National Governors Association.

tail, for there may be a relationship between national and state election results in presidential election years. "The great tides of presidential politics," V. O. Key, Jr., observed, "tend to engulf the affairs of states and often to determine the results of state elections."[40]

One reason for the relationship between presidential and gubernatorial voting is that many voters find it convenient to vote a straight party ticket by making a single mark or pulling a single lever (in states where they are permitted to do so). Even so, ticket splitting between candidates for president and governor is common, particularly in states where there is strong two-party rivalry.

Moreover, three-fourths of the gubernatorial races cannot be directly affected by the presidential campaign. A large number of states have scheduled gubernatorial elections in off-years to insulate themselves from the tides of national presidential politics. In 1992, a presidential year, twelve governors were elected, but in 1994, an off-year, thirty-seven governors' races were scheduled. (See Table 9–8.) This separation of gubernatorial and presidential races may help candidates of the party that is out of power nationally.[41]

PRESIDENTIAL '92: A CASE STUDY

In the election of 1992 Governor Bill Clinton of Arkansas, the Democratic nominee, won a decisive victory over President George Bush, the Republican candidate, and gave the Democratic party control of the presidency for the first time in twelve years. Clinton carried thirty-two of the fifty states, and won 370 electoral votes to 168 for George Bush. Clinton's victory marked the fifth time in this century that an incumbent president of the United States had been defeated. The results were:

	Popular Vote[42]	Electoral Vote	Popular Vote Percentage
Bill Clinton (D)	43,728,375	370	43.2%
George Bush (R)	38,167,416	168	37.8
Ross Perot (I)	19,237,247	0	19.0
Totals	101,133,038	538	100.0

The Republicans

As the 1992 presidential campaign year approached, President George Bush and his Republican supporters realized that three factors could have a powerful effect on their party's prospects:

In Republican circles it was almost unanimously assumed that President Bush would, at age 68, seek reelection to a second term in the White House in 1992. But the outcome of the election would depend on the

[40] V. O. Key, Jr., *Politics, Parties, and Pressure Groups*, 5th ed. (New York: Crowell, 1964), p. 304.

[41] In 1942 only ten states with four-year gubernatorial terms scheduled their election for governor midway through the president's term. By 1962 the number of such states stood at twenty; for 1990 it was thirty-four. Adapted from *Congressional Quarterly, Politics in America* (Washington, D.C.: Congressional Quarterly Service, May 1969), pp. 148–55; and *Congressional Quarterly, Weekly Reports*.

[42] Totals do not include minor-party votes, absentee ballots, or some scattered precincts. *New York Times*, November 5, 1992, p. B2.

answers to several questions. First, how popular would the president and his administration be in the summer and fall of 1992? If George Bush maintained high job approval ratings during the 1992 campaign, then a Bush victory was almost assured. Otherwise, the 1992 contest for the presidency could be close.

Second, would President Bush face opposition within his own party — and potentially damaging primary fights — as he sought renomination?

Third, and probably most important of all, what would economic conditions be like in the summer and fall of 1992? If the economy, which was faltering in 1991, appeared to be on the way to a robust recovery by late 1992, obviously the chances of a Republican victory would be greatly enhanced. But if the economy continued to sag, the Republican party would find itself on the defensive.

When President Bush and his advisers met in the summer of 1991 to discuss plans for the 1992 campaign, the possibility seemed remote that Bush's popularity would drop substantially or that he would face political opposition within his own party. In January and February of 1991, Bush had led an alliance of twenty-eight nations to a decisive military victory over Iraq and its dictator, Saddam Hussein, in the Persian Gulf War. In the aftermath of the war, the number of Americans who approved of the way George Bush was "handling his job as president" stood at 89 percent — the highest rating ever received by an American president in the history of the Gallup poll. (See Table 9-10.)

But after a series of triumphant victory parades and celebrations across the nation, the yellow ribbons and the memories of the Persian Gulf War began to fade. The ravages of the recession did not. The economy sank to its lowest point in October 1991. And during that autumn President Bush's job approval ratings began to drop — to 66 percent in October, to 56 percent in November, and to 50 percent (the danger zone for a president seeking re-election) in December. In the middle of January 1992, just one month before the New Hampshire presidential primary, Bush's approval rating fell to 46 percent. And in October 1992, less than one month before the presidential election, only 34 percent of those polled approved of the way Bush was handling his job. (See Table 9-10.)

Other factors worked against Bush. In 1991, the Senate held hearings on sexual harassment charges against Bush's controversial Supreme Court nominee, Clarence Thomas. The Senate confirmed Thomas, but many women were angry at the senators for their treat-

Table 9-9

Annual Rates of Inflation and Unemployment in the United States, 1980–92

	Inflation	Unemployment
1980	13.5%	7.1%
1981	10.4	7.6
1982	6.1	9.7
1983	3.2	9.6
1984	4.3	7.4
1985	3.6	7.1
1986	1.9	6.9
1987	3.6	6.1
1988	4.4	5.5
1989	4.6	5.3
1990	6.1	5.5
1991	3.1	6.7
1992*	3.2	7.4

*1992 figures are the annualized rate for the first ten months of the year.
SOURCE: U.S. Bureau of Labor Statistics.

ment of Anita Hill, his accuser, and at Bush for nominating Thomas. And December brought the departure from the White House of John H. Sununu, Bush's embattled chief of staff, who had been widely criticized for using official limousines and military aircraft on personal trips.

As the recession worsened, a few of Bush's advisers urged him to take strong steps to stimulate the economy and to speed up the rate of recovery. Their activist advice, however, ran counter to the advice the president was getting from his budget director, Richard Darman, his chief economic adviser, Michael Boskin, and his secretary of the Treasury, Nicholas Brady. The collective wisdom of these men "was that the economy would fix itself — that all the elements necessary to a recovery were in place and that discretion dictated leaving well enough alone." [43] Their advice coincided with the president's own preferences, and so, in the fall and winter of 1991–92, no major new economic policies were proposed. After that it would soon be too late for an economic stimulus program to take effect in time for the 1992 election.

On December 10, 1991, Patrick J. Buchanan, an articulate, staunchly conservative journalist, announced that he planned to challenge Bush for the Republican nomination in their party's primaries. Bu-

---

[43] *Newsweek, Special Election Issue*, November/December 1992, p. 61.

Table 9-10
President Bush's Job Rating, 1989–92*

Date of Interviews	Approve	Disapprove	No Opinion
Bush Elected with 54% of the Vote, November 1988			
Bush Inaugurated, January 1989			
January 24–26, 1989	51%	6%	43%
July 6–9, 1989	66	19	15
Panama Invasion, December 1989			
January 4–7, 1990	80	11	9
April 19–22, 1990	67	17	16
Bush Drops "No New Taxes" Pledge, June 1990			
October 18–21, 1990	53	37	10
Persian Gulf War Begins, January 1991			
January 17–20, 1991	82	12	6
Gulf War Victory, February 1991			
Feb. 28–Mar. 3, 1991	89†	8	3
July 25–28, 1991	71	21	8
Soviet Coup Fails, August 1991			
September 5–8, 1991	70	21	9
Recession's Low Point, October 1991			
October 17–20, 1991	66	26	8
November 14–17, 1991	56	36	8
December 12–15, 1991	50	41	9
January 16–19, 1992	46	48	6
April 20–22, 1992	42	48	10
Economic Recovery Stalls, Spring 1992			
June 26–30, 1992	38	55	7
July 31–August 2, 1992	29	60	11
Aug. 31–Sept. 2, 1992	39	54	7
Sept. 17–20, 1992	36	54	10
October 12–14, 1992	34	56	10

*Responses to the question: "Do you approve or disapprove of the way George Bush is handling his job as President?"
† Highest rating in Gallup poll annals.
SOURCE: Data provided by the Gallup poll.

chanan had worked in the White House in both the Nixon and the Reagan administrations. At first Buchanan had very little money to pay for television and radio advertising, and President Bush and his advisers did not seem to take his challenge very seriously.

The New Hampshire primary—as usual the nation's first—was held on February 18. The state had been particularly hard hit by the recession. As a result, the voters were receptive to Buchanan's increasingly sharp attacks on the president for not doing enough about the nation's ailing economy.

On primary day Bush got 53 percent of the vote to 37 percent for Buchanan. (Thousands of other Republicans wrote in the name of Paul Tsongas, a Democrat, rather than vote for either Buchanan or Bush.)[44] Bush had actually won the New Hampshire primary, but be-

cause of Buchanan's strong showing, the results were reported in the press as a major embarrassment for the president.

In Georgia, in one of the next Republican primaries, Buchanan polled 36 percent of the vote; on the same day he won 30 percent in Maryland and Colorado—two states where he had not even campaigned. The next contest, the most important of the primary season, would be Super Tuesday, March 10. Buchanan had entered his name in eight states, mostly in the South, that were to hold primary elections on that date. Now Bush's advisers took their Republican opponent seriously. In one meeting held to discuss the scripts for possible attack ads to be used on television and radio against Buchanan, Bush's usually mild-mannered campaign manager Robert Teeter exploded. "What this spot has to do," he said sharply, "is tell voters that this guy's a goddamn typewriter pusher, and the toughest thing

---

[44] Ibid., p. 64.

he's had to do in his whole life is change the ribbon on his goddamn Olivetti." [45]

On Super Tuesday Buchanan lost in all eight states by large margins. He received more than 30 percent of the vote only in Florida and Rhode Island, and after Super Tuesday he never became a serious threat to Bush's renomination.[46]

On August 19 Bush was formally nominated by the Republican National Convention in Houston. Buchanan continued to run in Republican primaries, however, all the way to the end in California in June. And the 15 to 25 percent of the vote that he polled in many of those primaries was a reminder that a substantial number of Republicans were dissatisfied with President Bush's leadership.

The Independent Candidacy of Ross Perot

As the Buchanan challenge receded, a new potential threat to Bush's reelection began to appear — a possible independent presidential candidacy by the Texas billionaire, Ross Perot. During the spring of 1992, Perot's thinking seemed to be "driven in part by his disdain for the leadership style of George Bush; he spoke of him privately as a hand-wringer and a whiner. . . ." [47] And he argued that neither of the two major-party candidates would offer the strong medicine that he said was required to fix a four trillion dollar debt.

On February 20, 1992, on the "Larry King Live" television show, Perot implied that he would indeed run for president if there were enough viewers who wanted him to run, and if they put him on the ballot in all fifty states. A flood of phone calls came in to Perot's offices in Dallas, and a Perot Petition Committee was organized. Eventually Perot's supporters, many of them paid volunteers, got his name on the ballot in all fifty states and the District of Columbia.

During the spring Perot's public support began to rise rapidly. By early June he was running first in the polls — ahead of George Bush, and ahead of Bill Clinton who was by then the certain Democratic nominee. (See Table 9–11.) By this time, however, Perot, like other candidates, began to encounter negative stories and scrutiny in the press. Perot's appearance in Nashville in July before the national convention of the NAACP was

a disaster. In his speech he offended many voters by referring to African Americans as "you" and "your people." [48] And his standing in the polls began to plummet. On July 16, the day that Bill Clinton accepted the Democratic nomination for the presidency, Ross Perot announced that he was withdrawing from the race.

The Democrats

During much of 1991, while President Bush's poll ratings stood at record or near-record highs, it seemed as though most leading Democrats were making news by announcing that they were *not* going to run for president. Among the potential presidential candidates who might have run but did not were Representative Richard Gephardt of Missouri, Senator Jay Rockefeller of West Virginia, Senator Bill Bradley of New Jersey, and Senator Albert Gore of Tennessee. Both Gephardt and Gore had pursued the Democratic presidential nomination in 1988.

[48] *New York Times*, July 17, 1992, p. A16.

[45] Ibid., p. 64.
[46] Ibid., p. 64.
[47] Ibid., p. 72.

Table 9-11

Voter Support for Clinton, Bush, and Perot: The Gallup Poll's Three-Way Trial Heats Between March and Election Eve, 1992

Date of Interviews	For Clinton	For Bush	For Perot	For Others, No Opinion
March 31–April 1	25%	44%	24%	7%
May 7–10	29	35	30	6
June 4–9	25	31	39	5
July 6–8	28	35	30	7
July 6–8*	40	48		12
Democratic Convention Meets, Perot Leaves Race, July 13–16, 1992				
July 17–18	56	34		10
August 8–10	56	37		7
Republican Convention Meets, August 17–20, 1992				
August 21–22	52	42		6
Aug 31–Sept. 2	54	39		7
September 17–18	51	42		7
Perot Re-enters Race, October 1, 1992				
October 7–8†	50	34	9	7
Televised Debates, October 11–19, 1992				
October 21–22§	43	34	16	7
October 26–27§	40	38	16	6
October 29–30§	42	39	14	5
November 1–2§	44	37	14	5
Election Results	43	38	19	—

* Perot voters assigned to candidate named as their second choice.

† Based on likely voters, responses to question: "If the presidential election were being held today, would you vote for the Republican candidates, George Bush and Dan Quayle, for the Democratic candidates, Bill Clinton and Al Gore, or for the independent candidates, Ross Perot and James Stockdale?"

§ One reason these results may have differed from other polls at the time is that for these surveys, Gallup sampled only "likely voters."

SOURCE: Data provided by the Gallup poll.

Then, late in 1991, two other leading Democrats announced that they would not run. On November 2, the Reverend Jesse Jackson, who had sought the presidency both in 1984 and 1988, declared that he would not be a candidate. And on December 20, New York's Governor Mario Cuomo, probably the Democratic party's best orator, announced that he, too, would not enter the race for president in 1992.

The Democrats who did come foward to seek their party's nomination were less well known nationally than several of the leading noncandidates. (Some political commentators unkindly characterized the candidates who entered the race as the "B List" of potential Democratic contenders.) The first to announce was Paul Tsongas, a former senator from Massachusetts. In time, five other candidates sought the nomination: Governor Douglas Wilder of Virginia, the first African American to be elected governor of a southern state in the twentieth century; Senator Tom Harkin of Iowa; Senator Bob Kerrey of Nebraska; Jerry Brown, the former governor of California; and Governor Bill Clinton of Arkansas. But Governor Wilder, criticized in his home state for spending too much time running for president, dropped out of the race very early, on January 9. As a result, for the first time in 12 years, there was no major black candidate seeking the Democratic nomination for president. As it turned out, Wilder's decision helped Clinton, who was to receive sizable majorities of the votes cast by African Americans in most of the state primaries.

The first Democratic primary took place February 18, 1992, in New Hampshire. As the campaign got under way, Clinton quickly emerged as the frontrunner in the polls.

Then came two startling developments that threatened to destroy the Clinton campaign almost before it began. The tabloid *Star* published a story in which Gennifer Flowers, a lounge singer, asserted that she had engaged in a twelve-year affair with Bill Clinton. Clinton and his wife, Hillary, went on the CBS television program "60 Minutes" to respond to the charges. The Arkansas governor declared that he had brought pain to his family by "marital wrongdoing" but he denied Flowers' allegations.

Then the *Wall Street Journal* raised a new issue: Clinton's draft record.[49] "A man who had been head of the ROTC program at the University of Arkansas said Clinton had promised to join the program in 1969 as a way of avoiding the draft when he was most vulnerable to being called—and then had reneged on his pledge."[50] After bypassing the ROTC program, Clinton drew a high number in the draft lottery and was not called. But questions about the draft, and about his varying explanations of what had occurred, were to plague Clinton throughout the 1992 campaign.

Within a few days Clinton had fallen behind Paul Tsongas in New Hampshire and was in danger of losing so badly that his campaign would be finished before it really started. The night before the election, when Clinton heard the final New Hampshire tracking poll numbers, he thought that his campaign was over. "We're going to get killed," Clinton declared.[51]

But Clinton ran much better in New Hampshire than he expected. Paul Tsongas was first, but the Arkansas governor was a strong second. The final tally was Tsongas 33 percent, Clinton 25, Kerrey 11, Harkin 10, Brown 8.[52] "See you down South, Paul," Clinton told Tsongas.

The South did indeed give a powerful lift to the Clinton candidacy. First there was a crucial primary in Georgia. Clinton won that with 57 percent of the vote to Tsongas's 24. On Super Tuesday, March 10, Clinton swept most of the rest of the South and the border states; Tsongas had victories only in Massachusetts and Rhode Island. The governor from Arkansas now had 800 delegates, more than a third of the number he needed to win the Democratic nomination.[53]

By now Harkin and Kerrey had joined Wilder in dropping out of the race, and a series of primaries in major northern states lay ahead. After Clinton won a decisive victory in Illinois, Tsongas also withdrew. Now Clinton's only announced Democratic opponent was Jerry Brown.

A Brown victory over Clinton in Connecticut—by one percentage point—gave special importance to the upcoming primary in New York state on April 7. Brown sought to strengthen his position among African American voters by promising that, if he won the nomination, he would select Jesse Jackson as his vice-presidential running mate. But Clinton still maintained considerable support among New York's black voters, and he won the New York primary with 40.9 percent of the vote. Tsongas pulled in 28.6 percent of the vote to finish second in New York, where his name remained on the ballot, followed by Brown with 26.2 percent. A Clinton nomination now seemed assured.

Nevertheless, during May and June, Clinton was running third—behind both Bush and Perot—in most of the national polls. Then, during the second and third weeks of July, the strategic outlook for the fall campaign changed dramatically. On July 9 Clinton announced that he had selected Senator Al Gore of Tennessee to be his vice-presidential running mate. The two Democrats were presented as a "New Generation" ticket. For the first time both candidates of a major party had been born after the Second World War—Gore was 44, Clinton was 46. And it was also the first all-southern presidential and vice-presidential ticket to be offered by a major political party since Andrew Jackson had run with John C. Calhoun in 1828. As two journalists noted as they watched Clinton and Gore make their first campaign appearance together, "Side by side they suddenly looked enormously attractive—far more potent than either had ever looked running alone."[54]

The next week, the Democrats dominated radio, television, and the newspapers for four days in what was generally perceived as a highly successful convention in New York City. And Ross Perot dropped out of the race. The first Gallup poll taken after the Democratic convention brought startling news—Clinton was now ahead of George Bush by twenty-two points, 56 percent to 34 percent. (See Table 9–11.) It had been a very good

[49] *Newsweek, Special Election Issue,* November/December 1992, p. 34
[50] Ibid., p. 34
[51] Ibid., p. 36.
[52] Ibid, p. 37.
[53] Ibid., p. 39.

[54] Peter Goldman and Tom Matthews, "America Changes the Guard," in *Newsweek, Special Election Issue,* November/December 1992, p. 56.

two weeks for the Democrats. During thirteen days in early and mid-July, Clinton had moved from last place in a three-way race to the point where he now had a commanding lead over the president.

The General Election Campaign

Part of the new Clinton lead was undoubtedly a temporary increase in support for a candidate whose party had held a successful convention — the so-called "convention bounce" in the polls. But three weeks later, shortly before the Republican convention, Clinton still led Bush by nineteen percentage points.

The Republicans now launched their counterattack at their national convention in Houston. Many convention speakers emphasized the theme of "family values," and Bush himself made a vigorous statement of the case against the Democrats in his acceptance speech. But a fiery convention speech by Pat Buchanan, who charged that the Democratic party was endangering fundamental cultural values, may have been more pleasing to the Republican party's right wing than it was to moderate and independent voters.

When the Republican convention was over, support for President Bush and his vice-presidential running mate Dan Quayle had risen by several percentage

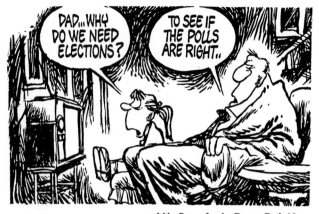

Mike Peters for the *Dayton Daily News*

points. And the support for the Clinton-Gore ticket had dropped about four points. But the Democrats still led in the Gallup poll by ten percentage points — a lead that they held through most of the remaining weeks of the campaign. (See Table 9–11.)

To many of those who watched the general election battle in September and October, the ebb and flow of the campaign suggested that the contest could be divided into four distinct phases. To be sure, the Democrats attempted throughout the campaign to focus attention on the poor performance of the economy under Republican rule. (A sign posted by Clinton campaign

"And now with a rebuttal. . ."

Drawing by Richter © 1979 The New Yorker Magazine, Inc.

THE CLINTON-BUSH-PEROT DEBATES: 1992

Bush: . . . I think character is a very important question. I said something the other day where I was accused of being like Joe McCarthy, because I questioned — I put it this way: I think it's wrong to demonstrate against your own country or organize demonstrations against your own country in foreign soil. I just think it's wrong.

Perot: . . . Certainly anyone in the White House should have the character to be there. But, I think it is very important to measure when and where things occurred. Did they occur when you were a young person in your formative years? Or did they occur while you were a senior official in the Federal Government? When you're a senior official in the Federal Government spending billions of dollars of taxpayers' money and you're a mature individual and you make a mistake, then that was on our ticket. If you make it as a young man, time passes. . . . Decide who you think will do the job, pick that person in November because believe me, as I've said before, the party's over and it's time for the cleanup crew.

Clinton: . . . I've got to respond directly to Mr. Bush. You have questioned my patriotism. You even brought some right-wing Congressmen into the White House to plot how to attack me for going to Russia in 1969–1970 when over 50,000 other Americans did. Now I honor your service in World War II. . . . But when Joe McCarthy went around this country attacking people's patriotism, he was wrong. . . . And a Senator from Connecticut stood up to him named Prescott Bush. Your father was right to stand up to Joe McCarthy. You were wrong to attack my patriotism. I was opposed to the war but I love my country and we need a President who will bring this country together, not divide it.

Bush: . . . Mr. and Mrs. America, when you hear him say 'We're going to tax only the rich,' watch your wallet. Because his figures don't add up and he's going to sock it right to the middle-class taxpayer and lower, if he's going to pay for all the spending programs he proposes. So we have a big difference on this trickle-down theory. I do not want any more trickle-down Government. It's gotten too big. I want to do something about that.

Perot: I grew up five blocks from Arkansas. Let's — let's put it in perspective. It's a beautiful state, it's a fairly rural state, it has a population less than Chicago or Los Angeles. . . . So I think probably we're making a mistake night after night after night to cast the nation's future on a unit that small. . . . I could say that I ran a small grocery store on the corner, therefore I extrapolate that into the fact that I could run Wal-Mart; that's not true.

Clinton: . . . I took a state that was one of the poorest states in the country and had been for 153 years and tried my best to modernize its economy and to make the kind of changes that had generated support from people like the presidents of Apple Computer and Hewlett Packard, and some of the biggest companies in this country. . . . I think it's important to elect a President who is committed to getting this economy going again and who realizes we have to abandon trickle-down economics and put the American people first again and who will send programs to the Congress in the first hundred days to deal with the critical issues that America is crying out for leadership on — jobs, incomes, the health care crisis, the need to control the economy. . . . They will be my first priority, not my election year concern.

Bush: . . . I am for the North American Free Trade Agreement. My problem with Governor Clinton once again, is that one time he's going to make up his mind he will see some merit in it, but then he sees a lot of things wrong with it. When you're President of the United States, you cannot have this pattern of saying well I'm for it but I'm on the other side of it.

Clinton: . . . Mr. Perot says it's a bad deal. Mr. Bush says it's a hunky dory deal. . . . I have a realistic approach to trade. I want more trade. And I know there are some good things in that agreement. But it can sure be made better. . . . I'll have a free and fair trade policy, a hardheaded realistic policy, and not get caught up in rubber-stamping everything the Bush Administration did.

Perot: Now that we've talked all around the problem about free trade, let's go, again, to the center of the bull's-eye. . . . foreign lobbyists, this whole thing, our country has sold out to foreign lobbyists. We don't have free trade. Both parties have foreign lobbyists on leaves and key roles in the campaigns. And if there's anything more unwise than that I don't know what it is.

—Excerpts from the televised Clinton-Bush-Perot debates, October 11, 1992, and October 19, 1992

adviser James Carville in the Democrats' campaign headquarters in Little Rock, Arkansas, reminded the campaign workers of their main theme: "The Economy, Stupid."[55])

But during the first half of September, President Bush and Vice-President Quayle focused on an attack theme of their own — Clinton's various explanations of his draft deferment during the Vietnam War. Clinton seemed to have difficulty giving a crisp, clear answer to

the charges, and for the first two weeks of September, he was on the defensive.

Then, about mid-September, the momentum of the campaign appeared to shift. The nonpartisan Commission on Presidential Debates had proposed that there be four televised debates during the campaign — three debates of presidential candidates between late September and mid-October; and a debate between the vice-presidential candidates on October 4. Clinton and Gore said that they would be happy to debate on the scheduled dates; but the Bush-Quayle campaign

---

[55] *Newsweek, Special Election Issue*, November/December 1992, p. 78.

THE GORE-QUAYLE-STOCKDALE DEBATE: 1992

Gore: . . . Bill Clinton and I stand for change, because we don't believe our nation can stand four more years of what we've had under George Bush and Dan Quayle. When the recession came they were like a deer caught in the headlights — paralyzed into inaction, blinded to the suffering and pain of bankruptcies and people who were unemployed.

Quayle: . . . At some time during these next four years there is going to be a crisis — there will be an international crisis. . . . We need a president who has the experience, who has been tested, who has the integrity and qualifications to handle the crisis. The president has been tested, the president has the integrity and the character. The choice is yours.

Stockdale: Who am I? Why am I here? I'm not a politician; everybody knows that. So don't expect me to use the language of the Washington insider. Thirty-seven years in the Navy, and only one of them up there in Washington. . . . I know how governments, how American governments can be — can be courageous, and how they can be callow. . . . Why am I here tonight? I am here because I have in my brain and in my heart what it takes to lead America through tough times.

Gore: This election is about the future of our country, not about personal attacks against one candidate or another. Our nation is in trouble and it is appalling to me that with 10 million Americans out of work, with the rest working harder for less money than they did four years ago, with the loss of 1.4 million manufacturing jobs in our nation, with the health care crisis, a crisis of crime and drugs and AIDS, substandard education, that George Bush would constantly try to level personal attacks at his opponent.

Quayle: . . . I agree with one thing on — with — Senator Gore, and that is that we ought to look to the future. And the future is, who's going to be the next president of the United States. And is it a negative attack and a personal attack to point out that Bill Clinton has trouble telling the truth? . . . I don't care whether he demonstrated or didn't demonstrate. The fact — the question — is, tell the truth.

Stockdale: I think the best justification for getting Ross Perot in the race again is to say that we're seeing this kind of chitchat back and forth about issues that don't concentrate on where our grandchildren — the living standards of our children and grandchildren. . . . I think I'm in a room with people that aren't living the life of reality. The United States is in deep trouble. We've got to have somebody that can get up there and bring out the firehoses and get it stopped, and that's what we're about in the Perot campaign.

—Excerpts from the televised Gore-Quayle-Stockdale debate, October 13, 1992

declined, proposing different formats. Hecklers began to turn up at Republican rallies dressed in bright yellow chicken costumes, thereby implying that Bush was afraid to debate — much to the annoyance of the president. And throughout September Clinton's lead in the polls over Bush continued to hold.

The third phase of the campaign season began on October 1. Ross Perot re-entered the presidential race, greatly altering the dynamics of the campaign for the remaining five weeks. About the same time, Bush suddenly challenged Clinton to a series of televised debates, which after intense negotiations were set for the middle of October. From October 11 to October 19 there would be four televised debates — three among the leading presidential nominees and one for the candidates for vice-president. And Ross Perot and his vice-presidential running mate, James B. Stockdale, would be in the debates.

Enormous audiences — some evenings as high as 93 million people — watched the debates. In the first encounter, in St. Louis, more people (31 percent) thought Clinton had "won" the debate than thought that Bush had come in first (19 percent). But Perot, with 43 percent, was the biggest winner.[56]

In the second debate, featuring the vice-presidential candidates, Dan Quayle was combative and hard hitting. The vice-president launched an all-out

[56] *Newsweek* poll, based on interviews conducted on October 11, 1992, *Newsweek*, October 19, 1992, p. 20.

1992: The presidential candidates answered questions from the audience in their second debate

assault on Clinton's character, questioning whether he was fit to serve in the presidency. Al Gore held his ground and assailed the Bush administration over the economy. Stockdale, by contrast, performed poorly. Uncomfortable in the spotlight, he did not help Perot's campaign.

Many Republican partisans responded warmly to Vice-President Quayle's aggressive performance, and it undoubtedly strengthened Quayle's standing within his own party. But there was evidence that Al Gore was the vice-presidential candidate who brought the greatest strength to his party's ticket. A *Newsweek* poll taken shortly after the vice-presidential debate asked the voters: "If you could vote separately for vice president, whom would you vote for?" The response was: Gore, 61 percent; Quayle, 28 percent; and Stockdale, 6 percent.[57]

The second presidential debate, in Richmond, Virginia, followed a more informal format. Members of

the audience, rather than journalists, asked most of the questions. Clinton seemed to thrive in this setting; Bush, by contrast, seemed to be less comfortable. At one point the president appeared to be stumped when a young African American woman asked him how the national debt affected him personally. "I'm not sure I get — " he said, "help me with the question and I'll try to answer it."[58]

In another room, James Carville, Clinton's senior campaign strategist, sat with other staff members watching an indicator that measured audience response to what each candidate was saying. The indicator had just reached its low point for the evening. "Bush just lost the election," Carville exclaimed as he watched the television screen. "Can you imagine if we had a candidate who did that? You'd be fanning me right now."[59]

But Bush had not yet lost the election. In the third and final presidential debate, in East Lansing, Michigan,

[57] *Newsweek* poll, based on interviews conducted on October 15–16, 1992. *Newsweek*, October 26, 1992, p. 27.

[58] *Washington Post*, October 16, 1992, p. A35.
[59] *Newsweek*, *Special Election Issue*, November/December 1992, p. 91.

"Well, George . . . I guess this answers the question . . . 'How has the recession affected you personally?'. . ."

Bill Schorr reprinted by permission of UFS, Inc.

on October 19, the president turned in a strong performance. He was clearly making one last, all-out effort to win. But the debates were over, and just two more weeks of the campaign remained. Perot had obviously made a favorable impression on many voters, and his standing in the polls began to rise rapidly. He held few campaign rallies; from his headquarters in Dallas he now launched a barrage of television ads and much lengthier "infomercials." Millions of Americans watched the Perot ads.

In the final days of the campaign, there were several dramatic developments. On October 25 Ross Perot claimed that he had pulled out of the race in July because he feared that if he stayed in, his daughter would be the victim of Republican "dirty tricks." Perot was unable to substantiate his charge, however, and the uproar that followed seemed for a time to blunt Perot's progress in the polls.

Meanwhile the president began to draw huge, enthusiastic crowds. He was obviously buoyed by their response; he also seemed to feel that he was closing the gap on Clinton, and some of the polls indicated he might be doing so. One Gallup poll reported that Clinton was now only two points ahead of the president.[60] Bush hit hard at the twin issues of "taxes and trust," arguing that his opponent would raise taxes and could not be trusted, in part because he had given varying

explanations of his draft deferment during the Vietnam War. And Bush seemed to be making an impact with his repeated charge that Clinton "waffled," was indecisive, and seemed to take all sides of some major policy issues.

As the campaign neared its end, Bush's attacks on his Democratic opponents became harsher. "My dog Millie knows more about foreign policy than these two bozos," Bush said, and he called Gore "Ozone Man," or just "Ozone." [61] Some campaign observers, however, thought that the president's more extreme personal attacks on his Democratic adversaries might backfire; calling the Democrats "bozos" seemed unpresidential.

Then, on Friday, October 30, Lawrence E. Walsh, the independent counsel investigating the Iran-contra affair, filed new evidence in court. The key document released was a handwritten note by then Defense Secretary Caspar W. Weinberger suggesting that Bush, while vice-president, had attended a high-level White House meeting and had not only known about, but had favored, exchanging arms with Iran for American hostages. [62] Over the final weekend the president and other

---

[60] Gallup poll October 28–29 for *Newsweek*, in *New York Times*, November 3, 1992, p. A13. One reason the result may have differed from other polls at the time is that for this survey, Gallup sampled only "likely voters."

[61] *Washington Post*, October 30, 1992, p. A1.

[62] *Washington Post*, October 31, 1992, p. A1.

Republicans were again on the defensive, denying that the president had been "in the loop." After he lost the election, Bush pardoned Weinberger and five other officials involved in the scandal.

On election day, a key question was: Will they vote? Both Clinton and Perot supporters contended that a large voter turnout would be a "pro-change" vote that could benefit their candidate. On election day, bright sunshine and balmy weather prevailed in most of the South and Southeast, and as far north as Philadelphia. There is an old belief among politicians that good weather usually means more voters will go to the polling places. But in New York City and New England, and in Chicago and other great cities of the Midwest, there was rain much of the day. And in the iron range of Minnesota, in Colorado, and elsewhere, snow had fallen. Everywhere, however, the people voted—the first day in the history of the nation when more than 100 million Americans went to the polls.

Despite the intense efforts of Bush and Perot to close the gap during the week before election, Clinton remained in the lead, as he had since the middle of July. He won by a margin of 5.4 percentage points over Bush and by more than 5,560,000 popular votes.

Several noteworthy features marked the voting patterns of 1992:

1. About 104 million voters went to the polls. The number of people who voted for president was up by more than 12 million from 1988, and the percentage turnout—about 55 percent—was the nation's highest since 1972.[63]

2. The 19.2 million votes (19 percent) polled by Ross Perot was the largest percentage received by a minor-party or independent candidate since Theodore Roosevelt ran as the candidate of the Progressive (Bull Moose) party in 1912. And it was the largest percentage ever received by a third-party or independent candidate who had not already served as president of the United States.

3. The impact of the recession—and of economic concerns—was strongly reflected in the returns. One-third of the voters (34 percent) reported that their families' financial situation was worse in 1992 than it had been in 1988. Among that large group of voters, Clinton led Bush by nearly 50 percentage points. (See Table 9-12).

---

[63] Data provided by the Committee for the Study of the American Electorate, Washington, D.C.

Table 9-12
Who Voted in 1992

	Clinton	Bush	Perot
All (100%)	44%	37%	19%
Men (46)	41	37	21
Women (54)	47	36	17
Whites (87)	40	39	21
Blacks (8)	83	11	7
Hispanics (3)	62	24	14
Didn't complete high school (6)	56	27	18
High school grad (25)	44	36	21
Some college (29)	43	36	21
College grad (24)	41	39	20
Postgrad (16)	50	35	15
Age 18–24 (11)	47	31	22
25–29 (11)	41	35	24
30–39 (25)	42	38	21
40–49 (24)	44	37	19
50–59 (13)	42	39	19
60 and up (16)	50	37	12
Family income*:			
Less than $15,000 (14)	59	22	19
$15,000–29,999 (24)	46	34	20
$30,000–49,999 (30)	42	37	21
$50,000–74,999 (20)	41	41	18
$75,000 or more (13)	38	46	16
Protestants (56)	34	45	21
Catholics (27)	42	37	21
Jews (4)	78	10	11
Family financial situation compared with 1988:			
Better (25)	25	60	15
Worse (34)	62	13	25
About the same (41)	42	41	18
Democrats (39)	78	10	13
Republicans (34)	11	72	18
Independents (28)	39	31	30
Liberals (22)	69	13	18
Moderates (50)	49	30	21
Conservatives (29)	18	64	17
1988 votes:			
Bush (53)	22	58	20
Dukakis (27)	83	5	12
Didn't vote (15)	50	24	26
First-time voters (11)	48	29	23
Union households (19)	56	23	22
Nonunion households (81)	42	39	19
Reagan voters in 1984 (44)	21	58	21

* Comparable income categories were used in 1988.
SOURCE: Voter Research and Surveys exit polls for 1992 in *National Journal*, November 7, 1992, p. 2543.

4. The Clinton tide extended across most regions of the country. In terms of states won and lost, however, there were important centers of Bush strength in four areas—most of the Southeast, Indiana, a string of six states in the center of the country running from Texas to the Canadian border, and four of the eight Rocky Mountain states.

5. Bush ran most strongly in the once heavily Democratic South. In the eleven states of the former Confederacy, Bush led Clinton—42.7 percent to 41.5 percent. In the rest of the country, Clinton led Bush by a sizable margin—44 percent to 36.5 percent.

6. Nevertheless, the Democrats' Clinton-Gore ticket, the first all-southern ticket since 1828, did make inroads into previous Republican strength in presidential voting in the South. In 1988, Bush led Dukakis by 17 percentage points in the South; in 1992 Bush's lead in the region was cut to less than two percent. Moreover, Clinton carried four southern states—Arkansas, Georgia, Louisiana, and Tennessee—and he came close to carrying two more, North Carolina and Florida.

7. In the presidential race, the most Democratic region was the Northeast, where Clinton outpolled Bush by 47 percent to 35 percent. In the Midwest the outcome was closer. Clinton ran ahead of Bush 42 percent to 37 percent.

8. One of the most striking regional trends was the improved showing by the Democrats in the West, a region where Ronald Reagan carried many of the states by landslide margins in the 1980s. Clinton won decisive victories in California, Oregon, and Washington; and among the eight Rocky Mountain states, Clinton was the winner in four—Colorado, New Mexico, Montana, and Nevada.

9. Despite Clinton's generally strong showing in the West, there was a substantial difference between the voting patterns in the Pacific Coast region and the pattern in the Rocky Mountain area. In the Pacific Coast states, Clinton ran ahead of Bush 46 percent to 32 percent. In the Rocky Mountain states, by contrast, the popular vote was close. It was Bush 38.6 percent and Clinton 36.9 percent—with nearly one vote in every four in the Rocky Mountain region (24.5 percent) going to Perot.

10. Clinton ran well among some traditionally Democratic groups in which the Democrats had suffered heavy losses to Reagan in the 1980s. Among members of union households, Clinton led Bush 56 percent to 23 percent; he also ran ahead of Bush among Hispanic Americans, 62 percent to 24 percent. Exit polls also showed Clinton doing well among two groups that had remained Democratic in 1984 and 1988: Clinton was backed by 83 percent of black voters and by 78 percent of Jewish voters.[64] Despite the attacks on his draft record, Clinton also won the votes cast by veterans of the nation's armed forces—by 41 percent to 37 percent.[65]

11. As in 1988, there was a substantial difference in the way women and men voted in the 1992 presidential race. Among male voters, Clinton had a modest lead over Bush. Among women who voted, Clinton led Bush by eleven percentage points. If all voters had voted the way American women cast their ballots in 1992, Clinton probably would have won the election by more than 10 million votes, instead of by 5,560,000.

12. The Democrats also made a net gain of two in the nation's governorships, leaving them with thirty governors to the Republicans' eighteen. (Two governors in 1992 were independents.)

13. Despite the Democratic presidential victory for Bill Clinton, in the battle for control of the House of Representatives, the Republicans slightly strengthened their position. The Republicans made a net gain of nine seats in the House. That still left the Democrats with a majority in the House of 259 to 175 (plus one independent from Vermont). Moreover, the 1992 results followed a post-1990 census reapportionment that had moved House seats from Democratic areas in the Northeast and Midwest to more Republican areas in the South and West. In part because of this reapportionment, at the beginning of the 1992 congressional campaigns the Republicans had hoped to do better.

14. The new House of Representatives elected in 1992 was also more representative of the American people. One-fourth of the new House that assembled in January 1993 were new members—

---

[64] Election Day exit polls of 15,241 voters conducted by Voter Research and Surveys. *National Journal*, November 7, 1992, p. 2543.
[65] Voter Research and Surveys exit polls. *Newsweek, Special Election Issue*, November/December 1992, p. 10.

men and women who had not served in the preceding Congress. Compared with the 102nd Congress, the new 103rd Congress was more diverse, had more minority members, was younger, and had fewer lawyers. There were many more women in the House — forty-seven in the new House compared with twenty-eight in the old. There were thirty-eight African Americans compared with twenty-five in the old House, and seventeen Hispanic Americans compared with ten in the previous House.

15. In the Senate, the balance of power between the parties remained the same — fifty-seven Democrats, and forty-three Republicans.[66] And like the House, the Senate became somewhat more diverse. Four more women were elected to the Senate, joining the two who served in that body before 1992. And in Colorado the victory of Ben Nighthorse Campbell, the Democratic candidate, sent the first Native American to the Senate in more than sixty years.

16. The 1992 elections left the Democratic party with a solid majority in the Senate, but it also left the Democrats with more seats than the Republicans to defend in the next battle for control of the Senate — the midterm congressional elections of 1994. One-third of the U.S. Senate seats (thirty-four seats) were to be filled in the midterm elections of 1994. Of those thirty-four seats, twenty-two were held by Democrats and only twelve were held by Republicans.

17. Perhaps the most important point of all about the 1992 election was that for a time, at least, there would be no more divided government, no more "partisan gridlock," and no more excuses for legislative or executive inaction. For the first time in twelve years, the presidency and the Congress would be controlled by the same party — the Democrats. How well the Democrats were perceived as *governing* would go a long way toward determining how their party would fare in future elections — whether they would be rewarded with additional electoral victories, or whether they, too, would encounter retribution at the polls.

---

[66] In 1992, two Senate contests were decided after election day in special elections held Nov. 24 in Georgia, won by the Republicans, and Dec. 4 in North Dakota, won by the Democrats.

THE ELECTORAL SYSTEM

The act of choice performed by the American voter on Election Day takes place within a legal and structural framework that strongly influences the result. The electoral system in the United States is not neutral — it affects the dynamics of voting all along the way. Before voters can step into the voting booths, they must meet a number of legal requirements. The candidates whose names appear on the ballot must have qualified under state law. The form of the ballot may influence voters' decisions — if they are allowed to pull a single lever, for example, they are more likely to vote a straight party ticket than if they must pull many levers to vote that way. How their votes count in a presidential election is controlled by custom, state law, and the Constitution, for all three affect the workings of the electoral college. In short, the structure, details, and workings of the electoral system affect the people's choice.

Suffrage

The Constitution provides for popular election of members of the House of Representatives, a provision extended to the election of senators by the Seventeenth Amendment, ratified in 1913. In electing a president, the voters in each state actually choose electors, who meet in December of the election year and cast their ballots for a chief executive. (See pp. 345–347.)

Voting is a basic right provided for by the Constitution. Under the Fourteenth Amendment, it is one of the privileges and immunities of national citizenship that the states may not abridge and that Congress has the power to protect by federal legislation. For example, in 1970 Congress limited state residence requirements for voting in presidential elections. The states, however, set many requirements for voting. State laws in part govern the machinery of choice — residence and other voting requirements, registration, primaries, and the form of the ballot. And state laws regulate political parties.

Until the age of Andrew Jackson, voting was generally restricted to men who owned property and paid taxes. Since then, suffrage has gradually been broadened. Most states lifted property requirements in the early nineteenth century. In 1869 Wyoming became the first state to enact women's suffrage, and three other western states did so in the 1890s. In 1917 the suffragettes began marching in front of the White House;

Exercise your right to vote. BE A VOTER!

they were arrested and jailed. In 1919 Congress passed the Nineteenth Amendment, making it unconstitutional to deny any citizen the right to vote on account of sex. The amendment was ratified by the states in time for women to vote in the presidential election of 1920.

The long struggle of African Americans for the right to vote is described in Chapter 5. As we have seen, even though the Fifteenth Amendment specifically gave black citizens the right to vote, it was circumvented when the South regained political control of its state governments following Reconstruction. Poll taxes, all-white primaries, phony literacy tests, intimidation, and violence were all effective in disenfranchising blacks in the South. In 1964 the Twenty-fourth Amendment eliminated the last vestiges of the poll tax in federal elections.[67] But blacks still faced many of the other barriers to voting; only 44 percent of voting-age black citizens in the South voted in the 1964 presidential election. The Voting Rights Act of 1965, which was extended in 1970, 1975, and in 1982 to the year 2007, sought to throw the mantle of federal protection

around these voters. It was followed by a dramatic increase in blacks voting in the South.

Residence Requirements When Congress extended the Voting Rights Act in 1970, it included a provision permitting voters in every state to vote in presidential elections after living in the state for thirty days. This uniform federal standard was designed to override state residence requirements, some of which had prevented millions of persons from voting for president. The Voting Rights Act also required states to permit absentee registration and voting. Subsequently, the Supreme Court ruled that states may not require residence of more than thirty days to vote in federal, state, and local elections,[68] although in 1973 the Court modified this standard to permit a state residency requirement of fifty days, at least in state and local elections.[69] But neither case changed the thirty-day maximum residence requirements for voting in presidential elections.

Literacy and Character Tests Historically, literacy tests were used to keep recent immigrants and blacks from voting. The Voting Rights Act of 1965 suspended literacy tests in the six southern states and all or part of four other states where less than half the voting-age population had registered or voted in the 1964 election. The law also suspended in those areas tests requiring voters to prove "good moral character."

Later amendments to the Voting Rights Act extended the ban against literacy and character tests to all states. Prior to passage of the law, twelve states — including California and New York — still listed literacy as a requirement for voting. Two states, Idaho and Connecticut, had "good character" tests. Under Idaho law, prostitutes, their customers and madams, bigamists, persons of Chinese or Mongolian descent, and persons who "lewdly or lasciviously cohabit together"[70] were banned from voting. And Connecticut had a law on its books requiring that voters be of "good moral character."

Although these anachronistic character tests were suspended along with literacy tests by the 1970 amendments to the Voting Rights Act, a number of states retained on the statute books other odd barriers to vot-

---

[67] Only five southern states still imposed a poll tax as a requirement for voting in federal elections when the Twenty-fourth Amendment went into effect on January 23, 1964. Under the Voting Rights Act of 1965, the United States Attorney General filed lawsuits against four of the twenty-seven states still imposing poll taxes in state and local elections. In 1966 the United States Supreme Court ruled in *Harper* v. *Virginia State Board of Elections*, 383 U.S. 633, that any state poll tax violated the Fourteenth Amendment. The decision outlawed the use of poll taxes at any level of election.

[68] *Dunn* v. *Blumstein*, 405 U.S. 330 (1972).
[69] *Marston* v. *Mandt*, 410 U.S. 679 (1973); *Burns* v. *Fortson*, 410 U.S. 686 (1973).
[70] Elizabeth Yadlosky, *Election Laws of the Fifty States and the District of Columbia*, Legislative Reference Service of The Library of Congress, June 5, 1968, p. 305.

ing. The laws of nine states, for example, disqualified paupers, and Louisiana law disqualified parents of illegitimate children. The laws of seven states disqualified persons engaging in duels. Such oddities were not affected by the Voting Rights Act or its various extensions, but they were generally not enforced by the states anyway.

Most states bar mentally incompetent persons and inmates of prisons from voting. Persons convicted of certain types of crimes lose the right to vote under the laws of forty-six states. Some states restore the right to vote on release from prison, or after a set number of years of imprisonment, or by executive or legislative clemency.

Age In the late 1960s, with young Americans fighting and dying in Vietnam — but denied the right to vote — pressure to lower the voting age to eighteen built up rapidly. After November 1970 eight states had lowered their legal voting age to below twenty-one. In all other states the minimum voting age was twenty-one years.

Efforts to amend the Constitution to allow people to vote at age eighteen had failed to pass Congress in the 1950s and 1960s. In 1970 Congress, by statute, lowered the voting age to eighteen in all elections, but later that year the Supreme Court ruled that Congress had power to do so only in *federal* elections.[71] The result was confusion. In 1971 Congress passed, and the necessary three-fourths of the states ratified, a constitutional amendment lowering the voting age to eighteen in all elections.

The new Twenty-sixth Amendment enfranchised approximately 10.5 million persons between the ages of eighteen and twenty-one in time to vote in the 1972 presidential election. Many political observers reasoned that the addition of so large a group of young voters could have an impact on the political system. But the lower voting age did not result in dramatic political change, in part because younger voters traditionally have had a low rate of turnout. In fact, in the first election in which all persons from eighteen through twenty could vote (1972), less than half (48 percent) voted.[72] In 1992, 11 percent of the total vote for president was cast by persons age 18 through 24.[73]

---

[71] *Oregon v. Mitchell*, 400 U.S. 112 (1970).
[72] U.S. Bureau of the Census, Current Population Reports, Population Characteristics, series P-20, no. 244, December 1972, p. 3.
[73] Voter Research and Surveys exit polls for 1992 in *National Journal*, November 7, 1992, p. 2543.

Citizenship Only United States citizens can vote. This was not always the case, however. In the nineteenth century, twenty-two states and territories gave aliens the right to vote; the last state to abolish alien voting was Arkansas, in 1926. As a result, the presidential election of 1928 was the first in which only United States citizens could vote. More than ten million United States residents reported that they could not vote in 1988 because they were not American citizens.

The Nominating Process: Primaries and Conventions

Voting requirements restrict the number of people who can step into the voting booth. The nominating process restricts choice, since the voter is effectively limited to those candidates nominated by parties or running as independents and placed on the ballot. (Write-in votes, where permitted, seldom elect anyone.)

State laws govern the nominating process and the selection of party leaders. Although the Constitution provides for election of members of Congress and the president, it makes no direct mention of how they shall be nominated and placed on the ballot. In the nineteenth century, candidates for public office were chosen by backroom caucuses of politicians or by local or state conventions. The abuses of that manner of selection led to demands for reform. By 1915 two-thirds of the states had some kind of law providing for primary elections to choose candidates for the general elections. Today every state has provisions for primary elections to choose some candidates who run in statewide contests. Party officials also may be chosen in primaries.

Currently most states hold direct primaries to nominate candidates for the House and Senate. In a handful of other states, nominations are by convention, party committee, or by a combination of methods. In states using primaries, the most common form is the closed primary, in which only registered members of a party or persons declaring their affiliation with a party can vote. Several states use the open primary, in which any voter may participate and vote for a slate of candidates of one political party.

Political parties still hold conventions to nominate candidates for president and vice-president. As noted in Chapter 7, in 1992 forty states and the District of Columbia held Democratic presidential primaries, and thirty-nine states plus the District of Columbia held Republican presidential primaries, in which voters in one or both parties chose all or some convention delegates. Other states chose delegates to national nominating conventions by different methods, including selection by state conventions, party caucuses, and party committees. But because most of the large states held presidential primaries in 1992, more than half of the national-convention delegates were selected in presidential primaries in that year.

Voter Registration

The old Tammany Hall slogan, "Vote Early and Vote Often," still brings nostalgic smiles to the faces of some political leaders in New York. But the use of "repeaters" to vote more than once, and of "tombstone" voters (using the names of deceased voters), and similar devices is made much more difficult—although by no means impossible—by modern systems of voter registration.

Before voters can vote, they must register. Under state laws, when voters register, their names are entered on a list of people qualified to vote. They may, if they wish, declare their party affiliation when they register. On Election Day, the registration list may be checked for each voter who comes to the polling place to ensure that he or she is qualified to cast his or her ballot.

Permanent registration, under which the voter registers only once in his or her district, prevails in all but a few states. *Periodic* registration, under which the voter must register every year or at other stated intervals, is used in a very small number of states. North Dakota requires no registration.

Like other forms of election machinery, registration procedures can affect the political result. For example, in Idaho, roving canvassers remind people to regis-

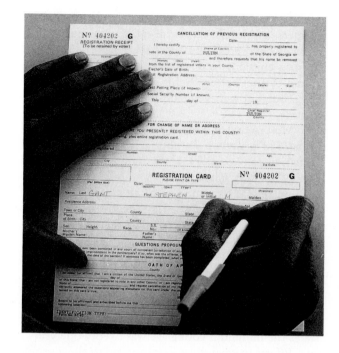

ter to vote, and the turnout has consistently been higher than the national average. No doubt other factors are at work in Idaho, but, as a presidential commission concluded: "The average American is far more likely to vote if few barriers stand between him and registration." [74]

A basic factor affecting registration and voting in the United States is that an American who wishes to register usually must take the initiative and appear in person at the local registration office. (In Great Britain and a number of European countries, the government

---

[74] *Report of the President's Commission on Registration and Voting Participation*, p. 32.

WINNING VOTES— MACHINE STYLE

I know every man, woman, and child in the Fifteenth District, except them that's been born this summer—and I know some of them, too. I know what they like and what they don't like, what they are strong at and what they are weak in, and I reach them by approachin' at the right side.

For instance, here's how I gather in the young men. I hear of a young feller that's proud of his voice, thinks he can sing fine. I ask him to come around to Washing-ton Hall and join our Glee Club. He comes and sings, and he's a follower of Plunkitt for life. Another young feller gains a reputation as a baseball player in a vacant lot. I bring him into our baseball club. That fixes him. You'll find him workin' for my ticket at the polls next election day. . . . I don't trouble them with political arguments. I just study human nature and act accordin'.

—Boss Plunkitt, in William L. Riordon, *Plunkitt of Tammany Hall*

takes the initiative in attempting to register eligible voters.) In more recent years, however, some attempts have been made to make it easier to register in the United States. In 1976 the House passed a bill that would allow registration by postcard in federal elections, but the Senate did not approve the measure. And in some states, potential voters may register at tables set up in stores, or with citizen registrars or party volunteers who go from door to door seeking new voters. In 1992 President Bush vetoed a bill that would have required states to register people to vote when they applied for a driver's license or other types of public permits — such as a marriage license — or when they picked up welfare checks or food stamps.

Ballots

The secret (so-called Australian) ballot was not adopted by every state in the United States until 1950. Early in American history the voter often orally announced his vote at the polling place. After the Civil War, this method was replaced by ballots printed by each political party; since the ballots were often of different colors, it was easy to tell how someone voted. Concern over voter intimidation and fraud led to pressure for secret ballots printed by public authorities. By 1900 a substantial number of states had adopted the secret ballot. This ballot has two chief forms:

1. The *party-column ballot*, or Indiana ballot, used in a majority of states, lists the candidates of each party in a row or column, beside or under the party emblem. In most cases, the voter can make one mark at the top of the column, or pull one lever, and thus vote for all the party's candidates for various offices. This ballot encourages straight-ticket voting.

2. The *office-column ballot*, or Massachusetts ballot, groups candidates according to the office for which they are running — all the presidential candidates of all the parties appear in one column or row, for example.

Research has demonstrated that the form of the ballot may influence the vote. Among independent voters, one study found that a party-column ballot increased straight-ticket voting by 60 percent.[75] (Examples of both kinds of ballots are shown on p. 344.)

---

[75] Campbell, Converse, Miller, and Stokes, *The American Voter*, p. 285.

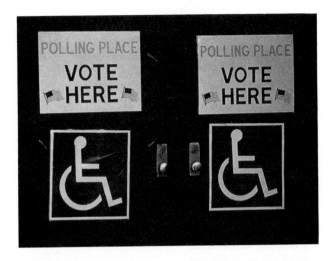

The first voting machine was used in 1892 by the city of Lockport, New York. By 1990 more than half the states used machines statewide or in most areas.

Counting the Votes

On election night the results in each state are tabulated by state and local election officials and reported to the nation through the News Election Service, a cooperative pool of the three major television networks and the Associated Press and United Press International, the two major wire services.

The drama of election night is in a sense entirely artificial. As the night wears on, one candidate may appear to lead, then fall behind, and perhaps forge ahead again. Actually, once the polls close, the popular vote result is already recorded inside the ballot boxes and voting machines.

In recent years the nation has no longer had to wait until the votes actually were counted to know the results of some elections, because the television networks have developed systems of *projecting* the vote with the aid of electronic computers. In 1992 NBC anchor Tom Brokaw predicted a victory for Bill Clinton at 10:49 P.M., EST, after Ohio, where the race had been close, had awarded its twenty-one electoral votes to Clinton. About that same time, the other networks were also predicting that the governor from Arkansas was now president-elect of the United States. In 1976, however, the election was so close that neither the computers nor the commentators were willing to make any predictions for many hours. Jimmy Carter was not declared the winner, by NBC, until 3:30 A.M., EST. In some instances

Figure 9–4
Sample Ballots

The party-column, or Indiana ballot.

The office-column, or Massachusetts ballot (used in a number of states, including Texas, as shown).

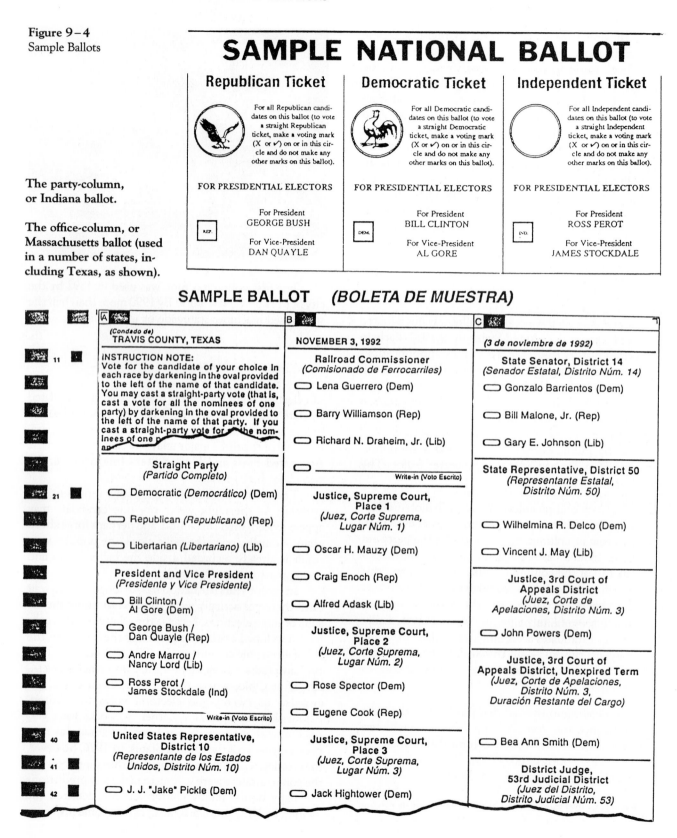

the computers have predicted the wrong winners in state contests.

The computerized vote-projection systems are based on analysis of key precincts in selected areas. Past election data about the sample precincts are coded and stored in the computers and compared with actual returns as they come in on election night. As the computer processes the data flowing in, it is able to make a statistical forecast of the probable outcome. In 1980 a number of western Democratic candidates as well as other political leaders complained sharply when the television networks declared Reagan the projected winner early in the evening, and President Carter conceded at 8:50 P.M., EST. These events, coming while the polls were still open on the West Coast, they argued, discouraged many potential voters from voting. Again in 1984, the television networks declared President Reagan the winner before the polls had closed on the West Coast.

In 1992, in order to deflect criticism, the television networks agreed that they would not project the winner in a state until the majority of the polls had closed in that state.

Fraud

With so much at stake on election night, it is not surprising that from time to time there are charges of voting fraud, even in presidential elections.

In 1960, after John Kennedy's narrow popular-vote victory over Richard Nixon, some Republicans charged that there had been election frauds in Cook County, Illinois; and in Texas. If Kennedy had failed to carry these two states, Nixon would have won in the electoral college. Kennedy carried Illinois by a mere 8,858 votes, but his margin in Texas was much larger, 46,257 votes. Nixon considered, but decided not to ask for, an investigation or a recount.[76]

It may well be that in the age of the computer, some form of electronic voting system will be developed so votes can be recorded and tallied quickly with a minimal possibility of tampering.

The Electoral College

The Constitution does not provide for the popular election of the president. Instead, it provides that each state "shall appoint, in such manner as the legislature thereof may direct," electors equal in number to the representatives and senators that each state has in Congress. Instead of voting directly for president, an American, in casting his or her ballot, votes for a slate of electors that is normally pledged to the presidential candidate of the voter's choice.

Many voters are unaware that they are voting for electors because their names do not even appear on the ballot in about two-thirds of the states. The slate of

---

[76] Richard M. Nixon, *Six Crises* (New York: Doubleday, 1962), p. 413.

electors that receives the most votes meets in the state capital in December of a presidential election year and casts its ballots. Each state sends the results to Washington, where the electoral votes are officially counted in a joint session of Congress early in January. The candidate with a majority of the electoral votes is elected president. (In 1992, when there were a total of 538 members of the electoral college, 270 electoral votes were required to win the presidency.) If no one receives a majority, the House of Representatives must choose the president from among the three candidates with the largest number of electoral votes, with each state delegation in the House having one vote. Members of the electoral college also vote for vice-president in a separate balloting procedure. If no candidate for vice-president receives a majority of the electoral votes, the Senate must choose the vice-president from one of the two candidates with the most electoral votes.[77]

Custom, not the Constitution, is the reason electors are chosen in each state by popular vote. In the first four presidential elections, state legislatures chose the electors in most cases. South Carolina was the last state to switch to popular election, in 1860. Although there is hardly any possibility that a state would discontinue the popular election of electors, legally, a state may select them any way it wishes.[78]

The framers of the Constitution had great difficulty in agreeing on the best way to elect the president. Some favored direct election by all of the voters, but others thought this would give an advantage to the more populous states. The provision for presidential electors represented a compromise between the big and little states. For, "only a few delegates to the Constitutional Convention felt that American democracy had matured

sufficiently for the choice of the President to be entrusted directly to the People."[79]

Over the decades, the electoral college has been severely criticized as an old-fashioned device standing between the people and their choice of a president. The criticism may be summarized as follows:

1. The "winner-take-all" feature of the electoral college means that if a candidate carries a state by even one popular vote, he wins all the state's electoral votes, distorting the will of the voters because the minority votes cast within a state count for nothing. As a result, a president may be elected who has lost the total popular vote. This actually happened in the elections of John Quincy Adams in 1824, Rutherford B. Hayes in 1876, and Benjamin Harrison in 1888.

2. The system, with its winner-take-all feature, gives an advantage to the populous states that have many electoral votes, and to the members of minority groups that constitute powerful voting blocs within those states. At the same time, very small states are overrepresented because every state has a minimum of three electoral votes.

3. Electors are not constitutionally bound to vote for the candidate to whom they are pledged. In 1988 Margaret Leach, a Democrat from West Virginia, voted for Lloyd Bentsen instead of Michael Dukakis, the Democratic party's presidential nominee. She did so even though Dukakis had carried the state of West Virginia for president. Since the nation began, eleven other electors have defected in similar fashion.

In 1968 major-party supporters feared that George Wallace would receive enough electoral votes to deprive Nixon or Humphrey of a majority; the third-party candidate then might be in a position to win concessions in return for his electoral votes, or force the election into the House of Representatives, where he might strike further bargains. Similar concerns were voiced early in 1992 when some observers thought that the independent candidacy of Ross Perot might throw the election into the House.

The closeness of the 1960 election, the Wallace campaign in 1968, and other factors all combined to create new pressures for electoral college reform. Past

---

[77] The House chose the president twice: after the election of 1800, when it elected Jefferson, and following the election of 1824, when it elected John Quincy Adams. The Senate chose the vice-president only once, when it elected Richard M. Johnson of Kentucky to that office in 1837. In the case of a tie in the presidential balloting in the House that is not resolved by Inauguration Day, January 20, the vice-president-elect becomes acting president. Since the Senate chooses the vice-president in the event of an electoral vote deadlock, the Senate, in effect, would select the new president on Inauguration Day; if no president or vice-president has been selected by January 20, the presidency would go to the Speaker of the House, or next to the president pro tempore of the Senate, or down through all the cabinet posts under the Presidential Succession Act.

[78] In fact, in 1969 Maine changed its system of choosing presidential electors; under a state law passed that year, two electors are chosen at large and two are chosen from Maine's two congressional districts. Nebraska has adopted a similar system. Other states elect their presidential electors on a statewide basis.

[79] Neal R. Peirce, *The People's President* (New York: Simon and Schuster, 1968), p. 41.

debates had centered on plans to choose presidential electors by district (as members of Congress are chosen), or to award each candidate electoral votes in proportion to his share of the popular vote within each state. In the 1960s, however, the idea of *direct election* of the president gained in popularity. It seemed closest to the principle of "one person, one vote" enunciated by the Supreme Court.

Proposals for Direct Election of the President

In September 1969 the House passed a proposed constitutional amendment to abolish the electoral college and substitute direct election of the president and vice-president. Under the amendment, if no candidate received 40 percent of the popular vote, a runoff election would be held between the top two presidential candidates. Congress would be authorized to set the date for the election and for any runoff. The states would continue to run the election machinery, but Congress reserved the right to set uniform nationwide residence requirements for voting in presidential elections. Although the states would still set the qualifications for candidates to appear on the ballot, Congress for the first time would have the power to override and change the relevant state laws. This provision was included to ensure that candidates of major parties would appear on the ballot in every state — if only to avoid the threat of intervention by Congress. As under the present system, however, minor parties could find it difficult to qualify for the ballot in many states.

In 1970 a filibuster by opponents of direct election prevented the Senate from voting on the proposal. Interest in direct election of the president waned for a time after the proposed amendment died in the Senate. One reason such an amendment did not pass in 1970 was a widespread reluctance, in and out of Congress, to change a fundamental aspect of the American political system. There were also a number of specific objections. Critics argued that it would encourage the growth of splinter parties. The result, they warned, could be fragmentation of American politics and destruction of the two-party system.[80] And the two-party system, these critics have contended, is a vital instrument in resolving social conflict and managing the transfer of power.

Those opposed to direct election also argued that the electoral college is compatible with the federal system and that direct election would (1) increase the temptation for fraud in vote counting, leading to prolonged recounts and chaos, (2) rob minority groups of their influence in big electoral-vote states, and (3) tempt states to ease voter qualification standards in order to fatten the voter rolls.

One Person, One Vote

During the 1960s the Supreme Court ruled in a series of *reapportionment* decisions that each person's vote should be worth as much as another's. Yet the decisions were controversial, for they upset the balance of political power between urban and rural areas in the United States. The result was a concerted but unsuccessful effort in Congress and the states to amend the Constitution to overturn the Supreme Court rulings.

A voter registering to vote in California

---

[80] See, for example, Irving Kristol and Paul Weaver, "A Bad Idea Whose Time Has Come," *New York Times Magazine*, November 23, 1969.

The State Legislatures All votes are equal when each member of a legislative body represents the same number of people. In the United States, however, successive waves of immigration and the subsequent growth of the cities resulted in glaring inequalities in the population of urban and rural state legislative districts by the turn of the century. The 1920 census showed that for the first time more Americans lived in urban than in rural areas. The rural state legislators, representing sparsely populated districts, passed state laws to maintain their advantage over the cities. By 1960, in every state the largest legislative district was at least twice as populous as the smallest district.

In Tennessee that year, the smallest district in the lower house had a population of 3,400 and the largest had 79,000. Obviously, the people in the biggest district were not equally represented with the voters in the smallest. Because the legislature had refused to do anything about it, a group of urban residents, including a county judge named Charles W. Baker, sued Joe C. Carr, Tennessee's secretary of state. The case went to the United States Supreme Court, which in 1946 had refused to consider a case involving malapportionment in Illinois (*Colgrove* v. *Green*). Justice Felix Frankfurter, in that earlier opinion, ruled that the Supreme Court "ought not to enter this political thicket." [81]

But in 1962, in *Baker* v. *Carr*, the Supreme Court ruled in favor of the voters who had challenged the established order in Tennessee.[82] In 1964, in *Reynolds* v. *Sims*, the Supreme Court made it clear that the Fourteenth Amendment required that seats in *both* houses of a state legislature be based on population. Second, the Court ruled that although legislative districts might not be drawn with "mathematical exactness or precision," they must be based "substantially" on population.[83] The Court had laid down the principle of "one person, one vote."

The reapportionment decisions had an immediate effect on the political map of America. The legislature of Oregon had reapportioned on the basis of population in 1961; between the *Baker* v. *Carr* ruling in 1962 and 1970, the other forty-nine states took similar steps.

Conservative and rural forces reacted strongly to the Supreme Court rulings. In 1965 and 1966 Senator Everett M. Dirksen proposed a constitutional amendment to allow a state to apportion one house of its legislature on a basis other than population. Although the "Dirksen amendment" received majority support in the Senate both years, it fell short of the needed two-thirds majority. Undaunted, Dirksen and his backers

encouraged the states to petition Congress for a constitutional convention, an alternate method of amending the Constitution that had never been used (see Chapter 2). On April 30, 1969, Iowa became the thirty-third state to pass a resolution requesting a constitutional convention, one short of the necessary two-thirds of the states. But even before the Iowa resolution, some states had moved to rescind their petitions, and the possibility of a constitutional convention to consider the Dirksen amendment appeared to have ended.

Congressional Districts It was not just the state legislatures that were malapportioned prior to the mid-1960s. Although the *average* congressional House district had a population of 410,000 in the 1960s, the actual population of these districts varied greatly. For example, in Georgia, one rural district had 272,000 people, but the Fifth Congressional District (Atlanta and its suburbs) numbered 823,000 people. In 1964, in the case of *Wesberry* v. *Sanders*,[84] the Supreme Court ruled that this disparity in the size of Georgia congressional districts violated the Constitution. As a result, the states were required to redraw the boundaries of their congressional districts to conform to the Court's ruling.

The Supreme Court's reapportionment decisions left open the question of how much the population of state legislative and congressional districts might vary from one another without violating the principle of "one person, one vote." In a series of decisions the Court shifted ground as it grappled with this difficult question, eventually ruling that deviations as high as 10 percent in state legislative districts were too small to merit attention by the courts.[85]

Under the Constitution and federal law, Congress determines the total size of the House of Representatives, which grew from 65 members in 1790 to 435 in 1912. Congress has kept the House membership at 435 since then, although it could change that semipermanent figure.[86] After each ten-year census, federal law requires that the *number of representatives for each state*

---

81 *Colgrove* v. *Green*, 328 U.S. 549 (1946).
82 *Baker* v. *Carr*, 369 U.S. 186 (1962).
83 *Reynolds* v. *Sims*, 377 U.S. 533 (1964).
84 *Wesberry* v. *Sanders*, 376 U.S. 1 (1964).
85 *Kirkpatrick* v. *Preisler*, 394 U.S. 526 (1969); *Mahon* v. *Howell*, *City of Virginia Beach* v. *Howell*, and *Weinberg* v. *Prichard*, 410 U.S. 315 (1973); *Gaffney* v. *Cummings*, 412 U.S. 735 (1973); and *White* v. *Regester*, 412 U.S. 755 (1973).
86 The membership of the House increased only briefly, to 436 in early 1959 and to 437 from late 1959 through 1962, as a result of the admission to statehood of Hawaii and Alaska.

be *reapportioned* on the basis of population. If a state gains or loses members of Congress, the state legislature *redistricts* by drawing new boundary lines for its House districts.[87] In 1972, for example, California gained a total of five seats as a result of the 1970 census, making its House delegation the largest in the nation. Previously, New York's was the largest. Again, after the 1980 and 1990 censuses, California, Florida, and Texas gained seats, and New York, Pennsylvania, Ohio, and Illinois lost seats. The average population of House districts had risen to about 584,000 by the time of the 1992 elections.

Following the 1990 census, state legislatures created a number of congressional districts in which the majority of the population was black or Hispanic. The lines of these new districts, subject to approval by the Justice Department, were drawn to conform with judicial interpretations of the Voting Rights Act requiring that minority voters have the maximum opportunity to elect minority members to Congress. In 1992, thirteen new African Americans and six new Hispanic Americans were elected to the House in these newly created districts. Also elected that year was Carol Moseley Braun of Illinois, who became the first African American woman and the first African American Democrat to serve in the Senate. In all, there were thirty-eight African American members and seventeen Hispanic Americans at the start of the 103rd Congress.

As a result of the reapportionment revolution of the 1960s, rural areas had been expected to lose power to the cities. But because of the population exodus from the cities, the *suburbs* have proven to be the areas that gained the most from reapportionment of state legislatures and congressional districts. As far back as 1965 an official of the National Municipal League noted that almost half of the big cities in the United States had less

population than their suburbs: "No center city contains the necessary 50 percent of the people to dominate the state. . . . The U.S. is an urban nation, but it is not a big-city nation. The suburbs own the future."[88]

Because the suburbs have grown much faster than the nation as a whole, in the 1970s, for the first time, there were more members of the House of Representatives from the suburbs than from the cities. And since then, this trend has continued. (See Table 9-13.) As the political battle shifts to the suburbs, Gerald M. Pomper has predicted, "Suburban power will influence the way both politics and government are conducted."[89]

ELECTIONS AND DEMOCRATIC GOVERNMENT

Who won the election? In the United States, with its federal system, the question must be asked on all levels — national (the president, Congress), state (the governor and state legislatures), and local (county and city governments). Since candidates of both major parties win these offices, the outcome of American elections is mixed. Which party won or lost is not always as simple as it might appear. In 1984, for example, Reagan, a Republican, won by a landslide in the presidential election and the GOP won a majority in the Senate for the third time in a row. But the Democrats retained control of the House of Representatives and a majority of the nation's statehouses and state legislatures. Yet there are differences in elections; the voice of the voter speaks more clearly in some years than in others.

Types of Elections

V. O. Key, Jr., has suggested three broad types of presidential elections.[90] A *landslide for the out-party* "expresses clearly a lack of confidence in those who have been in charge of affairs." Some observers felt that the defeat of President Bush in 1992 was fundamentally an election of this type. In other election years, however, the voters may approve an incumbent administration in a vote of confidence that amounts to a *reaffirmation of*

Table 9-13
Suburban, Central City, and Rural Congressional Districts in the United States House of Representatives, 1962–86

	1962	1966	1974	1986
Metropolitan districts	254	264	305	347
Central City	106	110	109	98
Suburban	92	98	132	167
Mixed Metropolitan	56	56	64	82
Rural Districts	181	171	130	88
Total	435	435	435	435

SOURCE: Data for 1962–1974 appear in Richard Lehne, "Suburban Foundations of the New Congress," *Annals of the American Academy of Political and Social Science*, November 1975, p. 143. Analysis extended for 1986 by Harvey L. Schantz, State University of New York, Plattsburgh.

[87] In some instances the new lines have been drawn by federal courts.
[88] William J. D. Boyd, in *Congressional Quarterly*, Weekly Report, November 21, 1969, p. 2342.
[89] Gerald M. Pomper, "Census '70: Power to the Suburbs," *Washington Monthly*, May 1970, p. 23.
[90] Key, *Politics, Parties, and Pressure Groups*, pp. 520–36.

support. Moreover, both in elections that oust the party in power and those that produce a reaffirmation of support, people appear to be engaged in *retrospective voting* —looking back and making a judgment on the way things have gone and the kind of government they have had during their political leaders' time in office.

A third type of election, a *realignment*, may return the party that controls the presidency to power, but with the support of a new coalition of voters. (There also may be a major realignment when the president's party loses control of the White House.) When the realignment within the electorate is "both sharp and durable," Key suggests that a "critical" election has taken place, one that results in "profound readjustments" in political power.[91]

Angus Campbell and his associates have classified presidential elections in somewhat similar fashion: they relate the election returns to the basic pattern of party identification. They speak of *maintaining elections*, which reflect the standing party-identification of the voters; of *deviating elections*, in which the majority party (according to party identification) is defeated in a temporary reversal; and of *realigning elections*, which may lead to a basic shift in the party identification of the electorate.[92]

The Meaning of Elections

Much of the discussion in this chapter has focused on the wide variety of reasons, sociological and psychological, that may cause different voters to vote for the same political candidate. Regardless of these individual reasons, the overall election verdicts have broad meaning for the political system as a whole.

First of all, elections decide which individuals shall govern. Who wins can make a difference—in the political philosophy and caliber of those appointed to the Supreme Court by the president and approved by Congress, to take but one example.

Second, elections can have important consequences for the broad direction of public policy. Naturally, many specific questions are not settled by elections, but 1936 was rather clearly a broad approval of the New Deal, just as 1964 was a repudiation of conservative

Republicanism in that year. The series of four Democratic presidential victories from 1936 to 1948 ("maintaining elections" in Angus Campbell's terminology, "reaffirmations of support" in Key's classification) served to ensure that most of the policy innovations of the New Deal would become established public programs.

The voice of the people is not always so clear. The meaning of a particular election, the "mandate" of the people to the president on specific issues, may be subject to varying interpretations. As we have noted, many different people vote for the same candidate for different reasons; this candidate, once elected, may make decisions that cause some of the voters to feel misled. For example, in 1964 Americans voted for a president who seemed to promise, among other things, to avoid an Asian war, but did not.[93] In the presidential election of 1968 some voters retaliated by voting Republican.

It is also true that issues may be warped and facts concealed from the public in campaign debate, so that people may cast their votes on the basis of inadequate information. For example, during the 1972 campaign, President Nixon, his press secretary, and spokespersons for the president's election committee all repeatedly denied responsibility for the burglary and bugging of the Democrats' Watergate headquarters. In the summer of 1973 Senate hearings disclosed in great detail the involvement of high government officials in the inci-

---

[91] V. O. Key, Jr., "A Theory of Critical Elections," *Journal of Politics*, vol. 17 (February 1955), pp. 3–18.

[92] Campbell, Converse, Miller, and Stokes, *The American Voter*, pp. 531–38.

---

[93] See Chapter 7, p. 255. At the start of the 1964 campaign there were 16,000 American troops in Vietnam as "advisers." Three months after his election in 1964, President Johnson ordered the bombing of North Vietnam. By June 1965 U.S. troops were admittedly fighting, not advising. By 1968 more than 500,000 American troops were in Vietnam. The last U.S. forces were pulled out by President Nixon in March 1973.

dent and in subsequent attempts to cover it up. And in the 1976 presidential election, Watergate, which had occurred during a Republican administration, worked to Gerald Ford's disadvantage.[94] Ford, the Republican incumbent, lost to Carter, the Democratic challenger.

To summarize, elections leave elected officials with a great deal of flexibility in governing. Yet elections also often set broad guidelines within which decision makers must stay — or risk reprisal by the voters.

Continuity and Change

It is true that most American elections have tended to be fundamentally centrist, or middle of the road in character. Parties and candidates have competed for the center ground in American politics because that is where the parties believed that the biggest bloc of voters were.[95] For this reason candidates do not as a rule endorse radical programs of social change. Yet the New Deal marked a considerable departure in government's approach to America's problems. Since 1932 government has intervened in the social and economic order to an unprecedented extent. Even President Reagan's conservative approach and extensive budget cuts did not fundamentally alter the major social role played by the federal government. Its role as economic regulator has been approved by many voters in elections for five decades. At the same time, on many public issues, the coming to power of the Reagan administration did change the terms of the debate over social policy in America. Elections do at times set broad parameters for change.

"The people," Key has observed, "may not be able to govern themselves but they can, through an electoral uprising, throw the old crowd out and demand a new order, without necessarily being capable of specifying exactly what it shall be. An election of this type may amount, if not to revolution, to its functional equivalent."[96]

Besides establishing a framework for change, elections also provide continuity and a sense of political community, for they are links in a chain that bind one generation of voters to the next. Every four years the voters come together in an act of decision that is influenced by the past and present, but designed to shape the future.

PERSPECTIVE

Voting is a fundamental way by which people influence government. For example, as the presidential election of 1992 demonstrated, one of the most potent weapons of popular control in a democracy is the ability of the electorate to remove a party from power. In that year, Governor Bill Clinton of Arkansas, the Democratic challenger, defeated the Republican incumbent, President George Bush.

In the federal system that exists in the United States, the voters choose public officials at all levels of government. In a presidential year, for instance, voters select the president and vice-president, 435 members of the House, one-third of the Senate, 12 state governors, and numerous other state and local officials. In a democracy, voting is an act of choice among alternative candidates, parties, and, depending on the election, alternative policies.

Half or more of the Americans of voting age have voted for president in each election since 1928. But in nonpresidential election years, considerably less than half have voted for members of Congress.

Two basic approaches have been followed in studying how the voters decide. The sociological method focuses on the social and economic background of the voters — their education, ethnic group, income, social class, and occupation — and attempts to relate these factors to how they vote. The psychological method attempts to go beyond socioeconomic factors and find out what is going on in the minds of the voters, to measure their perceptions of parties, candidates, and issues.

Voter studies of sociological factors, for example, have found that upper-class and middle-class voters are more likely to vote Republican than are voters of lower economic and social status, who tend to be Democrats. Professionals, business people, and college graduates are more likely to vote for Republicans than Democrats. Jews and Catholics have tended to vote Democratic. The support among African Americans for the

---

[94] On Election Day 1976, CBS News interviewed 14,836 persons as they left the polls. Those who voted for Jimmy Carter were given a list of ten possible issues and asked to check as many as three that "led you to vote for Jimmy Carter." By far the largest group — 49 percent — checked "Restoring trust in government." One in five checked "Watergate and the pardon." Source: *National Journal*, November 6, 1976, p. 1588.

[95] For a detailed statement of the view that elections are won and lost "in the center," see Richard M. Scammon and Ben J. Wattenberg, *The Real Majority* (New York: Coward-McCann, 1971).

[96] Key, *Politics, Parties, and Pressure Groups*, pp. 522–23.

party or the other and often do not change. However, the personal impressions that a candidate makes on the voters may also influence the election results. In the 1992 election year, for example, many voters, dissatisfied with the candidates and platforms of the major parties, turned their loyalties to independent candidate Ross Perot. Furthermore, on certain major issues, or on issues that affect them directly, the voters seem to "tune in" and form definite issue-based preferences. In most elections another factor also seems to be at work — many voters appear to make up their minds by looking back at what has happened under the country's current political leadership and making a rough judgment about their leaders' performance in office.

In a presidential election year, the vote for president may affect the vote for Congress and also can have an effect on state and local offices, although there are signs that in recent years the impact of the presidential vote on contests for other offices may be lessening. In the congressional races in years past, a president has sometimes helped to carry a majority of his own party into office with him through the "coattail" effect.

In the election of 1992 Bill Clinton won a decisive victory over President George Bush and gave the Democratic party control of the presidency for the first time in twelve years. Clinton carried thirty-two of the fifty states, and won 370 electoral votes to 168 for Bush. Clinton's victory marked the fifth time in this century that an incumbent president of the United States had been defeated.

Despite the Democratic presidential victory for Bill Clinton, in the battle for control of the House of Representatives, the Republicans slightly strengthened their position. The Republicans made a net gain of nine seats in the House. That still left the Democrats with a majority in the House of 259 to 175 (plus one independent from Vermont). The new House of Representatives elected in 1992 was also more representative of the American people. There were forty-seven women in the new House compared to twenty-eight in the old; thirty-eight African Americans compared with twenty-five in the old House; and seventeen Hispanic Americans compared with ten in the previous House. In the Senate, the balance of power between the parties remained the same — fifty-seven Democrats, and forty-three Republicans.

The electoral system in the United States is not neutral. It affects the dynamics of voting all along the way. Before voters can step into the voting booths, they must meet a number of legal requirements. The candi-

Democratic presidential nominee has usually been very strong. And, in general, the Democrats still draw their strength from the big cities of the North and East. From 1960 to 1980, the Democrats consistently got a higher percentage of the vote from those under age thirty than from voters fifty and older. In 1984 this pattern changed. Ronald Reagan, the oldest person ever to serve as president, showed surprising strength among the nation's youngest voters. And in 1984, the Democratic advantage in party identification narrowed considerably. In 1992 Bill Clinton was the third-youngest candidate to become president. Clinton polled 47 percent of the vote from those who were under twenty-five, and 42 percent among voters in their fifties. By 1992, 38 percent of the electorate considered themselves to be Democrats, compared with 29 percent who said they were Republicans and 33 percent who called themselves independents.

In measuring voter attitudes, three important factors have been identified: party identification, candidates, and issues. Voters may form an attachment to one

dates whose names appear on the ballot must have qualified under state law. The form of the ballot may influence voters' decisions. In short, the structure, details, and workings of the electoral system affect the people's choice.

Voting is a basic right provided for by the Constitution. Under the Fourteenth Amendment, it is one of the privileges and immunities of national citizenship that the states may not abridge. It is also a right that Congress has the power to protect by federal legislation. Until the age of Andrew Jackson, voting was generally restricted to men who owned property and paid taxes. Since then, suffrage has gradually been broadened, particularly by the Fifteenth Amendment which enfranchised black men, the Nineteenth Amendment which enfranchised women, and the Twenty-sixth Amendment which lowered the voting age to eighteen in all elections.

The Constitution does not provide for the popular election of the president. Instead, it provides that each state shall select electors equal in number to the representatives and senators it has in Congress. Instead of voting directly for president, an American voter casts his or her ballot for a slate of electors that normally is pledged to the presidential candidate of the voter's choice. The candidate who wins a majority of the electoral votes is elected president.

Following the 1990 census, state legislatures created a number of congressional districts in which the majority of the population was black or Hispanic. The lines of these new districts, subject to approval by the Justice Department, were drawn to conform with judicial interpretations of the Voting Rights Act requiring that minority voters have the maximum opportunity to elect minority members to Congress.

During the 1960s the Supreme Court ruled in a series of reapportionment decisions that each person's vote should be worth as much as another's.

The overall verdicts of elections have broad meaning for the political system as a whole. Elections decide which individuals shall govern. Elections can have important consequences for the direction of public policy. And elections often set broad guidelines within which decision makers must stay — or risk reprisal by the voters.

Suggested Reading

Berelson, Bernard R.; Lazarsfeld, Paul F.; and McPhee, William N. *Voting: A Study of Opinion Formation in a Presidential Campaign** (University of Chicago Press, 1954). An influential study of how voters decide for whom they will vote. Based on a series of interviews with about 1,000 residents of Elmira, New York, during the Truman-Dewey presidential contest of 1948.

Campbell, Angus; Converse, Philip E.; Miller, Warren E.; and Stokes, Donald E. *The American Voter** (University of Chicago Press, 1980). (Originally published in 1960; an abridged paperback edition was published in 1964.) A landmark study of voting behavior, based on interviews with national samples of the American electorate conducted by the Survey Research Center of the University of Michigan.

Fiorina, Morris, P. *Retrospective Voting in American National Elections** (Yale University Press, 1981). An important analysis of voting behavior in American elections. Emphasizes that many voters make a rough judgment — positive or negative — about the performance of the incumbent administration, and then cast their votes accordingly.

Flanigan, William H., and Zingale, Nancy. *Political Behavior of the American Electorate*, 7th edition* (Congressional Quarterly, 1991). Useful, concise analysis and summary of research on how and why Americans vote.

Jacobson, Gary C. *The Politics of Congressional Elections*, 3rd edition (HarperCollins, 1992). An illuminating general analysis of congressional elections. Focuses on the candidates, their campaigns, the voters, and the relationship between national politics and congressional elections.

Kelley, Stanley, Jr. *Interpreting Elections** (Princeton University Press, 1983). A thoughtful analysis of the way in which voters reach their decisions. Includes an illuminating discussion of the issues involved in the concept of electoral "mandates."

Key, V. O., Jr. *The Responsible Electorate* (The Belknap Press of Harvard University Press, 1966). An examination of American voting behavior in presidential elections, based primarily on analyses of Gallup poll data from 1936 to 1960. Key argues that the voters' views on issues and government policy are quite closely related to how they vote in such elections.

Key, V. O., Jr. *Southern Politics in State and Nation*, 2nd edition* (University of Tennessee Press, 1984). (Originally published in 1949.) A classic study of the politics of the South. Analyzes why the Democratic party dominated that region for nearly three generations after the Civil War, and what the political consequences were.

Lazarsfeld, Paul F.; Berelson, Bernard; and Gaudet, Hazel. *The People's Choice: How the Voter Makes Up His Mind in a Presidential Campaign* (Columbia University Press, 1968). (Originally published in 1944.) A classic in the study of voting behavior, based on a series of interviews with potential voters in Erie County, Ohio, during the Roosevelt-Willkie presidential contest of 1940. The book stresses the relationship between the voters' socioeconomic status and how they voted.

Mann, Thomas E. *Unsafe at Any Margin: Interpreting Congressional Elections* (American Enterprise Institute for Public Policy Research, 1978). A revealing analysis of the influence that local candidates and local events have in congressional elections. The author argues that members of the House are growing more independent of their party and the president, and that individual House candidates are becoming increasingly responsible for their own margins of victory or defeat.

Milbrath, Lester W., and Goel, M. L. *Political Participation: How and Why Do People Get Involved in Politics?*, 2nd edition* (University Press of America, 1982). A comprehensive, general analysis of who participates in politics and why.

Nelson, Michael, ed. *The Elections of 1984* (CQ Press, 1985). An interesting and informative analysis of the 1984 elections, by Michael Nelson and fourteen other scholars. Includes essays on the presidential contest, the strategies of the presidential candidates, the elections for Congress, and the possible effect of the 1984 election on the federal court system.

Nie, Norman H.; Verba, Sidney; and Petrocik, John R. *The Changing American Voter*, enlarged edition* (Harvard University Press, 1979). An important sequel to the classic 1960 study, *The American Voter*, based primarily on public opinion polls from 1956 to 1973. The authors concluded that, compared with the 1950s, issues were more visible and had a greater effect on voting in the elections from 1964 through 1972.

Page, Benjamin I. *Choices and Echoes in Presidential Elections: Rational Man and Electoral Democracy* (University of Chicago Press, 1978). An important and perceptive analysis of American voting behavior. Focuses on the policy stands that are taken by presidential candidates, as well as on the voters' response to the choices that are presented to them.

Peirce, Neal R., and Longley, Lawrence D. *The People's President: The Electoral College in American History and the Direct Vote Alternative*, revised edition* (Yale University Press, 1981). A detailed study of the history of the electoral college and its effect in past presidential elections. Presents the case for abolishing the electoral college and electing the president directly by popular vote.

Scammon, Richard M., and Wattenberg, Ben J. *The Real Majority* (Coward-McCann, 1970). A lively analysis of political attitudes and voting patterns in America. Argues that the majority of American voters are "unyoung, unpoor, and unblack," and contends that candidates who take moderate positions on issues — close to the "political center" — are more likely to be elected than candidates who take more extreme positions.

Sundquist, James L. *Dynamics of the Party System: Alignment and Realignment of Political Parties in the United States*, revised edition* (The Brookings Institution, 1983). A comprehensive historical analysis of the relative electoral strength of America's political parties over a 150-year period.

---

* Available in paperback edition.

PART THREE

THE
POLICYMAKERS

THE AMERICAN PRESIDENCY is a place of paradox. It is an office of enormous contrasts, of great power — and great limits. Over the past three decades, a number of factors and events have altered the public's perception of the presidency.

Although once viewed as extraordinarily powerful, the presidency more recently has seemed an institution of uncertain power. President Kennedy was assassinated in 1963, and his four immediate successors left office under adverse circumstances: President Johnson, criticized over the war in Vietnam, chose not to run; President Nixon was forced to resign over the Watergate scandal; Presidents Ford and Carter were defeated. Less than three months after his first inauguration, President Reagan was wounded in an assassination attempt. And President Bush failed in his bid for reelection.

Chapter 10

The President

Reagan's decisive re-election to a second term broke this pattern, marking the first time in twelve years that a president had been returned to office by the voters. In fact, it is possible that the desire of the American people for continuity in the White House was at least one factor working in Reagan's favor in 1984.

Reagan's victory was an impressive achievement. Until then, of the eight presidents who had served since the Second World War, only two others — Dwight Eisenhower and Richard Nixon — had been elected twice. And Nixon had failed to complete his second term.

Yet Reagan's own public approval eroded midway into his second term. The disclosure that he had approved a secret foreign policy, that he had allowed the sale of arms to Iran, and that millions of dollars had been diverted to the contras in Central America without the knowledge of the American people, tarnished his image. After the Iran-contra scandal, less was heard about

Reagan as a "Teflon" president to whom no adverse criticism would stick.

While the Iran-contra episode did not have the same impact on the public as did the Watergate affair more than a decade earlier during the Nixon presidency, it did weaken the Reagan presidency. For it revealed that secret operations, many of them illegal, were being run out of the White House by Marine Lt. Col. Oliver L. North, and concealed from Congress and the public. The tangled affairs of Reagan's attorney general and close friend and adviser, Edwin Meese, III, also proved a liability to the president. That a sitting attorney general was under investigation by a federal independent counsel seemed inappropriate to many voters, although it provided a field day for political cartoonists. Meese resigned in August 1988.

Reagan's political heir, Vice-President George Bush, was elected president in 1988. Bush's popularity, extraordinarily high after the Persian Gulf War early in 1991, dropped dramatically by the time he began his campaign for re-election in 1992 amid voter discontent and economic recession. Why had presidential power sometimes appeared so fragile? Perhaps one reason was that many of the problems faced by presidents had become more difficult to manage. The economy was a prime example; when Bush took office in 1989 he had to deal with soaring budget deficits, a legacy of the very economic policies he had supported as vice-president.

Bush's difficulties were compounded by his most famous campaign promise. As a candidate for president in 1988, he had proclaimed to the Republican National Convention: "Read my lips, no new taxes." The

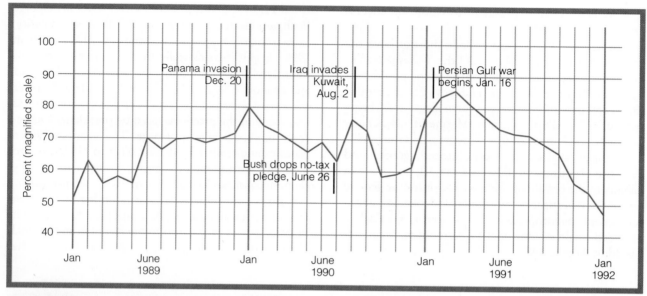

Figure 10-1
President Bush's Popularity During Times of Crisis

delegates cheered wildly. But two years later, he broke that celebrated pledge, agreed to raise taxes by $165 billion over five years, and thereby lost the trust of many voters.

As two former government officials noted in one study, economic problems do not easily yield to a president's decisions: "Fifteen years ago, the economy was a strong ally of presidential power. It appeared to respond magically to executive will, providing on a lavish scale the resources needed for a long agenda of social reforms. Today the economy is an adversary of presidential power — perhaps the greatest adversary. It appears to mock all executive ministrations, provides insufficient resources for a host of governmental objectives and vexes Presidents with choices between politically unacceptable evils."[1]

Against this background, some observers asked whether any chief executive, however able, could manage the nation's problems. And a number of scholars were exploring the question of how the presidency might be made more effective.

Only a little more than a decade earlier, many commentators and some voters had been concerned with a different problem. They worried about the expansion of presidential power and the emergence of what Arthur M. Schlesinger, Jr., termed "the imperial Presidency."[2] Particularly in the area of foreign and military policy, Schlesinger and others contended, the presidency had exceeded constitutional bounds and usurped congressional war powers.

The growth of the power of the presidency, many scholars noted, was accompanied by excessive reverence for the person of the president, a phenomenon that Louis W. Koenig has called "the Sun King complex."[3] In Schlesinger's view, "the age of the imperial Presidency had in time produced the idea that run-of-the-mill politicians, brought by fortuity to the White House, must be treated thereafter as if they had become superior and perhaps godlike beings."[4] Similarly, Thomas E. Cronin criticized the "textbook Presidency," the creation, he argued, of political scientists, journalists, and others who endow the chief executive with a "halo." Cronin perceived a "cult of the Presidency," in which the occupant of the White House becomes "benevolent, omnipotent, omniscient."[5]

---

[1] Ben W. Heineman, Jr., and Curtis A. Hessler, *Memorandum for the President: A Strategic Approach to Domestic Affairs in the 1980s* (New York: Random House, 1980), p. 56.

[2] Arthur M. Schlesinger, Jr., *The Imperial Presidency* (Boston: Houghton Mifflin, 1973).

[3] Louis W. Koenig, *The Chief Executive*, 4th ed. (New York: Harcourt Brace Jovanovich, 1981), p. 11.

[4] Schlesinger, *The Imperial Presidency*, p. 410.

[5] Thomas E. Cronin, *The State of the Presidency*, 2nd ed. (Boston: Little, Brown, 1980), pp. 76, 90.

"THE REVERENCE DUE A MONARCH"

The life of the White House is the life of the court. It is a structure designed for one purpose and one purpose only—to serve the material needs and the desires of a single man. It is felt that this man is grappling with problems of such tremendous consequence that every effort must be made to relieve him of the irritations that vex the average citizen. His mind, it is held, must be absolutely free of petty annoyances so that he can concentrate his faculties upon the "great issues" of the day.

To achieve this end, every conceivable facility is made available, from the very latest and most luxurious jet aircraft to a masseur constantly in attendance to soothe raw presidential nerves. Even more important, however, he is treated with all of the reverence due a monarch. No one interrupts presidential contemplation for anything less than a major catastrophe somewhere on the globe. No one speaks to him unless spoken to first. No one ever invites him to "go soak your head" when his demands become petulant and unreasonable.

—George E. Reedy, *The Twilight of the Presidency*

Even as the presidency was being criticized for an excess of power, however, it was simultaneously perceived as weakened by Vietnam and Watergate. Both of those traumatic events diminished public trust in the institution of the presidency, and—some analysts believed—diminished the actual power of that office as well.

The paradox of the presidency was vividly demonstrated by the Watergate drama and its central figure, Richard Nixon. A year after his triumphant re-election in 1972, Nixon was a beleaguered chief executive—the subject of an impeachment investigation in the House of Representatives, his ability to govern seriously impaired. The scandal had begun when burglars working for the president's re-election campaign broke into Democratic party headquarters in the Watergate office building. The president and his aides then tried to cover up the fact that the break-in had been ordered by high officials of the administration and the campaign. Less than two years after his re-election, Nixon had resigned in disgrace. Had he not been pardoned by his successor, Gerald Ford, Nixon might have faced criminal prosecution and prison.

Any discussion of the modern presidency is inevitably colored by Watergate. To some extent, that massive scandal may have resulted from political and institutional factors, among them the growth of presidential power in the twentieth century, increasing government secrecy, a lack of government credibility, a burgeoning national-security bureaucracy, and the use of intelligence agencies and techniques in domestic politics. Many of the same factors were responsible for the Iran-

contra scandal that began unfolding more than a decade later, in 1986, under President Ronald Reagan. But Watergate—and the Iran-contra affair as well—was a result of the policies and actions of a particular chief executive and his aides. Institutional factors may contribute to government corruption, but they do not absolve individual guilt; Watergate was in this sense the responsibility of one president and one administration.

In the wake of Vietnam and Watergate, Congress in the early 1970s moved to reassert its power within the political system. It enacted the War Powers Resolution in an effort to curb presidential military adventures; it imposed other restrictions on the president in the foreign policy and military fields; and it created a new structure to deal with the federal budget—an action designed to permit Congress to share power with the president over the budget process and the establishment of national priorities.

This effort to reassert congressional power coincided to some extent with the administration of President Ford. Most analysts regarded the Ford period as one of a weak presidency. However, Ford was an unelected president, the first to take office under the provisions of the Twenty-fifth Amendment, and he served only two and a half years. But his successor, Jimmy Carter, did not prove to be a strong chief executive either. Beset by foreign-policy problems and a lagging economy, he was decisively defeated by Ronald Reagan in 1980. Nor did Carter fare very well with Congress; although Democrats controlled both the House and Senate during Carter's presidency, major parts of his legislative program were not enacted. All this led the columnist Joseph Kraft to conclude that Arthur Schlesinger's "imperial Presidency" had, by 1980, become the "post-imperial Presidency." [6]

The opposing perceptions of the presidency—either as an office grown too powerful, or one in danger of being weakened by a reassertive Congress—leave unresolved the question of how the presidency can be controlled without so reducing its powers that the president cannot manage national problems and lead the nation. "The American democracy," Schlesinger has suggested, "must discover a middle ground between making the President a czar and making him a puppet. . . . we need a strong Presidency—but a strong Presidency *within the Constitution*." [7]

In the light of the nation's experience over the past two decades, a number of questions may be asked about the American presidency. Has the office grown too powerful? Are there enough checks on presidential power? Or is the presidency too weak? Does a president have enough control over the bureaucracy and policy formation, and enough influence with Congress, to solve the problems that come to him? Can the presidency be made more effective? Or will the president's impact always be marginal? Can any president govern? Are the public's expectations of presidential performance so high that any president is doomed to failure from the start? In exploring these questions, it might be useful to begin by examining the presidency as it appeared to two men who held that office.

THE AMERICAN PRESIDENCY

The day before he took the oath of office as thirty-fifth president of the United States, John F. Kennedy called upon President Eisenhower at the White House. "There are no easy matters that will ever come to you as President," Eisenhower told the younger man. "If they are easy, they will be settled at a lower level."

The accuracy of this parting advice had come home to President Kennedy when he told the story almost two years later during an interview over the three major television networks.[8] Kennedy's conversation with

"There are no easy matters that will ever come to you as President. . . ." President Kennedy (left) is visited by former President Eisenhower at Camp David, Maryland.

three newsmen in his Oval Office provided an unusual insight into the dimensions and perspectives of the American presidency. When asked how the job had matched his conception of it, Kennedy replied: "Well, I think in the first place the problems are more difficult than I had imagined they were. Secondly, there is a limitation upon the ability of the United States to solve these problems."

Although Kennedy was speaking of world problems, the same tone was apparent in his remarks about the president's domestic power. "The fact is," he said, "I think the Congress looks more powerful sitting here than it did when I was there in the Congress. . . . When you are in Congress you are one of a hundred in the Senate or one of 435 in the House, so that the power is so divided. But here I look at a Congress, and I look at

[6] Joseph Kraft, "The Post-Imperial Presidency," *The New York Times Magazine*, November 2, 1980, p. 31.

[7] Schlesinger, *The Imperial Presidency*, p. x.

[8] Television and radio interview: "After Two Years—a Conversation With the President," December 17, 1962, in *Public Papers of the Presidents of the United States, John F. Kennedy, 1962* (Washington, D.C.: U.S. Government Printing Office, 1963), pp. 889–904.

A PRESIDENT LOOKS TO THE FUTURE

It is not by any means the sole task of the Presidency to think about the present. One of the chief obligations of the Presidency is to think about the future. We have been, in our one hundred and fifty years of constitutional existence, a wasteful nation, a nation that has wasted its natural resources and, very often, wasted its human resources.

One reason why a President of the United States ought to travel throughout the country and become familiar with every State is that he has a great obligation to think about the days when he will no longer be President, to think about the next generation and the generation after that.

—Franklin D. Roosevelt, in Arthur Bernon Tourtellot, *The Presidents on the Presidency*

the collective power of the Congress . . . and it is a substantial power."[9]

In addition, Kennedy, an activist president impatient to get things done, fumed at the bureaucracy: "You know, after I met Mr. Khrushchev [the Soviet Premier] in Vienna and they gave us an *aide-mémoire*, it took me many weeks to get our answer out through the State Department. . . . This is a constant problem in various departments. . . . You can wait while the world collapses."[10]

Kennedy was well aware of an American president's enormous responsibility in the nuclear age. In the event of an atomic war, Kennedy observed in the interview, "this is the end, because you are talking about Western Europe, the Soviet Union, the United States, of 150 million fatalities in the first 18 hours. . . . One mistake can make this whole thing blow up."[11]

This candid discussion of the presidency illuminated both the power and limits of the office. It pointed up the fact that the president is not merely the symbolic and actual leader of more than 254 million Americans, sworn to "preserve, protect and defend" the Constitution — but also a world leader, whose decisions may affect the future of the more than 5 billion inhabitants of the globe.

Kennedy's sense of his power and its limits illustrates the paradox of the modern presidency, discussed at the start of this chapter. The core of the dilemma is that the technology of the nuclear age and the growth of government in a modern industrial society have combined to concentrate great power in the hands of a chief executive in some policy areas, while restricting his options in others. For example, the president's power to

use military force without a declaration of war by Congress was demonstrated during the 1960s in Southeast Asia and in the Persian Gulf in 1991, when President Bush took the country to war against Iraq. Yet, the Constitution provides that only Congress can declare war.

In 1973, over President Nixon's veto, Congress had enacted a law designed to attempt to recapture its war powers. But in the two decades that followed, the legislation, known as the War Powers Resolution, had not effectively limited presidential power. Even before the Persian Gulf War, President Bush had ordered the military into Panama in 1989. The invasion ousted dictator Manuel Noriega, who was arrested, brought back to Miami, tried, convicted of drug trafficking and sentenced to 40 years in prison. President Reagan sent the marines to Lebanon in 1982, dispatched American military forces to invade and capture the Caribbean island of Grenada in 1983, bombed Libya in 1986, sent the navy into the Persian Gulf in 1987, and during much of his presidency waged a covert war against the leftist government of Nicaragua. In none of these instances did the War Powers Resolution serve to restrict presidential power.

But these actions all took place abroad. Presidential power at home may be more limited. For example, although President Nixon was able to continue the war in Vietnam for five years and invade and bomb Cambodia with American forces, in the domestic sphere he could not get Congress to pass his plan to reform the welfare system.

Other presidents have faced the same dilemma. A president was able to bring the nation to the brink of nuclear disaster, as in the Cuban Missile Crisis of 1962, or involve America in war, as in the Persian Gulf, almost entirely by his own decisions and actions. Despite the war-powers legislation and the attempts by Congress to

---

[9] Ibid., p. 892.
[10] Ibid., p. 891.
[11] Ibid., pp. 897–898.

be more assertive in this area, the president's sheer military power, which he exercises as commander in chief of the armed forces, remains formidable. Yet the president may not be able to get a farm bill through Congress, reduce government spending, cut the deficit, or cope with a lagging economy.

The Institution, the Person

The presidency is both an institution and a person. The *institution* is the office created by the Constitution, custom, cumulative federal law since 1789, and the gradual growth of formal and informal tools of presidential power. The *person* is a human being, powerful yet vulnerable, compassionate or vain, ordinary or extraordinary. To the institution, the president brings the imprint of his personality and style. Under the Twenty-second Amendment, the incumbent must normally change at least once every eight years. The presidency is, then, both highly institutionalized and highly personal.

George Washington assumed the office feeling not unlike "a culprit who is going to the place of his execution." William Howard Taft thought it "the loneliest place in the world." Harry Truman declared that "being a President is like riding a tiger. A man has to keep on riding or be swallowed." Warren Harding thought the White House "a prison." Lyndon Johnson spoke of "the awesome power, and the immense fragility of executive authority," both of which he experienced. Jimmy Carter called it "the most difficult job, maybe, on earth." Ronald Reagan complained that "you live in a

fishbowl." And George Bush observed, "You have to have a fairly thick skin."

The strands of power have come together in the person and the institution of the modern presidency. When the president speaks to the nation, millions listen. His words are instantly transmitted around the globe by satellite and high-speed communications. When he pulls his beagle's ears, as Lyndon Johnson did, the bark of dog lovers is heard round the world. If he cancels a subscription to a newspaper, as John Kennedy did, a thousand thunderous editorials denounce him. When he says he does not like broccoli, as George Bush revealed, crates of the vegetable are shipped to the White House by indignant growers. Is his wife spending too much on her clothes? His kitten ill? His chef disloyal? Does he carry his own garment bag aboard the plane? Does he dye his hair? Does he consult astrologers? No detail in the life of a modern president (and these are real examples) escapes the eyes of the media,

"THE PRESIDENT WILL SEE YOU SHORTLY"

Copyright 1988 by Herblock in the *Washington Post*

"GOD, WHAT A JOB!"

I can't make a damn thing out of this tax problem. I listen to one side and they seem right, and then God! I talk to the other side and they seem just as right, and there I am where I started. I know somewhere there is a book that would give me the truth, but hell, I couldn't read the book. . . . God, what a job!

—Warren G. Harding, in Richard F. Fenno, Jr., *The President's Cabinet*

THE WHITE HOUSE ASTROLOGER

Virtually every major move and decision the Reagans made during my time as White House Chief of Staff was cleared in advance with a woman in San Francisco who drew up horoscopes to make certain that the planets were in a favorable alignment for the enterprise.

Nancy Reagan seemed to have absolute faith in the clairvoyant powers of this woman, who had predicted that "something bad" was going to happen to the President shortly before he was wounded in an assassination attempt in 1981. The First Lady referred to the woman as "My Friend."

Although I never met this seer—Mrs. Reagan passed along her prognostications to me after conferring with her on the telephone—she had become such a factor in my work, and in the highest affairs of the nation, that at one point I kept a color-coded calendar on my desk (numerals highlighted in green ink for "good" days, red for "bad" days, yellow for "iffy" days) as an aid to remembering when it was propitious to move the President of the United States from one place to another, or schedule him to speak in public, or commence negotiations with a foreign power . . .

Before I came to the White House, Mike Deaver had been the man who integrated the horoscopes of Mrs. Reagan's Friend into the Presidential schedule . . . "Humor her," Deaver advised. "At least this astrologer is not as kooky as the last one . . ."

But the President's schedule is the single most potent tool in the White House, because it determines what the most powerful man in the world is going to do and when he is going to do it. By humoring Mrs. Reagan we gave her this tool—or, more accurately, gave it to an unknown woman in San Francisco who believed that the zodiac controls events and human behavior and that she could read the secrets of the future in the movements of the planets.

—Donald T. Regan, *For the Record: From Wall Street to Washington*, 1988

which provide such information to a public apparently hungry for more.

Public disclosure of intimate details of a president's life is not limited to the press, or to the literary endeavors of White House cooks, seamstresses, and bottlewashers. His own distinguished, high-level staff assistants may be secret diarists, scribbling away nights for the sake of posterity and the best-seller lists. Indeed, presidents themselves write books, not only for money but to give their own version of events and, they hope, to secure their place in history. Truman, Eisenhower, Johnson, Nixon, Ford, Carter, and Reagan all published memoirs after they left the White House.

The intense public interest in the person and office of the president is a reflection of how the job of chief executive has become magnified in the twentieth century. The immense pressures on the human being who occupies the office of president have intensified because the institution of the presidency has evolved and grown with the nation.

THE EXPANDING PRESIDENCY

"We Never Once Thought of a King"

The framers of the Constitution who met at Philadelphia toiled in the greatest secrecy. No television cameras invaded their privacy in 1787. Yet even in that pre-electronic age, the framers felt it necessary to issue a press release (their only one) to counteract rumors that were circulating around the country. The statement was leaked to the *Pennsylvania Herald* in August: "Tho' we cannot, affirmatively, tell you what we are doing; we can, negatively, tell you what we are not doing—we never once thought of a king." [12]

The colonists who made the American Revolution were, perhaps understandably, prejudiced against kings. At the same time, the difficulties encountered under the Articles of Confederation had exposed the shortcomings of legislative government and demonstrated the need for a strong executive. But how strong?

James Wilson and Gouverneur Morris championed a single powerful chief executive, and James Madi-

son eventually adopted that view. Many of the framers considered legislatures to be dangerously radical; the blessings of liberty could best be enjoyed, they felt, if popular government was checked by a strong executive branch that could protect wealth, private property, and business. Support for a powerful single president was by no means unanimous, however; some of the framers had specifically proposed a plural executive, and some wanted the president to be chosen by Congress. The framers, as Thomas E. Cronin has observed, knew that the American presidency is always a "potentially dangerous institution. . . . The framers wanted a more authoritative and decisive national government, yet they were keenly aware that the American people were not about to accept too much centralized power vested in a single person." [13]

Out of the debates at Philadelphia emerged the basic structure of the presidency as we know it today: a single president who headed one of three separate branches of government and was elected independently for a four-year term. The great authority given to the president by the framers was limited by the separation of powers among three branches of government, by the checks and balances engraved in the Constitution, by the federal system, and, in time, by other informal controls generally unforeseen in 1787—the rise of political parties and mass media, for example.

The Growth of the American Presidency

"I prefer to supervise the whole operations of the government myself . . . and this makes my duties very great," President James Polk wrote in his diary in 1848. [14]

So great had those duties become in the twentieth century that by fiscal 1993 the president presided over a federal budget of more than $1.5 trillion and a bureaucracy of 3.1 million civilians and 2 million members of the armed forces. He would not have dreamed of attempting to "supervise the whole operations of the government" by himself.

Great crises and great presidents have contributed to the growth of the presidency since 1789. George Washington, Andrew Jackson, Abraham Lincoln,

---

[12] Carl Van Doren, *The Great Rehearsal* (New York: Viking Press, 1948), p. 145. Alexander Hamilton, however, did propose a virtual monarchy in the form of a lifetime chief executive, but his plan won no support.

[13] Thomas E. Cronin, in Thomas E. Cronin, ed., *Inventing the American Presidency* (Lawrence, Kan.: University Press of Kansas, 1989), p. ix.

[14] In Richard F. Fenno, Jr., *The President's Cabinet* (Cambridge: Harvard University Press, 1959), p. 217.

LYNDON JOHNSON LEAVES THE WHITE HOUSE

Of course I miss it. . . . President Nixon said to me, "How did you feel when you weren't President any more?" And I said, "I don't know whether you'll understand this now or not, but you certainly will later. I sat there on that platform and waited for you to stand up and raise your right hand and take the oath of office, and I think the most pleasant words . . . that ever came into my ears were 'So help me God' that you repeated after that oath. Because at that time I no longer had the fear that I was the man that could make the mistake of involving the world in war, that I was no longer the man that would have to carry the terrifying responsibility of protecting the lives of this country and maybe the entire world, unleashing the horrors of some of our great power if I felt that that was required. But that now I could ride back down that avenue, being concerned about what happened, being alarmed about what might happen, but just really knowing that I wasn't going to be the cause of it." . . . The real horror was to be sleeping soundly about three-thirty or four or five o'clock in the morning and have the telephone ring and the operator say, "Sorry to wake you, Mr. President" . . . there's just a second between the time the operator got me on the line until she could get . . . Mr. Bundy in the Situation Room, or maybe . . . Secretary McNamara. . . . And we went through the horrors of hell that thirty seconds or minute or two minutes. Had we hit a Russian ship? Had an accident occurred? We have another *Pueblo*? Someone made a mistake—were we at war? Well, those experiences are gone.

—Lyndon B. Johnson, Excerpts from a CBS Television News Special, "LBJ: Why I Chose Not to Run," December 27, 1969

Franklin D. Roosevelt influenced the modern presidency more than any other chief executive.

Theodore Roosevelt, Woodrow Wilson, and Franklin Roosevelt all placed their personal stamp on the presidency. When a president strengthens and reshapes the institution, the change may endure even after he leaves. The modern presidency, for example, is rooted in the style and approach of Franklin D. Roosevelt.

Although presidents and events have played a decisive role in the development of the presidency, several broad historical factors, discussed below, have combined to create a powerful chief executive today.

The Nuclear Age and the End of the Cold War For more than three decades after the end of the Second World War, the United States and the Soviet Union lived under the terrible shadow of nuclear war. Each possessed nuclear missiles that could destroy the other country in half an hour or less; given the time factor, the president, rather than Congress, of necessity became the one who had to decide whether to use such hideous, and ultimately irrational, weapons. (As Clinton Rossiter noted, the next wartime president "may well be our last." [15])

[15] Clinton Rossiter, *The American Presidency*, rev. ed. (New York: Harcourt Brace Jovanovich, 1960), p. 25.

In 1991, the collapse of the Soviet Union and the breakup of the communist central government into 15 separate nations marked the formal end to the Cold War. Although both sides were moving to cut strategic weapons drastically, as of 1992, the United States and Russia (and three other former Soviet republics) still possessed missiles with powerful nuclear warheads. At least five other countries were nuclear powers, and a number of third-world nations were attempting to develop nuclear arms. Despite the disintegration of the Soviet Union, the world was still a volatile place, and the president continued to control the "nuclear button."

In sum, the constitutional power of Congress to declare war has become eroded in the twentieth century by the power of the president to use nuclear weapons, to commit United States forces to meet sudden crises, and to fight so-called limited wars. As already noted, Congress sought to regain some of its control over the use of American military power and passed a war-powers law in 1973. (See pp. 374–375 and Chapter 14.) But even in a changed world, the president remains the dominant figure in responding to crisis with military force.

Foreign Affairs The president, under the Constitution, has the prime responsibility for conducting the foreign affairs of the United States. From its isolationism before the Second World War, the United States emerged in the postwar period as one of the two major world powers. During the Eisenhower administration, when John Foster Dulles exercised a powerful influence as secretary of state, the United States adhered to the principle of collective security to "contain" communism, and entered into a series of military alliances with other nations for this purpose. The wisdom of the role of the United States as a "world policeman" was seriously questioned in the 1960s and 1970s, when the United States became bogged down in the Vietnam War. By 1980, following the hostage crisis in Iran and Soviet intervention in Afghanistan, some of the post-Vietnam emphasis on détente and disarmament had given way to a renewed concern over national security and military strength. And in that year, and again in 1984, the voters in the presidential election chose Ronald Reagan, who increased defense spending and emphasized military preparedness. President Bush committed American forces to two wars between 1989 and 1991, while proclaiming a "new world order." Because the United States remains one of the most powerful nations in the world, the president is inevitably a world leader as well as a national leader.

Domestic Affairs The great increase in presidential power in the twentieth century has taken place in the domestic field as much as in foreign affairs. Roosevelt's New Deal, as Edward S. Corwin pointed out, brought "social acceptance of the idea that government should be active and reformist, rather than simply protective of the established order of things." [16]

With the tremendous growth of government as manager, the president directs a huge bureaucracy. Modern government is expected to "solve" or at least deal with social problems, from racial discrimination to health care, and the president has become the chief problem-solver. Although President Nixon cut back and dismantled some federal programs, the federal budget increased substantially during his presidency. President Ford attacked the federal bureaucracy during the 1976 campaign, but the budget and the number of persons on the federal payroll also went up during his period in office. Ronald Reagan, too, attacked the bureaucracy in his 1980 election campaign, but its size increased during his eight years in office. Reagan cut back or limited spending in a number of federal domestic areas, but he did not change such established major programs as social security, Medicare, or Medicaid. Nor did President Bush, who ran for re-election in 1992, attempt to tinker with these basic programs, on which millions of Americans depend. Any president's domestic responsibilities remain enormous, whatever his political philosophy about the role of the federal government.

The Mass Media Television and the other news media have helped to magnify the person and the institution of the presidency. (The relationship between the president and the press is discussed on pp. 390–392.) All the major networks, newspapers, magazines, and wire services have correspondents assigned full time to covering the president. These "White House regulars" accompany the chief executive wherever he travels, sending out a steady flow of news about his activities.

When a president wants to talk to the people, the networks (whose stations are licensed by the federal government) often make available free prime time. Presidential news conferences are frequently televised live. People identify with a president they see so often on television; his style and personality help to shape the times and the national mood.

---

[16] Edward S. Corwin, *The President, Office and Powers 1787–1957* (New York: New York University Press, 1957), p. 311.

Modern presidents, to a greater extent than the public is aware, often tailor their daily activities to television, scheduling events in time to appear in a "sound bite" on the evening news. Presidents and their media affairs experts attempt to orchestrate and dominate the news to the advantage of the White House.

THE IMPOSSIBLE BURDEN: THE MANY ROLES OF THE CHIEF EXECUTIVE

During George Bush's first week in office in 1989, he met with congressional leaders, gave fifteen lucky tourists a personal tour of the White House, conferred by telephone with West German Chancellor Helmut Kohl, received messages from several world leaders, presided over his first cabinet meeting, held his first formal news conference, appointed eight members of a commission to study ethical standards in the federal government, endorsed salary raises for members of

Congress, federal judges, and senior officials, attended an ecumenical service at the National Cathedral in Washington, and went jogging. That was only a sample of his first week's calendar.

The president is one individual but fills many separate roles: chief of state, chief executive, commander in chief, chief diplomat, chief legislator, chief of party, and popular leader. All but the last two are required of him by the Constitution; in addition, as one scholar of the presidency suggested, he is expected to be the voice of the people, protector of the peace, manager of prosperity, and world leader.[17] A modern president is presumed to be all these things and more. But of course, no human being can live up to such exalted expectations.

Moreover, it would be simplistic and misleading to think of the president as rapidly "changing hats" as he goes about filling these varied roles. Many of the presidential roles blend and overlap; some of the roles may

---

[17] Rossiter, *The American Presidency*, pp. 16–41.

"Okay, bring in the new guy . . ."

Cartoon by Auth ©1976 the *Philadelphia Inquirer*

collide with others. Being a vigorous party leader, for example, will often conflict with playing the role of chief of state, of being president of all the people. For a president's roles, as Cronin has noted, "are not compartmentalized, unrelated functions, but rather a dynamic, seamless assortment of tasks and responsibilities." [18]

For purposes of analysis, however, it is convenient to separate out the principal roles of the president. When we do so, we see that the "awesome burden" has identifiable parts.

Chief of State

The president of the United States is the ceremonial and symbolic *head of state*. In another role, he is also head of government, the official who presides over the machinery of the Executive Branch. See discussion of the president as Chief Executive, pp. 370–371.

In many countries, the two jobs are distinct; a figurehead king, queen, or president is head of state, but the premier or prime minister is head of government and exercises the real power. It is because the two functions are combined in the person of the American president that he finds himself declaring National Codfish Week or toasting the Grand Duchess of Luxembourg at a state dinner on the same day that he makes a vital foreign-policy decision or vetoes a major bill sent to him by Congress.

The distinction between head of state and head of government may seem trivial — of interest only to protocol officers and society columnists — but it is not. Much of the awe and mystery, the power and dignity that have surrounded the institution of the presidency are due precisely to the fact that the president *is* more than a prime minister; he is a symbol of nationhood as well as a custodian of the people's power. In Theodore Roosevelt's famous phrase, he is both "a king and a prime minister." [19]

As noted earlier in this chapter, some critics of presidential power have argued that presidents lose their perspective and their ability to make sound judgments because they are treated too much like monarchs and are isolated from the problems faced by ordinary citizens. In part, this may happen because a president is surrounded by the trappings of power — large staffs, private aircraft, and the Secret Service.

Because the chief executive is such a symbolic and familiar figure, when a president dies in office people often react as though they have suffered a great personal loss. Even the radio announcers wept as they told of Franklin Roosevelt's death. After President Kennedy's assassination, the nation went through a period of mourning; 250,000 people braved cold weather to line up to pass his bier in the Capitol rotunda; 100,000,000 people watched the funeral on television. Social scientists studying the impact of the assassination on children and adults found definite physical and psychological effects. [20] The nation again experienced a sense of loss when two former presidents, Harry Truman and Lyndon Johnson, died within a month of each other in December 1972 and January 1973.

---

[18] Cronin, *The State of the Presidency*, p. 156.

As the train bearing the body of Franklin D. Roosevelt left Warm Springs, a tearful Chief Petty Officer Graham Jackson played "Going Home."

---

[19] Letter to Lady Delamere, March 7, 1911.

[20] For example, among adults, one study found that "the assassination generally evoked feelings similar to those felt at the death of a close friend or relative." Of a sample of the adult population, 43 percent said they did not feel like eating, 29 percent smoked more than usual, 53 percent cried, 48 percent had trouble sleeping, and 68 percent felt nervous and tense. Source: Paul B. Sheatsley and Jacob J. Feldman, "A National Survey on Public Reactions and Behavior," in Bradley S. Greenberg and Edwin B. Parker, eds., *The Kennedy Assassination and the American Public* (Stanford: Stanford University Press, 1965), pp. 158, 168.

November 1963: President John F. Kennedy lies in state in the Capitol rotunda.

THE CASE OF THE WHITE HOUSE MOUSE

Little problems, like the White House mice, have proved as intractable as big ones. When a couple of mice scampered across the President's study one evening last spring, an alarm went out to the General Services Administration, housekeeper of Federal buildings. Some weeks later, another mouse climbed up inside a wall of the Oval Office and died. The President's office was bathed in the odor of dead mouse as Carter prepared to greet visiting Latin American dignitaries. An emergency call went out to G.S.A. But it refused to touch the matter. Officials insisted that they had exterminated all the "inside" mice in the White House and this errant mouse must have come from outside, and therefore was the responsibility of the Interior Department. Interior demurred, saying that the dead mouse was now inside the White House. President Carter summoned officials from both agencies to his desk and exploded: "I can't even get a damn mouse out of my office." Ultimately, it took an interagency task force to get rid of the mouse.

—*New York Times*, January 8, 1978

Chief Executive

"The executive Power shall be vested in a President of the United States of America." So reads Article II of the Constitution, which also states: " . . . he shall take Care that the Laws be faithfully executed. . . . "

Under this simply worded but powerful grant of executive authority, the president runs the executive branch of the government. As of fiscal 1991, the president headed a federal establishment with a total payroll of $102 billion. No executive in private industry has responsibilities that match the president's. The president receives a salary of $200,000 a year plus $50,000 in nontaxable expenses and up to $100,000 in travel expenses, also tax-free, as well as handsome retirement benefits, including a lifetime pension of $99,500 a year.[21] There are few legal qualifications for the office; the Constitution requires only that the president be a "natural-born" citizen, at least thirty-five, and fourteen years a resident of the United States.[22]

Obviously, there would be more than enough work in the president's in-basket to keep him busy if he did nothing else but administer the government. And, in fact, presidents do find themselves bogged down under a mountain of paper. Most presidents work at night to try to keep up; the sight of Franklin Roosevelt, a polio victim, being wheeled to his office at night, preceded by wire baskets full of paperwork, was a familiar one to White House aides during the New Deal era. President Eisenhower tried to solve the paperwork problem by ordering his staff to prepare memos no more than one page long. Lyndon Johnson took a swim and nap each afternoon, then began a second working day at 4 P.M., often summoning weary aides for conferences at the end of *their* working day.

Because administering the government is only one of seven major presidential roles, the president cannot spend all of his time running the executive branch. He has a White House staff, other agencies in the Executive Office of the President, and his cabinet to help him. He tries to confine himself to *presidential* decisions, such as resolving major conflicts within the bureaucracy, or among his own advisers, and initiating and approving major programs and policies.

Beneath the president in the executive branch are the fourteen cabinet departments (as of January 1993)

---

[21] Data provided by Office of Media Affairs, the White House, as of July 1992.

[22] A citizen born abroad of American parents might well be regarded as "natural-born." The question arose in 1968 because George Romney, a Republican hopeful, had been born in Mexico. The requirement of fourteen years' residence apparently does not mean that a president must have resided in the United States for fourteen *successive* years immediately prior to the election, since Herbert Hoover had not.

A PRESIDENT VIEWS HIS POWER

Power? The only power I've got is nuclear—and I can't use that.

—Lyndon Johnson, quoted in Hugh Sidey, *A Very Personal Presidency*

and about sixty major independent agencies, boards, and commissions. (See Figure 11–3, pp. 422–423.) These agencies are of two main types: *executive agencies* and *regulatory agencies*. The independent executive agencies are units of government under the president within the executive branch, but not part of a cabinet department. They are, therefore, "independent" of the departments, not of the president. The members of the major independent regulatory agencies are appointed by the president from both major parties to staggered, fixed terms, but do not report to him. The regulatory agencies, which exercise quasi-judicial and quasi-legislative powers, are administratively independent of both the president and Congress (although politically independent of neither).

The neat organizational charts do not show the overlapping and intricate real-life relationships among the three branches of government. Nor do they give any hint of the difficulties a president faces in controlling his own executive branch and in making the bureaucracy carry out his decisions.

President Truman understood the problems that Eisenhower would have as an army general elected president: "He'll sit here," Truman would remark (tapping his desk for emphasis), "and he'll say, 'Do this! Do that!' *And nothing will happen.* Poor Ike — it won't be a bit like the army. He'll find it very frustrating." [23]

Despite their vast constitutional and extraconstitutional powers, presidents are sometimes as much a victim of bureaucratic inertia as anyone else. "I sit here all day," Truman said, "trying to persuade people to do the things they ought to have sense enough to do without my persuading them. . . . That's all the powers of the President amount to." [24]

Richard Neustadt agrees with Truman that "Presidential *power* is the power to persuade." [25] In persuading people, however, the president can draw upon formidable resources, not the least of which is his power to appoint and remove officials. Under the Constitution, the president, "with the advice and consent of the Senate," appoints ambassadors, Supreme Court justices, other federal judges, the heads of regulatory agencies, and other senior officials. Under present law, the president names about 2,400 upper-level federal officials who are political appointees. (The great bulk of the 3.1

million federal civilian employees are appointed by department heads through the civil service system.)

The Constitution does not specifically give the president the power to remove government officials, but the Supreme Court has ruled that Congress cannot interfere with the president's right to fire officials whom he has appointed with Senate approval.[26] During Franklin Roosevelt's administration, the Court held that the president did *not* have the right to remove officials serving in administratively independent "quasi-legislative or quasi-judicial agencies." [27] Even though commissioners of regulatory agencies are thus theoretically immune from removal by presidential power, in practice they may not be. When scandal touched the chairman of the Federal Communications Commission in 1960, the incident embarrassed President Eisenhower; within a week the official resigned.

To the task of bureaucrat in chief, therefore, the president brings powers of persuasion that go beyond his formal, constitutional, and legal authority. By the nature of his job, he is the final decision maker in the executive branch. As the sign on Harry Truman's desk said: "The buck stops here."

The president also has the power to grant "reprieves and pardons for offenses against the United States," a power that seemed relatively unimportant in modern times until President Ford granted a pardon to his predecessor, Richard Nixon (who had appointed Ford vice-president). Ford noted that in the Watergate affair, the former president had "become liable to possible indictment and trial for offenses against the United States." Ford said that such a trial would divide the country, and he pardoned Nixon for all crimes that he "has committed or may have committed" as president. Ford later testified under oath that, prior to taking office, he had not entered into any arrangement with Nixon to grant the pardon.

Commander in Chief

When President Kennedy died at Parkland Hospital in Dallas on November 22, 1963, an army warrant officer named Ira D. Gearhart, armed but dressed in civilian clothes, picked up a locked briefcase known as the "football," or "black box," and walked down a hospital corridor to a small room where President Lyndon

---

[23] In Richard E. Neustadt, *Presidential Power* (New York: John Wiley & Sons, Inc., 1980), p. 9.

[24] Ibid., p. 9.

[25] Ibid., p. 10.

[26] *Myers v. United States,* 272 U.S. 52 (1926).

[27] *Humphrey's Executor v. United States,* 295 U.S. 602 (1935).

Lt. Comdr. Vivian Crea, U.S. Coast Guard, first woman military aide to the president, carries the "football."

coded orders. That such a person and such machinery exist is a reminder of the fact that, regardless of his other duties, the president is at all times commander in chief of the armed forces of the United States.

Although a president normally delegates most of this authority to his generals and admirals, he is not required to do so. During the Whiskey Rebellion of 1794, President Washington personally led his troops into Pennsylvania. During the Civil War, Lincoln often visited the Army of the Potomac to instruct his generals. Franklin Roosevelt and Prime Minister Winston Churchill conferred on the major strategic decisions of the Second World War. Truman made the decisions to drop the atomic bomb on Japan in 1945 and to intervene in Korea in 1950. Kennedy authorized the Bay of Pigs invasion of Cuba by Cuban exiles armed and trained by the Central Intelligence Agency. Johnson personally approved bombing targets in Vietnam. President Nixon made the decision to send American troops into Cambodia in 1970, to bomb North Vietnam, and to bomb Cambodia in 1973. President Reagan made the decision to send troops to invade Grenada in 1983 and to bomb Libya in 1986. President Bush dispatched 27,000 troops to invade Panama in 1989 and sent more than half a million men and women to the Persian Gulf in 1990.

The principle of *civilian supremacy* over the military is embodied in the clear constitutional power of the president as supreme commander of the armed forces.

Johnson was being guarded by Secret Service agents. The officer who carries the "football" must be near whoever is the president, to guard "a national security portfolio of cryptographic orders the president would send his military chiefs to authorize the launching of nuclear missiles. The orders can be dispatched by telephone, teletype, or microwave radio."[28]

In effect, the warrant officer has custody of the "nuclear button," which is not a button but a set of

---

[28] Bob Horton, Associated Press staff writer, "The Job of Guarding the President's Code Box," *Washington Star*, November 21, 1965. See also William Manchester, *The Death of a President* (New York: Harper & Row, 1967), pp. 62, 321.

LYNDON JOHNSON: VIETNAM VERSUS THE GREAT SOCIETY

I knew from the start," Johnson told me in 1970, describing the early weeks of 1965, "that I was bound to be crucified either way I moved. If I left the woman I really loved—the Great Society—in order to get involved with that bitch of a war on the other side of the world, then I would lose everything at home. All my programs. All my hopes to feed the hungry and shelter the homeless. All my dreams to provide education and medical care to the browns and blacks and the lame and the poor. But if I left that war and let the Communists take over South Vietnam, then I would be seen as a coward and my nation would be seen as an appeaser and we would find it impossible to accomplish anything for anybody anywhere on the entire globe.

"Oh, I could see it coming all right. History provided too many cases where the sound of the bugle put an immediate end to the hopes and dreams of the best reformers."

—Lyndon Johnson, quoted in Doris Kearns, *Lyndon Johnson and the American Dream*

President Ford, soon after leaving office, revealed his genuine disdain of the resolution. Ford told a University of Kentucky audience on April 11, 1977: "The United States was involved in six military crises during my presidency: The evacuation of U.S. citizens and refugees from DaNang, Phnom Penh, and Saigon in the Spring of 1975, the rescue of the *Mayagüez* in May 1975, and the two evacuation operations in Lebanon in June 1976. In none of those instances did I believe the War Powers Resolution applied. . . . I did not concede that the resolution itself was legally binding on the President on constitutional grounds."

—*Inquiry*, June 26, 1978

The principle was put to a severe test during the Korean War when General Douglas MacArthur repeatedly defied President Truman's orders. The hero of the Pacific theater during the Second World War, MacArthur enjoyed personal prestige to rival the president's and had a substantial political following of his own. Truman finally dismissed MacArthur in April 1951. In the most dramatic conflict in modern times between the military and the president, the president prevailed.

The Constitution declares that "Congress shall have Power . . . To declare War," but Congress has not done so since December 1941, when it declared war against Japan and Germany following the Japanese attack on Pearl Harbor.[29] In the intervening years the president has made the decision to go to war, although twice, in Vietnam and the Persian Gulf, he had

---

[29] Congress has declared war five times: in the War of 1812, the Mexican War, the Spanish-American War, the First World War, and the Second World War. It did not declare war in Korea, Vietnam, or the Persian Gulf. However, it authorized military action in Vietnam in the Tonkin Gulf Resolution in 1964, and against Iraq in the Authorization for Use of Military Force Against Iraq Resolution in 1991.

1991: President Bush visits troops in the Persian Gulf

congressional approval. By 1970, Congress was trying to regain some of its control over the war power. Congress repealed the Tonkin Gulf Resolution, which it had passed in 1964 to support President Johnson's Vietnam policy, and it restricted President Nixon's future use of American troops in Cambodia. Sentiment continued to grow in Congress to curb the president's power to wage undeclared war.

Then, in 1973, Congress passed legislation to attempt to limit presidential war-making power. President Nixon vetoed the measure as an unconstitutional restraint on his power as commander in chief. But Congress overrode the president's veto, and the War Powers Resolution became law. The measure provided:

1. Within forty-eight hours after committing armed forces to combat abroad, the president must report to Congress in writing, explaining the circumstances and scope of his actions.

2. Use of American forces in combat would have to end in 60 days unless Congress authorized a longer period, but the deadline could be extended for another thirty days if the president certified that the time was necessary for the safe withdrawal of the forces.

3. Within the sixty- or ninety-day period, Congress could order an immediate withdrawal of American forces by adopting a concurrent resolution—which is not subject to a presidential veto.

Some members of Congress and other persons who were against the expansion of presidential war power opposed the bill. They argued that the measure actually increased the president's power to make war by giving congressional authorization for "60-day wars." But most members of Congress disagreed; for them, the moment had come to attempt to reassert congressional authority over the combat use of American military power. In addition, Congress in 1974 required the CIA to report to it about covert operations, and in 1976 Congress enacted a law that gave it the right to veto arms sales by the executive branch.

Through the Reagan and Bush presidencies, however, the War Powers Resolution had not effectively restricted presidential military power. Presidents Nixon, Ford, Carter, Reagan, and Bush all took military actions that they did not report to Congress under the War Powers Resolution. In some instances, they did report military actions to Congress, but either said or implied that they had authority as president to deploy

1989: American troops in Panama

American forces, and that the reports were a matter of courtesy rather than a legal requirement. During the Nixon, Ford, Carter, Reagan, and Bush administrations, through 1992, presidents reported a total of twenty-five times in instances in which some type of American military intervention had taken place.

In September 1983, after President Reagan sent U.S. Marines to Lebanon, Congress invoked the War Powers Resolution for the first time since its passage ten years earlier. It enacted legislation declaring that the law applied to the conflict in Lebanon and authorizing continued deployment of the marines there for eighteen months. President Reagan signed the bill, but said this did not mean he accepted the principle that the War Powers Resolution applied in Lebanon.

In October 1983, when Reagan sent army troops and marines to Grenada, he informed Congress. But as previous presidents had done, he said he was acting voluntarily, not because he had to under the War Powers Resolution. The House and Senate each passed resolutions calling for withdrawal of the troops from Grenada within sixty days, but Congress did not formally invoke this provision of the law, and the combat troops were withdrawn before that deadline in any event.

The War Powers Resolution, or at least that portion of the law giving Congress authority to order a withdrawal of American forces, is a form of legislative veto, a device ruled unconstitutional by the Supreme Court in 1983.[30] As discussed in Chapter 12, however, a

---

[30] *Immigration and Naturalization Service v. Chadha*, 462 U.S. 919 (1983).

direct constitutional confrontation over the War Powers Resolution had not occurred by 1992, and was considered unlikely by some scholars.

The "military-industrial complex"—the term often used to describe the ties between the military establishment and the defense-aerospace industry—is another limit on the president's power as commander in chief. For example, a president may find it difficult to cancel production of a fighter plane, a bomber, an aircraft carrier, or some other weapons system that enjoys the strong support of the Joint Chiefs of Staff, Congress, and private industry.

Despite these limits, presidents have claimed and exercised formidable war powers during emergencies. In the ten weeks after the fall of Fort Sumter in April 1861, Lincoln called out the militia, spent $2 million without authorization by Congress, blockaded Southern ports, and suspended the writ of habeas corpus in certain areas. Lincoln declared: "I felt that measures otherwise unconstitutional might become lawful by becoming indispensable to the preservation of the Constitution through the preservation of the nation. Right or wrong, I assumed this ground and now avow it." [31]

During the Second World War, Franklin Roosevelt exercised extraordinary powers over food rationing and the economy, only partly with congressional authorization. And in 1942, with the consent of Congress, he permitted the forced removal of 112,000 persons of Japanese descent—most of them native-born citizens of the United States—from California and other western states to camps called "relocation centers" in the interior of the country.

During the Korean War, Truman seized the steel mills in the face of a strike threat, but the Supreme Court ruled he had no constitutional right to do so, even as commander in chief. [32] President Johnson expanded American forces in Vietnam after Congress passed the Tonkin Gulf Resolution, empowering the president to take "all necessary measures" in Southeast Asia. The president contended, however, that he did not need congressional approval to fight the war in Vietnam.

Chief Diplomat

"I make American foreign policy," President Truman declared in 1948. By and large, presidents do make foreign policy; that is, they direct the relations of the United States with the other nations of the world. The Constitution does not *specifically* confer this power on the president, but it does so indirectly. It authorizes him to receive foreign ambassadors, to appoint ambassadors, and to make treaties with the consent of two-thirds of the Senate. Because it requires that the president share some foreign-policy powers with Congress, the Constitution has been characterized as "an invitation to struggle for the privilege of directing American foreign policy." [33]

In this struggle the president usually enjoys the advantage. Because the State Department, the Pentagon, and the CIA report to him as part of the executive branch, the president—or so it is often assumed—has more information about foreign affairs available to him than do members of Congress. But senators and representatives also have sources of information—official briefings, background memoranda from the Library of Congress, data from the Congressional Budget Office, unofficial "leaks" from within the bureaucracy, and friends in the press and the universities. A president, therefore, does not have a monopoly of information. Much of the information he does receive is conflicting, because it represents different viewpoints within the bureaucracy; even with the best intelligence reports, a president may make decisions that prove to be misguided. Nevertheless, the information that flows in daily is a substantial source of power for the president.

Those who lack the information that the president has, or is presumed to have, including senators and representatives, find it difficult to challenge the president's actions. Often, at least in the short run, a foreign policy crisis may increase the public's support of the president's actions. This was true, for example, for President Bush when American forces in the Persian Gulf war drove Iraq's Saddam Hussein out of Kuwait, the Arab nation he had invaded. (See Figure 10–1.) Over a period of time, however, public opinion can change and Congress can chip away at a president's power in foreign affairs. The same crisis in the Persian Gulf that had been a public relations triumph for Bush in 1991 turned somewhat sour a year later when Bush sought re-election amid congressional charges that the White House had secretly supported Iraq in the years before Saddam invaded Kuwait. Many voters had second thoughts about the conflict, wondering why the Iraqi dictator was

[31] In Arthur Bernon Tourtellot, *The Presidents on the Presidency* (Garden City: Doubleday, 1964), p. 311.
[32] *Youngstown Sheet and Tube Co. v. Sawyer*, 343 U.S. 579 (1952).
[33] Corwin, *The President, Office and Powers 1787–1957*, p. 171.

"Presidents do make foreign policy." British Prime Minister Winston Churchill, President Truman, and Soviet Premier Stalin at Potsdam, 1945.

still in power in Baghdad if the United States had won the war.

The president has sole power to negotiate and sign treaties. The Senate may block a treaty by refusing to approve it, but it seldom does so. In 1920, however, it did refuse to ratify the Treaty of Versailles and its provision for United States membership in the League of Nations. Sometimes a president does not submit a treaty to the Senate because he knows it will not be approved, or he may modify the treaty to meet Senate opposition. In 1977 President Carter submitted two treaties to the Senate turning over the Panama Canal to Panama in the year 2000. After months of controversy, the Senate finally approved the treaties the following year, but with a reservation sponsored by Senator Dennis DeConcini, Democrat, of Arizona, asserting the right of the United States to send troops into Panama to keep the canal open. In January 1988, President Reagan asked the Senate to approve the INF (Intermediate-range Nuclear Forces) treaty that he had signed with the Soviet Union. The Senate approved the treaty in May 1988 just before Reagan left for a summit meeting in Moscow with Soviet leader Mikhail Gorbachev.

Executive agreements are international agreements between the president and foreign heads of state that do not require Senate approval. Today, they are employed by the president in the conduct of foreign affairs more often than treaties. Some executive agreements are made by the president with the prior approval of Congress. For example, in the Trade Act of 1974, Congress restored the president's power to negotiate tariff agreements with other countries. And sometimes, to gain political support, a president will submit an executive agreement to Congress after it is signed, although he is not legally required to do so.

Because a president can sign an executive agreement with another nation without the constitutional necessity of going to the Senate, the use of this device has increased enormously. This has been particularly true since the Second World War, as the United States' role in international affairs has expanded. Today, in a single year, a president may sign several hundred executive agreements.

The president also has sole power to recognize or not recognize foreign governments. The United States did not recognize the Soviet Union until November

1992: Russia's President Boris N. Yeltsin is greeted by President Bush at the White House

1933, sixteen years after the Russian Revolution. Since Wilson's day, presidents have used diplomatic recognition as an instrument of American foreign policy. President Nixon's historic journey to Peking early in 1972 marked the start of diplomatic contacts between the United States and the People's Republic of China. President Carter recognized China in 1979, and the two countries opened full diplomatic relations. In 1991, President Bush recognized the Baltic nations — Lithuania, Latvia, and Estonia — that had gained independence from the Soviet Union, and he established diplomatic relations with Boris N. Yeltsin, the new president of an independent Russia, and with the other former republics of what had been the Soviet Union.

In acting as chief diplomat, the president, as commander in chief, can back up his diplomacy with military power. Both the arrows and the olive branch depicted in the presidential seal are available to him, a good example of how presidential roles overlap.

Chief Legislator

"He shall from time to time give to the Congress Information of the State of the Union, and recommend to their Consideration such Measures as he shall judge necessary and expedient." With this statement in Article II, "the Constitution puts the President right square into the legislative business," as President Eisenhower observed at a 1959 press conference.

Today, presidents often use their televised State of the Union address, usually delivered to a joint session of Congress in January, as a public platform to unveil their annual legislative program. The details of proposed legislation are then filled in through a series of special presidential messages sent to Capitol Hill in the months that follow.

This was not always the case. Active presidential participation in the legislative process is a twentieth-century phenomenon, and the practice of presidents sending a comprehensive legislative package to Congress developed only after the Second World War during the Truman administration.[34]

The success of the president's role as chief legislator depends on the cooperation of Congress. A Republican president faced with a Democratic Congress, as was the case during the four years following Bush's election in 1988, or a Democratic president blocked by a coalition of Republicans and Southern Democrats (as in Kennedy's case), may find his role as chief legislator frustrating. As President Kennedy observed ruefully: "It is very easy to defeat a bill in the Congress. It is much more difficult to pass one. . . . They are two separate offices and two separate powers, the Congress and the Presidency. There is bound to be conflict."[35]

The conflict at times revolves around the doctrine of *executive privilege*. This doctrine is nowhere explicitly stated in the Constitution but rests on the separation of powers of the three branches of the federal government. By invoking executive privilege, presidents have claimed the inherent right to withhold information from Congress and the judiciary. Congress in turn has argued that its legislative powers include the right to make inquiries and investigations of the executive branch, and to obtain all necessary information from the president and his administration. Usually conflicts over executive privilege arise when a congressional committee demands documents from, or testimony by, presidential assistants.

As the Watergate scandal unfolded during the Nixon administration, the president was accused by his former counsel of participating in an illegal plot to cover

[34] Richard E. Neustadt, "Presidency and Legislation: Planning the President's Program," *American Political Science Review*, vol. 49 (December 1955), p. 981.

[35] "After Two Years — a Conversation With the President," *Public Papers*, p. 894.

up the break-in and bugging at the Democratic party's headquarters. Nixon's tapes of his own White House conversations became the crucial evidence, although an eighteen-and-a-half-minute segment of a key tape had apparently been erased. Eventually, the Watergate special prosecutor demanded the tapes for use in the trial of several high-ranking officials accused of covering up the break-in and the issue went to the United States Supreme Court. In ruling 8–0 that Nixon must surrender his tapes, the Court for the first time recognized the doctrine of executive privilege — but declared that the right of the president to keep some matters confidential must yield to the need for evidence in a criminal trial.[36]

Every president has staff assistants in charge of legislative liaison. Their job is to pressure Congress to pass the president's program. The senators or representatives who want the administration to approve a new federal building, or dam, or public-works project in their state or district may discover that the price is their vote on a bill that the president wants passed. There are other, more subtle pressures. A senator who opposes a president's foreign policies may no longer be invited to White House social functions. Often, on an important measure, the president himself takes charge of the "arm twisting" — telephoning members of Congress in their offices or inviting them to the White House for a chat about the merits of his program.

On the other hand, political scientist George C. Edwards III has argued, "while legislative skills may at times gain support for presidential policies, this is not typical." Examining the various resources available to a president, Edwards concluded that a chief executive "has relatively little influence to wield over Congress."[37]

As chief legislator, however, the president is not limited entirely to the arts of persuasion. He has an important constitutional weapon in the veto. The president, if he approves a bill, may sign it — often in front of news photographers and with much fanfare and handing out of pens. If he disapproves, however, he may veto the bill and return it with his objections to the branch of Congress in which it originated. By a vote of two-thirds of each house, Congress may pass the bill over the president's veto. If the president does not sign or veto a bill within ten working days after he receives it, the measure becomes law without his signature. If Congress adjourns during this ten-day period, the president can exercise his *pocket-veto* and kill the bill by taking no action. But the Constitution was unclear on whether a president could pocket-veto a bill anytime Congress was in recess. During the 1970s, Senator Edward M. Kennedy successfully challenged in court three pocket-vetoes by Presidents Nixon and Ford. The court rulings suggested that a president may not pocket-veto legislation when Congress is in recess but only when it adjourns for good at the end of the second session of a Congress. After Congress recessed in 1983, however, President Reagan pocket-vetoed a bill linking military aid to El Salvador to progress in human rights in that country. Except for joint resolutions, which are the same as bills, resolutions of Congress do not require presidential action since they are expressions of sentiment, not law. The War Powers Resolution of 1973 is an example of a law enacted in the form of a joint resolution.

Because Congress normally finds it difficult to override a presidential veto, merely the threat of a veto is often enough to force Congress to tailor a bill to conform to administration wishes. Only about 4 percent of presidential vetoes have been overridden by Congress. (See Table 10–1.)

The presidential veto power is limited by the fact that, unlike the governors of most states, the president does not possess the *item veto*, the power to disapprove particular parts of a bill. As a result, Congress is encouraged to pass *riders*, provisions tacked on to a piece of legislation that are not relevant to the bill. Sponsors of riders know that the president must swallow the legislation whole or veto the entire bill — he cannot veto just the rider. President Reagan asked Congress to propose a constitutional amendment giving the president an item veto over appropriations bills, or to permit him an item veto for a two-year trial period. Congress declined to act on his requests or on similar requests by President Bush.

Since the 1920s, until Congress legislated against the practice in 1974, modern presidents at times employed another weapon in dealing with Congress: *impoundment* of funds. The Constitution provides that Congress shall appropriate funds to run the government, but it does not specifically say the president must spend them. And presidents have periodically refused to spend money for programs they have opposed. In the Congressional Budget Act of 1974, however, Congress required the president to spend funds that had been appropriated.

---

[36] *United States* v. *Nixon*, 418 U.S. 683 (1974).

[37] George C. Edwards III, *Presidential Influence in Congress* (San Francisco: W.H. Freeman, 1980), pp. 10, 205.

Table 10-1
Presidential Vetoes, 1789–1992

	Regular Vetoes	Pocket Vetoes	Total Vetoes	Vetoes Overridden
Washington	2	—	2	—
Madison	5	2	7	—
Monroe	1	—	1	—
Jackson	5	7	12	—
Tyler	6	3	9	1
Polk	2	1	3	—
Pierce	9	—	9	5
Buchanan	4	3	7	—
Lincoln	2	4	6	—
A. Johnson	21	8	29	15
Grant	45	49	94	4
Hayes	12	1	13	1
Arthur	4	8	12	1
Cleveland	304	109	413	2
B. Harrison	19	25	44	1
Cleveland	43	127	170	5
McKinley	6	36	42	—
T. Roosevelt	42	40	82	1
Taft	30	9	39	1
Wilson	33	11	44	6
Harding	5	1	6	—
Coolidge	20	30	50	4
Hoover	21	16	37	3
F. Roosevelt	372	261	633	9
Truman	180	70	250	12
Eisenhower	73	108	181	2
Kennedy	12	9	21	—
L. Johnson	16	14	30	—
Nixon	24	19	43	5
Ford	44	22	66	12
Carter	13	18	31	2
Reagan	39	39	78	9
Bush	27	19	46	1
Total	1441	1069	2510	102

Source: Senate Library, *Presidential Vetoes* (U.S. Government Printing Office, 1969), p. 199. Data for L. Johnson from *Congressional Quarterly Almanac*, 1968 (Washington, D.C.: Congressional Quarterly Service, 1968), p. 23. Data for Nixon, Ford, Carter, and Reagan from Records Office, the White House. Data for Bush from Office of Media Affairs, the White House.

As chief legislator, the president may call Congress back into session. He also may adjourn Congress if the House and the Senate should disagree about when to adjourn, although no president has exercised this constitutional power.

The Supreme Court has held that Congress may not delegate legislative authority to the president, but Congress has in some cases passed legislation setting broad guidelines within which the president may act. For example, under such laws the president may be authorized to reduce tariffs. And since 1939 Congress has periodically passed a series of Reorganization Acts that permit the president to restructure federal agencies under plans that he must submit to Congress. Unless Congress *disapproves* the plans within sixty days, they go into effect.

The president's real ability to persuade Congress often rests on his personal popularity rather than on his formal or informal powers. The veto, "arm twisting," threats to withhold a public-works project, and social ostracism of a representative or senator are, over the long run, less important than the ability of a president to enlist public support for his programs and the extent of his prestige with both Congress and the electorate.

Chief of Party

"No President, it seems to me, can escape politics," John Kennedy said in 1960 when he sought the presidency. "He has not only been chosen by the Nation—he has been chosen by his party." [38]

Not every president has filled the role of party chief with the same enthusiasm that Kennedy brought to it. President Eisenhower, a career Army officer for most of his life, displayed a reluctance to engage in the rough-and-tumble of politics. As he told a press conference in 1955: "In the general derogatory sense . . . I do not like politics . . . the word 'politics' as you use it, I think the answer to that one, would be, no. I have no great liking for that." [39]

For many months in 1980, President Carter declined to campaign actively for re-election, claiming that the hostage crisis in Iran took precedence over his political duties and made it necessary for him to remain in the White House. "I am not going to resume business as usual as a partisan campaigner out on the campaign trail until our hostages are back here, free and at home," Carter declared.[40] Carter thus attempted to adopt a presidential "above politics" stance. But when, on April 30, Carter announced that the country's foreign and domestic problems "are manageable enough now for me to leave the White House," his statement brought hoots of disbelief from his critics.[41] President Reagan campaigned actively in 1984, and seemed to like doing so.

Whether or not a president enjoys his partisan role, he is the chief of his party. The machinery of the national committee reports to him; he can install his choice as national chairperson; he can usually demand his party's renomination and stage-manage the convention that acclaims him. Since success as chief legislator depends to a considerable degree on the political makeup of Congress, the president may find it advantageous to campaign for congressional candidates in off-year elections.

Given the decentralized nature of American political parties, a president's influence may not extend to state and local party organizations in every case. Nor does it prevail at all times with members of his party in Congress. In fact, his own leaders in Congress may not always bow to his political wisdom or policy wishes.

When a president makes decisions, he is, in the broadest sense, engaging in politics. A successful president must lead and gauge public opinion, must be sensitive to change, and must have a sure sense of the limits of the possible. All of these are *political* skills. As chief of party, the president is also the nation's number one professional politician. And, as Neustadt has suggested, "The Presidency is no place for amateurs." [42]

Popular Leader

The president also plays a vital role as the popular leader of the nation, the one person who speaks—in theory at least—for all of America. The president, aside from all of his more formal, constitutional, and political roles, is also expected to act as the national leader.

In times of crisis, the people tend to look to the president for reassurance. For example, when the president addresses the nation on television from the Oval Office to explain why he is sending American forces to some remote corner of the globe, as has often happened, he is technically acting as commander in chief, but in a larger sense he is acting as national leader, the powerful figure to whom the voters turn, perhaps as much for psychological support as for factual explanations.

To this role of popular leader, the president normally brings an ideology and a philosophy. Franklin D. Roosevelt was identified with the social welfare programs of the New Deal, Lyndon B. Johnson with their echo in the Great Society of the 1960s. Ronald Reagan, by contrast, was identified with limited government. To some extent, George Bush shared that view, often contending that individuals could accomplish more than government programs.

As national leader, the president does more, of course, than expound a philosophy. The policies of his administration, the legislative agenda he sends to Congress, and the actions of his bureaucrats often reflect his point of view. He may hope, although he may often be disappointed, that the justices he appoints to the Supreme Court will also march to his tune.

Today, presidential rhetoric—a chief executive's skills as an orator and persuader—powerfully affects his ability to govern. Indeed, "rhetorical leadership," in

---

[38] *Congressional Record,* January 18, 1960, pp. 710–12.
[39] Neustadt, *Presidential Power,* p. 166.
[40] *Weekly Compilation of Presidential Documents,* February 13, 1980, p. 310.
[41] See Dom Bonafede, "Who's He Trying to Kid?" *National Journal,* May 10, 1980, p. 781.

[42] Neustadt, *Presidential Power,* p. 180.

the view of Jeffrey K. Tulis, one presidential scholar, "is the essence of the modern presidency."[43] He adds: "Since the presidencies of Theodore Roosevelt and Woodrow Wilson, popular or mass rehetoric has become a principal tool of presidential governance. Presidents regularly 'go over the heads' of Congress to the people at large in support of legislation and other initiatives. . . . the doctrine that a president ought to be a popular leader has become an unquestioned premise of our political culture."[44] Presidents now are expected to inspire the public, Tulis notes. "And for many, this presidential 'function' is not one duty among many, but rather the heart of the presidency—its essential task."[45] President Reagan's "stunning string of partisan successes," including budget cuts and a military buildup, were due in no small measure to his skills as a popular leader, a "great communicator."[46]

But the president's role as popular leader is not without its perils. Modern presidents, Theodore J. Lowi has argued, are doomed to failure. Because of the "exalted rhetoric and high expectations surrounding the presidency," even a degree of success is considered a failure by the mass public, Lowi contends.[47] The presidency is thus a "no-win" situation, in Lowi's view, because for a successful presidential candidate, victory in November is the beginning of the end: ". . . his political career is finished before he can fully enjoy the prize."[48]

In this view, as soon as a president wins, he loses. This paradox is a direct result of the enormous attention focused on modern presidents in the American political system.

As Lowi puts it: ". . . since the president has become the embodiment of government, it seems perfectly normal for millions upon millions of Americans to concentrate their hopes and fears directly and personally upon him. It is no wonder that [the] United States has developed such a tremendous stake in the 'personal president' and his personal capacity to govern."[49]

The president, it must be emphasized again, fills all of these various presidential roles at once. The powers and duties of the office are not divisible. The roles conflict and overlap; in performing one role, the president may incur political costs that make it more difficult for him to perform another. In short, the presidency is a balancing act.

In addition to these basic roles, Americans expect the president to take on many other roles. In the event of a major civil disturbance, he is expected to act as a police officer and restore domestic tranquility. As the manager of the economy, he is expected to prevent a recession, ensure prosperity, and hold down the cost of butter and eggs. He is expected to set an example in his personal life—and woe unto the president who drives too fast or is photographed too often with a highball glass in his hand. He is expected to be a teacher, to educate the people about great public issues. In some mysterious way, the president is expected to speak for all the people and to give voice to their deepest aspirations and ideals. "The Presidency," Franklin Roosevelt said, "is not merely an administrative office. That is the least of it. It is preeminently a place of moral leadership."[50]

THE TOOLS OF PRESIDENTIAL POWER

In the exercise of power, the president of the United States has available a formidable array of tools, money, and people. In ever widening circles, this last category includes the White House staff (secretaries and advisers), the Executive Office of the President (a conglomerate of presidential substaffs), the vice-president, the cabinet, the fourteen cabinet departments, the many other agencies of the executive branch, and the five million employees of the federal bureaucracy and the military.

He has almost unlimited personal resources as well. When President Johnson had reviewed the marines in California on one occasion and was walking back to a helicopter, he was stopped by an officer who pointed to another helicopter and said, "That's your helicopter over there, sir." Johnson replied, "Son, they are all my helicopters."[51]

[43] Jeffrey K. Tulis, *The Rhetorical Presidency* (Princeton, N. J.: Princeton University Press, 1987) p. 4.
[44] Ibid.
[45] Ibid.
[46] Ibid.
[47] Theodore J. Lowi, *The Personal President: Power Invested, Promise Unfulfilled* (Ithaca, N.Y.: Cornell University Press, 1985), p. 11.
[48] Ibid., p. 10.
[49] Ibid., p. 96.

[50] Rossiter, *The American Presidency*, p. 148.
[51] Hugh Sidey, *A Very Personal Presidency* (New York: Atheneum, 1968), p. 98.

When the president travels, he has at his disposal not only helicopters, but a fleet of jets; aboard *Air Force One*, he can communicate with his aides or with the military anywhere in the world. If he flies to Kansas City to deliver a speech, a special switchboard, operated by a Pentagon communications unit that travels with the president, connects him with the White House.

In addition to the formal machinery of government at the president's command, he has other, informal resources — his reputation, personality and style, ability to arouse public opinion, political party, and informal advisers and friends.

As one leading presidential scholar, Thomas Cronin, has warned, however, listing the president's cabinet and all the other panels, staffs, and informal advisers that serve him might create the impression that a president "must have just about all the inside information and good advice anyone could want." As Cronin points out, one might even erroneously conclude that a president "can both set and shape the directions of public policy and can see to it that these policies *work as intended.*"[52] Yet, that is often not the case. As we have already seen, there are limitations on presidential power at almost every turn. Indeed, one of the measures of a president's power is how well he can use the tools at his command.

The Cabinet

The president, the vice-president, the heads of the major executive departments of the government, and certain other senior officials who may hold "cabinet rank" constitute the cabinet. But the cabinet is an informal institution. The Constitution speaks of "the principal Officer in each of the executive Departments" and of "Heads of Departments." The Twenty-fifth Amendment, ratified in 1967, allows for the possibility of the department heads acting as a group in case of presidential disability. But the cabinet as an organized body is nowhere specifically provided for by law or in the Constitution.

---

[52] Cronin, *The State of the Presidency*, p. 80.

CABINET MEETINGS: A SECRET RECORD

Cabinet meetings are normally secret, but in 1978 *The Nation* magazine somehow obtained and printed excerpts from the minutes of several cabinet meetings held during the Carter administration. The secret minutes suggested that the President and other members of the Carter cabinet often commented on press reports about themselves:

April 25, 1977: The President said that he regretted missing Dr. Schlesinger on *Face the Nation* yesterday, but he had watched the energy industry representatives on *Meet the Press.*

June 13: The President described a recent television show by Bill Moyers on CIA operations. . . .

July 11: Dr. Brzezinski noted a good editorial in Sunday's *New York Times* on U.S./Soviet relations. . . .

August 1: The President expressed his concern about recent leaks to the press regarding specific discussions at Cabinet meetings. He urged Cabinet members and White House staff *not* to characterize to the press what he and others say during the Cabinet meetings. . . .

August 1: The President said that some weekly summaries submitted by Cabinet members are superb, while others contain unnecessary information about travel plans, speeches and related items. . . . He noted that he will not complain about the brevity of reports. . . .

August 29: Mr. Blumenthal asked whether press reports that the new leadership in China is focusing more on economic development than on ideology were true. Mr. Vance said that it is true. . . . The President said that he is pleased that three Cabinet members appeared on Sunday television talk shows.

March 6: The President noted that there was a good article today in the *New York Times* on the Middle East. . . . Mr. Blumenthal said that today's *New York Times* editorial on the loan to New York City is also excellent.

—*The Nation*, September 30, 1978

The president, Richard F. Fenno points out, "is not required by law to form a Cabinet or to keep one," and the cabinet has become "institutionalized by usage alone." [53] Perhaps because the cabinet is entirely a creature of custom, it is a relatively weak institution. The weakness of the cabinet under a strong president is often illustrated by the story of how Lincoln counted when the entire cabinet was opposed to him: "Seven nays, one aye — the ayes have it."

In any case, a cabinet member may not be competent to discuss problems of a general nature, for "beyond his immediate bailiwick, he may not be capable of adding anything to the group conference." [54] For this reason, President Kennedy thought that cabinet meetings were "a waste of time." [55]

Modern presidents have made varied use of the cabinet. Lyndon Johnson met regularly with his cabinet, but the conduct of the war in Vietnam was normally discussed not in the cabinet, but at regular Tuesday luncheon meetings of the president and selected officials. Nixon sought, only briefly, to revitalize the cabinet as a formal advisory body, but seldom held cabinet meetings in his second term. President Ford tried to restore the cabinet to greater influence and held frequent cabinet meetings. Carter met with his cabinet more frequently than any president since Eisenhower. However, in one tumultuous week in 1979, he fired or accepted the resignations of five cabinet members. The shakeup brought considerable criticism of the president.

During the 1980 campaign, Ronald Reagan promised, if elected, to institute a "cabinet government," in which the president and the members of his cabinet arrived at decisions together. But in practice, it was the president and a small group of White House staff aides who usually made the real decisions. "Cabinet government is an illusion," one administration official acknowledged.[56] As one account put it, "Full Cabinet meetings, scornfully referred to as 'dog-and-pony shows' by one Cabinet member and as 'pep rallies' by another, were largely informational. The busier Cabinet members and White House staff members alike tended to regard them as a waste of time. 'I can't think of a single

Table 10-2
The President's Cabinet

The Executive Departments in Order of Formation[*]

State	1789
Treasury	1789
Interior	1849
Justice†	1870
Agriculture‡	1889
Commerce§	1913
Labor§	1913
Defense‖	1947
Housing and Urban Development	1965
Transportation	1966
Energy	1977
Education	1979
Health and Human Services¶	1979
Department of Veterans Affairs	1989

* As of 1992. The office of Postmaster General, created in 1789, received cabinet rank in 1829 and was made a cabinet department in 1872. In 1970 Congress abolished the Post Office as a cabinet department and replaced it with the United States Postal Service, an independent federal agency.
† The office of Attorney General, created in 1789, became the Department of Justice in 1870.
‡ Originally created in 1862 and elevated to a cabinet department in 1889.
§ The Department of Commerce and Labor, created in 1903, was divided into two separate departments in 1913.
‖ The Department of War (the army) created in 1789, and the Department of the Navy, created in 1798, were consolidated along with the air force under the Department of Defense in 1947.
¶ Originally created as the Department of Health, Education, and Welfare in 1953, it was divided into two separate cabinet departments in 1979.

major decision that has been made at the full Cabinet meeting,' said one secretary." [57]

When President Bush convened his first informal meeting with his cabinet members, he pulled a handwritten list from his pocket and read what he called "The Marching Orders." Bush instructed the assembled officials to "Fight hard for your position." But, he added, "When I make a call, we move as a team."[58] Bush thus sought to strike a balance in using his cabinet, attempting to give it a measure of independence without allowing the cabinet to dominate him.[59]

Although the cabinet is often considered to be a device to assist the president, it also limits his power to some extent. "The members of the Cabinet," Vice-President Charles G. Dawes said, "are a President's natural enemies." [60] In part, this is because cabinet members

[53] Fenno, *The President's Cabinet*, p. 19.
[54] Ibid., p. 137.
[55] "Conversation Between President Kennedy and NBC Correspondent Ray Scherer," broadcast over NBC television network, April 11, 1961, Stenographic Transcript, p. 17.
[56] *Washington Post*, July 18, 1982, p. 1.

[57] *Washington Post*, July 19, 1982, pp. 1, A8.
[58] William Safire, "Bush's Cabinet, Who's Up," *The New York Times Magazine*, March 25, 1990, p. 31.
[59] Ibid.
[60] Neustadt, *Presidential Power*, p. 39.

after a time tend to adopt the parochial view of their own departments. They may become narrow advocates of the programs and needs of their bureaucracies, competing with other cabinet members for bigger budgets and presidential favor. As Fenno has noted, a cabinet member's "formal responsibilities extend both upward toward the President and downward toward his own department."[61]

The White House Staff

Soon after the 1988 election, George Bush appointed John H. Sununu chief of staff at the White House. As governor of New Hampshire, Sununu had helped Bush win the presidential primary in that state, a crucial victory in Bush's drive for the presidential nomination. Now he was being rewarded. The announcement signaled to official Washington that Sununu would probably become one of the most powerful individuals in the capital during the Bush administration. Indeed he did, but Sununu's abrasive manner grated on his colleagues and members of Congress, and his high-living style caught the attention of the press. Stories appeared about Sununu using official limousines and military aircraft on personal trips, including ski trips and a visit to his dentist; soon the television networks were talking about "Air Sununu." At first, the pudgy, combative chief of staff weathered the storm, but by December of 1991 the criticism had become too intense to withstand; Sununu resigned.

The affair oddly echoed the fate of one of Sununu's predecessors during the Reagan administration. In his second term, Reagan named Donald T. Regan, a Wall Street broker who had been secretary of the treasury, as the new White House chief of staff. Regan, too, was known for his take-charge, aggressive manner. But after the Iran-contra scandal broke, a presidential panel named to investigate the matter found that Regan "must bear primary responsibility for the chaos that descended upon the White House"[62] following the disclosure of the affair. Regan's days were numbered even before the report was made public. Behind the scenes he had feuded with the influential Nancy Reagan, the president's wife, who led the campaign that resulted in Regan's ouster.

Modern presidents depend on large staffs. And great power is often wielded by those who surround the president, some of whom rise from relative obscurity to great influence. Wilson had his Colonel House, Franklin Roosevelt his Harry Hopkins, Eisenhower his Sherman Adams,[63] Johnson his Bill Moyers, and Nixon his H. R. (Bob) Haldeman and John D. Ehrlichman — both of whom went to jail in the Watergate scandal. Carter's aide, Hamilton Jordan, became a powerful figure in the White House. All modern presidents have come to rely on their advisers, and in every case, some aides have emerged as more influential than others.

The power of the president's assistants, however, flows from their position as extensions of the president. Seldom possessing any political prestige or constituency of their own, they depend entirely on staying in the president's good graces for their survival. Their power is derivative, though nonetheless real — it is not uncommon in the White House to see a cabinet member waiting to confer with a member of the president's staff.

In recent administrations, the president's assistant for national-security affairs has often taken a central role in foreign-policy formation and crisis management. With access to the president and the White House "Situation Room," the downstairs office into which all military, intelligence, and diplomatic information flows, the national-security adviser may emerge as a powerful rival to the secretary of state. Henry A. Kissinger, for example, took the post in the Nixon administration and quickly emerged as the most powerful White House adviser in the field of foreign affairs, overshadowing Secretary of State William P. Rogers. Eventually, Kissinger himself was named secretary of state by Nixon.[64]

The members of the president's staff fill a variety of functions that are essential to presidential decision making. Some act as gatekeepers and guardians of the president's time. Others deal almost exclusively with Congress. Still others serve as links with the executive departments and agencies, channeling problems and conflicts among the departments to the president. Some advise the president on political questions, patronage,

---

[61] Fenno, *The President's Cabinet*, p. 218.

[62] *Report of the President's Special Review Board* (Washington, D.C.: U.S. Government Printing Office, February 26, 1987), p. IV-11. The panel was generally known as the Tower Commission, after its chairman, the late Senator John Tower, Republican, of Texas.

[63] Much to Eisenhower's distress, Adams was forced to resign in 1958 for accepting a vicuña coat and other gifts from Bernard Goldfine, a Boston textile manufacturer for whom Adams had interceded with federal regulatory agencies.

[64] In a new departure, Nixon also permitted Kissinger to keep his title as assistant to the president for national security.

and appointments. Others may write his speeches. The press secretary issues presidential announcements on matters large and small and fences with correspondents at press briefings.

Presidents use their staffs differently. Eisenhower had a tight, formal system, with Sherman Adams, as chief of staff, screening all problems and deciding what the president should see. Kennedy favored a less structured arrangement, regarding his staff as "a wheel and a series of spokes" with himself in the center.[65] In his first term, Reagan relied on three senior advisers who seemed roughly equal in power. Bush returned to a more traditional White House staff system, with a single chief of staff, although the president's counsel, C. Boyden Gray, exercised considerable power as well.

The Office of Personnel Management in fiscal 1991 listed 376 persons under "The White House Office," with a payroll of $16.4 million. Of these presidential staff members, perhaps fewer than a dozen occupied top-ranking positions of policy influence. Inevitably,

the chief executive's vision, to a degree, is filtered through the eyes of his assistants. An Eisenhower or a Nixon, with a rigid staff system, may become isolated in the White House. A Lyndon Johnson, with an overpowering, demanding personality, may surround himself with deferential aides. In short, the president's staff may not let him hear enough, or it may tell him only what he wants to hear.

The Executive Office of the President

The White House staff is only a small part of the huge presidential establishment that has burgeoned since Franklin D. Roosevelt's day. Under the umbrella of the Executive Office of the President, there are more than half a dozen key agencies serving the president directly, with a combined payroll in fiscal 1991 of $85 million and a total staff of 1,752. (See Figure 10–2.) Many of these employees have offices in the Executive Office Building just west of the White House.

President Roosevelt established the Executive Office of the President in 1939 by executive order, after a committee of scholars had reported to him: "The

[65] "Conversation Between President Kennedy and NBC Correspondent Ray Scherer," p. 3.

Figure 10-2
Executive Office of the President, 1992

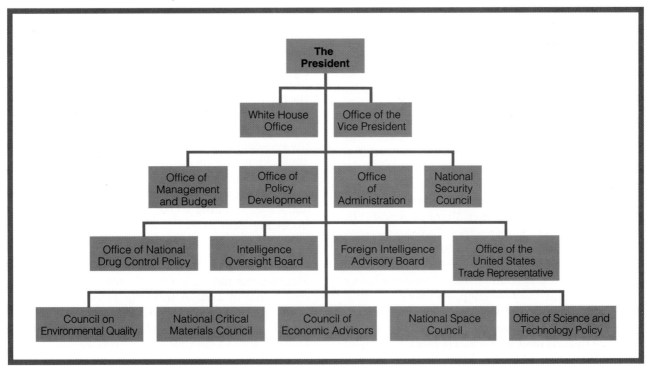

President needs help." Since that time, the office has grown substantially. As the Executive Office of the President existed in 1992, its major components included:

National Security Council When the United States emerged as a major world power after the Second World War, no central machinery existed to advise the president and help him coordinate American military and foreign policy. The National Security Council (NSC) was created under the National Security Act of 1947 to fill this gap. By statute, its four members are the president, the vice-president, and the secretaries of state and defense. The president's assistant for national security directs the NSC staff.

Like the cabinet, the NSC has been put to vastly different uses by different presidents. Eisenhower used the NSC extensively, and during his administration a substructure of boards and committees mushroomed beneath it. During the Cuban Missile Crisis in 1962, Kennedy established an informal body known as the Executive Committee of the National Security Council. Much larger than the statutory membership of the NSC, it consisted of some sixteen top officials and advisers in the foreign-policy, military, and intelligence fields whom the president felt it appropriate to consult. Nixon, an NSC member during the Eisenhower administration, sought as president to restore the NSC and its staff to its former place in the White House policy machinery. During the Nixon administration the NSC under Kissinger generated a steady flow of voluminous memoranda on foreign-policy problems, all of which helped to increase Kissinger's great influence and power in foreign affairs. Under President Reagan, the NSC played a central role in the events that became known as the Iran-contra scandal. A major covert operation — the barms sales to Iran and diversion of money to the contras — was run out of the White House itself by the National Security Council staff, an operational role that Congress had not intended for the NSC. Under President Bush's national security adviser, Brent Scowcroft, the NSC returned to its more traditional role.

In 1990, Admiral John M. Poindexter, who had been Reagan's national security adviser, was convicted of felonies in the Iran-contra affair and sentenced to six months in prison. His conviction was later overturned by a federal appeals court which ruled that Poindexter's testimony to a congressional investigating committee had been unfairly used against him in court. Poindexter

Admiral John M. Poindexter testifies at Iran-contra hearings

had admitted to Congress, however, that he had destroyed a secret and highly classified presidential finding about trading arms for hostages in Iran because he thought the document might be "politically embarrassing" to President Reagan. The entire episode illustrated that the president's national security adviser may wield great power, not only in foreign affairs, but in domestic politics as well.

Office of Policy Development All recent presidents have had a staff to assist them in formulating domestic policy. Creation of a formal staff for this purpose began under Lyndon Johnson in the 1960s. Nixon established a Domestic Council in 1970. President Carter renamed the panel the Domestic Policy Staff. To shape domestic policies, President Reagan redesignated the unit as the Office of Policy Development and named an assistant to the president for policy development. Below the assistant, several staff members specialized in such policy fields as energy, agriculture, natural resources, economic affairs, health and human resources, commerce and trade, and drug abuse. The office was continued under President Bush.

Office of Management and Budget The Office of Management and Budget (OMB) was created by President Nixon in 1970. A successor agency to what had been called the Bureau of the Budget, OMB was designed to tighten presidential control over the federal bureaucracy and improve its performance.

RONALD REAGAN ON THE IRAN-CONTRA SCANDAL

As the Iran-contra scandal began to unfold in 1986 President Reagan offered shifting interpretations of what had occurred: "We did not—repeat—we did not trade weapons or anything else for hostages."

—November 13, 1986

"I don't think a mistake was made."

—November 19, 1986

"I'm not going to lie about that. I didn't make a mistake."

—November 24, 1986

"It's obvious that the execution of these policies was flawed, and mistakes were made."

—December 6, 1986

"I told the American people I did not trade arms for hostages. My heart and my best intentions still tell me that's true. But the facts and the evidence tell me it is not . . . What began as a strategic opening to Iran deteriorated in its implementation into trading arms for hostages."

—March 4, 1987

—Washington Post

The OMB has two overlapping functions: preparing the federal budget and serving as a management tool for the chief executive. The director of the office advises the president on the allocation of federal funds, and attempts to resolve the competing claims of the departments and agencies for a larger share of the federal budget. The task of preparing and administering the annual budget gives OMB enormous power within the government.

National Economic Council This new body, modeled on the National Security Council, was created by President Clinton to coordinate all economic policy decisions at the presidential level. It deals with the budget, international trade, and other economic issues and programs

Council of Economic Advisers Since the Great Depression of the thirties, the president has been expected to manage the nation's efforts to achieve prosperity. Because few presidents are economic experts, presidents since 1946 have relied on a Council of Economic Advisers to assist them in the formation of national economic policy.

The three members, one of whom is designated chairperson by the president, are subject to Senate confirmation. The council is expected to give impartial professional advice, but since its members are also part of the president's administration, they perform a difficult task.

The Vice-President "I am Vice President," said John Adams. "In this I am nothing, but I may be everything." [66]

The remark remains apt today. Under the Constitution, the vice-president's only formal duties are to preside over the Senate, to vote in that body in case of a tie, and (under the Twenty-fifth Amendment) to help decide whether the president is disabled, and, if so, to serve as acting president.

If the president dies, resigns, or is removed from office, however, the vice-president becomes president. Through the 1992 presidential election this had occurred nine times as the result of the death or resignation of a president. In four of those cases, the president had been assassinated. Often in the past, the candidate for vice-president has been chosen by the presidential nominee to "balance the ticket," to add geographic or some other strength to the campaign. Thus, in 1984, Walter Mondale, the Democratic nominee, chose Geraldine Ferraro, the first woman ever to be nominated for vice-president by a major party, to add drama and excitement to his campaign. In 1992, however, Governor Bill Clinton chose a fellow Southerner, Senator Albert Gore, Jr., as his vice-presidential running mate. In this case, instead of seeking geographic balance, Clinton opted for a youthful image for the Democratic ticket by

---

[66] Donald Young, *American Roulette: The History and Dilemma of the Vice Presidency* (New York: Holt, Rinehart and Winston, 1965), p. 10.

SOME VICE-PRESIDENTS VIEW THEIR OFFICE

JOHN ADAMS

My country has in its wisdom contrived for me the most insignificant office that ever the invention of man contrived or his imagination conceived.

THOMAS JEFFERSON

The second office of this Government is honorable and easy, the first is but a splendid misery.

JOHN NANCE GARNER

The vice presidency isn't worth a pitcher of warm spit.

HARRY TRUMAN

Look at all the Vice Presidents in history. Where are they? They were about as useful as a cow's fifth teat.

THOMAS R. MARSHALL

Like a man in a cataleptic state [the vice-president] cannot speak; he cannot move; he suffers no pain; and yet he is perfectly conscious of everything that is going on about him.

SPIRO AGNEW

Now I know what a turkey feels like before Thanksgiving.

WALTER MONDALE

They know who Amy [Carter] is, but they don't know me.

GEORGE BUSH

If I fall out of favor at the White House, I might end up attending a lot of funerals in funny little countries.

DAN QUAYLE

The president gets the plums, and I get what's left.

—In Donald Young, *American Roulette*; Spiro Agnew quoted in the *Los Angeles Times West Magazine*, June 22, 1969; Walter Mondale quoted in the *Los Angeles Times*, January 13, 1978; George Bush quoted in the *Chicago Tribune*, August 18, 1981. Dan Quayle quoted in the *Washington Post*, August 17, 1992.

choosing a vice-presidential candidate who, like himself, was in his mid-forties.

In 1988, George Bush, the Republican presidential nominee, had selected Senator Dan Quayle of Indiana as his running mate in an effort to appeal to younger voters and conservatives. But Bush's choice was controversial from the start. As vice-president, Quayle was regarded by many voters, and widely in the media, as a lightweight. He soon became the butt of jokes by stand-up comics on late-night television. During the 1992 campaign, Quayle took on an aggressive role as Bush's point man, but he quickly became embroiled in controversy by attacking Murphy Brown, a fictitious character in a popular TV situation comedy, for her decision to

Vice President Dan Quayle teaches William Figueroa, 12, to spell

become a single parent. Quayle's difficulties reached an all-time peak later that spring when he encouraged an elementary school boy to spell potato with an unnecessary "e" at the end.

Bush's decision to choose Quayle as his running mate may well have stemmed from personal experience. In 1980 Ronald Reagan, then a sixty-nine-year-old conservative, had chosen Bush, a fifty-six-year-old Republican moderate, to give the ticket a somewhat younger look and solidify Reagan's ties to the eastern, internationalist wing of the party. Similarly, in 1968 Nixon chose Spiro Agnew of Maryland, a relatively obscure governor, in an effort to strengthen the national ticket's appeal in southern and border states.

Agnew quickly emerged as a controversial political figure. He attacked leaders of the protest against the Vietnam War and assailed network news commentators who had been critical of the president. It appeared that Nixon had found in his vice-president a useful political instrument to woo southern and conservative voters. In the midst of the Watergate crisis, however, at a time when Nixon was battling for his own political survival, it was disclosed that the vice-president was under investigation by a federal prosecutor in Baltimore for possible violation of criminal laws dealing with extortion, bribery, tax evasion, and conspiracy. The federal prosecutor gathered evidence that Agnew had asked for and accepted more than $100,000 in cash payments from highway engineering firms that were awarded state contracts while Agnew was governor of Maryland, and that one payoff was even made to Agnew in the office of the vice-president. Agnew resigned, pleaded no-contest to income-tax evasion, received a $10,000 fine, and was placed on probation for three years.

In the twentieth century, through the 1992 presidential election, seven vice-presidents had succeeded to the presidency through the death or resignation of an incumbent president, or by election.[67] These statistics would suggest that vice-presidents be carefully selected on merit rather than solely for political considerations.

Presidential Commissions From time to time, presidents appoint ad hoc "blue ribbon" commissions of prominent citizens to study special problems. Such panels can be helpful to a president by dealing with a

major crisis, by providing influential support for his programs, or by deflecting political pressure from the White House. But they also may cause him headaches by criticizing his administration, by proposing remedies he does not favor, or in other ways.

For example, in 1986 President Reagan named a special review board headed by former Senator John Tower, a Texas Republican, to investigate the Iran-contra affair. The panel strongly criticized the president personally as well as his administration, and some of its language was harsh. It concluded that top officials had lied to each other, and to the public, and had possibly broken the law.[68]

Similarly, in 1976 President Ford named the Rockefeller Commission to study published reports of spying within the United States by the CIA. But the commission also gathered information about CIA plots to assassinate foreign leaders, causing Ford political embarrassment.

After President Kennedy's assassination, the nation was torn by doubt and speculation over the facts of his death. President Johnson convinced the prestigious Chief Justice Earl Warren to head an investigating commission. The Warren Commission concluded that Lee Harvey Oswald shot the president and had "acted alone." At first this conclusion seemed to reassure much of the public that no conspiracy existed, but later the Warren Commission's conclusions were widely attacked by many critics who refused to accept the shooting as the act of one person.

The Informal Tools of Power Many factors affect a president's ability to achieve his objectives. The president is the chief actor on the Washington stage. He is carefully watched by bureaucrats, members of Congress, party leaders, and the press. The decisions he makes affect his professional reputation among these groups. In turn, his effectiveness as president depends on this professional reputation.[69]

In the exercise of presidential power, the president has available to him not only the formal tools of the office, but a broad range of *informal techniques.* Many presidents since Andrew Jackson have had a "kitchen cabinet" of informal advisers who hold no official position on the White House staff. Theodore Roosevelt had his "tennis cabinet," Warren Harding his "poker

---

[67] Through 1991, the vice-presidents who succeeded to the presidency in the twentieth century were Theodore Roosevelt, Calvin Coolidge, Harry S Truman, Lyndon B. Johnson, Gerald R. Ford, Richard M. Nixon, and George Bush. Nixon became president in 1969, eight years after serving as vice-president.

[68] *Report of the President's Special Review Board* (Washington, D.C.: U.S. Government Printing Office, February 26, 1987).

[69] Neustadt, *Presidential Power*, Chapter 4.

cabinet," and Herbert Hoover, who liked exercise, his "medicine ball cabinet." President Lyndon Johnson often called on friends such as Washington attorneys Abe Fortas, James H. Rowe, Jr., and Clark Clifford for advice. Ronald Reagan, too, had a "kitchen cabinet" of old friends who were for the most part California businessmen.

Television is another powerful tool of presidential power. With the development of electronic mass media, presidents can make direct appeals to the people. Roosevelt began the practice with his famous "Fireside Chats" over radio. Today, the president may schedule a live televised speech or press conference to publicize his policies. He may call a White House Conference to dramatize a major issue.

A president can take advantage of other perquisites of power. He may flatter key members of Congress by telephoning them for advice on key issues or inviting them to ride with him on Air Force One. He bargains with congressional leaders who frequently call on him at the White House, an informal arrangement that pays presidential homage to the importance of the leaders and incidentally allows them to make statements for the television cameras as they emerge from the executive mansion.

The President and the Press After George Bush became president in 1989, one of the most familiar faces in Washington was that of Marlin Fitzwater, the president's press secretary.

Fitzwater's style was low-key, almost deliberately dull. He managed, often but not always, to avoid controversy. But his predecessor, Larry Speakes, a former public relations executive, left the White House and wrote a book, in which he disclosed that as press secretary, he had made up quotes and attributed them to President Reagan.[70] The disclosure caused a storm, forcing Speakes to resign his job on Wall Street. Fitzwater called the practice of making up presidential quotes an "outrage."

The controversy focused attention on the important role of the White House press secretary. A modern president relies on a press secretary to speak for him in day-to-day dealings with the news media. Often, the press secretary acts as a buffer, standing between the president and the press and public, fielding questions that the president might prefer not to answer.

In recent years, most presidential press secretaries have held daily briefings for the White House press corps. The press secretary becomes a familiar personality to the public—but not always to the president's advantage. When the Watergate affair surfaced, President Nixon's press spokesman, Ronald L. Ziegler, repeatedly denied White House involvement and dismissed the break-in at Democratic headquarters as a "third-rate burglary attempt." After the truth began to emerge in April 1973, Ziegler announced that all previous White House denials were "inoperative," an explanation that did little to restore confidence in the administration's veracity—or Ziegler's. The White House had lied to the people, and the president found confidence in his administration shattered. (After Nixon left the White House, he told television interviewer David Frost: "I want to say right here and now, I said things that were not true." [71])

---

[70] Larry Speakes, *Speaking Out* (New York: The Macmillan Co., 1988).
[71] *New York Times*, May 5, 1977, p. 33.

THE PRESIDENT VERSUS THE PRESS

Every President, when he first enters the White House promises an "open Administration." He swears he likes reporters, will cooperate with them, will treat them as first-class citizens. The charade goes on for a few weeks or months, or even a couple of years. All the while, the President is struggling to suppress an overwhelming conviction that the press is trying to undermine his Administration, if not the Republic. He is fighting a maddening urge to control, bully, vilify, prosecute, or litigate against every free-thinking reporter and editor in sight. Then, sooner or later, he blows. Teddy Roosevelt sued newspapers. Franklin Roosevelt expressed his displeasure over a certain article by presenting its author with an Iron Cross. Lyndon Johnson . . . but there is no sense singling out a few. Every president from Washington on came to recognize the press as a natural enemy, and eventually tried to manipulate it and muzzle it.

—Timothy Crouse, *The Boys on the Bus*

The White House Office of Communications, first created during the Nixon administration, has often played a significant role in attempts at news management.[72] Administrations normally believe it to be in their self-interest to suppress embarrassing information. Mistakes, errors in judgment, or poorly conceived or badly executed policies are seldom brought to light unless discovered by the press or congressional investigators. Even then, White House spokespersons try to minimize unfavorable events. In describing military or intelligence operations, in particular, the government sometimes tends to conceal or distort. If the truth later becomes known, public confidence may be undermined.

Most presidents grant private interviews with a few syndicated columnists and influential Washington correspondents. They hope in that way to gain support for their views in the press and among readers. But the presidential press conference is a more direct device used by the chief executive to reach the public. Wilson began the practice by inviting reporters into his office. Harding, Coolidge, and Hoover accepted only written questions, and their press conferences were generally dull. Roosevelt held regular news conferences, canceled the requirement for written questions, and played the press like a virtuoso. Truman moved the press conference from his office to the Executive Office Building, establishing a more formal atmosphere.

Since Wilson's day, reporters could not quote the president directly without permission, but Eisenhower changed this, allowing his news conferences to be filmed and released to television after editing. Kennedy instituted "live," unedited TV press-conferences in the modern auditorium of the State Department, and he dazzled the press with his skill in fielding questions. Johnson had some full-dress press conferences, but often preferred to answer questions from reporters while loping rapidly around the White House South Lawn. Nixon reverted to formal, televised press conferences, but held very few. To an extent that exceeded any modern predecessors, the Nixon-Agnew administration considered the press a political target. President Ford's amiable personality helped him to maintain fairly good relations with the press. Carter also had reasonably good relations with the press during much of his presidency, although political cartoonists had a field

day, invariably caricaturing him with thick "blubber lips."

President Reagan, initially at least, enjoyed the traditional "honeymoon" from intense press criticism normally afforded to any new chief executive. But as Fred I. Greenstein has noted, it does not take the press very long to begin criticizing a president: "Media coverage of the President-elect and the first few months of an administration tends to emphasize the endearing personal touches — Ford's preparation of his own English muffins, Carter's fireside chat in informal garb. No wonder both of these Presidents enjoyed high poll ratings during their initial months in office. But the trend can only go downward . . . after idealizing Presidents, the media quickly search out their warts."[73]

And, in time, Reagan's relations with the press became somewhat less amicable. Reporters wrote stories pointing out that Reagan sometimes misstated facts and statistics. Other accounts suggested that Reagan napped, relaxed, or vacationed a good deal, leaving work to his aides, who hesitated to awaken him if a crisis developed in the middle of the night. Still other stories criticized Reagan for his relations with the press itself, for holding few press conferences, remaining isolated from correspondents, and often limiting his appearances for the press to "photo opportunities."

In his controversial book, Larry Speakes gave support to this image of Reagan. The president, he wrote, read few newspapers and preferred to "read the comics first."[74] Preparing Reagan for a news conference, the former press secretary added, was like "reinventing the wheel."[75] In his 8 years in office, Reagan held only 46 press conferences — 5.9 per year — an average lower than that of any other modern president. (See Table 10-3.) Despite some unfavorable news accounts during Reagan's first term, criticism of his policies or the errors of his subordinates did not seem to stick to him personally, so much so that Reagan's stewardship was frequently referred to in the press as "the Teflon presidency."[76]

---

[72] See John Anthony Maltese, *Spin Control: The White House Office of Communications and the Management of Presidential News* (Chapel Hill: University of North Carolina Press, 1992).

[73] Fred I. Greenstein, "Change and Continuity in the Modern Presidency," in Anthony King, ed., *The New American Political System* (Washington, D.C.: American Enterprise Institute for Public Policy Research, 1978), pp. 74–75.

[74] Larry Speakes, *Speaking Out*, p. 111.

[75] Ibid., p. 113.

[76] The phrase was coined by Representative Patricia Schroeder, Democrat, of Colorado, in a speech to the House in August 1983, in which she said that Reagan was "perfecting the Teflon-coated presidency. He sees to it that nothing sticks to him." *Washington Post*, April 15, 1984, p. 1.

Table 10-3
Presidential Press Conferences

President	Number	Years in Office*	Average Per Year*
Roosevelt	998	12	83
Truman	322	8	40
Eisenhower	193	8	24
Kennedy	64	3	21
Johnson	135	5	27
Nixon	37	5.5	7
Ford	39	2.5	16
Carter	59	4	15
Reagan	46	8	5.9
Bush	230	3.6†	64

*Figures rounded
† As of June 4, 1992

In Chapter 8, we discussed the advantages that a president normally enjoys as a political candidate, including the ability to dominate the news. But a president can wield that power day in and day out, even when no political campaign is under way. On the afternoon of March 16, 1988, the Iran-contra independent counsel, Lawrence E. Walsh, announced the indictments of President Reagan's former national security adviser, Rear Adm. John M. Poindexter; Marine Lt. Col. Oliver L. North, a former NSC aide; and two other key participants in the Iran-contra scandal. A few hours later, the president announced he was sending 3,200 troops to Honduras on a "training exercise." At the time, Nicaraguan forces had reportedly crossed the border into Honduras, and the president's action was undoubtedly designed to place pressure on the government of Nicaragua, and to try to persuade Congress to vote more aid to the contras. But some Reagan critics voiced suspicions that the dispatch of the troops was an obvious attempt to divert attention from, and overshadow, the unwelcome news of the indictments of the president's men.

As president, Reagan's successor George Bush did not always enjoy smooth sailing with the news media, which often delighted in describing how under pressure, in some of his public appearances, Bush's voice became high-pitched, and he tended to wave his arms and tangle his syntax.

By the 1992 election campaign, President Bush and his rival candidates, Arkansas governor Bill Clinton and Texas businessman Ross Perot, were finding new ways to use television to appeal to the electorate. Perot made repeated use of talk shows and morning television programs to reach voters directly. Both Clinton and Bush

did the same. At one point, President Bush sat in the Rose Garden on a warm day in July and chatted with bewildered tourists who had been plucked out of line at the White House to form an audience for the president's appearance on "CBS This Morning." A president's ability to gain almost constant access to the news media, especially television, is a vital instrument of presidential power in the electronic age.

WATERGATE: A CASE STUDY

It had begun shortly after 1 A.M. on the morning of June 17, 1972, when Frank Wills, a twenty-four-year-old, $80-a-week security guard at the Watergate office building, had pulled a piece of masking tape from the edge of a garage-level door. The tape presumably had been placed there to keep the door from latching shut. He left, but returned in a few minutes. To his astonishment, he found the door had been taped again— apparently by a persistent but foolish burglar. He called the police.

When Frank Wills pulled the tape off the door of the Watergate, it was as though one tiny strand of thread had unraveled a whole skein of corruption and criminal activity planned and condoned in what—until then—had seemed the least likely of places, the White House.

At first, however, the press treated the break-in as little more than a routine crime story. Five men had been arrested inside the headquarters of the Democratic National Committee in the Watergate office building, part of a high-rise complex along the Potomac River. But one of the men turned out to be James W. McCord, Jr., director of security for the Committee for the Re-election of the President (CREEP). Later two other suspects were arrested, E. Howard Hunt, Jr., and G. Gordon Liddy, both former White House aides. Liddy, like McCord, was an official of CREEP.

Several of the burglars had worked for the CIA— both Hunt and McCord were twenty-year veterans of the CIA—and it soon developed that the break-in had been ordered by high officials of the administration and of President Nixon's 1972 election campaign, and financed by money contributed to the campaign. Two young reporters on the *Washington Post*, Bob Woodward and Carl Bernstein, pursued the story.

As the scandal unfolded, it was disclosed that the burglars had "bugged" the Democratic headquarters and that telephone conversations of Democratic party officials had been broadcast by a concealed transmitter

"YOU COULD GET A MILLION DOLLARS"

On March 21, 1973, President Nixon, White House counsel John Dean, and H. R. Haldeman, Nixon's chief of staff, met in the Oval Office to discuss payoffs to buy the silence of the Watergate burglars. Their conversation, recorded by the President's secret taping system, became a crucial part of the evidence in the House Judiciary Committee's impeachment investigation of President Nixon. Following are excerpts from the March 21 conversation:

Nixon: How much money do you need?

Dean: I would say these people are going to cost a million dollars over the next two years.

Nixon: We could get that. . . . You could get a million dollars. You could get it in cash. I know where it could be gotten. It is not easy, but it could be done. But the question is who the hell would handle it? Any ideas on that?

Haldeman: . . . we thought [Former Attorney General John] Mitchell ought to be able to know how to find somebody who would know how to do all that sort of thing, because none of us know how to.

Dean: That's right. You have to wash the money. You can get $100,000 out of a bank, and it all comes in serialized bills.

Nixon: I understand.

Dean: And that means you have to go to Vegas with it or a book-maker in New York City. I have learned all these things after the fact. I will be in great shape for the next time around.

Haldeman: (Expletive deleted).

— From the White House transcripts, released April 30, 1974

to a room across the street at a Howard Johnson's motel. Reports of these conversations had been delivered to the president's re-election committee.

But the president publicly denied any knowledge of the break-in, and within the White House, his advisers took steps to cover up the links between the burglars and the president's campaign. Nixon was overwhelmingly re-elected in November. Watergate seemed to have been "contained."

In January 1973 five of the defendants pleaded guilty and two others who chose to stand trial were convicted by a federal jury. In March, McCord, facing a long prison term from Federal Judge John J. Sirica, suggested that White House and other officials had advance knowledge of the Watergate bugging. As public pressure mounted, President Nixon again denied prior knowledge of the Watergate bugging or the subsequent official cover-up. He accepted the resignations of his two principal aides, H. R. Haldeman and John Ehrlichman, and of his attorney general, Richard Kleindienst, and reshuffled the cabinet and the White House staff. He authorized the new attorney general to appoint a special prosecutor to investigate the Watergate case. But the storm did not abate.

Nixon admitted that he had established a special investigative unit in the White House, known as "the

Plumbers," to find the source of national-security news leaks. The Plumbers had been headed by none other than Howard Hunt and Gordon Liddy.

In the weeks that followed the break-in, the daily headlines brought one startling disclosure after another:

- In 1971 some of the same Watergate burglars, equipped by the Central Intelligence Agency— which by law has no internal police powers—had, on White House orders, traveled to Los Angeles and broken into the office of Dr. Lewis Fielding, a psychiatrist. They were ordered to search for and photograph the medical records of his patient, Daniel Ellsberg—the man who leaked the Pentagon Papers to the press.
- In 1970 President Nixon approved a plan for burglary, secret opening of first-class mail, and electronic surveillance of persons suspected of endangering national security, although he was warned, in writing, that burglary was "clearly illegal." The president said that he rescinded the plan after five days.
- From 1969 to 1971 the president ordered the secret wiretapping of seventeen persons, including a number of his own assistants and several journalists.

John W. Dean III

John N. Mitchell

Senator Sam J. Ervin, Jr., presides over Senate Watergate hearings in 1973.

- The president's personal attorney, Herbert W. Kalmbach, raised and secretly distributed $220,000 to the Watergate burglars and their attorneys.
- The acting director of the Federal Bureau of Investigation destroyed vital Watergate evidence — he burned the documents with his Christmas trash — and testified he had done so at the instigation of two of the president's top assistants.
- The president concealed secret microphones in his offices in the White House to record conversations on tape, in most cases without the knowledge of the persons being recorded.
- The president's assistants compiled an "enemies list" and requested tax audits of political opponents.
- The attorney general of the United States, John Mitchell, was present during a discussion of proposals for bugging the Watergate headquarters of the opposition political party, for kidnapping American citizens and taking them to Mexico, and for establishing a bordello on a yacht in Miami to gather political information by blackmail.
- The White House ordered the CIA to attempt to persuade the FBI to limit its investigation of the Watergate burglary.

In May 1973 a Senate select committee under chairman Sam J. Ervin, Jr., a North Carolina Democrat, began holding televised hearings into Watergate and the 1972 campaign. Within a few months, all seven of the Watergate burglars had been given jail sentences by Judge Sirica. Several other high administration officials pleaded guilty to crimes. In October Nixon dismissed the Watergate special prosecutor, but was forced by the tremendous public outcry to appoint another. The House of Representatives began its impeachment investigation. Nixon agreed to surrender some of the tapes of his conversations about Watergate.

Then came the climactic events of the summer of 1974. The Supreme Court ordered Nixon to surrender more tapes to the new Watergate special prosecutor, and the House Judiciary Committee voted to impeach the president. In addition, one of the newly released tapes showed that Nixon had lied when he denied he had participated in the cover-up of the Watergate burglary. On June 23, 1972, the tapes revealed, Nixon had ordered the CIA to try to confine the FBI investigation of the break-in, and he now admitted he knew he would gain political advantage from that order.

Nixon's support in Congress within his own Republican party crumbled almost totally. A delegation of Republican leaders from the House and Senate called on the president and told him the blunt truth: he did not have enough votes in Congress to avoid impeachment and removal from office.

Richard Nixon resigned on August 9, 1974, the first president in the nation's history ever to do so. A month later, he accepted a pardon from his successor, President Ford, and thus could not be prosecuted for acts committed while president. Many of Nixon's higher advisers were less fortunate. In 1975 John Ehrlichman, H. R. Haldeman, and John Mitchell were convicted of covering up the Watergate break-in. All three went to prison.

A total of nineteen persons were convicted or pleaded guilty in connection with Watergate-related crimes, including ten Nixon aides and three CREEP officials. All nineteen served prison sentences.

PRESIDENTIAL IMPEACHMENT, DISABILITY, AND SUCCESSION

Impeachment

Despite the enormous power of the president, under the Constitution he may be impeached by Congress and, if convicted of "Treason, Bribery or other high Crimes and Misdemeanors," removed from office.[76] Only the House can bring impeachment proceedings against a president, by majority vote. He is then tried by the Senate with the chief justice presiding. A two-thirds vote of the Senate is required to convict a president and remove him from office, a fate that Andrew Johnson escaped by one vote in 1868.

The unsuccessful attempt to remove Johnson from office grew out of the turmoil of the Civil War. The president hoped to carry out Lincoln's conciliatory Reconstruction policies toward the South after the war. This placed him in direct conflict with the Radical Republicans in Congress, who favored much harsher policies. When Johnson dismissed his secretary of war, the House charged he had violated the Tenure of Office Act and brought impeachment proceedings. The trial and balloting in the Senate went on for more than two months.

---

[77] Not only the president, but the vice-president and other federal officials and federal judges — as the Constitution puts it, all "civil officers of the United States" — are subject to impeachment. Members of Congress are subject to discipline and expulsion by their respective houses, but it is not clear whether they are "civil officers" subject to impeachment. At least some scholars believe that members of Congress are not exempt from removal by impeachment. See, for example, Raoul Berger, *Impeachment: The Constitutional Problems* (Cambridge: Harvard University Press, 1973), pp. 214–23.

Historically, Congress has hesitated to impeach and remove a president, for several reasons. First, there has been an understandable reluctance to act against the highest official in the land, who — unless he succeeds to his office — is elected by all the people. Second, there has been a fear that impeachment, as a political remedy, might become a partisan weapon to remove a president whenever he displeased a Congress controlled by the opposition political party or by political opponents in his own party.

Third, the language of the Constitution dealing with impeachment, scattered in four places, leaves many unanswered questions. For example, can officials be indicted before they are impeached, or in place of impeachment? Many legal scholars believe the answer is yes, for judges and officials up to and including the vice-president. But they also contend that a president must first be impeached and removed before prosecution. Otherwise the country might find itself in the untenable position of having its national leader behind bars while still holding office.

Yet another difficult problem is whether the "high crimes and misdemeanors" required as grounds for an impeachment conviction must literally be crimes in the legal sense — the breaking of specific laws — or whether that constitutional language encompasses serious abuses of the office of the president that might fall short of actual, indictable crimes.

Before 1973 it seemed most unlikely that any modern president could be impeached, but the Watergate scandal changed all that. A resolution to impeach President Nixon was introduced in the House on July 31 by the Rev. Robert F. Drinan, a Massachusetts Democrat. Some of those who might otherwise have favored such a course were dismayed at the prospect of the succession of Vice-President Agnew to the presidency in the event of Nixon's removal from office. But Agnew resigned the following October on the day he was convicted of criminal charges, and that same month the House Judiciary Committee began an inquiry into the possible impeachment of President Nixon. It was the first time since 1868 that Congress had taken steps to consider whether a president of the United States should be impeached.

The formal proceedings of the committee, under chairman Peter W. Rodino, Jr., began in February 1974. The committee staff amassed thirty-eight volumes of evidence, dealing with the Watergate break-in, Nixon's wiretapping of seventeen aides and news reporters, the White House "enemies list," and other abuses. The committee members, earphones clamped to their heads, listened for hours to the White House tapes. They also heard presentations by the president's attorney, James D. St. Clair, and by the committee's special counsel, John Doar. They heard witnesses in closed session, and then on July 24 began six historic days of public deliberation. The sessions were televised and watched by millions of Americans.

The Judiciary Committee voted three articles of impeachment. Article I accused Nixon of obstruction of justice by "using the powers of his high office" to "delay, impede, and obstruct" the investigation of the break-in at Democratic headquarters. The article specifically charged that Nixon had made false public statements "for the purpose of deceiving the people of the United States" into believing that the investigation had been thorough and that the president's campaign organization had not been involved. Article II accused the president of violating the constitutional rights of citizens by misusing the FBI, the CIA, the IRS, and other agencies, and by establishing a secret investigative unit, "the Plumbers," in the White House itself. Article III charged Nixon had defied the committee by failing to produce subpoenaed tapes and documents.

The full House had no opportunity to vote on these articles nor was there a Senate trial, as occurred in the case of Andrew Johnson. On August 9, 1974, ten days after the last of the articles had been approved by the Judiciary Committee, Nixon resigned.

Disability and Succession

Twice in American history, presidents were incapacitated for long periods. Garfield lived for eighty days after he was shot in 1881. Wilson never fully recovered from the illness that struck him in September 1919, yet he remained in office until March 1921. To a considerable extent, Edith Wilson was president. President Eisenhower suffered three serious illnesses, including a heart attack in 1955 that incapacitated him for four days and curtailed his workload for sixteen weeks. Sherman Adams, the White House chief of staff, and Press Secretary James Hagerty ran the executive-branch machinery during this period.

Eisenhower's heart attack in 1955 raised anew the question of presidential disability. The Constitution was exceedingly vague on the subject. It spoke of presidential "inability" and "disability," but left it up to Congress to define those terms and to decide when and how the vice-president would take over when a presi-

---

NOVEMBER 22, 1963: LYNDON JOHNSON LEARNS HE IS PRESIDENT

We arrived at Love Field in Dallas, as I remember, just shortly after 11:30 A.M. . . . The President and Mrs. Kennedy walked along the fence, shaking hands with people in the crowd that had assembled. . . .

Mrs. Johnson, Senator Ralph Yarborough, and I then entered the car which had been provided for us in the motorcade. . . . We were the second car behind the President's automobile. . . .

After we had proceeded a short way down Elm Street, I heard a sharp report. . . .

I was startled by the sharp report or explosion, but I had no time to speculate as to its origin because Agent Youngblood . . . shouted to all of us in the back seat to get down . . . he vaulted over the back seat and sat on me. I was bent over under the weight of Agent Youngblood's body. . . .

When we arrived at the hospital, Agent Youngblood told me to get out of the car, go into the building, not to stop, and to stay close to him and the other agents. . . .

In the hospital room to which Mrs. Johnson and I were taken, the shades were drawn—I think by Agent Youngblood. . . .

It was Ken O'Donnell who, at about 1:20 P.M., told us that the President had died. I think his precise words were "He's gone." . . .

I found it hard to believe that this had happened. The whole thing seemed unreal—unbelievable. A few hours earlier, I had breakfast with John Kennedy; he was alive, strong, vigorous. I could not believe now that he was dead. I was shocked and sickened.

—Statement of President Lyndon B. Johnson to the Warren Commission, July 10, 1964

Dallas, November 22, 1963: President Johnson takes the oath of office.

dent was unable to exercise his powers and duties. If a president became physically or mentally ill, or disappeared, or was captured in a military operation, or was under anesthesia in a hospital, what was the vice-president's proper role? Did he become president or only assume the "powers and duties" of the office? And for how long? Eisenhower and Nixon sought to cover these contingencies with an unofficial written agreement, a practice followed by Kennedy and Johnson, and Johnson and Humphrey.

But suppose a president were unable or unwilling to declare that he was disabled? Who would then decide whether he was disabled or when he might resume his duties? Could a scheming vice-president, with the help of psychiatrists, somehow have a perhaps temporarily unstable president permanently removed from office?

The Twenty-fifth Amendment, ratified in 1967, sought to settle these questions. It provides that the vice-president becomes *acting president* if the president informs Congress in writing that he is unable to perform his duties. Or, the vice-president may become acting president if the vice-president and a majority of the cabinet, or of some "other body" created by Congress, decide that the president is disabled. The president can reclaim his office at any time unless the vice-president and a majority of the cabinet or other body contend that he has not recovered. Congress would then decide the issue. But it would take a two-thirds vote of both houses within three weeks to support the vice-president; anything less and the president would resume office.

Until the Twenty-fifth Amendment was ratified, there was no constitutional provision for replacing a vice-president when that office became vacant.[78] So the amendment also provided that the president shall nominate a vice-president, subject to the approval of a majority of both houses of Congress, whenever that office becomes vacant. The provision reduces the possibility of presidential succession by the House Speaker or the Senate president pro tempore, or by cabinet members, unless the president and vice-president die simultaneously, or unless a president dies, resigns, or is impeached while the vice-presidency is vacant and before Congress has acted to approve a new vice-president.

The Twenty-fifth Amendment was used for the first time in October 1973 when President Nixon nominated Gerald R. Ford to succeed Agnew. Congress approved his choice, 92 to 3 in the Senate and 387 to 35 in the House. Until Ford was sworn in that December, the office of vice-president had remained vacant for fifty-seven days. During that period, if Nixon had ceased to be president, his successor would have been House Speaker Carl Albert.

The Twenty-fifth Amendment was used for the second time to fill a vice-presidential vacancy after

---

[78] As of 1992 the nation had been without a vice-president eighteen times for a total of thirty-seven years. Below the level of vice-president, the order in which other officials might succeed to the presidency is spelled out in the Presidential Succession Act of 1947.

Nixon resigned and Ford succeeded him as president. In August 1974 Ford nominated former New York governor Nelson A. Rockefeller to be vice-president. After lengthy hearings and approval by the House and Senate, Rockefeller took the oath of office in December.[79]

THE SPLENDID MISERY: PERSONALITY AND STYLE IN THE WHITE HOUSE

Thomas Jefferson conceived of the presidency as "a splendid misery." Others, like Franklin Roosevelt and Kennedy, brought great vigor and vitality to the job; they seemed to *enjoy* being president. The personality, style, and concept of the office that each president brings with him to the White House affect the nature of his presidency. William Howard Taft expressed the classic restrictive view of the presidency: "The President can exercise no power which cannot be fairly and reasonably traced to some specific grant of power."[80] Theodore Roosevelt adhered to the "stewardship" theory. He saw the chief executive as "a steward of the people" and believed that "it was not only his right but his duty to do anything that the needs of the Nation demanded unless such action was forbidden by the Constitution or by the laws."[81] Lincoln and Franklin Roosevelt went even further, contending that in great emergencies the president could exercise almost unlimited power to preserve the nation.

Louis W. Koenig has classified presidents as "literalist" (Madison, Buchanan, Taft, and, to a degree, Eisenhower) and "effective" (Washington, Jackson, Lincoln, Wilson, and the Roosevelts), adding that many chief executives fall somewhere in the middle. A literalist president, as defined by Koenig, closely obeys the letter of the Constitution; an effective president, who generally flourishes in times of crisis and change, interprets his constitutional powers as broadly as possible.[82]

A president's personality and approach to the office may leave a more lasting impression than his sub-

---

[79] Because of the extraordinary circumstances of a president and a vice-president resigning during the same term, the United States had four vice-presidents in a period of less than four years from 1973 to 1977: Spiro T. Agnew, Gerald R. Ford, Nelson A. Rockefeller, and Walter F. Mondale.

[80] Tourtellot, *The Presidents on the Presidency*, p. 426.

[81] Ibid., pp. 55–56.

[82] Koenig, *The Chief Executive*, pp. 16–19.

Figure 10-3
Presidential Greatness

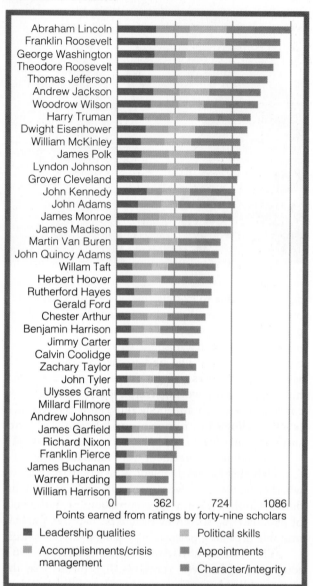

Points earned from ratings by forty-nine scholars

■ Leadership qualities   Political skills
Accomplishments/crisis management   ■ Appointments
■ Character/integrity

Source: The *Chicago Tribune*, p. 1, 4, January 11, 1982, from a *Chicago Tribune* survey conducted by 49 prominent historians, who found President Reagan ranked high above immediate predecessors but was given low marks for his political appointments.

stantive accomplishments or failures. We think of Teddy Roosevelt shouting "Bully!"; Wilson, austere and idealistic, in the end shattered by events; Franklin D. Roosevelt in a wheelchair, cigarette holder tilted at a jaunty angle, conquering paralysis with élan. We think of Eisenhower's golf, Kennedy's glamour, Johnson's

Left: Lyndon Johnson issues orders to a doubtful steer on his Texas ranch.
Center: Theodore Roosevelt in a typically exuberant pose   *Right:* John F. Kennedy
viewed the presidency as a "vital center of action."

William Howard Taft, who weighed 332 pounds,
displays a graceful follow-through.

"The presidency is both an institution
and a person. . . . "

President Bush lands a fish.

cowpuncher image, Nixon's isolation, Bush at the helm of his speedboat, churning across the waters at Kennebunkport, Maine — all say something about how they occupied the office of president.

James David Barber has attempted to systematize the study of presidential behavior by analyzing how childhood and other experiences may have molded a president's character and style. Barber has proposed four broad, general character-types into which presidents may be grouped, and has suggested that from such an analysis it might ultimately be possible to theorize about future presidential behavior.[83] Thus, Barber has contended that Eisenhower reluctantly ran for president because he was "a sucker for duty" as a result of his background; that Johnson ruled through "manipulative maneuvering"; and that Nixon "isolated himself."[84]

In an accurate prediction of Watergate and Nixon's downfall, Barber warned in 1972 that Nixon's character "could lead the President on to disaster. . . . The danger is that crisis will be transformed into tragedy. . . . The loss of power to forces beyond his con-

trol would constitute a severe threat. That would be a time to go down, if go down one must, in flames."[85]

Some observers contend that because of the many variables affecting human behavior, presidents may not act in ways that psychological analysis of their lives might suggest.[86] But because of the work of Barber and others, this approach has gained increasing attention.

THE AMERICAN PRESIDENCY: TRIUMPH AND TRAGEDY

Running for president in 1980, Ronald Reagan said he wanted to "bring our government back under control and make it acceptable to the people."[87] He would, he declared, eliminate "extravagance and fat in government."[88] Twenty years earlier, John F. Kennedy, seeking the presidency in 1960, viewed it as "the vital center

---

[83] James David Barber, *The Presidential Character: Predicting Performance in the White House*, 2nd ed. (Englewood Cliffs: Prentice-Hall, 1977). The four types that Barber identified are active-positive, active-negative, passive-positive, and passive-negative.

[84] Ibid., pp. 94, 159, 423–24, 441.

[85] Ibid., pp. 441–42.

[86] It is interesting to note in this connection that before President Kennedy met in Vienna in 1961 with Soviet Premier Khrushchev, he had access to an assessment of Khrushchev's character prepared for the CIA by a panel of psychiatrists and psychologists. See Bryant Wedge, "Khrushchev at a Distance — A Study of Public Personality," *Trans-Action*, October 1968.

[87] *Congressional Quarterly*, Weekly Report, July 19, 1980, p. 2064.

[88] *Congressional Quarterly*, Weekly Report, November 1, 1980, p. 3282.

THE PRESIDENT IS NOT ABOVE THE LAW

After the Watergate scandal, a Senate intelligence committee under Senator Frank Church, Democrat, of Idaho, investigated abuses by the FBI, CIA, and other federal intelligence and police agencies. Former President Nixon, responding to written questions from the committee, attempted to argue that a President was in some way above the law: "It is quite obvious," he said, "that there are certain inherently governmental actions which if undertaken by the sovereign in protection of the interest of the nation's security are lawful but which if undertaken by private persons are not." The committee emphatically rejected this concept of the President as "sovereign," and noted in its final report: "There is no inherent constitutional authority for the President or any intelligence agency to violate the law."

—Excerpt from the final report of the Senate Select Committee on Intelligence, Book IV, 1976

of action in our whole scheme of government." The problems of America, he said, "demand a vigorous proponent of the national interest — not a passive broker for conflicting private interests," a president who will "place himself in the very thick of the fight." [89]

Whether a president takes an activist approach, like Kennedy, or a more conservative approach, like

[89] *Congressional Record*, January 18, 1960, p. 711.

Reagan, the voters tend to look to the White House for solutions to major problems. Yet the president may not be able to solve the worst national problems that confront him. He cannot singlehandedly end environmental pollution, or control economic problems such as inflation, budget deficits, or unemployment. Nor can he easily use the nation's nuclear power in foreign-policy crises — to prevent the seizure of American hostages, for example. Koenig has suggested the concept of "the

Five former U.S. presidents: George Bush, Ronald Reagan, Jimmy Carter, Gerald Ford, Richard Nixon

imagined Presidency," which is "vested in our minds with more power than the Presidency really has." [90] The difference between the real and the imagined presidency, he contends, may lead to public frustration over presidential performance.

Although the great power of the presidency tends to overshadow its limitations, we have seen how, in many spheres, that power is circumscribed. As chief executive, the president faces an often intractable bureaucracy. As chief legislator, under the constitutional separation of powers, he faces an independent and often hostile Congress. As military and foreign-policy leader, his powers are enormous, but he must, at least to some extent, consider sentiment in Congress and the bureaucracy. The Twenty-second Amendment limits the president to two terms and thereby weakens his power in the second term (since everyone knows he will not be president again). Federal law may restrict his options. The Supreme Court may strike down his programs. The press may expose corruption in the bureaucracy or in the White House itself. Public opinion may turn against him. The necessities of politics may occasionally force him to weigh his actions in terms of their effect on his party. Finally, he may be impeached and removed from office.

Whether the presidency is too powerful, or not powerful enough, depends, then, to some extent not only on how a president uses his power but also on what he hopes to accomplish. Presidents have different goals. Most recent Democratic presidents have tried to press forward with energetic programs of social reform. Other presidents, such as Eisenhower and Ford, have tried to act with restraint. President Reagan cut back on government social programs.

The answer to the question of whether presidents have too much power depends ultimately on what one expects of the office and of the American political system. In the domestic arena, those who regard the presidency as an essential instrument to meet the social challenges and problems of the nation today do not necessarily tend to regard that office as too powerful. Others, alarmed at the size of the federal bureaucracy and opposed to social-welfare programs, may take a different view.

[90] Louis W. Koenig, *The Chief Executive,* 3rd ed. (New York: Harcourt Brace Jovanovich, Inc., 1975), p. 11.

In any event, presidential power fluctuates, depending in part on the situation in which it is being exercised. Franklin Roosevelt was able to wield extensive economic power during the early years of the New Deal because the nation was in the throes of an acute depression. By 1938 he was encountering substantial domestic opposition. When the Second World War came along, he was able to exercise great powers once more — people expected it.

The power a president exercises not only depends on the times and the circumstances but also on the policy area involved. Until the relatively ineffective War Powers Resolution of 1973, for several decades there had been few serious attempts to curb the president's power to commit American military forces abroad. In the field of domestic legislation, however, presidential powers may not be strong enough. For example, both Nixon and Carter were unable to get Congress to approve their welfare-reform programs. Reagan could not persuade Congress to shift responsibility for the welfare and food-stamp programs from the federal government to the states. And Bush was unable to get Congress to approve his "enterprise zones" for investment incentives in inner cities until after the riots in Los Angeles; he then vetoed the bill because it included new taxes.

The president (along with the vice-president) is the only official of the American government elected by all the people. The presidency, therefore, would seem to be the branch of government best situated to view and act on national problems in the interest of a national constituency. In a diverse democracy of conflicting interests and competing groups, the president is the one official who represents all the people, and who can symbolize their aspirations. He is the custodian of the future. Despite the limits on his powers, he can be the greatest force for national unity — or disunity. He can recognize the demands of minorities for social justice, or he can repress or ignore their rights. He can protect constitutional liberties or turn loose federal police power to wiretap, eavesdrop, and burglarize. He can lead the nation into war or preserve the peace. Such is his power that he leaves his indelible mark on the times, with the result that the triumph or tragedy of each presidency is, in some measure at least, also our own.

PERSPECTIVE

The American presidency is an office of enormous contrasts. A modern president may have great power in some policy areas, but limited options in others. Although once viewed as extraordinarily powerful, the presidency more recently has seemed an institution of uncertain power. Perhaps one reason is that many of the problems faced by presidents have become more difficult to manage.

The presidency is both an institution and a person. The institution is the office created by the Constitution, custom, federal laws since 1789, and the gradual growth of various tools of presidential power. The person is a human being who brings a particular personality and style to the White House. The presidency, then, is both highly institutionalized and highly personal.

Several broad historical factors have contributed to the growth of presidential power. For three decades, the United States and the Soviet Union lived under the shadow of nuclear war. The president, rather than Congress, became the one who had to decide whether to use nuclear weapons. In 1991, the collapse of the Soviet Union marked the end of the Cold War. Because the United States remains one of the most powerful nations in the world, the president is inevitably a world leader as well as a national leader. In addition, with the tremendous growth of the government's managerial role, the president directs a huge bureaucracy. Finally, television and other news media have helped to magnify the person and the institution of the presidency.

The president is one individual but fills many separate roles: chief of state, chief executive, commander in chief, chief diplomat, chief legislator, chief of party, and popular leader. All but the last two are required of him by the Constitution.

The president is the ceremonial and symbolic head of state. Under the authority granted by the Constitution, the president is also the head of government in his role as chief executive. The president runs the executive branch of government with the aid of a White House staff, the cabinet, and various agencies in the Executive Office of the President.

The president is commander in chief of the armed forces of the United States. The Constitution declares that "Congress shall have Power . . . To declare War," but Congress has not done so since 1941. In the intervening years the president has made the decision to go to war although twice, in Vietnam and the Persian Gulf, he had congressional approval. In 1973 Congress passed the War Powers Resolution to attempt to limit presidential war-making power. The resolution has not effectively restricted presidential military power, however.

Presidents make foreign policy; they direct the relations of the United States with other nations of the world. The Constitution does not specifically confer this power on the president, but it does so indirectly. It authorizes the president to receive foreign ambassadors, to appoint ambassadors, and to make treaties with the consent of two-thirds of the Senate. The president also can sign executive agreements with other nations.

Active presidential participation in the legislative process is a twentieth-century phenomenon. Modern presidents often use their televised State of the Union address, usually delivered to a joint session of Congress in January, as a public platform to unveil their annual legislative program. The president has many formal and informal powers at his disposal in his role as chief legislator, among them the veto, "arm twisting," and the use of television. But as chief legislator, the president's real ability to persuade Congress often rests on his personal popularity.

Whether or not a president enjoys his partisan role, he is also the chief of his political party. The machinery of the national committee reports to him; he can install his own choice as national chairperson; he can usually demand renomination by his party and stage-manage the convention that acclaims him. Given the decentralized nature of American political parties, a president's influence may not extend to state and local party organizations in every case. Nor does it prevail at all times with members of the president's own party in Congress.

The president is also the popular leader of the nation. His oratorical skills and ability to persuade and commuicate with the voters, particularly on television, may have a direct relation to his ability to govern.

The president, the vice-president, the heads of the major executive departments of the government, and certain senior officials who may hold "cabinet rank" constitute the cabinet. The cabinet as an organized body is not specifically provided for by law or in the Constitution. The cabinet has been a relatively weak institution.

A huge presidential establishment has burgeoned since Franklin D. Roosevelt took office in 1933. At its center is the White House staff, which guards the president's time, serves as a link with Congress and the executive departments, advises the president on political affairs, and deals with the press. The White House staff is part of the Executive Office of the President, which includes more than six key agencies that serve the president directly.

Under the Constitution, the vice-president's only formal duties are to preside over the Senate, to vote in that body in case of a tie, and (under the Twenty-fifth Amendment) to help decide whether the president is disabled, and, if so, to serve as acting president. However, if the president dies, resigns, or is removed from office, the vice-president becomes president.

Despite the enormous power of the president, under the Constitution he may be impeached by Congress and removed from office if convicted of "Treason, Bribery, or other high Crimes and Misdemeanors." Only the House can bring impeachment proceedings, by majority vote. The president is then tried by the Senate with the chief justice of the United States presiding. A two-thirds vote of the Senate is required to convict a president and remove him from office.

Suggested Reading

Barber, James David. *The Presidential Character: Predicting Performance in the White House*, 3rd edition* (Prentice-Hall, 1985). An important analysis of why presidents act as they do. Based on research on presidents from Taft to Carter, Barber's study explores the relationships between each president's personality type and his performance in office.

Burns, James MacGregor. *Roosevelt: The Lion and the Fox* (Harcourt Brace Jovanovich, 1963). (Originally published in 1956.) A political biography of Franklin D. Roosevelt, one of the foremost practitioners of the art of presidential leadership. Focuses primarily on Roosevelt's first two terms in office.

Corwin, Edward S. *The President: Office and Powers*, 5th revised edition* (New York University Press, 1984). A classic analysis of the American presidency. Stresses the historical development and the legal powers of the office.

Cronin, Thomas E. *The State of the Presidency*, 2nd edition* (Little, Brown, 1980). A comprehensive analysis of both the promise and limitations of the American presidency, based on interviews with White House staff members, cabinet officials, and department advisers. Includes discussions of presidential leadership, policymaking, and accountability, and explores the president's relations with Congress and the bureaucracy.

Cronin, Thomas E. *Inventing the American Presidency** (Lawrence, Kansas: University Press of Kansas, 1989). A useful collection of essays on the creation of the American presidency by the framers of the Constitution at Philadelphia. Contains analyses of the electoral college, impeachment, the president's executive and legislative powers, and other constitutional provisions.

Donovan, Robert J. *Conflict and Crisis: The Presidency of Harry S Truman, 1945–1948** (Norton, 1977); and *Tumultuous Years: The Presidency of Harry S Truman, 1949–1953** (Norton, 1982). A thorough review and analysis of the Truman presidency, written by a respected Washington journalist and author. Draws upon documents and diaries from Truman's years in the White House.

Edwards, George C. III. *At the Margins: Presidential Leadership of Congress* (Yale University Press, 1989). (Freeman, 1980). A detailed examination of the sources and weaknesses of presidential power in Congress.

Fenno, Richard F., Jr. *The President's Cabinet: An Analysis in the Period from Wilson to Eisenhower* (Harvard University Press, 1959). A thoughtful study of the development of the cabinet and its role as a distinct political institution. Examines the dual role of cabinet members as presidential advisers and department heads and the place of the cabinet in the larger political system.

Goldstein, Joel K. *The Modern American Vice Presidency: The Transformation of a Political Institution** (Princeton University Press, 1982). A study of the growth of the power and prestige of the vice-presidency from 1953 to 1978. Emphasizes that five vice-presidents have succeeded to the presidency in the twentieth century.

Greenstein, Fred I. *The Hidden-Hand Presidency: Eisenhower as Leader** (Basic Books, 1982). A study of the presidency of Dwight D. Eisenhower. Argues that Eisenhower exercised effective leadership behind the scenes while cultivating the appearance of being above the fray. Maintains that few observers recognized this "hidden-hand" technique.

Kearns, Doris. *Lyndon Johnson and the American Dream** (New American Library, 1977). (Originally published in 1976.) A revealing examination of the character and behavior of Lyndon Johnson. Assesses his public and private life, his early career, his years in the Senate, and his presidency.

Koenig, Louis W. *The Chief Executive*, 5th edition* (Harcourt Brace Jovanovich, 1986). An excellent, readable, and comprehensive study of the many facets of the presidency.

Light, Paul C. *The President's Agenda: Domestic Policy Choice from Kennedy to Reagan, 2nd revised edition** (Johns Hopkins University Press, 1991). An analysis of how specific policy proposals get on the agenda as part of the president's domestic program.

Lowi, Theodore J. *The Personal President: Power Invested, Promise Unfulfilled* (Ithaca, N.Y.: Cornell University Press, 1985). An analysis of the modern presidency that concludes that the president has become the personal embodiment of government in the United States. Argues that the high expectations surrounding today's presidents doom them to failure.

National Journal (Government Research Corporation). A very useful weekly report on American politics and government. Provides comprehensive detailed reports about current policy issues in many areas, and analyzes how Congress, the executive branch, and various interest groups interact on these issues.

Neustadt, Richard E. *Presidential Power: The Politics of Leadership from FDR to Carter** (Wiley, 1980). (Originally published in 1960.) A knowledgeable exploration of the problems faced by a modern president in seeking to exercise his power. The first edition of this book was influential in the Kennedy administration, in which its author served for a time as a special consultant.

Rossiter, Clinton. *The American Presidency*, rev. edition* (John Hopkins University Press, 1987). (Originally published in 1960.) A short, lucid analysis of the American presidency. Develops the concept of a varied, overlapping set of presidential roles and views the presidency as the central political force in the American system.

Schlesinger, Arthur M., Jr. *A Thousand Days** (Fawcett, 1977). (Originally published in 1965.) A well-written, detailed account of the Kennedy years by a scholar and former presidential aide. Although Schlesinger was not at the center of power in the Kennedy White House, he had the advantage of viewing events with the eye of a trained historian.

Tulis, Jeffrey K. *The Rhetorical Presidency* (Princeton, NJ: Princeton University Press, 1987) An important analysis suggesting that a president's skills as an orator and communicator, and as a popular leader, are directly related to his success. The development of the "rhetorical presidency," the author argues, has fundamentally transformed American politics in the twentieth century.

Wise, David. *The Politics of Lying: Government Deception, Secrecy, and Power* (Random House, 1973). An analysis, with detailed examples from several presidential administrations, of how government deception and official secrecy led to an erosion of confidence in the government during the late 1960s and early 1970s. Explores the relationship between the government and the press.

---

* Available in paperback edition.

As HE spoke to the cheering delegates at the
Democratic national convention in New York
in 1992 to accept their presidential nomination, Bill Clinton promised to "streamline the federal
government and change the way it works," and to "cut
100,000 bureaucrats" from the federal payroll. "We
have to change the way government does business, fundamentally," Clinton added.[1]

"The Republicans have campaigned against big
government for a generation," the Democratic nominee
continued. "But they've run big government for a generation and they haven't changed a thing, except from
bad to worse. They don't want to clean out the bureaucracy, they just want to run against it. . . . Big
bureaucracies, public and private, have failed."[2]

Chapter 11

The Bureaucracy

Clinton went on to finish his acceptance speech,
thousands of blue balloons floated down from the ceiling, and the delegates cheered. And once again, a candidate for high office had followed a time-honored practice of attacking bureaucrats.

The 1992 presidential campaign took place against
a background of widespread voter discontent with political leaders, political parties, and government. Aware
of these currents, Clinton sought to portray himself as
an outsider who would restore government as a servant
of the people. He would clean out all those bureaucrats,
at least 100,000 of them.

But during the campaign George Bush, as the incumbent president, defended his record. By doing so,
he was in effect praising the achievements of the federal
bureaucracy. The record of his administration, after all,
was largely the result of what bureaucrats had accom-

---

[1] *New York Times,* July 17, 1992, p. A14.
[2] Ibid., p. A15.

plished. So Bush extolled his policies and blamed the Democratic-controlled Congress for blocking his proposals for new federal programs.

As the debate illustrated, bureaucracy — and bureaucrats — are often handy political targets to blame for society's ills. By one dictionary definition, "bureaucrat" is a neutral word — it simply means an administrator — but its connotations are far from complimentary. "Bureaucrat" and "bureaucracy" are words that, to some people, conjure up an image of self-important but inefficient petty officials wallowing in red tape. It has been wryly suggested, and is widely believed, that once established, bureaucracies tend to mushroom under "Parkinson's Law": "Work expands so as to fill the time available for its completion."[3] The political theorist Hannah Arendt has described bureaucracy as "rule by Nobody," that is, "an intricate system of bureaus in which no men, neither one nor the best, neither the few nor the many, can be held responsible."[4]

There are checks on bureaucratic power, however, including the news media and congressional scrutiny. And government at every level — federal, state, and local — could not function without people to run it. Many government programs are highly complex and require experts and professional people to administer

[3] C. Northcote Parkinson, *Parkinson's Law* (Boston: Houghton Mifflin, 1957), p. 2.

[4] Hannah Arendt, *Crises of the Republic* (New York: Harcourt Brace Jovanovich, 1972), p. 137.

grow overnight, but developed gradually, largely in response to public needs. Most government departments and agencies have been created as a result of pressure from some segment of the population. And the same citizens who complain about "the bureaucracy" may protest the loudest if Washington proposes to close a defense installation that provides jobs in their local community.

Criticism of bureaucracy is not limited to attacks on the government in Washington. The student in the "multiversity" may feel crushed by an impersonal bureaucracy. So may an employee of a large corporation. The growth of computer technology and the tendency to assign numbers to individuals (credit cards, bank accounts, social security) has made many people feel that they are mere cogs in a vast bureaucratic machine. Voice mail and answering machines have replaced human beings; where once callers to companies, banks, or other institutions could talk to other people, today, as often as not, they must push buttons and leave messages.

them. *Public administration* is the term preferred by most political scientists to describe the bureaucratic process—the business of making government work—and bureaucrats are *public administrators*. The same bureaucrats who are blamed for red tape have also accomplished some remarkable tasks: NASA put men on the moon, and the Tennessee Valley Authority (TVA) brought about the greening of a large area of America.

Today, Americans frequently turn to the federal government to solve or alleviate problems of the economy, of the cities, of mass transportation, of poverty, pollution, public health, and energy. In all of these fields, public administrators—bureaucrats—make important decisions and bear great responsibilities.

The millions of persons who receive social security checks every month would not be getting them unless the Social Security Administration were part of the federal bureaucracy. The same "faceless bureaucrats" who are attacked in political campaigns process the social security checks. There is waste and red tape and inefficiency in the federal government, but, as in any large organization outside government, there are also thousands of honest, competent people.

Americans tend to be against "Big Government" in the abstract, but to demand all kinds of government services. The "bureaucracy in Washington" did not

DONALD DUCK GOES TO WASHINGTON

Washington — The General Accounting Office disclosed Thursday that it put Donald Duck's name on the payroll of the Department of Housing and Urban Development, and gave him a salary of $99,999 a year — without being challenged.

The department's computer, which is supposed to head off such shenanigans, not only failed to detect the "hiring" of the cartoon character, it raised no objections to a salary more than twice the legal limit, $47,500, for civil service pay.

It was not revealed what, if any, task the loquacious duck was supposed to perform at HUD, where 16,000 employees are charged with "providing for sound development of the nation's communities and metropolitan areas."

Officials of the GAO, Congress' watchdog over federal spending, disclosed the incident in testimony before the subcommittee on compensation and employee benefits of the House Post Office and Civil Service Committee. The subcommittee is looking into abuses of federal overtime pay.

— *Los Angeles Times*, October 27, 1978

"99,999 bucks! I've been working here in Washington for 30 years, and I only make 72,000!"

Editorial cartoon by Paul Conrad
Copyright © 1978, *Los Angeles Times*.
Reprinted by permission.

"I'm sorry, dear, but you knew I was a bureaucrat when you married me."

Drawing by Weber
© 1980 The New Yorker Magazine, Inc.

THE USES OF "BIG GOVERN-MENT"

Sometimes the government steps in and nobody minds.

When tropical storm Agnes hit eastern Pennsylvania in June 1972, the property damage came to $2 billion. In money terms, it was the worst natural disaster in the nation's history, and it called forth an unprecedented response from Federal, state and local governments. Among the details:

- More than 12,000 mobile homes were imported to the area to help house 20,000 people displaced by the flood.
- The Small Business Administration granted loans totaling $725 million to 81,000 homeowners and 9,000 businessmen.

- $108 million was spent to repair roads and bridges.
- Five devastated libraries, which lost 300,000 books, were almost fully restocked.
- About $550 million was allocated for urban renewal, with state bonds committed to pay $140 million of the total.

"Our work wasn't perfect, but I think we did a helluva job," says Jerome E. Parker, director of the U.S. Department of Housing and Urban Development's Office of Disaster Housing Management in Wilkes-Barre. "Big government does provide some use, there's no question about it."

—*Newsweek*, December 15, 1975

But the fattest bureaucratic target of all is the federal government. Some of the sentiment directed against the federal bureaucracy can be traced to the social-welfare programs of the New Deal, which vastly expanded the role of government in the lives of individual citizens. For three decades much of the criticism of the bureaucracy came from Republicans and conservatives opposed to the welfare state and the concentration of power in Washington. (Yet during eight years of Republican rule under President Eisenhower, the federal government increased in size.) In the late 1960s Democratic liberals began to voice similar thoughts. Ideological disenchantment with the federal bureaucracy had come full circle; conservatives and liberals joined in an anti-bureaucratic alliance of sorts.

Some critics, such as Peter F. Drucker, have gone so far as to conclude that "modern government has become ungovernable." Drucker contends that because of bureaucratic inertia and "administrative incompetence," government is unable to perform the tasks assigned to it. He adds, "There is no government today that can still claim control of its bureaucracy and of its various agencies. Government agencies are all becoming autonomous, ends in themselves, and directed by their own desire for power, their own rationale, their own narrow vision rather than by national policy."[5]

Even if such criticisms are overstated, they raise important, valid questions about the role of bureaucracy in modern society. But as long as people demand more and more services from their government — social security, Medicare, aid to education, housing, and the like — some form of bureaucracy is inevitable.

The classic concept of the bureaucracy was developed by the pioneering German sociologist Max Weber, who saw it as a strict hierarchy, with authority flowing from the top down within a fixed framework of rigid rules and regulations. In Weber's view, the bureaucracy draws its power from its expertise. Political rulers are in no position to argue with the technical knowledge of the trained bureaucrat: "The absolute monarch is powerless opposite the superior knowledge of the bureaucratic expert."[6] Even the Russian czar of old, Weber noted, could seldom act against the wishes of his bureaucracy.

In the nineteenth century, elected officials in the United States customarily rewarded their supporters with government jobs. Selection of bureaucrats on the basis of merit rather than politics was the goal of the civil-service reform movement of the late nineteenth century.

One result was that in the first third of the twentieth century, classic theories of public administration

---

[5] Peter F. Drucker, *The Age of Discontinuity* (New York: Harper & Row, 1969), p. 220.

[6] In H. H. Gerth and C. Wright Mills, *From Max Weber: Essays in Sociology* (New York: Oxford University Press, 1953), p. 234.

"Among the most familiar creatures of the political seas is the Bloated Bureaucracy . . . it cannot be hurried; it swims at its own pace."

Drawing by Jeff MacNelly from *A Political Bestiary* by Eugene J. McCarthy and James J. Kilpatrick, McGraw-Hill Book Company, 1979.

emerged that were rooted in the civil-service reform movement. As Dwight Waldo has noted, early theorists in the field of public administration concluded that "politics and administration are distinct" and that "politics in any 'bad' sense ought not to intrude upon administration."[7] Today, however, political scientists recognize that politics and bureaucracy are inseparable, and that bureaucratic decision making involves political as well as policy choices.

Since bureaucrats have great discretion in the decisions they make, a central problem is how to make bureaucracy accountable to popular control.[8] In short, how to reconcile bureaucracy and democracy.

Because civil servants are not elected and are free of direct control by the voters, the bureaucracy is semipermanent in character and, at times, an independent center of power. Can the president or Congress control it? In a democracy this is a serious question, for democratic institutions should be *responsive* to the people. But it is also important to ask, to whom is the bureaucracy responsive? A government agency may yield to pressure from an interest group or from some narrow segment of society rather than respond to broader public interests.

There is another danger, too. The executive branch may abuse its power and seek to misuse the bureaucracy — particularly police and intelligence agencies — against its political opponents. So, at the same time that it is responsive, bureaucracy, particularly in its law-enforcement and regulatory functions, must also, in some degree, be *independent*. If it is too responsive, it may yield to improper political pressures.

The bureaucracy also must be *effective* if government is to solve the social problems that face it. A poverty program that creates jobs for bureaucrats but fails to meet the needs of the poor, or a pollution program that issues regulations but fails to eliminate smog, adds to the taxpayers' burden without alleviating social ills. Today, many students of public administration contend that bureaucracy should be designed to serve people and to

---

[7] Dwight Waldo, "Public Administration," *Journal of Politics*, vol. 30, no. 2 (May 1968), p. 448.

[8] Wallace Sayre, "Premises of Public Administration: Past and Emerging," *Public Administration Review*, vol. 18, no. 2 (Spring 1958), p. 105.

BUREAU-CRATS: UNSUNG AND UNLOVED

In this century the bureaucracy has apparently inherited most of the animosity Americans have traditionally felt toward federal authority as such. Although the programs we like are . . . implemented by career officials, we seldom credit these bureaucrats for their accomplishments. We become interested in bureaucracy only when something does not get done, when red tape tangles the wheels of government, when seemingly mindless regulations impinge on our activities. Then the bureaucracy comes in for a brand of universal criticism that we seldom levy on even the worst of our elected officials. Bureaucracy arouses Americans to a level of intensity that some societies can achieve only when attacking religious opponents.

—Louis Galambos, ed., "By Way of Introduction," in *The New American State: Bureaucracies and Policies since World War II*

be sensitive to human needs and social inequality. They argue that the first goal of bureaucracy should not be efficiency and economy, but influencing and carrying out public policies "which more generally improve the quality of life for all."[9]

A number of complex questions are raised in assessing the role of public administration in a democratic political system. Can government really be "too big" when people demand increased services? Should the federal bureaucracy be broken up, decentralized? Closely tied to these questions is the important issue of whether the bureaucracy has been captured by industry or other interest groups, whether government regulators are tools of the regulated. Is the bureaucracy a responsive democratic institution, or does it make public policy solely by its own decisions? How effective are the checks on bureaucratic power?

BUREAUCRACY AND THE POLICY PROCESS

In theory, bureaucrats are simply public servants who administer policy decisions made by the accountable officials of the government—the president, his principal appointees, and Congress. In fact, government administrators by their actions—or inaction—often make policy. That is, they play an important role in choosing among alternative goals and selecting the programs to achieve those goals. As Francis E. Rourke has noted, "Bureaucrats themselves have now become a central factor in the policy process: in the initiation of proposals, the weighing of alternatives, and the resolution of conflict."[10]

Moreover, there is no single bureaucracy in America, and the term is not limited to the federal government: bureaucrats administer programs at every level, down to the smallest units of state and local government. Public administration in the United States is fragmented by the system of federalism. And at each level of government there are hundreds of bureaus and divisions.

Bureaucrats have great *discretionary powers*; what they decide to do, or not to do, constitutes a policy

output of the political system. A bureaucrat has discretion when the power he exercises leaves him "free to make a choice among possible courses of action or inaction."[11]

Bureaucrats also help to shape policy through the advice they give to elected officials. The elected officials have the final say on decisions, but their choices may be limited by the options presented to them by the bureaucrats. As a practical matter, elected officials are confined to choosing policies and programs that the bureaucracies are capable of carrying out.

Bureaucracy and Client Groups

The American bureaucracy is deeply involved in politics as well as policy. As in the case of the president and members of Congress, government agencies have *constituencies*. These are interest groups, or client groups, either directly regulated by the bureaucracy or vitally affected by its decisions.

Sometimes, through close political and personal association between a government agency and its client group, the regulating agency becomes a captive of the industry it is supposed to regulate. "In its most developed form," Rourke observes, "the relationship between an interest group and an administrative agency is so close that it is difficult to know where the group leaves off and the agency begins."[12] One reason for this close relationship is that a bureaucracy is often able to increase its political strength by building a constituency. As Rourke notes: "The groups an agency provides tangible benefits to are the most natural basis of . . . political support, and it is with these interest groups that agencies ordinarily establish the firmest alliances. Such groups have often been responsible for the establishment of the agency in the first place. Thereafter, the agency and the group are bound together by deeply rooted ties that may be economic, political, or social in character."[13]

Viewed in this light, the behavior of the bureaucracy becomes somewhat predictable. Thus, the Agriculture Department is a natural representative for farmers; the Commerce Department is friendly toward business;

[9] H. George Frederickson, "Toward a New Public Administration," in Frank Marini, ed., *Toward a New Public Administration: The Minnowbrook Perspective* (Scranton: Chandler, 1971), p. 314.

[10] Francis E. Rourke, ed., *Bureaucratic Power in National Politics* (Boston: Little, Brown, 1978), p. vii.

[11] Kenneth Culp Davis, *Discretionary Justice* (Baton Rouge: Louisiana State University Press, 1969), p. 4.

[12] Francis E. Rourke, *Bureaucracy, Politics, and Public Policy*, 2nd ed. (Boston: Little, Brown, 1976), p. 46.

[13] Ibid.

and the Pentagon is allied with defense contractors. These close relationships illustrate how some government agencies have mobilized the support of client groups.

Client groups do not always dominate, however. Although a government bureau may be influenced by its clients, it may at the same time be sensitive to, and responsive to, pressures from the public, Congress, and other actors in the political system. For example, often bureaucrats are particularly sensitive to the wishes of the congressional committees that monitor their activities and control their appropriations. At the same time, many senior bureaucrats complain that they are subject to so many pressures and controls that they are unable to do the work that the law requires their agency to perform.

The bureaucracy acts and reacts in a political way. It responds to a variety of pressures because it is at once accountable to several groups — its clients, the public at large, the press, Congress, and the president. Public administrators, in short, play a major role in the American political system, and their decisions are of crucial importance to government and society as a whole.

Bureaucracy and Congress

In addition to client groups, another source of bureaucratic power stems from the political support that an agency may enjoy in Congress, particularly among influential committee chairpersons. For a long time, the military services were able to count on the friendly support of powerful Democrats who chaired the House and Senate Armed Services committees — men like John Stennis of Mississippi, who for many years headed the Senate committee. Similarly, the FBI and the CIA have enjoyed the protection of a small group of influential representatives and senators.

Agencies that do not have cordial relations with important members of the legislative branch may find their power diminished. For years, the late Representative John J. Rooney, a Brooklyn Democrat, was the nemesis of the State Department, whose appropriations were handled by his House subcommittee. Rooney's hostility to "striped-pants cookie pushers" in the Foreign Service was legendary, and State Department officials dreaded their annual ordeal of testifying before his subcommittee.

The United States Corps of Engineers is a classic example of a federal agency that has won virtually inde-

pendent status by mobilizing political support in the legislative branch. Its river-and-harbor, navigation, and flood-control projects bring important benefits to local communities — and to members of Congress in those districts.[14]

Government agencies exert considerable effort to maintain cordial diplomatic relations with Capitol Hill. That task has become more complex in recent years because congressional reforms have resulted in the creation of many new subcommittees, and the agencies must deal with them. The cabinet departments employ hundreds of persons to engage in liaison with Congress. Liaison officers watch over legislation concerning their agencies; they also field requests made by members of Congress on behalf of constituents who have business

---

[14] See Arthur Maass, *Muddy Waters* (Cambridge: Harvard University Press, 1951); and "Congress and Water Resources," in Rourke, ed., *Bureaucratic Power in National Politics.*

pending before their agency. The large number of liaison officers, therefore, reflects congressional demands as well as an effort by government agencies to win support on Capitol Hill. At the same time, the mushrooming of subcommittees and the growth of legislative staff in Congress in recent years reflects, in part, efforts by Congress to oversee the agencies.

Political scientist Morris P. Fiorina has formulated an intriguing theory about the symbiotic relationship between Congress and the bureaucracy. He suggests that "the Washington System" follows a cycle: first, members of Congress earn credit from their constituents by establishing federal programs. Second, the legislation is drafted in very general terms, so that some government agency must create rules and regulations, which means "the trampling of numerous toes. At the next stage, aggrieved and/or hopeful constituents petition their members of Congress to intervene in the complex (or at least obscure) decision processes of the bureaucracy. The cycle closes when the congressman lends a sympathetic ear, piously denounces the evils of bureaucracy, intervenes in the latter's decisions, and rides a grateful electorate to ever more impressive electoral showings. Congressmen take credit coming and going. They are the alpha and the omega." As long as the bureaucracy responds to and accommodates members of Congress, Fiorina adds, Congress "will oblige with ever larger budgets and grants of authority. Congress does not just react to big government—it creates it."[15]

Of course, in the relationship between Congress and the bureaucracy, the bureaucracy is not without powerful resources. Members of Congress, for example, are particularly sensitive to any plans by the Defense Department to close military bases in their districts. And when some members of Congress talked about reducing the subsidies for rail lines, Amtrak countered by revealing plans for reduced operations. "Just coincidentally, lines to be eliminated seemed to run through the districts of critical members of the Appropriations and Commerce committees."[16]

Bureaucracy, Triangles, and Subgovernments

The bureaucracy, interest groups, and congressional committees interact. In some areas, such as agriculture

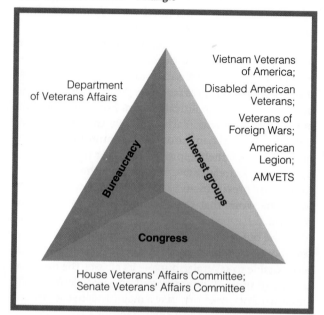

Figure 11-1
The Veterans' Affairs "Triangle"

Department of Veterans Affairs

Vietnam Veterans of America;
Disabled American Veterans;
Veterans of Foreign Wars;
American Legion;
AMVETS

Bureaucracy

Interest groups

Congress

House Veterans' Affairs Committee;
Senate Veterans' Affairs Committee

and defense, the relationship among the three actors is so close that it is often referred to as a *triangle*, an *iron triangle*, or a *subgovernment*. Although the terms may vary, they refer essentially to the same phenomenon: a powerful alliance of mutual benefit among an agency or unit of the government, an interest group, and a committee or subcommittee of Congress.

As Robert L. Lineberry has suggested, in such a situation, policymaking is a result of "close cooperation and interaction among these triads of power." Lineberry adds: "When a group becomes strong enough, it gets a part of the government, its own piece of the action. The measure of an interest group's strength is how many "shares" of the government it controls. "Little" interests, such as the fisheries or tobacco growers, may have only an agency or two within a cabinet department and only a subcommittee of Congress. "Big" interests, such as business and labor, have whole cabinet departments. . . ."[17]

There are numerous examples of triangles or subgovernments. In many cases the movement of people among the three corners of the triangle is also an important element; a Pentagon general may, after a required

[15] Morris P. Fiorina, *Congress: Keystone of the Washington Establishment* (New Haven: Yale University Press, 1977), pp. 48–49.
[16] Ibid., p. 78.

[17] Robert L. Lineberry, *American Public Policy: What Government Does and What Difference It Makes* (New York: Harper & Row, 1977), p. 55.

waiting period, end up as lobbyist for a missile manufacturer, or a staff member of the House Armed Services Committee may go to work for a defense contractor. Typically, in such triangles, many of the participants know one another and play "musical chairs," changing jobs within the triangle.

The existence of such triangles or subgovernments raises questions about the nature of the pluralist system. Instead of competing with one another, some analysts argue, interest groups merely capture a segment of the bureaucracy and call it their own.[18] For most government agencies today, however, Francis Rourke has argued, the "highly exclusionary" closed system of iron triangles "is long gone."[19] In Rourke's view, this is the result of greater openness in the bureaucracy enforced by Congress, the increase in the number of competing interest groups attempting to influence agency policies, and the increased power of the news media.[20] Moreover, client groups today, Rourke has observed, are "less supportive and considerably less deferential toward their administrative patrons than was once the case."[21]

Issue Networks: The Policy Activists

While the concept of iron triangles and subgovernments is helpful, it may not tell the whole story. Political scientist Hugh Heclo has suggested that "issue networks" play an important role in the shaping of public policy. As Heclo has defined it, "An issue network is a shared-knowledge group having to do with some aspect . . . of public policy."[22] As the term implies, issue networks are made up of "policy activists, those who care deeply about a set of issues and are determined to shape the fabric of public policy accordingly."[23]

In Heclo's model, an issue network is rather fluid, a loose grouping of people and organizations who seek to influence policy formation. Thus, an issue network is not as easily identifiable or as neatly categorized as an "iron triangle" or subgovernment. "Looking for the closed triangles of control, we tend to miss the fairly open networks of people that increasingly impinge upon government."[24]

These loose networks of policy activists not only help to shape the programs that the government adopts, Heclo contends, but increasingly they influence the appointment of the bureaucrats who administer those programs. Presidents today are less likely than in the past to appoint party politicians to fill cabinet posts. Instead, they tend to choose executives whose reputations have been established by word of mouth in the various "issue networks" that swirl and merge around the policy process in Washington.

THE POLITICS OF BUREAUCRACY

A new cabinet secretary in Washington often discovers that a title does not assure actual authority over his or her department. "I was like a sea captain who finds himself on the deck of a ship that he has never seen before," wrote one. "I did not know the mechanism of my ship; I did not know my officers — even by sight — and I had no acquaintance with the crew."[25]

As the cabinet member had quickly realized, the bureaucracy has its own sources of power that enable it to resist political authority. Cabinet secretaries come and go; the civil service remains. The expert technician in charge of a bureau within a department may have carved out considerable independence over the years and may resent the effort of a political appointee to take control of the bureau.

In his study of the politics of bureaucracy, Francis Rourke has developed three central themes: the bureaucracy exercises an *impact on policy*; it does so by *mobilizing political support* and *applying its expertise*.[26] As Rourke points out, the growth of the civil service and the removal of much of the appointment power from politics does not mean that politics has been removed from the bureaucracy. Quite the contrary; federal departments and bureaus are extremely sensitive to the winds of politics. A request or inquiry from a

---

[18] See Theodore J. Lowi, *The End of Liberalism: Ideology, Policy, and the Crisis of Public Authority* (New York: Norton, 1969), Chapter 3.

[19] Rourke, "American Bureaucracy in a Changing Political Setting," *Journal of Public Administration Research and Theory,* April 1991, p. 119.

[20] Ibid.

[21] Ibid., p. 112.

[22] Hugh Heclo, "Issue Networks and the Executive Establishment," in Anthony King, ed., *The New American Political System* (Washington, D.C.: American Enterprise Institute for Public Policy Research, 1978), p. 103.

[23] Ibid.

---

[24] Ibid., p. 88.

[25] In Richard F. Fenno, Jr., *The President's Cabinet* (Cambridge: Harvard University Press, 1959), p. 225. The cabinet secretary who voiced this nautical complaint was William Gibbs McAdoo, Wilson's secretary of the treasury.

[26] Rourke, *Bureaucracy, Politics, and Public Policy,* Chapter 3.

member of Congress usually brings speedy action by a government agency — the officials in that agency know where appropriations come from.

Furthermore, in mobilizing support, the bureaucracy practices politics, often in expert fashion. The bureaucracy draws support from three areas — the public, Congress, and the executive branch.[27]

Bureaucracy and Public Opinion

A government agency that enjoys wide public support has an advantage over agencies that do not. The president and Congress are both sensitive to public opinion, and a popular, prestigious agency may receive more appropriations and achieve greater independence than others. In the mid-1970s it was disclosed that the FBI under J. Edgar Hoover had committed burglaries to search for evidence or to gather intelligence, and in other ways had violated the constitutional rights of Americans.[28] But for more than four decades, the FBI had managed to build such a favorable image with the

general public that, until Hoover's death in 1972, both the bureau and its chief enjoyed a status of virtual independence. No president of the United States dared to fire J. Edgar Hoover.

During the 1960s the National Aeronautics and Space Administration (NASA) and its Apollo astronauts captured the public imagination. To enable it to place men on the moon in 1969, NASA received massive appropriations at a time when some Americans were demanding a reordering of national priorities to meet social needs on earth.

In order to improve their "image" and enlist public support for their programs, many federal agencies employ substantial numbers of public relations people and information officials. These information specialists issue news releases and answer questions from members of the press and the general public. One study estimated that the executive branch employed 5,599 people in

---

[27] Ibid.
[28] Frank J. Donner, *The Age of Surveillance: The Aims and Methods of America's Political Intelligence System* (New York: Knopf, 1980).

FIGHTING THE STATE DEPARTMENT WITH A TEASPOON

The State Department instructed me to survey Prague staffing needs, following the Communist seizure of the country, at which time the American staff, which I inherited, numbered 80. Six months after my recommendation, approved by the State Department, that personnel be reduced to 40, I had managed to get rid of two persons — two only. . . .

Today, a decade and a half later, it exhausts me to remember the struggle with Washington required to obtain that reduction from 80 to 78 persons. If I had started to dig the projected Nicaraguan Canal with a teaspoon, those 6 months might have shown a more impressive achievement. . . .

"Go cut the heads off somebody else's dandelions," was the gist of successive representations lodged in Foggy Bottom.

It was at that point that the Communists got into the act. Far as I know, they had no idea of the personnel war I was fighting — and losing — with Washington. They possibly thought they were dealing

the American Ambassador the most painful blow imaginable when they suddenly declared five-sixths of my staff persona non grata. They gave the Embassy 2 weeks to get 66 American employees and all their families over the border.

For 30 months thereafter, I ran the American Embassy in Prague with 12 individuals — 13, counting the Ambassador. No propaganda establishment. No country team. No Peace Corps. No Minister Counselor of Embassy for Administration.

The staff . . . included a deputy who acted as chargé d'affaires in the absence of the Ambassador, an extremely competent man who used to drive the Communists crazy by talking Eskimo over the telephone on a tapped line. . . .

It was the most efficient Embassy I ever had.

—Former Ambassador Ellis O. Briggs, testimony to Senate Subcommittee on National Security Staffing and Operations in *Administration of National Security*

Franklin Delano Roosevelt: "But the Treasury and the State Department . . . are nothing compared with the Na-a-vy."

public relations and spent nearly $337 million on public affairs activities.[29] In 1987 the Department of Defense alone listed 1,066 civilian and military public relations officials worldwide at a cost of $44.3 million.[30] And the actual cost and number of people performing public relations activities in the federal government are probably much higher than the "official" figures.

Bureaucracy and the President

The image of the department head as a sea captain aboard a strange ship with an unknown crew may be applied as well to a president seeking control over the bureaucracy. President Kennedy was particularly exasperated by vacillation and delay in the foreign-policy bureaucracy. "The State Department is a bowl of jelly," he once declared. "It's got all those people over there who are constantly smiling. I think we need to smile less and be tougher."[31]

Other presidents have voiced similar complaints. Franklin Roosevelt complained that it was "almost impossible" to get results from the Treasury Department.

> But the Treasury is not to be compared with the State Department. You should go through the experience of trying to get any changes in the thinking, policy, and action of the career diplomats. . . . But the Treasury and the State Department put together are nothing compared with the Na-a-vy. The admirals are really something to cope with—and I should know. To change anything in the Na-a-vy is like punching a feather bed. You punch it with your right and you punch it with your left until you are

finally exhausted, and then you find the damn bed just as it was before you started punching.[32]

Often, presidents attempt to gain tighter control of the bureaucracy by reorganizing its structure. Postwar efforts toward administrative reform led in 1947 to creation of the first of two Hoover Commissions. Formally entitled the Commission on Organization of the Executive Branch of the Government, the study panel was headed by former President Herbert Hoover. It first reported in 1949, and of its nearly 300 recommendations for streamlining the federal government, about half were adopted. Most of the commission's proposals emphasized centralization of authority and the need to simplify the organization of government.[33]

[29] United States General Accounting Office, *Public Affairs and Congressional Affairs Activities of Federal Agencies* (Washington, D.C.: General Accounting Office, February 1986), p. 2.

[30] Data provided by Department of Defense.

[31] Arthur M. Schlesinger, Jr., *A Thousand Days* (Boston: Houghton Mifflin, 1965), p. 406.

[32] Richard E. Neustadt, *Presidential Power* (New York: Wiley, 1960), p. 42.

[33] Commission on Organization of the Executive Branch of the Government, *Reports to Congress and Task Force Reports* (Washington, D.C.: U.S. Government Printing Office, 1949). The second Hoover Commission was established in 1953 and reported in 1955. Because it urged the government to eliminate many activities that competed with private enterprise, its proposals were more politically controversial. The second Hoover Commission report had little impact. See Commission on Organization of the Executive Branch of the Government, *Reports to Congress and Task Force Reports* (Washington, D.C.: U.S. Government Printing Office, 1955).

PRESIDENT KENNEDY'S STRUGGLE TO CONTROL THE BUREAUCRACY

Kennedy . . . was determined to . . . recover presidential control over the sprawling feudalism of government. This became a central theme of his administration and, in some respects, a central frustration. The presidential government, coming to Washington aglow with new ideas and a euphoric sense that it could not go wrong, promptly collided with the feudal barons of the permanent government, entrenched in their domains and fortified by their sense of proprietorship; and the permanent government, confronted by this invasion, began almost to function . . . as a resistance movement, scattering to the *maquis* in order to pick off the intruders. This was especially true in foreign affairs.

—Arthur M. Schlesinger, Jr.,
A Thousand Days

Since 1918 Congress has from time to time given presidents the right to restructure the executive branch. Presidents have made extensive use of this power under a series of Reorganization acts passed since 1939; this power was increased by the Reorganization Act of 1949. Under the law, reorganization plans prepared by the executive branch took effect in sixty days unless vetoed by Congress. From 1949 through 1972, seventy-two out of the ninety-one reorganization plans submitted by five presidents went into effect. Congress has since granted reorganization power to later presidents for varying lengths of time.

The creation in 1970 of the Office of Management and Budget (OMB) was designed to shift to the president and his budget officials tighter control over management of the federal bureaucracy. OMB absorbed the old Bureau of the Budget, which had been created in 1921 as part of a law that for the first time required the president to submit to Congress an annual budget for the federal government. OMB is a unit of the Executive Office of the President (see Chapter 10, pp. 386–387). The budget process, which OMB manages, can be a major tool of presidential control over the executive branch. The federal government runs on a fiscal year that starts October 1 and ends the following September 30. Each spring, agencies and departments begin planning their requests for the fiscal year starting seventeen months later. Matching these requests against economic forecasts and revenue estimates from his advisers, the president establishes budget guidelines; within this framework individual agency requests are studied by OMB and presented to the president for decision. The budget then goes to Congress in January.

The in-fighting and competition among government agencies for a slice of the budget pie give the president, through OMB, an important lever for bu-

Iran rescue mission, 1980: The advisers . . . the result

reaucratic control. Indeed, as Aaron Wildavsky has observed, "the budget lies at the heart of the political process."[34] Moreover, the bureaucrat "whose requests are continually turned down in Congress finds that he tends to be rejected in the Budget Bureau and in his own department as well. . . . The Bureau finds itself treating agencies it dislikes much better than those it may like better but who cannot help themselves nearly as much in Congress."[35]

Bureaucracy and Policymaking

In theory, presidents make policy and bureaucrats carry it out. In fact, officials often play a major role in policy formation. In large part, this is because presidents rely on bureaucratic *expertise* in making their policy decisions. Frederick C. Mosher has noted the tendency of professionals with "specialized knowledge, science, and rationality" to dominate many areas of the bureaucracy.[36] On the other hand, that kind of expertise is a less reliable source of bureaucratic power today. As Francis Rourke has observed, "the private sector now abounds with think tanks, consulting firms, and watchdog groups that are widely regarded as more reliable sources of information and advice than the government itself."[37]

Other factors have combined to reduce the influence of bureaucrats in setting policy agendas. For example, the "divided government" that has characterized the American political system during recent Republican administrations has reduced the influence of the bureaucracy. During the Reagan years, for example, Republicans controlled the White House and competed with the Democrats who controlled the House of Representatives and, for two years, the Senate. Under these circumstances, the White House sought to centralize executive power in the president's hands, while Congress tried to "micromanage" the bureaucrats. The result in each case was less power and discretion for the administrators.[38]

But presidents who rely too much on such expertise may get into trouble. For example, in April of 1980, President Carter ordered a military force to attempt to rescue the American hostages being held in the U.S. embassy in Iran. Although the secretary of defense, Harold Brown, and the Joint Chiefs of Staff had apparently assured the president the mission would have a

[34] Aaron Wildavsky, *The Politics of the Budgetary Process* (Boston: Little, Brown, 1964), p. 5.

[35] Ibid., pp. 41–42.

[36] Frederick C. Mosher, *Democracy and the Public Service* (New York: Oxford University Press, 1968), pp. 21, 109.

[37] Rourke, "American Bureaucracy in a Changing Political Setting," *Journal of Public Administration Research and Theory,* April 1991, p. 120.

[38] Ibid., pp. 113–114.

BORIS YELTSIN: MEET THE BUREAU-CRATS

Moscow — When Russian president Boris Yeltsin commandeered Communist party headquarters after the abortive coup last August, he threw the party apparatchiks out on their ears and hoisted the white, blue and red tricolor of the czars in place of the red flag of the international Communist movement. It seemed an era had ended.

Not yet.

Indeed, within weeks of the party's expulsion, a Yeltsin aide sought out an old Central Committee phonebook: the new regime needed to fill the now-vacant offices with experienced bureaucrats.

"The result is that most of the same people are sitting in the same offices as they did a year ago," said Aleksandr Sokolov, the new headquarters commandant, who watched the apparatchiks trickle back into the sprawling building on Moscow's Old Square. "When we were forming the new structures, we had to hire people from the old structures. Our supporters — the people who came to rallies and street demonstrations — didn't know anything about how to run a country. People who have never worked as bureaucrats will always lose out to people who have worked as bureaucrats."

—*Washington Post*, June 14, 1992

reasonable chance of success, it failed. It also cost the lives of eight American servicemen who died when a helicopter and a transport plane crashed into each other on the ground in a remote desert staging area. Of course, Carter was not only relying on his military experts. He undoubtedly felt that a successful rescue mission would be of enormous political benefit to him in an election year.

Other administrations have suffered similar setbacks. In 1961 President Kennedy approved a CIA plan to invade Cuba and topple Premier Fidel Castro. After the invasion of the Bay of Pigs proved a disaster, Kennedy publicly took responsibility for the mess, although privately he complained: "All my life I've known better than to depend on the experts. How could I have been so stupid, to let them go ahead?"[39] Of the Joint Chiefs of Staff, who had approved the CIA plan, Kennedy bitterly told a visitor: "They don't know any more about it than anyone else."[40]

Just as federal officials can promote policies that get the nation into trouble, they also can be instrumental in changing those policies. In 1968, during the war in Vietnam, several high-level Pentagon officials privately urged Clark M. Clifford, the secretary of defense, to try to bring about a reversal of President Johnson's Vietnam policy. As Clifford studied administration policy in Vietnam—and a request by the military for 206,000 more troops—he gradually became convinced of the folly of further escalation. Although his warm friendship with the president "grew suddenly formal and cool," Clifford and an advisory group of prestigious

civilians were apparently instrumental in persuading the president to reverse his policies.[41]

A PROFILE OF THE AMERICAN BUREAUCRACY

Who Are the Administrators?

In 1792 the federal government had 780 employees. Today there are approximately 3,105,690 civilian employees of the federal government.[42] A study of this total reveals some surprising facts. In the first place, "the bureaucracy in Washington" is not in Washington—at least most of it is not. One recent statistical breakdown, for example, showed that only 373,971 government employees—slightly more than 12 percent of the federal total—worked in the metropolitan Washington area. The rest were scattered throughout the fifty states and overseas. California alone had 314,590 federal workers, and some 131,884 employees worked overseas.[43]

In addition to workers on the federal payroll, however, there are several million persons working *indirectly* for the federal government. These are people working for defense contractors, as outside consultants, or in other programs funded by the government. Some of this outside consulting work has been criticized as wasteful or as a way of expanding the bureaucracy without seeming to do so.

[39] Theodore C. Sorensen, *Kennedy* (New York: Harper & Row, 1965), p. 309.
[40] David Wise and Thomas B. Ross, *The Invisible Government* (New York: Random House, 1964), p. 185.
[41] Townsend Hoopes, *The Limits of Intervention* (New York: David McKay, 1969), p. 181, Chapters 8–10.
[42] U.S. Office of Personnel Management, Federal Civilian Work Force Statistics, *Employment and Trends as of March 1992*, p. 10.
[43] Data provided by U.S. Office of Personnel Management, as of March 1992. Data for California as of December 1990.

Drawing by Ziegler © 1979 The New Yorker Magazine, Inc.

Figure 11-2
Government Employment — Federal, State, and Local

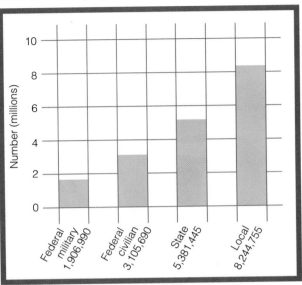

SOURCE: Department of Defense; U.S. Office of Personnel Management; U.S. Bureau of the Census. Data for state and local governments as of 1990; for federal military and civilian employment as of March 1992.

In 1992 almost one-third of the full-time civilian employees of the federal government worked for the Department of Defense. The 1,005,963 civilian workers in the Pentagon and other military installations, added to the 802,628 employees of the Postal Service, and the 258,476 in the Department of Veterans Affairs, comprised approximately 67 percent of the entire full-time federal bureaucracy. In other words, two-thirds of all federal employees worked in these three agencies. In contrast, the State Department employed only 25,990 persons.[44]

The federal civilian bureaucracy of some 3,105,690 persons is unquestionably large compared to private industry; General Motors, the biggest corporation in America, had about 751,000 employees in 1992. Yet federal workers comprise only 18.5 percent of total government employment — federal, state, and local — in the United States. More than four times as many people work for state and local governments as for the federal government. By 1990 local governments had some 8,244,755 employees (including 2,401,000 teachers) and state governments employed 5,381,445 persons.[45] A comparison of federal, state, and local bureaucracies is shown in Figure 11-2.

A rough portrait can be drawn of the "average" man or woman in the federal service: he or she is 42.7 years old, has worked for the government for 13.7 years, and earns an annual salary of $35,772.[46] The president receives $200,000 a year, the vice-president $166,200, and members of the cabinet $143,800. About two-thirds of the bureaucracy are members of the career civil service, with their salaries in many cases fixed on a General Schedule that ranges from a starting salary of $11,478 for clerks (GS-1) to $83,502 for a relative handful of top civil servants (GS-15).[47] However, members of the Senior Executive Service, a group of high-level managers within the government, can earn salaries ranging up to $112,100.[48]

What kinds of workers make up the bureaucracy? Although almost half a million fit the conventional image of bureaucrats — general administrative and clerical employees — the government also employs 172,825 engineers and architects; 146,006 accountants and budget personnel; 141,760 doctors and health employees; 56,135 social scientists, psychologists, and welfare workers; 9,763 librarians and archivists; and 2,411 veterinarians. Among federal white-collar workers, 826,500, or 49.7 percent, are women.[49]

---

44 U.S. Office of Personnel Management, Federal Civilian Work Force Statistics, *Employment and Trends as of March 1992*, pp. 17, 20.

45 Data provided by the U.S. Bureau of the Census.

46 Data provided by the U.S. Office of Personnel Management, as of March 1992.

47 Data provided by the U.S. Office of Personnel Management. Salaries as of January 1992.

48 Ibid.

49 Data provided by U.S. Office of Personnel Management, as of September 1989. Data for women as of 1990.

Figure 11-3
Executive Branch of the Government

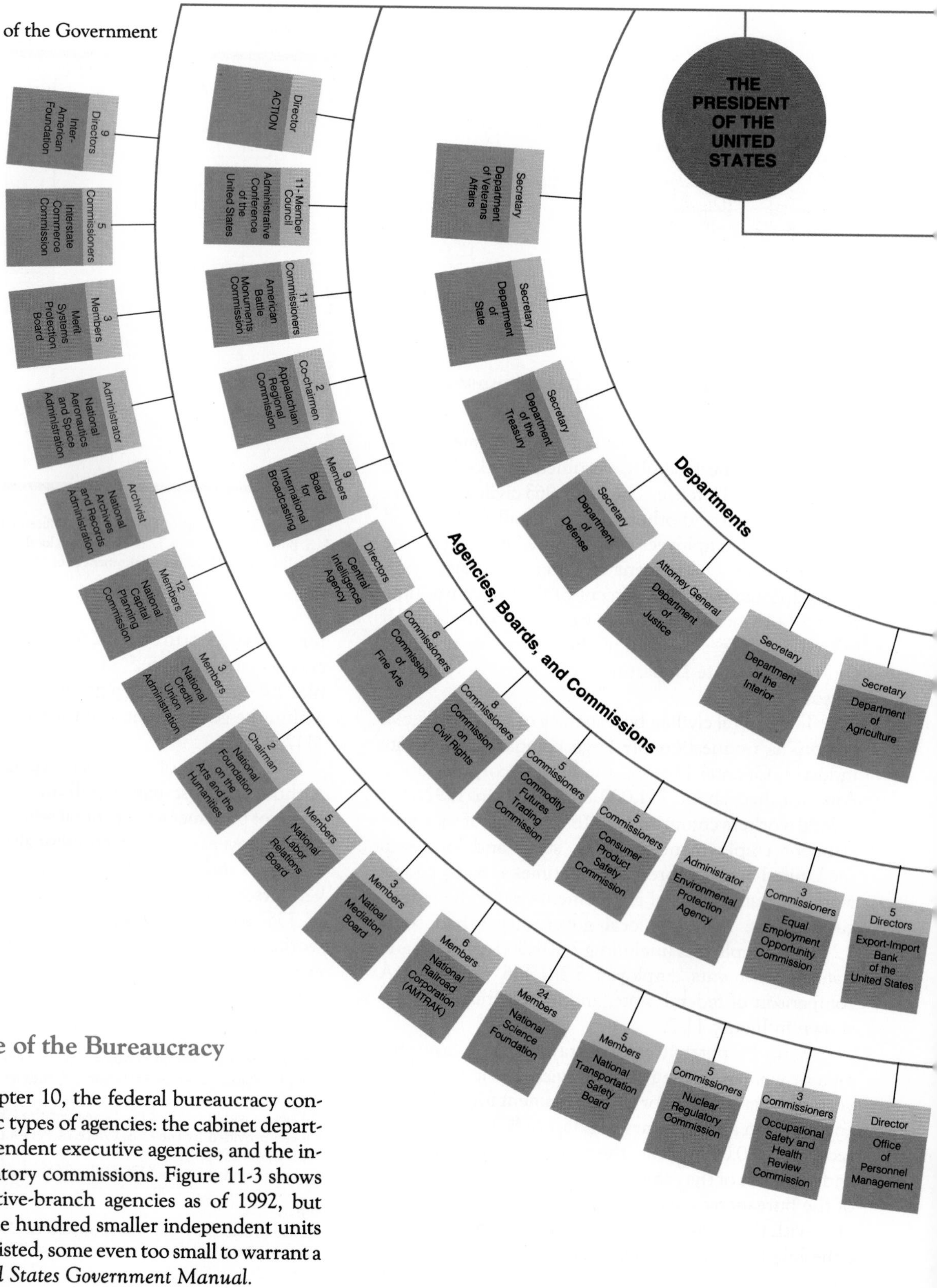

THE PRESIDENT OF THE UNITED STATES

Departments

Secretary Department of Veterans Affairs
Secretary Department of State
Secretary Department of the Treasury
Secretary Department of Defense
Attorney General Department of Justice
Secretary Department of the Interior
Secretary Department of Agriculture

Agencies, Boards, and Commissions

9 Directors Inter-American Foundation
5 Commissioners Interstate Commerce Commission
3 Members Merit Systems Protection Board
Administrator National Aeronautics and Space Administration
Archivist National Archives and Records Administration
12 Members National Capital Planning Commission
3 Members National Credit Union Administration

Director ACTION
11-Member Council Administrative Conference of the United States
11 Commissioners American Battle Monuments Commission
2 Co-chairmen Appalachian Regional Commission
9 Members Board for International Broadcasting
Directors Central Intelligence Agency
6 Commissioners Commission of Fine Arts
8 Commissioners Commission on Civil Rights
5 Commissioners Commodity Futures Trading Commission
5 Commissioners Consumer Product Safety Commission
Administrator Environmental Protection Agency
3 Commissioners Equal Employment Opportunity Commission
5 Directors Export-Import Bank of the United States

2 Chairman National Foundation on the Arts and the Humanities
5 Members National Labor Relations Board
3 Members National Mediation Board
6 Members National Railroad Corporation (AMTRAK)
24 Members National Science Foundation
5 Members National Transportation Safety Board
5 Commissioners Nuclear Regulatory Commission
3 Commissioners Occupational Safety and Health Review Commission
Director Office of Personnel Management

The Structure of the Bureaucracy

As noted in Chapter 10, the federal bureaucracy consists of three basic types of agencies: the cabinet departments, the independent executive agencies, and the independent regulatory commissions. Figure 11-3 shows the *major* executive-branch agencies as of 1992, but approximately one hundred smaller independent units of government existed, some even too small to warrant a line in the *United States Government Manual*.

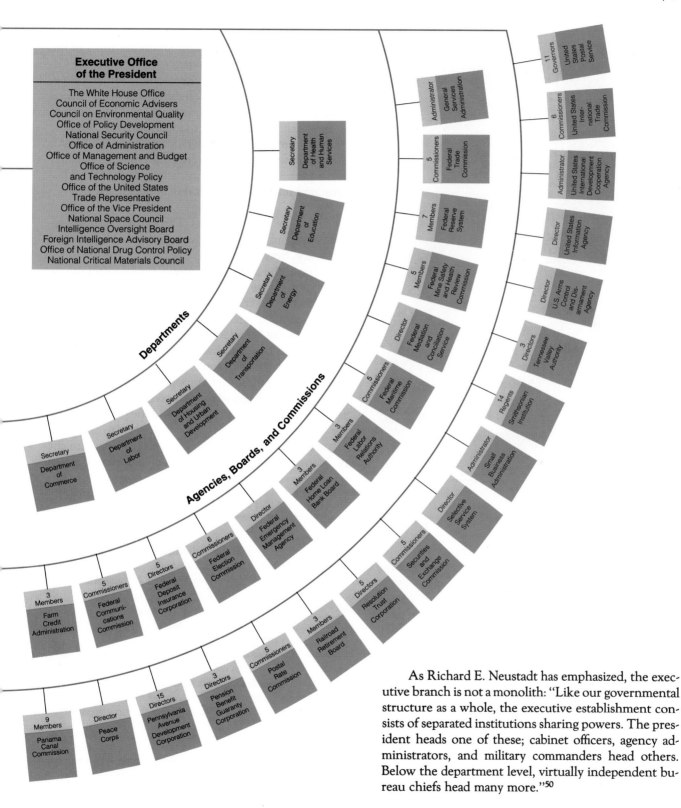

As Richard E. Neustadt has emphasized, the executive branch is not a monolith: "Like our governmental structure as a whole, the executive establishment consists of separated institutions sharing powers. The president heads one of these; cabinet officers, agency administrators, and military commanders head others. Below the department level, virtually independent bureau chiefs head many more."[50]

SOURCE: Adapted from *The United States Government Manual: 1991/92* (Washington, D.C.: U.S. Government Printing Office, 1991).

[50] Neustadt, *Presidential Power*, p. 39.

A president attempts to control the bureaucracy through his White House staff and other units of the Executive Office of the president — particularly the Office of Management and Budget — and through his department heads. Because of the sheer size of the federal government, however, no president can really hope to supervise all the activities of the administrators. And the effort to control the bureaucracy has led to the growth of the White House staff — creating a new bureaucracy at the presidential level. Thus, attempts to control bureaucracy may create new layers of bureaucracy.

The Cabinet Departments The fourteen cabinet departments are major components of the federal bureaucracy. Some idea of the structure of the executive branch and the problem of presidential control can be grasped by studying the organization chart of a cabinet department. At first glance, it might appear to be a tightly organized agency, with lines of authority flowing upward to the secretary, who in turn reports to the president. In fact, the chart masks entrenched bureaus and key civil servants, some of whom enjoy close outside ties with interest groups and congressional committees — relationships that give them power independent of the cabinet secretary and the president. The sheer size of most departments would seem to defy presidential control. To take one example, the Department of Transportation, formed in 1966, had some 109,000 employees in 1992. As shown in Figure 11-4, the

THE PAPER CHASE

The sheer volume of paper generated by the federal bureaucracy has long been the target of criticism. In one year, according to the government's own figures, it took Americans 913 million hours to fill out 4,900 different kinds of government forms. Congress, responding to public complaints about the amount of paperwork demanded by the government, established the Commission on Federal Paperwork. The task of the commission was to reduce the flood of official paper.

The commission acquired a staff of some three dozen people and issued 36 reports and 770 recommendations before it went out of business in 1977. Its major recommendation was that a new cabinet-level Department of Administration be created to manage federal paperwork.

Congress was less than enthusiastic over the idea of creating yet another bureaucracy to manage the bureaucracy. Representative Peter H. Kostmayer, a Pennsylvania Democrat, declared: "We can encourage each department to tighten up its operations without hiring thousands of more bureaucrats who, as we know, have an unsurpassed ability to produce paperwork." Congress did not establish the new department.

—Adapted from *Congressional Quarterly*, Weekly Report, December 10, 1977; and *New York Times*, December 1, 1979

HOLD THE PEPPERONI: BUREAUCRACY DEFINES PIZZA

There is no easy way to describe why Pizza Hut is locked in combat with the Agriculture Department. . . . Pizza Hut wants to be able to sell pepperoni pizzas to school lunch programs around the country. The Agriculture Department says the company can do that only if it puts no more than 20 slices of pepperoni on each one. . . .

What is a pizza? According to Agriculture Department reckoning, the cheese on a standard pizza makes it a dairy product unless the meat on top comes to more than 2 percent of its total weight. That translates to 20 slices of pepperoni per large pizza.

Pizza Hut can, in other words, legally sell pepperoni pizza to local schools. It just can't sell pizza with a lot of pepperoni on it, which is what it would like to do.

—*Washington Post*, October 11, 1991

Figure 11-4
Department of Transportation

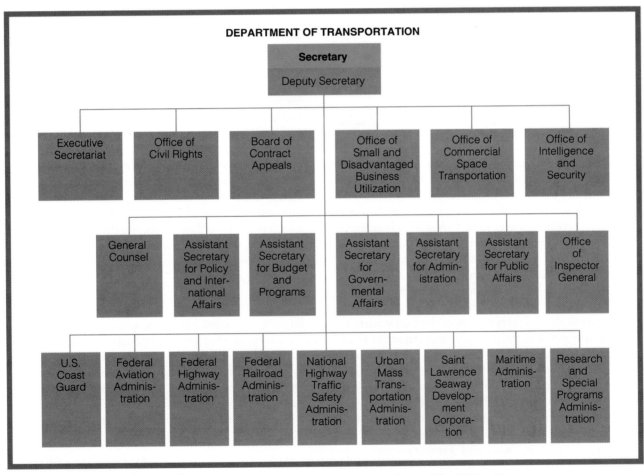

SOURCE: *The United States Government Manual: 1991/92* (Washington, D.C.: U.S. Government Printing Office, 1991), p. 448.

"It's the never-ending struggle between the State Department and the Department of Defense."

Drawing by Stevenson © 1982 The New Yorker Magazine, Inc.

department was headed by a secretary, a deputy secretary, and five assistant secretaries, each of whom had responsibility for several offices down the line.

In addition, several major agencies — with sometimes competitive client groups — were loosely grouped under the Department of Transportation, including the United States Coast Guard, the Federal Aviation Administration (FAA), the Federal Railroad Administration, the Urban Mass Transportation Administration, and the Federal Highway Administration. Although the organization chart does not show it, the Department of Transportation, like the other cabinet departments, is dispersed geographically. The air traffic controllers of the FAA operate airport towers across the United States; the Coast Guard and the Federal Highway Administration have field offices in several cities.

The creation of the cabinet departments parallels the growth of the American nation. Only three departments — State, War, and Treasury — were created in 1789. But new areas of concern have required the establishment of executive departments to meet

new problems. This fact is reflected in the names of the departments created in recent decades — Housing and Urban Development in 1965, Transportation in 1966, Energy in 1977, Education in 1979, and Health and Human Services also in 1979.[51]

The Executive Agencies   The *independent executive agencies* report to the president in the same manner as departments, even though they are not part of any cabinet department. They are not, therefore, independent of the president. Their heads are appointed by the president and may be dismissed by him. The executive agencies include several powerful units of the bureaucracy: NASA, the CIA, and the Selective Service System, to name a few.

Grouped with the executive agencies but somewhat different in status are *government corporations*. At one time these were semiautonomous, but through legislation since 1945 they have been placed under presidential control. In 1970 Congress abolished the Post Office as a cabinet department and established the U.S. Postal Service as an independent, government-owned corporation. The hope was to increase efficiency, remove postal employees from politics, and give the new service power to raise rates to meet expenses. But new forms of organization do not automatically solve bureaucratic problems. Many citizens complained that under the new system postal rates increased but the mail seemed slower than ever in reaching its destination. (As one result, several private delivery services, such as Federal Express, were competing actively with the government.) Some other examples of government corporations are the Federal Deposit Insurance Corporation, which protects bank deposits, and the Tennessee Valley Authority, which has built dams and provided hydroelectric power and other economic benefits to an area covering eight states.

The Regulatory Commissions   The *independent regulatory commissions* occupy a special status in the bureaucracy, for they are administratively independent of all three branches of the government. In fact, however, as has been made abundantly clear over the years, the regulatory commissions and agencies are sometimes susceptible to pressures from the White House, Congress, and the industries they regulate. The regulatory

---

[51] The Department of Education and the Department of Health and Human Services replaced the Department of Health, Education, and Welfare that had been created in 1953.

"All those in favor of establishing government regulatory agencies say 'Aye.'"

Drawing by Martins
© 1983 The New Yorker Magazine, Inc.

agencies decide such questions as who shall receive a license to operate a television station or build a natural gas pipeline to serve a large city. These licenses and franchises are worth millions of dollars, and the competition for them is fierce. As a result, the regulatory agencies are the target of intense pressures, including, at times, approaches by skillful and well-paid Washington lawyers who go in the "back door" to argue their clients' cases in private meetings with agency officials. Such *ex parte* (one-sided) contacts could become less useful, however; the Government-in-the-Sunshine Act (1976) opened up most agency meetings to the public and also prohibited secret contacts. In addition, a 1977 federal appeals court ruling in a case dealing with pay–cable television barred secret contacts with regulatory commission members when they were engaged in rule making in key cases. However, the Supreme Court, in another case, appeared to permit such backdoor approaches.[52]

The regulatory agencies were created because of the need for rule making and regulation in highly complex, technical areas involving the interests of the public. In awarding licenses, they also exercise a quasijudicial function. Despite the separation of powers provided for in the Constitution, regulatory agencies combine aspects of all three branches of government — legislative, executive, and judicial.

Commission members are appointed by the president with the consent of the Senate, but, unlike cabinet members, they do not report to the president. Although members of the regulatory commissions cannot, by law, all be drawn from the same political party, the president designates the chairperson. Through his appointive powers a president may in time gain political control of the commissions.

More than three decades ago, a House inquiry into regulatory agencies demonstrated during a dramatic series of hearings that the agencies had, in many cases, become servants of industry instead of regulating in the interest of the larger public. The hearings, and subsequent disclosures, revealed a pattern of fraternization by commissioners and regulated industries.

Some commission members have accepted free transportation, lecture fees, hotel rooms, and gifts from businesses subject to their authority.[53] Others have left the commissions for well-paying jobs in the regulated industry. Many have seemed more concerned with protecting pipeline companies, airlines, railroads, and television networks than with making sure the industries are serving the public satisfactorily. On the other hand,

---

[52] *Vermont Yankee Nuclear Power Corporation v. Natural Resources Defense Council, Inc.,* 435 U.S. 519 (1978).

[53] Bernard Schwartz, *The Professor and the Commissions* (New York: Knopf, 1959), p. 48.

at times, the regulatory agencies have been defenders of the public interest; for example, the Securities and Exchange Commission has protected investors from stock frauds, and the Federal Trade Commission has attempted to curtail false television advertising.

The major regulatory agencies, in order of their creation, are:

1. *The Interstate Commerce Commission* (1887): five members, five-year terms; regulates and fixes rates for railroads, trucking companies, bus lines, freight forwarders, oil pipelines, express agencies.

2. *The Federal Trade Commission* (1914): five members, seven-year terms; regulates industry; responsible for preventing unfair competition, price fixing, deceptive advertising, mislabeling of textile and fur products, false packaging, and similar abuses.

3. *The Federal Communications Commission* (1934): five members, five-year terms; licenses and regulates all television and radio stations in the United States; regulates frequencies used by police, aviation, taxicabs, citizens' band and "ham" operators, and others; fixes rates for telephone and telegraph companies in interstate commerce.

4. *The Securities and Exchange Commission* (1934): five members, five-year terms; created to protect the public from investing in securities on the basis of false or misleading claims; requires companies offering securities for sale to file an accurate registration statement and prospectus; registers brokers; regulates stock exchanges.

5. *The Federal Energy Regulatory Commission* (1978): five members, four-year terms; although within the Department of Energy, is an independent regulatory commission; fixes rates and has jurisdiction over natural gas companies, electric utilities, and interstate oil pipelines.

Many other government agencies have regulatory functions in whole or in part. For example, the Federal Maritime Commission regulates shipping; the National Labor Relations Board prohibits unfair labor practices; and the Board of Governors of the Federal Reserve System regulates the money supply, interest rates, and the banking industry. Many units of the regular cabinet departments also have regulatory functions. Examples include the Food and Drug Administration (FDA) in the Department of Health and Human Services; the Occupational Safety and Health Administration (OSHA) in the Labor Department; and the Antitrust Division of the Justice Department.

Deregulation: The Pattern Changes The government regulation of industry, which blossomed during the New Deal administration of Franklin D. Roosevelt, had, by the 1970s, become a target of criticism by many Republicans and Democrats alike. President Carter, for

example, called for deregulation of airlines, banking, trucking, railroads, and telecommunications.

Even before Carter took office in 1977, Congress had begun exploring deregulation of the airline and other industries. The rising tide of sentiment in Congress reflected complaints by business of excessive and costly government regulation, red tape, delay, and paperwork. A major target of deregulation was the Civil Aeronautics Board (CAB), the regulatory agency that granted domestic and overseas airline routes, set air fares, and approved airline mergers. The CAB was one of three major regulatory agencies created during Franklin Roosevelt's New Deal. In 1978 Congress enacted the Airline Deregulation Act, which ordered the CAB to emphasize competition and simplify its procedures. The CAB's powers were phased out by the law; it was allowed to grant routes until 1982 and set rates until 1983, and then went out of business, as scheduled, on January 1, 1985.

In 1980 Congress passed the Motor Carrier Act to deregulate the trucking industry. The law promoted competition among truckers, made it easier for new companies to enter the business, and reduced the powers of the Interstate Commerce Commission (ICC) over trucking. Also in 1980, Congress passed the Staggers Rail Act, substantially deregulating the railroads. The new law gave the railroads much more freedom to set the prices they charge their customers and reduced regulation by the ICC. That same year, Congress reduced the power of the Federal Trade Commission (FTC) to regulate certain industries. And in January 1981 President Reagan took office after an election campaign in which he frequently promised to reduce government regulation.

Pressures to deregulate continued after Reagan came to power. In 1982, the Federal Communications Commission reduced record-keeping requirements for broadcasters. And in 1987, the FCC abolished the fairness doctrine, which had required that broadcasters present all sides of important public issues.

In the rush to deregulate, some observers felt, the government may have gone too far. The airline industry is a case in point. After airlines were deregulated in 1978, they could, with some exceptions, fly where they pleased on domestic routes. As a result, major carriers dropped all service to 132 cities.[54] A number of smaller communities suffered severely because of these changes. New carriers sprang up to compete with the giants, and price wars broke out on transcontinental and other routes. The public sometimes benefited through lower air fares, and some airlines had a sharp increase in business at first. But after an initial surge of profits, the industry, beginning in 1981, operated at a loss for three years in a row. Eventually, Braniff, Pan Am, and Eastern Airlines all went out of business. Thousands of airline workers lost their jobs. In the airline industry, at least, deregulation proved a mixed blessing. Some airlines and other industries actually lobbied Congress for new regulation, asking that some rules that had been lifted be restored.

The Growth of Social Regulation   Although considerable deregulation of transportation, communications, and financial institutions has taken place in recent years, at the same time social regulation by the federal government has increased. Laws and rules to protect the employment rights of blacks, other minorities, and women; legislation to preserve the natural environment and to protect the public from air or water pollution; and laws and rules to guard the health and safety of employees in the workplace are all forms of *social regulation.*

Even as the authority of such old-line agencies as the ICC has been narrowed in recent years, that of the Environmental Protection Agency, the Equal Employment Opportunity Commission, and the Occupational Safety and Health Administration has been strengthened.

As Michael D. Reagan has observed, "Traditional economic regulation and the alphabet soup of New Deal regulatory commissions" were designed to control "abuses of private economic power. . . . There was . . . almost no concept of what we now call social regulation: programs designed to achieve positive social benefits in such areas as protection of health, safety, and individual rights."[55]

Those at the Top

When the president of the United States took office in January of 1993, he was viewed as the leader, not only of the nation, but of his "administration." But what,

---

[54] *National Journal*, March 6, 1982, p. 405.

[55] Michael D. Reagan, *Regulation: The Politics of Policy* (Boston: Little, Brown, 1987), p. v.

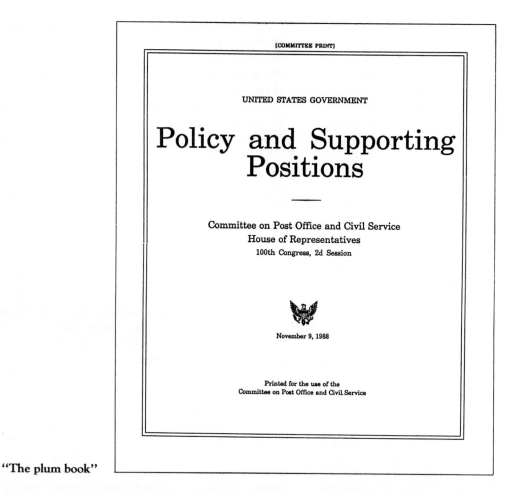

[COMMITTEE PRINT]

UNITED STATES GOVERNMENT

Policy and Supporting Positions

Committee on Post Office and Civil Service
House of Representatives
100th Congress, 2d Session

November 9, 1988

Printed for the use of the
Committee on Post Office and Civil Service

"The plum book"

exactly, did that mean? Although no formal definition of the term exists, in general a president's administration consists of the president, the heads of the fourteen cabinet departments, about 300 sub-cabinet officials and agency heads, 159 ambassadors, and 1,900 aides, assistants, and confidential secretaries.[56] In all, an incoming president makes approximately 2,400 key appointments, for the most part exempt from civil service requirements. Of this total, perhaps 700 are important policy–advisory posts.

Most of the nearly 3,105,690 federal workers are civil servants, not "the president's men" or women. They are not appointed by him to the key policy jobs in the bureaucracy.

In presidential election years, the House or Senate Post Office and Civil Service Committee has obligingly published something known affectionately in Washing-

ton as "the plum book" (as in "political plum"), a listing of the non-civil-service jobs that the incoming president may fill.[57] For White House aides assigned to screen patronage appointees for the new administration, the plum book is an indispensable reference guide. Jobseekers in the Bush administration who studied the new edition published after the 1988 presidential election found 7,779 positions listed in the 230-page book — beginning with the White House staff.

The Civil Service

Today the vast majority of government jobs are filled through the competitive civil service system. Yet presidents have always rewarded their political supporters

---

[56] Data provided by the Office of Media Affairs, White House, as of March 1992.

[57] U.S. Congress, House Committee on Post Office and Civil Service, United States Government *Policy and Supporting Positions*, 100th Cong., 2nd sess. (Washington, D.C.: U.S. Government Printing Office, 1988).

and friends with government jobs. (In many cases, of course, presidents appoint persons recommended by powerful senators or House members.) Although George Washington declared that he appointed officials on the basis of "fitness of character," he favored members of his own party, the Federalists. Jefferson dismissed hundreds of Federalists when he became president, replacing them with members of his own party.

The Spoils System After Andrew Jackson was elected in 1828, he dismissed more than a third of the 612 presidentially appointed officeholders and 10 to 20 percent of the 10,000 lesser government officials. Although Jackson thereby continued a practice started by Jefferson, he is generally credited with introducing the "spoils system" to the national government. (Jackson preferred to call it "rotation in office.") In 1832 Senator William Learned Marcy of New York, defending a Jackson ambassadorial appointment, declared: "To the victor belong the spoils." The phrase became a classic statement of the right of victorious politicians to reward their followers with jobs. Political workers expected such rewards; when Lincoln became president, officeseekers prowled the White House stairways and hallways.

The Road to Reform Inefficiency and corruption in the federal government led to the first efforts at reform in the 1850s. After the Civil War the reform movement gathered momentum. Although President Grant's administration was riddled by corruption, it was Grant who persuaded Congress in 1871 to set up the first Civil

Chester A. Arthur

Service Commission. But the reform efforts had faltered by 1875, partly because Congress declined to appropriate new funds for the commission.

In 1880 the Republican party was divided into two factions, for and against civil service reform. James A. Garfield, the Republican presidential candidate, ran on a reform platform. To appease the "Stalwarts," or antireform faction, Chester A. Arthur was chosen for vicepresident.

After Garfield's election, Charles J. Guiteau, an eccentric evangelist and lawyer, decided he deserved the post of ambassador to Austria or at least the job of Paris consul. In 1881 it was easy to get into the White House, and Guiteau actually had an unsuccessful interview with President Garfield. Brooding over his failure to join the diplomatic service, Guiteau purchased a revolver. On July 2, he approached Garfield at the railroad station in Washington and shot him in the back, crying: "I am a Stalwart and now Arthur is President!" Garfield died eighty days later, and his assassin was hanged.

To the dismay of his political cronies, Chester Arthur became a champion of civil service reform. In the wake of public indignation over the assassination, Congress passed the Civil Service Reform Act of 1883 (the Pendleton Act). It established a bipartisan Civil Service Commission under which about 10 percent of federal employees were chosen through competitive examinations.

The basic purpose of the 1883 act was to transfer the power of appointment from politicians to a bipartisan commission that would select federal employees on merit. In this century Congress has placed more and more government workers under the protective umbrella of civil service. Today 88 percent of the federal bureaucracy is appointed under the merit system. During the Carter administration, Congress enacted the Civil Service Reform Act of 1978, which replaced the Civil Service Commission with the Office of Personnel Management (OPM) and two other agencies.

To a degree, the removal of civil service appointments from politics has done the president a favor. No matter who a president selects for a government post, he may antagonize others. William Howard Taft complained that every time he made an appointment he created "nine enemies and one ingrate."[58]

In 1992 1.3 million government jobs were exempt from the civil service system. But many of these were in

---

[58] In Louis W. Koenig, *The Chief Executive*, 4th ed. (New York: Harcourt Brace Jovanovich, 1981), p. 132.

HOW TO FIRE A BUREAUCRAT IN 21 MONTHS

What has 21 feet and 85 boxes and makes you want to pull your hair out?

Answer: A chart of the procedure for dismissing one Government clerk for being late or absent from work all the time.

Looking like a diagram of the circuitry for an intercontinental ballistic missile, its 21 feet (one foot for each month the process took) of boxes, triangles and zigzagging lines chronicle the memos, warnings, suspensions and conferences needed to dismiss one lowly Federal employee. . . .

The 21-foot chart represented the case of a clerk-typist in an unnamed agency. In Government parlance, he or she was a GS-4, near the bottom of the [15]-grade Federal pay scale. . . .

According to a report accompanying the diagram, the process demonstrates "why so many supervisors would rather put up with a marginal employee than subject themselves to the discomforts of the firing process. . . ."

But all the streamlined procedures in the world will not make it easier to dismiss high-level workers. "If a GS-4 cannot type, that's pretty clear," said Howard M. Messner of the budget office. "But if a GS-15 cannot think, what can you do?"

—*New York Times*, February 22, 1978

agencies such as the Postal Service, the Foreign Service of the Department of State, and the FBI, which have their own merit systems.

Recruiting the Bureaucrats The OPM acts as an employment agency for the bureaucracy. It does so through Federal Job Information Centers located in many states. At these centers, a person interested in federal employment can find out what jobs are available. The applicant contacts OPM or applies directly to the agency with openings and fills out the necessary forms. In some cases, examinations for various kinds of positions are held by OPM boards located in major population areas. When a job opens up in a federal agency, OPM may refer a list of names of eligible persons to the agency, which then selects the applicant from among the three names at the top of the list. Or the agency may fill the job itself from its own resources and lists. Under a system of "veteran preference," disabled veterans and certain members of their families receive up to ten extra points on their examination scores; some other honorably discharged veterans receive five points.

Before being accepted for government employment, applicants are told that an investigation will be made of their reputation, character, and loyalty to the United States. OPM conducts most of these investigations, but if the job is in the national security area, in which the applicant has access to classified material, the FBI usually conducts the background check. New government employees must swear or affirm that they will support and defend the Constitution. Employees must also swear that they will not participate in a strike against the government or any agency of the government. Within that framework, they are free to join one of the numerous unions and employee organizations that represent federal workers. Unions of government workers at the federal, state, and local level have in recent years advocated a national law to give full collective-bargaining rights to their members. But in a number of cases, the courts have ruled against the position favored by the unions.

Government workers receive annual vacations that increase from two to five weeks with length of

Civil-service reform: applicants taking exams for government jobs at the New York City Customs House

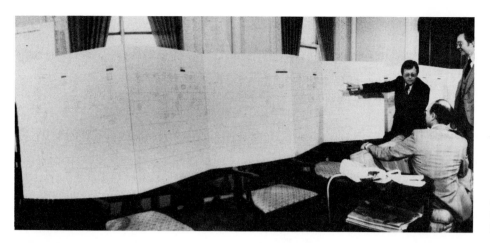

An official explains the number of steps necessary to fire a federal employee.

service, and liberal sick leave and fringe benefits. Under the merit system, they almost certainly will be promoted if they remain in the career service. Federal employees may express political opinions, contribute to political parties, vote, badger their representatives in Congress, wear a campaign button, display a bumper sticker on their cars, and attend political rallies, but under the Hatch Act they may not take an *active* part in party politics or campaigns, or run for political office. Many federal workers consider the law a violation of their rights of free speech. In 1973, however, the Supreme Court upheld the constitutionality of the Hatch Act; the Court noted that Congress had passed the law because of the danger that a political party might use federal workers in campaigns and that promotions and job security might depend on party loyalty.[59]

There is no mandatory retirement age for federal employees, but they can voluntarily retire with a pension on reaching the age range of fifty-five to sixty-two, depending on length of service. Retired government workers drawing a pension receive from 7.5 percent to 80 percent of their salaries for the rest of their lives, depending on length of service. On average, federal employees retire after thirty years and receive slightly more than half their pay.

Federal workers hired after 1983 must usually join the Federal Employees' Retirement System (FERS), a new pension program that combines social security, an annuity, and a savings plan.

For most of the bureaucracy below the level of political appointees, a government career has offered a relatively high degree of security. It is true that federal

employees may be fired for cause (such as misconduct or inefficiency), or if they are adjudged a security risk. Or employees may be given little to do, or dull work, or be transferred to the bureaucratic equivalent of Siberia, if they offend a superior. But, by and large, they are protected from arbitrary dismissal. Firing most career federal workers is difficult because it still entails a complex and lengthy series of hearings and appeals. On the other hand, Congress may end a government program or cut the appropriation, resulting in a "reduction in force" in the bureaucracy. Workers who are thus "riffed" may be transferred to another job in their agency or to some other government unit, or they may be fired. About 21 percent of federal employees leave or retire each year, representing a turnover of more than 657,086 employees annually.[60]

The Carter Reforms

"We want a government that can be trusted," President Carter said in a speech in 1978, " . . . that will be efficient, not mired in its own red tape."

Carter went on to propose major changes in the civil service system, designed, he said, to reward merit and penalize incompetence. Before the year was out, Congress had passed, and the president had signed, the Civil Service Reform Act of 1978.

This new law, the first major overhaul of the government civil service system in almost a century, established three new agencies: the Office of Personnel

[59] *Civil Service Commission v. National Association of Letter Carriers,* AFL-CIO, 413 U.S. 548 (1973).

[60] U.S. Office of Personnel Management, Federal Civilian Work Force Statistics, *Employment and Trends as of September 1991,* p. 51.

Management, to act as the president's personnel arm, handling recruitment, examinations, pay policy, job classification, and retirement; the Merit Systems Protection Board, to hear appeals and conduct investigations, including inquiries into complaints by "whistle-blowers" about corruption and waste; and the Federal Labor Relations Authority, to oversee labor-management relations and arbitrate labor disputes between federal agencies and employee unions.

Under the law, federal officials were given somewhat more flexibility in firing employees for incompetence, although not nearly as much as Carter had requested. The appeals process still gave employees substantial job protection. For the first time, a system of merit pay increases, rather than entirely automatic raises, was established at the upper-middle levels of the bureaucracy.

The Senior Executive Service (SES) Perhaps the most important feature of the reform act was the establishment of the Senior Executive Service, a corps of about 8,100 high-level administrators and managers at the top of the government bureaucracy. Those senior executives who chose to join the SES knew they would have less job tenure and could be transferred more easily within an agency or to another agency. At the same time, they became eligible for substantial cash bonuses for merit. Well over 90 percent of eligible government executives joined the SES.

The idea behind the creation of the SES was to establish a nucleus of top executives in the government in a way that would balance career risk-taking against rewards for high performance, and at the same time would emphasize mobility, managerial discretion in assignments, and accountability.[61]

But difficulties soon developed in carrying out the Carter reforms. In 1980, NASA gave almost half of its senior managers merit bonuses. Alarmed, Congress for a time restricted the number and size of the awards. Many senior executives were angered, and there were complaints that favoritism and politics had distorted the cash bonus system. Over time, however, many of these early difficulties faded and the senior executives received substantially higher pay. In enacting the reform law, Congress had sought to apply the carrot-and-stick incentives of private industry to the massive federal bureaucracy. To an extent, at least, the experiment had succeeded.

Bureaucracy and Society

During his campaign for president in 1976, Jimmy Carter promised to make drastic reductions in the size of the federal bureaucracy if elected. But as president, he scaled down the scope of his plans to reorganize the government. He did propose and achieve reorganization of the civil service system, as already discussed. And Congress at his request established the Department of Energy and created the Department of Education and the Department of Health and Human Services, largely by splitting the old Department of Health, Education, and Welfare. The Carter administration also reorganized some other parts of the bureaucracy, including agencies dealing with civil rights, civil defense, and international communications.

Ronald Reagan promised during the 1980 campaign to abolish the Department of Energy and the Department of Education if elected. But as president, he found it easier said than done. Twelve years later, in 1992, the two cabinet departments still existed.

Reagan had campaigned against the bureaucracy, however, and as president he moved to try to control the bureaucracy and to reduce its power. In this effort, Reagan relied on presidential counselor Edwin Meese III, later attorney general, to oversee the administration's personnel policies. Meese sent a memo to all departments and agencies saying that job performance ratings for federal workers could be used "to insure that administration . . . policies are appropriately carried out."[62] Critics immediately charged that the White House was attempting to use the performance appraisal system "to enforce ideological discipline among career civil service employees."[63]

When the nation's air traffic controllers went on strike in August of 1981, Reagan fired some 12,000 of them. The strikers were members of the Professional Air Traffic Controllers Organization (PATCO), ironically one of the few unions to have endorsed Reagan in the 1980 presidential campaign. Supervisory personnel of the Federal Aviation Administration and military air

---

[61] James P. McGrath, *Civil Service Reform Act: Implementation* (Washington, D.C.: The Library of Congress, Congressional Research Service, 1980), p. 9.

[62] Dick Kirschten, "Administration Using Carter-Era Reform to Manipulate the Levers of Government," *National Journal*, April 9, 1983, p. 733.

[63] Rep. Patricia Schroeder, D., Colo., Ibid.

INDIVIDUAL CONSCIENCE AND BUREAUCRACY

The overriding concern with institutions should be how we as individuals can tell our institutions that they are not going to have a momentum of their own . . . that they are going to reflect individual inputs . . . that the individual in these large institutions, whether they are companies or government agencies or other organizations, must reassert his rights . . . and that every person who is part of a large organization must have that line drawn for himself beyond which he will no longer subserve himself to the dictates of the organization, beyond which he will say . . . my loyalty to mankind, to my society, to my fellow citizen, overrides my loyalty to my organization and that is where I must place my commitment and knowledge. Unless every individual somewhere in his mind draws that line when he will no longer simply take orders . . . unless every individual has that line drawn for himself, he will have within him a potential slice of the Nuremberg problem.

—Ralph Nader,
commencement address at
Franklin Pierce College, 1970

controllers manned the radar screens, and many flights were curtailed. But, in time, the strike was broken. Reagan emphasized that the walkout was illegal, since the strikers had defied a court order to return to their jobs, but his tough stance was a message to the bureaucracy as a whole.

Rational Decision Making

One of the criticisms of bureaucracy is that its decision making tends to be "incremental" — that is, what was decided yesterday limits the scope of choice today. New policies, instead of replacing old ones, tend to be "added on" to existing programs because government officials are usually wary of sweeping change or policy innovations.

Peter Drucker has suggested: "Certain things are inherently difficult for government. Being by design a protective institution, it is not good at innovation. It cannot really abandon anything. The moment government undertakes anything it becomes entrenched and permanent."[64]

Because of the obstacles to innovation, bureaucracy may overlook problems that do not fit into established forms. A former surgeon general of the United States, Dr. William H. Stewart, once told a Senate subcommittee on poverty that the federal government did not know the extent of hunger and malnutrition in

America. "We just don't know," he said. "It hasn't been anybody's job."

On the other hand, bureaucracy is sometimes able to use its resources to attack the problems of society. For example, earlier than many private employers, the federal government was active in helping minorities, women, and the disadvantaged through "affirmative action" hiring policies and programs.

Often, when government is confronted with a new task, a new agency is established to handle it. For example, during the Kennedy administration, the Peace Corps was made independent of the State Department, and during the Johnson administration, the poverty program was created as a separate agency. The tendency to start new agencies for new programs to some extent reflects resistance to change on the part of old-line, existing agencies.

In an attempt to break through traditional forms of bureaucratic decision making, the federal government beginning in the 1960s tried to apply newer techniques of management technology to policy problems. The goal of the "rationalists," as advocates of the new techniques were sometimes called, was to arrive at decisions on the basis of systematic analysis, rather than on the basis of guesswork or custom.

The new methods often utilized electronic computers to analyze masses of data. One of the new management tools, known as "cost effectiveness," or "systems analysis," was inaugurated at the Pentagon in 1961 by former Defense Secretary Robert S. McNamara, who said that the technique helped to measure the benefits

---

[64] Drucker, *The Age of Discontinuity*, p. 226.

THE CLOCK-WATCHERS

The request from an Upper West Side restaurant to erect a large clock on a Broadway sidewalk had proceeded smoothly through the city's complicated approval process.

Only one defect marred the project's otherwise orderly flow through the city bureaucracy: The black, 19-foot-high clock has been standing in front of the Ancora Restaurant at Broadway and 85th Street off and on for more than a year. When city officials discovered that last month, they issued an ultimatum to the restaurant's owners. If you want permission to erect the clock, you must first remove it.

But discussions produced a less severe solution. The restaurant's owners agreed to donate to a community cause the $5,000 it would have cost to tear down and then reinstall the clock. In addition, they agreed to remove the restaurant's name from above the clock.

"You would think 18 months would be enough to finish the normal planning process," [Douglas] Griebel [one of the partners in the restaurant] said. "I'm not putting up Trump Tower, after all."

—Adapted from *New York Times*, August 5, 1986

Clock in front of Ancora Restaurant

of alternative policies against their dollar costs. Presidents Johnson, Nixon, Ford, and Carter also sought to apply such management systems to control the federal budget.

Efforts to apply the tools and techniques of rational decision making to reform the management of the executive branch have been both praised and criticized. The system works best for areas in which goals can be "quantified"—expressed in dollar amounts. Thus, within limits, the Pentagon can use this technique to measure the relative merits and cost of weapons systems and military hardware. But in areas like welfare, education, and foreign policy, correct choices cannot so easily be arrived at by measuring benefits against costs. The long-range benefits to American society from an improved educational system, for example, cannot be evaluated wholly by a computer.

Checks on Bureaucratic Power

Bureaucracy is big, and powerful. There are, however, some visible checks on that power. First, government agencies must share power with other elites in the political system, not only competing agencies in the executive branch, but also Congress, the courts, and groups and leaders outside the government. When government agencies mobilize political support among private industry or other "client" groups, they give up some of their independence and power in the process. In addition to sharing power with other parts of government and with interest groups, officials are held in check to some degree by the press. Fear of adverse publicity is a powerful factor in decision making in Washington, as well as in state and local government. Moreover, in recent years some government employees have become

WHISTLE BLOWING: A DANGEROUS OCCUPATION

When Victor McKay tried to warn the government that it was wasting millions on a foreign aid program, he says his memo was thrown into a trash can and he was later fired.

When Clif McKenzie complained that the Bureau of Indian Affairs in Oklahoma was authorizing illegal travel advances, his supervisors soon found his work performance "unacceptable" and he, too, lost his job.

And when Shirley Stoll exposed instances of patient abuse at a Veterans Administration hospital in Missouri, she was labeled a troublemaker, she says, and confined to a tiny room at work where she could receive no visitors and make no phone calls. Four months later she, too, was fired.

McKay, McKenzie, and Stoll are a sampling of the nation's "whistle-blowers," federal workers who see and report what they believe is government waste, mismanagement and fraud. Their fates, and those of others who have "gone public," reflect the adage about killing the messenger with the bad news. Blowing the whistle can be tantamount to professional suicide, and some who tell all end up wishing they had never opened their mouths.

—*Washington Post*, October 3, 1982

"whistle-blowers"; that is, they have publicly exposed evidence of waste or corruption that they learned about in the course of their duties.

Whistle-blowers   Whistle-blowing can sometimes turn out to be a significant factor within the bureaucracy. For example, in 1968, A. Ernest Fitzgerald, a Pentagon official, exposed a $2-billion cost overrun in the C-5A aircraft program. After this, Fitzgerald was forced out of his $32,000-a-year job; he was not reinstated until 1973. His reinstatement followed the disclosure in Senate Watergate testimony that a White House aide had complained about Fitzgerald's revelations in a memo that said, "only a basic no-goodnik would take his official business grievances so far from normal channels." Later it was revealed that President Nixon had personally ordered Fitzgerald fired.

And whistle-blowers often pay a high price for their actions. Although Fitzgerald was reinstated, he was not, at first, reassigned to the same level of work as he had done before his dismissal. Finally, in 1982, a federal court ordered Fitzgerald reinstated to his original job in the air force.

Other whistle-blowers, less well known, also have been fired. Consider, for example, the case of Dr. J. Anthony Morris, a government virologist. In 1976 a soldier at Fort Dix, New Jersey, died of swine flu. Fearing a nationwide epidemic, the director of the federal Centers for Disease Control called for a national program of immunization. Two weeks later, President Ford told the nation he was asking for $135 million to launch a massive inoculation program.[65] Alone within the government, Dr. Morris opposed the program; he had been questioning the value of flu shots for several years. He vigorously protested that there was no evidence the swine flu would cause an epidemic like the one that had occurred in 1918. And, he warned, the vaccine was

A. Ernest Fitzgerald, cost-minded Pentagon employee

[65] See Richard E. Neustadt and Harvey V. Fineberg, M.D., *The Swine Flu Affair* (Washington, D.C.: U.S. Department of Health, Education, and Welfare, 1978).

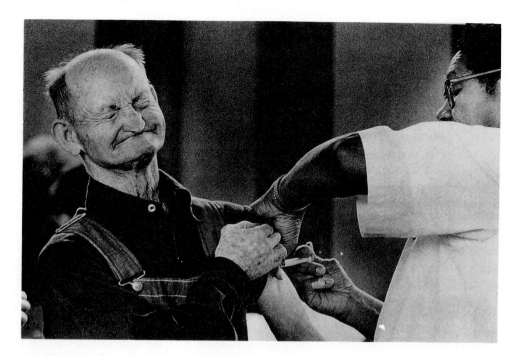

Some 50 million Americans were given swine flu vaccine, despite the risks.

dangerous. At age fifty-eight, Dr. Morris was fired from his $32,000 research job by the head of the Food and Drug Administration, who found him guilty of "insubordination and inefficiency."[66]

Inoculations started in October 1976, were suspended for a time, and then cut off entirely in February 1977. Some 50 million Americans were given swine flu vaccine, but the program was halted after several persons became seriously ill with Guillain-Barré syndrome, a rare paralytic disease. By January 1988, 4,178 claims totaling $3.2 billion had been filed against the government. The lawsuits also claimed that at least 360 deaths and more than 1600 cases of Guillain-Barré disease had resulted from the flu shots.[67]

There have been many similar stories. When John Kartak, an Army recruiter in Minneapolis discovered his office had forged high school diplomas and concealed criminal records to meet recruiting quotas, he called the Army whistle-blower hotline. The Army responded by ordering two psychological evaluations of Kartak, whose superior said he had been filing a lot of complaints lately and was "highly unstable." But Kartak was vindicated when the Army eventually determined

his charges were true and found 58 people in the office guilty of engaging in illegal acts.[68] Less fortunate was Joseph Setepani of the Food and Drug Administration, who protested the use of carcinogens and mutagens in food supplies. Setepani "was reassigned to long-term research in a trailer on an experimental farm."[69]

In 1978, Congress created an Office of Special Counsel to protect whistle-blowers, but it proved ineffective; government workers who exposed waste were still subject to retaliation. In 1988, Congress enacted— but President Reagan pocket-vetoed—a new law to make the office independent and strengthen its powers. In 1989, however, Congress reenacted the Whistleblower Protection Act, and President Bush signed it into law. Although whistle-blowers may pay a high price, the possibility of exposure from within the bureaucracy sometimes acts to curb potential abuses.

Other Checks on Bureaucracy In addition, there are certain "inner checks" on the bureaucracy. To some extent at least, bureaucrats may be inhibited from abusing their power by the social and political system in which they operate. Like other citizens, bureaucrats have been politically socialized, and in many cases they

[66] Helen Dudar, "The Price of Blowing the Whistle," *New York Times Magazine,* October 30, 1977, pp. 48–49.
[67] Data provided by Torts Division, Department of Justice; and *New York Times,* June 10, 1979, p. 1.

[68] *Washington Post,* August 25, 1989, p. A19.
[69] Ibid.

may tend to adhere to standards of fair play and respect for individual rights. But relying on individual conscience is rather uncertain, and the search continues for institutionalized methods of control. The device of the *ombudsman*, for example, has proved popular in Sweden and in some other countries. The *ombudsman* is an official complaint-taker who tries to help citizens wronged by the actions of government agencies.

The courts and the legal system also play a role in controlling bureaucracy. Ten officials of the Nixon administration were convicted and jailed in the Watergate scandal. In 1980 two former high-ranking FBI officials were tried in federal court on charges of violating the constitutional rights of citizens by authorizing FBI break-ins in the search for radical fugitives in the early 1970s. They were convicted, but later pardoned by President Reagan. Several high-level officials of the Reagan administration and other individuals were charged with crimes as a result of the Iran-contra scandal; some were convicted.

More than one hundred officials of the Reagan administration were accused of illegal or unethical conduct, forced to resign, indicted, or convicted.[70] The unusual number of aides involved in improprieties of one sort or another gave the Democrats a "sleaze factor" that they sought to exploit in the 1988 presidential campaign.

Despite these checks, the problems posed by bureaucracy remain. Yet as long as government has responsibility for allocating things of value, for deciding who gets what in American society, there will be bureaucrats to help make and carry out those decisions. Bureaucrats are convenient political targets, vulnerable to attack, and their shortcomings will no doubt continue to be criticized. Nevertheless, the government could not function without bureaucrats. At the same time, the problem of controlling bureaucracy and making it serve the people is a continuing challenge to the American system.

PERSPECTIVE

Bureaucracy and bureaucrats are handy political targets to blame for society's ills. Yet government at every level — federal, state, and local — could not function without bureaucrats, or public administrators, to run it.

[70] *Washington Post*, February 9, 1988, p. E7.

Today, Americans frequently turn to the federal government to solve or alleviate problems of the economy, of the cities, of mass transportation, of poverty, pollution, public health, and energy. As long as people demand more and more services from their government, some form of bureaucracy is inevitable.

In theory, bureaucrats are simply public servants who administer policy decisions made by the accountable officials of the government, including the president and Congress. In fact, public administrators by their actions — or inaction — often make policy. Bureaucrats have discretionary powers; what they decide to do, or not to do, constitutes a major policy output of the political system.

Bureaucrats help to shape policy through the advice they give to elected officials. As a practical matter, elected officials are confined to choosing policies and programs that the bureaucracies are capable of carrying out.

The American bureaucracy is deeply involved in politics. Bureaucrats have constituencies; these are interest groups, or client groups, either directly regulated by the bureaucracy or vitally affected by its decisions. Sometimes, through close political and personal association between a government agency and its client group, the agency becomes a captive of the industry it is supposed to regulate. A bureaucracy is often able to increase its political strength by building a constituency of such client groups.

Another source of bureaucratic power stems from the political support an agency may enjoy in Congress, particularly among influential committee chairpersons. Agencies that do not enjoy cordial relations with important members of the legislative branch may find their power diminished. The cabinet departments employ hundreds of persons to engage in liaison with Congress. The large number of liaison officers reflects congressional demands as well as an effort by government agencies to win support on Capitol Hill.

The bureaucracy, interest groups, and congressional committees interact, sometimes forming an especially powerful alliance of mutual benefit known as a "triangle." But today "issue networks" made up of activists may also play an important role in shaping public policy in a specific area.

A government agency that enjoys wide public support has an advantage over agencies that do not. The president and Congress are both sensitive to public opinion, and a popular, prestigious agency may receive more appropriations and achieve greater independence than others. To improve their "image" and enlist public support for their programs, many federal agencies employ public relations people and information specialists.

Since 1918, Congress has from time to time given presidents the right to restructure the executive branch. The creation in 1970 of the Office of Management and Budget gave the president an important lever for bureaucratic control.

Today there are approximately 3.1 million civilian employees of the federal government. Yet, more than four times as many people work for state and local governments as for the federal government.

The federal bureaucracy consists of three basic types of agencies: cabinet departments, independent executive agencies, and independent regulatory commissions. In 1992 there were fourteen cabinet departments. At first glance, a cabinet department might appear to be a tightly organized agency, with lines of authority flowing upward to the secretary, who in turn reports to the president. In fact, each department has entrenched bureaus and key civil servants, some of whom enjoy close outside ties with interest groups and congressional committees — relationships that give them power independent of the cabinet secretary and the president.

Independent executive agencies report to the president in the same manner as departments, but are separate from the cabinet departments. Their heads are appointed by the president and may be dismissed by him.

Independent regulatory commissions occupy a special status in the bureaucracy, for they are administratively independent of all three branches of government. However, they are susceptible to pressures from the White House, Congress, and the industries they regulate. These agencies were created because of the need for rule making and regulation in highly complex technical areas involving the interests of the public.

In recent years Congress has reduced government control over the airline, trucking, and railroad industries. The rising tide of deregulation sentiment reflected complaints by business of excessive and costly government regulation, red tape, delay, and paperwork. Deregulation brought new problems, however. Three major airlines went out of business and thousands of airline workers lost their jobs.

Even as economic regulation has been relaxed in some industries in recent years, social regulation by the federal government has increased in such areas as civil rights, the environment, and safety in the work place.

Presidents have always rewarded their political supporters and friends with government jobs. But the vast majority of government jobs are filled through the competitive civil service system, which was reorganized under President Carter in 1978. The Office of Personnel Management acts as a recruiting agency for the bureaucracy. The Senior Executive Service offers top-level federal officials cash incentives for high performance, but less job security.

Although the bureaucracy is powerful, there are external checks on that power. Government agencies must share power with other elites in the political system, including Congress, the courts, and interest groups. Officials are also held in check to some degree by the press. In recent years some government employees, acting as "whistle-blowers," have publicly exposed evidence of waste or corruption in government, sometimes at the cost of their jobs. There are also inner checks on the bureaucracy. Like other citizens, bureaucrats have been politically socialized and may tend to adhere to standards of fair play and respect for individual rights. And bureaucrats who break the law may be punished by the courts. Nevertheless, controlling the bureaucracy remains a continuing challenge.

Suggested Readings

Altshuler, Alan A., and Thomas, Norman C., eds. *The Politics of the Federal Bureaucracy,* 2nd edition* (Harper & Row, 1977). A useful examination of the role of the federal bureaucracy in the political system. Stresses the political dynamics of how the bureaucracy operates.

Chubb, John E. *Interest Groups and the Bureaucracy: The Politics of Energy* (Stanford University Press, 1983). A study of the relationship between interest groups and bureaucracy and of the effects of that interaction on public policy. Argues that much of the contact between interest groups and government agencies is initiated by the agencies.

Heclo, Hugh. *A Government of Strangers** (The Brookings Institution, 1977). An important analysis of the relations between political leaders and the bureaucracy. Heclo identifies weaknesses in the nation's political structure and suggests reforms to bring about more effective executive leadership.

Kaufman, Herbert. *Are Government Organizations Immortal?** (The Brookings Institution, 1976). An interesting and thought-provoking exploration of the factors that work for or against the survival of governmental agencies once they have been established.

Mosher, Frederick C. *Democracy and the Public Service,* 2nd edition* (Oxford University Press, 1982). An excellent and readable discussion of various trends in the public service, including professionalization, unionization, and the merit system. Discusses their implications for democratic government.

Rourke, Francis E. *Bureaucracy, Politics, and Public Policy*, 3rd edition* (Scott, Foresman & Co., 1984). A concise and valuable general introduction to the role of the bureaucracy in the making of public policy. Among other topics, the book analyzes the sources of power of government bureaucracies, and new approaches to policymaking in bureaucratic agencies.

Seidman, Harold, and Silmoor, Robert S. *Politics, Position, and Power: From the Positive to the Regulatory State*, 4th edition* (Oxford University Press, 1986). An enlightening discussion of the operations of government agencies and the political realities affecting proposals for their reorganization.

Simon, Herbert A. *Administrative Behavior: A Study of Decision-Making Processes in Administrative Organizations*, 3rd edition* (Free Press, 1976). A classic theoretical and empirical analysis of decision making in government bureaucracies. This book, first published in 1947, has influenced modern scholarly work on bureaucratic organizations.

White, Leonard D. *The Federalists* (Greenwood, 1978). (Originally published in 1948); *The Jeffersonians, 1801–1829* (Macmillan, 1951); *The Jacksonians, 1829–1861* (Macmillan, 1954); and *The Republican Era, 1869–1901* (Macmillan, 1958). A notable and detailed study, in four volumes, of the historical development of the American public service from 1789 to the turn of the twentieth century.

Wildavsky, Aaron. *The New Politics of the Budgetary Process*, 2nd edition (New York: HarperCollins, 1992). A revealing analysis of the nature of the federal budgetary process and its relationship to the making of public policy. Discusses and summarizes the important changes in the 1990 budget reconciliation act.

Wilson, James Q. *Bureaucracy: What Government Agencies Do and Why They Do It* (Basic Books, 1989). A comprehensive survey of why government agencies in the United States behave in the ways they do. Stresses the important differences that can be found among various agencies.

Wilson, James Q. *The Politics of Regulation** (Basic, 1980). A valuable collection of nine case studies on public policymaking and the relationship between the public and private sectors in Washington regulatory agencies. Includes a discussion of the political and historical origins of a wide range of agencies—from state public utility commissions to the Federal Trade Commission.

---

* Available in paperback edition.

ON AUGUST 3, 1987, Senator Daniel K. Inouye, the chairman of the Senate committee investigating the Iran-contra affair, delivered his closing remarks to the television cameras and the American people.

For 250 hours, the committee and a House panel had taken testimony from twenty-eight witnesses who unfolded a tale of how the Reagan administration had secretly sold arms to Iran to try to free American hostages in the Middle East, then siphoned off the profits to the contras in Nicaragua. Somehow, even more millions of dollars had also ended up in the Swiss bank accounts of the private individuals involved.

Marine Lt. Col. Oliver L. North, who ran the secret operation from the White House, had, briefly, cap-

Chapter 12

The Congress

tured the imagination of the American public; he wore his uniform when he testified and was perceived by many viewers as a hero. But he admitted to the congressional committees that he had misled Congress and shredded key documents. Rear Adm. John M. Poindexter, the president's national security adviser, also said he had destroyed evidence to save the president embarrassment.

"The story has now been told," Inouye said. "I see it as a chilling story, a story of deceit and duplicity and the arrogant disregard of the rule of law. . . . Vigilance abroad does not require us to abandon our ideals or the rule of law at home. On the contrary, without our principles and without our ideals, we have little that is special or worthy to defend."

In the end, the senator said, "a great nation betrayed the principles which have made it great, and thereby became hostage to the hostage-takers."[1]

---

[1] *New York Times*, August 4, 1987, p. 1.

More than a decade earlier, on the evening of July 24, 1974, under the bright television lights, Congressman Peter W. Rodino, Jr., the silver-haired chairman of the House Committee on the Judiciary, slowly began reading a statement as the nation watched. An American flag and the oil portraits of Rodino's predecessors on the wall formed a backdrop in the dark-paneled committee room on Capitol Hill.

"Almost two centuries ago," he said, "the Founding Fathers of the United States reaffirmed . . . that here all men are under the law, and it is only the people who are sovereign. So speaks our Constitution, and it is under our Constitution, the supreme law of the land, that we proceed through the sole power of impeachment. We have reached the moment when we are ready to debate . . . whether or not the Committee on the Judiciary should recommend that the House of Representatives adopt articles calling for the impeachment of Richard M. Nixon."

"Make no mistake about it. This is a turning point, whatever we decide. Our judgment is not concerned with an individual but with a system of constitutional government. . . . Let us leave the Constitution as unimpaired for our children as our predecessors left it to us."

For six days the thirty-eight members of the committee debated the question of the impeachment of the president. Although the committee was deeply divided, the debate was conducted with dignity and, at times, with great eloquence. Many citizens might hold

Congress in low esteem, but on this occasion the committee and its chairman earned the nation's respect.

Three articles of impeachment were adopted by the committee. The articles accused President Nixon of covering up the burglary of the Democratic headquarters in the Watergate office building; of abuse of power by using the FBI, the CIA, the Internal Revenue Service, and other federal agencies in an illegal manner; and of failing to surrender tapes and documents subpoenaed by the committee. Within ten days of the final vote of the committee, Richard Nixon had resigned his office.

In 1991, the American public was outraged at disclosures that members of the House of Representatives had written 8,331 bad checks on the private bank maintained for members. But unlike checks written by ordinary citizens who overdraw their accounts, those written by the representatives did not bounce, but were honored by the bank. As the House bank scandal grew, eventually the names of 247 members of Congress and 56 former members who wrote overdrafts were made public. Some individual legislators had written hundreds of bad checks totalling hundreds of thousands of dollars.

For example, Representative Stephen J. Solarz, a New York Democrat, wrote 743 overdrafts totalling $594,646; Representative Robert W. Davis, a Michigan Republican, wrote 878 overdrafts totalling $344,450; and Representative Robert J. Mrazek, a New York Democrat, held the record for the largest number of checks, 920, totalling $351,609. As the names of the offenders were publicized, many chose to retire from the House rather than to try to explain their actions to the voters. By mid-1992, forty-eight House members and seven senators had announced their retirements.

The check scandal focused attention on other "perks" or privileges enjoyed by representatives and senators, including their own dining rooms, hideaway offices, health facilities, medical services, barber shops, and a cut-rate store. On top of the check scandal, irregularities were uncovered in the House Post Office. These disclosures came soon after widespread publicity about "the Keating 5," five senators accused of intervening on behalf of Charles H. Keating, Jr., a big contributor to their campaigns who was eventually imprisoned for his role in the scandal that surrounded the collapse of many of the nation's savings and loan banks.

All of these scandals contributed to the voter disillusion with politics and politicians that was apparent during the 1992 election year. But it was not only the voters who were disenchanted with the process — many members of Congress, including some who retired, also expressed frustration with their own jobs and complained of the difficulty of getting anything done on Capitol Hill.

DIARY OF A DROPOUT

After 18 years on Capitol Hill, Senator Tim Wirth, Democrat of Colorado, described how his illusions were shattered and why, within one week, he chose not to run for a second term in the United States Senate:

I am leaving the Senate now because I have become frustrated with the posturing and paralysis of Congress. I even fear that the political process has made me a person I don't like.

. . . all the time it took to raise funds was time not spent talking with constituents, not tending to legislative business and not actually campaigning. That style of grass-roots, county-courthouse politics was, for me, more myth than memory.

Unhappily, the first loyalty of any candidate is too often to self and re-election, rather than to any broad political organization or community of like-minded activists.

Politics was consuming us all. A basic reason our institution was in trouble, I said, was that we were too often engaged in trivia and not performing the work for which we were elected.

The truth was that I dreaded the campaign that lay ahead and . . . of having to spend another six years . . . hating to go to work every morning. One reason the Senate had become such a dispiriting place to work was that most of its members felt the same impotence I did in the face of the staggering deficits that had turned the United States Government into a holding operation, rather than an arena for innovation.

—*New York Times Magazine*, August 9, 1992

"Perhaps the witness would care to reconsider his answer to the last question?"

Drawing by Stevenson
©1979 The New Yorker Magazine, Inc.

Mike Peters reprinted by permission of UFS, Inc.

The hearings on the Iran-contra affair by the Senate and House investigating committees, and the actions of the House Judiciary Committee during the impeachment inquiry, contrasted with the behavior of some lawmakers in the House bank scandal.

These events tell something both about Congress and public perceptions of Congress. In the Iran-contra affair, the televised hearings and the later final report of the two committees helped to lay the facts before the American people. And in the impeachment debate, the House committee acted in a manner worthy of a great deliberative body. In the House bank scandal, by

"I'm sorry, sir, Congressman Clayborne isn't in at the moment. He's doing two to five for mail fraud."

Drawing by Mulligan ©1979 The New Yorker Magazine, Inc.

contrast, many members of Congress appeared to be abusing their power by engaging in a practice beyond the reach of ordinary voters. The contrast in the way members of Congress acted in these and other episodes is reflected in the public's varying views of Congress.

Fundamental questions may be asked about the performance of Congress in the American political system. Are too many members of Congress insensitive to ethical standards? Can Congress meet the social needs of the American people in the twentieth century? Or is it a hopelessly outmoded institution, hobbled by powerful special interests and undesirable fragmentation? How well does Congress represent the voters and should it lead or follow them? What is the role of Congress in the American political system as a whole? How well does it perform that role?

Congress is a much-criticized institution. At the outset, therefore, we shall discuss Congress within the framework of the controversy that swirls around it. We shall examine in some detail the case for and the case against Congress.

CONGRESS: CONFLICT AND CONTROVERSY

The Case Against Congress

For more than twenty years, until the enactment of Medicare in 1965, Congress declined to pass health care legislation for the elderly. Yet the need for such help

was clear enough: in March 1965, a few months before passage of Medicare, the median income of Americans aged sixty-five and over was *$1,355 a year*.[2] Obviously, on such incomes most older Americans were unable to afford adequate health care in the face of rising medical costs. What is more, the public supported such legislation; a Gallup poll in 1962 showed 69 percent in favor of Medicare.[3] By 1940 every Western European country had some form of government health insurance. Yet the United States, the richest country in the world, had failed to act. A powerful interest group, the American Medical Association, fought Medicare as "socialized medicine," and for two decades Congress would not be moved.

Nor was Medicare an isolated example. President Kennedy was killed by gunfire in 1963, his brother Robert in 1968, and Martin Luther King, Jr., that same year. While campaigning for the Democratic presidential nomination, Alabama Governor George Wallace was shot and severely wounded in 1972. In 1981, President Reagan was shot and seriously wounded after only a little more than two months in office. Despite the hue and cry for gun control after each tragedy, America in 1992 had no broadly effective federal gun-control legis-

[2] U.S. Bureau of the Census, *Statistical Abstract of the United States*, 1969, p. 279.
[3] Peter A. Corning, *The Evolution of Medicare*, U.S. Department of Health, Education, and Welfare (Washington, D.C.: U.S. Government Printing Office, 1969), p. 93.

GUNS AND VIOLENCE: "A PUBLIC HEALTH EMERGENCY"

WASHINGTON, June 9—Gunshot wounds are the second-leading cause of death among all high-school-age children in the United States, and they are increasing faster than any other cause in that age group among both whites and blacks, according to Federal statistics published today. One third of high school students say they have easy access to handguns, and six percent of them say they bring handguns to school. About six percent of high school students say they actually own handguns, and among those about one third have fired them at someone.

General owners of handguns give as their chief reason for owning one "protec-

tion from crime," but gun owners kill themselves and family members 43 times as often as they shoot down a criminal at home.

. . . homicide and suicide deaths by gunshot rose from 12 per 100,000 [people age 15 to 19] in 1979 to 18 per 100,000 in 1989.

The studies overall, said Dr. [George] Lundberg, "paint a grotesque picture of a society steeped in violence, especially by firearms, with such ubiquity and prevalence as to be seemingly accepted as inevitable." It is not inevitable, he said, adding, "Violence in America is a public health emergency."

—*New York Times*, June 10, 1992

As President Bush and Congress prepare for the November [1992] elections, few can recall a time when relations between the two branches of government have been more contentious in manner, barren of substance and infuriating to the American people.

More often than not, Congress's Democratic majority rejects Bush's proposals, Bush vetoes proposals from the Democrats, and Congress cannot override the vetoes.

Bills are delayed or killed, and vital matters are ignored, trivialized or manipulated for partisan advantage.

The more Bush and Congress slide in the polls, the more they harden their positions, seeking political salvation in blaming the other side. And the more they engage in what lawmakers of both parties describe as a "blame game," the more they slide in the polls.

As a way to describe it, Americans have embraced a word more often associated with traffic jams than governance — "gridlock."

—*Washington Post*, August 3, 1992

---

lation. In the more than two decades since Robert Kennedy's assassination, an estimated 600,000 persons were killed by handguns in the United States.[4] In the nation's cities, including the capital, Washington, D.C., "drive-by" shootings among inner-city youths, often drug-related, have become commonplace. Yet Congress, under pressure by the gun lobby, passed only limited legislation to deal with this major national problem.

When Representative Richard Bolling, a Missouri Democrat, served in the House, he put the question bluntly: "Is the Congress to continue as the least responsible organ of Government, acting, if at all, ten and twenty and thirty years late?"[5] Too often, Congress has seemed caught in a "gridlock," unable to act. This has especially been true during periods of "divided government," when a Republican president has faced a Democratic-controlled Congress.

Not every analyst believes that divided government always blocks the passage of important legislation, however. After studying 267 major laws enacted from 1947 through 1990, political scientist David R. Mayhew concluded that in recent times when one party controls both Congress and the White House it "has not made an important difference" in congressional investigations or the output of major legislation. Mayhew added: "From the Taft-Hartley Act and Marshall Plan of 1947–48 through the Clean Air Act and $490 billion

deficit-reduction package of 1990, important laws have materialized at a rate largely unrelated to conditions of party control."[6]

Although Congress has reformed and modernized its procedures in recent years and has opened up most of its committee meetings, some argue that the reforms have diluted the power of the committee chairpersons and left Congress fragmented and undirected. Until the mid-1970s, under the workings of the seniority system, those members of Congress with longest continuous service on a committee automatically became heads of committees. The seniority system was criticized for rewarding age, rather than merit, and for concentrating too much power in the hands of a few old, often conservative, committee chairpersons who were accountable to no one. That is no longer true. Chairpersons are

---

[6] David R. Mayhew, *Divided We Govern* (New Haven: Yale University Press, 1991), p. 4.

Mike Peters reprinted by permission of UFS, Inc.

---

[4] In 1989, there were 35,000 firearm deaths in the United States, including 18,000 suicides, 15,000 homicides, and 1,500 accidents. Source: *New York Times*, April 3, 1992, p. 1.

[5] Richard Bolling, *Power in the House* (New York: Dutton, 1968), p. 269.

now elected by their party colleagues. They still tend to be the older members with longer years of service, but because their selection is no longer automatic, they now must be much more responsive to the wishes of other members of their committee, and to other legislators.

Congress also has sometimes been assailed in the past, although less frequently today, for rules and procedures designed to block rather than facilitate the passage of legislation. In the Senate, the filibuster is the traditional weapon of obstruction and delay. In the House, until 1961 and even beyond, the Rules Committee exercised rigid control over what bills were brought to the floor for debate. Nor does Congress always get its work done on time. On several occasions, for example, it has failed to act on the federal budget in time for the government to meet its payroll. When that happens, Congress has resorted to "continuing resolutions" to fund the departments and keep federal workers on the job.

And in the past many of the norms and customs of the House and Senate tended to reward conformity. Although today it is no longer true that the newcomer to Congress is expected to be seen and not heard, the paternalistic atmosphere of the not-too-distant past was best summarized by then Speaker Sam Rayburn's advice to his colleagues in the House: "If you want to *get* along, *go* along."[7]

In the field of foreign affairs, Congress has often been criticized for yielding too much power to the president. Under the Kennedy, Johnson, and Nixon administrations, the United States engaged in a major, divisive military conflict in Vietnam, although Congress never declared war. The War Powers Resolution, passed in 1973, was an important attempt by Congress to reassert its authority. In the two decades since the resolution was passed, however, the law had not effectively restricted the president's military power. In the Persian Gulf, President Bush embarked on a major war against Iraq in 1991 without a declaration of war by Congress, although Congress did pass a resolution authorizing the use of military force.

As congressional investigations in the mid-1970s revealed, Congress (and the executive branch) failed to exercise proper control over the activities of the federal intelligence agencies. Although intelligence committees were established in the House and Senate in the wake of those investigations, they have performed their task of overseeing the intelligence agencies with mixed results. In the 1980s, for example, the Reagan administration covertly continued to support the contra rebels in Nicaragua despite a congressional ban on such activity, action that led to the Iran-contra affair. Congress was unable or unwilling to prevent the law-breaking that took place.

In the domestic field, many critics have asserted, Congress has largely approved or disapproved programs proposed by the chief executive, but has not initiated or innovated very much. In the twentieth century, there has been a discernible loss of power by legislatures and parliaments to presidents and prime ministers, and the United States has not been exempt from this "shift of initiative toward the executive."[8]

And, as already noted, Congress has been tarnished by scandal and by the questionable ethics and activities of some of its members. Some members of Congress travel abroad on "junkets" for dubious legislative purposes. Some have relatives on their office payroll. Many have accepted speaking fees from lobbyists. However, since 1991, members of the House and Senate have been prohibited from accepting fees for articles or speeches.

Since 1970, more than twenty-five members of Congress have been the subject of criminal charges.[9] Several members were prosecuted on charges that they had used their influence as legislators in return for bribes. (See Table 12-1.) Even the Speaker of the House, Representative Jim Wright of Texas, found it necessary to resign from Congress in 1989 after the House Ethics Committee accused him of evading limits on outside income by selling copies of his book, *Reflections of a Public Man*, and of taking $145,000 in improper gifts from a Texas developer.

The Case for Congress

Many political scientists who have studied the operation of Congress have concluded that Congress does a fairly good job on the whole. Those who defend Congress argue that it is a generally representative assembly that broadly mirrors the desires of the people. If it fails to act "fast enough" to meet social needs, perhaps it is because

[7] In Roger H. Davidson, *The Role of the Congressman* (New York: Pegasus, 1969), p. 180. The slogan was often heard in the Senate as well.

[8] David B. Truman, *The Congressional Party* (New York: Wiley, 1959), p. 7.

[9] Data provided by Library of Congress.

Table 12-1

Selected Conduct Cases in the House of Representatives

Following are examples of some well-known instances in which members of the House have been investigated by their colleagues:

Year	Allegations	Committee Action	House Action	Further Action
1798	Representative Matthew Lyon of Vermont, having been taunted, spat on Representative Roger Griswold of Connecticut on the House floor	Committee of the Whole heard evidence and recommended expulsion	Motions for censure and expulsion failed	Lyon wrote a letter of apology
1798	Representative Griswold hit Representative Lyon with a cane on the House floor. Representative Lyon responded with fireplace tongs	Committee on Privileges heard evidence and recommended against expulsion	Committee report adopted; motion to censure failed	House ordered both members to pledge to keep the peace
1838	Representative William J. Graves of Kentucky killed Representative Jonathan Gilley of Maine in a duel	Special committee recommended expulsion of Representative Graves and censure of two other members who had acted as seconds	The matter was tabled and reports and testimony were ordered printed	—
1856	Representative Preston S. Brooks of South Carolina assaulted Senator Charles Sumner of Massachusetts with a walking stick on the Senate floor over "certain language used by Mr. Sumner in [Senate] debates . . . which Mr. Brooks considered libelous of the State of South Carolina and slanderous of his near kinsman, Mr. [Andrew Pickens] Butler, a Senator from that State"	Special committee recommended expulsion	Resolution for expulsion failed to achieve the necessary two-thirds vote	Brooks resigned after vote
1983	Representative Gerry E. Studds of Massachusetts, relationship with House page	Committee on Standards held investigation and recommended reprimand	Censured by House	—
1988	Representative Mario Biaggi of New York, illegal gratuities: accepting free trips in return for official action	Committee on Standards held inquiry and disciplinary hearing; unanimously recommended expulsion	House deferred action on expulsion resolution while member was defending against second prosecution	Member resigned from the House and went to prison after conviction
1990	Representative Robert Garcia of New York, bribery, extortion, accepting illegal gratuities, conspiracy	After conviction, Committee on Standards initiated preliminary inquiry	—	Member convicted of extorting money from Wedtech Corporation; resigned from the House and served time in prison
1990	Representative Gus Savage of Illinois, improper sexual advances toward a female Peace Corps volunteer while traveling in his capacity as a member of Congress	Committee on Standards issued public report disapproving of the member's conduct	—	Member wrote letter of apology to volunteer
1990	Representative Barney Frank of Massachusetts, attempting to use political influence to affect probation of a male prostitute with whom he had a personal relationship	Committee on Standards initiated preliminary inquiry; committee recommended reprimand	House defeated resolutions of expulsion and censure; adopted resolution to reprimand member	—

SOURCE: Adapted from *Historical Summary of Conduct Cases in the House of Representatives*, Committee on Standards of Official Conduct, U.S. House of Representatives, April 1992.

the people do not want it to act any faster. And one may ask: "How fast is fast enough?"

To some extent, at least, Congress mirrors the diversity of American society. And often when Congress is divided on an issue and fails to act, it is because the country is divided on that issue. Ralph K. Huitt, a leading student of the congressional process, noted that at one time much criticism of Congress as being "obstructive" has come from liberals. As presidents such as Truman and Kennedy encountered obstacles to liberal programs, he argued, the critics urged reform of the structure and procedures of Congress to make it more responsive to the president. But Huitt also suggested that "elections do count and representation does work." For example, in 1965, "in the first session of the Eighty-ninth Congress, with a top-heavy Democratic majority that included some seventy generally liberal freshmen, President Johnson got approval of a massive domestic legislative program that might normally have taken twenty years."[10]

It may be argued that, to some degree, an internal system that places substantial power in the hands of individual committee and subcommittee chairpersons is necessary for Congress to function at all. Richard F. Fenno, Jr., studying the House of Representatives,

noted that a body of 435 people "must process a workload that is enormous, enormously complicated and enormously consequential. . . . To meet the more general problems, the House has developed a division of labor—a system of standing committees."[11] And the workload of Congress, measured by hours in session and the number of committee meetings, has increased dramatically since Fenno's study.[12]

Fenno concluded that the House enjoys stability as a result of "internal processes which have served to keep the institution from tearing itself apart while engaged in the business of decision making." For example, it is generally assumed that members will not "pursue internal conflicts to the point where the effectiveness of the House is impaired."[13]

In short, the House operates under a set of rules that may be necessary for *system maintenance*—that is, to keep a diverse, unwieldy institution functioning. From this basic premise has flowed the defense of such congressional procedures as the committee system and the tradition of elaborate courtesy that senators nor-

[10] Ralph K. Huitt, "Congress, the Durable Partner," in Ralph K. Huitt and Robert L. Peabody, eds., *Congress: Two Decades of Analysis* (New York: Harper & Row, 1969), p. 219.

[11] Richard F. Fenno, Jr., "The Internal Distribution of Influence: The House," in David B. Truman, ed., *The Congress and America's Future*, prepared for the American Assembly, Columbia University (Englewood Cliffs: Prentice-Hall, 1965), p. 53.

[12] Samuel C. Patterson, "The Semi-Sovereign Congress," in Anthony King, ed., *The New American Political System* (Washington, D.C.: American Enterprise Institute for Public Policy Research, 1978), pp. 158–59.

[13] Fenno, "The Internal Distribution of Influence: The House," p. 70.

TO SENATE WING

mally, although not always, display in addressing one another on the floor.

A case also may be made for some of the other procedures of Congress that are often condemned. Much of the earlier criticism of Congress originated with liberals and activists who were impatient for the national legislature to get on with the business of meeting social needs. And certainly the filibuster was used by southern senators to impede major civil-rights legislation. Yet, beginning in the 1970s, northern liberals discovered that they, too, were able to use the filibuster to oppose legislation. Moreover, congressional procedures sometimes protect the country in a crisis against hasty or misguided action that could result from bowing to popular emotion.

More than three decades ago, Senator Joseph S. Clark of Pennsylvania took the floor to denounce the "Senate establishment," and journalist William S. White wrote of an "Inner Club." Both terms described an elite group of leaders that was said to run the Senate.[14] Today, the picture has changed substantially; the old guard is gone and in its place has emerged a younger breed, many of whom have become highly visible as first-term senators. Yet no one who has spent any amount of time watching the United States Senate in action can doubt that some senators are a good deal more influential than others. As Nelson W. Polsby has

noted, however, each United States senator "enjoys high social status, great visibility, a large staff, and substantial powers in his own right."[15]

Some of the institutional factors that have distorted the representative nature of Congress have changed dramatically. In particular, the seniority system has been modified and made less rigid (see p. 461). As will be discussed, Congress in recent years also has made other important internal reforms. The abuses of malapportionment in the makeup of the House have been declared unconstitutional by the Supreme Court. As a result, the ideal of equal representation in terms of population is coming closer to being a reality. (Even though congressional districts now must be nearly equal, the problem remains of how the district lines should be drawn. Where these lines are drawn by state legislatures for political advantage, in order to favor one party or group over another, the district is said to be *gerrymandered*.) In addition, as discussed in Chapter 9, following the 1990 census, state legislatures created a number of congressional districts in which the majority of the population was black. The lines of these new districts were drawn to conform with the provisions of the Voting Rights Act.

To the charge that Congress no longer legislates effectively and has become a "rubber stamp" for the

---

[14] William S. White, *Citadel* (New York: Harper & Row, 1957), p. 84.

[15] Nelson W. Polsby, *Congress and the Presidency* (Englewood Cliffs: Prentice-Hall, 1964), p. 36.

chief executive, one can reply that this was certainly not President Bush's view as he clashed with the Democratic-controlled Congress over his legislative proposals and vetoed many of the bills that Congress had enacted.

Nor could it have been Richard Nixon's view. Congress rejected two of his nominees for the Supreme Court and passed the War Powers Resolution over his veto. And in 1974 it was the threat of impeachment by Congress that forced Nixon to resign—the first president ever to do so.

The War Powers Resolution is discussed in detail on pp. 374–375. That measure requires the president to report to and, where possible, consult with Congress when committing American combat troops overseas. The resolution has not proved as effective as its sponsors had hoped. Nevertheless, it represented a significant attempt by Congress to exercise more authority over foreign policy.

Certainly Congress does not confine itself to saying "yes" or "no" to presidential programs. To an extent that is perhaps underemphasized, Congress innovates and initiates, sometimes on matters of great importance. And since the passage of the Congressional Budget and Impoundment Control Act of 1974, Congress has taken a greater role in the entire budget process—the way in which the government decides how its money is spent.

Finally, those who view Congress in a more favorable light argue that scandal and dishonesty among its members are the exception and not the rule, and that the vast majority of senators and representatives are both hardworking and honest. Not every lawmaker junkets to the French Riviera at the taxpayers' expense, and if the Senate produced Warren Harding, whose presidency was tarnished by the Teapot Dome scandal, it also produced Robert A. Taft, Hubert H. Humphrey, and John F. Kennedy. In fact, four out of five presidents elected between 1948 and 1972, and every presidential nominee of a major party between 1960 and 1972, had served in the United States Senate. In recent years, state governors, such as Jimmy Carter, Ronald Reagan, Michael Dukakis, and Bill Clinton have played a prominent role as presidential candidates, but Congress remains an important source of political leaders. In 1992, the Republican candidate for re-election was President George Bush, a former member of the House of Representatives; the Republican nominee for vice-president was former Senator Dan Quayle of Indiana, and the Democratic candidate for vice-president was the junior senator from Tennessee, Albert Gore, Jr.

The Varied Roles of Congress

Congress plays a central and crucial role in the political system by making laws—the general rules that govern American society. It is called upon to deal with all of the major issues confronting the nation—the economy, the budget deficit, the tax structure, protection of the environment, and many other problems. No less than the president, Congress, by legislating, makes and implements national policy.

Most of the controversy over how well or how badly Congress performs focuses on this lawmaking function. But Congress plays other important roles. It has several nonlegislative functions: it proposes amendments to the Constitution; it may declare war; it can impeach and try the president or other civil officers of the United States, including judges; it may rule on presidential disability; it regulates the conduct of its members, and can punish, censure, or expel them; and it has power to decide whether a prospective member has been properly elected or should be seated. The House may choose the president in the event of electoral deadlock. The Senate approves or rejects treaties and presidential appointments, and, through the unwritten custom of *senatorial courtesy*, individual senators who belong to the same political party as the president exercise an informal veto power over presidential appointments in their states.

In addition, Congress oversees and supervises the operations of the executive branch and the independent regulatory agencies. For example, when bureaucrats are closely questioned at appropriations hearings, Congress is exercising its supervisory powers. The power of the purse, which the Constitution grants to Congress, carries with it the power to monitor how well the money is spent. For this purpose Congress conducts investigations and holds hearings. These are ostensibly tied to a legislative purpose, but often they serve a broader function of focusing public attention on specific social problems. During the early 1950s, Senator Joseph R. McCarthy achieved formidable personal political power by using the Senate's investigatory function to conduct "witch hunts" in search of alleged Communists in government. McCarthy succeeded in creating an atmosphere of fear in which the rights of witnesses were frequently violated. But congressional investigations also have been used to publicize the risks of birth-control pills, the problems of American policy in Southeast Asia, the tragedy of hunger in the midst of plenty, the political corruption of Watergate, the violation of individual rights by government intelligence agencies, and the conduct of a secret foreign policy in the Iran-contra scandal.

Perhaps even more important than some of these formal roles is the function of Congress in "legitimizing" the outputs of the political system. People are more likely to accept the policy decisions of a political system if major decisions are made by representative institutions. Congress, therefore, at times plays a key role in the *resolution of conflict* in American society. As in the case of all political institutions, Congress is subject to external pressures by organized interest groups, unorganized public opinion, the press, and individual constituents. Not every problem can be solved by passing a law. But in responding to social needs with legislation, Congress can at least help to ease the friction points.

In thus managing conflict (or making conflict manageable), Congress helps to *integrate* various groups and interests within the community by acting, to some extent, as a referee. However, as was noted in Chapter 6, not all groups in a pluralistic society have equal power. And highly organized, well-financed, single-issue lobbies may exercise an influence out of proportion to their number of supporters. Disadvantaged groups—the poor and African Americans, for example—may find it more difficult to influence Congress than does the oil industry. Consequently, in resolving conflict, Congress may still leave many groups unsatisfied. Yet Congress does provide one of several points of access to the political system for many individuals and groups. The inputs, in the form of demands and supports by segments of the community, are transformed by Congress through the legislative process into policy outputs and binding decisions for all of society.

But Congress is more than just a machine for making decisions. It is also a group of 535 men and women, and who they are is worth examining in some detail, for it may affect what they do.

THE LEGISLATORS

Portrait of a Lawmaker

When the 102nd Congress convened in January 1991, the average age of its members was 54 years.[16] Senators and representatives were, on the average, 13.3 years older than other adult Americans.

In part, the age level of Congress is slightly higher because of constitutional restrictions: a member of the House must be at least twenty-five (and a citizen for seven years) and a senator must be at least thirty (and a citizen for nine years). In part, of course, it is explained by the fact that senators and representatives usually do not achieve their office without considerable prior experience in politics or other fields.

More than half the nation's population are women, but the 102nd Congress had only thirty-one women members. All but two, Senator Nancy Landon Kassebaum, a Kansas Republican, and Senator Barbara A. Mikulski, a Maryland Democrat, served in the House. Only twenty-six African Americans, and one Native American, Representative Ben Nighthorse Campbell, served in the 102nd Congress, all in the House.

In many other respects, the socioeconomic makeup of Congress is not representative of the general population. For example, almost half of the 102nd Congress, or 244 out of 535 members, were lawyers. In the population as a whole, lawyers compose just over one half of one percent of the labor force. Other major occupational groups of members of Congress were: business or banking, 189; education, 67; journalism, 35; and agriculture, 28.[17] As Roger Davidson has suggested, representatives "are recruited almost wholly from the same relatively high-status occupations."[18]

Although today America is a highly urbanized society, Congress historically has been predominantly Main Street and rural. Donald Matthews reported in a study some years ago that about half of all senators were born in towns of 2,500 to 50,000 people.[19] Congress is also mostly Protestant; for example, of the members of the 102nd Congress, 47 percent were Protestants, 27 percent were Catholics, and 8 percent were Jews.[20]

If one were to draw a portrait of a typical member of Congress, that person might turn out to be about fifty-four, male, white, Protestant, and a lawyer.

How significant is it that in many ways Congress is not literally a cross section of America? Obviously, Congress does not have to be an exact model of the

---

[16] *Congressional Quarterly*, Weekly Report, January 12, 1991, p. 118.

[17] Norman J. Ornstein, Thomas E. Mann, and Michael J. Malbin, *Vital Statistics on Congress 1991–1992* (Washington, D.C.: Congressional Quarterly, Inc., 1992), pp. 22–29.
[18] Davidson, *The Role of the Congressman*, p. 69.
[19] Donald R. Matthews, *U.S. Senators and Their World* (Chapel Hill: University of North Carolina Press, 1960), pp. 14–18.
[20] Ornstein, Mann, and Malbin, *Vital Statistics on Congress 1991–1992*, pp. 34–37.

A member of Congress
among other jobs, must
find time to visit with constituents.

Representative Norm
Dicks of Washington

population in order to represent its constituents. Nor is
it entirely surprising that lawyers are overrepresented in
a body that makes laws. Yet it is not hard to see how
blacks, other minorities, women, blue-collar workers,
the poor, and members of under-represented socioeconomic groups in general may feel "left out" of a system
that produces a predominantly white, male, Protestant,
and upper-middle-class national legislature.

The Life of a Legislator

"It is true that we just don't have much time to legislate
around here."[21] The complaint was voiced by a Republican congressman who participated in a series of
round-table discussions about life on Capitol Hill. It
could easily have come from almost any one of the 435
members of the House or the 100 senators. There are so
many demands on members of Congress that lawmakers soon discover they cannot possibly do all that is
expected of them. One House member attempted some
years ago to list all the aspects of his job. Only a sample is
quoted here: "a Congressman has become an expanded

messenger boy, an employment agency . . . ward-
heeler . . . kisser of babies, recoverer of lost lug-
gage . . . contributor to good causes—cornerstone
layer . . . bridge dedicator, ship christener."[22]

Although members of Congress differ in how they
choose to allocate their time, it is constituents who elect
legislators, and most of those elected spend a fair portion of their day trying to take care of their constituents'
problems. Many lawmakers bounce back and forth between Washington and their districts like Ping-Pong
balls.

As of 1992, members of the House and Senate
received salaries of $129,500 a year, plus funds to hire a
staff (senators from populous states are permitted to
hire more assistants), and certain other allowances for
office supplies, telephone calls, and travel, as well as the
franking privilege for their official mail. Although the
basic salary and benefits are considerable, members of
Congress also have substantial expenses—many maintain residences both in Washington and their home-
towns, for example.

The mail pours in from constituents, and it must,
somehow, be answered. Because the volume of mail is so

[21] Charles L. Clapp, *The Congressman: His Work as He Sees It*
(Washington, D.C.: The Brookings Institution, 1963), p. 61.

[22] Luther Patrick, "What Is a Congressman?" *Congressional Record*,
May 13, 1963, p. A2978.

Representative Constance Morella of Maryland

great, many lawmakers use computers to churn out personalized form letters. Thanks to the franking privilege, members of Congress are entitled to send mail to constituents without charge by putting their frank, or mark, on the envelope. A 1973 law restricts use of the frank to official business and forbids its use to solicit votes or money, or for mass mailings sixty days before an election. Even so, the privilege is widely abused by members who are simply puffing their accomplishments. As one observer put it, "with the coming of the computer, the swift creation of sophisticated mailing lists and laser devices capable of printing individualized letters at the speed of 20,000 lines a minute, there is almost no limit to the letters that members can now generate."[23] In an election year, the House and Senate combined may send out more than seven hundred million letters under the frank.[24]

And computers enable senators and representatives to target specialized groups with their mailings. All of this technology has increased the advantages that incumbents enjoy over their challengers, who do not have free mailing privileges. Staff members and legislators, however, defend their use of the mail as "outreach programs" designed to keep members of Congress in close touch with their constituents.

Not all of the incoming mail is friendly, of course. Few senators and representatives dare to reply to abusive letters as Congressman John Steven McGroarty of California did. He wrote to a constituent: "One of the countless drawbacks of being in Congress is that I am compelled to receive impertinent letters from a jackass like you in which you say I promised to have the Sierra Madre mountains reforested and I have been in Congress two months and haven't done it. Will you please take two running jumps and go to hell."[25]

On a typical day, a member of Congress may spend an hour reading mail, making calls, dictating memos, then rush off to a 10 A.M. committee meeting, eat lunch (if there is time), dash to the floor for a vote, and then return to a committee hearing. Perhaps late in the afternoon the member manages to get back to the office, where a group of constituents is waiting. A powerful interest group (a labor union or business association, for

[23] David Burnham, "Computer Is Leaving a Wide Imprint on Congress," *New York Times*, April 13, 1984, p. B10.

[24] Ibid., and Roger H. Davidson and Walter J. Oleszek, *Congress and Its Members* (Washington, D.C.: Congressional Quarterly Press, 1981), pp. 140–41.

[25] In John F. Kennedy, *Profiles in Courage* (New York: Harper & Row, 1956), p. 30.

example) has invited the member to one or more cocktail receptions, and he or she must dutifully put in an appearance, have a drink, and chew on a rubbery shrimp before getting home for dinner — that is, on the nights not spent at a dinner in some hotel banquet hall. And some nights members must remain on Capitol Hill; for the past several years, the House has held afternoon legislative sessions on Wednesdays that often last into the late evening. Members spend many weekends in their home state or district, flying there to march in the Veterans Day parade or listen to constituents' woes. All of this can be difficult for the family of a representative or senator.

Studies of how senators and representatives spend their time show that both groups average eleven-hour days or more and work at least a third of their time on the floor or in committee or subcommittee meetings.[26] "We're like automatons," one senator said. "We spend our time walking in tunnels to go to the floor to vote."[27]

Although members of Congress do spend a great deal of time handling problems of constituents, 77 percent of House members questioned in one study listed legislative work as their most time-consuming job; only 16 percent listed "Errand Boy; lawyer for constituents."[28] Members of Congress must choose among alternative roles open to them — whether, for example, to concentrate on working for the interests of their districts, on seeking to become party leaders, on running for higher office, on specializing in a committee, or on seizing an issue that may bring them national recognition.

The Image of the Legislator

Congress and its individual members enjoy a rather mixed public image. In recent years, voters have had a generally negative view of Congress, although this was not always the case. Voter attitudes toward Congress fluctuate markedly. For example, in 1965, after Congress passed landmark Great Society legislation, 64 percent of the public rated its performance "Excellent to pretty good."[29] (See Table 12-2.) By 1991, however, the percentage of those who had confidence in Congress was at an all-time low. Only 18 percent of the public said they had "a great deal or quite a lot of confidence" in Congress.[30] Low public confidence in Congress was reflected in demands to limit the terms of senators and representatives. In 1992, voters in 14 states approved term limits for members of both houses of Congress.

Table 12-2
Public Attitudes Toward Congress, 1965–92

	Approve	Disapprove	Don't Know
1965	64%	26%	10%
1967	38	55	7
1968	46	46	8
1969	34	54	12
1970	34	54	12
1971	26	63	11
1974	38	54	8
1978	34	63	3
1982	29	54	17
1987	42	49	9
1990	24	68	8
1991	32	53	15
1992	19	78	3

SOURCE: Louis Harris, "Congress Gets Poor Ratings," *Washington Post*, March 1, 1971, p. A13; "Congress Rating Improves," *Washington Post*, September 23, 1974, p. 4; "Job Rating for Congress Is Higher Than Carter's," *Washington Post*, August 28, 1978, p. A3; Gallup Poll, August 1, 1982; Gallup Poll, October 1, 1987; and Gallup *Newsweek* Survey, March 13, 1992. In some of the earlier years reported in this table, Gallup used the headings, "Positive, Negative, Not Sure" for this survey.

However, most legal scholars said that term limitations were unconstitutional.

But there is a paradox; public opinion of Congress as a whole may be negative, but individual lawmakers are often popular and frequently re-elected. For example, 71 percent of those surveyed in a 1992 poll were critical of Congress, but only 30 percent were critical of their own representative.[31] And, through 1990, normally more than 90 percent of the members of Congress who sought re-election were victorious. As Richard F. Fenno, Jr., has asked: "How come we love our Congressmen so much more than our Congress?"[32]

After the 1992 elections, the new 103rd Congress was younger and more diverse, with more women, African Americans, and members of other minority groups.

[26] Davidson and Oleszek, *Congress and Its Members*, pp. 110–11.
[27] Ibid., p. 110.
[28] Davidson, *The Role of the Congressman*, pp. 98–99.
[29] Louis Harris, "Public Gives Congress Mixed Rating for Year's Work," *Philadelphia Inquirer*, January 13, 1969. Respondents were asked: "How would you rate the job Congress did this past year . . . excellent, pretty good, only fair, or poor?"
[30] *The Gallup Poll Monthly*, October 1991, p. 36.
[31] CBS News Poll, July 1992, in *New York Times*, August 9, 1992, p. E5.
[32] Richard F. Fenno, Jr., "If, As Ralph Nader Says, Congress Is 'The Broken Branch,' How Come We Love Our Congressmen So Much?", in *Congress in Change*, Norman J. Ornstein, ed. (New York: Praeger Publishers, 1975), pp. 277–87.

Representation: The Legislators and Their Constituents

Should members of Congress lead or follow the opinions of their constituents? The question poses the classic dilemma of legislators, mixing as it does the problems of the proper nature of representation in a democracy with practical considerations of the lawmaker's self-interest and desire for re-election.

One answer was provided by Edmund Burke, the eighteenth-century British statesman, in his famous speech to the voters of Bristol, who had just sent him to Parliament. As Burke defined the relationship of a representative to his constituents, "Their wishes ought to have great weight with him; their opinion high respect. . . . But his unbiased opinion, his mature judgment, his enlightened conscience, he ought not to sacrifice to you. . . . Your representative owes you, not his industry only, but his judgment."[33] Parliament, Burke contended, was an assembly of one nation, and local interests must bow to the general, national interest.

The Burkean concept of the legislator as trustee for the people clashes with the concept of the representative as *instructed delegate*, who automatically mirrors the will of the majority of his constituents. (Burke encountered political difficulties with his own constituents; those who cite his independence as a role model for legislators seldom note that six years after his speech, he withdrew as the member from Bristol.) On the other hand, members of Congress who attempted faithfully to follow opinion in their districts would soon discover that it was very difficult to measure opinion accurately. They would find that on some issues many voters had no strong opinions. Even when opinions could be discerned and measured, they also would find that a constituency is made up of competing interests and is in actuality several constituencies. Often they could please one group only at the expense of offending another.

A large proportion of House and Senate members, therefore, reject the role solely of trustee or that of instructed delegate. Instead they try to combine the two by exercising their own judgment *and* representing constituency views. As Roger Davidson has suggested, "Many congressmen observe that their problem is one of balancing the one role against the other."[34] In interviews with eighty-seven members of the House of Representatives, Davidson found that almost half, by far the largest group of respondents, sought to blend the trustee and delegate conceptions.[35]

---

[33] Edmund Burke, *The Works of the Right Honourable Edmund Burke*, vol. 2 (London: Oxford University Press, 1930), pp. 164–65.

[34] Davidson, *The Role of the Congressman*, p. 119.
[35] Ibid., pp. 117–19.

"THIS IS HOW REPRESENTATIVES GET WHIPSAWED"

WASHINGTON, May 3 — For Dennis E. Eckart, a second-term Democratic Congressman from Ohio, it came down to a choice, a tough choice, between the economic burdens of his constituents and his longstanding concern about the environment. In the end, the local issues proved more important, causing him to cast a vote that may well have doomed any prospect for adoption of legislation this year to reauthorize the Clean Air Act and control acid rain.

Mr. Eckart, a liberal whose voting record has been strongly in favor of environmental issues, voted Wednesday for a motion introduced by Republicans to kill a proposal that would have sharply reduced the emissions from coal-burning power plants that are regarded as the chief sources of acid rain. . . .

Mr. Eckart said his vote was "an extremely difficult and agonizing decision." . . . he represents a district in a state that would bear a large burden in complying with the acid rain regulations, since they would require installation of expensive scrubbers on smokestacks. . . .

As for the consequences of his vote, "I can't win either way," he said.

"This is how Representatives get whipsawed," Mr. Eckart said. "I vote one way and people say, 'Aren't you supposed to represent the national interest?' I vote the other way and people say, 'We sent you there to represent us.'"

—*New York Times*, May 4, 1984

Sometimes a member of Congress faces the dilemma of local versus national interest. Constituents may feel foreign aid is a waste of money, but the legislator may decide it is in the best interests of the United States and vote accordingly. Often, however, local interests are put first — that is where the voters are. And some members of Congress feel that their first obligation is to the constituency that elected them.

Political scientists have studied the process of how legislators make up their minds on an issue. David R. Mayhew has suggested that the "electoral connection," the relationship between members of Congress and their constituents, profoundly influences congressional behavior. "United States congressmen are interested in getting reelected," Mayhew emphasizes, and that basic fact, he adds, influences the kinds of activities congressmen find it "electorally useful to engage in."[36] And Richard F. Fenno, Jr., has emphasized that the re-election prospects of members of Congress depend greatly on their "home style" — the way they present themselves to constituents back in the district.[37]

Aage R. Clausen has concluded that members of Congress generally vote according to their known policy positions and display substantial stability and continuity in their voting patterns.[38] Donald R. Matthews and James A. Stimson have reported that when members of Congress must cast a vote on a complex issue about which their knowledge is limited, they search "for cues provided by trusted colleagues" who may possess more information about the legislation in question.[39]

To an extent the dilemma faced by the members of Congress may be artificial. One major study of constituent influence discovered that average voters know little about their representative's activities — a finding that contrasted with the view of most members of Congress, who regard their voting record as important to their re-election.[40] Approximately half the voters surveyed in one House election year had heard *nothing* about either the incumbent or the opposing candidate. The study, based on interviews with both members of Congress and voters, also indicated that, while legislators tend to think that the views of their constituents match their own, there is often a gap between the actual opinions of constituents and the member's *perception* of their views.[41]

Polling Constituents Even if members of Congress want to sample opinion among their constituents to help them in making up their minds on an issue, they face the practical problem of how to go about it. To gauge the thinking back home, members of Congress rely on conversations with friends, party leaders, and journalists in their states or districts; the mail (particularly personal letters); local newspapers; and political polls published in their states. In recent years increasing numbers of lawmakers have been using questionnaires mailed to the voters, or have turned to professional polling organizations for help. Without professional assistance, congressional polls are likely to be amateurish and the results distorted. In fact, such polls may be taken not so much to gauge constituency thinking as to promote legislators by flattering their constituents with a questionnaire.[42]

THE HOUSE

Although Congress is one branch of the federal government, the House and Senate are distinct institutions, each with its own rules and traditions and each jealous of its own powers and prerogatives. (See Table 12-3.)

One basic difference, of course, was established by the Constitution, which provided two-year terms for members of the House and staggered six-year terms for senators. The result is that all members of the House, but only one-third of the Senate, must face the voters every other year.

Because the House has 435 members compared to 100 in the Senate, the House is a more formal institution with stricter rules and procedures. For example, the Senate permits unlimited debate most of the time, but representatives in the House may be limited to speaking for five minutes or less during debate.

[36] David R. Mayhew, *The Electoral Connection* (New Haven: Yale University Press, 1974), pp. 13, 49.

[37] Richard F. Fenno, Jr., *Home Style: House Members in Their Districts* (Boston: Little, Brown, 1978).

[38] Aage R. Clausen, *How Congressmen Decide: A Policy Focus* (New York: St. Martin's, 1973), pp. 9, 53.

[39] Donald R. Matthews and James A. Stimson, *Yeas and Nays: Normal Decision-Making in the U.S. House of Representatives* (New York: Wiley, 1975), p. 45.

[40] Warren E. Miller and Donald E. Stokes, "Constituency Influence in Congress," *American Political Science Review*, vol. 57 (March 1963), pp. 53-54.

[41] Ibid.

[42] V. O. Key, Jr., *Public Opinion and American Democracy* (New York: Knopf, 1961), pp. 492-93.

Table 12-3

Major Differences Between the House and Senate

House	Senate
Larger (435 members)	Smaller (100 members)
Shorter term of office (2 years)	Longer term of office (6 years)
Less flexible rules	More flexible rules
Narrower constituency	Broader, more varied, constituency
Policy specialists	Policy generalists
Power less evenly distributed	Power more evenly distributed
Less prestige	More prestige
More expeditious in floor debate	Less expeditious in floor debate
Less reliance on staff	More reliance on staff
Less press and media coverage	More press and media coverage

SOURCE: Adapted from Walter J. Oleszek, *Congressional Procedures* and *the Policy Process*, 3rd ed. (Washington, D.C.: Congressional Quarterly Press, 1984), p. 22.

And because there are so many representatives, they generally enjoy less prestige than senators. At Washington dinner parties where protocol is observed, House members sit below the salt, ranking three places down the table from their Senate colleagues. (House members are outranked not only by senators, but by governors and former vice-presidents.[43]) In the television age, some senators, especially those who are presidential aspirants, have become celebrities, instantly recognizable to the spectators in the galleries. By contrast, visitors in the House galleries find it difficult to pick out their own representative, let alone any other.

In one survey, only 46 percent of adult Americans were able to name their representative.[44] While the figure is low, it does not give the whole picture. Although many voters cannot *remember* the name of their own representative, a much higher percentage can *recognize* the name from those on a list. In a selected group of congressional districts, "virtually all voters recognized the name of the incumbent when they heard it," and "most had a positive or negative response."[45]

Despite its size, the House has achieved a stability of tenure and a role never envisioned by the Founding Fathers. The men who framed the Constitution distrusted unchecked popular rule, and provided an indi-

rectly elected Senate to restrain the more egalitarian House of Representatives (the Seventeenth Amendment in 1913 provided for the direct election of the Senate). As Gouverneur Morris put it: "The second branch [the Senate] ought to be a check on the first [the House]. . . . The first branch, originating from the people, will ever be subject to precipitancy, changeability, and excess. . . . The second branch ought to be composed of men of great and established property—an aristocracy. . . . Such an aristocratic body will keep down the turbulency of democracy."[46]

Ironically, the House and Senate have on some issues exchanged places in terms of these expectations of the framers. One reason is that House seats are safer; in recent decades the turnover in the House of Representatives has been relatively small. A commonly cited standard for a "safe" congressional district is one in which the winner receives 55 percent of the vote or more. Less than that is considered "marginal." And recent House elections have shown a pattern of what David Mayhew has called "vanishing marginals."[47] That is, the number of unsafe, marginal districts appears to be declining. In 1976 only 17.9 percent of members of the House were elected with less than 55 percent of the vote. A decade later, in 1986, only 10.6 percent of House members were elected from marginal districts. In 1990, the figure rose to 13.7 percent.[48]

---

[43] Virginia F. Depew, ed., *The Social List of Washington, D.C., and Social Precedence in Washington* (Kensington: Jean Shaw Murray, 1980).

[44] Gallup poll, August 1, 1982.

[45] Thomas E. Mann, *Unsafe at Any Margin: Interpreting Congressional Elections* (Washington, D.C.: American Enterprise Institute for Public Policy Research, 1978), p. 30.

---

[46] In Robert A. Dahl, *Pluralist Democracy in the United States: Conflict and Consent* (Chicago: Rand McNally, 1967), p. 35.

[47] David R. Mayhew, "Congressional Elections: The Case of the Vanishing Marginals," *Polity*, vol. 6 (Spring 1974), pp. 295–317.

[48] *Congressional Quarterly*, Weekly Report, November 6, 1976, pp. 3114–54; Weekly Report, March 14, 1987, pp. 486–93; and *Congressional Quarterly*, Weekly Report, February 23, 1991, p. 486.

THE ART OF PORK-BARREL POLITICS

In an angry election year, when the worst name a politician can be called is "incumbent," Rep. Steny H. Hoyer (D-Md.) has found something good about that awful condition. In fact, Hoyer has come up with millions of good things.

There's the $10 million Hoyer wedged into the federal budget for a new aircraft testing facility at Patuxent River Naval Air Station. There's the $5 million for research on airplane ejection seats at Indian Head Naval Surface Warfare Center. And there's the $2 million for a new day-care center there.

Those projects have three things in common. They are in southern Maryland, three largely rural counties that the state legislature placed in Hoyer's district earlier this year. They are included in the House's defense appropriations bill at least in part

because of Hoyer's lobbying. And they offer solid proof that, even at a time when voters seem eager to throw the bums out, being one of the bums ain't all bad.

Hoyer, the House's fourth-ranking Democrat and a senior member of the Appropriations Committee, is dramatically demonstrating to his new constituents the art of pork-barrel politics. He unabashedly declares that one man's pork is another man's national priority.

" 'Pork' is an epithet that applies to projects that are not in one's district," Hoyer says. "It's politics. I'm trying to represent my area as effectively as I can. And I plead guilty to representing my area very effectively."

—*Washington Post*, July 5, 1992

Morris P. Fiorina has suggested one possible explanation for these "vanishing marginals." He contends that "the Washington system" (discussed in Chapter 11) may be responsible. Under it, members of Congress create new bureaucracies in the executive branch and then gain credit by helping constituents deal with the complex rules issued by the new agencies. As this system has developed, Fiorina concludes, representatives from marginal districts have increasingly found it possible to base their re-election on such casework for constituents and on "procuring the pork."[49]

Senate seats are less safe. In 1976, for example, 33.3 percent of those running were elected with less than 55 percent of the vote. In 1986, however, the total had increased to 45.4 percent. In 1990, the total had dropped to 30.3 percent. Since Senate races often tend to be close, there is a greater possibility of dramatic shifts in party strength in the Senate, such as occurred in 1980.[50]

Because members of the House are more likely to come from safe districts than their colleagues in the

Senate, the House is often less responsive than the Senate to pressures for change in the status quo. Senators have statewide constituencies that are frequently dominated by urban areas with powerful labor and minority-group vote blocs; as a result, the Senate at times has proved to be the *more* "liberal" branch of Congress.[51] But not always. In 1981, Reagan's victory, the Republicans took control of the Senate, and several conservative members became chairmen of important committees. The House, which remained Democratic, emerged as the more liberal branch.

Another result of the greater stability of House seats has been the "institutionalization" of that body. For many representatives, being a member of the House has become a career, with predictable steps up the ladder. Because the House is decentralized, a number of rewards, such as chairing committees and subcommittees, usually await career members; and as an institution, the House can gain the loyalty of its members.[52]

On the other hand, despite the relative safety of House seats, there has been a dramatic turnover in the membership of the House over the past decade. Some

[49] Morris P. Fiorina, *Congress: Keystone of the Washington Establishment* (New Haven: Yale University Press, 1977), p. 50.

[50] *National Journal*, November 6, 1976, p. 1599; *Congressional Quarterly, Weekly Report*, March 14, 1987, pp. 486–93; and *Congressional Quarterly, Weekly Report*, January 12, 1991, pp. 127–130.

[51] Lewis A. Froman, Jr., *Congressmen and Their Constituencies* (Chicago: Rand McNally, 1963), pp. 69–84.

[52] Nelson W. Polsby, "The Institutionalization of the U.S. House of Representatives," *American Political Science Review*, vol. 62 (March 1968), pp. 144-68.

members, tired of constituent pressures and election campaigns every two years, have quit. Others, of course, have been defeated. As already noted, in 1992, in the wake of the House bank scandal, a record number of lawmakers decided to seek other employment.

Power in the House: The Leadership

In the House, the Speaker is the most powerful member. But the Speaker must contend with the chairpersons of the twenty-two standing committees of the House, many of whom are powerful in their own right.

The Speaker exercised great power until 1910 when the rules were revised to strip the Speaker of much of his formal power, including the right to appoint members to committees of the House. But a Speaker with a strong personality and great legislative skill can still exert great influence in the House, as Sam Rayburn of Texas demonstrated during his seventeen-year tenure between 1940 and 1961. Over bourbon and branch water in a small room in the Capitol, Rayburn and his intimates would plan strategy for the House and swap political stories in an informal institution known as the "Board of Education."[53] Today, the Speaker remains a key figure, exercising more formal powers than at any time since 1910.

For ten years, until he retired in 1987, Thomas P. "Tip" O'Neill, Jr., of Massachusetts reigned as Speaker, and he made a considerable impact on both Congress and the nation. As a member of the House, he had succeeded John F. Kennedy. He became majority leader in 1972 and Speaker in 1977. O'Neill, a huge barrel-chested man with a thatch of shaggy white hair and a booming, easy laugh, proved to be a colorful Speaker. He looked exactly like what he was — an old-time Irish politician from Boston. But he was more than that. Early in his career as a House leader, he was called upon to take actions of historic importance for the nation. As

---

[53] Neil MacNeil, *Forge of Democracy: The House of Representatives* (New York: David McKay, 1964), pp. 82–83.

majority leader, O'Neill played a key role in the decision to hold the impeachment hearings that became an important factor in Nixon's decision to resign as president in 1974. During the Carter administration, O'Neill proved to be an accomplished legislative leader, and in Reagan's first term, an effective voice of the Democratic opposition in Congress. But on some major domestic and foreign-policy issues, he gave bipartisan support to the Republican president.

His successor, Representative Jim Wright, a Texas Democrat from Fort Worth, was controversial from the start. A pugnacious, often quick-tempered man, he did not hesitate to plunge into turbulent political waters. He drew criticism from the Reagan White House, for example, when he dealt directly with Central American leaders who were seeking to bring peace in Nicaragua. By 1988, Wright found himself under serious criticism over a book that earned him $55,000 in royalties and had been published by a Texas supporter who received $250,000 from the Wright election campaign committee. Republicans hoped to exploit Wright's book deal to divert attention from the "sleaze factor," a term Democrats used to characterize questionable dealings by members of the Reagan administration. As criticism of Wright mounted, the House Ethics Committee voted to investigate the Speaker. As noted earlier, Wright resigned in 1989 after the committee charged him with violating House rules.

The House then chose Representative Thomas S. Foley, a liberal Democrat from Spokane, Washington, as the new Speaker. Six-foot-four, white-haired and distinguished-looking, Foley was a mild-mannered congressional veteran with a low-key personality. Although he projected an image of integrity, he was publicly criticized by his Democratic colleagues for not reacting more aggressively to contain the damage done by the House check-overdraft scandal.

The position of Speaker is provided for in the Constitution ("The House of Representatives shall chuse their Speaker and other Officers"). The Speaker has a number of official powers: to preside over the House, to recognize or ignore members who wish to speak, to appoint the chairperson and all members of the Rules Committee, to appoint members of special or select committees that conduct special investigations, to refer bills to one or more committees, and to exercise other procedural controls. Much of the Speaker's real power, however, stems from the combination of these formal duties with that of *political leader* of the majority

House Speaker Thomas Foley

party in the House. Technically, the Speaker is elected by the House, with each party offering a candidate. In practice, the Speaker is chosen at the start of each Congress by a caucus, or meeting, of the majority party. Since in the past, at least, the formal voting in the House has been strictly along party lines, the majority party's candidate for Speaker has automatically won.

The Speaker has two chief assistants, the majority leader and the majority whip, both elected by the party caucus. The majority leader is the party's floor leader and a key strategist. Together with the Speaker and the members of the House Rules Committee, the majority leader schedules debate and negotiates with committee chairpersons and party members on procedural matters. The majority whip, along with a number of deputy whips, is responsible for rounding up party members for important votes and counting noses. (The term "whip" comes from "whipper-in," the person assigned in English fox hunts to keep the hounds from straying.) The minority party also elects a minority leader and a minority whip. Republican members of the House receive committee assignments from a Committee on Committees. The Democratic members are nominated for committee assignments by the Democratic Steering and Policy Committee, which is chaired and heavily influenced by the Speaker (when Democrats control the

House). These nominations are routinely ratified by a vote of all Democratic members of the House.

The established Democratic leadership of the House has faced challenges from party liberals. A number of the liberals banded together in 1959 in an informal organization known as the Democratic Study Group. In 1973 House reformers, led by members of the Democratic Study Group, succeeded in achieving a number of changes in Democratic party rules in the House. These included modification of the seniority system, opening up more bills to floor amendment, and new provisions to limit committee secrecy.

Then early in 1975 the House and Senate made a number of significant internal reforms. In the House, Democrats, finally departing from the seniority system, ousted three committee chairmen and granted more power to subcommittees and increased their staffs. The Senate changed its rules to make it easier to end debate; and Senate Democrats, too, modified the seniority system for the selection of committee chairpersons. Other changes and reforms modernized and liberalized the more restrictive procedures of both houses.

The Rules Committee

The House Committee on Rules exercises considerable control over what bills are brought to the floor. Most major legislation cannot be debated without a "special rule" from the Rules Committee that limits the time for floor debate and the extent to which a bill may be amended. The whole House must adopt each special rule before it goes into effect.[54]

In 1961 President Kennedy and Speaker Sam Rayburn barely won a fight to enlarge the House Rules Committee and thus curb the power of its conservative chairman. Democrats at that time controlled the House, but a coalition of southern Democrats and Republicans frequently succeeded in blocking passage of liberal legislation. In the 1961 change, the committee's size was increased, and the new members were chosen for their support of the administration's position on controversial bills.[55] By the 1970s, the Rules Committee was no

longer a bottleneck to legislation. The most important change made during the early 1970s empowered the Speaker of the House to nominate all majority-party members of the Rules Committee. As a result, for some two decades, the Committee has operated as an arm of the House Democratic leadership.[56]

The Legislative Labyrinth: The House in Action

The basic power structure of the House, then, consists of the Speaker, the floor leaders and whips of the two major parties, the Rules Committee, and the chairpersons of the twenty-one other standing committees. How these individuals and committees interact powerfully affects the fate of legislation. But the business of making laws is also governed by a complicated, even Byzantine, set of rules and procedures. Although most citizens are not familiar with them, these procedures can affect policy outcomes. Whether a bill is successfully steered through the legislative labyrinth or gets lost along the way often depends on how the rules and procedures are applied.

About 7 percent of all bills and joint resolutions introduced in Congress become public law. In the 101st Congress in 1989–90, 10,352 public bills and joint resolutions were introduced but only 650 became public law.[57]

After a bill is introduced by a House member, it is referred to a committee by the Speaker. Often the choice is limited by the jurisdictions of the standing committees, but when jurisdictions overlap or when new kinds of legislation are introduced, the Speaker may have considerable discretion in deciding where to assign a bill.

Only about 16 percent of bills get out of committee in the House. The committee chairperson may assign

54 For a detailed study of the complex rules and procedures of the House and Senate, see Walter J. Oleszek, *Congressional Procedures and the Policy Process*, 3rd ed. (Washington, D.C.: Congressional Quarterly Press, 1988); and text of the Legislative Reorganization Act of 1970.

55 Milton C. Cummings, Jr., and Robert L. Peabody, "The Decision to Enlarge the Committee on Rules: An Analysis of the 1961 Vote," in Robert L. Peabody and Nelson W. Polsby, eds., *New Perspectives on the House of Representatives* (Chicago: Rand McNally, 1963), p. 193.

56 Since 1989, the minority leader of the House has had the power to nominate minority party members of the Rules Committee.

57 Ilona B. Nickels, *Guiding a Bill Through the Legislative Process: Considerations for Legislative Staff*, (Washington, D.C.: Congressional Research Service, 1987), p. 5; and Ornstein, Mann, and Malbin, *Vital Statistics on Congress 1991–1992*, pp. 151, 153, and 154.

"There are days, Hank, when I don't know who's President, what state I'm from, or even if I'm a Democrat or a Republican, but, by God, I still know how to bottle up a piece of legislation in committee."

Drawing by Stan Hunt © 1977 The New Yorker Magazine, Inc.

Table 12-4
Regulating Legislative Traffic: The House Calendars

Union
Bills that directly or indirectly appropriate money or raise revenue are placed on the Union Calendar.

House
Bills that do not appropriate money or raise revenue go on the House Calendar. Most bills go either to the Union or House calendars.

Private
Bills that affect specific individuals and deal with private matters, such as claims against the government, immigration, or land titles, are placed on the Private Calendar and are called on the first and third Tuesdays of each month.

Consent
For noncontroversial bills passed without debate. Bills on the Consent Calendar are called on the first and third Mondays of each month, but debate may be blocked by the objection of any member. The second time a bill is called in this manner, three members must object to block consideration. All bills on the Consent Calendar originate on either the House or Union calendars.

Discharge
Motions to force a bill out of committee are placed on the Discharge Calendar if they receive the necessary 218 signatures from House members. The procedure is rarely successful.

the measure to one of the 135 subcommittees of the standing committees.[58] If the bill is reported out of committee, it is placed on one of five calendars, or lists of business eligible for House floor consideration. The various House *calendars* and the kinds of bills referred to them are shown in Table 12-4.

Certain bills from the Appropriations Committee may be taken on the floor without going through the Rules Committee. On specified days, bills on the Con-

sent Calendar and Private Calendar may be called up directly for House action. And if two-thirds of the members who are voting agree, any bill may be debated under a procedure, permitted every Monday and Tuesday, called "suspension of the rules." No floor amendments are permitted and a two-thirds vote is required for passage.

A quorum consisting of a majority of the House, 218 members, is required for general debate. When the House is considering legislation that deals with taxes and spending, however, it sits as a Committee of the Whole, a device that allows the House to conduct its business with fewer restrictions on debate (and a quorum of only one hundred members).

Before 1970, but rarely since, one kind of vote in the Committee of the Whole was a "teller vote," in which members filed down the aisle and were counted. As a result, a representative's vote was secret unless reported by a watching journalist — no easy feat since members filed down the aisle *away* from the press gallery, with their backs to the news reporters. Under this practice, as old as the Congress itself, constituents usually had no way of knowing how their representative had voted. Growing pressures for reform led the House in 1970 to provide for recorded votes, if enough representatives demand them. A recorded vote is one in which the position of each member is noted and pub-

---

[58] Data as of June 1992. Source: *Congressional Quarterly, Weekly Report*, June 6, 1992, p. 1584.

lished in the *Congressional Record*. Under this procedure, members vote electronically.

The system of electronic voting was installed in the House in 1973. Under it, when an electronic vote is taken, members insert a plastic identification card in one of forty-four voting stations on the floor and press one of three buttons. If the member votes "yes," a green light appears on a display board over the Speaker's head; for "no," a red light appears, and for "present," an amber light. The use of electronic voting has greatly reduced the time needed for recorded votes; under the old system, the clerk called the roll and each member present had to answer by name. The changes in voting procedure in the Committee of the Whole and the inauguration of electronic voting in the House itself have greatly increased the number of on-the-record votes by representatives. The number of recorded votes in the Committee of the Whole and the House increased from 266 in 1970 to 536 in 1990.[59] The increase in recorded votes kept legislators running from committee meetings to the House floor to cast their votes and brought complaints.

Supporters or opponents of a bill sometimes request recorded votes as a delaying tactic to gain time to round up their forces. Often, however, such votes are demanded to place members on the spot. Representatives know that in a roll-call vote their position must become a matter of public record. Some interest groups regularly rate the records of members on the basis of their roll-call votes. Constituents may not pay much attention to how representatives vote, but opponents in an election campaign may use the legislator's roll-call votes on a key issue against them.

When debate is concluded in the Committee of the Whole, the House may vote on final passage. On rare occasions, the House may vote instead to send the bill back to its committee of origin (thereby killing it permanently), or it may send the bill back to the committee with instructions to make further changes in the bill (thereby delaying it temporarily).

Televising Congress

In March 1979, amid much controversy, the House began live television and radio broadcasts of floor debate. The broadcasts are carried gavel-to-gavel by a network of about 4,218 cable television systems in all 50 states, with a potential audience of 57.2 million homes in 1992. In addition, excerpts are sometimes carried by local stations and the major networks. The stations and networks are permitted to carry up to two minutes a day of debate.

When the television coverage began, there were dire predictions that publicity-seeking members would engage in ham-acting and long-winded oratory. Although some members did play to the cameras, a majority of House members—65 percent—reported they were satisfied with the results. Nevertheless, the opportunity to posture for audiences at home has lengthened House sessions. "There are an awful lot of added speeches that we wouldn't have without television," Speaker O'Neill complained.[60]

Not all members of the public have been impressed by watching the House in action on television. "The results of government in action are disgusting enough without having to have it aired," a woman in Winston-Salem, North Carolina, wrote to the House. But a man in Chelsea, Massachusetts, wrote: "This has given me much more knowledge of the manner in which the laws of this great nation are devised, debated, amended and finally resolved."[61]

Many viewers do not know, however, that television in the House operates under restrictions. The cameras are operated by employees of the House, not by the cable networks. And during regular debate the cameras are not permitted to pan around the floor and show members sleeping, fidgeting, or walking around. In 1984, however, Speaker O'Neill became infuriated at Republican attacks upon him and other Democrats during a period known as "special orders," at the end of the legislative day after most members had gone home. He changed the rules to permit the cameras to pan and show that the House chamber was almost empty during the Republican attacks. But during regular floor debate, the old rule remained in effect, and cameras were required to focus on the person speaking.

The Senate, after resisting television for many years, finally voted in 1986 to permit the deliberations on the Senate floor to be televised. Since the 1950s, Senate committee meetings, particularly important investigations that attracted widespread public interest, have often been televised.

Even those who had initially opposed televising floor debate in the Senate, however, later conceded that

---

[59] Ornstein, Mann, and Malbin, *Vital Statistics on Congress 1991–1992*, p. 154.

[60] *Congressional Quarterly*, Weekly Report, March 15, 1980, p. 735.
[61] Boris Weintraub, "TV in Congress—Measuring the Impact," *Washington Star*, March 19, 1980, p. C5.

television did not appear to have had a major impact on the way the Senate conducted its business. "My fears did not materialize," said Senator J. Bennett Johnston, a Louisiana Democrat, who had originally resisted TV cameras in the Senate but later decided it was a good idea. "Senators, mindful of the prying eye of television, are not talking as long as I feared," he said. "They may speak more often, but they're a little more succinct."[62]

THE SENATE

The Senate may not be "the most exclusive club in the world" nor a "rich man's club," although it has been called both. (In 1991, there were at least twenty-one millionaires in the Senate.[63]) It may not have an "Inner Club." But it certainly has both the atmosphere and appearance of a club. Its membership is relatively small; its quarters are ornate and gilded; its ways are slow.

But the folkways and customs of the Senate have changed markedly since the days, more than three decades ago, when William S. White, then Senate correspondent of the *New York Times*, wrote of the "Inner Club" run by southerners.[64] Around the same period, Donald Matthews, a political scientist, described the

Senate's "unwritten rules of the game, its norms of conduct." The freshman senator, Matthews wrote, was expected to serve a silent apprenticeship, to be one of the Senate "work horses" rather than one of the "show horses," to develop a legislative specialty, pay homage to the institution, and observe its folkways.[65] At the time, these included the elaborate courtesy with which senators, even bitter enemies, customarily addressed each other on the floor.

A decade later Nelson W. Polsby argued that "the role of the Senate in the political system has changed over the last 20 years," decreasing the importance of Senate norms. He contended that television, with its ability to publicize individual senators, had made the Senate "an incubator of presidential hopefuls" and eroded the significance of its rules of behavior.[66] And Ralph K. Huitt observed that the Senate has always had a place for "mavericks" and "independents."[67]

Today, newcomers to the Senate often speak up and speak out, sometimes gaining national recognition very rapidly. Many of the old ways have faded. As political scientist Barbara Sinclair has noted, senators now seek "broad involvement across multiple issues and

---

[62] *Washington Post*, June 3, 1987, p. A17.
[63] *USA Today*, June 17, 1991, p. 6A.
[64] White, *Citadel*, pp. 2, 82-84.

[65] Matthews, *U.S. Senators and Their World*, pp. 92–117.
[66] Nelson W. Polsby, "Goodbye to the Inner Club," *Washington Monthly*, August 1969, pp. 30–34.
[67] Ralph K. Huitt, "The Outsider in the Senate: An Alternative Role," in Huitt and Peabody, *Congress: Two Decades of Analysis*, pp. 159-78.

presidential candidates," they suggest, has affected the behavior of "a wider circle of senators." For example, when Senator John F. Kennedy set his sights on the presidency, he spoke out on a variety of subjects "beyond the jurisdictions of his original committee assignments." Kennedy was contributing to the decline of the silent apprenticeship as a Senate norm. Soon other senators with presidential ambitions began to speak out, adding to "the breakdown of apprenticeship."[73]

As more senators run for president, they can be expected to ignore the norm of "legislative work," the authors argue. And the tradition that senators should specialize in certain subjects has been weakened by the need for presidential contenders to be generalists, with a wide knowledge of public-policy questions.[74]

Another reason that senators today are more vocal even as newcomers is that they have become much more vulnerable to electoral challenges. In a sense, they must begin working for re-election from day one. To the public, "senators are right out front as visible targets for the expression of voter dissatisfaction."[75]

Power in the Senate: The Leadership

Just as the Speaker is elected by the House, the Senate elects a president pro tempore, who presides in the absence of the vice-president. Although the office is provided for in the Constitution, it has little formal power.

The closest parallel to the Speaker is the Senate majority leader, who is the most powerful elected leader of the Senate — although, as in most political offices, a great deal depends on the person and political circumstances. Lyndon Johnson, the Democratic Senate leader from 1953 to 1960, was widely regarded as an extraordinarily skillful and powerful floor leader. Johnson's power to persuade was formidable. A big man, he towered over most other senators as, on occasion, he subjected them to "The Treatment" — a prolonged exercise in face-to-face persuasion that combined

arenas."[68] She adds: "In the contemporary Senate, freshmen are not expected to remain on the sidelines, nor even to be restrained in their participation in committee or on the floor."[69] Thus, a "new Senate style" has emerged, replacing the old behavior.[70] Although courtesy is still observed in floor debate, "it seems to be breached more often than it used to be."[71] For example, during one Senate debate, Senator Lowell Weicker of Connecticut suggested that his Republican colleague, John Heinz of Pennsylvania, was "an idiot."[72]

Political scientists Robert L. Peabody, Norman J. Ornstein, and David W. Rohde have also analyzed the decline of folkways and norms in the Senate. The emergence of the Senate as "a major breeding ground for

---

[68] Barbara Sinclair, *The Transformation of the U.S. Senate* (Baltimore: The Johns Hopkins University Press, 1989), p. 79.
[69] Ibid., p. 94.
[70] Ibid., p. 101.
[71] Ibid., p. 99.
[72] Ibid.

[73] Robert L. Peabody, Norman J. Ornstein, and David W. Rohde, "The United States Senate as Presidential Incubator: Many Are Called but Few Are Chosen," *Political Science Quarterly*, vol. 91, no. 2 (Summer 1976), pp. 252–53.
[74] Ibid., pp. 253–56.
[75] Charles O. Jones, "The New, New Senate," in Ellis Sandoz and Cecil V. Crabb, Jr., eds., *A Tide of Discontent: The 1980 Elections and Their Meaning* (Washington, D.C.: Congressional Quarterly Press, 1981), p. 100.

Senate Minority
Leader Robert J.
Dole

elements of a police "third degree" with Johnson's flair
for dramatic acting.

In addition to his powerful personality, Johnson
had several tangible tools at his disposal. He could assist
a senator in getting legislation passed; he controlled
committee assignments; and, above all, he built an intelligence system known as "the Johnson Network." At its
heart was Bobby Baker, "a country boy from Pickens,
South Carolina, who had come to Washington as a
teen-aged Senate page" and whom Johnson made his
top assistant.[76] Baker knew how to count noses; because
Johnson was well informed of sentiment in the Senate,
he was able to anticipate the outcome of close votes. The
effect was cumulative, for after a while "it was taken for
granted that 'Lyndon's got the votes.' "[77] Through his
network, Johnson came to know the strengths and
weaknesses of each senator, and he used that knowledge
to further his goals; his was a highly personal leadership.

In contrast, Johnson's successor as majority leader,
soft-spoken Mike Mansfield of Montana, did not attempt to exercise power in the way that Johnson had.
When Mansfield was accused of not providing sufficient leadership for the Senate, he declared: "I am neither a circus ringmaster, the master of ceremonies of a
Senate nightclub, a tamer of Senate lions, or a wheeler
and dealer."[78] When Mansfield retired from the Senate
in January 1977, Robert C. Byrd of West Virginia was
elected as the majority leader.

Byrd, who rose from rural poverty in the hills of
West Virginia, played country music on his fiddle for
the voters and even released a record album. Extremely
hardworking, Byrd, when he served as majority leader,
concentrated more on making the Senate work than on
influencing legislation ideologically.[79]

Senator George J. Mitchell of Maine succeeded
Byrd in 1988. He grew up in Waterville, Maine, in modest circumstances; his father was a janitor at Colby College and his mother was a Lebanese immigrant. He rose
through the ranks in state Democratic politics, ran for
governor and lost, but was named a federal judge. First
appointed to the Senate in 1980, he was elected in an
upset two years later. Mitchell projected a personal
image of calm and confidence and soon emerged as "one
of the operational leaders and leading spokesmen of the
Democratic Party."[80] As majority leader, he played a
crucial role in passage of the Clean Air Act of 1990,
denounced Marine Lt. Col. Oliver North at the Iran-
contra hearings, and opposed the use of force in the
Persian Gulf in 1991.

There has been a parallel on the Republican side to
these changes in Senate leadership style. Senator Everett McKinley Dirksen, the Senate minority leader from
1959 to his death in 1969, was a flamboyant personality
who wielded considerable power. Howard H. Baker, Jr.,
who became Senate minority leader in 1977 and majority leader in 1981, had a quieter style.

Baker gained national attention during the televised Senate Watergate hearings in 1973, repeatedly
asking about President Nixon: "What did the President
know and when did he know it?" When Baker stepped
down as majority leader in January 1985, he was replaced by Senator Robert J. Dole, Republican of Kansas,
who in 1987 became minority leader.

[76] Rowland Evans and Robert Novak, *Lyndon B. Johnson: The Exercise of Power* (New York: New American Library, 1966), pp. 68,
99. When it later developed that Bobby Baker had used his Senate position to amass a personal fortune, the scandal became an
issue in the 1964 presidential election campaign and embarrassed
Lyndon Johnson, who by then was president. Baker was convicted in 1967 of income tax evasion, theft, and conspiracy to defraud the federal government, and served sixteen months in prison.
[77] Ralph K. Huitt, "Democratic Party Leadership in the Senate,"
in Huitt and Peabody, *Congress: Two Decades of Analysis*, p. 147.

[78] *Congressional Record*, November 27, 1963, p. 22862.
[79] Mark Green, with Michael Calabrese *et al.* and Ralph Nader
Congress Watch, *Who Runs Congress*, 3rd ed. (New York: Bantam Books, 1979), pp. 100–01.
[80] Michael Barone and Grant Ujifusa, *The Almanac of American
Politics 1992* (Washington, D.C.: National Journal, 1992), p. 530.

Senate Majority Leader George J. Mitchell

teen standing committees of the Senate. The Democratic counterpart is known as the Democratic Steering Committee.

Although the organization of each party appears to be much the same, there are important differences in how the machinery operates. The Democratic party leadership tends to be centralized in the hands of the floor leader. The Republicans tend to spread the party posts around.

The Senate in Action

Unlike the House, with its complex procedures, calendars, and tight restrictions on debate, the Senate is more informal and less bound by rules. In part this is so because the Senate is smaller than the House.

Senate bills appear on only one legislative calendar, and they are usually called up by *unanimous consent*. Since a single senator may object to this procedure, the majority leader, in conducting floor business, consults with the minority leader across the aisle on most major matters to avoid objections.

The Senate does not have electronic voting as the House does; instead, the clerk calls the roll, reading out the name of each senator.

The Filibuster Most of the time, the Senate allows unlimited debate. Because of this, a single senator, or a group of senators, may stage a *filibuster* to talk a bill to death.[81] Usually, the filibuster is employed to defeat a bill by tying up the Senate so long that the measure will never come to a vote. But a number of factors, including the 1975 rule change making it easier to cut off debate, have combined to diminish the importance of the filibuster as a weapon to block legislation.

To filibuster, all that senators must do is remain on their feet and keep talking. For the first three hours, their comments must relate to the subject of the debate, but after that, they may, if they wish, read the telephone book. The record for such marathon performances by a single senator was set by Senator Strom Thurmond of South Carolina, who spoke against the Civil Rights Act of 1957 for twenty-four hours and eighteen minutes. A group filibuster may go on for many days or even

Dole, a veteran politician, and the Republican vice-presidential candidate in 1976, was known for his sharp tongue and skills at legislative infighting. As minority leader, he helped the president win a number of important battles in Congress. However, in 1990 he urged Bush to abandon his campaign pledge and raise taxes. Bush did, at considerable political cost.

The Senate majority and minority leaders represent their party in the Senate. But they may not represent majority sentiment in their party nationally. While the majority or minority leaders are nominally responsible for steering their party's program through the Senate, they may oppose parts of it.

Senate Democrats and Republicans are organized along party lines for both political and legislative purposes:

The *floor whips*. As in the House, the leader of each party is assisted by a whip, and in the case of the Democrats, assistant whips, to round up senators for key votes.

The *party conference*. The conference, or caucus, of each party consists of all the senators who are members of that party. Both party conferences elect leaders, who assume the title of majority or minority leader, depending on which party controls the Senate.

The *policy committee*. The policy committee of each party provides a forum for discussion of party positions on legislative issues.

The *assignment committee*. The Republican Committee on Committees appoints Republicans to the six-

---

[81] The word "filibuster" originally meant a privateer or pirate, and its origin in American politics is not certain. See William Safire, *The New Language of Politics* (New York: Random House, 1968), p. 143.

NIGHT OF THE FILIBUSTER

For nine days in September of 1977, Senators James Abourezk of South Dakota and Howard M. Metzenbaum of Ohio staged a filibuster against a gas deregulation bill that was part of President Carter's energy package. The filibuster included an all-night session, described in this newspaper account:

The usually decorous Senate chamber was not very dignified early Wednesday morning as senators jumped up from folding cots every half hour or so to answer yet another roll-call vote demanded by Metzenbaum and Abourezk.

Under normal circumstances, senators wear ties and jackets on the Senate floor, but Wednesday some removed their ties and left their shirt-tails hanging out over their trousers. Sen. Ernest F. Hollings (D-S.C.) showed up in a jogging costume.

Shoeless, Sen. Barry Goldwater (R-Ariz.) padded onto the floor in his socks and asked, "Isn't it time to go home?"

Sen. Robert J. Dole (R-Kan.) said the Senate was looking ridiculous and quoted a tourist who had remarked to him Wednesday, "I'm so happy the Senate is open because the zoo is closed."

—*Los Angeles Times,* September 29, 1977

"Listen, pal! I didn't spend seven million bucks to get here so I could yield the floor to you."

Drawing by Dana Fradon © 1987 The New Yorker Magazine, Inc.

months. When one senator tires, he or she merely "yields" to a fresher colleague, who takes over. To counter these tactics, the Senate may meet round-the-clock in the hope of wearing down the filibusterers. But the senators conducting the filibuster may retaliate by suggesting the absence of a quorum (fifty-one senators). Such a demand voiced at, say, 4 A.M. is inconvenient for other senators. So, senators attempting to break the filibuster set up cots in the halls and straggle in to answer the roll; then they try to go back to sleep.

Today, however, more often than not, the Senate permits "gentleman's filibusters" that run from 9 A.M. to 5 P.M. and allow senators to get home in time for dinner. This was not always the case. Donald A. Ritchie, the associate historian of the Senate, recalled the days when senators such as Huey Long, the Louisiana Democrat, would take the floor for marathon filibusters. "He used to read recipes for gumbo and for pot liquor and greens, the Bible and Shakespeare," Ritchie said.[82]

Under Rule XXII of the Senate, a filibuster may be ended if sixteen members petition, and three-fifths of the entire Senate (sixty members) vote, for *cloture*. Until 1959 the vote of two-thirds of the entire Senate was required to impose cloture. In 1959 the cloture rule was eased to require only two-thirds of those present and voting. As a result, northern liberals were able several times to vote cloture to cut off the debate of southern senators on civil rights legislation in the 1960s. Then in 1975 the rule was eased even further, to require only sixty senators to end debate.[83] Even with the less restrictive rule, cloture is difficult to impose. From 1919 through 1991, cloture was voted only 109 times in 311 attempts.

Although filibusters have often been used by southern conservatives, northerners and liberals have used them, too. For example, northern liberals filibustered in the early 1970s against funds for the Vietnam War and extension of the military draft.

In 1976 Senator James Allen of Alabama used a loophole in the filibuster rules to stage a new kind of post-cloture filibuster. Under the then-existing rules, once cloture was invoked, debate was limited to one hundred hours, one for each senator. But quorum calls, roll-call votes, and other procedural devices did not count against a senator's hour. Allen, with the help of forty roll calls, managed to delay action on a civil rights bill for two weeks. Then in 1977 Senators James Abourezk and Howard M. Metzenbaum staged a post-cloture filibuster against the natural gas bill, tying the Senate up into a pretzel and forcing the first all-night session in thirteen years. Since 1986, when the Senate allowed its debates to be televised, post-cloture filibusters have been further limited to thirty hours.

One of the most dramatic—some thought comic—episodes surrounding a filibuster took place early in 1988, when Senate Republicans tried to block a Democratic bill to limit the cost of Senate campaigns. Senator Robert C. Byrd invoked a rule to compel the attendance of senators in the chamber. He ordered the sergeant-at-arms to arrest any senators who could be found and bring them to the floor. The sergeant-at-arms and a posse of Capitol police began scouring the buildings. "They spotted Sen. Steven D. Symms (R-Idaho), but he fled before they could apprehend him."[84] Then the police "forced their way into the office of Sen. Bob Packwood (R-Ore.), arrested him and carried him feet-first into the Senate chamber in a flamboyant climax to a bitter all-night filibuster."[85] Angry Republicans accused the Democrats of turning the Senate into a "banana republic." The Democrats failed in their effort to invoke cloture to end the filibuster, and the bill was set aside.

THE COMMITTEE SYSTEM

Committees and subcommittees are where Congress does most of its work. Policies are shaped, interest groups heard, and legislation hammered out.

Long before Woodrow Wilson became president, he described what he called "government by the chairmen of the Standing Committees of Congress." Wilson saw congressional committees as "little legislatures," and added that the House sat "not for serious discussion, but to sanction the conclusions of its Committees" as rapidly as possible. "Congress in its committee-rooms," Wilson concluded, "is Congress at work."[86]

The growth of the modern presidency has modified the Wilsonian view of the power of Congress and

---

[82] *New York Times*, February 25, 1988, p. A26.
[83] To cut off debate on changes in Senate rules, a vote of two-thirds of the senators present is still required.

[84] *Washington Post*, February 25, 1988, p. A4.
[85] Ibid., p. A1.
[86] Woodrow Wilson, *Congressional Government* (New York: World, Meridian Books, 1956), pp. 69, 82-83. Originally published in 1885.

COMMITTEE ROOM

its committees. The committees are, nevertheless, vital centers of congressional activity.

The standing committees of Congress are the permanent committees that consider bills and conduct hearings and investigations. In the 102nd Congress there were sixteen standing committees of the Senate and twenty-two standing committees of the House. (The thirty-eight standing committees of Congress are listed in Table 12-5.)

The standing committees constitute the heart of the committee system. At times, Congress also creates special or *select committees* to conduct special investigations. In addition, there are *joint committees* of the House and Senate dealing with such subjects as the economy and taxes.[87]

The Subcommittees and Decentralization

The thirty-eight chairpersons of the standing committees of the House and Senate still wield substantial power. Yet here, too, Congress is changing. As Anthony King has observed, "by the late 1970s, committee chairmen, although still very influential people, had lost much of their former power. They felt bound to defer to the other members of the committee; much of the committees' work had been devolved onto subcommittees, often chaired by junior, even freshman, congressmen, and senators."[88]

As a result of these changes, Congress has become substantially *decentralized*. "The most striking feature of congressional organization is decentralization," Samuel C. Patterson has observed, and "congressional government by subcommittee" increased in the 1970s.[89] The proliferation of subcommittees is, in fact, one of the most dramatic changes in the structure of Congress over the past two decades.

Representative David R. Obey of Wisconsin, who has studied the organization of the House, observed that in the past the House was run by its committee chairmen, "a few old bulls" who held onto their power because of seniority.[90] The reforms of the 1970s stripped the chairmen of some of their power and dispersed it to the subcommittees, each with its own chairperson. The heads of the subcommittees enjoyed their newfound power and liked the system of divided authority. Under this system, Obey pointed out, every interest group has "a port of entry into Congress, but the bulwark of strong central leadership is lacking."[91]

The subcommittee explosion can be clearly traced by studying the subcommittee totals in the House over the past three-and-a-half decades. In 1951 there were only 69 subcommittees in the House; by 1971 the number had climbed to 120; and by 1992 it had reached 135 — an increase since 1951 of 96 percent. The Senate in 1992 had 87 subcommittees, a decrease from some earlier years, but still a large number.[92]

[87] In the 102nd Congress, there were four special or select committees in the Senate and five in the House, and four joint committees.

[88] Anthony King, "Introduction," in Anthony King, ed., *The New American Political System*, p. 2.
[89] Samuel C. Patterson, "The Semi-Sovereign Congress," in King, ed., *The New American Political System*, p. 160.
[90] *New York Times*, November 13, 1978, p. B9.
[91] Ibid.
[92] U.S. Congress, House of Representatives, Select Committee on Committees, *Final Report*, 96th Cong., 2nd sess. (Washington, D.C.: U.S. Government Printing Office, 1980), p. 321; and Ornstein, Mann, and Malbin, *Vital Statistics on Congress 1991–1992*, pp. 111-12. There were also eleven subcommittees of the select or special committees in the House, for a total of 146. In addition, there were eight joint House and Senate subcommittees. When added to the total of 146 House subcommittees (135 standing, 11 select) and 87 Senate subcommittees, the grand total of subcommittees in both houses in 1992 was 241. But no one knew the precise total, since the number of subcommittees changed frequently.

Table 12-5
Standing Committees of the 102nd Congress

Senate Committees	Chairperson	State	Age*
Agriculture, Nutrition, and Forestry	Patrick J. Leahy	Vt.	52
Appropriations	Robert C. Byrd	W.Va.	74
Armed Services	Sam Nunn	Ga.	53
Banking, Housing, and Urban Affairs	Donald W. Riegle, Jr.	Mich.	54
Budget	Jim Sasser	Tenn.	55
Commerce, Science, and Transportation	Ernest F. Hollings	S.C.	70
Energy and Natural Resources	J. Bennett Johnston	La.	60
Environment and Public Works	Quentin N. Burdick†	N.Dak.	84
Finance	Lloyd Bentsen	Tex.	71
Foreign Relations	Claiborne Pell	R.I.	73
Governmental Affairs	John Glenn	Ohio	70
Judiciary	Joseph R. Biden, Jr.	Del.	49
Labor and Human Resources	Edward M. Kennedy	Mass.	60
Rules and Administration	Wendell H. Ford	Ky.	67
Small Business	Dale Bumpers	Ark.	66
Veterans' Affairs	Alan Cranston	Calif.	78

House Committees	Chairperson	State	Age*
Agriculture	E. (Kika) de la Garza	Tex.	64
Appropriations	Jamie L. Whitten	Miss.	82
Armed Services	Les Aspin	Wis.	53
Banking, Finance and Urban Affairs	Henry B. Gonzalez	Tex.	76
Budget	Leon E. Panetta	Calif.	54
District of Columbia	Ronald V. Dellums	Calif.	56
Education and Labor	William D. Ford	Mich.	64
Energy and Commerce	John D. Dingell	Mich.	65
Foreign Affairs	Dante B. Fascell	Fla.	75
Government Operations	John Conyers, Jr.	Mich.	63
House Administration	Charlie Rose	N.C.	52
Interior and Insular Affairs	George Miller	Calif.	47
Judiciary	Jack Brooks	Tex.	69
Merchant Marine and Fisheries	Walter B. Jones§	N.C.	78
Post Office and Civil Service	William Clay	Mo.	61
Public Works and Transportation	Robert A. Roe	N.J.	68
Rules	John Joseph Moakley	Mass.	65
Science, Space and Technology	George E. Brown, Jr.	Calif.	72
Small Business	John J. LaFalce	N.Y.	52
Standards of Official Conduct	Louis Stokes	Ohio	67
Veterans' Affairs	G.V. Montgomery	Miss.	71
Ways and Means	Dan Rostenkowski	Ill.	64

*Names and ages of chairpersons as of July 1, 1992.
†Senator Daniel Patrick Moynihan of New York, 65, became chairman on September 15, 1992, following the death of Senator Burdick.
§Representative Gerry E. Studds of Massachusetts, 55, succeeded Representative Jones, who died on September 15, 1992.

All of this made Congress a place of "buzzing confusion," confronting outside groups with "a bewildering array of access points."[93] Where lobbies or executive-branch agencies could once deal with a handful of members of Congress, "large numbers of legislators must now be contacted."[94]

The Committees at Work

Committees perform the valuable functions of division of labor and specialization in Congress. No member of

[93] Roger H. Davidson, "Subcommittee Government: New Channels for Policy Making," in Thomas E. Mann and Norman J. Ornstein, eds., *The New Congress* (Washington, D.C.: American Enterprise Institute for Public Policy Research, 1981), pp. 130–31.

[94] Ibid., p. 130.

the House or Senate could hope to know the details of all of 10,352 bills introduced, for example, in the 101st Congress in 1989–90.[95] For that reason, senators and representatives tend to rely on the expert knowledge that members of committees may acquire. If a committee has approved a bill, other members generally assume that the committee has considered the legislation carefully, applied its expertise, and made the right decision. That is why Congress, for the most part, approves the decisions of its committees.

As a result of the committee system, members of Congress specialize in various fields. Sometimes they become more knowledgeable in their areas than the bureaucrats in the executive branch. Finally, many scholars argue that a legislative body should have some forum where members of competing parties can resolve their differences. Committees serve this purpose; they are natural arenas for political bargaining and legislative compromise.

Not all committees are alike. Richard F. Fenno, Jr., has identified a number of factors that may affect a committee's degree of independence, influence in Congress, and success in managing legislation. Fenno found

five key variables in committee behavior: *Member goals* reflect the benefits desired by each committee member; for instance, members of the Post Office Committee are primarily interested in improving their own chances of re-election by getting new post offices for their districts, but members of the House Education and Labor Committee are oriented more toward making public policy for the nation as a whole. *Environmental constraints* are the outside influences that affect a committee — primarily the other members of the House, the executive branch, client groups, and the two major political parties. *Strategic premises* are the basic rules of the game for a committee — the Appropriations Committee often tries to reduce presidential budget requests, for example, and thus appears more responsible with taxpayers' money, but other committees may find it more to their advantage to agree to the president's requests. *Decision-making processes* are the internal rules for each committee. Finally, *decisions* of committees vary; the Appropriations Committee, for example, generally does cut the president's budget, but the Foreign Affairs Committee tends to respond to the president's wishes.[96]

In their more recent analysis of the congressional committee system, Steven S. Smith and Christopher J.

---

[95] It should be noted that many of the bills introduced were either private bills for the benefit of individuals or duplicated another bill. A public law applies to whole classes of citizens.

[96] Richard F. Fenno, Jr., *Congressmen in Committees* (Boston: Little, Brown, 1973).

IRAN-CONTRA: "DISDAIN FOR THE LAW"

The common ingredients of the Iran and Contra policies were secrecy, deception, and disdain for the law. . . . [Marine Lt. Col. Oliver L.] North admitted that he and other officials lied repeatedly to Congress and to the American people about the Contra covert action and Iran arms sales, and that he altered and destroyed official documents. . . .

Secrecy became an obsession. Congress was never informed of the Iran or the Contra covert actions, notwithstanding the requirement in the law that Congress be notified of all covert actions in a "timely fashion.". . .

The President's N.S.C. [National Security Council] staff secretly diverted millions of dollars in profits from the Iran arms sales to the Contras, but the President said he did not know about it and [Vice Adm. John M.] Poindexter claimed he did not tell him.

The Chairman of the Joint Chiefs of Staff was not informed of the Iran arms sales, nor was he ever consulted regarding the impact of such sales on the Iran-Iraq war or on U.S. military readiness.

The Secretary of State was not informed of the millions of dollars in Contra contributions solicited by the N.S.C. staff from foreign governments with which the State Department deals each day.

Congress was told almost nothing — and what it was told was false.

—Report of the Congressional Committees Investigating the Iran-Contra Affair, 1987

A hearing of the Senate Watergate investigating committee. The committee members are at left; the witness sits at the table facing them.

Deering concluded that "two decades of change have produced committees that are less powerful and autonomous."[97] At the same time, they emphasize that there are important differences between House and Senate committees. For example, Senate committees do not rely on subcommittees to draft legislation nearly as much as do House committees. " 'Subcommittee government' therefore is an accurate depiction of decision-making patterns within most House committees but very few Senate committees."[98]

Congressional Investigations

Although committees basically process legislation, they perform other tasks, such as educating the public on important issues through hearings and investigations. In 1973 the Senate Select Committee on Presidential Campaign Activities began its far-reaching inquiries into the Watergate affair. Those hearings revealed that President Nixon had tape-recorded his White House conversations, a disclosure that precipitated the legal confrontation between the president and the courts over access to the tapes.

More than anything that had gone before, the Watergate hearings revealed the inside workings of the executive branch at that time. The hearings demonstrated the tremendous power of a congressional investigation, particularly a televised Senate investigation, to

[97] Steven S. Smith and Christopher J. Deering, *Committees in Congress*, 2nd edition (Washington, D.C.: CQ Press, 1990), p. xi.
[98] Ibid., p. 162.

focus the nation's attention on its political process. In 1974, the hearings were followed by the House Judiciary Committee's impeachment investigation and Nixon's resignation. Again, in 1987, the televised hearings on the Iran-contra scandal were viewed by millions of Americans and revealed a great deal of information about the secret foreign policies of the Reagan administration.

Some congressional investigations, such as those conducted by Senator Joseph R. McCarthy, have trampled on individual rights. But a series of Supreme Court decisions, starting in 1957, has attempted to give some protection to witnesses before committees. For example, the Supreme Court has ruled that Congress has no power to "expose for the sake of exposure" and that questions asked by a congressional investigating committee must be relevant to its legislative purpose.[99] On the other hand, the Supreme Court has ruled that witnesses cannot refuse under the First Amendment to answer questions about their political beliefs if the questions are pertinent to the committee's legislative purpose.[100] Of course, witnesses before a committee can invoke the Fifth Amendment on the grounds that their answers might tend to incriminate them. But many people infer that witnesses who invoke this constitutional privilege are guilty of something, and the witnesses may lose their jobs or suffer other social penalties as a result.

Committee Chairpersons

The party that controls the House or Senate selects the chairpersons and that party's members of the standing committees for that house. Most committee chairpersons still achieve their power and position by seniority, but the system has been modified in recent years. Today, in both the Senate and the House, members can no longer count on length of service to promote them automatically to committee chairs.

Beginning in the early 1970s, both Democrats and Republicans in the House passed reforms that allowed party members to vote by secret ballot to select committee chairpersons and ranking minority members. In the Senate, both parties also provided for election of committee chairpersons and ranking minority members. Republican members of Senate committees select their chairpersons, when Republicans control the Senate, or

ranking members when they do not, subject to approval by the party conference. Senate Democrats vote as a group for committee chairpersons or ranking members, and by secret ballot when 20 percent of Democratic senators request it. These congressional reforms ended the long-standing practice of selecting committee chairpersons automatically by seniority. Until these reforms were adopted, no aspect of Congress had been criticized more often than the seniority system (sometimes assailed as "the senility system"). The system has not been entirely abandoned, however, since older members usually are selected as chairpersons.

Despite the reforms, as of 1992, the seniority principle had been set aside only rarely in the House. It had never been violated in the Senate. Seniority is still the leading factor in choosing committee chairpersons. In mid-1992 the average age of the chairpersons of the standing committees of Congress was 64.6 years, more than 10 years older than the average for Congress as a whole. (See Table 12-5 for the ages of the individual chairpersons.)

The chief argument against seniority has been that it bestowed power not necessarily on the most qualified, but on the longest-lived; that the power of committee chairpersons diluted party responsibility and congressional support for presidential programs; and that committee chairpersons returned by "safe" constituencies tend to be more conservative than the nation as a whole. In the past, for example, the seniority system resulted in the selection of many older, conservative southern Democrats who had been re-elected from safe districts.

But the same seniority system that historically has benefited southerners also has rewarded those northerners and liberals who are regularly returned to Capitol Hill. In 1992, for example, there were four African American standing-committee chairmen in the House. In addition, one select committee of the House was also headed by an African American.

Members of the House and Senate are assigned to committees by the party machinery discussed earlier in this chapter. By tradition, each party is usually allotted seats on committees roughly in proportion to its strength in each house of Congress.

Members are assigned to committees partly on the basis of seniority, but other factors are taken into account, including the party standing of members, willingness to vote with the leadership, geographical balance, the number of available vacancies, the interests of the legislators' districts, and whether the assignment will help their re-election. Certain committees are more

---

[99] *Watkins v. United States*, 354 U.S. 178 (1957).
[100] *Barenblatt v. United States*, 360 U.S. 109 (1959).

important than others. In the House, members compete for places on Appropriations, Rules, and Ways and Means. In the Senate, particularly desirable committees include Appropriations, Finance, Foreign Relations, and Armed Services.

Committee chairpersons still wield considerable influence. They schedule meetings, decide what bills will be taken up, and usually control the hiring and firing of the majority committee staff. In some cases a committee chairperson can pigeonhole a bill simply by refusing to hold hearings.

In recent years, however, there has been a trend toward greater democracy within some of the committees. Rules have been adopted by some committees giving rank-and-file members a greater voice in committee operations and providing for regularly scheduled meetings. In the House, a majority of members can file a discharge petition to dislodge a bill from any committee, including Rules, but the device is little used and seldom successful.[101]

Congressional Staffs

Congress has become a bureaucracy. In recent years, the number of people on the congressional payroll has increased enormously.

In addition to staff members on their office payrolls, senators and representatives have large committee and subcommittee staffs to serve them. Office staffs are likely to concentrate on legislative and constituent services, while on the committees, staff members draft and analyze bills, coordinate with officials in the executive branch, and prepare for hearings. In 1957 congressional staffs totaled 4,489. By 1992 the figure had more than quadrupled to 20,460.[102]

Although congressional staff members have been criticized for having too much influence, one study concluded that members of the staff "do much of the congressional work and . . . in many instances, this work could not be done without staff."[103] The staffs have grown because of "a greater congressional workload" and the desire of senators and representatives to have "the assistance of skilled experts."[104]

Staff members on some key committees wield power almost comparable to that of White House staff members. Along with the explosion in congressional staff there has been a corresponding increase in cost. Between 1970 and 1990 the cost of running Congress rose from $361 million to $1.9 billion.[105]

Senator Nancy Kassebaum, Republican of Kansas, confers with staff aide.

In addition to their staffs, members of Congress have several legislative support agencies that help them do their jobs. The Congressional Research Service of the Library of Congress provides quick answers and long-range studies on a wide range of issues and has computerized data bases available to members and their staffs. The General Accounting Office (GAO) serves as an important watchdog into waste or fraud in the bureaucracy and conducts investigations at the request of congressional committees. The Congressional Budget Office provides Congress with an independent analysis of the president's budget and economic assumptions. Finally, the Office of Technology Assessment helps Congress deal with scientific and technological issues, from the safety of nuclear reactors to the risks of genetic engineering.

Congress and the Budget

Before Congress passed the Congressional Budget and Impoundment Control Act of 1974, it was hard for members to keep track of the dollar total of the various

[101] The Senate, too, has a discharge procedure, but it is almost never invoked.
[102] Federal Civilian Workforce Statistics, *Employment and Trends as of March 1992* (Washington, D.C.: U.S. Office of Personnel Management, 1992), p. 16.
[103] Harrison W. Fox, Jr., and Susan Webb Hammond, *Congressional Staffs* (New York: Free Press, 1977), p. 2.
[104] Ibid., p. 27.
[105] Ornstein, Mann, and Malbin, *Vital Statistics on Congress 1991–1992*, pp. 136–37.

appropriations bills it passed. Certain programs were favored by members of Congress, and, partly as a result, the lawmakers proved unable to control federal spending. Conflict over the budget on the one hand, and soaring costs on the other, were the twin factors that helped to bring about passage of the 1974 act.[106] The new law required Congress to adopt budget *resolutions* each year setting target figures for total spending. The act also created a House Budget Committee, a Senate Budget Committee, and a Congressional Budget Office within Congress to provide the experts, the computers, and the data needed by the members. Moreover, the law established a timetable for Congress and its committees to act on spending bills. This schedule was an attempt to give Congress time to evaluate the president's budget and to choose among competing programs.

In 1985, Congress, worried by growing budget deficits and a $2 trillion national debt, passed a sweeping new law designed ostensibly to eliminate all deficits and providing for the use, if necessary, of unprecedented automatic budget cuts. The law was sponsored by two freshmen senators, Phil Gramm, a Texas Republican, and Warren Rudman, a New Hampshire Republican, and by a more senior Democrat, Ernest F. Hollings of South Carolina. Only eight months later, however, in July of 1986, the United States Supreme Court struck down the Gramm-Rudman provision for automatic budget cuts. The Court held that the provision for automatic cuts violated the constitutional principle of separation of powers because the cuts would have been enforced by the Comptroller General—an official who can be removed by Congress. That provision, the Court held, encroached on the president's authority.

In 1987, Congress rewrote Gramm-Rudman to restore the requirement for automatic cuts by giving the Office of Management and Budget power to make the reductions, a change designed to meet the constitutional objections raised by the Supreme Court. The new law required that the deficit be eliminated by 1993, a goal that was not met.

Gramm-Rudman also revised the annual timetable for the budget process. On October 1, the federal fiscal year begins, running until the following September 30. On more than one occasion, however, Congress has failed to meet the October 1 deadline and has been forced to enact stopgap measures to keep the government operating.

In 1990, Congress again tackled the huge federal deficit, and revised the budget process once more. The new procedures emerged in the wake of a memorable power struggle between President Bush and Congress, sometimes known as the budget "summit." In the process Bush reneged on his 1988 campaign promise— "read my lips, no new taxes"—and agreed to $164 billion in new taxes over five years as part of a compromise that included spending limits. The complex new legislation, known as the Omnibus Budget Reconciliation Act of 1990, set caps on appropriations for domestic, international, and defense programs. It placed such mandatory spending programs as Medicare on a "pay as you go" basis. Under the law's new timetables for the budget process, the president's budget request is due the first Monday in February each year. As before, Congress is required to adopt a budget resolution by April 15, and the fiscal year begins on October 1.

The complex provisions of the 1990 act created what political scientist Aaron Wildavsky has termed a "budgetary wonderland."[107] The 1985 Gramm-Rudman budget act, as Wildavsky noted, "has been left partly in place, the new rising somewhat shakily atop the old."[108]

The earlier 1974 budget act, as modified by a later Supreme Court decision, also provided that a president cannot "impound" or refuse to spend money that Congress has appropriated, unless Congress approves that action by law.[109] This provision was included because President Nixon had withheld billions of dollars appropriated by Congress.

As part of the overall budget process, Congress, as in the past, also authorizes spending programs. In separate legislation, it then enacts appropriations to pay for them. Many members of Congress have complained that the procedural demands of the budget act have proved burdensome. On the other hand, the new process has "helped Congress overcome its image of fiscal irresponsibility."[110] And the creation of the Congressional Budget Office meant that Congress no longer had

[106] Allen Schick, *Congress and Money: Budgeting, Spending and Taxing* (Washington, D.C.: The Urban Institute, 1980), p. 42.

[107] Aaron Wildavsky, *The New Politics of the Budgetary Process*, 2nd edition (New York: HarperCollins, 1992), p. 516.

[108] Ibid.

[109] As originally enacted, the 1974 law permitted either branch of Congress to force the president to release money. Under the decision of the Supreme Court and of a lower federal court, Congress can now only do so by law. The cases are *Immigration and Naturalization Service* v. *Chadha*, 462 U.S. 919 (1983), and *City of New Haven* v. *United States*, 809 F. 2d 900 (d.c. cir. 1987).

[110] Joel Havemann, *Congress and the Budget* (Bloomington: Indiana University Press, 1978), p. 205.

to rely on the executive branch for fiscal facts and figures.

These changes have shifted more power to Congress in dealing with the federal budget. Allen Schick, a student of the congressional budget process, concluded that the 1974 law has given Congress the tools it needs to manage conflict over the budget, if it has the will to do so.[111] At the same time, the new budget procedure "concentrates enormous power in the Budget Committees."[112]

A BILL IS PASSED

All of these institutions, people, and procedures — the formal organization of Congress, the party leadership, the floor maneuvering, the committee system, staff work — bear some relationship to whether a bill will make its way into law. To do so, it must cross hurdles every step of the way.

The formal route that a bill must follow is shown in Figure 12-1. Any member may introduce a bill. (Some legislation is introduced as a "Joint Resolution," which becomes law in the same manner as a bill.[113]) After a bill is introduced in either the House or the Senate, or both, it is referred to a committee, which may hold hearings or assign the bill to a subcommittee. Hearings are almost always open to the public. They may be closed by an open vote of the committee, but this normally occurs only when national security or classified information is being discussed. After receiving the subcommittee's recommendations, the full committee meets to decide what action to take on the bill. It may do nothing, or it may rewrite the bill completely, or it may report out the original bill to the House or Senate, with or without

[111] Allen Schick, *Congress and Money: Budgeting, Spending and Taxing*, pp. 566–79.

[112] Allen Schick, *Reconciliation and the Congressional Budget Process* (Washington, D.C.: American Enterprise Institute for Public Policy Research, 1981), p. 37.

[113] There are two other kinds of congressional resolutions. A "simple" resolution is passed by one branch of Congress and relates to matters entirely within the jurisdiction of that house. A concurrent resolution must be passed by both houses. Neither a simple nor a concurrent resolution goes to the president for his signature and neither has the force of law.

Figure 12-1
How a Bill Becomes Law

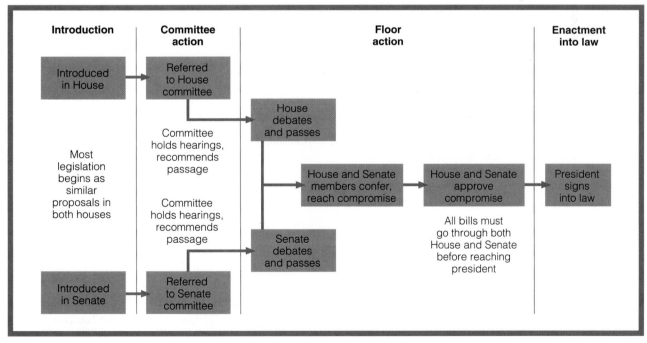

amendments. A written report, often with minority views, accompanies the bill from committee.[114] The bill is placed on one of the House calendars or the Senate calendar to await floor action.

If a bill is passed by one house, it is sent to the other chamber, which may pass the bill as is, send it to committee, or ignore it and continue to press its own version of the legislation. If there are major differences in the final bill passed by each house, one house may ask for a *conference*. The presiding officer of each house names a conference committee usually composed of senior members of the standing committees or subcommittees that have considered the bill. The selection of members to serve on the conference committee may influence whether any legislation emerges, or the nature of the legislation that is reported out. The conferees attempt to iron out disagreements and reconcile the two versions. Usually, they reach some form of agreement and report back to their respective houses. But agreement is not always reached, or it may be reached only after important changes in the legislation are made. Each house then approves or rejects the conference report. If both houses approve, the final version is signed by the Speaker and the president of the Senate and is sent to the president, who may sign the bill into law, let it become law without his signature, or veto or pocket veto the bill, as described in Chapter 10. If Congress overrides a presidential veto by a two-thirds vote in both houses, the bill becomes law without the president's signature.

Legislative Vetoes

In recent years, Congress has enacted many laws containing a "legislative veto" over acts of the executive branch. A legislative veto, as the term suggests, is a provision of law in which Congress asserts the power to override or strike down an action by the executive branch. Presidents have consistently opposed such provisions as being unconstitutional, and in 1983 the Supreme Court agreed. In the landmark *Chadha* case, the Court ruled 7–2 that the legislative veto violated the constitutional requirement of separation of powers among the branches of the government.[115]

At the time of the Supreme Court ruling, more than two hundred statutes had been passed containing some form of legislative veto. The practice dates back to 1932.

The Court's decision, although historic, left a great deal of uncertainty in its wake. One of the most important legislative vetoes is contained in the War Powers Resolution, which Congress passed in 1973 to limit the president's authority to commit troops to combat overseas. Many constitutional scholars thought it unlikely that any president would directly challenge Congress over the war powers law.

Even after the *Chadha* decision, Congress continued to pass laws containing legislative veto provisions. President Reagan signed the bills, with disclaimers concerning the legislative vetoes. Both Congress and the president found it convenient to compromise rather than fight over the issue. "'It may come as a surprise to some observers in town that Congress has continued to enact legislative vetoes after the *Chadha* decision,' said Louis Fisher, a specialist in the government division of the Congressional Research Service of the Library of Congress, who has written extensively about the legislative veto.

"'Are they unconstitutional?' Mr. Fisher asked rhetorically of the post-*Chadha* legislative vetoes. 'By the court's definition they are. Will this change the behavior between committees and agencies? Probably not.'"[116]

Gradually, in the wake of *Chadha*, however, Congress on a piecemeal basis began rewriting laws containing legislative vetoes to require action by both houses of Congress and a signature by the president—in other words, passage of a new law—before a legislative veto could take effect.

CONGRESS AND THE AMERICAN POLITICAL SYSTEM

Congress is a major battleground of American democracy. But in attempting to manage the external demands placed on it, it is caught among the crosscurrents of a restless and rapidly changing society.

---

[114] The minority section of the report sets forth the views of those opposed to the majority recommendation of the committee. Typically, but not always, the minority view is signed primarily by members of the committee who belong to the minority party in that house of Congress.

[115] *Immigration and Naturalization Service v. Chadha*, 462 U.S. 919 (1983).

[116] Martin Tolchin, "In Spite of the Court, the Legislative Veto Lives On," *New York Times*, December 21, 1983, p. B10.

Its decentralized pattern of organization, with power allocated among various committees and subcommittees, may work against innovative leadership on Capitol Hill. Moreover, programs enacted by Congress may not fit together as a coherent whole. This policy fragmentation is particularly visible in the House, where bills on major subjects such as energy and health are sometimes referred to well over a dozen committees and subcommittees. In recent years, the House has formed temporary ad hoc committees to deal with energy and welfare reform. These temporary arrangements are symptoms of "the difficulties the House has in attempting to come to grips with major policy questions that cut across the dispersive power structure of subcommittee governments."[117]

On the other hand, the Congressional Budget and Impoundment Control Act of 1974, the Gramm-Rudman Act in 1985, as modified in 1987, and the Omnibus Budget Reconciliation Act of 1990 represented a major effort by Congress to adopt a more coherent approach to federal spending. "Most important, budget reform forced Congress to confront the budgetary consequences of its own actions."[118]

[117] Patterson, "The Semi-Sovereign Congress," in King, *The New American Political System,* p. 163.
[118] Havemann, *Congress and the Budget,* p. 205.

For many years, Congress failed to exercise a leadership role in the field of foreign policy; it tended to defer to the president in the exercise of its war powers. One result was Vietnam: the longest war in American history, fought without a declaration of war by Congress. But starting in 1973, Congress began to try to reassert its power in the field of foreign policy. It ended the bombing of Cambodia, enacted the War Powers Resolution, and ordered the Central Intelligence Agency to report to Congress on covert operations.

Some scholars have argued that the American political system is not designed to cope with change, that the checks and balances embedded in the Constitution, combined with differences between the president and Congress, make the legislative branch unable to act. Others have criticized the procedures of Congress itself.

Certainly there is still room for reform in Congress. The behavior of some members who violate ethical standards casts a cloud over all members. For many years Congress showed little desire to institute reforms. Its prevailing attitude was reflected by the late senator Everett Dirksen, who, when asked about prospects for a reform measure, replied: "Ha, ha, ha; and I might add, ho, ho, ho."

In the wake of scandals, however, both the House and Senate established ethics committees, and in 1968 both houses adopted weak codes of conduct for their

Congress: "rule-making for society . . . "

members. In 1977 the House and Senate strengthened their ethics codes, requiring financial disclosure by members and limiting outside earned income. Beginning in 1991, members of the House and Senate could no longer accept fees for speeches or articles.

In the 1970s, both the Democrats and the Republicans modified the seniority system and adopted many other important reforms. The changes in the seniority system—such as the election of committee chairpersons by the majority party caucus—have altered power relationships by making chairpersons more responsive to the majority sentiment in their party and more representative of the country as a whole. Committee chairpersons now have to seek the support of their colleagues to ensure their re-election as chairpersons—a major departure from the autocratic ways of the past.

In addition, as already noted, Congress does more than approve legislation. At times it does innovate and initiate, and it serves to give a measure of legitimacy to the process of rule-making for society. Many of the innovative measures that a president finally adopts as his own have first been proposed by individual legislators.

There are times when Congress seems to be still operating in the nineteenth century. But at other times it is perhaps slow to act because the consensus in the country that Congress needs to act and to innovate is slow to develop. To a great extent, Congress reflects the decentralization and pluralism that characterize the American political system as a whole. A powerful argument can be made that Congress does act when the people demand it, their voice is clear, and the need unmistakable. E. E. Schattschneider has described American government as a political system "in which the struggle for democracy is still going on."[119] Viewed in that context, Congress is neither ideal nor obsolete, but rather an enduring arena for political conflict and a crucible for democratic change.

PERSPECTIVE

Congress plays a central and crucial role in the political system by making laws. By legislating, Congress makes and implements national policy. Congress has nonlegislative functions as well, such as proposing amendments to the Constitution, declaring war, ruling on presiden-

tial disability, and regulating the conduct of its members. Congress oversees and supervises the operations of the executive branch and the independent regulatory agencies. Congress also acts, to some extent, as a referee in resolving conflict among groups, and it provides one of several points of access to the political system for many individuals and groups.

Congress is a much-criticized institution. It has been tarnished by scandal and by the questionable ethics and activities of some of its members. Since 1970, for example, more than twenty-five members of Congress have been the subject of criminal charges.

On the other hand, Congress has instituted a number of procedural reforms in recent years. For example, in response to criticism that it has rewarded age rather than competence, it has modified the seniority system. Most committee chairpersons still achieve their power and position by seniority, but members with the longest service no longer automatically chair committees. As a result, chairpersons are now more responsive to the wishes of committee members.

Congress was also long criticized for failure to exercise power over foreign affairs; it tended to defer to the president in the exercise of its war powers. In response, Congress in 1973 passed the War Powers Resolution and has taken a greater role in the conduct of foreign policy. In the two decades since the resolution was passed, however, the law had not effectively restricted the president's military power. In the Persian Gulf, President Bush embarked on a major war against Iraq in 1991 without a declaration of war by Congress, although Congress did pass a resolution authorizing the use of military force.

The socioeconomic makeup of Congress is not representative of the general population. When the 102nd Congress convened in January 1991 there were only thirty-one women, twenty-six African Americans, and one Native American. A typical member of Congress might be a person about fifty-four years old, male, white, Protestant, and a lawyer.

Legislators must choose among alternative roles open to them. They must decide whether, for example, to work for the interests of their districts, seek to become party leaders, run for higher office, specialize in a committee, or seize an issue that may bring them national recognition.

Congress and its individual members enjoy a rather mixed public image. Public opinion of Congress as a whole may be negative, but individual lawmakers are often popular and frequently re-elected.

---

[119] E. E. Schattschneider, *The Semisovereign People* (New York: Holt, Rinehart and Winston, 1960), p. 102.

The classic dilemma of legislators is whether they should lead or follow the opinion of their constituents. Should they follow their own judgment and serve as trustees for the people? Or should they act as instructed delegates who automatically mirror the will of the majority of their constituents? Most House and Senate members try to combine the two roles by exercising their own judgment and representing constituency views as well.

Although Congress is one branch of the federal government, the House of Representatives and Senate are distinct institutions. The 435 members of the House of Representatives serve two-year terms. Despite the relative safety of House seats, there has been a dramatic turnover in the membership of the House over the past decade. For example, in 1992, in the wake of the House bank scandal, a record number of lawmakers decided to retire.

Because of its larger size, the House is a more formal institution than the Senate, with stricter rules and procedures. In the House, the Speaker is the most powerful member. The Speaker's formal duties include the power to preside over the House and to recognize or ignore members who wish to speak. Much of the Speaker's power comes from the combination of these official duties with the Speaker's position as political leader of the majority party in the House. But the Speaker must share power with the chairpersons of the twenty-two standing committees of the House, many of whom are powerful in their own right. The Speaker has two chief assistants, the majority leader and the majority whip. Most legislation in the House must be cleared by the Rules Committee before it can be debated on the floor.

The Senate has one hundred members who serve staggered six-year terms. The closest parallel in the Senate to the Speaker of the House is the Senate majority leader, who is the most powerful elected leader of the Senate. The Senate majority and minority leaders represent their party in the Senate. But they may not represent majority sentiment in their party nationally. As in the House, the leader of each party in the Senate is assisted by a whip.

Unlike the House, the Senate is more informal and less bound by rules. Most of the time, the Senate allows unlimited debate. Because of this, a single senator or group of senators may stage a filibuster and talk at length to prevent a bill from coming to a vote. A filibuster may be ended if sixteen members petition, and three-fifths of the entire Senate (sixty members) vote, for cloture.

Once cloture is invoked, debate is limited to thirty hours. The norms and rules—for example, silent apprenticeship, specialization—that once characterized the Senate have been weakened as more senators have emerged as presidential candidates. Today, senators seek broad involvement in multiple issues, and newcomers often speak up, sometimes rapidly gaining national recognition.

Committees and subcommittees are where Congress does most of its work. It is here that policies are shaped, interest groups heard, and legislation hammered out. The thirty-eight standing committees of Congress are the permanent committees that consider bills and conduct hearings and investigations. The standing committees are the heart of the committee system. At times, Congress may create special or select committees to conduct special investigations.

The chairpersons of the standing committees of the House and Senate wield considerable power. But power in Congress has become substantially decentralized. Much committee work is now dispersed to subcommittees, each with its own chairperson. In 1992 there were 135 House subcommittees, and the Senate had 87 subcommittees. The proliferation of subcommittees is one of the most dramatic changes in the structure of Congress over the past two decades.

Although committees basically process legislation, they perform other tasks, such as educating the public on important issues through hearings and investigations. In 1973 the Senate Select Committee on Presidential Campaign Activities began its far-reaching inquiries into the Watergate affair. And in 1987 the televised hearings on the Iran-contra scandal were viewed by millions of Americans and revealed a great deal of information about the secret foreign policies of the Reagan administration.

In 1974 Congress passed the Congressional Budget and Impoundment Control Act. The new law made it easier for members to keep track of the dollar total of the various appropriations bills it passed. The act required Congress to adopt budget resolutions each year setting target figures for total spending. The act also created a House Budget Committee, a Senate Budget Committee, and a Congressional Budget Office within Congress to provide the experts, the computers, and the data needed by the members. The law established a timetable for Congress and its committees to act on spending bills. This schedule was an attempt to give Congress time to evaluate the president's budget and to choose among competing programs.

By 1985, Congress was worried by growing budget deficits and a $2 trillion national debt. Senators Phil Gramm, Warren Rudman, and Ernest F. Hollings sponsored a new law designed to eliminate all deficits, and providing for the use of automatic budget cuts. However, in July of 1986, the United States Supreme Court struck down the law and held that the provision for automatic cuts was unconstitutional because it encroached on the president's authority. In 1987, Congress rewrote Gramm-Rudman to restore the provision for automatic cuts by giving the Office of Management and Budget power to make reductions. The new law required that the deficit be eliminated by 1993, a goal that was not met. In 1990, after a struggle with President Bush over taxes and the budget, Congress again revised the budget process by enacting the Omnibus Budget Reconciliation Act. This complex new legislation set caps on appropriations for domestic, international, and defense programs.

Any member of Congress may introduce a bill. After a bill is introduced in either the House or the Senate, or both, it is referred to a committee, which may hold hearings or assign the bill to a subcommittee. After receiving the subcommittee's recommendations, the full committee may do nothing with the bill, rewrite the bill completely, or report out the original bill with or without amendments. If a bill is passed by one house, it is sent to the other chamber. If both houses pass different versions of the bill, the differences may be resolved by a conference committee usually composed of senior members of the committees that have considered the bill. If agreement is reached, and both houses approve the conference report, the bill is sent to the president. The president may sign the bill into law, let it become law without his signature, or veto or pocket veto the bill. If Congress overrides a presidential veto by a two-thirds vote in both houses, the bill becomes law without the president's signature.

Since 1932, Congress has passed many laws containing a "legislative veto" over acts of the executive branch. In 1983, however, the Supreme Court ruled the practice unconstitutional, but Congress has continued to pass such laws.

Suggested Reading

Barone, Michael, and Ujifusa, Grant. *The Almanac of American Politics* 1992,* published biennially (National Journal, 1991). An extremely useful, comprehensive guide to political leaders at the local, state, and national levels. Includes political profiles of the governors, senators, and representatives, their districts, voting records on major issues, and ratings from various interest groups.

Congressional Quarterly, Weekly Report and annual *Almanac* (Congressional Quarterly, Inc.). A comprehensive and very useful report on American politics, with special emphasis on Congress and current legislation. Published weekly, with an annual almanac that contains much of the material from the weekly reports.

Davidson, Roger H., and Oleszek, Walter J. *Congress and Its Members*, 3rd edition* (Congressional Quarterly Press, 1989). A very useful general introduction to Congress and to the men and women who are elected to it.

Fenno, Richard F., Jr. *Congressmen in Committees** (Little, Brown, 1973). A revealing and important comparative analysis of how congressional committees make decisions. Based on a detailed examination of six different committees in the House of Representatives, and their six Senate counterparts.

Fenno, Richard F., Jr. *Home Style** (Little, Brown, 1978). A thoughtful analysis of a very important aspect of the political behavior of House members — their relationships with the constituents in their home district.

Fiorina, Morris P. *Congress: Keystone of the Washington Establishment** (Yale University Press, 1989). A lively and interesting discussion of how Congress creates new bureaucracies in Washington and then gains credit at home by helping voters to deal with those agencies. The author argues that House seats are safer as a result.

Fox, Harrison W., Jr., and Hammond, Susan Webb. *Congressional Staffs* (Free Press, 1977). A detailed and informative analysis of the professional, nonelected men and women who work for Congress. Focuses on their backgrounds, personalities, and work-related roles, and assesses the impact of staffs on Capitol Hill.

Huitt, Ralph K., and Peabody, Robert L., eds. *Congress: Two Decades of Analysis* (Greenwood Press, 1979). (Originally published in 1969.) Peabody presents an excellent summary and analysis of research on Congress from the mid-1940s to the mid-1960s, and Huitt offers a series of perceptive and influential articles on congressional behavior. Contains a useful bibliography of books and articles on Congress.

Mann, Thomas E., and Ornstein, Norman J., eds. *The New Congress** (American Enterprise Institute for Public Policy Research, 1981). An interesting collection of essays on important changes in the way Congress operates. Analyzes the effects of decentralization and the greater independence of members of Congress.

Mayhew, David R. *Congress: The Electoral Connection** (Yale University Press, 1974). A stimulating and thoughtful analysis of congressional behavior. Argues that a member of Congress's basic motivation is to win re-election, and traces the effects this has on a member's legislative behavior and the way Congress makes policy.

Oleszek, Walter J. *Congressional Procedures: The Policy Process*, 3rd edition* (Congressional Quarterly Press, 1988). An extremely useful, clearly written examination of the rules and procedures in the Senate and the House of Representatives. Describes the congressional legislative process in detail, from the introduction of a bill to final presidential action.

Peabody, Robert L. *Leadership in Congress* (Little, Brown, 1976). An important study of party leadership in Congress. Examines the personalities, activities, and recruitment of House and Senate leaders through a series of case studies of leadership contests from 1955 to 1974.

Peabody, Robert L., and Polsby, Nelson W., eds. *New Perspectives on the House of Representatives*, 4th revised edition* (Johns Hopkins University Press, 1992). A useful series of articles on various aspects of the House, including specific congressional committees, leadership contests, and legislative-executive relations.

Polsby, Nelson W. *Congress and the Presidency*, 4th edition* (Prentice-Hall, 1986). A concise, readable analysis of the legislative and executive branches of government. Polsby makes useful observations on the Senate and House of Representatives as distinct political institutions, and traces the budgetary process in the executive branch and Congress.

Sinclair, Barbara. *The Transformation of the U.S. Senate* (Johns Hopkins University Press, 1989). An interesting analysis of how and why Senate norms have been transformed in recent decades. Argues that senatorial folkways have changed because senators are now rewarded for broad involvement in multiple issues and policy arenas.

Smith, Steven S., and Deering, Christopher J. *Committees in Congress*, 2nd edition* (Congressional Quarterly Press, 1990). A detailed, recent analysis of the dynamics of congressional committees. Argues that over the past two decades, for a variety of reasons, committees of Congress have become less powerful and less autonomous.

Sundquist, James L. *The Decline and Resurgence of Congress* (The Brookings Institution, 1981). A major study that focuses on the efforts made by Congress in the early 1970s to recapture some of the powers it had lost to the presidency. Discusses the expansion of congressional staff, procedural changes, the strengthening of legislative oversight, and reforms in the congressional budget process.

Wilson, Woodrow. *Congressional Government: A Study in American Politics** (Peter Smith, 1958). (Originally published in 1885.) A classic study of congressional government in the late nineteenth century by a scholar who later became president of the United States. Stresses the separation of powers in the American political system, the importance of congressional committees and committee chairpersons, and what Wilson viewed as the predominance of congressional power over that of the president in that era.

---

* Available in paperback edition

I N THE high-ceilinged marble chamber of the Supreme Court late in June 1992, the marshal of the Court rapped his gavel on a wooden block and cried: "The honorable, the Chief Justice and the Associate Justices of the Supreme Court of the United States. Oyez, oyez, oyez. All persons having business before the honorable, the Supreme Court of the United States, are admonished to draw near."

As the marshal spoke, Chief Justice William H. Rehnquist and the associate justices, wearing their black robes, filed in through the red velvet curtains behind the bench. It was the last day of the Court's term before the summer adjournment, and decisions were announced in a number of important cases.

In its most significant ruling, the Supreme Court reaffirmed but modified its 1973 decision in *Roe* v.

Chapter 13

Justice

Wade which had established abortion as a fundamental right. Now, nearly two decades later, the Court gave the states much wider power to regulate abortion. Its decision came in the landmark case of *Planned Parenthood of Southeastern Pennsylvania* v. *Casey*.[1]

Earlier that month, the Court decided several other major cases. It ruled that prayer at a public school graduation violated the constitutional prohibition against establishment of religion.[2] It held that the health warning on cigarette packs did not protect tobacco companies from lawsuits by persons claiming that their health had been injured by smoking.[3] And it ruled that a criminal defendant can be kidnapped abroad by the United States government and brought back for trial in this country.[4]

[1] *Planned Parenthood of Southeastern Pennsylvania* v. *Casey*, 112 S.Ct. 2791 (1992).
[2] *Lee* v. *Weisman*, 112 S.Ct. 2649 (1992).
[3] *Cipollone* v. *Liggett Group*, 112 S.Ct. 2608 (1992).
[4] *United States* v. *Alvarez-Machain*, 112 S.Ct. 2188 (1992).

Despite its school prayer decision, by 1992 the Rehnquist Court tended to be a generally conservative body, reflecting appointments to the Court by two Republican presidents, Ronald Reagan and George Bush. First, Reagan, elected in 1980 as a conservative Republican, was able, over time, to place his imprint on the Court. During his first term, he filled only one vacancy on the high court, choosing Sandra Day O'Connor in 1981 to become the first woman ever to serve on the Supreme Court.

But in Reagan's second term, two more vacancies occurred. First, in 1986, Chief Justice Warren E. Burger retired. That allowed Reagan to promote Justice Rehnquist to chief justice, and to appoint Antonin Scalia, like Rehnquist a conservative, to the Court. The following year, Justice Lewis F. Powell, Jr., retired, and Reagan

named Anthony M. Kennedy, a federal appeals-court judge in San Francisco, to the Court. Kennedy was confirmed by the Senate in 1988, ending a bitter seven-month battle over the vacant seat.[5]

Reagan's successor, George Bush, had additional opportunities to attempt to shape the Court's conservative majority. When Justice William J. Brennan, Jr., the last of the two remaining liberals on the Court, retired

---

[5] Before approving Justice Kennedy, the Senate had rejected Judge Robert H. Bork, a controversial conservative, after a stormy political battle. Reagan then nominated another conservative judge of the Washington, D.C., appeals court, Douglas H. Ginsburg, but his nomination went up in a puff of smoke when it was disclosed that he had used marijuana both as a student and as a professor at Harvard Law School. For an administration pledged to a war against drugs, it was too much; within two days Ginsburg asked the president to withdraw his nomination.

in July of 1990, Bush nominated David H. Souter, a little-known federal appeals court judge from New Hampshire. A year later, Justice Thurgood Marshall, a giant of the civil rights movement before he was named to the high court by President Johnson, also stepped down at the age of eighty-two, citing his advanced years and medical condition. Bush named Clarence Thomas, a conservative federal appeals court judge, to succeed him.

Thomas, a forty-three-year-old African American born in rural Georgia and raised in poverty, was on his way to Senate confirmation when Anita F. Hill, an Oklahoma law professor, accused him of sexual harassment. Hill's charges, aired on television for days by the Senate Judiciary Committee, errupted into a major political controversy and an extraordinary drama.

Hill said that at the Department of Education and later at the Equal Employment Oppportunity Commission, Thomas had repeatedly asked her for dates and engaged in explicit sexual conversations with her about pornographic movies and his own sexual abilities. She testified in a calm, matter-of-fact manner.

For his part, Thomas categorically denied Hill's charges, said he had never talked to her about pornographic films, and accused the committee of a "high-tech lynching for uppity blacks." The committee, unable to resolve the conflicting stories, approved the Thomas nomination, and he was narrowly confirmed by the full Senate, fifty-two to forty-eight.

But, aside from the question of who was telling the truth, many persons watching the televised hearings were outraged by the treatment of Hill by the all-white, male, Senate committee. The hearings mobilized an unprecedented number of women to run for political office in 1992 and to participate in the election campaigns that year. And criticism of Hill by some committee members became a pivotal issue in more than one primary and congressional race.

Yet, well before 1992, the Supreme Court had gradually been moving in a conservative direction. More than two decades earlier, in 1969, Chief Justice Earl Warren, a liberal, had retired, and Chief Justice Burger had been named by President Nixon to succeed him. Over the next three years, Nixon had appointed three more justices to the Court, and in 1975 President Ford chose one justice. Thus by 1976 a majority of the nine-member Court had been appointed since Earl Warren's retirement.

By the mid-1980s, the Court under Burger displayed a more conservative tendency. It had, in previous

years, upheld the death sentence in certain circumstances, narrowed the reach of the Fourth Amendment's protections against unreasonable search and seizure, and limited the rights of criminal defendants. The Court's decisions in these cases were hailed by conservatives, who argued that police should be given latitude in dealing with crime.

By no means did all of the Burger Court's decisions narrow and restrict the interpretations of the Warren Court, however. In some areas, such as desegregation and privacy, the Burger Court extended and even broadened the decisions of the Warren Court. It held, for example, that all-male groups can be compelled to admit women — a ruling that the Rehnquist Court later extended to include private clubs.[6]

Nevertheless, it was clear that the Supreme Court, under Chief Justice Burger, had moved on a generally different path than it had followed under Chief Justice Warren. And this became even more apparent in the Rehnquist era.

The more conservative trend represented a major change from the Warren Court era. During Earl

---

[6] *Roberts v. U.S. Jaycees*, 468 U.S. 609 (1984); *New York State Club Association v. New York City*, 487 U.S. 1 (1988).

Warren's sixteen years as chief justice, the Supreme Court had a profound impact on politics and government in America. The Warren Court was an extraordinarily activist, innovative tribunal that wrought far-reaching change in the meaning of the Constitution. Among its major decisions, the Warren Court outlawed official racial segregation in public schools, set strict national standards to protect the rights of criminal defendants, required the equal apportionment of state legislatures and the House of Representatives, and ruled that prayers and Bible-reading in the public schools were unconstitutional. And it handed down other dramatic decisions that won it both high praise and sharp criticism — and engulfed it in great controversy.

Riding the crest of the tidal wave of social change that swept through America in the 1950s and 1960s, the Court became a natural target of those who felt it was moving too fast and too far. The political reaction to its bold decisions was symbolized by automobile bumper stickers that read "Impeach Earl Warren."

During the 1968 presidential campaign, Richard M. Nixon promised to appoint to the Supreme Court "strict constructionists who saw their duty as interpreting law and not making law. They would see themselves as caretakers of the Constitution and servants of the people, not super-legislators with a free hand to impose their social and political viewpoints upon the American people."[7]

Nixon's campaign comments clearly reflected one side of the historical argument over the "proper" role of the Supreme Court. Although the argument was as old as the republic itself, it had, by 1968, taken on new political meaning; the Warren Court had become linked in the minds of many voters with black militancy, urban riots, rising crime, and the volatile issue of "law and order" and justice in America. By contrast, others viewed the Warren Court as a humanitarian force that had revitalized American democracy.

In Chief Justice Burger, Nixon made it clear, he believed he had found a "strict constructionist" who would fit his political and philosophical requirements. After appointing Burger, Nixon sought to change the political balance on the Court further by nominating a conservative federal appeals-court judge, Clement F. Haynsworth, Jr., of South Carolina, to be an associate justice. When the Senate rejected Haynsworth in 1969 after a prolonged battle centering on conflict-of-interest

charges, Nixon in 1970 nominated another conservative southerner, G. Harrold Carswell, a federal-appeals-court judge in Florida. Carswell, too, was rejected after another dramatic fight in the Senate over charges that Carswell had shown racial bias and was a mediocre jurist. Finally, Nixon nominated Harry Andrew Blackmun, a Minnesota Republican and federal-appeals-court judge. Blackmun, a moderate, was confirmed. Over time, however, Blackmun often voted with the Court's liberal bloc.

In 1971 Nixon nominated two more Supreme Court justices whom he said shared his "conservative" philosophy. They were Lewis F. Powell, Jr., a prominent Richmond, Virginia, attorney, and William Rehnquist, then an assistant attorney general. Both were confirmed, giving President Nixon four appointees on the highest court. Since Byron R. White, a Kennedy appointee, and Potter Stewart, an Eisenhower appointee, voted in a number of important cases with the four new justices, from that point forward, in some decisions at least, Nixon had an effective majority in the highest tribunal. By the mid-1980s, however, Powell had emerged as the important "swing vote" on the Supreme Court, sometimes siding with conservatives, sometimes with liberals. Thus, in a number of important cases, Powell's vote was decisive.

In 1975 Justice William O. Douglas, an outspoken champion of individual liberties, retired after more than thirty-six years on the Court when a stroke left him unable to carry on his work. President Ford chose as his replacement a moderate, John Paul Stevens, a federal-appeals-court judge from Chicago. In 1981, Potter Stewart resigned and to replace him President Reagan named the first woman ever to serve on the Supreme Court, Judge Sandra Day O'Connor of the Arizona Court of Appeals. During the 1980 presidential

---

[7] Campaign speech, November 2, 1968, quoted in *Congressional Quarterly*, Weekly Report, May 23, 1969, p. 798.

campaign, the National Organization for Women and other feminist groups had denounced candidate Ronald Reagan for "medieval stances" on women's issues. Reagan countered by promising, if elected, to name a woman to fill one of the first Supreme Court vacancies in his administration.

With the O'Connor appointment, the associate justices of the Supreme Court found it necessary to drop the traditional title of "Mr. Justice." From then on, their title became "Justice." As a member of the Supreme Court, O'Connor at first generally allied herself with the Court's conservative wing, often voting with Chief Justice Burger, Justice Rehnquist, and Justice Powell. Reagan's appointment of Justice Scalia, the elevation of William Rehnquist to chief justice, the appointment of Anthony Kennedy in 1987, and Bush's appointments of Justices Souter in 1990 and Thomas in 1991, meant that, of the nine members of the Court, eight had been appointed by Republican presidents.

In the space of a relatively few years, the members and political philosophy of one of the three branches of the federal government had changed measurably. And, given the advanced ages of some of the justices, there would be further change. Reagan and Bush may have been able to shape the character of the Court, perhaps for years to come.

Yet the decisions of the Supreme Court are often unpredictable, and its direction not always easily categorized. For example, in 1992, after the ruling in the controversial Pennsylvania abortion case, it became clear that three justices—Sandra Day O'Connor, Anthony M. Kennedy, and David H. Souter—all moderately conservative, held the balance of power in the Court. The three justices often took a center position and voted together in a number of important close cases, including those dealing with abortion and school prayer. Souter in particular, an unknown quantity when he was appointed, had emerged as a key figure. As one observer put it, "Justice Souter's home is at the center of the Court, a center that to a striking degree he is anchoring and helping to define."[8]

THE SYSTEM OF JUSTICE

The Supreme Court stands at the pinnacle of the American judiciary, but it is only one part of the fragmented, decentralized system of justice in America, a system that encompasses a network of federal courts,

state and local courts and prosecutors, the United States Department of Justice, state and local police, the FBI, prisons and jails, probation and parole officers, and parole boards.

During a time of political activism, as in the 1960s and early 1970s, the police and the courts became the cutting edge and the enforcement arm of the "Establishment" in the eyes of dissident groups. To the mass of Americans, however, the police and courts represent the forces of "law and order."

Today, crime and its prevention influences American life in a variety of ways. Closed-circuit television guards stores and the lobbies of apartment buildings. Airline passengers must routinely pass through metal detectors, and submit their baggage to be x-rayed, in order to prevent highjackers from taking weapons aboard a plane. Many private homes, especially in more affluent areas, have burglar alarms. Armed, uniformed security guards are commonplace in shopping malls and office buildings. Gas-station cashiers sit behind protective glass windows, talking to customers through microphones. Many of these practices were unheard of little more than a decade ago. They grew so gradually that we now tend to accept them as a normal part of the landscape. But they are symbols of how crime affects the quality of life.

In recent years, the nature of justice in America, the crime rate, and the actions of the police have sometimes themselves become political issues. Decisions of the Warren Court favoring the rights of criminal defendants, and the backlash from conservatives, played a part in this. But, in addition, events during the Vietnam

[8] Linda Greenhouse, "Souter: Unlikely Anchor at Court's Center," New York Times, July 3, 1992, p. A1.

THE LAW / 491

War focused widespread public attention on the American system of justice and raised important questions about its operations, adequacy, and fairness. For example, in prosecuting antiwar protesters, the government sometimes relied on informers who encouraged or committed the same acts for which their associates were later tried. During the same period, federal grand juries were used to gather intelligence against the peace movement and to suppress political dissent. The Federal Bureau of Investigation conducted a domestic counterintelligence program (COINTELPRO), in which the FBI secretly harassed American citizens and in some cases even endangered lives.

In 1973 the extraordinary developments in the Watergate scandal led to the appointment of a special prosecutor, operating outside regular Justice Department channels, to handle the case. The appointment symbolized public skepticism over whether the normal machinery of justice could be relied on in a case involving the highest officials of the government. When Nixon fired the special prosecutor for demanding presidential tapes, the strong public reaction forced him to name another. For months, Nixon and his attorneys resisted the courts; Nixon yielded his tapes only after the Supreme Court had ruled 8–0 that he was required to produce them, and then only in the face of the growing sentiment in the House of Representatives for his impeachment.[9] In time, Attorney General John Mitchell and several high officials of the White House went to prison. The president himself was named by a federal grand jury as an unindicted co-conspirator in the cover-up of the Watergate burglary and eventually resigned and received a presidential pardon. It was clear that the president and his aides had tried to block the investigation of a crime. The Watergate controversy intensified the doubts sometimes raised about the system of justice in America.

Again, in 1986 and afterward, the Iran-contra scandal cast a shadow over the final years of the Reagan presidency and led to the indictment and trial of senior presidential aides and other participants. Once again, the attorney general of the United States, in this case Edwin Meese III, was the subject of investigation by grand juries and by a special prosecutor for a wide variety of alleged unethical or improper dealings. Several of his top aides quit in disgust, and Meese had difficulty filling senior posts in his own Department of Justice.

---

[9] *United States v. Nixon*, 418 U.S. 683 (1974).

Finally, in August 1988, Meese resigned after the special prosecutor had filed his report. Although it found no grounds to indict the attorney general on criminal charges, the report concluded he had been insensitive to the ethical requirements of his office. Against this background, a number of questions may be asked about the courts and the law.

What is the "proper" role of the Supreme Court in the American political system? Since the Constitution created three separate branches of the federal government, can the Supreme Court, as head of the judicial branch, overrule the other two branches—the president and Congress? Since its members are appointed and not accountable to the voters, should the Supreme Court "legislate" and make social policy? What has been the political impact of the Court's decisions? How is the system of criminal justice supposed to operate? How does it really operate? Is it stacked against African Americans and other minorities? Do the rich have a better chance under the system than the poor? Should America continue to have capital punishment? What steps can be taken to protect against corrupt officials at the highest level of the government? Who can investigate impartially if a president, other White House officials, or cabinet members are potential targets of a criminal investigation?

THE LAW

In a political sense, law is the body of rules made by government for society, interpreted by the courts, and backed by the power of the state. While this is a simple, dictionary-type definition, there are conflicting theories of law and little agreement on precisely how it should be defined.

If law were limited to what can be established and enforced by the state, then Louis XIV would have been correct in saying, "It is legal because I wish it." The founders of the American nation were influenced by another tradition, rooted in the philosophy of John Locke and in the principle of natural rights. This was the theory that human beings, living in a state of nature, possessed certain fundamental rights that they brought with them into organized society. The tradition of natural rights was used by the American revolutionaries of 1776 to justify their revolt against England, in modern times by Dr. Martin Luther King, Jr. and by others who practiced "civil disobedience" against laws they believed to be unjust, unconstitutional, or immoral.

Still another approach to law is sociological. In this view, law is seen as the gradual growth of rules and customs that reconcile conflict among people in societies; it is as much a product of culture, religion, and morality as of politics. There is always a problem of incorporating majority morality into criminal law; if enough people decide to break a law, it becomes difficult to enforce. One example was Prohibition, which was widely ignored and finally repealed.

Much American law is based on English *common law*. In twelfth-century medieval England, judges began to dispense law, and their cumulative body of decisions, often based on custom and precedent, came to be called common law, or judge-made law (as opposed to written law made by legislatures). In deciding cases, judges have often relied on the principle of *stare decisis*, the Latin phrase meaning "stand by past decisions." In other words, judges generally attempt to find a *precedent* for a decision in an earlier case involving similar principles. Most law that governs the actions of Americans is *statutory law* enacted by Congress, or by state legislatures or local legislative bodies, but many statutes embody principles of English common law.

Laws do not always ensure fairness. If a man discovers that his apple trees are gradually being cut down by a neighbor, he can sue for damages, but by the time the case is decided the trees may all be felled. Instead, he may, under the legal principle of *equity*, seek an immediate injunction to prevent any further tree-chopping. Equity, or fair dealing, may provide preventive measures and legal remedies unavailable under ancient principles of common law.

Cases considered by federal and state courts are either *civil* or *criminal*. Civil cases concern relations between individuals or organizations, such as a divorce action, or a suit for damages arising from an automobile accident or for violation of a business contract. The government is often party to a civil action — when the Justice Department files a civil antitrust suit against a corporation, for example. Criminal cases concern crimes committed against the public order. Most crimes are defined by local, state, and federal statutes, which set forth a range of penalties as well.

A growing body of cases in federal courts concerns questions of *administrative law*, the rules and regulations made and applied by federal regulatory agencies and commissions. Corporations and individuals can go into federal court to challenge the rulings of these agencies.

Supreme Court Justice Robert Jackson once observed that people are governed either by the will of one person, or group of persons, or by law. He added, "Law, as the expression of the ultimate will and wisdom of a people, has so far proven the safest guardian of liberty yet devised."[10]

THE SUPREME COURT

The Supreme Court is a *political institution* that makes both policy and law. Although insulated by tradition and judicial tenure from the turmoil of everyday politics, the Supreme Court lies at the heart of the ongoing struggle in the American political system. "We are very quiet there," said Justice Oliver Wendell Holmes, Jr., "but it is the quiet of a storm centre."

In giving the Constitution contemporary meaning, the Supreme Court inevitably makes political and policy choices. "To consider the Supreme Court of the United States strictly as a legal institution," Robert A. Dahl has suggested, "is to underestimate its significance in the American political system. For it is also a political institution, an institution, that is to say, for arriving at decisions on controversial questions of national policy."[11]

The Supreme Court: Politics, Policy, and Public Opinion

A basic reason for the political controversy surrounding the Supreme Court is that its precise role in the American political system was left ambiguous by the framers of the Constitution. The Supreme Court is at the apex of the judicial branch, one of the three independent, constitutionally coequal branches of the federal government. But does it have the constitutional right to resolve conflicts among the three branches? The Court may be seen, on the one hand, as one of three "coordinate" branches of the federal government, or it may be viewed as the final arbiter of constitutional questions. As Robert G. McCloskey noted, "The fact that the Constitu-

[10] Robert H. Jackson, *The Supreme Court in the American System of Government* (Cambridge: Harvard University Press, 1955), p. 27.

[11] Robert A. Dahl, "Decision-Making in a Democracy: The Role of the Supreme Court as a National Policy-Maker," in Raymond E. Wolfinger, ed., *Readings in American Political Behavior* (Englewood Cliffs: Prentice-Hall, 1966), p. 166.

tion is supreme does not settle the question of who decides what the Constitution means." [12]

This was dramatically illustrated during the 1974 court battle over the tape recordings that President Nixon secretly made of his White House conversations. When the Watergate special prosecutor subpoenaed tape recordings of certain presidential conversations for use in the criminal trial of Nixon's former subordinates, the White House announced that the president would comply only with a "definitive" Supreme Court ruling, a term that was not explained. The president cited the doctrine of separation of powers and claimed executive privilege; he argued that because the Constitution established three independent branches of government, the Supreme Court could not compel the president to release the tapes. The Court held otherwise; it recognized the existence of executive privilege, but ruled that the president could not hold back evidence needed for the criminal trial of his subordinates. [13] Despite his threats of possible defiance, Nixon yielded to the Supreme Court.

[12] Robert G. McCloskey, *The American Supreme Court* (Chicago: University of Chicago Press, 1960), p. 8.

[13] *United States* v. *Nixon* (1974).

Judicial Review Since Chief Justice John Marshall's day, the Supreme Court has exercised the right of *judicial review*, the power to declare acts of Congress or actions by the executive branch — or laws and actions at any level of local, state, and federal government — unconstitutional. Lower federal courts and state courts may exercise the same power, but the Supreme Court normally has the last word in deciding constitutional questions. "We are under a Constitution," Charles Evans Hughes declared, "but the Constitution is what the judges say it is."[14]

Yet why, it is often asked, should nine justices who are appointed for life and not elected by the people have the power in a democratic system to strike down the laws and decisions of popularly elected legislatures and leaders? The question is asked most often by people who disapprove of what the Supreme Court is doing at a particular time. Those who approve of the philosophy of a given Court seldom complain that it is overstepping its power.

And judicial review is in effect a coin with two sides. Although the Supreme Court may exercise judicial review and strike down a law as unconstitutional, it may also affirm that a law or executive act is constitutional. To date, only a little more than one hundred acts have been declared unconstitutional; thousands more have been sustained by the Court.

One view of the Supreme Court holds that, because the justices are not popularly elected, the Court should move cautiously and interpret the Constitution "strictly." Popular democracy and the principle of majority rule are more consistent, in this view, with legislative supremacy. An opposite view holds that the Court is the cornerstone of a system of *checks and balances* and restraints on majority rule provided by the Constitution. In this view, the Supreme Court often may be the *only* place in the political system where minorities are protected from the majority.

The debate over the role of the Supreme Court in the American system is sharpened by the fact that the Constitution is written in broad and sometimes ambiguous language. As a result, the Supreme Court has interpreted the meaning of the Constitution very differently at different times.

Felix Frankfurter

Justice Felix Frankfurter once observed:

> The meaning of "due process" and the content of terms like "liberty" are not revealed by the Constitution. It is the justices who make the meaning. They read into the neutral language of the Constitution their own economic and social views. . . . Let us face the fact that five Justices of the Supreme Court are the molders of policy rather than the impersonal vehicles of revealed truth.[15]

The Supreme Court must, however, operate within the bounds of public opinion, and, in the long run, within the political mainstream of the times. The Court possesses no armies, and it must finally rely on the executive branch to enforce many of its rulings. It was this truth that supposedly led President Andrew Jackson to declare of his chief justice, "John Marshall has made his decision — *now let him enforce it*."[16] The Court cannot completely ignore the reactions to its decisions in Congress and in the nation because, ultimately, as a political institution its power rests on public opinion.

The Road to Judicial Review

The Constitution gives the Supreme Court power to consider "all Cases . . . arising under this Constitution." The principle of judicial review traces back to

---

[14] Alpheus T. Mason, *The Supreme Court: Palladium of Freedom* (Ann Arbor: University of Michigan Press, 1962), p. 143. Hughes, later chief justice of the United States, made this comment in 1907 as governor of New York.

[15] Felix Frankfurter, "The Supreme Court and the Public," *Forum*, vol. 83 (June 1930), pp. 332–34.

[16] Quoted in Robert H. Jackson, *The Supreme Court in the American System of Government*, p. 11.

English common law, although the Constitution nowhere explicitly gives this power to the Court. The question of the framers' intent is still debated, but in 1788 Alexander Hamilton argued in *The Federalist* that the judicial branch did in fact have the right to judge whether laws passed by Congress were constitutional.[17] James Madison made the same point during the debate in Congress over the Bill of Rights. Later, so did James Wilson, another influential framer of the Constitution. And, according to Henry J. Abraham, "a vast majority" of the delegates to the constitutional convention favored the idea of judicial review.[18] The principle of judicial review was largely taken for granted in the debates of the convention and in the state conventions that ratified the Constitution.

During the colonial period, the British Privy Council in London exercised judicial review over laws passed by the colonial legislatures. And during the first decade of the new nation's existence, the Supreme Court, in a few cases, ruled on whether federal laws were constitutional. It invalidated one federal statute, for example, and at least twice struck down minor state laws.[19]

The power of judicial review, however — although it had already been exercised — was not firmly enunciated and established by the Supreme Court until 1803 in the case of *Marbury v. Madison*.[20] When Jefferson became president in 1801 he was angered to find that his Federalist predecessor, John Adams, had appointed a number of federal judges just before leaving office, among them one William Marbury as a justice of the peace in the District of Columbia. When Jefferson discovered that Marbury's commission had not actually been delivered to him, he ordered Secretary of State James Madison to hold it up. Under a provision of the Judiciary Act of 1789, Marbury sued in the Supreme Court for a writ of mandamus compelling the delivery of his commission. The Supreme Court under Chief Justice John Marshall dismissed the case, saying it lacked jurisdiction to issue such a writ. The Court held that the section of the Judiciary Act under which Marbury had sued was unconstitutional, since the Constitution did not empower the Court to issue a writ of mandamus, as

the act provided. The ruling thus avoided an open political confrontation with the executive branch over Marbury's commission but at the same time established the power of the Court to void acts of Congress. "The Constitution is superior to any ordinary act of the legislature," Marshall wrote, and "a law repugnant to the Constitution is void."[21]

Although the Court's power of judicial review was thus established, the question of *how* the Court should apply its great power has remained a subject of controversy up to the present day. The debate has centered on whether the Court should practice *judicial activism* or *judicial restraint*.

As one scholar has posed the central questions: "Should the Court play an active, creative role in shaping our destiny, equally with the executive and legislative branches? Or should it be characterized by self-restraint, deferring to the legislative branch whenever there is room for policy judgment and leaving new departures to the initiative of others?"[22]

The philosophy of judicial restraint is associated with Justices Felix Frankfurter, Louis D. Brandeis, and Oliver Wendell Holmes, Jr. Briefly stated, that philosophy requires the Court to avoid constitutional questions where possible and to uphold acts of Congress unless they clearly violate a specific section of the Constitution. Frankfurter held that the Court should avoid deciding "political questions" that could involve it in conflicts with other branches of the federal government.

The philosophy of judicial activism was embraced on many issues by a majority of the members of the Warren Court, which boldly applied the Constitution to social and political questions. For example, in protecting the rights of criminal defendants and in its reapportionment decisions, the Court moved into controversial areas that earlier Supreme Court justices had avoided.

The Changing Role of the Supreme Court

Although John Marshall had set forth the right of judicial review in 1803, the Supreme Court did not declare another act of Congress unconstitutional until the *Dred*

[17] Edward Mead Earle, ed., *The Federalist*, No. 78 (New York: The Modern Library), p. 506.

[18] Henry J. Abraham, *The Judicial Process*, 4th ed. (New York: Oxford University Press, 1980), p. 322.

[19] Ibid., pp. 324–36.

[20] *Marbury v. Madison*, 1 Cranch 137 (1803).

[21] Ibid.

[22] Archibald Cox, *The Warren Court* (Cambridge: Harvard University Press, 1968), p. 2.

Scott case in 1857. Under Marshall's successor, Roger B. Taney (1836–1864), the Court protected states' rights and stressed the power of the states over that of the federal government.

After the Civil War, the Court refused to apply the Fourteenth Amendment to protect the rights of black Americans, even though Congress had passed the amendment for this specific purpose (see Chapter 5). Instead, the Court used the amendment's "due process" clause to protect business from state regulation. The Fourteenth Amendment provides that no state shall "deprive any person of life, liberty, or property, without due process of law." The Court accepted the argument that a corporation was a "person" within the meaning of the amendment. In a series of cases, it used the Fourteenth and Fifth amendments to protect industry, banking, and public utilities from social regulation. In the 1890s the Supreme Court struck down the federal income tax and emasculated the federal antitrust laws. In general, the Court during this era served as a powerful guardian of the "robber barons" — the businessmen who amassed great fortunes in the late nineteenth century — as well as a champion of *laissez-faire* capitalism, a philosophy that government should interfere as little as possible in the affairs of business.

The Court continued to expound a conservative philosophy under Chief Justice William Howard Taft in the 1920s. The election of Franklin D. Roosevelt in 1932 was followed by vast social change in America, but a majority of the Supreme Court was not in sympathy with the programs of the New Deal. Between 1933 and 1937 the Court struck down one after another of Roosevelt's programs.

In 1936 the average age of members of the Court was seventy-one, and the justices were dubbed the "nine old men."[23] Reelected by a landslide that year, Roosevelt risked his prestige in 1937 when he proposed his famous "court-packing" plan. His objective was to put younger justices on the Court who would be more sympathetic to the New Deal. Roosevelt's plan to bring the Supreme Court out of what he termed "the horse and buggy age" provided that whenever a justice refused to retire at age seventy, the president could appoint an additional justice. Under the plan, the Court could have been expanded to a maximum of fifteen members.

The debate raged in and out of Congress all that spring, but in less than six months the proposal was dead. Although Roosevelt's plan failed, by the time the Court recessed that summer it had already begun to shift to a more liberal position and to uphold New Deal programs. As a result, 1937 is regarded as a watershed year in the history of the Supreme Court. From that date on, the Court for many years emerged as the protector, not of big business, but in many cases, of the individual.

The Warren Court

Before he retired as chief justice, Earl Warren was asked to name the most important decisions of the Warren Court.[24] He singled out those dealing with reapportionment, school desegregation, and the right to counsel, in that order.[25] Each of these cases symbolized one of three broad fields in which the Warren Court brought about far-reaching changes in America: the political process itself, civil rights, and the rights of the accused.

In its reapportionment decisions, the Warren Court required that each citizen's vote count as much as

---

[24] *1968 Congressional Quarterly Almanac*, p. 539.
[25] *Baker* v. *Carr*, 369 U.S. 186 (1962); *Brown* v. *Board of Education of Topeka, Kansas*, 347 U.S. 483 (1954); *Gideon* v. *Wainwright*, 372 U.S. 335 (1963), respectively.

---

[23] A phrase popularized by columnists Drew Pearson and Robert S. Allen. See William Safire, *The New Language of Politics* (New York: Random House, 1968), p. 286.

Former Chief Justice Earl Warren

another's. If the quality of a democracy can be gauged, certainly the individual's vote is a basic unit of measurement. Until the reapportionment revolution of the Warren Court, voters were often powerless to correct basic distortions in the system of representation itself.

The *Brown* decision has not eliminated racial segregation in American schools or American society. But by striking down the officially enforced dual school system in the South, the Court implied that "all racial discrimination sponsored, supported, or encouraged by government is unconstitutional."[26] Thus the decision foreshadowed a social upheaval. The civil rights movement, the civil rights legislation of the 1960s, and the continuing controversy over the busing of public-school children all followed in the Supreme Court's wake.

By the 1980s, "integration" in itself appeared to be less important to many African Americans than freedom, dignity, and a full share of the economic opportunities of American society. Nevertheless, the *Brown* decision remains a judicial milestone; by its action at a time when much of white America was complacent and satisfied with the existing social order, the Supreme Court provided moral as well as political leadership — it reminded the nation that the Constitution applies to *all* Americans.

The third broad area of decision by the Warren Court — the protection of the rights of criminal defendants — was discussed in Chapter 4. In a series of controversial decisions, including *Miranda, Escobedo, Gideon,* and *Mapp,* the Court, bit by bit, threw the mantle of the Bill of Rights around persons accused by state authorities of crimes. In so doing, the Court collided directly with the electorate's rising fear of crime; it was accused of "coddling criminals" and "handcuffing the police." Under the Burger Court the pendulum swung back substantially, in favor of the police and prosecutors.

The Warren Court moved aggressively in several other areas as well — banning prayers in the public schools, curbing the anti-Communist legislation of the 1950s, and easing the laws dealing with "obscenity." All this activity provided ample ammunition to the Warren Court's conservative critics: the Court, they charged, had tinkered with legislative apportionment, forced school integration, overprotected the rights of crimi-

nals, banished prayer from the classroom, tolerated Communists, and encouraged pornography. Moreover, as many of the Court's critics frequently pointed out, it decided many important cases by a narrow 5 – 4 margin. The Burger Court and the Rehnquist Court moved more cautiously in the 1970s and 1980s and narrowed the sweep of some of the Warren Court's decisions, particularly in the fields of criminal justice and pornography. The Supreme Court might do so even more dramatically in the future. Yet one leading scholar predicted that

> the doctrines of equality, freedom, and respect for human dignity laid down in the numerous decisions of the Warren Court cannot be warped back to their original dimensions. . . . Generations hence it may well appear that what is supposedly the most conservative of American political institutions, the Supreme Court, was the institution that did the most to help the nation adjust to the needs and demands of a free society.[27]

The Burger Court

As noted at the outset of this chapter, even before the 1980s it had become clear that the Burger Court was moving in a different direction than the Warren Court. In decisions involving the rights of criminal defendants, for example, the Burger Court usually sought to strengthen the hand of the police and prosecutors. The Court restricted the landmark *Miranda* decision,

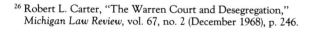

[26] Robert L. Carter, "The Warren Court and Desegregation," *Michigan Law Review,* vol. 67, no. 2 (December 1968), p. 246.

[27] William M. Beaney, "The Warren Court and the Political Process," *Michigan Law Review,* vol. 67, no. 2 (December 1968), p. 352.

narrowed the Fifth Amendment's protection against self-incrimination, made it easier for police to stop and frisk suspects, and handed down a number of other decisions more favorable to police than to defendants. Thus, one of the Burger Court's most significant actions was to chip away at the "exclusionary rule" in a series of decisions making it easier for state and local prosecutors to use illegally seized evidence to convict defendants. (See Chapter 4.) And, of course, as previously noted, the Burger Court restored the death penalty. In addition, the Court ruled that journalists had no First Amendment privilege to protect confidential sources and that journalists must answer questions about what they were thinking when they prepared reports resulting in libel suits. Many observers concluded that the Burger Court was more conservative than its predecessor and could be characterized as being to the right of center.

On a number of important issues this was certainly true, but it was not the whole picture. In some policy areas, the Burger Court gave little comfort to conservatives: it legalized abortion, declined to stop the publication of the Pentagon Papers, extended the right to counsel to poor defendants even in misdemeanor cases, outlawed wiretapping of domestic groups without a court warrant, limited the power of local communities to ban pornography, and ruled that even the president must yield evidence to the courts. In the field of civil rights, the Burger Court banned racial discrimination in private schools, declared that federal courts can require low-cost public housing for African Americans in the white suburbs, ordered busing to desegregate schools in several cities, and upheld affirmative action in education, jobs, and in federal contracts.

Thus, even as the Supreme Court shifted to the right, many of its decisions still protected individual liberties and minority groups. But, clearly, the Burger Court had developed its own style and philosophy as it carried out its task of interpreting the Constitution.

The Rehnquist Court

When William Rehnquist was sworn in as Chief Justice of the United States in September 1986, many political observers expected that his elevation would usher in an era of conservative decisions by the highest court.

But that was not the case initially, at least. During the Rehnquist Court's first term, the liberals won all but two of the major cases and the conservatives prevailed only in the area of criminal law. A moderate-liberal coalition, led by Justice William J. Brennan, Jr., decided cases on affirmative action, teaching creationism in the public schools, protection for pregnant workers, and political asylum for illegal aliens. Justice Powell's "swing vote," as previously noted, often proved decisive in closely argued cases.

For much of its second term, during 1987–88, members of the liberal-moderate wing formed the majority in a number of important cases. Moreover, the Court, by a vote of 8–0, threw out the Rev. Jerry Falwell's suit against *Hustler* magazine.[28] In so doing, the Court declined to curb criticism of public figures. The justices, on procedural grounds, declined to uphold a New Jersey law requiring public schools to set aside a moment of silence each day.[29]

But by 1988 the Rehnquist Court appeared to be moving in a somewhat more conservative direction, giving public school officials the right to censor school newspapers and plays, for example.[30] And after the appointment of Justice Anthony M. Kennedy, the Court in several decisions made it more difficult for workers to sue employers for discrimination.[31] The Court's action alarmed liberals and led to speculation that a conservative majority had finally emerged. In May 1988, in another decision that to some analysts seemed to reflect a more conservative trend, the Court ruled 6–2 that police may, without a warrant, search through trash that people leave outside their home to be collected.[32] But, as always, the decisions varied; the Court in 1990 struck down the federal law that sought to ban flag-burning.[33] And in 1991, it invalidated New York's "Son of Sam" law which had barred criminals from earning money from books about their crimes; the Court said the state law violated the First Amendment's provisions of free press and free speech.[34]

The President and the Court

Historically, presidents have picked Supreme Court justices for their politics more than for their judicial talents. By nominating justices whose political views

---

[28] *Hustler Magazine, Inc. v. Rev. Jerry Falwell*, 485 U.S. 46 (1988).
[29] *Karcher v. May*, 484 U.S. 72 (1987).
[30] *Hazelwood School District v. Kuhlmeier*, 484 U.S. 260 (1988).
[31] Among the cases were *Patterson v. McLean Credit Union*, 491 U.S. 164 (1988) and *Wards Cove Packing Co. Inc. v. Atonio*, 490 U.S. 642 (1988) The series of decisions was overturned by the civil rights bill passed by Congress in 1991.
[32] *California v. Greenwood*, 486 U.S. 35 (1988).
[33] *U. S. v. Eichman; U. S. v. Haggerty*, both 496 U. S. 310 (1990).
[34] *Simon and Schuster v. New York State Crime Victims Board*, 112 S.Ct. 501 (1991).

appear compatible with their own, they try to gain political control of the Supreme Court.

When Franklin Roosevelt unsuccessfully attempted to "pack" the Supreme Court, he was aiming not so much at the age of its members as at their political views. As Justice Hugo Black put it, "Presidents have always appointed people who believed a great deal in the same things that the President who appoints them believes in."[35]

This practice is not necessarily bad if it does not lead to the appointment of mediocre judges. In fact, it is one important way in which the Supreme Court is at least *indirectly* responsive to the electorate. Along with the power of public opinion and the power of the Senate to confirm or reject the president's nominee, the presidential appointment power to some degree links the Court to the voters and the rest of the political system.

Approximately 90 percent of all Supreme Court justices in American history have belonged to the appointing president's political party; some have been selected from the president's inner circle of political advisers. In 1965, for example, President Johnson named Washington attorney Abe Fortas—a Democrat who had been his lawyer and political confidant for many years—to the Supreme Court.[36] The requirement that a majority of the Senate approve a Supreme Court nominee restricts the president's ability to shape the Court completely to his political liking. Up to 1992 the Senate had failed to approve twenty-eight, or almost 20 percent, of the 139 Supreme Court nominations sent to it.[37]

Nor do justices always act as presidents expect. Supreme Court justices have a way of becoming surprisingly independent once they are on the bench; more than one president has been disappointed to find that he misjudged his appointee. As governor of California, Earl Warren helped to elect President Eisenhower. There was nothing in Warren's background as a moderate Republican to make the president think his chief

Table 13-1
The Supreme Court, 1992

Justices	Appointed by	Date
Byron R. White	Kennedy	1962
Harry A. Blackmun	Nixon	1970
William H. Rehnquist*	Nixon	1971
John Paul Stevens	Ford	1975
Sandra Day O'Connor	Reagan	1981
Antonin Scalia	Reagan	1986
Anthony M. Kennedy	Reagan	1987
David H. Souter	Bush	1990
Clarence Thomas	Bush	1991

* Chief Justice of the United States. Rehnquist was elevated to chief justice by President Reagan on June 17, 1986. Members of the Court as of October, 1992.

justice would preside over a social upheaval. Later, Eisenhower reportedly called the Warren appointment "the biggest damn-fool mistake I ever made."[38] And President Nixon was bitterly disappointed when Chief Justice Burger, joined by two other Nixon appointees, voted with the rest of the Court to require the president to yield his crucial tape recordings, a decision that set the stage for Nixon's resignation.[39]

At times, presidential nominations of Supreme Court justices touch off memorable political battles. Such was the case in 1991, when President Bush nominated Clarence Thomas, and in 1987, when President Reagan nominated Robert Bork. A coalition of liberal and moderate forces sought to block the nomination of Bork, a former Yale University law professor who had opposed the Supreme Court's landmark 1973 ruling permitting abortions, and who had taken other outspoken conservative positions. Opponents charged that Bork would attempt to undo rulings favoring women's rights, civil rights, privacy, and other individual rights. After televised Senate hearings and acrimonious debate, the Senate rejected Bork, fifty-eight to forty-two.

President Reagan then nominated another conservative, Douglas Ginsburg, to the court vacancy. As already noted, Ginsburg's admission that he had smoked marijuana while a law professor at Harvard, together with other ethical and personal questions

[35] "Justice Black and the Bill of Rights," interview broadcast over CBS television network, December 3, 1968, transcript in *Congressional Quarterly*, Weekly Report, January 3, 1969, p. 9.
[36] In 1968 the Senate declined to approve Johnson's elevation of Fortas to be chief justice. In 1969 Fortas resigned from the Court when it developed that three years earlier he had accepted a $20,000-a-year retainer from a foundation controlled by Louis E. Wolfson, a financier who went to prison for his stock dealings shortly before the Fortas resignation.
[37] Douglas H. Ginsburg withdrew from consideration before the president sent his nomination to the Senate.

[38] In Joseph W. Bishop, Jr., "The Warren Court Is Not Likely to Be Overruled," *New York Times Magazine*, September 7, 1969, p. 31.
[39] J. Anthony Lukas, *Nightmare: The Underside of the Nixon Years* (New York: Viking, 1976), p. 518. Associate Justice William H. Rehnquist disqualified himself and did not participate in the tapes decision, since he had served in the Justice Department under Nixon.

about his background, combined to force his withdrawal as a nominee. It was then that Reagan named Anthony Kennedy, who was confirmed in February 1988.

Congress and the Court

As Supreme Court Justice Jackson once suggested, conflict among the branches of the federal government is always latent, "ready to break out again whenever the provocation becomes sufficient."[40] The Supreme Court, in deciding cases, must worry not only about public opinion, but about how Congress may react. Walter F. Murphy has suggested that the Court's conflicts with Congress ebb and flow in a three-step pattern: First, the Court makes decisions on important aspects of public policy. Second, the Court receives severe criticism coupled with threats of remedial or retaliatory action by Congress. The third step, according to Murphy, has generally been "judicial retreat."[41]

Robert A. Dahl has concluded that the dominant policy views of the Court "are never for long out of line" with the dominant views of the legislative majority.[42] Or, as humorist Finley Peter Dunne's "Mr. Dooley" put it, "the Supreme Court follows the election returns."

Under the Constitution, Congress can control the *appellate jurisdiction* of the Supreme Court as well as its *size*. In its early history the Court had five, six, seven, and ten justices. Congress did not fix the number at nine until 1869.

After the Civil War, Congress blocked the Court from reviewing Reconstruction laws. During the late 1950s, a coalition in Congress of southern Democrats and conservative Republicans mounted a legislative assault to curb the power of the Supreme Court and limit its jurisdiction. That effort failed, but the threat of congressional retaliation is always present.

Indeed, in the 1980s, conservatives in Congress led by Senator Jesse Helms, the North Carolina Republican, introduced "court-stripping" bills designed to restrict the Supreme Court's jurisdiction and remove its

power over cases dealing with abortion and school prayer. These attempts were defeated and did not become law.

Congress (in conjunction with the states) also possesses the power to overturn Supreme Court decisions by amending the Constitution.[43] The Sixteenth Amendment, establishing the federal income tax, passed by Congress in 1909 and ratified in 1913, was adopted as a direct result of a Supreme Court decision; in 1895 the Court had ruled unconstitutional an attempt by Congress to levy a national income tax.[44] And the Twenty-sixth Amendment, giving persons eighteen and over the right to vote in all elections, was passed by Congress in 1971 and ratified that year because the Supreme Court had ruled that Congress could lower the voting age only in federal, not in state and local, elections. More recently, "pro-life" groups have tried to get Congress to propose a constitutional amendment to overturn the Supreme Court's decision legalizing abortion. And groups favoring school prayer have lobbied Congress to propose a constitutional amendment to overrule the Court's ban on prayers in the public schools.

Finally, Congress may attempt to overturn specific Supreme Court rulings by legislation. For example, Title II of the Omnibus Crime Bill of 1968 sought to overturn three major decisions of the Warren Court dealing with the rights of accused persons.[45] Police continued to be guided by the Court rulings, however.

In 1988, Congress, over President Reagan's veto, reinstated civil rights protections that had been narrowed by the Supreme Court's 1984 decision in the *Grove City* case.[46] The Civil Rights Restoration Act expanded civil rights for women, minorities, the elderly, and the disabled. The new law stated that federal antidiscrimination laws apply to an entire institution even if it accepts federal aid for only one program. The law directly overturned the Supreme Court decision. And Congress in 1991 passed a civil rights law that overturned a series of Supreme Court decisions that had made it more difficult for workers to sue employers for discrimination.

[40] Jackson, *The Supreme Court in the American System of Government*, p. 9.

[41] Walter F. Murphy, *Congress and the Court* (Chicago: University of Chicago Press, 1962), pp. 246–47.

[42] Dahl, "Decision-Making in a Democracy: The Role of the Supreme Court as a National Policy-Maker," pp. 171, 180.

[43] The Eleventh, Fourteenth, Sixteenth, and Twenty-sixth amendments to the Constitution reversed specific Supreme Court rulings.

[44] *Pollock* v. *Farmers' Loan and Trust Co.*, 158 U.S. 601 (1895).

[45] *Miranda* v. *Arizona*, 384 U.S. 436 (1966); *Mallory* v. *United States*, 354 U.S. 449 (1957); *United States* v. *Wade*, 388 U.S. 218 (1967).

[46] *Grove City* v. *Bell*, 465 U.S. 555 (1984).

THE DEATH PENALTY: THE SUPREME COURT DELIBERATES

In 1972 the Supreme Court, by a vote of 5–4, struck down the death penalty as then administered in the United States. (Four years later, the Court approved new, more carefully drawn capital punishment laws.) Here is an account of the conference at which the justices reached their 1972 decision:

> Marshall was opposed to the death penalty in any form. . . . It almost seemed a penalty designed for poor minorities and the undereducated. The rich and well-educated were rarely sentenced to death. They hired fancy lawyers. With his experience in the South, and a year spent during the Korean War investigating the cases of black GIs sentenced to death, Marshall knew very well how the system worked. The death penalty was the ultimate form of racial discrimination. . . .

The conference met on the death cases on January 21, 1972. . . . The Chief began. He observed that if he were a legislator, he would vote against the death penalty, but he was not. He would uphold. Clearly the penalty was constitutional.

Douglas and Brennan argued to strike the death penalty as Marshall had expected.

Then, there was a surprise. . . . Stewart indicated that he was inclined to vote to strike the current capital punishment laws. He would not go along with a sweeping Eighth Amendment abolition of the death penalty. But the randomness and arbitrariness of the sentencing decisions made the laws "cruel and unusual."

Marshall was pleased. He now had four votes. But White and the three Nixon appointees had not spoken.

Then came another surprise. White said that he too was troubled by the infrequency [of the death penalty's use]. It had changed his perspective. Infrequency nullified the state interest in deterrence. He too was inclined to vote to strike.

Blackmun and Powell voted tentatively to uphold the laws. Rehnquist voted firmly to uphold. . . .

"Boys, it is a surprise to me, but the death cases seem to be coming out 5 to 4 against the death penalty," Brennan told his clerks after conference.

—Bob Woodward and Scott Armstrong, *The Brethren: Inside the Supreme Court*

The Supreme Court in Action

Unlike Congress and the presidency, institutions that are the subject of continual scrutiny by the press, the Supreme Court has usually operated in secrecy. Its internal workings and deliberations have, until recently, gone largely unreported, although oral arguments and decisions in major cases are given wide publicity.

Some of this traditional secrecy was stripped away in 1979 with the publication of *The Brethren*, a controversial book by two investigative reporters about the operations of the Supreme Court.[47] The book, which covered the years 1969 through 1975, published internal memoranda of the justices and reported in great detail on the private weekly conferences in which justices discuss pending cases. A number of scholars criticized the book because its material was unsourced, and some lawyers and judges argued that the judicial process was not served by exposing the Court's internal deliberations.[48]

Nevertheless, in one area, *The Brethren* seemed persuasive — it revealed a degree of conflict and intense competition among the justices that had previously been suggested but not reported in as great detail.[49] As already noted, the Supreme Court is a political institution. According to the book, the justices engage in

---

[47] Bob Woodward and Scott Armstrong, *The Brethren: Inside the Supreme Court* (New York: Simon and Schuster, 1979).

[48] See, for example, Alpheus Thomas Mason, "Eavesdropping on Justice," in *Political Science Quarterly*, vol. 95, no 2 (Summer 1980), pp. 295–304.

[49] For two earlier analyses of conflict and decision making in the Supreme Court, see J. Woodford Howard, Jr., *Mr. Justice Murphy: A Political Biography* (Princeton: Princeton University Press, 1968); and Walter F. Murphy, *Elements of Judicial Strategy* (Chicago: University of Chicago Press, 1964).

trade-offs and deals, and form shifting alliances, much as do political participants in the executive and legislative branches.

Nor should it have been surprising that in the period from 1969 to 1975 there was sharp conflict and controversy inside the Court. It was precisely during those years that a Republican president was appointing justices with a very different philosophy from that of the Supreme Court's liberals, some of whom had been on the Court since the administration of Franklin D. Roosevelt.

The Brethren was particularly harsh on Chief Justice Warren Burger, whom it portrayed as a jurist of distinguished bearing, but a man of personal pomposity and shallow intellect. It quoted Justice William J. Brennan, Jr., as calling Burger a "dummy," and quoted Justice Lewis F. Powell, Jr., as saying of Burger's draft in a busing case: "If an associate in my law firm had done this . . . I'd fire him."[50]

The book's gossipy style and its emphasis on personalities are of less value to the scholar and student than the light it sheds on the ways that justices determine which cases reach the Court's docket and how those cases are decided.

In recent years, Supreme Court justices have been less reluctant to speak out about the Court's operations and on public issues. Chief Justice Rehnquist even wrote a book about the history and procedures of the Court.[51]

How Cases Reach the Court   Most cases never get to the Supreme Court. Those that do usually reach the Court in one of three ways. Under the Constitution, the Court has *original jurisdiction* to hear certain kinds of cases directly. These include cases involving foreign diplomats or cases in which one of the fifty states is a party. But the Court rarely exercises original jurisdiction; many more cases reach the Supreme Court under its *appellate jurisdiction*. That is, they are appealed on the grounds that they concern violations of constitutional rights. But the Court, which theoretically is obliged to hear such cases, can in practice dismiss them if it decides that no substantial federal question is involved. The overwhelming majority of cases presented to the Court come in the form of petitions for a writ of

certiorari (a Latin term meaning "made more certain"). The Court can choose which of the cases it wants to hear by denying or granting certiorari. The votes of four justices are needed to grant "cert." Between 85 and 90 percent of all such applications are denied.[52]

Cases may reach the Supreme Court for review either from *state* or *federal* courts. The cases come from a state court of last resort (usually a state supreme court), or from federal courts of appeals, U.S. district courts, or special-purpose federal courts.

Of the more than 10 million cases tried annually in American courts, only some 7,000 are taken to the Supreme Court. Of this total, the Court customarily hears argument on fewer than 200. In the 1991 term the Supreme Court disposed of a total of 6,770 cases. But the Court heard oral arguments in only 127. It handed down signed opinions in 107 of these.[53] The rest of the cases on the Court's docket were dismissed, affirmed, or reversed by written "memorandum orders." In choosing whether even to consider a case, the Supreme Court makes law (because, usually, the Supreme Court's refusal to take a case means that a lower-court decision stands).

Court Tradition   The Court normally sits from October through June. The Court building on Capitol Hill is a majestic structure of white marble, built in 1935 and modeled after the Greek Temple of Diana at Ephesus, one of the seven wonders of the ancient world. The great bronze doors weigh six and a half tons each; the courtroom seats 300 and has a ceiling forty-four feet high. Tradition is observed; some federal government lawyers appearing for oral argument still wear morning clothes—a formal cutaway coat with tails and striped pants—as do a few private attorneys, although rarely. Most attorneys simply wear dark suits. The rather grandiose setting of the building and the formal atmosphere are designed to preserve the dignity of the nation's highest tribunal, but they also provide some comfort to its critics, particularly political cartoonists, who find it easy to lampoon the Court's elaborate Grecian setting.

Lawyers arguing before the Court usually have one-half hour to make their case. Five minutes before their time expires a white light comes on; when a red light flashes on they must stop. But the justices often use up some of the precious time by interrupting to question the attorneys, a procedure that can be totally un-

---

[50] Woodward and Armstrong, *The Brethren: Inside the Supreme Court*, p. 284.

[51] William H. Rehnquist, *The Supreme Court: How It Was, How It Is* (New York: Morrow, 1988).

[52] Abraham, *The Judicial Process*, p. 187.

[53] U.S. Supreme Court, Statistical Sheet No. 27, June 29, 1992.

around a conference table. Behind each justice is a cart on which law clerks have placed all the legal documents the justices may need to expound their positions on the various cases. During these deliberations, no one other than the nine justices is allowed in the conference room, not even a clerk. The chief justice himself takes notes to record the actions of the Court.

The Chief Justice Although theoretically equal to the other eight justices, "the Chief" has four important tools available to him: prestige, the power to influence the Court's selection of cases through his position of leadership, the power to chair the conference, and the power to assign the writing of opinions by the justices. The chief justice, therefore, may play a very important role as "Court unifier."[54] Or the chief justice may be a source of disunity.

Leadership styles among chief justices differ. Charles Evans Hughes, chief justice during the 1930s, was popular among the justices on the Court even though he ran the conference with a firm hand. His successor, Harlan Fiske Stone, was much less reserved, and delighted in joining in the debate. "'Jackson,' he would say, 'that's damned nonsense.' 'Douglas, *you* know better than that.'"[55]

nerving for lawyers making their initial appearance before the Supreme Court.

On Fridays when the Court is sitting, the justices meet in *conference* to discuss and vote on pending cases and petitions for certiorari. The justices, by a tradition established in 1888, shake hands as they file into the oak-paneled conference room. The meetings are secret and presided over by the chief justice. Beneath a portrait of Chief Justice John Marshall, which hangs over the marble fireplace, the members of the Court gather

---

54 David J. Danelski, "The Influence of the Chief Justice in the Decisional Process," in Walter F. Murphy and C. Herman Pritchett, eds., *Courts, Judges and Politics: An Introduction to the Judicial Process*, 3rd ed. (New York: Random House, 1979), pp. 695–703.
55 In Danelski, "The Influence of the Chief Justice in the Decisional Process," p. 698.

The chief justice, if in the majority, decides who will write the Court's opinion; otherwise, the ranking justice among the majority assigns the writing of the opinion. According to *The Brethren*, Chief Justice Burger often maneuvered in conference to assign opinions (and thus perhaps influence their content) even when he was not in the majority on a case. In one such instance, the authors reported, Justice William O. Douglas complained in a 1972 memo that Burger should not have assigned a group of major abortion cases to Justice Harry A. Blackmun:

> When . . . the minority seeks to control the assignment, there is a destructive force at work in the Court. When a Chief Justice tries to bend the Court to his will by manipulating assignments, the integrity of the institution is imperiled.
>
> Historically, this institution has been composed of fiercely independent men with fiercely opposed views. . . . But up to now the Conference, though deeply disagreeing on legal and constitutional issues, has been a group marked by goodwill. . . . Perhaps the purpose of the Chief Justice, a member of the minority in the *Abortion Cases*, in assigning the opinions was to try to keep control of the merits. If that was the aim, he was unsuccessful.[56]

According to *The Brethren*, Douglas eventually withdrew his threat to publish the explosive memo. But clearly, the interaction among the justices on the Court is a political process, in which votes are sometimes traded and positions compromised. Shortly after Justice Lewis F. Powell, Jr., retired in 1987, he granted an interview in which he talked frankly about this process.

"Whenever you're assigned to write a 5-to-4 decision, you know that you cannot afford to lose a vote," he said. "And sometimes you end up on the short end of a case when you started out with five votes, and that makes you more than a little unhappy."[57]

He added: "You receive memos from other Justices, saying 'Dear Lewis, I'm inclined to join your opinion but it would help me if you changed so and so.' And sometimes a Justice will suggest language . . ."[58]

The justices, Powell added, call uninteresting cases "dogs." " 'A dog is a case that you wish the Chief Justice had assigned to some other justice' — a deadly dull case, 'a tax case, for example.' "[59]

Dissenting Opinions   Once an opinion is assigned, justices are free to write dissenting opinions if they disagree with the majority, or concurring opinions if they reach the same conclusion as the majority, often for different reasons. Important bargaining takes place backstage among the justices as the opinions are written and circulated informally, and justices may trade their votes to influence the shape of an opinion. Some legal experts believe that dissents, because they publicly reveal disunity, weaken the prestige of the Court — the large number of 5-4 decisions by the Warren Court, for example, provided fuel for its enemies. But many of the most eloquent arguments of the Supreme Court have been voiced in dissents by justices such as John Marshall Harlan, Sr.; Holmes; Brandeis; Stone; Black; and Douglas. Today's dissent may become tomorrow's majority opinion when the Court, as it has frequently done, overrules past decisions to meet new problems.

When it is in session, the Court usually hands down its opinions in the first part of each week. The justices read or summarize their opinions in the courtroom, sometimes adding informal comments. The words that echo through the marble chamber, often with enormous consequences for society, become the law of the land and renew the meaning of constitutional government.

THE AMERICAN COURT SYSTEM

Because the United States encompasses both a federal government and fifty state governments, it has a *dual* court system. "In effect, this means that there exist, side by side, two major court systems — one could even say fifty-one — which are wholly distinct. . . ."[60]

At the top of the system is the United States Supreme Court. But as we have seen, relatively few cases get there. The average citizen has neither the time nor the money to fight a case all the way to the highest tribunal. In any event, the Court only considers cases involving a substantial federal question or constitutional issue, and normally after all remedies in the state courts have been exhausted.

The Federal Courts

The bulk of the cases that come before the judicial branch of the federal government are handled in the "inferior" courts created by Congress under the Con-

[56] Woodward and Armstrong, *The Brethren: Inside the Supreme Court*, pp. 187–88.
[57] *New York Times*, July 11, 1987, p. 18.
[58] Ibid.
[59] Ibid.

[60] Abraham, *The Judicial Process*, p. 146.

stitution. Immediately below the Supreme Court are the United States *courts of appeals*, also known as *circuit courts*. The nation is divided geographically into twelve judicial circuits, each with a court of appeals. Every state and territory falls within the jurisdiction of one of these circuit courts. (In addition, there is a thirteenth circuit court that has jurisdiction nationwide.) Each court of appeals has from four to twenty-three judges, but usually three judges hear a case. The circuit courts hear appeals from lower federal courts and review the decisions of federal regulatory agencies. In 1992 there were a total of 179 circuit-court judges. Each year about 35,000 cases reach the circuit courts.

Below the circuit courts are the *federal district courts*. In 1992 there were eighty-nine district courts in the fifty states, plus one each for the District of Columbia, Puerto Rico, the Virgin Islands, Guam, and the Mariana Islands, making a total of ninety-four. Each district has from one to twenty-eight judges, making a total of 649 district judgeships. More than half of the federal judicial districts coincide with state lines, but some populous states, such as California, Texas, and New York, are divided into as many as four districts. The federal district courts are trial courts; they handle cases involving disputes between citizens of different states, and violations of federal law — for example, of civil rights, patent and copyright, bankruptcy, immigration, counterfeiting, antitrust, and postal laws. In 1991, 254,777 cases were commenced in the federal district courts, of which 47,035 were criminal and the rest civil.[61]

Special Federal Courts

Congress has created special-purpose courts to deal with certain kinds of cases. These include the United States Claims Court, which has jurisdiction over such cases as claims for compensation for property taken by the government, claims for income-tax refunds, or claims by government workers for back pay; the United States Court of International Trade, which hears civil actions arising under the tariff laws; the United States Court of Appeals for the Federal Circuit, which hears copyright, trademark, and patent cases; the United States Tax Court, which hears a variety of tax cases; and the United States Court of Military Appeals, often termed the "GI Supreme Court."

---

[61] Data provided by the Legislative and Public Affairs Office, Administrative Office of the United States Courts.

Lt. William Calley, Jr.

The Court of Military Appeals, whose three judges are civilians, is the final appellate tribunal in court-martial convictions. It was established by Congress in 1950, along with a Uniform Code of Military Justice. The code represented the first major overhaul of the system of military justice since the early nineteenth century.

The Vietnam War focused new attention on the process of military justice. The most controversial case growing out of that war was the murder conviction of 1st Lt. William L. Calley, Jr. In 1968 American soldiers swept through the South Vietnamese hamlet of My Lai and killed somewhere between 102 and 347 men, women, and children, all civilians. The tragedy was covered up for more than a year, until journalist Seymour M. Hersh publicized the story, for which he won a Pulitzer Prize. The government brought charges in connection with the massacre and the cover-up against twenty-five officers and enlisted men, including the general who commanded the division at the time of the murders. But only Lieutenant Calley, who led his platoon through My Lai, was convicted. In 1971 an army court found Calley guilty of the premeditated murder of at least twenty-two South Vietnamese civilians at My Lai. He was sentenced to life imprisonment, but the army later reduced the sentence to ten years. Calley was paroled by the army after he had served one-third of his sentence.

The cases occurring in Vietnam dramatized the fact that many Americans—almost two million by 1992—were subject to military justice and therefore were at least temporarily outside the civilian system of justice as it has evolved under the Constitution. Moreover, there is always the danger that justice in military trials will be swayed by command influence; that is, that the decisions of prosecutors, and officers who serve on military juries, may be affected by the views of their commanding officers.

In 1983, Congress empowered the Supreme Court to review certain decisions of the Court of Military Appeals. Even before that, the Supreme Court had asserted a limited right to review some military cases.[62] Moreover, in the past several years, the Court of Military Appeals itself has moved to broaden the legal rights of servicemen and women. For example, it held that the Supreme Court's *Miranda* decision, ruling out involuntary confessions, must also apply in military cases.[63]

In 1969 the Supreme Court ruled that military personnel must be tried in civilian courts for crimes not connected with the service and committed in peacetime while on leave or off duty.[64] However, in 1987 the Supreme Court, reversing itself, ruled that military personnel suspected of a crime of any type must be tried in military courts, whether or not the crime was committed at a military installation.[65]

In 1974 the Supreme Court upheld the controversial Article 134, the "general article" of the Uniform Code of Military Justice, which permitted the military to impose criminal penalties for any offense that imperiled "good order and discipline" in the armed forces.[66] Although the Supreme Court thus declined to do away with the "general article," reforms were gradually taking place in the system of military justice. Beginning in 1980, for example, by presidential order, the rules of evidence used in federal criminal trials also apply to military courts-martial.

The State Court System

State and local courts, not the federal courts, handle most cases in the United States. The quality and structure of the court system in the states vary tremendously with each state, but most states have several layers of courts:

1. *Magistrates' courts* are courts in which justices of the peace, or magistrates, handle minor offenses (misdemeanors), such as speeding, and perform civil marriages. Most "J.P."'s do not have law degrees, but what they may lack in legal training they make up for in their well-known zeal for convictions, which average 80 percent in criminal cases.[67]

2. *Municipal courts* are known variously as police courts, city courts, traffic courts, and night courts. These courts, generally one step up from the magistrates' courts, usually hear civil and lesser criminal cases.

3. *County courts*, also called superior courts, try serious criminal offenses (felonies) and major civil cases. At this level, jury trials are held in some cases.

4. *Special jurisdiction courts* are sometimes created at the county level to handle domestic relations, juveniles, probate of wills and estates, and other specialized tasks.

5. *Intermediate courts of appeals*, or appellate divisions, exist in some states to hear appeals from the county and municipal courts.

6. *Courts of appeals*, often called state supreme courts, are the final judicial tribunals in the states.

The Judges

Federal Court Judges All federal court judges are appointed by the president, subject to Senate approval. Historically, federal judges have been selected under a Senate patronage system that has often drawn criticism. The system changed briefly under Carter, but traditionally it has worked this way: senators present the president with the names of three candidates for federal judgeships; from these, the president selects one; the Justice Department and the FBI check the background of the person selected; the American Bar Association files a report; and the name is submitted to the Senate for confirmation.

[62] *Burns v. Wilson*, 346 U.S. 137 (1953).
[63] *United States v. Tempia*, 16 USCMA 629 (1967).
[64] *O'Callahan v. Parker*, 395 U.S. 258 (1969).
[65] *Solorio v. U.S.*, 483 U.S. 435 (1987).
[66] *Parker v. Levy*, 417 U.S. 733 (1974); *Secretary of the Navy v. Avrech*, 418 U.S. 676 (1974).
[67] Abraham, *The Judicial Process*, p. 148.

"God forbid some poor wretch should throw himself on the mercy of the court today."

Drawing by Whitney Darrow ©1975 The New Yorker Magazine, Inc.

During the 1976 presidential campaign, however, Jimmy Carter promised to appoint all federal judges "strictly on the basis of merit without any consideration of political aspect or influence." As president, Carter issued two executive orders, one creating merit commissions to recommend circuit-court judges, and another encouraging the creation of such commissions in the states to recommend candidates for federal district courts.

Commissions were established in about half the states. Despite the loose, partly voluntary nature of the merit system, Carter's orders had an impact. And more women and members of minority groups were appointed to the federal bench. President Reagan canceled both Carter orders and returned to the Senate patronage system. Fewer women and minority judges were named; in Reagan's eight years in office, he appointed 385 judges, of whom seven were African American, fifteen were Hispanic, and thirty-two were women.[68] President Bush, through September of 1992

appointed 182 judges, of whom twelve were African American, eight Hispanic and thirty-three were women.[69]

State and Local Judges　A majority of the 28,748 state judges in the United States are elected, as are many local judges.[70] Judges are elected in eighteen states, appointed in seven, and selected by both methods in eight states. Most of the other seventeen states employ the merit system for the selection of judges, patterned after the "Missouri plan."[71] The basic elements of that plan, which went into effect in Missouri in 1940, are as follows:

1. Nomination of the judges by a nonpartisan commission made up of lawyers, a judge, and citizens.

2. Appointment by the governor.

3. Approval by the voters after an initial term on the bench.

Despite the efforts to bring about judicial reform, in most cases "it is the politicians who select the judges. The voters only ratify their choices."[72] Political parties sometimes do not run competing candidates for the judiciary; rather, political leaders of both major parties get together and carve up the available judgeships. The nominees then run with the endorsement of both parties. In the process, political hacks are sometimes elevated to the bench.

But a presidential commission has warned: "The quality of the judiciary in large measure determines the quality of justice."[73] Bad judges do more than administer bad law; in the process they erode public respect for the entire system of criminal justice and the political system of which it is a vital part.

[68] Data provided by Office of Public Affairs, U.S. Department of Justice.

[69] Ibid.

[70] *State Court Caseload Statistics, Annual Report 1990*, State Justice Institute, National Center for State Courts, February 1992, p. 275.

[71] *The Book of the States*, 1991–92 edition (Lexington, Ky.: The Council of State Governments, 1992), pp. 233–34.

[72] Glenn R. Winters and Robert E. Allard, "Judicial Selection and Tenure in the United States," in Harry W. Jones, ed., *The Courts, the Public, and the Law Explosion*, prepared for the American Assembly, Columbia University (Englewood Cliffs: Prentice-Hall, 1965), p. 157.

[73] *The Challenge of Crime in a Free Society*, report by the President's Commission on Law Enforcement and Administration of Justice (Washington, D.C.: U.S. Government Printing Office, 1967), p. 146.

THE CRIMINAL JUSTICE TREADMILL

Half of all major crimes are never reported to police.

Of those that are, less than 25 percent are solved by arrests.

Half of these arrests result in dismissal of charges.

90 percent of the rest are resolved by a plea of guilty.

The fraction of cases that do go to trial represent less than 1 percent of all crimes committed.

About 25 percent of those convicted are sent to prison; the rest are released on probation.

Nearly everyone who goes to prison is eventually released.

Between half and two-thirds of those released are arrested and convicted again; they become repeat criminals known as recidivists.

—Adapted from *To Establish Justice, To Insure Domestic Tranquility*, Final Report of the National Commission on the Causes and Prevention of Violence

CRIMINAL JUSTICE IN AMERICA

A high-level presidential commission has observed, " . . . the poor—like the rich—can go to court. Whether they find satisfaction there is another matter. . . . Too frequently courts . . . serve the poor less well than their creditors. . . . The poor are discouraged from initiating civil actions against their exploiters. Litigation is expensive; so are experienced lawyers."[74]

The commission that issued this critical report included a mixture of liberals, moderates, and conservatives. The report went on to criticize the nation's criminal justice system in words that were often harsh. In fact, the commission said, there is no real *system* of criminal justice.

There is, instead, a reasonably well-defined criminal *process* . . . through which each accused offender may pass: from the hands of the police, to the jurisdiction of the courts, behind the walls of a prison, then back onto the street. . . . Criminal courts themselves are often poorly managed and . . . seriously backlogged. . . . Prisons . . . are . . . schools in crime. . . . The typical prison experience is degrading . . . and the outlook of most ex-convicts is bleak.[75]

Most criticism of the administration of justice in the United States is directed not at the principles of the system — the presumption that a defendant is innocent until proven guilty and the protections of the Bill of Rights — but at the failure of the system to work the way it is supposed to work.

Americans, Edward L. Barrett, Jr., has noted, tend to think that the procedure of the criminal courts protects the dignity of the individual against the power of the government.

Such is the general image we have of the administration of criminal justice. But if one enters the courthouse in any sizeable city and walks from courtroom to courtroom, what does he see? One judge, in a single morning, is accepting pleas of guilty from and sentencing a hundred or more persons charged with drunkenness. Another judge is adjusting traffic cases with an average time of no more than a minute per case. A third is disposing of a hundred or more other misdemeanor offenses in a morning. . . .

Suddenly it becomes clear that for most defendants in the criminal process, there is scant regard for them as individuals. They are numbers on dockets, faceless ones to be processed and sent on their way. The gap between the theory and the reality is enormous.[76]

A Profile of Crime in America

In 1991 there were an estimated 14.9 million violent and property crimes reported to law-enforcement agencies in the United States, of which 1,911,767, or 13 percent,

---

[74] "Violence and Law Enforcement," in *To Establish Justice, To Insure Domestic Tranquility*, Final Report of the National Commission on the Causes and Prevention of Violence (Washington, D.C.: U.S. Government Printing Office, December 1969), pp. 143–44.

[75] Ibid., pp. 149–52, 155.

[76] Edward L. Barrett, Jr., "Criminal Justice: The Problem of Mass Production," in Jones, *The Courts, the Public, and the Law Explosion*, pp. 86–87.

Table 13-2
Crime in the United States, 1991

Crime Offenses	Estimated Number of Crimes	Rate per 100,000 Inhabitants
Total	14,872,883	5,897.8
Violent	1,911,767	758.1
Property	12,961,116	5,139.7
Murder	24,703	9.8
Forcible rape	106,593	42.3
Robbery	687,732	272.7
Aggravated assault	1,092,739	433.3
Burglary	3,157,150	1,252.0
Larceny-Theft	8,142,228	3,228.8
Auto theft	1,661,738	659.0

SOURCE: Adapted from *Crime in the United States 1991*, Uniform Crime Reports, Federal Bureau of Investigation (Washington, D.C.: U.S. Government Printing Office, 1992), pp. 5–49.

Figure 13-1
Crime Clocks—1991

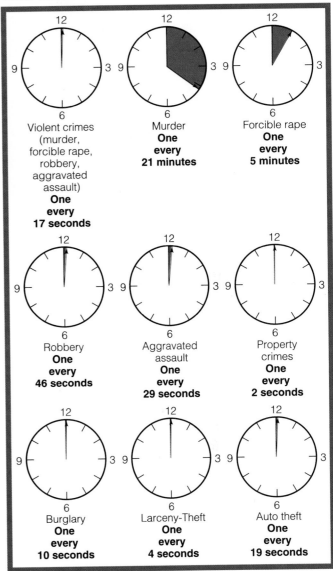

SOURCE: Adapted from *Crime in the United States 1991*, Federal Bureau of Investigation (Washington, D.C.: U.S. Government Printing Office, 1992), p. 4.

fell into the category of crimes that people fear the most: murder, forcible rape, robbery, and aggravated assault. (See Table 13–2.) In the United States in 1991, 24,703 persons were murdered, an all-time high and an increase of 23 percent in four years.[77] There were more than 3.2 million burglaries reported, 66.6 percent of these in homes. Over 1.6 million cars were stolen. Put another way, on the average a violent crime was committed every seventeen seconds, a murder every twenty-one minutes, a rape every five minutes, a robbery every forty-six seconds, and a car stolen every nineteen seconds.[78] (See Figure 13–1.)

But these figures, compiled annually by the FBI from reports received by law-enforcement agencies, do not reflect the full magnitude of crime in the United States. A presidential commission estimated that, based on population sampling, the actual amount of crime committed is "several times" greater than the amount of crime reported to the authorities.[79] People fail to report crime for a variety of reasons, including a reluctance to "get involved," doubt that police can do anything about it, or fear of reprisal by the criminal.[80]

There are some popular misconceptions about crime. As the president's commission noted, "the risks of personal harm are spread very unevenly," because it is much higher for residents of the inner city than for

---

[77] In 1991, guns were the weapon of choice in 7 out of 10 murders, the highest number of murders occurred in the month of August, the lowest number in February, and 78 percent of all murder victims were males. Among the geographic regions of the country, the South had the greatest number of murders. Almost half of all murder victims were related to or acquainted with their assailants. Source: *Crime in the United States 1991*, Uniform Crime Reports, Federal Bureau of Investigation (Washington, D.C.: U.S. Government Printing Office, 1992), pp. 14–17.

[78] Ibid., pp. 4–49.

[79] *The Challenge of Crime in a Free Society*, pp. 21–22.

[80] *Task Force Report: Crime and Its Impact—An Assessment*, The President's Commission on Law Enforcement and Administration of Justice (Washington, D.C.: U.S. Government Printing Office, 1967), pp. 93–94.

most other Americans.[81] Author Richard Harris has observed that for a black resident of Chicago's inner city, "the chance of being physically assaulted, on the basis of reported crimes, was one in seventy-seven, whereas for the white resident of a nearby suburb the chance was one in ten thousand."[82]

Crime by youths accounts for a substantial share of all crime. In 1991, for example, 29 percent of the arrests for violent and property crimes were of persons under age eighteen.[83] Narcotics addiction is another source of crime. Estimates vary greatly as to how much crime is committed by heroin addicts in order to get money to support their habit. Some estimates attribute as much as three-quarters of all serious crime in New York City and Washington, D.C., to drug addicts.[84]

In 1991 the rate of violent and property crimes in America rose by 10 percent over the 1987 rate.[85] Even if the crime rate remained level, there would be more crime because the population is increasing.

The Prisons

In 1991 there were 804,103 persons in prisons and jails in the United States in federal, state, and local institutions.[86] Of the total, 69,504 persons were inmates of federal prisons.[87] The bulk of prisoners were in the state prison systems, where uprisings, often violent, and the seizure of hostages have become increasingly frequent in recent years.

Prison overcrowding is recognized as a serious problem in America. In more than a third of the states, prisoners were sleeping on floors, and at least twenty-one states had passed laws providing for early release of prisoners when overcrowding reached certain levels. In many areas, two and three prisoners were jammed into cells built for one. Overpopulation was a major factor in the increased number of riots and cases of hostage-taking in the prisons.

Yet the United States Supreme Court has ruled 8–1 that prison overcrowding is not forbidden by the Constitution. In a 1981 decision, the Burger Court held that "harsh" prison conditions are the price of crime, "part of the penalty that criminal offenders pay for their offenses against society." Although prison conditions may not be "grossly disproportionate to the severity of the crime . . . persons convicted of serious crimes cannot be free of discomfort."[88] The case challenged the housing of two men in cells of sixty-three square feet in an Ohio prison. And in 1984 the Court held that the Constitution protected prisoners far less than other citizens.[89] In 1992, the Supreme Court ruled that federal courts are no longer obliged to hear appeals by state prison inmates.[90] In the same year, however, the Court decided an important case strengthening prisoners' rights when it ruled that beatings or other excessive use of force by guards may violate the Constitution even when there is no serious injury to the prisoner.[91]

The nation's prisons, instead of rehabilitating offenders, may contribute to the crime rate by serving in many instances as "human warehouses" for the custody

[81] *The Challenge of Crime in a Free Society*, p. 19.
[82] Richard Harris, *Justice: The Crisis of Law, Order, and Freedom in America* (New York: Dutton, 1970), pp. 27–28.
[83] *Crime in the United States 1991*, Uniform Crime Reports, Federal Bureau of Investigation (Washington, D.C.: U.S. Government Printing Office, 1992), p. 212.
[84] Harris, *Justice: The Crisis of Law, Order, and Freedom in America*, p. 44.
[85] *Crime in the United States 1991*, p. 6.

[86] Bureau of Justice Statistics, U.S. Department of Justice, *National Update*, April 1992, p. 4. A private research organization, the Sentencing Project, reported in 1991 that the United States had the highest incarceration rate in the world. Source: *Washington Post*, January 5, 1991, p. A3.
[87] *National Update*, p. 4.
[88] *Rhodes v. Chapman*, 452 U.S. 337 (1981).
[89] *Hudson v. Palmer*, 468 U.S. 517 (1984); *Block v. Rutherford*, 468 U.S. 576 (1984).
[90] *Keeney v. Tamayo-Reyes*, 112 S. Ct. 1715 (1992).
[91] *Hudson v. McMillian*, 112 S.Ct. 995 (1992).

of convicts. Close to half of felons released from prison commit new crimes. In many cases little is done to prepare prisoners for their return to the outside world. More than half of all state prisons have no vocational training programs. A presidential study commission concluded that "for a great many offenders . . . corrections does not correct."[92] Moreover, state and federal parole systems are badly overburdened. As a result, the decision on when to release prisoners is often

arbitrary and unfair, creating further bitterness among those who must remain behind bars.

As noted earlier, tensions in America's prisons frequently run so high that they explode in prison riots, in which guards or other hostages are seized and inmates demand better conditions. One of the most dramatic and tragic outbreaks occurred in 1971 at Attica, a maximum-security state prison in New York State. The dismal conditions at Attica were typical of many state prison systems: old and overcrowded buildings, with guards who are often poorly trained and sometimes

[92] *The Challenge of Crime in a Free Society*, p. 159.

CRIME AND DRUGS: THE HIGH COST FOR SOCIETY

Among all age groups, close to ninety percent of those arrested for violating the laws on addictive drugs had criminal records, and seventeen percent of them were armed, presumably to enable them to commit crimes to support their habit.

It is an exceedingly expensive one. A heroin addict . . . needs between fifty and sixty dollars a day to keep himself supplied. Since an addict is rarely able to hold down an ordinary job, let alone a job paying that kind of money, he must steal money or else merchandise that can easily be converted into money. As a rule, stolen goods bring

about ten percent of their value in cash, so, theoretically, the country's sixty-three thousand known addicts must steal three and a half million dollars a day in cash or thirty-five million dollars a day in merchandise, or a combination of the two, in order to survive. In trying to raise funds, the addict most often relies on muggings, holdups, or burglaries, and in the course of committing them he not infrequently assaults or murders his victims.

—Richard Harris, *Justice: The Crisis of Law, Order, and Freedom in America*

brutal. Racial tensions ran high at Attica, as at other prisons where many inmates are African American and most of the guards white.

For four days, convicts took control of the courtyard of a cell block and held hostages. Governor Nelson Rockefeller ordered 200 state troopers to storm the prison. Thirty-two inmates and eleven hostages died. Almost all of them had been killed in the hail of troopers' bullets. A special New York State commission that investigated the bloodshed at Attica concluded that the conditions that sparked the revolt were, in a sense, universal: "Attica is every prison; and every prison is Attica."[93]

The Police

Police in the United States walk a tightrope; often underpaid, with inadequate personnel and resources, they are expected to fight crime, enforce the law, keep the peace, and provide a wide variety of social and community services.

Police must spend much of their time performing such community services—from directing traffic to rescuing stray cats. These duties greatly reduce the amount of time police can spend fighting crime. As the armed embodiment of the law, police are sometimes caught between the established order and dissident or minority groups seeking change. Mutual hostility be-

tween police and militant minorities or political protesters erupted in tragic violence and bloodshed in the 1960s. And police face violence in fighting crime. From 1970 through 1991, 2,079 police officers in the United States were killed in the line of duty.

"The policeman," in the words of a task force report to a presidential commission, "lives on the grinding edge of social conflict, without a well-defined, well-understood notion of what he is supposed to be doing

[93] *Attica: The Official Report of the New York State Special Commission on Attica* (New York: Bantam Books, 1972), p. xii.

AMERICA'S PRISONS: "THE LETHAL CRUCIBLES"

We Americans have made our prisons disappear from sight as if by an act of will. We locate them mostly in places remote from view, and far removed from the homes of the inmates; we emphasize security almost to the exclusion of rehabilitation; and we manage to forget inmates and custodians alike by pretending that the prisoners will not return to our cities and our villages and our farms. . . .

The Atticas of this country have become lethal crucibles in which the most explosive social forces of our society are mixed with the pettiness and degradation of prison life, under intense pressure of maintaining "security." . . .

There was no escape within the walls from the growing mistrust between white middle America and the residents of urban ghettos. Indeed, at Attica racial polarity and mistrust were magnified by the constant reminder that the keepers were white and the kept were largely African American and Hispanic.

—*Attica: The Official Report of the New York State Special Commission on Attica, 1972*

there."[94] And differences in the social and cultural background of police and minorities or dissidents may contribute to tension between them.

Many Americans strongly support and defend the police. Even when police employed violence against young antiwar demonstrators at the 1968 Democratic National Convention in Chicago, 56 percent of the public approved of the way the police had acted.[95] Later, a staff study of a presidential commission adjudged the events at Chicago "a police riot."[96] But in times of turmoil and fear of violence, many Americans appear to regard "law and order" as a requirement that takes precedence over all other considerations, including the constitutional right of peaceful dissent.[97]

On the other hand, when a state jury acquitted four white Los Angeles police officers in the beating of Rodney King, 77 percent of respondents thought that

the jury verdict was "not justified."[98] In this instance, the beating had been videotaped by a citizen and shown repeatedly on television. The acquittal touched off the devastating riots in Los Angeles in April of 1992. Three months later, a federal grand jury indicted the same four police officers on federal charges of violating the civil rights of Rodney King. Because so many Americans had viewed the brutal beating on TV, the episode, the trials, and the riots focused new attention on the controversial question of how far police may go in enforcing the law before they themselves become lawbreakers.

The controversy over the role of the police in responding to social protest has to some extent tended to obscure the conventional role of the police officer in the system of criminal justice. Police officers are, after all, highly visible and important public officials. As "the cop on the beat" dealing with everyday social conflict and crime, they exercise great discretionary powers.[99] Should a fight be broken up, a speeding car stopped, a street-corner crowd dispersed? The police officer must decide. To a great extent, law-enforcement policy is made by the police.

Police do not capture most lawbreakers, however. There is a huge gap between the number of crimes reported and the number of criminals arrested. In 1991, for example, only 21 percent of known serious offenses were "cleared" from police record-books by arrests

[94] James S. Campbell, Joseph R. Sahid, and David P. Stang, *Law and Order Reconsidered*, Report of the Task Force on Law and Law Enforcement to the National Commission on the Causes and Prevention of Violence (Washington, D.C.: U.S. Government Printing Office, 1969), p. 290.

[95] Gallup poll, September 17, 1968. The question asked of 1,507 persons was, "Do you approve or disapprove of the way the Chicago police dealt with the young people who were registering their protest against the Vietnam war at the time of the Chicago Convention?" The nationwide findings were: Approve, 56%, Disapprove, 31%, No Opinion, 13%.

[96] Daniel Walker, *Rights in Conflict*, Report of the Chicago Study Team to the National Commission on the Causes and Prevention of Violence (New York: Bantam Books, 1968), p. 5.

[97] For example, 76 percent of the people questioned in a telephone survey by the Columbia Broadcasting System said extremist groups should not be allowed to "organize protests" against the government; 55 percent said news media should not report stories that the government considers harmful to the national interest; and 58 percent thought that a suspect in a serious crime should be held in jail by police until they can get enough evidence to charge him with the crime. *The CBS News Poll*, Survey Operations Department, CBS News Election Unit, March 20, 1970, pp. 1–6.

[98] *The Gallup Poll*, April 30-May 1, 1992.

[99] See, for example, James Q. Wilson, *Varieties of Police Behavior* (Cambridge: Harvard University Press, 1968), pp. 7, 278.

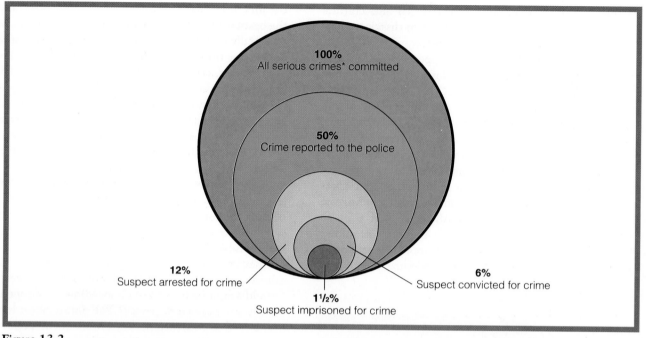

Figure 13-2
Crime and Law Enforcement
* Homicide, forcible rape, robbery, aggravated assault, burglary, larceny over $50, auto theft. Based on estimates.
SOURCE: *To Establish Justice, To Insure Domestic Tranquility*, Final Report of the National Commission on the Causes and Prevention of Violence (Washington, D.C.: U.S. Government Printing Office, December 1969), p. xviii.

(although for certain crimes, such as murder, 67 percent were cleared by arrests).[100] Crime can be viewed as a series of concentric circles, in which the smallest, innermost circle represents persons actually convicted and sent to prison. (See Figure 13–2.)

The Department of Justice

Although criminal justice and law enforcement are primarily the responsibility of state and local authorities, the federal government wields substantial power in this field. The Department of Justice in recent years has emerged as a major policymaking agency in relation to a broad range of political, legal, and social issues. The department is headed by the attorney general, who is both a cabinet officer and the president's chief legal adviser.

One of the Justice Department's basic responsibilities is to conduct criminal prosecutions in the federal

courts. This means that the attorney general has tremendous power to make political decisions about who will be prosecuted and who will not.

And the attorney general is often a powerful political figure in Washington. This was dramatically illustrated by the controversy swirling around Attorney General Edwin Meese III during the twilight of the Reagan administration. For months, Meese's finances and his possible link to a scandal surrounding a military contractor, the Wedtech Corp.—as well as other ventures—were under investigation. An independent counsel was appointed to probe the allegations. The news media focused heavily on the Meese case, and the nation was treated to the spectacle of an attorney general spending the bulk of his time testifying before grand juries, answering questions by investigators, and defending his record. The beleaguered attorney general was under constant attack.

By the spring of 1988, Meese had clearly become a liability to Vice-President George Bush, who was already assured of the Republican presidential nomination. Finally, Meese resigned in midsummer, after the independent counsel had filed his report. In disclosing that he would leave office, Meese announced he had

---

[100] *Crime in the United States 1991*, Uniform Crime Reports, Federal Bureau of Investigation (Washington, D.C.: U.S. Government Printing Office, 1992), pp. 6, 22.

been "completely vindicated" because the report found no basis to prosecute the attorney general of the United States on criminal charges. Meese's argument was criticized; it seemed an unusual new standard by which to judge the nation's highest law-enforcement officer. And, although the report did not recommend prosecution, it blamed Meese for failure to avoid the appearance of impropriety as attorney general. Meese's decision to resign was greeted with relief by the Bush camp.

As noted earlier, during the Watergate inquiries more than a decade before, there was deep public suspicion about the willingness of the Justice Department to prosecute high officials of the Nixon administration who had participated in wrongdoing or helped to cover it up.

Against this background, a special prosecutor, Harvard law professor Archibald Cox, was named to pursue the Watergate case and related cases. When Cox sought presidential tape recordings to learn whether Nixon himself had participated in covering up the burglary of Democratic headquarters and in obstructing justice, Nixon dismissed the special prosecutor. Attorney General Elliot L. Richardson then resigned, along with the deputy attorney general.[101] But many members of Congress and the public were dismayed that the Watergate investigation had been removed from the hands of the special prosecutor. How could the president's Justice Department investigate the president? There were immediate demands for the appointment of a new special prosecutor. Responding to these pressures, Nixon named Texas attorney Leon Jaworski to the post. The appointment, dismissal, and replacement of the special Watergate prosecutor was a dramatic illustration of the politically sensitive nature of the Justice Department. In the wake of Watergate, Congress in 1978 passed the Ethics in Government Act, providing for appointment of a special prosecutor — formally known as an "independent counsel" — in cases involving possible crimes by high officials. In 1992, the section of the law allowing the appointment of independent counsels expired, and in that year Congress did not reenact it.

An attorney general might publicly disclaim any suggestion that the decisions of that office were political. But the attorney general is a cabinet officer responsible to the president. As a result, both the attorney general and the Justice Department play a significant political role. The attorney general's political viewpoint

is normally an important factor weighed by the president in selecting an individual for that post. In exercising discretion about whom to prosecute, the attorney general may also reflect personal ideology and outlook. Should an antitrust suit be brought against a major American corporation? Should the vice-president of the United States be brought to trial on criminal charges? Should the department crack down on organized crime? The attorney general may decide.

In 1980, for example, Attorney General Benjamin Civiletti was widely criticized when he admitted that he had privately advised President Carter that his brother, Billy, would not be prosecuted by the Justice Department if he registered as a foreign agent. Before making his admission, Civiletti had denied that he had ever discussed the case with the president.

The Justice Department prosecutes persons accused of federal crimes through its United States attorneys in each of the federal judicial districts. Although United States attorneys are appointed by the president, subject to Senate approval, they serve under the attorney general. Under the supervision of the department's criminal division, the United States attorney in each district initiates investigations and decides whether to prosecute or to seek a grand jury indictment in criminal cases.

Separate divisions of the Justice Department deal with criminal, civil, antitrust, tax, civil rights, and natural resources cases. A special unit in the criminal division handles cases involving organized crime. The Justice Department also includes the Immigration and Naturalization Service, the Drug Enforcement Administration, the Law Enforcement Assistance Administration — created in 1968 to distribute federal funds through the states to local police — and the Bureau of Prisons, which is in charge of federal prisons and youth centers.

The FBI

Best known of all the arms of the Justice Department is the Federal Bureau of Investigation. In 1992 the FBI had a budget of almost two billion dollars and employed 21,773 people (almost 23 percent of all the Justice Department's employees). Of the total, 9,477 were FBI agents; most of the rest were laboratory technicians, clerks, and secretaries. The FBI is the investigative arm of the Justice Department, and its jurisdiction is limited to suspected violations of federal law. It has fifty-six field offices and twenty offices abroad for liaison with foreign

---

[101] A separate confrontation over Nixon's tapes in 1974 resulted in the Supreme Court ruling requiring him to surrender additional tape recordings.

police and intelligence services. In its files are the fingerprints of 199.5 million people.[102]

Senate and House investigations of the FBI in the wake of the Watergate scandal revealed that for years — while the FBI enjoyed a highly favorable public image — the bureau had systematically engaged in illegal activities that violated the constitutional rights of American citizens. FBI agents, for example, engaged in hundreds of burglaries of individuals and groups to plant microphones or to photograph documents. From 1956 to 1971, the bureau, through its counter-intelligence program (COINTELPRO), harassed American citizens and disrupted their organizations through a wide variety of clandestine techniques, some of which broke up marriages or endangered lives. Moreover, since the administration of Franklin D. Roosevelt, the FBI had gathered intelligence on domestic groups and individuals with only the shakiest legal authority to do so. For years the bureau compiled various indexes or lists of politically unreliable persons to be rounded up in an emergency. And as the congressional investigations also disclosed, the FBI opened first-class mail in violation of the law.[103] All of these disclosures of FBI abuses surfaced several years after the death of the bureau's longtime chief, J. Edgar Hoover, but many of the illegal practices had taken place under his leadership.

For forty-eight years, until his death in 1972 at the age of seventy-seven, Hoover was director of the FBI. Under eight presidents, Hoover and the FBI acquired an unprecedented degree of power and independence. One major source of Hoover's power was the secret dossiers and files of the FBI. A member of Congress who had a drinking problem, or who had accepted a campaign contribution from someone rumored to have connections with organized crime, or who was having an extramarital affair, might have good reason to fear the contents of the FBI's file on him or her.

Even presidents respected Hoover's power, and under his reign, the FBI, although an arm of the Justice Department, became largely independent of the attorney general. With a masterful gift for publicity, Hoover invented the "Ten Most Wanted" list and helped to project the image of the "G-man" as square-jawed,

J. Edgar Hoover

clean-cut, and infallible. Through movies, a television series, and guided tours of its headquarters for the millions of tourists who visit Washington each year, the FBI became the most publicized agency of the federal government. During Hoover's years, it was able to obtain almost anything it wanted from Congress, including a new $126-million headquarters building named for Hoover that opened in 1975.

Even before Hoover's death, the FBI had become controversial. The majority of Americans traditionally thought of it in favorable terms, as an agency adept at catching bank robbers and spies. But other Americans worried about the concentration of power in the hands of the FBI, and they feared that its wiretaps and dossiers might be used for political ends, or to enhance the power of the director. Because Hoover's political views

[102] Data provided by the Federal Bureau of Investigation.
[103] For details of these and other abuses by the intelligence agencies, see U.S. Congress, Senate, Select Committee to Study Governmental Operations with Respect to Intelligence Activities, *Intelligence Activities and the Rights of Americans, Book II*, 94th Cong., 2nd sess., Final Report (Washington, D.C.: U.S. Government Printing Office, 1976).

were generally conservative, liberals feared that the FBI was more concerned about pursuing domestic radicals than organized crime.

The FBI's reputation suffered after President Nixon named an old political associate, L. Patrick Gray, as acting director to succeed Hoover. According to evidence published by congressional investigating committees, Gray — at Nixon's request, relayed through the Central Intelligence Agency — slowed down and restricted the FBI investigation of the Watergate burglary. And Gray admitted that he had burned key files in the Watergate case.

After Gray, Nixon appointed Clarence M. Kelley, the police chief of Kansas City, Missouri, as FBI director. In 1976 Congress enacted a law that limits the director of the FBI to one ten-year term of office. President Carter named a federal judge, William Webster of Missouri, as head of the FBI in 1978. The FBI's image improved under Webster, who remained director until 1987, when President Reagan named him to head the CIA. Reagan appointed another federal judge, William S. Sessions of Texas, as the new director of the FBI.

The FBI's entanglement in the Watergate case had raised a question exactly the opposite of that posed by Hoover's independence. Gray's actions had illustrated the danger of an FBI chief who was *too* responsive to political control. In the early 1980s, some critics questioned whether the FBI had improperly entrapped members of Congress in its "Abscam" investigation, in which seven lawmakers were indicted and convicted for taking bribes from agents posing as wealthy Arabs. Clearly the role and power of a secret police agency raises disturbing problems in a democracy.

The Criminal Courts

Americans who have never had a brush with the law may tend to think of the system of criminal justice in terms of "due process of law," trial by jury, and the right to counsel — in short, the *adversary system* of justice, in which the power of the state is balanced by the defendant's constitutional rights and by the presumption, not specifically written in the Constitution, but deeply rooted in Anglo-Saxon law, that a person is innocent until proven guilty beyond a reasonable doubt.[104]

Plea Bargaining These protections may prevail *when* a case goes to trial. But in fact, the great majority of cases never go to trial. According to one report, "Most defendants who are convicted — as many as 90 percent in some jurisdictions — are not tried. They plead guilty,

---

[104] The Supreme Court has held that the "due process clause" of the Constitution requires the presumption that a criminal defendant is innocent until proven guilty beyond a reasonable doubt. *Davis* v. *United States*, 160 U.S. 469 (1895); *Coffin* v. *United States*, 156 U.S. 432 (1895); *In the Matter of Samuel Winship*, 396 U.S. 885 (1970).

THE CRIMINAL COURT: A SYSTEM IN COLLAPSE

New York City's Criminal Court is in chaos, according to judges, prosecutors, defense lawyers, police officials, witnesses, crime victims and defendants.

Rarely has any public institution been held in such open contempt by those who work in it and those who pass through it.

Judges call it a sham and a fraud. Lawyers say that justice is unpredictable at best and that the tawdry surroundings and atmosphere of deal making deprive the court of even a feeling of justice.

"It's impossible to afford justice in these circumstances," said Joseph B. Williams, the administrative judge in charge of the court. "I think the quality of justice is almost nil." . . . Many Criminal Court lawyers meet their clients for the first time only moments before they face the judge. Six times between 9:45 A.M. and 12:20 P.M., one $25-an-hour court-appointed defense attorney went up and down the aisle of Judge Frank Brenner's Brooklyn courtroom, calling a client's name.

The missing client, an 18-year-old woman charged with petty theft, finally answered. The lawyer took her out in the hallway and screamed at her for being late. Her tardiness, he said, might have exposed her to a bench warrant and was "stupid" because the court was a "revolving door."

"Everybody called in here knows how the system works," he said later. "They know how to use it."

—*New York Times*, June 26, 1983

"Since you have already been convicted by the media,
I imagine we can wrap this up pretty quickly."

Drawing by Mischa Richter; © 1991 The New
Yorker Magazine, Inc.

often as the result of negotiations about the charge or
the sentence."[105] In other words, the machinery of the
adversary system of justice exists—but it may not be
used. Most guilty pleas are the result of backstage discussions between the prosecutor and defense counsel.
The practice is commonly known as "plea bargaining,"
or, less elegantly, as "copping a plea."

The practice sometimes serves everyone's needs
but the defendant's. The government is saved the time
and expense of a public prosecution; the defense attorney can collect a fee and move on to the next client; the
judge can keep the business of the court moving along.
But the guilt or innocence of the accused person is not
proven.

Usually, the plea bargaining process works this
way: a defendant agrees to plead guilty to a less serious
charge than might be proven at a trial; in return the
prosecutor agrees to reduce the charges or recommend
leniency. Often, the accused person will get a lighter
sentence this way than if the case went to trial and
resulted in a conviction. There is no guarantee, however, that the judge will act as the prosecutor has promised. And, an innocent person may be persuaded to
plead guilty to a crime he or she did not commit.

In 1970 the Supreme Court upheld the practice of
plea bargaining.[106] The Court ruled that a guilty plea,
entered voluntarily and intelligently with the advice of
counsel, was constitutional.

Sometimes an accused person will simply plead
guilty without plea bargaining, perhaps in the hope of
receiving a lighter sentence. If the accused pleads not
guilty, a trial date is set.

Court Delay American courts do not have enough
judges to handle the volume of cases that come before
them. In a single year the courts may dispose of more
than three million cases.[107]

The high caseload, the lack of judges, and poor
administration of the courts all result in major delays in
the criminal process. The courts are badly backlogged;
in many large cities the average delay between arrest and
trial is close to a year. In Great Britain the period from
arrest to final appeal frequently takes four months, but
the same process in many states in America averages ten
to eighteen months.

Bail Reform During the long wait for their trials,
accused persons may be free on bail or detained. Bail is a
system designed to ensure that defendants will appear in
court when their cases are called; typically, arrested persons go before a judge or magistrate who fixes an
amount of money to be "posted" with the court as
security in exchange for the defendant's freedom. If
defendants do not have the money, a bondsman may
post bail for them, but the defendants must pay the
bondsman a premium of 5 to 20 percent. If the accused
persons cannot raise bail either way, they may have to
remain in jail until their case comes up. If they go free on
bail but fail to appear for their trial, the bail is forfeited.

The rights of the individual and the community
conflict during the pretrial period. The accused person
may have a job and a family to support, and he or she
needs to be free in order to prepare a defense. On the
other hand, the community demands that the accused
appear for trial; that, after all, is the rationale of the bail
system.

Such a system obviously discriminates against the
poor, who may not be able to buy their way out of jail.
"Millions of men and women are, through the American bail system, held each year in 'ransom' in American
jails, committed to prison cells often for prolonged periods before trial," Ronald Goldfarb has written. "Because they are poor or friendless, they may spend days,

[105] *The Challenge of Crime in a Free Society*, p. 134.
[106] *Brady v. United States*, 396 U.S. 809 (1970).
[107] *Attica: The Official Report of the New York State Special Commission on Attica*, p. xiii.

weeks, or months in confinement, often to be acquitted of wrongdoing in the end."[108]

Until the Bail Reform Act of 1966, federal judges had often deliberately set a high bail for defendants they considered dangerous, in the hope that the bail could not be paid; the practice was an illegal but widespread system of pretrial detention. Under the 1966 act this subterfuge was no longer possible. *Federal* judges were required to release defendants before trial except in capital cases—in which death was the possible punishment—and unless there were good reasons to believe that the defendant would flee if released. A federal judge might still set bail, but defendants could no longer be held because they did not have the money. The reform legislation does not apply to *state* or *local* courts, however, where the amount of bail remains up to the judge. And in those courts, many defendants are still imprisoned because they lack bail money.

The Trial Under the Fifth Amendment, a person charged with a serious *federal* crime must first be accused in an *indictment* by a grand jury. The Supreme Court has not applied this requirement to the states, where defendants are more often brought to trial on an *information* issued by a judge. The grand jury, so named because it is larger than the trial jury, does not determine guilt or innocence. It does seek to establish

whether there is enough evidence to justify a criminal trial.

Within the states, although procedures vary in different jurisdictions, in general, arrested persons are brought before a magistrate for a preliminary hearing at which they are either held or released on bail. They may be assigned counsel if they cannot afford a private attorney. The district attorney or prosecutor next may seek a grand-jury indictment or may present the case to a judge who may issue an information. Now formally accused, defendants are arraigned—which means that the formal charges in the indictment or information are read to them—and they plead guilty or not guilty. (In some cases they may plead "no contest" and put themselves at the mercy of the court.) At every critical stage, a criminal suspect is entitled to have the advice of a lawyer, and defendants too poor to hire one must be offered or assigned counsel in all criminal cases where conviction might mean imprisonment.

Jury trials are required in *federal* courts in all criminal cases and in all common-law civil suits where the sum involved is larger then $20. Under a 1968 Supreme Court decision, *states* must also provide jury trials in "serious" criminal cases,[109] which the Supreme Court defined in 1970 as all cases in which the penalty for conviction could exceed six months.[110] However, in

---

[108] Ronald Goldfarb, *Ransom* (New York: Harper & Row, 1965), p. 1.

[109] *Duncan* v. *Louisiana*, 391 U.S. 145 (1968).
[110] *Baldwin* v. *New York*, 399 U.S. 66 (1970).

"Of course everybody is looking at you accusingly. You are, after all, the accused."

Drawing by Ross
©1976 The New Yorker Magazine, Inc.

"We find the defendant
not guilty but not all that
innocent, either."

Drawing by Modell ©1986
The New Yorker Magazine, Inc.

1971 the Supreme Court held 6–3 that juveniles do not have a constitutional right to a trial by jury in state courts.[111] (In a federal court, if a defendant wishes to waive the right of a jury trial and have the judge try the case, it is usually possible, but many states do not permit this practice.)

Federal juries must render a unanimous verdict in criminal and civil cases, but more than two-thirds of the states permit a less-than-unanimous verdict (usually by three-fourths of the jurors) in civil cases. In 1972 the Supreme Court ruled that unanimous jury verdicts were not required even in state criminal cases.[112] But only two states permit split verdicts in certain criminal cases that do not carry a possible death penalty.[113]

In a number of states, juries may consist of fewer than the traditional number of twelve persons. The Supreme Court in 1970 upheld the constitutionality of juries with fewer than twelve members.[114] Federal criminal juries contain twelve members. But most federal civil cases may be tried with juries of six persons.[115]

Although courtroom procedures vary on the federal, state, and local levels, in general the pattern is the same. First, the jury is chosen, with the prosecution and the defense each having the right to challenge and replace prospective jurors. Then the prosecution presents its case, and the defense cross-examines the witnesses for the prosecution. After that, the defense presents its own witnesses, who are cross-examined in turn by the prosecutor. A defendant does not have to take the stand to testify on his or her own behalf. A trial may be over in a few hours or drag on for months. Finally, the judge delivers a charge to the jury, explaining the law and emphasizing that the defendant's guilt must be proven beyond a reasonable doubt. The jury deliberates, and renders its verdict.

Capital Punishment   On July 2, 1976, there were 611 men and women in death-row cells in the United States awaiting execution. On that day the United States Supreme Court ruled 7–2 that the death penalty was constitutional.[116] The majority specifically held that capital punishment, if administered under adequate guidelines, did not violate the Eighth Amendment's prohibition against "cruel and unusual punishments." Approximately half of the inmates on death row faced possible execution as a result of the Court's decision. They were imprisoned either in the three states whose laws were upheld or in states with similar statutes. The Supreme Court held that judges and juries could impose the death sentence as long as they had sufficient information to determine whether the sentence was appropriate in each case. The Court upheld state laws providing for capital punishment in Georgia, Florida, and Texas, but it struck down two other state statutes requiring automatic death sentences for murder.[117]

[111] *McKeiver v. Pennsylvania*, 403 U.S. 528 (1971).
[112] *Johnson v. Louisiana*, 406 U.S. 356 (1972); *Apodaca v. Oregon*, 406 U.S. 404 (1972).
[113] Data provided by the Center for Jury Studies, National Center for State Courts.
[114] *Williams v. Florida*, 399 U.S. 78 (1970).
[115] *Colgrove v. Battin*, 413 U.S. 149 (1973).

[116] *Gregg v. Georgia*, 428 U.S. 153 (1976).
[117] *Woodson v. North Carolina*, 428 U.S. 280 (1976); *Roberts v. Louisiana*, 428 U.S. 325 (1976).

"We now hold that the punishment of death does not invariably violate the Constitution," the Supreme Court declared. And it noted that the framers of the Constitution accepted capital punishment: "At the time the Eighth Amendment was ratified, capital punishment was a common sanction in every state. Indeed, the first Congress of the United States enacted legislation providing death as the penalty for specified crimes."

In 1972, four years earlier, the Supreme Court had ruled out executions under any law then in effect. In a 5–4 decision that year, the Court held that capital punishment, as then administered, was unconstitutional.[118] At that time, thirty-eight states, the federal government, and the District of Columbia had laws authorizing the death penalty for various crimes. But no one had been executed in the United States since 1967.

By the time the Supreme Court faced the constitutional issue in 1972, thirty-seven nations had abolished the death penalty in peacetime. In Western Europe, for example, only France and Spain retained capital punishment. In the years following the 1972 decision, thirty-six states and the federal government passed new laws providing for capital punishment and designed to satisfy the standards set forth by the Supreme Court. (Federal law provided the death penalty for air hijacking

[118] *Furman v. Georgia*, 408 U.S. 238 (1972).

Table 13-3
Public Support for the Death Penalty, 1960–91

Year	Favor	Opposed
1960	51%	36%
1971	49	40
1978	62	27
1981	66	25
1986	70	22
1988	79	16
1991	76	18

SOURCE: Gallup poll, June 26, 1991, p. 2.

resulting in death, and for murder linked to drug trafficking.) Most of the state laws prescribed death sentences for such crimes as mass murder; killing a police officer, fire fighter, or prison guard; and murder while committing rape, kidnapping, arson, or hijacking.

The new laws were enacted during a period when public support for the death penalty was rising sharply in American society. In a 1971 Gallup poll, for example, 49 percent of those interviewed were "in favor of the death penalty for persons convicted of murder." By 1991, 76 percent of Americans favored the death penalty. (See Table 13–3.)

Since the federal government began keeping statistics on executions in 1930, 3,859 persons had been

THE DEATH PENALTY: PRO AND CON

Many people, including advocates as well as opponents of the death penalty, assume that there are innocent people on death row and some of their sentences will be carried out.

"I don't think my case is exceptional—I just lived to tell about it," said Joseph Green Brown. . . . He was freed from prison this year, 14 years after he was sentenced to die for a murder he did not commit. "Any time the Government has all the resources and you have none, you're going to be in deep trouble," he said. "If you're black you're in deeper trouble, particularly if the victim is white.". . . .

Even some proponents of the death penalty, like Dr. Ernest van den Haag of Fordham University, admit the likelihood of error. "If you want to punish people, mistakes will be made, and some people will be executed who are innocent," he said, adding that judicial safeguards make such errors extremely rare. "If you believe that justice requires that murderers will be executed and if you further believe that the death penalty deters murders, then I think the advantages more than offset the disadvantages."

Recent court rulings and popular sentiment seem to indicate more use of the death penalty, not less. "There is a lot of public outrage," said Attorney General David Lee of Oklahoma. . . . "People are very upset nobody's been executed," Mr. Lee said. "There have been a lot of horrible murders throughout the years, and we have a real large death row population for the size of our state. People are critical of the length of time it takes."

—*New York Times*, November 1, 1987

executed by civil authority in the United States prior to the Supreme Court's ruling in 1972. Increasingly, however, the death penalty came under attack for moral and legal reasons. Nevertheless, in upholding capital punishment in 1976, the Court concluded: "It is an extreme sanction, suitable to the most extreme of crimes." In 1977 Gary Gilmore, a convicted killer who had demanded to die, was shot by a Utah firing squad in the first execution in America in a decade. On May 25, 1979, as demonstrators outside the Florida State Prison chanted "Death Row Must Go," John Arthur Spenkelink, a thirty-year-old drifter and convicted murderer, became the second person to be executed in America since 1967. And on November 2, 1984, Margie Velma Barfield, fifty-one, became the first woman to be executed in the United States in twenty-two years. As the executions continued, the Supreme Court did set a minimum age for capital punishment; in 1988, it declared unconstitutional the death penalty for juveniles who are under sixteen when they commit murder.[119]

[119] *Thompson v. Oklahoma,* 487 U.S. 815 (1988).

By the mid-1980s, the pace of executions in America had increased. And by 1992, there were 2,588 prisoners on death row.[120] By April of that year, there had been 168 executions since 1977, forty-six in Texas alone. Executions, at first carried out only in southern states after the Supreme Court restored the death penalty, had taken place by 1992 in every region of the country. California, which had not executed anyone since capital punishment was reinstated, sent Robert Alton Harris to the gas chamber in San Quentin in April of that year. Among the states with laws providing for the death penalty, lethal injection was the most common method, then electrocution, hanging, the gas chamber, and the firing squad.

Intense legal battles were fought to save some of the condemned men. In Texas, James D. Autry was scheduled to die in 1983. "Already strapped to the execution table, with the intravenous needles stuck in place and only twenty-four minutes before the poison was to flow at midnight, Autry was rescued by a stay order from Associate Justice Byron R. White."[121] The reprieve was only temporary; Autry was executed on March 14, 1984. In 1992, the state of Virginia executed Roger Keith Coleman for the murder of his sister-in-law. Coleman, who was electrocuted, went to his death protesting his innocence.

Proponents of capital punishment argue that it is appropriate punishment by society for terrible, brutal crimes, including serial murders. Moreover, the proponents contend, the death penalty may deter other murders. They also argue that persons convicted of murder may in time be released from prison and may kill again. A number of studies, however, have concluded that capital punishment is not an effective deterrent — there have been about 240,000 murders in the United States since the death penalty was restored — and opponents also argue that there is always the possibility that innocent persons will be executed if justice miscarries. One study of hundreds of capital cases between 1900 and 1985 concluded that in 350 of these cases an innocent person had been convicted, and that twenty-three of these prisoners were executed.[122] Since 1972, the study found, twenty-four innocent persons had been

[120] Data as of April 1992. Source: *New York Times,* May 22, 1992, p. A14.
[121] Robert Sherrill, "Death Row on Trial," *The New York Times Magazine,* November 13, 1983, p. 80.
[122] The study by Michael L. Radelet and Hugo Adam Bedau was published in the *Stanford Law Review* of November 1987.

sentenced to death; one was executed and the others eventually released from prison.[123]

ORGANIZED CRIME

In April of 1992, John Gotti, the head of the Gambino crime family based in New York City, was convicted in federal court on murder and racketeering charges. Gotti was found guilty of arranging the slaying of Paul Castellano, his predecessor as crime boss of the Gambinos, who was gunned down on the streets of Manhattan seven years earlier. He was sentenced to life in prison without parole.

With his $1,000 double-breasted suits, his smile, and his mobster's swagger, Gotti had become a sort of media celebrity, a real-life "Godfather." Previously acquitted in three other trials, Gotti had seemed so immune to prosecution that he had earned the sobriquet of "the Teflon don." But this time, his underboss, Salvatore ("Sammy the Bull") Gravano testified against his chief. Gotti's conviction symbolized both the government's increased success in fighting organized crime and the gradual deterioration of crime families in many cities across the country. In Los Angeles, New Jersey, New England, New Orleans, Kansas City, Detroit, and St.

Louis, the conviction of top crime bosses had weakened but not destroyed the mob, which remained strong in New York City.

One important tool the federal government employed in fighting the mob was the 1970 Racketeer Influenced and Corrupt Organizations Act (RICO). In addition, the FBI had successfully used electronic surveillance to penetrate the crime families, and it relied on the federal witness-protection program to provide safety and new identities for mobsters willing to testify.

The conviction of John Gotti was a dramatic event, but earlier court cases had revealed to the public the power of organized crime in America. For example, many years earlier, in 1970, a flurry of federal indictments, along with tape recordings of "bugged" conversations made public by the FBI, suggested that mobsters virtually dominated the government of Newark, New Jersey. Much of the power in Newark, at least according to these documents, was wielded not by the elected mayor, Hugh Addonizio, but by the local crime chieftain, Anthony ("Tony Boy") Boiardo, heir to a crime empire built by his father, Ruggiero ("Richie the Boot") Boiardo.[124]

The FBI transcripts included this conversation between Angelo ("Gyp") De Carlo, identified as "Ray," and an associate named "Joe":

Joe: You know . . . it's going to take three weeks but we'll own this Hughie [Addonizio]. This guy here, I'll guarantee we'll own him. I'll use that term — in three or four weeks. . . .
Ray: Hughie [Addonizio] helped us along. He give us the city.[125]

According to another tape-recorded conversation, "Tony Boy" and De Carlo discussed an important question — who should be appointed police director of Newark. "Tony Boy" said the decision was up to De Carlo.[126] Summoned before a federal grand jury, the mayor of Newark invoked his constitutional immunity and declined to answer any questions about his alleged ties with the mob. In July, after losing the mayoralty race to Kenneth Gibson (who became the first African American mayor of Newark), Addonizio, along with four codefendants, was convicted of extorting money from a contractor doing work for the city. Addonizio was sentenced to ten years in prison and fined $25,000.

John Gotti

---

[123] Ibid. Source: *New York Times,* May 3, 1989, p. A18.

[124] Fred J. Cook, "The People v. the Mob; Or, Who Rules New Jersey?" *The New York Times Magazine,* February 1, 1970.
[125] *New York Times,* January 7, 1970, p. 28.
[126] Cook, "The People v. the Mob; Or, Who Rules New Jersey?" p. 36.

IF YOU VIOLATE THE RULES, "THEY KILL YOU"

A rare glimpse inside the world of organized crime was offered in 1980 by Aladena (Jimmy the Weasel) Fratianno, a government witness in a federal court trial:

> The witness . . . described . . . a secret organization that was divided into "families" that conducted criminal activities in major cities throughout the country. In his testimony last week, he said he became a member of the Los Angeles group in 1948.
>
> Recalling the initiation ceremony, he said: "They took me in a room by myself. There was a long table where all of the members were; most of the members were sitting. There was a gun and a sword crossing one another in the middle of the table."
>
> "They all stood up," he continued. "We held hands; the boss said something in Italian. It lasts about two or three minutes.
>
> "Then they prick your finger with a needle or a sword until blood draws. Then you go around and meet each member of the family. You kiss them on the cheek and you're a member."

Mr. Fratianno testified that the organization operated in 20 cities, with one family in each city except New York, which had five.

> Each family is headed by a boss elected by all of its members, the witness said. He added that the boss appointed an underboss and a consiglieri, or counselor, to assist him and that capos, or captains, supervised the members, called soldiers.
>
> There is also a "national commission" composed of the five New York City bosses and the Chicago boss, he said, adding that "they more or less handle disputes with other families." . . .
>
> The prosecutor questioned him about the requirements for becoming a member. . . . "You are more or less proposed by somebody," he answered. "Sometimes you do something significant. Sometimes you have a brother or a father in it."
>
> He said one of its main rules was "never divulge anything about the organization." If you violate the rules, he said, "they kill you."

—*New York Times*, November 2, 1980

There is still argument over whether organized crime in America should be called the Mafia, the mob, or the syndicate, but there is little doubt that it has existed on a major scale. (Some Italian-American groups have objected to the term "Mafia" on the grounds that if reflects unfairly on the majority of law-abiding Italian Americans.) Organized crime controls illegal gambling, loan sharking, narcotics, and other unlawful activities. It also owns legitimate businesses and infiltrates labor unions. In some instances it corrupts public officials by paying them to permit the mob to operate.

A presidential commission estimated, more than two decades ago, that the mob operated in 80 percent of all cities of more than one million residents.[127] One White House statement declared, "Investigations of the national crime syndicate . . . show its membership at some 5,000 divided into twenty-four 'families' around the nation."[128] According to the presidential commission, each "family" is organized to resemble the structure of the Mafia that has operated for more than a century in Sicily: a "boss" at the top; an underboss; a

counselor; several lieutenants; beneath them, the "soldiers" or "button men"; an "enforcer" whose job is "the maiming and killing of recalcitrant members"; and a "corrupter" who buys off public officials. "The highest ruling body of the twenty-four families is the "commission,'" a combination supreme court and board of directors composed of nine to twelve of the most powerful bosses.[129]

"All available data indicate that organized crime flourishes only where it has corrupted local officials," the presidential commission emphasized.[130] Donald R. Cressey, an expert on organized crime, reports that in one instance a United States congressman resigned when ordered to do so by a crime boss. In this district, the crime syndicate "also 'owns' both judges and the

---

[127] *The Challenge of Crime in a Free Society*, p. 191.
[128] President Nixon's message to Congress on organized crime, *New York Times*, April 24, 1969, p. 30.
[129] *The Challenge of Crime in a Free Society*, pp. 193–94.
[130] Ibid., p. 191.

Narcotics dealers, gamblers and businessmen make illicit payments of millions of dollars a year to policemen of New York, according to policemen, law-enforcement experts and New Yorkers who make such payments themselves. . . .

A detective with many years of experience in the narcotics division said one of his colleagues had arranged payoffs to the police from major heroin dealers of up to $50,000, in return for such favors as the destruction of evidence gathered on secret wiretaps. . . .

A report by the Joint Legislative Committee on Crime . . . charged that gambling in the slums of New York "could not function without official tolerance induced by corruption . . . ghetto residents are

perfectly aware of the corrupt relationship between racketeers and certain elements in the Police Department, and, for this reason, have a deep cynicism concerning the integrity of the police in maintaining law and order in the community."

Putting an exact price tag on corruption is impossible. . . . however . . . the city's 10,000 small Puerto Rican grocery stores were estimated to give the police $6.2 million a year. . . . Numbers operators, according to federal and state agencies and private researchers' estimates, make payoffs between $7 million and $15 million a year.

—David Burnham, "Graft Paid to Police Here Said to Run Into Millions," *New York Times*, April 25, 1970

officials who assign criminal cases to judges. About 90 percent of the organized crime defendants appear before the same few judges."[131]

The Justice Department's Organized Crime and Racketeering Section is the government unit in charge of attempts to curb the power of the crime syndicate. Despite the diminishing power of the mob in many cities, and the conviction every year of hundreds of organized crime figures, no one in Washington claimed that the federal government had succeeded in controlling the problem.

Organized crime could not thrive if the public did not demand the services it provides, and if law-enforcement and elected officials refused to be bought. Corruption of the political system is the most disturbing threat posed by the mob. "The extraordinary thing about organized crime," the presidential commission concluded, "is that America has tolerated it for so long."[132]

JUSTICE AND THE AMERICAN POLITICAL SYSTEM

Although the Supreme Court and the Constitution may seem remote from the lives of most citizens, the decisions of the Court — the ultimate outputs of the system of justice — have direct, immediate relevance for

the individuals involved and much broader meaning for the political system as a whole. As Chief Justice Earl Warren noted in his last words from the bench, " . . . the Court develops the eternal principles of our Constitution in accordance with the problems of the day."[133]

In 1992, for example, the power of the Supreme Court meant that the families of persons who died of lung cancer after smoking cigarettes could sue the to-

[131] Donald R. Cressey, *Theft of the Nation* (New York: Harper & Row, 1969), pp. 252–53.
[132] *The Challenge of Crime in a Free Society*, p. 209.
[133] Woodward and Armstrong, *The Brethren: Inside the Supreme Court*, p. 26.

The Court is and always will be a storm center of controversial issues. For to it come most of the troublesome, contentious problems of each age, problems that mirror the tensions, fears and aggressiveness of the people. It will be denounced by some group, whatever it does.

—William O. Douglas, *The Court Years: 1939–1975*

bacco companies on grounds that the industry knew the hazards of smoking but had conspired to cover up the risks.[134] For African American students, the power of the Court meant that state college systems that were still segregated might have to open their doors wider to minority students.[135] And for women living in the state of Pennsylvania, it meant they would not have to inform their husbands of their intention to have an abortion.[136]

The list is much longer. Although each case sometimes affected only one person directly, the Supreme Court's decisions had wider implications for the nation. The victory for the family of Rose Cipollone, for example, meant that other smokers or their heirs could sue the tobacco companies. It raised the possibility that corporations in other industries, such as automobiles and pesticides, might be held more accountable for their products. The Court's rulings often affect society as a whole.

The decisions of the Supreme Court have great *political* significance as well. In the field of civil rights, for example, the Warren Court was well ahead of the executive branch or Congress. Because its power rests on public opinion, the Court cannot get too far ahead of the country, but it can, in the words of Archibald Cox, attempt to respond to the "dominant needs of the time."[137] And it can also serve as the conscience of the nation and a guardian of minorities, the poor, and the forgotten.[138]

There are serious inequalities and flaws in the American system of justice, as we have seen — backlogged criminal courts and a bail system that often penalizes poor defendants; plea bargaining in the place of trial by jury; some judges and officials who are puppets of organized crime; prisons that do not rehabilitate.

[134] *Cipollone* v. *Liggett Group* (1992). Five months after the Supreme Court ruled in favor of the heirs of Rose Cipollone, who had smoked cigarettes for 42 years, lawyers handling the case dropped it, apparently because it was too expensive to continue the litigation. But other cases against the tobacco industry were expected to go forward as a result of the Supreme Court's ruling.

[135] *U.S.* v. *Fordice; Ayers* v. *Fordice*, 112 S.Ct. 2727 (1992). The Supreme Court ruled in a case brought against Mississippi by African American students. In the wake of the Court's decision, however, the future of some of the historically black colleges in Mississippi was uncertain. But civil rights lawyers believed the ruling would make it more difficult in the long run for states to maintain segregated college systems.

[136] *Planned Parenthood of Southeastern Pennsylvania* v. *Casey* (1992).

[137] Cox, *The Warren Court*, p. 5.

[138] See, for example, Justice Black's opinion in *Chambers* v. *Florida*, 309 U.S. 227 (1940).

Some of these problems can, of course, be solved by specific reforms — bringing defendants to trial more rapidly by appointing more judges, strengthening law enforcement, improving facilities for handling juvenile offenders, and so forth. At the same time, a presidential commission has concluded: "The most significant action that can be taken against crime is action designed to eliminate slums and ghettos, to improve education, to provide jobs. . . . We will not have dealt effectively with crime until we have alleviated the conditions that stimulate it."[139]

[139] *The Challenge of Crime in a Free Society*, p. 15.

THE
CHIEF
JUSTICES
OF THE
UNITED
STATES

John Jay (1789–1795)
John Rutledge (1795)
Oliver Ellsworth (1796–1800)
John Marshall (1801–1835)
Roger B. Taney (1836–1864)
Salmon P. Chase (1864–1873)
Morrison R. Waite (1874–1888)
Melville W. Fuller(1888–1910)
Edward D. White (1910–1921)
William Howard Taft (1921–1930)
Charles Evans Hughes (1930–1941)
Harlan F. Stone (1941–1946)
Fred M. Vinson (1946–1953)
Earl Warren (1953–1969)
Warren E. Burger (1969–1986)
William H. Rehnquist (1986–)

Ultimately, as Justice Robert Jackson observed, the third branch of government, the judiciary, maintains "the great system of balances upon which our free government is based"—the balances among the various parts of the federal system, between authority and liberty, and between the rule of the majority and the rights of the individual.[140] Chief Justice Earl Warren confessed on the day he retired that performing this task is extremely difficult, "because we have no constituency. . . . We serve only the public interest as we see it, guided only by the Constitution and our own conscience."[141]

The resolution of conflict in American society through law, rather than through force, depends on public confidence in the courts and in the process of justice. And confidence in the system of justice requires that the words "Equal Justice Under Law," carved in marble over the entrance to the Supreme Court, be translated into reality at every level of the system.

PERSPECTIVE

The United States Supreme Court stands at the pinnacle of the American judiciary, but it is only one part of the fragmented, decentralized system of justice in America, a system that encompasses a network of federal courts, state and local courts and prosecutors, the United States Department of Justice, state and local police, the FBI, prisons and jails, probation and parole officers, and parole boards.

In a political sense, law is the body of rules made by government for society, interpreted by the courts, and backed by the power of the state. Another approach to law is sociological. Law can be seen as the gradual growth of rules and customs that reconcile conflict among people. In applying the law and deciding cases, judges often rely on *stare decisis*, or precedent. Most American law is statutory law enacted by Congress, or by state or local legislative bodies, but many statutes are based on English common law.

Cases considered by federal and state courts are either civil or criminal. Civil cases concern relations between individuals or organizations. Criminal cases concern crimes committed against the public order. Most crimes are defined by local, state, and federal statutes, which set forth a range of penalties as well.

The United States has a dual court system, consisting of federal courts and the courts in the fifty states. At the top of the judicial system is the Supreme Court. Its nine members are appointed by the president, subject to Senate approval. The Supreme Court is a political institution that makes both policy and law. Although insulated from everyday politics, the Supreme Court lies at the heart of the ongoing struggle in the American political system.

The Supreme Court is at the apex of one of the three independent, constitutionally coequal branches of the federal government. How the Court should apply its power has always been a subject of controversy. Much of the Supreme Court's power stems from its exercise of *judicial review*: the power to declare acts of Congress or actions by the executive branch—or laws and actions at any level of local, state, and federal government—unconstitutional.

Most cases never reach the Supreme Court. Those that do usually reach the Court through original jurisdiction, appellate jurisdiction, or, as in the majority of cases, through the granting of a writ of certiorari. Cases may reach the Supreme Court for review either from state or federal courts. The cases come from a state court of last resort (usually a state supreme court), or from federal courts of appeals, U.S. district courts, or special-purpose federal courts.

Most federal cases are handled by the inferior courts created by Congress under the Constitution—

---

[140] Jackson, *The Supreme Court in the American System of Government*, p. 61.
[141] *New York Times*, June 24, 1969, p. C24.

federal courts of appeals, federal district courts, and special-purpose courts, such as the Court of Military Appeals, which deal with specific kinds of cases. The states also have several layers of courts, including magistrates' courts, municipal courts, county courts, special jurisdiction courts, intermediate appellate divisions, and courts of appeals.

All federal court judges are appointed by the president, subject to Senate approval. A majority of state and local judges are elected.

Police in the United States are the armed embodiment of the law. Often underpaid, with inadequate personnel and resources, they are expected to fight crime, enforce the law, keep the peace, and provide a wide variety of social and community services. Police are sometimes caught between the established order and dissident or minority groups seeking change.

Criminal justice and law enforcement are primarily the responsibility of state and local authorities. However, in recent years, the federal Department of Justice has emerged as a major policymaking agency for a broad range of political, legal, and social issues. The department is headed by the attorney general. The Justice Department conducts criminal prosecutions in the federal courts. Separate divisions of the department deal with criminal, civil, antitrust, tax, civil rights, and natural resources cases. A special unit in the criminal division handles cases involving organized crime. The Federal Bureau of Investigation is the investigative arm of the Justice Department.

In processing criminal cases, the machinery of the adversary system of justice is available, but often it is not used. Instead, plea bargaining is more often used to avoid a trial. Widespread court delays, a discriminatory bail system, and serious overcrowding in the prisons are other flaws in the system.

Although the Supreme Court may seem remote from the lives of most citizens, its decisions affect not only the individuals involved in specific cases, but also society as a whole. The resolution of conflict in American society through law, rather than through force, depends on public confidence in the courts and in the process of justice.

Suggested Reading

Abraham, Henry J. *The Judicial Process,* 5th edition* (Oxford University Press, 1986). A very useful general introduction to the American judicial process. Explains the operations of local, state, and federal courts and the legal system, and compares the United States judicial system with that of other countries.

Berger, Raoul. *Government by Judiciary** (Harvard University Press, 1977). An interesting, historical study of the Fourteenth Amendment and the intentions of its framers. Berger argues that the original meaning attached to the amendment must still be binding on the Court.

Bickel, Alexander. *The Supreme Court and the Idea of Progress** (Yale University Press, 1978). (Originally published in 1970.) A critical and detailed assessment of some of the major areas of judicial decision making by the Warren Court. Argues that the Court went further than was prudent in a number of decisions that had controversial public-policy consequences.

Cressey, Donald R. *Theft of the Nation* (Harper & Row, 1969). A comprehensive study of organized crime in the United States by a sociologist who served as consultant to the President's Crime Commission. Describes the corruption of law enforcement and government by organized crime.

Howard, J. Woodford, Jr. *Courts of Appeals in the Federal Judicial System** (Princeton University Press, 1981). An innovative study of three U.S. courts of appeals. Analyzes the political values, role perceptions, and judicial opinions of the judges and examines the flow of litigation to and from the courts of appeals.

McCloskey, Robert G. *The American Supreme Court** (University of Chicago Press, 1961). A lucid and penetrating analysis of the role of the Supreme Court in the American system of government.

Murphy, Walter F. *Elements of Judicial Strategy** (University of Chicago Press, 1973). An informative study of the nature of judicial decision making and its consequences for public policy. Analyzes the Supreme Court's role as a major decision maker in the political system.

Murphy, Walter F., and Pritchett, C. Herman, eds. *Courts, Judges, and Politics,* 4th edition* (McGraw-Hill, 1986). A comprehensive collection of cases, documents, and essays on the role of judges and the courts in the policy-making process.

Schubert, Glendon. *Judicial Policy-Making,* 2nd edition (Scott Foresman, 1974). An introduction to the role the judiciary plays in the making of public policy. Applies systems theory to the activities of the courts.

The Supreme Court, Justice and the Law, 2nd edition (Congressional Quarterly, 1977). A useful study of the Supreme Court and federal judiciary from 1969 to 1977. Includes summaries of the Court's major decisions and biographical sketches of the justices who served on the Court during those nine years.

Ungar, Sanford J. *FBI* (Atlantic-Little, Brown, 1976). A detailed analysis of the Federal Bureau of Investigation — its history and development, and its personnel, procedures, and power. Examines J. Edgar Hoover's forty-eight-year reign as director, as well as events since his death, including the Watergate investigation.

Wilson, James Q., ed. *Crime and Public Policy** (Institute for Contemporary Studies, 1983). A collection of thirteen articles that examines crime-control policies in America. Proposes a number of new initiatives that might be used in the effort to combat crime.

Wise, David. *The American Police State* (Random House, 1976). Details and summarizes the abuse of power and violation of constitutional rights of individuals by the federal intelligence agencies, including the FBI, CIA, and others. Includes the major findings of the Senate and House select committees on intelligence, and additional case studies.

Woodward, Bob, and Armstrong, Scott. *The Brethren: Inside the Supreme Court** (Avon, 1981). (Originally published in 1979.) An account by two Washington journalists of the internal workings of the Supreme Court from 1969 to 1976. Examines the Court's step-by-step decision-making process, from preliminary votes to the final drafts of written opinions.

---

* Available in paperback edition.

PART FOUR

GOVERNMENT
IN
OPERATION

I N AN UNCERTAIN world of nuclear weapons and regional conflicts, foreign policy often plays an important role when the voters, every four years, choose their president. Who has more experience in foreign affairs? Which candidate should be trusted with control of nuclear weapons? Which candidate will be most likely to keep America out of war? Whose policies seem best in such trouble spots such as the Middle East, the Balkans, or Central America?

In the fall of 1992, when President George Bush campaigned for re-election against Governor Bill Clin-

Chapter 14

Foreign Policy and National Security

ton of Arkansas, the Democratic candidate, the lagging economy and other domestic issues dominated, but the candidates also clashed over foreign-policy questions. Indeed, George Bush, widely regarded as stronger in diplomacy than in domestic affairs, sought to focus the debate on foreign policy, where his advisers felt he had an advantage.

For example, in his acceptance speech at the Republican National Convention that renominated him in Houston in 1992, Bush declared: "My opponents say I spend too much time on foreign policy. As if it didn't matter that schoolchildren once hid under their desks in drills to prepare for nuclear war. I saw the chance to rid our children's dreams of the nuclear nightmare, and

I did." [1] Under his administration, he said, the Cold War had ended with the collapse of communism in the Soviet Union and in Eastern Europe, Germany had been united, the American hostages in the Middle East were free, and Arabs and Israelis were holding peace talks. By emphasizing these events, Bush sought to persuade the voters that his opponent, the governor of a small southern state, could not match his experience on the world stage.

---

[1] *Congressional Quarterly*, Weekly Report, August 22, 1992, p. 2556.

As Bush fell further behind in the polls, he questioned Clinton's patriotism, assailing him for participating or organizing demonstrations in England against the Vietnam War while a student there. Bush also wondered why Clinton had visited Moscow as a student in 1969, but he dropped that line of attack when he was criticized for unfair innuendo.

Clinton, in turn, emphasized domestic issues, but he countered in the foreign policy arena by citing evidence suggesting that as vice-president Bush had played a more prominent role in the Iran-contra scandal than

he had ever admitted. If so, Clinton charged, it called into question Bush's "veracity," and "his support for illegal conduct" in the scandal.[2]

As the presidential candidates debated the issues in the campaign of 1992, the setting for the discussion was no longer the same. The world as Americans had known it since the Second World War had changed almost beyond recognition in the previous four years.

• • •

At 7:32 P.M. on December 25, 1991, the red flag of the Soviet Union with hammer-and-sickle fluttered in the wind for the last time as it was slowly lowered over the Kremlin in Moscow, marking the formal end to the Soviet Union. The breakup of the Communist empire had seemed inconceivable in 1988 when Bush had defeated Massachusetts Governor Michael S. Dukakis. For four decades, the United States and the Soviet Union had been locked in a seemingly insoluble era of conflict, somewhere between peace and war. With both sides possessing unimaginably destructive nuclear missiles and bombs, the possibility of Armageddon was never far in the background. Indeed, in the Cuban missile crisis of 1962, the world went to the brink of nuclear war.

But in the fall of 1989, the tide of history once more swept across eastern Europe. In one country after another, democratic forces were able to break the grip of the Communist dictatorships, closely allied with Moscow, that had come to power in the aftermath of the

_____

[2] *Washington Post*, September 9, 1992, p. A12.

Taking down the Berlin Wall, November 1991

Second World War. In Hungary, Poland, East Germany, Czechoslovakia, and Bulgaria, governments toppled, often after mass demonstrations by ordinary citizens. In Romania, the revolt was bloody as security forces fired into the crowds, and dictator Nicolae Ceausescu and his wife, who attempted to flee by helicopter, were caught and shot.

In November, East Germany opened its borders to the West, and on television the world watched the memorable scene of crowds dancing in joyful celebration atop the Berlin Wall, the symbol of divided Ger-

---

RUSSIA'S "TIME TRAVELER"

Moscow, March 25—Cosmonaut 3rd Class Sergei Krikalev's return to Earth today was one small step for a man, followed by one giant whiff of smelling salts.

Krikalev, stuck in a space station as an orbiting hostage to budget problems on the ground in Russia, returned to a bewilderingly different country than he left 10 months ago. The cosmonaut, who was blasted into space 313 days ago by the Soviet Union, landed safely in Kazakhstan—one of the independent states formed in December.

While he was circling the Earth in the Mir space station, the Soviet Union fought off a coup, changed leaders and went out of existence. . . . Krikalev now is being called Russia's "Time Traveler" and compared to science fiction characters who suddenly find themselves catapulted into a new century.

Even his home town changed its name while he was in space—from Leningrad to St. Petersburg.

Originally scheduled to return in October, Krikalev continued to spin around the Earth 16 times a day while economic, territorial and bureaucratic battles raged below.

—*Washington Post*, March 26, 1992

A WORLD AT WAR

The Center for Defense Information, a nonprofit research organization in Washington, periodically publishes a survey of armed conflicts taking place around the globe. In 1992, it counted twenty-four major and minor wars then in progress, involving approximately 6.4 million soldiers and paramilitary fighters. The total loss of lives in these conflicts is unknown, but it is estimated that more than 6 million people have been killed. The following were rated as the ten most violent wars:

Conflict	Number of Deaths	Year Started
1. Afghanistan	1,300,000	1978
2. Cambodia	1,300,000	1963
3. Mozambique	1,000,000	1975
4. Sudan	1,000,000	1963
5. Uganda	310,000	1961
6. Angola	300,000	1974
7. Indonesia	200,000	1975
8. Lebanon	150,000	1975
9. Guatemala	100,000	1967
10. Kurdish wars	100,000	1961

— Data provided by Center for Defense Information

many. Soon afterward, the wall itself came down, and chunks of its stones became souvenirs of a vanished and unlamented era.

Still, the mighty Soviet Union stood, seemingly impervious to change. But Mikhail Gorbachev, who had come to power in 1985, had unleashed *glasnost*, or change, and *perestroika*, or restructuring, of Soviet society, which had become much more open in just a few years. But the new policies had some unexpected results. On May Day of 1990, something extraordinary happened in Red Square — the crowds jeered President Gorbachev and the Kremlin leaders atop Lenin's tomb. As the loudspeakers blared out martial music, demonstrators marched across the cobblestones carrying banners that said "Down with the Politburo! Resign!" and calling for freedom for Lithuania.

In August of 1991, a cabal of hardliners led by Vladimir A. Kryuchkov, the chairman of the KGB, the Soviet secret police, briefly held Gorbachev prisoner at his dacha on the Black Sea. As demonstrators in Moscow rallied in support of President Gorbachev, Boris N. Yeltsin, the President of Russia, climbed on a tank and defied the coup-plotters. The tide turned, the plotters were arrested, and a weakened Gorbachev returned briefly to power. But within four months, the republics of the Soviet Union had declared their independence of central control, Gorbachev resigned, and Yeltsin, as president of Russia, emerged as the most important leader in the former Soviet empire, which had broken up into fifteen independent states. But Yeltsin himself faced an uncertain future as he struggled to impose a free market economy on the rubble of the Soviet system. The Russians, once America's adversaries, were seeking billions of dollars in aid from the United States. Both sides drastically reduced their nuclear arsenals. All of these changes — political, military, and economic — had come so fast as to be breathtaking.

In the 1992 election campaign, President Bush also sought to reap political advantage from the fact that he had confronted Iraq's dictator, Saddam Hussein, in the Persian Gulf War of 1991. After Iraq had invaded Kuwait in 1990, threatening Saudi Arabia's oilfields, Bush had dispatched more than half a million troops to the Persian Gulf and, with the support of the United Nations and a coalition of twenty-eight nations, forced Iraq to withdraw.

Bush had proclaimed a "new world order," in which, as he envisioned it, the United States and other nations would cooperate to keep the peace. But even the American military triumph in the Gulf contained

Vietnam peace accords are
signed in Paris, January 1973.

"Thanks a lot"

Don Wright, *The Miami News*

political pitfalls for Bush; Saddam Hussein was still in power in Baghdad during the 1992 American presidential election campaign, and a congressional investigation and news reports disclosed that in the 1980s Washington had contributed secretly and substantially to Iraq's military buildup during that country's war against Iran.

The 1992 and previous presidential elections illustrated the fact that American foreign policy and national security are closely related to, and interwoven with, domestic politics. Presidents may be reluctant to admit

that their foreign policy is affected by domestic political considerations. They usually prefer to describe their actions in terms of national security and global complexities. But they are always well aware of the impact of foreign policy on politics at home. Often, they consider how a particular policy abroad may affect their chances for reelection. During the 1992 campaign, for example, President Bush went to Fort Worth, Texas, to announce at a General Dynamics plant that he had approved the sale of up to 150 F-16 fighter jets to Taiwan,

gress to try to reassert its authority in the conduct of foreign policy, much of the time the president remains the dominant figure in foreign and military matters. The great power of the president over foreign policy has disturbed many Americans and people in other countries because of the new and terrifying dimension added to the conduct of international relations since the Second World War. For the first time in human history, nations possess the technological power to destroy each other. Even after the collapse of the Soviet Union, the threat of nuclear war remained, even if substantially diminished.

Along with the United States, Britain, and France, Russia and China still retained nuclear weapons, and several smaller, third-world nations were actively attempting to acquire such weapons. The threat of nuclear proliferation — the spread of weapons of mass destruction to other nations — continued. Even small wars carry the potential of growing out of control into nuclear war. Although political candidates and leaders debate about America's military strength and the best way to ensure "national security," it is also possible to

an action that reversed ten years of U.S. policy. It also provided thousands of jobs in a state considered crucial to Bush's election strategy.

Although the long and tragic war in Vietnam had ended two decades earlier, that conflict had a far-reaching influence on domestic politics in the United States. The Vietnam War also demonstrated the overriding importance of American foreign policy, not only to Americans, but to the world in which the United States plays so powerful a role. Vietnam and the Persian Gulf War also illustrated the central role of the president in the conduct of foreign relations. The Constitution gives Congress the power to declare war, but Congress never did so in either Vietnam or the Gulf. In both instances a president made the decision to go to war.

In the 1990s Americans had become increasingly aware that the United States, while still a superpower — indeed the only surviving superpower — was but one nation in an increasingly interdependent, multipolar world; that is, a world in which there are many competing centers of power. The American who watches television on a Sony, drives a Honda, and uses a computer that runs on a Japanese memory chip, could hardly fail to understand that fact. Nor was it possible to separate military and diplomatic policies from domestic economic policies. Economic factors, such as large federal budget deficits, affected the strength of the dollar abroad and the balance of trade.

Today, the American president faces a complex mix of foreign policy problems. Despite actions by Con-

ask whether nations and people can ever really achieve security in the nuclear age.

The dramatic political changes in the world also raised fundamental questions about the concept of national security. Put simply, the United States had lost its principal "enemy," the Soviet Union. That central fact suggested the need for a major re-evaluation of America's foreign-policy goals, the size of its vast military establishment, and the allocation of its resources at home. As one analysis suggested, "failure to make progress on a domestic economic and social agenda now threatens America's long-term national security more than the traditional preoccupations of security and foreign policy. . . ."[3]

Nor were the problems confined to home. As the Cold War faded into history, new global issues had come to the fore, centering on challenges that transcended national boundaries. The global environment, nuclear proliferation, overpopulation, famine, disease, including the AIDS epidemic, a rising tide of nationalism, and ethnic and religious conflicts — all were issues that, in a global context, were broader than the old

rivalry of competing political systems. They were also issues that in many cases involved the future of humanity and the survival of the planet.

Against this background, we may ask: What is foreign policy? Who makes it? What role should the president play? The Congress? And how, in a democratic society, can people make their views felt and influence foreign policy? What should America's objectives be in its relations with the rest of the world? Should it attempt to be the world's police force, intervening in conflicts around the globe? How much of the nation's resources should go into military spending? What dangers are posed to U.S. institutions by a multibillion-dollar defense budget? What are the responsibilities of richer nations toward less developed nations?

THE UNITED STATES AND WORLD AFFAIRS

American Foreign Policy

Foreign policy is the sum of the goals, decisions, and actions that govern a nation's relations with the rest of the world. But the world changes, and so does foreign policy. A president may adopt one policy only to discard

[3] Peter G. Peterson with James K. Sebenius, "The Primacy of the Domestic Agenda," in Graham Allison and Gregory F. Treverton, eds., *Rethinking America's Security: Beyond Cold War to New World Order* (New York: W. W. Norton & Co., 1992), p. 69.

Albert Gore, at the environmental summit meeting in Rio de Janeiro, 1992

KISSINGER: "THE NATURE OF POWER"

The most ominous change that marked our period was the transformation in the nature of power. Until the beginning of the nuclear age it would have been inconceivable that a country could possess too much military strength for effective political use; every addition of power was — at least theoretically — politically useful. The nuclear age destroyed this traditional measure. A country might be strong enough to destroy an adversary and yet no longer be able to protect its own population against attack. By an irony of history a gargantuan increase in power had eroded the relationship of power to policy. Henceforth, the major nuclear powers would be able to devastate one another. But they would also have great difficulty in bringing their power to bear on the issues most likely to arise. They might be able to deter direct challenges to their own survival; they could not necessarily use this power to impose their will. The capacity to destroy proved difficult to translate into a plausible threat even against countries with no capacity for retaliation. The margin of the superpowers over non-nuclear states had been widening; yet the awesomeness of their power had increased their inhibitions. As power had grown more awesome, it had also turned abstract, intangible, elusive.

—Henry Kissinger, *White House Years*

it later; a new president may reverse the policies of his predecessor. Alliances shift; the Soviet Union, America's ally against Nazi Germany in the Second World War, became its principal adversary in the "Cold War" that began soon afterward, and lasted more than four decades. Japan, which had been America's wartime enemy, became its peacetime ally, as did West Germany.

So "foreign policy" is a changing and elusive concept. Roger Hilsman, a former assistant secretary of state, has suggested that the problem of foreign policy is not so much one of relating decisions to a single set of goals as it is "precisely one of choosing goals" in the midst of onrushing events and crises, and of reconciling the advocates of competing goals and policies. "The making of foreign policy," he concluded, "is a political process."[4]

The preservation of national security is a basic consideration in the formulation of foreign policy. But "national security" is so broad and vague a term that it can be used to justify almost any action that a nation or a president takes. President Nixon, for example, invoked it to attempt to justify a broad range of abuses of power that eventually led to his resignation.

After the Second World War, there were two approaches to the question of national security and American foreign policy. One view emphasized threats to United States security posed by the power of Communist or unfriendly nations. Another regarded the security of the United States as dependent on some form of world order "compatible with our values and interests."[5] This second view of American foreign policy holds that there can be no real security for the United States without world peace and security for all people.

Yet security proved a relative term in the thermonuclear age. During the Cuban Missile Crisis of 1962, President Kennedy's advisers knew that their decisions, if wrong, "could mean the destruction of the human race."[6] So any description of national security and foreign policy must take into account the changed nature of the world since the beginning of the atomic age.

During the years of the Cold War, the growth of Soviet power and the spread of nuclear weapons to several countries brought with it a decline in the relative military strength of the United States. Nevertheless, the United States and the Soviet Union dominated the world stage. The two superpowers confronted each other and sometimes clashed in Europe, the Middle East, Africa, Cuba, and other parts of the world. And twice after 1945, in Korea and Vietnam, the United States fought a protracted war against Communist

[4] Roger Hilsman, *To Move a Nation* (Garden City: Doubleday, 1967), pp. 12–13, 541.

[5] Paul H. Nitze, "The Secretary and the Execution of Foreign Policy," in Don K. Price, ed., *The Secretary of State*, prepared for the American Assembly, Columbia University (Englewood Cliffs: Prentice-Hall, 1960), pp. 6–7.

[6] Robert F. Kennedy, *Thirteen Days* (New York: Norton, 1969), p. 44.

power in Asia. Faced with often hostile, armed Communist nations, the United States sought to maintain a high level of military strength. American policymakers argued that this costly arms burden was necessary to protect the national security, American liberties at home, and the freedom of other nations. Only the shield of American power, they contended, prevented Communist expansion to a degree that would threaten American security.

Critics of this view maintained that the United States often used its vast power to support military governments in Asia, Latin America, and elsewhere in the world, including some that violated human rights and civil liberties, and tortured or killed political opponents. For example, the United States supported the government of El Salvador despite the operations of right-wing "death squads" that murdered thousands of persons and seemed to have the approval of high-ranking Salvadoran military and civilian officials.

Some critics argued that the United States already had enough nuclear weapons to destroy any adversary several times over and therefore did not need to continue such a high level of defense spending. But these arguments made little headway until after the collapse of the Soviet Union in 1991, when cutbacks in defense spending finally gained bipartisan political support.

During the Cold War, Marxist economists and others contended that America had become a modern imperial power, intervening on the world stage to protect its own political and economic interests. For example, Harry Magdoff suggested that there was a link between "the aggressive United States foreign policy aimed at controlling . . . as much of the globe as possible, and on the other hand, an energetic international expansionist policy of U.S. business." [7] In Magdoff's view, American foreign policy was designed to keep areas of the world open for investment and to make certain that underdeveloped countries provide the raw materials needed by American industry.

But this point of view is sharply challenged by other scholars, who argue that the radical economists have failed to show that governments conduct foreign policy to serve corporate interests. Business interests may influence governments, Benjamin J. Cohen has suggested, but "economics cannot account for everything." [8] The United States' "traditional support of Israel against the Arab states runs in diametric opposition to the interests of major U.S. oil companies," Cohen argued. And he cited the lengthy war in Southeast Asia as another example. "Can United States policy

in Vietnam possibly be explained in terms of concern for the economic advantages of American business?" [9]

Some scholars and political leaders have turned their attention to another phenomenon on the international stage — the powerful multinational corporations, many of them based in the United States, whose activities cut across national borders. Richard J. Barnet and Ronald E. Muller argue that these giant corporations are primarily concerned with profits, ignoring the social or environmental effects of their activities. They ask: " . . . by what right do a self-selected group of druggists, biscuit makers, and computer designers become the architects of the new world?" [10]

Within the United States, the high degree of military spending that characterized the Cold War years created several paradoxes. America faced, and still faces, the problem of how to balance its military needs against social needs at home. Billions of dollars that might, in part at least, have been used for education, housing, transportation, and similar programs were siphoned off into arms.

A "military-industrial complex" spawned to protect American security has created numerous problems for American society. Even when the United States lost its main adversary, with the disintegration of the Soviet Union, the question remained of whether, and to what extent, the vast defense and aerospace industry would retool for peace, and how much money previously earmarked for the military would find its way into education or other social programs.

Indeed, some analysts argued that the continued high level of military spending by the United States was in itself leading to the possible relative decline of the nation. Yale professor Paul Kennedy, in his widely read book, *The Rise and Fall of the Great Powers*, advanced just such a thesis: "If . . . too large a proportion of the state's resources is diverted from wealth creation and allocated instead to military purposes, then that is likely to lead to a weakening of national power over the longer term. In the same way, if a state overextends itself strategically — by, say, the conquest of extensive terri-

---

[7] Harry Magdoff, *The Age of Imperialism: The Economics of U.S. Foreign Policy* (New York: Modern Reader Paperbacks, 1969), p. 12.
[8] Benjamin J. Cohen, *The Question of Imperialism: The Political Economy of Dominance and Dependence* (New York: Basic Books, 1973), p. 130.
[9] Ibid., p. 126.
[10] Richard J. Barnet and Ronald E. Muller, *Global Reach: The Power of the Multinational Corporations* (New York: Simon and Schuster, 1974), p. 25.

tories or the waging of costly wars — it runs the risk that the potential benefits from external expansion may be outweighed by the great expense of it all — a dilemma which becomes acute if the nation concerned has entered a period of relative economic decline." [11]

The creation of a "garrison state" at times threatened liberties at home. During the Watergate scandal, President Nixon argued that the wiretapping of his own aides and of journalists, the formation of a special White House investigative unit known as "the Plumbers" to plug news leaks, and a plan to open first-class mail and burglarize the homes or offices of suspected persons were all justified by "national security."

At times, critics of American foreign policy have focused on what former Senator J. William Fulbright has called an "excessive moralism." [12] In the 1950s, when John Foster Dulles served as secretary of state under President Eisenhower, the rhetoric and sometimes the reality of American foreign policy took on the aspect of a missionary crusade against communism. It was the height of the Cold War — the period of intense East-West rivalry after the Second World War. There were echoes of this period again in the early 1980s, when President Reagan repeatedly denounced the Soviet Union.

By 1987, however, Reagan had signed a major arms limitation treaty with the Soviet Union and had met three times with Soviet leader Mikhail Gorbachev. Thus many of the concepts and attitudes of the Cold War began to change, even before the end of communism. During the 1960s American policymakers came to recognize that communism was not a monolith, but contained many variations and conflicts — particularly in the case of the Soviet Union and mainland China. President Nixon was able to open doors to Moscow and Beijing because, in both America and the Soviet Union, there was gradual recognition that the arms race not only threatened the survival of humanity, but also was distorting the economies of both nations, and diverting energies and resources into military hardware that might better be used to serve people. The Vietnam War illustrated the limits of American world power, and in its wake much of the crusading zeal that had marked the nation's foreign policy gave way to a more cautious, pragmatic approach.

One of the legacies of Vietnam, therefore, was a reluctance on the part of many Americans and their political leaders to undertake another foreign venture that might embroil the United States in a war. By 1980,

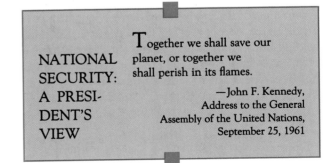

---

[11] Paul Kennedy, *The Rise and Fall of the Great Powers: Economic Change and Military Conflict from 1500 to 2000* (New York: Random House, 1987), p. xvi.

[12] J.W. Fulbright, *Old Myths and New Realities* (New York: Random House, 1964), p. 45.

however, at the end of the Carter presidency, there was a new mood of frustration over the limits of American power, triggered to a great extent by the seizure of American hostages in Iran and by the Soviet invasion of Afghanistan.

In the 1980 presidential election, the American electorate chose Ronald Reagan, who had promised to strengthen the nation's diplomacy and its military power. True to his word, Reagan presided over a major buildup of American military strength.

Some analysts and political leaders have viewed the United States as a special power, pursuing a foreign policy designed to create and support a world order based on the principles of freedom. Others, such as political scientist Richard Rosecrance, argue that "America has become an ordinary country in foreign relations. The trauma over Vietnam, the radical reduction of American economic influence, the greatly increased independence of traditional allies in Europe and East Asia—all these have brought about an end to distinctively American leadership of the international system. The *Pax Americana* is over." [13]

The Historical Setting

A nation's foreign policy is rooted in its politics and in its past. In discussing the history of American foreign policy, we can identify some recurring strands and major themes that are relevant to today's changed world.

One fundamental historical characteristic of American foreign policy was that of *isolationism*. President George Washington declared that it was the nation's policy "to steer clear of permanent alliance," and Jefferson said that America wanted peace with all nations, "entangling alliances with none."

During the nineteenth century, the diplomats of Europe maneuvered to preserve the "balance of power" in the Old World; America, protected by the broad Atlantic, could afford to remain relatively aloof from the problems of Europe. In 1823 the Monroe Doctrine warned European powers to keep out of the Western Hemisphere and pledged that the United States would not intervene in the internal affairs of Europe. American isolation, of course, was only relative. The United

States fought a war with Great Britain in 1812; it acquired Texas in a war with Mexico in 1846; and it took possession of Puerto Rico, Guam, and the Philippines under the treaty ending the Spanish-American War in 1898. (The Philippines gained independence in 1946.) However, the United States did not become a major colonial power, with vast overseas territories, on a scale comparable with Great Britain or some of the nations of Europe.

By the end of the nineteenth century, an opposite strand of American foreign policy, that of *interventionism*, was visible. In the early twentieth century, the United States practiced "gunboat diplomacy," intervening militarily in Mexico, the Caribbean, and Latin America. The First World War brought major United States military involvement in Europe for the first time. After the war, however, the United States declined to join with other countries in the League of Nations. President Woodrow Wilson's dream of world order was shattered, and America retreated "back to normalcy" and isolationism.

But during the Second World War, the United States and its allies defeated Nazi Germany and Japan, and America emerged in the position of a great world power. The United States traded its former position of isolationism for one of *internationalism*.

A world weary of war and destruction centered its hopes for peace on the United Nations (UN), created in 1945. It quickly became clear, however, that the future of the postwar world would be shaped not in the UN but in the relations between the two major powers, the United States and the Soviet Union. In a speech at Fulton, Missouri, in March 1946, British Prime Minister Winston Churchill declared that from the Baltic to the Adriatic seas, "an iron curtain has descended across the continent." In retrospect, it became clear that a Cold War had begun.

During this period, the United States adopted a policy of *containment* of the Soviet Union, first elaborated in the quarterly *Foreign Affairs* by George F. Kennan, a senior American diplomat who later became ambassador to Russia. Kennan, who was a State Department official in 1947 when the article was published, signed his name "Mr. X" to preserve his anonymity. The article set forth a doctrine that became "the Bible of Western foreign policy in the mid-twentieth century." [14] Kennan argued that the Soviet Union

[13] Richard Rosecrance, ed., *America as an Ordinary Country: U.S. Foreign Policy and the Future* (Ithaca: Cornell University Press, 1976), p. 11.

[14] H. Bradford Westerfield, *The Instruments of America's Foreign Policy* (New York: Crowell, 1963), p. 165.

President Truman, Secretary of State George C. Marshall (center), and Acting Secretary of Defense Robert A. Lovett

would expand its power wherever it could to challenge western institutions. He advocated that United States policy toward the Soviet Union be one of "firm and vigilant containment of Russian expansive tendencies." [15]

In the immediate aftermath of the Second World War, the United States moved to counterbalance Soviet power. Under the "Truman Doctrine," Washington began a program of military aid to Greece, which was fighting Communist guerrillas, and Turkey, which was under pressure to cede military bases to the Soviet Union. As enunciated by President Truman, the doctrine declared that American security and world peace depended on United States protection for the "free peoples of the world." [16]

In the summer of 1947, the United States launched the Marshall Plan (named for its creator, Secretary of State George C. Marshall) and poured more than $13 billion in four years into Western Europe to speed its

postwar economic and social recovery. The Soviet Union and other Eastern European nations declined to join the Marshall Plan.

In 1949 the United States and many of the nations of Western Europe formed the North Atlantic Treaty Organization (NATO), whose members were pledged to defend each other against attack. NATO was the first and most important of a series of postwar collective security pacts signed by the United States. These

---

[15] Mr. X, "The Sources of Soviet Conduct," *Foreign Affairs*, July 1947, pp. 566–82.

[16] Harry S Truman, *Memoirs by Harry S Truman*, vol. 2, *Years of Trial and Hope* (Garden City: Doubleday, 1958), p. 106.

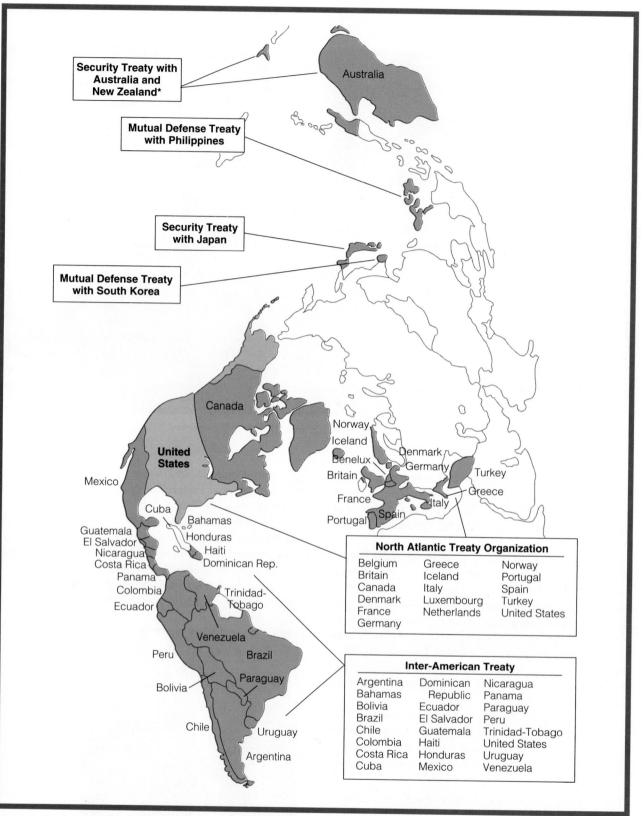

Security Treaty with Australia and New Zealand*

Mutual Defense Treaty with Philippines

Security Treaty with Japan

Mutual Defense Treaty with South Korea

Australia

Canada

Norway

Iceland

Benelux

Denmark

Germany

Britain

France

Portugal

Spain

Italy

Turkey

Greece

United States

Mexico

Cuba

Bahamas

Guatemala

Honduras

El Salvador

Haiti

Nicaragua

Dominican Rep.

Costa Rica

Panama

Colombia

Trinidad-Tobago

Ecuador

Venezuela

Brazil

Peru

Paraguay

Bolivia

Chile

Uruguay

Argentina

North Atlantic Treaty Organization

Belgium	Greece	Norway
Britain	Iceland	Portugal
Canada	Italy	Spain
Denmark	Luxembourg	Turkey
France	Netherlands	United States
Germany		

Inter-American Treaty

Argentina	Dominican	Nicaragua
Bahamas	Republic	Panama
Bolivia	Ecuador	Paraguay
Brazil	El Salvador	Peru
Chile	Guatemala	Trinidad-Tobago
Colombia	Haiti	United States
Costa Rica	Honduras	Uruguay
Cuba	Mexico	Venezuela

* As of 1986, the United States suspended its treaty obligation with New Zealand.

SOURCE: Department of State, Treaties in Force. Data as of 1987

Figure 14–1 United States Security Pacts

arrangements were greatly expanded during the Eisenhower administration. In 1992 the United States was pledged under security pacts to defend forty-two nations. (See Figure 14-1.)

Although America was preoccupied with European recovery and collective security, and with containing Soviet expansion, it was in the Pacific that a new war broke out only five years after the end of the Second World War. During the Korean War (1950-53), the United States became involved for the first time in a land war in Asia.

New forces, sometimes obscured by the rhetoric of the Cold War, were loose in the world. The United States, the sole nuclear power at the end of the Second World War, lost that advantage when the Soviet Union acquired atomic weapons in 1949. About the same time, however, world Communist unity began to come apart. As early as 1948, Yugoslavia's President Tito had broken with the Soviet Union. In 1956 Soviet tanks crushed a revolt against Communist rule in Hungary. By 1961 Russia and its former ally, Communist China, were open and bitter adversaries. In 1968 Soviet and Warsaw Pact troops invaded Czechoslovakia in order to put down a movement toward democratic reforms in that country.

During the same postwar period, a rising tide of *nationalism* brought independence to various nations in Africa, Asia, and the Middle East, and stirred political currents in Latin America. In 1947 India and Pakistan gained their independence from Britain, and in 1949 Indonesia became free of Dutch control. The 1960s saw a second wave of nationalism, in Africa. As European powers withdrew from what remained of their nineteenth-century colonial empires, the "Third World" became a new battleground in which the United States, the Soviet Union, and Communist China competed for influence and power. In the 1970s the United States and the Soviet Union vied for power in the Middle East and Africa. In many of these areas of the globe, poverty, hunger, disease, illiteracy, and political instability were combined in a volatile mixture.

Not all relationships that cut across national boundaries are controlled by governments. Modern scholars have also focused on *transnationalism*, which includes such global activities as trade, personal contacts, communications between private groups, and business relationships. Transnational relations may be defined as "contacts, coalitions, and interactions across state boundaries that are not controlled by the central foreign policy organs of governments." [17]

---

[17] Joseph S. Nye, Jr., and Robert O. Keohane, eds., *Transnational Relations and World Politics* (Cambridge: Harvard University Press, 1972), pp. x-xi.

1956: Soviet tanks in Hungary

In addition, foreign policy analysts today often speak of *interdependence*, or mutual dependence among nations. Sometimes this mutual dependence is cooperative, as when several nations agree to combat an environmental problem. Or it can be involuntary, as was the case of the United States and the Soviet Union, whose strategic interdependence derived "from the mutual threat of nuclear destruction." [18]

Vietnam and Its Aftermath

In Vietnam, the United States gradually moved into the power vacuum created when the French withdrew from Indochina following their defeat in 1954 by Ho Chi Minh. Presidents Eisenhower and Kennedy supported the government of South Vietnam, and Kennedy sent 16,000 troops there as "advisers." But it was President Johnson who, in 1965, committed the United States to a full-scale war against Communist North Vietnam and the National Liberation Front, or Vietcong. Eventually, Johnson sent more than 500,000 combat troops to Vietnam. The war proved divisive and increasingly unpopular at home, and it was a major factor in Johnson's decision to announce, in March 1968, that he would not seek the presidency again.[19]

Richard Nixon's promise to end the war helped to bring about his election in November 1968. Yet it took Nixon four years to redeem his pledge. By the time the peace agreement was signed in Paris in January 1973, more than 47,000 Americans had died in combat in eight years, and more than 303,000 had been wounded. Perhaps a million Vietnamese soldiers, North and South, were killed. At least 415,000 civilians died in

Vietnam: the costs were high.

South Vietnam. The United States dropped more than 7 million tons of bombs in Southeast Asia in eight years, three times the total bomb tonnage dropped in the Second World War. In money, even excluding billions in veterans' benefits, the cost of the war was more than $140 billion.

For almost a decade the Vietnam issue divided the nation and cast a shadow over the quality of American life. The lengthy war caused many Americans to become disillusioned with the workings of the political system itself. For that reason alone, the cost of the Vietnam War may be felt for many years to come.

From Détente to the End of the Cold War

Even before the United States had disengaged from Vietnam, a period of détente, or relaxation of tensions, between the two superpowers had begun in May 1972,

---

[18] Robert O. Keohane and Joseph S. Nye, *Power and Interdependence: World Politics in Transition* (Boston: Little, Brown, 1977), p. 9.

[19] Polls indicated that a majority of Americans considered the United States' involvement in Vietnam to have been an error. For example, a Gallup poll of June 1970 reported that 56 percent of the public considered that the United States had made "a mistake" in sending troops to Vietnam. The percentage of people who answered "yes" when asked "Do you think the United States made a mistake sending troops to fight in Vietnam?" rose above 50 percent for the first time in August 1968 and remained above 50 percent thereafter.

when President Richard Nixon held a summit meeting in Moscow with Soviet party chief Leonid Brezhnev. In Moscow, Nixon signed the SALT (Strategic Arms Limitation Talks) agreement placing a measure of control over nuclear weapons. The meeting followed Nixon's historic trip to China, the first by an American president.

Secretary of State Henry A. Kissinger was the architect of the new policy of détente. But in 1973 the Soviet Union became involved in the war in the Middle East and later in the conflict in Angola. These Soviet actions gave critics an opportunity to argue that *détente* had failed to restrain Moscow.

President Jimmy Carter, elected in 1976, achieved a major foreign policy breakthrough in the Middle East. In March of 1979, Carter brought about the signing of a peace treaty between Israel and Egypt after a generation of hostility between those two nations. The agreement followed a summit meeting between the leaders of Egypt and Israel that had taken place six months earlier at Camp David, the presidential retreat near Washington. The treaty provided for the withdrawal of Israeli troops from the Sinai Peninsula and for talks on autonomy for Palestinians on the West Bank of the Jordan River and in the Gaza Strip.

Also in 1979, the United States under President Carter entered into full diplomatic relations with the People's Republic of China and ended diplomatic relations with the Republic of China (Taiwan). But the pro-democracy movement that swept through Eastern Europe and ended with the collapse of the Soviet Union had more difficulty taking root in China, whose leaders continued to practice police-state repression against those who challenged the Communist leadership. In May and June of 1989, hundreds of thousands of students and other citizens demonstrated for democracy in Beijing's Tiananmen Square. The students erected a replica of the Statue of Liberty. The army opened fire on the demonstrators, and tanks crushed some of them. Thousands were killed or injured and there were mass arrests in the wake of the demonstrations. For the moment, at least, democracy had been crushed in China.

A decade earlier, in 1979, Soviet troops invaded Afghanistan and established a pro-Soviet government. Through the Central Intelligence Agency, the United States provided money and arms in support of the Afghan rebels fighting the more than 100,000 Soviet troops in that country. By 1992, the United States had spent more than $2 billion to arm the rebels.[20] The war in Afghanistan proved to be costly and unpopular for the Soviets, evoking parallels to the U.S. experience in Vietnam. In 1988, the Soviets began pulling their armed forces out of Afghanistan. Within four years, the rebels marched into Kabul, the capital.

---

[20] *Washington Post*, July 19, 1992, p. A24.

1989: Tiananmen Square, Beijing

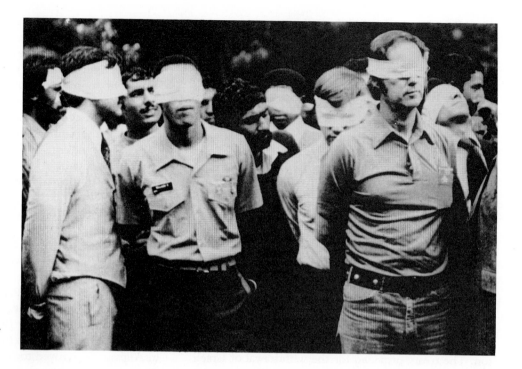

Iran, November 1979: American hostages are seized at U.S. embassy in Teheran.

During the 1980s, the United States pursued policies in Central America aimed at defeating forces in Nicaragua and El Salvador that were supported, President Reagan charged, by the Soviet Union and Cuba. In El Salvador, the administration poured in millions of dollars to shore up the government against pressure from left-wing guerrillas. In Nicaragua, through the Central Intelligence Agency, Reagan supported a covert war against that country's leftist Sandinista rulers.

Reagan soon found himself caught in a scandal growing out of crises in Iran and Nicaragua. In November 1979 Iranian militants had forced their way into the American embassy in Teheran and seized more than sixty Americans as hostages. The militants demanded that the deposed Shah of Iran, then in New York, be returned to Iran by the United States. Their demands were backed by the Ayatollah Khomeini, leader of Iran's Islamic revolution.

In April 1980 President Jimmy Carter approved a military rescue mission to Iran that turned into a disaster in the desert, leaving eight American servicemen dead and the hostages still imprisoned. Election Day 1980—the first anniversary of the seizure of the Americans—came and went with the hostages still in Iran. Carter lost to Reagan. Finally, on Inauguration Day 1981, only moments after Ronald Reagan had taken the oath of office, all fifty-two remaining hostages

were flown out of Iran, ending their 444 days in captivity.

But other American hostages had been seized in Lebanon, and President Reagan wanted them out. As a result, under Reagan, the staff of the National Security Council, operating from within the White House itself, conducted a secret foreign policy. Arms were sold to Iran to try to free the hostages seized in Lebanon, and millions of dollars in profits from those arms sales were diverted to support the contra rebels in Nicaragua, at a time when Congress had banned such aid. Even larger sums ended up in the Swiss bank accounts of the private individuals who ran the secret operations for Marine Lt. Col. Oliver North, a staff member of the National Security Council. By turning to private citizens to conduct such operations, the White House attempted to circumvent the constitutional requirement that Congress as well as the president play a role in the conduct of foreign policy.

The Iran-contra scandal, as it became known, created a dilemma for Bush when he first ran for president in 1988. As vice-president, he had emphasized his importance within the Reagan White House. He had presented himself as an official who was completely informed on the great affairs of state. Yet he professed to have only marginal knowledge of the Iran-contra affair, claiming he was "out of the loop," a position that seemed contradictory and opened him to attack by his Democratic opponent.

Bush had served as vice-president under Ronald Reagan, a president who emphasized military power. In the Reagan years, relations with the Soviet Union had improved substantially after initial tensions. Early in his presidency, Reagan had denounced the Soviet Union as an "evil empire." [21]

But in 1987 Reagan and Gorbachev signed the first treaty in history reducing the size of their nations' nuclear arsenals. Moreover, both countries agreed for the first time to allow inspectors at sensitive sites on their own soil to monitor the treaty. The two leaders also began a dialogue about reducing their long-range, strategic nuclear weapons.

After Israel invaded Lebanon in 1982, President Reagan dispatched 1,200 Marines to serve as part of a multinational peacekeeping force in Beirut, the Lebanese capital. In 1983, a terrorist drove a truck laden with explosives into the U.S. Marine barracks in a suicide attack that killed 241 servicemen. After the bombing, criticism of the administration increased at home. An independent Defense Department commission blamed the tragedy on failures in the chain of command from top to bottom.[22] In the face of eroding public support for the Marine mission, Reagan in February 1984 pulled the troops out.

The Middle East remained unstable. In 1986, U.S. warplanes under orders from President Reagan bombed Libya in retaliation for suspected terrorist acts by Libya and its leader, Muammar Qaddafi. In 1987 and 1988, Palestinian youths attacked Israeli troops on the West Bank and in the Gaza Strip, leading to even greater tensions in that area of the world.

The United States and its Western European allies depended on the oil fields on the Persian Gulf to fuel their economies. In 1987, President Reagan sent the navy into the Persian Gulf to protect Kuwaiti oil tankers. Later, he extended U.S. protection to ships of neutral nations.

The bombing of the Marine barracks in Lebanon by terrorists who may have received support from Syria and Iran was an example of the increasing use of terrorism in the world, sometimes with the support of governments. The murder or kidnapping of diplomats, businesspersons, educators, or others; embassy take-overs and bombings; aircraft hijackings, and other forms of terror were becoming increasingly familiar. These violent actions have been carried out by a wide range of political groups for a variety of reasons. By 1991, 8,022 persons had been killed in 11,598 terrorist incidents since 1968.[23] Some of the American and other hostages seized by terrorist groups in Lebanon were held for years. Late in 1991, the terrorists began releasing the hostages, and in December, Terry Anderson of the Associated Press, the last of the hostages, was set free after more than six years in captivity.

Not only terrorism, but international drug trafficking had an increasing impact on foreign policy. The drug overlords had gained extraordinary power in some countries, such as Colombia, a major cocaine producer, and the best efforts of American authorities had done relatively little to stem the flow of illegal drugs into the United States. In 1988 the federal government indicted General Manuel Antonio Noriega, the military dictator of Panama, for drug dealing. In 1989, President Bush had sent troops into Panama. They toppled Noriega, who was arrested, brought back to Miami, placed on trial, convicted of drug trafficking and sentenced to 40 years in prison.

Regional conflicts, such as the war in the Persian Gulf, and the agony of the people of Yugoslavia as that country splintered into a terrible civil war, demonstrated that the world was still not a peaceful place. Yet the superpower conflict that had most threatened the survival of humanity was history. On February 1, 1992, President Bush and President Boris Yeltsin of Russia met at Camp David, Maryland, and formally declared what was already apparent to the world: the Cold War was over.

HOW FOREIGN POLICY IS MADE

The President and Foreign Policy

In the field of foreign affairs, as President Kennedy once remarked, "the President bears the burden of the responsibility. . . . The advisers may move on to new advice." [24]

---

[21] *Weekly Compilation of Presidential Documents*, March 14, 1983, p. 369.
[22] *New York Times*, December 29, 1983, p. 1.

[23] Data provided by U.S. Department of State.
[24] Television and radio interview: "After Two Years—a Conversation with the President," December 17, 1962, in *Public Papers of the Presidents of the United States: John F. Kennedy, 1962* (Washington, D.C.: U.S. Government Printing Office, 1963), p. 889.

As noted in Chapter 10, the president is both chief diplomat and commander in chief. Particularly in the twentieth century, the two roles overlap. National security, foreign policy, and domestic programs are closely related because the president must decide how much money to allocate for each area within the overall framework of his annual budget.

A large defense budget means less money for meeting priorities at home, and the level of defense expenditures affects the economy. As a Senate subcommittee on national security put it: "The boundary between foreign and domestic policy has almost been erased." [25]

The president has the responsibility of deciding whether to use nuclear weapons. The collapse of the Soviet system has diminished, but not eliminated, that terrible responsibility. During the Cold War, Richard Neustadt could write that the president "lives daily with the knowledge that at any time he, personally, may have to make a human judgment . . . which puts half the world in jeopardy." [26] Although this fear eased after the breakup of the Soviet Union, several nations still possess the bomb, and others hope to acquire nuclear

weapons. As a result, the president's finger remains on the nuclear "button." The vast power of the president in the realm of foreign policy carries with it great risks —risks that a president will exercise his judgment unwisely or that he will act without public or congressional support.

In conducting the nation's foreign and military policies, the president must often choose among conflicting advice as he makes his decisions. "The State Department wants to solve everything with words, and the generals, with guns," President Johnson was quoted as saying.[27] A president's background, experience, and beliefs may strongly influence his attitude toward foreign affairs. President Nixon, for example, had long been identified with international affairs as vice-president; as president he put great emphasis on foreign policy and negotiations. In time, however, a domestic event—Watergate—beclouded his diplomatic initiatives and ended his presidency.

President Reagan's strong anti-Communist philosophy colored his early rhetoric against the Soviet Union, but his views appeared to have softened substantially by the time of his fourth summit meeting with Mikhail Gorbachev in the spring of 1988. Reagan also took a strong stance against dealing with terrorists. Yet he secretly sold arms to Iran to try to persuade terrorists

[25] "Basic Issues," Subcommittee on National Security Staffing and Operations, Committee on Government Operations, United States Senate, in *Administration of National Security* (Washington, D.C.: U.S. Government Printing Office, 1965), p. 7.

[26] Richard E. Neustadt, testimony to Subcommittee on National Security Staffing and Operations, Committee on Government Operations, United States Senate, March 25, 1963, in *Administration of National Security*, p. 76.

[27] Eric F. Goldman, *The Tragedy of Lyndon Johnson* (New York: Knopf, 1969), p. 383.

JFK: A STRATEGY OF PEACE

What kind of peace do I mean? What kind of peace do we seek? Not a Pax Americana enforced on the world by American weapons of war. . . . I am talking about genuine peace, the kind of peace that makes life on earth worth living, the kind that enables men and nations to grow and to hope and to build a better life for their children— not merely peace for Americans but peace for all men and women—not merely peace in our time but peace for all time. . . . Total war makes no sense . . . in an age when the deadly poisons produced by a nuclear exchange would be carried by wind and water and soil and seed to the far corners of the globe and to generations yet unborn. . . .

First: Let us examine our attitude toward peace itself. Too many of us think it is impossible. . . .
We need not accept that view. Our problems are manmade—therefore, they can be solved by man. . . . No problem of human destiny is beyond human beings. . . . And if we cannot end now our differences, at least we can help make the world safe for diversity. For, in the final analysis, our . . . common link is that we all inhabit this small planet. We all breathe the same air. We all cherish our children's future. And we are all mortal.

—John F. Kennedy, Commencement Address at American University in Washington, June 10, 1963

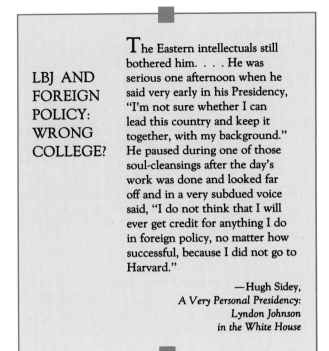

who had seized American hostages to release them. As a result, the disclosure of the arms transactions undermined public confidence in his leadership to a greater extent than might otherwise have been the case.

Like both Reagan and Nixon, President Bush also appeared more confident dealing with foreign rather than domestic issues. He met frequently with foreign leaders both in Washington and abroad and emphasized his expertise in foreign policy when he ran for reelection. But, in a time of economic difficulties, Bill Clinton hammered away at domestic issues, and won.

Congress and Foreign Policy

Under the Constitution, power to conduct foreign and military affairs is divided between Congress and the president. While the Constitution gave the president power to appoint ambassadors and command the armed forces, Congress was given power to declare war, raise and support armies, and appropriate money for defense; and the Senate was granted power to approve or disapprove treaties and ambassadorial nominations made by the president.

But the Constitution does not spell out the boundaries of the power that each branch shall exercise. The result has been intermittent conflict between the presi-

dent and Congress over foreign policy. For example, it took months of controversy before Congress, in 1978, finally agreed with President Carter and ratified two treaties turning over the Panama Canal to Panama in the year 2000. Congress' action ended an era that had begun 75 years before when President Theodore Roosevelt acquired the land to build the waterway. The Senate voted to approve the two treaties only after adding a "reservation" specifying that the United States could intervene militarily to keep the canal open.

In the struggle between Congress and the president over foreign policy, at various times in history one branch has dominated. After the Second World War, Congress lost to the president much of its war power and control over foreign policy. In the late 1960s and early 1970s, as a result of the increasing unpopularity of the war in Vietnam, a movement began in Congress to try to restore some of the war power to the legislative branch. (These efforts are traced in Chapter 10, on pp. 374–375.)

It was not until 1973 that Congress succeeded in placing any significant restrictions on presidential power to wage war. The first congressional victory was a bill barring any combat in, or bombing of, Cambodia after August 15, 1973. That same year, Congress passed the War Powers Resolution, designed to limit to sixty or ninety days the president's ability to commit American troops to combat without congressional authorization. The bill became law over President Nixon's veto. The War Powers Resolution failed to restrict presidential use of military power in several instances, however. It was clear in the early 1990s that the president remained the dominant partner in the conduct of foreign policy.

Congress also made efforts to gain greater control over secret intelligence operations. Beginning in 1974, Congress required that before a covert operation can take place the president issue a "finding" that the proposed operation is important to the national security. Congress also provided that the Central Intelligence Agency (CIA) could not spend money on covert operations without reporting them to six (later eight) congressional committees "in timely fashion." In 1980 Congress reduced to two the number of committees to which the CIA must report, but required prior notice of most secret operations. President Reagan circumvented this provision in 1986, however, when he ordered his CIA director, William J. Casey, to conceal the Iranian arms sales from Congress. As a result, Congress in 1991 enacted a new law tightening the provisions requiring the president to notify the congressional committees of

"THIS CHAMBER REEKS OF BLOOD"

On September 1, 1970, the United States Senate rejected an amendment sponsored by Senators George McGovern, Democrat of South Dakota, and Mark O. Hatfield, Republican of Oregon, to withdraw U.S. troops from Vietnam. Just before the vote, Senator McGovern arose on the Senate floor to plead for an end to a war that Congress had never declared:

> Every senator in this chamber is partly responsible for sending 50,000 young Americans to an early grave. This chamber reeks of blood. Every senator here is partly responsible for the human wreckage at Walter Reed and Bethesda Naval and all across our land — young boys without legs, or arms, or genitals, or faces, or hopes. There aren't very many of these blasted and broken boys who think this war is a glorious venture. Don't talk to them about bugging out, or national honor, or courage. It doesn't take courage at all for a congressman, or a senator, or a President to wrap himself in the flag and say we're staying in Vietnam. Because it isn't our blood that is being shed. But we are responsible for those young men and their lives and their hopes. And if we don't end this foolish, damnable war, those young men will someday curse us for our pitiful willingness to let the Executive carry the burden the Constitution puts on us.

—Quote in Robert Sam Anson, *McGovern:*
A Biography

covert actions, including operations carried out through other countries or private citizens.

Between 1950 and 1992, eight American presidents committed United States troops to foreign soil (in Korea, Lebanon, the Dominican Republic, Vietnam, Cambodia, Iran, Grenada, Honduras, Panama, the Persian Gulf, and Somalia) without any declaration of war by Congress. In six instances, however, Congress had passed resolutions broadly supporting presidential action in various geographic areas: the Formosa Resolution (1954); the Middle East Resolution (1957); the Cuba Resolution (1962); the Tonkin Gulf Resolution (1964), the Multinational Force in Lebanon Resolution (1983), and the Authorization for Use of Military Force Against Iraq Resolution (1991).

But, because the president has substantial control over the channels of information about military actions — the news that the Pentagon releases to the public and

Early each morning officials meet at CIA to prepare the president's daily intelligence briefing on world developments

to Congress—he may be able to shape the congressional response. Congress passed the Tonkin Gulf Resolution after President Johnson announced on nationwide television on August 4, 1964, that two United States destroyers, the *Maddox* and the *Turner Joy*, had been attacked in the Gulf of Tonkin off Vietnam. Secretary of Defense Robert S. McNamara declared that the two ships had been under "continuous torpedo attack." Up to this point 163 Americans had died in Vietnam and there were 16,000 troops there as "advisers." After passage of the Tonkin Gulf Resolution, President Johnson—beginning early in 1965—vastly expanded the war.

It developed, however, that reports of the attack in the Tonkin Gulf had been considerably exaggerated. For example, the captain of the *Maddox*, Commander Herbert L. Ogier, later said he thought that two torpedoes were fired but that subsequent reports of torpedoes were actually sonar readings caused by the destroyer's own propellers.[28] Indeed, the task force commander warned Washington that, "Freak weather effects and over-eager sonarman may have accounted for many reports." [29] At a Senate hearing four years later, Senator Albert Gore, Democrat, of Tennessee (whose son and namesake was elected vice-president in 1992), told Secretary McNamara to his face: "I feel that I have been misled, and that the American people have been misled." [30]

As the Tonkin Gulf episode illustrates, one major reason Congress has lost to the president so much of its power over foreign affairs is that diplomatic, military, and intelligence information flows directly to the president. As a result, Congress and the public have tended to assume that the president "has the facts" and is acting on the basis of expert advice. Second, foreign policy decisions are often made in crisis situations, in "an atmosphere of real or contrived urgency." [31] This, too, puts pressure on Congress to defer to presumed presidential wisdom. More recently, however, there has been

an increasing realization that the extensive flow of information to the president does not guarantee that his foreign policy decisions will necessarily prove correct or wise.

The Machinery

Today the president of the United States has powerful tools available to him for the conduct of foreign policy, including his personal staff and that of the National Security Council, the State Department, the Pentagon, the CIA, and other agencies. (The existence of this machinery does not mean, however, that the United States can always influence, let alone control, the course of international events. American policymakers may not be able to affect the price of OPEC oil, stop the seizure of American diplomats by Islamic revolutionaries, or prevent terrorist attacks on U.S. installations.) Until 1947 no formal centralized machinery existed to aid the president in his foreign-policy tasks. In that year, Congress attempted to give the president the tools to match his responsibilities.

The National Security Council The National Security Act of 1947 created the National Security Council (NSC) to advise the president on the integration of "domestic, foreign, and military policies relating to the national security." In one sense the act, amended and expanded in 1949, was an effort to institutionalize the power that had been wielded over military–diplomatic affairs by President Roosevelt in the Second World War. It was also an effort to provide continuity from one administration to the next in the conduct of national security affairs. The NSC, however, has been used very differently by a succession of presidents.

Eisenhower made frequent use of the NSC. But by the time President Kennedy was inaugurated in 1961, the NSC had spawned such a formidable growth of subcommittees and coordinating groups that paperwork was beginning to overwhelm policy formation. President Kennedy's national security adviser, McGeorge Bundy, "promptly slaughtered committees right and left." [32] Kennedy used the NSC infrequently and informally, and some critics contended that the result was a lack of foreign policy coordination. During both the Kennedy and Johnson administrations, the

---

[28] David Wise, "Remember the Maddox!" *Esquire*, April 1968, p. 126. See also, Joseph C. Goulden, *Truth Is the First Casualty* (New York: Rand McNally, 1969).

[29] U.S. Congress, Senate, Committee on Foreign Relations, *The Gulf of Tonkin, The 1964 Incidents*, Hearings, 90th Cong., 2nd sess. (Washington, D.C.: U.S. Government Printing Office, 1968), p. 54.

[30] Ibid., p. 91. Albert Gore, Jr., elected to the Senate from Tennessee in 1984, was a candidate for the Democratic presidential nomination in 1988, became the Democratic nominee for vice-president in 1992, and was elected.

[31] U.S. Congress, Senate, Committee on Foreign Relations, *National Commitments*, Report, 90th Cong., 1st sess. (Washington, D.C.: U.S. Government Printing Office, 1967), p. 14.

[32] Arthur M. Schlesinger, Jr., *A Thousand Days* (Boston: Houghton Mifflin, 1965), p. 210.

NSC was occasionally used for "window-dressing" during a crisis to give the appearance of somber decisions being made by the president with his highest national security advisers. Real decisions were sometimes reached in less formal meetings. But even Kennedy and Johnson promulgated major national security decisions *within* the administration in the form of NSC directives.

President Nixon directed that the NSC "be reestablished as the principal forum for presidential consideration of foreign policy issues." [33] Various interagency groups, special panels, and review committees began to flourish once again under Nixon and his adviser for national security, Henry A. Kissinger. The basic structure Kissinger had established remained in effect under President Ford, Nixon's successor. President Carter named Columbia University professor Zbigniew Brzezinski as his national security adviser. President Reagan named Richard V. Allen, formerly of Stanford University's Hoover Institution, as his national security adviser. Allen resigned under fire after one year for receiving $1,000 in cash that a group of Japanese journalists had sought to give to Mrs. Reagan after interviewing her at the White House, and for taking three watches in a related gift. He was replaced by William P. Clark, Jr., a longtime aide to Reagan, who was in turn succeeded by his deputy, former Marine Colonel Robert C. McFarlane.

Under McFarlane, Marine Lt. Col. Oliver L. North coordinated the secret operations that burgeoned into the Iran-contra scandal. When McFarlane left the NSC in 1985, he was succeeded by Vice Adm. John M. Poindexter, who worked closely with North in carrying out and concealing the Iran arms sales and the diversion of profits to the contras in Nicaragua.

In 1988, McFarlane pleaded guilty to misleading Congress about the affair. After an investigation by an independent counsel, North, Poindexter, and others were indicted for conspiring to defraud the government and then covering up their actions. North was convicted in 1989 on federal charges of preparing false documents and destroying documents, but his conviction was overturned by a federal appeals court, which questioned whether his testimony to congressional investigators had been unfairly used against him. The independent counsel then dropped all charges. But in North's testimony to Congress he had admitted shredding documents sought by investigators. Poindexter

"Let me guess—It's a proclamation for National Apple Pie Week"

Herblock at Large (Pantheon Books, 1987)

was convicted of deceiving Congress and lying to Congress, but the appeals court also overturned his conviction on similar grounds. At the congressional hearings into the scandal, however, Admiral Poindexter, calmly puffing on his pipe, admitted that he had destroyed a presidential "finding," a statement permitting the covert arms-for-hostages sales. He also asserted that he had never informed Reagan of the diversion of millions of dollars to the contras. Thus, under Reagan, the NSC and the post of national security adviser fell, for a time, into disrepute. After George Bush was elected president, he named former Air Force General Brent Scowcroft to head the NSC staff.

The State Department George F. Kennan has described the American State Department in a less turbulent era: "The Department of State . . . in the 1920s when I entered it, was a quaint old place, with its law-office atmosphere, its cool dark corridors, its swinging doors, its brass cuspidors, its black leather rocking chairs, and the grandfather's clock in the Secretary of State's office." [34]

Today the State Department is huge; it occupies a large, antiseptically modern building that houses a third of its 26,000 employees. Department couriers hand-

---

[33] *Congressional Quarterly*, Weekly Report, February 20, 1970, p. 518.

[34] George F. Kennan, *American Diplomacy* (Chicago: University of Chicago Press, 1951), pp. 91–92.

carry diplomatic documents 10,000,000 miles a year in travels between Washington and the 159 U.S. embassies abroad.[35] High-speed coded communications link the secretary of state to American embassies overseas, handling more than 300,000 words daily. In the Operations Center on the seventh floor, behind a locked door that is opened by a buzzer, the secretary can monitor a developing crisis. A device flashes incoming cables on a screen; the center can reach any U.S. post abroad in two minutes.

Despite all this, the State Department's level of efficiency has been the target of periodic criticism. As the United States became a world power, the size of the department increased vastly; bureaus and assistant secretaries proliferated. One reason that the State Department is slow to form policy is the "clearance factor" — the tendency of each branch of the department to check and clear matters with other branches and bureaus and other agencies of government. The department's snail-like replies to President Kennedy's requests were a constant source of frustration in the White House. According to Arthur M. Schlesinger, Jr., Kennedy would say, " 'Damn it, Bundy and I get more done in one day in the White House than they do in six months at the State Department. . . . They never have any ideas over there,' he complained, "never come up with anything new.' "[36]

The role of the secretary of state varies greatly according to the secretary's personal relationship with the president. In theory the principal foreign-policy adviser and the ranking officer of the cabinet, the secretary in practice may be overshadowed by the president's national security assistant and the secretary of defense, or even by prestigious subordinates. As national security adviser, Henry Kissinger was far more powerful than Secretary of State William P. Rogers during the first Nixon administration. Rogers was often kept in the dark about major foreign policy decisions, which were concealed from him by Kissinger and Nixon.[37] Later Nixon appointed Kissinger as secretary of state.

Under President Carter, Secretary of State Cyrus Vance clashed with the national security adviser, Zbigniew Brzezinski. Vance resigned in protest when,

against his advice, President Carter dispatched a military mission that failed in an attempt to rescue the American hostages in Iran. Ronald Reagan's first secretary of state, former Army General Alexander M. Haig, battled frequently with President Reagan's national security adviser and other White House aides, and he resigned after only a year and a half in office. As his successor, Reagan chose George Shultz, a business executive who had also served in the Nixon cabinet. Under Shultz, the State Department regained at least some of the power it had lost to the White House in previous administrations. For the first time in many years, the secretary of state was not overshadowed by the president's national security adviser. Shultz's stature increased when the NSC staff was tarnished by the Iran-contra affair.

Bush named his campaign chairman, James A. Baker III, secretary of state. Under Baker, a powerful figure in the Bush administration, the State Department once more enjoyed more prestige than the NSC staff. When Bush slipped in the polls during 1992, he brought Baker to the White House to serve as chief of staff and chief strategist for his presidential reelection campaign.

To help administer the State Department and its annual budget of about $5.2 billion,[38] the secretary of state has the Executive Secretariat, which controls the flow of paper work and tries to keep the secretary from being drowned in a sea of words. There are five geographic bureaus: African Affairs, East Asian and Pacific Affairs, European and Canadian Affairs, Inter-American Affairs, and Near Eastern and South Asian Affairs. Within the geographic bureaus are more than a hundred country desks. In addition, there are functional bureaus dealing with subjects such as consular affairs; public affairs; human rights and humanitarian affairs; economic and business affairs; intelligence and research; politico-military affairs; refugee programs; oceans and international environmental and scientific affairs; administration; and international organization (the bureau that manages United States policy at the United Nations).

The United States Foreign Service consists of the professional diplomats who represent the United States overseas and staff key policy posts in the State Department in Washington. Most foreign service officers are stationed abroad as ambassadors, ministers, and political and consular officials. Posts are normally rotated, and

---

[35] Data provided by Bureau of Consular Affairs, U.S. Department of State.

[36] Schlesinger, A Thousand Days, p. 406.

[37] For details of this and other aspects of Kissinger's role, see Seymour M. Hersh, The Price of Power: Kissinger in the Nixon White House (New York: Summit Books, 1983); and Walter Isaacson, Kissinger: A Biography (New York: Simon & Schuster, 1992).

[38] The $5.2 billion was the budget request for the Department of State in Fiscal Year 1993.

members of the foreign service periodically return to Washington between tours of duty overseas. In 1992 the foreign service numbered more than 12,425 men and women, of whom 4,240 were foreign service "officers" — the professional diplomats.

Overseas, the ambassador is the president's personal representative to the chief of state and government to which he or she is accredited. Appointed by the president and subject to Senate confirmation, the ambassador is formally in charge of the entire United States mission in a foreign capital. The mission may include representatives of the Agency for International Development (AID) and the United States Information Agency (USIA), the military service attachés, military assistance advisory groups, and officers of the CIA, all of whom make up the so-called "country team." Often it is a team in name only, however, with each element reporting back to its own headquarters in Washington and some officials working at cross-purposes to the ambassador. "To a degree," a Senate subcommittee concluded, "the primacy of the ambassador is a polite fiction." [39]

In addition to problems of coordination with other agencies of government, the State Department also faces competition from those agencies. In the past it has competed for the president's attention, not only with

the White House national security adviser but with other agencies involved in foreign policy — the Office of International Security Affairs in the Defense Department, for example, and the CIA. To some extent the State Department must even compete with outside sources of advice in foreign policy — defense research firms, universities, presidential task forces, private organizations interested in foreign policy, and former government officials who may be called in and consulted by the president.

Intelligence and Foreign Policy: The CIA During the 1992 presidential campaign, President Bush was questioned about the extent of his knowledge of the Iran-contra affair. That controversy had begun in the Reagan administration, in which Bush served as vice-president. Under Reagan, the Central Intelligence Agency had supported what eventually grew into an army of 15,000 "contras," exiles dedicated to overthrowing the leftist Sandinista government of Nicaragua. In 1979, the Sandinistas had overthrown the regime of Anastasio Somoza, whose family had ruled Nicaragua for decades. Many of the exiles financed by the CIA had served in Somoza's feared national guard.

President Reagan, concerned over what he saw as Communist expansion in Central America, vigorously pursued what had begun as a secret war but soon became widely discussed and debated. Although Reagan

[39] "Basic Issues," in *Administration of National Security,* p. 16.

Don Wright, *The Miami News*

> ## CIA: DON'T TALK ABOUT ASSASSI- NATIONS
>
> . . . the difficulty with this kind of thing, as you gentlemen are all painfully aware, is that nobody wants to embarrass a President of the United States by discussing the assassination of foreign leaders in his presence. This is something that has got to be dealt with in some other fashion. Even though you use euphemisms you've still got a problem. . . . I think any of us would have found it very difficult to discuss assassinations with a President of the U.S. I just think we all had the feeling that we're hired to keep those things out of the Oval Office.
>
> —Richard M. Helms, former CIA director, testifying to Senate Intelligence Committee, June 13, 1975

said the purpose of the CIA-backed war was to stop the flow of arms from Nicaragua to guerrillas in neighboring El Salvador, the contras clearly hoped to regain power in Nicaragua. Critics both in and out of Congress warned that the CIA operation might open the way to a wider war involving U.S. combat troops. The controversy boiled over in April 1984 when Senator Barry Goldwater, Republican chairman of the Senate Intelligence Committee, charged that the CIA had not clearly informed the committee that it had mined Nicaraguan ports, an action that caused damage to several foreign ships. Disturbed over the secret war in Nicaragua, Congress passed restrictions on CIA participation—the "Boland amendments."

It was in an effort to circumvent these laws that the Reagan White House, through the NSC staff, took control of the contra operation. But CIA director William Casey worked closely with Lt. Col. Oliver North in the resupply effort, and some CIA personnel took part despite the congressional ban. In an effort to free American hostages seized in the Middle East, the administration sold arms to Iran and diverted the profits to aid the contras. The chief of covert operations retired in the wake of the Iran-contra scandal and the new CIA director, former FBI chief William Webster, disciplined seven CIA officers for their roles.[40]

The activities in Central America were examples of CIA covert operations — secret political action in other countries. And it was certainly not the first time that the intelligence agency's covert actions had stirred controversy.

During the 1970s Senate and House investigating committees disclosed a series of startling actions by the Central Intelligence Agency: the CIA had hired two underworld figures, Sam Giancana and Johnny Rosselli (both of whom were later murdered), to assassinate Cuban Premier Fidel Castro with poison. During four presidential administrations, the CIA had also plotted the assassination of, or coups against, seven other foreign leaders.[41] The congressional committees also disclosed abuses by the FBI and other branches of the intelligence community.

The congressional inquiries were launched after Seymour M. Hersh, an investigative reporter for the *New York Times*, disclosed that for several years, beginning in the late 1960s, the CIA had, in violation of its charter, spied on American citizens at home and infiltrated antiwar and other dissident groups.[42] These

---

[40] *Washington Post*, December 18, 1987, p. A12.
[41] U.S. Congress, Senate, Select Committee to Study Governmental Operations with Respect to Intelligence Activities, *Alleged Assassination Plots Involving Foreign Leaders*, Interim Report, 94th Cong., 1st sess. (Washington, D.C.: U.S. Government Printing Office, 1975). In addition to describing the efforts to assassinate Castro, the report also details CIA plots against Patrice Lumumba of the Congo; Rafael Trujillo of the Dominican Republic; President Salvador Allende and General René Schneider of Chile; President Ngo Dinh Diem of South Vietnam; President François Duvalier of Haiti; and President Achmed Sukarno of Indonesia.
[42] *New York Times*, December 22, 1974, p. 1.

"INTEL- LIGENCE AGENCIES MUST BE MADE SUBJECT TO THE RULE OF LAW."

The Committee's fundamental conclusion is that intelligence activities have undermined the constitutional rights of citizens. . . . we do not question the need for lawful domestic intelligence. We recognize that certain intelligence activities serve perfectly proper and clearly necessary ends of government. Surely, catching spies and stopping crime, including acts of terrorism, is essential to insure "domestic tranquility" and to "provide for the common defense." . . .

[But] we must be wary about the drift toward "big brother government." . . .

Through a vast network of informants, and through the uncontrolled or illegal use of intrusive techniques — ranging from simple theft to sophisticated electronic surveillance — the Government has collected, and then used improperly, huge amounts of information about the private lives, political beliefs and associations of numerous Americans. . . . intelligence agencies must be made subject to the rule of law.

— Final report of the Senate Intelligence Committee, 1976

charges were later documented in a report of a presidential commission headed by Vice-President Nelson A. Rockefeller, which found that some of the CIA's actions were "plainly unlawful."[43]

The Rockefeller report and the congressional committees disclosed that the CIA had photographed and followed American citizens; engaged in break-ins, wiretapping, and bugging of Americans; and for twenty years had opened, read, and photographed first-class mail in violation of federal law. The agency had also experimented with mind-altering drugs; one subject, an army civilian researcher, committed suicide several days

The Central Intelligence Agency, Langley, Virginia

after the CIA had laced his after-dinner drink with LSD. He was not told about the drug until twenty minutes after it was administered.

Activities of this sort were not mentioned in the law passed by Congress in 1947 establishing the CIA. The law said that the agency was to advise the National Security Council and to acquire and analyze political, military, and economic knowledge about other countries on which the president could base his foreign policy decisions. But, in addition to collecting intelligence, the CIA has engaged in covert operations, such as those in Central America. In 1984, for example, the CIA was reported to be conducting 50 covert operations around the globe.[44] The law establishing the CIA makes no specific reference to such covert operations abroad, although the statute does permit the CIA to perform such "other functions and duties" as the National Security Council may direct. But the Senate Intelligence Committee concluded, "Authority for covert action cannot be found in the National Security Act."[45] Yet the committee reported that the CIA had carried out 900 major covert operations between 1961 and 1975. And it found that the CIA's widespread domestic spying, to which it gave the code name Operation CHAOS, violated the provisions of the 1947 act designed to prohibit the agency from acting as a domestic police force.

Prior to the Japanese attack on Pearl Harbor in 1941, the United States had no central intelligence-gathering agency. After Pearl Harbor, President Roosevelt created the Office of Strategic Services (OSS) to gather intelligence, conduct secret political warfare, and sabotage operations behind enemy lines during the Second World War. The CIA was the direct descendant of the wartime OSS. The director of the CIA wears one hat as head of the agency. But the director is simultaneously chairperson of the National Foreign Intelligence Board and thus is responsible for coordinating

[43] *Report to the President by the Commission on CIA Activities within the United States* (Washington, D.C.: U.S. Government Printing Office, 1975), p. 10.
[44] *New York Times*, June 11, 1984, p. 1.

[45] U.S. Congress, Senate, Select Committee to Study Governmental Operations with Respect to Intelligence Activities, *Foreign and Military Intelligence*, Final Report, 94th Cong., 2nd sess. (Washington, D.C.: U.S. Government Printing Office, 1976), Book 1, p. 128.

the work of the other government intelligence agencies, including the National Security Agency (NSA), the code-making and code-breaking arm of the Pentagon; the Defense Intelligence Agency (DIA), the military rival to the CIA; the FBI; and the State Department's Bureau of Intelligence and Research (INR). Together, these agencies spend more than $30 billion a year.[46]

The CIA has two principal divisions. An *Intelligence Directorate* engages in overt collection, research, and analysis of foreign intelligence. Most of the criticism of the CIA has been directed at its *Operations Directorate*, which engages in the secret collection of intelligence (espionage) and in secret political action (covert operations). On occasion this directorate has helped to overthrow governments — in Iran in 1953 and Guatemala in 1954, for example. It was this clandestine arm of the CIA that plotted the assassination of such leaders as Cuba's Fidel Castro and Patrice Lumumba in the Congo (now Zaire), launched the invasion of Cuba at the Bay of Pigs in 1961, and supported a secret army of 30,000 persons in Laos.

Although, unlike the FBI, the CIA has no police power within the United States, in 1967 it was disclosed that the agency was subsidizing the National Student Association and dozens of foundations and private groups *within* this country. President Johnson ordered that most of the secret funding be ended.

In 1972 the CIA again became enmeshed in domestic activities. Most of the burglars caught in the Watergate break-in had CIA backgrounds, and one was on the intelligence agency's payroll at the time of the break-in. A year earlier, at the request of the White House, the CIA had secretly assisted E. Howard Hunt, Jr., a former CIA operative and White House "plumber," and one of the men eventually convicted in the Watergate burglary. And President Nixon tried to use the CIA to block the FBI from probing the burglary of Democratic headquarters.

The CIA's size and budget are secret, but it has been unofficially estimated that the agency spends about $3.5 billion a year and employs some 20,000 people. The CIA has its headquarters in a secluded, wooded area of Langley, Virginia, just across the Potomac River from Washington.

During the 1950s, the CIA, under its director, Allen W. Dulles, toiled largely out of the limelight. The loss of a U-2, a CIA spy plane, on a flight over the Soviet Union in 1960 and the disaster at the Bay of Pigs in 1961 thrust the CIA into the headlines and focused attention on its activities. By 1964 critics charged that the CIA stood at the center of what had become "an invisible government."[47] Former Assistant Secretary of State Roger Hilsman wrote: "The root fear was that the CIA represented . . . a state within a state, and certainly the basis for fear was there."[48]

On the other hand, because the CIA is a secret agency, and usually does not make any public comment, it is sometimes blamed for things it does not do. Defenders of the CIA argue that it operates under sufficient control and does not carry out any covert operations abroad "without appropriate approval at a high political level in our government *outside the CIA.*"[49] This approval usually comes from an interagency board that has responsibility for authorizing covert operations. However, in the mid-1970s the Senate Intelligence Committee (known at the time as the Church Committee for its then chairman, Senator Frank Church, Democrat, of Idaho) reported that the interagency board seldom met. And former CIA director Richard Helms conceded in testimony to the committee that the board has acted as a "circuit breaker" to insulate the president from responsibility for covert CIA operations.[50] Nor has the interagency board always been advised of CIA covert operations.

The CIA's defenders have argued that despite the agency's mistakes, it is an essential arm of the government. Allen Dulles wrote, for example, that an intelligence service "is the best insurance we can take out against surprise." As for covert CIA operations inside other countries, Dulles contended that the United States could not limit its activities "to those cases where we are invited in."[51]

In the wake of the various investigations of the CIA and the FBI, Congress finally moved to strengthen its control over the intelligence establishment. The Senate and the House each created a permanent Select Committee on Intelligence with authority over the CIA

---

[46] *Washington Post*, July 5, 1991, p. A9.

[47] David Wise and Thomas B. Ross, *The Invisible Government* (New York: Random House, 1964), p. 3.

[48] Hilsman, *To Move a Nation*, pp. 64–65.

[49] Allen Dulles, *The Craft of Intelligence* (New York: Harper & Row, 1963), p. 189.

[50] U.S. Congress, Senate, Select Committee to Study Governmental Operations with Respect to Intelligence Activities, *Foreign and Military Intelligence*, p. 46.

[51] Dulles, *The Craft of Intelligence*, pp. 48–51, 235–36.

and the other intelligence agencies. By 1980, however, following the crises in Iran and Afghanistan, the CIA's supporters charged that the various investigations had weakened the intelligence agency. In the new, more militant atmosphere, Congress declined to enact detailed reform bills to control the intelligence agencies. Instead, in 1980 it passed a more limited bill requiring the president to furnish information to the intelligence committees and to notify them in advance of covert operations in most circumstances.

When President Reagan appointed William J. Casey, a millionaire New York lawyer, as director of the CIA, the choice proved controversial, in part because Casey had managed Reagan's 1980 presidential campaign. Concern over a political figure directing the intelligence agency was heightened by reports that it was Casey who had obtained President Carter's briefing book before the 1980 televised debate with Reagan, a charge that Casey denied. The CIA director was also criticized for stock-market transactions and other business dealings.

Casey died in May 1987, before he could be fully questioned by Congress about his role in the Iran-contra scandal. After Casey's death, it was revealed that he had gone outside normal CIA channels and arranged with the Saudi Arabian intelligence service to undertake covert operations; one, an assassination attempt, mistakenly killed 80 innocent people when a car bomb exploded in Beirut in 1985.[52] When William Webster retired as CIA director in 1991, President Bush named Robert M. Gates to succeed him. Because Gates had worked closely with William Casey during the time of the Iran-contra operation, his nomination was controversial. Additional controversy centered around charges by CIA analysts that Gates had slanted intelligence estimates to please his superiors in the CIA and the White House. After protracted hearings that fall, Gates was confirmed by the Senate. In 1992, the CIA was criticized for failure to disclose to federal prosecutors its knowledge of a scandal involving billions of dollars in loans to Iraq by the Atlanta branch of an Italian bank. After Clinton's election as president that year, Gates announced he would resign.

However necessary it may be to protect American security, the existence of a clandestine intelligence and espionage establishment creates special problems in a free society. The operations of the CIA and the other United States intelligence agencies pose the continuing dilemma of how secret intelligence machinery can be made compatible with democratic government.[53]

Other Instruments: AID, USIA, the Peace Corps, and the Arms Control and Disarmament Agency

Today the State Department must compete in the foreign policy field not only with the president's NSC staff, the CIA, and the Pentagon, but with many other agencies and units of the federal government.

One of the agencies with foreign policy responsibilities both in Washington and in the field is the Agency for International Development (AID). AID, as its initials imply, is responsible for carrying out programs of financial and technical assistance to less economically developed nations.

Since the initiation of the Marshall Plan, the United States has spent more than $200 billion on foreign aid, contributions to international organizations, and military assistance. For fiscal 1993, for example, the president's budget request for foreign aid totaled $7.4 billion, and included economic assistance for more than 100 countries in Latin America, Asia, Africa, the Near East, Eastern Europe, and the former republics of the Soviet Union. In recent years, the United States has placed greater emphasis on channeling aid through multilateral financial institutions, and it has increased its participation in the International Bank for Reconstruction and Development (World Bank), which makes loans to and promotes foreign investments in underdeveloped nations.

AID is politically unpopular because many Americans regard it as a "give-away" program with little visible benefit to the taxpayers. But the aid program can be defended both on humanitarian grounds and, more narrowly, on political grounds. As the richest nation in the world, the United States has felt a moral obligation to try to alleviate poverty, disease, and malnutrition in other nations. At the same time, supporters of the aid program contend, peace and stability are unlikely to be achieved for the United States or the world as a whole as long as such conditions exist in the poorer nations.

Despite some popular misconceptions, most foreign aid is not given to other countries in the form of cash. Most AID dollars are spent in the United States to buy commodities and to hire technical experts for projects overseas. AID provides technical assistance by

[52] Bob Woodward, *Veil: The Secret Wars of the CIA 1981–1987* (New York: Simon and Schuster, 1987), pp. 395–98.

[53] See David Wise, *The American Police State* (New York: Random House, 1976).

sending abroad specialists in such fields as health, education, and agriculture. Through development loans, repayable in dollars, AID offers other countries long-term, low-interest financing for such projects as highways, dams, schools, and hospitals. In addition, the United States donates and sells agricultural commodities at low cost to other countries.

The United States Information Agency (USIA), according to an official description, helps to achieve the objectives of United States foreign policy by trying "to strengthen foreign understanding of American society" and to bring about "greater support of U.S. policies."[54] The USIA is, in short, the propaganda agency of the United States government.

Wary that such an agency might be used by a president to influence domestic opinion, Congress has generally restricted the USIA to operations overseas. The agency has 8,784 employees and branches in 128 countries. Its libraries and information centers in foreign countries are sometimes visible and popular targets of anti-American mob violence. The Voice of America, a part of USIA, beams abroad news broadcasts, music, and feature programs in forty-seven languages. As a government radio station, it operates under policy restrictions and guidelines set by the State Department.

The Peace Corps was created under President Kennedy in 1961 to provide a trained corps of highly motivated American volunteers, many of them young, to help people in developing nations. In 1992 about 6,100 Peace Corps volunteers were in training or serving abroad in ninety-four countries as teachers, agricultural aides, doctors, and in many other capacities. In 1990, after democratic governments emerged in the former Soviet Union and Eastern Europe, the Peace Corps sent volunteers for the first time to many of those countries, including Czechoslovakia, Hungary, Poland, Russia, and the Ukraine. Peace Corps volunteers, who must be U.S. citizens and at least eighteen, serve abroad for two years and typically receive about $150 per month as allowance for food, clothing, and housing, and other living expenses. Upon completing a tour, Peace Corps volunteers receive an additional $200 for each month served. By 1992, 135,000 persons had served in the Peace Corps.

The Arms Control and Disarmament Agency was established in 1961 during the Kennedy administration.

Although technically not a division of the State Department, the director is an adviser to the secretary of state and the president. The agency prepares and manages United States participation in international arms control and disarmament negotiations, but it also has important responsibilities in conducting long-range research on techniques of arms control. The agency played an active role in negotiations leading to a United States–Soviet agreement in 1971 to reduce the danger of accidental nuclear war, and to an eighty-five-nation pact, ratified by the Senate in 1972, to prohibit implanting of nuclear weapons on the ocean floor. In addition, the agency participated in talks that resulted in the 1972 and 1979 SALT agreements on nuclear arms. It also took part in separate negotiations that led to the signing by the United States in 1972 of an international convention to ban germ warfare. In addition, the arms control agency played a key role in the drafting of the treaty signed in 1987 to bar intermediate-range nuclear weapons, and in the START treaty signed in 1991 to reduce strategic arms.

AID, USIA, the Peace Corps, and the disarmament agency all receive policy guidance from the State Department. The State Department itself must share the foreign policy field with dozens of other agencies of the federal government involved in various aspects of foreign affairs. These include the departments of Defense, Agriculture, Labor, Commerce, Justice, Transportation, and the CIA.

The United Nations

The United Nations was founded in San Francisco in 1945 to fulfill the dream of a community of nations, a world body that could take collective action to keep the peace and work for the betterment of humanity. The opening words of the UN charter declare its principal goal: "We the peoples of the United Nations determined to save succeeding generations from the scourge of war, which twice in our lifetime has brought untold sorrow to mankind. . . ."

During the Cold War years, however, the United Nations (UN) was generally unable to keep the peace on issues that divided the major world powers. Decisions affecting world peace were made in Washington, Moscow, Beijing, and other capitals, but less often at UN headquarters in New York City. In part, this was predictable from the structure of the UN and the nature of international relations. The UN Security Council, with

---

[54] *United States Government Manual, 1991–92* (Washington, D.C.: U.S. Government Printing Office, July 1991), p. 737.

fifteen members, cannot act over the veto of any of the five permanent members—as of 1992, the United States, Russia, Britain, France, and the People's Republic of China. Other countries, including Germany and Japan, were pressing to become members of the Security Council. Because the Soviet Union frequently exercised a veto in the Security Council, UN members sought a way to circumvent the council. In November 1950, the UN General Assembly decided that it could act to meet threats to peace when the Security Council failed to do so because the permanent members lacked unanimity. There is no veto power in the General Assembly, to which all member nations belong. Although the General Assembly has thus increased somewhat in importance, it, too, has proved unable to cope with many major conflicts.

The UN has acted with varying success in several world crises: in Korea in 1950, Suez in 1956, the Congo in 1961, and Cyprus in 1964. And in the Arab-Israeli War of October 1973, the UN played a significant role in reducing tensions and avoiding a military confrontation between the United States and the Soviet Union. At the height of the 1973 Mideast crisis, the Security Council passed a resolution to send a multinational peacekeeping force to the war zone. Ultimately, two UN peacekeeping forces were dispatched to the Middle East, one to the Sinai Peninsula and, later, a second to the Golan Heights at the time of the disengagement of Israeli and Syrian troops in 1974. In its actions following the 1973 war, the UN provided an alternative to direct intervention by the big powers. But the UN was not able to end the tragic war in Nigeria or the fighting in Vietnam; and it had scant success in the Middle East during the Arab-Israeli Six-Day War in 1967. The UN failed in its efforts to mediate in the dispute between Argentina and Britain over the Falkland Islands in 1982, and its attempt to end Israel's invasion of Lebanon that year was also unsuccessful.

On the other hand, the UN played a role in bringing about the Soviet withdrawal from Afghanistan and in halting the long war between Iran and Iraq. And it provided the umbrella for the coalition of nations, led by the United States, that forced Iraq to withdraw from Kuwait in 1991. The following year UN teams, at great risk and with casualties, brought relief supplies by air and land to beleaguered Sarajevo in the civil war that followed the breakup of Communist Yugoslavia. The UN also voted trade sanctions against Yugoslavia in an effort to promote peace among the warring factions. In 1992, there were more than 45,000 UN peacekeeping forces deployed around the world. (These are detailed in Table 14–1).

The United States, which provides one-quarter of the UN's budget, lost much of its influence in that organization in the 1960s as the UN shifted from a pro-Western to a neutralist stand. As many of the former colonial territories of Africa and Asia gained independence, they joined the UN, and the United

Table 14-1

United Nations Peacekeeping Forces, 1992

Member states of the United Nations provide troops and officers for UN peacekeeping forces that are periodically sent to crisis areas around the world. In 1992, there were more than 45,000 UN forces in the field.

UN Force (year created)	Location	Troops
UN Truce Supervision Organization (1948)	Israel	298
UN Military Observer Group in India and Pakistan (1949)	India-Pakistan	38
UN Peacekeeping Force in Cyprus (1964)	Cyprus	2,361
UN Disengagement Observer Force (1974)	Golan Heights (Syria-Israel Border)	1,338
UN Interim Force in Lebanon (1978)	Southern Lebanon	5,812
UN Iraq-Kuwait Observation Mission (1991)	Iraq-Kuwait	550
UN Angola Verification Mission (1991)	Angola	440
UN Observer Mission in El Salvador (1991)	El Salvador	543
UN Mission for the Referendum in Western Sahara (1991)	Western Sahara	375
UN Transitional Authority in Cambodia (1992)	Cambodia	19,500
UN Protection Force in Bosnia and Herzegovina (1992)	Bosnia-Herzegovina	15,000
UN Operation in Somalia (1992)	Somalia	550
		Total 46,805

SOURCE: United Nations

States could no longer count on winning its political battles in that body.

With the loss of American leadership in the UN, criticism of the world body increased in the United States, particularly during the 1980s among conservatives associated with the Reagan administration. At the same time, public support for the UN diminished; a 1985 Gallup poll, for example, found only 38 percent of Americans felt the UN was doing a "good job."[55]

In 1983, discontented with anti-American and anti-Western sentiments in the United Nations Educational, Scientific and Cultural Organization (UNESCO), the United States announced it would withdraw from UNESCO at the end of 1984. In Washington's view, UNESCO had become a forum to blame Israel and the West for many of the problems of the developing world. The U.S. was also opposed to a UNESCO plan backed by third-world nations to place tighter government controls over journalists.

By 1992 the UN had expanded from its original fifty to 179 members, with a budget of $15.6 billion and a staff of 51,600 around the world. The UN is administered by a Secretariat, staffed by the member nations, and headed by a secretary general, who in 1992 was Boutros Boutros Ghali of Egypt. The United States is represented by an ambassador who heads a United States mission in New York. Although the UN has had somewhat limited success as a peacekeeping agency, it has served several other constructive purposes. It provides a forum for discussion, a place where new and small nations can be heard. It sometimes helps to defuse world crises by allowing nations to talk instead of fight. And its economic, social, and health agencies have made significant contributions in improving the lives of millions of people all over the world. In the 1990s, the UN was also having some success in dealing with such international environmental issues as the peaceful use of outer space and seabeds, pollution of the oceans, and overpopulation. Finally, the UN, for all its inadequacies, still remains a symbol of hope, the tangible embodiment of humanity's fragile dream of peace.

The Politics of Foreign Policymaking

Over a period of time, widespread or intense domestic reaction to foreign policy may have an impact on government. During the late 1960s, there was domestic

protest against the war in Vietnam by students, professors, and many other citizens. Some Americans reacted against the protesters, but others were undoubtedly favorably influenced by the peace movement. Eventually, a majority of Americans felt the war was a mistake, and a climate developed in which President Johnson felt it prudent not to run for reelection. The growing opposition to the war provided the political backdrop for President Nixon's decision in 1969 to begin the withdrawal of American troops and for the lengthy peace negotiations, conducted initially in secret, that finally brought an end to United States participation in the war in 1973.

The Role of the Public Despite public awareness of highly publicized issues like Vietnam or the seizure of American diplomats in Iran, some political scientists have argued that on most foreign policy issues, the public is both uninterested and uninformed. Gabriel A. Almond has observed that "Americans tend to exhaust their emotional and intellectual energies in private pursuits." While members of the public may develop well-defined views on domestic questions that affect them directly, he has argued, on questions of foreign policy they tend to react in changeable, "formless and plastic moods."[56] Almond has suggested that relatively small leadership groups play the major role in the making of

[56] Gabriel A. Almond, *The American People and Foreign Policy* (New York: Praeger, 1960), p. 53.

---
[55] Data provided by the Gallup Poll.

most specific foreign policy decisions, and that the public's role is largely confined to the expression of mass attitudes that provide a framework within which officials may work.[57]

James N. Rosenau has also differentiated between public response to domestic issues and foreign policy issues, but he emphasizes that when a foreign policy question becomes so big that it involves "a society's resources and relationships," it quickly turns into a domestic political issue — and he cites the war in Vietnam as an example.[58]

Nevertheless, a president has wide latitude in conducting foreign policy. Kenneth N. Waltz has suggested that as a rule, "The first effect of an international crisis is to increase the president's popular standing." But,

Waltz points out, a president sometimes risks political unpopularity in a foreign policy crisis no matter what he does.[59] And a president who responds too readily to public opinion may be pushed into dangerous choices if public sentiment is running high for quick or simple solutions. Just as the public may demand peace, at other times it may demand retaliation that risks war.

Domestic influence on foreign policy is not limited to mass public opinion as reflected in polls, letters, or protest demonstrations. Congress, individual legislators or committee chairpersons, interest groups, private organizations concerned with foreign policy, opinion leaders, the press, TV commentators, and proximity to an election all may have some effect on policy outcomes. Some foreign policy questions are of special importance to particular groups. A president who is interested in carrying New York, California, and Illinois, for example, in his re-election campaign may frame United States policy toward Israel with some thought to the likely reaction among the many Jewish voters in those states. On Polish patriotic days, members of Congress from heavily Polish areas such as Buffalo or Chicago stand in the House and Senate and carefully pay homage to the contribution of Polish heroes to the nation's heritage.

Presidential Credibility A president's conduct of foreign policy depends in large measure on whether he is able to carry the public along with him on big decisions. Without public trust in his leadership, he may fail.

President Reagan's approval rating plummeted after the disclosure in 1986 that — despite his stated public policy of never dealing with terrorists — he had secretly sold arms to Iran to try to extricate American hostages seized by terrorists in Lebanon.

Other presidents have encountered credibility problems. Since the Second World War, the government has on more than one occasion told official lies designed to protect secret intelligence operations. Under President Eisenhower, for example, the administration claimed at first that the U-2 spy plane shot down 1,200 miles inside the Soviet Union was a "weather research" aircraft that had strayed off course. Under President Kennedy, the government initially denied, but later admitted, that it was responsible for the CIA-backed invasion of Cuba at the Bay of Pigs.

---

[57] Ibid., pp. 4–6.
[58] James N. Rosenau, "Foreign Policy as an Issue-Area," in James N. Rosenau, ed., *Domestic Sources of Foreign Policy* (New York: Free Press, 1967), p. 49.

[59] Kenneth N. Waltz, "Electoral Punishment and Foreign Policy Crises," in Rosenau, ed., *Domestic Sources of Foreign Policy*, pp. 273, 283.

President Johnson suffered from a "credibility gap" that seriously hampered his presidency. The Tonkin Gulf episode, discussed on page 553, was one example of an event during his presidency that took on a far different coloration after the fact. During the Watergate scandal, President Nixon claimed he had concealed certain information for "national security" reasons, but he later admitted political motivation as well; "national security" had been used as a pretext to cover up a crime.[60] Official statements about foreign policy and national security, in short, have contributed to an erosion of public confidence in government honesty.

Political Parties, Campaigns, and Foreign Policy

The two-party system tends to push both major parties toward the center on foreign-policy issues. Kenneth N. Waltz explains that "failure to do so will give a third party the chance to wedge itself in between its two larger competitors. . . . The policy positions of two competing parties begin to approach one another, and the candidates even begin to look and talk very much alike."[61]

Nevertheless, foreign-policy questions often become campaign issues. In 1992, for example, President Bush sought to emphasize his own experience in foreign affairs, and his Democratic opponent's relative inexperience, by talking about the success of the military in the Persian Gulf and about how the threat of nuclear war had diminished during his presidency.

Advocates of *bipartisanship* in foreign policy contend that both major political parties should broadly support the president, and that foreign-policy issues should not be sharply debated in political campaigns. They argue that it is in the nation's interest to appear united to the rest of the world. Opponents of bipartisanship have argued that foreign-policy issues must be discussed in political campaigns precisely because those issues are so important. Bipartisanship flourished particularly in the period shortly after the Second World War. It was symbolized by the phrase "Politics stops at the water's edge," a concept popularized in 1950 by Senator Arthur H. Vandenberg, a Michigan Republican who had served as chairman of the Senate Foreign Relations Committee under a Democratic president, Harry Truman.

[60] "President Nixon's August 5, 1974 Statement," and "The June 23, 1972 Nixon–Haldeman Transcripts," in the *New York Times, The End of a Presidency* (New York: Bantam Books, 1974), pp. 324–53.

[61] Kenneth N. Waltz, *Foreign Policy and Democratic Politics* (Boston: Little, Brown, 1967), p. 86.

The Economics of Foreign Policymaking

Across the industrial heartland of America, more and more workers have lost their jobs to foreign competition in the last decade. Layoffs, plant closings, and unemployment have become all too familiar in what some have called "the rust belt."

Why has American industry, once the world's proud leader, fallen on such hard times? An obvious answer is that the United States has become less competitive with the rest of the world. Not only are the wages of its workers higher, thanks to strong unions, but the salaries and benefits of its executives have skyrocketed. It is not unusual for CEOs of major corporations to earn salaries and stock options in the millions of dollars a year.

In Japan, Korea, Taiwan, and other countries, industry, often heavily subsidized by government, has been turning out products that are frequently better and cheaper than those produced in California, Ohio, or Pennsylvania. And Americans are buying those products. The result has been devastating to many industries in the United States, including automobiles, steel, computers, clothing, electronics, and others.

Europe, dependent on America for foreign assistance after the destruction of the Second World War, had emerged as an economic rival. The twelve-nation European Community, founded in 1967, eliminated most tariffs among the member states, even if it stumbled in 1992 in its efforts to create a common currency for the EC.

In a world in which the American economy is so directly affected by trade, foreign policy cannot be concerned with political and military power alone. As the nation moved further into the last decade of the twentieth century, foreign policy increasingly involved major economic questions, such as trade restrictions, import quotas, the balance of trade, "domestic content" legislation, and interest rates.

When American corporations are hurt by foreign competition, it often creates pressures to protect industries at home by setting high tariffs, which are taxes on imported goods. That makes the price of foreign products higher, and may encourage people to buy domestically manufactured products instead. But protectionism works two ways; other countries can and do retaliate by setting up trade barriers of their own. As a result, most presidents favor free trade.

The American auto industry can be studied as an example of the larger problem facing the nation and its

Reprinted with permission of Doug Marlette, New York Newsday

work force. For many years, Detroit did not have to worry about significant competition from foreign auto manufacturers. General Motors, Ford, and Chrysler could compete at home for the domestic auto market.

Gradually, however, German Volkswagens and then Japanese small cars began appearing on U.S. highways, until today it would almost seem as if every fourth car is a Toyota, a Honda, or a Nissan. The statistics bear out the impression: in 1990, 6.9 million American-made passenger cars were sold in the United States, but another 2.4 million foreign cars were sold in the U.S., including 1.7 million from Japan and 266,775 from West Germany. In other words, 25.8 percent of cars sold in America that year were foreign.[62]

To the extent that Americans buy cars made in Japan, for example, American auto workers lose jobs, which in turn creates protectionist pressures on the American government to erect trade barriers against imports. At the same time, the flow of U.S. dollars to Japan adversely affects the U.S. *balance of trade*, the relationship between the total cost of foreign goods imported to this country and sales of U.S. products overseas. In 1991, for example, the U.S. spent $73.4 billion more to buy foreign goods than it earned from sales abroad. Foreign policy also is concerned with the *balance of payments*, the net balance or relationship between total income and total expenditures by the nation in its dealings with the rest of the world.

[62] Source: Motor Vehicle Manufacturers Association.

So complex is the trade picture, however, that even citizens who want to "buy American" to support the economy at home may find themselves frustrated. Some Japanese car manufacturers, for example, have opened plants in the United States, employing American workers. Is a Japanese car made in Kentucky a "foreign" car?

Because some foreign manufacturers enjoy help from their governments, Congress has legislated against "dumping," a term that means the sale of goods in the U.S. at prices below their cost of production, usually because of subsidies by a foreign government to its own industries. Brazil, for example, subsidizes its steel industry, and American steelmakers complained that this gave Brazilian steel an "unfair advantage" over the U.S. steel industry. The Trade Act of 1974 protects American industries from foreign competitors who may engage in dumping. Under the 1974 law, the United States International Trade Commission determines whether a domestic industry is facing "serious injury" because of dumping. Once the commission so decides, the president has the power to take various actions to bring relief to the industry involved.

In 1984 the commission ruled that American steel makers were being injured by foreign imports. The panel called on President Reagan to restrict the sale of foreign steel to give the domestic industry time to recover. The steel industry advocated legislation to limit steel imports to 15 percent of the American market for five years. Reagan turned down the commission's call for import protections and instead pledged to seek "voluntary" agreements with steel-exporting nations.

In 1988, Congressman Richard A. Gephardt, Democrat of Missouri, sponsored what became known as the "Gephardt amendment" to a trade bill then pending in Congress. The amendment would have opened the way to retaliation by Washington against countries that had a trade surplus with the United States. Congress rejected the amendment but passed a major trade bill to stiffen the U.S. response to unfair trading practices by other countries. It was signed into law by President Reagan.

Even interest rates in the United States affect foreign policy. During the 1980s, for example, third-world nations sought some relief from repayment of loans to American banks. Interest rates in America, which were then high, made it difficult for the poorer nations to repay their debts.

All of these interlocking problems affected foreign-policy decisions as well. Indeed, the line between domestic and foreign policy was often hard to find.

THE DEFENSE ESTABLISHMENT

On August 2, 1990, Iraqi troops invaded the desert sheikdom of Kuwait, seizing control of the capital and its oilfields. For President Bush, the surprise invasion posed a major dilemma. To respond with military force risked a war in which there might be many thousands of American casualties. To do nothing, the policymakers in Washington reasoned, might encourage Iraq's dictator, Saddam Hussein, to move farther south into Saudi Arabia, jeopardizing a major source of oil supplies for the United States and the West.

Bush ordered American forces into the Persian Gulf. With the backing of the United Nations and a coalition of twenty-eight countries, Washington went to war, eventually sending 527,000 men and women to the Gulf. When Iraq did not back down, on January 16, 1991, Bush launched Operation Desert Storm with massive air and missile attacks on targets in Iraq and Kuwait. Saddam Hussein responded: "The mother of all battles has begun." [63]

Iraq began firing Scud missiles at Saudi Arabia and Israel, and the United States destroyed a number of them with Patriot missiles. When repeated bombing

---

[63] *Washington Post*, January 17, 1991, p. A1.

failed to dislodge Iraqi forces from Kuwait, Bush ordered a ground war to begin on February 23. Four days later, the war was over, with Iraqi forces in full retreat.

U.S. casualties were remarkably light. A total of 146 Americans were killed in action and 467 were wounded. It was a war that Americans at home watched on television. CNN correspondent Peter Arnett reported from Baghdad even as the bombs were dropping around him. Viewers watched Scud missiles arcing into Israel, and videotapes of American "smart bombs" literally dropping into the smokestacks of enemy targets. The commander of Desert Storm, General H. Norman Schwarzkopf, became an instant celebrity, and after he retired, a millionaire from his memoirs. President Bush's popularity soared.

A year later, as already discussed, the war had to a large extent faded from public memory. Bush, facing voters worried about their jobs and futures, saw his approval rating plummet. And in the aftermath of war, the public learned that some of what had occurred had been concealed and that some of the information that was released had been misleading. For example, almost 24 percent of American battle deaths were from so-called "friendly fire." Only 6 percent of all bombs dropped in the war were "smart," that is, guided to their targets by lasers, and most of the rest missed their targets. [64] Leading scientists testified to Congress that the

---

[64] Barton Gellman, "One Year Later: War's Faded Triumph," *Washington Post*, January 16, 1992, p. A10.

1991: American soldiers in Kuwait

THE PERSIAN GULF WAR: FRAYED YELLOW RIBBONS

SAVANNAH, Ga., Jan. 15—The yellow ribbons, now frayed and faded, are still wrapped around the oak trees near the Hunter Army Air Field here where horn-honking, flag-waving crowds lined the streets in the early morning hours last March to greet the first troops returning from the Persian Gulf war.

But here as elsewhere, the war seems like something from another era these days, and the talk is of other things: the sluggish economy, the dreary stretch of empty buildings on Broughton Street downtown, the record-breaking local murder rate.

A year after it began in fear and ambiguity and ended in relief and jubilation, the Persian Gulf war has receded to a degree that few people expected, replaced by fears about the economy and doubts about the country's ability to handle problems at home as easily as it dispatched Saddam Hussein's overmatched military forces.

At the Raytheon plant in Andover, Mass., where the Patriot missiles that helped decide the war are manufactured, the talk is of possible layoffs.

"This seems to be the Andy Warhol war," said John Shy, a history professor at the University of Michigan. "A quarter-hour of fame and maximum attention and, in retrospect, horrendous losses of life on the other side, but remarkably trivial in its consequences otherwise."

—*New York Times*, January 16, 1992

THE PRESS V. THE PENTAGON

On the anniversary of Iraq's invasion of Kuwait, many journalists described also falling in defeat to the U.S. Government due to censorship and Pentagon propaganda.

Painful examples abound, including buying into exaggerated figures on Iraqi troop strength, inflating the success and significance of "smart bombs" and Patriot missiles and hiding the thousands of Iraqi dead by confining reporters and camera crews to press pools that—with few exceptions—never got to the scene of actual fighting. Overall, Americans got a more realistic view of the war from a few journalists who remained in Baghdad (and who were widely denounced for it!) than they did from the press corralled far from the battlefield.

—John R. MacArthur, Op Ed article, *New York Times*, July 27, 1992

Patriots may have caused more damage from explosive debris than if they had never been fired. This was true, the scientists said, because when a Patriot anti-missile successfully intercepted a Scud, the broken pieces from both missiles inflicted great damage when they fell to the ground. And since the Patriot system fired more than one interceptor missile at each incoming Scud, the number of explosive warheads that fell to earth in Israel was larger than if the defensive system had not been deployed.[65] One study found that Patriot missiles had intercepted Iraqi Scud missiles only 9 percent of the time.[66] And the war had cost the taxpayers at least $7.3 billion.[67]

Nevertheless, as a purely military exercise, it was an impressive performance. More than half a million men and women had been moved across the ocean to the Middle East, along with hundreds of planes, tanks, missiles, bombs, and other military equipment. The United States had rolled up Iraq's army, considered the best in the region, in four days, with relatively low casualties.

To an extent, the success of American forces on the battlefield was a reflection of the enormous expenditures for defense by the United States in recent decades. Since the Second World War the United States has spent more than $2 trillion on national defense; in fiscal 1993 the Defense Department's budget request was $277.9 billion. Because of expanding technology, however, some weapons systems become obsolete even as they are deployed. And during the years when the Soviet Union stood as a rival superpower, a strong argument could be made that, because of the threat of nu-clear war, as spending for armaments increased, national security actually diminished. Aside from this paradox, the existence of a multibillion-dollar military machine has created numerous problems for American society. Within the "military-industrial complex," whole industries depend on government defense contracts; aerospace industry lobbyists attempt to guard their clients' interests in Washington; and some universities compete for classified military research contracts. A society that devotes close to 25 percent of its total national budget to defense-related spending cannot allocate as much as it otherwise might to eliminate poverty, or improve health, schools, and the natural environment. The "cost" of a defense economy cannot be measured simply in terms of the size of the annual Pentagon budget.

Thus far, America's nuclear weapons have remained in their underground silos and beneath the sea in submarines. With the end of the Cold War, their use seems even less likely. But since the Second World War, the United States has fought a series of "limited" or conventional wars in Korea, Vietnam, and the Persian Gulf. Despite its vast weaponry, manpower, and technology, the United States learned in Vietnam that superior size and resources were of little advantage against an elusive and politically dedicated enemy skilled in guerrilla warfare.

The United States could not employ nuclear weapons against a smaller nation without being morally condemned by most of the rest of the world as well as by millions of citizens at home. The use of such weapons has been considered, however. During the Korean War, for example, President Eisenhower discussed with his advisers the possible employment of nuclear arms.[68] But

---

[65] *New York Times*, April 17, 1991, p. A11.
[66] The study was conducted for Congress by the General Accounting Office. Source: *Washington Post*, September 30, 1992, p. A4.
[67] *USA Today*, May 6, 1992, p. 1A.

[68] *New York Times*, June 8, 1984, p. 8.

Strategic Air Command's
underground control center

the use of tactical or strategic nuclear weapons in a conventional "limited war" may carry with it the threat of escalation into a larger war. To an extent, therefore, the "usable power" of the United States has been limited. Furthermore, domestic opposition to the United States' involvement in Southeast Asia, the Middle East, Central America, and the Persian Gulf demonstrated the potential political risks and limitations for American leaders pursuing military solutions to foreign-policy problems.

Foreign policy and defense policy are intimately linked. Ideally, as Burton M. Sapin notes, "Foreign policy establishes the broad outlines within which the defense establishment must do its work." [69] A modern president must contend with the problems of controlling a huge, powerful military establishment with its friends and protectors in Congress and its clients in private industry. The president must see that the generals serve his foreign-policy goals, rather than the other way around.

The Department of Defense

The principle of civilian control over the American military establishment is deeply rooted in the Constitution and the nation's tradition. The president is com-

mander in chief of all the armed forces, and the secretary of defense, by law, must be a civilian. Yet the effectiveness of civilian control of the military has sometimes been open to question.

Across the Potomac River from Washington, in Arlington, Virginia, lies the Pentagon. Completed in 1943 at a cost of $83 million, the Pentagon houses some 23,000 civilian and military employees. In its concourse

[69] Burton M. Sapin, *The Making of United States Foreign Policy* (New York: Praeger, for the Brookings Institution, 1966), p. 136.

The Pentagon

is a shopping center large enough for most suburban cities. The Pentagon has its own bank, post office, barbershop, department stores, florist—even an optometrist and medical and dental clinics. The secretary of defense is the Western world's biggest employer, in charge of more than 1,000,000 civilians and 1,906,990 members of the armed forces as of 1992. (Indirectly, the Pentagon is also the biggest private employer in America; by 1991, for example, the Defense Department's contracts were running at a level of $137 billion a year.[70]

The National Security Act of 1947, as amended in 1949, unified the armed forces under the control of a single secretary of defense. The army, navy, and air force continue to exist as separate entities within the Defense Department, each with its own secretary. The secretaries of the armed services do not control their military operations, however; that is the responsibility of the president, acting through the secretary of defense and the Joint Chiefs of Staff. The Pentagon has its own "little State Department," the Office of International Security Affairs (ISA), which serves both as the Defense Department's link with the State Department and as a competing source of foreign-policy formulation. The Pentagon also has its own intelligence organization, the Defense Intelligence Agency (DIA), created in 1961, as well as the supersecret National Security Agency (NSA), which intercepts the codes of other nations and conducts electronic espionage.

The Joint Chiefs of Staff

The members of the Joint Chiefs of Staff are the chairman, the chiefs of staff of the three armed services, and, when Marine corps matters are under consideration, the commandant of the Marines. By law the chairman, whose powers were greatly strengthened by the Defense Reorganization Act of 1986, advises the president and the secretary of defense.

The chairman and other members of the Joint Chiefs are appointed by the president. Sometimes the president may skip over senior officers to appoint a more dynamic, younger service chief. The chairman of the Joint Chiefs outranks the other members. Together, the Joint Chiefs are responsible for day-to-day conduct of military operations as well as long-range strategic planning. They are assisted by a Joint Staff of not more

than 400 officers selected about equally from the three services. Although the president relies on the chairman of the Joint Chiefs for military advice, he may choose to disregard the chairman's views. The president has the responsibility to weigh military risks against the nation's total foreign-policy objectives.

Robert Kennedy has related that during the Cuban Missile Crisis in 1962, one member of the Joint Chiefs advocated the use of nuclear weapons. "I thought, as I listened, of the many times that I had heard the military take positions which, if wrong, had the advantage that no one would be around at the end to know." [71]

But not every military officer is a "hawk." A whole series of leading military figures in recent decades, generals like George Marshall, Omar Bradley, Matthew Ridgway, James Gavin, and Maxwell Taylor, proved themselves capable of viewing foreign policy in its broadest context—not merely in narrow, military terms. Another career military man, General Eisenhower, successfully resisted the advice of some of his military advisers and refused, for example, to intervene in Southeast Asia in 1954. And some high-ranking military officers and ex-officers criticized the war in Vietnam.

Selective Service

Although in peacetime the United States has usually relied on a volunteer army, the government has registered or drafted men for military service during times of international tension or war. During the Second World War, the Korean War, and the Vietnam War, for example, men were conscripted for military duty.

Early in 1980, in response to events in Iran and Afghanistan, President Carter asked Congress to resume draft registration. Congress approved the legislation, and registration at 34,000 post offices began that summer. The Selective Service System did not issue draft cards or classify those who registered. There could not be an actual draft unless Congress approved a call-up. Although Carter had asked for authority to register both men and women, Congress refused to approve draft registration for women. In 1981, the Supreme Court ruled that a draft of men only was constitutional.[72] Draft registration of men continued under Presidents Reagan and Bush.

---

[70] Data provided by the Center for Defense Information.

[71] Kennedy, *Thirteen Days*, p. 48.
[72] *Rostker* v. *Goldberg*, 453 U.S. 57 (1981).

Strategic Arms: The Balance of Terror

Near Great Falls, Montana, Aberdeen Angus cattle grazed placidly on a grassy hillside. Some sixty feet below, two officers of the Strategic Air Command (SAC) controlled ten Minuteman missiles, each tipped with a hydrogen bomb. Within two minutes and thirty seconds after receiving an order, the two officers could fire the missiles. A nuclear war, with devastation beyond imagination, would have begun.

With the disappearance of the Soviet Union, the chief adversary of the United States, this horrible scenario seemed much less likely to occur. But the chilling setting in Montana was described to readers of the *Washington Post* some years ago in a story that captured the atmosphere of the time. The Department of Defense had permitted a reporter to visit the two-man crew at the Minuteman launch control center at Malmstrom Air Force Base. The story explained:

> Air Force lieutenants Peter N. Micale and Michael J. Wallace are seated in oversized couch chairs. . . . Sixty feet below the Montana prairie, the credibility of America's nuclear deterrent comes down to one question: are Micale and Wallace willing to turn the key if the order comes? . . .
>
> Wallace has seen pictures of nuclear destruction. His undergraduate degree from Texas A & M University was in physics. He understands the power at his fingertips. And, yes, he has seen "The Day After." What would the world be like? "I don't know," he says. . . . "I honestly don't want to think about it." . . .
>
> This is the Minuteman launch procedure that Micale and Wallace would complete. . . . They receive a coded message, containing the "enabling" code, which allows the

missiles to be unlocked. . . . Micale and Wallace then each open a combination lock on the red metal box above Wallace's desk. Inside is a book telling them if the code they received is genuine. The box also contains two keys. . . . On Micale's order, he and Wallace insert the keys into the locks—located roughly 12 feet apart . . . far enough apart that one man cannot turn both keys. . . . When Micale and Wallace turn their keys, they "vote" to fire the missiles. . . . Once any two crews in the squadron have "voted," the missiles will be launched according to a computer program. Once launched, the missiles cannot be stopped.[73]

At the time this story was written, across the Arctic Circle, the Soviet equivalent of the two SAC officers sat in their missile silos ready to launch huge SS-18 ICBMs at the United States. A study by the federal government estimated that in a nuclear exchange as many as 260 million American and Soviet citizens would have been killed.[74]

In the decades since the 1950s, the world lived with the knowledge that it was less than thirty minutes away from nuclear disaster. Even with the end of the Cold War, and major cutbacks in strategic arms, a nuclear war—even one started by accident—while much less likely, is not an impossibility.

The American nuclear monopoly was broken when the Soviet Union exploded an atomic bomb in 1949. In 1957 the Soviet Union launched the first

---

[73] Lawrence Meyer, "The Men Who Would Finish World War III But Who Might Refuse to Start It," *Washington Post Magazine*, June 3, 1984, pp. 9, 17–18.

[74] Adapted from Congress of the United States, Office of Technology Assessment, "The Effects of Nuclear War," Summary, April 1980, p. 18.

Figure 14–2 Potential Destruction from Nuclear Weapons

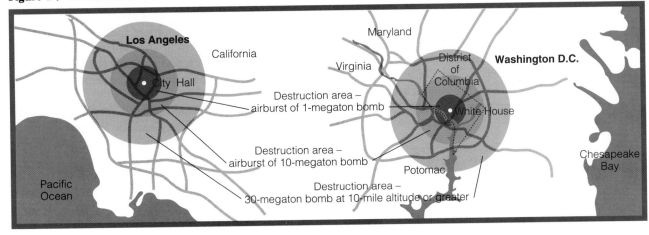

Sputnik, or earth satellite. The military implications were clear; if Russia possessed the technology to boost a satellite into outer space, it had long-range missiles that could be targeted on American cities. In October 1964 Communist China exploded its first nuclear bomb, and the "nuclear club" then had five members — the United States, the Soviet Union, Britain, France, and China. India became the sixth member when it exploded a nuclear device in May 1974. Israel is also widely believed to possess nuclear weapons.

Since the Second World War, the United States has adopted a policy of *strategic deterrence*. The theory of deterrence, developed in the Pentagon with the assistance of defense "think tanks" such as the Rand Corporation and the Institute of Defense Analyses (IDA), involved deploying enough nuclear weapons so that an enemy would not, in theory, attack the United States, for fear of being attacked in retaliation.

But how, if it relied on nuclear arms alone, could the United States respond to nonnuclear military challenges? President Kennedy believed it was necessary for the United States to supplement its nuclear power by expanding its capacity to fight "conventional" wars. During the 1960s, the policy of massive nuclear retaliation changed to one of "limited" or "flexible" response, and the Pentagon trained its Special Forces in guerrilla warfare and "counterinsurgency." In Vietnam, at least, the new theory and techniques did not prove to be very successful.

Henry A. Kissinger argued in 1957 that the United States must be able to fight a "limited nuclear war," [75] a position from which he later retreated. [76]

Some defense intellectuals shocked many people by their attempts at rational analysis of an essentially irrational process — thermonuclear war. For example, Herman Kahn wrote in 1961 that a nuclear war "would not preclude normal and happy lives for the majority of survivors and their descendants." [77] The picture of nuclear survivors living happy lives amid the debris did not convince everyone. Other analysts, such as Ralph E. Lapp, argued that the nation's arsenal of weapons had grown into "a monstrous stockpile which could not only kill, but overkill, any possible enemy." [78]

The strategy of deterrence had a language all its own. Military theorists spoke of "first-strike capability" and "second-strike capability," "stable deterrent," or "counterforce." By the late 1960s the jargon included ominous new acronyms: MIRV (Multiple Independently Targetable Re-entry Vehicle), MAD (Mutually Assured Destruction), and ABM (antiballistic missile). Whatever parity had been achieved in the "balance of terror" was threatened by new technology — the simultaneous development of the ABM as a defense against ballistic missiles, and the MIRV, designed to overwhelm the ABM system by firing from one missile a cluster of real and dummy warheads to confuse radar defenses.

The spiraling arms race, in short, threatened to go out of control. The history of United States development of the ABM illustrates the problem: in 1967 the Johnson administration disclosed that the Soviet Union had deployed an antiballistic-missile system around Moscow. The administration opposed deployment of the ABM by the United States, arguing that Soviet countermeasures would leave both countries with no net increase in security.

But the Joint Chiefs of Staff and powerful members of Congress favored an ABM program. So the United States in 1969 embarked on a round of strategic spending for the Safeguard ABM system that would cost the taxpayers many billions of dollars.

On October 1, 1975, the enormous complex of radars, missiles, and computers, located in the wheat fields near Grand Forks, North Dakota, was completed, at a cost of $5.7 billion. The Pentagon announced that Safeguard was fully operational. By an irony of history, the next day the House of Representatives voted to dismantle the project. The Senate concurred and the missile facilities were shut down. Even before its completion, the ABM had become obsolete when the Soviets developed MIRV: multiple independently targetable warheads that could overwhelm the antimissile defense system. [79] This was precisely the argument that critics of the ABM had used during a Senate debate over the ABM in 1968.

The 1972 SALT agreement limited ABM deployment by the United States and the Soviet Union and included a five-year freeze on production of offensive

[75] Henry A. Kissinger, *Nuclear Weapons and Foreign Policy* (New York: Harper & Row, 1957), pp. 174–202. Published for the Council on Foreign Relations.

[76] Henry A. Kissinger, *The Necessity for Choice* (New York: Harper & Row, 1961), p. 81.

[77] Herman Kahn, *On Thermonuclear War* (Princeton: Princeton University Press, 1961), p. 21.

[78] Ralph E. Lapp, *Kill and Overkill* (New York: Basic Books, 1962), p. 10.

[79] *Washington Post*, November 20, 1975, p. 1; and *New York Times*, November 25, 1975, p. 1.

nuclear weapons. At the time of the agreement, however, the United States had 1,054 intercontinental ballistic missiles (ICBMs) and 656 submarine-launched missiles; the Soviet Union had 1,618 ICBMs and 650 submarine-launched missiles.[80] Both sides, in other words, continued to possess immense destructive power despite the agreement, and despite the later accords signed in 1974 at Vladivostok in the Soviet Union, and the intermediate-range-missile treaty signed in Washington in 1987.

In 1977 President Carter cancelled full production of the controversial neutron, or Enhanced Radiation (ER) bomb which kills people but spares buildings. A year later, however, he ordered the Department of Energy to begin building components of the neutron bomb. And in 1981 President Reagan ordered full production and stockpiling. Under President Bush, production of the neutron bomb was halted and the weapon phased out of the U.S. arsenal. Carter also announced plans for a $33 billion system of 200 ten-warhead mobile MX intercontinental nuclear missiles, to be deployed in the Utah–Nevada area, where they would shuttle on giant launchers among 4,600 underground shelters along roads shaped in loops, like racetracks. The theory behind MX was that with so many shelters, the Soviets could not know which shelters contained the missiles. The MX would be eliminated under an agreement reached in June of 1992 by President Bush and President Boris N. Yeltsin of Russia.

American strategic deterrence has long rested on a "triad" of nuclear weapons—land-based missiles, nuclear missile-firing submarines, and the Strategic Air Command's bombers. But the theories of how these deadly weapons should be used have changed over the years. For example, in 1980 President Carter signed Presidential Directive 59, which adopted a new nuclear strategy. The new strategy placed greater emphasis on destroying Soviet military forces and missiles, rather than cities.[81]

Then in 1983, President Reagan announced a new Strategic Defense Initiative (SDI), better known as "Star Wars." The $26 billion five-year program was designed to develop and test components for tracking and shooting down Soviet nuclear missiles. SDI assumed the development of such advanced technology as lasers or particle beams that could intercept incoming missiles. The Reagan strategy thus meant a shift from the traditional doctrine of "massive retaliation" to a defensive posture. Critics of the program said it would be overwhelmed by countermeasures, would cost vast sums of money, and, most of all, might encourage an enemy to attack first, before such a defensive net could be deployed. With the end of the Cold War, the program was scaled down. The newer version envisioned interceptors in space called "Brilliant Pebbles" to destroy incoming missiles, backed up by ground-launched missiles to intercept any missiles that slipped through. Proponents of the scheme argued that it was necessary

---

[80] *New York Times*, May 27, 1972, p. 1.

[81] *Washington Post*, August 6, 1980, p. 10.

"General Hoskins, I don't care if you are in charge of our star-wars defense. You must wear a regulation uniform."

Drawing by Dana Fradon © 1984 The New Yorker Magazine, Inc.

because more nations were acquiring nuclear weapons and ballistic missiles, increasing the chance of accidental or intentional use.

Even as the arms race spiraled, scientists raised new questions about whether a nation that launched a nuclear attack, even a "successful" attack, might destroy itself and the planet. A 1983 study presented by Carl Sagan and other scientists concluded that an atomic war could trigger a "nuclear winter." The cloud of debris, the study said, would create a temporary ice age, blocking out 90 percent of the sun's light and plunging temperatures to −13 Farenheit for three months. Nothing would grow, and human beings who survived the blast and radiation would freeze or starve to death.[82] Other scientists have strongly disputed these conclusions, and believe that the chilling effect was overstated. In light of such studies, however, it might be asked whether *any* nuclear strategy could provide true security for any nation.

Some idea of the dimensions of the danger during the Cold War were suggested by a 1984 Pentagon study, which estimated that the Soviet Union possessed about 34,000 nuclear warheads and the United States 26,000, for a total of 60,000 warheads — each containing many times the explosive power of the atomic bombs that destroyed Hiroshima and Nagasaki in the Second World War.[83] A few months before the Pentagon study was made public, the chief of staff of the United States Air Force, Gen. Charles A. Gabriel, declared: "I don't think anyone in his right mind would argue that nuclear war is winnable."[84] As will be seen, these warhead totals were being greatly reduced in the aftermath of the Soviet collapse.

Arms Control and Disarmament

In June of 1992, President Bush and President Yeltsin of Russia met in Washington and announced agreement to reduce sharply their stocks of nuclear weapons and to eliminate all land-based intercontinental ballistic missiles with multiple warheads. The agreement required each country to reduce its total of missiles to 3,500 for the United States and 3,000 for Russia by the year 2003 or sooner.

The desire of both countries to cut back on their nuclear arsenals was outpacing diplomacy, for the Bush-Yeltsin agreement went far beyond the formal treaties and agreements reached over the previous decade, including the Strategic Arms Reduction Treaty (START) signed in 1991, and ratified by the Senate the following year. In the fall of 1991, Bush had announced sweeping unilateral reductions in U.S. nuclear weapons. In the wake of the dissolution of Soviet power, disarmament — long a goal — was finally on its way to becoming a reality.

For years, leaders on both sides realized that the arms race and the strategy of deterrence, however "logical," could lead to disaster. One obvious but elusive alternative is arms control and disarmament, the subject of intermittent negotiations between Moscow and Washington since the Second World War. But progress was slow, until the global political framework changed so suddenly and surprisingly.

The march toward disarmament began in 1963 when the United States and the Soviet Union reached agreement on a nuclear test-ban treaty. The treaty, banning tests in the air, underwater, and in outer space — but not underground — was signed in Moscow and ratified by the United States Senate. More than one hundred nations signed the treaty, but two atomic powers — France and Communist China — refused to do so.

Despite progress between Washington and Moscow, "nuclear proliferation," the spread of atomic weapons to more countries, continues to complicate the picture. Even as the superpowers were cutting back, smaller nations were busily attempting to acquire nuclear weapons and join the "nuclear club." If that should happen, some analysts worried, global stability might be threatened even more than it had been during the Cold War era.

In 1968 the United Nations General Assembly voted approval of a draft treaty banning the spread of nuclear weapons to states not already possessing them. The United States, the Soviet Union, and sixty other nations signed, and the Senate ratified, the Nonproliferation Treaty in March 1969. But Israel, India, and Japan — all potential nuclear powers at the time — did not sign, nor did France or Communist China.

In 1972 the United States and the Soviet Union signed the SALT treaty to limit strategic arms. Seven years later, in 1979, a second agreement, known as SALT II, was reached which would have set a ceiling on

---

[82] "A Cold, Dark Apocalypse," *Time*, November 14, 1983.
[83] *New York Times*, June 18, 1984, p. A8.
[84] *Seattle Times*, August 26, 1983, p. B2.

33 YEARS OF SUMMITRY WITH MOSCOW

September 1959 Dwight D. Eisenhower and Nikita S. Khrushchev meet at Camp David, Md. The talks result in the "spirit of Camp David," an effort to press for scientific and cultural exchanges and disarmament.

June 1961 Khrushchev and John F. Kennedy have heated exchanges in Vienna. There are no formal agreements. A year later, the Soviets send nuclear missiles to Cuba; the United States forces their removal.

May 1972 Richard M. Nixon and Leonid I. Brezhnev, in Moscow, sign the first treaties setting limits on strategic nuclear arms, known as SALT I, and on curbing antiballistic missile systems. They agree to keep negotiating on arms, but regional issues divide them.

June 1979 Jimmy Carter and Brezhnev, in Vienna, sign the second treaty limiting strategic arms, or SALT II. Although the Senate never approves the treaty because of the Soviet sweep into Afghanistan in December 1979, both sides agree informally to observe its limits.

October 1986 Ronald Reagan and Mikhail S. Gorbachev meet in Reykjavik, Iceland, to provide momentum to arms-control talks. The two sides speak of vast cuts in strategic arms and medium-range missiles, but the accord falls through because of disagreements over the American plan for a space-based missile defense system, or "Star Wars," and over Moscow's insistence on putting all arms issues in one package.

December 1987 Reagan and Gorbachev meet in Washington. They sign a treaty to destroy intermediate-range nuclear forces, known as I.N.F., and agreee to seek a treaty cutting long-range nuclear arsenals. But "Star Wars" remains a sticking point.

December 1988 Gorbachev says farewell to Reagan and greets President-elect George Bush at a two-hour luncheon on Governors Island in New York harbor.

December 1989 Bush, now President, and Gorbachev meet in Malta. They say they will strive to conclude treaties on long-range nuclear weapons and conventional arms in 1990.

May – June 1990 Bush and Gorbachev meet in Washington. They pledge to cut stockpiles of long-range nuclear arms and chemical weapons. They also sign a trade treaty.

February 1992 Bush and Boris N. Yeltsin, president of Russia, meet in Washington and declare the formal end to the Cold War.

June 1992 Bush and Yeltsin meet again in Washington and announce drastic reductions in their nuclear arsenals.

—Adapted from *New York Times*, July 30, 1991

---

the numbers of strategic missiles and bombers for both sides. But that treaty was never ratified by the United States Senate.

In the summer of 1982, a new round of arms-control talks began in Geneva. SALT was renamed START (Strategic Arms Reduction Talks) by the Reagan administration. Finally in 1987, the United States and the Soviet Union agreed to dismantle all of their intermediate- and shorter-range missiles, and Gorbachev journeyed to Washington to sign the treaty in December. The agreement, sometimes known as the INF (Intermediate-range Nuclear Forces) treaty, was historic because it marked the first time that the two countries had agreed to reduce their nuclear arsenals. Under it, the United States pledged to destroy the nuclear missiles it had deployed in Western Europe as well as all other intermediate- and shorter-range weapons, and the Soviets in turn promised to destroy their intermediate- and shorter-range missiles. And in 1991, both sides signed the START agreement to reduce strategic, long-range missiles.

During the war in the Persian Gulf, Israel and the UN allies feared that Iraq might arm its missiles with chemical weapons. That did not occur, but the world

SIXTY
THOUSAND
NUCLEAR
WARHEADS: A
COLD WAR
LEGACY

Between 1945 and 1985 the United States manufactured an estimated sixty thousand nuclear warheads for 116 weapons systems, an average production rate of four per day. These ranged from huge thermonuclear city busters to an atomic warhead for a jeep-mounted bazooka. In a 1985 essay, three critics of the American arsenal, Robert S. Norris, Thomas B. Cochran, and William M. Arkin, concluded: "Bureaucratic competition and inertia have led to nuclear warheads for every conceivable military mission, arm of service, and geographic theater — all compounded by a technological momentum that overwhelmed what should have been a more sober analysis of what was enough for deterrence. The result is a gigantic nuclear weapons system — laboratories, production facilities, forces, and so on — that has become self-perpetuating, conducting its business out of public view and with little accountability."

—Seymour M. Hersh, *The Samson Option*

still faced the threat of chemical and biological warfare. In 1969 President Nixon announced that the United States was renouncing germ warfare and would no longer stockpile biological weapons. But he said the United States would continue to engage in "defensive research" in biological weapons. At that time the United States did not renounce chemical warfare, including the production of deadly nerve gases like GB, or Sarin — a tiny drop of which kills instantly. But in 1970 President Nixon submitted to the Senate the Geneva Protocol outlawing chemical and biological warfare among nations. The United States had signed the treaty in 1925, but the Senate had never ratified it. It finally did so in 1974. In 1972 the United States, the Soviet Union, and some seventy other nations signed an international agreement to outlaw biological weapons. This treaty, too, was ratified by the Senate in 1974. Thus, today, the United States is formally pledged not to use chemical or biological weapons.

But the treaties did not prohibit the production or stockpiling of chemical weapons. In 1980 Congress approved $3 million to build a plant at Pine Bluff, Arkansas, that could produce a new generation of deadly nerve-gas weapons. Congress voted funds only for construction of the plant, not for production of nerve gas. Actual production would require a presidential directive. In that event, the plant could turn out binary nerve-gas shells for the army — devices in which two harmless chemicals are kept separate inside a projectile but then mixed during flight to create the lethal gas. In 1982 President Reagan asked Congress to vote funds for the production of binary Bigeye bombs and artillery shells, both containing nerve gas. In April 1984, Reagan proposed a new international treaty to ban the use,

production, or stockpiling of chemical weapons. Congress later voted to approve the nerve-gas bombs, and production began in early 1988 at the army's arsenal in Pine Bluff, Arkansas. Still, the U.S. continued to participate in multilateral negotiations to bar chemical weapons.

THE MILITARY-INDUSTRIAL COMPLEX

In his final speech to the nation, President Eisenhower warned against what he called "unwarranted influence" by the "military-industrial complex."[85] Eisenhower thus focused attention on the consequences for America of a vast military establishment linked to a huge arms industry. In the years after Eisenhower's 1961 warning, the concept of the "military-industrial complex" was expanded to encompass universities conducting defense research, scientists, laboratories, aerospace-industry contractors, and research firms.

Entire communities in some areas were dependent on defense industries or military installations. In fiscal 1991 the McDonnell Douglas Corporation received $8.1 billion in defense contracts from the government, heading the list of the hundred largest defense contractors in the United States.[86] The top ten defense contractors in America are shown in Table 14–2.

Defense spending fattens the congressional "pork barrel." Powerful individual legislators can, and do, ob-

[85] Dwight D. Eisenhower, *The White House Years, Waging Peace 1956–1961* (New York: Doubleday, 1965), p. 616.
[86] *New York Times*, April 3, 1988, p. E-5.

Table 14-2
Top Ten Defense Contractors in 1991

Rank	Company*	Amount of Defense Contracts (in billions)
1	McDonnell Douglas Corp.	$8.1
2	General Dynamics Corp.	7.8
3	General Electric Co.	4.9
4	General Motors Corp.	4.4
5	Raytheon Co.	4.1
6	Northrop Corp.	3.3
7	United Technologies Corp.	2.8
8	Martin Marietta Corp.	2.7
9	Lockheed Corp.	2.7
10	Grumman Corp.	2.4

* Includes subsidiaries.
SOURCE: Data provided by the Center for Defense Information.

The Stealth bomber

tain multimillion-dollar contracts for their states and districts. Another example of the interrelationships within the military-industrial complex is the fact that retired military officers are frequently hired by aerospace industry contractors.

The effect of the military-industrial complex is pervasive and difficult to measure. But with many billions of dollars at stake, the scramble for contracts, the pressure on Congress and the Pentagon, and the political and economic rewards involved have given some Americans a substantial interest in an economy geared to defense production.

The debate over the controversial B-1 bomber provided an example of the enormous economic stakes in a new weapons system. For years the air force, backed by the aerospace industry and influential members of Congress, had pushed for production of the supersonic missile-firing bomber. In 1976, Congress, at President Ford's urging, approved funds to build three prototype models. Soon after taking office in 1977, President Carter announced that he had decided not to proceed with production of the B-1 bomber.

The B-1 took wing again under President Reagan, however. In 1981, Reagan announced plans to produce 100 of the supersonic aircraft, and Congress began voting billions of dollars to fund production. By 1986, the cost of the B-1 had jumped to $280 million for each plane, and the bomber was the single most expensive weapons system in the federal budget. Moreover, the B-1 was produced only as an interim plane until the

EISEN-
HOWER'S
WARNING:
THE
MILITARY-
INDUSTRIAL
COMPLEX

This conjunction of an immense military establishment and a large arms industry is new in the American experience. The total influence — economic, political, even spiritual — is felt in every city, every statehouse, every office of the federal government. We recognize the imperative need for this development. Yet we must not fail to comprehend its grave implications. Our toil, resources, and livelihood are all involved; so is the very structure of our society.

In the councils of government, we must guard against the acquisition of unwarranted influence, whether sought or unsought, by the military-industrial complex.

The potential for the disastrous rise of misplaced power exists and will persist.

We must never let the weight of this combination endanger our liberties or democratic processes. We should take nothing for granted. Only an alert and knowledgeable citizenry can compel the proper meshing of the huge industrial and military machinery of defense with our peaceful methods and goals, so that security and liberty may prosper together.

—Dwight David Eisenhower, Farewell Radio and Television Address to the American People, January 17, 1961

THE GUN THAT SHOOTS FANS

To understand some of the priorities of military procurement, consider the Army's new Sergeant York air-defense gun.

The weapon is a computerized, radar-guided pair of guns mounted on a tank chassis. Designed to shoot down planes and helicopters, the weapon is programmed to fire at whirring blades. In recent tests . . . the first production model ignored all the targets presented to it. But the weapon is no dummy. Instead, it zeroed in on what it considered a more promising target: the exhaust fan in a nearby latrine. . . .

But a man with a machine gun can bring down a helicopter. The Army should know: it lost 4,643 of them in Vietnam, nearly all to rifles and machine guns. Why does it need radar-guided guns, which cost $6.5 million each?

Because . . . in 1973 the Israelis captured a Soviet radar-controlled gun called the Shilka. Tested by the Army, the Shilka proved a poor weapon, incapable of hitting maneuvering aircraft. But the Army was envious. Ten years later it has a high-tech, armor-plated lemon all its own. . . .

—*New York Times*, March 7, 1984

Stealth bomber, which was designed to evade enemy radar, was developed for the 1990s.

The first B-1 rolled off the production line in October of 1986. But accidents and serious flaws in the plane's performance raised questions about whether the costly plane really worked. As author Nick Kotz wrote in 1988, "By now the B-1 is more than a bomber. It has become a cause. . . . Decisions about the American defense arsenal are influenced as much by psychological, political, and economic factors as by military analy-

THE B-1 BOMBER: "THE FLYING EDSEL"?

On October 1, 1986, the U.S. Air Force proudly hailed a victory for which its generals had valiantly fought for 30 years: A new strategic bomber called the B-1 was taking its place in the American nuclear arsenal. Precisely on schedule, the first squadron of fifteen planes stood poised for action at an airbase in the mesquite-covered hills of north Texas. . . . At a cost of more than $28 billion for the hundred-plane force, the B-1 was the most expensive airplane in aviation history . . .

Months later, however, the Air Force admitted that despite the fanfare, not a single bomber had been battle-ready that October day. The B-1 had problems of flight-control stability, which caused difficulty with aerial refueling—which in turn limited its range. The terrain-following radar-navigation system malfunctioned, limiting the bomber's ability to attack at ground-hugging altitudes. . . . The mechanism for firing the bomber's twenty-four nuclear-armed short-range attack missiles did not work well. Added weight kept the B-1 from cruising at an altitude high enough for best fuel consumption. . . .

Some defense analysts labeled the bomber the Flying Edsel, alluding to the highly touted 1950s Ford car that flopped . . . Retired Air Force Colonel James Boyd . . . sardonically told a fellow officer that the best use for the B-1 was "to paint it yellow and use it as a line taxi," to carry equipment and crews from hangars to aircraft. When an Air Force general declared that the B-1 was "the best war plane in the world today," Democratic Congressman Sam Stratton of New York, normally a strong military supporter, responded, "That's a lot of baloney." . . .

In September 1987, one year after the first fifteen-plane squadron was scheduled to join the nuclear force, only a single B-1 stood a lonely and symbolic alert. The other sixty-six bombers already delivered were undergoing testing, repairs and revisions.

—Nick Kotz, *Wild Blue Yonder*

sis."[87] Whether a weapons system gets built may depend as much on political factors as on military necessity, Kotz argued. The result may be "billions wasted on weapons and military facilities we don't need," and an arms program "totally out of control."[88] A total of 97 B-1 bombers was built, but the aircraft was never used in the war in the Persian Gulf; the Air Force depended on older, more reliable aircraft.

One result of the military-industrial complex is that the United States has become arms merchant to the world. In 1987, for example, the government and commercial arms dealers in the U.S. sold nearly $9.3 billion in armaments to other nations, with more than 76 percent of the total representing sales by the Pentagon.[89] In addition, the United States ships war materiel, ranging from rifles to jet planes, to other nations under a military assistance program.

The military-industrial complex also has had social and political effects. Demographically, it has been partly responsible for increased population in states such as California, Texas, and Florida with large defense or aerospace industries. This, in turn, has increased the political power of those states. Influential committee chairmen in Congress have channeled huge defense expenditures to their states, bringing economic benefits to those states and political benefits to the legislators. Conversely, in the early 1990s, cutbacks in defense spending caused by the end of the Cold War led to increased unemployment among defense workers in these states.

Finally, the huge amounts of money flowing into defense contracts can lead to corruption. In 1988, it was revealed that for two years federal agents had been in-

vestigating fraud and bribery in the Pentagon's procurement of military weapons. The investigation focused on the relationship between Defense Department officials, outside consultants, and major contractors. There were charges that billions of dollars in contracts had been awarded to companies improperly and that some Pentagon officials had been bribed.

AMERICA'S WORLD ROLE IN THE 1990S

By the 1990s, as we have seen, foreign policy issues had arisen in many new forms. They tended, perhaps even more than in the past, to involve economic issues—world trade, import restrictions, oil reserves and prices, the threat of oil embargoes, the multinational corporations, raw materials, the international environment and the ocean bed, hunger, overpopulation, disease, including the AIDS epidemic, and nuclear proliferation.

In the environmental area alone, the United States and other countries faced the daunting challenges of global warming, acid rain, depletion of the ozone layer, oil spills, controlling pesticides, preserving the rain forests that help to provide oxygen, and ensuring biodiversity, that is, maintaining the diversity of animals and plants in a world that humans share with other species. These global problems suggest a new definition of the

---

[87] Nick Kotz, *Wild Blue Yonder: Money, Politics, and the B-1 Bomber* (New York: Pantheon Books, 1988), p. 234.
[88] Ibid., p. 235.
[89] Data provided by U.S. Department of Defense and other sources.

THIS ENDANGERED PLANET

The scale of modern technology is overflowing every political boundary. Whether it is a matter of radioactive fallout, carbon monoxide, or other poison effluents, multinational corporations, computer technology, satellite broadcasting, or air and space travel, we constantly witness a drive toward operations on a planetary scale. And yet most political behavior continues to be dominated by the territorial state. States compete with one another for power, wealth, and prestige, and jealously guard their sovereign prerogatives. This competitive pattern generates conflict, waste, and distrust. Huge amounts of resources are devoted to national defense, collective violence is persistent and pervasive, and wars occur at many points of the planet. . . . Governments at all levels have not demonstrated a great capacity to solve the most urgent problems of human society. Violence and misery persist in most national societies of the world.

—Richard A. Falk, *This Endangered Planet*

term "national security." As one study concluded, "the new concept of security in terms of common global threats, including threats to the environment, now presents an alternative to the traditional definition." [90]

Yet the old tensions among nations continued to exist, even if their shape had changed, in addition to these newer concerns. The United States emerged from the Second World War as a major power, and it cannot wish away its power and global responsibility. But it can honestly redefine its foreign-policy goals and reorder its priorities in a world become less dangerous by the end of superpower rivalry.

As the nation moved further into the 1990s, many changes had taken place in the relations among nations. In the 1970s, American forces had come back from Vietnam, an American president had opened the door to the People's Republic of China, and Congress had at least tried to reassert its voice in the conduct of foreign policy. In the 1980s, the United States and the Soviet Union had moved part of the way down the road to limiting nuclear armaments. In the 1990s, both sides, now with Russia as the new player on the world stage, pledged drastic cuts in their nuclear arsenals. Democracy had come to Eastern Europe. But the collapse of communism had created new ethnic strife, for example, among nationalities in the former Soviet republics, in Yugoslavia, and in Germany. The Middle East remained volatile.

In the immediate aftermath of the Vietnam War, the conviction grew among many Americans that the nation should exercise great caution in intervening in armed conflicts beyond its borders. There was concern over the danger of United States involvement in "another Vietnam." Yet only a few years later, in the wake of Afghanistan and the seizure of American hostages in Iran, a new issue had arisen in the debate over foreign policy—whether the United States was sufficiently strong militarily to protect its interests in the Persian Gulf and elsewhere around the globe. The Reagan administration's emphasis on a military buildup reflected this concern. In the Gulf War, President Bush reaped the benefits of these policies.

At the same time, economic recession and other domestic problems increased the pressures on the policymakers in Washington to weigh the legitimate concerns of American national security against needs at home. And it was increasingly clear that in addition to

military power alone, a revival of America's domestic economy—and with it, an increased ability to compete in world markets—would be the true measure of the nation's strength and its position in the world. It was no longer really possible to separate economic and foreign policies.

America in the last years of the twentieth century remained a major international power. The United States' relations with the rest of the world were both broad-ranging and highly complex. And the formation of American foreign policy continued to be a major challenge to the nation's political leadership. The survival of the planet might depend on the decisions made in America.

PERSPECTIVE

By the 1992 presidential election campaign, the world as Americans had known it since the Second World War had changed almost beyond recognition. For four decades, the United States and the Soviet Union had been locked in a seemingly insoluble era of conflict, somewhere between peace and war. With both sides possessing unimaginably destructive weapons the possibility of nuclear war was never far in the background.

But in the fall of 1989, the tide of history once more swept across eastern Europe. In one country after another, democratic forces were able to break the grip of the Communist dictatorships, closely allied with Moscow, that had come to power in the aftermath of the Second World War. The Berlin Wall, a symbol of divided Germany, came down.

In the Soviet Union itself, Mikhail Gorbachev, who had come to power in 1985, had unleashed a series of reforms. In August of 1991, Gorbachev was briefly held prisoner during an unsuccessful coup. Four months later, in December, the Soviet Union formally ended. President Boris N. Yeltsin, the President of Russia, emerged as the most important leader in the former Soviet empire, which had broken up into fifteen independent states.

The Middle East remained unstable. After Iraq invaded Kuwait in 1990, threatening Saudi Arabia's oilfields, President Bush dispatched more than half a million troops to the Persian Gulf and, with the support of the United Nations and a coalition of twenty-eight nations, forced Iraq to withdraw.

Even after the collapse of the Soviet Union, the threat of nuclear war remained, although substantially

[90] Gareth Porter and Janet Welsh Brown, *Global Environmental Politics* (Boulder, Co.: Westview Press, 1991), p. 141.

diminished. Along with the United States, Britain, and France, Russia and China still retained nuclear weapons, and several smaller, third-world nations were actively attempting to acquire such weapons. The threat of nuclear proliferation—the spread of weapons of mass destruction to other nations—continued.

As the Cold War faded into history, new global issues—such as the environment, nuclear proliferation, overpopulation, famine, disease, including the AIDS epidemic, a rising tide of nationalism, and ethnic and religious conflicts—had come to the fore, centering on problems that often transcended national boundaries.

Foreign policy is the sum of the goals, decisions, and actions that govern a nation's relations with the rest of the world. The preservation of national security is a basic consideration in the formulation of foreign policy. The dramatic political changes in the world raised fundamental questions about the concept of national security. Many political leaders and analysts felt that national security required not only military forces but strengthening the nation's economy and meeting social needs at home.

The president is both chief diplomat and commander in chief. Particularly in the twentieth century, the two roles overlap. National security, foreign policy, and domestic programs are closely related because the president must decide how much money to allocate for each area within the overall framework of his annual budget. The vast power of the president in the realm of foreign policy carries with it great risks—risks that a president or his subordinates will exercise judgment unwisely, or act without public or congressional support. During the Reagan administration, for example, the Iran-contra scandal took place. The scandal arose when it was disclosed that the government secretly traded arms to Iran, hoping to free American hostages in the Middle East, and used the profits to support the contra rebels in Nicaragua despite a ban by Congress on such aid.

Under the Constitution, power to conduct foreign and military affairs is divided between Congress and the president. While the Constitution gave the president power to appoint ambassadors and command the armed forces, Congress was given power to declare war, raise and support armies, and appropriate money for defense; and the Senate was granted power to approve or disapprove treaties and ambassadorial nominations made by the president.

After the Second World War, Congress lost to the president much of its war power and control over foreign policy. In 1973, as one result of the increasing unpopularity of the war in Vietnam, Congress passed the War Powers Resolution, designed to limit to sixty or ninety days the president's ability to commit American troops to combat without congressional authorization. The law failed to restrict presidential use of military power in several instances, however. Between 1950 and 1992, eight American presidents committed United States troops to foreign soil without any declaration of war by Congress. In six instances Congress had passed resolutions broadly supporting presidential action, including the Authorization for Use of Military Force Against Iraq Resolution in 1991.

Today the president has powerful tools available to him for the conduct of foreign policy, including his personal staff and that of the National Security Council, the State Department, the Pentagon, the CIA, and other agencies. Until 1947 no formal centralized machinery existed to aid the president in his foreign-policy tasks. The existence of this machinery does not mean, however, that the United States can always influence, let alone control, the course of international events.

The United Nations, founded in 1945 as a world body that could take collective action to work for the betterment of humanity, was generally unable during the Cold War years to keep the peace on issues that divided the major world powers. But UN peacekeeping forces have helped to reduce tensions in the Middle East and to provide relief supplies in the civil war that followed the breakup of Yugoslavia. The UN also played a role in bringing about the Soviet withdrawal from Afghanistan and in halting the long war between Iran and Iraq. By 1992 the UN had expanded from its original fifty to 179 members.

Foreign-policy questions often become campaign issues. Advocates of *bipartisanship* in foreign policy contend that both major political parties should broadly support the president, and that foreign-policy issues should not be sharply debated in political campaigns. Opponents of bipartisanship argue that foreign-policy issues must be discussed in political campaigns precisely because those issues are so important.

To an extent, the success of American forces in the Persian Gulf War was a reflection of the enormous expenditures for defense by the United States in recent decades. Since the Second World War, the United States has spent more than $2 trillion on national defense. In fiscal 1993 the Defense Department's budget request was $277.9 billion. Because of expanding technology, however, some weapons systems become obsolete even as they are deployed. And during the years when the Soviet Union stood as a rival superpower, a strong argument could be made that, because of the threat of nuclear war, as spending for armaments increased, national security actually diminished. A society that devotes close to 25 percent of its total national budget to defense-related spending cannot allocate as much as it otherwise might to eliminate slums and poverty, or improve health, schools, and the natural environment. The "cost" of a defense economy cannot be measured simply in terms of the size of the annual Pentagon budget. In 1961, for example, President Eisenhower spoke of the "military-industrial complex," warning of the consequences for America of a vast military establishment linked to a huge arms industry.

Today, the secretary of defense is the Western world's biggest employer, in charge of more than 1,000,000 civilians and 1,906,990 members of the armed forces. The National Security Act of 1947, as amended in 1949, unified the armed forces under the control of a single secretary of defense. The army, navy, and air force continue to exist as separate entities within the Defense Department, each with its own secretary.

During the Cold War years, the United States adopted a policy of *strategic deterrence*. The theory of deterrence involved deploying enough nuclear weapons so that an enemy would not, in theory, attack the United States, for fear of being attacked in retaliation.

In 1992, President Bush and President Yeltsin of Russia announced agreement to sharply reduce their stocks of nuclear weapons and to eliminate all land-based intercontinental ballistic missiles with multiple warheads. The desire of both countries to cut back on their nuclear arsenals was outpacing diplomacy, for the Bush-Yeltsin agreement went far beyond the formal treaties and agreements reached over the previous decade, including the Strategic Arms Reduction Treaty (START) signed in 1991, and the two SALT agreements signed in the 1970s. In 1987, President Reagan and Soviet leader Mikhail Gorbachev signed the Intermediate-range Nuclear Forces (INF) treaty, under which both nations agreed to dismantle all intermediate- and shorter-range missiles.

In the environmental area alone, the United States and other countries faced the daunting challenges of global warming, acid rain, depletion of the ozone layer, oil spills, controlling pesticides, preserving the rain forests that help to provide oxygen, and ensuring biodiversity.

At the same time, economic recession and other domestic problems increased the pressures on the policymakers in Washington to weigh the legitimate concerns of American national security against needs at home. And it was increasingly clear that in addition to military power alone, a revival of America's domestic economy — and with it, an increased ability to compete in world markets — would be the true measure of the nation's strength and its position in the world. It was no longer really possible to separate economic and foreign policies.

Suggested Reading

Allison, Graham, and Treverton, Gregory F., eds. *Rethinking America's Security: Beyond Cold War to New World Order* (New York: W. W. Norton & Co., 1992). A valuable collection of essays on foreign policy, by several contributors, in the wake of the end of the Cold War. The editors and some of the authors argue that repairing America's social ills is the first priority in preserving America's national security.

Almond, Gabriel A. *The American People and Foreign Policy*, 2nd edition (Greenwood, 1977). (Originally published in 1950.) An influential and valuable study of public opinion on foreign-policy questions and how it relates to the formulation and conduct of American policy overseas.

Halberstam, David. *The Best and the Brightest** (Random House, 1972). A detailed account of the men and the policies that led the United States into the costly war in Vietnam. Written in a highly readable, anecdotal style by a leading journalist who was one of the first to challenge the optimistic official reports on the progress of the war.

Hersh, Seymour M. *The Price of Power: Kissinger in the Nixon White House* (Summit Books, 1983). A detailed, highly critical account of Henry Kissinger's role as the architect of foreign policy during the Nixon administration. By a Pulitzer-prize-winning investigative reporter.

Kennedy, Paul. *The Rise and Fall of the Great Powers: Economic Change and Military Conflict from 1500 to 2000** (Random House, 1987). An important analysis of the shifts in global power over the past five centuries and how historical patterns are reflected in modern times. The author argues that nations actually lose power by "overextending" militarily and not allocating enough resources to the creation of wealth.

Kennedy, Robert F. *Thirteen Days** (Norton, 1971). (Originally published in 1969.) A short, fascinating account of the Cuban Missile Crisis of 1962 as it appeared to a key participant in the crucial decisions made by the Kennedy administration. Reflects the great tension during the world's first nuclear confrontation.

Kissinger, Henry A. *White House Years* (Little, Brown, 1979). An important, personal account of foreign policy during the first four years of the Nixon administration. Kissinger, who served as assistant to the president for national security affairs from 1969 to 1973, covers the first SALT negotiations, the Vietnam peace talks, diplomacy in the Middle East, and the historic summit meetings in Peking and Moscow.

Kotz, Nick. *Wild Blue Yonder: Money, Politics and the B-1 Bomber** (Random House, 1988). An excellent, detailed case study of the development of the B-1 Bomber over thirty years. The author argues that the country's defense programs depend less on military merit than on the demands of dozens of interlocking special interests.

Porter, Gareth, and Brown, Janet Welsh. *Global Environmental Politics* (Boulder, Co.: Westview Press, 1991), p. 141. A brief but useful exploration of global environmental issues, such as acid rain and depletion of the ozone layer, that transcend national boundaries. The authors argue that threats to the global environment are replacing traditional definitions of national security.

Rosecrance, Richard, ed. *America as an Ordinary Country: U.S. Foreign Policy and the Future* (Cornell, 1976). An important collection of essays expressing the view that, for a variety of reasons, the era of American world dominance as a superpower has ended. The contributors argue that as an "ordinary" power, the U.S. cannot be expected to act as a world peacekeeper with special global responsibilities.

Rosenau, James N., ed. *Domestic Sources of Foreign Policy* (Free Press, 1967). A useful series of essays on the interrelations between domestic politics and American foreign policy, written by a number of specialists in the field.

Waltz, Kenneth N. *Foreign Policy and Democratic Politics: The American and British Experience* (Little, Brown, 1967). A thoughtful analysis of the problems faced by democratic states in making foreign policy. Contains useful comparative data on Great Britain and the United States.

---

* Available in paperback edition.

THE 1992 PRESIDENTIAL CAMPAIGN offered the voters a choice about the role of government in America.

President George Bush, the Republican nominee, defended the record of his four years in office and promised to improve the economy — but with minimal participation by Washington. Campaigning for reelection in Detroit, he said: "I want to empower people to make their own choices, not yoke them to new bureaucracies. I want a government that spends less, regulates less and taxes less." [1]

The words, in just a sentence or two, summarized Bush's philosophy. As his party's candidate for president, Bush espoused a relatively limited role for the

Chapter 15

Promoting the General Welfare

federal government in managing the economy and in all other areas. Like his predecessor, President Reagan, Bush argued that free enterprise and individual initiative, with the least possible interference from government, was best for the country.

Governor Bill Clinton of Arkansas, Bush's Democratic opponent, brought to the campaign a different approach, rooted in the belief that government, when necessary, should intervene to manage the economy and to provide social programs for people. Clinton, it is true, believed that too much emphasis on such programs had cost the Democrats elections. As a result he was cautious in his approach, and his proposals were more moderate than some previous Democratic

---

[1] *Washington Post*, September 11, 1992, p. A1.

standard-bearers. For example, he proposed a $6 billion job training program but said he would require persons on welfare to work after two years. The work provision was designed to appeal to those blue-collar and middle-class Americans who resented the high cost of government welfare programs.

In this way, Clinton sought to avoid the "liberal" label and to move closer to the political center than had Democrats of the recent past. Nevertheless, there were substantial differences between the two major parties in their approach to governing. Bush argued that affluent Americans are taxed too much; Clinton favored higher taxes for the rich. Bush believed in cutting social programs and public works. Clinton favored government spending for roads, bridges, and transportation and communications systems. Bush argued for less government regulation of business. Clinton proposed more regulations to protect the environment and preserve energy.

The differences between the parties over the role of government in promoting the general welfare could be seen in even sharper focus during the Reagan era, when Bush had served as vice-president.

Reagan and his advisers came into office in 1981 advocating economic policies that were a sharp departure from the past. These policies, known as "supply side" economics, called for a program of tax cuts and federal spending cuts to try to assure growth without

A soup kitchen in the nation's capital

inflation and to end recessions. The money moving into the economy because of the tax reductions, it was hoped, would be used by industry to build new factories and machinery to provide jobs and growth. The benefits would thus flow to the public, in theory. Congress went along with Reagan's program, enacting massive tax and spending cuts.

The Reagan cutbacks had an immediate impact on millions of Americans. Government welfare aid, job-training programs for the poor, education, legal services, unemployment benefits, Medicaid, food stamps, and many other social services were cut.

Economic conditions worsened. Unemployment reached 10.7 percent in 1982, the highest figure since the Second World War, and 12 million people were jobless. By the time Reagan ran for a second term in 1984, however, the economy had improved dramatically, and he had no difficulty defeating Walter Mondale, the Democratic candidate, that year.

But there were danger signs for the economy as well. The government's budget deficits were soaring to unprecedented multibillion-dollar levels, in part because the Reagan administration increased the proportion of money spent on defense. In the fall of 1987 the stock market plunged, and the dollar fell against many foreign currencies.

Taken together, the Reagan budget and tax cuts reduced the income of the poor and increased the income of the rich.[2] Moreover, the percentage and number of poor people increased substantially under Reagan.[3]

Clinton proposed to tax wealthy Americans to help pay for new programs. Beneath the campaign rhetoric in 1992 the questions were both moral and pragmatic: whether one segment of society should pay for the needs of another, and beyond that, whether even with the best of intentions, federal social programs can achieve their objectives.

By the 1990s, it was not only conservatives who criticized government social-welfare programs and "Big Government." Some liberals, too, wondered whether federal social-welfare programs inevitably created so much regulation and so many controls that they failed to help the people they were designed to help. The Democrats, defeated in the 1980, 1984, and 1988 presidential elections, recognized the electorate's caution toward government programs. Bill Clinton symbolized the new, moderate approach by the Democrats. And in 1992, he won.

---

[2] Congressional Budget Office, "The Combined Effects of Major Changes in Federal Taxes and Spending Programs Since 1981," Staff Memorandum, April 1984, table 5; and *Washington Post*, July 26, 1984, p. A7.

[3] U.S. Bureau of the Census, Current Population Reports, *Money Income and Poverty Status of Families and Persons in the United States: 1983*, August 1984, p. 1; and *New York Times*, July 26, 1984, p. A19.

By the 1992 presidential campaign, the large social programs begun by President Franklin D. Roosevelt during the New Deal and expanded by John F. Kennedy and Lyndon B. Johnson had clearly come under increasing scrutiny. One observer, Anthony King, has pointed to what he called "the decline of the ideas of the New Deal as the principal organizing themes of American political life. The central idea of the New Deal was a simple one: that the federal government could, and should, solve the country's economic and social problems." [4]

By contrast, the Reagan and Bush administrations sought to restrict the government to a more limited role; where possible, social programs were eliminated or cut back. Many of the conservatives who staffed the Reagan administration believed that government programs had not worked, and that the federal bureaucracy, and the rules and regulations spawned by these programs, had proved burdensome to individuals. To the Reagan conservatives, government was not the solution, it was the problem. As president, Bush adopted much the same philosophy.

Often, the rhetoric does not match the reality. Although views about the proper role of government vary greatly, no modern president would propose to shut down a program like social security, on which millions of retired persons depend. The responsibility of the national government to make *social policy* was recognized at the beginning of the American nation, for the Constitution was established, among other purposes, to "promote the general welfare."

To take one example of the need for federal intervention, it would be very difficult, if not impossible, for people, or even for groups, to compel American industry to reduce pollution of the environment. But government, supported by public opinion and public demands, possesses the power to accomplish that task. Whether government can be expected to exercise that power, however, and intervene to regulate corporate power on behalf of consumers and individuals is not always clear. Government regulation, no matter how desirable and necessary, is a source of potential and actual tension in a largely free-enterprise capitalist economy such as that of the United States. Many of the conflicts of American politics concern the degree to which government should intervene in the private sector.

For example, in 1992 "family leave" emerged as an important political issue. The Democratic-controlled Congress passed legislation that would permit workers to take up to twelve weeks of unpaid leave each year to care for a sick or new child, to receive medical treatment, or to care for a seriously ill spouse or parent. President Bush vetoed the measure, arguing that the federal government should not decree leave policies for employers and workers, and Congress failed to override his veto.

Some political theorists have even contended that political liberty exists only where there is a free market system and private enterprise, with a minimum of government intervention. In the view of Charles E. Lindblom, for example, "much of the fuller development of personal liberty that men have sought is freedom to engage in trade . . . freedom also to move about, to keep one's earnings and assets. . . ." [5]

On the other hand, E. E. Schattschneider has suggested that "the struggle for power is largely a confrontation of two major power systems, government and business." The function of democracy, he argued, has been "to provide the public with a second power system, an alternative power system, which can be used to counterbalance the economic power." [6]

To "promote the general welfare," the federal government fills several major roles. It is regulator, promotor, manager, and protector. It performs these roles in a wide variety of ways, and with a degree of zeal that varies with the political climate and the administration in power. It regulates business and labor. But it also promotes business and labor. It assists farmers. It runs such agencies as the Food and Drug Administration and the Tennessee Valley Authority. It tries to manage the economy through fiscal and monetary policies and, at times, through wage and price controls. It acts, to some extent—and with varying success—as protector in consumer affairs, health, education, welfare, science, poverty, hunger, and the environment.

The government does not necessarily perform all of its roles well. By the presidential election of 1992 the nation was in a prolonged and scary period of economic recession. It was a time of high unemployment and

[4] Anthony King, "The American Polity in the Late 1970s: Building Coalitions in the Sand," in Anthony King, ed., *The New American Political System* (Washington, D.C.: American Enterprise Institute for Public Policy Research, 1978), p. 371.

[5] Charles E. Lindblom, *Politics and Markets: The World's Political-Economic Systems* (New York: Basic Books, 1977), pp. 163–64.
[6] E. E. Schattschneider, *The Semisovereign People* (New York: Holt, Rinehart and Winston, 1960), pp. 118, 121.

economic hardship. Layoffs, plant closings, high food prices in the supermarket, the difficulties many people faced in buying a house, and the growing problem of the homeless might have led many Americans to take a rather dim view of the ability of the government to manage the economy. As noted throughout this book, there are many areas in which American government and society have failed to live up to American expectations. So in discussing government in operation, a careful distinction must be made between the various roles of the government and its actual performance.

A government like that of the United States, which exercises responsibility for the welfare of its citizens in such areas as social security, housing, and education, is sometimes described as a "welfare state." The term is often used as one of criticism. But the role of the federal government in making social policy has been well established in this century, particularly since the days of the New Deal. As one study suggested, "social welfare programs substantially improve the well-being of most beneficiaries and . . . retrenchment does have serious repercussions . . . there is no reason to abandon the aim of providing a minimal level of support for all who remain in need." [7]

Despite the cutbacks in government social programs under President Reagan, and the sharply differing philosophy of his administration from that of Democratic administrations in the past, Washington did not ignore its domestic role. Programs such as social security, public assistance, and Medicare continued to aid millions of Americans.

Today, regardless of who occupies the White House, the terms of the argument usually concern the proper *extent* of government intervention in domestic problems, as well as *how* government should respond to national needs. Government services require government spending, and the size of government programs is directly related to the level of taxes. The level of government taxing and spending for welfare and social programs is a volatile *political* issue, directly affecting votes. That is why the question of how much the government should spend on such programs is often an important issue in presidential campaigns.

For example, substantial numbers of Americans are persuaded that welfare "chiselers" are "getting something for nothing." But many poor people, and

other citizens as well, believe government welfare programs are inadequate. Each group tends to vote for political leaders who appeal to its view. Where people stand on social-welfare issues may be related to their economic, social, and political background. The homeowner in a comfortable suburb may have less sympathy for federal welfare-assistance programs than the mother of four children living in a rat-infested Harlem tenement.

How and to what extent should the federal government "promote the general welfare"? How well does it do so? How efficiently does government regulate corporate power on behalf of the consumer? How does government attempt to manage the economy? How well has it performed in the field of social welfare, in eliminating poverty and hunger, in coping with rising medical costs and educational needs, in protecting the environment?

GOVERNMENT AS REGULATOR AND PROMOTER

Government and Business

The Constitution, as Justice Oliver Wendell Holmes, Jr., once wrote, "is not intended to embody a particular economic theory." [8] But the Supreme Court, which interprets the meaning of the Constitution, has often embodied the particular economic theory of its time. For half a century, from the late 1880s until 1937, during Franklin Roosevelt's New Deal, the Court generally interpreted the Constitution in such a way as to prevent government from regulating industry. It adopted the prevailing laissez-faire philosophy, which held that government should intervene as little as possible in economic affairs.

During the late nineteenth century, economic power was concentrated in the "trusts" and in the hands of the "robber barons." But a rising tide of populism created public demands that led to the passage of state and federal laws regulating industry. Nevertheless, the Supreme Court, as was noted in Chapter 13, interpreted the Fourteenth Amendment to protect business from social regulation by the states and by Congress.

Justice Holmes made the comment quoted at the beginning of this section in his famous dissent in

---

[7] Sar A. Levitan and Robert Taggart, *The Promise of Greatness* (Cambridge: Harvard University Press, 1976), pp. 283, 293.

[8] *Lochner v. New York*, 198 U.S. 45 (1905).

the *Lochner* case. In that 1905 decision the majority of the Supreme Court struck down a New York State law that had limited bakery employment to "sixty hours in any one week" and "ten hours in any one day." Today it might seem incredible that the Supreme Court would permit a bakery owner to work his employees more than sixty hours a week. But in 1905 the Supreme Court refused to approve the use of the power of the state to regulate private property — in this case a bakery.

The Great Depression and the New Deal brought about a reversal of Supreme Court thinking. Since 1937 the Court has upheld laws policing business; the right of government to regulate wages, hours, and working conditions of employees is now firmly established. Indeed, some of the regulations of the Occupational Safety and Health Administration (OSHA) have been so detailed and stringent that they have brought a storm of protests from business and industry. And corporate power often counterbalances government power. As one scholar has suggested, the scope and effectiveness of the federal government's efforts "have been sharply limited by business's success in weakening the content and constraining the enforcement of the new legislation." [9]

But business, even as it protests government regulation, asks for government protection. "A powerful campaign has been mounted [by industry] to contain government; reduce its size — or rate of growth — especially as regards social welfare functions; and diminish its regulatory encroachments. . . . On the other hand, business clamors for government protection, decisive efforts to control inflation. . . . This is a whipsaw treatment of government." [10]

Regulating Business: Antitrust Policy In 1890 Congress passed the Sherman Antitrust Act, which was designed to encourage competition in business and prevent the growth of monopolies. The Supreme Court severely limited the scope of the act, however, by ruling that it was up to the states to control industrial monopolies. Then in 1914 Congress passed the Clayton Act, which sought to put teeth into the federal antitrust law by defining illegal business practices, by providing the remedy of court injunctions, and by giving the Federal Trade Commission power to issue cease-and-desist

orders. The same measure exempted labor unions from antitrust actions.

Subsequent legislation has strengthened the antitrust laws, and both the antitrust division of the Justice Department and the Federal Trade Commission have blocked many large corporate mergers. But the degree of enforcement of the antitrust laws varies with the attitudes of the administration in power in Washington.

Nevertheless, there have been a number of landmark cases in which the government has changed the shape of major industries. In a famous case in 1957, the Supreme Court, under the Clayton Act, forced du Pont to divest itself of 23 percent of the stock of General Motors. [11]

In 1982, the Justice Department settled an antitrust case it had begun in 1974 against the giant American Telephone & Telegraph Company. AT&T, the biggest company in the world, with $150 billion in assets, was forced to give up ownership of its twenty-two local telephone companies, which were then consolidated into seven independent regional firms. In turn, AT&T was free to enter the data-processing and computer fields previously denied to it. But the breakup meant that AT&T became only one of many telephone companies competing with each other in long-distance rates and new services and technologies.

Encouraging competition sometimes brings disadvantages to the consumer, however. Although long-distance rates went down because of the price war among the competing companies, charges for local service increased dramatically. And, in the beginning at least, phone service deteriorated.

Although government regulation has had some success at blocking *monopoly*, the control of a market by a single company, it has not been able to prevent *oligopoly*, the concentration of economic power in the hands of a relatively few large companies. Economist John Kenneth Galbraith has noted that "in the characteristic market of the industrial system, there are only a handful of sellers." [12]

Among the five hundred largest corporations in the United States in 1991, the top ten corporations earned 43 percent of the profits. In one recent year, the revenues of General Motors were more than six times

[9] Edward S. Herman, *Corporate Control, Corporate Power*, A Twentieth Century Fund Study (New York: Cambridge University Press, 1981), p. 177.
[10] Ibid., p. 185.

[11] *United States v. E. I. du Pont de Nemours and Co.*, 353 U.S. 586 (1957).
[12] John Kenneth Galbraith, *The New Industrial State* (Boston: Houghton Mifflin, 1967), p. 179.

Table 15-1
The Ten Largest Industrial Corporations in the United States, 1991

Rank (by sales volume)	Company	Sales (in billions)	Assets (in billions)
1	General Motors	$123.8	$184.3
2	Exxon	103.2	87.6
3	Ford Motor	89.0	174.4
4	International Business Machines	64.8	92.5
5	General Electric	60.2	168.3
6	Mobil	56.9	42.2
7	Philip Morris	48.1	47.4
8	E.I. du Pont de Nemours	38.0	36.1
9	Texaco	37.6	26.2
10	Chevron	36.8	34.6

SOURCE: *Fortune*, April 20, 1992, p. 220.

those of the state of Ohio.[13] But in a lagging economy, the company dismissed thousands of employees and went through a management upheaval. Only one of the top ten, Exxon, increased its profits in 1991. The ten largest corporations in the United States are shown in Table 15-1.

Despite government regulation, some American corporations have increased in both size and diversity. Nothing illustrates the trend better than the rise in recent years of giant *conglomerates*; multi-interest, and often multinational, corporations may, under one corporate roof, manufacture products ranging from missiles to baby bottles.

---

[13] Data for 1987.

Because conglomerates are formed by mergers of companies in unrelated fields, they have been long considered exempt from most antitrust regulation.

The ordinary consumer cannot keep up with the complexities of corporate ownership in what Galbraith has called "the new industrial state." As ownership of industry becomes more and more impersonal and remote, it is increasingly difficult for the private citizen to fix responsibility for corporate actions. In some instances, individuals have turned to the courtroom.

In 1978 the Ford Motor Company recalled 1.5 million Pintos to improve the safety of their fuel tanks. That same year, three young women died after their Pinto caught on fire when hit by a van. The owners of the car destroyed in the accident had not received a

Ford Pinto in which three young women died in 1978; the auto company was acquitted.

recall notice. In 1980 the state of Indiana prosecuted Ford for reckless homicide in the deaths. The case was tried under a state law making corporations liable for the safety of their products. Ford spent a million dollars on its defense and was acquitted.

But the issue of corporate responsibility extends beyond the individual to the larger question of the responsibility of corporations toward society as a whole. The consumer movement, public concern over pollution by industry, and similar pressures have led a number of corporations to take steps to improve their public image in the area of corporate responsibility.

Ralph Nader's crusade for auto safety brought federal legislation and prodded the automobile industry to produce safer cars and to recall those with suspected defects. Increasing awareness of the issue of corporate responsibility led in the 1960s and 1970s to the emergence of *public-interest law firms* composed of young law school graduates. Instead of joining traditional, old-line law firms representing large corporations, the graduates offered their skills to protect consumers, minorities, and the poor. Today, however, these public-interest firms are much fewer in number, although some conventional law firms perform a limited amount of public-interest work.

The Regulatory Agencies Although the Justice Department has responsibility for fostering competition through the antitrust laws, much of the day-to-day contact between government and industry is carried on through federal regulatory agencies, including the major commissions discussed in Chapter 11. Thus the Securities and Exchange Commission (SEC) has responsibility for regulating the stock market; the Federal Communications Commission (FCC), the broadcast industry; the Interstate Commerce Commission (ICC), the transportation industry; the Federal Energy Regulatory Commission (FERC), power companies and pipelines; and the Federal Trade Commission (FTC), industry as a whole. Other federal agencies, such as the Food and Drug Administration, the Environmental Protection Agency, the Federal Maritime Commission, and the Consumer Product Safety Commission, have played an important role in regulating business.

As pointed out in Chapter 11, many of the commissions have, to varying degrees, become captives of their client industries, and deregulation has reduced the authority of some of these agencies. Nor has regulation always been successful. A case in point is the railroad industry, which has long asserted that its passenger

operations lose money while its freight operations make money. The great increase in air and highway travel in the past few decades was a major factor in reducing railroad revenues. Poor management by some railroads was certainly another factor. But some would argue that the government also bears part of the responsibility for the deterioration of the railroads. The ICC, although responsible for regulating the railroads in the public interest, permitted passenger service to decline to a point approaching extinction. Americans visiting Japan or Europe found better rail service in cleaner, more modern trains than was the case in many parts of their own country. On the other hand, the railroads have complained that government regulation forced the railways to continue service on unwanted passenger routes and in other ways made it difficult for them to compete with the airlines.

In 1970 Congress passed legislation to establish a federally subsidized national rail network of passenger trains. The law created a government-sponsored corporation to run many of the nation's intercity passenger trains (but not commuter lines). The National Railroad Passenger Corporation, better known as Amtrak, lost money. But the corporation expanded its Metroliner service between Washington, New York, and New Haven, providing comfortable high-speed train service at frequent intervals. Because the Metroliner was well run and competitive with the airlines in the heavily traveled northeast corridor, the Metroliner initially made a profit, even though Amtrak as a whole did not. Congress later enacted legislation increasing Amtrak's authority, independence, and budget. The railroad's excellent safety record was marred, however, by a series of accidents in the 1980s that caused a number of deaths and injured hundreds.

In 1973 Congress established a new federal agency to reorganize the Penn Central and six other bankrupt rail lines; it also created Conrail, a new federally financed corporation, to run the freight lines of the reorganized railroads. The Reagan administration, ideologically opposed to government ownership, returned Conrail to private hands. But the fact that the government found itself in the railroad business was at least partially a result of the failure of previous government policies. In 1980, as part of a general trend toward deregulation, Congress passed the Staggers Rail Act, which substantially deregulated the nation's railroads, giving them more freedom to set rates and drop routes.

Aiding Business Related to the concept of government as regulator is that of government as promoter. Government promotes commerce by providing services and direct and indirect subsidies to producers and farmers. Many business firms and farmers benefit from government aid. Appropriations for highways are indirect subsidies to truckers, bus lines, and automobile manufacturers and users. The federal government pays the airlines and the railroads to carry the mail; it helps support the merchant marine through subsidies to shipbuilders and ship operators; and it finances airport construction.

In the "alphabet soup" of government agencies in Washington there are several service agencies for industry — the Commerce Department and the Small Business Administration (SBA), for example — as well as the Department of Agriculture, which serves farmers.

At times the government has even extended direct aid to large corporations in financial trouble. In 1979, for example, Congress authorized a massive $3.5 billion aid package for the ailing Chrysler Corporation, the nation's third largest automobile manufacturer. Chrysler had miscalculated the extent of consumer demand for small cars that would use less gasoline and started building them too late; by 1979 the company's losses had mounted to $1.1 billion for the year. Congress acted, and President Carter signed the bill, because of growing concern over the impact on the economy if the government permitted the huge auto manufacturer to go under. By 1983, Chrysler had turned the corner, showing a profit of $927 million.

In addition to subsidies and services, the federal government assists industry through its *trade and tariff* policies. In the United States a tariff is a federal tax on imports. A high tariff discourages other nations from sending goods to U.S. markets and is therefore "protective" of American manufacturers. But a tariff wall can work two ways; other countries have retaliated by raising their tariffs on imports from the United States. Pressure from American industry seeking foreign markets for its products, and from consumers wanting lower prices for imported goods, has resulted in a gradual reduction of United States tariff barriers since the 1930s. In 1947 the United States and twenty-two other nations signed the General Agreement on Tariffs and Trade (GATT), which provided a formal framework for international tariff reductions. The Trade Expansion Act of 1962 gave President Kennedy broad tariff-cutting authority, and more trade barriers fell during the 1960s after the Kennedy round of trade talks in Geneva.

During the same period, however, industry in Japan and the growth of the Common Market in Western Europe threatened the competitive advantage previously enjoyed at home by American business. Protectionist sentiment succeeded in placing many restrictions on tariff reductions — for example, by imposing quotas on certain categories of imports. Another broad tariff agreement was signed by major trading nations in Geneva in 1979, however. As noted in Chapter 14, the president can restrict imports when the United States International Trade Commission finds that a particular U.S. industry faces serious injury because of unfair foreign competition. In 1988 Congress passed and the president signed a trade bill that provided protection for industries seriously injured by imports.

In 1992, the United States, Mexico, and Canada completed negotiations on an agreement to create a single free trade bloc for the three countries. President Bush sent the North American Free Trade Agreement (NAFTA) to Congress for approval. But in an election year, many members of Congress were cautious about the pact, fearing that some U.S. companies would move their plants to Mexico, where labor is cheaper. Opponents also feared that the pact would lead to expanded competition with Mexico, since products manufactured there could now enter the United States more freely.

The economic relations among nations can greatly affect the quality of life around the globe. One scholar has concluded, for example, that because of global economic interdependence, understanding international trade and monetary relations "is essential to understanding the prospects of individual countries." [14] Yet the system of liberal trade policies among nations and of

---

[14] John Williamson, *The Open Economy and the World Economy* (New York: Basic Books, Inc., 1983), p. 400.

stable currencies has given way to competition and instability. As Robert Gilpin notes, "The spread of protectionism, upheavals in monetary and financial markets, and the evolution of divergent national economic policies among the dominant economies have eroded the foundations of the international system." [15]

Aiding Agriculture Since the New Deal administration of Franklin D. Roosevelt, the federal government has attempted to stabilize farm prices. It has done so through a program of price supports, acreage controls, cash subsidies, and buying and storing of surplus crops. Under the price support program, when farm prices fall below certain minimums, known as "target prices," the government steps in and pays the farmer the difference. The government has also required farmers to hold acreage out of production. And over the years the government has bought up huge farm surpluses. In the early 1970s, however, market prices for agricultural

[15] Robert Gilpin, with the assistance of Jean M. Gilpin, *The Political Economy of International Relations* (Princeton: Princeton University Press, 1987), p. 3.

products were so high that for several years the government did not have to intervene. One reason for the high price levels was the 1972 wheat deal with the Soviet Union, in which the Russians bought nineteen million tons of grain from the United States for more than $1 billion.

Early in 1980, however, after the Soviet invasion of Afghanistan, President Carter announced an embargo on the seventeen million tons of grain, mostly feed corn, that American firms had planned to sell to the Soviet Union. Although the administration budgeted almost $3 billion to support grain prices to make up for the embargo, the move in a presidential election year dismayed most farmers in the Corn Belt. Two weeks before the election, the United States signed an agreement to sell up to thirty-two million tons of grain to China over four years. Both the embargo and the timing of the sale to Beijing were reminders that the government's actions as promoter and regulator often have political implications. In 1981 President Reagan ended the embargo on grain sales to the Soviet Union.

But with the nation's 2.9 million farmers producing more than they can sell profitably, there were still

Farmers demonstrate in Washington for higher prices.

enormous problems in agriculture. In 1983, the Reagan administration tried a one-year experiment, spending $12 billion on a Payment in Kind (PIK) program that gave farmers government surplus grain in return for not planting their land.

Two years later, Congress tried another approach. The Food and Agricultural Security Act of 1985 gradually lowered government price supports to discourage farmers from overproducing. Under the act, farmers were also compensated for planting trees and grass instead of crops on some lands, in order to prevent soil erosion. In 1991, 63.9 million acres, or 16 percent of the total available farmland, was taken out of production as a result of the act.

The Food, Agriculture, Conservation, and Trade Act of 1990, which revised the 1985 law, allows farmers to plant up to one-quarter of their acreage with the crop best suited to their region in order to bring the highest market price. The law was designed to encourage farmers to produce for profit rather than growing crops to collect government subsidies.

Government and Labor

As in the case of business, labor is both regulated and assisted by the federal government. Today organized labor wields great economic and political power in the United States. This was not always the case; the history of the labor movement in America is one of long struggle, intermittent violence, and only gradual recognition.

The industrialization of the nineteenth century brought American laborers job opportunities in factories but scant bargaining power with employers. As a result they worked long hours at low wages and under hazardous working conditions. In 1881 Samuel Gompers, a London-born cigarmaker, founded what became the American Federation of Labor (AFL). The Federation fought for "bread-and-butter" improvements — the eight-hour day, higher pay, fringe benefits, and restrictions on child labor. The AFL was largely a federation of craft unions — groups of skilled workers organized by trades: construction, printing, mining, clothing manufacturing, and others.

The Great Depression, which threw millions of people out of work, and the liberal policies of the New Deal created a favorable climate for the labor movement. In the mid-1930s a group of labor leaders within the AFL began to organize industrial unions in the mass-production industries, thus bringing unskilled workers into a labor movement dominated until then by craft unions. Led by John L. Lewis, head of the United Mine Workers, the dissidents formed a new labor organization that became known in 1938 as the Congress of Industrial Organizations (CIO). The CIO rapidly won recognition from the automotive, steel, rubber, and other industries. In 1955 the AFL merged with the CIO. By 1992 there were 16.6 million union members in the United States, of which about fourteen million belonged to unions in the AFL-CIO.

In its early years the labor movement was unable to gain protection in the courts, so in the 1920s it turned to Congress for help. As early as 1926, the Railway Labor Act stated labor's right to organize and established a National Mediation Board to assist in settling rail strikes. The Norris-LaGuardia Act of 1932 sharply restricted the power of the courts to issue injunctions in labor disputes. Up to that time employers were frequently able to break strikes by obtaining court injunctions against the unions. The National Labor Relations Act of 1935 was labor's great milestone. Sponsored by Senator Robert F. Wagner, Democrat, of New York, it established labor's right to collective bargaining and barred employers from setting up "company unions" (unions controlled by the employer) or discriminating against any worker for union activity or membership. The act also established the National Labor Relations Board (NLRB), an independent regulatory agency that supervises union elections and determines unfair labor practices. The Fair Labor Standards Act of 1938 established a minimum wage for American workers, a maximum forty-hour workweek, and time-and-a-half for overtime. It also outlawed child labor. Over the years, the minimum wage law has been amended by Congress and its coverage expanded. By 1992 the federal minimum wage was $4.25 per hour, and the law covered more than eighty million workers.

The power gained by labor during the New Deal inevitably brought a political reaction. The National Labor Relations Act had placed restrictions on employers but none on unions. In 1947 Congress passed the Taft-Hartley Act, which sought to shift some of labor's newly won power back to management. The act prohibited the "closed shop," under which only union members may be hired, but it did permit the "union shop," under which any person may be hired provided he or she joins the union within a specified time. Under Section 14B of the Taft-Hartley Act, twenty-one states (ten in the South) passed state "right to work" legislation to outlaw the union shop. The act also defined and

prohibited unfair labor practices by unions; expanded the membership of the NLRB, an agency that employers had considered too favorable to labor; barred labor unions from making political contributions; and outlawed strikes by government employees. Finally, the law provided that in strikes creating a national emergency, the president can seek a court injunction against a union during an eighty-day "cooling off period."

Big labor unions continued to prosper and grow, despite the restrictions of the Taft-Hartley Act. And the legislation had one result that its Republican sponsors had not intended: because passage of the law demonstrated to labor that legislation aimed at unions could

win support in Congress, it had the effect of increasing the political activity of labor unions. Often, although not always, that labor support went to Democrats.

In the late 1950s a Senate committee held a series of hearings to investigate labor racketeering. Two successive Teamsters Union presidents, Dave Beck and James R. Hoffa, eventually went to jail after the disclosures, and the AFL-CIO expelled the Teamsters. The televised hearings brought national recognition to the Senate committee's chief counsel, Robert F. Kennedy. It also led to demands for reform legislation.

The Labor Reform Act of 1959 (Landrum-Griffin Act) grew out of the hearings. The act (1) required unions to file elaborate financial reports, constitutions, and bylaws with the Secretary of Labor; (2) granted union members the right to elect officers by secret ballot; (3) barred ex-convicts from holding union office; and (4) tightened Taft-Hartley provisions against secondary boycotts, organizational picketing, and other labor practices that employers felt gave unions an unfair advantage.

Despite provisions for injunctions that sometimes avert or delay major strikes, the public is often unprotected against walkouts that may inconvenience millions of people — airline, rail, and garbage strikes, for example. Compulsory arbitration to settle major labor disputes has not won wide acceptance, and the problem of disruptive strikes in an industrial society remains.

Garbage strike, New York City

Because unions have concentrated on bread-and-butter gains through collective bargaining, organized labor has made great economic progress in the United States. The extent of labor's *political* power is less clear. Unlike many industrial nations, the United States has never had a major, enduring "labor party." Rather than run its own candidates for political office, labor has usually worked through the two-party system. Since the New Deal era, labor has usually supported the national Democratic party, but it carefully watches the records of members of Congress in both parties and supports those whom it considers friendly to labor.

Although labor support is vital to many political candidates, the concept of a deliverable "labor vote" is dubious since union members are also Republicans and Democrats as well as members of other groups. In the 1972 presidential campaign, for example, the organization's executive council failed to support the Democratic nominee and instead voted to remain neutral in the presidential race. That November, union members voted 54 percent for Nixon to 46 percent for McGovern.[16] In 1984, Walter Mondale, the Democratic candidate, enjoyed strong support from organized labor, so much so that critics charged he was overly obligated to special interests, and particularly labor unions. In 1992, Bill Clinton, the Democratic candidate, also enjoyed the support of organized labor.

Union membership has been declining, however, as the nation has shifted from manufacturing to service industries. As a result, labor's base of blue-collar workers has been shrinking. By the 1990s, unsuccessful strikes in some industries reflected the weakened position of organized labor.

The Department of Labor, which achieved cabinet status in 1913, administers and enforces laws relating to the welfare of wage earners in the United States. Its responsibilities include manpower and job-training programs, administering the wages and hours law, and enforcing the safety and health standards for workers set by various federal laws.

MANAGING THE ECONOMY

Although America is a nation that prides itself on its system of "free enterprise," most voters, whether conservative or liberal, look to the government in Washington to provide remedies to the country's economic

---

[16] Gallup poll, *Washington Post*, December 14, 1972, p. A4.

problems. Those problems vary with the times, but whether they are inflation, unemployment, high interest rates, or foreign competition, the president and his advisers are expected to provide solutions. Today most people expect the federal government to exercise a major responsibility for the health, stability, and growth of the national economy.

The federal government took a major role in economic affairs with the coming of Franklin D. Roosevelt's New Deal. When Roosevelt was inaugurated in 1933, at the height of the Great Depression, 13 million people—25 percent of the labor force—were unemployed. And unemployment remained high until the rapid recovery of the economy during the Second World War. National growth with full employment became a major goal in the postwar world.

The Employment Act of 1946 spelled out in law the responsibility of the federal government for the economy and required it "to promote maximum employment, production, and purchasing power." The law directed the president to submit an annual economic report to Congress; it created a three-member Council of Economic Advisers to assist the president; and it established a Joint Economic Committee, made up of members of the House and Senate, to study the president's report and the economy.

In making economic policy, the president has a number of tools and advisers available to him—the Council of Economic Advisers, the Office of Management and Budget, the secretary of the treasury, the Department of Labor, and the economists and experts who staff these government agencies. He can invoke his powers to delay major strikes under the Taft-Hartley Act. Various presidents have had power to negotiate and alter U.S. tariffs. Through his appointment power, the president can influence the makeup of the Federal Reserve Board. And, of course, the president is free to consult outside economists and experts in the private sector, including the universities. The president can also impose economic controls or voluntary guidelines on prices and wages. He may call upon all of these resources in shaping the fiscal and monetary policies of the federal government. Yet presidents in recent years have not always been successful in controlling inflation, recession, or high unemployment. In part, this may be due to world economic conditions—factors that are beyond any president's control. But it also may stem from the nature of the American economic system, in which there are limits on the government's ability to manage the economy.

The United States operates predominantly under an economic system of free enterprise, or capitalism. Under capitalism, there is private ownership of the means of production. In such a system, in its purest form, there is little room for government; people own private property, either directly or as shareholders; and as consumers they participate in a free marketplace that responds to the laws of supply and demand. In practice, however, the United States has a *mixed*, or modified, free-enterprise system in which both private industry and government play important roles.

The individual's economic freedom is sharply limited by federal, state, and local economic policies. To begin with, the higher the federal, state, and local taxes a person pays, the less money he or she will have to spend on consumer goods. If government fails to prevent a recession, the person may be out of work. If government fails to prevent inflation, the dollar buys less; and retired people living on pensions and savings may find their fixed incomes inadequate.

In general, Democrats have favored a larger role for government in regulating the welfare of society and the individual, and Republicans generally have favored less government intervention. But the basic responsibility of government for economic policy is now well established.

Economic Controls

Most presidents have been reluctant to take the drastic step of imposing compulsory controls on the economy, although President Nixon did so. In 1971 Nixon announced a program of sweeping economic controls. His economic policy amounted to a sharp reversal of traditional Republican philosophy and of his own previous statements. There was precedent for Nixon's actions; economic controls were imposed during the First World War, the Second World War, and the Korean War. There was also some peacetime precedent, since for a time controls were kept on prices and rents during the Truman administration.

The economic stabilization measures imposed by President Nixon were extraordinary rules issued to meet an inflationary crisis. Usually, the federal government has attempted to influence the total shape of the economy through two sets of tools: *fiscal policy* and *monetary policy*. The fiscal tools of the government are primarily spending and taxation. The monetary tools are control of the supply of money and control of the supply of credit through the Federal Reserve System.

Fiscal Policy

Since the New Deal, many government economists have been influenced by the thinking of the British economist John Maynard Keynes. Keynes argued that when people did not consume and invest enough to maintain national income at full employment levels, government must step in and regulate the economy through *fiscal policy*—by cutting taxes or increasing spending in the public sector, or both. (As discussed at the outset of this chapter, the "supply side" economists of the Reagan administration took a different view of fiscal policy, emphasizing both tax and budget cuts.) Keynesian economists and their modern successors place major emphasis on fiscal policy to guide the economy, although they recognize the role of monetary policy.

The Budget The federal budget reflects an allocation of resources by the national government. But the budget is also an important tool of fiscal policy. During a time of inflation, the president may cut spending and ask for higher taxes to cool down the economy. In a recession he may propose a bigger budget, more public works spending, and lower taxes. Or, as Reagan did in 1981, a president may call for both lower taxes and less spending. By planning a budget surplus or deficit, the federal government attempts to pump money into or out of the economy, to stimulate it or slow it down. In recent years, however, repeated federal deficits became part of the problem, rather than a solution to the nation's economic worries.

But the president must share with Congress his fiscal control over the economy. Only Congress can vote to spend federal funds. It does so in a three-step process. First, it passes *budget resolutions* to set overall spending targets. Second, it passes *authorizations* to spend federal money. Third, it passes *appropriations* bills to pay for the spending it has authorized. Under this system legislative committees deal with the substance of programs and, by authorizing funds, set forth their view of what *ought* to be spent. Within that framework, the appropriations committees decide what *actually* may be spent.

The idea behind this system is that appropriations committees have an overview of expenditures by Congress—which legislative or "program" committees do not have—and are therefore in a better position to allocate funds. Since an authorization without an appropriation is meaningless, the system places great power in the hands of the House and Senate appropriations committees and subcommittees. Congress may increase or cut the president's appropriations requests.

Once money is appropriated, Congress has its own accountant to check up on how it is spent — the Comptroller General of the United States, who heads the General Accounting Office (GAO).

The Congressional Budget and Impoundment Act of 1974 established the budget committees in the House and Senate and created a new framework for Congress to deal with the president's budget. In an attempt to eliminate mounting deficits, the congressional budget process was further modified by the Gramm-Rudman Act of 1985, and the later version passed in 1987. (See Chapter 12.)

Three years later, Congress again modified the budget process, enacting the complicated Omnibus Budget Reconciliation Act of 1990. The new law set limits on appropriations for domestic, international, and defense programs. It put mandatory spending programs such as Medicare on a "pay as you go" basis. Under the act, the president submits his budget request on the first Monday in February each year. Congress is required to adopt a budget resolution by April 15, and the fiscal year begins on October 1. The 1990 law supplemented, but did not repeal, the Gramm-Rudman acts.

None of these laws made much of a dent on the huge annual federal deficit, which by 1993 had reached

Table 15-2

The Federal Budget: Where the Money Comes From

Source	1993 Estimate (in billions)	Percent
Individual income taxes	519.6	34
Corporation income taxes	103.2	7
Social insurance taxes and contributions	446.7	29
Excise taxes	48.1	3
All other receipts	51.6	4
Borrowing	352.1	23
Total budget receipts	$1,521.3	100%

SOURCE: Adapted from *Budget of the United States Government Fiscal Year 1993*, pp. 1–290, 2–3.

an estimated $352.1 billion. The deficit, which represents the difference between revenues and spending by the federal government, was not only an economic problem; it had also become a political issue. In 1992, for example, both major-party presidential candidates were criticized for failing to explain how they would reduce the deficit.

Taxes "The Congress shall have Power to lay and collect Taxes." And Congress, as every taxpayer knows, exercises this constitutional authority. Under the budget for fiscal 1993 the federal government planned to spend $1,517 billion, most of it raised from taxes. Of every dollar the government expected to take in during fiscal 1993, 34 cents came from individual income taxes, 7 cents from corporate income taxes, 29 cents from social-insurance taxes, 3 cents from excise taxes (taxes on commodities), and 4 cents from other revenue sources. Borrowing accounted for another 23 cents.[17] Estimated tax receipts for 1993 appear in Table 15-2.

As these figures show, individual income taxes are the federal government's largest single source of revenue. The federal income tax is graduated — although less sharply since passage of the 1986 tax reform law — on the theory that persons with higher incomes should be taxed at a higher rate. But taxpayers at all levels grumble about the tax squeeze; not many people enjoy paying their taxes or consider them low.

Until this century the Constitution required the federal government to collect income taxes in proportion to state population. The Sixteenth Amendment, ratified in 1913, permitted the government to levy a

"I'm afraid I must concur with Dr. Hamilton and Dr. Movin. The cause of death was taxes."

Drawing by Henry Martins © 1977 The New Yorker Magazine, Inc.

---

[17] Adapted from *Budget of the United States Government Fiscal Year 1993*, p. 1–290.

general income tax. Since that time, however, various interest groups have lobbied Congress and won special tax advantages. Until 1975 the major oil producers had their "depletion allowance." Business executives still enjoy certain "expense account" deductions. There are also other "loopholes" in the tax law. A rich person can afford to hire a high-priced tax attorney to find them. People in high-income brackets may set up foundations, invest in tax-free municipal bonds or various types of "tax shelters," or take business losses that enable them to avoid high taxes.

By the end of the 1960s growing public awareness of inequalities in the federal tax laws led to talk of "a taxpayers' revolt." Congress responded by passing tax reform legislation in 1969, 1976, 1981, and 1986.

The 1986 tax-reform measure, passed during the Reagan administration, was the most extensive revision in the nation's tax laws in forty years. The Tax Reform Act of 1986 cut individual rates to 15, 28, and 33 percent and reduced corporate rates to 34 percent. The measure ended the preferential treatment for capital gains, and ended or modified a wide variety of taxpayer deductions.

The politics of taxation result in intense pressures on Congress from interest groups when changes in the structure of the tax laws are under consideration. And Congress and the president often fight political battles over how tax policy should be used as a fiscal tool to slow down or stimulate the economy. The use of fiscal policy to control the economy depends, in theory, on delicate timing; but Congress tends to move very slowly in passing tax legislation.

And tax and spending policies are often at the center of the nation's political debate. President Bush broke his famous 1988 campaign promise, "read my lips, no new taxes," two years later when he agreed to $164 billion in new taxes over five years as part of a compromise with the Democratic-controlled Congress. The broken promise came back to haunt Bush in the 1992 presidential campaign, when he again pledged, if elected, not to raise taxes. Bush sought to make "trust" a central issue in the campaign, asking repeatedly who could better be trusted to run the country. That theme was undercut by Bush's own broken promise on taxes.

Borrowing When the federal government spends more than it earns, it has to borrow. The national debt stood at $16.2 billion in 1930, or almost 18 percent of the nation's Gross National Product (GNP), the total national output of goods and services; by 1992 the na-

"**The Gross National Product . . . Its favorite drink is oil . . .**"

Drawing by Jeff MacNelly, from *A Political Bestiary* by Eugene J. McCarthy and James J. Kilpatrick, McGraw-Hill Book Company, 1979

tional debt was more than $4 trillion, or 67 percent of the Gross National Product. The government borrows by selling federal securities to individuals, corporations, and other institutions. In 1917 Congress passed a statutory debt limit, or ceiling, on government borrowing, but the limit has been revised upward many times. Borrowing costs money; in fiscal 1993 the government expected to spend $237 billion, or 15.6 percent of the federal budget, on interest payments.

Monetary Policy

Government also attempts to regulate the economy by monetary policy — controlling the supply of money and the cost and availability of credit. It does this through the operations of the Federal Reserve System. "The Fed," as the system is often called, was established in 1913. Prior to that time, the United States had no way in which to expand and contract the money supply according to the needs of the economy. To provide such an elastic system, Congress created the Federal Reserve.

The Fed is headed by a Board of Governors. Although the board's seven members are appointed by the president with the approval of the Senate, they serve overlapping fourteen-year terms and are largely independent of both Congress and the White House. The chairperson, appointed by the president for a term of four years, can, and sometimes does, oppose the policies of the administration. During the Reagan administration, for example, there was frequent tension between the president and the chairman of the Fed.

The Federal Reserve is the central banking system of the United States; it operates through twelve Federal Reserve Banks and twenty-five branches across the nation. All national banks and about 10 percent of state banks are members of the system.

When individuals or corporations need money, they normally borrow from a bank. When banks need money, they may borrow from the Federal Reserve System. The Federal Reserve is, therefore, a banker's bank. When it lends to the banks, it can, in effect, create new money.

Through its control of the flow of money and credit within the United States, the Fed attempts to pump more money into the economy when a recession threatens. In a time of rising prices and excessive spending, the Fed normally tries to tighten the supply of money and credit so that people will have less to spend. As one chairman remarked, the Fed tries "to lean against the prevailing economic winds." It does so chiefly in four ways:

1. Open Market Operations. Banks lend money to people in relation to the amount of reserves the banks have on deposit with the Federal Reserve. When the Fed sells government bonds on the open market, the effect is to reduce bank reserves and tighten credit; banks then have less money to lend to people. Or, the Federal Reserve can buy government securities and expand credit.

2. The Fed can raise or lower the "discount rate" that it charges member banks for loans. This affects interest rates in the economy generally.

3. It can raise or lower the size of the reserves that member banks must keep in the Federal Reserve banks against their deposits and thus tighten or expand credit.

4. It can raise or lower the "margin requirements" for persons buying securities. The margin requirement defines how much money people can borrow to purchase stocks.

In recent years, the "Chicago school" of economists, led by Milton Friedman of the University of Chicago, has suggested that the money supply — the quantity of money in circulation — is the key to government regulation of the economy. Friedman has argued that interest rates, which are one aspect of monetary policy, and fiscal policy — taxes and spending — have little impact or importance. He also has argued that the money supply should be increased at a constant rate. Friedman received the Nobel Prize in 1976.

His views have won increasing, but by no means universal, acceptance in the United States and abroad. Most United States economists believe that a stock market crash and a depression as severe as that which began in 1929 are unlikely to happen again because there are more built-in economic stabilizers today. Even so, the sharp dip in the stock market in October of 1987, when the Dow Jones Industrial Average fell a record 508 points in one day, caused great concern in Wall Street, in Washington, and in the country, and had repercussions in markets around the world.

And economists and politicians widely disagree over the best way to maintain price stability, full employment, and economic growth. Some measures are politically safer to take than others; for example, it is easier for government to spend money on public works to combat recession than it is to impose wage–price controls to fight inflation. Whatever steps an administration takes carry great political risks if they fail. Normally both the president and Congress try to steer a safe course between the twin reefs of recession and inflation. Prosperity and "bread-and-butter" concerns are often key election issues, as was illustrated in 1992, when the faltering economy dominated the presidential campaign.

GOVERNMENT AS PROTECTOR

During the 1992 presidential campaign, both major-party candidates talked about the crisis in health care in America. In that year, there were about 36 million Americans without any health insurance.

Bill Clinton, the Democratic candidate, promised if elected to sponsor a program to guarantee health care for all Americans. Clinton said he would require private employers to provide and pay for 80 percent of the cost of health insurance, with the federal government helping to pay for health care protection for the unemployed. President Bush, seeking reelection, proposed a program of vouchers and tax credits to make it easier for people to purchase health insurance. Both plans would have barred insurance companies from excluding pre-existing medical conditions from their coverage.

The Democratic and Republican candidates for the highest office in the land clashed over the health insurance issue in speeches, and in their televised debates. Their exchanges were of intense personal interest to millions of viewers who could not afford health insurance to protect their families.

In the past four decades the national government has enacted multibillion-dollar social-welfare programs — ranging from school breakfasts for the young to social security for the aged. By the late 1970s, however, a degree of disillusionment had set in among liberals and conservatives alike about the ability of government to solve social problems with government programs. Even so, while many Americans might criticize specific programs — the welfare system, for example — by and large people expect the government to act as protector of the general welfare. Proposing to tamper with or modify established social programs that enjoy broad public support carries a high political risk.

In the rest of this chapter, we shall explore some of the important aspects of government as protector. It should be kept in mind, of course, that the government does not always successfully fulfill its role as protector of the public. Despite screening by the Food and Drug Administration, dangerous prescription drugs have been sold to the public. Hazardous nuclear waste

escaped into the atmosphere and into the ground for years from the government's plutonium plant in Rocky Flats, Colorado, which was finally shut down for safety violations in 1988. Radioactive materials escaped from other government nuclear facilities as well. Congress has passed laws to clean up the air we breathe, but the executive branch has sometimes enforced those laws in ways that favor the polluters, not the public. As always, in studying the operations of government we should remember that there is often a gap between the goal and the reality.

Government and the Consumer

Today, most Americans would agree that government has a responsibility to protect ordinary consumers from the perils of the marketplace. Three decades ago few citizens were aware of consumer issues. That the picture changed dramatically was, to a considerable extent, the work of a single crusader for consumer protection, attorney Ralph Nader.

In his book, *Unsafe at Any Speed*, published in 1965, Nader charged that the automobile industry bore partial responsibility for many highway accidents and deaths by making cars that emphasized style over safety. Nader was then investigated by private detectives hired by attorneys for the General Motors Corporation (GM).

UNSAFE TO ATTACK GENERAL MOTORS

In 1965, Ralph Nader, then a thirty-one-year-old Connecticut attorney, criticized the safety of American automobiles, particularly the General Motors Corvair, in his book *Unsafe at Any Speed*. General Motors, through an attorney in Washington, hired a "private eye" to investigate Nader. Senate investigators found that the New York detective agency, Vincent Gillen Associates, Inc., had issued the following instructions to its "gumshoes":

> [Nader] apparently is a freelance writer and attorney. Recently he published a book *Unsafe at Any Speed*, highly critical of the automotive industry's interest in safety. Since then our clients' client apparently made some cursory inquiries into Nader to ascertain his expertise, his interest, his background, his

backers, etc. They have found out relatively little about him, and that little is detailed below. Our job is to check his life and current activities to determine "what makes him tick," such as his real interest in safety, his supporters, if any, his politics, his marital status, his friends, his women, boys, etc., drinking, dope, jobs — in fact all facets of his life. This may entail surveillance which will be undertaken only upon the OK of Vince Gillen as transmitted by him to the personnel of Vincent Gillen Associates, Inc.

—Hearings before the Subcommittee on Executive Reorganization, Committee on Government Operations, United States Senate, *Federal Role in Traffic Safety*, March 22, 1966

Consumer advocate Ralph Nader

A Senate subcommittee disclosed that the private detectives had put Nader under surveillance and had even checked into his sex life. As a result of the Senate investigation, James M. Roche, the president of GM, found it prudent to apologize publicly to Nader at a committee hearing.[18]

The congressional investigation of GM's flagrant action against a private citizen made Nader a national figure overnight. In the years that followed, he played a vital role in the passage of five major federal consumer laws. GM removed the Corvair from production after Nader charged that the car was hazardous to drive under certain conditions. Today, major auto companies routinely recall cars from consumers to correct safety defects. Ralph Nader's crusades found a response among the public, the press, Congress, and the executive branch.

The basic demand of the consumer movement is that government step in to protect buyers from hazardous products, shoddy merchandise, mislabeling, fraudulent sales techniques, consumer credit abuses, and other deceptive or dangerous practices. "Consumer-

---

[18] In 1970, four years after the Senate hearings, GM paid Nader $425,000 in an out-of-court settlement of his invasion-of-privacy suit. See *New York Times*, August 14, 1970, p. 1.

ism" holds that when business will not police itself, government must act.

The person who must return a coffeepot to the repair shop three times before it is fixed properly; the child playing with an inflammable toy; the inner-city resident talked into buying an overpriced bedroom suite for "only $799"; the family injured in an auto crash because of defective tires — all are victims of consumer abuses. Many products that Americans buy seem to have "built-in" obsolescence — that is, they are designed to wear out after a certain amount of time.

Consumer frauds victimize the most those who can afford it the least. Various studies have shown that "the poor pay more." Residents of the inner city often buy low-quality merchandise at high prices. Why? One reason is that neighborhood merchants extend "easy" credit terms to poor people who may not be able to buy on credit in major department stores. And, as David Caplovitz has noted in his study of poverty areas in Manhattan, "neighborhood merchants . . . compensate for extending credit to poor risks by high markups."[19] The result is that poor families often end up paying higher prices for appliances such as television sets and washing machines than do more affluent families.[20] To deal with customers who cannot keep up the payments, the merchant can use the weapons of repossession and salary garnishment, backed by the power of the law. During the 1960s and 1970s, legislation was

---

[19] David Caplovitz, *The Poor Pay More* (New York: Free Press of Glencoe, 1963), p. 85.
[20] Ibid., p. 84.

"Granted the public has a *right* to know what's in a hot dog, but does the public really *want* to know what's in a hot dog?"

Drawing by Richter © 1978 The New Yorker Magazine, Inc.

passed to deal with consumer problems, and limited machinery to deal with those problems was established within the executive branch. Presidents Kennedy, Johnson, Nixon, Ford, Carter, Reagan, and Bush all appointed staff assistants for consumer affairs. Several federal agencies are involved in consumer matters, but the principal responsibility is in the hands of the Federal Trade Commission.

The principal consumer laws include:

1. *Auto safety* (1966). One law requires manufacturers to meet federal standards for automobile and tire safety, and another requires each state to establish federally approved highway safety programs or lose 10 percent of federal highway construction funds.

2. *Truth-in-packaging* (1966). To help shoppers make price comparisons, a law was passed requiring manufacturers to label their products more clearly. But it does not require standard package sizes, which would aid shoppers in threading their way through the supermarket jungle of "jumbo," "family," and "large economy" sizes.

3. *Meat and poultry inspection* (1967 and 1968). Two laws were designed to tighten consumer protection against poor-quality meat and poultry. Prior to this legislation these products were subject to federal inspection when shipped between states, but products consumed within a state were subject only to state inspection. And, seven states had no meat inspection at all.

4. *Truth-in-lending* (1968). This legislation requires merchants and lenders to provide full, honest, and understandable information about credit terms. For example, a customer who agrees to pay "only 3 percent per month" must now be told that the *annual* interest rate is actually 36 percent.

5. *Product safety* (1972). The law establishes an independent five-member Consumer Product Safety Commission. The commission has broad power to act against hazardous products that by 1991 caused an estimated 12 million consumer injuries each year.

In almost every case, industry has lobbied against consumer bills and has often succeeded in weakening the final versions. There is some danger, therefore, that the passage of consumer legislation may create the appearance of government regulation without the reality. Consumer advocates in the 1990s were increasingly focusing their attention on how consumer laws are put into effect and on their real impact once enacted. At the same time, the power of the consumer movement had diminished as Congress and the electorate became preoccupied with economic and other issues.

The General Welfare

By 1993, 45 million Americans — retired or disabled workers and their dependents — received about $299.7 billion in social security payments. Another 4.4 million

---

ACCELERATING PROBLEMS OF THE CONSUMER

The gas gauge was nearing "empty" so the University of Arizona co-ed pulled off the freeway into the nearest service station. All went routinely enough until suddenly she noticed white smoke billowing out from under the open hood. The attendant, standing over it with a properly concerned expression, informed her that the car needed "a new accelerator in its generator" and that if she tried to drive out of the station without having it fixed, the car would be ruined.

One tank of gas and $119 later the student was back on the freeway, heading for the university campus. To confirm her growing suspicion, she took the car to her regular mechanic for a recheck. His verdict: Potassium powder had been used to simulate smoke, and she had been "conned" (a generator does not have an accelerator).

The case is not as exceptional as one might think. Despite stepped-up efforts by law-enforcement agencies and more widespread and vehement complaining on the part of car owners, deceptive auto-repair practices persist as a major consumer problem.

— *Christian Science Monitor*, January 29, 1970

"IT'S ALL TURNING TO RUST"

"This is your 'shining city,'" Art Bensley, a Baltimore steelworker, said as he drove about the crumbling ruins of plants and factories that had been shut down in recent years as the nation's industrial base steadily declined.

"Our grandfathers and our fathers — they all worked in these mills," he continued. "They built America down here in a sense. Now it's all turning to rust. They say that next they're going to shut my mill."

In the distance, hard by another closed mill, a ship was unloading foreign-made cars.

"I don't blame the Japanese or the Germans for working hard and shipping cars over here," Mr. Bensley said. "What I want to know is how and why we got to the point that we don't make so many of our own cars. Whose fault is this? Don't we need some new policies? Isn't it time we stopped this?"

He waved his hand at the rusting mills that spread as far as the eye can see, to a road spur leading to Interstate 70, the concrete belt that stretches across the waist of the country, from Baltimore through Kansas City and on to the west, almost to the Pacific. On each side of Interstate 70, there is almost endless evidence of the economic and political trouble that afflicts America, and there is anguish in the voices of the people who live along the way.

—*New York Times*, February 9, 1992

families received public assistance (welfare) payments totaling about $20.4 billion, of which the federal government paid half (with state and local governments paying the rest). Another $17.9 billion a year in federal benefits went to 4.8 million persons under the Supplemental Security Income program. In addition, it was estimated that a weekly average of 3.1 million jobless workers would collect $28.9 billion in unemployment insurance.[21]

Yet prior to 1935 these programs did not exist. The hardships of old age, ill health, poverty, unemployment, blindness, or disability were problems for individuals, their families, private charity, states, and local communities.

The Depression of the 1930s changed all that. Millions lost their jobs, and a blight of hunger and poverty descended on the land. "Brother, can you spare a dime?" was a popular song of 1932. America realized that individuals needed help from the national government to maintain their income in hard times. In the midst of the Great Depression, Franklin D. Roosevelt proposed, and Congress passed, the landmark Social Security Act of 1935. Although to some Americans it seemed a revolutionary step at the time, the United States was the last major industrial nation in the world to adopt a general system of social security.

There are two kinds of social-welfare programs in operation, both designed to guarantee personal economic security to individuals. One is called *social insurance*. The social security program is, in effect, a compulsory national insurance program, in theory self-financed by taxes on employers and employees. The other kind of program, *public assistance*, has no pay-as-

---

[21] Data provided by Social Security Administration; Office of Family Assistance, U.S. Department of Health and Human Services; and Unemployment Insurance Claims Office, U.S. Department of Labor.

you-go features; it simply distributes public funds to people who are poor. (Recipients are usually said to be "on welfare.") The distinction is important, because each approach has significant political consequences.

Social insurance is widely accepted because it is "earned." People assume they have a "right" to retirement income after a lifetime of work. But "welfare" programs do not enjoy the same acceptance by the public. Many Americans who receive welfare payments, and many others who do not, believe society has a responsibility to care for those who are less fortunate. However, as Gilbert Y. Steiner points out, some Americans

> resent supporting those who can't make their own way. . . . The idea of "toughening up" is forever popular. Toughening up, it is argued, will drive the cheaters out, the slackers to work, the unwed mothers into chastity; and it will save money. It is this clash between the ideas of public aid as a right and public aid as a matter of sufferance, to be granted with suspicion, with strings, and with restraints, that is reflected in public policy debates and political action.[22]

Social Security The Social Security Act of 1935 and its later amendments provide for both social insurance and public assistance programs. The insurance aspects fall into four categories: old-age and survivors insurance, disability insurance, Medicare, and unemployment insurance.

When people talk about receiving "social security," they generally mean the monthly cash payments received by retired, older people. A man or woman who reaches the age of sixty-two may draw partial social security payments if he or she has worked enough years to qualify — ten years in 1992. Men and women who have worked long enough to qualify may receive social security at the full, higher rate beginning at age sixty-five, a figure that will gradually rise to age sixty-seven by the year 2027. The payments depend on a person's average earnings over a period of years. In September 1992 the average monthly benefit for a retired worker was $632.19. (Examples of social security payments are shown in Table 15–3.)

As originally passed, social security payments provided only retirement benefits. In 1939 the program was expanded to provide payments to dependents and survivors of workers covered by the system. And in 1956 it was expanded to include disabled workers.

---

[22] Gilbert Y. Steiner, *Social Insecurity: The Politics of Welfare* (Chicago: Rand McNally, 1966), pp. 7–8.

Table 15-3
Examples of Average Monthly Cash Payments Under Social Security

Retired worker, all ages	$632.19
Retired worker, age 62–64	$543.63
Retired worker, age 65+	$641.84
Retired men, all ages	$712.49
Retired women, all ages	$544.09
Wives and husbands of retired workers, all ages	$326.11
Children of retired workers	$275.41
Disabled workers, all ages	$607.45

SOURCE: Data provided by Social Security Administration, U.S. Department of Health and Human Services. Data as of September 1992.

Over the years, Congress has extended social security coverage to virtually all types of workers. The system is financed by a social security tax levied equally on employers and employees. Self-employed persons also must pay a social security tax. In 1993 employers and employees each paid 7.65 percent of an employee's income up to a ceiling of $57,600 (earnings beyond this amount were not taxed for social security purposes); self-employed persons paid 15.3 percent.

Inflation hits hardest at persons living on fixed incomes, such as retired workers who depend on social security payments. Because of this, Congress has linked social security benefits to the cost of living; increases in the amounts paid out under the program are now as a rule automatic.

SOMEDAY SON, NONE OF THIS WILL BE YOURS...

SOCIAL SECURITY
10100-000

Drawing by Mike Peters for the *Dayton Daily News*. Reprinted by permission of United Features Syndicate, Inc.

Social Security is the largest of the federal *entitlement programs*, which are programs mandated by law and not subject to annual review by Congress or the president. By fiscal 1993, these entitlement programs, including interest, accounted for 64 percent of the total federal budget. Since mandatory programs cannot be cut, unless Congress changes the law, their continuing growth made it even more difficult to control the deficit.

By the time President Reagan took office in 1981, the social security program was in crisis. The expansion of the social security system, coupled with continuing inflation, had created enormous financial strain on the system. To put it simply, social security was running out of money. Social security taxes go into trust funds so that the program can be self-sustaining. But payments to recipients were outpacing the growth of the system's reserves. Part of the problem was demographic: compared to when the program started, there were, proportionately, fewer people of working age to pay taxes and more people of retirement age to draw benefits, and this trend can be expected to continue.

In the spring of 1981, the Reagan administration proposed a delay in social security cost-of-living increases as part of an $88 billion program of social security cuts. A storm of controversy erupted. The president and the leaders of the House and Senate then appointed a special bipartisan commission, which proposed legislation to save the system. In March of 1983, Congress passed the compromise rescue plan, which provided $165 billion more for the program through increased payroll taxes and other measures, and cut benefits for those who chose to retire early. The legislation was designed to give workers reasonable assurance

that old-age benefits through social security would be available into the next century. Because people were living longer, further changes probably would have to be made in the system; for example, Congress might decide to reduce benefits for wealthier persons.

Medicare In 1965 Congress added health insurance for persons sixty-five and over to the social security program.[23] Medicare helps to pay hospital bills, and for those who choose to pay an extra amount ($31.80 a month in 1992), it also pays part of doctor bills. In 1992 there were an estimated thirty-five million people on Medicare, most of whom had also enrolled in the voluntary insurance program for doctor bills.

The program cost $145.9 billion in fiscal 1993 and will undoubtedly cost more in the future, even if it is merged into a general program of national health insurance. Some of the proposed bills to create a national health-insurance system would keep Medicare; others would absorb Medicare into a general plan covering all persons.

In 1988, Congress passed a new law to pay for more of the costs of catastrophic illness for persons eligible for Medicare. It was immediately controversial. The expanded Medicare coverage was to pay for most hospital costs, doctors bills, and prescription drugs, although it did not cover nursing homes. The new law would have meant an extra tax for many older Americans, as much as $1,600 a year in the case of the wealthiest 5 percent. Highly vocal opposition led by this affluent minority killed the measure in little more than a year; Congress repealed the law in 1989 before it could go into effect.

Unemployment Insurance The social security benefits discussed above are paid directly by the federal government. But the Social Security Act of 1935 also virtually forced the states to set up unemployment insurance programs to pay benefits to people out of work. The program is financed by federal and state taxes on employers (and on employees in three states). Every state has an unemployment insurance program, but the size of benefits and the amount of time they are granted vary greatly. Most, but by no means all, workers are covered. In 1992, under emergency legislation, states paid unemployment benefits of twenty-six to forty-six weeks (up to fifty-two weeks in areas of high unemployment). But a weekly payment in 1992 of $171 — the national average

---

[23] In 1992 Medicare also covered three million disabled persons *under* age sixty-five.

— was scarcely enough to support a jobless worker with a family.

Welfare: Politics and Programs The Social Security Act of 1935 created three public assistance or "welfare" programs: old-age assistance; aid to the blind; and the largest program, known later as Aid to Families with Dependent Children (AFDC). In 1950 a fourth program was added — aid to the permanently and totally disabled. Then in 1974 the Supplemental Security Income program (SSI) was established to provide uniform federal benefits to needy aged, blind, or disabled persons.

The federal government provides most of the money for the welfare system in the form of grants to the states. In some states, local governments also assume part of the cost. State and local welfare agencies run the programs.

The welfare system has come under attack on several grounds. First, it does not cover all the poor. Moreover, because the states control the programs, benefits vary sharply. Southern states pay lower welfare benefits than do the big-industrial states of the North.

For many years, more than one-third of the states had some kind of rule barring welfare payments to families in which there was a "man in the house" who was not married to the mother. Welfare recipients objected strongly to this attempt by the states to regulate moral behavior. The United States Supreme Court has ruled that states may no longer restrict welfare payments to dependent children just because there is a "man in the house," unless it can be shown that he is actually contributing some of his income to the support of the children.[24]

The welfare system has frequently been criticized on the grounds that it degrades those whom it is attempting to help. Welfare agencies regularly investigate those receiving payments, and poor people often regard welfare workers as unwelcome detectives. Behind all this is the public suspicion that many welfare recipients are "loafers" and "chiselers."

The welfare program that emerged from the New Deal had been criticized on the basis that it "creates a class of dependent persons and then sustains them in their dependency."[25] During the 1960s an alternative approach evolved, sometimes called a "guaranteed annual income" or a "negative income tax." This concept, if put into action, would guarantee everyone a minimum

---

[24] *King v. Smith,* 392 U.S. 309 (1968); *Lewis v. Martin,* 397 U.S. 552 (1970).

[25] Daniel P. Moynihan, "One Step We Must Take," *Saturday Review of Literature,* May 23, 1970, p. 22.

WELFARE: "IT IS VERY HUMILIATING"

Virginia Velazquez works two days a week at MFY Legal Services, a federally financed group of lawyers and social workers. She juggles calls on a dozen lines with friendly efficiency. Her deep, soft voice moves easily between Spanish and English. She concludes a conversation with "Adiosbyebye!"

With her income of $142 every two weeks, Velazquez would be eligible for supplemental welfare payments. She went on welfare last year but withdrew after three months, preferring poverty.

"It is very frustrating to deal with welfare," she said. "The caseworkers like to downgrade people. It is very humiliating."

The family also receives $205 a month in food stamps, and [daughter] Juanita collects $172 in Aid to Families with Dependent Children every two weeks, part of which she contributes to her mother for room and board.

"It's not easy living this way," . . . "How can they think $205 is enough for six people? We have to buy milk for the children every other day. How do you come up with $65 for a doctor's bill?" . . .

Faced with eviction last January, she struggled with the bureaucracy for a month, including seven days spent at a welfare office, to arrange the $932 emergency grant to pay back rent. . . .

Velazquez's experience is not unusual. A 1981 Ford Foundation study of Puerto Rican women reported that some spent up to three days a week in appointments, shuttling among housing, Medicaid, job services, Supplemental Security Income, food stamps and day-care offices.

—*Washington Post,* April 15, 1984

income, making the existing welfare system unnecessary. In 1972 Congress established the first guaranteed minimum income program, which began in 1974. This Supplemental Security Income program (SSI) replaced a web of state and local programs to provide uniform federal payments to the needy, aged, blind, or disabled. SSI supplemented but did not replace social security payments to such persons.

Congress did not approve welfare reform plans submitted by both President Nixon and President Carter. The Reagan administration proposed, but later abandoned, a plan to transfer welfare and food stamp programs to the states in exchange for the federal government paying the full cost of Medicaid, the program of medical care for needy persons.

In 1988, Congress enacted the first major revision of the nation's welfare laws since their creation in 1935. In an effort to break what critics called the "cycle of dependency," the new law required some able-bodied welfare recipients, except those caring for children under age three, to work or to enroll in job-training programs. The measure also provided for child care for one year for families that lost their eligibility for welfare payments because their earnings had increased.

As noted earlier in this chapter, during the 1992 presidential campaign Bill Clinton proposed a plan to limit persons on welfare to no more than two years.

After that, under Clinton's plan, recipients would have to work in the private sector or in a program of community service. Clinton said the program would eventually cost an additional $6 billion a year in increased funds for job training and tax credits for the working poor.

The Politics of Poverty

"This administration," President Lyndon B. Johnson declared in his first State of the Union message, "today here and now declares unconditional war on poverty in America." [26]

When President Johnson spoke these words in January 1964, many Americans might have wondered what he was talking about. Through the picture window of split-level suburbia, the poor could not be seen. Yet they were there, millions of people living in poverty in the mountains of Appalachia and in the nation's inner cities. When the black urban neighborhoods exploded in flames during the second half of the decade, the poor became more visible.

The federal antipoverty program resulted in part from the publication in 1962 of Michael Harrington's *The Other America*, a book that described in forceful

---

[26] *1964 Congressional Quarterly Almanac*, p. 862.

Job-training session, California Conservation Corps

language the extent of poverty in the United States and had a substantial impact among segments of the public and within the federal government. The poor, he noted, were "across the tracks," out of view of more comfortable Americans.[27] The poor lived, in Ben H. Bagdikian's words, "in the midst of plenty," occupying "a world inside our society in which the American dream is dying." Yet poor people "are not made so differently from their fellow Americans."[28]

Who are the poor?

The federal government answers the question in terms of how many people have incomes below a certain "poverty" level. But to some extent poverty is a relative term; people may feel poor if they have a good deal less than most other people have. And with affluence no farther away than the commercials shown on television, the poor in American society are constantly reminded of their poverty.

In statistical terms the Census Bureau estimated that in 1990 there were 33.6 million poor people in the United States. The government defined poverty in that year as an income of less than $13,359 for a nonfarm family of four.[29] The profile of the poor included these facts:

1. There were more than twice as many poor white people as poor African Americans — 22.3 million as compared with 9.8 million. But a higher percentage of African Americans were poor — almost one out of every three African Americans as opposed to about one out of every nine whites.

2. About 13.5 percent of the nation's population was poor.[30]

In response to President Johnson's "war on poverty," Congress in 1964 passed legislation creating the Office of Economic Opportunity (OEO). Community-action programs became a highly controversial aspect of the antipoverty program. They were designed to give federal grants to a wide range of programs organized and administered by local public or private groups, "with maximum feasible participation" of the poor. While successful in some areas, the community-action programs led in some other cases to what one critic, Daniel P. Moynihan, termed a "maximum feasible misunderstanding."[31]

Supporters of the poverty program argued that through community action the poor could be organized *politically* to express their grievances to the "power structure." But in some cases the strategy led to widely publicized confrontations between the poor and established political leaders. Big-city mayors and other critics charged that the federal government was funding community-action groups to march on City Hall and challenge the entrenched power of local political organizations. Conflict over the program was inevitable. Perhaps one of the problems as well was that President Johnson, by promising, in effect, to end poverty in the United States, had created public expectations that exceeded the ability of the program to achieve its goal.

President Nixon did not support the poverty program. He dissolved OEO and dispersed its functions to

[27] Michael Harrington, *The Other America* (New York: Macmillan, 1962), p. 4.

[28] Ben H. Bagdikian, *In the Midst of Plenty* (Boston: Beacon Press, 1964), pp. 6–7.

[29] U.S. Bureau of the Census, Current Population Reports, *Poverty in the United States: 1990*, series P-60, no. 175, August, 1991, p. 1. In 1991, the number of poor persons had increased to 35.7 million, or 14.2 percent of the population. Source: Census data reported in *New York Times*, September 3, 1992, p. A1. The number and percent of poor persons was lower if noncash government benefits, such as food stamps, school lunches, public housing, and medical programs were counted.

[30] Ibid., pp. 1, 4.

[31] Daniel P. Moynihan, *Maximum Feasible Misunderstanding: Community Action in the War on Poverty* (New York: Free Press, 1969).

other government units. In 1971, Nixon created AC-TION, an umbrella agency for various volunteer programs. ACTION took over VISTA, a part of the poverty program in which volunteers live and work for one year in poor urban or rural areas.

The Politics of Hunger

In the midst of the 1992 election campaign, a small, four-paragraph news story moved on the wires of the Associated Press. The *Washington Post* carried the story on page eight under this headline: "30 Million Hungry in U.S., Report Says." [32] Perhaps it was a measure of how accustomed Americans had become to the problem of hunger that the news item caused no great stir either in the campaign or the country.

The story said that the figure of 30 million persons in America who were too poor to eat enough food was contained in a report prepared at Tufts University at the

request of Representative Tony P. Hall, the Ohio Democrat who chaired the House Select Committee on Hunger. According to the report, hunger had increased by 50 percent since the mid-1980s, the result of increasing poverty and declining incomes. [33]

Although hunger is a social problem, it is also a political issue, because it is caught up in the different approaches of the two major parties to the larger problem of poverty in America. For example, a decade ago, in 1983, Edwin Meese III, White House counselor to a Republican president, Ronald Reagan, touched off a storm of political controversy when he told reporters: "Well, I don't know of any authoritative figures that there are hungry children. I've heard a lot of anecdotal stuff . . ." Meese added: "I think some people go to soup kitchens voluntarily. I know we've had considerable information that people go to soup kitchens because the food is free and that's easier than paying for it." [34]

---

[32] *Washington Post*, September 10, 1992, p. A8.

[33] Ibid.
[34] *Washington Post*, December 10, 1983, p. A8.

To critics, Meese's remarks seemed particularly insensitive in a nation in which the number of officially defined poor had increased by six million people in three years. The impact of the remarks was compounded by the fact that Meese himself was sleek and jowly and appeared personally well-fed.

Moreover, the president's counselor, one of Reagan's two highest advisers, spoke against a background of news stories that told of poor people lining up in subfreezing weather for surplus government cheese, and of increasing numbers of men and women, some recently unemployed, seeking food and shelter from public and private agencies.

A month after Meese's comments, a presidential Task Force on Food Assistance reported on the status of hunger in America. The panel said it had taken forceful testimony "about the existence of widespread and growing hunger in this country" although it could neither refute nor prove these claims. But the panel's chairman issued a statement declaring hunger "a real and significant problem throughout our nation" and calling for "immediate action to remedy this problem." [35] The task force recommended that federal food assistance benefits be increased by $500 million a year. The Reagan budget for fiscal 1985 asked instead that such assistance be decreased by that amount.[36]

Various private study groups agreed with or went even beyond the presidential task force in assessing the problem. In 1986, the Physicians Task Force on Hunger in America, a Harvard-based group, concluded, ". . . hunger in America is a national health epidemic." [37]

To some extent, the problem of hunger in America was related to what seemed to be a growing population of homeless people. Estimates of the size of that population vary, however. As far back as 1983, Margaret M. Heckler, the secretary of health and human services, said she was leading a campaign "to house and feed an estimated two million homeless Americans." [38] Seven months later, the Department of Housing and Urban Development said there were 250,000 to 300,000 homeless people in the United States.[39] President Reagan, commenting on the problem on the television program "Good Morning America," said that people sleeping on outdoor grates in cities are homeless "by choice." [40]

Figures on the extent of hunger in America also vary, since hunger is more easily felt by an individual than defined by a government agency. But studies have agreed that millions of Americans go hungry every day in the midst of affluence.[41] Today, many low-income

Americans benefit from a massive federal food-stamp program. Even so, hunger had not been eliminated.

In 1961 President Kennedy, by executive order, initiated the food stamp program to increase the buying power of low-income families. Congress established a food stamp system by law in 1964. Most recipients of food stamps have incomes well below the national poverty level.

From its modest beginnings, the food stamp program rapidly spiraled into one of the federal government's largest welfare programs. By 1992 an estimated $22.7 billion a year was budgeted for food stamps for 25.4 million persons.[42] In other words, nearly one person in ten in the United States depended on food stamps. In addition to food stamps, the federal government

---

[35] *New York Times*, January 11, 1984, p. 1.
[36] *New York Times*, February 2, 1984, p. B10.
[37] *New York Times*, April 20, 1986, p. 28.
[38] *New York Times*, May 2, 1984, p. 1.
[39] Ibid.
[40] *Washington Post*, February 1, 1984, p. 1.
[41] Nick Kotz, *Let Them Eat Promises* (Englewood Cliffs: Prentice-Hall, 1969), p. 23.
[42] *Budget of the United States Government Fiscal Year 1993*, A1–12; and *Washington Post*, May 24, 1992, p. A1.

distributed surplus food crops to the poor through local welfare agencies, and it financed a school lunch program and a special milk program for children. The school lunch program was cut sharply and the milk program drastically reduced under President Reagan.

Health

In 1992 the federal government spent an estimated $230 billion, or 15 percent of the national budget, for health services.[43] The funds were allocated for research, training and education, hospital construction, Medicare and Medicaid, and prevention of disease.

The *Medicare* program, discussed earlier in the chapter, provides hospital and medical services to older persons through the social security program. *Medicaid*, also established in 1965, is a public assistance program to

---

[43] Data provided by Office of Management and Budget.

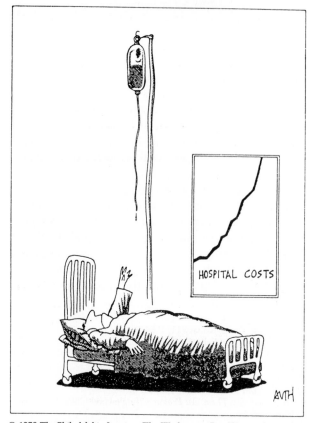

© 1978 *The Philadelphia Inquirer*, The Washington Post Writers Group. Reprinted with permission.

help pay hospital, doctor, and medical bills for persons with low incomes. It is financed through general federal, state, and local taxes. Under a current law, Washington pays 58 percent of the cost of state programs established under Medicaid. It was estimated that Medicaid would pay out $84.4 billion in federal dollars to aid more than thirty million people in 1993. Annual federal and state Medicaid costs had reached a combined total of more than $145 billion.[44]

While federal programs have assisted the aged and the needy, they have not helped the majority of Americans to obtain adequate health care at a reasonable cost. The cost of hospital rooms, physicians' care, and other health services has increased at an alarming rate. Major illness could easily wipe out the financial resources of the average American family, and private insurance plans often fail to cover the cost of prolonged hospitalization or medical treatment, or long-term care for older persons. The expanded Medicare coverage for catastrophic illness enacted in 1988 helped the elderly but did not assist the general population, and, in any event, was repealed the following year.

As a result of spiraling health costs, pressure for a general federal program of health insurance grew in the 1970s and emerged as a major issue in the 1980s. By the 1992 presidential election, about 36 million Americans were without any health insurance, and as noted earlier, both candidates offered plans to deal with the problem.

Much of the debate over national health insurance to provide universal access to health care for all Americans centered on the question of who would pay for such a multibillion-dollar program — for an estimated twenty-nine million operations and more than one billion prescriptions a year.

Education

By the early 1990s, Americans of all political persuasions seemed to agree that the nation's educational system was in crisis. Many parents, students, and other citizens were concerned that America's public schools were not doing a good enough job of educating the nation's children in a world where the United States faced increasing economic competition with other countries. The recession had compounded the problem, forcing many

---

[44] Adapted from *Budget of the United States Government Fiscal Year 1993*, p. A1–57; and data provided by Health Care Finance Administration, U.S. Department of Health and Human Services.

Table 15-4
Federal Outlays for Education, 1968–93 (in billions of dollars)

	1968	1972	1976	1979	1983	1985	1989	1993
Elementary and secondary education	3.2	5.4	4.7	5.9	5.6	6.2	9.8	12.6
Higher education	4.4	4.9	2.6	4.5	7.2	7.2	9.6	14.1
Adult and other education	1.2	1.6	.8	2.0	1.8	2.1	1.4	1.2
Total	$8.8	$11.9	$8.1	$12.4	$14.6	$15.5	$20.8	$27.9

SOURCE: Adapted from *Budget of the United States Government*, for fiscal years 1968–1993.

states — even large states like California — to make deep cuts in their education budgets. Across the nation, teachers were often underpaid, their status not equal to that of other important professions. Political candidates vied with one another in offering solutions to the challenge.

In 1989, more than 62 million students were enrolled in the nation's schools and colleges. Of the total, 13.4 million were enrolled in colleges, 16.8 million in high schools, 29.2 million in elementary schools, and 2.9 million in nursery schools.[45]

In fiscal 1993 the federal government budgeted $27.9 billion for various kinds of direct aid to education. (See Table 15–4.) This aid was channeled in two ways: to *educational institutions* and to *individuals*.

As far back as 1862, Congress had passed the Morrill Act to establish "land-grant" colleges. And millions of veterans of the Second World War went to college under the federally financed GI Bill of Rights. In 1958, the year after the Soviet Union launched its Sputnik earth satellite, Congress enacted the National Defense Education Act to provide loans for college students in the fields of science, engineering, mathematics, and foreign languages. In 1963 Congress began appropriating funds for the construction of college classrooms.

Not until 1965, however, did Congress pass a law providing for general federal aid to education. In that year, the high-water mark of President Johnson's "Great Society," it enacted the Elementary and Secondary Education Act and the Higher Education Act. Until 1965 the church-state controversy had blocked passage of a general aid to education bill. (See Chapter 4, pp. 108–109.) The Elementary and Secondary Education Act bypassed that dispute by providing aid to children in both public and private (including religious-affiliated) schools on the basis of economic need. Although most counties in the nation were eligible, the bulk of the money was concentrated in urban and rural areas with a high percentage of children from poor families. Under the law, the federal government also provided general-purpose grants, plus money for textbooks, library books, special programs for handicapped children, and teacher training.

In 1981, Congress passed the Education Consolidation and Improvement Act, which continued about half of the education aid programs contained in the 1965 law but dropped the rest. A new system of block grants was established for most of the programs that continued, giving the states more power over spending.

The Higher Education Act of 1965 for the first time provided federal scholarships, called educational opportunity grants, for undergraduates. These were later revised and renamed Pell grants for their sponsor, Senaor Claiborne Pell, Democrat, of Rhode Island. The law also provided federally insured loans for college students, federal subsidies to pay the interest on student loans from private lenders, and a work-study program to help the colleges pay the wages of students with part-time jobs obtained through the schools. It channeled money to colleges to buy library books and created a program of fellowships for graduate students. It also established a Teacher Corps in which future teachers who received federal aid while studying agreed, after graduating, to teach in schools in inner cities and poor rural areas. In 1992, Congress extended the Higher Education Act, providing $100 billion over a five-year period for student financial aid, and making more middle-class students eligible for aid. By 1992, the government was spending $11.7 billion a year to assist six million college undergraduate and graduate students. An estimated 2.4 million more students were expected to benefit under the 1992 act.

[45] U.S. Bureau of the Census, *Statistical Abstract of the United States 1991*, pp. 132, 137.

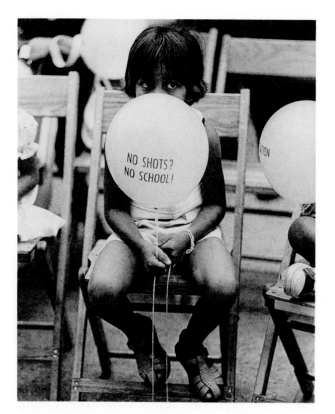

NO SHOTS? NO SCHOOL!

But federal spending has failed to avert continuing problems in the nation's public schools. Political battles continue over school desegregation and busing. The quality of education in many big-city public school systems has deteriorated. As large numbers of middle-class residents have moved to the suburbs, big cities have found their tax dollars dwindling; one result is that schools are often poorest where their services are needed most — in low-income, inner-city communities.

In 1979 Congress created a new Department of Education at the cabinet level. The department, which was given responsibility for the entire federal educational effort, absorbed the education branches of the old Department of Health, Education, and Welfare, as well as units concerned with education in several other government departments. The department had long been advocated by the National Education Association, the influential teachers' lobby. Ronald Reagan opposed the new department, and during the 1980 campaign he called for its abolition. However, as president, Reagan in 1981 appointed a secretary of education to his cabinet and the department survived his presidency.[46]

---

[46] A cabinet department can only be abolished by Congress, and not solely by a president.

Science

In an age of science and technology some people have come to feel that, more and more, decisions affecting their lives are being made not by elected political leaders, but by "faceless technocrats in long, white coats." [47]

Should American astronauts try to land on Mars? Should a new weapons system, such as the Strategic Defense Initiative, or "Star Wars," be developed? What should government medical researchers be doing about AIDS? For the answers to such questions, the president must turn to scientists. Government today has become far too complicated for political leaders to know all the scientific data they need to make policy decisions.

The federal government spends billions of dollars every year on scientific research and development. In fiscal 1993, more than $76 billion was budgeted for this purpose. Of the total, over $43 billion went to military programs. The National Aeronautics and Space Administration accounted for $15 billion. More than $14 billion was spent on basic research, most of it in colleges and universities. This level of spending has raised questions about the relationship of science and government. For instance, what is the proper role of science within the political system? Today, some critics regard science as "something very close to an *establishment* . . . a set of institutions supported by tax funds, but largely on faith, and without direct responsibility to political control." [48] Another question is whether universities can accept government funds for research without restricting or losing their academic independence.

The president has a science adviser within the White House. The adviser heads the Office of Science and Technology Policy, which has broad responsibility for advising the president on scientific affairs. In addition, the National Science Foundation, a government agency established in 1950, supports basic and applied research.

In the years after 1957 the federal science effort in large part was geared to responding to Soviet space accomplishments, particularly the launching of Sputnik, the world's first earth satellite. American scientists were called on to solve scientific, military, and technological problems, and America soon surpassed the Soviet Union in outer space. In 1969 the Apollo 11 astronauts landed on the moon. In 1976 America's Viking robot

---

[47] Senator E. L. Bartlett, D., Alaska, in Don K. Price, *The Scientific Estate* (Cambridge: Belknap Press of Harvard University Press, 1965), p. 57.
[48] Price, *The Scientific Estate*, p. 12.

Protecting the Environment

During the 1992 campaign, President Bush, seeking votes in the timber country of the Pacific Northwest, took aim at the spotted owl in a speech in Colville, Washington. "It is time," Bush declared, "to make people more important than owls." [49]

Bush was well aware that preserving the old-growth forests that are the habitat of the spotted owl, an endangered species, had cost thousands of jobs in Oregon and Washington. Calling the owl "that little furry, feathery guy," [50] Bush said he would not sign an extension of the Endangered Species Act, unless it were changed to balance economic costs against wildlife protection. Although he had promised four years earlier to serve as the "environmental president," Bush calculated in 1992 that owls don't vote. But in appealing to the economic self-interest of workers in the northwest, he risked the wrath of pro-environment voters, also an important constituency in the Western states, and particularly in California.

The northern spotted owl, while not the only endangered species in America, had perhaps become the most celebrated. Although there were other reasons that the timber industry faced hard times, preserving the owl cost jobs, and that stark fact symbolized the larger conflict between the environment and the economy.

---

[49] *Washington Post,* September 15, 1992, p. A8.
[50] Ibid.

spacecraft landed on Mars and transmitted photographs back to earth. And in 1980, Voyager I photographed the rings of Saturn almost a billion miles away in outer space. But there have been disasters as well, notably the explosion that sent the space shuttle Challenger plunging into the ocean shortly after launch in 1986, killing all six persons aboard.

Often, political controversy surrounds expensive scientific projects. Should America spend billions on a space station, and to what end? In recent years, congressional support for NASA has been waning, because of the high cost of its projects and because of highly publicized technical failures such as the Hubble telescope's malfunctioning mirror in 1990. NASA's proposed space station is expected to cost at least $40 billion and once built, another $100 billion over 30 years to operate and service. The ambitious and expensive project would be an orbiting laboratory where scientists would live and study how human beings react to long periods in outer space. It would also serve as a launch platform for manned rockets embarking on other space flights and exploration. NASA also proposed a $3-billion program to build a more powerful rocket motor for use on the space shuttle.

©1992 Toles/Buffalo News

THE POLLUTED LAND

Those of us who were born after 1900, or even after 1920, inherited a land that was generally pleasant, livable, and lovely to look at. To be sure, there were slums and tenements and soft coal soot, and quite a lot of mud mixed with the horse manure, but the quality of life, as measured in clean air, clean water, and verdant hills, was something to remember with wonder — and with dismay.

For the generations of this century have squandered that inheritance. Never was so great a trust so grossly violated. We turned our valleys into dust bowls and our rivers into sewers, killed the lakes, fouled the air, choked the cities. With the brute efficiency of systematic vandals, we combined stupidity and greed. Now we measure the quality of our life by the tons of litter we leave behind. The hallmark of our society is stamped on 10 million roadside bottles: No deposit, no return.

—James J. Kilpatrick, *Washington Star*,
January 8, 1970

The owl itself is about two feet tall and weighs 22 ounces, its chocolate-colored plumage marked with white spots. There are perhaps 2,000 pairs left. Officials of the Bush admininistration estimated that saving the bird could cost 20,000 jobs in the Pacific Northwest. At the Coos County fair in the heart of Oregon's timber country, the sentiments of the loggers and their families could be read on their T-shirts: "Save a Logger — Eat an Owl," and "I Love Spotted Owls . . . Fried." [51]

To try to resolve the controversy, the Bush administration convened a cabinet-level Endangered Species Committee, nicknamed "the God Squad," which recommended in May of 1992 that the law be suspended to allow logging on about 1,700 acres of federal land in Oregon, but not on other tracts of land in dispute, action that would still cost thousands of timber jobs.

Two decades ago, words and phrases like pollution, the environment, and energy crisis were unfamiliar. By the 1990s, however, Americans were acutely aware of the danger to the environment posed by technology. At the same time, they wanted to enjoy the benefits of that technology. Americans wanted clean air and water — but they were also aware that cars that met clean-air standards would cost more money. They were

[51] *Washington Post*, July 6, 1990, p. A6.

BATTLE OF HASTINGS

MAGNA CARTA SIGNED

COLUMBUS REACHES AMERICA

DECLARATION OF INDEPENDENCE

LOUISIANA PURCHASE

LINCOLN SHOT

ATTACK ON PEARL HARBOR

GEORGE BUSH ELECTED the ENVIRONMENTAL PRESIDENT

concerned about oil spills polluting their beaches — but they wanted plenty of gasoline for their automobiles at the lowest possible price. There was a conflict, in other words, between the environment and energy.

In the winter of 1973–74 the nation found itself facing a major energy crisis. The president appointed an "energy czar" to allocate oil supplies; gasoline stations were closed on Sundays; speed limits were lowered; the federal government ordered cutbacks in deliveries of heating oil to homes and offices; and airlines laid off thousands of pilots, flight attendants, and other employees as a shortage of jet fuel forced the cancellation of many flights. Other industries that depended on oil were adversely affected. The immediate shortages were the result of a cutoff of oil shipments by the Arab states after the Arab-Israeli War in October 1973. But the crisis forced the nation to reassess its entire approach to the use of energy; the long lines of cars at gas stations left little choice.

Americans in large numbers had begun to understand that humanity in the technological age was slowly destroying nature and the earth itself — and endangering its own survival. Scientists warned that economic growth combined with overpopulation might end in disaster for the world. In the United States, cities had become enveloped in smog, rivers clogged with human and industrial waste, sea birds and shorelines ravaged by oil spills and litter. Alarmed and concerned, the public focused on the science of ecology, which deals with the relationship between living organisms and their environment.

The upsurge of interest in the quality of the natural environment was soon reflected in the political environment. Political leaders of both major parties scrambled to stake out a position. Public pressure for a cleanup led rapidly to major legislation. First, the Clean Air Act amendments of 1970 set federal air-quality standards to control automobile and industrial pollution. Legislation to clean up the nation's waterways followed two years later. A new government unit, the Environmental Protection Agency (EPA), began operating in 1970.

Pollution is a result of industrialization and increased consumption, combined with population growth. The close relationship between pollution and "the population bomb" has been emphasized by Barry Commoner, a leading ecologist (and a minor-party presidential candidate in 1980). He has predicted that the population of the earth, which was 5.3 billion people in 1990, will grow by the year 2000 to between 6 and 8 billion. Somewhere near that population level is what Commoner has called "the crash point," at which, he argues, the air, water, and earth can no longer support human life.

As with most major national problems, progress toward restoring the environment requires cooperation by individuals, corporations, and institutions — but it also requires coercion in the form of government legislation and enforcement. For that reason, many organizations and individuals who supported environmental causes were concerned when the Reagan administration came to power in 1981. They feared that protection of the environment would be given a lower priority than either the search for new energy sources or the effort to reduce government regulation of business.

Criticism of the Reagan administration's environmental policies quickly focused on the person of James G. Watt, a conservative lawyer from Wyoming who fought for business against environmentalists, and whom the president appointed as secretary of the interior. Watt was eventually forced to resign from the cabinet because of indiscreet remarks about minorities. His departure followed by several months a major scandal at the Environmental Protection Agency over the government's handling of toxic wastes. After many years of concern over toxic waste dumps, especially the contamination of Love Canal near Buffalo, New York, Congress in 1980 had created a $1.6-billion "superfund" to clean up such sites. The dangers of hazardous industrial waste were underscored even more sharply early in 1983 when residents of the entire town of Times Beach,

"I don't see why all the fuss over dioxin. . . . Shoot, it didn't even kill the chickens. . . ."

Drawing by Schorr for the *Los Angeles Herald Examiner*. Reprinted by permission: Tribune Media Services, Inc.

THE THROWAWAY SOCIETY

The USA is tossing out more trash than ever — despite an emphasis on recycling, a new EPA report says.

Each person produced an average of 4.3 lbs. of trash daily in 1990 — up from 4 lbs. in 1988, says the Environmental Protection Agency. Total: 196 million tons annually.

The report also found:

• Recycling increased 4% overall; the big-

gest increases came in yard waste recycling.
• Each year, 500,000 tons of telephone books are thrown away — along with 13 million tons of newspapers and 2.6 million tons of disposable diapers.

The largest paper product discarded: 24 million tons of corrugated cardboard.

Also tossed are 8 million tons of beer, wine, liquor and soft drink bottles.

Copyright 1992, *USA Today*.
Reprinted with permission.

Missouri, had to be moved because of deadly dioxin contamination.

The dollar cost of a cleaner environment, the personal inconvenience caused by new laws and regulations, and the competing pressures for development of energy sources have combined to create many conflicts. Despite counterpressures, the environmental movement became firmly rooted in only a few years, with some visible results. In 1971, for example, Congress cancelled plans to build an American supersonic jet transport (SST) in part because of the danger that the plane's exhaust would deplete the ozone layer in the stratosphere. The ozone layer filters out ultraviolet sunlight, and some studies concluded that because damage to the ozone layer would expose more people to ultraviolet radiation, the SST exhaust might lead to an increase in skin cancer in human beings. The environmentalists do not always win, however; the federal government permitted the British Concorde, a supersonic plane, as well as the French Concorde, to fly regular routes to the United States.

On the other hand, by the 1990s Americans were much more aware of the need to preserve the environment, and some tried to do something about it in their daily lives. For example, many Americans voluntarily separated their trash for recyling, and in a number of cities the law now requires it.

With the competing pressures in American society, environmentalists will inevitably lose many battles. Energy needs will often prevail over environmental concerns. Nevertheless, the political power of the environmental supporters is tangible. Millions of people belong to an estimated 2,000 to 3,000 environmental organizations across the country. Public interest in the environment has been followed by legislation and ex-

pansion of the government's role as environmental regulator. Clean air, clean water, land use, and other similar issues are significant factors in political campaigns. And a major new concern has been added to the government's policy agenda.

The Environmental Protection Agency The controversy that enveloped the Environmental Protection Agency during the Reagan administration was not surprising. The environment is a major arena of conflict, with competing interest groups clashing over policy. EPA was established in 1970 as an independent unit of the executive branch. The creation of EPA pulled together under one roof various regulatory powers that had been scattered through a dozen bureaus and agencies. EPA's administrator is often called on to make hard and controversial decisions — whether to grant the auto industry more time to manufacture cars with cleaner engines, for example.

In recent years Congress has passed major legislation dealing with the environment. The laws have dealt with clean air, clean water, and endangered species.

Air Pollution The Clean Air Act amendments of 1970, steered through the Senate by Edmund Muskie of Maine, set strict federal air-quality standards governing major forms of pollution by industry, including automobile emissions. The law provides heavy fines for violators. Under the 1970 act, auto manufacturers were required by 1975 to reduce by 90 percent the levels of carbon monoxide, hydrocarbons, and nitrogen oxides in engine exhaust. When the big auto companies in Detroit claimed they needed more time to comply, Congress and the administrator of EPA granted extensions. The act was amended again in 1977, under Presi-

AIR POLLUTION AT EPA

Since 1985, Bobbie Lively-Diebold has worked at the Environmental Protection Agency mapping out a strategy to clean up the nation's most polluted industrial dump sites.

Now the pollution has hit closer to home. When she enters her office at EPA headquarters in Southwest Washington, Lively-Diebold might as well be knee deep in toxic waste. Her lips, ear canals, throat and eyes burn. Her vocal chords swell so that she cannot speak. The room seems to spin in slow motion as she strains for every breath, wheezing like an asthmatic.

Lively-Diebold and dozens of her colleagues are suffering from indoor pollution at the headquarters of the agency dedicated to clean air.

. . . The situation at EPA adds an ironic twist to a growing public health problem known as "sick building syndrome," which is believed to account for millions of lost workdays each year through the exposure of a captive work force to insidious chemical gases and fibers . . .

Unlike the factory smoke stacks and auto exhaust normally associated with air pollution, the indoor version is invisible and often odorless. It comes in the form of microscopic fungi and bacteria spun out of dirty ventillation systems; molecules of formaldehyde and other toxic substances that rise from new carpets and room partitions; ozone and hydrocarbons that seep from copying machines; asbestos fibers that flake off from damaged insulation, and cigarette smoke.

—*Washington Post*, May 25, 1988

dent Carter; the auto emission deadlines were extended through 1979 but tightened beginning in 1980 and 1981. The act also required cities to meet national clean-air standards by 1982, except for cities with severe pollution problems, which were given until 1987. Most cities failed to meet the deadline, which was extended in 1988 for another five years until 1993.

In 1990, Congress passed major revisions to the Clean Air Act. The law would gradually phase out the use of chlorofluorocarbons and the chemicals used in aerosol sprays that deplete the ozone layer, it would significantly reduce automobile emissions, and set new rules to reduce urban smog, to curb the chemicals that produce acid rain, and to regulate toxic pollutants. Environmentalists complained, however, that the Bush administration had sabotaged the law by failing to enforce it.

Acid rain is an increasing problem that has caused friction between the United States and Canada, which has complained that sulfur dioxide and nitrogen oxides from U.S. factories cause acid rain that destroys lakes, forests, and fish and other wildlife. Acid rain knows no geographic boundaries, however, and similar damage has been caused by this form of pollution in the United States. In 1988, President Reagan agreed to freeze U.S. emission levels of nitrogen oxides at 1987 levels, a decision that cleared the way for the United States to join

Acid rain knows no geographic boundaries: North Carolina

with twenty-three other nations in signing an international treaty, in November 1988, aimed at controlling acid rain.

Air pollution is a global, not merely a national, problem. Increasingly, scientists warned that the fragile ozone layer protecting the earth had been damaged by the chlorofluorocarbons used in air conditioning, aerosol sprays, and elsewhere. As noted, the ozone layer blocks some of the ultraviolet radiation from the sun that causes skin cancer in humans; the radiation also damages crops and forests. In 1987, twenty-four nations met in Montreal to sign a pact designed to protect the ozone layer by restricting the use of the chemicals causing the damage. Scientists also detected a global warming trend that some attributed to the "greenhouse effect," a process that causes heat to be trapped on the earth by pollutants in the atmosphere. A major pollutant, for example, is carbon dioxide, a product of the burning of fossil fuels such as oil and coal. Health officials and scientists have warned that even if alternative sources of energy are developed, temperatures on earth may rise to unacceptable levels. The extraordinary heat wave and drought suffered by the United States in the summer of 1988 caused extensive damage to crops, and led to devastating forest fires in many western states. The heat and drought were seen by some scientists as evidence that the "greenhouse effect" had already begun.

Water Pollution On March 24, 1989, the 987-foot super tanker Exxon *Valdez* ran aground on a reef 25 miles south of Valdez, Alaska, spilling nearly eleven million gallons of crude oil into Prince William Sound. It was the largest oil spill from a tanker in United States history, and it had a devastating effect on fish, birds and other wildlife, and on the beaches of Alaska. The spill also caused great hardship among those who lived in the area, especially the Alaska natives and others who fished the sea or depended upon its bounty for their livelihood. Exxon spent about $2.5 billion to clean up the spill. Two years later, Exxon paid $1.1 billion as part of a plea bargain in which federal criminal and state charges were dropped. The captain of the tanker, Joseph J. Hazelwood, was dismissed by Exxon, acquitted of operating the vessel while drunk, but convicted of negligence. However, in 1992, an Alaska appeals court overturned his conviction.

The Exxon *Valdez* episode was only the most dramatic example of a larger problem that had begun to cause concern some two decades earlier. By the start of the 1970s, all across America, rivers, lakes, and streams were getting dirtier. Cities and towns were dumping their waste into rivers. Industrial plants pumped chemical wastes and toxic compounds into once-clear waters. The result: fouled drinking water, polluted beaches unfit for swimming, dead fish, and algae-clogged streams.

Cleaning up the Exxon *Valdez* oil spill, April 1989

Congress responded by passing the Water Pollution Control Act of 1972, which had as its goal the complete elimination of discharges of pollutants into the nation's waterways by 1985. The law allotted $18 billion to the states to build the waste treatment plants they needed to clean up the water. Within five years pollution began to diminish in at least some of the nation's waterways. According to one federal report, of twelve major rivers studied, five, including the Colorado and the Ohio, showed significant reductions in bacterial counts.[52]

Oil spills from drilling rigs or tankers like the Exxon *Valdez* are also a major form of pollution that has fouled the nation's beaches and endangered wildlife. One major oil spill occurred off Santa Barbara, California, in 1969. In 1976 an oil tanker, the SS *Argo Merchant*, ran aground off Nantucket, Massachusetts,

[52] *Seventh Annual Report*, Council on Environmental Quality (Washington, D.C.: U.S. Government Printing Office, 1976), p. 272.

spilling 7.5 million gallons of thick, gummy oil and threatening New England beaches, birds, and marine life. And in 1979, 140 million gallons of oil spilled into the Gulf of Mexico after a blowout on a Mexican oil rig.

In 1987, Congress, overriding a veto by President Reagan, passed a $20-billion Clean Water Act to help communities build sewage treatment plants and carry out other programs to reduce water pollution. In the summer of 1988 many East Coast beaches were closed because of a new type of pollution — syringes, blood bags, and other forms of medical waste dumped by hospitals and laboratories.

Environmental Impact and Endangered Species
The National Environmental Policy Act of 1969 required the government to assess the impact on the environment of all new projects involving the federal government. The provision is important because it has since been adopted by many states and communities; in addition, it has provided the basis for environmental lawsuits. The 1969 act also established a three-member Council on Environmental Quality to advise the president, and required the president to submit an annual "state of the environment" report to Congress.

The Endangered Species Act was passed by Congress in 1973 to protect wildlife and plants that might otherwise vanish forever from the earth. The law helped to save the American bald eagle, the national symbol, and more than 700 other species.[53] But long

---

[53] *New York Times*, May 26, 1992, p. A1.

before the northern spotted owl became a presidential campaign issue, the law proved controversial.

The battle over the tiny snail darter, a rare fish in the Little Tennessee River, is a case in point. In 1973 David Etnier, a University of Tennessee zoologist, discovered the three-inch fish in an area where the Tennessee Valley Authority (TVA) planned to build the Tellico Dam. The fish was placed on a list under the Endangered Species Act, entitling it to protection from actions of the government. Opponents of the dam took their case to the United States Supreme Court and won a ruling in 1978 requiring the TVA to halt the project. A special board created by Congress studied the problem and also sided with the fish. But in 1979 Congress voted to finish construction of the dam and also voted to allow exemptions to the Endangered Species Act in the future. Reluctantly, President Carter signed the bill. The snail darter had lost.

But the story had a happy ending. In 1976, 710 snail darters were transplanted to a tributary of the Little Tennessee, ten miles downstream from the dam, and the species thrived there. In 1980, fourteen baby snail darters were unexpectedly discovered eighty miles below the dam in the South Chickamauga Creek. And in July of 1984, the tiny fish was removed from the endangered species list. By 1992, however, the political battle over the spotted owl had made the law itself an endangered species, its future uncertain.

Energy Policy Even before the 1990s, the nuclear power industry in America was in serious trouble. Five

---

BIRD VS. AIR FORCE

A confrontation on Guam between a tiny bird that does not fly and the United States Air Force found the Air Force backing off . . .

Under a Strategic Air Command directive to bolster defenses against terrorists, Andersen Air Force Base on the island had moved to clear an area of heavy shrubbery near the flight line that attackers might use for cover. But when environmentalists protested that the shrubbery was the last known habitat of the small Guam rail, the United States Fish and Wildlife Service placed the bird on its emergency endangered-species list.

The action blocked the Air Force land-clearing for 240 days while the two sides considered the plight of the Guam rail, believed left with but 50 survivors after suffering thousands of losses since 1968.

Maj. James McGuire, a spokesman for the Strategic Air Command's headquarters near Omaha, says the command has temporarily waived its security order while it seeks to "develop a coordinated approach" with United States and Guam wildlife officials to protect the rail.

—*New York Times*, June 24, 1984

plants, including Seabrook in New Hampshire and another in Midland, Michigan, had shut down in one two-month period because of excessive cost or safety reasons. Orders for about one hundred other reactors had been cancelled, representing a loss of billions of dollars, and there had been no orders for new nuclear plants since 1978.

A combination of skyrocketing costs and public opposition because of accidents, such as that at Three Mile Island, had turned many of the nuclear construction projects into financial disasters. Groups such as the Clamshell Alliance and other foes of nuclear power did not always win every round, however: in 1984, after massive and prolonged protests, the Nuclear Regulatory Commission gave the Diablo Canyon nuclear plant near San Luis Obispo, California, permission to open.

All told, there were 110 nuclear plants in operation in the United States in 1992 producing almost 21 percent of the nation's electricity and 9 percent of total energy use in the United States. Nuclear plants have become the most important source of electric power after coal.

But the public continued to fear the release of deadly radiation in the event of an accident at a nuclear power plant. The Nuclear Regulatory Commission conceded in 1982 that 100,000 people could be killed in a worst-case accident at the Salem plant in New Jersey, assuming a total meltdown of the nuclear core and adverse weather conditions.[54]

The problems besetting the nuclear power industry meant higher prices for consumers, but beyond that, disappointment for those who hoped that nuclear power would solve the nation's future energy needs.

What quickly became known as the "energy crisis" hit home in America during the winter of 1973–74 when long gas lines formed across the nation; again in the summer of 1979 the shortage recurred in many areas. Its reminders were everywhere at the time: in the steadily rising gasoline prices at the pump, in the higher costs faced by consumers to heat their homes in winter or cool them in summer, in the soaring profits of the oil companies, and in the frequent announcements of price increases by the Organization of Petroleum Exporting Countries (OPEC). In the 1980s, the war between Iraq and Iran in the Middle East again had the potential of reducing oil supplies to the West; even Americans who normally paid little attention to foreign policy were

[54] *USA Today*, November 2, 1982, p. 3A.

aware that their ability to take the family out for a Sunday drive might depend on what happened six thousand miles away in the Persian Gulf. America's dependence on foreign oil from the Middle East was never more apparent than in 1990–91 when the United States went to war against Iraq's Saddam Hussein, who had seized Kuwait and was then in a position to threaten Saudi Arabia and its vast oilfields.

For the ordinary citizen, the energy crisis that emerged two decades before was difficult to understand. Some argued that there had been no shortage at all, that gas lines and the crisis were artificial, created by the actions of "Big Oil." Many Americans were reluctant to adjust their affluent life-styles to the energy crisis — to commute to work in car pools or turn down their thermostats in winter. Energy legislation was extremely complex, and even concerned citizens were bewildered by the explanations.

Some of the basic facts were not all that complicated, however. The United States has abundant petroleum deposits in Texas, Louisiana, Oklahoma, California, and offshore in the oceans and the Gulf of Mexico. Before the Second World War, domestic fields supplied about 95 percent of the oil used in this country. By 1992, however, the United States was using almost seventeen million barrels of oil a day, and domestic sources were providing about 50 percent of the total. The other 50 percent was imported, a little more than half of that amount from OPEC nations in the Middle East.

Although the United States had only 5 percent of the world's population, it consumed 25 percent of the world's energy.[55]

The dependence on foreign oil created problems at home. Rising fuel prices contributed to inflation and unemployment. The billions of dollars paid annually to import oil accounted for a substantial share of the U.S. trade and balance-of-payments deficits. And energy problems were directly linked to the nation's foreign policy, as the war in the Persian Gulf illustrated.

Over the years, the federal government and Congress have attempted to deal with the energy problem. For example, President Carter proposed a number of measures, ranging from increased conservation to the use of alternative energy sources, such as synthetic fuels (called *synfuels*) and solar power.

He also decontrolled oil prices and asked Congress to enact a stiff windfall profits tax to recoup the "huge and undeserved windfall profits" that the oil companies would reap from his action.

Congress responded only in part to the president's program. In 1980 it created a Synthetic Fuels Corporation, which could spend $20 billion to promote the production of synfuels from such materials as coal, vegetation, and garbage. It also approved a windfall profits tax of from 30 to 70 percent of new oil company profits after decontrol.

One of Carter's requests did go through Congress substantially intact. In 1977 he asked for and got a new cabinet-level Department of Energy. The creation by Congress of the new department underscored the importance of a problem that the nation had been slow to recognize, but that would doubtless continue to have an enormous impact on the political system and the lives of individual Americans.

Nuclear Power: Three Mile Island March 28, 1979, was a routine night in the control room of the nuclear power plant on Three Mile Island in the Susquehanna River, eleven miles southeast of Harrisburg, Pennsylvania. Inside the control room, a horseshoe-shaped panel stretched forty feet along three walls. It was lined with dials, gauges, and 1,200 red and green warning lights.

Suddenly, at 4 A.M., a Klaxon sounded. A voice on a loudspeaker intoned: "Turbine trip in Unit 2." It was

Drawing by Mike Peters for the *Dayton Daily News*. Reprinted by permission of United Features Syndicate, Inc.

the beginning of the worst accident in the history of nuclear power production in the United States.

A valve had failed in the nuclear reactor's cooling system, and the nuclear core of the reactor was rapidly overheating, raising the possibility of a "meltdown." If that happened, the nuclear core would burn through steel and concrete walls and would release lethal levels of radioactivity into the atmosphere. What opponents of nuclear power had always warned against — a nuclear disaster in a populated urban area — seemed close at hand.

The governor of Pennsylvania closed nearby schools and advised pregnant women and preschool children within five miles of the site to leave and people within ten miles to stay indoors. An evacuation of up to 300,000 people was planned, but not ordered. Many residents left on their own.

It took technicians and government experts seven days to bring the danger under control. Although the feared "meltdown" did not take place, some radiation was released. There were no reported injuries to the public, but the incident sowed fear and confusion among residents of the area and alerted millions of Americans to the dangers of nuclear power. A presidential commission studied the accident and recommended that new nuclear plants be built in areas remote from population centers.

Despite the dangers dramatized by the accident at Three Mile Island, advocates of nuclear power argued that nuclear plants were an important element in the nation's energy supply. Opponents maintained that the

---

[55] Data provided by the American Petroleum Institute; and *BP Statistical Review of World Energy*, British Petroleum Company, June 1992, p. 33.

disaster averted at Three Mile Island would surely come, sooner or later.

In 1986, it did. The meltdown of a reactor in a Soviet nuclear plant at Chernobyl, near Kiev, released high levels of radiation into the air. At least twenty-three people were killed, hundreds were hospitalized, and 40,000 persons were evacuated from the area. European nations banned the import of food from Eastern Europe for fear of contamination. It was the worst nuclear power disaster in history.

By the mid-1980s, abundant supplies of oil on the world market and declining demand had led OPEC to cut its prices. Americans appeared much less worried about the prospect of gas shortages or energy problems in general. But the Persian Gulf War was a dramatic

reminder that events in the Middle East could quickly endanger the flow of oil to the rest of the world. Well before the war, one study warned, "the world oil supply framework is very fragile . . . most of all, in the critical Middle East . . . if loading facilities in the Persian Gulf were to be destroyed or its waters made inaccessible to shipping . . . the world would quickly draw down its accumulated stocks of crude and refined products, prices would skyrocket, and the economies of the oil-importing countries would once again come under stress." [56]

---

[56] Joel Darmstadter, Hans H. Landsberg, Herbert C. Morton, with Michael J. Coda, *Energy Today and Tomorrow: Living with Uncertainty* (Englewood Cliffs: Prentice-Hall, 1983), p. 86.

Three Mile Island: a frightening accident

IS GOVERNMENT THE PROBLEM?

Ten years ago a review of major economic and social problems would have concentrated on asking how government might best deal with them. In today's climate of public opinion, the same kind of review must begin by asking whether government is capable of dealing with them. Ten years ago, government was widely viewed as an instrument to solve problems; today government itself is widely viewed as the problem.

—Charles Schultze and Henry Owen, *Setting National Priorities: The Next Ten Years*

CAN GOVERNMENT MEET THE CHALLENGE?

This discussion of government in operation has examined a number of crucial areas in which government—and therefore American society—has attempted to solve urgent social and economic problems. The results have been mixed.

In some policy areas, the government has had only limited success. Complex fiscal and monetary policies—even direct economic controls—have not consistently avoided the evils of recession or inflation. Economic stability has been endangered by soaring budget deficits, even as Congress struggled to control them. Government was slow to develop new and alternative sources of energy to meet the nation's future needs. In many cases, regulatory agencies have served corporate power and have failed to protect the public. In a free enterprise economy, it was not always clear whether government had the will or the power to regulate industry on behalf of consumers.

In the field of social welfare, the federal government has promised much and delivered less. President Johnson declared his "war on poverty" in 1964, but some decades later over thirty-three million Americans were still poor. The public assistance program has helped millions of people, but has been widely criticized. Under President Reagan, deep cuts were made in many social programs.

Despite government programs, there is a wide gap between rich and poor in the United States, and the number of persons living in poverty has increased steadily in recent years. Indeed, Benjamin I. Page, a political scientist, concluded that government welfare programs do little to redistribute wealth and have been largely offset by other government policies that favor the rich: ". . . after all government actions are taken into account . . . after New Deals and Fair Deals and Wars on Poverty, the incomes of Americans remain very unequal. The welfare state may help establish a minimum level of existence for its citizens, but . . . it does not produce a substantial degree of equality." [57]

On the other hand, Congress had continued to fund a wide variety of programs to assist those in need. Environmental legislation and the creation of new federal agencies dealing with the environment are an example of government responding to public demands and societal needs. And the social security program was providing benefits to more than forty-five million Americans.

Achieving desirable social and economic ends requires money, however, and not all Americans want to or can afford to pay the price in higher taxes and other costs, especially in troubled economic times. How to deal with the complex social and economic problems confronting America is by no means clear. Not every problem may have an answer. But massive programs at any level of government may mean hard choices, high taxes, and other sacrifices. In the area of social policy, the real dilemma facing Americans today is whether they are willing to pay the costs of "promoting the general welfare" and attempting to build a better society.

PERSPECTIVE

By the presidential election of 1992 the nation was in a prolonged period of economic recession. The presidential campaign that year offered the voters a choice about the role of government in America. As his party's candidate for president, President Bush espoused a relatively limited role for the federal government in managing the economy and in all other areas. Like his

[57] Benjamin I. Page, *Who Gets What from Government* (Berkeley: University of California Press, 1983), p. 19.

predecessor, President Reagan, Bush argued that free enterprise and individual initiative, with the least possible interference from government, was best for the country. Governor Bill Clinton of Arkansas, Bush's Democratic opponent, brought to the campaign a different approach, rooted in the belief that government, when necessary, should intervene to manage the economy and to provide social programs for people. Clinton's proposals, however, were more moderate than some previous Democratic standard-bearers.

The differences between the parties over the role of government in promoting the general welfare could be seen in even sharper focus in the 1980s, when Reagan called for a program of massive tax and federal spending cuts. Many government social services, such as unemployment benefits, Medicaid, and food stamps, were cut. Studies showed that the percentage and number of poor people increased substantially under Reagan.

The Constitution was established, among other purposes, to "promote the general welfare." In doing so, the federal government acts as regulator, promoter, manager, and protector. It regulates, as well as promotes, business and labor. It tries to manage the economy through fiscal and monetary policies. And government acts with varying success as protector in the areas of consumer affairs, health, education, welfare, science, poverty, hunger, and the environment.

From the late 1880s until 1937, the Supreme Court adopted a laissez-faire philosophy, which held that government should intervene as little as possible in economic affairs. The Great Depression and Franklin D. Roosevelt's New Deal, however, brought about a reversal of Supreme Court thinking. Since 1937 the Supreme Court has upheld laws policing business and the right of government to regulate wages, hours, and working conditions of employees.

To regulate business, Congress enacted antitrust laws designed to encourage competition in business and to prevent the growth of monopolies. The Justice Department and the Federal Trade Commission have responsibility for carrying out antitrust policy. Although the government has had some success at blocking *monopoly*, the control of a market by a single company, it has not been able to prevent *oligopoly*, the concentration of economic power in the hands of a relatively few large companies. Despite government regulation, some American corporations have increased in both size and diversity.

Government promotes commerce by providing services and direct and indirect subsidies to producers and farmers. At times the government has even given direct aid to large corporations in financial trouble, such as the Chrysler Corporation. American industry receives indirect aid from federal trade and tariff policies as well.

Organized labor wields great economic and political power in the United States and, as in the case of business, labor is both regulated and assisted by the federal government. The National Labor Relations Act of 1935 established labor's right to collective bargaining and barred employers from setting up company unions or discriminating against union workers. The Fair Labor Standards Act of 1938 established a minimum wage for American workers, a maximum forty-hour workweek, and time-and-a-half for overtime. It also outlawed child labor. The Taft-Hartley Act of 1947 sought to curb some of labor's power and shift it back to management. The law defined and prohibited unfair labor practices by unions, and provided that in strikes creating a national emergency, the president can seek a court injunction against a union during an eighty-day "cooling off period." Union membership has been declining, however, as the nation has shifted from manufacturing to service industries. By the 1990s, unsuccessful strikes in some industries reflected the weakened position of organized labor.

In making economic policy, the president has a number of tools and advisers available to him—the Council of Economic Advisers, the Office of Management and Budget, the secretary of the treasury, the Department of Labor, and the economists and experts who staff these government agencies. Yet presidents in recent years have not always been successful in controlling inflation, recession, or high unemployment. In part, this may be due to world economic conditions—factors that are beyond any president's control. But it also may stem from the nature of the American economic system, in which there are limits on the government's ability to manage the economy.

The federal government has attempted to influence the total shape of the economy through *fiscal policy* and *monetary policy*. The fiscal tools of the government are primarily spending and taxation. The monetary tools are control of the supply of money and control of the supply of credit through the Federal Reserve System.

The federal budget reflects an allocation of resources by the national government. The president must share with Congress fiscal control over the economy. Only Congress can vote to spend federal funds.

Despite several attempts at legislation to modify the budget process, none of the laws made much of a dent on the huge annual federal deficit, which by 1993 had reached an estimated $351 billion.

Individual income taxes are the federal government's largest single source of revenue. The Tax Reform Act of 1986 was the most extensive revision in the nation's tax laws in forty years. The measure reduced individual and corporate rates, ended the preferential treatment for capital gains, and ended or modified a wide variety of taxpayer deductions. President Bush broke his 1988 campaign promise of "no new taxes" when he agreed to $164 billion in new taxes over five years as part of a compromise with the Democratic-controlled Congress.

Today, most Americans agree that government has a responsibility to protect consumers from the perils of the marketplace. The work of consumer advocate Ralph Nader and his associates contributed to the passage of a wide range of consumer laws during the 1960s and the 1970s.

In the past four decades the national government has enacted multibillion-dollar social-welfare programs — ranging from school breakfasts for the young to social security for the aged. During the Great Depression, Franklin D. Roosevelt proposed, and Congress passed, the landmark Social Security Act of 1935. This was the beginning for two types of social-welfare programs: *social insurance* and *public assistance*. The social security program is a compulsory national insurance program, in theory self-financed by taxes on employers and employees. The other kind of program, public assistance, has no pay-as-you-go features; it simply distributes public funds to people who are poor.

By the 1990s Americans were acutely aware of the danger to the environment posed by technology. At the same time, they wanted to enjoy the benefits of that technology. Americans wanted clean air and water — but they were also aware that cars that met clean-air standards would cost more money. They were concerned about oil spills polluting their beaches — but they wanted plenty of gasoline for their automobiles at the lowest possible price. There was a conflict, in other words, between the environment and energy. There also was a large conflict between the environment and the economy. For example, preserving the old-growth forests that are the habitat of the spotted owl, an endangered species, had cost thousands of jobs in Oregon and Washington state. The upsurge of interest in the quality of the natural environment was soon reflected in the political environment. Congress in 1970 created the Environmental Protection Agency, and has since passed several laws to protect the air and water, and the wildlife and plants that might otherwise vanish forever from the earth.

Even before the 1990s, the nuclear power industry in America was in serious trouble. Five plants had shut down in a two-month period because of excessive cost or safety reasons. About one hundred other reactors had been cancelled, representing a loss of billions of dollars. The problems besetting the nuclear power industry meant higher prices for consumers, but beyond that, disappointment for those who hoped that nuclear power would solve the nation's future energy needs. But opponents emphasized the danger of nuclear power, illustrated by the accident at Three Mile Island in 1979.

America's dependence on foreign oil from the Middle East was never more apparent than in 1991 when the United States went to war against Iraq's Saddam Hussein, who had seized Kuwait and was then in a position to threaten Saudi Arabia and its vast oilfields. Iraq was defeated in the Persian Gulf War and withdrew from Kuwait. By 1992 the United States was using almost seventeen million barrels of oil a day, and domestic sources were providing about 50 percent of the total. The other 50 percent was imported, a little more than half of that amount from OPEC nations in the Middle East. The dependence on foreign oil created problems at home. Rising fuel prices contributed to inflation and unemployment. The billions of dollars paid annually to import oil accounted for a substantial share of the U.S. trade and balance-of-payments deficits.

Government social-welfare programs have not always achieved their objectives, but they have helped millions of people. The real question facing Americans today is whether they are willing to pay the costs of "promoting the general welfare" and attempting to build a better society.

Suggested Reading

Browning, Robert X. *Politics and Social Welfare Policy in the United States** (University of Tennessee Press, 1986). A detailed analysis of the development of the federal government's social-welfare programs since the 1940s. Emphasizes the effects that various economic and political factors have had on the growth of welfare programs.

Darmstadter, Joel; Landsberg, Hans H.; Morton, Herbert C.; and Coda, Michael J. *Energy, Today and Tomorrow: Living with Uncertainty* (Prentice-Hall, 1984). A concise primer on energy problems faced by the United States and the world. Discusses such issues as oil pricing, nuclear power, and alternative energy sources.

Davies, Barbara S., and Davies, J. Clarence III. *The Politics of Pollution*, 2nd edition (Pegasus, 1975). A useful analysis of pollution as a political issue, covering federal antipollution legislation, the role of Congress, public opinion, and interest groups. The authors emphasize that improvement of the environment depends upon public pressure on the executive branch and on Congress.

Derthick, Martha. *Policymaking for Social Security** (The Brookings Institution, 1979). A comprehensive study of policymaking for social security. Examines the basic policies that have shaped the program, the small group of people who influence decisions, and the future of the social security system.

Donovan, John C. *The Politics of Poverty*, 3rd edition (University Press of America, 1980). A comprehensive examination of attempts by government to alleviate poverty in the United States. Discusses the various political forces that affect policymaking in this area.

Dubos, Renné J. *Reason Awake: Science for Man* (Columbia University Press, 1970). A collection of essays by a distinguished microbiologist focusing on the threat to people and the environment caused by the technological and population explosions. Analyzes a whole range of problems — from nuclear weapons to urban sprawl — that have resulted from a constantly expanding technology.

Harrington, Michael. *The Other America** (Penguin, 1971). (Originally published in 1962.) One of the most widely read introductory surveys of the nature and extent of poverty in the United States in the early 1960s.

Herman, Edward S. *Corporate Control, Corporate Power* (Cambridge University Press, 1981). A comprehensive analysis of the power of corporations and their relationship to government. Argues that government power is checked and limited by corporate power.

Levitan, Sar A., and Taggart, Robert. *The Promise of Greatness** (Harvard University Press, 1976). A careful, detailed examination of recent social-welfare programs, including Medicare and Medicaid, CETA, and Aid to Families with Dependent Children. The authors argue that the federal programs and policies of the 1960s moved the nation toward a better, more equitable society and urge renewed government efforts to achieve social reform.

Meyer, Jack A., and Lewin, Marion Ein, eds. *Charting the Future of Health Care: Policy, Politics, and Public Health** (American Enterprise Institute, 1987). An informative anal-ysis of one of the major public policy issues facing the United States in the late 1980s and the 1990s.

Nader, Ralph; Green, Mark; and Seligman, Joel. *Taming the Giant Corporation* (Norton, 1977). A critical analysis of the political, economic, and social consequences of large corporations. Argues that big corporations should be chartered by the federal government and made to reveal far more information about their activities to the public.

Nivola, Pietro S. *The Politics of Energy Conservation** (The Brookings Institution, 1986). A comprehensive examination of energy problems faced by the United States. Stresses the importance of conservation in efforts to meet the nation's energy needs and discusses the influence that interest groups and public opinion have on policymaking in this area.

Page, Benjamin I. *Who Gets What from Government** (University of California Press, 1983). An analysis of the redistributive effect of government economic and social programs. Concludes that significant inequality persists in the United States and that recent governmental policies have been making it worse.

Piven, Frances Fox, and Cloward, Richard A. *The New Class War: Reagan's Attack on the Welfare State and Its Consequences** (Pantheon, 1982). An analysis of the welfare state and the efforts of business-oriented leaders of the Reagan administration to dismantle some of its protections. Argues that despite budget cutbacks, the welfare state will survive.

Price, Don K. *The Scientific Estate* (Belknap Press of Harvard University Press, 1965). A thoughtful and perceptive analysis of science and scientists, and their relation to public policymaking in the United States.

Schlesinger, Arthur M., Jr. *The Coming of the New Deal** (Houghton Mifflin, 1959). A revealing and highly readable historical account of the inauguration of Franklin Roosevelt's New Deal, which established the basis for much of the nation's current economic welfare legislation. Part of the multivolume historical study by Schlesinger of Roosevelt and New Deal politics.

Steiner, Gilbert Y. *The State of Welfare** (The Brookings Institution, 1971). A detailed analysis of major government welfare programs in the United States. Includes a discussion of proposed changes in federal welfare policies and considers the political factors affecting welfare reform.

Sundquist, James L. *Politics and Policy: The Eisenhower, Kennedy, and Johnson Years* (The Brookings Institution, 1968). An informative and valuable study of the battles in Congress and in the country to pass what became the new domestic social-welfare programs of the Johnson administration.

---

* Available in paperback edition.

PART FIVE

THE AMERICAN COMMUNITY

I N THE WASHINGTON suburb of Suitland, Maryland, five miles southeast of the Capitol dome and far from familiar paths trod by tourists, a complex of federal buildings houses a group of men and women whose business, in part, is to peer into the future.

The building is the headquarters of the United States Bureau of the Census, a division of the Commerce Department. By using electronic computers, and calculating birth and death rates and other factors, the Census Bureau is able to make population projections for the future. It cannot do so with precision, because there is a wide margin for error in such tabulations. Nevertheless, the Census Bureau is able to guess that

Chapter 16

State and Local Government

the population of the United States, which was more than 248 million after the 1990 census, may stand, by the year 2010, somewhere around 302 million.[1]

Although this projection is only an estimate, an increase of about 54 million people in twenty years would be like adding the populations of Sweden, Austria, Switzerland, Angola, Nicaragua, and Nepal to the United States. And, by the year 2040, the population of the United States may reach 372 million, according to Census Bureau estimates.[2] In other words, there is a

---

[1] U.S. Bureau of the Census, Current Population Reports, Supplement to *Projections of the Population of the United States, by Age, Sex, and Race: 1988 to 2080*, series P-25, no. 1018, January 1989, p. 39; figures rounded.

[2] Data provided by Populations Projections Branch, U.S. Bureau of the Census.

possibility that the 1990 population of more than 248 million will increase by 124 million in fifty years.

Today American society is burdened with multifold, interlocking problems — the varying state of the economy, environmental pollution, limited energy resources, racial discrimination, unemployment, poverty, homelessness, drug abuse, and crime. If, as seems possible, the population increases substantially in five decades, will the American political system and American society be able to cope with these problems? To take a random example — and assuming there is enough gasoline or other fuel to go around — would anyone care to visualize what it might be like driving along the San Bernardino Freeway during the morning rush hour in

the year 2040? It is bad enough now, as Los Angeles commuters can attest.

But one does not have to wait until the next century to see the problems facing states and localities. By the 1992 presidential election year, states and local governments across America were facing a budget crunch. Reduced revenues because of a lagging economy meant that one state after another had been forced to raise taxes and cut services drastically. Schools, libraries, health facilities, and other basic needs suffered as a result.

One of the most dramatic examples occurred in California that summer. For 64 days, Governor Pete Wilson and state legislators were unable to agree on a

budget, and the mighty state of California had to issue IOUs of uncertain worth to pay its own employees. The fiscal package finally approved meant increased fees for students at community colleges and universities, reduced hours for many public facilities, and closing of trauma centers in many counties. Six other states besides California each had budget shortfalls of more than $1 billion in 1992–93.

Clearly, a growing population combined with economic problems spells trouble for the taxpayers. Not only the size of the population but its geographic distribution affect the nature of a society. In the United States, almost 70 percent of the people are crowded into just over 10 percent of the land area. More than half of the population of the United States lives in just nine states.[3] Since 1920 the population of the United States has been more urban than rural. In 1990, when the population stood at 248.7 million, 192.7 million Americans, or 77 percent, lived in metropolitan areas. Of this total, 77.6 million lived in central cities and about 115 million lived outside the cities, mostly in the suburbs. About 56 million lived in rural or other nonmetropolitan areas.[4] (See Figure 16–1).

In 1990 more than 124 million people, or just over half the population of the United States, lived in metropolitan areas of at least one million.[5] As America has become urbanized, many of the nation's difficult problems have developed in their most acute form in urban areas — in the central "core" cities and the surrounding suburbs. Obviously, the decisions and actions of state, city, and other local governments have a direct impact on the quality of American life.

Much of this book has focused on the national government and national politics, but at last count there

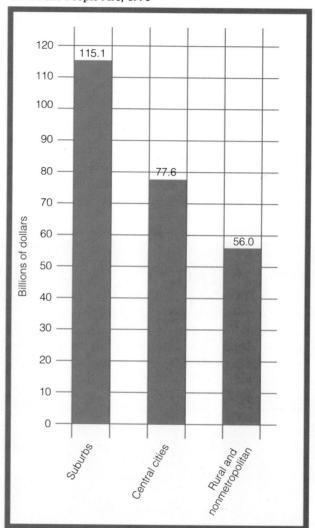

Figure 16–1
Where the People Are, 1990

SOURCE: Data provided by Statistical Information Office, Population Division, U.S. Bureau of the Census.

were, in addition to the government in Washington, 83,185 units of state and local government in the United States.[6] The performance of these governments is often criticized for failure to keep pace with the complex problems they face — transportation, housing, pollution, welfare services, schools, drugs, crime — to name some of the major ones. This inability to keep pace is not always the fault of the state or community; many of the

---

[3] California, New York, Texas, Pennsylvania, Florida, Illinois, Ohio, Michigan, and New Jersey. Together these large states, ranked above in order of population in 1990, comprise 51.8 percent of the population. U.S. Bureau of the Census, *Statistical Abstract of the United States 1991*, p. 22.

[4] Data provided by Statistical Information Office, Population Division, U.S. Bureau of the Census. The terms urban, rural, metropolitan, and suburban are subject to varying definitions. The federal government in 1983 divided the nation into Metropolitan Statistical Areas (MSAs), each of which contains at least one city of 50,000 persons, or an urban area of that size, and a total population of 100,000 (75,000 in New England). Suburbs are defined here as areas outside central cities but within the Census Bureau definition of a metropolitan area. Not all the 115 million people in the suburbs, so defined, might feel that they live in suburbia; suburban population obviously depends on how one defines a "suburb."

[5] News release, U.S. Bureau of the Census, February 21, 1991.

[6] U.S. Bureau of the Census, *1987 Census of Governments*, vol. 1, no. 1, p. VI.

problems that exist have been compounded by urbanization and patterns of population migration in recent decades. These factors have interacted to place a serious strain on the federal system.

Since the Second World War, for a variety of reasons, large numbers of low-income African Americans and whites have migrated from rural areas to big cities. At the same time, many middle-class families and business firms have moved out to the suburbs, taking the city tax base with them. The newcomers to the inner city have required costly government services — schools, welfare, police and fire protection, for example — but have not had sufficient taxable incomes and property to finance these services.

By the early 1970s the flow of black migrants to the cities had declined sharply.[7] And by that time African Americans were also migrating to the suburbs. Nevertheless, in 1990 only 8 percent of suburban residents were black. Some of the outward migration by African Americans represented a spilling over of city neighborhoods into adjoining suburbs. Moreover, many African Americans in the suburbs continued to live in highly segregated neighborhoods. About 83 percent of African Americans lived in metropolitan areas, and the percentage living in the central cities was more than twice that of whites.[8]

But the 1990 census revealed new patterns of population change. For example, the census data showed that the African American population in metropolitan areas of the North and Midwest remained about the same or declined in the previous decade but increased dramatically in the Sun Belt and in areas of economic growth. Chicago and Pittsburgh lost black population, but the number of African Americans in Sacramento increased by 65 percent and in Seattle by 40 percent.[9]

For the most part, cities rely on the property tax to finance the bulk of municipal services. Suburban governments now collect the taxes on the property of families and industries that have left the cities — and suburban residents have little desire to "bail out" City Hall. Big-city mayors look to Washington and the statehouses for relief. But, the mayors maintain, what limited federal funds are available have been siphoned off in part by the states for use in the suburbs and in rural areas.

A "mismatch" exists not only between urgent problems and state and local financial resources, but between the magnitude of the problems and the performance of state and local governments. Two overriding conclusions may be drawn from many of the studies of state and local problems:

1. *Many of the problems are larger than the boundaries of the governmental units that are attempting to deal with them.* Smog, for example, respects no city lines, and the issue of commuter transportation in a metropolitan area may involve two dozen local communities.

2. *The solutions frequently cost more than the governmental units have available or are willing to spend.* A

[7] Karl E. Taeuber, "Racial Segregation: The Persisting Dilemma," *Annals of the American Academy of Political and Social Science,* November 1975, p. 93.

[8] U.S. Bureau of the Census, 1990 Census of Population, "Race, Hispanic Origin, and Group Quarters Population: Metropolitan Areas, 1990," p. 4. Preliminary data, percentage rounded.

[9] *Washington Post,* July 5, 1991, p. A1.

suburban area cannot possibly afford, for example, to build a mass-transit line to carry its residents to downtown offices, nor can the central cities raise the tax revenues to provide adequate social services for those inner-city residents who need them most.

Against this background, we may ask: How well are the state and local governments meeting their responsibilities? How are state and local governments organized? What is the relationship among federal, state, and local governments? What are the major problems of the cities and the suburbs? Given the politics and existing structure of state and local governments, can they hope to solve problems that are larger than their geographic boundaries and financial resources? What are the implications of these problems for America's future?

THE STATES

America is a nation of states. The political institutions of the thirteen colonies foreshadowed the shape of the federal system created under the Constitution. The states, in short, were here *before* the American nation. They grew in number as the frontier was pushed westward to the Pacific. They are not mere administrative or geographic units established for the convenience of the central government. Rather, the states are key political institutions rooted in the nation's historical development, sharing power under the federal system with the national government in Washington. But the federal system was constructed when the United States was a small, rural nation. In today's predominantly urban America, a nation of congested cities, neighborhoods devastated by poverty and drugs, and sprawling suburbs, are the states any longer relevant? Can they meet the new demands placed on them by urbanization?

Many critics of state government feel that the states are not doing as much as they should, particularly in the crucial area of urban problems. However, the states have been making an effort to meet their responsibilities. For example, state and local spending has been increasing at an even faster rate than federal spending. In the four years between 1986 and 1990, total federal spending increased by 27 percent. But during the same period, state and local expenditures increased by 36 percent. In addition, in recent years the staffs of the bureaucracies that run the state governments, and the staffs of the state legislatures, have become more professional; that is, they tend to be better educated, better

trained, and to have a longer-term commitment to their government jobs than in the past. The states and localities do not, of course, spend as much as the federal government, but their level of spending for domestic programs often actually exceeds that of the federal government.

As the budget woes of the states in the early 1990s illustrated, however, often a serious imbalance, or income gap, has existed between the demands on state and local governments and the revenues they raise through taxes. One reason for this is that state and local governments rely heavily on property and consumer taxes, which do not reflect the general growth of the economy as rapidly as the federal income tax does. At present, the federal government collects more than half of all taxes; the states and communities divide the remainder.

During the late 1960s and in the 1970s, in an effort to find new sources of revenue, states raised taxes and imposed new taxes on a massive scale. Despite some state tax reductions in the late 1970s, the trend toward higher state taxes continued. Between 1990 and 1991, for example, thirty-seven states increased their taxes. Although the amount of the increases and the particular taxes affected varied from state to state, the changes included higher taxes on sales, personal income, corporations, motor fuel, cigarettes, and alcohol.[10]

By that time, however, there had been a significant tax revolt in several states, most notably in California. In 1978 California voters approved by 2 – 1 a constitutional amendment that appeared on the ballot as Proposition

---

[10] *The Book of the States, 1992–93 Edition* (Lexington, KY: The Council of State Governments, 1992), p. 390.

13. It limited real estate taxes in the state to 1 percent of previous property values and was approved by the electorate despite warnings that it would result in cuts in government services. In Washington, and across the nation, political leaders read the election returns as a general "taxpayers' revolt" and a demand for lower taxes.

One result of the passage of Proposition 13 was to increase the power of the state and the state legislature because "local governments in California . . . now have less political capacity, as well as less fiscal capacity, with which to shape the futures of their communities."[11]

At first, the impact of Proposition 13 was cushioned by a $5 billion state surplus that had accumulated in California. Two years later, in 1980, a new proposition, which would have cut the state's income tax in half, was offered to the voters. By now, however, the atmosphere in California had changed somewhat. People had begun to feel the pinch in government services brought about by the passage of Proposition 13. This time, the new tax-cutting initiative was defeated by a margin of 5–3. In Colorado in 1992, however, the voters passed Amendment 1, a sweeping tax-limitation measure that required any state tax increase or debt to be approved by the voters.

In 1991 seven states still had no personal income tax, however, and many other states taxed incomes at relatively low rates.[12] States are cautious in taxing in part because they must compete with one another. They "must be wary of increasing taxes or redistributing income in a way that will enable neighboring states to attract away industry."[13]

The federal government provides some financial help. In fiscal 1993 federal aid to the states was budgeted at $199.1 billion, or 13 percent of the federal budget. But the cuts in the federal budget imposed by President Reagan in the early 1980s had a particularly severe impact on state governments. One study calculated that in the administration's first year, "grants to state and local governments were cut by 13.1 percent."[14] And as a percentage of the total federal budget, grant spending by 1983 "had returned to the levels of the early 1960s."[15]

Some states were forced to use their own funds to replace the loss of federal revenues during this period. But relatively few states and localities did so. "Most federal aid cuts were 'ratified,' that is, passed along to the recipients of the federally aided benefits and services."[16]

During the early Reagan years, the states felt the effects of economic recession and tax and revenue limitations perhaps even more than the cuts in aid from Washington. In California in the early 1980s, after Proposition 13 had limited the property tax rate to 1 percent, voters also limited personal income taxes and abolished inheritance and gift taxes. "The recession weakened the state's ability to absorb these revenue losses. . . ."[17] The result of this combination of factors was to increase fiscal strain in the federal system.

What do the states do? They have major responsibilities in the fields of education, welfare, transportation, the administration of justice, the prisons, housing, public health, and the environment. (See Figure 16–2.) States share with local governments responsibility for the delivery of these and many other vital public services. And this responsibility is the source of many of the difficulties faced by the states, as well as by local governments.

To provide these services, state and local governments employ more people than does the federal government — with all of the accompanying problems of unionization, strikes, and control of bureaucracy. Even though states are spending more money on public services, they have not always been successful in attacking the urban problems they face. There is a wide variation in the performance and effectiveness of the fifty states, just as there are substantial differences in state politics and state political institutions.

As noted in Chapter 3, however, many states have adopted innovative programs in education and other

[11] John J. Kirlin, The Political Economy of Fiscal Limits (Lexington, MA: Lexington Books, D. C. Heath, 1982), p. 4.
[12] Data provided by Advisory Commission on Intergovernmental Relations. The seven states without a general income tax were Alaska, Florida, Nevada, South Dakota, Texas, Washington, and Wyoming.
[13] James Q. Wilson, "Urban Problems in Perspective," in James Q. Wilson, ed., The Metropolitan Enigma (Washington, D.C.: U.S. Chamber of Commerce, 1967), p. 395.

[14] George E. Peterson, "Federalism and the States: An Experiment in Decentralization," in John L. Palmer and Isabel V. Sawhill, eds., The Reagan Record: An Assessment of America's Changing Domestic Priorities, An Urban Institute Study (Cambridge: Ballinger Publishing, 1984), p. 227.
[15] Ibid.
[16] Richard P. Nathan, Fred C. Doolittle, and Associates, The Consequences of Cuts: The Effects of the Reagan Domestic Program on State and Local Governments (Princeton: Princeton Urban and Regional Research Center, 1983), p. 6.
[17] Ibid., p. 77.

Figure 16–2

Major Expenditures of State and Local Governments, 1989–90 (in millions of dollars)

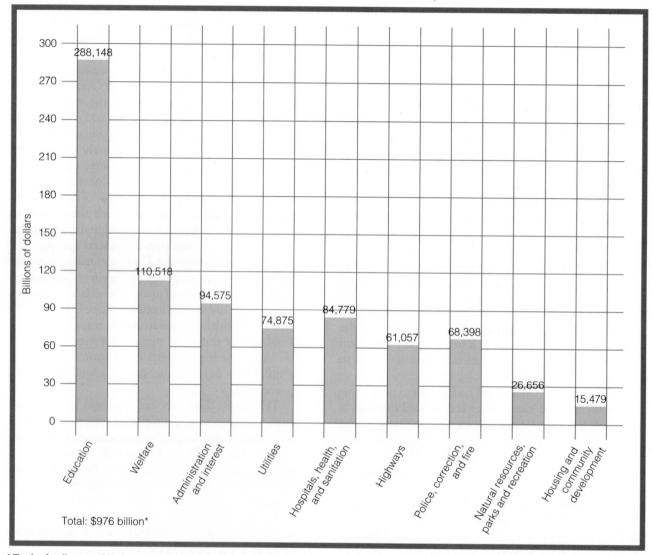

Total: $976 billion*

* Total is for all state and local expenditures, including items not shown.
SOURCE: U.S. Bureau of the Census. *Government Finances: 1989–90*, December 1991, p. 10.

areas that have later been copied by the federal government. Particularly during the 1980s, when Washington cut back on social programs, the states experimented with their own programs. Wisconsin introduced the first welfare plan linking payments to school attendance; Illinois introduced self-management of public-housing projects; Vermont proposed a system of universal access to health care; and Minnesota, the state of Washington, and Alaska established programs to target parents who evade child support by changing jobs fre-

quently. Arkansas, Bill Clinton's home state, made its teachers accountable for their classroom performance.

Beyond providing services, states have a major impact on people's lives. It is the states, not the federal government, that regulate marriage, divorce, child custody, drivers' licenses, auto inspection, transfer of property, wills and estates, and many other matters. And it is the states, as well as the federal government, that determine the penalty for possession of marijuana, or whether capital punishment shall be applied for certain crimes. The federal courts may eventually review state cases that involve constitutional questions, but initially at least, in cases that do not involve federal laws, the states decide.

The State Constitutions

State constitutions spell out the basic structure of each state government. Every state constitution provides for an executive, legislative, and judicial branch. Although each includes a bill of rights, some state constitutions are more liberal than others. For example, the constitutions of the newest states, Alaska and Hawaii, have strong civil rights provisions.

State constitutions tend to be lists of what the state cannot do; they limit the power of the governor and of the legislature—to levy taxes and borrow money, for example. As a result, state constitutions are often condemned as restrictive, negative documents that impede the ability of states to meet modern problems.

In the late 1960s and early 1970s, many states streamlined their constitutions. But modernizing state constitutions does not in itself improve governmental performance; there also must be changes in the political climate in which those governments operate. In many areas of the nation, however, there is political resistance to massive, costly undertakings by governments to solve urban problems. For example, New Jersey has one of the most modern state constitutions, but it has not surpassed other states in responding to urban problems.

The state constitutions, as Duane Lockard pointed out, "have been amended more than 3000 times and in some instances it is necessary to read the constitution backwards like a Chinese newspaper, in order to see what the last word is on an original provision." [18] Lockard also found a number of oddities; the California Constitution, for example, limited the power of the legislature to regulate the length of wrestling matches, and the Georgia Constitution provided a $250,000 reward for the first person to strike oil within the borders of the Peach State. [19]

The most common means of amending state constitutions is by a majority or two-third vote of the legislature and approval of a majority of the voters at the next election. [20] In addition, four-fifths of the states permit constitutional conventions to amend their constitutions, with the changes subject to approval of the voters. In some states, the legislature may appoint a commission to recommend constitutional changes, again subject to voter approval. And seventeen states permit their constitutions to be amended by *initiative*. [21] Under this method, proposed constitutional amendments can be placed on the ballot if enough signatures are obtained on a petition. California's Proposition 13 was an example of a constitutional amendment approved by the voters in this fashion. In addition, almost half the states —23 in 1992, mostly in the West and Midwest— permit voters to enact legislation by majority vote. In 1992, for example there were sixty-six initiatives on the ballot in various states, permitting voters to enact or repeal taxes, and dealing with issues such as abortion, gay rights, state lotteries, banning trucks with triple trailers, requiring employers to provide health insurance, and outlawing the hunting of nursing mother bears. [22]

The Governors

At first glance, it might appear as though the fifty states are federal governments in miniature. Each has the familiar three branches with checks and balances. The governors are usually reasonably prestigious figures, at least within their states; like the president, they head an executive branch. And, like the president, they have armed forces under their command in the form of the state police and the National Guard. Appearances are deceptive, however, for the position of governor in some states is much less powerful than is popularly imagined.

In the first place, the states have come to occupy a less prominent position within the federal system than they enjoyed in years past. The actions of a governor, and of other state officials, and the laws passed by state legislatures cannot conflict with federal law and are subject to judicial review by the United States Supreme Court. At Little Rock, Arkansas, and elsewhere in the South, federal power has prevailed over that of state

[18] Duane Lockard, *The Politics of State and Local Government*, 2nd ed. (New York: Macmillan, 1969), p. 85.
[19] Duane Lockard, *The Politics of State and Local Government*, 3rd ed. (New York: Macmillan, 1983), p. 94.
[20] *The Book of the States, 1992–93 Edition*, pp. 3, 22. In Delaware, only the legislature can ratify and propose amendments.
[21] Ibid., p. 24.
[22] *New York Times*, October 16, 1992, p. A10.

governors in confrontations over public school deseg-regation.

Beyond this, the position of governor has been weakened by historical and political factors. During the colonial period, the royal governors clashed with the elected legislatures. The state constitutions written at the time of the American Revolution reflected the pre-vailing distrust of executive power; in most states, the legislature chose the governor. During the nineteenth century, popular election of governors spread through the states, but the power of the governors remained relatively weak. Not until the twentieth century were state governments reorganized and executive power in-creased in some states. But even today, the office of governor is weak in a number of states.

At the same time, political scientists have noted marked improvements in the abilities and stature of American governors in recent decades. Larry Sabato has suggested that the political hacks of the past have faded away: "The good-time Charlies are gone." [23] In their place, Sabato observes, there has arisen "a new breed of governor," more highly skilled, better trained, and bet-ter able to lead their states in the modern age. [24]

Variations in the power of state governors were shown in a study published by a federal commission. In only ten states was the governor said to be "very strong." [25] Another study, by Thad L. Beyle, a political scientist, ranked the states according to the formal powers of the governors—including tenure, appoint-ment, removal, budget, legislative budget-changing, or-ganization, veto powers, and party control—and con-cluded that governors were "very strong" in four states, "strong" in twenty-one, "moderate" in fourteen, "weak" in nine, and "very weak" in two states. [26]

Beyle found that the governors' formal powers were stronger in the larger and wealthier states—such as New York, Massachusetts, Pennsylvania, New Jersey, and Ohio—with a large concentration of urban popu-lation. He found no governors with very strong powers in the South. The governors of California, New York,

Governor Ann Richards of Texas

and other large states, Beyle noted, "are important and powerful in political circles. They often are elevated to potential presidential candidacy just because they are the governors of these states. The national press covers them closely. . . . In short, these governors have na-tional power because of the states they head." [27] In re-cent years, a number of states have taken steps to strengthen the power of the governor. In twenty-two states, the governor now has power to reorganize the executive branch by executive order, subject to veto by the legislature. [28] Several governors have been given broader power to appoint department heads and other state officials. [29]

In most states, the governor shares executive power with at least one other popularly elected official. Typically, the officials elected by the voters along with the governor may include the lieutenant governor, at-torney general, secretary of state, treasurer, auditor, and

[23] Larry Sabato, *Goodbye to Good-time Charlie: The American Gov-ernorship Transformed*, 2nd ed., (Washington, D.C.: CQ Press, 1983), p. 201.

[24] Ibid.

[25] *Fiscal Balance in the American System*, vol. 1, Advisory Commis-sion on Intergovernmental Relations (Washington, D.C.: U.S. Government Printing Office, October 1967), pp. 233–34.

[26] Thad L. Beyle, "Governors," in Virginia Gray, Herbert Jacob, and Robert B. Albritton, eds., *Politics in the American States: A Comparative Analysis*, 5th ed. (Glenview, IL: Scott, Foresman & Company, 1990), p. 228.

[27] Ibid., p. 217. The study measured potential formal powers of the governors, not how those powers were actually utilized.

[28] *The Book of the States, 1992–93 Edition*, pp. 49–50.

[29] Data provided by National Governors Association.

superintendent of education. The governor's difficulties are increased if one or more of these elected executive-branch officials belong to the opposing political party. The power of governors to appoint important officials (in states where they are not elected independently) varies from state to state; in some cases their choices are subject to approval by the state senate.

All states except North Carolina grant their governors the power to veto state legislation. The veto is one of the few areas in which governors actually have more power than the equivalent power of the president. In 1992, governors in forty-three states could exercise an *item veto* over single parts of appropriations bills.[30] The president could only veto entire bills (see Chapter 10, p. 378).

More than half the states limit the term of office of the governor, restricting the governor either to one or two four-year terms. But seventeen states have four-year terms with unlimited succession. In 1992 only three states had two-year terms for governor.[31] In general, a governor's power and ability to develop long-range policies are greater if the term in office is four years and he or she is permitted to seek reelection. Otherwise, to some extent, the governor becomes a "lame duck" as soon as the inauguration takes place.

The governor's control over the state budget is another index of power. In all but a few states, the governor prepares an executive budget and submits it to the legislature. While this usually serves to increase the governor's strength, much still depends on the skill a governor shows in managing the state bureaucracy and on other fiscal and political practices within the state. Since federal grants provide a substantial share of state revenues, the power of governors also varies with the degree of control they have over state participation in federal programs. Even so, the power of governors to use federal grants is limited by the administrative "strings" attached to money flowing from Washington; states receiving grants must comply with federal laws — such requirements as affirmative action, for example — and with various federal reporting and record-keeping rules.

The Legislatures

When the American nation began, state legislatures were powerful and prestigious political institutions. Today, they are sometimes described in unflattering terms. During the nineteenth century, in the era of Jacksonian democracy and again after the Civil War, voters in many states wrote into the state constitutions various restrictions on legislative power — limiting state expenditures and borrowing power, for example. Many of these curbs are still in effect.

Public respect for state legislators and legislatures also has been eroded by occasional disclosures of bribes and corruption among the lawmakers. One result has been a suspicion that some state legislators manage to use their position for private gain. Closely tied to this assumption is the belief that lobbyists and special-interest groups can work their will at the statehouse more easily than in Washington. An industry, utility, or labor union that exercises great power within a state capital sometimes achieves its legislative aims more easily at the state level than in Congress, where its power may be diffused and it must compete with many other interest groups.

Finally, until the Supreme Court's reapportionment decisions of the 1960s, overrepresentation of rural areas in the state legislatures diminished legislative prestige in urban areas. City dwellers grumbled about state legislatures controlled by "appleknockers" and "farmers" who primarily served rural interests.

There have been some signs of improvement, however. By the 1980s, a number of state legislatures had begun modernizing both their procedures and facilities — for example, strengthening their committee system, installing computers, and initiating other reforms. As noted, this has been accompanied by a trend toward greater professionalism in the staffing of state legislatures.

Every state has a two-house legislature except Nebraska, which has a unicameral legislature. The 7,461 state lawmakers serve in legislatures that range in size from sixty in Alaska to 424 in New Hampshire. Typically, the upper house has about forty members and the lower house about one hundred members. Most state senators serve four-year terms; most state representatives in the lower house serve for two years. In forty-three states the legislature meets annually. In most of the other states, the legislatures meet regularly only every two years, normally in January.[32]

For the majority of state legislators, public service is only a part-time job. In almost two-thirds of the states

---

[30] *The Book of the States, 1992–93 Edition*, pp. 49–50.
[31] Ibid., pp. 44–45. The states were New Hampshire, Rhode Island, and Vermont.
[32] Ibid., pp. 137–141.

Table 16-1
The State Legislatures, 1992

	Senate Members	Length of Term	House Members	Length of Term	Years Sessions Are Held	Salary*
Alabama	35	4	105	4	annual	$10(d)
Alaska	20	4	40	2	annual	24,012
Arizona	30	2	60	2	annual	15,000
Arkansas	35	4	100	2	odd	7,500
California	40	4	80	2	annual	52,500
Colorado	35	4	65	2	annual	17,500
Connecticut	36	2	151	2	annual	16,760
Delaware	21	4	41	2	annual	24,213
Florida	40	4	120	2	annual	22,560
Georgia	56	2	180	2	annual	10,509
Hawaii	25	4	51	2	annual	27,000
Idaho	42	2	84	2	annual	12,000
Illinois	59	4#	118	2	annual	37,230
Indiana	50	4	100	2	annual	11,600
Iowa	50	4	100	2	annual	18,100
Kansas	40	4	125	2	annual	60(d)
Kentucky	38	4	100	2	even	100(d)
Louisiana	39	4	105	4	annual	16,800
Maine	35	2	151	2	annual	7,125
Maryland	47	4	141	4	annual	27,000
Massachusetts	40	2	160	2	annual	30,000
Michigan	38	4	110	2	annual	45,450
Minnesota	67	4	134	2	annual	27,979
Mississippi	52	4	122	4	annual	10,000
Missouri	34	4	163	2	annual	22,870
Montana	50	4	100	2	odd	56(d)
Nebraska	49	4	**	**	annual	12,000
Nevada	21	4	42	2	odd	130(d)
New Hampshire	24	2	400	2	annual	100
New Jersey	40	4	80	2	annual	35,000
New Mexico	42	4	70	2	annual	75(d)
New York	61	2	150	2	annual	57,500
North Carolina	50	2	120	2	annual	12,504
North Dakota	53	4	106	2	odd	90(d)
Ohio	33	4	99	2	annual	42,426
Oklahoma	48	4	101	2	annual	32,000
Oregon	30	4	60	2	odd	11,868
Pennsylvania	50	4	203	2	annual	47,000
Rhode Island	50	2	100	2	annual	5(d)
South Carolina	46	4	124	2	annual	10,400
South Dakota	35	2	70	2	annual	4,267(o)
						3,733(e)
Tennessee	33	4	99	2	annual	16,500
Texas	31	4	150	2	odd	7,200
Utah	29	4	75	2	annual	65(d)
Vermont	30	2	150	2	annual	90(m)
Virginia	40	4	100	2	annual	18,000
Washington	49	4	98	2	annual	23,200
West Virginia	34	4	100	2	annual	6,500
Wisconsin	33	4	99	2	annual	33,622
Wyoming	30	4	64	2	annual	75(d)

* Salaries as of 1992. Amounts are annual unless otherwise noted as (d) per day, (m) per month, (o) odd year, or (e) even year.
# Terms vary from two to four years.
** Unicameral legislature.
SOURCE: Adapted from *The Book of the States*, 1992–93 Edition (Lexington: Council of State Governments, 1992), pp. 137–139, 141, 151–152.

the length of regular legislative sessions is constitution-ally limited, sometimes to sixty days. Even then, the legislators may spend only a few days in the capital each week, often ending the session with a great flurry of last-minute legislation. Sometimes the clock is literally stopped to permit the passage of bills within the time limit.

In 1992, New York legislators were paid $57,500 a year, the highest state legislative salaries in the nation. Although five states—California, Michigan, New York, Ohio, and Pennsylvania—paid legislators $40,000 or more annually, eleven states paid only a per diem rate. The average annual salary of state legislators was about $22,000.[33]

Who are the legislators? State lawmakers tend to come from a higher-than-average social and economic background. As Samuel C. Patterson has noted:

> The largest occupational group among state legislators is that of lawyers. . . . few white- and blue-collar workers serve in the legislatures, even in the industrial states with large labor union memberships. . . . In the last decade women have been winning legislative seats in increasing numbers, but the percentages are not very large.[34]

By 1991 the number of state legislators who were women had increased from 10 percent in 1980 to just over 18 percent.[35] Perhaps the most important aspect of

state legislatures today is their changing nature as a re-sult of the "reapportionment revolution" discussed in Chapter 9 (pp. 347–349). In *Baker v. Carr* in 1962, the Supreme Court held that the voters of Tennessee did have the right to challenge unequal representation in the state's legislature.[36] And in *Reynolds v. Sims* in 1964, it ruled that apportionment of both houses of state leg-islatures must be based closely on population and the principle of "equal representation for equal numbers of people."[37]

The Court's decisions did not, despite popular ex-pectations, shift the base of state political power from rural areas to the central cities. Instead, the main bene-ciary has proved to be the suburbs. And suburban legis-lators have often proved to be just as conservative on many social welfare and urban issues as lawmakers from a state's rural areas.

As a result of voter discontent with politicians, a number of states have amended their constitutions to limit the terms of elected officials and legislators. Voters in California, Oklahoma, and Colorado adopted such term limits in 1990. And the movement was growing. In 1992, voters in 13 states approved limits on the terms of state officials. In 12 of those states, plus two other states, voters approved limits on the terms of members of Congress, restricting senators to two terms and repre-sentatives to two or three terms. But most constitu-tional scholars doubted that states could impose such limits without an amendment to the United States Constitution.

The Judges

Most Americans never see the inside of the United States Supreme Court, or even of a federal district court. But many have been to state and local courts—for example, traffic court to pay a fine, or divorce court—where most criminal and civil cases are handled. The quality of justice in America, therefore, depends to a great extent on the quality of justice in the states and communities. These courts, rather than federal courts, are most visible to the average citizen.

[33] Ibid., pp. 85–87.
[34] Samuel C. Patterson, "State Legislators and Legislatures" in Gray, Jacob, and Albritton, eds., *Politics in the American States*, 5th ed., p. 176.
[35] Data provided by the National Conference of State Legislatures.
[36] *Baker v. Carr*, 369 U.S. 186 (1962).
[37] *Reynolds v. Sims*, 377 U.S. 533 (1964).

Just as the Supreme Court may strike down federal, state, or local laws that conflict with the United States Constitution, state courts often strike down state laws that conflict with their state constitutions. But the decisions of state and local courts must conform to the U.S. Constitution as interpreted by the Supreme Court.

State and local judgeships can be important political prizes. Young lawyers who "go into politics" may serve in the legislature or in a state or municipal administration. But often their hope is to be appointed a judge, as their safe, prestigious, and ultimate political reward.

The structure of the state and local judiciary and the problems of the nation's criminal justice system are discussed in detail in Chapter 13.

Politics and Parties

In Chapter 7 we examined the structure of state political party organizations, their relation to national parties, the geographic cleavage that exists between "upstate" and "downstate" urban–rural areas in many states, and the decline of big-city political machines. In Chapter 9 we mentioned the various national influences on state politics and the increasing effort of states to isolate themselves from the tides of presidential politics by scheduling elections for governor in the off-years. In the American federal system, state politics and state political parties cannot be separated from any discussion of politics and government at the national level.

In the five presidential elections from 1976 through 1992, three former or incumbent governors were elected president: Jimmy Carter of Georgia in 1976, Ronald Reagan of California in 1980 and 1984,

and Bill Clinton of Arkansas in 1992. Thirteen other presidents also had served as governors.

The states are the building blocks of the national political parties. But among the states, the pattern of party competition differs widely. For example, for many years in the one-party states of the Deep South, competition was largely *within* the Democratic party. The real battles were fought for the Democratic nomination; the winner of the nomination was virtually assured of victory over a Republican opponent in the general election.

The emergence of Alabama Governor George Wallace's third party in the 1960s, combined with major Republican inroads in the "Solid South," changed the face of southern politics. In 1968 President Nixon carried five southern states, and in 1972 he won the entire South. Four years later a southerner, Jimmy Carter, headed the Democratic ticket and carried all but one southern state. But in 1980 the Republican candidate, Ronald Reagan, accomplished exactly the reverse, carrying the entire South except for Carter's home state of Georgia. And in 1984, Reagan carried every southern state, as George Bush did in 1988. In 1992, however, the Democratic ticket was headed by Bill Clinton, a southern governor, and Albert Gore, a southern senator, and the Democrats captured four of the eleven states of the old Confederacy.

Some states have vigorous two-party competition. Other states have modified two-party competition — one party is on the average stronger than the other. But in both types of states, control of the statehouse and the legislature can swing back and forth. A study measuring party competition for state offices from 1981 to 1988 characterized one state as one-party Democratic, twenty-one as modified one-party Democratic, twenty-two as two-party, and six as modified one-party Republican.[38] (See Figure 16–3.) Since then, the pattern may have changed in some states, but not in most.

---

[38] John F. Bibby, Cornelius P. Cotter, James L. Gibson, Robert J. Huckshorn, "Parties in State Politics," in Gray, Jacob, and Albritton, eds., *Politics in the American States*, 5th ed., p. 92. The measure of interparty competition used in this study is based entirely on elections for *state* offices. The authors point out that "every state is now competitive in presidential elections." The study gave "more weight to partisan control of the state legislature then it [did] to winning the governorship. As a result, recent Republican successes in gubernatorial elections in such traditionally Democratic states as Arkansas, Florida, North Carolina, South Carolina, and Texas" carried less weight than "the heavy Democratic dominance of the state legislatures in these states" (p. 91).

Figure 16–3
Party Competition in the States

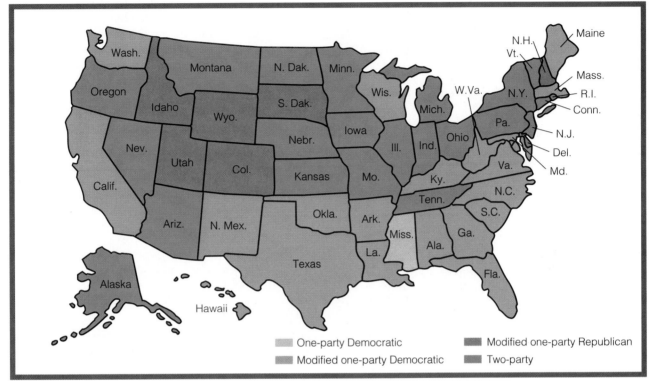

SOURCE: Adapted from data from John F. Bibby, Cornelius P. Cotter, James L. Gibson, Robert J. Huckshorn, "Parties in State Politics," in Virginia Gray, Herbert Jacob, and Robert B. Albritton, eds., *Politics in the American States: A Comparative Analysis*, 5th ed., p. 92. Data for states from 1981 through 1988. Copyright © 1990 by Scott, Foresman & Co.

Within the states, political parties show considerable ideological variation. A Democrat from rural Florida may be much closer to a Republican in ideological hue than to a Wisconsin Democrat. The Republican party in Mississippi bears little resemblance to the Republican party in Massachusetts.

The rise of the direct primary for state political nominations (discussed in Chapter 9) has weakened control of state political machines by party leaders. The primary has at least partially shifted control over nominations to the voters, in those states where they care to exercise that power.

LOCAL GOVERNMENTS

The cartoon in *The New Yorker* showed a woman sitting at a table on her apartment terrace, calling to her husband, "Hurry, dear, your soup is getting dirty." For most city dwellers, air pollution is no joke. And a city's laws and regulations affect the battle for cleaner air. Whether a person lives in a skyscraper, a tenement, or a small town, the quality of local government is likely to have immediate impact on that person's life. In this sense, local government is "closer" to the citizen, even though the federal government may have a greater effect on one's life in the long run.

New York City is a case in point. Its residents have lived through financial crises and strikes by sanitation workers, transit workers, and teachers. One way or another, these inconveniences involved the city government. If New Yorkers watch noxious trash piling up on the sidewalks, if they must walk several miles to work, or if they cannot send their children to school, they have ample reason to be aware of the impact of local government on their lives.

Although the connection is not always well understood, local governments are in actuality legal creatures

of the states. The state constitutions vest power in the state governments; local governments only exercise the power that the state gives to them.

Cities

Cities are municipal corporations chartered by the states. The charters define the municipal powers. About half the states have widely varying provisions for local *home rule.* As the term implies, home rule empowers municipalities to modify their charters and run their affairs without approval by the legislature, subject to the constitution and laws of the state. While home rule may give municipalities more freedom in choosing their *form* of government, in most states their freedom is not much greater than that of other localities in such fields as education, police power, and other substantive areas. Home rule, in other words, may not help cities solve problems. At a time when so many urban problems cut across the boundaries of local government units, many urban specialists believe there is a need for greater inter-

dependence and cooperation among local governments, not greater autonomy and independence.

There are three basic forms of city government:

The Mayor-Council Plan Today, most of the nation's cities of half a million people or more employ a strong mayor-council form of government. Under it, the mayor has substantial formal power over the executive agencies of government and in dealings with an elected city council. In some cities, however, a weak mayor-council form is still in use. Under it, the mayor is merely a figurehead and must share administrative power with the council and other elected officials. Some cities employ a mixture of the two systems. Nearly half the cities of 2,500 or more people use the mayor-council plan.

The Council-Manager Plan The council-manager form of government was first adopted before the First World War by the communities of Staunton, Virginia, and Sumter, South Carolina. Under this system a council, usually elected on a nonpartisan ticket, hires a professional city manager, who runs the city government and has power to hire and fire city officials. The council in turn has power to fire the city manager (although the city council is not supposed to interfere in the day-to-day administration of city affairs).

City managers often bring professional skills to the business of running a city and may frequently receive high salaries. Although city managers are nominally "nonpolitical," they may be dismissed as a result of a political battle within the community. Almost half of all cities with populations of 2,500 or more have city managers. The plan is employed all across the nation, from Portland, Maine, to San Jose, California, but it is particularly popular in California and other western states. It is also used widely in Virginia and Ohio.

The Commission Plan When a hurricane and high waves smashed Galveston, Texas, in 1900, more than five thousand people were killed and property damage was estimated to be in the millions. In the emergency, while the city government was paralyzed, the Texas State Legislature appointed a commission of five local businessmen to run Galveston.

The plan caught on and for a time, at least, was extremely popular in American cities. Under it, a board of city commissioners, usually five, is popularly elected (on a nonpartisan ballot in a majority of cities that use the system). The commissioners make policy as a city council, but they also run the city departments as administrators. One commissioner is usually designated mayor but often has no extra power. In time, the commission plan proved disappointing to reformers. Responsibility was diffused under the system, and commissioners frequently lacked the skills needed to administer city departments. Some 94 cities of 2,500 or more people still use this form of local government. But the number of cities using the commission plan is declining. In 1960 it was abandoned by Galveston, which turned to the council-manager plan.

Counties

In rural areas the county is the most important geographic unit of local government. There are 3,141 counties in the United States. Their size and power vary, but typically the elected officials include the sheriff, county prosecutor, coroner, clerk, and treasurer. These officials share governing power with elected county boards, most frequently called a "board of commissioners" or a "board of supervisors." Some large counties elect a county executive to act as chief administrator, and others appoint an administrator, much like city managers. The county courthouse is usually the local center of political power, the gathering place of those local officials, political leaders, and hangers-on referred to in some counties as "the courthouse gang." But county governments are changing. Of the total, 2,042 counties were run by commissioners, 422 counties were run by professional county administrators, 391 counties were governed by elected county executives, and the rest were administered in other ways.[39]

Towns and Townships

The New England town meeting has long stood as a symbol of direct participatory democracy. These meetings are still held in many New England towns: the townspeople come together for an annual meeting in the spring, at which they elect a board of selectmen and settle local policy questions. But today, urbanization and a vastly increased population have sapped the town meeting of much of its former strength.

In New England and New York, the "town" includes the village and the surrounding countryside. In the Middle Atlantic states and the Midwest, counties are often subdivided into townships. By order of Congress, many Midwest townships were laid out early in the nation's history in six-by-six-mile checkerboard fashion. For this reason, many townships today are thirty-six square miles in area. Rural townships are declining in importance and number. But in a number of urban areas, townships perform the function of cities.

Special Districts

Special districts are established within states to deal with problems that cut across the boundary lines of local units of government or to spread the tax burden over a geographic area larger than that of the pre-existing local units. They are created for such purposes as fire protection, sewage, water, schools, transportation, and parks.

---

[39] Data for 1987, provided by Government Division, U.S. Bureau of the Census.

The number of special districts has been growing at a rapid rate.

The existence of so many different kinds and layers of local government results in fragmentation and overlapping, contributing to the inability of local governments to respond effectively to their problems. For example, the existence in so many states of a separate system of government control for schools often makes it difficult for local governments to coordinate education with other programs. Special districts often mean that problems will be dealt with by experts and specialists. But such districts may also mean that local governments give up control over those programs. And the tax revenues raised by special districts cannot be used by other units of government to meet other needs.

CITIES AND SUBURBS: THE METROPOLITAN DILEMMA

For more than a decade, the suburbs, by Census Bureau estimates, have formed the largest segment of the American population. It was one day in 1970—no one knows the exact date—that the number of people living in suburbia exceeded the population living in the central cities or rural areas.[40]

There were no ceremonies to mark the occasion, no presidential ribbon-cutting, no television coverage. But the date was a milestone, nevertheless.

One political result can be measured in the increase in suburban representation in Congress and in state legislatures. Another result has been to sharpen the conflict between the suburbs and the cities on issues where their interests differ. Even before the suburbs had outgrown the cities in population, the urban-suburban rift was clearly visible. In state after state, suburban legislators, sometimes in alliance with rural forces, defeated legislation to aid central cities.

At the turn of the century, George Washington Plunkitt, the Tammany district leader, complained that rural legislators had imposed an unfair tax burden on New York City:

> This city is ruled entirely by the hayseed legislators at Albany. . . . In England . . . they make a pretense of givin' the Irish some self-government. In this state, the Republi-

can government makes no pretense at all. It says right out in the open: "New York City is a nice big fat goose. Come along with your carvin' knives and have a slice." They don't pretend to ask the Goose's consent.[41]

Today, the white suburban resident has largely replaced the "hayseeds" of yesteryear as the adversary of the city dweller. If Boss Plunkitt were around today, he probably would be complaining about the "commuters" in New York City's suburban Nassau and Westchester counties.

The picture of conflict between cities and suburbs might be even bleaker but for two emerging factors. First, the pattern of metropolitan growth has created an *interdependence* among all governments in the area, especially in such fields as air pollution, mass transit, and land use, where no single government's boundaries conform to the size of the problem. Suburbs and cities can, and have, cooperated on problems in which their mutual benefit is at stake. Second, many of the problems of the cities—crime, overcrowding, welfare rolls, traffic, housing—have begun to appear in the suburbs as their population has increased. Suburban residents are discovering that, to some extent, they "took the city with them."

As a result, more and more suburbs and cities may come to realize that, on certain issues at least, they are in the same boat. This happened in Georgia; urban and suburban legislators, formerly political enemies, joined in an "Urban Caucus"—in part because the area around Atlanta, including Cobb County, began experiencing many of the same problems afflicting the core city. With the population shift to suburbia, the "urban crisis" in America has become the "urban-suburban crisis," or, more accurately, a "metropolitan crisis."

The Problems of the Cities

In Greece more than 2,000 years ago planners dreamed of a new city-state called Megalopolis. *Polis* was the Greek word for city-state (from which "politics" is derived), and "mega" comes from the word for "large," so Megalopolis meant a very large city. In 1961 Jean Gottmann used the word to describe "the unique cluster of metropolitan areas of the northeastern seaboard of the United States." [42] Stretching six hundred miles through

---

[40] *New York Times*, June 21, 1970, p. 1. As noted in footnote 4 of this chapter, the suburbs are defined here as areas outside central cities but within the Census Bureau definition of a metropolitan area.

[41] In William L. Riordon, *Plunkitt of Tammany Hall* (New York: Dutton, 1963), p. 21. The original edition was published in 1905.

[42] Jean Gottmann, *Megalopolis* (New York: Twentieth Century Fund, 1961), p. 4.

"Help!"

From *The Herblock Gallery* (Simon and Schuster, 1968)

eleven states and the District of Columbia in a band thirty to one hundred miles wide, this region in 1990 contained about fifty-five million people and included the cities of Boston, New York, Philadelphia, Baltimore, and Washington.[43] Driving through the area seemed almost like one continuous community. Some urban experts foresee the time when the United States will have three megalopolises, "Boswash" (the corridor from Boston to Washington), "Chipitts" (a strip from Chicago to Pittsburgh), and "San-San" (San Francisco to San Diego) along the West Coast.

But is this how people were meant to live? Since the beginning of civilization, people have clustered together in cities, which have served as magnets of communication, commerce, and culture. But critics of megalopolis have deplored the effect of the modern city on the quality of life. Lewis Mumford has asked: "Will the whole planet turn into a vast urban hive?"[44] Mumford argued that the modern metropolis has grown in "a continuous shapeless mass" and that its residents are subject to constant frustration and harassment in their daily lives while becoming increasingly removed from nature.[45]

On the other hand, Edward C. Banfield has argued that most city dwellers "live more comfortably and con-

veniently than ever before." In Banfield's view, many urban problems — congestion, for example — are overstated: "people come to the city . . . precisely *because* it is congested. If it were not congested, it would not be worth coming to." In defending the city, Banfield adds: "To a large extent, then, our urban problems are just like the mechanical rabbit at the racetrack, which is set to keep just ahead of the dogs no matter how fast they may run. Our performance is better and better but because we set our standards and expectations to keep ahead of performance, the problems are never any nearer to solution."[46] Despite Banfield's defense of urban life, a more general view is that the nation's cities *are* in difficulty and that problems such as poverty, crime, drugs, racial inequalities, housing, transportation, and the quality of public education are not being solved fast enough in what is often perceived as the world's richest society.

Part of the problem is that cities are no longer performing the same role they performed in the past. In the nineteenth and early twentieth centuries, America's cities were great socializing engines, taking unskilled immigrants from Europe and, in a generation or two, turning many of them into middle-class or even affluent Americans. Some of this is still taking place; the Cubans in Miami and the Mexicans and Hispanics in Texas, California, and other areas have become a political

---

[43] Adapted from U.S. Bureau of the Census, 1990 Census of Population.

[44] Lewis Mumford, *The City in History: Its Origins, Its Transformations, and Its Prospects* (New York: Harcourt Brace Jovanovich, 1961), p. 3.

[45] Ibid., pp. 543–48.

[46] Edward C. Banfield, *The Unheavenly City* (Boston: Little, Brown, 1970), p. 5.

force, and in the past two decades Asian immigrants have contributed significantly to the urban mix.

But to an extent, the socializing process has stopped. Many of the migrants to the cities in recent decades have been African Americans who, historically, especially those with lower incomes, have not been integrated into American society in the same way as the Irish, Italians, Jews, Poles, and other groups; African Americans have faced greater and more persistent discrimination.

Who will pay for the cost of providing schools, housing, and other social services for residents of the inner city? That remains the core of the dilemma: the cities say they cannot, and many residents of the suburbs either have little desire to do so or feel they cannot afford higher taxes. City mayors complain that the federal government has simply not allocated enough money to bridge the gap. And many taxpayers — 78 percent in one survey — either do not want an increase in services that would require higher taxes, or they favor a decrease in taxes and services.[47]

President Bush proposed to revitalize the inner cities by creating "enterprise zones." Businesses would be encouraged through tax breaks and other assistance to move into these areas. Congress did not act on the concept until 1992 following the riots in Los Angeles that spring. After that, Congress passed and sent to President Bush a bill to create fifty such zones, half in cities, half in rural areas, at a cost of $2.6 billion over five years. But the provision for enterprise zones was contained in a broader bill that included some tax increases, and the legislation was a casualty of the presidential campaign. In October, it became apparent that Bush, behind in the polls in his campaign for re-election — and already in trouble for having broken his 1988 "no new taxes" pledge — would veto the bill. After election, he did so, saying the measure would have raised taxes. Since Congress had adjourned, it could not try to override the president's veto.

Although enterprise zones had become an issue for Congress only in the 1990s, thirty-six states and the District of Columbia had already established more than 1,000 such zones. Many local governments in these areas combined tax benefits to businesses in the zones with increased police and fire protection and street improvements.[48]

---

[47] *Changing Public Attitudes on Governments and Taxes 1983*, Advisory Commission on Intergovernmental Relations, table 2, 1982, p. 17. The poll showed that 42 percent of respondents wanted governments to "keep taxes and services about where they are," while 36 percent favored a decrease, for a total of 78 percent; 8 percent favored increased services and taxes, and 14 percent had no opinion.

---

[48] *Congressional Quarterly*, Weekly Report, August 8, 1992, p. 2354.

Harborplace, Baltimore

Urban problems are complex and often have resulted in physical deterioration of the cities. Some cities have attempted to reverse the trend by building attractive new commercial or residential complexes in the downtown area. Baltimore's impressive Harborplace complex, which opened in 1980, is one example, and similar projects have been developed in Boston and Philadelphia. But some critics have argued that expensive downtown centers, catering mainly to business executives, visitors, and the affluent, may only serve to mask the continuing and serious social and economic problems of the cities.

Population Trends Census Bureau figures tell much of the story of the "sorting out" of city and suburban population. During the past two decades, the white population of the central cities *declined* even as the white population of the suburbs increased dramatically. By 1990, 57 percent of all African Americans lived in central cities, and only 27 percent lived in suburbs surrounding the cities. By contrast, only 26 percent of the white population lived in central cities, and 50 percent lived in suburbia. (See Figure 16–4.)

More African Americans were migrating to the suburbs. Between 1970 and 1990, according to Census Bureau data, the African American suburban population more than doubled to eight million. But more than ninety-nine million whites lived in the suburbs.[49]

Despite the popular image of poor whites and African Americans pouring into the cities to go on welfare, one study of urban migration indicates that people come to the cities for jobs, not social services, and that, compared to the nonwhite population already living in the cities, the average nonwhite who comes to the city has a higher occupational and educational background.[50] But the newcomers face job and housing discrimination; they are not in the same position as whites moving to a pleasant suburban neighborhood. As one observer put it, "the Welcome Wagon rarely calls in the ghetto."[51]

Housing, HUD, and Community Development Officials of the federal government and others who have studied urban problems differ widely on how to break the circle of poverty in the inner city. Where should government begin in attempting to eliminate poverty?

---

[49] U.S. Bureau of the Census, 1990 Census of Population, "Race, Hispanic Origin, and Group Quarters Population: Metropolitan Areas, 1990," p. 4. Preliminary data, numbers are rounded.
[50] Charles Tilly, "Race and Migration to the American City," in Wilson, ed., *The Metropolitan Enigma*, pp. 129–31.
[51] Ibid., p. 142.

Figure 16–4
Distribution of White and African American Population: 1990

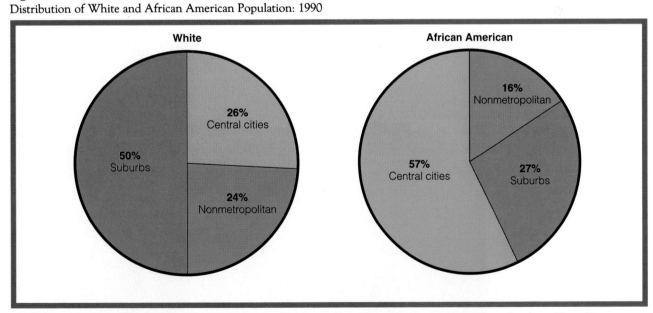

SOURCE: Adapted from U.S. Bureau of the Census, 1990 Census of Population, "Race, Hispanic Origin, and Group Quarters Population: Metropolitan Areas, 1990," p. 4. Preliminary data, percentages rounded.

With housing? Schools? Jobs? All of those things at once? Nobody really knows the answer.

The difficulties of making progress in attacking the overall problem can be illustrated by a close look at just one aspect of urban needs: housing. Substandard housing exists in rural as well as urban areas. Nevertheless, deteriorating inner-city neighborhoods were and are a highly visible, urgent social problem.

How well has government coped with that problem? In the Housing Act of 1949, Congress proclaimed the goal of "a decent home and a suitable living environment for every American family." That goal, the law states, shall be met "as soon as feasible." Yet in 1989, four decades later, there were 7.6 million dwellings listed as physically inadequate in the United States.[52]

As one example of the scope of the urban housing problem, in New York City a few years ago a family that asked for an apartment in a public housing project became about No. 200,000 on the waiting list. At the existing turnover rate, the family could expect to move into a project in *forty* years.[53] The government has spent billions on housing, yet the federal effort has nowhere near kept pace with the need for better housing. And many public housing projects tend to be institutional-looking sterile places plagued by crime and vandalism. In St. Louis, the government blew up the Pruitt-Igoe housing project, which had been built with federal support, because vandals and the high crime rate had led to the abandonment of most of the apartments.

In many cities — most notably in St. Louis and the South Bronx in New York — whole neighborhoods have become wastelands of rubble-strewn streets, boarded-up and abandoned buildings, vacant lots, and stripped automobiles. Across the nation, tens of thousands of deteriorated housing units have been abandoned.

Sometimes federal programs appear to have conflicting goals. More than eight hundred communities and practically every large city in America participated in the federal urban renewal program that began in 1949. Under the program, the federal government defrayed two-thirds to three-fourths of the cost. In many cases, however, urban renewal has *added* to inner-city tensions by forcing poor people from their homes to make way for middle- or upper-income housing and commercial centers. Fannie Lou Hamer, an outspoken African American civil rights leader in Mississippi, made this observation on the subject of urban renewal: "We're already living nowhere, and now they're going to move us out of that."[54]

The responsibility of the federal government for housing was given recognition at the cabinet level in 1965 when Congress established the Department of

---

[52] Data provided by Division of Housing and Demographic Analysis, U.S. Department of Housing and Urban Development.

[53] *New York Times*, April 10, 1986, p. B6.

[54] Speech, Robert F. Kennedy Memorial Journalism Awards dinner, Washington, D.C., June 19, 1969.

The Pruitt-Igoe housing project is dynamited in St. Louis.

THE MYTH OF MONEY

There is a wistful myth that if only we had enough money to spend—the figure is usually put at a hundred billion dollars—we could wipe out all our slums in ten years, reverse decay in the great, dull, gray belts that were yesterday's and day-before-yesterday's suburbs, anchor the wandering middle class and its wandering tax money, and perhaps even solve the traffic problem.

But look what we have built with the first several billions: Low-income projects that become worse centers of delinquency, vandalism, and general social hopelessness than the slums they were supposed to replace. Middle-income housing projects which are truly marvels of dullness and regimentation, sealed against any buoyancy or imagination, sealed against any buoyancy or

vitality of city life. Luxury housing projects that mitigate their inanity, or try to, with a vapid vulgarity. Cultural centers that are unable to support a good bookstore. Civic centers that are avoided by everyone but bums, who have fewer choices of loitering place than others. Commercial centers that are lackluster imitations of standardized suburban chainstore shopping. Promenades that go from no place to nowhere and have no promenaders. Expressways that eviscerate great cities. That is not the rebuilding of cities. This is the sacking of cities.

—Jane Jacobs, *The Death and Life of Great American Cities*

Housing and Urban Development (HUD). The same year, Congress passed a comprehensive housing bill, including for the first time a program of rent supplements for low-income families.

In 1966 Congress approved a major new Model Cities program under the direction of HUD. The goal of the program was to rebuild entire poverty neighborhoods in selected cities and to attack social problems as well as the physical problem of decaying buildings. Model Cities was one of the major legislative programs passed under President Johnson's "Great Society." Over a period of several years Congress provided almost $4 billion for Model Cities in 150 communities, but the

program became embroiled in controversy. Even supporters of the Model Cities program were disappointed in its record. Representative Charles L. Weltner, a Georgia Democrat, reported that the number of housing units in the Atlanta program had actually decreased and the percentage of families on welfare had gone up. "For the most part," he said, "things . . . are about the same, except maybe a little worse." [55]

President Nixon curtailed or ended a number of federal housing programs, including Model Cities,

---

[55] William Raspberry, "Model Cities: Learning from Their Failure," *Washington Post*, January 9, 1978, p. A23.

WELFARE IN THE LAND OF PLENTY

Marshalltown, Iowa—This city of 25,000 sits amid cornfields and factories in the center of a state that has been riding out the recession with one of the lowest unemployment levels in the country. Yet around 2,000 poor people here are getting help of some kind from the welfare system, from vouchers to heat a house to a regular welfare check.

This is not the South Bronx or Appalachia, where poverty often gets blamed on culture or behavior, on racism or reckless childbearing.

But Marshalltown shows with unusual clarity other powerful forces that make welfare and poverty hard to escape anywhere: the nation's proliferation of low-wage jobs and two decades of falling wages, especially for the least skilled, in terms of what they can buy. . . .

But no one can blame racism for poverty here. Ninety-eight percent of the 38,000 people of Marshall County, of which Marshalltown is the seat, are white, as are nearly all the families on welfare.

—*New York Times*, July 7, 1992

public housing, and urban renewal, and proposed to consolidate these and other programs into one large community development package. Nixon argued that federally aided public housing had often failed. "All across America, the federal government has become the biggest slumlord in history," Nixon said.[56]

In 1974 Congress approved a program of block grants as well as rent supplements and various forms of housing rehabilitation, and subsidies for apartments and mortgage interest. Two years later Congress revived public housing construction on a limited scale, ending a three-year moratorium that had been imposed by Nixon.

Some middle-class voters have opposed spending tax money for low-income housing for the poor. Yet middle-income and more affluent homeowners receive what amounts to a federal housing subsidy because they can deduct the interest they pay on their mortgage loans in figuring their federal income taxes. Low- and middle-income homeowners benefit as well from the fact that the Federal Housing Administration (FHA) insures the mortgages of many homes.

Federal housing policy is closely related to civil rights issues; in 1976 the Supreme Court ruled that in certain circumstances, the federal government might be required to finance federal housing projects in white suburban neighborhoods — not just in black areas within cities.[57] But in 1977 the Supreme Court held that suburban communities could not be compelled to change their zoning to permit low- and middle-income housing unless the "intent" of the zoning was to keep out African Americans or other minorities.[58]

The net result of these two Supreme Court decisions was that suburbs had considerable power to exclude public housing. "For large numbers of suburbanites," Michael N. Danielson has observed, "subsidized housing is a threat, the incarnation of everything in urban society they have sought to insulate themselves from in politically autonomous communities."[59] Danielson suggests that racial prejudice is an important factor in such suburban resistance to housing projects, but he argues that many suburbanites are also concerned

about the socioeconomic impact in their communities of low-income families; they fear lower property values, crime, and higher taxes for social services.[60]

The goal of the Reagan administration, from the start, was to end construction of low-cost public housing. Although Congress funded some public housing during the eight Reagan years, total outlays for new public housing dropped by 80 percent.[61] Under President Reagan, housing officials argued that subsidies to enable people to occupy existing housing would serve more people at a lower cost. But critics contended that in many cities there are not enough affordable rental units to meet demand.

In 1986, Congress passed a law providing nearly $1 billion for housing for homeless people. A year later, the Housing and Community Development Act of 1987 barred landlords from evicting poor tenants in order to sell or upgrade the property to make more money.

In fiscal 1993 the federal government had budgeted $20.4 billion for housing programs, including funds designed to allow persons with low incomes to buy their own homes, and a block grant to help state and local governments to assist low-income families. About 4.4 million households were receiving assistance from HUD. But an estimated 8 million other households had

---

[56] President Nixon's message to Congress on community development, September 19, 1973, quoted in *Congressional Quarterly, Weekly Report*, September 22, 1973, p. 2522.

[57] *Hills v. Gautreaux*, 425 U.S. 284 (1976).

[58] *Village of Arlington Heights* v. *Metropolitan Development Corporation*, 429 U.S. 252 (1977).

[59] Michael N. Danielson, *The Politics of Exclusion* (New York: Columbia University Press, 1976), p. 83.

---

[60] Ibid., pp. 83–92.

[61] *National Journal*, April 9, 1988, p. 977.

LIFE AND DEATH IN A HOUSING PROJECT

Herman Everett bounded down the stairs, his grandmother's voice filling the graffiti-smeared hallway behind him. "Be safe," she called. "Be safe."

In Mr. Everett's neighborhood these days, people don't usually say, "See you later" or "Have a nice day." They say, "Be safe."

Mr. Everett's neighborhood is the Martin Luther King Jr. Towers, a sprawling public housing project that rises from the faded Harlem checkerboard of tenements lived-in, tenements abandoned and lots now vacant but for the weeds and the rats. . . .

A few days after Thanksgiving, as they walked through King Towers to a store out on Lenox Avenue, the 19-year-old Mr. Everett and two boyhood friends were attacked by an armed mugger who was after Mr. Everett's black shearling coat — the current dangerous-to-wear status symbol on the city's fast and hard streets.

Only Mr. Everett escaped unharmed.

One of his friends, 18-year-old Desmond Lawrence, was wounded in the shoulder. The other, Bernard Richardson, a quiet young man of 20 with a wisp of a goatee, was shot in the back and killed. . . .

Just after 1 A.M., the three friends left the apartment and began walking across the project. . . . a young man, not much past his teens, stepped away from a group on the street and said, "Give me your shearlings."

The three friends ignored him and kept on walking. . . . "I looked back, and that's when I saw the gun," Mr. Lawrence recalled. "Then I heard the shot. Then I fell to the ground. It was like a numbness in my arm. It was like my chest was on fire. Then I heard two or three more shots. I thought he was trying to kill me real bad."

The next shot hit Mr. Richardson in the back. . . . And when it was over, the killer walked back into the project, leaving the coats.

—*New York Times*, February 4, 1991

housing problems.[62] In other words, the number of people living in inadequate housing was almost double the number receiving help from the federal government.

Taken as a whole, the federal housing program illustrates the difficulties confronting the nation in meeting the urban crisis. Although housing has finally been recognized as a cabinet-level problem, the provision of decent housing for all Americans remains a goal rather than a reality.

Urban Transportation   The reporter in the traffic helicopter seldom broadcasts good news; getting in and out of the nation's cities during morning and evening rush hours, or getting to work within the city limits, is often an ordeal. Americans spend a substantial part of their lives commuting to and from their jobs; and time spent in a crowded subway, as Lewis Mumford has suggested, takes its toll: "Emerson said that life was a matter of having good days, but it is a matter of having good minutes too. Who shall say what compensations are not necessary to the metropolitan worker to make up for the strain and depression of the twenty, forty, sixty, or more minutes he spends each night and morning passing through these metropolitan man-sewers?" [63]

Metropolitan transportation in the United States has been dominated by the automobile and the highway. Commuter railroads and other forms of mass transit were permitted to decline during the 1950s and 1960s. Federal policy has to some extent influenced the dominance of highways over rails. The federal government pays 90 percent of the cost of the huge interstate highway program, a massive incentive for states and cities to build roads rather than transit lines. The federal funds come from highway user taxes on trucks and buses, tires, and gasoline; the program, passed by Congress in 1956, was designed to link the nation's cities with 41,000 miles of super-highways, almost all of them

---

[62] Morton J. Schussheim, "Current Issues in Housing," Congressional Research Service, the Library of Congress, March 11, 1992, Summary.

[63] Mumford, *The City in History: Its Origins, Its Transformations, and Its Prospects*, pp. 549–50.

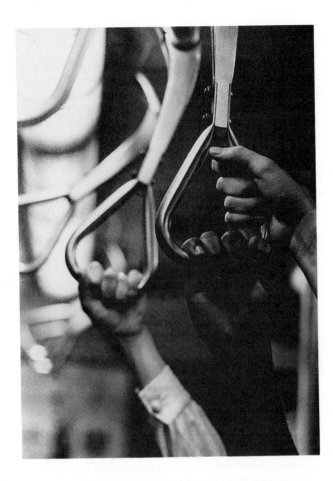

"I'm supposed to be in the new U.S. Department of Transportation—if I can get to it."

From *The Herblock Gallery* (Simon and Schuster, 1968)

four-lane. Powerful interest groups have major stakes in highway politics. But the nation has not developed an overall transportation policy, one that would balance highways and rapid transit, and ease congestion in metropolitan centers. The nation's dependence on the automobile became painfully obvious when Americans were confronted in 1973 and 1979 with a shortage of oil and gasoline.

The Urban Mass Transportation Act of 1970 authorized a ten-year, $12 billion program to enable cities to build or improve rapid rail, subway, and bus commuter lines. Congress in 1973 raised the federal share of urban mass-transit funds to 80 percent, and for the first time approved the use of millions of dollars in the Highway Trust Fund for urban transit needs. In the two decades since then, Congress has provided more billions for urban mass transit and highways, including bridge repairs and highway construction, financed in part from an increase in the tax on gasoline. In 1991 Congress provided $151 billion for transportation over six years, $119 billion of the total for highways and $32

billion for mass transit. The measure gave states much more flexibility than in the past in deciding whether to spend the funds for highways or mass transit.

San Francisco's gleaming BART subway system, Washington, D.C.'s Metro subway, and Atlanta's MARTA are examples of both the benefits and limitations of mass transit. BART has provided modern transportation for many residents of the San Francisco Bay area, but it has not—as its sponsors hoped— substantially reduced traffic jams on the highways. The commuters who now use BART instead of cars to get to work appear to have been replaced by other drivers. And the system, originally built at a cost of $1.6 billion and opened in 1972, has been running at a deficit.[64] The first segment of Washington's 103-mile Metro opened in 1976 and provided fast, comfortable, and esthetically pleasing downtown transportation for the nation's capital. By 1992, 81 miles had been completed. But Metro

---

[64] See Robert Lindsey, "Mass Transit, Little Mass," *New York Times Magazine*, October 19, 1975, p. 17.

construction costs were expected to soar to almost $10 billion by the project's scheduled completion date near the year 2000, and the system has been losing money. Atlanta's MARTA opened in 1979 and by 1992 had cost $4.6 billion and covered 32 miles. Just over half of the total was paid by the federal government. By 1996, new extensions were scheduled to be completed to serve the city's north-side commuters.

As attractive as these systems are, they are unsuitable for many cities, which cannot afford them. Because commuters travel to widely scattered destinations, rail lines do not take most people where they want to go. As a result, urban rail links are often difficult to justify in economic terms. And for most people the automobile still offers the most convenient form of transportation.

Problems interlock. The dominance of the automobile and the highway is directly related both to the energy crisis and to the problem of pollution, since automobiles produce at least 60 percent of total air pollution in the United States (electric power plants and industry account for most of the rest).

Poverty Poverty remains a pervasive problem in American cities, overshadowing or underlying almost all other problems. In 1990 about 73 percent of all poor people lived in metropolitan areas. Of these, more than 48 percent of poor whites lived in the central cities, but for African Americans the total was more than 76 percent.[65]

This does not mean that urban and racial problems are synonymous. However, the African American, Mexican American, or Puerto Rican child in the inner-city is caught up in a circle of poverty from which there is often no exit. Education may be one key to eliminating poverty, but inner-city schools often occupy the oldest buildings and have the least experienced teachers, since many teachers with seniority shun assignments to those classrooms. African Americans and other minorities face discrimination in employment and housing as well. Unlike such physical problems as transportation or air pollution, racial bias involves social attitudes that work against certain minority groups. Many of the problems of the nation's cities, therefore, are bound up with the larger problem of ensuring full equality for all Americans.

Urban Fiscal Problems: The Case of New York City

On a bleak day in October 1975, New York City stood literally only two hours away from financial default. The

[65] U.S. Bureau of the Census, Current Population Reports, *Poverty in the United States: 1990*, series P-60, no. 175, August 1991, p. 6.

proud eastern city, which considers itself America's cultural and business leader, the city that is the home of Wall Street and the great television networks, stood on the brink of insolvency. It was unable to meet its fiscal obligations to its bondholders.

At that perilous moment, Albert Shanker, the leader of the city's teachers' union, came forward and saved New York from default by investing $150 million in union pension funds in the bonds of the Municipal Assistance Corporation, known colloquially as "Big Mac."

There was widespread fear at the time that if New York went under, other cities facing similar financial problems might find it impossible to sell their bonds to investors, which in turn could have serious effects on the already troubled United States economy. In addition to New York, other major cities had found it necessary to cut back city services, freeze wages, or lay off municipal workers while attempting to cope with inadequate tax revenues and increasing costs.

The crisis faced by New York City had historical roots. For many years, the city, which has a liberal political tradition, spent billions for social services and welfare programs. At the same time, its expenditures were rising much faster than its revenues.[66] Increasingly, the city turned to short-term borrowing to raise money.

But mounting city deficits—despite heavy borrowing—had shaken the municipal bond market. Put simply, the city found that no one wanted its bonds. New York state moved to help the city and also established an emergency financial control board to monitor city spending. That meant that Governor Hugh Carey and a state-dominated board, rather than Mayor Abraham Beame, were then in control of the city's finances.[67]

President Ford, sensing a profitable political issue, campaigned for a time against New York City. "I am prepared to veto any bill that has as its purpose a federal bailout of New York City to prevent a default," he said.[68] By November the hostility toward New York had given way to fear; bankers, economists, and politicians worried that the snowballing effect of default by the city might cause a more general financial crisis. Ford reversed course and proposed a $2.3 billion package of aid to New York City, which Congress approved. The immediate crisis was over.

Donald H. Haider has suggested that New York's fiscal problems follow a pattern; he has concluded that higher taxes were usually imposed in the city in the one year in four in which there was no city, state, or national election. The mayor, the governor, the state legislature, and the city labor unions all bargained for advantage within this "election-tax cycle." In Haider's view, the city had "an insufficient tax base to carry out the range of services and redistributive programs to which it gradually had become wedded."[69] By 1987, however, New York City had paid off all of its loans and was considered one of the most stable economic regions in the country. But the crisis a decade earlier, the precarious situation that had been faced by the nation's largest city and its more than seven million residents, had served as a dra-

[66] Donald H. Haider, "Fiscal Scarcity: A New Urban Perspective," in Louis H. Masotti and Robert L. Lineberry, *The New Urban Politics* (Cambridge: Ballinger Publishing, 1976), p. 187.

[67] Ibid., p. 202.
[68] Ibid., p. 204.
[69] Ibid., pp. 186–200.

"You should have been here in the old days, before the budget cutbacks. . . . There were cops and fire engines and planes buzzing around . . ."

Mike Peters for the *Dayton Daily News*

matic reminder of the serious nature of the problems confronting America's cities.

Urban Politics: Governing the Cities

The term "power structure" was popularized more than three decades ago by Floyd Hunter, a sociologist who studied community leadership in Atlanta, Georgia.[70] Hunter concluded that a group of about forty people, mostly top businessmen, determined policy in Atlanta and used the machinery of government to attain their own goals.

But in a study of New Haven, Connecticut, Robert A. Dahl concluded that the city was not run by a power elite of economic or social notables, and that policy decisions were made by changing coalitions of leaders drawn from different segments of the community.[71] As noted in Chapter 6, scholars have provided diverse answers to the question of "Who governs?" Some scholars argue that power elites make public policy, but other political scientists see American society as pluralistic, with many — although not all — groups sharing in the decision making.

Edward C. Banfield and James Q. Wilson have contended that, regardless of how decisions are made in various American cities, all cities have one thing in common: "Persons not elected to office play very considerable parts in the making of many important decisions." [72] Banfield and Wilson have suggested the term "influentials" for powerful citizens who hold no official position.

When most people think of city government, however, they usually think of decisions being made by officials elected to political office by the voters. As on the national and state levels, parties, politics, and the ballot box play a central role in the decisions made at the city level that affect people's lives.

But cities are not nations. Paul E. Peterson has argued that cities "cannot make war or peace; they cannot issue passports or forbid outsiders from entering their territory" and as a result are limited in the policies they can adopt.[73]

Moreover, cities are limited in size and geographical jurisdiction and they must compete with each other for new industry. As a result, Peterson maintains, cities tend to favor policies that "enhance the economic position of a community in its competition with others." [74] They do not favor policies that benefit the poor but cost money and create economic risks for the cities. If cities attempt to redistribute income — to raise taxes to finance large-scale social programs — they face the danger that businesses and employees will leave. Given these constraints, Peterson concludes, the cities are, for the most part, unable to redistribute income effectively to help the disadvantaged.[75]

Population trends, as well as economic factors, affect city government. One result of the migration of many whites to the suburbs has been that more cities with a large African American electorate have chosen African American officials. In 1992, for example, African American mayors served in 14 major cities, including New York, Los Angeles, Detroit, New Orleans,

[70] Floyd Hunter, *Community Power Structure* (Chapel Hill: University of North Carolina Press, 1953).

[71] Robert A. Dahl, *Who Governs?* (New Haven: Yale University Press, 1961).

[72] Edward C. Banfield and James Q. Wilson, *City Politics* (Cambridge: Harvard University Press, 1963), pp. 244–45.

[73] Paul E. Peterson, *City Limits* (Chicago: University of Chicago Press, 1981), p. 4.

[74] Ibid., p. 41.

[75] Ibid., pp. 167–83.

Mayor Sharon Pratt Kelly, Washington, D.C.

The late Mayor
Richard J. Daley
of Chicago

Atlanta, Newark, Baltimore, Denver, Kansas City, Seattle, and Washington, D.C.. In several of these cities the African American population exceeded the white population. In all, 314 American cities had African American mayors, of whom 65 were women.[76]

Historically, the big-city political machine has characterized urban politics. The political machines traded jobs and social services for the votes of immigrants. But with the changing nature of American society, urban political machines have declined. The power of Tammany Hall was broken in New York City in the early 1960s by a Democratic reform movement. In Chicago the reign of Chicago's powerful political leader, Mayor Richard J. Daley, often described as the last of the big-city bosses, ended with his death in 1976.

As the tightly structured, old-style political machines have faded away, mayors of large cities have found it more difficult to govern. Their power has become diffused. One reason for this is the growth of "functional fiefdoms," specialized government agencies that operate specific programs, such as urban renewal or highway construction.[77] As these agencies have increased in number, they have often made independent decisions, bypassing mayors and city councils.

Just as public administrators exercise great power in the federal government, bureaucracies on the local level influence and limit the power of a big-city mayor —as do other factors. One study of urban politics noted that the mayor of New York must share his power with party leaders, appointed and elected public officials, the bureaucracy, nongovernmental associations, the media, and officials and agencies of governments outside New York City. Since no one group dominates, decisions are actually the result of "mutual accommodation."[78] In short, the business of governing a metropolis usually means that mayors are constantly striving to build and maintain workable coalitions of interest groups; their power is limited and they are handy targets when things go wrong. Another study of how mayors govern found at least five distinct mayoral styles and concluded that no one approach was necessarily the "best." And the study noted that mayors, because of the difficulties and frustrations of their jobs, may not ever achieve any higher political office.[79]

[76] *Black Elected Officials: A National Roster 1991* (Washington, D.C.: Joint Center for Political Studies, 1991).

[77] John J. Harrigan, *Political Change in the Metropolis* (Boston: Little, Brown, 1976), pp. 139–46.

[78] Wallace S. Sayre and Herbert Kaufman, *Governing New York City: Politics in the Metropolis* (New York: Norton, 1965), pp. 710–12.

[79] John P. Kotter and Paul R. Lawrence, *Mayors in Action: Five Approaches to Urban Governance* (New York: Wiley, 1974).

"HONEST GRAFT": BOSS PLUNKITT'S PHILOSOPHY

Nobody thinks of drawin' the distinction between honest graft and dishonest graft. There's all the difference in the world between the two. . . . My party's in power in the city, and it's goin' to undertake a lot of public improvements. Well, I'm tipped off, say, that they're going to lay out a new park at a certain place.

I see my opportunity and I take it. I go to that place and I buy up all the land I can in the neighborhood. Then the board of this or that makes its plan public, and there is a rush to get my land, which nobody cared particular for before.

Ain't it perfectly honest to charge a good price and make a profit on my investment and foresight? Of course, it is. Well, that's honest graft.

—Boss Plunkitt, quoted in William L. Riordon, *Plunkitt of Tammany Hall*

The Face of the Suburbs

The 1990 census figures confirmed the existence of a trend that urban specialists had begun to suspect several years earlier — some suburbs closest to central cities were actually losing population.

"This is a national phenomenon," Dr. George Sternlieb of Rutgers University said. "It is a pattern that is occurring within every large metropolitan area." Blue- and white-collar workers, he said, are "leapfrogging" farther out into "exurbia" to find housing they can afford.[80]

The changing population pattern in the suburbs in the 1990s was in marked contrast to the massive migration to the closer-in suburbs after the Second World War. One of the phenomena of that migration was the construction of whole new communities by a single builder. In 1958 Herbert J. Gans, a young sociologist, moved with his family into one such instant suburb, Levittown, New Jersey. His purpose was to study the community as a participant and observer. In recording the quality of social life in this suburb of Philadelphia, Gans quoted one woman describing her next-door neighbor: "We see eye to eye on things, about raising kids, doing things together with your husband, living the same way; we have practically the same identical background."[81]

Although most suburbs are not modeled on Levittown, the quote summarizes both sides of the argument about suburbia. In an impersonal society, where people toil on assembly lines or in beehive offices of large corporations, many Americans long for a sense of identity and belonging. In part, people have moved to the suburbs in "a search for community." To some extent, the migration to the suburbs may be seen as a turning back to the grass roots, a yearning for the small-town America celebrated by Booth Tarkington and Mark Twain. On the other hand, the suburbs have been assailed as centers of conformity and homogeneity, in which community pressures tend to produce narrow social and political attitudes among suburbanites and massive unconcern for urban and national problems.

Why do people move to the suburbs in the first place? According to Peter H. Rossi, they are both "pushed" and "pulled."[82] The "push" reasons are often emphasized: crime in the cities, bad schools, deteriorat-

ing housing. But the "pull" reasons are also highly important: the desire for more space and to "own our own home" and the attraction of suburban schools, for example. The automobile and FHA mortgage guarantees, allowing lower- and middle-income families to purchase their own homes, have been powerful factors as well.

The move to suburbia has brought change to the center of America's cities. Despite the efforts of a number of cities to revitalize their downtown districts, in many metropolitan areas not only people, but jobs and industry, have moved to the suburbs. Suburban residents no longer need to go to the city to shop; the department stores have moved to suburban shopping malls to be near *them*. There is still a need for downtown business areas, but often less as centers of retail trade than as places for the conduct of businesses that require face-to-face contact — banking, finance, and communications, for example.

Not all suburbs are alike. Some of the older, more affluent suburbs have been able to preserve their residential character. But the newer suburbs have mammoth retail shopping centers, office buildings, industrial parks, and other hallmarks of cities. Thus, as Louis H. Masotti has noted, suburbia is "becoming increasingly less suburban and more urban."[83]

In the popular image, however, life in the suburbs tends to be centered around home and family. And the stereotype of the suburban father happily barbecuing steaks on his outdoor grill or fussing with his lawn

[82] Peter H. Rossi, *Why Families Move* (New York: Free Press of Glencoe, 1955).
[83] Louis H. Masotti and Jeffrey K. Hadden, eds., *The Urbanization of the Suburbs* (Beverly Hills: Sage Publications, 1973), p. 17.

[80] *New York Times*, October 7, 1980, p. 1.
[81] Herbert J. Gans, *The Levittowners* (New York: Pantheon Books, 1967), p. 155.

sometimes reflects the reality. But what about his less fortunate fellow citizens back in the city? Gans suggests that the Levittowners "deceive themselves into thinking that the community, or rather the home, is the single most influential unit in their lives. . . . the real problem is that the Levittowners have not yet become aware of how much they are a part of the national society and economy."[84]

Today, however, the suburbs face many of the same problems that are faced by cities. The suburbanites who take pride in their shrubs, homes, and communities are also part of a larger American community with many unpleasant problems that cannot be wished away. Particularly the older suburbs, closest to the central cities, are experiencing difficulties, including rising welfare costs, crime, and physical deterioration. Sooner or later — and it may be happening sooner — the quality of life in the nation as a whole will be reflected in the suburbs. For example, it might surprise most Americans to know that the majority of welfare recipients live in suburbs, small towns, and rural areas — not in the inner cities.[85]

Although social problems such as inferior education, poor housing, crime, and inadequate health care have greatest impact in the cities, "they are not unknown to the suburbs and are increasingly being found there. . . . more and more suburban communities have city-like characteristics and all the problems asso-

---

[84] Gans, *The Levittowners*, p. 418.
[85] *New York Times*, July 7, 1992, p. A1.

ciated with those characteristics."[86] There is, in short, no place to hide from the problems faced by American society as a whole.

The Politics of Suburbia

The fact that more Americans — more than 115 million now — live in what could be termed "the suburbs" might be expected to have a major impact on the political system. A closely related question is whether people who live in the suburbs really hold different political views from residents of other areas, or whether the suburbs are merely experiencing the first stages of urbanization — growing into cities, as it were.

One way to measure the political impact of the population shift to suburbia is to study the reflection of that growth in the Congress. Richard Lehne has noted that in 1974, following the redistricting in Congress after the 1970 census, the 132 representatives from suburban areas for the first time composed the largest single group in Congress. In other words, there were more legislators from the suburbs than from the cities or from rural areas. That trend has continued. By 1986, following the redistricting after the 1980 census, there were 167 suburban legislators, 98 from the central cities, 88 from the rural districts, and 82 from mixed metropolitan areas.[87]

"The election of large and increasing numbers of suburban representatives to Congress means that, today

---

[86] Alan K. Campbell and Donna E. Shalala, "Problems Unsolved, Solutions Untried: The Urban Crisis," in Alan K. Campbell, ed., *The States and the Urban Crisis* (Englewood Cliffs: Prentice-Hall, 1970), p. 21.
[87] Richard Lehne, "Suburban Foundations of the New Congress," in *Annals of the American Academy of Political and Social Science*, November 1975, p. 143. Data for 1986 provided by Harvey L. Schantz, State University of New York, Plattsburgh.

and in the future, Congress must come to grips with the policy positions and reform preferences of suburbanites," Lehne suggested.[88] Analyzing ratings of representatives by interest groups, Lehne concluded that central-city legislators take liberal policy positions, rural representatives favor conservative policies, and men and women who represent suburban constituents "strike a moderate balance between the other two groups."[89]

But Lehne also discovered that members of Congress from older, established suburbs tend to take more liberal positions on most issues than representatives from the newer suburbs. These findings, Lehne concluded, support those who contend that the process of urbanization has extended to the suburbs. The members of Congress from older suburbs tended to vote much like their city cousins.[90]

Another study of emerging suburban political power, by Thomas P. Murphy and John Rehfuss, found great diversity among the suburbs and their representatives in Congress. "Despite the increase in the number of congressmen representing suburban districts," the authors said, "a strong suburban bloc has not emerged." One reason they cite is that "different types of suburbs have different needs." The study concluded: ""Suburban power' remains a paper tiger, but it has the potential to exert great influence."[91]

EXPLODING METROPOLIS AND AMERICA'S FUTURE

Metropolitan Solutions

If metropolitan problems are larger than the boundary lines of local governments, why not create larger political units to solve these problems? The approach might seem logical, but there are many obstacles to metropolitan government. Not the least of these is the reluctance of suburban areas to give up their political independence and to pay for services for residents of the central cities. And African American residents of the cities, having finally achieved greater political power — and with African American mayors elected in several cities

— are equally reluctant to lose that hard-won power to a metropolitan government.

Some efforts at "metro" solutions are being made, however, including the creation of special districts to handle specific functions, interstate compacts, area-wide planning agencies, consolidated school and library systems, and various informal intergovernmental arrangements. Annexation of outlying areas by the central city and the consolidation of cities and surrounding counties have all been tried; in many cases, they have been found wanting. Another approach has been the plan adopted in Los Angeles, under which the county has assumed responsibility for many area-wide functions, but local communities have retained their political autonomy.

Some urban experts have advocated metropolitan federalism as the best solution. Toronto, Canada, and its suburbs have operated under this system since 1953. Mass transit, planning, highways, and many other functions are run by a council made up of elected officials from the central city and surrounding suburbs. London also had a federated system encompassing the thirty-two boroughs of Greater London.

In Florida, Miami and Dade County narrowly opted for "Metro" government in 1957. Under the plan, Miami and twenty-seven suburban cities retain control of local functions, but have ceded to "Metro" area-wide functions such as fire and police protection and transportation. Political control is vested in an elected board of commissioners, which appoints a county manager.

Varying degrees of area-wide consolidation have been established in Nashville, Tennessee; Jacksonville, Florida; Baton Rouge, Louisiana; Indianapolis, Indiana; Columbus and Athens, Georgia; Lexington, Kentucky, and Butte, Montana. By 1992 there had been twenty consolidations.[92]

Despite steps toward consolidation and metropolitan government in many areas of the country, some scholars have strongly disputed the "reformist" belief that a single metropolitan government, by eliminating overlapping jurisdictions, will promote greater efficiency. For example, one study has concluded that since individuals have different preferences in government services, "a system of government composed of many different units will be more responsive to the interests

[88] Ibid., p. 142.
[89] Ibid., p. 144.
[90] Ibid., p. 150.
[91] Thomas P. Murphy and John Rehfuss, *Urban Politics in the Suburban Era* (Homewood: The Dorsey Press, 1976), pp. 29, 40, 42.

[92] Data provided by Geography Division, U.S. Bureau of the Census.

of citizens than a single government for any one urban region." [93]

As urban growth continues, however, old concepts of metropolitan areas may change. The cities of the industrial Northeast, for example, may indeed come closer to the concept of "Boswash". One scholar has suggested that tomorrow's metropolis may look less like a fried egg, with a clearly defined center and outer ring, and more like "a thin layer of scrambled eggs over much of the platter." [94]

Intergovernmental Relations

Although this chapter has focused on state and local problems, any real solution to metropolitan ills depends in large measure on the relationship among federal, state, and local governments.

State and local governments frequently do not have enough revenues to meet the social demands of both urban and rural areas. The confusing, overlapping programs of federal grants have been widely criticized. At the same time, state and local revenues have often lagged behind national economic growth. The federal system, insofar as intergovernmental fiscal relations are concerned, has become rather creaky at the joints.

The American Challenge

The problems discussed in this chapter involve the question of what kind of nation America wants to be. How people live in their local communities reflects the quality of American life.

Do Americans have a sense of national community? Will comfortable or affluent Americans be willing to pay higher taxes for better schools and for other social services for the poor? There is no constitutional requirement that an affluent majority take such steps on behalf of a less affluent minority. But the future of the

[93] Robert L. Bish and Vincent Ostrom, *Understanding Urban Government: Metropolitan Reform Reconsidered* (Washington, D.C.: American Enterprise Institute for Public Policy Research, 1973), p. 73.

[94] York Willbern, *The Withering Away of the City* (Tuscaloosa: University of Alabama Press, 1964), p. 33.

nation's democratic institutions may be affected by the answer. John Gardner, a former cabinet member, has suggested:

> If Americans continue on their present path their epitaph might well be that they were a potentially great people—a marvelously dynamic people—who forgot their obligations to one another, who forgot how much they owed one another.[95]

A further question is whether political institutions created when America was a rural nation can respond to, and cope with, the demands and problems of a highly urbanized, changing society. American democracy is under pressure; its institutions are being tested. Yet, the problems of American society—economic ills, crime, drugs, protection of the environment, racial discrimination, health care, education, poverty, the homeless, political corruption, energy resources, and all the rest— are not necessarily beyond solution if Americans, acting through the political process, insist on change. To a great extent, the America of tomorrow can be what the American people make it.

More than one hundred years ago, the English philosopher John Stuart Mill voiced much the same thought in his essay, *On Liberty*: "The worth of a State, in the long run, is the worth of the individuals composing it."

PERSPECTIVE

By the 1992 presidential election year, states and local governments across America were facing a budget crunch. Reduced revenues because of a lagging economy meant that one state after another had been forced to raise taxes and cut services drastically. Schools, libraries, health facilities, and other basic needs suffered as a result.

Not only the size of the population but its geographic distribution affect the nature of a society. Since 1920 the population of the United States has been more urban than rural. In 1990, when the population stood at 248.7 million, 192.7 million Americans, or 77 percent, lived in metropolitan areas. The Census Bureau has estimated that by the year 2040, the population of the United States may reach 372 million. As America has become urbanized, many of the nation's difficult prob-

lems have developed in their most acute form in urban areas—in the central "core" cities and the surrounding suburbs.

Two conclusions emerge from the numerous studies that have been made of state and local problems. First, many of the problems are larger than the boundaries of the governmental units that are attempting to deal with them. And second, the solutions frequently cost more money than the governmental units have available or are willing to spend.

Many critics of state government feel that the states are not doing as much as they should, particularly in the crucial area of urban problems. However, the states have been making an effort to meet their responsibilities. In the four years between 1986 and 1990, total federal spending increased by 27 percent. But during the same period, state and local expenditures increased by 36 percent. The states have major responsibilities in the fields of education, welfare, transportation, the administration of justice, the prisons, housing, public health, and the environment. States share with local governments responsibility for the delivery of these and many other vital public services.

Each state has a constitution that provides for an executive, legislative, and judicial branch. State constitutions may be amended by the legislature and approved by the voters, but seventeen states also permit initiatives to place proposed amendments on the ballot. Almost half of the states permit voters to enact or repeal legislation by majority vote.

Each state has a governor who heads the executive branch. The actions of a governor, and of other state officials, and the laws passed by state legislatures cannot conflict with federal law and are subject to judicial review by the United States Supreme Court. The veto is one of the few areas in which governors actually have more power than the equivalent power of the president. In 1992, governors in forty-three states could exercise an item veto over single parts of appropriations bills. The president could only veto entire bills. In forty-three states the legislature meets annually. For the majority of state legislators, public service is only a part-time job. By 1991 the number of state legislators who were women had increased to just over 18 percent.

The states are the building blocks of national political parties, but among the states the pattern of party competition varies widely. Some states have vigorous two-party competition. Other states have modified two-party competition—one party is on the average stronger than the other. But in both types of states,

---

[95] Text of speech prepared for delivery to the Illinois Constitutional Convention, Springfield, Ill., May 13, 1970.

control of the statehouse and the legislature can swing back and forth.

Cities are municipal corporations chartered by the states. *Home rule* empowers municipalities to modify their charters and run their affairs without approval by the legislature, subject to the constitution and laws of the state. There are three basic forms of city government: the mayor-council plan, used by most larger cities, the council-manager plan, and the commission plan. Other units of local government are counties, towns, townships, and special districts—created for such purposes as schools or fire protection—that extend beyond the boundary lines of local jurisdictions.

The nation's cities face problems such as poverty, crime, drugs, racial inequalities, housing, transportation, and the quality of public education. At the core of the urban dilemma is the question of who will pay the cost of providing social services for residents of the inner city. City mayors complain that the federal government does not provide enough money, and taxpayers either do not want an increase in services that would require higher taxes, or they favor a decrease in taxes and services.

President Bush proposed to revitalize the inner cities by creating "enterprise zones." Businesses would be encouraged through tax breaks and other assistance to move into these areas. Congress did not act on the concept until 1992, following the riots in Los Angeles that spring. Congress passed and sent to President Bush a bill to create fifty such enterprise zones, half in cities, half in rural areas. After the election, Bush vetoed the measure on the grounds that it was part of a larger bill that included tax increases.

Substandard housing exists in rural as well as urban areas. Nevertheless, deteriorating inner-city neighborhoods are a highly visible, urgent social problem. The responsibility of the federal government for housing was given recognition at the cabinet level in 1965 when Congress established the Department of Housing and Urban Development. Federal housing policy is closely related to civil rights issues; the net result of two Supreme Court decisions in the 1970s was that suburbs had considerable power to exclude public housing. In fiscal 1993 the federal government had budgeted $20.4 billion for housing programs. But the number of people living in inadequate housing was almost double the number receiving help from the federal government.

Metropolitan transportation in the United States has been dominated by the automobile and the highway. The federal government pays 90 percent of the cost of the interstate highway program, a massive incentive for states and cities to build roads rather than transit lines. Congress, however, has appropriated billions of dollars to enable cities to build or improve rapid rail, subway, and bus commuter lines.

Poverty remains a pervasive problem in American cities, overshadowing or underlying almost all other problems. Education may be one key to eliminating poverty, but inner-city schools often occupy the oldest buildings and have the least experienced teachers.

Population trends, as well as economic factors, affect city government. One result of the migration of many whites to the suburbs has been that more cities with a large African American electorate have chosen African American officials.

Many cities have been facing serious financial difficulties. Historically, the big-city political machine has characterized urban politics. The political machines traded jobs and social services for the votes of immigrants. But with the changing nature of American society, urban political machines have declined. As the tightly structured, old-style political machines have faded away, mayors of large cities have found it more difficult to govern. Their power has become diffused.

Despite the efforts of a number of cities to revitalize their downtown districts, in many metropolitan areas not only people, but jobs and industry, have moved to the suburbs. The suburbs, however, face many of the same problems that are faced by cities: rising welfare costs, crime, and physical deterioration. The majority of welfare recipients live in suburbs, small towns, and rural areas—not in the inner cities.

One possible solution to urban problems is to create larger units of government to deal with them. Some efforts at "metro" solutions have been made, including the creation of special districts to handle specific functions, interstate compacts, area-wide planning agencies, and various informal intergovernmental arrangements. Annexation of outlying areas by the central city and the consolidation of cities and surrounding counties have all been tried. But any real solution to metropolitan ills depends to a great extent on the relationship among federal, state, and local governments.

How people live in their local communities reflects the quality of American life. Will comfortable or more affluent Americans be willing to pay for social services for the poor? The answer to that question will influence the shape of the American future.

Suggested Reading

Banfield, Edward C., and Wilson, James Q. *City Politics* (Harvard University Press, 1963). A comprehensive examination of politics in American cities.

Beyle, Thad L., and Muchmore, Lynn, eds. *Being Governor: The View from the Office* (Duke University Press, 1983). An interesting and revealing collection of articles on the way governors view their office and responsibilities. Based on surveys of governors, former governors, and their staffs.

Bradbury, Katharine L.; Downs, Anthony; and Small, Kenneth A. *Urban Decline and the Future of American Cities** (The Brookings Institution, 1982). An examination of metropolitan population and economic trends. Assesses the extent of urban decline in 153 American cities.

Danielson, Michael N. *The Politics of Exclusion** (Columbia University Press, 1976). An examination of the development and impact of exclusionary policies in the nation's suburbs. Analyzes the economic, social, and racial isolation of individual communities and discusses the role of suburban politics in perpetuating that isolation.

Gottmann, Jean. *Megalopolis* (Kraus Reprint & Periodicals). (Originally published in 1961.) A pioneering study of the geographical, economic, social, and cultural characteristics of America's northeastern urban corridor.

Gray, Virginia; Jacob, Herbert; and Albritton, Robert B., eds. *Politics in the American States: A Comparative Analysis*, 5th edition (Scott, Foresman & Co., 1990). A useful collection of essays on various aspects of the political systems in the states, written by a number of leading authorities in the field.

Harrigan, John J. *Political Change in the Metropolis*, 4th edition* (Scott, Foresman & Co., 1989). A detailed assessment of political change in urban America. Harrigan focuses on the decline of the old-style political machine and on the growth of specialized government agencies that operate specific programs and often bypass the power of elected officials.

Kotter, John P., and Lawrence, Paul R. *Mayors in Action: Five Approaches to Urban Governance** (Wiley, 1974). An informative study of how mayors govern in urban areas. The authors found at least five distinct types of mayoral styles; they concluded that no one approach to the job is necessarily the best.

Lockard, Duane. *The Politics of State and Local Government*, 3rd edition (Macmillan, 1983). A comprehensive analysis of the politics of U.S. state and local governments.

Meltsner, Arnold J. *The Politics of City Revenue* (University of California Press, 1971). A useful study emphasizing the political factors that make it difficult to raise money to pay for urban public services.

Mollenkopf, John H. *The Contested City** (Princeton University Press, 1983). A comprehensive analysis of the ways the federal government has tried to aid American cities since the New Deal. Discusses the consequences of these policies for urban development in the United States.

Murphy, Thomas P., and Rehfuss, John. *Urban Politics in the Suburban Era* (The Dorsey Press, 1976). A comprehensive and valuable study of the growth of suburban political power. Murphy and Rehfuss found great diversity among American suburbs in their purpose, size, politics, and representation in Congress. The authors concluded that despite increases in the number of suburban district representatives in Congress, a strong suburban bloc has not yet emerged.

Peirce, Neal R. *The Megastates of America* (Norton, 1972); *The Pacific States of America* (Norton, 1972); *The Mountain States of America* (Norton, 1972); *The Great Plains States of America* (Norton, 1973); *The Deep South States of America* (Norton, 1974); *The Border South States* (Norton, 1975); *The New England States* (Norton, 1976); *The Mid-Atlantic States of America* (Norton, 1977); *The Great Lake States of America* (Norton, 1980); and *The Book of America: Inside Fifty States Today* (Warner Books, 1984). An unusually comprehensive and richly detailed sociopolitical guide to America, state by state.

Peterson, Paul E. *City Limits** (University of Chicago Press, 1981). An important analysis of city government and politics. Argues that a city will tend to favor policies that strengthen its own economic position in its competition with other cities, counties, and states.

Peterson, Paul E., ed. *The New Urban Reality** (The Brookings Institution, 1985). A useful series of essays on various aspects of city life. Topics covered include population changes in urban areas, urban crime problems, and transportation policies in urban areas.

Rivlin, Alice M. *Reviving the American Dream: The Economy, the States, and the Federal Government* (The Brookings Institution, 1992). A comprehensive examination of America's economy. Proposes a major restructuring of responsibilities between the federal and state governments.

Sabato, Larry. *Goodbye to Good-time Charlie: The American Governorship Transformed*, 2nd edition* (CQ Press, 1983). A comprehensive study of modern American governors. Concludes that the political hacks who sometimes served as governors in the past have departed, their place taken by a new breed of better-prepared, better-trained governors.

Wilson, James Q. *Thinking About Crime*, revised edition* (Random House, 1985). A discussion of the problems of crime and law enforcement that are faced by many urban and suburban areas. Includes an analysis of the ways local communities attempt to deal with crime and offers some suggestions for improving public policies in this area.

---

* Available in paperback edition

THE DECLARATION OF INDEPENDENCE

In Congress, July 4, 1776.
A DECLARATION
By the Representatives of the
United States of America,
In General Congress Assembled.

WHEN in the Course of human Events, it becomes necessary for one People to dissolve the Political Bands which have connected them with another, and to assume among the Powers of the Earth, the separate and equal Station to which the Laws of Nature and of Nature's God entitle them, a decent Respect to the Opinions of Mankind requires that they should declare the causes which impel them to the Separation.

We hold these Truths to be self-evident, that all Men are created equal, that they are endowed by their Creator with certain unalienable Rights, that among these are Life, Liberty, and the Pursuit of Happiness — That to secure these Rights, Governments are instituted among Men, deriving their just Powers from the Consent of the Governed, that whenever any Form of Government becomes destructive of these Ends, it is the Right of the People to alter or to abolish it, and to institute new Government, laying its Foundation on such Principles, and organizing its Powers in such Form, as to them shall seem most likely to effect their Safety and Happiness. Prudence, indeed, will dictate that Goverments long established should not be changed for light and transient Causes; and accordingly all Experience hath shewn, that Mankind are more disposed to suffer, while Evils are sufferable, than to right themselves by abolishing the Forms to which they are accustomed. But when a long Train of Abuses and Usurpations, pursuing invariably the same Object, evinces a Design to reduce them under absolute Despotism, it is their Right, it is their Duty, to throw off such Government, and to provide new Guards for their future Security. Such has been the patient Sufferance of these Colonies; and such is now the Necessity which constrains them to alter their former Systems of Government. The History of the present king of Great-Britain is a History of repeated Injuries and Usurpations, all having in direct Object the Establishment of an absolute Tyranny over these States. To prove this, let Facts be submitted to a candid World.

He has refused his Assent to Laws, the most wholesome and necessary for the public good.

He has forbidden his Governors to pass Laws of immediate and pressing Importance, unless suspended in their Operation till his Assent should be obtained; and when so suspended, he has utterly neglected to attend to them.

He has refused to pass other Laws for the Accommodation of large Districts of People, unless those People would relinquish the Right of Representation in the Legislature, a Right inestimable to them, and formidable to Tyrants only.

He has called together Legislative Bodies at Places unusual, uncomfortable, and distant from the Depository of their public Records, for the sole Purpose of fatiguing them into Compliance with his Measures.

He has dissolved Representative Houses repeatedly, for opposing with manly Firmness his Invasions on the Rights of the People.

He has refused for a long Time, after such Dissolutions, to cause others to be elected; whereby the Legislative Powers, incapable of Annihilation, have returned to the People at large for their exercise; the State remaining in the mean time exposed to all the Dangers of Invasion from without, and Convulsions within.

He has endeavoured to prevent the Population of these States; for that Purpose obstructing the Laws for Naturalization of Foreigners; refusing to pass others to encourage their Migrations hither, and raising the Conditions of new Appropriations of Lands.

He has obstructed the Administration of Justice, by refusing his Assent to Laws for establishing Judiciary Powers.

He has made Judges dependent on his Will alone, for the Tenure of their Offices, and the Amount and Payment of their Salaries.

He has erected a Multitude of new Offices, and sent hither Swarms of Officers to harrass our People, and eat out their Substance.

He has kept among us, in Times of Peace, Standing Armies, without the consent of our Legislatures.

He has affected to render the Military independent of and superior to the Civil Power.

He has combined with others to subject us to a Jurisdiction foreign to our Constitution, and unacknowledged by our Laws; giving his Assent to their Acts of pretended Legislation:

For quartering large Bodies of Armed Troops among us:

For protecting them, by a mock Trial, from Punishment for any Murders which they should commit on the Inhabitants of these States:

For cutting off our Trade with all Parts of the World:

For imposing Taxes on us without our Consent:

For depriving us, in many Cases, of the Benefits of Trial by Jury:

For transporting us beyond Seas to be tried for pretended Offences:

For abolishing the free System of English Laws in a neighbouring Province, establishing therein an arbitrary Government, and enlarging its Boundaries, so as to render it at once an Example and fit Instrument for introducing the same absolute Rule into these Colonies:

For taking away our Charters, abolishing our most valuable Laws, and altering fundamentally the Forms of our Governments:

For suspending our own Legislatures, and declaring themselves invested with Power to legislate for us in all Cases whatsoever.

He has abdicated Government here, by declaring us out of his Protection and waging War against us.

He has plundered our Seas, ravaged our Coasts, burnt our Towns, and destroyed the Lives of our People.

He is, at this Time, transporting large Armies of foreign Mercenaries to compleat the Works of Death, Desolation, and Tyranny, already begun with circumstances of Cruelty and Perfidy, scarcely paralleled in the most barbarous Ages, and totally unworthy the Head of a civilized Nation.

He has constrained our fellow Citizens taken Captive on the high Seas to bear Arms against their Country, to become the Executioners of their Friends and Brethren, or to fall themselves by their Hands.

He has excited domestic Insurrections amongst us, and has endeavoured to bring on the Inhabitants of our Frontiers, the merciless Indian Savages, whose known Rule of Warfare, is an undistinguished Destruction, of all Ages, Sexes and Conditions.

In every stage of these Oppressions we have Petitioned for Redress in the most humble Terms: Our repeated Petitions have been answered only by repeated Injury. A Prince, whose Character is thus marked by every act which may define a Tyrant, is unfit to be the Ruler of a free People.

Nor have we been wanting in Attentions to our British Brethren. We have warned them from Time to Time of Attempts by their Legislature to extend an unwarrantable Jurisdiction over us. We have reminded them of the Circumstances of our Emigration and Settlement here. We have appealed to their native Justice and Magnanimity, and we have conjured them by the Ties of our common Kindred to disavow these Usurpations, which, would inevitably interrupt our Connections and Correspondence. They too have been deaf to the Voice of Justice and of Consanguinity. We must, therefore, acquiesce in the Necessity, which denounces our Separation, and hold them, as we hold the rest of Mankind, Enemies in War, in Peace, Friends.

We, therefore, the Representatives of the UNITED STATES OF AMERICA, in GENERAL CONGRESS, Assembled, appealing to the Supreme Judge of the World for the Rectitude of our Intentions, do, in the Name, and by Authority of the good People of these Colonies, solemnly Publish and Declare, That these United Colonies, are, and of Right ought to be, FREE AND INDEPENDENT STATES; that they are absolved from all Allegiance to the British Crown, and that all political Connection between them and the State of Great-Britain, is and ought to be totally dissolved; and that as FREE AND INDEPENDENT STATES, they have full Power to levy War, conclude Peace, contract Alliances, establish Commerce, and to do all other Acts and Things which INDEPENDENT STATES may of right do. And for the support of this Declaration, with a firm Reliance on the Protection of divine Providence, we mutually pledge to each other our Lives, our Fortunes, and our sacred Honor.

Signed by ORDER *and in* BEHALF *of the* CONGRESS,
JOHN HANCOCK, PRESIDENT.
ATTEST.
CHARLES THOMSON, SECRETARY.

PHILADELPHIA: PRINTED BY JOHN DUNLAP.

SIGNERS OF THE
DECLARATION OF INDEPENDENCE
According to the Authenticated List Printed by
Order of Congress of January 18, 1777*
John Hancock.

New-Hampshire.
   Josiah Bartlett,
   W^m. Whipple,
   Matthew Thornton.†

Massachusetts-Bay.
   Saml. Adams,
   John Adams,
   Robt. Treat Paine,
   Elbridge Gerry.

Rhode-Island and
Providence, &c.
   Step. Hopkins,
   William Ellery.

Connecticut.
   Roger Sherman,
   Saml. Huntington,
   W^m. Williams,
   Oliver Wolcott.

New-York.
   W^m. Floyd,
   Phil. Livingston,
   Fran^s. Lewis,
   Lewis Morris.

New-Jersey.
   Rich^d. Stockton,
   Jno. Witherspoon,
   Fra^s. Hopkinson,
   John Hart,
   Abra. Clark.

Pennsylvania.
   Robt. Morris,
   Benjamin Rush,
   Benja. Franklin,
   John Morton,
   Geo. Clymer,
   Ja^s. Smith

Geo. Taylor,
James Wilson,
Geo. Ross.

Delaware.
   Caesar Rodney,
   Geo. Read,
   (Tho. M:Kean.)‡

Maryland.
   Samuel Chase,
   W^m. Paca,
   Thos. Stone,
   Charles Carroll,
     of Carrollton.

Virginia.
   George Wythe,
   Richard Henry Lee,
   Th^s. Jefferson,
   Benj^a. Harrison,

Thos. Nelson, J^r.
Francis Lightfoot Lee,
Carter Braxton.

North-Carolina.
   W^m. Hooper,
   Joseph Hewes,
   John Penn.

South-Carolina.
   Edward Rutledge,
   Thos. Heyward, jun^r
   Thomas Lynch, jun^r
   Arthur Middleton.

Georgia.
   Button Gwinnett,
   Lyman Hall,
   Geo. Walton.

---

* Spelling and abbreviation of names conform to original printed list.

† Matthew Thornton's name was signed on the engrossed copy following the Connecticut Members, but was transferred in the printed copy to its proper place with the other New Hampshire Members.

‡ Thomas McKean's name was not included in the list of signers printed by order of Congress on January 18, 1777, as he did not sign the engrossed copy until some time thereafter, probably in 1781.

THE CONSTITUTION OF THE UNITED STATES OF AMERICA*

We the people of the United States, in Order to form a more perfect Union, establish Justice, insure domestic Tranquility, provide for the common defence, promote the general Welfare, and secure the Blessings of Liberty to ourselves and our Posterity, do ordain and establish this Constitution for the United States of America.

Article I

Section 1. All legislative Powers herein granted shall be vested in a Congress of the United States, which shall consist of a Senate and House of Representatives.

Section 2. The House of Representatives shall be composed of Members chosen every second Year by the people of the several States, and the Electors in each State shall have the Qualifications requisite for Electors of the most numerous Branch of the State Legislature.

No Person shall be a Representative who shall not have attained to the Age of twenty-five Years, and been seven Years a Citizen of the United States, and who shall not, when elected, be an Inhabitant of that state in which he shall be chosen.

[Representatives and direct Taxes shall be apportioned among the several States which may be included within this Union, according to their respective Numbers, which shall be determined by adding to the whole Number of free persons, including those bound to Service for a Term of Years, and excluding Indians not taxed, three fifths of all other Persons.][1] The actual Enumeration shall be made within three Years after the first Meeting of the Congress of the United States, and within every subsequent Term of ten Years, in such Manner as they shall by Law direct. The Number of Representatives shall not exceed one for every thirty Thousand, but each State shall have at Least one Representative; and until such enumeration shall be made, the State of New Hampshire shall be entitled to chuse three, Massachusetts eight, Rhode-Island and Providence Plantations one, Connecticut five, New-York six, New Jersey four, Pennsylvania eight, Delaware one, Maryland six, Virginia ten, North Carolina five, South Carolina five, and Georgia three.

When vacancies happen in the Representation from any State, the Executive Authority thereof shall issue Writs of Election to fill such Vacancies.

The House of Representatives shall chuse their Speaker and other Officers; and shall have the sole Power of Impeachment.

Section 3. The Senate of the United States shall be composed of two Senators from each State, [chosen by the Legislature threof,][2] for six Years; and each Senator shall have one Vote.

Immediately after they shall be assembled in Consequence of the first Election, they shall be divided as equally as may be into three Classes. The Seats of the Senators of the first Class shall be vacated at the Expiration of the second Year, of the second Class at the Expiration of the fourth Year, and of the third Class at the Expiration of the sixth Year, so that one-third may be chosen every second year; [and if Vacancies happen by Resignation, or otherwise, during the Recess of the Legislature of any State, the Executive thereof may make temporary Appointments until the next Meeting of the Legislature, which shall then fill such Vacancies].[3]

No Person shall be a Senator who shall not have attained to the Age of thirty Years, and been nine Years a Citizen of the United States, and who shall not, when elected, be an Inhabitant of that State in which he shall be chosen.

The Vice-President of the United States shall be President of the Senate, but shall have no vote, unless they be equally divided.

---

* The Constitution and all amendments are shown in their original form. Parts that have been amended or superseded are bracketed and explained in the footnotes.

[1] Modified by the Fourteenth and Sixteenth amendments.

[2] Superseded by the Seventeenth Amendment.

[3] Modified by the Seventeenth Amendment.

The Senate shall chuse their other Officers, and also a President pro tempore, in the absence of the Vice-President, or when he shall exercise the Office of the President of the United States.

The Senate shall have the sole Power to try all Impeachments. When sitting for that purpose, they shall be on Oath or Affirmation. When the President of the United States is tried, the Chief Justice shall preside: And no person shall be convicted without the Concurrence of two thirds of the Members present.

Judgment in Cases of Impeachment shall not extend further than to removal from Office, and disqualification to hold and enjoy any Office of honor, Trust, or profit under the United States: but the Party convicted shall nevertheless be liable and subject to Indictment, Trial, Judgment, and punishment, according to Law.

Section 4. The Times, Places and Manner of holding Elections for Senators and Representatives, shall be prescribed in each state by the Legislature thereof; but the Congress may at any time by Law make or alter such Regulations, except as to the Places of Chusing Senators.

The Congress shall assemble at least once in every Year, and such Meeting shall [be on the first Monday in December,]⁴ unless they shall by Law appoint a different Day.

Section 5. Each House shall be the Judge of the Elections, Returns and Qualifications of its own Members, and a Majority of each shall constitute a Quorum to do Business; but a smaller number may adjourn from day to day, and may be authorized, to compel the Attendance of absent Members, in such Manner, and under such Penalties, as each House may provide.

Each House may determine the Rules of its Proceedings, punish its Members for disorderly Behavior, and, with the Concurrence of two thirds, expel a Member.

Each House shall keep a Journal of its Proceedings, and from time to time publish the same, excepting such Parts as may in their Judgment require Secrecy; and the Yeas and Nays of the Members of either House on any question shall, at the Desire of one fifth of those present, be entered on the journal.

Neither House, during the Session of Congress, shall, without the Consent of the other, adjourn for more than three days, nor to any other Place than that in which the two Houses shall be sitting.

Section 6. The Senators and Representatives shall receive a Compensation for their Services, to be ascertained by Law, and paid out of the Treasury of the United States. They shall in all Cases, except Treason, Felony, and Breach of the Peace, be privileged from Arrest during their Attendance at the Session of their respective Houses, and in going to and returning from the same; and for any Speech or Debate in either House, they shall not be questioned in any other place.

No Senator or Representative shall, during the Time for which he was elected, be appointed to any civil Office under the Authority of the United States, which shall have been created, or the Emoluments whereof shall have been increased, during such time; and no person holding any Office under the United States shall be a Member of either House during his continuance in Office.

Section 7. All Bills for raising Revenue shall originate in the House of Representatives; but the Senate may propose or concur with Amendments as on other bills.

Every Bill which shall have passed the House of Representatives and the Senate, shall, before it become a Law, be presented to the President of the United States; If he approve he shall sign it, but if not he shall return it, with his Objections, to that House in which it shall have originated, who shall enter the Objections at large on their Journal, and proceed to reconsider it. If after such Reconsideration two thirds of that House shall agree to pass the bill, it shall be sent, together with the objections, to the other House, by which it shall likewise be reconsidered, and if approved by two thirds of that House, it shall become a Law. But in all such Cases the Votes of both Houses shall be determined by Yeas and Nays, and the Names of the Persons voting for and against the Bill shall be entered on the Journal of each House respectively. If any Bill shall not be returned by the President within ten Days (Sundays excepted) after it shall have been presented to him, the Same shall be a Law, in like Manner as if he had signed it, unless the Congress by their Adjournment prevent its Return, in which Case it shall not be a Law.

Every Order, Resolution, or Vote to which the Concurrence of the Senate and House of Representatives may be necessary (except on a question of Adjournment) shall be presented to the President of the United States; and before the Same shall take Effect, shall be approved by him, or being disapproved by him, shall be repassed by two thirds of the Senate and House of Representatives, according to the Rules and Limitations prescribed in the Case of a Bill.

Section 8. The Congress shall have Power to lay and collect Taxes, Duties, Imposts and Excises, to pay the Debts and provide for the common Defence and general Welfare of the United States; but all Duties, Imposts and Excises shall be uniform throughout the United States;

To borrow money on the credit of the United States; To regulate Commerce with foreign Nations, and among the several States, and with the Indian Tribes;

To establish an uniform Rule of Naturalization, and uniform Laws on the subject of Bankruptcies throughout the United States;

To coin Money, regulate the Value thereof, and of foreign Coin, and fix the Standard of Weights and Measures;

To provide for the Punishment of counterfeiting the Securities and current Coin of the United States;

To establish Post Offices and Post Roads;

To promote the Progress of Science and useful Arts, by securing for limited times to Authors and Inventors the exclusive Right to their respective Writings and Discoveries;

To constitute Tribunals inferior to the Supreme Court;

To define and punish Piracies and Felonies committed on the high Seas, and Offenses against the Law of Nations;

To declare War, grant Letters of Marque and Reprisal, and make Rules concerning Captures on Land and Water;

To raise and support Armies, but no Appropriation of Money to that Use shall be for a longer Term than two Years;

To provide and maintain a Navy;

To make Rules for the Government and Regulation of the land and naval forces;

To provide for calling forth the Militia to execute the Laws of the Union, suppress Insurrections and repel Invasions;

To provide for organizing, arming, and disciplining the Militia, and for governing such part of them as may be employed in the Service of the United States, reserving to the States respectively, the Appointment of the Officers, and the Authority of training the Militia according to the discipline prescribed by Congress;

To exercise exclusive Legislation in all Cases whatsoever, over such District (not exceeding ten Miles square) as may, by Cession of particular States, and the acceptance of Congress, become the Seat of

---

⁴ Superseded by the Twentieth Amendment.

the Government of the United States, and to exercise like Authority over all places purchased by the Consent of the Legislature of the State in which the Same shall be, for the Erection of Forts, Magazines, Arsenals, dock-Yards, and other needful Buildings; — And

To make all Laws which shall be necessary and proper for carrying into Execution the foregoing Powers, and all other Powers vested by this Constitution in the Government of the United States, or in any Department or Officer thereof.

Section 9. The Migration or Importation of such Persons as any of the States now existing shall think proper to admit shall not be prohibited by the Congress prior to the Year one thousand eight hundred and eight, but a tax or duty may be imposed on such Importation, not exceeding ten dollars for each person.

The privilege of the Writ of Habeas Corpus shall not be suspended, unless when in Cases of Rebellion or Invasion the public Safety may require it.

No Bill of Attainder or ex post facto Law shall be passed.

[No capitation, or other direct, Tax shall be laid unless in proportion to the Census or Enumeration herein before directed to be taken.]5

No Tax or Duty shall be laid on Articles exported from any State.

No Preference shall be given by any Regulation of Revenue to the ports of one State over those of another: nor shall Vessels bound to, or from, one State, be obliged to enter, clear, or pay Duties in another.

No Money shall be drawn from the Treasury, but in Consequence of Appropriations made by Law; and a regular Statement and Account of the Receipts and Expenditures of all public Money shall be published from time to time.

No Title of Nobility shall be granted by the United States: And no Person holding any Office of profit or Trust under them, shall, without the Consent of the Congress, accept of any present, Emolument, Office, or Title, of any kind whatever, from any King, Prince, or foreign State.

Section 10. No State shall enter into any Treaty, Alliance, or Confederation; grant Letters of Marque and Reprisal; coin Money; emit Bills of Credit; make any Thing but gold and silver Coin a Tender in payment of Debts; pass any Bill of Attainder, ex post facto Law, or Law impairing the Obligation of Contracts, or grant any Title of Nobility.

No State shall, without the Consent of the Congress, lay any Imposts or Duties on Imports or Exports, except what may be absolutely necessary for executing its inspection Laws: and the net Produce of all Duties and Imposts, laid by any State on Imports or Exports, shall be for the Use of the Treasury of the United States; and all such Laws shall be Subject to the Revision and Control of the Congress.

No State shall, without the Consent of Congress, lay any duty of Tonnage, keep Troops, or Ships of War in time of peace, enter into any Agreement or Compact with another State, or with a foreign power, or engage in War, unless actually invaded, or in such imminent Danger as will not admit of delay.

Article II

Section 1. The executive Power shall be vested in a President of the United States of America. He shall hold his Office during the Term of four years, and, together with the Vice-President, chosen for the same Term, be elected, as follows:

Each State shall appoint, in such Manner as the Legislature thereof may direct, a Number of Electors, equal to the whole Number of Senators and Representatives to which the State may be entitled in the Congress: but no Senator or Representative, or person holding an Office of Trust or profit under the United States, shall be appointed an Elector.

[The Electors shall meet in their respective States, and vote by Ballot for two persons, of whom one at least shall not be an Inhabitant of the same State with themselves. And they shall make a List of all the Persons voted for, and of the Number of Votes for each; which List they shall sign and certify, and transmit sealed to the Seat of the Government of the United States, directed to the President of the Senate. The President of the Senate shall, in the Presence of the Senate and House of Representatives, open all the Certificates, and the Votes shall then be counted. The person having the greatest Number of Votes shall be the President, if such Number be a Majority of the whole Number of Electors appointed; and if there be more than one who have such Majority, and have an equal Number of Votes, then the House of Representatives shall immediately chuse by Ballot one of them for president; and if no person have a Majority, then from the five highest on the List the said House shall in like Manner chuse the President. But in chusing the President, the Votes shall be taken by States, the Representation from each State having one Vote; a quorum for this Purpose shall consist of a Member or Members from two-thirds of the States, and a Majority of all the States shall be necessary to a Choice. In every Case, after the Choice of the President, the Person having the greatest Number of Votes of the Electors shall be the Vice-President. But if there should remain two or more who have equal votes, the Senate shall chuse from them by Ballot the Vice-President.]6

The Congress may determine the Time of chusing the Electors, and the Day on which they shall give their Votes; which Day shall be the same throughout the United States.

No person except a natural-born Citizen, or a Citizen of the United States, at the time of the Adoption of this Constitution, shall be eligible to the Office of President; neither shall any Person be eligible to that Office who shall not have attained to the Age of thirty-five years, and been fourteen Years a Resident within the United States.

[In Case of the Removal of the President from Office, or of his Death, Resignation, or Inability to discharge the powers and Duties of the said Office, the same shall devolve on the Vice-President, and the Congress may by Law provide for the Case of Removal, Death, Resignation, or Inability, both of the President and Vice-President, declaring what Officer shall then act as President, and such Officer shall act accordingly, until the disability be removed, or a President shall be elected.]7

The President shall, at stated Times, receive for his Services a Compensation, which shall neither be increased nor diminished during the period for which he shall have been elected, and he shall not receive within that Period any other Emolument from the United States, or any of them.

Before he enter on the execution of his Office, he shall take the following Oath or Affirmation: — "I do solemnly swear (or affirm) that I will faithfully execute the Office of President of the United

---

5 Modified by the Sixteenth Amendment.

6 Superseded by the Twelfth Amendment.

7 Modified by the Twenty-fifth Amendment.

States, and will, to the best of my Ability, preserve, protect, and defend the Constitution of the United States."

Section 2. The president shall be Commander in Chief of the Army and Navy of the United States, and of the Militia of the several States, when called into the actual Service of the United States; he may require the Opinion, in writing, of the principal Officer in each of the executive Departments, upon any subject relating to the Duties of their respective Offices, and he shall have Power to Grant Reprieves and Pardons for Offenses against the United States, except in Cases of Impeachment.

He shall have Power, by and with the Advice and Consent of the Senate, to make Treaties, provided two thirds of the Senators present concur; and he shall nominate, and by and with the Advice and Consent of the Senate, shall appoint Ambassadors, other public Ministers and Consuls, Judges of the supreme Court, and all other Officers of the United States, whose Appointments are not herein otherwise provided for, and which shall be established by Law: but the Congress may by Law vest the Appointment of such inferior Officers, as they think proper, in the President alone, in the Courts of Law, or in the Heads of Departments.

The President shall have Power to fill up all Vacancies that may happen during the Recess of the Senate, by granting Commissions which shall expire at the End of their next Session.

Section 3. He shall from time to time give to the Congress Information of the State of the Union, and recommend to their Consideration such Measures as he shall judge necessary and expedient; he may, on extraordinary occasions, convene both Houses, or either of them, and in Case of Disagreement between them, with respect to the Time of Adjournment, he may adjourn them to such Time as he shall think proper; he shall receive Ambassadors and other public Ministers; he shall take Care that the Laws be faithfully executed, and shall Commission all the Officers of the United States.

Section 4. The President, Vice-President and all civil Officers of the United States, shall be removed from Office on Impeachment for, and Conviction of, Treason, Bribery, or other high Crimes and Misdemeanors.

Article III

Section 1. The judicial power of the United States, shall be vested in one supreme Court, and in such inferior Courts as the Congress may from time to time ordain and establish. The Judges, both of the supreme and inferior Courts, shall hold their Offices during good Behaviour, and shall, at stated Times, receive for their Services, a Compensation, which shall not be diminished during their Continuance in Office.

Section 2. The judicial Power shall extend to all Cases, in Law and Equity, arising under this Constitution, the Laws of the United States, and treaties made, or which shall be made, under their Authority;—to all Cases affecting ambassadors, other public ministers and consuls;—to all cases of admiralty and maritime Jurisdiction;—to Controversies to which the United States shall be a Party;—to Controversies between two or more States;—[between a State and Citizens of Another State;][8]—between Citizens of different States,—between Citizens of the same State claiming Lands under Grants of different States, and between a State, or the Citizens thereof, and foreign States, Citizens or Subjects.

In all Cases affecting Ambassadors, other public Ministers and Consuls, and those in which a State shall be Party, the supreme Court shall have original Jurisdiction. In all the other Cases before mentioned, the supreme Court shall have appellate Jurisdiction, both as to Law and Fact, with such Exceptions, and under such Regulations as the Congress shall make.

The trial of all Crimes, except in Cases of Impeachment, shall be by Jury; and such Trial shall be held in the State where the said Crimes shall have been committed; but when not committed within any State, the Trial shall be at such Place or Places as the Congress may by Law have directed.

Section 3. Treason against the United States, shall consist only in levying War against them, or in adhering to their Enemies, giving them Aid and Comfort. No person shall be convicted of Treason unless on the Testimony of two Witnesses to the same overt Act, or on Confession in open Court.

The Congress shall have power to declare the Punishment of Treason, but no Attainder of Treason shall work Corruption of Blood, or Forfeiture except during the Life of the Person attained.

Article IV

Section 1. Full Faith and Credit shall be given in each State to the public Acts, Records, and judicial Proceedings of every other State. And the Congress may by general Laws prescribe the Manner in which such Acts, Records and Proceedings shall be proved, and the Effect thereof.

Section 2. The Citizens of each State shall be entitled to all Privileges and Immunities of Citizens in the several States.

A Person charged in any State with the Treason, Felony, or other Crime, who shall flee from Justice, and be found in another State, shall on demand of the executive Authority of the State from which he fled, be delivered up, to be removed to the State having Jurisdiction of the crime.

[No person held to Service or Labour in one State, under the Laws thereof, escaping into another, shall, in Consequence of any Law or Regulation therein, be discharged from such Service or Labour, but shall be delivered up on Claim of the party to whom such Service or Labour may be due.][9]

Section 3. New States may be admitted by the Congress into this Union; but no new State shall be formed or erected within the Jurisdiction of any other State; nor any State be formed by the Junction of two or more States, or parts of States, without the Consent of the Legislatures of the States concerned as well as of the Congress.

The Congress shall have power to dispose of and make all needful Rules and Regulations respecting the Territory or other property belonging to the United States; and nothing in this Constitution shall be so construed as to prejudice any Claims of the United States, or of any particular State.

Section 4. The United States shall guarantee to every State in this Union a Republican Form of Government, and shall protect each of them against Invasion; and on Application of the Legislature, or of the Executive (when the Legislature cannot be convened) against domestic Violence.

---

[8] Modified by the Eleventh Amendment.

[9] Superseded by the Thirteenth Amendment.

Article V

The Congress, whenever two-thirds of both Houses shall deem it necessary, shall propose Amendments to this Constitution, or, on the Application of the Legislatures of two-thirds of the several States, shall call a Convention for proposing Amendments, which, in either Case, shall be valid to all Intents and Purposes, as part of this Constitution, when ratified by the Legislatures of three-fourths of the several States, or by Conventions in three-fourths thereof, as the one or the other Mode of Ratification may be proposed by the Congress; provided that no Amendment which may be made prior to the Year One thousand eight hundred and eight shall in any Manner affect the first and fourth Clauses in the Ninth Section of the first Article; and that no State, without its Consent, shall be deprived of its equal Suffrage in the Senate.

Article VI

All Debts contracted and Engagements entered into, before the Adoption of this Constitution, shall be as valid against the United States under this Constitution, as under the Confederation.

This Constitution, and the Laws of the United States which shall be made in Pursuance thereof; and all Treaties made, or which shall be made, under the Authority of the United States, shall be the supreme Law of the Land; and the Judges in every State shall be bound thereby, any Thing in the Constitution or Laws of any State to the Contrary notwithstanding.

The Senators and Representatives before mentioned, and the Members of the several State Legislatures, and all executive and judicial Officers, both of the United States and of the several States, shall be bound by Oath or Affirmation to support this Constitution; but no religious Test shall ever be required as a qualification to any Office or public Trust under the United States.

Article VII

The Ratification of the Conventions of nine States shall be sufficient for the Establishment of this Constitution between the States so ratifying the same.

Done in Convention by the Unanimous Consent of the States present the Seventeenth Day of September in the Year of our Lord one thousand seven hundred and Eighty seven, and of the Independence of the United States of America the Twelfth. In Witness whereof We have hereunto subscribed our Names.

Articles in Addition to, and Amendment of, the Constitution of the United States of America, Proposed by Congress, and Ratified by the Legislatures of the Several States, Pursuant to the Fifth Article of the Original Constitution.

Amendment I[10]

Congress shall make no law respecting an establishment of religion, or prohibiting the free exercise thereof; or abridging the freedom of speech, or of the press; or the right of the people peaceably to assemble, and to petition the Government for a redress of grievances.

Amendment II

A well regulated Militia, being necessary to the security of a free State, the right of the people to keep and bear Arms shall not be infringed.

Amendment III

No Soldier shall, in time of peace, be quartered in any house, without the consent of the Owner, nor in time of war, but in a manner to be prescribed by law.

Amendment IV

The right of the people to be secure in their persons, houses, papers, and effects, against unreasonable searches and seizures, shall not be violated, and no Warrants shall issue, but upon probable cause, supported by Oath or affirmation, and particularly describing the place to be searched, and the persons or things to be seized.

Amendment V

No person shall be held to answer for a capital, or otherwise infamous crime, unless on a presentment or indictment of a Grand Jury, except in cases arising in the land or naval forces, or in the Militia, when in actual service in time of War or public danger; nor shall any person be subject for the same offence to be twice put in jeopardy of life or limb; nor shall be compelled in any criminal case to be a witness against himself, nor be deprived of life, liberty, or property, without due process of law; nor shall private property be taken for public use without just compensation.

Amendment VI

In all criminal prosecutions, the accused shall enjoy the right to a speedy and public trial, by an impartial jury of the State and district wherein the crime shall have been committed, which district shall have been previously ascertained by law, and to be informed of the nature and cause of the accusation; to be confronted with the witnesses against him; to have compulsory process for obtaining witnesses in his favor, and to have the Assistance of Counsel for his defence.

Amendment VII

In suits at common law, where the value in controversy shall exceed twenty dollars, the right of trial by jury shall be preserved, and no fact tried by a jury, shall be otherwise reexamined in any Court of the United States, than according to the rules of the common law.

Amendment VIII

Excessive bail shall not be required, nor excessive fines imposed, nor cruel and unusual punishments inflicted.

[10] The first ten amendments were passed by Congress September 25, 1789. They were ratified by three-fourths of the states December 15, 1791.

Amendment IX

The enumeration in the Constitution, of certain rights, shall not be construed to deny or disparage others retained by the people.

Amendment X

The powers not delegated to the United States by the Constitution, nor prohibited by it to the States, are reserved to the States respectively, or to the people.

Amendment XI (1795)[11]

The Judicial power of the United States shall not be construed to extend to any suit in law or equity, commenced or prosecuted against one of the United States by Citizens of another State, or by Citizens or Subjects of any Foreign State.

Amendment XII (1804)

The Electors shall meet in their respective States and vote by ballot for President and Vice-President, one of whom, at least, shall not be an inhabitant of the same State with themselves; they shall name in their ballots the person voted for as President, and in distinct ballots the person voted for as Vice-President, and they shall make distinct lists of all persons voted for as President, and of all persons voted for as Vice-President, and of the number of votes for each, which lists they shall sign and certify, and transmit sealed to the seat of the government of the United States, directed to the President of the Senate; — The President of the Senate shall, in the presence of the Senate and House of Representatives, open all the certificates and the votes shall then be counted; — The person having the greatest number of votes for President, shall be the President, if such number be a majority of the whole number of Electors appointed; and if no person have such majority, then from the persons having the highest numbers not exceeding three on the list of those voted for as President, the House of Representatives shall choose immediately, by ballot, the President. But in choosing the President, the votes shall be taken by states, the representation from each state having one vote; a quorum for this purpose shall consist of a member or members from two-thirds of the states, and a majority of all the states shall be necessary to a choice. [And if the House of Representatives shall not choose a President whenever the right of choice shall devolve upon them, before the fourth day of March next following, then the Vice-President shall act as President, as in the case of the death or other constitutional disability of the President.][12] — The person having the greatest number of votes as Vice-President, shall be the Vice-President, if such number be a majority of the whole number of Electors appointed, and if no person have a majority, then from the two highest numbers on the list, the Senate shall choose the Vice-President; a quorum for the purpose shall consist of two-thirds of the whole number of Senators, and a majority of the whole number shall be necessary to a choice. But no person constitutionally ineligible to the Office of President shall be eligible to that of Vice-President of the United States.

[11] Date of ratification.
[12] Superseded by the Twentieth Amendment.

Amendment XIII (1865)

Section 1. Neither slavery nor involuntary servitude, except as a punishment for crime whereof the party shall have been duly convicted, shall exist within the United States, or any place subject to their jurisdiction.

Section 2. Congress shall have power to enforce this article by appropriate legislation.

Amendment XIV (1868)

Section 1. All persons born or naturalized in the United States, and subject to the jurisdiction thereof, are citizens of the United States and of the State wherein they reside. No State shall make or enforce any law which shall abridge the privileges or immunities of citizens of the United States; nor shall any State deprive any person of life, liberty, or property, without due process of law; nor deny to any person within its jurisdiction the equal protection of the laws.

Section 2. Representatives shall be apportioned among the several States according to their respective numbers, counting the whole number of persons in each State, excluding Indians not taxed. But when the right to vote at any election for the choice of electors for President and Vice-President of the United States, Representatives in Congress, the Executive and Judicial Officers of a State, or the members of the Legislature thereof, is denied to any of the male inhabitants of such State, being twenty-one years of age, and citizens of the United States, or in any way abridged, except for participation in rebellion, or other crime, the basis of representation therein shall be reduced in the proportion which the number of such male citizens shall bear to the whole number of male citizens twenty-one years of age in such State.

Section 3. No person shall be a senator or Representative in Congress, or elector of President and Vice-President, or hold any Office, civil or military, under the United States, or under any State, who, having previously taken an oath, as a member of Congress, or as an Officer of the United States, or as a member of any State legislature, or as an executive or judicial Officer of any State, to support the Constitution of the United States, shall have engaged in insurrection or rebellion against the same, or given aid or comfort to the enemies thereof. But Congress may by a vote of two-thirds of each House, remove such disability.

Section 4. The validity of the public debt of the United States, authorized by law, including debts incurred for payment of pensions and bounties for services in suppressing insurrection or rebellion, shall not be questioned. But neither the United States nor any State shall assume or pay any debt or obligation incurred in aid of insurrection or rebellion against the United States, or any claim for the loss or emancipation of any slave; but all such debts, obligations, and claims shall be held illegal and void.

Section 5. The Congress shall have the power to enforce, by appropriate legislation, the provisions of this article.

Amendment XV (1870)

Section 1. The right of citizens of the United States to vote shall not be denied or abridged by the United States or by any State on account of race, color, or previous condition of servitude —

Section 2. The Congress shall have power to enforce this article by appropriate legislation.

Amendment XVI (1913)

The Congress shall have power to lay and collect taxes on incomes, from whatever source derived, without apportionment among the several States, and without regard to any census or enumeration.

Amendment XVII (1913)

The Senate of the United States shall be composed of two Senators from each State, elected by the people thereof, for six years; and each Senator shall have one vote. The electors in each State shall have the qualifications requisite for electors of the most numerous branch of the State legislatures.

When vacancies happen in the representation of any State in the Senate, the executive authority of such State shall issue writs of election to fill such vacancies: *Provided,* That the legislature of any State may empower the executive thereof to make temporary appointments until the people fill the vacancies by election as the legislature may direct.

This amendment shall not be so construed as to affect the election or term of any Senator chosen before it becomes valid as part of the Constitution.

Amendment XVIII (1919)[13]

Section 1. After one year from the ratification of this article the manufacture, sale, or transportation of intoxicating liquors within, the importation thereof into, or the exportation thereof from the United States and all territory subject to the jurisdiction thereof for beverage purposes is hereby prohibited.

Section 2. The Congress and the several States shall have concurrent power to enforce this article by appropriate legislation.

Section 3. This article shall be inoperative unless it shall have been ratified as an amendment to the Constitution by the legislatures of the several States, as provided in the Constitution, within seven years from the date of the submission hereof to the States by the Congress.

Amendment XIX (1920)

The right of citizens of the United States to vote shall not be denied or abridged by the United States or by any State on account of sex.

Congress shall have power to enforce this article by appropriate legislation.

Amendment XX (1933)

Section 1. The terms of the President and Vice-President shall end at noon on the 20th day of January, and the terms of Senators and Representatives at noon on the 3d day of January, of the years in which such terms would have ended if this article had not been ratified; and the terms of their successors shall then begin.

Section 2. The Congress shall assemble at least once in every year, and such meeting shall begin at noon on the 3d day of January, unless they shall by law appoint a different day.

[13] Repealed by the Twenty-first Amendment.

Section 3. If, at the time fixed for the begining of the term of the President, the President elect shall have died, the Vice-President elect shall become President. If a President shall not have been chosen before the time fixed for the beginning of his term, or if the President elect shall have failed to qualify, then the Vice-President elect shall act as President until a President shall have qualified; and the Congress may by law provide for the case wherein neither a President elect nor a Vice-President elect shall have qualified, declaring who shall then act as President, or the manner in which one who is to act shall be selected, and such person shall act accordingly until a President or Vice-President shall have qualified.

Section 4. The Congress may by law provide for the case of the death of any of the persons from whom the House of Representatives may choose a President whenever the right of choice shall have devolved upon them, and for the case of the death of any of the persons from whom the Senate may choose a Vice-President whenever the right of choice shall have devolved upon them.

Section 5. Sections 1 and 2 shall take effect on the 15th day of October following the ratification of this article.

Section 6. This article shall be inoperative unless it shall have been ratified as an amendment to the Constitution by the legislatures of three-fourths of the several States within seven years from the date of its submission.

Amendment XXI (1933)

Section 1. The eighteenth article of amendment to the Constitution of the United States is hereby repealed.

Section 2. The transportation or importation into any State, Territory, or possession of the United States for delivery or use therein of intoxicating liquors, in violation of the laws thereof, is hereby prohibited.

Section 3. This article shall be inoperative unless it shall have been ratified as an amendment to the Constitution by conventions in the several States, as provided by the Constitution, within seven years from the date of the submission hereof to the States by the Congress.

Amendment XXII (1951)

No person shall be elected to the Office of the President more than twice, and no person who has held the Office of President, or acted as President, for more than two years of a term to which some other person was elected President shall be elected to the Office of the President more than once.

But this Article shall not apply to any person holding the Office of President when this Article was proposed by the Congress, and shall not prevent any person who may be holding the Office of President, or acting as President, during the term within which this Article becomes operative from holding the Office of President or acting as President during the remainder of such term.

Amendment XXIII (1961)

Section 1. The District constituting the seat of Government of the United States shall appoint in such manner as the Congress may direct:

A number of electors of President and Vice-President equal to the whole number of Senators and Representatives in Congress to which the District would be entitled if it were a State, but in no event more than the least populous State; they shall be in addition to those appointed by the States, but they shall be considered, for the purposes of the election of President and Vice-President, to be electors appointed by the State; and they shall meet in the District and perform such duties as provided by the twelfth article of amendment.

Section 2. The Congress shall have power to enforce this article by appropriate legislation.

Amendment XXIV (1964)

Section 1. The right of citizens of the United States to vote in any primary or other election for President or Vice-President, for electors for President or Vice-President, or for Senator or Representative in Congress, shall not be denied or abridged by the United States or any State by reason of failure to pay any poll tax or other tax.

Section 2. The Congress shall have power to enforce this article by appropriate legislation.

Amendment XXV (1967)

Section 1. In case of the removal of the President from Office or of his death or resignation, the Vice-President shall become President.

Section 2. Whenever there is a vacancy in the Office of the Vice-President, the President shall nominate a Vice-President who shall take Office upon confirmation by a majority vote of both Houses of Congress.

Section 3. Whenever the President transmits to the President pro tempore of the Senate and the Speaker of the House of Representatives his written declaration that he is unable to discharge the powers and duties of his Office, and until he transmits to them a written declaration to the contrary, such powers and duties shall be discharged by the Vice-President as Acting President.

Section 4. Whenever the Vice-President and a majority of either the principal Officers of the executive department or of such other body as Congress may by law provide, transmit to the President pro tempore of the Senate and the Speaker of the House of Representatives their written declaration that the President is unable to discharge the powers and duties of his Office, the Vice-President shall immediately assume the powers and duties of the Office as Acting President.

Thereafter, when the President transmits to the President pro tempore of the Senate and the Speaker of the House of Representatives his written declaration that no inability exists, he shall resume the powers and duties of his Office unless the Vice-President and a majority of either the principal Officers of the executive department or of such other body as Congress may by law provide, transmit within four days to the President pro tempore of the Senate and the Speaker of the House of Representatives their written declaration that the President is unable to discharge the powers and duties of his Office. Thereupon Congress shall decide the issue, assembling within forty-eight hours for that purpose if not in session. If the Congress, within twenty-one days after receipt of the latter written declaration, or, if Congress is not in session, within twenty-one days after Congress is required to assemble, determines by two-thirds vote of both Houses that the President is unable to discharge the powers and duties of his Office, the Vice-President shall continue to discharge the same as Acting President; otherwise, the President shall resume the powers and duties of his Office.

Amendment XXVI (1971)

Section 1. The right of citizens of the United States, who are eighteen years of age or older, to vote shall not be denied or abridged by the United States or by any State on account of age.

Section 2. The Congress shall have power to enforce this article by appropriate legislation.

Amendment XXVII (1992)

No law varying the compensation for the services of the Senators and Representatives shall take effect, until an election of Representatives shall have intervened.

PRESIDENTS OF THE UNITED STATES

Year	President	Party	Vote	Electoral Vote	Percentage of Popular Vote
1789	George Washington	no designation		69	
1792	George Washington	no designation		132	
1796	John Adams	Federalist		71	
1800	Thomas Jefferson	Democratic-Republican		73	
1804	Thomas Jefferson	Democratic-Republican		162	
1808	James Madison	Democratic-Republican		122	
1812	James Madison	Democratic-Republican		128	
1816	James Monroe	Democratic-Republican		183	
1820	James Monroe	Democratic-Republican		231	
1824	John Quincy Adams	Democratic-Republican	108,740	84	30.5
1828	Andrew Jackson	Democratic	647,286	178	56.0
1832	Andrew Jackson	Democratic	687,502	219	55.0
1836	Martin Van Buren	Democratic	765,483	170	50.9
1840	William H. Harrison	Whig	1,274,624	234	53.1
1841	John Tyler*	Whig			
1844	James K. Polk	Democratic	1,338,464	170	49.6
1848	Zachary Taylor	Whig	1,360,967	163	47.4
1850	Millard Fillmore*	Whig			
1852	Franklin Pierce	Democratic	1,601,117	254	50.9
1856	James Buchanan	Democratic	1,832,955	174	45.3
1860	Abraham Lincoln	Republican	1,865,593	180	39.8
1864	Abraham Lincoln	Republican	2,206,938	212	55.0
1865	Andrew Johnson*	Democratic			
1868	Ulysses S. Grant	Republican	3,013,421	214	52.7
1872	Ulysses S. Grant	Republican	3,596,745	286	55.6
1876	Rutherford B. Hayes	Republican	4,036,572	185	48.0
1880	James A. Garfield	Republican	4,453,295	214	48.5
1881	Chester A. Arthur*	Republican			
1884	Grover Cleveland	Democratic	4,879,507	219	48.5
1888	Benjamin Harrison	Republican	5,447,129	233	47.9
1892	Grover Cleveland	Democratic	5,555,426	277	46.1
1896	William McKinley	Republican	7,102,246	271	51.1
1900	William McKinley	Republican	7,218,491	292	51.7
1901	Theodore Roosevelt*	Republican			
1904	Theodore Roosevelt	Republican	7,628,461	336	57.4
1908	William H. Taft	Republican	7,675,320	321	51.6
1912	Woodrow Wilson	Democratic	6,296,547	435	41.9
1916	Woodrow Wilson	Democratic	9,127,695	277	49.4
1920	Warren G. Harding	Republican	16,143,407	404	60.4
1923	Calvin Coolidge*	Republican			
1924	Calvin Coolidge	Republican	15,718,211	382	54.0
1928	Herbert C. Hoover	Republican	21,391,993	444	58.2
1932	Franklin D. Roosevelt	Democratic	22,809,638	472	57.4
1936	Franklin D. Roosevelt	Democratic	27,752,869	523	60.8
1940	Franklin D. Roosevelt	Democratic	27,307,819	449	54.8
1944	Franklin D. Roosevelt	Democratic	25,606,585	432	53.5
1945	Harry S Truman*	Democratic			
1948	Harry S Truman	Democratic	24,105,812	303	49.5
1952	Dwight D. Eisenhower	Republican	33,936,234	442	55.1
1956	Dwight D. Eisenhower	Republican	35,590,472	457	57.6
1960	John F. Kennedy	Democratic	34,227,096	303	49.9
1963	Lyndon B. Johnson*	Democratic			
1964	Lyndon B. Johnson	Democratic	43,126,506	486	61.1
1968	Richard M. Nixon	Republican	31,785,480	301	43.4
1972	Richard M. Nixon	Republican	47,169,905	520	60.7
1974	Gerald R. Ford†	Republican			
1976	Jimmy Carter	Democratic	40,827,394	297	50.0
1980	Ronald Reagan	Republican	43,899,248	489	50.8
1984	Ronald Reagan	Republican	54,450,603	525	58.8
1988	George Bush	Republican	47,946,422	426	53.9
1992	Bill Clinton	Democratic	43,728,375	370	43.2

* Succeeded to presidency upon death of the incumbent.
† Succeeded to presidency upon resignation of the incumbent.

GLOSSARY

administrative law The rules and regulations made and applied by federal regulatory agencies and commissions.

adversary system of justice A judicial system in which the power of the state is balanced by the defendant's constitutional rights and by the presumption that a person is innocent until proven guilty beyond a reasonable doubt.

affirmative action programs Programs of government, universities, and businesses that are designed to favor minorities and remedy past discrimination.

agenda setting The power to determine which public policy questions will be debated or considered.

Antifederalists Those who opposed ratification of the Constitution.

appellate jurisdiction The right of the Supreme Court to hear cases that are appealed from lower state or federal courts on the grounds that they concern violations of constitutional rights.

appropriations bills Bills passed by Congress to pay for the spending it has authorized.

arraignment The proceeding before a judge in which the formal charges of an indictment or information are read to an accused person, who may plead guilty or not guilty.

Articles of Confederation (1781–89) The written framework for the government of the original thirteen states before the Constitution was adopted. Under the Articles of Confederation, the national government was weak and dominated by the states. There was a unicameral legislature, but no national executive or judiciary.

backgrounder A meeting in which government officials discuss policies and plans with reporters with the mutual understanding that the information can be attributed only to unnamed "officials" or sometimes not attributed to any source.

bail An amount of money "posted" with the courts as security in exchange for a defendant's freedom until the case comes to trial.

balancing test The view of the majority of the Supreme Court that First Amendment rights must be weighed against the competing needs of the community to preserve order.

bandwagon effect The possible tendency of some voters or convention delegates to support the candidate who is leading in the polls and seems likely to win.

bicameral legislature A two-house legislature.

bill of attainder A law aimed at a particular individual. Prohibited by the Constitution.

Bill of Rights The first ten amendments to the Constitution that set forth basic protections for individuals. (Some scholars define the Bill of Rights as only the first eight or nine amendments.)

bipartisanship A view that both major political parties should broadly support the president on foreign policy issues.

block grants Federal grants to state and local communities that are for general use in a broad area, such as community development.

Brown v. Board of Education of Topeka, Kansas Ruling by the Supreme Court in 1954 that racial segregation in public schools violated the Fourteenth Amendment's requirement of equal protection of the laws for all persons.

budget resolutions Overall spending targets set by the Congress.

bureaucrats Public administrators.

cabinet The president, the vice-president, the heads of the major executive departments of the government, and certain other senior officials who may hold "cabinet rank."

capitalism An economic system of free enterprise with private ownership of the means of production.

caucus A group or a meeting of a group of a political party or organization in which such matters as selection of candidates, leaders, or positions on issues are decided.

***certiorari*, writ of** A writ which, if granted by the Supreme Court, means that it agrees to hear a case.

charter colonies Colonies in which freely elected legislatures chose the governors, and laws could not be vetoed by the king.

checks and balances The provisions of the Constitution that divide power among three constitutionally equal and independent branches of government—legislative, executive, and judicial—in the hope of preventing any single branch from becoming too powerful.

civil cases Court cases that concern relations between individuals and organizations, such as a divorce action or a suit for damages arising from an automobile accident or for violation of a business contract.

civil disobedience The conscious refusal to obey laws that are believed to be unjust, unconstitutional, or immoral.

civil liberties The fundamental rights of a free society that are protected by the Bill of Rights against the power of the government, such as freedom of speech, religion, press, and assembly.

civil rights The constitutional rights of all individuals, and especially of African Americans and other minorities, to enjoy full equality and equal protection of the laws.

civil service The civilian employees of the government and the administrative system in which they work.

clear and present danger test A test established by Supreme Court Justice Oliver Wendell Holmes in 1919 to define the point at which speech loses the protection of the First Amendment.

closed primary A form of primary election in which only registered members of a political party or persons declaring their affiliation with a party can vote.

closed shop A place of work in which only union members may be hired.

cloture A Senate procedure to cut off a filibuster by a vote of three-fifths (sixty members) of the entire Senate.

cluster sampling A technique used by polling organizations in which several people from the same neighborhood are interviewed.

coalitions Alliances of segments of the electorate, interest groups, and unorganized masses of voters who coalesce behind a political candidate or party.

coattail effect The ability of a major candidate, such as a presidential or gubernatorial candidate, to help carry into office lesser candidates from the same party who are also on the ballot.

COINTELPRO The "counterintelligence program" of the FBI that harassed American citizens and disrupted their organizations through a wide variety of clandestine techniques.

Cold War The period after the Second World War marked by superpower rivalry and tension between the United States and the communist government of the Soviet Union. The Cold War ended with the collapse of the Soviet government in 1991.

collective security A principle embraced by the United States during the Truman and Eisenhower administrations, under which the nation attempted to "contain" communism and entered into a series of military alliances with other countries for this purpose.

commission plan A form of city government under which a board of city commissioners is popularly elected (often on a nonpartisan ballot). The commissioners make policy as a city council, but they also run city departments as administrators.

Committee of the Whole A device used by the House of Representatives when it considers legislation sent to it by the Rules Committee. When the House sits as a Committee of the Whole, it is able to conduct business with less formality, and with a quorum of only 100 members.

Committees of Correspondence A political communications network established in 1772 by Samuel Adams to unite the colonists in their fight against British rule.

common law The cumulative body of law as expressed in judicial decisions and custom rather than by statute.

concurrent powers Powers of government exercised independently by both the federal and state governments, such as the power to tax.

conference committee A committee composed of senior members of the House and Senate that tries to reconcile disagreements between the two branches of Congress over differing versions of a bill.

conglomerates Multi-interest and often multinational corporations that, under one corporate roof, may manufacture a wide variety of products.

Connecticut Compromise The plan adopted during the Constitutional Convention of 1787 providing for a House of Representatives based on population and a Senate with two members from each state. (Also known as the Great Compromise.)

constituencies Voters in a political district; interest groups or client groups either directly regulated by the bureaucracy or vitally affected by its decisions.

Constitution The written framework for the United States government that established a strong national government of three branches—legislative, executive, and judicial—and provided for the control and operation of that government.

constitutional amendment A change to the Constitution proposed by a two-thirds vote of both houses of Congress or a constitutional convention, and ratified by legislatures or ratifying conventions in three-fourths of the states.

containment The foreign policy of the United States in the period after the Second World War, designed to contain the expansion of Soviet power.

cooperative federalism A view that the various levels of government in America are related parts of a single governmental system, characterized by cooperation and shared functions.

council-manager plan A form of city government under which a council, usually elected on a nonpartisan ticket, hires a professional city manager, who runs the city government and has power to hire and fire officials.

court-packing plan A plan proposed by President Franklin D. Roosevelt in 1937, which Congress rejected, to add younger justices to the Supreme Court who would be more sympathetic to the New Deal.

covert operations Secret political action within other countries.

creative federalism A term coined by President Lyndon B. Johnson to describe his own view of the relationship between Washington and the states.

credentials committee The body of a political convention that decides which delegates should be seated, subject to approval of the entire convention.

criminal cases Court cases that concern crimes committed against the public order.

dark horse A political candidate who is initially thought to have only an outside chance of gaining the nomination.

delegates The men and women formally entitled to select the presidential nominees of the two major parties at their party's presidential nominating convention.

demands What people and groups want from the political system.

democracy Rule by the people.

deregulation The elimination or reduction of government regulation of industry.

desegregation The process of ending separation of persons by race.

détente A relaxation of international tensions.

deviating elections Elections in which the majority party (according to party identification) is defeated in a temporary reversal.

direct mail fund raising A technique to raise money directly from the public with the aid of computerized mailing lists.

discharge petition A petition which can be filed by a majority of House members in order to dislodge a bill from a House committee.

distributive policy A public policy that is meant to benefit everyone.

double jeopardy More than one prosecution for the same offense. Prohibited by the Constitution.

Dred Scott decision A ruling by the Supreme Court in 1857 — reversed by the Fourteenth Amendment in 1868 — that black Americans were not citizens under the Constitution.

dual federalism The concept — accepted until 1937 — of the federal government and the states as competing power centers, with the Supreme Court as referee.

due process of law A phrase, contained in the Fifth and Fourteenth amendments, that protects the individual against the arbitrary power of the state. _Substantive due process_ means that laws must be reasonable. _Procedural due process_ means that laws must be administered in a fair manner.

elastic clause Article I, Section 8 of the Constitution, which allows Congress to make all laws that are "necessary and proper" to carry out the powers of the Constitution.

elections The procedure by which voters choose, usually among competing candidates, to determine who shall hold public office. _See also_ deviating elections, maintaining elections, and realigning elections.

electoral college The body composed of electors from the fifty states, who formally have the power to elect the president and vice-president of the United States. Each state has a number of electors equal to its number of senators and representatives in Congress.

elite theory The view that power in America is held by the few, not by the masses of people.

enabling act A congressional act that allows the people of a territory desiring statehood to frame a state constitution.

enterprise zones Urban or rural areas in which businesses would be encouraged to locate because of tax breaks and other incentives. In 1992 President Bush vetoed a bill containing enterprise zones.

entitlement programs Programs mandated by law and not subject to annual review by Congress or the president.

enumerated powers Powers of government that are specifically granted to the three branches of the federal government under the Constitution.

equal protection clause The provision of the Fourteenth Amendment that seeks to guarantee equal treatment for all persons.

Equal Rights Amendment (ERA) A proposed amendment to the Constitution, aimed at ending discrimination against women, that stated: "Equality of rights under the law shall not be denied or abridged by the United States or by any state on account of sex." The proposal was defeated in 1982.

equal time provision A provision of the Federal Communications Act that requires broadcasters to provide "equal time" to all legally qualified candidates.

equality A concept that all people are of equal worth, even if not of equal ability.

equalization A formula for federal matching requirements that takes into account the state's or community's ability to pay.

equity A legal principle of fair dealing, which may provide preventive measures and legal remedies that are unavailable under ancient principles of common law.

establishment clause The First Amendment provision that "Congress shall make no law respecting an establishment of religion."

exclusionary rule A doctrine established by the Supreme Court that, with some exceptions, bars the federal government from using illegally seized evidence in court.

executive agencies Units of government under the president, within the executive branch, that are not part of a cabinet department.

executive agreements International agreements between the president and foreign heads of state that, unlike treaties, do not require Senate approval.

executive privilege A doctrine under which presidents have claimed the right to withhold information from Congress and the judiciary.

exit polls Polls taken as people leave the voting booths. Sometimes have been used by the television networks to predict election outcomes before the polls close.

ex parte contacts One-sided contacts, such as an approach to a regulatory agency by a lawyer representing one side in a case.

ex post facto laws Laws that punish an act that was not illegal at the time it was committed.

extradition A constitutional provision allowing a state to request another state to return fugitives.

fairness doctrine A requirement by the Federal Communications Commission, abolished in 1987, that radio and television broadcasters present all sides of important public issues.

Federal Election Campaign Act of 1974 An act to regulate campaign finance by providing for public funding of presidential elections and by placing limits on campaign contributions.

Federal Election Commission A six-member commission created in 1974 to enforce campaign finance laws and administer public financing of presidential elections.

federalism A system of government characterized by a constitutional sharing of power between a national government and regional units of government.

The Federalist Papers A series of letters published in the late 1780s by Alexander Hamilton, James Madison, and John Jay to explain and help bring about ratification of the Constitution.

Federalists Those who supported the Constitution during the struggle over its ratification following the Constitutional Convention of 1787.

feedback The response of the rest of society to decisions made by the authorities of a political system.

felony A major crime, such as murder, arson, or rape.

filibuster The process by which a single senator, or a group of senators, can sometimes talk a bill to death and prevent it from coming to a vote.

fiscal policy Government regulation of the economy through its control over rates of taxation and government spending.

flexible construction The principle, established by Chief Justice Marshall in 1819 in the case of *McCulloch* v. *Maryland*, that the Constitution must be interpreted flexibly to meet changing conditions.

foreign policy The sum of the goals, decisions, and actions that govern a nation's relations with the rest of the world.

franking privilege A system entitling members of Congress to send mail to constituents without charge by putting their frank, or mark, on the envelope. The law forbids this privilege for soliciting money or votes, or for mass mailings 60 days before an election.

Freedom of Information Act A law passed in 1966 which requires federal executive branch and regulatory agencies to make information available to journalists and the public unless it falls into one of several confidential categories.

free exercise clause The First Amendment provision that Congress shall make no law "prohibiting the free exercise" of religion.

full faith and credit A clause in Article IV of the Constitution, requiring that each state respect the laws, records, and court decisions of another state.

gender gap A difference, such as that in the 1992 elections, in the voting behavior of men and women.

gerrymandering The drawing of the lines of congressional districts, or of any other political district, in order to favor one political party over another.

government The individuals, institutions, and processes that make the rules for society and possess the power to enforce them.

government corporations Agencies that were at one time semiautonomous, but that through legislation have been placed under presidential control since 1945.

grants-in-aid Federal aid to states and localities that is earmarked for specific purposes only. Also known as categorical grants.

Gross National Product The total national output of goods and services.

guaranteed annual income A proposed alternate approach to welfare that would guarantee everyone a minimum income, making the existing welfare system unnecessary.

Hatch Act A federal law that prevents federal employees from taking an active part in party politics or campaigns, or from running for political office.

home rule The power of some municipalities to modify their charters and run their affairs without approval by the state legislature.

impeachment Under the Constitution, the formal proceedings against the president or other federal officials or federal judges, who may be removed from office if convicted of "Treason, Bribery or other high Crimes and Misdemeanors."

implementation The action, or actions, taken by government to carry out a policy.

implied powers Powers of the national government that flow from its enumerated powers and the "elastic clause" of the Constitution.

impoundment The practice, curtailed in 1974, whereby a president refused to spend funds appropriated by Congress.

independent counsel A special federal prosecutor appointed under the 1978 Ethics in Government Act in cases involving possible crimes by high officials. Formerly known as a "special prosecutor."

independent executive agencies Agencies that report to the president in the same manner as departments, even though they are not part of any cabinet department.

independent expenditures Funds spent for or against a candidate by committees not formally connected to a candidate.

independent regulatory commissions *See* regulatory agencies.

Indiana ballot Also known as the party-column ballot. Used in a majority of states, it lists the candidates of each party in a row or column, beside or under the party emblem. Allows for and encourages straight-ticket voting.

indictment A finding by a grand jury that there is enough evidence against an individual to warrant a criminal trial.

inherent powers Powers of government that the national government may exercise simply because it exists as a government, such as the right to conduct foreign relations.

initiative A method of amending state constitutions, used in seventeen states, under which proposed constitutional amendments can be placed on the ballot if enough signatures are obtained on a petition. Almost half the states also employ the initiative on the ballot to allow voters to enact or repeal laws.

injunction An order from a court to prevent or require an action.

inputs The demands upon and supports for a political system.

instructed delegate A legislator who automatically mirrors the will of the majority of his or her constituents.

interest groups Private groups that attempt to influence the government to respond to the shared attitudes of their members.

interstate compacts Agreements between or among states made with the approval of Congress.

interventionism A strand of American foreign policy that was visible by the end of the nineteenth century; it included "gunboat diplomacy" and other forms of military involvement in various parts of the world.

isolationism A policy of avoiding foreign entanglements.

issue network A loose grouping of people and organizations who seek to influence policy formation.

item veto The power of most governors to disapprove particular parts of appropriations bills.

Jim Crow laws Laws that were designed to segregate black and white Americans.

Joint Chiefs of Staff The chairman, the chiefs of staff of the three armed services, and, when Marine Corps matters are under consideration, the commandant of the marines. By law, the Joint Chiefs of Staff advise the president and the secretary of defense and are the chiefs of their respective military services.

joint committees Committees composed of both representatives and senators.

judicial activism A philosophy, often embraced by a majority of the members of the Warren Court, that boldly applies the Constitution to social and political questions.

judicial restraint A philosophy often associated with Justices Frankfurter, Brandeis, and Holmes, that requires the Supreme Court to avoid constitutional questions when possible, and to uphold acts of Congress unless they clearly violate a specific section of the Constitution.

judicial review The power of the Supreme Court to declare acts of Congress or actions by the executive — or laws and actions at any level of local, state, and federal government — unconstitutional.

jus sanguinis Right of blood. Under this principle, the citizenship of a child is determined by that of the parents.

jus soli Right of soil. Under this principle, citizenship is conferred by place of birth.

kitchen cabinet Informal advisers to the president who hold no official position on the White House staff.

laissez faire The philosophy that government should intervene as little as possible in economic affairs.

"lame duck" A legislator or other official whose term of office extends beyond an election at which he or she has been defeated.

legislative veto A provision of law in which Congress asserts the power to nullify actions of the executive branch. In 1983 the Supreme Court ruled that the "legislative veto" was unconstitutional, but Congress continued to pass laws containing such provisions.

liaison officers Employees of government agencies whose job is to maintain good relations with Congress.

literacy tests Tests of a voter's ability to read and write, which were often used to keep recent immigrants and blacks from voting.

lobbying Communication with legislators or other government officials to try to influence their decisions.

magistrates' courts Courts in which justices of the peace, or magistrates, handle minor offenses (misdemeanors), such as speeding, and perform civil marriages.

Magna Carta A historic British document, signed by King John in 1215, in which the nobles confirmed that the power of the king was not absolute.

maintaining elections Elections that reflect the basic party identification of the voters.

majority leader A leader elected by the majority party in a legislative house.

majority rule A concept of government by the people under which everyone is free to vote, but normally whoever gets the most votes wins the election and represents all the people (including those who voted for the losing candidate).

Mallory rule A rule established by the Supreme Court in *Mallory v. United States* (1957) requiring that a suspect in a federal case be arraigned without unnecessary delay.

management by objective (MBO) A program for managing the executive branch that required federal agencies to make periodic checks to be sure they were achieving their objectives.

Marbury v. Madison The 1803 case in which the Supreme Court first firmly set forth and established the power of judicial review, by declaring an act of Congress unconstitutional.

marginal district A congressional district in which the winning candidate receives less than 55 percent of the vote.

Massachusetts ballot Also known as the office-column ballot. This ballot groups candidates according to the office for which they are running.

matching requirements The federal government's requirement that state or local governments put up some of their own funds in order to be eligible for federal aid for a program.

mayor-council plan A form of city government under which power is divided between a mayor and an elected city council.

McCulloch v. Maryland An important decision of the Supreme Court in 1819 that established the key concepts of implied powers, broad construction of the Constitution, and supremacy of the national government.

Medicaid A public assistance program established in 1965 to help pay hospital, doctor, and medical bills for persons with low incomes. It is financed through general federal, state, and local taxes.

Medicare A federal program established in 1965 that provides hospital and medical services to older persons through the social security program.

megalopolis By definition, a very large city. The term has also been used to describe the cluster of metropolitan areas of the northeastern seaboard of the United States.

merit commissions Commissions set up to recommend candidates for federal district and circuit courts on the basis of merit.

military-industrial complex A term often used to describe the economic and political ties between the military establishment and the defense-aerospace industry.

minority leader A leader elected by the minority party in a legislative house.

minor party A political party other than one of the major parties; also known as a third party.

Miranda warnings Warnings that police must give suspects to advise them of their constitutional rights. Under the Supreme Court decision in *Miranda v. Arizona* (1966), before suspects are questioned, they must be warned that they have the right to remain silent, that any statements they make may be used against them, and that they have the right to a lawyer.

misdemeanor A minor offense.

mixed (or modified) free enterprise system An economic system, such as that of the United States, in which both private industry and government play important roles.

Model Cities A controversial program approved by Congress in 1966, and ended in 1973, that sought to rebuild entire poverty neighborhoods in selected cities.

monetary policy Government regulation of the economy through its control over the supply of money and the cost and availability of credit.

money supply The quantity of money in circulation.

monopoly Control of a market by a single company.

national chairperson The head of a national political party.

national committee Between conventions, the governing body of a major political party. Members of the national committee are chosen in the states and formally elected by the party's national convention.

national convention The formal source of all authority in each major political party. It nominates the party candidates for president and vice-president, writes a platform, settles disputes, writes rules, and elects the members of the national committee.

national presidential primary A proposed new form of primary in which voters could directly choose the presidential candidates of the major parties.

National Security Council A White House council created in 1947 to help the president coordinate American military and foreign policy.

negative advertising Political commercials that strongly attack a rival candidate.

negative campaigning Political campaigning in which the candidates appear to spend more time attacking each other than discussing policies and programs.

neutron bomb A controversial bomb that kills people but spares buildings.

new federalism President Richard Nixon's effort to return federal tax money to state and local governments. The term was also adopted by President Reagan.

New Jersey Plan A plan offered at the Constitutional Convention of 1787 by William Paterson of New Jersey, and favored by the small states, which called for one vote for each state in the legislature, an executive of more than one person to be elected by Congress, and a Supreme Court to be appointed by the executive.

New York Times **rule** A rule established by the Supreme Court in the case of *New York Times Company* v. *Sullivan* (1964), which makes it almost impossible to libel a public official unless the statement is made with "actual malice" — that is, unless it is deliberately or recklessly false.

nuclear proliferation The spread of atomic weapons to more countries.

oligopoly The concentration of economic power in the hands of a relatively few large companies.

ombudsman An official complaint taker who tries to help citizens who have been wronged by the actions of government agencies.

open primary A form of primary election in which any voter may participate and vote for a slate of candidates of one political party.

original jurisdiction The right of the Supreme Court, under the Constitution, to hear certain kinds of cases directly, such as cases involving foreign diplomats.

out party A major political party that functions as an opposition party because it does not control the presidency.

outputs The binding decisions that a political system makes, whether in the form of laws, regulations, or judicial decisions.

party activists People who ring doorbells or serve as delegates to political conventions. They perform the day-to-day, grass-roots work of politics.

party identification Attachment to one political party by a voter.

Pentagon Papers A forty-seven volume study of the Vietnam war compiled by the Defense Department and leaked to the press by a former Pentagon official in 1971.

periodic registration A system of voter registration in which the voter must register every year or at other stated intervals.

permanent registration A system of voter registration in which the voter registers only once in his or her district.

planning-programming budgeting system (PPBS) A management tool that required federal departments to define their goals precisely and measure the costs and benefits of alternative programs to achieve those goals.

plea bargaining A bargain in which a defendant in a criminal case agrees to plead guilty to a less serious charge than might be proven at a trial. In return, the prosecutor agrees to reduce the charges or recommend leniency.

plum book A listing of the non-civil-service jobs that an incoming president may fill.

pluralism A system in which many conflicting groups within the community have access to government officials and compete with one another in an effort to influence policy decisions.

pocket veto A power of the president to kill a bill by taking no action (if Congress adjourns during the ten-day period after the president receives the bill). Some court rulings have suggested that a president may exercise a pocket veto only when Congress adjourns for good at the end of a second session, and not during a recess.

policy A course of action decided upon by a government — or by any organization, group, or individual — that usually involves a choice among competing alternatives.

political action committees (PACs) Independent organizations, but more often the political arms of corporations, labor unions, or interest groups, established to contribute to candidates or to work for general political goals.

political opinion Opinions on political issues, such as a choice among candidates or parties.

political participation The involvement of citizens in the political process of a nation.

political party, major A broadly based coalition that attempts to gain control of the government by winning elections, in order to exercise power and reward its members.

political socialization The process through which an individual acquires a set of political attitudes and forms opinions about social issues.

poll tax A tax on voting repealed by the Twenty-fourth Amendment in 1964, long used by Southern states to keep blacks (and, in some cases, poor whites) from participating in elections.

power The possession of control over others.

power structure A term popularized by sociologist Floyd Hunter to describe the community leaders who he said determined policy in Atlanta, Georgia. More broadly, the term is used to describe "power elites" generally.

precedent An earlier court case that serves as a justification for a decision in a later case. Also known as *stare decisis*.

presidential primary Method used by more than three-quarters of the states in which voters in one or both parties express their preference for a presidential nominee and choose all or some convention delegates.

press secretary, presidential The White House official who speaks for the president in day-to-day meetings with the news media.

primary group A group that a person comes into face-to-face contact with in everyday life; for example, friends, office associates, or a local social club.

prior restraint The censoring of printed material by the government prior to publication.

proportional representation A system of multimember election districts that encourages the existence of many parties by allotting legislative seats to competing parties according to the percentage of votes that they win.

Proposition 13 A constitutional amendment approved by California voters in 1978 that limited real estate taxes in the state to one percent of previous property values.

proprietary colonies Colonies in which the proprietors (who had obtained their patents from the king) named the governors, subject to the king's approval.

psychological method An approach in studying how voters decide that attempts to find out what is going on inside the minds of the voters and to measure their perceptions of parties, candidates, and issues.

public administration The term preferred by political scientists to describe the bureaucratic process — the business of making government work.

public assistance A welfare program that distributes public funds to people who are poor.

public interest law firms Law firms, often staffed by young lawyers, that represent consumers, minorities, and the poor.

public opinion The expression of attitudes about government and politics.

public policy A course of action chosen by government officials.

quota sample A method of polling, considered less reliable than a random sample, in which interviewers are instructed to question members of a particular group in proportion to their percentage in the population as a whole.

random sample A group, chosen by poll takers, that is representative of the universe that is being polled.

realigning elections Elections which may lead to a basic shift in the party identification of the electorate.

redistributive policy A public policy that takes something away from one person and gives it to someone else.

redistricting The drawing of new boundary lines for legislative districts based on the results of a census of the population.

reference group A group whose views serve as guidelines to an individual's opinion.

regulatory agencies Government agencies that exercise quasi-judicial and quasi-legislative powers. They are administratively independent of both the president and Congress (although politically independent of neither).

regulatory federalism The emergence of federal programs aimed at, or implemented by, state and local governments.

representative democracy A democracy in which leaders are elected to speak for and represent the people.

retrospective voting Voting based upon looking back and making judgments about the way things have gone and the kind of government experienced during a political leader's time in office.

revenue sharing, general A program that ended in 1986, under which federal grants were made to local communities, with few or no strings about how the money was to be used.

riders Provisions tacked on to a piece of legislation that are not relevant to the bill.

right to work laws State legislation designed to outlaw the union shop, passed by twenty-one states acting under Section 14B of the federal Taft-Hartley Act.

Roe v. *Wade* A 1973 Supreme Court decision affirming that no state may interfere with a woman's right to have an abortion during the first three months of pregnancy.

roll-call vote A method of voting in a legislature in which all members present at a session must vote, and their positions become a matter of public record.

royal colonies Colonies controlled by the British king through governors appointed by him and through the king's veto power over colonial laws.

safe congressional district As usually defined, a district in which the winner receives 55 percent or more of the vote.

secondary group An organization or group, such as a labor union, or a fraternal, professional, or religious group, that may influence an individual's opinion.

Secret Service The government agency that guards the president, the vice-president, the major presidential and vice-presidential candidates, and their spouses.

segregation The separation of persons by race.

select committees *See* special committees.

senatorial courtesy An unwritten custom by which individual senators who belong to the same political party as the president exercise an informal veto power over presidential appointments in their states.

Senior Executive Service (SES) A corps of about 8,100 high-level administrators and managers at the top of the government bureaucracy who have less job tenure but who are eligible for substantial cash bonuses for merit.

seniority system A system, until modified and reformed in the 1970s, that automatically resulted in the selection as committee chairperson of those members of the majority party in a house of Congress who had the longest continuous service on a committee.

separate but equal A doctrine established by the Supreme Court in 1896 under which "Jim Crow" segregation laws were held to be constitutional.

separation of powers The principle that each of the three branches of government is constitutionally equal to and independent of the others.

shared powers The fusing or overlapping of powers and functions among the separate branches of government.

shield laws Laws passed by state legislatures that are designed to protect reporters from being forced to reveal their news sources.

smoke-filled room A phrase that grew out of the 1920 Republican Convention in Chicago, symbolizing the selection of a candidate by political bosses operating in secret.

social security A compulsory national insurance program, financed by taxes on employers and employees. The insurance falls into four categories: old-age and survivors insurance, disability insurance, Medicare, and unemployment insurance.

sociological method An approach in studying how the voters decide that focuses on the social and economic background of the voters, their income, social class, ethnic group, education, and similar factors.

soft money Funds raised by the two major political parties, not subject to the limits of federal law, and spent by them in the states to aid candidates *indirectly* in a variety of ways.

Speaker of the House The presiding officer and most powerful member of the House of Representatives. The Speaker is technically elected by the full House but in practice is chosen by the majority party.

special committees Committees created by Congress to conduct special investigations.

special prosecutor An independent federal prosecutor appointed under the 1978 Ethics in Government Act in cases involving possible crimes by high officials. Later known formally as an "independent counsel."

special publics A concept developed by political scientists to describe those segments of the public with views about particular issues.

special rule A rule from the House Rules Committee that limits the time to be allowed for floor discussion of a bill and the extent to which it may be amended.

spoils system A practice under which victorious politicians reward their followers with jobs.

standing committees The permanent committees of a legislature that consider bills and conduct hearings and investigations.

stare decisis A Latin phrase meaning "stand by past decisions," a principle that is often, but not always, used by judges in deciding cases.

START A treaty to reduce strategic arms signed by the United States and the Soviet Union in 1991.

statutory law Law enacted by Congress, or by state legislatures or local legislative bodies.

steering committee A committee appointing senators to standing committees. Also known as assignment committee.

straight-ticket voting Voting for all candidates of a single party for all offices.

Strategic Arms Limitation Talks (SALT) Negotiations between the United States and the Soviet Union that resulted in the signing of two arms agreements in 1972 and the SALT II agreement in 1979. SALT II was not ratified by the Senate.

strategic deterrence A policy followed by the United States since the Second World War that assumes that if enough nuclear weapons are deployed by the United States, an enemy would not attack for fear of being destroyed by a retaliatory blow.

subcommittees Small committees formed from the members of a larger committee.

subpoena A written document issued by a court that orders a person to appear in court or to produce evidence.

subsidy A government grant of money.

suffrage The right to vote.

supply-side economics Tax cuts or other economic measures designed to increase work effort, savings, and investment in order to expand the total supply, or output, of the nation's goods and services.

supports The attitudes and actions of people that sustain and buttress the political system at all levels and allow it to continue to work.

supremacy clause The clause in Article VI of the Constitution declaring that the Constitution and the laws of Congress are "the supreme Law of the Land" and shall prevail over any conflicting state constitutions or laws.

suspension of the rules A procedure permitted two days each week under the rules of the House of Representatives that allows any bill to be debated if two-thirds of the members who are voting agree.

system maintenance The process of keeping a diverse, unwieldy institution, such as the House of Representatives, functioning.

tariff A federal tax on imports.

teller vote A vote in the Committee of the Whole in which members file down the aisle of the House and are counted. Now rarely used.

third party A minor party that is an alternative to the two major parties; for example, the Know-Nothings of the 1850s, a party that exploited fear of Irish immigrants and other "foreigners," or the Populists of the 1890s, a protest party of Western farmers favoring "free silver."

ticket-splitter A voter who may be a Republican or Democrat, but who occasionally votes for a candidate of another party.

tombstone voters Persons who vote illegally by using the names of deceased voters.

town meeting An annual meeting held in the spring in many New England towns, at which the townspeople come together to elect a board of selectmen and to discuss local policy questions. The town meeting has become a symbol of participatory democracy.

transnational relations Contacts, coalitions, and interactions across national boundaries — such as personal contacts or business relationships — that are not controlled by the central foreign policy organs of governments.

triangle A powerful alliance of mutual benefit among an agency or unit of the government, an interest group, and a committee or subcommittee of Congress. Also called an iron triangle or a subgovernment.

Truman Doctrine As enunciated by President Truman, a doctrine declaring that American security and world peace depended on United States protection for the "free peoples of the world."

trustee Concept of the British statesman Edmund Burke that legislators should act according to their own consciences.

unanimous consent A time-saving procedure under which bills may be called up for consideration in the Senate unless one or more members objects.

unicameral legislature A legislature with only one house.

union shop A place of work in which any person may be hired provided he or she joins the union within a specified time.

unitary system of government A centralized system of government, such as that of France, where most of the important policy decisions are made by a central government.

United Nations A world organization founded in 1945 for the purpose of collectively keeping the peace and working for the betterment of humanity.

unit rule A procedure at national political conventions which in some cases allowed the majority of a state delegation to cast the state's entire vote.

universe The total group from which poll takers may select a random sample in order to measure public opinion.

unreasonable searches and seizures Searches prohibited by the Fourth Amendment, often because they take place without a search warrant issued by a court.

vanishing marginals An electoral trend in which the number of unsafe, marginal districts in House elections appears to be declining.

veto Disapproval of a bill by a chief executive, such as the president, or a state governor.

Virginia Plan A plan offered at the Constitutional Convention of 1787, and favored by the large states, which called for a two-house legislature, the lower house chosen by the people and the upper house chosen by the lower; and a national executive and a national judiciary chosen by the legislature.

War Powers Resolution A law passed by Congress in 1973 that sets a time limit on the use of combat forces abroad by a president.

welfare state A government like that of the United States that exercises responsibility for the welfare of its citizens in such areas as social security, housing, and education.

whips Legislative leaders of each party who are responsible for rounding up party members for important votes.

whistle-blowers Government employees who publicly expose evidence of official waste or corruption that they have learned about in the course of their duties.

winner-take-all primaries Presidential primaries in which the victorious candidate could win all of a state's convention delegates, no matter how slim the margin of victory.

COPYRIGHTS AND ACKNOWLEDGMENTS

The authors are indebted to the following for permission to reprint from copyrighted material.

Allyn and Bacon. For data published in *Political Behavior of the American Electorate*, 4th edition, 1979, and 5th edition, 1983 by William H. Flanigan and Nancy H. Zingale. Reprinted with permission.

Congressional Quarterly, Inc. For excerpts from *Weekly Report* and *Politics in America*, 1969 and 1979. Used with permission.

The Gallup Organization, Inc. For data from *Gallup Report* and *Gallup Opinion Index*. Copyright © The Gallup Organization and reprinted by permission.

Harcourt Brace Jovanovich. For excerpt from Donald T. Regan, *For The Record: From Wall Street to Washington*. Copyright © and reprinted by permission of Harcourt Brace Jovanovich, Inc.

Los Angeles Times. Copyright © 1977,78,79 by *Los Angeles Times*. Reprinted by permission.

The New York Times Company. For excerpts from the *New York Times*. Copyright © 1970,73,74,78,80,83,84,87,91,92 by The New York Times Company. Reprinted by permission.

Pantheon Books, a division of Random House, Inc. For excerpt from Nick Kotz, *Wild Blue Yonder: Money, Politics and the B-1 Bomber*. Pantheon Books, © 1988.

Simon and Schuster, Inc. For excerpts from *The Brethren: Inside The Supreme Court*. Copyright © 1979 by Bob Woodward and Scott Armstrong. Reprinted by permission of Simon and Schuster, Inc.

USA Today. For excerpt from story in *USA TODAY*, copyright © 1992, USA TODAY. Reprinted with permission.

Washington Post. For excerpts from stories in the *Washington Post*, Copyright © 1973,79,82,83,84,87,88,89,91,92 by The Washington Post. Reprinted by permission.

Illustration Credits
Part One: © Davidson/Magnum
Part Two: AP/Wide World
Part Three: © Paul Conklin
Part Four: © 1992 Peter Turnley/Black Star/Newsweek
Part Five: © Stephen Meyers/International Stock Photography

Chapter 1: **Page 5:** © Olympia/PhotoEdit; **6:** (top) Reuters/Bettmann; (bottom) Reuters/Bettmann; **7:** © John Barr/Gamma Liaison; **8:** (top) UPI/Bettmann; (bottom) © Robin Layton Kinsley; **9:** (bottom) © Dennis Brack/Black Star; (top) © Donald McCullin/Magnum; **12:** D. Gorton/NYT Pictures; **13:** © Kim Johnson/Sygma; **15:** Sovfoto; **16:** © Kristin L. Kenney; **18:** Fred R. Conrad/NYT Pictures; **19:** © Kathy Brownell; **20:** © Rhoda Sidney/PhotoEdit; **22:** (top) H. Darr Beiser/USA Today; (bottom) AP/Wide World; **24:** AP/Wide World.

Chapter 2: **Page 29:** Comstock; **30:** courtesy Bridget C. Mergens Mayhew; **31:** © Bob Kusel/SIPA; **33:** (top) The Granger Collection; (bottom) Smithsonian Institution; **36:** (top) Historical Picture Service; (bottom) Library of Congress; **37;** Culver Pictures; **38;** The Granger Collection; **39:** Culver Pictures; **40:** The Granger Collection; **50:** George Tames/NYT Pictures; **52:** © Trippet/SIPA; **54:** The Granger Collection; **57:** © Jesse Nemerofsky/Picture Group.

Chapter 3: **Page 61:** Reuters/Bettmann; **65:** UPI/Bettmann; **66:** UPI/Bettmann; **70:** Boston Athenaeum; **74:** © John Pickerell/TSW; **75:** (left) © Topham/Image Works; (right) © Dan Ford Connolly/Picture Group; **76:** © F. Lee Corkran/Sygma; **77:** AP/Wide World; **78:** UPI/Bettmann; **83:** © Fred Lyon/Photo Researchers.

Chapter 4: **Page 87:** © Comstock, Inc.; **88:** AP/Wide World; **90:** Culver Pictures; **93:** (top) © Stone/Sygma; **96:** (both) AP/Wide World; **107:** © Miro Vintoniv/Stock, Boston; **110:** © Phillips/Black Star; **112:** NYT Pictures; **117:** Arizona Republic; **119:** © Flip Schulke/Black Star; **122:** © Andrew Popper/Picture Group; **124:** © Steve Sapp/Sygma.

Chapter 5: **Page 129:** © Steve Sapp/Sygma; **130:** © Robert Brenner/PhotoEdit; **133:** (left) © John Running/Stock, Boston; (right) © Budnick/Woodfin Camp & Associates; **135:** UPI/Bettmann; **137:** © Curt Gunther/Camera 5; **140:** © David Young-Wolff/PhotoEdit; **141:** © Rob Crandall/Picture Group; **147:** (left) © Jeff Markowitz/Sygma; (right) © Dennis Brack/Black Star; **148:** (top) © David R. Swanson/Gamma Liaison; (bottom) © Mike Theiler/SIPA; **149:** (top) Uniphoto; (bottom) Mike Mills/Wide World; **150:** © Jesse Nemerofsky/Picture Group; **153:** © Randy Taylor/Sygma; **155:** © Rob Crandall/Picture Group; **156:** © David Butow/Black Star; **157:** Mark Elias/Wide World; **159:** (top) American Antiquarian Society; (bottom) National Archives; **160:** Library of Congress; **161:** Carl Iwasaki, Life Magazine. © 1954, Time, Inc.; **163:** UPI/Bettmann; **165:** AP/Wide World; **166:** Ebony Magazine; **169:** © James Karales/DPI.

Chapter 6: **Page 180:** © Shepard Sherbell/SABA; **183:** © Jerome Delay/Gamma Liaison; **185:** © Jim Heemstra/Picture Group; **187:** © Bart Bartholomew/Black Star; **189:** (top) © Ray Ellis/Photo Researchers; (bottom) UPI/Bettmann; **195:** AP/Wide World; **199:** courtesy *Star Magazine*; **204:** (left) © 1991 Cable News Network, Inc. All Rights Reserved; (right) © Dennis Brack/Black Star; **209:** Reprinted by permission from *Time* magazine; **213:** © Franklin Wing/Stock, Boston; **214:** courtesy Handgun Control, Inc.

Chapter 7: **Page 223:** Charlie Archambault/USN&WR; **224:** (left) courtesy Bush/Quayle '92; (right) courtesy Clinton/Gore; **226:** (top) University of Hartford Collection; (bottom) Ralph E. Becker Collection/Smithsonian Institution; **227:** (top) The Hermitage; (bottom) courtesy of the Indiana Historical Society and the Smithsonian Institution; **228:** Ralph E. Becker Collection/Smithsonian Institution; **229:** (top left) Library of Congress; (top right) Ralph E. Becker Collection/Smithsonian Institution; (bottom left) Stanley King Collection; (bottom right) Ralph E. Becker Collection/Smithsonian Institution; **231:** Smithsonian Institution; **235:** Ralph E. Becker Collection/Smithsonian Institution; **237:** Bill Snead; **243:** © Paul Conklin; **244:** © Shepard Sherbell/Picture Group; **246:** Larry Downing/Newsweek; **248:** (left) AP/Wide World; (right) © Paul Conklin; **249:** (bottom) © Paul Conklin; (top) © Paul Conklin; **252:** Chick Harrity/USN&WR; **254:** James Keyser/Time Magazine.

Chapter 8: **Page 261:** Cynthia Johnson/*Time* magazine; **262:** courtesy Clinton/Gore; **263:** (top) AP/Wide World; (bottom) © Cornell Capa/Magnum; **267:** (top) © David Hume Kennerly/Gamma Liaison; (bottom) AP/Wide World; **269:** AP/Wide World; **271:** Harvard University Library/Theodore Roosevelt Collection; **272:** Andrew Sacks; **273:** AP/Wide World; **276:** UPI/Bettmann; **278:** Copyright 1992 *Time.* Reprinted by permission; **279:** With permission of Doyle, Dane, Bernbach, Inc./photos courtesy Tony Schwartz; **280:** CBS Photo; **283:** AP/Wide World; **284:** Reuters/Bettmann; **287:** (left); © Starr/Stock, Boston; (right) courtesy United We Stand, America; **289:** AP/Wide World; **292:** © Dennis Brack/Black Star; **293:** (left) UPI/Bettmann; (center) Reuters/Bettmann; (right) AP/Wide World; **294:** © Michael Grecco/Picture Group; **297:** Cynthia Johnson, *Time* magazine; **299:** © Allan Tannenbaum/Sygma; **301:** courtesy Republican National Committee; **303:** Sygma.

Chapter 9: **Page 307:** © Jim Anderson/Woodfin Camp; **319:** © Bob Daemmrich/Image Works; **320:** © Allan Tannenbaum/Sygma; **323:** AP/Wide World; **325:** Cynthia Johnson/*Time* magazine; **328:** Reuters/Bettmann; **331:** © Larry Downing/Sygma; **335:** © Roger Sandler/Picture Group; **342:** © Thomas S. England/Photo Researchers; **343:** © Rob Crandall/Picture Group; **345:** Smithsonian Institution; **347:** © Rob Crandall/Picture Group; **350:** © Choplin/Black Star; **352:** Barton Silverman/NYT Pictures; **353:** The New York Historical Society.

Chapter 10: **Page 357:** courtesy White House; **360:** George Tames/NYT Pictures; **363:** AP/Wide World; **365:** AP/Wide World; **368:** Clark/*Life* magazine © Time, Inc.; **369:** UPI/Bettman; **372:** UPI/Bettman; **373:** AP/Wide World; **374:** Allan Tannenbaum/Sygma; **376:** Bettman Archive; **377:** © Larry Downing/Woodfin Camp & Associates; **386:** UPI/Bettman; **388:** © Mike Mancuso/Sygma; **394:** (top left) © Fred Ward/Black Star; (bottom left) © Laffont/Sygma; (right) © Laffont/Sygma; **397:** UPI/Bettman; **399:** (top left) AP/World Wide; (top middle) Brown Brothers; (top right) UPI/Bettman; (bottom left) Brown Brothers; (bottom right) UPI/Bettman; **400:** AP/World Wide; **401:** AP/World Wide; **402:** © Ira Wyman/Sygma.

Chapter 11: **Page 407:** © Richard Pasley/Stock, Boston; **408:** (top) NASA; (bottom) AP/Wide World; **413:** UPI/Bettman; **417:** Culver Pictures; **418:** (left) UPI/Bettman; (right) J.T. Atlan/Sygma; **420:** Dennis Brack/Black Star; **424:** © Bob Daemmrich/Stock, Boston; **428:** © Richard Cash/PhotoEdit; **431:** Bettman Archive; **432:** Culver Pictures; **433:** © Dennis Brack/Black Star; **437:** UPI/Bettman; **438:** UPI/Bettman.

Chapter 12: **Page 443:** UPI/Bettmann; **450:** (left) Wolf von dem Bussche; (right) George Tames/NYT Pictures; **451:** Wolf von dem Bussche; **454:** courtesy George Behan; **455:** © Paul Conklin; **459:** © 1991 Jake McGuire; **461:** © Dennis Brack/Black Star; **462:** UPI/Bettmann; **466:** © Paul Conklin; **467:** © Paul Conklin; **468:** UPI/Bettmann; **469:** UPI/Bettmann; **475:** (top) © Little/Camera 5; *(bottom)* © Alex Webb/Magnum; **477:** © Paul Conklin; **481:** © Archambault/Picture Group.

Chapter 13: **Page 487:** AP/Wide World; **488:** © Dennis Brack/Black Star; **489:** © Okamoto/Photo Researchers; **490:** NYT Pictures; **493:** © Declan Haun/Black Star; **494:** UPI/Bettmann; **496:** © Fred Ward/Black Star; **497:** © Dennis Brack/Black Star; **503:** (top) © Larry Downing/Woodfin Camp & Associates; (bottom) © Fred Ward/Black Star; **505:** UPI/Bettmann; **510:** Larry Morris/Washington Post; **511:** © Cornell Capa/Magnum; **512:** © Dain/Magnum; **513:** © George Gardner; **516:** © Okamoto/Photo Researchers; **522:** © Forden/Sygma; **523:** © Graubard/Sygma; **526:** © Rob Crandall/Picture Group.

Chapter 14: **Page 533:** Steve Liss/*Time* magazine; **534:** © Christopher J. Wise; **536:** (top) AP/Wide World; **537:** (top) Charlie Archambault/USN&WR; (bottom) © Nick Del Calzo/Documentary Portraits; **538:** © Carlos Humberto/Contact/Woodfin Camp; **543:** (top) U.S. Army; (bottom) © Skoogfors/Woodfin Camp & Associates; **545:** Bettman Archive; **546:** (top) © Bill Strode/Woodfin Camp & Associates (bottom) © Richard Brummett, 1980; **547:** AP/Wide World; **548:** UPI/Bettman; **552** © Roger Ressmeyer/Starlight; **557:** © Tretick/Sygma; **558:** © Roger Ressmeyer/Starlight; **564:** © Bert Glinn/Magnum; **565:** Michael Geissinger/NYT Pictures; **569:** © Bruno Barbey/Magnum; **571:** (top) © Herman Kokojan/Black Star; (bottom) © Malloch/Magnum; **579:** AP/Wide World.

Chapter 15: **Page 587:** © Tannenbaum/Sygma; **588:** © J.L. Atlan/Sygma; **592:** AP/Wide World; **593:** © Brody/Stock, Boston; **595:** Zabala/NYT Pictures; **597:** (top) © Owen Franken/Stock, Boston; (bottom) UPI/Bettmann; **604:** UPI/Bettmann; **606:** Dorothea Lange/Culver Pictures; **607:** © Paul Conklin/Monkmeyer; **610:** © Liane Enkalis/Stock, Boston; **612:** © Rob Crandall/Picture Group; **613:** Bernard Gotfryd/Newsweek; **616:** Boenzi/NYT Pictures; **617:** NASA; **621:** © Judy Canty/Stock, Boston; **623:** (top) AP/Wide World; (bottom) © Leif Skoogfors/Woodfin Camp & Associates; **625:** © Dejean/Sygma; **627:** (left) © Rick Smolan/Woodfin Camp & Associates; (right) © Skoogfors/Gamma Liaison.

Chapter 16: **Page 635:** Photo Researchers; **637:** © Springman/Black Star; **638:** UPI/Bettmann; **642:** AP/Wide World; **645:** © Black Star; **646:** Photo Researchers; **646:** Aero Service Division/Geophysical Company of America;

INDEX

Page numbers in *italics* refer to captions.

1964

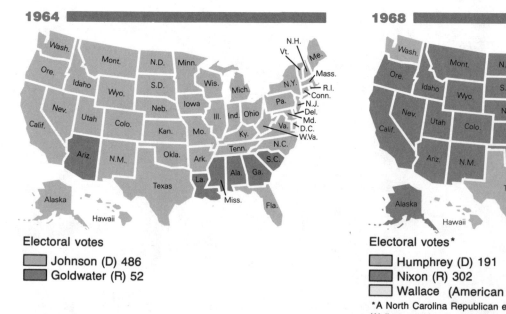

Electoral votes

■ Johnson (D) 486
■ Goldwater (R) 52

1968

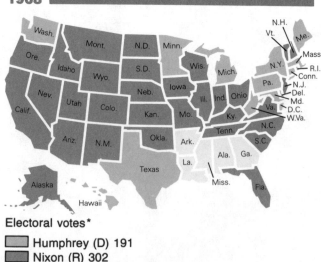

Electoral votes*

■ Humphrey (D) 191
■ Nixon (R) 302
■ Wallace (American Independent) 45

*A North Carolina Republican elector cast his vote for George Wallace, making the official count: Nixon, 301; Humphrey, 191, Wallace, 46.

1980

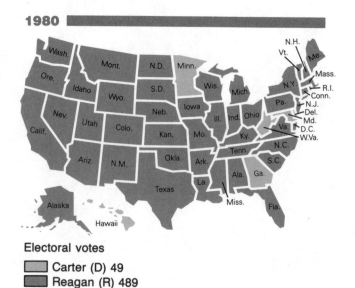

Electoral votes

■ Carter (D) 49
■ Reagan (R) 489

1984

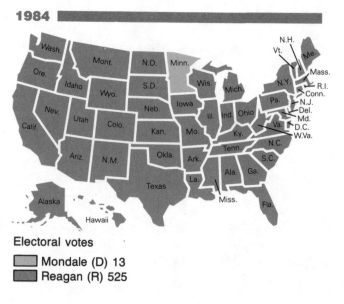

Electoral votes

■ Mondale (D) 13
■ Reagan (R) 525